Advanced Mathematics

An Incremental Development

Second Edition

Advanced Mathematics

An Incremental Development

Second Edition

John H. Saxon, Jr.

SAXON PUBLISHERS, INC.

Advanced Mathematics: An Incremental Development
Second Edition

Copyright © 2003 by Saxon Publishers, Inc.

All rights reserved.

No part of this publication may be reproduced, stored in a retrieval system, or transmitted in any form or by any means, electronic, mechanical, photocopying, recording, or otherwise, without the prior written permission of the publisher.

Printed in the United States of America.
ISBN: 978-1-56577-039-3
ISBN: 1-56577-039-0

Production Supervisor: David Pond

Production Coordinator: Joan Coleman

Graphic Artist: John Chitwood

4 5 6 7 8 0868 12 11 10 09

> *Reaching us via the Internet*
>
> www.saxonpublishers.com

Contents

Preface

This book is the second edition of the third book in a three-book series designed to teach the concepts and skills necessary for students to succeed in calculus and in disciplines that are mathematically based, such as chemistry and physics. Because of the emphasis on problem solving and the development of productive thought patterns, it also is an excellent book for students who will study the social sciences. New lessons on functions, matrices, statistics, and the graphing calculator have been added. The review of algebra and the beginning concepts of trigonometry presented in the six review lessons in the front of the first edition have been spread out over nineteen lessons. The geometry topics have been moved to the front of the book and presented in these same nineteen lessons. Two-column proofs and paragraph proofs are presented in Lesson 15, and at least one proof is required in every problem set in the first half of the book.

This book contains an in-depth coverage of trigonometry, logarithms, analytic geometry, and upper-level algebraic concepts. It also completes the study of geometry, which is spread over four years in the Saxon math series. It contains 125 lessons which cover all topics normally addressed in an advanced math book and the topics of a precalculus book. It can be taught in two 5-semester-hour courses at the college level. **For high school students who complete *Algebra 2* in the ninth grade, this is a three-semester book. These students can begin their study of calculus the second semester of their junior year. The book is a two-semester book only for the top third of high school students, i.e., those who complete *Algebra 2* in the ninth grade and are highly motivated. They can begin their study of calculus in the fall of their junior year. For high school students who complete *Algebra 2* in the tenth grade, this is a four-semester book. This will assure high college board scores and will prepare these students for calculus as college freshmen.** In the past, many publishers have watered down the books used by the less gifted and less motivated students. Schools that have used the first edition of this book have proven that these students can learn the advanced concepts if the presentation is slowed down. **This book provides for long-term practice with the fundamental concepts and skills of precalculus mathematics, and its use will produce a significant increase in the number of students who succeed in calculus, physics, and chemistry either in high school or in college.**

Primary emphasis is on a continuation of the practice of intermediate algebraic concepts and skills while the upper-level algebraic concepts and skills are introduced. The study of trigonometry begun in the middle of *Algebra 2* is continued, and heavy emphasis is placed on the study of trigonometric functions, common and natural logarithms, and the equations of conics.

The dramatic gains in student math achievement in schools that have used the Saxon books can be attributed directly to the philosophy used to construct these books. The philosophy is that mathematics is not difficult. Mathematics is just different, and long-term practice with concepts that are different turns the concepts into familiar concepts which are not troublesome but are instead friendly and helpful. This book covers all of the concepts that must be mastered before students can be successful in calculus and other advanced mathematics courses. These concepts are upper-level concepts, and even the brightest students cannot absorb upper-level concepts quickly and place them in their long-term memory. The amount of practice required depends on the ability and motivation of the student. In the past, students who were slow to assimilate the concepts of mathematics were forced out of mathematics, not because they were incapable, but because they were not quick. Pace adjustment has proven to be the answer to this problem.

Students who have used Saxon's *Algebra 2* and take four semesters to complete *Advanced Mathematics* will have worked at least two trigonometry problems in each problem set for over two and one half years. They will have worked three algebra-of-logarithm problems in each problem set for almost two years. They will be expert problem solvers because they have finished a program that builds problem-solving skills gently and patiently over a long period of time. Success with these problems is the result of long-term practice in the use of the concepts. Some people have asked that this book be separated into two books. If we did this, it would be difficult to provide the pacing necessary for both the quick and the slow to get the practice needed for success in calculus.

This book uses an incremental development to permit long-term practice of concepts. One facet, or increment, of a concept is introduced and practiced for a time until the next increment of the concept is presented. The understanding achieved through practice on the first increment allows the second increment to be understood. Thus, every problem set contains a problem that permits the practice of every concept previously presented. The traditional development of topics in chapters requires that all facets of a concept be presented in a chapter and then a chapter test given. This development is almost a "flash card" presentation. The student is given insufficient time to assimilate the abstraction and is almost encouraged to forget what has been learned because provision for long-term practice is not provided.

Teachers who use this book must remember that it is designed to teach by letting the students **do,** and that understanding a concept comes after the concept has been used for a long time. Therefore, the long, involved explanations that have been necessary in the past will not be necessary because only one increment of a concept is being presented. The teacher's presentations should be succinct. Understanding will come in time with practice.

The emphasis in Saxon's *Algebra 1* was on providing a foundation in the basic concepts and skills of algebra, with special attention to signed numbers, positive and negative exponents, linear equations, and word problems. In *Algebra 2*, practice in the topics of Algebra I was provided for, while middle-level algebra skills were introduced and practiced. Also in *Algebra 2*, emphasis was given to systems of linear equations, quadratic equations, and systems of nonlinear equations. Area and volume problems were in most of the problem sets. Similar triangles were introduced early, and problems involving similar triangles appeared often. Right-triangle trigonometry was introduced at the one-third point and continued in every problem set in *Algebra 2*. The types of word problems and their level of difficulty were selected with the aim of automating the use of the fundamental concepts and procedures required in the solutions of word problems.

This book continues the development begun in *Algebra 1* and *Algebra 2*. Practice in the fundamental skills of algebra, geometry, and trigonometry is provided for, while advanced topics are introduced and practiced. Logarithms are introduced early, and three or four problems that involve logarithms or exponentials are contained in every problem set until the end of the book. Emphasis is on the algebra of logarithms. Heavy emphasis is given to all phases of trigonometry, including trigonometric equations, trigonometric identities, and the equations and graphs of sinusoids. Other topics that are covered in-depth include matrices, determinants, arithmetic series, geometric series, conic sections, roots of higher-order polynomial equations, and functions, including curve sketching.

The emphasis on fundamental word problems in *Algebra 1* and *Algebra 2* provides the foundation necessary for the in-depth development of rate problems in this book. This, in turn, permits the introduction and automation of the use of the concepts and procedures necessary to solve abstract rate problems. This three-year development of word problem skills and other skills explains the high college board scores attained by students who have completed this series. These students have been carefully led through a program that develops the higher-order thought processes required by the word problems of upper-level mathematics and science courses. Teachers of these courses have remarked on the improved preparation of their "Saxon students."

The problems in this book deal with advanced concepts and are no longer one-step or two-step problems. These problems must be worked repetitively if the use of the concepts they contain is to be automated. **Thus, all the problems in all the problem sets must be worked by every student to get the full effect of the repetition.**

To the Student

This book is designed to automate the use of the many skills necessary for calculus and other upper-division mathematics courses. Historically, these courses have been difficult for students because they contain many problems that require several levels of skills. Students have not had the practice necessary to automate the use of many advanced-level skills and are forced to "reinvent the wheel" each time one of these skills is required. Thus, the time that should be spent on the new concept is expended in trying to recall middle- and advanced-level skills that have been forgotten. Instant redevelopment of these skills is often beyond the student's capability. Thus, comprehension of the new concept is impossible because this comprehension requires a complete understanding of concepts and the use of skills that the student does not possess.

Automation of the use of advanced skills is not more difficult than the automation of the use of lower-level skills. Automation of advanced skills, however, requires an awareness of the task and concentration on the process of automation. **It is most important to work every problem in every problem set.** Work the problems with the realization that similar problems will appear again and again. Try to develop the ability to recognize the concept being reviewed and to develop a supply of productive methods of attack that can be called on automatically. This automatic application of productive responses will ensure success when more advanced concepts are being studied. If the use of the requisite advanced-level skills becomes automated, the problems encountered in calculus and physics will at least seem reasonable, if not easy.

Acknowledgments

I thank Frank, Mark, and Cindy Wang for their help on the first edition of this book. I thank Smith Richardson and Charles Nunley for their extensive help on this edition. I thank Julie Webster, Lorijayne Stephens, and Steve Johnson for typesetting the book and John Chitwood for creating the graphics. I thank the following people for proofreading the book: Joan Coleman, Travis Rose, Paul Kerr, Seung Chung, Lisa Sawyer, Russ Gibson, Jason Perkins, Sarah Leming, Burt Albers, Terry Liu, and Kitt Thompson. Special thanks goes to Diana Stolfus, who has taught from the first edition of this book for nine years and taught out of the manuscript of the revision last year. Her insight and suggestions smoothed many rough places and enhanced the flow of the many strands. Thank you again, Diana.

John Saxon
Norman, Oklahoma
January 1996

LESSON 1 *Geometry Review*

1.A

points, lines, and rays

Some fundamental mathematical terms are impossible to define exactly. We call these terms **primitive terms** or **undefined terms.** We define these terms as best we can and then use them to define other terms. The words **point, curve, line,** and **plane** are primitive terms.

A point is a location. When we put a dot on a piece of paper to mark a location, the dot is not the point because a mathematical point has no size and the dot does have size. We say that the dot is the **graph** of the mathematical point and marks the location of the point. A curve is an unbroken connection of points. Since points have no size, they cannot really be connected. Thus, we prefer to say that a curve defines the path traveled by a moving point. We can use a pencil to graph a curve. These figures are curves.

A mathematical line is a straight curve that has no ends. **Only one mathematical line can be drawn that passes through two designated points.** Since a line defines the path of a moving point that has no width, a line has no width. The pencil line that we draw marks the location of the mathematical line. When we use a pencil to draw the graph of a mathematical line, we often put arrowheads on the ends of the pencil line to emphasize that the mathematical line has no ends.

We can name a line by using a single letter (in this case, p) or by naming any two points on the line in any order. The line above can be called line *AB*, line *BA*, line *AM*, line *MA*, line *BM*, or line *MB*. Instead of writing the word *line*, a commonly used method is to write the letters for any two points on the line in any order and to use an overbar with two arrowheads to indicate that the line continues without end in both directions. All of the following notations name the line shown above. These notations are read as "line *AB*," "line *BA*," etc.

$$\overleftrightarrow{AB} \qquad \overleftrightarrow{BA} \qquad \overleftrightarrow{AM} \qquad \overleftrightarrow{MA} \qquad \overleftrightarrow{BM} \qquad \overleftrightarrow{MB}$$

We remember that a part of a line is called a **line segment** or just a **segment.** A line segment contains the endpoints and all points between the endpoints. A segment can be named by naming the two endpoints in any order. The following segment can be called segment *AB* or segment *BA*.

Instead of writing the word *segment*, we can use two letters in any order and an overbar with no arrowheads to name the line segment whose endpoints are the two given points. Therefore, $\overline{AB}$ means "segment *AB*" and $\overline{BA}$ means "segment *BA*." Thus, we can use either

$$\overline{AB} \qquad \text{or} \qquad \overline{BA}$$

to name a line segment whose endpoints are *A* and *B*.

1

The length of a line segment is designated by using letters without the overbar. Therefore, *AB* designates the length of segment *AB* and *BA* designates the length of segment *BA*. Thus, we can use either

$$AB \quad \text{or} \quad BA$$

to designate the length of the line segment shown below whose endpoints are *A* and *B*.

The words **equal to, greater than,** and **less than** are used only to compare numbers. Thus, when we say that the measure of one line segment is equal to the measure of another line segment, we mean that the number that describes the length of one line segment is equal to the number that describes the length of the other line segment. Mathematicians use the word **congruent** to indicate that designated geometric qualities are equal. In the case of line segments, the designated quality is understood to be the length. Thus, if the segments shown here

are of equal length, we could so state by writing that segment *PQ* is congruent to segment *RS* or by writing that the length of $\overline{PQ}$ equals the length of $\overline{RS}$. We use an equals sign topped by a wavy line (≅) to indicate congruence.

CONGRUENCE OF LINE SEGMENTS		EQUALITY OF LENGTHS
$\overline{PQ} \cong \overline{RS}$	or we could write	$PQ = RS$

Sometimes we will use the word *congruent* and at other times we will speak of line segments whose *measures* are equal.

A **ray** is sometimes called a **half line.** A ray is part of a line with one endpoint—the beginning point, called the **origin**—and extends indefinitely in one direction. The ray shown here begins at point *T*, goes through points *U* and *X*, and continues without end.

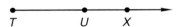

When we name a ray, we must name the origin first and then name any other point on the ray. Thus we can name the ray above by writing either "ray *TU*" or "ray *TX*." Instead of writing the word *ray*, we can use two letters and a single-arrowhead overbar. The first letter must be the endpoint or origin, and the other letter can be any other point on the ray. Thus, we can name the ray shown above by writing either

$$\overrightarrow{TU} \quad \text{or} \quad \overrightarrow{TX}$$

These notations are read as "ray *TU*" and "ray *TX*."

Two rays of opposite directions that lie on the same line (rays that are **collinear**) and that share a common endpoint are called **opposite rays.** Thus, rays *XM* and *XP* are opposite rays, and they are both collinear with line *MX*.

If two geometric figures have points in common, we say that these points are points of **intersection** of the figures. We say that the figures intersect each other at these points. If two different lines lie in the same plane and are not parallel, then they intersect in exactly one point. Here we show lines *b* and *e* that intersect at point *Z*.

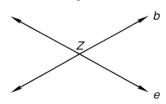

1.B
planes

A mathematical line has no width and continues without end in both directions. A mathematical plane can be thought of as a flat surface like a tabletop that has no thickness and that continues without limit in the two dimensions that define the plane. Although a plane has no edges, we often picture a plane by using a four-sided figure. The figures below are typical of how we draw planes. We label and refer to them as plane *P* and plane *Q*, respectively.

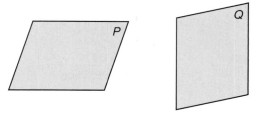

Just as two points determine a line, three noncollinear points determine a plane. As three noncollinear points also determine two intersecting straight lines, we can see that two lines that intersect at one point also determine a plane.

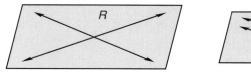

On the right, we see that two parallel lines also determine a plane. We say that lines that lie in the same plane are **coplanar.**

A line not in a plane is parallel to the plane if the line does not intersect the plane. If a line is not parallel to a plane, the line will intersect the plane and will do so at only one point. Here we show plane *M* and line *k* that lies in the plane. We also show line *c* that is parallel to the plane and line *f* that intersects the plane at point *P*.

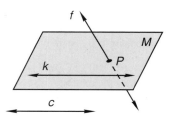

Skew lines are lines that are not in the same plane. Skew lines are never parallel, and they do not intersect. However, saying this is not necessary because if lines are parallel or intersect, they are in the same plane. Thus, lines *k* and *f* in the diagram above are skew lines because they are not both in plane *M*, and they do not form another plane because they are not parallel and they do not intersect.

1.C
angles

There is more than one way to define an angle. An angle can be defined to be the **geometric figure** formed by two rays that have a common endpoint. This definition says that the angle is the set of points that forms the rays, and that the measure of the angle is the measure of the opening between the rays. A second definition is that the angle is the **region** bounded by two radii and the arc of a circle. In this definition, the measure of the angle is the ratio of the length of the arc to the length of the radius.

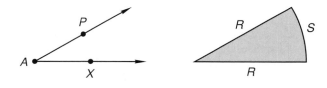

Using the first definition and the left-hand figure on the preceding page, we say that the angle is **the set of points that forms the rays $\overrightarrow{AP}$ and $\overrightarrow{AX}$.** Using the second definition and the right-hand figure on the preceding page, we say that the angle is **the set of points that constitutes the shaded region,** and that the measure of the angle is *S* over *R*. A third definition is that an angle is the **difference in direction** of two intersecting lines. A fourth definition says that an angle is the **rotation of a ray about its endpoint.** This definition is useful in trigonometry. Here we show two angles.

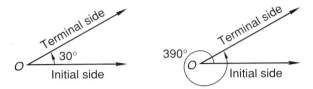

The angle on the left is a 30° angle because the ray was rotated through 30° to get to its terminal position. On the right, the terminal position is the same, but the angle is a 390° angle because the rotation was 390°. Because both angles have the same initial and terminal sides, we say that the angles are **coterminal.** We say the measure of the amount of rotation is the measure of the angle. We can name an angle by using a single letter or by using three letters. When we use three letters, the first and last letters designate points on the rays and the center letter designates the common endpoint of the rays, which is called the **vertex** of the angle. The angle shown here could be named by using any of the notations shown on the right.

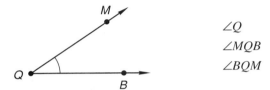

$\angle Q$

$\angle MQB$

$\angle BQM$

We use the word *congruent* to mean "geometrically identical." Line segments have only one geometric quality, which is their length. Thus, when we say that two line segments are congruent, we are saying that their lengths are equal. When we say that two angles are congruent, we are saying that the angles have equal measures. If the measure of angle *A* equals the measure of angle *B*, we may write

CONGRUENCE OF ANGLES		EQUALITY OF ANGLE MEASURE
$\angle A \cong \angle B$	or we could write	$m\angle A = m\angle B$

We will use both of these notations.

If two rays have a common endpoint and point in opposite directions, the angle formed is called a **straight angle.** A straight angle has a measure of 180 degrees, which can also be written as 180°. If two rays meet and form a "square corner," we say that the rays are **perpendicular** and that they form a **right angle.** A right angle has a measure of 90°. Thus, the words *right angle*, *90° angle*, and *perpendicular* all have the same meaning. As we show below, a small square at the intersection of two lines or rays indicates that the lines or rays are perpendicular.

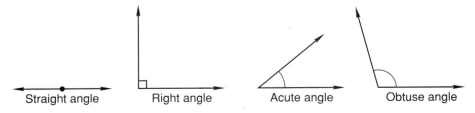

Acute angles have measures that are greater than 0° and less than 90°. **Obtuse angles** have measures that are greater than 90° and less than 180°. If the sum of the measures of two angles is 180°, the two angles are called **supplementary angles.** If the sum of the measures of

two angles is 90°, the angles are called **complementary angles.** On the left we show two adjacent angles whose measures sum to 180°. We can use this fact to write an equation to solve for x.

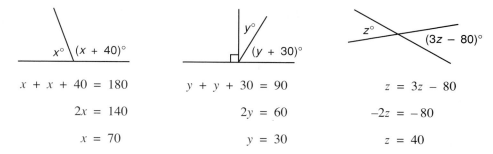

$$x + x + 40 = 180 \qquad y + y + 30 = 90 \qquad z = 3z - 80$$
$$2x = 140 \qquad\qquad 2y = 60 \qquad\qquad -2z = -80$$
$$x = 70 \qquad\qquad y = 30 \qquad\qquad z = 40$$

In the center we show two adjacent angles whose measures sum to 90°. We can use this fact to write an equation and solve for y. Two pairs of **vertical angles** are formed by intersecting lines. Vertical angles have equal measures. On the right we show two vertical angles, write an equation, and solve for z.

1.D
betweenness, tick marks, and assumptions

One point is said to lie **between** two other points only if the points lie on the same line (are collinear). When three points are collinear, one and only one of the points is between the other two.

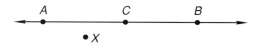

Thus, we can say that point C is between points A and B because point C belongs to the line segment determined by the two points A and B and is not an endpoint of this segment. Point X is not between points A and B because it is not on the same line (is not collinear) that contains points A and B.

We will use **tick marks** on the figures to designate segments of equal length and angles of equal measure.

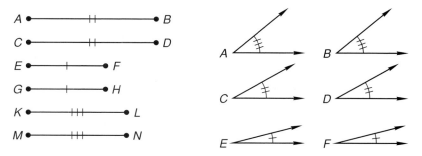

Here we have indicated the following equality of segment lengths: $AB = CD$, $EF = GH$, and $KL = MN$. The equality of angle measures indicated is $m\angle A = m\angle B$, $m\angle C = m\angle D$, and $m\angle E = m\angle F$.

In this book we will consider the formal proofs of geometry. We will use geometric figures in these proofs. When we do, some assumptions about the figures are permitted and others are not permitted. **It is permitted to assume that a line that appears to be a straight line is a straight line, but it is not permitted to assume that lines that appear to be perpendicular are perpendicular. Further, it is not permitted to assume that the measure of one angle or line segment is equal to, greater than, or less than the measure of another angle or line segment.** We list some permissible and impermissible assumptions on the following page.

PERMISSIBLE	NOT PERMISSIBLE
Straight lines are straight angles	Right angles
Collinearity of points	Equal lengths
Relative location of points	Equal angles
Betweenness of points	Relative size of segments and angles
	Perpendicular or parallel lines

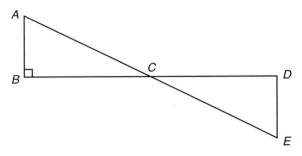

In the figure above we may assume the following:

1. That the four line segments shown are segments of straight lines
2. That point C lies on line BD and on line AE
3. That point C lies between points B and D and points A and E

We may not assume:

4. That $\overline{AB}$ and $\overline{DE}$ are of equal length
5. That $\overline{BC}$ and $\overline{CD}$ are of equal length
6. That $\angle D$ is a right angle
7. That $m\angle A$ equals $m\angle E$
8. That $\overline{AB}$ and $\overline{DE}$ are parallel

1.E

triangles

Triangles have three sides and three angles. The sum of the measures of the angles in any triangle is 180°. Triangles can be classified according to the measures of their angles or according to the lengths of their sides. If the measures of all angles are equal, the triangle is **equiangular.** The Greek prefix *iso-* means "equal" and the Greek word *gonia* means "angle." We put them together to form *isogonic*, which means "equal angles." An **isogonic triangle** is a triangle in which the measures of at least two angles are equal. If one angle is a right angle, the triangle is a **right triangle.** If all angles have a measure less than 90°, the triangle is an **acute triangle.** If one angle has a measure greater than 90°, the triangle is an **obtuse triangle.** An **oblique triangle** is a triangle that is not a right triangle. Thus, acute triangles and obtuse triangles are also oblique triangles.

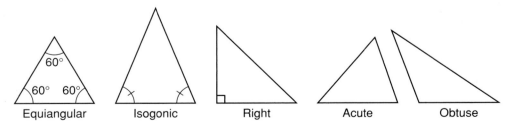

Triangles are also classified according to the relative lengths of their sides. The Latin prefix *equi-* means "equal" and the Latin word *latus* means "side." We put them together to form *equilateral*, which means "equal sides." An **equilateral triangle** is a triangle in which the lengths of all sides are equal. Since the Greek prefix *iso-* means "equal" and the Greek word *skelos* means "leg," we can put them together to form *isosceles*, which means "equal legs." An **isosceles triangle** is a triangle that has at least two sides of equal length. If all the sides of a triangle have different lengths, the triangle is called a **scalene triangle.**

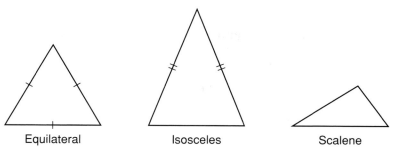

| Equilateral | Isosceles | Scalene |

The lengths of sides of a triangle and the measures of the angles opposite these sides are related. If the lengths of the sides are equal, then the measures of angles opposite these sides are also equal. This means that every isogonic triangle is also an isosceles triangle and that every isosceles triangle is also an isogonic triangle. Every equilateral triangle is also an equiangular triangle and every equiangular triangle is also an equilateral triangle. If the measure of an angle in a triangle is greater than the measure of a second angle, the length of the side opposite the angle is greater than the length of the side opposite the second angle. The sum of the measures of the angles of any triangle is 180°.

1.F

transversals; alternate and corresponding angles

We remember that two lines in a plane are called **parallel lines** if they never intersect. A **transversal** is a line that cuts or intersects one or more other lines in the same plane. **When two parallel lines are cut by a transversal, two groups of four angles whose measures are equal are formed. The four small (acute) angles have equal measures, and the four large (obtuse) angles have equal measures. If the transversal is perpendicular to the parallel lines, all eight angles are right angles.**

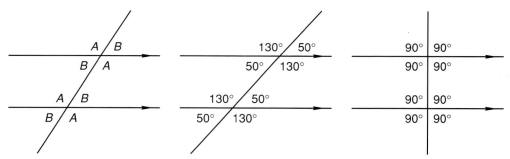

In the figures above, note the use of arrowheads to indicate that lines are parallel. In the left-hand figure, we have named the small angles *B* and the large angles *A*. In the center figure, we show a specific example where the small angles are 50° angles and the large angles are 130° angles. Also, note that **in each case, the sum of the measures of a small angle and a large angle is 180° because together the two angles always form a straight line.** The angles have special names that are useful. The four angles between the parallel lines are called **interior angles,** and the four angles outside the parallel lines are called **exterior angles.**

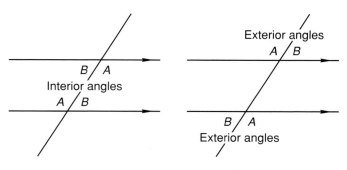

Angles on opposite sides of the transversal are called **alternate angles.** There are two pairs of **alternate interior angles** and two pairs of **alternate exterior angles,** as shown below. It is important to note that **if two parallel lines are cut by a transversal, then each pair of alternate interior angles has equal measures and each pair of alternate exterior angles also has equal measures.**

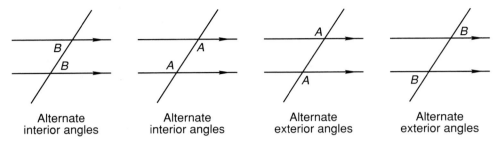

| Alternate interior angles | Alternate interior angles | Alternate exterior angles | Alternate exterior angles |

Corresponding angles are angles that have corresponding positions. There are four pairs of corresponding angles, as shown below. It is important to note that **if two parallel lines are cut by a transversal, then each pair of corresponding angles has equal measures.**

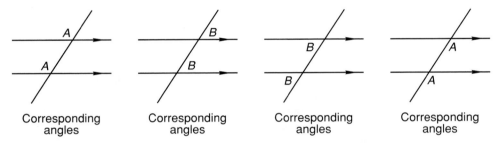

| Corresponding angles | Corresponding angles | Corresponding angles | Corresponding angles |

We summarize below some properties of parallel lines. In the statements below, remember that saying two angles are congruent is the same as saying that the angles have equal measures.

PROPERTIES OF PARALLEL LINES

1. If two parallel lines are cut by a transversal, then each pair of corresponding angles is congruent.
2. If two parallel lines are cut by a transversal, then each pair of alternate interior angles is congruent.
3. If two parallel lines are cut by a transversal, then each pair of alternate exterior angles is congruent.

We also state below the conditions for two lines to be parallel.

CONDITIONS FOR LINES TO BE PARALLEL

1. If two lines are cut by a transversal so that a pair of corresponding angles is congruent, then the lines are parallel.
2. If two lines are cut by a transversal so that a pair of alternate interior angles is congruent, then the lines are parallel.
3. If two lines are cut by a transversal so that a pair of alternate exterior angles is congruent, then the lines are parallel.

Some geometry textbooks will **postulate,** or in other words assume true without proof, one of the statements in each of the boxes and then prove the other statements as theorems. We decide to postulate all the statements in the boxes and use these statements to prove other geometric facts later.

When two transversals intersect three parallel lines, the parallel lines cut the transversals into line segments whose lengths are proportional, as we will show in Lesson 8. This fact will allow us to find the length of segment x in the diagram on the left. These segments are proportional. This means that the ratios of the lengths are equal.

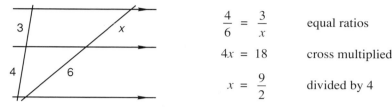

$$\frac{4}{6} = \frac{3}{x}$$ equal ratios

$$4x = 18$$ cross multiplied

$$x = \frac{9}{2}$$ divided by 4

We decided to put the lengths of the segments on the left on the top and the lengths of the segments on the right on the bottom.

1.G

area and sectors of circles

The area of a rectangle equals the product of the length and the width. The **altitude,** or **height,** of a triangle is the perpendicular distance from either the base of the triangle or an extension of the base to the opposite vertex. Any one of the three sides can be designated as the base. The altitude can (a) be one of the sides of the triangle, (b) fall inside the triangle, or (c) fall outside the triangle. When the altitude falls outside the triangle, we have to extend the base so that the altitude can be drawn. This extension of the base is not part of the length of the base. The area of any triangle equals one half the product of the base and the altitude.

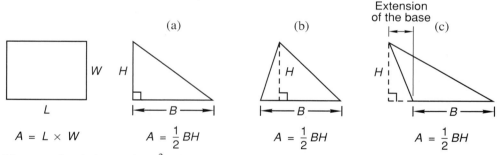

Extension of the base   (c)

$$A = L \times W \qquad A = \frac{1}{2}BH \qquad A = \frac{1}{2}BH \qquad A = \frac{1}{2}BH$$

The area of a circle equals πr^2, where r represents the **radius** of the circle. The perimeter of a circle is called the **circumference** of the circle and equals the product of π and the diameter of the circle. The length of the diameter equals twice the length of the radius.

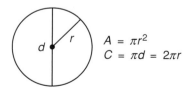

$$A = \pi r^2$$
$$C = \pi d = 2\pi r$$

An **arc** is two points on a circle and all the points on the circle between them. If we draw two radii to connect the endpoints of the arc to the center of the circle, the area enclosed is called a **sector** of the circle.

We define the degree measure of the arc to be the same as the degree measure of the **central angle** formed by the two radii. There are 360° in a circle. One degree of arc is $\frac{1}{360}$ of the circumference of the circle. Eighteen degrees of arc is $\frac{18}{360}$ of the circumference of the circle. The sector designated by 18° of arc is $\frac{18}{360}$ of the area of the circle. The length of an 18° arc is $\frac{18}{360}$ of the circumference of the circle. The radius of the circle shown below is 5 cm, so the area of the 18° sector is $\frac{18}{360}$ times the area of the whole circle. The length of an 18° arc is $\frac{18}{360}$ times the circumference of the whole circle.

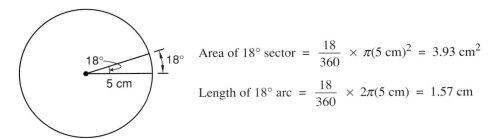

Area of 18° sector $= \dfrac{18}{360} \times \pi(5 \text{ cm})^2 = 3.93 \text{ cm}^2$

Length of 18° arc $= \dfrac{18}{360} \times 2\pi(5 \text{ cm}) = 1.57 \text{ cm}$

example 1.1   The measure of the central angle of the unshaded sector is 126°. The radius of the circle is $2\sqrt{5}$ m. Find the area of the shaded region of the circle.

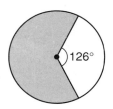

solution   Since the full measure of a circle is 360°, the measure of the central angle of the shaded sector of the circle is 360° minus 126°, or 234°. The area of the shaded sector equals the product of the fraction of the central angle that is shaded and the area of the whole circle.

$$\text{Area of 234° sector} = \frac{234}{360} \times \pi(2\sqrt{5} \text{ m})^2 = \mathbf{13\pi \text{ m}^2}$$

1.H

concept review problems

Virtually all the problems in the problem sets are designed to afford the student practice with concepts or skills. Often, a problem may be contrived so that it requires the use of a particular technique or the application of a particular concept. However, there are some problems that defy simple classification. These may be problems that appear very difficult but can be easily solved with clever reasoning or a "trick." These may be problems that can be solved using either very long and tedious calculations or may be very easily solved through some "shortcut" requiring a deep understanding of the underlying concepts. Knowing what "shortcuts" and "tricks" to use requires experience. We do not believe one can become a good problem solver by reading about the philosophy of problem solving. One learns the art of problem solving by solving problems. What we will do is provide conceptually oriented review problems at the end of many problem sets to permit exposure to a wide spectrum of problems, many of which appear in some similar form on standardized exams such as the ACT and SAT. Through time and practice, students gain confidence, experience, and competence solving these types of problems.

Problems that compare the values of quantities come in many forms and can be used to provide practice in mathematical reasoning. In these problems, a statement will be made about two quantities A and B. **The correct answer is A if quantity A is greater and is B if quantity B is greater. The correct answer is C if the quantities are equal and is D if insufficient information is provided to determine which quantity is greater.**

example 1.2   Let x and y be real numbers. If $x > 0$ and $y < 0$, compare: A. $x + y$ B. $x - y$

solution   We will subtract expression B from expression A. If the result is a positive number, then A is greater. If the result is a negative number, then B is greater. If the result is zero, the expressions have equal value and the answer is C. If insufficient information is provided to determine which quantity is greater, the answer is D. Therefore, we have

$$(x + y) - (x - y) = 2y$$

We were told that $y < 0$, so $2y$ is a negative number. Thus,

$$(x + y) - (x - y) < 0 \qquad \text{expression}$$
$$x + y < x - y \qquad \text{added } x - y \text{ to both sides}$$

Therefore, quantity B is greater, so the answer is **B**.

example 1.3   Let x and y be real numbers. If $1 < x < 6$ and $1 < y < 6$, compare: A. $x - y$ B. $y - x$

solution   We are given that x is greater than 1 and less than 6 and y is greater than 1 and less than 6. There are three cases that we must consider:

1. If $x < y$, then $x - y$ is a negative number and $y - x$ is a positive number.
2. If $x > y$, then $x - y$ is a positive number and $y - x$ is a negative number.
3. If $x = y$, then $x - y = 0$ and $y - x = 0$.

We can see that if $1 < x < 6$ and $1 < y < 6$, then all three cases are possible. Therefore, insufficient information is provided to determine which quantity is greater, so the answer is **D**.

example 1.4   Given two intersecting lines with angles k, l, m, and n, as shown, compare:
A. $(k + l + m)^\circ$ B. $(180 - n)^\circ$

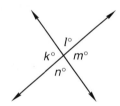

solution   We know that a straight angle has a measure of 180°. Therefore, we have

$$
\begin{array}{ll}
k + l = 180 & \text{straight angle} \\
\underline{m + n = 180} & \text{straight angle} \\
k + l + m + n = 360 & \text{added}
\end{array}
$$

Thus,

$$k + l + m = 360 - n = 180 + (180 - n)$$

Thus,

$$k + l + m > 180 - n$$

Therefore, quantity A is greater, so the answer is **A**.

example 1.5   Given $\overline{ZW}$ and $\overline{XY}$ are parallel, as shown.

Compare: A. Area of $\triangle WXY$

    B. Area of $\triangle ZXY$

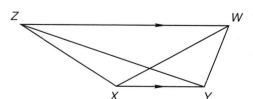

solution   We know that the area of any triangle equals one half the product of the base and the altitude. For both triangles, $\overline{XY}$ is the base. Also, since $\overline{ZW}$ is parallel to $\overline{XY}$, the altitudes of the two triangles are of equal length. Thus, the areas of the two triangles $\triangle WXY$ and $\triangle ZXY$ are equal. Therefore, the quantities are equal, so the answer is **C**.

**problem set
1**

1. Find the measure of angle A if five times the complement of angle A is $150°$ greater than the supplement of angle A. Remember that the complement of angle A has a measure of $90° - A$ degrees and the supplement of angle A has a measure of $180° - A$ degrees.

2. Find the measure of angle B if seven times the complement of angle B exceeds twice the supplement of angle B by $220°$.

3. Find an angle such that 4 times its complement equals $200°$.

4. Twenty percent of the molybdenum fused. If 1420 grams did not fuse, what was the total mass of molybdenum used?

5. The ratio of pusillanimous brave men to oxymorons on the battlefield is 17 to 2. If the total of both on the battlefield is 342, how many are oxymorons?

Simplify:

6. $\dfrac{2^{-3}x^{0}(x^{2})}{x^{-3}xy^{-3}y}$

7. $-(-3 - 2) + 4(-2) + \dfrac{1}{-2^{-3}} - (-2)^{-3}$

8. Simplify by adding like terms: $\dfrac{xy}{y^{-2}} - \dfrac{3x^{4}y^{4}}{x^{3}y} + \dfrac{7xy^{-2}}{xy^{-3}}$

9. Expand: $\dfrac{x^{0}y^{-2}x}{x^{3}y}\left(\dfrac{x^{2}y}{m} - \dfrac{3x^{4}y^{2}}{m^{-2}}\right)$

10. Solve: $3^{0}(2x - 5) + (-x - 5) = -3(x^{0} - 2)$

11. Evaluate: $xy - x(x - y^{0})$ if $x = 2$ and $y = -\dfrac{1}{2}$

12. Add: $\dfrac{2}{x} + \dfrac{x}{x + 1}$

13. Multiply: $(2x + 3)(2x^{2} + 2x + 2)$

14. Use elimination to solve: $\begin{cases} N_{N} + N_{D} = 50 \\ 5N_{N} + 10N_{D} = 450 \end{cases}$

15. Use substitution to solve: $\begin{cases} N_{P} + N_{D} = 50 \\ N_{P} + 10N_{D} = 140 \end{cases}$

16. Use N_{N} as the variable for the number of nickels and N_{D} as the variable for the number of dimes to write two equations that correspond to the following statement and solve for N_{N} and N_{D}:

    The number of nickels exceeds the number of dimes by 7. The total value of the coins is $1.55.

17. What do we mean when we say that two line segments are congruent?

18. What is an acute angle?

19. Find x and y.

20. Find A, B, and C.

21. Find A, B, and C.

22. Find x.

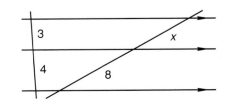

23. The radius of the circle is π cm. The base of the triangle is π cm. The area of the circle equals the area of the triangle. What is the height of the triangle?

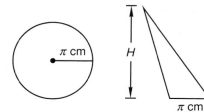

24. An equilateral triangle has an altitude of $2\sqrt{3}$ in. and a perimeter of 12 in. What is the area of the triangle?

25. An equilateral triangle has an altitude of $3\sqrt{6}$ cm and an area of $18\sqrt{3}$ cm^2. What is the perimeter of the triangle?

26. The central angle of the shaded sector measures 40°. The radius of the circle is $3\sqrt{3}$ meters. Find the area of the shaded sector.

27. In this figure, points A and B are the centers of two smaller circles and lie on a diameter of the big circle. The two smaller circles are tangent to the larger circle and to each other. Find the area of the shaded region of this figure. Dimensions are in centimeters.

28. In the figure shown, all adjacent circles are tangent to each other and the outer circles are tangent to the square. The sum of the areas of the nine circles is 52π m^2. The circles have equal areas. What is the area of the shaded portion of the figure?

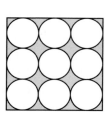

CONCEPT REVIEW PROBLEMS **29.** Compare: A. $\sqrt{\dfrac{1}{4}} + \sqrt{\dfrac{1}{25}}$ B. $\sqrt{\dfrac{1}{4} + \dfrac{1}{25}}$

30. Let x and y be real numbers. If $x > 0$ and $y > 0$, compare: A. $y - x$ B. $y + x$

LESSON 2   *More on Area • Cylinders and Prisms •*
Cones and Pyramids • Spheres

2.A

more on area   On the left below we show a rectangle whose length is 3 units and whose width is 2 units. On the right we use this information to draw parallel and perpendicular lines so that the rectangle is separated into six squares whose sides are 1 unit long.

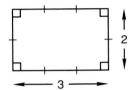   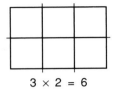

If we do this for many rectangles whose lengths and widths are different, we note that every time the number of squares we get equals the product of the length times the width. So we see that every rectangle has a property that can be associated with a number that equals the product of the length and the width. Mathematicians have decided to call this number the **area** of the rectangle. **We define the area of a rectangle to be the number that equals the product of the length of the rectangle and the width of the rectangle.** If we use centimeters as the measure of length and width, the area will tell us the number of square centimeters that will cover the surface of the rectangle. If we use feet as the measure of length and width, the area will tell us the number of square feet necessary to cover the surface of the rectangle.

We can use the definition of the area of a rectangle to help us find the areas of other planar (flat) geometric figures. We have been told that the area of any triangle equals one half the product of the base and the altitude regardless of the shape of the triangle. The proof of this is interesting and not difficult. We remember that if two figures are geometrically identical, we say that the figures are congruent.

In the figure below we show a rectangle whose sides have lengths B and H, so the area of the rectangle is BH. The diagonal D divides the rectangles into two right triangles whose bases are B and whose heights are H. We remember (and will discuss again in Lesson 9) that two triangles are geometrically identical (congruent) if the lengths of the sides in one triangle are the same as the lengths of the sides in the other triangle. Thus, the triangles are congruent by the side-side-side congruency postulate. Therefore, the area of each triangle is $\frac{1}{2}BH$.

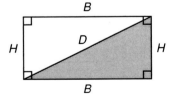

Triangles are congruent by *SSS*.

Area of each triangle is $\dfrac{1}{2}BH$.

This proves that the area of a right triangle is one half the product of the lengths of the sides that form the right angle.

$$\text{Area of a right triangle } = \frac{1}{2}BH$$

For all triangles, the area equals one half the product of the side that is chosen as the base and the perpendicular distance from the base to the opposite vertex. Any one of the three sides can be called the base. Sometimes the altitude falls in the interior of the triangle and sometimes it falls outside the triangle. If we choose side B as the base in the triangle on the left, the altitude falls in the interior of the triangle, as we show in the center figure.

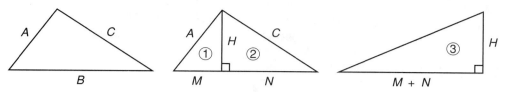

The altitude H forms two right triangles named ① and ②. We note that B equals $M + N$. We can show that the sum of the areas of triangles ① and ② equals the area of triangle ③ on the right.

$$\text{Area of } \Delta① \;=\; \frac{1}{2}MH$$

$$\text{Area of } \Delta② \;=\; \frac{1}{2}NH$$

$$\text{Total area} \;=\; \frac{1}{2}MH + \frac{1}{2}NH$$

Next, we factor $\frac{1}{2}H$ from each term on the right and get

$$\text{Total area} \;=\; \frac{1}{2}H(M + N) \qquad \text{factored}$$

But $M + N$ equals B, and if we substitute B for $M + N$, we get

$$\text{Total area} \;=\; \frac{1}{2}H(B) \qquad \text{substituted}$$

$$\;=\; \frac{1}{2}BH \qquad \text{switched } B \text{ and } H$$

If we choose side B as the base in the triangle on the left below, we see that the altitude is measured from an extension of the base, as we show in the center figure.

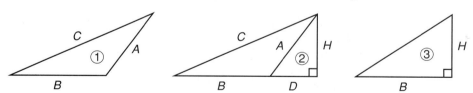

We can show that the area of triangle ① equals the area of the big right triangle in the center figure diminished by the area of triangle ② and equals the area of triangle ③, which equals $\frac{1}{2}BH$.

$$\text{Area of large right triangle} \;=\; \frac{1}{2}(B + D)H$$

$$\;=\; \frac{1}{2}BH + \frac{1}{2}DH$$

The area of triangle ② equals $\frac{1}{2}DH$. If we subtract the area of triangle ② from the area of the big right triangle, we get the area of triangle ①.

$$\text{Area of triangle } ① \;=\; \frac{1}{2}BH + \frac{1}{2}DH - \frac{1}{2}DH \;=\; \frac{1}{2}BH$$

Thus we have proved that the area of any triangle equals one half the product of the base and the altitude or height.

$$\text{Area of any triangle} \;=\; \frac{1}{2}BH$$

2.B
cylinders and prisms

We define a **cylindrical surface** to be the surface swept out by a line which is always parallel to a given line and moves along a curved path called the **directrix.** Every position of the moving line is called an **element** of the surface. If the directrix is an open curve, as we show in the third figure, the surface is called an **open surface.** If the directrix is a closed curve, the surface is called a **closed surface,** as we show on the right.

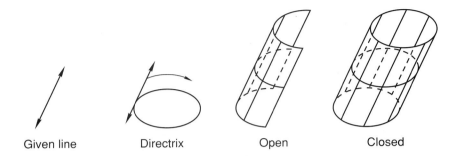

Given line   Directrix   Open   Closed

A *cylinder* is a geometric solid determined by two **parallel planes** that intersect all the elements of a closed cylindrical surface. The end surfaces of the cylinder are called the **bases** of the cylinder. The bases of a cylinder are congruent (geometrically identical).

If the bases are perpendicular to the cylindrical surface, the cylinder is called a **right cylinder** or a **right solid.** The shapes of bases determine the shape of the cylinder. If each base is a circle, we have a **circular cylinder.** If the base is an ellipse, we have an **elliptical cylinder.** On the left below we show a **right circular cylinder.** If the base is symmetrical about a point, the point is called the **center** of the base. The line that connects the centers of the two bases is called the **axis** of the cylinder. **Oblique cylinders** are cylinders whose bases are not perpendicular to the sides. On the right we show an oblique circular cylinder.

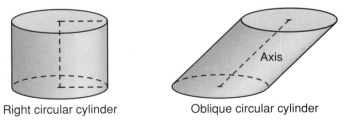

Right circular cylinder   Oblique circular cylinder

If the bases of a cylinder are polygons, the cylinder can also be called a **prism.**

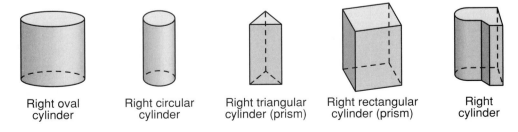

Right oval cylinder   Right circular cylinder   Right triangular cylinder (prism)   Right rectangular cylinder (prism)   Right cylinder

The right cylinder on the left is a **right oval cylinder** because the top and bottom surfaces (faces) are identical ovals whose surfaces are parallel. The next cylinder is a **right circular cylinder.** The bases of this cylinder are identical circles whose surfaces are parallel. The third cylinder is a **right triangular cylinder** with identical bases that are triangles whose surfaces are parallel. This cylinder can be called a **prism** because its base is a polygon. The **right rectangular cylinder** is also a prism.

We describe in the box below how to compute the volume of a cylinder. Since a prism is a special type of cylinder, what is stated also applies to prisms.

VOLUME OF CYLINDERS AND PRISMS

The volume of a cylinder or a prism is equal to the product of the area of a base and the perpendicular distance between the bases.

The statement above applies to all cylinders, whether or not the cylinder is a right cylinder. For example, the statement applies to all the cylinders shown below.

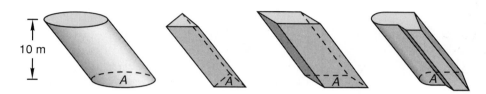

If the perpendicular distance between the base of each cylinder shown above is 10 m and if the area of each base is 9 m², the volume of each cylinder is 90 m³.

$$\text{Volume of cylinder (prism)} \ = \ \text{area of base} \ \times \ \text{height}$$

$$= \ 9 \, \text{m}^2 \ \times \ 10 \, \text{m} \ = \ 90 \, \text{m}^3$$

We define the **lateral surface area** of a cylinder or a prism to be the area of all external surfaces except the bases. Unfortunately, there is no simple way of determining the lateral surface area of an oblique cylinder or oblique prism. However, we are able to easily compute the lateral surface area of a right cylinder or a right prism, as we show in the box below.

LATERAL SURFACE AREA OF
RIGHT CYLINDERS AND RIGHT PRISMS

The lateral surface area of a right cylinder or a right prism is the perimeter of a base multiplied by the height (where the height is defined to be the perpendicular distance between the bases).

To find the total surface area of a cylinder or a prism, we add the areas of the bases to the lateral surface area.

example 2.1 The base of a right cylinder 10 centimeters high is shown. Find the surface area of the right cylinder. Dimensions are in centimeters.

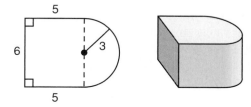

solution The surface area equals the sum of the areas of the two equal bases and the lateral surface area.

Area of one base =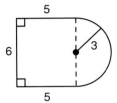

$$= (l \times w) + \frac{\pi r^2}{2}$$

$$= (5 \text{ cm} \times 6 \text{ cm}) + \frac{\pi(3 \text{ cm})^2}{2}$$

$$= 30 \text{ cm}^2 + \frac{9\pi}{2} \text{ cm}^2 = 44.14 \text{ cm}^2$$

The lateral surface area of any right cylinder equals the perimeter of a base times the height. We can see this if we cut our solid and mash it flat. We get

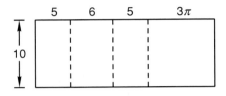

The length of the curved side equals the circumference of a whole circle divided by 2.

$$\text{Length of curve} = \frac{\pi d}{2} = \frac{\pi(2r)}{2} = \pi r = 3\pi \text{ cm}$$

The perimeter of the figure is

$$\text{Perimeter} = 5 \text{ cm} + 6 \text{ cm} + 5 \text{ cm} + 3\pi \text{ cm} = 25.425 \text{ cm}$$

Thus, the lateral surface area is the area of the rectangle.

$$\text{Lateral surface area} = (10 \text{ cm})(25.425 \text{ cm}) = 254.25 \text{ cm}^2$$

We add this to the surface area of both bases to get the total surface area,

Base area	44.14 cm²
Base area	44.14 cm²
Lateral surface area	254.25 cm²
Total surface area	**342.53 cm²**

example 2.2 Find the surface area of this right prism.

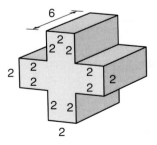

solution The total surface area of a right prism is the sum of all the surface areas of the right prism. Each base can be divided into 5 squares and the area of one base can be found by adding the areas of the squares.

$$\text{Area of one base} = 5(2 \times 2)$$

$$= 20 \text{ square units}$$

The lateral surface area is that of 12 sides that measure 2 × 6.

Lateral surface area = 12(2 × 6) = 144 square units

The total surface area is the area of both bases plus the lateral surface area.

Surface area = (2 × 20) + 144 = **184 square units**

For those who like formulas, we remember that the lateral surface area is the perimeter of a base times the height. The perimeter is 24 units and the height is 6 units, so we check our lateral surface area as follows.

Lateral surface area = 24 × 6 = 144 square units

2.C

cones and pyramids

The area of the rectangle on the left is the product of the length, 6 units, times the width, 4 units, which equals 24 square units.

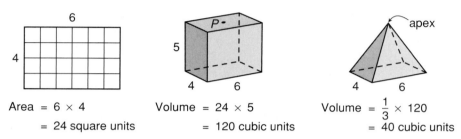

Area = 6 × 4   Volume = 24 × 5   Volume = $\frac{1}{3}$ × 120
    = 24 square units   = 120 cubic units   = 40 cubic units

The **right solid** or **right cylinder** shown in the center figure has the 6-by-4 rectangle as the upper base and the lower base. The volume of the right cylinder (right solid) equals the area of a base times the height, which is 5 units, so the volume of the right cylinder (right solid) is 24 times 5, or 120 cubic units.

If a point P is selected in the plane of the upper base and connected to the points on the lower base with an infinite number of lines, the **cone** shown on the right is formed. **The volume of any cone is one third the volume of the right cylinder that contains it,** so the volume of this cone is 40 cubic units. A polygon is a planar closed geometric figure whose sides are straight line segments, as we will discuss again in Lesson 3. If the base of a cone is a polygon, the cone is also called a **pyramid.** Since a rectangle is a polygon, this cone is also a pyramid. Since the volume of a right solid equals the product of the area of the base and the height, the volume of any cone or pyramid is one third of this product.

VOLUME OF A CONE OR PYRAMID

The volume of any cone or pyramid equals one third the product of the area of the base and the height.

The figure on the left below is the lower base and the upper base of the right solid (right cylinder) shown in the center. The dimensions of the base are shown in inches and the height of the solid is 12 inches.

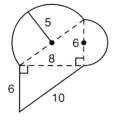   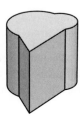   

The area of the base can be computed to be

$$\text{Area of base} = 24 \text{ in.}^2 + 24 \text{ in.}^2 + \frac{9\pi}{2} \text{ in.}^2 + \frac{25\pi}{2} \text{ in.}^2 = 101.41 \text{ in.}^2$$

To find the volume of the right solid, we multiply by 12 inches.

$$\text{Volume of right solid} = \left(101.41 \text{ in.}^2\right)(12 \text{ in}) = 1216.92 \text{ in.}^3$$

The apex of the cone can be any point in the plane of the top base, and the volume of any of these cones so formed is one third the volume of the right solid.

$$\text{Volume of cone} = \frac{1}{3}\left(1216.92 \text{ in.}^3\right) = 405.64 \text{ in.}^3$$

example 2.3   The base of a cone is shown. The dimensions are in meters. If the cone is 6 meters high, what is its volume?

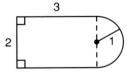

solution   The area of the base is the sum of the area of the 3-meter-by-2-meter rectangle and the semicircle whose radius is 1 meter.

$$\text{Area of base} = (3 \text{ m} \times 2 \text{ m}) + \frac{\pi(1 \text{ m})^2}{2}$$

$$= 6 \text{ m}^2 + \frac{\pi}{2} \text{ m}^2 = 7.57 \text{ m}^2$$

The volume of the cone is equal to one third the product of the area of the base and the height.

$$\text{Volume} = \frac{1}{3}(7.57 \text{ m}^2)6 \text{ m} = \textbf{15.14 m}^3$$

surface area of cones   The base of the cone on the left is a circle and the apex lies on the perpendicular segment that passes through the center of the circle. This cone is called a **right circular cone.** The shortest distance from the apex to a point on the circle is called the **slant height** l of the cone. The lateral surface area of a right circular cone is the product of pi, the radius of the circle, and the slant height, or $\pi r l$.

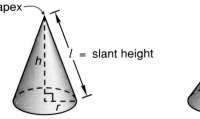 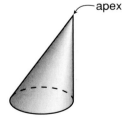 

Right circular cone
Lateral surface area = $\pi r l$ Oblique circular cone   Cone

The apex of the cone in the center is not directly above the center of the circle and this cone is called an **oblique circular cone.** The cone on the right has no special name. There is no general method for determining the lateral surface area of a cone that is not a right circular cone.

A pyramid is classified by the shape of its base. We will confine our discussion of pyramids to regular pyramids, which are pyramids whose bases are regular polygons (all sides of equal length and all angles of equal measure) and whose apex is directly above the center of the base of the pyramid. The altitude or height of a pyramid is the perpendicular distance from the base to the apex.

Regular	Regular	Regular
triangular	quadrilateral	pentagonal
pyramid	pyramid	pyramid

The lateral surfaces of a pyramid are called the **faces** of the pyramid. The **slant height** of a regular pyramid is the distance from the apex to the midpoint of any side of the base.

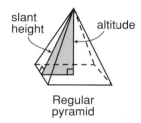

Regular
pyramid

The surface area of a pyramid is the sum of the area of the base and the triangular faces of the pyramid.

example 2.4   The radius of the base of a right circular cone is 8 cm. The slant height of the cone is 10 cm. Find the surface area of the cone.

solution   The surface area of the right circular cone is the area of the base plus the lateral surface area. We note that the area of the base is the area of a circle. Also, the formula for the lateral surface area of a right circular cone is $\pi r l$, where l is the slant height of the cone. Therefore, we have

$$\text{Surface area} = \pi r^2 + \pi r l$$
$$= \pi(8\text{ cm})^2 + \pi(8\text{ cm})(10\text{ cm})$$
$$= \mathbf{144\pi \text{ cm}^2}$$

example 2.5   The volume of a right circular cone is 6π cm^3. The height of this right circular cone is 2 cm. Find the radius of the base of the cone.

solution   We remember that the volume of a right circular cone is equal to one third the product of the area of the base and the height.

$$\text{Volume} = \frac{1}{3}bh$$

Substituting in known values, we get

$$6\pi\text{ cm}^3 = \frac{1}{3}b(2\text{ cm})$$
$$b = 9\pi\text{ cm}^2$$

The area of the base is the area of a circle, πr^2, so we have

$$9\pi \text{ cm}^2 = \pi r^2$$

Solving for r (note that we only take the positive value of r as only the positive value makes sense), we get

$$r^2 = 9 \text{ cm}^2$$

$$r = 3 \text{ cm}$$

The radius of the base of the cone equals **3 cm.**

example 2.6   The base of a regular pyramid is a square with each side measuring 4 cm. The slant height of the pyramid is 5 cm. Find the surface area of the pyramid.

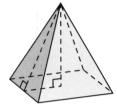

solution   The surface area of the pyramid is the area of the base added to the lateral surface area. The area of the base is simply the area of a square with sides of length 4 cm.

$$\text{Area of base} = (4 \text{ cm})^2 = 16 \text{ cm}^2$$

The lateral surface area is four times the area of a lateral face. Each lateral face looks as follows:

The area of each lateral face is the area of a triangle whose height is of length 5 cm and whose base is of length 4 cm.

$$\text{Area of a lateral face} = \text{area of triangle} = \frac{1}{2}(4 \text{ cm})(5 \text{ cm}) = 10 \text{ cm}^2$$

Thus, the lateral surface area is $4 \cdot 10 \text{ cm}^2 = 40 \text{ cm}^2$. Therefore, we have

$$\text{Total surface area} = \text{area of base} + \text{lateral surface area}$$

$$= 16 \text{ cm}^2 + 40 \text{ cm}^2$$

$$= \textbf{56 cm}^2$$

2.D

spheres   A **sphere** is a perfectly round, three-dimensional shape. All points on the surface of a sphere are the same distance from the center. This distance is the radius of the sphere.

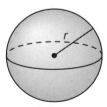

Sphere

The surface area of the sphere shown is equal to $4\pi r^2$, and the volume of the sphere shown is equal to $\frac{4}{3}\pi r^3$. Proof of these formulas is beyond the scope of this book and most people find them difficult to remember as they are not used often. A **mnemonic** is a memory aid. To remember the formula for the surface area of a sphere, we think of the sphere as a grapefruit. The surface area of the grapefruit is the same as the sum of four cross-sectional areas of a grapefruit.

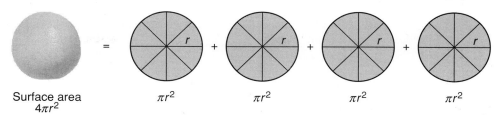

Surface area πr^2 πr^2 πr^2 πr^2
$4\pi r^2$

The volume of a sphere is exactly two thirds the volume of the smallest right circular cylinder into which the sphere fits. The radius of the cylinder equals the radius of the sphere, and the height of the cylinder is twice the radius of the sphere.

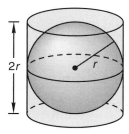

Volume of the sphere equals $\frac{2}{3}$ the volume of the cylinder

Area of base $= \pi r^2$

Volume of cylinder $= (2r)\pi r^2$

$\qquad\qquad\qquad = 2\pi r^3$

Volume of sphere $= \dfrac{2}{3}\left(2\pi r^3\right)$

$\qquad\qquad\qquad = \dfrac{4}{3}\pi r^3$

Close your eyes and try to remember this diagram. It will help you remember the formula for the volume of a sphere. The first proof of this method of finding the volume of a sphere is attributed to the Greek philosopher Archimedes (287–212 B.C.).

example 2.7   Find the surface area and volume of a sphere of radius 9 meters.

solution   For a sphere of radius r,

$$\text{Surface area} = 4\pi r^2$$

$$\text{Volume} = \frac{4}{3}\pi r^3$$

Substituting 9 meters for r, we get

$$\text{Surface area} = 4\pi(9 \text{ m})^2 = \mathbf{324\pi \ m^2}$$

$$\text{Volume} = \frac{4}{3}\pi(9 \text{ m})^3 = \mathbf{972\pi \ m^3}$$

example 2.8   Find the surface area of a sphere whose volume is $288\pi \text{ cm}^3$.

solution   The volume of a sphere of radius r is given by

$$\text{Volume} = \frac{4}{3}\pi r^3$$

Thus,

$$288\pi \text{ cm}^3 = \frac{4}{3}\pi r^3$$

$$216 \text{ cm}^3 = r^3$$

Solving for r, we get

$$r = 6 \text{ cm}$$

We are asked for the surface area, so we substitute 6 cm for r below.

$$\text{Surface area} = 4\pi r^2$$
$$= 4\pi(6 \text{ cm})^2$$
$$= 144\pi \text{ cm}^2$$

Therefore, the surface area of the sphere is **144π cm^2**.

problem set 2

1. The complement of angle A is 20° less than half the supplement of angle A. Find the measure of angle A.

2. Find an angle such that 3 times its supplement equals 450°.

3. Three times the number of reds is one less than twice the number of blues. If the sum of the reds and the blues is 13, how many are red and how many are blue?

4. The ratio of tulips to roses is 17 to 11. If there are 3444 tulips and roses in the garden, how many are tulips?

5. Forty percent of the fuel was consumed. If 1215 gallons of fuel remain, how much fuel was present initially?

Simplify:

6. $\dfrac{5^2\, a^3 b^{-2} a}{5^1 a^{-3} b^2 b^0}$

7. $-(-3 - 2) + 4(-5) - \dfrac{1}{4^{-2}} + (-4)^2$

8. Simplify by adding like terms: $\dfrac{4r^3 s}{r} - \dfrac{2s^2}{r^{-1}} - \dfrac{3r^3 s}{r^2 s^{-1}} + \dfrac{2r^4}{r^2 s^{-1}}$

9. Expand: $\dfrac{c^1 d^2 c}{c^{-1} d} \left(\dfrac{cd^3 f}{d^2 c^2} - \dfrac{c^{-1} dcd}{c^2 d} \right)$

10. Solve: $2^2(x - 7) + (3 - 2x) = -5(2x + 1)$

11. Evaluate: $x^2 + y^2 - xy(x + y)$ if $x = 1$ and $y = 2$

12. Multiply: $(3x - 2y)(x^2 + xy - y^2)$

13. Use elimination to solve: $\begin{cases} N_R + N_B = 70 \\ 2N_R + 3N_B = 190 \end{cases}$

14. Use substitution to solve: $\begin{cases} N_W + 2N_G = 7 \\ 3N_W - 5N_G = 10 \end{cases}$

15. The average of six numbers is 22. The numbers are 20, 17, 24, 18, 29, and x. Find x.

16. What is a scalene triangle?

17. Find x and y.

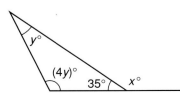

18. Find x, y, and z.

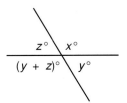

19. Find A, B, and C.

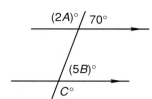

20. Find x.

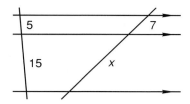

21. An equilateral triangle has a perimeter of 24 m and an area of $16\sqrt{3}$ m^2. Find the altitude of the triangle.

22. In the circle shown, O is the center. The radius of the circle is 5 meters. Find the area of the shaded sectors.

23. In this figure, points C and D are the centers of two smaller circles and lie on a diameter of the big circle. The two smaller circles are tangent to the larger circle and to each other. Find the area of the shaded region of this figure. Dimensions are in meters.

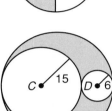

24. The volume of a sphere equals two thirds the volume of the smallest right circular cylinder into which the sphere fits. The first proof of this method of finding the volume of a sphere is attributed to the Greek philosopher Archimedes (287–212 B.C.). Find the volume of the smallest right circular cylinder that will hold a sphere whose radius is 4 meters. Find the volume of the sphere.

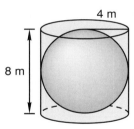

25. The volume of this circular cylinder is 588π cm^3. What is the height of the circular cylinder? Dimensions are in centimeters.

26. The base of a right cylinder is a right triangle joined by a 60° sector of a circle, as shown. The volume of this right cylinder is 9π cm^3. What is the height of the right cylinder? Dimensions are in centimeters.

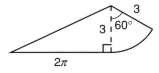
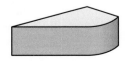

27. Find the volume of the cone whose base is shown and whose altitude is 8 meters.

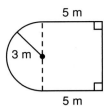

5 m

3 m

5 m

28. The figure below shows the base of a right cylinder that is 9 centimeters high. Find the volume of the right cylinder in cubic centimeters. Find the surface area of the right cylinder in square centimeters. Find the volume of a cone in cubic centimeters with the same height and base. Dimensions are in centimeters.

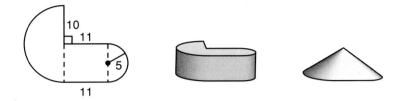

10

11

5

11

**CONCEPT REVIEW
PROBLEMS**

29. Compare: A. $\sqrt{\dfrac{4}{9}} + \sqrt{\dfrac{9}{16}}$ B. $\sqrt{\dfrac{4}{9} + \dfrac{9}{16}}$

30. Given: Rectangle *ABCD* and triangle *AED*, where *E* is arbitrarily chosen on segment *BC*

Compare: A. Area of △*AED*

B. Area of △*ACD*

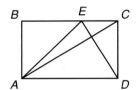

LESSON 3 *Pythagorean Theorem • Triangle Inequalities (1) •
Similar Polygons • Similar Triangles*

3.A

**Pythagorean
theorem**

The relationship of the lengths of the sides of a right triangle is attributed to the Greek mathematician Pythagoras who lived in the sixth century B.C. He was born on the Aegean island of Samos and was later associated with a school or brotherhood in the town of Crotona on the Italian peninsula. His statement of the Pythagorean theorem was geometric because algebra had not yet been invented. The geometric statement of the Pythagorean theorem was that the area of the square drawn on the hypotenuse of a right triangle equals the sum of the areas of the squares drawn on the other two sides. At the top of the next page on the left, we show a right triangle whose hypotenuse is 5 units long and whose sides have lengths of 3 units and 4 units, respectively. The area of the big square is 25 square units and the sum of the areas of the other two sides is also 25 square units.

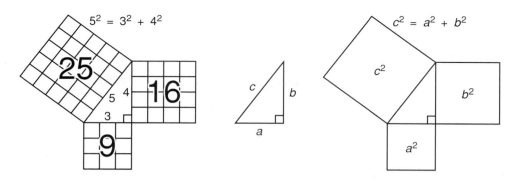

In the center we show a right triangle whose hypotenuse is c units long and whose sides have lengths of a units and b units, respectively. Above the figure on the right, we show the algebraic statement of the Pythagorean theorem.

3.B
triangle inequalities (1)

The sum of the lengths of any two sides of any triangle is greater than the length of the third side. This statement is called the **triangle inequality postulate** and applies to every triangle. In the triangle on the left below, we see that the sum of the lengths of any two sides is greater than the length of the third side. The other two triangle inequalities are illustrated in the center figure and in the figure on the right. If the area of the square drawn on the longest side of a triangle is greater than the sum of the areas of the squares drawn on the other two sides, the angle opposite the longest side has a measure greater than 90° and the triangle is an obtuse triangle, as we show in the center figure.

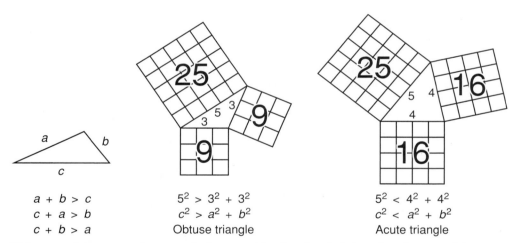

$a + b > c$	$5^2 > 3^2 + 3^2$	$5^2 < 4^2 + 4^2$
$c + a > b$	$c^2 > a^2 + b^2$	$c^2 < a^2 + b^2$
$c + b > a$	Obtuse triangle	Acute triangle

If the area of the square drawn on the longest side of a triangle is less than the sum of the areas of the squares drawn on the other two sides, the angle opposite the longest side has a measure less than 90° and the triangle is an acute triangle, as we show on the right. The inequalities

$$c^2 > a^2 + b^2 \qquad \text{and} \qquad c^2 < a^2 + b^2$$

are called the **Pythagorean inequalities.**

example 3.1   The lengths of the sides of a triangle are 7, 5, and 4, respectively. Is the triangle a right triangle, an acute triangle, or an obtuse triangle?

solution   The longest side is 7 and its square is 49. The squares of the other sides are 25 and 16. Since 49 is greater than the sum of 25 and 16, we know that the triangle is an **obtuse triangle.**

$$7^2 > 5^2 + 4^2$$

$$\text{or} \quad c^2 > a^2 + b^2$$

3.C

similar polygons

Polygons are simple, closed, coplanar geometric figures whose sides are straight lines. These figures are not polygons.

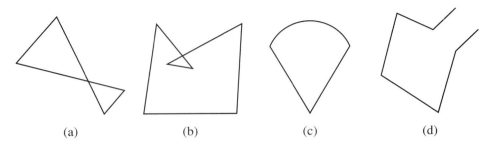

(a)   (b)   (c)   (d)

The sides of figures (a) and (b) cross, so these are not simple geometric figures. One "side" of (c) is not a straight line, and figure (d) is not a closed figure. The five figures shown below are all polygons. **Note that in each figure the number of vertices (corners) is the same as the number of sides.**

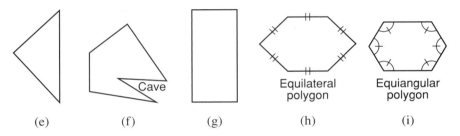

(e)   (f)   (g)   (h)   (i)

Figure (f) has an indentation that we can think of as a cave. Thus we call this a **concave polygon.** Any polygon that does not have a cave is a **convex polygon.** Any two points in the interior of a convex polygon can be connected with a line segment that does not cut a side of the polygon.

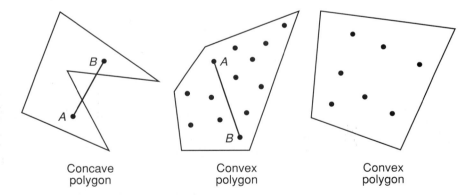

Concave   Convex   Convex
polygon   polygon   polygon

Informally, we say that two polygons are **similar** if each is a magnification or reduction of the other because they have the property of "sameness of shape." If we place the figure on the left on a copy machine whose magnification is set at 1.4, we get the figure on the right.

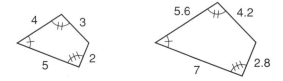

The measures of the corresponding angles in both figures are equal and the lengths of the corresponding sides are proportional. This means that the lengths have equal ratios. If we place the lengths of the sides in the right-hand figure over the lengths of the corresponding sides in the left-hand figure, the ratio is 1.4 in each case.

$$\frac{5.6}{4} = 1.4 \qquad \frac{4.2}{3} = 1.4 \qquad \frac{2.8}{2} = 1.4 \qquad \frac{7}{5} = 1.4$$

We say that the **scale factor** from left to right is 1.4 because we can multiply the length of any side in the left-hand figure by 1.4 and get the length of the corresponding side in the right-hand figure. The scale factor from right to left is the reciprocal of 1.4. If we multiply the sides in the right-hand figure by 1.4 "upside down," we get the length of the corresponding side in the left-hand figure.

$$5.6 \times \frac{1}{1.4} = 4 \qquad 4.2 \times \frac{1}{1.4} = 3 \qquad 2.8 \times \frac{1}{1.4} = 2 \qquad 7 \times \frac{1}{1.4} = 5$$

We remember that we define a polygon to be a closed path in a plane formed by the connected line segments $AB, BC, CD, \ldots$, which does not cut across itself. We call the defining points $A, B, C, D, \ldots$, the **vertices** of the polygon, and the connecting segments are called the **sides** of the polygon. On the left we show polygon $ABCDE$. On the right we draw a similar polygon $PQRST$.

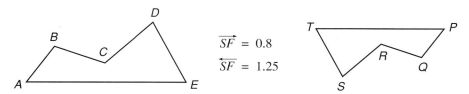

We note that the orientation of the polygon on the right is not the same as that of the polygon on the left, but the figures are still similar because the measure of angle P equals the measure of angle A. The measures of all other corresponding angles are equal. Also, the lengths of all corresponding sides are proportional. In these figures the scale factor from left to right is 0.8 and the scale factor from right to left is the reciprocal of 0.8, which is 1.25. If the angles in one polygon have the same measures as the angles in another polygon, the lengths of corresponding sides do not have to be proportional.

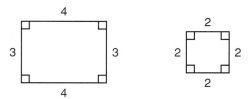

All the angles in the rectangle on the left and in the square on the right are right angles, but the lengths of the sides are not proportional because the ratios of the lengths of corresponding sides are not equal. For two polygons to be similar, there are two conditions: **The measures of corresponding angles must be equal, and the lengths of corresponding sides must also be proportional.**

3.D
similar triangles

Triangles are special polygons because if the corresponding angles in two triangles have equal measures, the lengths of the corresponding sides in the two triangles will be proportional. If the lengths of the corresponding sides in two triangles are proportional, the corresponding angles in the two triangles will have equal measures. Since one statement guarantees the other, we can use either statement as a definition of triangle similarity. **Mathematicians have decided to define similar triangles to be triangles whose corresponding angles have equal measures.** Because the properties of triangles are so important, much of the study of geometry is devoted to the study of these properties.

Consider the two triangles shown here.

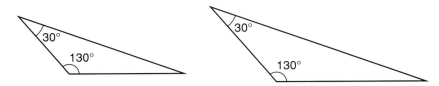

Both triangles have a 30° angle and a 130° angle. The sum of the measures of the angles of any triangle is 180 degrees, so we see that both unmarked angles must have measures of 20° because 30 plus 130 plus 20 equals 180. **From this we see that if two angles in one triangle have the same measures as two angles in another triangle, the triangles are similar because the other angles must also have equal measures.**

example 3.2   Find x and y.

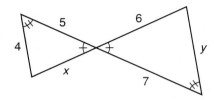

solution   The triangles are similar because the tick marks tell us that two angles in the left-hand triangle have the same measures as two angles in the right-hand triangle. We can use the scale factor or equal ratios to find the missing parts. We will solve this problem by using both methods.

The sides opposite the unmarked angles are 5 and 7, so these sides are corresponding sides. We can use this fact to find the scale factor from the left-hand triangle to the right-hand triangle.

$$5 \cdot \overrightarrow{SF} = 7 \qquad \overrightarrow{SF} \text{ is scale factor}$$

$$\overrightarrow{SF} = \frac{7}{5} \qquad \text{solved}$$

Thus the scale factor from left to right is $\frac{7}{5}$. We use this to find y.

$$y = 4 \cdot \overrightarrow{SF} \qquad \text{used scale factor}$$

$$y = 4 \cdot \frac{7}{5} \qquad \text{substituted}$$

$$y = \frac{28}{5} \qquad \text{multiplied}$$

The scale factor from right to left is $\frac{5}{7}$. We can use this to find x.

$$x = 6 \cdot \overleftarrow{SF} \qquad \text{used scale factor}$$

$$x = 6 \cdot \frac{5}{7} \qquad \text{substituted}$$

$$x = \frac{30}{7} \qquad \text{multiplied}$$

To use the ratio method we write the ratios of corresponding sides, which are the sides opposite angles of equal measure. From left to right, we write the ratios of the sides opposite the single tick-mark angles, the sides opposite the double tick-mark angles, and the sides opposite the unmarked angles. We decide to put the sides from the left-hand triangle on top.

$$\frac{4}{y} \qquad \frac{x}{6} \qquad \frac{5}{7}$$

All of the ratios have equal values. The third ratio has two numbers. We can equate the first ratio with the third ratio and solve for y.

$$\frac{4}{y} = \frac{5}{7} \qquad \text{equated ratios}$$

$$28 = 5y \qquad \text{cross multiplied}$$

$$y = \frac{28}{5} \qquad \text{solved}$$

Now we equate the center ratio with the third ratio and solve for x.

$$\frac{x}{6} = \frac{5}{7} \qquad \text{equated ratios}$$

$$7x = 30 \qquad \text{cross multiplied}$$

$$x = \frac{30}{7} \qquad \text{solved}$$

example 3.3   Find x, y, and z.

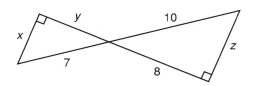

solution   The two angles in the center of the figure are vertical angles. Vertical angles have equal measures and both triangles have a right angle, so the triangles have two corresponding angles whose measures are equal. Thus the triangles are similar triangles. To solve, we decide to use the ratio method and put the sides from the triangle on the right on top. The ratios are

$$\frac{10}{7} \qquad \frac{8}{y} \qquad \frac{z}{x}$$

All of these ratios are equal. If we equate the two on the left, we can solve for y.

$$\frac{10}{7} = \frac{8}{y} \qquad \text{equated ratios}$$

$$10y = 56 \qquad \text{cross multiplied}$$

$$y = \mathbf{5.6} \qquad \text{solved}$$

We cannot use the ratio on the right because we do not know the value of either z or x. If we check the triangle on the right again, we see that we can use the Pythagorean theorem to solve for z.

$$c^2 = a^2 + b^2 \qquad \text{Pythagorean theorem}$$

$$10^2 = 8^2 + z^2 \qquad \text{substituted}$$

$$z^2 = 36 \qquad \text{simplified}$$

$$z = \mathbf{6} \qquad \text{solved}$$

Now we can use 6 for z in the right-hand ratio. We can equate the first ratio with the third ratio and solve for x.

$$\frac{10}{7} = \frac{6}{x} \qquad \text{equated ratios}$$

$$10x = 42 \qquad \text{cross multiplied}$$

$$x = \mathbf{4.2} \qquad \text{solved}$$

example 3.4   Find A, B, and C.

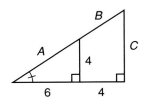

solution   This is an interesting problem because it allows us to practice using the Pythagorean theorem and also allows us to practice using similar triangles. There are two right triangles that also contain the angle with the single tick mark. Thus the triangles are similar triangles. It helps to draw the triangles separately.

  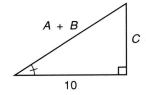

First we use the Pythagorean theorem to find A.

$$A^2 = 6^2 + 4^2 \qquad \text{used Pythagorean theorem}$$

$$A^2 = 52 \qquad \text{simplified}$$

$$A = \sqrt{52} = \mathbf{2\sqrt{13}} \qquad \text{solved}$$

Now we have the lengths shown below.

  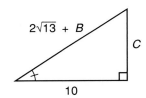

Next we write the ratios and put the sides from the triangle on the left on top. The ratios are

$$\frac{6}{10} \qquad \frac{4}{C} \qquad \frac{2\sqrt{13}}{2\sqrt{13} + B}$$

We equate the first two ratios and solve for C.

$$\frac{6}{10} = \frac{4}{C} \qquad \text{equated ratios}$$

$$6C = 40 \qquad \text{cross multiplied}$$

$$C = \frac{\mathbf{20}}{\mathbf{3}} \qquad \text{solved}$$

Now we equate the first ratio and the last ratio and solve for B.

$$\frac{6}{10} = \frac{2\sqrt{13}}{2\sqrt{13} + B} \qquad \text{equated ratios}$$

$$12\sqrt{13} + 6B = 20\sqrt{13} \qquad \text{cross multiplied}$$

$$6B = 8\sqrt{13} \qquad \text{simplified}$$

$$B = \frac{\mathbf{4\sqrt{13}}}{\mathbf{3}} \qquad \text{solved}$$

example 3.5   Find a, b, and h.

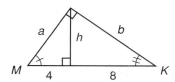

solution   This figure is unique and famous because it contains three similar triangles. On the left below
we show the big right triangle. On the right below we break out the two smaller right triangles.

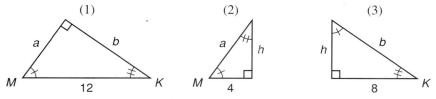

The big triangle shown on the left has a right angle and angles M and K. The small triangle in
the center has a right angle and angle M. Thus the measure of the upper angle must be the same
as that of angle K. The triangle on the right contains a right angle and angle K, so the other
angle must have the same measure as angle M. Therefore, the two smaller right triangles are
similar to the original right triangle and to each other. Thus, we can pair up any two of these
triangles, write the ratios, and solve for one of the unknown sides. Then we can use the
Pythagorean theorem to find the other two unknown sides. We will demonstrate that all three
of the pairings will permit us to solve the problem. On the left we write the equal ratios of
triangles (1) and (2) and put the sides from triangle (1) on top. In the center we write the ratios
from triangles (1) and (3) and put the sides of triangle (1) on top. On the right we write the
ratios from triangles (2) and (3) and put the sides of triangle (2) on top.

Triangles (1) and (2)	Triangles (1) and (3)	Triangles (2) and (3)
$\dfrac{a}{4}\quad\dfrac{12}{a}\quad\boxed{\dfrac{b}{h}}$	$\boxed{\dfrac{a}{h}}\quad\dfrac{12}{b}\quad\dfrac{b}{8}$	$\dfrac{4}{h}\quad\boxed{\dfrac{a}{b}}\quad\dfrac{h}{8}$

We have boxed one ratio in each set of ratios. These ratios have two variables and will not be
useful in the solution. If we equate the remaining ratios, cross multiply, and solve, we can find
a, b, and h.

$$\frac{a}{4} = \frac{12}{a} \qquad\qquad \frac{12}{b} = \frac{b}{8} \qquad\qquad \frac{4}{h} = \frac{h}{8}$$

$$a^2 = 48 \qquad\qquad b^2 = 96 \qquad\qquad h^2 = 32$$

$$a = \sqrt{48} \qquad\qquad b = \sqrt{96} \qquad\qquad h = \sqrt{32}$$

$$a = 4\sqrt{3} \qquad\qquad b = 4\sqrt{6} \qquad\qquad h = 4\sqrt{2}$$

It was not necessary to use all three pairs of triangles. The length of the side found by using
one pair of triangles could be used to find the other sides. On the left above we have found that
the length of side a is $4\sqrt{3}$ units. We can use the Pythagorean theorem and triangles (1) and (2)
to find b and h, as we show here.

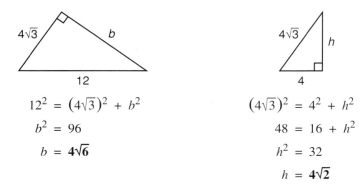

$$12^2 = \left(4\sqrt{3}\right)^2 + b^2 \qquad\qquad \left(4\sqrt{3}\right)^2 = 4^2 + h^2$$

$$b^2 = 96 \qquad\qquad\qquad 48 = 16 + h^2$$

$$b = 4\sqrt{6} \qquad\qquad\qquad h^2 = 32$$

$$\qquad\qquad\qquad\qquad\qquad h = 4\sqrt{2}$$

**problem set
3**

1. Find the measure of angle A if the supplement of angle A is $20°$ greater than twice the complement of angle A.

2. Words that were ubiquitous appeared seven times more often than words that appeared seldom. If 296 words were considered, how many words were classified as ubiquitous?

3. Fourteen percent were belligerent while the rest were merely eristic. If 4300 were eristic, how many were belligerent?

4. Use N_N and N_D to represent the number of nickels and the number of dimes in this problem. There were 13 more nickels than dimes and the total value of the coins was $1.85. Find the number of nickels and the number of dimes.

5. The lengths of the sides of a triangle are 7 cm, 12 cm, and 6 cm, respectively. Is the triangle a right triangle, an acute triangle, or an obtuse triangle?

6. In the two triangles shown, find the scale factor from right to left. What is the scale factor from left to right? Using scale factors, find x and y.

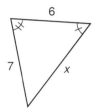

7. Find x and y.

8. Find x, y, and z.

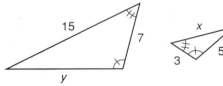
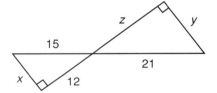

9. Find a, b, and c.

10. Find x, y, and z.

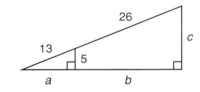
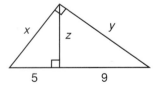

Simplify:

11. $\dfrac{7^4 p^4 q^{-1} pq^{-2}}{7^3 p^{-2} q^4}$

12. $\dfrac{6^3 a^0 b^{-3} a^2}{6^2 a^{-4} b^2 b^{-4}}$

Solve:

13. $\begin{cases} x - 3y = -6 \\ 2x + 5y = 21 \end{cases}$

14. $2\frac{1}{4}x - 3\frac{1}{2} = -\dfrac{1}{16}$

15. $-2(-x^0 - 4^0) - 3x(2 - 6^0) = x(-2 - 3^2 - 2) - x(-2 - 2^0)$

16. Add: $\dfrac{3}{x - 2} + \dfrac{4}{x - 1} - \dfrac{1}{x}$

17. Multiply: $(x^2 - 1)(4x^3 - 3x^2 + 5)$

18. Expand: $\dfrac{4x^{-2}y^{-2}}{z^2}\left(\dfrac{3x^2 y^2 z^2}{4} + \dfrac{2x^0 y^{-2}}{z^2 y^2}\right)$

19. Evaluate: $-2^0 - 3^0(-2 - 5^0) - \dfrac{1}{-2^{-2}} + x^2 y - xy$ if $x = -2$ and $y = 3$

20. Find x.

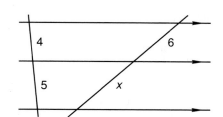

21. In the circle shown, O is the center. The radius of the circle is $\sqrt{3}$ cm. Find the area of the shaded sectors.

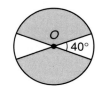

22. In this figure, points P and Q are the centers of two smaller circles and lie on a diameter of the big circle. The two smaller circles are tangent to the larger circle and to each other. Find the area of the shaded region of this figure. Dimensions are in centimeters.

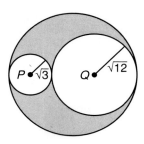

23. In the figure shown, each circle is tangent to the square. All adjacent circles are tangent to each other. If all circles are congruent, find the area of the shaded region.

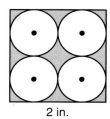

2 in.

24. Three equal semicircles are drawn on the diameter of a circle with a center Q, as shown in the diagram. If the area of the big circle Q is 9π square inches, find the area of the shaded region.

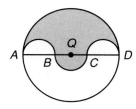

25. Find the perimeter of the figure. All angles that look like right angles are right angles. Dimensions are in feet.

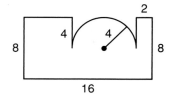

26. In the regular pentagon shown, O is the center. Draw line segments connecting each vertex to O to break the figure into five congruent triangles. Find the area of the figure.

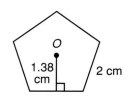

27. A steel ball whose radius is 18 cm is placed in a right circular cylinder. The radius of the right circular cylinder is 18 cm and the height is 36 cm. What is the difference in the volumes?

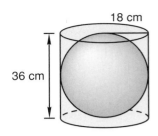

28. Find the volume of the cone whose base is shown and whose altitude is 5 meters.

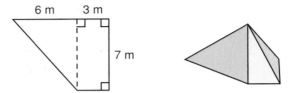

CONCEPT REVIEW PROBLEMS

29. Compare: A. $7^{26} - 7^{25}$ B. $7^{25}(6)$ (*Hint*: Begin by factoring A.)

30. Given: O is the center of the circle shown and $OP = 4$ and $OQ = 8$

Compare: A. Area of outer circle   B. Twice the area of inner circle

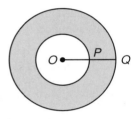

LESSON 4 *Construction*

construction   We can use a plastic device called a *protractor* to measure angles. To measure an angle, we align the baseline of the protractor with one side of the angle and move the protractor left or right as necessary to place the angle vertex under the origin at the center of the baseline. We read the measure of the angle where the other ray passes through the scale.

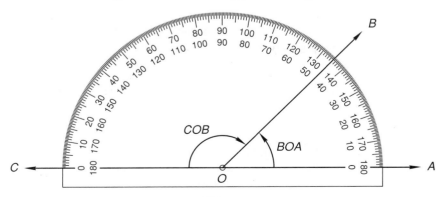

The angle *BOA* shown here has a measure of 45°, as we read on the inner scale. The measure of angle *COB* is read on the outer scale as 135°.

To construct geometric figures, we will use a compass and a straightedge.

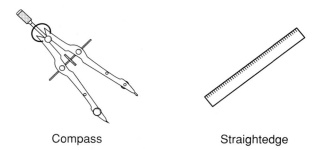

Compass   Straightedge

The ancient Greeks were the first to do geometric constructions. The straightedge of the Greeks did not have markings as do our rulers, so the Greek straightedge could only be used to draw a line segment between or through two points or to extend a given line segment. Sometimes we will use the ruler as a straightedge, and at other times we will use a ruler to measure distances. The modern compass shown above has capabilities that the Greek compasses did not have. We can use a modern compass to copy a given length, to draw a full circle, or to draw an arc of a circle.

The most useful constructions are copying line segments, copying angles, bisecting angles, bisecting line segments, and erecting perpendiculars. These basic constructions can be used in combination to perform more involved constructions, as we shall see. We will learn to do the constructions first. Then we will practice their use.

copying line segments   To copy a line segment, we use a compass. On the left is segment *AB*. To copy this segment, we use a straightedge to draw ray *XY*. Then we place one end of the compass on point *A* and adjust the compass so that the other end is at point *B*.

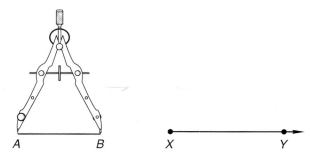

Then we place one end of the compass at *X* and draw an arc that intersects $\overrightarrow{XY}$ at a point we call *P*.

The distance *XP* is equal to the distance *AB*, so segments *AB* and *XP* have equal lengths.

copying angles   To copy angle *BAC* on the left, we first draw ray *XY* on the right. Then we use the compass to draw equal arcs with center at *A* and *X*, respectively.

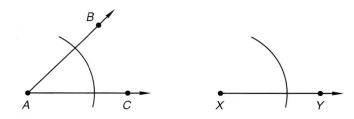

In the figure on the left below, the arc intersects the sides of the angle at points we call M and N. In the figure on the right, the arc intersects $\overrightarrow{XY}$ at Z.

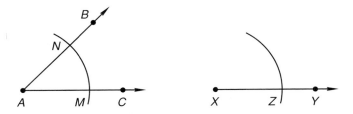

Next, we adjust the compass to length MN and draw from Z an arc whose radius is MN.

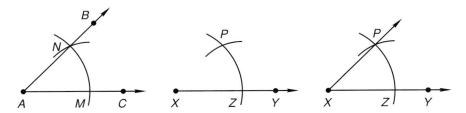

As the last step, we use the straightedge to draw ray XP. Angle PXY has the same measure as angle BAC, so the angles are congruent.

bisecting angles To bisect angle BAC on the left below, we first draw an arc whose center is A, as we show in the center figure. This arc intercepts the sides of the angle at points we call X and Y.

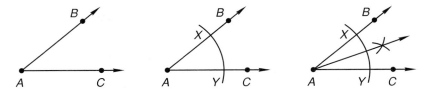

Then we draw arcs of equal radii whose centers are X and Y. The intersection of these arcs lies on the ray that is the bisector of the angle.

bisecting line segments To construct the perpendicular bisector of segment BK, we draw equal intersecting arcs from both B and K as shown. We note that the lengths of the arcs must be greater than half the length of segment BK for the arcs to intersect.

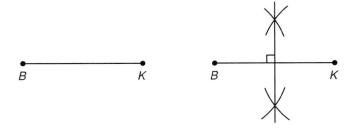

The line segment that connects the points of intersection of the arcs is the perpendicular bisector of segment BK.

erecting perpendiculars To erect a perpendicular from point P on line AC below, we draw equal arcs on either side of point P that intersect $\overleftrightarrow{AC}$ at points we label M and N, as we see on the right.

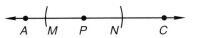

Then we widen the compass and construct the perpendicular bisector of $\overline{MN}$.

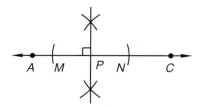

To demonstrate the method of erecting a perpendicular from a line to a point not on the line, we will use point P and line EF on the left below. First we draw two equal arcs whose center is P that intersect the line at R and S, as shown on the right.

Then we construct the perpendicular bisector of $\overline{RS}$. This line segment will pass through point P.

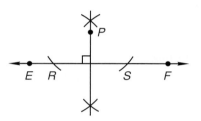

constructing triangles   Given segments BC, AX, and MN, construct a triangle whose sides have these lengths.

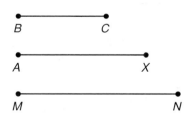

There is only one triangle whose sides have these lengths. First we draw a ray. Then we draw on this ray an arc whose length is either MN, AX, or BC. We decide to use length MN, so we label the origin of the ray as M. The other end is N. M and N will be two vertices of the triangle.

From one end of $\overline{MN}$ we draw an arc whose length is AX. From the other end of $\overline{MN}$ we draw an arc whose length is BC. The intersection of these arcs is the other vertex of the triangle.

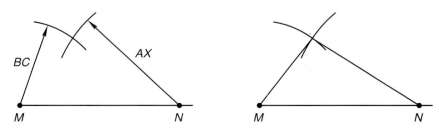

constructing parallels

We can construct a line that is parallel to a given line and that passes through a point not on the line. On the left below, we show the line and the point. The first step is to pick a point X on the line and draw the new line $\overrightarrow{PX}$. We do this on the right and call the angle formed angle A.

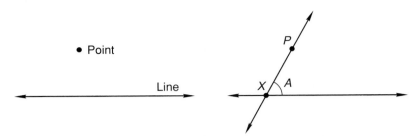

Next we copy angle A at point P.

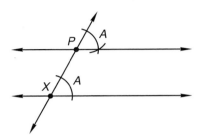

We remember from Lesson 1 that if two lines are cut by a transversal so that a pair of corresponding angles is congruent, then the lines are parallel. Therefore, the constructed line that passes through P is parallel to the given line.

equal segments

We can use construction to divide a line segment into any number of segments of equal lengths. To illustrate, we will divide a line segment into three segments of equal lengths. On the left, we show segment AB. On the right, we draw ray AP at a convenient angle to $\overline{AB}$.

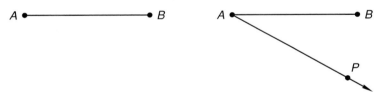

Next, on $\overrightarrow{AP}$ we use a compass to mark off three equal segments $\overline{AR}$, $\overline{RS}$, and $\overline{ST}$. Lastly, we connect T and B and construct line segments parallel to this segment from R and S.

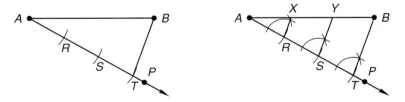

Since parallel lines separate transversals into proportional segments, $AX = XY = YB$. The same procedure could be used to divide $\overline{AB}$ into any desired number of segments of equal lengths by laying off on $\overrightarrow{AP}$ the necessary number of equal segments and drawing the required parallel line segments.

problem set 4

1. Three times the complement of angle A is 40° more than the supplement of angle A. Find the measure of angle A.

2. The ratio of sycophants to mere flatterers was 10 to 7. If there were 1106 who were mere flatterers, how many sycophants were there?

3. A poll was conducted with 594 respondents favoring the new bill. If this was 72% of all respondents, how many respondents were there?

4. Shannon had a total of twenty dimes and quarters. If the value of the coins was $3.35, how many of each coin did she have?

5. The total number of orange football helmets and blue football helmets is 44. If twice the number of blue football helmets exceeds the number of orange football helmets by 4, how many are there of each color?

6. The lengths of the sides of a triangle are 10 m, 9 m, and 3 m, respectively. Is the triangle a right triangle, an acute triangle, or an obtuse triangle?

7. Construct a segment congruent to $\overline{AB}$.

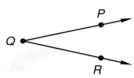

8. Construct an angle which is congruent to $\angle PQR$.

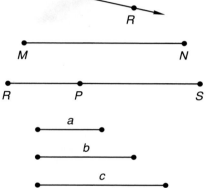

9. Construct the perpendicular bisector of segment MN.

10. Construct a perpendicular to $\overline{RS}$ at P.

11. Construct a triangle whose sides have lengths a, b, and c.

Solve:

12. $\begin{cases} 2x - 3y = 5 \\ 3x + y = 35 \end{cases}$

13. $\frac{3}{2}x + \frac{1}{5} = \frac{3}{10}$

14. $-3(-x^0 - 4) + 2(-x)^0 = 7(x - 3^2 + 4^2)$

15. Add: $\frac{3}{x^2} + \frac{1}{x} - \frac{2}{x + 1}$

16. Expand: $\frac{9s^2t^{-3}}{s^{-2}t}\left(\frac{3^{-1}s^{-1}t}{s^2} - \frac{s^3t^4}{t^{-1}} \right)$

17. Evaluate: $\frac{3^0 4^{-1}}{2^{-4}}x^{-1}y + 2^{-1}xy^0 - 3x + y^2$ if $x = 1$ and $y = 2$

18. Find x and y.

19. Find a, b, and c.

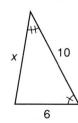

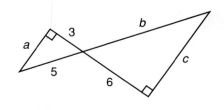

20. Find a, b, and c.

21. Find a, b, and h.

22. Find *d*.

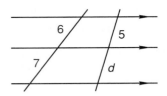

23. Find the perimeter of the figure. All angles that look like right angles are right angles. Dimensions are in meters.

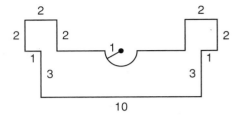

24. In the regular hexagon shown, *O* is the center. Draw line segments connecting each vertex to *O* to break the figure into six congruent triangles. Find the area of the figure.

25. The radius of the right circular cylinder is 3 meters and the height is 12 meters. The measure of the central angle of the shaded sector is 60°. Find the volume of the slice of the cylinder that has the 60° sector as its top surface.

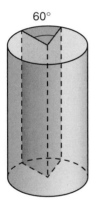

26. The base of a right circular cone has a radius of 10 cm. The height of the cone is 10 cm. Find the volume and surface area of the cone.

27. A sphere has a radius of 10 m. Find the volume and surface area of the sphere.

28. The base of a regular pyramid is a square whose perimeter is 20 cm. The height of the pyramid is 5 cm. Find the volume of the pyramid.

CONCEPT REVIEW PROBLEMS

29. Given: $\triangle ABC$ where $m\angle A < m\angle C$

Compare: A. *AB*   B. *BC*

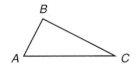

Note: Figure not drawn to scale

30. Let *x* and *y* be real numbers. If $y > 1$, compare: A. $\dfrac{x+1}{y+1}$ B. $\dfrac{x}{y} + 1$

LESSON 5 *Exponents and Radicals • Complex Numbers • Areas of Similar Geometric Figures • Diagonals of Rectangular Solids*

5.A

exponents and radicals

We remember that the square root of a number is another number which, when used as a factor twice, equals the number. Thus

$$\sqrt{4}\sqrt{4} = 4 \qquad \sqrt{3}\sqrt{3} = 3$$

Because we add exponents when we multiply powers of the same base, we can use one half as an exponent that indicates the square root.

$$4^{\frac{1}{2}} \cdot 4^{\frac{1}{2}} = 4^1 = 4 \qquad 3^{\frac{1}{2}} \cdot 3^{\frac{1}{2}} = 3^1 = 3$$

For the same reason, the exponent $\frac{1}{3}$ can be used to indicate the cube root and the exponent $\frac{1}{4}$ can be used to represent the fourth root, etc.

$$3^{\frac{1}{3}} \cdot 3^{\frac{1}{3}} \cdot 3^{\frac{1}{3}} = 3 \qquad 3^{\frac{1}{4}} \cdot 3^{\frac{1}{4}} \cdot 3^{\frac{1}{4}} \cdot 3^{\frac{1}{4}} = 3$$

When we simplify radical expressions, it is often helpful to replace the radicals with parentheses and fractional exponents.

example 5.1   Simplify: $\sqrt{x^3 y}\ \sqrt[4]{xy^3}$

solution   First we replace the radicals with parentheses and fractional exponents and multiply exponents where indicated.

$$\left(x^3 y\right)^{\frac{1}{2}} \left(xy^3\right)^{\frac{1}{4}} = x^{\frac{3}{2}} y^{\frac{1}{2}} x^{\frac{1}{4}} y^{\frac{3}{4}}$$

Now we rearrange the bases and simplify by adding the exponents of like bases.

$$x^{\frac{3}{2}} x^{\frac{1}{4}} y^{\frac{1}{2}} y^{\frac{3}{4}} = x^{\frac{7}{4}} y^{\frac{5}{4}}$$

example 5.2   Simplify: $\dfrac{a^{\frac{x}{2}} \left(y^{2-x}\right)^{\frac{1}{2}}}{a^{3x} y^{-2x}}$

solution   We simplify and write all exponentials in the numerator.

$$a^{\frac{x}{2}} a^{-3x} y^{\left(1-\frac{x}{2}\right)} y^{2x}$$

Now we simplify by adding the exponents of like bases.

$$a^{\left(\frac{-5x}{2}\right)} y^{\left(\frac{2+3x}{2}\right)}$$

example 5.3   Simplify: $\dfrac{x^{-2} + y^{-2}}{(xy)^{-1}}$

solution   We begin by eliminating the negative exponents, and then we add the two expressions in the numerator.

$$\dfrac{\dfrac{1}{x^2} + \dfrac{1}{y^2}}{\dfrac{1}{xy}} = \dfrac{\dfrac{y^2 + x^2}{x^2 y^2}}{\dfrac{1}{xy}}$$

We finish by multiplying above and below by the reciprocal of the denominator.

$$\dfrac{\dfrac{y^2 + x^2}{x^2 y^2} \cdot \dfrac{xy}{1}}{\dfrac{1}{xy} \cdot \dfrac{xy}{1}} = \dfrac{x^2 + y^2}{xy}$$

example 5.4   Simplify: $3\sqrt{\dfrac{3}{2}} - 4\sqrt{\dfrac{2}{3}} + 2\sqrt{24}$

solution   First we change the form of the radicals and use multiplication as necessary to rationalize the denominators.

$$3\dfrac{\sqrt{3}}{\sqrt{2}} \cdot \dfrac{\sqrt{2}}{\sqrt{2}} - 4\dfrac{\sqrt{2}}{\sqrt{3}} \cdot \dfrac{\sqrt{3}}{\sqrt{3}} + 2\sqrt{4}\sqrt{6}$$

Next we simplify.

$$\dfrac{3\sqrt{6}}{2} - \dfrac{4\sqrt{6}}{3} + 4\sqrt{6}$$

We finish by finding a common denominator and adding.

$$\dfrac{9\sqrt{6}}{6} - \dfrac{8\sqrt{6}}{6} + \dfrac{24\sqrt{6}}{6} = \dfrac{\mathbf{25\sqrt{6}}}{\mathbf{6}}$$

example 5.5   Simplify: $\left(\sqrt{2} + \sqrt{x}\right)\left(1 - \sqrt{x}\right)$

solution   We multiply as indicated.

$$
\begin{array}{r}
\sqrt{2} + \sqrt{x} \\
1 - \sqrt{x} \\
\hline
\sqrt{2} + \sqrt{x} \\
-\sqrt{2x} - x \\
\hline
\sqrt{2} + \sqrt{x} - \sqrt{2}\sqrt{x} - x
\end{array}
$$

If we factor the two middle terms, we can write the answer with only 3 terms.

$$\mathbf{\sqrt{2} + \left(1 - \sqrt{2}\right)\sqrt{x} - x}$$

We note that the coefficient of the second term is the sum $1 - \sqrt{2}$.

5.B
complex numbers

In mathematics, we use the letter i to represent the positive square root of -1.

$$i = \sqrt{-1}$$

The square root of -1 is encountered often in the solution of quadratic equations. This "shorthand" symbol for $\sqrt{-1}$ was first used by the Swiss mathematician Leonard Euler (1707–1783). It may be that i was first used to represent $\sqrt{-1}$ because i can be written with one stroke of the pen (if the dot is neglected) while $\sqrt{-1}$ requires three strokes of the pen. Square roots of negative numbers can be written as the product of a real number and i, as we show here.

$$\sqrt{-13} = \sqrt{13(-1)} = \sqrt{13}\sqrt{-1} = \sqrt{13}\,i$$

Since $i = \sqrt{-1}$, then $i^2 = -1$.

$$i^2 = -1 \qquad \text{because} \qquad \sqrt{-1}\sqrt{-1} = -1$$

A complex number is made up of two real numbers a and b and the letter i. If the number with i as a factor is written last as **$a + bi$,** the complex number is said to be in **standard form.** A complex number has a real component a and an imaginary component. In the past, the combination bi was considered to be the imaginary component, but recently more than a few authors have said that the real number b is the imaginary component of the complex number. Note that all of the following numbers are complex numbers in the standard form $a + bi$.

(a) $4 + 2i$ (b) $3.01 - \dfrac{\sqrt{2}}{3}i$ (c) 4.06 (d) $3i$ (e) $\dfrac{\sqrt{13}}{5.6} + \sqrt{2}i$

In (a) both components are integers. In (b) one component is a terminating decimal and the other component is an irrational number. We note that the complex number (c) has only the real component. We can write (c) as $4.06 + 0i$. Thus, every real number is a complex number whose imaginary component is zero. The imaginary number (d) can be written as $0 + 3i$. Thus, every imaginary number is a complex number whose real component is zero. In (e) both components are irrational numbers.

example 5.6   Simplify: $3i^3 + 2i^5 - 3i + 2i^2$

solution   First we expand the i terms and pair the i's.

$$3i(ii) + 2i(ii)(ii) - 3i + 2(ii)$$

Now we replace each pair of i's with -1.

$$3i(-1) + 2i(-1)(-1) - 3i + 2(-1)$$

We finish by simplifying and writing the result in standard form.

$$-3i + 2i - 3i - 2 = \mathbf{-2 - 4i}$$

example 5.7   Simplify: $\sqrt{-3}\sqrt{4} + 3\sqrt{-2}\sqrt{-9} + \sqrt{-16} + \sqrt{16}$

solution   We begin by using the i notation.

$$(\sqrt{3}i)(2) + (3\sqrt{2}i)(3i) + 4i + 4$$

Now we simplify $2\sqrt{3}i - 9\sqrt{2} + 4i + 4$ and finish by grouping the real parts and the imaginary parts.

$$\mathbf{\left(4 - 9\sqrt{2}\right) + \left(2\sqrt{3} + 4\right)i}$$

5.C
areas of similar geometric figures

The ratio of the areas of similar two-dimensional geometric figures equals the square of the scale factor between the figures. This is easy to say but difficult to internalize and to remember. Many people find that specific examples can be a great help in remembering this relationship.

example 5.8   The scale factor between two rectangles is 4. What is the ratio of the areas?

solution   We could use the square of the scale factor, but let's figure it out. On the left we draw a rectangle of dimensions L and W, and on the right we draw a rectangle of dimensions $4L$ and $4W$.

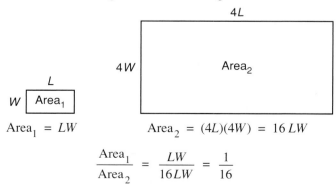

$$\text{Area}_1 = LW \qquad\qquad \text{Area}_2 = (4L)(4W) = 16\,LW$$

$$\frac{\text{Area}_1}{\text{Area}_2} = \frac{LW}{16LW} = \frac{1}{16}$$

Thus, we see that the ratio of the areas is **16 to 1,** or **1 to 16.**

example 5.9   The radius of one circle is R, and the radius of a second circle is $\frac{3R}{5}$. What is the ratio of the area of the first circle to the area of the second circle?

solution

$$\frac{\text{Area}_1}{\text{Area}_2} = \frac{\pi R^2}{\pi \left(\dfrac{3R}{5}\right)^2} = \frac{\pi R^2}{\pi \left(\dfrac{9R^2}{25}\right)} = \frac{25}{9}$$

We could have tried to use the fact that the ratio of the areas equaled the square of the scale factor, but we might have ended up with $\frac{9}{25}$. If we work it out each time, we can be accurate and have a better feel for what we are doing.

5.D
diagonals of rectangular solids

We can use the Pythagorean theorem twice to find a formula for the length of a diagonal of a rectangular solid, as we show in the following example.

example 5.10   Find the length of the diagonal that connects corners B and H in the rectangular solid shown.

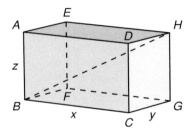

solution   The solution is in two steps. The first step is to find the length of line segment BG. To do this we will look at the floor of the rectangular solid from above. We can see that line segment BG is the hypotenuse of the right triangle whose sides are $\overline{BC}$ and $\overline{GC}$. The length of $\overline{BC}$ is given as x and the length of $\overline{GC}$ is given as y. Now, we can use the Pythagorean theorem to find the length of line segment BG.

$$(BG)^2 = (BC)^2 + (GC)^2 \qquad \text{Pythagorean theorem}$$
$$(BG)^2 = x^2 + y^2 \qquad \text{substituted}$$
$$BG = \sqrt{x^2 + y^2} \qquad \text{solved}$$

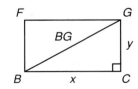

The second step is to find the length of diagonal BH, which is the hypotenuse of the right triangle whose sides are $\overline{BG}$ and $\overline{HG}$, as shown. We found the length of $\overline{BG}$ in the first step and the length of $\overline{HG}$ is given as z. Now, we can use the Pythagorean theorem to find the length of diagonal BH.

$$(BH)^2 = (BG)^2 + (HG)^2 \qquad \text{Pythagorean theorem}$$
$$(BH)^2 = \left(\sqrt{x^2 + y^2}\right)^2 + z^2 \qquad \text{substituted}$$
$$(BH)^2 = x^2 + y^2 + z^2 \qquad \text{simplified}$$
$$BH = \sqrt{x^2 + y^2 + z^2} \qquad \text{solved}$$

example 5.11   Find the length of diagonal AC in the rectangular solid shown. Do a two-step development and do not use the formula in example 5.10.

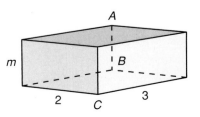

solution   We will do the solution in two steps. The first step is to find the length of the base diagonal BC. In the figure below, we show the floor of the rectangular solid as seen from above. We can see that the base diagonal BC is the hypotenuse of the right triangle whose sides have lengths of 2 units and 3 units, respectively. Now we can use the Pythagorean theorem to find the length of the base diagonal BC.

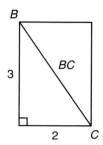

$$(BC)^2 = 2^2 + 3^2 \qquad \text{used Pythagorean theorem}$$
$$(BC)^2 = 13 \qquad \text{simplified}$$
$$BC = \sqrt{13} \qquad \text{solved}$$

The second step is to find the length of diagonal AC, which is the hypotenuse of the right triangle whose sides are $\overline{BC}$ and $\overline{AB}$, as shown. We found the length of $\overline{BC}$ in the first step and the length of $\overline{AB}$ is given as m. Now, we can use the Pythagorean theorem to find the length of diagonal AC.

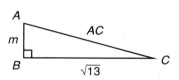

$$(AC)^2 = (BC)^2 + (AB)^2 \qquad \text{Pythagorean theorem}$$
$$(AC)^2 = (\sqrt{13})^2 + m^2 \qquad \text{substituted}$$
$$(AC)^2 = 13 + m^2 \qquad \text{simplified}$$
$$AC = \sqrt{13 + m^2} \qquad \text{solved}$$

problem set 5

1. Twice the supplement of angle θ is 104° greater than four times the complement of angle θ. Find θ.

2. The alloy is 35% titanium. If there are 1508 grams of other elements in the alloy, how much titanium does it contain?

3. There are a total of 24 dimes and quarters and the value of the coins is \$3.90. How many quarters and how many dimes are there?

4. The lengths of the sides of a triangle are 11 cm, 7 cm, and 9 cm, respectively. Is the triangle a right triangle, an acute triangle, or an obtuse triangle?

5. The ratio of blues to whites is 7 to 5 and the number of blues exceeds the number of whites by 12. How many are blue and how many are white?

6. The radius of the big circle is R meters and the radius of the small circle is $\frac{2}{5}R$ meters. What is the ratio of the area of the small circle to the area of the large circle?

Simplify:

7. $\sqrt{x^3 y^2} \sqrt[4]{xy^3}$

8. $x^{\frac{1}{2}} x^{\frac{3}{4}} \sqrt{xy} \sqrt[3]{x^4}$

9. $\dfrac{a^{\frac{x}{2}} \left(y^{2-x}\right)^{\frac{1}{2}}}{a^{4x} y^{-2x}}$

10. $\dfrac{y^{x+3} y^{\left(\frac{x}{2}-1\right)} z^a}{y^{\left(\frac{x-a}{2}\right)} z^{\left(\frac{x-a}{3}\right)}}$

11. $2\sqrt{\dfrac{3}{2}} - 3\sqrt{\dfrac{2}{3}} + 2\sqrt{24}$

12. $(\sqrt{3} + \sqrt{x})(\sqrt{3} + \sqrt{x})$

13. $(\sqrt{2} - \sqrt{x})(1 - \sqrt{x})$

14. $\dfrac{x^{-2} + y^{-2}}{(xy)^{-1}}$

15. $3i^4 + 2i^5 + 3i^3 + 2i^2$

16. $\sqrt{-3}\sqrt{4} + 3\sqrt{-2}\sqrt{-9}$

17. $2\sqrt{-2}\sqrt{2} + 3i\sqrt{2}$

18. Find *x* and *y*.

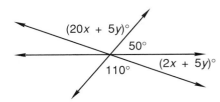

19. Find the length of diagonal *AC* in the rectangular solid shown.

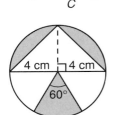

20. The diameter of the circle is 8 cm, as shown. The sum of the areas of the top two shaded regions is equal to the area of half the circle minus the area of the big triangle. The shaded region below is a 60° sector of the circle. Find the sum of the three shaded areas.

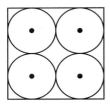

21. Find the area of the shaded region. Dimensions are in meters.

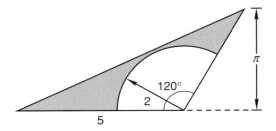

22. In the figure shown, each circle is tangent to the square. All adjacent circles are tangent to each other. The sum of the areas of the four circles is 36π m^2. The circles have equal areas. Find the area of the square.

23. Find *a*, *b*, and *c*.

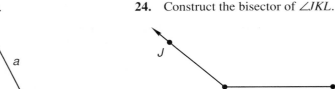

24. Construct the bisector of $\angle JKL$.

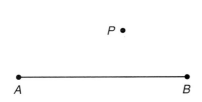

25. Construct a line through *P* parallel to segment *AB*.

26. Draw a large scalene triangle on a full sheet of paper. Construct the perpendicular bisector of each side of the triangle. The bisectors will meet at a point equidistant from the vertices of the triangle. Use a compass to draw a circle centered at the point and that passes through all three vertices. We say that the triangle is **inscribed** in the circle, or the circle is **circumscribed** about the triangle.

27. The base of a cone is a right triangle joined by a 30° sector of a circle, as shown. The altitude of the cone is 12 meters. Find the volume of the cone. Dimensions are in meters.

28. The base of a regular pyramid is a regular hexagon, as shown. The altitude of the pyramid is 14 centimeters. Find the volume and the surface area of the pyramid. Dimensions are in centimeters.

CONCEPT REVIEW PROBLEMS

29. If $x = 0$, $y > 1$, and $z > 1$, compare: A. $2y(x + z)$ B. $x(y + z)$

30. Given: $a = 3$ and $b = \dfrac{1}{6}$. Compare: A. $2a - 18b$ B. $3a - 36b$

LESSON 6   *Fractional Equations • Radical Equations • Systems of Three Linear Equations*

6.A
fractional equations

A good first step in the solution of a fractional equation is to multiply the numerator in each term on both sides of the equation by the least common multiple of the denominators. This will permit the denominators to be eliminated, and the resulting equation can then be solved. Of course, values of the variable that would cause one or more denominators to equal zero are unacceptable as solutions. In the following example, x cannot equal -2 because replacing x with -2 would cause the second denominator to equal zero.

example 6.1   Solve: $\dfrac{4}{7} + \dfrac{3}{x + 2} = \dfrac{5}{3}$

solution   By writing $x \neq -2$ we note the unacceptable value of the variable. Next, we multiply each numerator by $21(x + 2)$, which is the least common multiple of the denominators. Then we cancel the denominators and solve.

$$21(x + 2) \cdot \frac{4}{7} + 21(x + 2) \cdot \frac{3}{x + 2} = 21(x + 2) \cdot \frac{5}{3} \qquad \text{multiplied}$$

$$3(x + 2)4 + 21 \cdot 3 = 7(x + 2)5 \qquad \text{canceled}$$

$$12x + 24 + 63 = 35x + 70 \qquad \text{multiplied}$$

$$23x = 17 \qquad \text{simplified}$$

$$x = \frac{17}{23} \qquad \text{divided}$$

example 6.2   Solve: (a) $\begin{cases} \dfrac{3}{7}x + \dfrac{2}{5}y = 11 \\ 0.03x - 0.2y = -0.37 \end{cases}$
              (b)

solution   If we multiply the top equation by 35, we can eliminate the denominators. If we multiply the bottom equation by 100, we can make all the numbers in the bottom equation whole numbers.

MULTIPLYING   SIMPLIFIED EQUATIONS

$$\text{(a)} \quad 35 \cdot \frac{3}{7}x + 35 \cdot \frac{2}{5}y = 35 \cdot 11 \qquad \longrightarrow \qquad 15x + 14y = 385 \quad \text{(c)}$$

$$\text{(b)} \quad 100(0.03x) - 100(0.2y) = 100(-0.37) \quad \longrightarrow \quad 3x - 20y = -37 \quad \text{(d)}$$

Now if we multiply equation (d) by –5, we can add the equations and eliminate x.

$$\text{(c)} \quad 15x + 14y = 385 \quad \longrightarrow \quad (1) \quad \longrightarrow \quad 15x + 14y = 385 \qquad \text{multiplied by 1}$$

$$\text{(d)} \quad 3x - 20y = -37 \quad \longrightarrow \quad (-5) \quad \longrightarrow \quad \underline{-15x + 100y = 185} \qquad \text{multiplied by } -5$$

$$114y = 570 \qquad \text{added}$$

$$y = \frac{570}{114} \qquad \text{divided}$$

$$y = 5 \qquad \text{solved}$$

Now we use equation (c) to solve for x.

$$15x + 14y = 385 \qquad \text{equation (c)}$$

$$15x + 14(5) = 385 \qquad \text{substituted 5 for } y$$

$$15x + 70 = 385 \qquad \text{multiplied}$$

$$x = \frac{315}{15} \qquad \text{simplified}$$

$$x = 21 \qquad \text{solved}$$

So our solution is the ordered pair **(21, 5)**.

6.B

radical equations

Radicals in equations can be eliminated by isolating the radical on one side of the equation and then raising both sides of the equation to the power that will eliminate the radical. When the radical is a square root radical, both sides are raised to the second power. When the radical is a cube root radical, both sides are raised to the third power, and so on. **When an equation contains two radicals, it is sometimes necessary to repeat the procedure.**

example 6.3   Solve: $\sqrt[3]{x - 5} - 2 = 2$

solution   We first isolate the radical by adding +2 to both sides of the equation. To eliminate the cube root radical, we raise both sides of the equation to the third power. Then we solve the resulting equation.

$$\sqrt[3]{x - 5} = 4 \qquad \text{added +2 to both sides}$$

$$x - 5 = 64 \qquad \text{raised both sides to third power}$$

$$x = \mathbf{69} \qquad \text{solved}$$

Now we check our answer in the original equation because raising expressions to a power sometimes generates an equation that has extraneous solutions.

$$\sqrt[3]{(69) - 5} - 2 = 2 \qquad \text{substituted}$$

$$\sqrt[3]{(69) - 5} = 4 \qquad \text{rearranged}$$

$$\sqrt[3]{64} = 4 \qquad \text{simplified}$$

$$4 = 4 \qquad \text{check}$$

example 6.4   Solve: $\sqrt{s - 48} + \sqrt{s} = 8$

solution   First we isolate $\sqrt{s - 48}$ and square both sides to eliminate this radical.

$$\sqrt{s - 48} = 8 - \sqrt{s} \qquad \text{added } -\sqrt{s} \text{ to both sides}$$

$$s - 48 = 64 - 16\sqrt{s} + s \qquad \text{squared both sides}$$

$$-48 = 64 - 16\sqrt{s} \qquad \text{simplified}$$

Now we rearrange the equation to isolate $\sqrt{s}$, and then we square both sides of the equation again.

$$16\sqrt{s} = 112 \qquad \text{rearranged}$$

$$\sqrt{s} = 7 \qquad \text{divided both sides by 16}$$

$$s = \mathbf{49} \qquad \text{squared both sides}$$

We finish by checking our solution in the original equation.

$$\sqrt{(49) - 48} + \sqrt{(49)} = 8 \qquad \text{substituted}$$

$$\sqrt{1} + 7 = 8 \qquad \text{simplified}$$

$$8 = 8 \qquad \text{check}$$

6.C

systems of three linear equations

Systems of linear equations can be solved by using either the substitution method or the elimination method. Some systems are most easily solved if both methods are used.

example 6.5   Solve: (a) $\begin{cases} 2x + 2y - z = 14 \\ 3x + 3y + z = 16 \\ x - 2y = 0 \end{cases}$
(b)
(c)

solution   In this book, systems of linear equations of three unknowns will be designed so that the numbers are easy to handle and so that most of the answers will be integers. These problems are studied to allow practice in the concepts of solving equations, and not for practice in arithmetic. Even though the numbers in these problems are integers, a calculator can often be used to prevent mistakes in arithmetic. For the first step, we solve equation (c) for x and find that $x = 2y$. Then in equations (a) and (b) we replace x with $2y$, simplify, and use elimination to solve for y.

$$\text{(a) } 2(2y) + 2y - z = 14 \quad \longrightarrow \quad 6y - z = 14 \qquad \text{substituted } 2y \text{ for } x$$

$$\text{(b) } 3(2y) + 3y + z = 16 \quad \longrightarrow \quad \underline{9y + z = 16} \qquad \text{substituted } 2y \text{ for } x$$

$$15y = 30 \qquad \text{added}$$

$$y = 2 \qquad \text{solved}$$

Now we know that $x = 4$ because equation (c) tells us that $x = 2y$. We finish by using 2 for y and 4 for x in equation (a) and solving for z.

$$2(4) + 2(2) - z = 14 \qquad \text{substituted 2 for } y \text{ and 4 for } x$$

$$12 - z = 14 \qquad \text{simplified}$$

$$z = -2 \qquad \text{solved}$$

Thus, the solution is the ordered triple **(4, 2, –2)**.

example 6.6   Solve: (a) $\begin{cases} x + 2y + z = 4 \\ 2x - y - z = 0 \\ 2x - 2y + z = 1 \end{cases}$
           (b)
           (c)

solution   We decide to begin by eliminating z. Thus, we first add equations (a) and (b) to get equation (d), which has no z term. Now we must use equation (c). We can add equation (c) to either equation (a) or (b) and eliminate z again. We decide to add equation (c) to equation (b).

(a) $x + 2y + z = 4$	(b) $2x - y - z = 0$
(b) $\underline{2x - y - z = 0}$	(c) $\underline{2x - 2y + z = 1}$
(d) $3x + y \quad\ = 4$	(e) $4x - 3y \quad\ = 1$

Now we have the two equations (d) and (e) in the two unknowns x and y. We will use elimination and add equation (e) to the product of equation (d) and 3.

$$(3)(d) \quad 9x + 3y = 12$$

$$(e) \quad \underline{4x - 3y = 1}$$

$$13x \qquad\ = 13$$

$$x = 1$$

Now we can use $x = 1$ in either equation (d) or (e) to find y. This time we will do both to show that either procedure will yield the same result.

(d) $3(1) + y = 4$	(e) $4(1) - 3y = 1$
$3 + y = 4$	$4 - 3y = 1$
$y = 1$	$-3y = -3$
	$y = 1$

Now we can use $x = 1$ and $y = 1$ in either (a), (b), or (c) to find z. This time we will use all three equations to show that all three will produce the same result.

USING EQUATION (a)	USING EQUATION (b)	USING EQUATION (c)
$(1) + 2(1) + z = 4$	$2(1) - (1) - z = 0$	$2(1) - 2(1) + z = 1$
$1 + 2 + z = 4$	$2 - 1 - z = 0$	$2 - 2 + z = 1$
$3 + z = 4$	$1 - z = 0$	$0 + z = 1$
$z = 1$	$z = 1$	$z = 1$

Thus, the solution is the ordered triple **(1, 1, 1)**.

problem set 6

1. Ten percent of the reds are added to twenty percent of the blues, and the total is 24. Yet the product of the number of reds and 3 exceeds the number of blues by 20. How many are red and how many are blue?

2. Four times the supplement of angle A exceeds 8 times the complement of angle A by 28. Find the measure of angle A.

3. The ratio of reds to greens was 5 to 16 and six times the number of reds exceeded the number of greens by 112. How many were red and how many were green?

4. The lengths of the sides of a triangle are 5 cm, 13 cm, and 12 cm, respectively. Is the triangle a right triangle, an acute triangle, or an obtuse triangle?

Solve:

5. $\dfrac{4}{7} + \dfrac{3}{x+3} = \dfrac{5}{3}$

6. $\dfrac{5}{3} - \dfrac{2}{x-4} = \dfrac{1}{2}$

7. $\dfrac{1}{x-7} + \dfrac{1}{4} = \dfrac{1}{3}$

8. $\sqrt{s-7} + \sqrt{s} = 7$

9. $\sqrt{s-27} + \sqrt{s} = 9$

10. $\begin{cases} \dfrac{3}{7}x + \dfrac{2}{5}y = 11 \\ 0.03x - 0.2y = -0.37 \end{cases}$

11. $\begin{cases} 2x + 3y = -1 \\ x - 2z = -3 \\ 2y - z = -4 \end{cases}$

12. $\begin{cases} x - 2y + z = -2 \\ 2x - 2y - z = -3 \\ x + y - 2z = 1 \end{cases}$

Simplify:

13. $\sqrt[3]{ab^4}\left(ab^3\right)^{\frac{1}{5}} b^2$

14. $\dfrac{x^{\left(\frac{a}{3}-2\right)} y^{\left(\frac{b-2}{3}\right)}}{x^{2a}\left(y^{\frac{1}{3}}\right)^{2a}}$

15. $2\sqrt{\dfrac{7}{3}} - \sqrt{\dfrac{3}{7}} - 2\sqrt{84}$

16. $\dfrac{x^{-1} + y^{-1}}{x^{-1}y}$

17. $\left(\sqrt{2} - x\right)\left(2 - \sqrt{x}\right)$

18. $\sqrt{-3}\sqrt{3} - \sqrt{2}i - \sqrt{-3}\sqrt{-2} - 2$

19. $2i^3 + 3i^2 + 2i - 2\sqrt{2}i$

20. Find the length of diagonal AC in the rectangular solid shown.

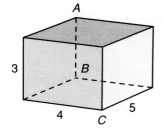

21. Construct a perpendicular to $\overline{BD}$ at P.

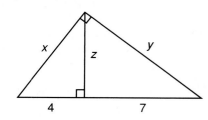

22. Construct a triangle whose sides have lengths r, s, and t.

23. Construct a line through P parallel to segment RS.

24. Find a and b.

25. Find x, y, and z.

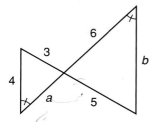

26. The radius of the big circle is 6 cm, as shown. The radius of each of the two small semicircles is 3 cm. Find the area of the shaded region. Dimensions are in centimeters.

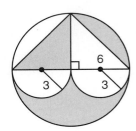

27. Find the volume of the pyramid whose base is shown and whose altitude is 12 cm. Dimensions are in centimeters.

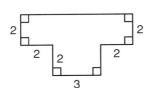

28. Find the surface area of the regular pyramid whose base is shown. The altitude of the triangular base is $\sqrt{3}$ meters and the slant height of the pyramid is 5 meters. Dimensions are in meters.

CONCEPT REVIEW
PROBLEMS

29. Compare: A. $\dfrac{6 + \dfrac{3}{4}}{2 - \dfrac{5}{4}}$ B. 3^2

30. Compare: A. The average of $\sqrt{0.49}$, $\dfrac{3}{4}$, and 0.8   B. 75%

LESSON 7 *Inductive and Deductive Reasoning • Logic • The Contrapositive • Converse and Inverse*

7.A

inductive and deductive reasoning

Inductive reasoning is the process of trying to find a rule. Many times a rule formulated by induction is not true. Suppose we flip a coin 100 times and it comes up heads 40 times and comes up tails 60 times. We might take this data and **induce** a rule that says if we flip a coin 100 times we will always get more tails than heads. Then we repeat the experiment and this time we get more heads than tails. This means that the first rule we induced was not true, but now we surely can induce the rule that we will get either a head or a tail every time we flip the coin. But if we flip the coin millions of times we find that once or twice the coin will stand on edge. Then our second attempt to induce a rule was also a failure. Thus we see that inductive reasoning is a process of gathering data, making observations, and then guessing. **Deductive reasoning** is the process of using a rule once it has been formulated. If the rule is a false rule and the rule is used properly, the conclusion reached can be false. We can also reach a false conclusion by using a true rule improperly. Thus there are two ways we can reason to a false conclusion. The study of logical reasoning is a study of the proper use of the rules and the truth or falsity of the rule is not a consideration.

7.B
logic

The ancient Greeks formalized the study of logic by using **syllogisms** in their investigation of deductive reasoning. A syllogism is a formal reasoning process in which a conclusion is reached by using two statements called **premises.** We will begin by looking at syllogisms in which the premises are called **categorical propositions** because they place things in categories. We will concentrate on premises called **universal affirmatives** because these premises affirm that all members of a particular set possess a certain property. This premise is often called the **major premise.** The other premise is often called the **minor premise** and identifies a member of the set. The conclusion follows that this member has the property possessed by all the members of the set. We demonstrate by using one of the oldest syllogisms known. The first premise is as follows:

> **1.** All men are mortal.   (Major premise)

This statement establishes mortality as a property possessed by every member of the set of all men.

> **2.** Aristotle is a man.   (Minor premise)

This statement identifies Aristotle as a member of the set of all men.

> Therefore, Aristotle is mortal.   (Conclusion)

This conclusion is a logical consequence because if Aristotle is a member of the set of all men, then he possesses the properties possessed by every member of this set. This is the type of reasoning we use in the geometric proofs in this book. Observe:

> The sum of the exterior angles of a convex polygon is 360°.
>
> Triangle *ABC* is a convex polygon.
>
> Therefore, the sum of the exterior angles of triangle *ABC* is 360°.

The major premise identifies a property of every member of the set of convex polygons. The minor premise identifies triangle *ABC* as a member of that set. Thus, triangle *ABC* has all the properties possessed by every member of the set. The entire three-step process is called an **argument.** In our investigation of syllogistic reasoning, we will concentrate on the argument and will not consider the truth or falsity of the premises. Consider the following syllogism:

> All frogs are green.   Major premise
>
> Henry is a frog.   Minor premise
>
> Therefore, Henry is green.   Valid conclusion

The argument is a valid argument because the major premise stated a property possessed by all frogs (they are green), and the minor premise identified Henry as a member of the set of all frogs. The major premise is false because some frogs are not green and thus Henry might be brown or red or some other color. But, because the argument is a valid argument, we will say that the conclusion is a valid conclusion. **This does not mean that the conclusion is true but means only that the argument is a valid argument.**

The conclusion in the following syllogism is invalid because the argument is faulty, as the minor premise does not identify a member of the set defined by the major premise.

> If it rains, I will go to town.   Major premise
>
> It did not rain.   Minor premise
>
> Therefore, I did not go to town.   Invalid conclusion

The major premise identified a result on each member of the set of days on which rain occurred. It made no statement about the set of days on which there was no rain. Thus, the day in question is not a member of the established set and may or may not possess the property in question.

example 7.1   Is the following argument a valid argument? Why or why not?

> All normal dogs have four legs.
>
> That dog has four legs.
> _____
> Therefore, that dog is a normal dog.

solution   **The argument is invalid.** The set described is the set of normal dogs. For a valid argument, the minor premise should have stated that a particular dog was a member of this set.

example 7.2   Is the following argument a valid argument? Why or why not?

> All boys are good.
>
> That child is a good child.
> _____
> Therefore, that child is a boy.

solution   **The argument is invalid.** The major premise made a statement about the set of all boys. The minor premise talked about a member of the set of good children. For a valid argument, the minor premise would have to identify a member of the set of all boys.

example 7.3   Is the following argument a valid argument? Why or why not?

> All chickens have three legs.
>
> Henny Penny is a chicken.
> _____
> Therefore, Henny Penny has three legs.

solution   **The argument is valid.** All chickens do not have three legs, but we still say that the argument is a valid argument. This does not mean that the conclusion is true. It means that the argument is valid because the major premise identified a property of the set of all chickens and the minor premise identified Henny Penny as a member of the set.

7.C
the contrapositive

The major premise implies an if-then statement that has two parts called the **hypothesis** and the **conclusion.** The hypothesis begins with the word *if* and the conclusion begins with the word *then*. When the words *if* and *then* are not written, the premise can be written so that these words are used. For example, the major premise "Rabbits are fast runners" can be written as an if-then statement by writing

---

PREMISE

HYPOTHESIS		CONCLUSION
If an animal is a rabbit,	→	then the animal is a fast runner.

The premise is a **one-way process** as indicated by the arrow. **The premise did not say that all fast runners are rabbits.**

If we change the sense of the if-statement by using the word *not* or the prefix *non-*, we have the **negation** of the if-statement.

If an animal is a rabbit,	if-statement
If an animal is not a rabbit,	negation
If an animal is a non-rabbit,	negation

If we change the sense of the then-statement by using the word *not* or the prefix *non-*, we have the negation of the then-statement.

then the animal is a fast runner.	then-statement
then the animal is not a fast runner.	negation
then the animal is a non-fast runner.	negation

The **contrapositive** is a "double negative" way to make the same statement as the premise. To form the contrapositive of a premise, we replace the if-statement with the **negative** of the then-statement and replace the then-statement with the **negative** of the if-statement.

If an animal is a rabbit,	→	then the animal is a fast runner.	premise
If the animal is not a fast runner,	→	then the animal is not a rabbit.	contrapositive

If a premise is true, its contrapositive is also true. If a premise is false, its contrapositive is also false. This is easy to see if we use a Venn diagram.

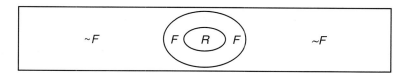

We place all rabbits (*R*) inside the smaller curve and all fast animals (*F*) inside the larger curve. This puts all animals who are not fast (~*F*) outside the larger curve. From this we can see that if an animal is a rabbit, it is also inside the *F* curve and is a fast runner. Also, we see that if an animal is not a fast runner, it is outside the larger curve and thus cannot be a rabbit.

example 7.4   Is the following argument valid?

All nonathletes are vegetarians.	Major premise
Jim is a nonvegetarian.	Minor premise
Therefore, Jim is an athlete.	Conclusion

solution   Many people find premises easier to understand when they are written in if-then form. If we rewrite the major premise in if-then form, we get: If a person is a nonathlete, then the person is a vegetarian.

If nonathlete,	→	then vegetarian.	Major premise
Jim is a nonvegetarian.			Minor premise
Therefore, Jim is an athlete.			Conclusion

The major premise makes a statement about a property of the members of the set of nonathletes and the minor premise says that Jim is a member of the set of nonvegetarians. We remember that a premise can always be replaced with its contrapositive. Thus we decide to replace the major premise with its contrapositive. We reverse the nouns and replace each noun with its negation.

If nonvegetarian,	→	then athlete.	Contrapositive
Jim is a nonvegetarian.			Minor premise
Therefore, Jim is an athlete.			Conclusion

This is a valid argument, so the original argument is also **valid.** The conclusion is not necessarily true, but the argument is valid.

7.D
converse and inverse

Let's look at two of our premises in abbreviated form.

$$\text{If} \quad \text{normal dog,} \qquad \text{then} \quad \text{four legs}$$
$$\text{If} \quad \text{rabbit,} \qquad \text{then} \quad \text{fast}$$

We can generalize both of these premises by using P for the if-statement, replacing *then* with an arrow, and using Q for the then-statement.

$$P \quad \rightarrow \quad Q \qquad \text{premise}$$

We read this by saying "If P, then Q." The symbol $\sim P$ is read as "not P" and the symbol $\sim Q$ is read as "not Q." We can write the contrapositive, which has the same truth or falsity as the premise, by writing

$$\sim Q \quad \rightarrow \quad \sim P \qquad \text{contrapositive}$$

which we read by saying "If not Q, then not P." We will devote almost all of our attention to the premise and the contrapositive and remember that if one of them is true, the other is true. If one is false, the other is false. There are two other forms of interest to the logician and we will mention them here. The first is the "other way" statement of the premise, which is called the **converse,**

$$Q \quad \rightarrow \quad P \qquad \text{converse}$$

and its "reverse negation" called the **inverse,** which has the same truth or falsity as the converse.

$$\sim P \quad \rightarrow \quad \sim Q \qquad \text{inverse}$$

Many of our difficulties in using logical reasoning come from our tendency to assume that the converse is true if the premise is true. Sometimes we falsely assume that a one-way premise also goes the other way.

$$\text{All normal dogs have four legs.}$$
$$P \quad \rightarrow \quad Q$$

This does not tell us that all four-legged dogs are normal dogs because some four-legged dogs have only one eye and thus are not normal dogs.

Some statements, however, are true in both directions and these statements are called **if-and-only-if statements.** We abbreviate *if and only if* by writing "iff." **All definitions are true in both directions.** For example, we define a right angle as follows: If an angle has a measure of 90°, then it is a right angle. Since definitions are "both way" statements, this also means that if an angle is a right angle, then it has a measure of 90°. We use two arrowheads to indicate that a statement is true in both directions.

$$\text{Measure of } 90° \quad \Leftrightarrow \quad \text{right angle}$$

To make a general statement about "iff" statements, we can use P and Q and write

$$P \quad \Leftrightarrow \quad Q$$

problem set 7

Write each of the following statements as if-then statements:

1. Elephants are large animals.

2. Advanced math students are intelligent.

Write the contrapositive of the following statements:

3. If an animal is green, then it is not a seal.

4. If the team won, then the coach is happy.

5. Is the following argument valid or invalid?

All students study at home.

Lori is studying at home.

Therefore, Lori is a student.

6. Write the contrapositive of the major premise of this syllogism to help determine whether the following argument is valid or invalid:

If the car is not moving, then the motor is off.

The motor is on.

Therefore, the car is moving.

7. The ratio of reds to greens was 4 to 11 and 60 percent of the greens exceeded the number of reds by 52. How many were red and how many were green?

8. There were 220 nickels and dimes in the bowl and the total value of the coins was $17.50. How many were nickels and how many were dimes?

9. To review the concept of consecutive integers, we remember that we can designate an unspecified integer with the letter N and greater consecutive integers with $N + 1$, $N + 2$, etc.

Consecutive integers $N, N + 1, N + 2$, etc.

Consecutive odd integers are 2 units apart, and consecutive even integers are also 2 units apart. Thus, we can designate both of them with the same notation.

Consecutive odd integers $N, N + 2, N + 4, N + 6$, etc.

Consecutive even integers $N, N + 2, N + 4, N + 6$, etc.

Now find three consecutive even integers such that 6 times the sum of the first and the third is 24 greater than 11 times the second.

Solve:

10. $\dfrac{2}{5} - \dfrac{3}{x - 4} = \dfrac{5}{6}$

11. $\begin{cases} \dfrac{4}{5}x - \dfrac{2}{3}y = \dfrac{7}{30} \\ 0.01x + 0.1y = 0.03 \end{cases}$

12. $\sqrt{2x - 7} + \sqrt{25} = 7$

13. $\begin{cases} 2x + 3y - z = 6 \\ 3x - y + z = 1 \\ x + y + z = 1 \end{cases}$

Simplify:

14. $yx^{\frac{2}{3}} \sqrt[3]{x^2} \left(x^2 y\right)^{\frac{1}{5}}$

15. $\left(\sqrt{2} + \sqrt{x}\right)\left(\sqrt{2} + \sqrt{x}\right)$

16. $\dfrac{a^{-2} + b^{-1}}{a^{-1}b}$

17. $\left(x^{\frac{1}{2}} + y^{\frac{1}{2}}\right)^2$

18. $\sqrt{2}\sqrt{-2} + \sqrt{-3}\sqrt{-3} + \sqrt{-4} - i$

19. $\left(3 - i + \sqrt{-4}\right)\left(2 - i - \sqrt{-9}\right)$

20. $3i^4 - 2i^3 + 4i - 5\sqrt{-16}$

21. Two 12-sided polygons are similar. A side of the larger polygon is 3 times as long as the corresponding side of the smaller polygon. What is the ratio of the area of the larger polygon to the area of the smaller polygon?

22. Find the length of diagonal AC in the rectangular solid shown.

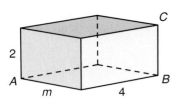

23. Construct a 45° angle.

24. Find a, b, and c.

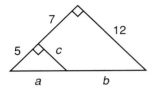

25. Construct a perpendicular from $\overline{PQ}$ that passes through M.

$M \bullet$

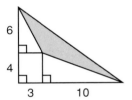

26. The measure of the central angle of the unshaded sector is 162°. The radius of the circle is $2\sqrt{15}$ m. Find the area of the shaded region of the circle.

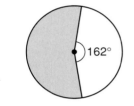

27. Find the area of the shaded region of this figure. Dimensions are in meters.

28. The radius of the right circular cylinder is 4 cm and the height is 16 cm. The measure of the central angle of the shaded sector is 45°. Find the volume of the slice of the cylinder that has the 45° sector as its top surface.

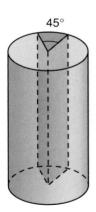

CONCEPT REVIEW PROBLEMS

29. Let a and b be real numbers. If $a - b = a + b$, compare: A. b B. 1

30. Compare: A. Surface area of a sphere with radius 1 cm

B. Area of a circle with radius 2 cm

LESSON 8   *Statements of Similarity • Proportional Segments • Angle Bisectors and Side Ratios*

8.A

statements of similarity

When we use the vertices of triangles to write statements of triangle similarity, we must be careful to list the vertices so that the angles in the triangles are corresponding angles. Consider the triangles shown here.

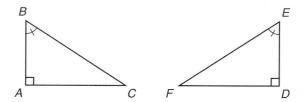

Both triangles have a right angle and the angles at B and E have equal measures, as indicated by the tick marks. Thus the triangles are similar triangles. We can use the symbol ~ for *similar* to write a statement of similarity.

$$\triangle ABC \sim \triangle DEF$$

Note that A and D are the first vertices listed in the name of each triangle. The angles at A and D are right angles, so their measures are equal. The second vertices listed are B and E, the vertices of the single tick-mark angle. The last vertices, C and F, are the other angles. We could also write that

$$\triangle CBA \sim \triangle FED$$

because the angles at C and F have equal measures and the angles at B and E also have equal measures. It would be incorrect to write that

$$\triangle ABC \sim \triangle DFE \qquad \textbf{No!}$$

because angles at B and F do not have equal measures and the angles at C and E do not have equal measures. We know that the ratios of the corresponding sides in similar triangles are equal. Often the proportional sides are difficult to identify. We can tell which sides are proportional by using a statement of triangle similarity. We repeat the first statement of similarity shown above. We connect the first two letters on each side with curves, connect the second two with an angle, and the first and last with square corners.

$$\triangle \overset{\frown\wedge}{A\,B\,C} \sim \triangle \overset{\frown\wedge}{D\,E\,F}$$

We can use the first two, the last two, and the first and the last letters to write the three ratios that have equal values. We put the letters from the left triangle on top.

$$\frac{AB}{DE} \qquad \frac{BC}{EF} \qquad \frac{AC}{DF}$$

Each pair of letters indicates the length of the segment between the indicated vertices. All three of these ratios have equal values.

example 8.1   In $\triangle ABC$, segment BD is the altitude to the hypotenuse AC.

Show the following: $\dfrac{AD}{AB} = \dfrac{AB}{AC}$

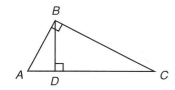

solution   **When we are asked to show that two ratios are equal, we look for similar triangles.** There are two right triangles in the figure that also contain the angle at vertex A, so these triangles are similar. Using the vertices in a correct order, we write

$$\triangle ADB \sim \triangle ABC$$

Then we write the three ratios and put the sides of $\triangle ADB$ on top.

$$\frac{AD}{AB} \qquad \frac{DB}{BC} \qquad \frac{AB}{AC}$$

All of these ratios are equal. The problem asks us to equate the first and last ratios. We do and get

$$\frac{AD}{AB} = \frac{AB}{AC}$$

8.B

proportional segments

In this section we will prove that two parallel lines cut proportional segments from any two intersecting transversals. First, we must prove the following algebraic fact:

$$\frac{a + b}{a} = \frac{c + d}{c} \qquad \text{which means that} \qquad \frac{b}{a} = \frac{d}{c} \quad \text{(where } a, c \neq 0\text{)}$$

We begin by rewriting both sides of the equation $\frac{a+b}{a} = \frac{c+d}{c}$ as the sum of two fractions.

$$\frac{a + b}{a} = \frac{a}{a} + \frac{b}{a} \qquad \text{and} \qquad \frac{c + d}{c} = \frac{c}{c} + \frac{d}{c}$$

Simplifying, we get

$$\frac{a + b}{a} = 1 + \frac{b}{a} \qquad \text{and} \qquad \frac{c + d}{c} = 1 + \frac{d}{c}$$

Now, we substitute into the original equation to get

$$1 + \frac{b}{a} = 1 + \frac{d}{c}$$

Now, we subtract 1 from both sides of the equation to get

$$\frac{b}{a} = \frac{d}{c}$$

In the diagram on the left below, we see a small triangle and a large triangle, both of which contain angle M. The arrowheads tell us that the base of the small triangle is parallel to the base of the large triangle, so the base angles of the two triangles are congruent as marked because they are corresponding angles formed by transversals and a pair of parallel lines. Thus the triangles are similar.

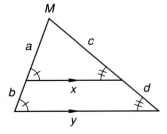 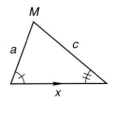 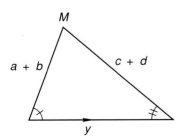

On the right we have drawn the triangles separately. If we write the ratios of the corresponding sides and put the sides from the large triangle on top, we get

$$\frac{a + b}{a} \qquad \frac{c + d}{c} \qquad \frac{y}{x}$$

We will not use the third ratio. If we equate the first two ratios, we get

$$\frac{a + b}{a} = \frac{c + d}{c} \quad \text{which means that} \quad \frac{b}{a} = \frac{d}{c}$$

The thought process involved in this proof can be extended to any number of parallel lines, as we indicate on the left and on the right.

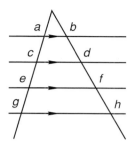 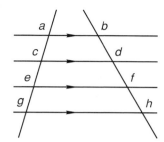

The intersection of the transversals is not shown in the diagram on the right, but since the lines are not parallel, we know that they do intersect. **So we see that parallel lines cut proportional segments from any two intersecting transversals.**

example 8.2   Find x.

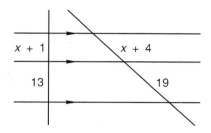

solution   We write the proportion, cross multiply, and solve.

$$\frac{x + 1}{13} = \frac{x + 4}{19} \qquad \text{proportion}$$

$$19x + 19 = 13x + 52 \qquad \text{multiplied}$$

$$6x = 33 \qquad \text{simplified}$$

$$x = \frac{11}{2} \qquad \text{solved}$$

8.C

angle bisectors and side ratios

If a line segment bisects an angle of a triangle, it also divides the opposite side into segments proportional to the other two sides. In the figure on the left, angle 1 and angle 2 have equal measures. There are two ways to write the equal proportions. One way is to equate side ratios by writing "a is to b as c is to d," as we show in the center figure.

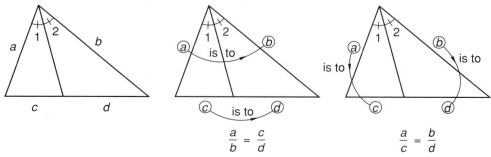

The other way is to equate the side-segment ratio of one triangle to the side-segment ratio of the other triangle, as we show in the figure on the right.

optional proof   The proof shown below is tricky because it requires that two line segments be added to form another triangle. On the left below, we form this triangle by drawing m as an extension of b and by drawing line segment k parallel to the angle bisector. The angles 1, 2, 3, and 4 are congruent. Angle 1 is congruent to angle 2 because they are halves of the bisected angle. Angle 1 is congruent to angle 3 because they are alternate interior angles, and angle 2 is congruent to angle 4 because they are corresponding angles. Using substitution, we see that angle 3 is congruent to angle 4.

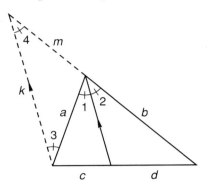 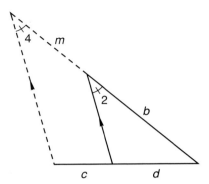

The fact that angle 3 is congruent to angle 4 makes the leftmost triangle an isosceles triangle, so the length of side m equals the length of side a. From the simplified figure on the right, we can write the ratios of the corresponding sides. If in these ratios we replace m with a, we get our final result.

$$\frac{c}{d} = \frac{m}{b} \xrightarrow{\text{replace } m \text{ with } a} \frac{c}{d} = \frac{a}{b}$$

example 8.3   In $\triangle ABC$, segment BD is the angle bisector of angle B. Find x.

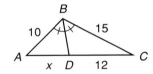

solution   If a line segment bisects an angle of a triangle, it also divides the opposite side into segments proportional to the other two sides.

$$\frac{x}{12} = \frac{10}{15} \qquad \text{proportion}$$

$$15x = 120 \qquad \text{multiplied}$$

$$x = \mathbf{8} \qquad \text{solved}$$

example 8.4   In $\triangle ABC$, segment AD is the angle bisector of angle A. Find x.

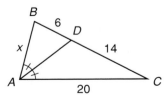

solution   If a line segment bisects an angle of a triangle, it also divides the opposite side into segments proportional to the other two sides.

$$\frac{6}{14} = \frac{x}{20} \qquad \text{proportion}$$

$$14x = 120 \qquad \text{multiplied}$$

$$x = \mathbf{\frac{60}{7}} \qquad \text{solved}$$

problem set 8

1. Thirty percent of the greens were added to fifteen percent of the purples and the total was 21. Four times the number of purples was ten more than three times the number of greens. How many were green and how many were purple?

2. The ratio of whats to hows was 7 to 3, and three times the number of hows was 40 less than twice the number of whats. How many were whats?

3. Joe Bob was amazed when he opened the drawer because it contained 173 coins whose value was $11.25. If all the coins were either nickels or quarters, how many of each were in the drawer?

4. The sum of twice the supplement of angle A and three times the supplement of angle B equaled 500°. The measure of angle B was 10° greater than the measure of angle A. What were the measures of angles A and B?

Are the following arguments valid or invalid?

5. All authors wear gold watches.

   John wears a gold watch.
   _____
   Therefore, John is an author.

6. All reds are blue.

   Joe Bob is red.
   _____
   Therefore, Joe Bob is blue.

7. Write the contrapositive of the major premise of this syllogism to help determine whether the following argument is valid or invalid:

   All nondogs are not blue.

   Jim is blue.
   _____
   Therefore, Jim is a dog.

8. Find three consecutive odd integers such that three times the sum of the first two equals four times the third.

9. Given: $\triangle XYZ$ is a right triangle

   $\overline{YM}$ is the altitude to the hypotenuse XZ

   Show the following: $\dfrac{XY}{XM} = \dfrac{YZ}{MY}$

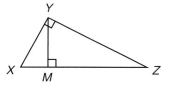

10. Find x.

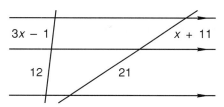

11. In $\triangle ABC$, $\overline{BD}$ is the angle bisector of angle B. Find x.

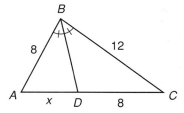

Solve:

12. $\begin{cases} x - y = 1 \\ y - 2z = 1 \\ 3x - 4z = 7 \end{cases}$

13. $\begin{cases} 2x + 2y - z = 9 \\ 3x + 3y + z = 16 \\ x - 2y = -1 \end{cases}$

14. $\begin{cases} \dfrac{2}{3}x + \dfrac{1}{4}y = \dfrac{49}{12} \\ 0.05x + 0.2y = 0.85 \end{cases}$

15. $\dfrac{3}{2} + \dfrac{4}{x + 1} = \dfrac{1}{3}$

16. $\sqrt{3x + 1} + \sqrt{9} = 7$

Simplify:

17. $5\sqrt{\dfrac{5}{2}} - 6\sqrt{\dfrac{2}{5}} + 3\sqrt{40}$

18. $\left(3x^{\frac{a}{2}} + 2y^{\frac{b}{3}}\right)\left(2x^{\frac{a}{2}} - 2y^{\frac{b}{3}}\right)$

19. $\dfrac{x^{\left(\frac{a}{4}+1\right)} y^{\left(\frac{c+3}{2}\right)}}{\left(x^2\right)^b y^{-c+1}}$

20. $\sqrt{3}\sqrt{-3} - \sqrt{-2}\sqrt{-2} + \sqrt{-4} + 5i + \sqrt{-3}$

21. $7i^6 - 3i^4 + 5i^3 + \sqrt{16}\,i^5$

22. Use construction to divide $\overline{AB}$ into 3 congruent segments.

23. Construct an equilateral triangle with sides that have length AB.

24. Draw a large scalene triangle on a full sheet of paper. Construct the bisector of each of the angles. The bisectors will meet at a point P that is equidistant from the sides of the triangle. Next, construct a perpendicular segment from point P to one of the sides of the triangle. Then use a compass to draw a circle with point P as its center and the perpendicular segment as its radius. This circle will be tangent to the sides of the triangle. We say that the circle is **inscribed** in the triangle.

25. Find a and b.

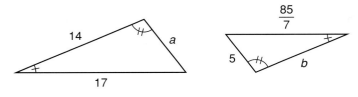

26. Solve for x and y.

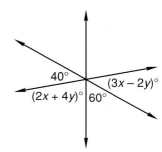

27. A sphere has a radius of 4 centimeters. Find the volume and surface area of the sphere.

28. Find the volume of the cone whose base is shown and whose altitude is 10 cm.

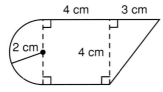

CONCEPT REVIEW PROBLEMS   **29.** If $a * b = a - 3b$ and $a \# b = 2a + 3b$, evaluate the expression $(4 * 3) \# 5$.

30. If $x \# y = 2x + 3y$ and $x * y = 5x + 4y$, evaluate the expression $2 \# (4 * 3)$.

LESSON 9   *Congruent Figures   •   Proof Outlines*

9.A
congruent figures

We remember that in mathematics we use the words **equal to, greater than,** and **less than** to compare real numbers.

$$4 = 2 + 2 \qquad 4 > 2 \qquad 4 < 6$$

Four is equal to 2 plus 2. Four is greater than 2, and 4 is less than 6. We use the number line to define what we mean when we use the words *equal to, greater than,* and *less than* by saying that one number is greater than another number if its graph is farther to the right on the number line than the graph of the other number.

We see that the graph of 4 and the graph of 2 + 2 are at the same place, so these symbols represent the same number, not different numbers. The symbols 2 + 2 and 4 are called **numerical expressions** or **numerals** and the number is the **idea** that they represent. The graph of 4 is to the right of the graph of 2 and to the left of the graph of 6, so we say that 4 is greater than 2 and less than 6.

We remember that we use the word **congruent** when we want to say that two figures are **geometrically equivalent.** On the left we show two line segments that are 2 units long. In the center we show two angles whose measures are 27°, and on the right we show two triangles in which the corresponding angles have equal measures and the corresponding sides have equal lengths.

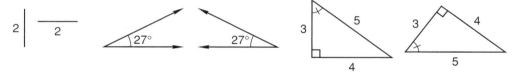

We say that the two line segments are congruent because they are geometrically equivalent. The only quality of a line segment that can be measured is its length, and the lengths are equal. The two angles are congruent because they are geometrically equivalent. The only quality of these angles that can be measured is the measure of the angles, and both angles have a measure of 27°. The two triangles are congruent because they are geometrically equivalent. All corresponding sides have equal lengths and all corresponding angles have equal measures. **If one geometric figure can be picked up mentally, flipped and turned as necessary, and placed on top of another geometric figure so that the figures match exactly, the figures are said to be congruent.**

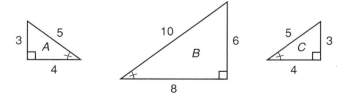

All three of these triangles are similar because they contain the same three angles. The lengths of the sides in triangle *B* are twice as long as the lengths of corresponding sides in triangle *A*, so the scale factor from triangle *A* to triangle *B* is 2 and the scale factor from triangle *B* to triangle *A* is $\frac{1}{2}$. The lengths of the sides in triangle *C* have the same lengths as the corresponding sides in triangle *A*, so the scale factor between triangle *C* and triangle *A* is 1. **From this we see that congruent triangles are similar triangles whose scale factor is 1.**

There are four ways or methods that we use to convince ourselves that two triangles are congruent. We will not prove these methods; instead, we will **postulate** that the methods are correct. We remember that a **postulate** is a statement that everyone accepts without proof. We will discuss definitions, postulates, and proofs in detail in a later lesson. We now proceed to try to justify our four postulates of triangle congruence. We hope you agree and accept the reasonableness of our postulates. The first postulate of triangle congruence is called **side-side-side,** abbreviated *SSS.* In Lesson 4 we noted that only one triangle can be constructed with three sides of designated lengths. Consider the segments whose lengths are 2, 3, and 4, as shown on the left.

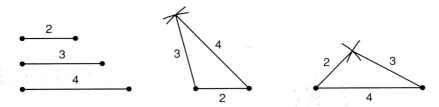

In the center figure we constructed a triangle by using side 2 as a base and arcs that have the lengths 3 and 4. In the right-hand figure we used side 4 as a base and let the arcs have lengths 2 and 3. If we mentally slide over and rotate the right-hand triangle, it will cover the triangle on the left exactly and we see that the two triangles are geometrically equivalent. The same thing would happen if we used side 3 as a base and used arcs that have lengths 2 and 4. Thus, all triangles constructed whose sides have the same lengths as the given segments are congruent.

A second postulate of triangle congruence is called **side-angle-side,** abbreviated *SAS.* If two sides and the included angle in one triangle have the same measures as two sides and the included angle in another triangle, the triangles are congruent. Consider the figures shown here.

To complete the triangle on the left, we need to draw segment *BC*. The length of segment *BC* is fixed by the location of points *B* and *C* and the measures of the angles that will be formed at *B* and *C* are also fixed. The triangle *ABC* will be congruent to triangle *DEF* because specifying the lengths of two sides and the angle between them completely determines the length of the missing side and the measures of the missing angles.

A third postulate of triangle congruence is usually called **angle-side-angle,** abbreviated *ASA.* This is often confusing to students because they believe that the given side must be between the given angles. But this is not true. Consider the two triangles shown here.

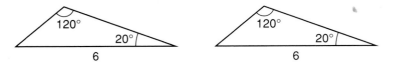

The triangles are congruent even though the side designated is not between the angles designated. The sum of the measures of the angles in any triangle is 180°, so the unmarked angle in both of these triangles must have a measure of 40°. Since the triangles have the same angles, the triangles are similar, and because the sides opposite the 120° angle are both 6 units long, the scale factor is 1 and the triangles are congruent. For this reason, the author prefers the notations **angle-side-angle-angle** or **angle-angle-angle-side,** abbreviated *ASAA* or *AAAS,* for if we know the measures of any two angles in a triangle, we know the measure of the other angle.

A fourth postulate of triangle congruence is called **hypotenuse-leg,** abbreviated *HL*, and pertains only to right triangles because only right triangles have a hypotenuse. Consider the two figures shown here.

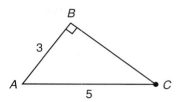 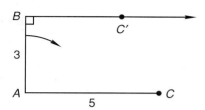

In the figure on the right, we show the right angle connecting the leg of length 3 units to ray *BC'*. If we rotate segment *AB* about point *A*, we hope you agree that ray *BC'* will intersect the 5-unit segment at *C*. If you do, you will agree with our postulate that if the length of the hypotenuse and the length of one leg in a right triangle are the same as the length of the hypotenuse and the length of one leg in another right triangle, the triangles are congruent. The four postulates of triangle congruency (*SSS*, *SAS*, *AAAS*, and *HL*) will be used as major postulates in the deductive reasoning process we will use to do geometric proofs.

9.B
proof outlines

In a later lesson we will discuss and learn how to do formal geometric proofs. Many of these proofs will require that we prove that two triangles are congruent. Before we begin formal proofs, we must do a **proof outline.** Then the formal proof will consist of fleshing out the proof outline. We remember that we use an equals sign topped by a wavy line ($\cong$) as our symbol for *congruent*. Also, we remember that two letters topped by a bar is our symbol for *segment*.

$$\overline{AB} \cong \overline{DB} \qquad \overline{DC} \perp \overline{AB} \qquad \overline{MP} \parallel \overline{QR}$$

We read these from left to right as "Segment *AB* is congruent to segment *DB*," "Segment *DC* is perpendicular to segment *AB*," and "Segment *MP* is parallel to segment *QR*." Two letters written without the overbar indicate the length of the segment. If segment *PQ* is 5 centimeters long, we may write

$$PQ = 5 \text{ cm}$$

The notation

$$\triangle ABC \cong \triangle DEF$$

is read "Triangle *ABC* is congruent to triangle *DEF*." This means that angle *A* has the same measure as angle *D*, angle *B* has the same measure as angle *E*, angle *C* has the same measure as angle *F*, and the scale factor is 1. **When we write statements of triangle similarity or triangle congruence, we must be careful to list vertices in the correct order so that angles at the vertices are corresponding angles.**

example 9.1   Given: $\overline{AD} \cong \overline{BD}$

$\qquad\qquad\quad \overline{DC} \perp \overline{AB}$

Outline a proof that shows:

$\qquad\qquad\quad \overline{AC} \cong \overline{BC}$

solution   When we are asked to prove that two line segments are congruent, almost always the way to do it is to prove that two triangles are congruent. If we can prove that $\triangle ADC$ is congruent to $\triangle BDC$, segment *AC* is congruent to segment *BC* because these segments are corresponding parts of congruent triangles. This proof outline is very short because it requires only three steps. The first step is to copy the figure and use tick marks to indicate sides and angles whose measures are equal. We use a circle to mark the segment that is a side in both triangles.

1.

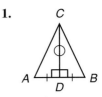

2. $\triangle ADC \cong \triangle BDC$ SAS

3. $\overline{AC} \cong \overline{BC}$ CPCTC

The second step is to note that the triangles are congruent by side-angle-side. The third step is to note that $\overline{AC} \cong \overline{BC}$. This statement of congruency can also be written as a statement that two lengths are equal by writing $AC = BC$. The statement of congruency is followed by *CPCTC*, a shorthand notation that means "corresponding parts of congruent triangles are congruent." This proof uses *SAS*. There are other ways to state this problem so that *SSS*, *AAAS*, and *HL* can be used as the reason for congruence. We will see these problems in the homework problem sets.

example 9.2   Given: $\angle E \cong \angle H$

                $\overline{EF} \cong \overline{HG}$

Outline a proof that shows:

                $\overline{DF} \cong \overline{DG}$

solution   This proof outline has only three steps, but the first step has two parts. First we copy the figure and use tick marks to indicate the parts of the figure that have equal measures.

1.A.

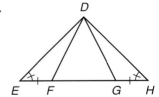

We note that angles *E* and *H* have equal measures. They are the base angles of the big triangle, so the big triangle is isosceles and the sides opposite these congruent angles have equal lengths, which we note by placing tick marks on them in the figure below.

1.B.

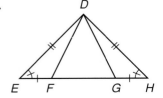

2. $\triangle EDF \cong \triangle HDG$ SAS

3. $\overline{DF} \cong \overline{DG}$ CPCTC

In this figure we can see that the small triangles on the left and right are congruent by *SAS*, as we note in step 2. This permits step 3.

example 9.3 In this problem we will remember that if two segments have equal lengths, the halves of the segments have equal lengths.

Given: $\overline{AG} \cong \overline{EF}$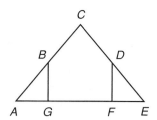

$\overline{CA} \cong \overline{CE}$

B is the midpoint of $\overline{CA}$

D is the midpoint of $\overline{CE}$

Outline a proof that shows:

$\overline{BG} \cong \overline{DF}$

solution There is no format for proof outlines. We have to know exactly what we are going to do before we begin a formal proof, as we will discuss in Lesson 15. In the last two examples we used three short steps. In this proof outline we will again copy the figure and use tick marks as the first step.

1.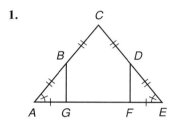

Now we will discuss a method that can be used to do the required proof.

2. To show that $\overline{BG} \cong \overline{DF}$, we need to show that the two small triangles are congruent. We were given that $\overline{AG} \cong \overline{EF}$. Angle A is congruent to angle E because $\overline{CA} \cong \overline{CE}$ and the base angles of an isosceles triangle have equal measures. Now $\overline{AB} \cong \overline{ED}$ because B and D are midpoints, and halves of congruent segments are congruent. Thus

$$\triangle ABG \cong \triangle EDF \qquad SAS$$

3. We were careful to list the vertices in corresponding order. Now we can state that $\overline{BG} \cong \overline{DF}$ because they are corresponding parts of congruent triangles.

$$\overline{BG} \cong \overline{DF} \qquad CPCTC$$

We will do proof outlines in the problem sets until we get to Lesson 15, where we begin to do formal proofs.

problem set 9

1. The ratio of goods to bads was 2 to 5 and the number of bads exceeded twice the number of goods by 40. How many were good and how many were bad?

2. Fourteen percent of the blues were added to 20 percent of the greens for a total of 54. Also, 5 times the number of blues exceeded twice the number of greens by 100. How many were blue and how many were green?

3. Write the following statement as an if-then statement:

    Sides opposite congruent angles in a triangle are congruent.

4. Is the following argument valid or invalid?

    All well-educated people know algebra.

    Lao Tzu knows algebra.
    _____

    Therefore, Lao Tzu is well-educated.

5. Write the contrapositive of the major premise of this syllogism to help determine whether the following argument is valid or invalid:

   > If the switch is on, then the light is not on.
   >
   > The light is on.
   > ─────────────────────────────────
   > Therefore, the switch is on.

6. Leonard found four consecutive integers such that 3 times the sum of the first and the fourth was 114 less than the product of −5 and the sum of the first two. What were the integers?

7. Two triangles are similar. A side of the larger triangle is 4/3 times as long as the corresponding side of the smaller triangle. What is the ratio of the area of the smaller triangle to the area of the larger triangle?

8. The sides of a triangle have lengths 4 cm, 5 cm, and 7 cm, respectively. Is the triangle a right triangle, an acute triangle, or an obtuse triangle?

9. Triangles can be shown to be congruent by the *SSS* congruency postulate, *SAS* congruency postulate, *AAAS* congruency postulate, or *HL* congruency postulate. The triangles in each pair shown below are congruent. State the congruency postulate that can be used to prove them congruent.

   (a) $\triangle ABC \cong \triangle DEF$ (b) $\triangle WXZ \cong \triangle YXZ$

   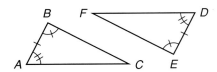   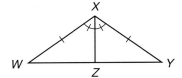

   (c) $\triangle PQR \cong \triangle PSR$ (d) $\triangle ABC \cong \triangle ADC$

   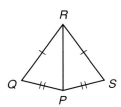   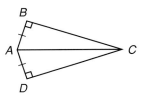

10. Given: $\overline{AB} \cong \overline{CB}$
    $\angle ABD \cong \angle CBD$

    Outline a proof that shows:
    $\triangle ABD \cong \triangle CBD$

    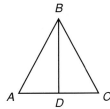

11. Given: $\overline{BC} \cong \overline{DC}$
    $\overline{AB} \cong \overline{AD}$

    Outline a proof that shows:
    $\angle ABC \cong \angle ADC$

    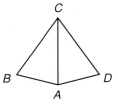

Simplify:

12. $7\sqrt{\dfrac{2}{3}} - 3\sqrt{\dfrac{3}{2}} + 2\sqrt{24}$

13. $\sqrt{-2}\sqrt{2} + \sqrt{-4}i - 2i^6 + \sqrt{-2}i^2$

14. $\left(2x^{\frac{a}{2}} + y^{\frac{b}{2}}\right)\left(2x^{\frac{a}{2}} - y^{\frac{b}{2}}\right)$

15. $\dfrac{x^{\left(\frac{a}{2}-3\right)}y^{\left(\frac{b-3}{2}\right)}}{x^{3a}\left(y^{\frac{1}{3}}\right)^{2b}}$

Solve:

16. $\sqrt{3x - 5} + \sqrt{3x} = 5$

17. $\dfrac{1}{2x - 8} + \dfrac{1}{5} = \dfrac{1}{7}$

18. $\begin{cases} 2x + 2y - z = -1 \\ x + y - 3z = -8 \\ 2x - y + z = 8 \end{cases}$

19. $\begin{cases} 2x - z = 10 \\ y + 2z = -2 \\ 3x - 2y = 8 \end{cases}$

20. Find a, b, and h.

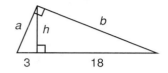

21. Given: $\triangle ABC$ is a right triangle

$\overline{BD}$ is the altitude to the hypotenuse AC

Show the following: $\dfrac{AB}{BD} = \dfrac{AC}{BC}$

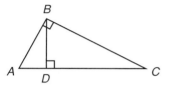

22. In $\triangle ABC$, $\overline{BD}$ is the angle bisector of angle B. Find x.

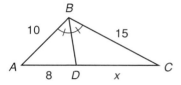

23. Use construction to divide $\overline{PQ}$ into 5 congruent segments.

$\bullet\!\!\!-\!\!\!\rule{8cm}{0.4pt}\!\!\!-\!\!\!\bullet$

P $\qquad\qquad\qquad\qquad\qquad\qquad\qquad\qquad\qquad Q$

24. Construct a 30° angle. (*Hint*: Construct an equilateral triangle.)

25. In the figure shown, the arrowheads tell us that the pairs of opposite sides are parallel. Find x and y.

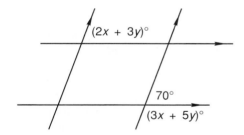

26. Find a and b.

27. Find a, b, and c.

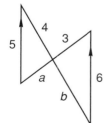

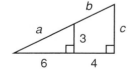

28. The base of a regular pyramid is a square whose perimeter is 40 centimeters. The height of the pyramid is 6 centimeters. Find the volume of the pyramid.

CONCEPT REVIEW PROBLEMS **29.** Let $x \mathbin{\#} y = 2x - 3y$ and $x \mathbin{*} y = x - y$. If $x = 10$ and $y = 12$, evaluate $(x \mathbin{\#} y) \mathbin{*} y$.

30. If $a > 0$ and $b > 0$, compare: A. $a + b$ B. $\sqrt{a^2 + b^2}$

LESSON 10 Equation of a Line • Rational Denominators • Completing the Square

10.A

equation of a line

A horizontal line has a slope of zero. A horizontal line does not cross the x axis and crosses or intersects the y axis at only one point. The y coordinate of that point is called the **y intercept** of the line. The equation of a horizontal line contains the letter y, an equals sign, and a number. The equation of the horizontal line in the figure on the left below contains no x because the value of y is +4 for every value of x. We list the coordinates of several points on the line and note that the y coordinate is +4 for each of the points. The equation of the line is $y = 4$.

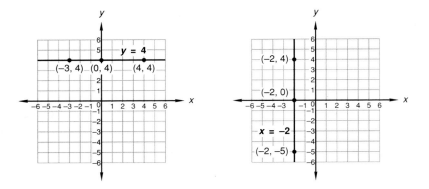

A vertical line has an undefined slope. A vertical line does not cross the y axis and crosses or intersects the x axis at only one point, called the **x intercept,** as we show in the figure on the right. The equation of this line contains an x, an equals sign, and a number. The equation does not contain the letter y because the x coordinate of every point on the line is –2 regardless of the value of the y coordinate. The equation of the line is $x = -2$.

A line that is not vertical has a slope and has a y intercept. If you can determine the slope of a line and know where the line crosses the y axis, the line is defined and can be drawn.

If the equation of a line is written in the form $y = mx + b$, we say that the line is written in **slope-intercept form.** The constant term b in the equation is the y intercept and the letter m, the coefficient of x, is the slope. The slope is the change in the y coordinate divided by the change in the x coordinate as we move from any point on the line to any other point on the line. The sign of the slope can be determined visually by remembering the following diagrams. **The little man always comes from the left side, as we show here.** He sees the first set of lines as uphill lines with positive slopes and the second set of lines as downhill lines with negative slopes.

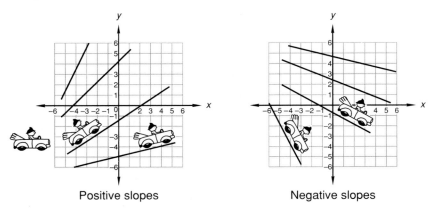

Positive slopes   Negative slopes

example 10.1   Find the slope-intercept form of the equation of the line that passes through the points $(-3, 2)$ and $(4, -3)$.

solution   We graph the points and draw the line and a right triangle whose hypotenuse is the segment connecting the points.

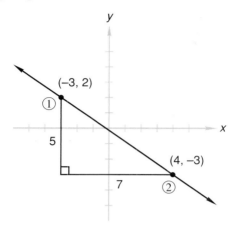

Slope is negative

Slope $= -\dfrac{5}{7}$

If we move from point 1 to point 2, the y coordinate changes from $+2$ to -3, a change of -5; and the x coordinate changes from -3 to $+4$, a change of $+7$. Thus, the slope is

$$m = \frac{\text{change in } y}{\text{change in } x} = \frac{-5}{+7} = -\frac{5}{7}$$

We get the same result if we move from point 2 to point 1. The y coordinate changes from -3 to $+2$, a change of $+5$; and the x coordinate changes from 4 to -3, a change of -7.

$$m = \frac{\text{change in } y}{\text{change in } x} = \frac{+5}{-7} = -\frac{5}{7}$$

The line appears to cross the y axis near the origin, so the y intercept should be a number close to zero. We can find the exact value of the y intercept if we replace m in the linear equation $y = mx + b$ with $-\frac{5}{7}$ and then use the coordinates of either of the given points as replacements for x and y to solve for b.

$$y = -\frac{5}{7}x + b \qquad \text{slope-intercept form of equation}$$

$$2 = -\frac{5}{7}(-3) + b \qquad \text{used } (-3, 2) \text{ for } x \text{ and } y$$

$$\frac{14}{7} = \frac{15}{7} + b \qquad \text{simplified}$$

$$b = -\frac{1}{7} \qquad \text{solved}$$

We find that b is $-\frac{1}{7}$, so we can write the equation of the line as

$$y = -\frac{5}{7}x - \frac{1}{7}$$

example 10.2   Find the equation of the line that passes through the point $(-2, 5)$ and is perpendicular to the line $3y + 4x = 2$.

solution   First we write the given line in slope-intercept form by solving for y.

$$y = -\frac{4}{3}x + \frac{2}{3}$$

A line that is perpendicular to this line would have a slope of $+\frac{3}{4}$ because the slopes of perpendicular lines are negative reciprocals of each other. So we have

$$y = \frac{3}{4}x + b$$

Now we can use $(-2, 5)$ for x and y and solve for b.

$$5 = \frac{3}{4}(-2) + b \qquad \text{used } (-2, 5) \text{ for } x \text{ and } y$$

$$\frac{10}{2} = -\frac{3}{2} + b \qquad \text{simplified}$$

$$b = \frac{13}{2} \qquad \text{solved}$$

Now we have both the slope and the y intercept, so we can write the equation of the line as

$$y = \frac{3}{4}x + \frac{13}{2}$$

example 10.3 Find the equations of lines (a) and (b).

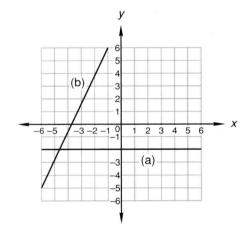

solution (a) Remember that vertical lines have the same x coordinate at every point on the line regardless of the value of the y coordinate. The equation of a vertical line passing through the point (h, k) is $x = h$. Also, horizontal lines have the same y coordinate at every point on the line regardless of the value of the x coordinate. The equation of a horizontal line passing through the point (h, k) is $y = k$. Line (a) is a horizontal line and every point on the line is two units below the x axis. Therefore, the equation of line (a) is

$$y = -2$$

(b) The equations of lines that are neither horizontal nor vertical contain two variables and have the form

$$y = mx + b$$

We note that line (b) passes through the points $(-6, -5)$ and $(-1, 6)$ and that the slope is positive. Thus, the slope is

$$m = \frac{\text{change in } y}{\text{change in } x} = +\frac{11}{5}$$

Therefore, we can write $y = \frac{11}{5}x + b$.

When we know the slope and the coordinates of any point on the line, we can find the exact value of the y intercept by replacing x and y with the coordinates of the point in the equation. We decide to use the coordinates of the point $(-1, 6)$.

$$y = \frac{11}{5}x + b \qquad\qquad \text{slope-intercept form of equation}$$

$$6 = \frac{11}{5}(-1) + b \qquad\qquad \text{used } (-1, 6) \text{ for } x \text{ and } y$$

$$\frac{30}{5} = -\frac{11}{5} + b \qquad\qquad \text{simplified}$$

$$b = \frac{41}{5} \qquad\qquad \text{solved}$$

Now we have both the slope and the y intercept, so we can write the equation of line (b) as

$$y = \frac{11}{5}x + \frac{41}{5}$$

We note that this equation is really not an exact equation for line (b) because we estimated that the line passed through the points $(-6, -5)$ and $(-1, 6)$. Thus, the equation $y = \frac{11}{5}x + \frac{41}{5}$ is an estimate for line (b).

10.B
rational denominators

When we divide a counting number by the number one, the result (quotient) is the counting number itself. When we divide a counting number by another counting number, the quotient is a decimal number whose digits terminate or repeat in a fixed pattern that has no end.

$$\frac{4}{1} = 4 \qquad \frac{4}{2} = 2 \qquad \frac{1}{4} = 0.25 \qquad \frac{13}{3} = 4.3333\ldots$$

We can use an overbar to represent the pattern of digits that repeat. If we divide 111 by 99, we get the repeating pattern on the left, which we indicate by using an overbar, as we show on the right.

$$\frac{111}{99} = 1.1212121212\ldots \qquad\qquad \frac{111}{99} = 1.\overline{12}$$

A **ratio** can be written as a fraction and we say that real numbers that can be written as fractions of integers are ratio numbers or **rational numbers.** Thus, all of the following are rational numbers.

$$-6.4 \qquad 0.0021 \qquad -122 \qquad 4.16\overline{32} \qquad 8.\overline{3} \qquad 0.0$$

The ratio of the circumference of a circle to the diameter of a circle is called *pi* and is represented by the symbol π. Pi is not a rational number because it cannot be written as a fraction of counting numbers and its decimal representation is infinite in length and does not have a pattern that repeats. Thus, we say that π is an irrational number. Here we show the first forty digits in the decimal representation of π.

$$\pi = 3.1415926535897932384626433832795028841971\ldots$$

In later lessons we will discuss the number used as the base for natural logarithms, which we designate with the letter e. This number is also an irrational number. Here we show the first forty digits in the decimal representation of e.

$$e = 2.7182818284590452353602874713526624977757\ldots$$

If the square root, cube root, fourth root, or any counting number root of a counting number is not a counting number, the root is an irrational number. Thus, all of the following numbers are irrational numbers.

$$\sqrt{142} \qquad \sqrt[3]{13} \qquad \sqrt[4]{65} \qquad \sqrt[5]{17} \qquad \sqrt[12]{143}$$

Only real numbers (the numbers whose graphs are on the number line) can be rational numbers, so any complex number with a nonzero imaginary part cannot be a rational number. It is customary to write numbers with rational denominators. For example, the four numbers

(a) $\dfrac{2}{\sqrt{3}}$ (b) $\dfrac{6}{2i}$ (c) $\dfrac{4 + \sqrt{3}}{2 - 3\sqrt{3}}$ (d) $\dfrac{2 - i^3 + 2i^5}{-2i + 4}$

can be written with rational denominators as

(a') $\dfrac{2\sqrt{3}}{3}$ (b') $-3i$ (c') $\dfrac{-17 - 14\sqrt{3}}{23}$ (d') $\dfrac{1}{10} + \dfrac{4}{5}i$

The process of converting a denominator to a rational number is called **rationalizing the denominator.** In (a) we multiplied above and below by $\sqrt{3}$. In (b) we multiplied above and below by $-i$. We will show the procedure for rationalizing the denominators of (c) and (d) in the next two examples.

example 10.4   Simplify: $\dfrac{4 + \sqrt{3}}{2 - 3\sqrt{3}}$

solution   We remember that **an expression that contains square roots of counting numbers is in simplified form when no radicand has a perfect square (other than 1) as a factor and no radicals are in the denominator.** We can rationalize the denominator if we multiply above and below by $2 + 3\sqrt{3}$, which is the **conjugate of the denominator.**

$$\frac{4 + \sqrt{3}}{2 - 3\sqrt{3}} \cdot \frac{2 + 3\sqrt{3}}{2 + 3\sqrt{3}}$$

We have two multiplications to perform, one above and one below. Many people find it easier to do these multiplications separately and then to write the answer. We will do this.

ABOVE	BELOW
$4 + \sqrt{3}$	$2 - 3\sqrt{3}$
$2 + 3\sqrt{3}$	$2 + 3\sqrt{3}$
$8 + 2\sqrt{3}$	$4 - 6\sqrt{3}$
$12\sqrt{3} + 9$	$6\sqrt{3} - 27$
$8 + 14\sqrt{3} + 9 = 17 + 14\sqrt{3}$	$4 \qquad - 27 = -23$

Thus, our simplification is

$$\frac{17 + 14\sqrt{3}}{-23} \qquad \text{or} \qquad \frac{\mathbf{-17 - 14\sqrt{3}}}{\mathbf{23}}$$

example 10.5   Simplify: $\dfrac{2 - i^3 + 2i^5}{-2i + 4}$

solution   First we write both complex numbers in standard form and get

$$\frac{2 + 3i}{4 - 2i}$$

We can change the denominator of this expression to a rational number if we multiply above and below by $4 + 2i$, which is the **conjugate of the denominator.** We have two multiplications indicated, one above and one below. We will use the vertical format for both of the multiplications.

ABOVE	BELOW
$2 + 3i$	$4 - 2i$
$4 + 2i$	$4 + 2i$
$8 + 12i$	$16 - 8i$
$4i + 6i^2$	$8i - 4i^2$
$8 + 16i - 6 = 2 + 16i$	$16 \qquad + 4 = 20$

Thus, we can write our answer as

$$\frac{2 + 16i}{20} = \frac{1 + 8i}{10}$$

This answer is not in the preferred form of $a + bi$. We can write this complex number in standard form if we write

$$\frac{1}{10} + \frac{4}{5}i$$

10.C
completing the square

If a quadratic equation is in the form of the two equations shown here, the solution can be found by taking the square root of both sides of the equation.

(a) $\left(x + \dfrac{1}{2}\right)^2 = 3$ (b) $(x - 4)^2 = 5$ equation

$\qquad x + \dfrac{1}{2} = \pm\sqrt{3}$ $\qquad x - 4 = \pm\sqrt{5}$ square root of both sides

$\qquad x = -\dfrac{1}{2} \pm \sqrt{3}$ $\qquad x = 4 \pm \sqrt{5}$ solved for x

The process of rearranging a quadratic equation into the form $(x - h)^2 = p$ is called **completing the square.** The basis for this procedure comes from observing the patterns of the coefficients when binomials are squared. Here we give four examples.

(c) $(x + 3)^2 = x^2 + 6x + 9$ (d) $(x - 5)^2 = x^2 - 10x + 25$

(e) $\left(x - \dfrac{1}{2}\right)^2 = x^2 - x + \dfrac{1}{4}$ (f) $\left(x + \dfrac{2}{5}\right)^2 = x^2 + \dfrac{4}{5}x + \dfrac{4}{25}$

We note that, in each example, the constant term of the trinomial is a positive number and is the square of one half the coefficient of the x term in the trinomial. Thus, if we have

$$x^2 + \frac{3}{5}x$$

and want to add a constant so that the result is the square of a binomial, we multiply the coefficient of x by $\frac{1}{2}$ and square the result.

$$\left(\frac{3}{5} \cdot \frac{1}{2}\right)^2 = \frac{9}{100}$$

Now if we add $\frac{9}{100}$ to the expression under consideration, we can write the result as the square of a binomial.

$$x^2 + \frac{3}{5}x + \frac{9}{100} \qquad \xrightarrow{\text{which can be written as}} \qquad \left(x + \frac{3}{10}\right)^2$$

We also note that the constant in the binomial is one half the coefficient of x in the trinomial.

Finding the answers to many problems in mathematics, physics, and engineering requires that we solve a quadratic equation. We are fortunate that the solutions to these equations can be found by the straightforward process of completing the square or by using the quadratic formula, which we will review in the next lesson.

example 10.6   Solve $-x + 3x^2 = -5$ by completing the square.

solution   As the first step we write the equation in standard form.

$$3x^2 - x + 5 = 0$$

Then we divide every term by 3 so that the coefficient of x^2 will be 1.

$$x^2 - \frac{1}{3}x + \frac{5}{3} = 0$$

Next we write the parentheses and move the constant term to the right-hand side.

$$\left(x^2 - \frac{1}{3}x \qquad\right) = -\frac{5}{3}$$

Now we multiply the coefficient of x by $\frac{1}{2}$ and square this product.

$$\left(-\frac{1}{3} \cdot \frac{1}{2}\right)^2 = \frac{1}{36}$$

Then we add $\frac{1}{36}$ to both sides of the equation.

$$\left(x^2 - \frac{1}{3}x + \frac{1}{36}\right) = -\frac{5}{3} + \frac{1}{36}$$

Now we simplify and solve for x.

$$\left(x - \frac{1}{6}\right)^2 = -\frac{59}{36} \qquad\qquad \text{simplified}$$

$$x - \frac{1}{6} = \pm\sqrt{-\frac{59}{36}} \qquad\qquad \text{square root of both sides}$$

$$x = \frac{1}{6} \pm \frac{\sqrt{59}}{6}i \qquad\qquad \text{solved}$$

problem set 10

1. Forty percent of the bigs exceed sixty percent of the smalls by 128 and the ratio of the bigs to the smalls is 17 to 6. How many are big and how many are small?

2. The value of 142 dimes and quarters is $29.20. How many are dimes and how many are quarters?

3. The ratio of the area of the small circle to the area of the big circle is 1 to 64. What is the ratio of the radius of the small circle to the radius of the big circle?

4. Find three consecutive even integers such that 4 times the product of the first and the third is 28 greater than the product of −10 and the sum of the second and the third.

5. Find the equation of the line that passes through (1, 0) and (0, 1).

6. Find the equation of the line that passes through $(4, 1)$ and is parallel to the line $y = 2x - 1$.

Simplify:

7. $-2i^5 + 3i^3 - 3i^6$

8. $2i^3 + 4i^5 - 6i^7 + 8i^9$

9. $\dfrac{2 + i}{3 - 2i}$

10. $\dfrac{2 + i - 2i^3}{2i^3 + 4}$

11. $\dfrac{2 + 2\sqrt{3}}{1 - \sqrt{3}}$

Solve by completing the square:

12. $x^2 - 4x - 12 = 0$

13. $x + 3x^2 = -5$

14. Is the following argument valid or invalid?

> If the light is on, then the switch is on.
>
> The switch is not on.
> _____
> Therefore, the light is not on.

15. Triangles can be shown to be congruent by the *SSS* congruency postulate, *SAS* congruency postulate, *AAAS* congruency postulate, or *HL* congruency postulate. The triangles in each pair shown below are congruent. State the congruency postulate that can be used to prove them congruent.

(a) $\triangle ABC \cong \triangle DEF$

(b) $\triangle PRS \cong \triangle RPQ$

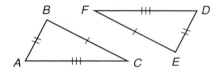

(c) $\triangle STU \cong \triangle WVU$

(d) $\triangle PSR \cong \triangle QSR$

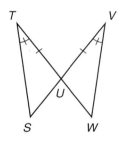

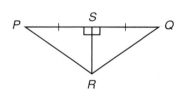

16. Given: $\angle C \cong \angle E$

$\overline{CD} \cong \overline{ED}$

Outline a proof that shows:

$\triangle BCD \cong \triangle AED$

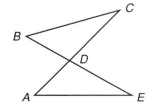

17. Given: $\overline{AD} \cong \overline{BD}$

$\overline{DC} \perp \overline{AB}$

Outline a proof that shows:

$\angle A \cong \angle B$

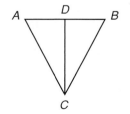

18. Given: $\triangle PQR$ is a right triangle

$\overline{QS}$ is the altitude to the hypotenuse PR

Show the following: $\dfrac{SR}{SQ} = \dfrac{QR}{PQ}$

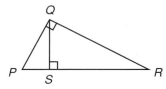

19. Find a, b, and c.

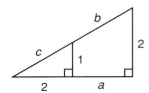

20. Find x.

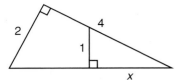

Solve:

21. $\sqrt{2x - 7} + \sqrt{2x} = 7$

22. $\begin{cases} \dfrac{3}{4}x + \dfrac{5}{2}y = 8 \\ 0.25y - 0.4z = 0.1 \\ -\dfrac{x}{2} - \dfrac{z}{2} = -\dfrac{5}{2} \end{cases}$

Simplify:

23. $\dfrac{x^{-3} + y^{-6}}{x^{-6}y^2}$

24. $\dfrac{x^3 \sqrt{x^3} \left(yx^2\right)^{\frac{a}{3}}}{x^a y^{2a}}$

25. Construct a line through P perpendicular to $\overline{EF}$.

$P \bullet$

E F

26. Construct an equilateral triangle whose sides have length $\frac{1}{2}AB$.

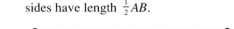

A B

27. Find the surface area of this right prism. Dimensions are in meters.

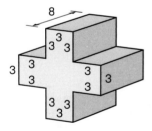

28. A sphere has a radius of 3 inches. Find the volume and surface area of the sphere.

CONCEPT REVIEW PROBLEMS **29.** Given: $x * y = 5x + y$ and $x \# y = x + 3y$. Compare: A. $3 * 4$ B. $3 \# 4$

30. If x, y, z, and t are as shown, compare: A. $x - z$ B. $t - y$

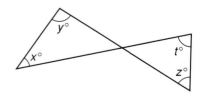

LESSON 11   *Circles • Properties of Circles • The Quadratic Formula*

11.A
circles

A **circle** is the locus of all points in a plane that are equidistant from a point called the **center** of the circle. The **radius** of a circle is a line segment that connects a point on the circle to the center or is the length of such a segment. A **chord** is a line segment that connects any two points on a circle. A **diameter** is a chord that passes through the center of the circle or is the length of such a chord. A **secant** is a line that intersects a circle at two points. A **tangent** to a circle is a line, coplanar with the circle, that intersects (touches) the circle at only one point.

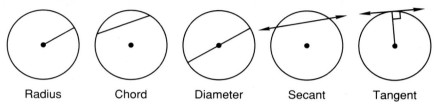

Radius   Chord   Diameter   Secant   Tangent

All of the foregoing statements are definitions and we remember that definitions are true in both directions. The figure on the right above shows that a tangent is perpendicular to the radius at the point of intersection. This fact can be proved by using an argument called an *indirect proof*, so this fact is a theorem. Many authors at this level simply postulate this fact. We will also postulate the perpendicularity of the tangent and the radius.

The **perimeter** of a circle is called the **circumference** of the circle. An **arc** is two points on a circle and all the points on the circle between them. A **semicircle** is an arc whose length is half the circumference. The **central angle** of an arc is formed by two radii connecting the endpoints of the arc with the center of the circle. **We define the angular measure of an arc to be the same as the measure of its central angle.** Thus the angular measure of the arc that we call a semicircle is 180° because the two radii to the endpoints of the arc form a straight angle, as we show on the left below. The angular measure of the total arc of a circle is 360°. The circle on the right is divided into a **major arc** and a **minor arc**. If the measures of two arcs are not equal, we call the larger arc the *major arc* and the smaller arc the *minor arc*. The minor arc has a measure of 100° since its central angle has a measure of 100°. The major arc and its central angle both have a measure of 260°.

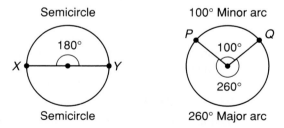

As we see, two points on a circle determine both a major arc and a minor arc. It is customary to use two letters to designate a minor arc and to use three letters to designate a major arc. The symbol $\overarc{BC}$ is read "arc *BC*" and the symbol $\overarc{ABC}$ is read "arc *ABC*."

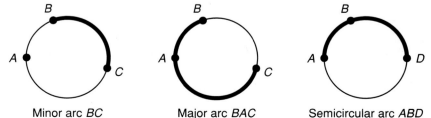

Minor arc *BC*   Major arc *BAC*   Semicircular arc *ABD*

We define **congruent circles** to be circles that have the same radii. Congruent arcs are arcs that have the same angular measure that are on one circle or on congruent circles.

When we speak of the **measure of an arc,** we are speaking of the **angular measure of the arc,** which is the same as the angular measure of the central angle of the circle. The measure of an arc is not the length of the arc.

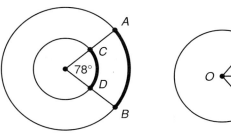

In the figure on the left, the measure of arc AB equals the measure of arc CD because both arcs have the same central angle.

$$m\overset{\frown}{AB} = m\overset{\frown}{CD}$$

For the figure on the right we can write that

$$m\overset{\frown}{XY} + m\overset{\frown}{YZ} = m\overset{\frown}{XZ}$$

because $m\angle XOY + m\angle YOZ = m\angle XOZ$

11.B
properties of circles

Properties of circles are important. Students who have completed a standard geometry book or the *Algebra 2* book of this series have been exposed to the proofs of these properties, but both the properties and the proofs have been forgotten by many. We will review several major properties here.

An angle whose vertex lies on a circle and whose sides are chords of the circle is called an **inscribed angle.** In Lesson 128 in the *Algebra 2* book we proved that **the measure of an inscribed angle is equal to one half the measure of its intercepted arc.** In the figure on the left below, the arc and the central angle have a measure of 44°. In the next figure we see that every inscribed angle that intercepts the 44° arc has a measure of 22°.

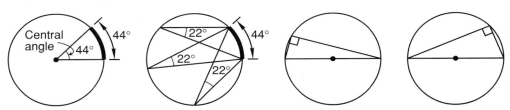

The endpoints of a diameter of a circle intercept an arc whose measure is 180°. **Thus, any inscribed angle that intercepts a diameter has a measure of 90°,** as we see in the two figures on the right above. **To construct a right angle, we can draw a circle, draw a diameter, and inscribe an angle whose endpoints are the ends of the diameter.**

The fact that an inscribed angle has half the measure of the arc it intercepts tells us that the sum of the measures of any pair of opposite angles in a quadrilateral inscribed in a circle is 180°. Consider the following figure:

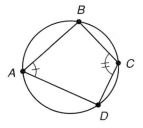

Angle A intercepts $\overset{\frown}{BD}$ and angle C intercepts $\overset{\frown}{BAD}$. Since the sum of the measures of the arcs is 360°, the sum of the measures of the angles is 180°.

If two chords of a circle intersect, each chord is divided into two segments. **The product of the lengths of the segments of one chord equals the product of the lengths of the segments of the other chord, as we show in the figure on the left.**

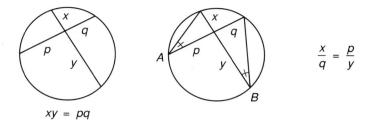

$$xy = pq \qquad\qquad \frac{x}{q} = \frac{p}{y}$$

We can see the reason if we draw additional chords to form similar triangles, as we show in the figure on the right. The angles at A and B have equal measures because they intercept the same arc. The vertical angles in the center also have equal measures, so the triangles are similar. If we put sides x and p from the left-hand triangle on the top and the corresponding sides from the right-hand triangle on the bottom, we form the two equal ratios we show on the right. Then we can cross multiply to form the equation shown below the figure on the left.

Two tangent segments from a point outside a circle have equal lengths. We will do a formal proof of this statement in a later lesson. The proof is straightforward. On the left we show tangent segments m and n from a point P outside the circle.

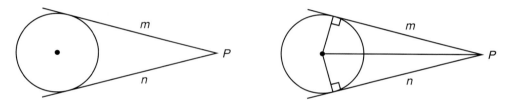

We remember that we postulated the fact that if a line segment is tangent to a circle, then the line segment is perpendicular to the radius at the point of tangency. Therefore, the radii are perpendicular to the tangents. Thus, the two triangles formed are right triangles that share the same hypotenuse. Thus, the two triangles are congruent by the hypotenuse-leg congruency postulate. Thus, m and n have equal lengths because they are corresponding parts of congruent triangles.

example 11.1   Find x and y.

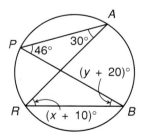

solution   Angles A and B have equal measures because they intercept the same arc, $\overset{\frown}{PR}$. Angle A has a measure of $30°$ and angle B has a measure of $(y + 20)°$. Thus we can write the following equation and solve for y.

$$y + 20 = 30 \quad\longrightarrow\quad y = \mathbf{10}$$

Angles P and R have equal measures because they intercept the same arc, $\overset{\frown}{AB}$, so we can write the following equation and solve for x.

$$x + 10 = 46 \quad\longrightarrow\quad x = \mathbf{36}$$

example 11.2   Find x, y, and z.

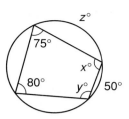

solution   This problem gives us practice with the fact that the measure of an intercepted arc has twice the measure of the inscribed angle and with the fact that the sum of the measures of two opposite angles in an inscribed quadrilateral is 180°. Also, the sum of the measures of the interior angles of any quadrilateral is 360°.

$$z + 50 = 2 \times 80 \qquad (\text{arc})° = 2 \times (\text{inscribed angle})°$$
$$z + 50 = 160 \qquad \text{multiplied}$$
$$z = \mathbf{110} \qquad \text{solved}$$

Since the sum of the measures of opposite angles in an inscribed quadrilateral is 180°, we can solve for x and y.

$$x + 80 = 180 \qquad\qquad y + 75 = 180$$
$$x = \mathbf{100} \qquad\qquad\quad y = \mathbf{105}$$

example 11.3   Find x, y, and z.

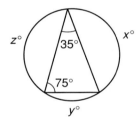

solution   The measure of arc x is twice the measure of the 75° inscribed angle, so x equals **150.** In the same way, y must equal **70,** so x and y sum to 220. Then z makes up the rest of 360°, so z equals **140.**

example 11.4   Find x.

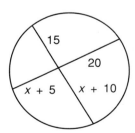

solution   The products of the segments of the chords are equal.

$$20(x + 5) = 15(x + 10) \qquad \text{equal products}$$
$$20x + 100 = 15x + 150 \qquad \text{multiplied}$$
$$5x = 50 \qquad\qquad\quad \text{simplified}$$
$$x = \mathbf{10} \qquad\qquad\quad \text{solved}$$

example 11.5   The triangle and the circle are tangent at three points, as shown. Find x and y.

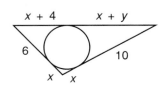

solution   Two tangent segments to a circle from a point outside the circle have equal length. Thus

$$x + 4 = 6 \quad \longrightarrow \quad x = 2$$

$$x + y = 10 \quad \longrightarrow \quad y = 8$$

11.C
the quadratic formula

By completing the square, any quadratic equation can be written in the form of $(x - h)^2 = p$ and then can be solved by taking the square root of both sides. This process is time-consuming, and it is a little faster to use the quadratic formula. This formula can be derived by completing the square on a general quadratic equation. We begin by writing a general quadratic equation that uses the letters a, b, and c as constants.

$$ax^2 + bx + c = 0$$

Next we give x^2 a unity coefficient by dividing every term by a, and we get

$$x^2 + \frac{b}{a}x + \frac{c}{a} = 0$$

Now we move c/a to the right-hand side and use parentheses on the left-hand side.

$$\left(x^2 + \frac{b}{a}x \qquad \right) = \qquad -\frac{c}{a}$$

Note that we placed the $-c/a$ well to the right of the equals sign. Now we multiply the coefficient of x, which is b/a, by $1/2$ and square the result.

$$\left(\frac{b}{a} \cdot \frac{1}{2} \right)^2 = \frac{b^2}{4a^2}$$

Next we add $b^2/\left(4a^2\right)$ inside the parentheses and also to the other side of the equation. On the right we are careful to place $b^2/\left(4a^2\right)$ in front of $-c/a$.

$$\left(x^2 + \frac{b}{a}x + \frac{b^2}{4a^2} \right) = \frac{b^2}{4a^2} - \frac{c}{a}$$

Now we write the parentheses term as a squared term and combine $b^2/\left(4a^2\right)$ and $-c/a$.

$$\left(x + \frac{b}{2a} \right)^2 = \frac{b^2 - 4ac}{4a^2}$$

Finally, we take the square root of both sides and then solve for x.

$$x + \frac{b}{2a} = \pm\sqrt{\frac{b^2 - 4ac}{4a^2}} \qquad \text{took square roots}$$

$$x = -\frac{b}{2a} \pm \frac{\sqrt{b^2 - 4ac}}{2a} \qquad \text{solved for } x$$

$$x = \frac{-b \pm \sqrt{b^2 - 4ac}}{2a} \qquad \text{added}$$

The derivation of the quadratic formula will be required in future problem sets. This derivation requires only simple algebraic manipulations, and the requirement that a student be able to perform this derivation is not unreasonable.

example 11.6   Use the quadratic formula to find the roots of the equation $3x^2 - 2x + 5 = 0$.

solution   The formula is

$$x = \frac{-b \pm \sqrt{b^2 - 4ac}}{2a}$$

If we write the given equation just below the general quadratic equation,

$$ax^2 + bx + c = 0 \qquad \text{general quadratic equation}$$

$$3x^2 - 2x + 5 = 0 \qquad \text{given equation}$$

we note the following correspondences between the equations.

$$a = 3 \qquad b = -2 \qquad c = 5$$

If we use these numbers for a, b, and c in the quadratic formula, we get

$$x = \frac{-(-2) \pm \sqrt{(-2)^2 - 4(3)(5)}}{2(3)} \qquad \text{substituted}$$

$$x = \frac{2 \pm \sqrt{-56}}{6} \qquad \text{simplified}$$

$$x = \frac{1}{3} \pm \frac{\sqrt{14}}{3}i \qquad \text{solved}$$

problem set 11

1. The ratio of those included to those excluded is 4 to 7. If five times the number of excluded is 62 greater than the number included, how many are included and how many are excluded?

2. Forty percent of the number of beavers is 9 greater than the number of skunks. If the ratio of beavers to skunks is 3 to 1, how many beavers and how many skunks are there?

3. Find four consecutive even integers such that six times the sum of the first two exceeds twice the sum of the first and the fourth by 416.

4. Is the following argument valid or invalid?

   All well-educated people study algebra.

   Homer Lee is not well-educated.

   Therefore, Homer Lee does not study algebra.

5. Find x and y.

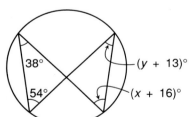

6. Find x.

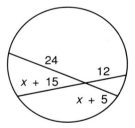

7. The triangle and the circle are tangent at three points, as shown. Find x and y.

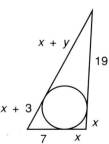

8. Begin with $ax^2 + bx + c = 0$ and derive the quadratic formula.

Use the quadratic formula to solve:

9. $3x^2 + 2x + 5 = 0$

10. $-x = -3x^2 + 4$

11. Find the equation of the line that passes through $(3, -2)$ and is perpendicular to the line $2y + 6x = 5$.

Simplify:

12. $\dfrac{3i^3 + 2 - 2i^3}{i - 4}$

13. $\dfrac{3 + 2\sqrt{3}}{2 - 3\sqrt{3}}$

Solve by completing the square:

14. $2x^2 = -x - 5$

15. $2x + 7 = 3x^2$

Solve:

16. $\begin{cases} 3x - 2y + z = -1 \\ x + 2y - z = 9 \\ 2x - y + 2z = 2 \end{cases}$

17. $\sqrt{2x + 20} + \sqrt{2x} = 10$

18. $\dfrac{x + 1}{x - 1} - \dfrac{1}{x} = \dfrac{2}{x(x - 1)}$ (*Hint*: Check solutions.)

19. Triangles can be shown to be congruent by the *SSS* congruency postulate, *SAS* congruency postulate, *AAAS* congruency postulate, or *HL* congruency postulate. The triangles in each pair shown below are congruent. State the congruency postulate that can be used to prove them congruent.

(a) $\triangle HIJ \cong \triangle HKJ$

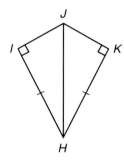

(b) $\triangle WXZ \cong \triangle YZX$

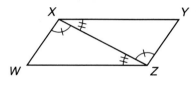
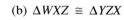

(c) $\triangle PQR \cong \triangle TSR$

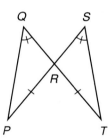

(d) $\triangle ABD \cong \triangle CBD$

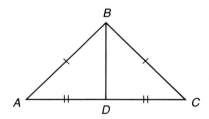
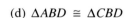

20. Given: $\angle Q$ and $\angle S$ are right angles

$\overline{QR} \cong \overline{SR}$

Outline a proof that shows:

$\triangle PQR \cong \triangle PSR$

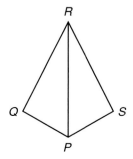

21. Given: $\angle B \cong \angle D$

$\overline{AC} \cong \overline{EC}$

Outline a proof that shows:

$\overline{BC} \cong \overline{DC}$

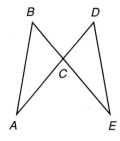

22. In $\triangle JKL$, $\overline{KM}$ is the angle bisector of angle K. Find x.

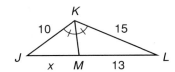

23. Find x.

24. Find x and y.

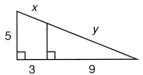

25. Construct a circle. Then construct a line tangent to the circle. (*Hint*: Draw a ray starting at the center of the circle. At the point where the ray intersects the circle, the tangent must be perpendicular to the ray.)

Simplify:

26. $\dfrac{a^{-7} + b^{-3}}{a^4 b^{-5}}$

27. $\dfrac{x^{3a+2}\left(\sqrt{x^3}\right)^{2a}}{y^{2a-4}\left(\sqrt{x}\right)^{2a+1}}$

28. $\left(6x^{\frac{3}{2}} - 2y^{\frac{1}{2}}\right)\left(6x^{\frac{3}{2}} + 2y^{\frac{1}{2}}\right)$

CONCEPT REVIEW PROBLEMS

29. Let x and y be real numbers. If $x^2 + y^2 = 1$, compare: A. xy B. 2

30. Given: $\triangle ABC$

Compare: A. AC B. $AB + DC$

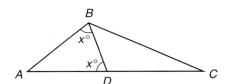

LESSON 12   *Angles and Diagonals in Polygons • Proof of the Chord-Tangent Theorem*

12.A

angles and diagonals in polygons

Both concave polygons and convex polygons have the same number of sides as they have vertices. The pentagons shown here have five sides labeled 1 through 5 and five angles labeled A through E.

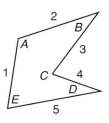

Concave polygon

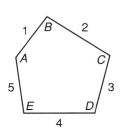

Convex polygon

At each vertex of both concave and convex polygons, there is an angle "inside" the polygon and an angle "outside" the polygon. The sum of these two angles at any vertex is 360°. **Convex polygons have both interior and exterior angles at each vertex.** There are two exterior angles at each vertex of a convex polygon and only one interior angle. An exterior angle is formed by extending one side of the convex polygon at the vertex. On the left below we show a scalene triangle. The interior angles are designated by the tick marks. In the center figure we have extended one side at a vertex and used *I* to designate the interior angle and *E* to designate the exterior angle.

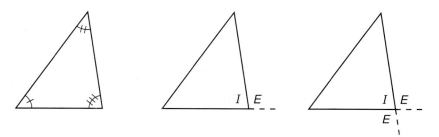

We note that angles *I* and *E* form a straight line, so the sum of the measures of an interior angle and an exterior angle is 180°. In the right-hand figure we extend the other side and form the second exterior angle *E*. The exterior angles *E* have equal measures since they are vertical angles.

The triangle on the left below has 3 sides and 3 vertices and the sum of the measures of the interior angles is 180°. We can find the sum of the interior angles of any convex polygon by drawing diagonals from one vertex to **triangulate** the polygon. The five-sided polygon (pentagon) shown can be triangulated into three triangles from any vertex, as we show. Thus, the sum of the measures of the interior angles of a convex pentagon is 3(180°), or 540°.

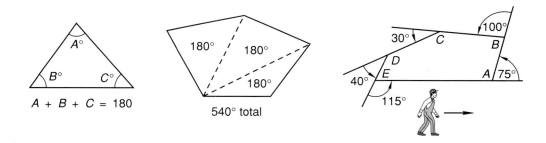

The sum of the measures of the exterior angles of any convex polygon is 360°, as we see in the figure on the right. If the little man walks all the way around the polygon and adds the number of degrees he turns at each corner, he will return to his starting place and find that he has turned all the way around, an angular measure of 360°.

For the following figure we see that a total of 5 diagonals can be drawn in a convex pentagon.

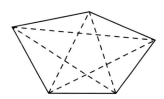

To develop a general expression for the total number of diagonals that can be drawn in a convex polygon of N sides, we note in the following figure that a diagonal can be drawn from vertex B to every vertex except B and the two adjacent vertices A and C.

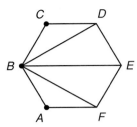

Thus, a total of $N - 3$ diagonals can be drawn from each vertex in a convex polygon of N sides. Since there are N vertices, the number of diagonals is $N(N - 3)$. But the diagonal from B to D is the same as the diagonal from D to B. Thus we have counted this diagonal and every other diagonal twice. To eliminate this duplication, we divide by 2 and get

$$\text{Number of diagonals} = \frac{N(N - 3)}{2}$$

This gives us an idea of how formulas for geometric properties can be developed. To develop an expression that will give us the sum of the measures of the interior angles of a convex polygon, we note that a convex polygon can be triangulated into $N - 2$ triangles from any vertex. The triangle has 3 sides, so this works for the triangle on the left. Every time we add a side to the convex polygon, we get another triangle. N for the quadrilateral is 4 and $4 - 2$ is two triangles, as we show in the center. A hexagon has 6 sides and $N - 2$ equals four triangles, as we show in the figure on the right.

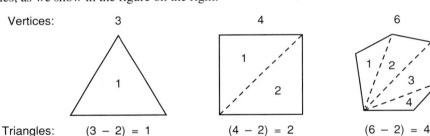

So a convex polygon can be triangulated into $N - 2$ triangles, and since the sum of the measures of the interior angles of any triangle is 180°, we can write

Sum of the measures of the interior angles of a convex polygon of N sides $= (N - 2)180°$

example 12.1   Find the sum of the measures of (a) the interior angles and (b) the exterior angles of a seven-sided convex polygon.

solution   (a) Some people like to stick numbers into formulas and turn the crank. We do this below.

$$(N - 2)180° = (7 - 2)180°$$
$$= (5)180°$$
$$= \mathbf{900°}$$

$$5 \times 180° = 900°$$

We often forget formulas and trying to remember too many clutters up the mind. On the right we draw a seven-sided convex polygon and triangulate it from one vertex. We count the triangles and multiply by 180°. We get the same answer without using the formula.

(b) The sum of the measures of the exterior angles of any convex polygon is **360°**.

12.B

proof of the chord-tangent theorem

We have stated that the measure of an inscribed angle is equal to one half the measure of its intercepted arc.

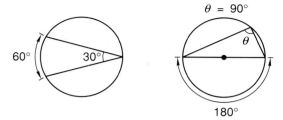

Thus the measure of a 30° inscribed angle will intercept an arc whose measure is 60°, as we show on the left. On the right we note that the measure of any inscribed angle θ that intercepts a diameter must have a measure equal to 90° because a diameter intercepts an arc whose measure is 180°. In the four figures below, from left to right, we note that if we fix one side of an inscribed angle and rotate the other side, the chord formed by the rotated side becomes shorter and shorter. Finally, the ends of the chord (A and C) are almost together and the rotated side is tangent to the circle. From this, we see that the angle formed by a chord and a tangent segment has the same characteristics as the angle formed by two chords.

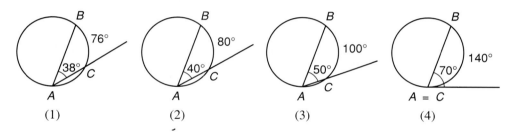

We can prove that the measure of the angle formed by a chord and a tangent segment that intersect at the tangent's point of contact is equal to one half the measure of the intercepted arc. This is called the **chord-tangent theorem.** There are three possible configurations of the proof, as we see in the following figures. In Case I, the chord intersects the center of the circle; in Case II, the center is included in the angle; and in Case III, the center is outside the angle.

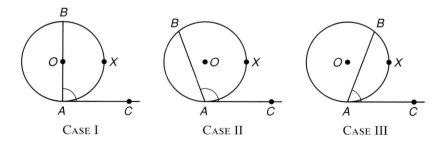

example 12.2   Prove Case I of the chord-tangent theorem

solution   For this proof, we use the Case I diagram. We have postulated that a tangent to a circle is always perpendicular to the radius, so tangent AC is perpendicular to radius OA and the measure of angle BAC equals 90°. The arc BXA intercepted by the diameter AB measures 180°. Therefore, the measure of angle BAC equals one half the measure of arc BXA. So we have our proof.

$$m\angle BAC = \frac{1}{2}m\widehat{BXA}$$

example 12.3   Prove Case II of the chord-tangent theorem.

solution   For this proof, we use the Case II diagram and draw diameter *AOY*, as shown in the left-hand figure below.

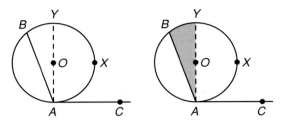

In the right-hand figure, we see that the measure of angle *BAY* equals one half the measure of arc *BY*. From Case I, we know that the measure of angle *YAC* equals one half the measure of arc *YXA*. Thus,

$$m\angle BAY = \tfrac{1}{2}m\widehat{BY} \qquad \text{inscribed angle}$$

$$m\angle YAC = \tfrac{1}{2}m\widehat{YXA} \qquad \text{from Case I}$$

$$\rule{7cm}{0.4pt}$$

$$m\angle BAY + m\angle YAC = \tfrac{1}{2}\left(m\widehat{BY} + m\widehat{YXA}\right)$$

But $m\angle BAY + m\angle YAC = m\angle BAC$ and $m\widehat{BY} + m\widehat{YXA} = m\widehat{BXA}$, so we have our proof.

$$m\angle BAC = \tfrac{1}{2}m\widehat{BXA}$$

example 12.4   Prove Case III of the chord-tangent theorem.

solution   For this proof, we use the Case III diagram and draw diameter *AOY*, as shown in the left-hand figure below.

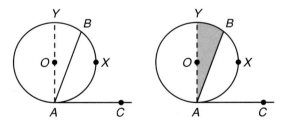

In the right-hand figure, we see that the measure of angle *YAB* equals one half the measure of arc *YB*. From Case I, we know that the measure of angle *YAC* equals one half the measure of arc *YXA*. Thus,

$$m\angle YAB = \tfrac{1}{2}m\widehat{YB} \qquad \text{inscribed angle}$$

$$m\angle YAC = \tfrac{1}{2}m\widehat{YXA} \qquad \text{from Case I}$$

$$\rule{7cm}{0.4pt}$$

$$m\angle YAC - m\angle YAB = \tfrac{1}{2}\left(m\widehat{YXA} - m\widehat{YB}\right)$$

But $m\angle YAC - m\angle YAB = m\angle BAC$ and $m\widehat{YXA} - m\widehat{YB} = m\widehat{BXA}$, so we have our proof.

$$m\angle BAC = \tfrac{1}{2}m\widehat{BXA}$$

problem set 12

1. Two animals out of seven believed Chicken Little. If 85 animals did not believe Chicken Little, how many animals were there in all?

2. A total of 52 gophers and badgers lived in the valley. If three times the number of badgers exceeded the number of gophers by four, how many of each lived in the valley?

3. Zinc made up 30% of the alloy and tin made up 50%. If there were 183 grams of zinc, how much tin was there?

4. Find the sum of the measures of the interior angles and the sum of the measures of the exterior angles of a six-sided convex polygon.

5. How many diagonals can be drawn in a nine-sided convex polygon?

6. The triangle and the circle are tangent at three points, as shown. Find x and y.

7. Find x, y, and z.

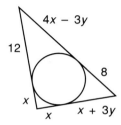

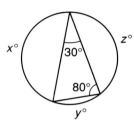

8. In the figure shown, quadrilateral $ABCD$ is inscribed in circle O. Find x.

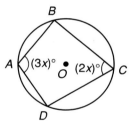

9. Begin with $ax^2 + bx + c = 0$ and derive the quadratic formula.

Use the quadratic formula to solve:

10. $2x^2 = x - 5$

11. $4 + 3x^2 = -2x$

12. Find the equation of the line that passes through $(2, 3)$ and $(5, 9)$.

Simplify:

13. $3i^3 + 2i^2 - 3i + 4$

14. $\dfrac{3 - \sqrt{2}}{4 + 2\sqrt{2}}$

Solve by completing the square:

15. $3x^2 = -6 - x$

16. $4x + 7 = 2x^2$

Solve:

17. $\begin{cases} \dfrac{1}{3}x - \dfrac{1}{4}y = 2 \\ 0.4y + 0.2z = 2 \\ \dfrac{1}{6}x + \dfrac{1}{2}z = \dfrac{5}{2} \end{cases}$

18. $\sqrt{4x - 12} + \sqrt{4x} = 6$

Simplify:

19. $\sqrt{6}\sqrt{3}\sqrt{-2}\sqrt{-16} + \sqrt{2}\sqrt{-2} - 6\sqrt{-8}\sqrt{2}$

20. $\dfrac{8i^4 - 4i^3 - 6i}{-3i^3 + 5i - \sqrt{-16}}$

21. $\dfrac{x^{-3}y^{-1} + y^{-5}}{x^{-4}y^5}$

22. Triangles can be shown to be congruent by the *SSS* congruency postulate, *SAS* congruency postulate, *AAAS* congruency postulate, or *HL* congruency postulate. The triangles in each pair shown below are congruent. State the congruency postulate that can be used to prove them congruent.

(a) $\triangle PQR \cong \triangle XYZ$

(b) $\triangle XVW \cong \triangle XYZ$

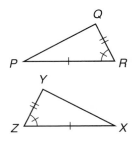

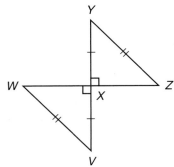

(c) $\triangle DEF \cong \triangle DGF$

(d) $\triangle HIJ \cong \triangle KLM$

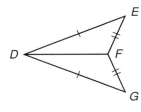

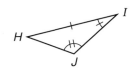

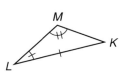

23. In this problem, we will remember that if two sides of a triangle are congruent, then the angles opposite these sides are congruent.

Given: $\overline{AB} \cong \overline{CB}$

$\overline{XY} \cong \overline{XZ}$

$\angle AXY \cong \angle CXZ$

Outline a proof that shows:

$\triangle AYX \cong \triangle CZX$

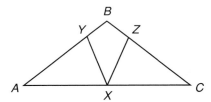

24. In this problem, we will remember that if two angles of a triangle are congruent, then the sides opposite these angles are congruent.

Given: $\angle A \cong \angle C$

$\overline{AE} \cong \overline{CD}$

Outline a proof that shows:

$\triangle ABE \cong \triangle CBD$

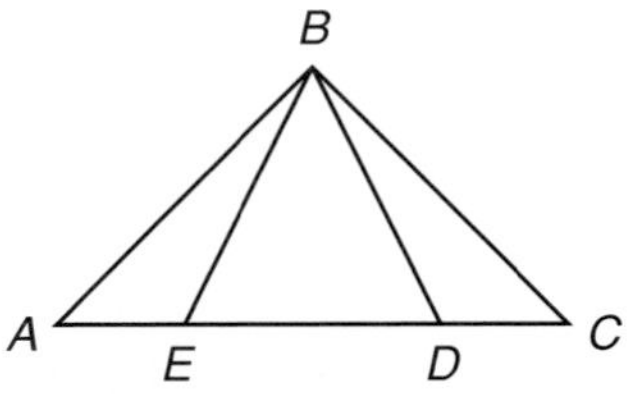

25. Find x, y, and z.

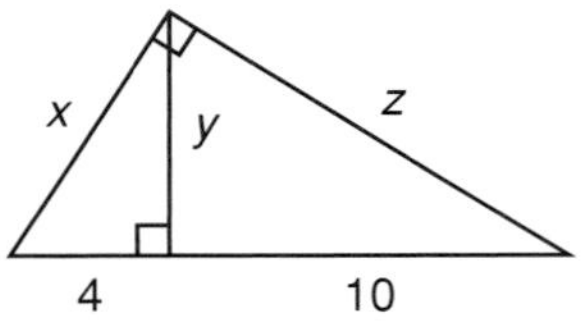

26. In $\triangle ABC$, $\overline{BD}$ is the angle bisector of angle B. Find x.

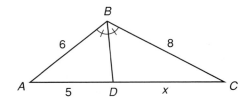

27. Construct a regular hexagon as follows: Use a compass to construct a circle. Choose a point on the circle and call it A. Without changing the compass setting, start at A and draw a series of arcs on the circle. Then connect the adjacent points with line segments.

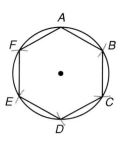

28. A small sphere is contained inside a larger sphere. The surface area of the small sphere is π cm^2 and the surface area of the larger sphere is 36π cm^2. Find the volume of the region inside the large sphere but outside the small sphere.

CONCEPT REVIEW PROBLEMS

29. In the figure shown below, three parallel lines are intersected by a transversal.

Compare: A. x B. y

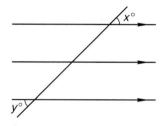

30. If x is a real number and $-1 < x < 1$, compare: A. x^4 B. x^2

LESSON 13 ***Intersecting Secants • Intersecting Secants and Tangents • Products of Chord Segments • Products of Secant and Tangent Segments***

13.A

intersecting secants

We remember that a line that intersects (touches) a circle at only one point is called a **tangent**. A **secant** is a line that intersects a circle at two points. **If two secants intersect inside a circle, the measures of the angles formed equal one half the sum of the measures of the intercepted arcs.** We illustrate this in the figure below.

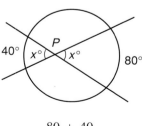

$$x = \frac{80 + 40}{2} = 60$$

example 13.1 Prove that the measure of an angle formed by two secants that intersect inside a circle is equal to one half the sum of the measures of the intercepted arcs.

solution   The proof that the measure of an angle formed by two secants that intersect inside a circle equals one half the sum of the measures of the intercepted arcs requires that we remember that the measure of an exterior angle of a triangle equals the sum of the measures of the remote interior angles. In the figure on the left below, we show two chords that intersect at a point P in the interior of the circle. We draw chord CB and label the angles 1, 2, and 3.

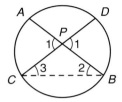 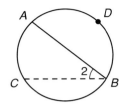 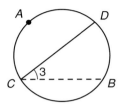

In the figure on the left above, the vertical angles labeled 1 are exterior angles of the triangle and thus their measures are equal to the sum of the measures of the angles labeled 2 and 3. Thus, we can write

$$m\angle 1 = m\angle 2 + m\angle 3 \qquad \text{equation}$$

As we emphasize in the two figures on the right above, the measure of angle 2 equals one half the measure of $\overset{\frown}{AC}$ and the measure of angle 3 equals one half the measure of $\overset{\frown}{BD}$. Thus,

$$m\angle 2 = \frac{1}{2}m\overset{\frown}{AC} \qquad \text{inscribed angle}$$

$$m\angle 3 = \frac{1}{2}m\overset{\frown}{BD} \qquad \text{inscribed angle}$$

Now we substitute these values in the equation above and get

$$m\angle 1 = \frac{1}{2}m\overset{\frown}{AC} + \frac{1}{2}m\overset{\frown}{BD} \qquad \text{substituted}$$

$$m\angle 1 = \frac{1}{2}\left(m\overset{\frown}{AC} + m\overset{\frown}{BD}\right) \qquad \text{factored}$$

13.B

intersecting secants and tangents   The measure of an angle formed by two secants, a secant and a tangent, or two tangents that intersect at a point outside a circle is equal to one half the difference of the measures of the intercepted arcs. We illustrate this in the three figures below.

Two Secants   A Secant and a Tangent   Two Tangents

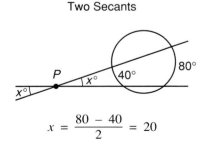 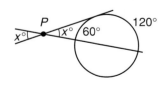 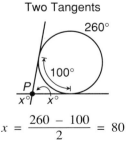

$$x = \frac{80 - 40}{2} = 20 \qquad\qquad x = \frac{120 - 60}{2} = 30 \qquad\qquad x = \frac{260 - 100}{2} = 80$$

example 13.2   Prove that the measure of an angle formed by two secants that intersect outside a circle is equal to one half the difference of the measures of the intercepted arcs.

solution   The proof that the measure of an angle formed by two secants that intersect outside a circle equals one half the difference of the measures of the intercepted arcs also requires that we remember that the measure of an exterior angle of a triangle equals the sum of the measures of the remote interior angles. In the figure on the left below, we show two secants that form an angle at P. In the figure on the right below, we draw chord AD and label the four angles 1, 2, 3, and 4.

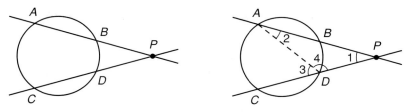

We note that angle 3 is an exterior angle of the triangle and, therefore, equals the sum of the measures of angles 1 and 2. Thus, we can write

$$m\angle 1 + m\angle 2 = m\angle 3 \qquad \text{equation}$$

$$m\angle 1 = m\angle 3 - m\angle 2 \qquad \text{rearranged}$$

Now the measure of angle 2 equals one half the measure of $\overset{\frown}{BD}$ and the measure of angle 3 equals one half the measure of $\overset{\frown}{AC}$. Thus,

$$m\angle 2 = \frac{1}{2}m\overset{\frown}{BD} \qquad \text{inscribed angle}$$

$$m\angle 3 = \frac{1}{2}m\overset{\frown}{AC} \qquad \text{inscribed angle}$$

Now we substitute these values in the rearranged equation above and get

$$m\angle 1 = \frac{1}{2}m\overset{\frown}{AC} - \frac{1}{2}m\overset{\frown}{BD} \qquad \text{substituted}$$

$$m\angle 1 = \frac{1}{2}\left(m\overset{\frown}{AC} - m\overset{\frown}{BD}\right) \qquad \text{factored}$$

example 13.3   Prove that the measure of an angle formed by a secant and a tangent that intersect outside a circle is equal to one half the difference of the measures of the intercepted arcs.

solution   The proof that the measure of an angle formed by a secant and a tangent that intersect outside a circle equals one half the difference of the measures of the intercepted arcs also requires that we remember that the measure of an exterior angle of a triangle equals the sum of the measures of the remote interior angles. In the figure on the left below, we show a secant and a tangent that form an angle at P. In the figure on the right below, we draw chord AB and label the four angles 1, 2, 3, and 4.

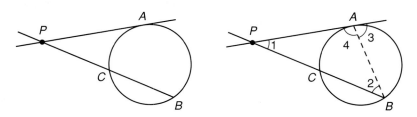

We note that angle 3 is an exterior angle of the triangle and, therefore, equals the sum of the measures of angles 1 and 2. Thus, we can write

$$m\angle 1 + m\angle 2 = m\angle 3 \qquad \text{equation}$$

$$m\angle 1 = m\angle 3 - m\angle 2 \qquad \text{rearranged}$$

Now the measure of angle 2 equals one half the measure of $\overset{\frown}{AC}$. We have proved that the measure of the angle formed by a chord and a tangent drawn to the point of tangency is equal to one half the measure of the intercepted arc. Therefore, the measure of angle 3 equals one half the measure of $\overset{\frown}{AB}$. Thus,

$$m\angle 2 = \frac{1}{2}m\overset{\frown}{AC} \qquad \text{inscribed angle}$$

$$m\angle 3 = \frac{1}{2}m\overset{\frown}{AB} \qquad \text{chord and tangent}$$

Now we substitute these values in the rearranged equation above and get

$$m\angle 1 = \frac{1}{2}m\overset{\frown}{AB} - \frac{1}{2}m\overset{\frown}{AC} \qquad \text{substituted}$$

$$m\angle 1 = \frac{1}{2}\left(m\overset{\frown}{AB} - m\overset{\frown}{AC}\right) \qquad \text{factored}$$

example 13.4 Prove that the measure of an angle formed by two tangents that intersect outside a circle is equal to one half the difference of the measures of the intercepted arcs.

solution The proof that the measure of an angle formed by two tangents that intersect outside a circle equals one half the difference of the measures of the intercepted arcs also requires that we remember that the measure of an exterior angle of a triangle equals the sum of the measures of the remote interior angles. In the figure on the left below, we show two tangents that form an angle at P. In the figure on the right below, we draw chord AB and label the four angles 1, 2, 3, and 4.

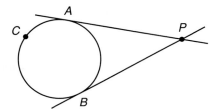 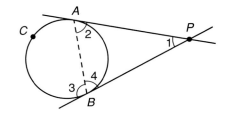

We note that angle 3 is an exterior angle of the triangle and, therefore, equals the sum of the measures of angles 1 and 2. Thus, we can write

$$m\angle 1 + m\angle 2 = m\angle 3 \qquad \text{equation}$$

$$m\angle 1 = m\angle 3 - m\angle 2 \qquad \text{rearranged}$$

Now we have proved that the measure of the angle formed by a chord and a tangent drawn to the point of tangency is equal to one half the measure of the intercepted arc. Therefore, the measure of angle 2 equals one half the measure of $\overset{\frown}{AB}$ and the measure of angle 3 equals one half the measure of $\overset{\frown}{BCA}$. Thus,

$$m\angle 2 = \frac{1}{2}m\overset{\frown}{AB} \qquad \text{chord and tangent}$$

$$m\angle 3 = \frac{1}{2}m\overset{\frown}{BCA} \qquad \text{chord and tangent}$$

Now we substitute these values in the rearranged equation above and get

$$m\angle 1 = \frac{1}{2}m\overset{\frown}{BCA} - \frac{1}{2}m\overset{\frown}{AB} \qquad \text{substituted}$$

$$m\angle 1 = \frac{1}{2}\left(m\overset{\frown}{BCA} - m\overset{\frown}{AB}\right) \qquad \text{factored}$$

example 13.5   Find x.

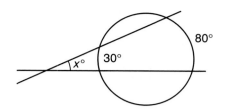

solution   The measure of angle x is equal to one half the difference of the measures of the intercepted arcs. One intercepted arc has a measure of 80° and the other intercepted arc has a measure of 30°. Thus,

$$x = \frac{1}{2}(80 - 30) \qquad \text{equation}$$

$$x = 25 \qquad \text{solved}$$

example 13.6   Find x.

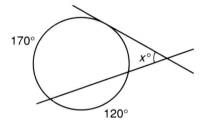

solution   The measure of angle x is equal to one half the difference of the measures of the intercepted arcs. One intercepted arc has a measure of 170°. Since the full measure of a circle is 360°, we can calculate that the other intercepted arc has a measure of 360° minus 290°, or 70°. Thus,

$$x = \frac{1}{2}(170 - 70) \qquad \text{equation}$$

$$x = 50 \qquad \text{solved}$$

13.C

products of chord segments   We remember that a chord is a line segment that connects any two points on a circle. If two chords of a circle intersect in the interior of the circle, each chord is divided into two segments. We can use the property of similar triangles to prove that the products of the lengths of the segments of each chord are equal. We illustrate this in the figure below where the product of the lengths of the segments of chord AB is 24, and the product of the lengths of the segments of chord CD is also 24.

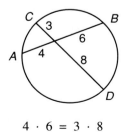

$$4 \cdot 6 = 3 \cdot 8$$

example 13.7   Prove that if two chords of a circle intersect in the interior of the circle, then the product of the lengths of the segments of one chord is equal to the product of the lengths of the segments of the other chord.

solution   In the figure on the left below, we show two chords of a circle that intersect at a point P in the interior of the circle. In the figure on the right below, we connect the endpoints of the chords to form the two triangles $\triangle APC$ and $\triangle DPB$.

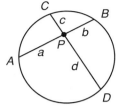 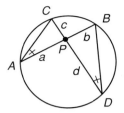

First we note that the vertical angles formed by the intersecting chords have equal measures. The inscribed angles at A and D in the right-hand figure also have equal measures because both intercept arc BC. Therefore, the third angles in the two triangles have equal measures. Thus the triangles $\triangle APC$ and $\triangle DPB$ are similar. This means that the ratios of the corresponding sides in the two triangles will be equal. If we put sides a and c from $\triangle APC$ on the top and the corresponding sides from $\triangle DPB$ on the bottom, we form the two equal ratios shown below.

$$\frac{a}{d} = \frac{c}{b} \qquad \text{equated ratios}$$

$$ab = cd \qquad \text{cross multiplied}$$

example 13.8   Find x.

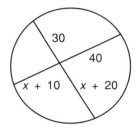

solution   The products of the lengths of the two segments of each chord are equal. Thus,

$$30(x + 20) = 40(x + 10) \qquad \text{equal products}$$

$$30x + 600 = 40x + 400 \qquad \text{multiplied}$$

$$200 = 10x \qquad \text{simplified}$$

$$x = \mathbf{20} \qquad \text{solved}$$

13.D

products of secant and tangent segments   We remember that a secant is a line that intersects a circle at two points. We call the segment from a point outside the circle to the second point of intersection a **secant segment** and the segment from the point outside the circle to the first point of intersection an **external secant segment**. We illustrate this in the figure below, where $\overline{PAB}$ is the secant segment and $\overline{PA}$ is the external secant segment.

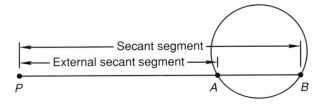

If two secant segments are drawn to a circle from a point outside the circle, the products of the lengths of the secant segments and the lengths of their external secant segments are equal. We illustrate this in the figure below where the length of the upper secant segment is 8 and the length of its external secant segment is 3. Three times 8 equals 24. The length of the lower secant segment is 12 and the length of its external secant segment is 2. Two times 12 is also equal to 24.

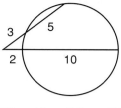

$$3(3 + 5) = 2(2 + 10)$$

example 13.9   Prove that if two secant segments are drawn to a circle from a point outside the circle, then the product of the length of one secant segment and the length of its external secant segment is equal to the product of the length of the other secant segment and the length of its external secant segment.

solution   In the figure on the left, we show two secant segments that are drawn to a circle from a point P outside the circle. In the figure on the right, we draw dotted lines to connect both R and T to the ends of arc SU. Then we look at the two triangles $\triangle RPU$ and $\triangle TPS$ separately in the figures below.

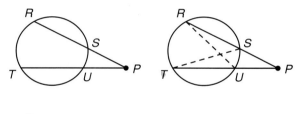

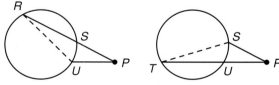

The inscribed angles at R and T in the two triangles have equal measures because both intercept arc SU. Both triangles also contain angle P. Therefore, the third angles in the two triangles have equal measures. Thus, triangles $\triangle RPU$ and $\triangle TPS$ are similar. This means that the ratios of the corresponding sides in the two triangles will be equal. If we put sides PR and PU from $\triangle RPU$ on the top and the corresponding sides from $\triangle TPS$ on the bottom, we form the two equal ratios shown below.

$$\frac{PR}{PT} = \frac{PU}{PS} \qquad \text{equated ratios}$$

$$PR \cdot PS = PT \cdot PU \qquad \text{cross multiplied}$$

Each of these products has two factors. One factor is the length of the secant segment, and the other factor is the length of its external secant segment.

example 13.10   Find x.

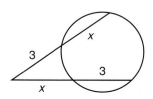

solution The products of the lengths of the secant segments and the lengths of their external secant segments are equal.

$$3(x + 3) = x(x + 3) \qquad \text{equation}$$
$$3x + 9 = x^2 + 3x \qquad \text{multiplied}$$
$$x^2 = 9 \qquad \text{rearranged}$$
$$x = 3, -3 \qquad \text{solved}$$

We reject the solution –3 because a length is always represented by a positive number. Thus, the solution is **3**.

When a secant segment and a tangent segment are drawn to a circle from a point outside the circle, the product of the length of the secant segment and the length of its external secant segment equals the square of the length of the tangent segment. We illustrate this in the figure below where the length of the secant segment is 16 and the length of its external secant segment is 4. Four times 16 equals 64. The length of the tangent segment is 8. Eight squared is also equal to 64.

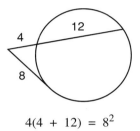

$$4(4 + 12) = 8^2$$

We can develop this rule by studying the three diagrams below. Then we will prove this result more formally in example 13.11. In the left-hand figure below, we show two secant segments that are drawn to a circle from a point P outside the circle. Thus the product of the length of one secant segment and the length of its external secant segment is equal to the product of the length of the other secant segment and the length of its external secant segment.

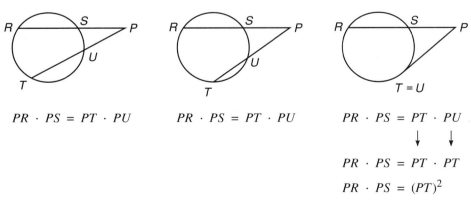

$$PR \cdot PS = PT \cdot PU \qquad PR \cdot PS = PT \cdot PU \qquad PR \cdot PS = PT \cdot PU$$
$$\downarrow \qquad \downarrow$$
$$PR \cdot PS = PT \cdot PT$$
$$PR \cdot PS = (PT)^2$$

In the center figure above, we rotate the secant segment PT counterclockwise about point P. As we do this, T and U move closer together and the equation is the same. In the right-hand figure above, the secant segment PT has been rotated counterclockwise about point P until T and U designate the same point. Therefore, $\overline{PT}$ becomes a tangent and the length of the secant segment is the same as the length of the external secant segment. So we replace the secant segment length with the tangent segment length PT and also replace the external secant segment length with the tangent segment length PT, as shown.

example 13.11 Prove that if a secant segment and a tangent segment are drawn to a circle from a point outside the circle, then the product of the length of the secant segment and the length of its external secant segment equals the square of the length of the tangent segment.

solution   In the figure on the left below, we show a secant segment and a tangent segment that are drawn to a circle from a point P outside the circle. In the figure on the right, we draw chord RT and chord ST. Then we look at the two triangles $\triangle RPT$ and $\triangle TPS$ separately in the figures below.

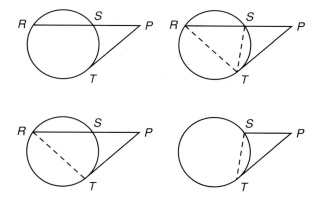

Now angle TRS is an inscribed angle and so its measure is equal to one half the measure of $\overset{\frown}{ST}$. Also, angle STP is an angle formed by a chord and a tangent drawn to the point of tangency and so its measure is equal to one half the measure of $\overset{\frown}{ST}$. Thus,

$$m\angle TRS = \frac{1}{2}m\overset{\frown}{ST} \qquad \text{inscribed angle}$$

$$m\angle STP = \frac{1}{2}m\overset{\frown}{ST} \qquad \text{chord and tangent}$$

So $m\angle TRS = m\angle STP$ by substitution. Both triangles also contain angle P. Therefore, the third angles in the two triangles have equal measures. Thus triangles $\triangle RPT$ and $\triangle TPS$ are similar. This means that the ratios of the corresponding sides in the two triangles will be equal. If we put sides PR and PT from $\triangle RPT$ on the top and the corresponding sides from $\triangle TPS$ on the bottom, we form the two equal ratios shown below.

$$\frac{PR}{PT} = \frac{PT}{PS} \qquad \text{equated ratios}$$

$$PR \cdot PS = (PT)^2 \qquad \text{cross multiplied}$$

example 13.12   Find x.

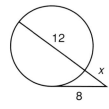

solution   The product of the length of the secant segment and the length of its external secant segment equals the square of the length of the tangent segment.

$$x(x + 12) = 8^2 \qquad \text{equation}$$

$$x^2 + 12x = 64 \qquad \text{multiplied}$$

$$x^2 + 12x - 64 = 0 \qquad \text{rearranged}$$

$$(x + 16)(x - 4) = 0 \qquad \text{factored}$$

$$x = -16, 4 \qquad \text{solved}$$

We reject the solution -16 because a length is always represented by a positive number. Thus, the solution is **4**.

problem set 13

1. LeAnn's test scores are 88, 100, 72, and 94, respectively. What does she need on the last test in order to average 90 on her tests?

2. The ratio of successes to failures was 7 to 3. If there were 1026 failures, how many successes were there?

3. Find three consecutive even integers such that four times the sum of the first and second equals twice the third.

4. Find x.

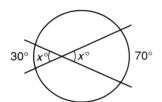

5. Find x.

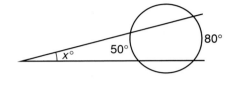

6. Find x.

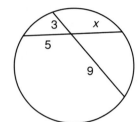

7. Find x.

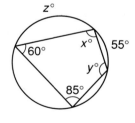

8. How many diagonals can be drawn in a 10-sided convex polygon?

9. Find the sum of the measures of the interior angles and the sum of the measures of the exterior angles of a 10-sided convex polygon.

10. Is the following argument valid or invalid?

> All non-octopi are orange.
>
> Shannon is not orange.
> _____
>
> Therefore, Shannon is an octopus.

11. In the figure shown, O is the center of the circle. Find x and y.

12. Find x, y, and z.

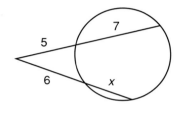

Solve by completing the square:

13. $2x - x^2 = 1$

14. $5x^2 - 2x + 1 = 0$

Use the quadratic formula to solve:

15. $2x^2 - 3x + 1 = 5$

16. $2 + 3x = x^2$

17. Find the equation of the line that passes through $(3, 6)$ and is parallel to the line $y = 3x - 8$.

Solve:

18. $\begin{cases} 2x + 3y - z = 17 \\ 3x - y + 2z = 11 \\ x - 3y + 3z = -4 \end{cases}$

19. $\sqrt{3x + 6} + \sqrt{3x - 1} = 7$

20. $\dfrac{x - 6}{x^2 - 9x + 20} = \dfrac{2}{x - 4} - \dfrac{x}{x - 5}$ (*Hint*: Check solutions.)

Simplify:

21. $\dfrac{3 - 2i + i^3}{1 - i}$

22. $\dfrac{2 - \sqrt{5}}{2 + \sqrt{5}}$

23. $\dfrac{3 - 2i}{4 + 6i}$

24. In this problem, we will remember that a midpoint divides a segment into two congruent segments.

Given: $\angle A \cong \angle C$

D is the midpoint of $\overline{AC}$

Outline a proof that shows:

$\triangle ABD \cong \triangle CBD$

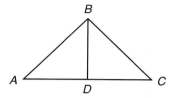

25. In this problem, we will remember that if two parallel lines are cut by a transversal, then each pair of alternate interior angles is congruent.

Given: $\overline{PQ} \cong \overline{SR}$

$\overline{PQ} \parallel \overline{SR}$

Outline a proof that shows:

$\triangle PQR \cong \triangle RSP$

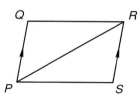

26. In $\triangle PQR$, $\overline{QS}$ is the angle bisector of angle Q. Find x.

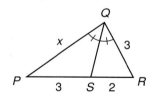

27. Construct a right triangle given the hypotenuse of length m and a leg of length n.

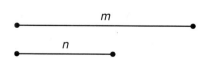

28. Find the volume of the right cylinder whose base is shown and whose altitude is 3 meters. Dimensions are in meters.

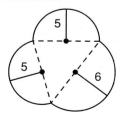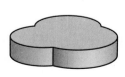

29. Compare: A. $\dfrac{\frac{1}{2} - \frac{1}{3}}{\frac{1}{2} + \frac{1}{3}}$ B. $\dfrac{1}{5}$

30. Let x and y be real numbers. If $x > y > 0$, compare: A. $2x - y$ B. $x - 2y$

LESSON 14 *Sine, Cosine, and Tangent • Angles of Elevation and Depression • Rectangular and Polar Coordinates • Coordinate Conversion*

14.A
sine, cosine, and tangent

A right triangle has one right angle and two acute angles. If we select one of the acute angles, we call the ratio of the side opposite this angle to the hypotenuse the **sine** of the angle. The ratio of the side adjacent to the selected angle to the hypotenuse is called the **cosine** of the angle. The ratio of the side opposite the selected angle to the side adjacent to the selected angle is called the **tangent** of the angle. These ratios are the same for every acute angle whose measure is the same as that of the selected angle. To remember which ratio corresponds to which name requires pure memorization, and mnemonics are helpful for memorizing these ratios. To the right of the equations below, we use the first letters of the words *opposite*, *hypotenuse*, and *adjacent* to form the first letters of a sentence that is easy to remember.

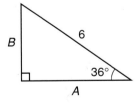

$$\sin A = \frac{\text{opposite}}{\text{hypotenuse}} \qquad \frac{\text{Oscar}}{\text{had}}$$

$$\cos A = \frac{\text{adjacent}}{\text{hypotenuse}} \qquad \frac{\text{a}}{\text{heap}}$$

$$\tan A = \frac{\text{opposite}}{\text{adjacent}} \qquad \frac{\text{of}}{\text{acorns}}$$

Thus, if we can remember to write *sine*, *cosine*, and *tangent*, in that order, and then write "Oscar had a heap of acorns," we have the definitions memorized. Some people take the first letters of the words *sine*, *opposite*, *hypotenuse*; *cosine*, *adjacent*, *hypotenuse*; and *tangent*, *opposite*, *adjacent* to form the expression

Soh   Cah   Toa

and say that it sounds like an American Indian phrase.

We can use the sine, cosine, and tangent ratios to solve for unknown values in right triangles, as we show in the following examples.

example 14.1   Find *A* and *B*.

solution   We can find *A* and *B* by using the cosine and sine of 36°.

$$\frac{A}{6} = \cos 36° \qquad\qquad \frac{B}{6} = \sin 36°$$

$$A = 6 \cos 36° \qquad\qquad B = 6 \sin 36°$$

We can use a scientific calculator to find the values of cos 36° and sin 36°. First we ensure that the calculator is in the degree mode. Then we press [3] [6] [cos] to find the cosine of 36° and press [3] [6] [sin] to get the value of sin 36°. If we insert these values and then multiply, we get the following numbers for *A* and *B*.

$$A = 6 \cos 36° \qquad\qquad B = 6 \sin 36°$$

$$A = 6(0.809017) \qquad\qquad B = 6(0.5877853)$$

$$A = \mathbf{4.854102} \qquad\qquad B = \mathbf{3.5267115}$$

It is not necessary to copy the numerical value of cos 36° and sin 36° to find the answer. We can press [6] [×] [3] [6] [cos] [=] and [6] [×] [3] [6] [sin] [=] and get the answers directly.

$$A = 6 \cos 36° \qquad\qquad B = 6 \sin 36°$$

$$A = 4.854102 \qquad\qquad B = 3.5267115$$

$$A = \mathbf{4.85} \qquad\qquad B = \mathbf{3.53}$$

A calculator is accurate to more digits than we need, so we normally round our answers to a more convenient number of digits, as we did here.

example 14.2   Find angle M and side x.

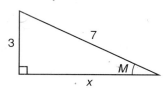

solution   We use the sine ratio to find angle M.

$$\sin M = \frac{3}{7}$$

We use a calculator to divide and get

$$\sin M = 0.4285714$$

To find the angle whose sine is this number, we press [inv] [sin] and get 25.376934, which we round and get

$$M = \mathbf{25.38°}$$

We used a calculator and then rounded to a more reasonable number. To find side x, we could use a trigonometric function of 25.38° or we could use the Pythagorean theorem. We decide to use the Pythagorean theorem.

$$x^2 + 3^2 = 7^2 \qquad\qquad \text{used Pythagorean theorem}$$

$$x^2 = 49 - 9 \qquad\qquad \text{rearranged}$$

$$x = \sqrt{40} = \mathbf{6.32} \qquad\qquad \text{solved}$$

We used a calculator and rounded.

14.B

angles of elevation and depression

Angles of elevation and **angles of depression** are measured from the horizontal. On the left below we show that an angle of elevation is measured upward from the horizontal, and on the right below we show that an angle of depression is measured downward from the horizontal.

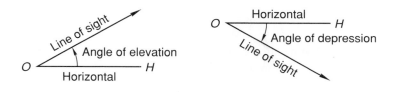

example 14.3 A man 6 feet tall is 200 feet from a tree, and he measures the angle of elevation to the top of the tree as 11°. How tall is the tree?

solution We draw a diagram of the problem. This diagram is not drawn to scale. The angle of elevation is 11°. Now we solve for y.

$$\frac{y}{200} = \tan 11°$$

$$y = 200 \tan 11° = 38.88$$

We used a calculator and rounded. The man is 6 feet tall, so the total height of the tree is

$$\text{Height} = 38.88 \text{ ft} + 6 \text{ ft} = \textbf{44.88 ft}$$

example 14.4 An airplane is flying at an altitude of 3000 feet above the ground. The pilot sights an object on the ground at an angle of depression of 26°. What is the slant range from the airplane to the object?

solution We draw a diagram of the problem. This diagram is not drawn to scale. The angle of depression is 26°, so the angle in the triangle is $90° - 26° = 64°$. Now we solve for s.

$$\cos 64° = \frac{3000}{s}$$

$$s = \frac{3000}{\cos 64°} = \textbf{6843.52 ft}$$

We used a calculator and rounded.

14.C
rectangular and polar coordinates

We can use two different methods to describe the location of a point on the coordinate plane with respect to the origin. One method of locating a point on the coordinate plane is called the method of **rectangular coordinates** and uses two numbers. One number indicates the distance of the point to the right or the left of the origin, and the other number indicates the distance of the point above or below the origin. We tell which number is which either by writing the numbers as an ordered pair enclosed in parentheses or by writing a letter with each number to designate directions. Any letters can be used, but the customary letters are i and j, where i is used to indicate the positive x direction and j is used to indicate the positive y direction. However, in this book we use the letter i to represent $\sqrt{-1}$. Therefore, in order to avoid confusion, we will write i and j with a **carat,** a mark that students often call a *hat*. Because $\hat{i}$ and $\hat{j}$ indicate directions and have length 1, they are called **unit vectors.** Thus, the location of a point 3 units to the right of the origin and 4 units below the origin can be designated by using one of these notations.

$$(3, -4) \qquad \text{or} \qquad 3\hat{i} - 4\hat{j}$$

The notation on the left is an **ordered pair** (x, y) and the notation on the right is a **vector notation** meaning +3 in the x direction and -4 in the y direction. In this book, we will use the notations interchangeably.

Another method of locating a point on the coordinate plane is called the method of **polar coordinates,** which uses a distance and an angle. **Positive angles are measured counterclockwise from the positive *x* axis and negative angles are measured clockwise from the same axis.** If a point is a distance of 6 units from the origin at a positive angle of 50°, we can designate the location by using parentheses and an ordered pair of *r* and *θ*, as shown on the left, or by giving the distance and then the angle, as shown on the right.

$$(6, 50°) \quad \text{or} \quad 6\underline{/50°}$$

Measuring counterclockwise 50° from the positive *x* axis brings one to the same direction as measuring 310° in the clockwise direction, so the point could also be designated by writing either (6, −310°) or 6$\underline{/−310°}$.

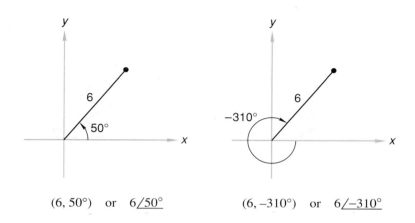

$$(6, 50°) \quad \text{or} \quad 6\underline{/50°} \qquad\qquad (6, −310°) \quad \text{or} \quad 6\underline{/−310°}$$

We must remember that when we use *r* and *θ* that *r* is a **directed distance.** If we turn through either −130° or +230° **and then back up 6 units,** we find that we are standing on the same point designated in the diagrams above.

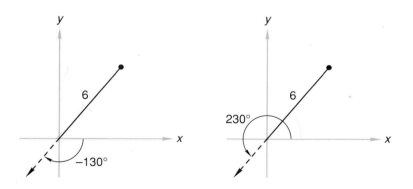

Thus, the point we are discussing can also be designated by writing either

$$-6\underline{/−130°} \quad \text{or} \quad -6\underline{/230°}$$

It is less confusing if one can remember to turn through the angle first and then go in the indicated direction if *r* is a positive number and back up if *r* is a negative number.

14.D
coordinate conversion

To convert from rectangular coordinates to polar coordinates, we first draw a diagram. Next, we determine the length of the hypotenuse of the right triangle and the measure of the angle. Then we measure the polar angle from the positive *x* axis.

example 14.5   Convert $-3\hat{i} + 2\hat{j}$ to polar coordinates. Write four forms of polar coordinates for this point.

solution   On the left we graph the point and draw the triangle. **Note that one side of the triangle is perpendicular to the *x* axis.**

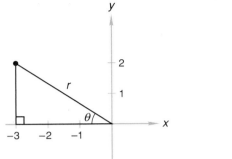

$$r^2 = 3^2 + 2^2 = 13$$

$$r = \sqrt{13}$$

$$\tan \theta = \frac{2}{3} = 0.6667$$

$$\theta = 33.69°$$

On the right, we find that the length of *r* is $\sqrt{13}$ and that the small angle is 33.69°. If we measure counterclockwise from the positive *x* axis, the polar angle is 146.31°; and if we measure clockwise from the positive *x* axis, the polar angle is –213.69°. If we use negative magnitudes, as shown in the right-hand figures below, we find the corresponding polar angles are fourth-quadrant angles.

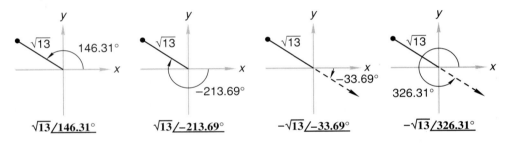

$$\sqrt{13}\underline{/146.31°} \qquad \sqrt{13}\underline{/-213.69°} \qquad -\sqrt{13}\underline{/-33.69°} \qquad -\sqrt{13}\underline{/326.31°}$$

example 14.6   Convert $-13\underline{/-253°}$ to rectangular form.

solution   We always draw the angle first, as we show on the left.

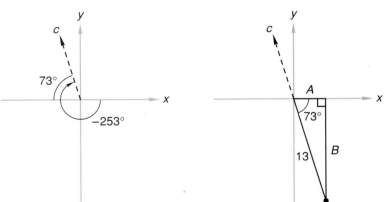

Now, facing in the direction the arrow *c* is pointing, **we back up 13 units** to locate the designated point. Then we find *A* and *B*.

$$A = 13 \cos 73° \qquad\qquad B = 13 \sin 73°$$

$$A = 3.80 \qquad\qquad B = 12.43$$

Now we can write the rectangular coordinates using either ordered pairs or the unit vectors $\hat{i}$ and $\hat{j}$.

$$\textbf{(3.80, –12.43)} \qquad \text{or} \qquad \textbf{3.80}\hat{i} - \textbf{12.43}\hat{j}$$

1. The ratio of ups to downs is 7 to 5 and ten percent of the ups is three less than twenty percent of the downs. How many are up and how many are down?

2. Find three consecutive odd integers such that three times the first is 9 greater than six times the third.

3. Find the sum of the measures of the interior angles and the sum of the measures of the exterior angles of a seventeen-sided convex polygon.

4. An airplane is flying at an altitude of 5000 feet above the ground. The pilot sights an object on the ground at an angle of depression of 28°. What is the slant range from the airplane to the object?

Convert to polar coordinates. (Write four forms for each point.)

5. $3.06\hat{i} - 2.75\hat{j}$

6. $-2.41\hat{i} + 7.3\hat{j}$

Convert to rectangular coordinates:

7. $-8.6\underline{/265°}$

8. $7.42\underline{/-143°}$

9. Find x and y.

10. Find x, y, and z.

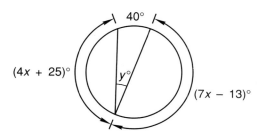

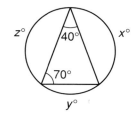

11. Find x and y.

12. Find x.

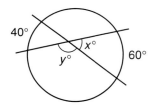

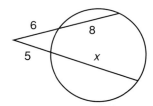

Solve by completing the square:

13. $4x^2 = -5 - 2x$

14. $3x + 7 = 4x^2$

Use the quadratic formula to solve:

15. $3x^2 = -4 + 2x$

16. $5x^2 = -2x + 6$

17. Find the equation of the line that passes through $(-3, 1)$ and is perpendicular to the line $2x - 3y - 5 = 0$.

Simplify:

18. $\sqrt{3}\sqrt{3}\sqrt{-3} - \sqrt{-2}\sqrt{-2}\sqrt{-2} - 5\sqrt{-9} + 3i$

19. $\dfrac{a^{2x}b^{3x}\left(\sqrt{a^3}\right)^x}{b^{x-y}a}$

20. $\dfrac{3i^3 - 2i^2 - i^5}{2 - 4i^2 + \sqrt{-4}}$

21. $\dfrac{a^{-5} + a^3b^{-2}}{a^4b^{-7}}$

22. In this problem, we will remember that if two parallel lines are cut by a transversal, then each pair of corresponding angles is congruent.

Given: $\angle BAC \cong \angle DCE$

$\overline{BC} \parallel \overline{DE}$

C is the midpoint of $\overline{AE}$

Outline a proof that shows:

$\triangle ABC \cong \triangle CDE$

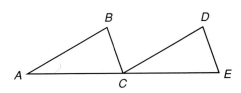

Simplify:

23. $\dfrac{5 - \sqrt{3}}{4 - 2\sqrt{3}}$

24. $\left(2x^{\frac{1}{3}} - 4y^{-\frac{1}{5}} \right)\left(2x^{\frac{1}{3}} + 4y^{-\frac{1}{5}} \right)$

Solve:

25. $\begin{cases} \dfrac{x}{2} - \dfrac{y}{3} = \dfrac{1}{6} \\[2mm] \dfrac{x}{3} + \dfrac{2z}{5} = 2\dfrac{3}{5} \\[2mm] \dfrac{y}{3} + \dfrac{2z}{3} = 4 \end{cases}$

26. $\sqrt{x + 10} - 2 = \sqrt{x}$

27. Find a, b, and h.

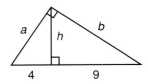

28. The base of a regular pyramid is a regular hexagon, as shown. The volume of this regular pyramid is 2160 cm^3. Find the height of the pyramid. Dimensions are in centimeters.

**CONCEPT REVIEW
PROBLEMS**

29. Given: $\triangle ABC$ and $\triangle DEF$

Compare: A. x B. y

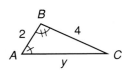
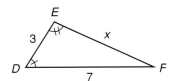

30. In the figure shown, O is the center of the circle and $PQ > QR$.

Compare: A. x B. y

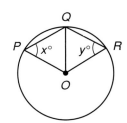

LESSON 15 Assumptions • Proofs

15.A
assumptions

We remember that definitions are the names we give to ideas or things and that all definitions are reversible. We define parallel lines to be lines that are in the same plane that do not intersect. Thus, if two lines lie in the same plane and do not intersect, the lines are parallel lines. We also remember that postulates and axioms are assumptions we make and accept without proof. **Theorems** are statements that we can prove by using definitions, postulates, and axioms in a deductive reasoning process.

We make a distinction between the meanings of the words *axiom* and *postulate*. **We say that an *axiom* is an assumption that is true in all areas of mathematics. A *postulate* is an assumption that is applicable to a particular branch of mathematics, such as geometry.**

The first recorded postulates are the geometric postulates of the Greek scholar Eukleides, whom we now call Euclid. Euclid probably lived in Alexandria, Egypt, during the reign of the first Greek king of Egypt, Ptolemy I, circa 300 B.C. Euclid was able to reduce his list of postulates to 10. The essence of Euclid's postulates is contained in the following statements. The wording of Postulate 5 shown here is attributed to John Playfair (1748–1819) and was the wording usually used in high school geometry texts in the early 1900s.

> **Postulate 1.** **Two points determine a unique straight line.**
> **Postulate 2.** **A straight line extends indefinitely far in either direction.**
> **Postulate 3.** **A circle may be drawn with any given center and any given radius.**
> **Postulate 4.** **All right angles are equal.**
> **Postulate 5.** **Given a line *n* and a point *P* not on that line, there exists in the plane of *P* and *n* and through *P* one and only one line *m*, which does not meet the given line *n*.**

> **Postulate 6.** **Things equal to the same thing are equal to each other.**
> **Postulate 7.** **If equals be added to equals, the sums are equal.**
> **Postulate 8.** **If equals be subtracted from equals, the remainders are equal.**
> **Postulate 9.** **Figures which can be made to coincide are equal.**
> **Postulate 10.** **The whole is greater than any part.**

The modern wording of some of these postulates is different, and mathematicians have found it necessary to add other postulates to the 10 postulates of Euclid. One of the postulates concerns betweenness and another concerns continuity. We will not discuss these additional postulates in this book.

15.B
proofs

In our proofs we will use Euclid's ten postulates as necessary and will also use the four postulates of triangle congruency, *SSS, SAS, AAAS,* and *HL,* which we discussed in Lesson 9. The proofs of mathematics are almost always presented in paragraph form where the reason for each step in the proof is justified. An exception to this rule is made in beginning geometry books where two-column proofs are used because this format emphasizes the fact that each step must be justified and is easy for beginning students to use. Two-column proofs are almost never encountered in higher-level mathematics courses. We will use the two-column format in this book for the reason stated. Later on, perhaps your teacher will ask you to use the paragraph format for a few proofs even though the paragraph format is harder to grade.

It is helpful, but not necessary, to begin proofs of triangle congruency by using tick marks as we did for proof outlines. Then the two-column proof consists only of a detailed recording of the steps in the left-hand column with a justification of the steps recorded in the right-hand column.

example 15.1 **A median of a triangle is a segment that connects a vertex with the midpoint of the side opposite the vertex.** Prove that the median drawn from the vertex formed by the equal sides of an isosceles triangle bisects the angle at this vertex.

solution In the left-hand figure we draw an isosceles triangle and mark the sides whose lengths are equal with single tick marks.

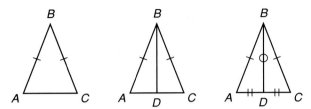

In the center figure we draw the median that connects B with D, the midpoint of $\overline{AC}$, which divides $\overline{AC}$ into two segments of equal length. In the figure on the right we use double tick marks to note that $\overline{AD}$ and $\overline{CD}$ have equal lengths. We draw a circle on $\overline{BD}$ to note that it is a side of both small triangles. We can see that $\triangle ABD$ is congruent to $\triangle CBD$ because three sides in one triangle have the same lengths as the three sides in the other triangle. Thus angles ABD and CBD have equal measures because they are corresponding parts of congruent triangles. This proves that the median bisects the angle at vertex B.

The proof just presented is called a **paragraph proof.** It took a lot of words to write this proof, and now we will use the short-hand notation of a two-column proof to prove the same theorem.

STATEMENTS	REASONS
1. In isosceles $\triangle ABC$, $\overline{AB} \cong \overline{CB}$.	1. Given in the definition of isosceles triangle.
2. Draw median $\overline{BD}$ to side $\overline{AC}$.	2. Given
3. $\overline{AD} \cong \overline{CD}$	3. A median in a triangle divides the side to which it is drawn into two congruent segments.
4. $\overline{BD} \cong \overline{BD}$	4. Reflexive axiom
5. $\triangle ABD \cong \triangle CBD$	5. SSS congruency postulate
6. $\angle ABD \cong \angle CBD$	6. CPCTC

The fourth step was justified by the reflexive axiom. **The *reflexive axiom* is a formal recognition of the fact that everything is equal to itself.** The word *reflexive* comes from the Latin word *reflexere*, which means "to reflect." When you stand in front of a mirror, the reflection in the mirror is of you. The sentence "The duck bathed itself" is a reflexive sentence because the subject and the direct object are the same thing.

example 15.2 Prove that if two tangents to a circle intersect at a point outside the circle, then the lengths of the tangent segments are equal.

solution On the left below we show two lines that are tangent to circle O at A and B and that intersect at point P. Euclid's first postulate tells us that two points determine a unique straight line. So in the right-hand figure we draw radii OA and OB and segment OP.

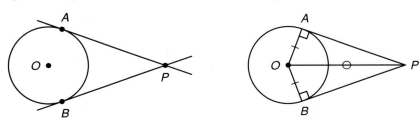

In Lesson 11 we postulated the fact that if a line is tangent to a circle, then the line is perpendicular to the radius at the point of tangency. Therefore, the radii OA and OB are perpendicular at A and B to $\overline{AP}$ and $\overline{BP}$, respectively. Thus, $\angle OAP$ and $\angle OBP$ are right angles. Therefore, we see that we have two right triangles, $\triangle OAP$ and $\triangle OBP$, that share the same hypotenuse OP. The two legs, $\overline{OA}$ and $\overline{OB}$, are congruent because they are radii of the circle. Therefore, $\triangle OAP$ and $\triangle OBP$ are congruent by the HL congruency postulate. Thus, the segments AP and BP are congruent because they are corresponding parts of congruent triangles. Therefore, $AP = BP$ because congruent segments have equal lengths. This proves that the lengths of the tangent segments are equal. Now we will rewrite the paragraph proof as a two-column proof of the same theorem.

STATEMENTS	REASONS
1. $\overline{AP}$ and $\overline{BP}$ are tangent to circle O at A and B, respectively.	1. Given
2. Draw radii OA and OB and segment OP.	2. Two points determine a unique straight line. (Euclid's first postulate)
3. $\overline{OA} \perp \overline{AP}$ and $\overline{OB} \perp \overline{BP}$	3. If a line is tangent to a circle, then the line is perpendicular to the radius at the point of tangency.
4. $\angle OAP$ and $\angle OBP$ are right angles.	4. Perpendicular lines intersect to form right angles.
5. $\triangle OAP$ and $\triangle OBP$ are right triangles.	5. A triangle which contains a right angle is a right triangle.
6. $\overline{OP} \cong \overline{OP}$	6. Reflexive axiom
7. $\overline{OA} \cong \overline{OB}$	7. All radii of a circle are congruent.
8. $\triangle OAP \cong \triangle OBP$	8. HL congruency postulate
9. $\overline{AP} \cong \overline{BP}$	9. CPCTC
10. $AP = BP$	10. Definition of congruent segments

example 15.3   Prove that the sum of the measures of the angles of a triangle is 180°.

solution   The proof that the sum of the measures of the angles of a triangle is 180° is a simple proof that uses Euclid's fifth postulate and the knowledge we have about the angles formed when transversals intersect parallel lines. On the left below we show triangle ABC. Euclid's fifth postulate tells us that through a point not on a line, there is exactly one line parallel to the given line. So in the figure on the right below, we draw a line BD through vertex B that is parallel to side AC. We also use arrowheads to indicate that $\overleftrightarrow{BD}$ and $\overline{AC}$ are parallel, and label the top three angles 1, 2, and 3, as shown.

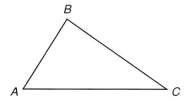
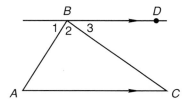

In the figure on the right above, at vertex B we see that the angles 1, 2, and 3 form a straight angle whose measure is 180°. Thus, we can write

$$m\angle 1 + m\angle 2 + m\angle 3 = 180° \qquad \text{equation}$$

We know that $\angle 2$ and $\angle B$ are two different notations for naming the same angle. Therefore, we substitute $m\angle B$ for $m\angle 2$ in the above equation and get

$$m\angle 1 + m\angle B + m\angle 3 = 180° \qquad \text{substituted}$$

The angle at vertex A and the angle labeled 1 have equal measures because they are alternate interior angles formed by the parallel lines and a transversal. The angle at vertex C and the angle labeled 3 have equal measures because they are alternate interior angles formed by the parallel lines and a transversal. Thus,

$$m\angle 1 = m\angle A \qquad \text{alternate interior angles}$$

$$m\angle 3 = m\angle C \qquad \text{alternate interior angles}$$

Now we substitute these values in the equation above and get

$$m\angle A + m\angle B + m\angle C = 180° \qquad \text{substituted}$$

This proves that the sum of the measures of the angles of a triangle is 180°. Now we will rewrite the paragraph proof as a two-column proof of the same theorem.

STATEMENTS	REASONS
1. $\triangle ABC$	1. Given
2. Through vertex B, draw line BD parallel to side AC.	2. Through a point not on a line, there is exactly one line parallel to the given line. (Euclid's fifth postulate)
3. $m\angle 1 + m\angle 2 + m\angle 3 = 180°$	3. Angles 1, 2, and 3 form a straight angle whose measure is 180°.
4. $\angle 2 = \angle B$	4. We know that $\angle 2$ and $\angle B$ are two different notations for naming the same angle.
5. $m\angle 1 + m\angle B + m\angle 3 = 180°$	5. Substitution
6. $m\angle 1 = m\angle A$ $m\angle 3 = m\angle C$	6. If two parallel lines are cut by a transversal, then each pair of alternate interior angles is equal in measure.
7. $m\angle A + m\angle B + m\angle C = 180°$	7. Substitution

example 15.4   Use the sixth and eighth postulates of Euclid to prove that vertical angles are equal in measure.

solution   We will use the short-hand notation of a two-column proof to prove the theorem. We begin by drawing two intersecting lines and labeling the four angles A, B, C, and D whose measures are $A°$, $B°$, $C°$, and $D°$, as shown.

STATEMENTS	REASONS
1. $\angle A$ and $\angle C$ are vertical angles.	1. Given
2. $m\angle A + m\angle B = 180°$	2. Angles A and B form a straight angle whose measure is 180°.
3. $m\angle B + m\angle C = 180°$	3. Angles B and C form a straight angle whose measure is 180°.
4. $m\angle A + m\angle B = m\angle B + m\angle C$	4. Things equal to the same thing are equal to each other. (Euclid's sixth postulate)
5. $m\angle A = m\angle C$	5. If equals are subtracted from equals, the remainders are equal. (Euclid's eighth postulate)

The same procedure can be used to prove that $m\angle B = m\angle D$. Thus, we have used two postulates of Euclid and reasoned deductively from these postulates to prove a theorem.

example 15.5   Given: $\overline{BD}$ is the angle bisector of angle B

$\overline{AB} \cong \overline{CB}$

Write a two-column proof to prove:

$\overline{AD} \cong \overline{CD}$

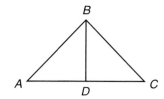

solution   Now we will write a two-column proof to prove $\overline{AD} \cong \overline{CD}$.

STATEMENTS	REASONS
1. $\overline{AB} \cong \overline{CB}$	1. Given
2. $\overline{BD}$ is the angle bisector of angle B.	2. Given
3. $\angle ABD \cong \angle CBD$	3. An angle bisector divides an angle into two congruent angles.
4. $\overline{BD} \cong \overline{BD}$	4. Reflexive axiom
5. $\triangle ABD \cong \triangle CBD$	5. *SAS* congruency postulate
6. $\overline{AD} \cong \overline{CD}$	6. *CPCTC*

example 15.6   Given: $\angle Q \cong \angle S$

$\overline{PQ} \parallel \overline{SR}$

Write a two-column proof to prove:

$\triangle PQR \cong \triangle RSP$

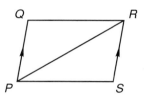

solution   Now we will write a two-column proof to prove $\triangle PQR \cong \triangle RSP$.

STATEMENTS	REASONS
1. $\angle Q \cong \angle S$	1. Given
2. $\overline{PQ} \parallel \overline{SR}$	2. Given
3. $\angle QPR \cong \angle SRP$	3. If two parallel lines are cut by a transversal, then each pair of alternate interior angles is congruent.
4. $\angle QRP \cong \angle SPR$	4. If two angles in one triangle are congruent to two angles in a second triangle, then the third angles are congruent.
5. $\overline{PR} \cong \overline{PR}$	5. Reflexive axiom
6. $\triangle PQR \cong \triangle RSP$	6. *AAAS* congruency postulate

problem set 15

1. Zollie found four consecutive odd integers such that 5 times the sum of the first and the third was 22 greater than the product of 8 and the sum of the second and the fourth. What were the integers?

2. The mixture was of zinc and cobalt and 430 tons of zinc were required to make 700 tons of the mixture. How many tons of cobalt were required to make 2800 tons of the mixture?

3. Find the equation of the line that passes through $(-4, 5)$ and $(-6, 3)$.

4. A woman stood on the top of a 500-ft building and measured a 20° angle of elevation to an airplane flying at an altitude of 2500 ft. What was the straight-line distance from the woman to the airplane?

5. Given: $\overline{AC} \cong \overline{BC}$

    $\angle ACD \cong \angle BCD$

    Write a two-column proof to prove:

    $\triangle ACD \cong \triangle BCD$

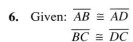

6. Given: $\overline{AB} \cong \overline{AD}$

    $\overline{BC} \cong \overline{DC}$

    Write a two-column proof to prove:

    $\triangle ABC \cong \triangle ADC$

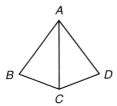

Convert to polar coordinates. (Write four forms for each point.)

7. $-7.08\hat{i} + 4.2\hat{j}$ 8. $4.2\hat{i} - 3\hat{j}$

Convert to rectangular coordinates:

9. $-15\underline{/-335°}$ 10. $-42\underline{/138°}$

11. Find x.   12. Find x.

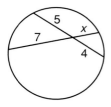   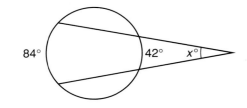

Solve by completing the square:

13. $3x^2 = -4 + 3x$ 14. $-6x - 9 = 2x^2$

15. Solve $-5x - 8 = 3x^2$ by using the quadratic formula.

16. Find the equations of lines A and B.

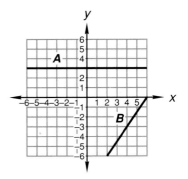

17. Solve: $\begin{cases} \dfrac{1}{2}x - \dfrac{1}{4}y = \dfrac{1}{2} \\ 0.2y - 0.2z = 1 \\ -\dfrac{1}{8}x + \dfrac{1}{4}z = -\dfrac{1}{4} \end{cases}$

Simplify:

18. $4i^3 - 3i^7 + 6i^5 - \sqrt{-4} - 3\sqrt{-9}$ 19. $\dfrac{2 + 3\sqrt{2}}{2\sqrt{2} - 1}$

20. $\dfrac{2x^{-1} + 3y^{-1}}{9x^2 - 4y^2}$

21. $\sqrt{2}\sqrt{-2}\sqrt{3}\sqrt{-3} + \sqrt{3}\sqrt{-3} - 7\sqrt{-8}\sqrt{2}$

22. $\dfrac{a^{2z-3}\left(\sqrt[4]{b^4}\right)^{4z+8}}{a^{4z+2}b^{2z-3}}$

23. $\left(3x^{\frac{1}{2}} - 2z^{\frac{1}{4}}\right)\left(3x^{\frac{1}{2}} + 2z^{\frac{1}{4}}\right)$

24. The circle is inscribed in the triangle. Find x, y, and z.

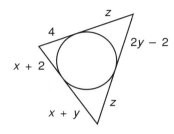

25. In the figure shown, quadrilateral $ABCD$ is inscribed in circle O. Find $m\angle A$ and $m\angle C$.

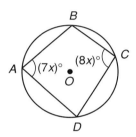

26. In $\triangle ABC$, $\overline{BD}$ is the angle bisector of angle B. Find x.

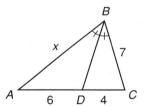

27. Find the length of diagonal AC in the rectangular solid shown.

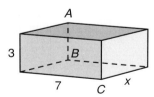

28. The base of a regular pyramid is a square whose perimeter is 32 m. The surface area of this regular pyramid is 144 m^2. Find the slant height and height of the pyramid.

CONCEPT REVIEW PROBLEMS

29. Let a, b, and c be real numbers. If $a + b > c + b$, compare: A. a B. c

30. Let a, b, and c be real numbers. If $ab > cb$, compare: A. a B. c

LESSON 16   *Complex Fractions* • *Abstract Equations* • *Division of Polynomials*

16.A

complex fractions

A **complex fraction** is a fraction that contains more than one fraction line. We can simplify complex fractions easily if we can remember that any expression retains its original value if multiplied by another expression that has a value of 1. We can multiply 5 by 10 over 10 without changing the value

$$5 \cdot \frac{10}{10} = \frac{50}{10}$$

because 5 and 50 over 10 are expressions that designate the same number. In the same way, we can multiply b by d over d (if d does not have a value of zero) without changing the value of the expression because d over d has a value of 1.

$$b \cdot \frac{d}{d} = \frac{bd}{d}$$

If we wish to add the two terms

$$b + \frac{c}{d}$$

we have a problem because fractions cannot be added unless the denominators are the same. But we can overcome this difficulty by multiplying b by d over d. Then the terms can be added, as we show here.

$$\frac{bd}{d} + \frac{c}{d} = \frac{bd + c}{d}$$

We say that we multiplied b by a **"well-chosen one"** because d over d had a value of 1 and was therefore "well chosen" because it allowed us to make the denominators equal so that the fractions could be added. If we had multiplied b by z over z, we would have multiplied by an expression that had a value of 1, but it would not have been "well chosen" because doing this would not have resulted in a denominator of d, which we needed.

We remember that the product of a number and its reciprocal is the number 1.

$$\frac{1}{2} \cdot 2 = 1 \qquad a \cdot \frac{1}{a} = 1 \qquad \frac{a}{b} \cdot \frac{b}{a} = \frac{ab}{ba} = 1$$

We can use this fact to select a "well-chosen one" and to simplify an expression that has a fraction in the denominator such as

$$\frac{m}{\dfrac{bd + c}{d}}$$

If we multiply the denominator by its reciprocal, the result will be a 1 in the denominator. But we must also multiply the numerator by the same quantity. It is helpful to write m as m over 1 when we do this.

$$\frac{\dfrac{m}{1} \cdot \dfrac{d}{bd + c}}{\dfrac{bd + c}{d} \cdot \dfrac{d}{bd + c}} = \frac{\dfrac{md}{bd + c}}{1} = \frac{md}{bd + c}$$

example 16.1   Simplify: $\dfrac{x}{a + \dfrac{m}{b + \dfrac{c}{d}}}$

solution We begin by writing $b + \frac{c}{d}$ as a simple fraction and get

$$\frac{x}{a + \cfrac{m}{\cfrac{bd + c}{d}}}$$

Now we simplify the triple-decker fraction and get

$$\frac{x}{a + \cfrac{\cfrac{m}{1}}{\cfrac{bd + c}{d}} \cdot \cfrac{\cfrac{d}{bd + c}}{\cfrac{d}{bd + c}}} = \frac{x}{a + \cfrac{md}{bd + c}}$$

Now we add the two terms in the denominator and get

$$\frac{x}{\cfrac{a(bd + c) + md}{bd + c}}$$

and finish by multiplying above and below by the reciprocal of the denominator.

$$\frac{\cfrac{x}{1}}{\cfrac{a(bd + c) + md}{bd + c}} \cdot \frac{\cfrac{bd + c}{a(bd + c) + md}}{\cfrac{bd + c}{a(bd + c) + md}} = \boldsymbol{\frac{x(bd + c)}{a(bd + c) + md}}$$

example 16.2 Simplify: $\dfrac{\cfrac{a}{x^2} + \cfrac{b}{x}}{\cfrac{m}{x^2} + \cfrac{k}{xc}}$

solution We can simplify this expression in two steps by first writing both the numerator and denominator as simple fractions.

$$\frac{\cfrac{a + bx}{x^2}}{\cfrac{mc + kx}{x^2c}}$$

Then we can multiply above and below by the reciprocal of the denominator.

$$\frac{\cfrac{a + bx}{x^2}}{\cfrac{mc + kx}{x^2c}} \cdot \frac{\cfrac{x^2c}{mc + kx}}{\cfrac{x^2c}{mc + kx}} = \boldsymbol{\frac{c(a + bx)}{mc + kx}}$$

This type of problem is encountered often and there is a shortcut that we can use to simplify the expression in just one step. This shortcut cannot be used on the problem in example 16.1. **Whenever a complex fraction has the sum of fractions in the numerator and the denominator, the fraction can be simplified in one step by multiplying above and below by the least common multiple of all denominators.** The least common multiple of the denominators is x^2c.

$$\frac{\left(\cfrac{a}{x^2} + \cfrac{b}{x}\right)}{\left(\cfrac{m}{x^2} + \cfrac{k}{xc}\right)} \cdot \frac{\cfrac{x^2c}{1}}{\cfrac{x^2c}{1}} = \boldsymbol{\frac{ac + bxc}{mc + kx}}$$

This shortcut is helpful because problems like this one are ubiquitous on college entrance examinations where time is limited.

16.B

**abstract
equations**

We can use the process of multiplying by a well-chosen one to change the form of an expression if the expression either is in an equation or is not in an equation. The expression

$$\frac{a}{b + \dfrac{c}{x + y}}$$

does not contain an equals sign. Thus we do not have an equation and the rules for equations cannot be used. When we see an equals sign, we can change the form of any expression in the equation and we can also use the addition rule for equations and the multiplication rule for equations, as we show in the following example.

example 16.3   Solve $y = v\left(\dfrac{a}{x} + \dfrac{b}{mc}\right)$ for c.

solution   **This problem has an equals sign and the multiplication rule for equations can be used.** As the first step, we use the distributive property to clear the parentheses on the right-hand side of the equation and get

$$y = \frac{va}{x} + \frac{vb}{mc}$$

Next, we can use the multiplication rule for equations to get rid of the denominators. To do this we multiply every numerator by xmc, which is the least common multiple of the denominators.

$$xmc \cdot y = xmc \cdot \frac{va}{x} + xmc \cdot \frac{vb}{mc}$$

Now we can cancel the denominators and get

$$xmcy = mcva + xvb$$

Since we are solving for c, we put all terms with c on one side of the equals sign (either side).

$$xmcy - mcva = xvb$$

Next we factor out c,

$$c(xmy - mva) = xvb$$

and finish by dividing both sides of the equation by the coefficient of c.

$$\frac{c(xmy - mva)}{xmy - mva} = \frac{xvb}{xmy - mva} \quad \longrightarrow \quad c = \frac{xvb}{xmy - mva}$$

16.C

**division of
polynomials**

When polynomials are divided, the division can be checked by adding the quotient and the remainder fraction. We demonstrate this procedure in the following example.

example 16.4   Divide $x^3 - 2$ by $x - 1$ and check the result by adding the quotient and the remainder fraction.

solution   First we perform the indicated division and remember to insert $0x^2$ and $0x$ to help with spacing.

$$
\begin{array}{r}
x^2 + x + 1 \\
x - 1 \overline{\smash{\big)}\, x^3 + 0x^2 + 0x - 2} \\
\underline{x^3 - x^2} \\
x^2 + 0x \\
\underline{x^2 - x} \\
x - 2 \\
\underline{x - 1} \\
-1
\end{array}
$$

Thus, we find that

$$\frac{x^3 - 2}{x - 1} = x^2 + x + 1 - \frac{1}{x - 1}$$

To check, we must write both parts of the answer with a denominator of $x - 1$ so the parts can be added. Thus we must multiply $x^2 + x + 1$ by $(x - 1)$ over $(x - 1)$.

$$\left(x^2 + x + 1\right) \cdot \frac{(x - 1)}{(x - 1)} - \frac{1}{(x - 1)}$$

We perform the multiplication on the left and get

$$\frac{x^3 + x^2 + x - x^2 - x - 1}{x - 1} - \frac{1}{(x - 1)}$$

and we simplify the numerators and get

$$\frac{x^3 - 2}{x - 1} \qquad \text{check}$$

problem set 16

1. A total of 13 cheetahs and rhinoceroses lived in the park. If twice the number of cheetahs exceeded three fourths the number of rhinoceroses by four, how many of each animal lived in the park?

2. Pierre and Ernst found three consecutive even integers such that 7 times the sum of the first and third was 48 less than 10 times the second. What were the integers?

3. Find the equation of the line that passes through $(-4, 2)$ and is perpendicular to the line $3y - 2x - 18 = 0$.

4. An airplane is flying at an altitude of 6 miles above the ground. The pilot sights the airport at an angle of depression of $3°$. What is the ground distance from the airplane to the airport?

Simplify:

5. $\dfrac{\dfrac{x}{a^2} + \dfrac{b}{a}}{\dfrac{1}{a^2} - \dfrac{k}{ac}}$

6. $\dfrac{p}{m + \dfrac{m}{1 + \dfrac{b}{c}}}$

7. $\dfrac{a}{x + \dfrac{y}{p + \dfrac{m}{c}}}$

8. Solve $x = pm\left(\dfrac{1}{y} + \dfrac{a}{bd}\right)$ for d.

9. Solve $y = m\left(\dfrac{a}{x} + \dfrac{b}{mc}\right)$ for c.

10. Divide $x^3 - 1$ by $x - 2$ and check the result by adding the quotient and the remainder fraction.

11. Given: $\angle A \cong \angle B$

  $\overline{CD} \cong \overline{CE}$

  Write a two-column proof to prove:

  $\triangle ACD \cong \triangle BCE$

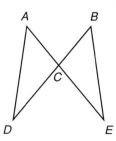

12. Given: $\angle Q$ and $\angle S$ are right angles

  $\overline{PQ} \cong \overline{PS}$

  Write a two-column proof to prove:

  $\triangle PQR \cong \triangle PSR$

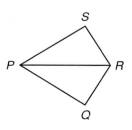

Convert to polar coordinates. (Write four forms for each point.)

13. $4\hat{i} - 6\hat{j}$ **14.** $-6\hat{i} - 8\hat{j}$

Convert to rectangular coordinates:

15. $4.2\underline{/-75°}$ **16.** $-42\underline{/-75°}$

17. Solve $-3x^2 + 2x = 5$ by completing the square.

18. Solve $-5x^2 - x = 7$ by using the quadratic formula.

19. Find the equations of lines A and B.

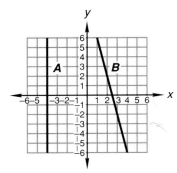

Solve:

20. $\begin{cases} 2x - z = 5 \\ 3x + 2y = 13 \\ y - 2z = 0 \end{cases}$

21. $\dfrac{x + 2}{x^2 - 3x + 2} - \dfrac{x - 6}{x^2 - 5x + 6} = \dfrac{1}{x - 1}$ (*Hint*: Check solutions.)

Simplify:

22. $\dfrac{2i^2 - 3i + 4i^3}{2i^5 - 3i - 2i^2}$ **23.** $\dfrac{3 + 2\sqrt{3}}{4 - 12\sqrt{3}}$

24. $\sqrt{-2}\sqrt{2} - \sqrt{2}i - \sqrt{-4} + i$ **25.** $\dfrac{a^3b^{-4} + b^2a^5}{a^{-3}b}$

26. Find x, y, and z.   **27.** Find a, b, and h.

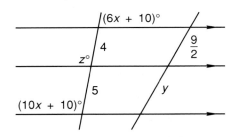
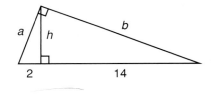

28. The base of a right circular cone has a radius of 6 cm. The height of the cone is 4 cm. Find the volume and surface area of the cone.

CONCEPT REVIEW PROBLEMS   **29.** If z is a real number and $-10 < z < -1$, compare: A. $\dfrac{1}{z^5}$ B. $\dfrac{1}{z^4}$

30. In the figure shown, quadrilateral $ABCD$ is inscribed in circle O.

Compare: A. x B. y

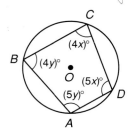

LESSON 17   *Proofs of the Pythagorean Theorem* • *Proofs of Similarity*

17.A

proofs of the Pythagorean theorem

The discussion of the Pythagorean theorem in Lesson 3 showed that this theorem has both geometric and algebraic properties. Many different proofs have been developed for the Pythagorean theorem, including original proofs by Leonardo da Vinci and the twentieth president of the United States, James A. Garfield. This theorem has probably been proven more different ways than any other theorem in geometry. We will show two of these proofs.

Proof (1)

We remember that the perpendicular drawn from the hypotenuse to the right angle in a right triangle forms two smaller right triangles that are similar to the original right triangle and to each other. On the left below we have the big right triangle with sides a, b, and c and note that side c can also be written as $x + y$. On the right below we break out the two smaller right triangles. We will use the three similar right triangles below to do an easy proof of the Pythagorean theorem. We want to show that $c^2 = a^2 + b^2$.

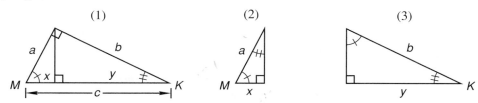

Now on the left below, we equate the ratios of the sides opposite the right angles to the sides opposite the angles whose measure is K in triangle (1) and triangle (2) and put the sides of triangle (1) on top. On the right below, we equate the ratios of the sides opposite the right angles to the sides opposite the angles whose measure is M in triangle (1) and triangle (3) and put the sides of triangle (1) on top.

Triangles (1) and (2)   Triangles (1) and (3)

$$\frac{c}{a} = \frac{a}{x} \qquad\qquad \frac{c}{b} = \frac{b}{y}$$

Next we cross multiply in both equations and get

$$cx = a^2 \qquad\qquad cy = b^2$$

If we add these equations, we get

$$cx + cy = a^2 + b^2$$

Now, on the left-hand side, we factor out c and get

$$c(x + y) = a^2 + b^2$$

Then we replace $(x + y)$ with c. Thus the left-hand side becomes c^2 and we have our proof.

$$c(c) = a^2 + b^2 \qquad \text{replaced } x + y \text{ with } c$$
$$c^2 = a^2 + b^2 \qquad \text{multiplied}$$

Proof (2)

Another proof of the Pythagorean theorem that we will show uses a simple argument involving the areas of right triangles and squares. We begin with the right triangle on the left below that has sides a, b, and c. Then we make three exact copies of this triangle, as shown.

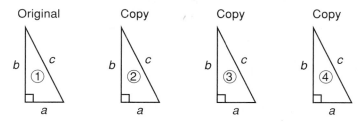

The area of each right triangle is $\frac{1}{2}ab$ and there are four of them, so their total area is $2ab$.

$$\text{Total area of the four right triangles} = 4\left(\frac{1}{2}ab\right) = 2ab$$

Now we arrange the four congruent right triangles as follows so that $ABCD$ is a square and label the four angles 1, 2, 3, and 4, as shown.

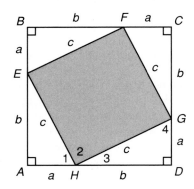

Now we must show that the shaded quadrilateral $EFGH$ in the center is a square. Since the four right triangles are congruent, $EF = FG = GH = HE$. So quadrilateral $EFGH$ is equilateral. In the figure above, the angles labeled 3 and 4 are complementary angles because they are acute angles of right triangle HGD. Thus $m\angle 3 + m\angle 4 = 90°$. Now $m\angle 1 = m\angle 4$ since they are corresponding angles of congruent triangles. Therefore, $m\angle 3 + m\angle 1 = 90°$ by substitution. Also, we see that the angles labeled 1, 2, and 3 form a straight angle whose measure is 180°. Thus, we can write

$$
\begin{array}{ll}
m\angle 1 + m\angle 2 + m\angle 3 = 180° & \text{straight angle} \\
\underline{\phantom{m\angle 1 + {}}m\angle 1 + m\angle 3 = 90°} & \text{equation} \\
\phantom{m\angle 1 + m\angle 1 + {}}m\angle 2 = 90° & \text{subtraction}
\end{array}
$$

In the same way, it can be shown that the measure of each of the other three angles of quadrilateral $EFGH$ is 90°. So quadrilateral $EFGH$ is equiangular. Since quadrilateral $EFGH$ is equilateral as well as equiangular, it is a square. Thus, we can write

$$\text{Area of shaded square} = c^2$$

$$\text{Area of big square} = (a + b)^2$$

We see that the area of the shaded square equals the area of the big square reduced by the total area of the four right triangles.

$$
\begin{array}{ll}
\begin{array}{c}\text{Area of}\\\text{shaded}\\\text{square}\end{array} = \begin{array}{c}\text{Area of}\\\text{big square}\end{array} - \begin{array}{c}\text{Total area of}\\\text{the four right}\\\text{triangles}\end{array} & \text{equation} \\
c^2 = (a + b)^2 - 2ab & \text{substituted} \\
c^2 = \left(a^2 + 2ab + b^2\right) - 2ab & \text{multiplied} \\
c^2 = a^2 + b^2 & \text{simplified}
\end{array}
$$

17.B
proofs of similarity

We remember that triangles are called *similar triangles* if the measures of the three angles in one triangle are equal to the measures of the three angles in the other triangle. We use the notation *AAA* to note that the angles have equal measures. We also remember that if two angles in one triangle have the same measures as two angles in a second triangle, the measures of the third angles must also be equal because the sum of the measures of the angles of a triangle is 180°. Thus, *AA* implies *AAA*, or *AA* → *AAA*. We also remember that congruent triangles are similar triangles whose scale factor is one. The three angles in these triangles have equal measures, as indicated by the tick marks.

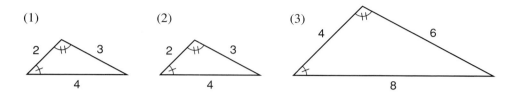

Thus all three triangles are similar. The lengths of the sides opposite corresponding angles in similar triangles are proportional. This means that the ratios of corresponding sides are equal. On the left below we write the ratios of the corresponding sides of triangles (1) and (2) and note that they all have a value of one.

Triangles (1) and (2)   Triangles (1) and (3)

$$\frac{2}{2} \quad \frac{3}{3} \quad \frac{4}{4} \qquad \frac{2}{4} \quad \frac{3}{6} \quad \frac{4}{8}$$

On the right we have written the ratios of corresponding sides in triangles (1) and (3) and we note that the ratios all have a value of one half because the sides in triangle (1) are half as long as the corresponding sides in triangle (3).

We have postulated that we can state that triangles are congruent by *SSS*, *SAS*, *AAAS*, and *HL*. The *SSS* and *SAS* postulates hold for proofs of similarity, but the letter *S* means that sides are proportional instead of congruent.

SSS   When we give *SSS* as the reason for triangle congruence, we mean that the corresponding sides have equal lengths. When we give *SSS* as the reason for triangle similarity, we mean that the lengths of corresponding sides are proportional.

SAS   When we give *SAS* as the reason for triangle congruence, we mean that the two corresponding sides that form the angle have equal lengths. When we give *SAS* as the reason for triangle similarity, we mean that the lengths of the two corresponding sides are proportional.

example 17.1   Prove △*ABC* ~ △*EDC*.

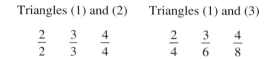

solution   We will write a two-column proof to prove △*ABC* ~ △*EDC*. We will use *AAA* as the basis for this proof.

STATEMENTS	REASONS
1. ∠*A* ≅ ∠*E*	1. Given
2. ∠*ACB* ≅ ∠*ECD*	2. Vertical angles are congruent.
3. ∠*B* ≅ ∠*D*	3. *AA* → *AAA*
4. △*ABC* ~ △*EDC*	4. *AAA*

example 17.2   Prove △*ABC* ~ △*DEC*.

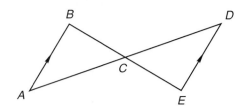

solution   We will write a two-column proof to prove △*ABC* ~ △*DEC*. We will use *AAA* as the basis for this proof. The arrowheads tell us that $\overline{AB}$ is parallel to $\overline{ED}$ and we note that both $\overline{AD}$ and $\overline{BE}$ are transversals that intersect parallel lines.

STATEMENTS	REASONS
1. $\overline{AB} \parallel \overline{ED}$	1. Given
2. ∠*ACB* ≅ ∠*DCE*	2. Vertical angles are congruent.
3. ∠*A* ≅ ∠*D*	3. If two parallel lines are cut by a transversal, then each pair of alternate interior angles is congruent.
4. ∠*B* ≅ ∠*E*	4. *AA* ⟶ *AAA*
5. △*ABC* ~ △*DEC*	5. *AAA*

example 17.3   Prove △*GHI* ~ △*JKL*.

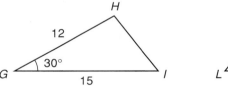
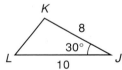

solution   Almost all useful proofs of triangle similarity are *AAA* proofs like the last two proofs. Proofs of similarity that use the *SSS* similarity postulate and the *SAS* similarity postulate are seldom encountered. This problem was carefully fabricated to permit an *SAS* proof. We will write a two-column proof to prove △*GHI* ~ △*JKL*.

STATEMENTS	REASONS
1. ∠*G* ≅ ∠*J*	1. Both angles measure 30°.
2. $\dfrac{GH}{JK} = \dfrac{12}{8}$	2. Given
3. $\dfrac{GI}{JL} = \dfrac{15}{10}$	3. Given
4. $\dfrac{GH}{JK} = \dfrac{GI}{JL}$	4. $\dfrac{12}{8} = \dfrac{3}{2} = \dfrac{15}{10}$
5. △*GHI* ~ △*JKL*	5. *SAS* similarity postulate

The *SAS* similarity postulate tells us that the angles have equal measures and that the ratios of the lengths of the sides that form these angles are equal.

problem set 17

1. Find three consecutive even integers such that twice the product of the first and last numbers is 28 more than the square of the second number.

2. The ratio of sonnets to odes was 15 to 4. If six times the number of odes was 12 less than twice the number of sonnets, how many were odes and how many were sonnets?

3. Find the equation of the line that passes through $(1, -1)$ and is perpendicular to the line $x + 4y = 3$.

Determine whether each pair of triangles shown below are similar and justify your answer. Write the ratio of corresponding sides when possible.

4.

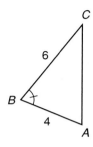

5.

 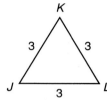

6.

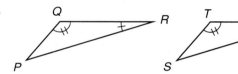

7. Determine if $\triangle ABC \sim \triangle DEF$ and justify your answer.

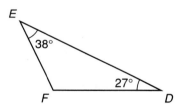

8. Given: $\overline{BC} \parallel \overline{AE}$

   Write a two-column proof to prove:

   $$\triangle ADE \sim \triangle CDB$$

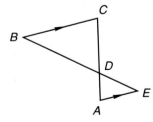

Simplify:

9. $\dfrac{\dfrac{a}{bc} - \dfrac{x}{c^2}}{\dfrac{c}{a} + \dfrac{b}{ax}}$

10. $\dfrac{x}{4 + \dfrac{x}{1 + \dfrac{1}{x}}}$

11. Solve for k: $a = b\left(\dfrac{1 + k}{2k}\right)$

12. Solve for r: $t = ax\left(\dfrac{b}{x^2} - \dfrac{2}{br}\right)$

13. Divide $x^3 + 2x - 1$ by $x + 3$ and check.

14. Given: $\overline{AD} \cong \overline{BD}$
$\overline{ED} \cong \overline{CD}$

Write a two-column proof to prove:

$\triangle ADE \cong \triangle BDC$

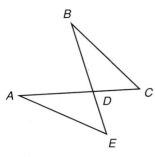

Convert to polar coordinates. (Write four forms for each point.)

15. $5\hat{i} + 7\hat{j}$ **16.** $-12\hat{i} + 2\hat{j}$

17. Convert to rectangular coordinates: $-20\underline{/80°}$

18. Solve $-3 = x - 4x^2$ by completing the square.

19. Find the equations of lines A and B.

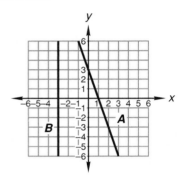

Solve:

20. $\begin{cases} x + 2y + z = 0 \\ 3x - y - z = 5 \\ 5x - 2y - 3z = 12 \end{cases}$ **21.** $\sqrt{x + 2} = 2x + 1$

Simplify:

22. $\dfrac{2i^2 + 4i^3 - 1}{i^8 + i^3 - 2}$ **23.** $\dfrac{3 - 2\sqrt{5}}{\sqrt{5} - 1}$

24. $\left(3x^{\frac{1}{2}} + y^{\frac{3}{2}}\right)\left(x^{\frac{1}{2}} - 2y^{\frac{3}{2}}\right)$ **25.** $\dfrac{\left(x^{3a+2}\right)\left(\sqrt[3]{b}\right)^{2y}}{x^{4a-1}\left(b^{3a}\right)^{\frac{1}{2}}}$

26. Find x.

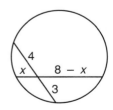

27. In $\triangle ABC$, $\overline{BD}$ is the angle bisector of angle B. If $AB = 10$, $CB = 14$, and $AC = 12$, find AD and DC.

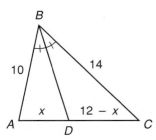

28. The base of a right circular cone has a perimeter of 12π cm. The surface area of this right circular cone is 96π cm^2. Find the slant height and height of the cone.

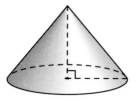

CONCEPT REVIEW PROBLEMS

29. Let x and y be real numbers. If $x - 2y > 0$, compare: A. x B. y

30. In the figure shown, two parallel lines are intersected by a transversal.

Compare: A. $n - 3m$ B. -11

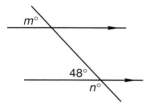

LESSON 18   *Advanced Word Problems*

Word problems are worked by transforming written statements into mathematical equations and then solving the equations. Percent and ratio problems can be solved by using any one variable. Nickel and dime problems can be solved by using two variables. Many problems require the use of three or more variables for their solution. **As many variables may be used as are convenient. For a unique solution of a system of linear equations, we must have as many independent equations as we have variables.**[†] The variables x, y, and z should be avoided because it is difficult to remember what they represent in a particular problem. Subscripted variables should be used because their meanings are easier to remember.

Word problems tend to be categorized into types according to the different thought processes required to find their solutions. Thus far, we have looked at simple problems whose solutions required the use of at most two variables. In this lesson, we will review the solution of problems that require the use of three variables in three equations. We also will review other types of problems. Some of these problems were selected because they require procedures that have a wide variety of applications. Other problems were selected because they represent types of problems that will be encountered in almost the same forms in chemistry and physics courses.

example 18.1   The number of blues was 4 less than the sum of the whites and the greens. Also, the number of greens equaled the sum of the blues and the whites. How many of each were there if there were twice as many blues as whites?

solution   This problem can be worked by using three equations in three unknowns. We will use N_B, N_W, and N_G as the variables. The three equations are as follows:

(a) The number of blues was 4 less than the sum of the whites and the greens.

$$N_B + 4 = N_W + N_G$$

(b) The number of greens equaled the sum of the blues and the whites.

$$N_G = N_B + N_W$$

(c) There were twice as many blues as whites.

$$N_B = 2N_W$$

[†]This is true for systems of linear equations if the domain for all variables and all coefficients is the set of real numbers.

Note that in (a) we added 4 to the number of blues because there were 4 fewer blues. Also, in (c) we multiplied the number of whites by 2 to equal the number of blues. When a statement tells how much greater or less a quantity is, addition or multiplication is required so that an equation (statement of equality) may be written. We begin by substituting $2N_W$ for N_B in equations (a) and (b).

(a) $(2N_W) + 4 = N_W + N_G$ $\longrightarrow$ $N_W - N_G = -4$

(b) $N_G = (2N_W) + N_W$ $\longrightarrow$ $\dfrac{-3N_W + N_G = 0}{-2N_W = -4}$

$$N_W = 2$$

Now N_B equals $2N_W$, so $N_B = 4$; and N_G equals $N_B + N_W$, so $N_G = 6$. Thus

$$N_W = 2 \qquad N_B = 4 \qquad N_G = 6$$

example 18.2   The quarters, nickels, and dimes totaled 20, and their value was $1.90. How many of each kind were there if there were 4 times as many nickels as quarters?

solution   There were 20 coins in all,

(a) $N_N + N_D + N_Q = 20$

and their value was $1.90.

(b) $5N_N + 10N_D + 25N_Q = 190$

There were 4 times as many nickels as quarters.

(c) $N_N = 4N_Q$

We begin by using (c) to substitute for N_N in (a) and (b).

(a) $(4N_Q) + N_D + N_Q = 20$ $\longrightarrow$ $N_D + 5N_Q = 20$ (a′)

(b) $5(4N_Q) + 10N_D + 25N_Q = 190$ $\longrightarrow$ $10N_D + 45N_Q = 190$ (b′)

Now we multiply (a′) by -10 and add to (b′).

$(-10)(a') \quad -10N_D - 50N_Q = -200$

(b′) $\quad \dfrac{10N_D + 45N_Q = 190}{-5N_Q = -10}$

$$N_Q = 2$$

$N_N = 4(2) = 8$, and since there were 20 in all, **10 were dimes.**

example 18.3   Reds varied directly as blues squared and inversely as greens. When there were 80 reds, there were 4 blues and 2 greens. How many reds were there when there were 8 blues and 10 greens?

solution   The problem can be worked as a variation problem. This approach is often used in physics books. The first sentence gives us the basic equation.

(1) $R = \dfrac{kB^2}{G}$ \qquad (2) $R = \dfrac{kB^2}{G}$

Writing the equation twice is a mnemonic to help us remember that this is a two-step problem. The first step is to use the numbers given in the second sentence in the left-hand equation and find that k equals 10. Then we replace k with 10 in the right-hand equation.

$$80 = \dfrac{k(4)^2}{2} \quad \longrightarrow \quad k = 10 \quad \longrightarrow \quad R = \dfrac{10B^2}{G}$$

To finish, we use the second set of numbers in the right-hand equation and find that R equals 64.

$$R = \frac{10(8)^2}{10} \quad \longrightarrow \quad R = \mathbf{64}$$

The ratio method can also be used to work this problem. This approach is often used in chemistry books. The first sentence gives us the basic equation.

$$\frac{R_1}{R_2} = \frac{B_1^2 G_2}{B_2^2 G_1}$$

Now we make the required replacements and solve.

$$\frac{80}{R_2} = \frac{(4)^2(10)}{(8)^2(2)} \quad \longrightarrow \quad \frac{80}{R_2} = \frac{160}{128} \quad \longrightarrow \quad R_2 = \mathbf{64}$$

example 18.4   The sum of the digits of a two-digit counting number is 5. When the digits are reversed, the number is 9 greater than the original number. What was the original number?

solution   The counting numbers are the positive integers. The sum of the digits is 5. If we use U for the units' digit and T for the tens' digit, we get

$$\text{(a) } U + T = 5$$

The value of the units' digit is U and of the tens' digit is $10T$, but when the digits are reversed the values will be $10U$ and T.

	ORIGINAL NUMBER		NEW NUMBER MINUS 9
(b)	$10T + U$	$=$	$T + 10U - 9$

which simplifies to

$$9T - 9U = -9 \quad \longrightarrow \quad T - U = -1$$

Now we substitute from equation (a) and solve.

$$(5 - U) - U = -1 \qquad \text{substituted for } T$$

$$5 - 2U = -1 \qquad \text{added}$$

$$-2U = -6 \qquad \text{added } -5 \text{ to both sides}$$

$$U = 3 \qquad \text{solved}$$

Since $U + T = 5$, $T = 2$, and the original number was **23.**

example 18.5   To get 1000 gallons (gal) of a mixture that was 56% alcohol, it was necessary to mix a quantity of 20% alcohol solution with a quantity of 80% alcohol solution. How much of each was required?

solution   We decide to make the statement about alcohol.

$$\text{Alcohol}_1 + \text{alcohol}_2 = \text{alcohol total}$$

Next, we use parentheses as mixture containers.

$$(\ ) + (\ ) = (\ )$$

We pour in P_N gallons of the first mixture and dump in D_N gallons of the second mixture for a total of 1000 gallons.

$$(P_N) + (D_N) = (1000)$$

Now we multiply by the proper decimals so that each entry represents gallons of alcohol.

$$\text{(a) } 0.2(P_N) + 0.8(D_N) = 0.56(1000)$$

This equation has two unknowns, so we need another equation, which is

$$\text{(b) } P_N + D_N = 1000$$

Now we substitute to solve.

$$0.2\left(1000 - D_N\right) + 0.8D_N = 0.56(1000) \qquad \text{substituted}$$

$$200 - 0.2D_N + 0.8D_N = 560 \qquad \text{multiplied}$$

Now we eliminate the decimals by multiplying by 10.

$$2000 - 2D_N + 8D_N = 5600 \qquad \text{multiplied by 10}$$

$$6D_N = 3600 \qquad \text{added}$$

$$D_N = \textbf{600 gal of 80\% alcohol} \qquad \text{solved}$$

Since the total was 1000 gallons, we need **400 gallons of 20% alcohol.**

example 18.6   How many liters of a 64% glycol solution must be added to 77 liters of a 23% glycol solution to get a 42% glycol solution?

solution   The solution to this problem is not difficult if a calculator is used to help with the arithmetic. We will make the statement about glycol and then insert the indicated quantities in the parentheses used as mixture containers.

$$\text{Glycol}_1 + \text{glycol added} = \text{glycol final}$$

$$(77) \quad + \quad \left(P_N\right) \quad = \left(77 + P_N\right)$$

The mixture entries indicate the amount of mixture. It is important to use symbols such as P_N or D_N for the amount of solution added. **Avoid using G for glycol added because the mixture added was not all glycol.** Next, we multiply each of the mixture container entries by the proper decimal number so that the product will equal the amount of glycol for each step.

$$0.23(77) + 0.64\left(P_N\right) = 0.42\left(77 + P_N\right)$$

We use a calculator to permit a quick solution to this equation.

$$17.71 + 0.64P_N = 32.34 + 0.42P_N \qquad \text{multiplied}$$

$$0.22P_N = 14.63 \qquad \text{rearranged}$$

$$P_N = \textbf{66.5 liters} \qquad \text{divided}$$

example 18.7   The weight of the carbon (C) in the container of C_3H_7Cl was 113 grams. What was the total weight of the compound? (C = 12; H = 1; Cl = 35)

solution   This is a ratio problem. The gram atomic weights are given above in parentheses.

Carbon	$12 \times 3 =$	36
Hydrogen	$1 \times 7 =$	7
Chlorine	$35 \times 1 =$	35
Total		78

Thus, the ratio of the carbon to the total weight is 36 to 78, and the carbon weighed 113 grams.

$$\frac{C}{T} = \frac{36}{78} \quad \longrightarrow \quad \frac{113}{T} = \frac{36}{78} \quad \longrightarrow \quad T = \textbf{244.83 grams}$$

**problem set
18**

1. The number of blues is 7 less than the sum of the whites and the greens. The number of greens is 1 greater than the sum of the blues and the whites. How many of each kind are there if there are 3 times as many greens as blues?

2. The quarters, nickels, and dimes totaled 20, and their value was $2.05. How many of each kind were there if there were 3 times as many dimes as quarters?

3. Reds varied directly as blues and inversely as greens squared. When there were 5 reds, there were 2 blues and 4 greens. How many reds were there when there were 4 blues and 4 greens?

4. Find the equation of the line that passes through the point $(-2, 3)$ and is perpendicular to the line $5x - 2y + 4 = 0$.

5. The sum of the digits of a two-digit counting number is 13. When the digits are reversed, the new number is 45 greater than the original number. What was the original number?

6. How much of a 14% iodine solution should be added to 89 ounces of a 47% iodine solution to get a 29% solution?

7. The weight of the chlorine (Cl) in the container of C_3H_7Cl was 400 grams. What was the total weight of the compound? (C = 12; H = 1; Cl = 35)

8. For $\triangle PQR$ and $\triangle STU$, write the ratios of corresponding sides. Determine if $\triangle PQR \sim \triangle STU$ and justify your answer.

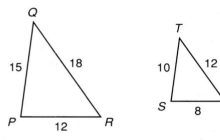

Simplify:

9. $\dfrac{\dfrac{m^2}{a^2} + \dfrac{7y}{x}}{\dfrac{p^2}{ax} - \dfrac{3}{a^2}}$

10. $\dfrac{m}{a + \dfrac{b}{1 + \dfrac{c}{d}}}$

11. Solve for c: $x = kb\left(\dfrac{1}{c} - \dfrac{a}{x}\right)$

12. Solve for k: $mc = p\left(\dfrac{a}{cm} + \dfrac{2}{kc}\right)$

13. Divide $x^4 - 2$ by $x^2 - 1$ and check.

14. Given: $\angle Q \cong \angle S$
    $\overline{PQ} \parallel \overline{SR}$

    Write a two-column proof to prove:
    $\triangle PQR \cong \triangle RSP$

Convert to polar coordinates. (Write four forms for each point.)

15. $-15\hat{i} + 3\hat{j}$

16. $14\hat{i} - 3\hat{j}$

Convert to rectangular coordinates:

17. $-32\underline{/-50°}$

18. $46\underline{/215°}$

19. Solve $4 = -3x^2 + 5x$ by using the quadratic formula.

20. Solve $-x + 2x^2 = 3$ by completing the square.

21. Solve: $\begin{cases} \dfrac{x}{2} - \dfrac{3y}{4} = \dfrac{5}{2} \\ 0.4y - 0.05z = -0.95 \\ \dfrac{x}{3} - \dfrac{2z}{5} = -\dfrac{8}{15} \end{cases}$

Simplify:

22. $\sqrt{5}\sqrt{-5} + \sqrt{-3}\sqrt{-3} + \sqrt{-4} - i$ **23.** $\dfrac{4 + 2\sqrt{12}}{6 - \sqrt{48}}$

24. $b^2 \sqrt[3]{ab^4} \left(ab^3\right)^{\frac{1}{5}}$

25. Find a.

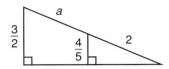

26. In right triangle JKL, angle K is a right angle and $\overline{KM}$ is the altitude to the hypotenuse JL. If $KM = 6$, find the length of the hypotenuse JL.

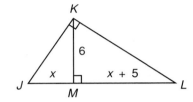

27. In the figure shown, square $ABCD$ is inscribed in circle O. Also, $\overline{OE} \perp \overline{AD}$ and $OE = 5$ cm. Find the area of the shaded region.

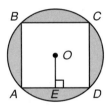

28. A sphere has a volume of 2304π cm^3. Find the diameter of the sphere.

CONCEPT REVIEW
PROBLEMS   **29.** Let x, y, and z be the lengths of the sides of a triangle whose area is 20 square units. Compare: A. x B. $y + z$

30. If x is a real number and $x^2 - x^4 > 0$, compare: A. x B. 1

LESSON 19   *Nonlinear Systems • Factoring Exponentials • Sum and Difference of Two Cubes*

19.A

nonlinear systems

The variables in a linear equation have an understood exponent of 1. Thus $y - x = 1$ is a linear equation and $3x + 2y + z = 5$ is a linear equation. The equations $y = 4^x$, $xy = 4$, and $x^2 - y = 6$ are nonlinear equations. A **nonlinear system of equations** contains one or more nonlinear equations. Nonlinear systems are sometimes solved by using substitution and elimination just as we do when we solve systems of linear equations. Solving nonlinear systems may involve the solution of a quadratic equation as the final step. These quadratic equations are seldom solved by factoring, and we usually solve them by using the quadratic formula.

example 19.1   Solve: (a) $\begin{cases} x^2 + y^2 = 9 & \text{(circle)} \\ y - x = 1 & \text{(line)} \end{cases}$

solution   This system of equations can be solved by using either substitution or elimination. We decide to use substitution. We will begin by solving equation (b) for y and then we will square both sides.

$$y - x = 1 \qquad \text{equation (b)}$$

$$y = x + 1 \qquad \text{solved for } y$$

$$y^2 = x^2 + 2x + 1 \qquad \text{squared both sides}$$

Now we will substitute $x^2 + 2x + 1$ for y^2 in equation (a).

$$x^2 + y^2 = 9 \qquad \text{equation (a)}$$

$$x^2 + (x^2 + 2x + 1) = 9 \qquad \text{substituted } x^2 + 2x + 1 \text{ for } y^2$$

$$2x^2 + 2x - 8 = 0 \qquad \text{simplified}$$

$$x^2 + x - 4 = 0 \qquad \text{divided by 2}$$

We will use the quadratic formula to solve this equation.

$$x = \frac{-b \pm \sqrt{b^2 - 4ac}}{2a} \qquad \text{quadratic formula}$$

$$x = \frac{-1 \pm \sqrt{(1)^2 - 4(1)(-4)}}{2(1)} \qquad \text{substituted}$$

$$x = -\frac{1}{2} \pm \frac{\sqrt{17}}{2} \qquad \text{simplified}$$

$$\text{which means} \quad x = -\frac{1}{2} + \frac{\sqrt{17}}{2} \quad \text{and} \quad x = -\frac{1}{2} - \frac{\sqrt{17}}{2}$$

Now we could use either equation (a) or equation (b) to find the values of y. We will use equation (b) to find the values of y because this equation has no squared terms and is easier to use.

$$y = x + 1 \qquad\qquad y = x + 1 \qquad\qquad \text{equation (b)}$$

$$y = \left(-\frac{1}{2} + \frac{\sqrt{17}}{2}\right) + 1 \qquad y = \left(-\frac{1}{2} - \frac{\sqrt{17}}{2}\right) + 1 \qquad \text{substituted}$$

$$y = \frac{1}{2} + \frac{\sqrt{17}}{2} \qquad\qquad y = \frac{1}{2} - \frac{\sqrt{17}}{2} \qquad \text{simplified}$$

Thus, the ordered pairs of x and y that satisfy the given system of equations are

$$\left(-\frac{1}{2} + \frac{\sqrt{17}}{2}, \frac{1}{2} + \frac{\sqrt{17}}{2}\right) \quad \text{and} \quad \left(-\frac{1}{2} - \frac{\sqrt{17}}{2}, \frac{1}{2} - \frac{\sqrt{17}}{2}\right)$$

The graph of the circle and the line are shown here. We will study the graphs of circles and other conics in later lessons. Here we are concentrating on the algebra of the solutions.

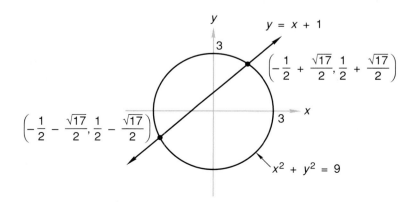

example 19.2   Solve: (a) $\begin{cases} x^2 + y^2 = 9 & \text{(circle)} \\ 2x^2 - y^2 = -6 & \text{(hyperbola)} \end{cases}$

solution   This system of equations can be solved by using either substitution or elimination. We must be careful to get all the answers because this circle and hyperbola intersect at four different points. We decide to use elimination. We can eliminate the y^2 terms if we add equations (a) and (b) just as they are. If we do this, we get

$$3x^2 = 3 \qquad \text{added}$$

$$x^2 = 1 \qquad \text{divided by 3}$$

$$x = \pm\sqrt{1} \qquad \text{solved}$$

which means $x = 1$ and $x = -1$

Now we could use either equation (a) or equation (b) to find the values of y. We will use equation (a) to find the values of y because this equation is easier to use. We begin by letting x equal $+1$ and solve for the values of y.

$$x^2 + y^2 = 9 \qquad \text{equation (a)}$$

$$(1)^2 + y^2 = 9 \qquad \text{substituted (1) for } x$$

$$y^2 = 8 \qquad \text{added } -1 \text{ to both sides}$$

$$y = \pm 2\sqrt{2} \qquad \text{solved}$$

Thus, there are two points of intersection when $x = 1$. So two solutions of our system of equations are

$$(1, 2\sqrt{2}) \qquad \text{and} \qquad (1, -2\sqrt{2})$$

Next, we let x equal -1 and solve for the values of y.

$$x^2 + y^2 = 9 \qquad \text{equation (a)}$$

$$(-1)^2 + y^2 = 9 \qquad \text{substituted } (-1) \text{ for } x$$

$$y^2 = 8 \qquad \text{added } -1 \text{ to both sides}$$

$$y = \pm 2\sqrt{2} \qquad \text{solved}$$

Thus, there are two points of intersection when $x = -1$. So our other two solutions of our system of equations are

$$(-1, 2\sqrt{2}) \qquad \text{and} \qquad (-1, -2\sqrt{2})$$

Here we show the graph of the circle and the hyperbola and note that there are four points where the two curves intersect. Do not worry about the graphs now. They will be discussed in later lessons.

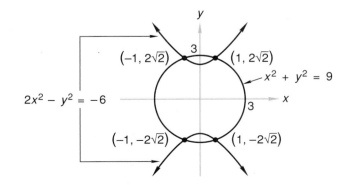

example 19.3   Solve: (a) $\begin{cases} xy = -4 & \text{(hyperbola)} \\ (b) \end{cases}$
                      (b) $\begin{cases} y = -x - 2 & \text{(line)} \end{cases}$

solution   This system of equations can be solved by using either substitution or elimination. We decide to use substitution. We will begin by substituting $-x - 2$ for y in equation (a).

$$xy = -4 \qquad \text{equation (a)}$$

$$x(-x - 2) = -4 \qquad \text{substituted } -x - 2 \text{ for } y$$

$$-x^2 - 2x = -4 \qquad \text{multiplied}$$

$$x^2 + 2x - 4 = 0 \qquad \text{rearranged}$$

We will use the quadratic formula to solve this equation.

$$x = \frac{-b \pm \sqrt{b^2 - 4ac}}{2a} \qquad \text{quadratic formula}$$

$$x = \frac{-2 \pm \sqrt{(2)^2 - 4(1)(-4)}}{2(1)} \qquad \text{substituted}$$

$$x = -1 \pm \sqrt{5} \qquad \text{simplified}$$

which means $\quad x = -1 + \sqrt{5} \quad$ and $\quad x = -1 - \sqrt{5}$

Now we could use either equation (a) or equation (b) to find the values of y. We will use equation (b) to find the values of y because this equation is linear and is easier to use.

$y = -x - 2$	$y = -x - 2$	equation (b)
$y = -(-1 + \sqrt{5}) - 2$	$y = -(-1 - \sqrt{5}) - 2$	substituted
$y = 1 - \sqrt{5} - 2$	$y = 1 + \sqrt{5} - 2$	simplified
$y = -1 - \sqrt{5}$	$y = -1 + \sqrt{5}$	simplified

Thus, the ordered pairs of x and y that satisfy the given system of equations are

$$\left(-1 + \sqrt{5}, -1 - \sqrt{5}\right) \qquad \text{and} \qquad \left(-1 - \sqrt{5}, -1 + \sqrt{5}\right)$$

The graph of the hyperbola and the line are shown below.

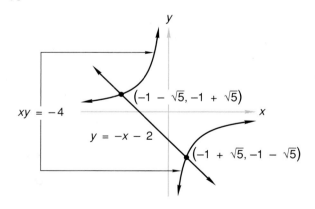

19.B
factoring exponentials

Expressions in which a base is raised to a power are often called **exponential expressions** or just **exponentials.** The word *exponential* also has a more restrictive definition that is explained in Lesson 23. When two quantities are multiplied, each of the quantities is called a **factor.** The reverse process is called **factoring** because when we factor, we break up an algebraic sum into an indicated product of two or more factors.

example 19.4   Factor: $3x^{2n+2} + 12x^{3n+3}$

solution   Sometimes it helps if we rewrite exponential expressions whose exponents are complicated. We can rewrite the given expression as

$$3 \cdot x^n \cdot x^n \cdot x^2 + 3 \cdot 4 \cdot x^n \cdot x^n \cdot x^n \cdot x^3$$

We see that the common factor is $3x^n x^n x^2$. Thus, we can write the expression in factored form as

$$3x^{2n}x^2\left(1 + 4x^n x\right) = 3x^{2n+2}\left(1 + 4x^{n+1}\right)$$

example 19.5   Simplify: $\dfrac{x^{2a} - y^{2b}}{x^a + y^b}$

solution   We recognize that the numerator is really the difference of two squares and can be factored.

$$\frac{\left(x^a\right)^2 - \left(y^b\right)^2}{x^a + y^b} = \frac{\left(x^a + y^b\right)\left(x^a - y^b\right)}{x^a + y^b} = x^a - y^b$$

19.C

sum and difference of two cubes

The sum of two cubes can be factored and the difference of two cubes can be factored.

$$a^3 + b^3 = (a + b)\left(a^2 - ab + b^2\right) \qquad a^3 - b^3 = (a - b)\left(a^2 + ab + b^2\right)$$

Using the forms for factoring the sum or difference of two cubes is required, and disuse encourages one to forget the factored forms. Yet, if one can remember that $a^3 + b^3$ is divisible by $a + b$ and $a^3 - b^3$ is divisible by $a - b$, it is possible to do the long divisions to find the other factors, as we show here.

$$
\begin{array}{r}
a^2 - ab + b^2 \\
a + b\,\overline{)a^3 \qquad\qquad\quad + b^3} \\
a^3 + a^2b \\ \hline
-a^2b \\
-a^2b - ab^2 \\ \hline
ab^2 + b^3 \\
ab^2 + b^3 \\ \hline
\end{array}
\qquad
\begin{array}{r}
a^2 + ab + b^2 \\
a - b\,\overline{)a^3 \qquad\qquad\quad - b^3} \\
a^3 - a^2b \\ \hline
a^2b \\
a^2b - ab^2 \\ \hline
ab^2 - b^3 \\
ab^2 - b^3 \\ \hline
\end{array}
$$

Thus, we see that we can factor as follows:

$$(1) \quad a^3 + b^3 = (a + b)\left(a^2 - ab + b^2\right)$$

$$(2) \quad a^3 - b^3 = (a - b)\left(a^2 + ab + b^2\right)$$

To extend these forms to more complicated expressions, some people find that it is helpful to think F for *first thing* and S for *second thing* instead of a and b. If we do this in the above equations, we get

$$(1') \quad F^3 + S^3 = (F + S)\left(F^2 - FS + S^2\right)$$

$$(2') \quad F^3 - S^3 = (F - S)\left(F^2 + FS + S^2\right)$$

example 19.6   Factor: $x^3y^3 - p^3$

solution   We recognize that this expression can be written as the difference of two cubes

$$(xy)^3 - (p)^3$$

and note that the first thing that is cubed is xy and that the second thing that is cubed is p. Thus, if we use form (2′),

$$(2') \quad F^3 - S^3 = (F - S)(F^2 + FS + S^2)$$

and replace F with xy and S with p, we can write the given expression in factored form.

$$x^3y^3 - p^3 = (xy - p)(x^2y^2 + xyp + p^2)$$

example 19.7 Factor: $8m^3y^6 + x^3$

solution We recognize that this expression can be written as the sum of two cubes

$$(2my^2)^3 + (x)^3$$

and note that the first thing that is cubed is $2my^2$ and that the second thing that is cubed is x. Thus, if we use form (1′),

$$(1') \quad F^3 + S^3 = (F + S)(F^2 - FS + S^2)$$

and replace F with $2my^2$ and S with x, we can write the given expression in factored form.

$$8m^3y^6 + x^3 = (2my^2 + x)(4m^2y^4 - 2my^2x + x^2)$$

problem set 19

1. Two 14-sided polygons are similar. A side of the larger polygon is 4 times as long as the corresponding side of the smaller polygon. What is the ratio of the area of the larger polygon to the area of the smaller polygon?

2. Four times the sum of the number of reds and browns exceeded three times the number of greens by 10. Three less than four times the number of browns was seven greater than the number of greens. If the total number of reds, browns, and greens was 20, how many were red, brown, and green?

3. There were 50 nickels, quarters, and dimes in the pot. Their total value was $6.40. There were four more quarters than nickels. How many coins of each kind were there?

4. Find the equation of the line that passes through $(5, -3)$ and is parallel to the line $5y - 2x - 30 = 0$.

5. The number of coaches varied directly as the number of ringleaders squared and inversely as the number of scholars cubed. When there were 6 coaches present, there were 4 ringleaders and 2 scholars. How many coaches were present when there were 6 ringleaders and only 1 scholar?

6. The sum of the digits of a two-digit counting number is 11. When the digits are reversed, the new number is 9 greater than the old number. What is the old number?

7. Two solutions are to be mixed to make 50 ml of a solution that is 16% bromine. One solution is 10% bromine and the other solution is 40% bromine. How much of each solution should be used?

Solve:

8. $\begin{cases} x^2 + y^2 = 9 \\ y - x = 1 \end{cases}$

9. $\begin{cases} x^2 + y^2 = 9 \\ 2x^2 - y^2 = -6 \end{cases}$

10. $\begin{cases} xy = -4 \\ y = -x - 2 \end{cases}$

11. Factor: $4x^{3n+2} - 6x^{4n+1}$

12. Simplify by factoring the numerator: $\dfrac{x^{4a} - y^{4b}}{x^{2a} + y^{2b}}$

Factor:

13. $27x^{12}y^6 - z^9$

14. $8x^6y^3 + p^3$

15. For $\triangle UVW$ and $\triangle XYZ$, write the ratios of the two corresponding sides that form the angle. Determine if $\triangle UVW \sim \triangle XYZ$ and justify your answer.

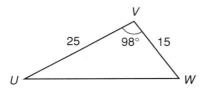
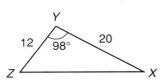

Simplify:

16. $\dfrac{\dfrac{3a}{b^2} + \dfrac{2c}{ab}}{\dfrac{a}{c} - \dfrac{b}{d}}$

17. $\dfrac{3i^4 - 2i^2 + i^3}{1 - 3i^2 + \sqrt{-9}}$

18. $\dfrac{3 - 2\sqrt{12}}{5 + 4\sqrt{27}}$

19. $\dfrac{1 - 3i}{5i + 4}$

20. $\left(3a^{\frac{x}{3}} - b^{\frac{y}{2}}\right)\left(3a^{\frac{x}{3}} + b^{\frac{y}{2}}\right)$

21. $\dfrac{x^{3c-1}y^{2-4d}}{x^{c+d}y^{c-d}}$

22. Divide $x^4 - 2x + 1$ by $x - 2$ and check.

23. Solve for z: $\quad 2t = \dfrac{1}{3s^2}\left(\dfrac{5z}{6} - \dfrac{4m}{n}\right)$

24. Given: $\overline{UV} \cong \overline{WV}$
$\qquad\quad \overline{VX} \perp \overline{UW}$

Write a two-column proof to prove:
$\qquad \triangle UVX \cong \triangle WVX$

25. Given: $\overline{HK} \cong \overline{IJ}$
$\qquad\quad \overline{HI} \cong \overline{KJ}$

Write a two-column proof to prove:
$\qquad \triangle HIK \cong \triangle JKI$

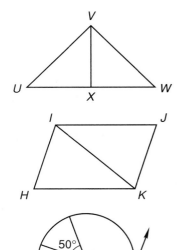

26. In the figure shown, $\overrightarrow{AB}$ is tangent to circle O. Find x.

27. In the figure shown, O is the center of the circle. Find x.

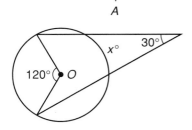

28. (a) A sphere has a surface area of 2916π square meters. Find the volume of the sphere.

(b) Find the length of a radius of a sphere whose volume in cubic centimeters is equal to its surface area in square centimeters.

CONCEPT REVIEW PROBLEMS

29. In the figure shown, $\triangle ABC$ is inscribed in circle O.

Compare: A. $m\angle B$ B. $m\angle C - m\angle A$

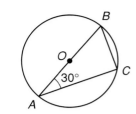

30. Given: $\triangle ABC$

Compare: A. AC B. $BC + AD$

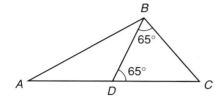

LESSON 20 Two Special Triangles

We have found that the trigonometric ratios that we call the cosine, the sine, and the tangent can be used to help us solve right triangles for unknown sides or angles. We have used a calculator to find numerical approximations of the values of these trigonometric functions. In this lesson we will explain how to obtain the trigonometric function values without using a calculator for the acute angles having measures 30°, 45°, and 60°. The trigonometric function values of these angles can easily be memorized, or they can be recalled when associated with two special right triangles in which the shortest side of each triangle has a length of one unit. Using the Pythagorean theorem and basic geometric facts, we can figure out the lengths of the other sides.

To find the trigonometric function values of a 45° angle, we begin by drawing an isosceles right triangle whose legs are one unit long, as shown below. We know that the base angles of an isosceles triangle are equal. Therefore, the two angles marked θ are equal angles. We also know that the sum of the measures of the angles of a triangle is 180°. Therefore, the two angles marked θ are 45° angles because they and the right angle must sum to 180°. Now we use the Pythagorean theorem to solve for c and find that c equals $\sqrt{2}$. Thus, the length of the hypotenuse is $\sqrt{2}$.

$c^2 = a^2 + b^2$	Pythagorean theorem
$c^2 = 1^2 + 1^2$	substituted
$c^2 = 2$	simplified
$c = \sqrt{2}$	solved

We draw the completed triangle below. Right triangles whose acute angles are 45° are often called *45°-45°-90° triangles*. We use this 45°-45°-90° triangle to find the cosine, sine, and tangent of 45°.

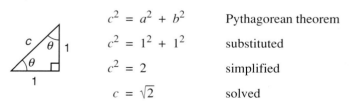

$$\cos \theta = \frac{\text{adj}}{\text{hyp}} \qquad \cos 45° = \frac{1}{\sqrt{2}}$$

$$\sin \theta = \frac{\text{opp}}{\text{hyp}} \qquad \sin 45° = \frac{1}{\sqrt{2}}$$

$$\tan \theta = \frac{\text{opp}}{\text{adj}} \qquad \tan 45° = \frac{1}{1} = 1$$

To find the trigonometric function values of a 30° or 60° angle, we begin by drawing an equilateral triangle whose sides are two units long, as shown below. The three angles in an equilateral triangle are equal angles. Since the sum of the measures of the angles of a triangle is 180°, the measure of each angle must be 60°. In the equilateral triangle $\triangle ABC$, we also draw the angle bisector of angle A, as shown. We know that an angle bisector in an equilateral triangle is perpendicular to the side opposite the angle and also bisects that side. Therefore, the equilateral triangle $\triangle ABC$ can be separated into two congruent right triangles whose acute angles are 30° and 60°.

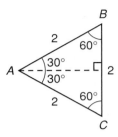

We discard the lower half of the triangle, and the remaining triangle is a right triangle whose sides are 2, 1, and x. Now we use the Pythagorean theorem to solve for x and find that x equals $\sqrt{3}$.

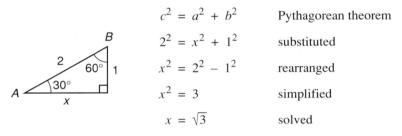

$$c^2 = a^2 + b^2 \qquad \text{Pythagorean theorem}$$
$$2^2 = x^2 + 1^2 \qquad \text{substituted}$$
$$x^2 = 2^2 - 1^2 \qquad \text{rearranged}$$
$$x^2 = 3 \qquad \text{simplified}$$
$$x = \sqrt{3} \qquad \text{solved}$$

We draw the completed triangle below. Right triangles whose acute angles are 30° and 60° are often called *30°-60°-90° triangles*. We use this 30°-60°-90° triangle to find the cosine, sine, and tangent of 30° and 60°.

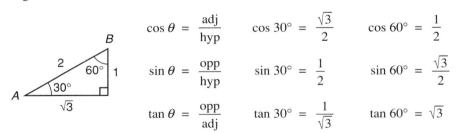

$$\cos \theta = \frac{\text{adj}}{\text{hyp}} \qquad \cos 30° = \frac{\sqrt{3}}{2} \qquad \cos 60° = \frac{1}{2}$$
$$\sin \theta = \frac{\text{opp}}{\text{hyp}} \qquad \sin 30° = \frac{1}{2} \qquad \sin 60° = \frac{\sqrt{3}}{2}$$
$$\tan \theta = \frac{\text{opp}}{\text{adj}} \qquad \tan 30° = \frac{1}{\sqrt{3}} \qquad \tan 60° = \sqrt{3}$$

We remember that right triangles whose acute angles are 45° are often called *45°-45°-90° triangles* and right triangles whose acute angles are 30° and 60° are often called *30°-60°-90° triangles*. In this book, we will refer to 45°-45°-90° triangles and 30°-60°-90° triangles as *reference triangles*.

example 20.1   Draw the necessary reference triangle and evaluate tan 30°.

solution   We begin by drawing the 30°-60°-90° reference triangle and then find tan 30°.

$$\tan \theta = \frac{\text{opp}}{\text{adj}}$$

$$\tan 30° = \frac{1}{\sqrt{3}}$$

REFERENCE TRIANGLE

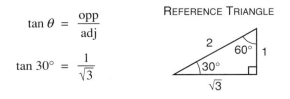

Therefore, we have $\tan 30° = 1/\sqrt{3}$. It is customary to write answers that do not have a radical in the denominator, so we multiply $1/\sqrt{3}$ above and below by $\sqrt{3}$ to rationalize the denominator.

$$\frac{1}{\sqrt{3}} = \frac{1}{\sqrt{3}} \cdot \frac{\sqrt{3}}{\sqrt{3}} = \frac{\sqrt{3}}{3}$$

Therefore, we have

$$\tan 30° = \frac{\sqrt{3}}{3}$$

Some modern authors have suggested that rationalizing the denominator is an unnecessary procedure. Perhaps it is, but we will continue to rationalize denominators for the practice the procedure provides in handling radical expressions.

example 20.2   Draw the necessary reference triangle and evaluate $7 \sin 45°$.

solution   We begin by drawing the 45°-45°-90° reference triangle and then find $\sin 45°$.

$$\sin \theta = \frac{\text{opp}}{\text{hyp}}$$

$$\sin 45° = \frac{1}{\sqrt{2}}$$

REFERENCE TRIANGLE

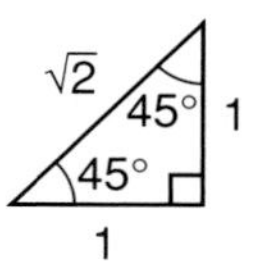

Therefore, we have $\sin 45° = 1/\sqrt{2}$. Now we multiply $1/\sqrt{2}$ above and below by $\sqrt{2}$ to rationalize the denominator.

$$\frac{1}{\sqrt{2}} = \frac{1}{\sqrt{2}} \cdot \frac{\sqrt{2}}{\sqrt{2}} = \frac{\sqrt{2}}{2}$$

Therefore, we have $\sin 45° = \sqrt{2}/2$. Since we want $7 \sin 45°$, we multiply by 7. Therefore, we have

$$7 \sin 45° = \frac{7\sqrt{2}}{2}$$

example 20.3   Draw the necessary reference triangle and evaluate $4\sqrt{3} \cos 60°$.

solution   We begin by drawing the 30°-60°-90° reference triangle and then find $\cos 60°$.

$$\cos \theta = \frac{\text{adj}}{\text{hyp}}$$

$$\cos 60° = \frac{1}{2}$$

REFERENCE TRIANGLE

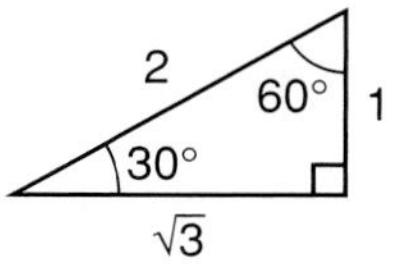

Therefore, we have $\cos 60° = 1/2$. Since we want $4\sqrt{3} \cos 60°$, we multiply by $4\sqrt{3}$. Therefore, we have

$$4\sqrt{3} \cos 60° = 4\sqrt{3}\left(\frac{1}{2}\right) = 2\sqrt{3}$$

example 20.4   Draw the necessary reference triangle and evaluate $10/\sqrt{5}\ \tan 45°$.

solution   We begin by drawing the 45°-45°-90° reference triangle and then find tan 45°.

$$\tan \theta = \frac{\text{opp}}{\text{adj}}$$

REFERENCE TRIANGLE

$$\tan 45° = \frac{1}{1} = 1$$

Therefore, we have $\tan 45° = 1$. Since we want $10/\sqrt{5}\ \tan 45°$, we multiply by $10/\sqrt{5}$. Therefore, we have

$$\frac{10}{\sqrt{5}}\ \tan 45° = \frac{10}{\sqrt{5}}$$

Now we multiply $10/\sqrt{5}$ above and below by $\sqrt{5}$ to rationalize the denominator.

$$\frac{10}{\sqrt{5}} = \frac{10}{\sqrt{5}} \cdot \frac{\sqrt{5}}{\sqrt{5}} = \frac{10\sqrt{5}}{5} = 2\sqrt{5}$$

Therefore, we have

$$\frac{10}{\sqrt{5}}\ \tan 45° = \mathbf{2\sqrt{5}}$$

problem set 20

1. A kite is flying at the end of a straight string that has a length of 250 meters. The string makes an angle of 65° with the ground. How high above the ground is the kite?

2. Find the equation of the line that passes through the point $(-2, 0)$ and is perpendicular to the line $5x + 3y + 2 = 0$.

3. Forty percent of the reds added to 60 percent of the greens numbered 56. If the ratio of the number of reds to the number of greens was 1 to 4, how many were red and how many were green?

4. Twice the number of reds exceeded 3 times the number of blues by 8. The ratio of the reds to the sum of the reds and blues was 5 to 7. How many were red and how many were blue?

5. There are 12 nickels, dimes, and quarters whose total value is $1.55. If the number of nickels exceeds the number of quarters by 1, how many coins of each kind are there?

6. The sum of the digits of a two-digit counting number is 12 and the ratio of the units' digit to the tens' digit is 1 to 2. What is the number?

7. An alloy of copper and tin is 20% copper. How many pounds of copper must be added to 20 pounds of the alloy to get an alloy that is 50% copper?

8. A pharmacist has 100 ounces of a solution that is $3\frac{1}{2}$% iodine and $96\frac{1}{2}$% alcohol. How much alcohol should the pharmacist add to get a $1\frac{1}{2}$% iodine solution?

9. Draw the necessary reference triangle and evaluate $6\sqrt{2}\ \cos 30°$. Do not use a calculator.

10. Draw the necessary reference triangle and evaluate $6\sqrt{3}\ \sin 45°$. Do not use a calculator.

11. Draw the necessary reference triangle and evaluate $4\ \tan 60°$. Do not use a calculator.

12. In the figure shown below, $VW = 35$, $WZ = 28$, $WX = 12$, $VZ = 21$, $YX = 20$, and $YZ = 12$. For $\triangle VWZ$ and $\triangle YXZ$, write the ratios of corresponding sides. Determine if $\triangle VWZ \sim \triangle YXZ$ and justify your answer.

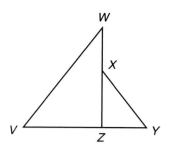

13. Given: $\overline{AB} \parallel \overline{DE}$
$\qquad \overline{BC} \parallel \overline{EF}$

Write a two-column proof to prove:

$\qquad \triangle ABC \sim \triangle DEF$

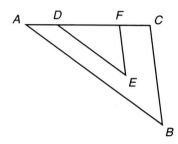

Solve:

14. $\begin{cases} \dfrac{3}{4}x - \dfrac{5}{2}z = -2 \\ 0.4x + 0.3z = 2.2 \\ -\dfrac{1}{2}x + \dfrac{3}{2}y = \dfrac{5}{2} \end{cases}$

15. $\begin{cases} x^2 + y^2 = 9 \\ y - 2x = 1 \end{cases}$

16. $\dfrac{x}{x-3} - \dfrac{2}{x+1} = \dfrac{x+9}{x^2 - 2x - 3}$ (*Hint*: Check solutions.)

Factor:

17. $27x^3y^6 + 8p^3$

18. $8x^3y^{12} - 27z^9$

Simplify:

19. $\dfrac{x}{2y - \dfrac{6z}{3 + \dfrac{s}{t}}}$

20. $\left(2x^5y\right)^{-2}\left(\dfrac{2x^3y^2}{xy^{-1}}\right)^{-1}$

21. $\sqrt{7}\sqrt{7}\sqrt{-7} + \sqrt{-5}\sqrt{-5}\sqrt{-5} - 3\sqrt{-4} + 2i$

22. Solve for y: $s^2 = \dfrac{1}{df}\left(\dfrac{4y}{3} - \dfrac{7x^3}{g}\right)$

23. Divide $x^4 - 6$ by $x^2 - 1$ and check.

24. Convert $7\hat{i} - 13\hat{j}$ to polar coordinates. (Write four forms for this point.)

25. Solve $-5x - 8 = 3x^2$ by completing the square.

26. Given: $\overline{PQ} \parallel \overline{ST}$
$\qquad \overline{PQ} \cong \overline{ST}$

Write a two-column proof to prove:

$\qquad \triangle PRQ \cong \triangle TRS$

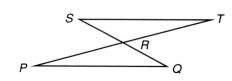

27. In the figure shown, O is the center of the circle. Find the radius of the circle. Dimensions are in meters.

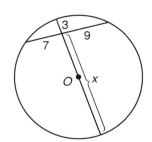

28. The base of a regular pyramid is a square with each diagonal measuring $12\sqrt{2}$ cm. The surface area of this regular pyramid is 384 cm^2. Find the slant height and altitude of the pyramid.

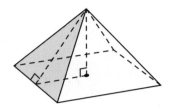

CONCEPT REVIEW PROBLEMS

29. Let x and y be real numbers. If $x > 0$ and $y < 0$, compare: A. $x - y$ B. $y - x$

30. In the figure shown, two lines l_1 and l_2 are intersected by a transversal. Lines l_1 and l_2 meet when extended to the right.

Compare: A. 180   B. $x + y$

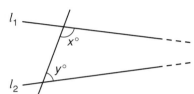

LESSON 21 *Evaluating Functions • Domain and Range • Types of Functions • Tests for Functions*

21.A

evaluating functions

In Lesson 20 we said that the trigonometric ratios that we call the cosine, the sine, and the tangent are called *trigonometric functions*. In this lesson we will explore what we mean when we use the word **function**. The essence of the word function is *single-valued*. For example, if we replace x with 3 in the expression

$$x^2 - 4x + 7$$

the expression will have a value of 4. If we replace x with -2, the expression will have a value of 19.

LET $x = 3$		LET $x = -2$	
$(3)^2 - 4(3) + 7$	substituted	$(-2)^2 - 4(-2) + 7$	substituted
$9 - 12 + 7$	multiplied	$4 + 8 + 7$	multiplied
4	simplified	19	simplified

Because we will get exactly one value for the expression for any number we use as a replacement for x, and because the value depends on the number we use, we say that the value of the expression is a function of x. If we let y designate the value of the expression, we can write an equation as we show here.

$$y = x^2 - 4x + 7$$

In this equation we can replace x with any real number we choose, so we call x the **independent variable.** The value of y depends on the number we use to replace x, so we call *y* the **dependent variable.** Mathematicians have developed a notation called *functional notation* that is most useful. If we write *f(x)*, read "*f* of *x*," instead of writing *y*, the equation becomes

$$f(x) = x^2 - 4x + 7$$

We tend to use *f(x)* because this reminds us that the value of the expression is a function of the value of *x*. But we don't have to use *f(x)*. We can use *g(x)*, read "*g* of *x*," or *h(x)*, read "*h* of *x*," or any other letter we choose. We can even use Greek letters and write *θ(x)*, read "theta of *x*," or *ψ(x)*, read "psi of *x*." This lets us name functions, as we will demonstrate. Consider the equations

$$\text{(a)}\ y = x^2 + 2 \qquad \text{(b)}\ y = x^3 - x + 3 \qquad \text{(c)}\ y = x - 13$$

Instead of calling these equations (a), (b), and (c), we could speak of the *f* function, the *g* function, and the *h* function, and write

$$f(x) = x^2 + 2 \qquad g(x) = x^3 - x + 3 \qquad h(x) = x - 13$$

Now we can ask someone to find *h*(20), read "*h* of twenty." This means to find the value of the *h* function when *x* is replaced with 20.

$$h(x) = x - 13 \qquad\qquad h \text{ function}$$

$$h(20) = (20) - 13 \qquad\qquad \text{replaced } x \text{ with } 20$$

$$h(20) = 7 \qquad\qquad \text{simplified}$$

This answer tells us that we used the *h* function, replaced *x* with 20, and that the answer was 7.

example 21.1   If $f(x) = x^2 + x - 10$, find *f*(5).

solution   To find *f*(5), we replace *x* everywhere with 5.

$$f(x) = x^2 + x - 10 \qquad\qquad \text{function}$$

$$f(5) = (5)^2 + (5) - 10 \qquad\qquad \text{replaced } x \text{ with } 5$$

$$f(5) = \mathbf{20} \qquad\qquad \text{simplified}$$

example 21.2   If $f(x) = x^2 + 1$, find *f(x + 2)*.

solution   To find *f(x + 2)*, we replace *x* everywhere with *x + 2*.

$$f(x) = x^2 + 1 \qquad\qquad \text{function}$$

$$f(x + 2) = (x + 2)^2 + 1 \qquad\qquad \text{replaced } x \text{ with } x + 2$$

$$f(x + 2) = \mathbf{x^2 + 4x + 5} \qquad\qquad \text{simplified}$$

example 21.3   If $h(\theta) = \sin \theta$, find $4\sqrt{3}h(30°)$.

solution   We begin by drawing the 30°-60°-90° reference triangle and then find sin 30°.

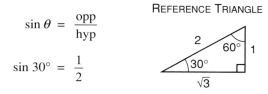

$$\sin \theta = \frac{\text{opp}}{\text{hyp}}$$

$$\sin 30° = \frac{1}{2}$$

REFERENCE TRIANGLE

Therefore, we have

$$h(\theta) = \sin \theta \qquad\qquad \text{function}$$

$$h(30°) = \sin (30°) \qquad \text{replaced } \theta \text{ with } 30°$$

$$h(30°) = \frac{1}{2} \qquad\qquad \text{simplified}$$

Now we can find $4\sqrt{3}h(30°)$.

$$4\sqrt{3}h(30°) = 4\sqrt{3} \cdot \frac{1}{2} = 2\sqrt{3}$$

21.B

domain and range

We usually use only the real numbers (zero and all positive and negative numbers) as replacements for x, and we accept only values of $f(x)$ that are real numbers. **So we cannot use numbers as replacements for x that indicate division by zero or that require that we take square roots of negative numbers.** If a number is an acceptable replacement for x, we say that the number is a member of the **domain** of the function. We call the set of all possible outputs of a function the **range.** We state formally the definition of a function below.

DEFINITION OF FUNCTION

A **function** is a mapping or correspondence between one set called the **domain** and a second set called the **range** such that for every member of the domain there corresponds exactly one member in the range.

---

example 21.4   If $f(x) = \sqrt{10 - x}$, find the domain of f.

solution   If we replace x with 10 in the f function, we find that $f(10)$ equals zero, and since zero is a real number, the number 10 is an acceptable replacement value for x.

$$f(x) = \sqrt{10 - x} \qquad f \text{ function}$$

$$f(10) = \sqrt{10 - (10)} \qquad \text{substituted}$$

$$f(10) = \sqrt{0} = 0 \qquad \text{acceptable}$$

But any number greater than 10 is not acceptable because this will cause the value of the f function to be an imaginary number and imaginary numbers are not acceptable. Let's try 10.01 for x.

$$f(x) = \sqrt{10 - x} \qquad f \text{ function}$$

$$f(10.01) = \sqrt{10 - (10.01)} \qquad \text{substituted}$$

$$f(10.01) = \sqrt{-0.01} \qquad \text{simplified}$$

$$f(10.01) = 0.1i \qquad \text{NO!   } 0.1i \text{ is imaginary}$$

The domain of the f function is the set of all real numbers that will result in a real number answer, so the domain of the f function contains all real numbers x such that $10 - x \geq 0$. This means that x must be less than or equal to 10. To designate domains, we can use set notation; that is, we can use {   } to designate the set, use the symbol $\in$ to mean *an element of*, and use the symbol $\mathbb{R}$ to represent the real numbers. We use a vertical line to mean *such that*. Therefore, using set notation, we can write

$$\text{Domain of } f = \left\{ x \in \mathbb{R} \mid x \leq 10 \right\}$$

We can read this as follows: "The domain of f is the set of all real numbers x such that x is less than or equal to ten."

example 21.5   If $g(x) = \dfrac{1}{x - 2}$, find the domain of g.

solution   From the denominator of the function, we see that x cannot equal 2 because this would make the denominator equal zero. Any other real number used for x will give us a real number for $g(x)$, so the domain of g is the set of all real numbers not equal to 2. Therefore, using set notation, we can write

$$\text{Domain of } g = \{x \in \mathbb{R} \mid x \neq 2\}$$

example 21.6   Find the domain and range of the function $y = \sqrt{x}$ and graph the function.

solution   All values of x and y for the function must be real numbers. The square root of a negative number is an imaginary number. For example, $\sqrt{-4}$ is equal to $2i$, which is an imaginary number. Therefore, we cannot use negative numbers for x because $\sqrt{x}$ will be an imaginary number. Thus the only numbers we can use for x are zero and the positive numbers, so the domain of the function is the set of all real numbers that are equal to or greater than zero. Using set notation, we can write

$$\text{Domain of } \sqrt{x} = \{x \in \mathbb{R} \mid x \geq 0\}$$

Finding the range of this function is easier if we graph the function first. On the left we make a table and choose 0, 1, and 4 as values of x. Then we use these values to find the paired values of y, which we place in the table. Then we graph the three points and sketch the graph of the function.

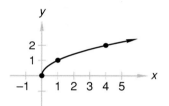

x	y
0	
1	
4	

$\sqrt{0} = 0$
$\sqrt{1} = 1$
$\sqrt{4} = 2$

x	y
0	0
1	1
4	2

On the graph we see that there are no negative values of y and that the values of y increase as x increases, so the range of the function is the set of all real numbers that are equal to or greater than zero. Using set notation, we can write

$$\text{Range of } \sqrt{x} = \{y \in \mathbb{R} \mid y \geq 0\}$$

We can read this as follows: "The range of $\sqrt{x}$ is the set of all real numbers y such that y is equal to or greater than zero."

example 21.7   Find the domain and range of the function $y = \sqrt{x + 4}$ and graph the function.

solution   We cannot use numbers that will cause $\sqrt{x + 4}$ to be an imaginary number, which means that $x + 4$ cannot be negative. Therefore, we see that the domain of the function is the set of all real numbers that are equal to or greater than -4. Using set notation, we can write

$$\text{Domain} = \{x \in \mathbb{R} \mid x \geq -4\}$$

Finding the range of this function is easier if we graph the function first. On the left we make a table and choose -4, 0, and 5 as values of x. Then we use these values to find the paired values of y, which we place in the table. Then we graph the three points and sketch the graph of the function.

x	y
-4	0
0	2
5	3

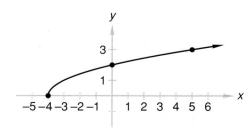

On the graph we see that there are no negative values of y and that the values of y increase as x increases, so the range of the function is the set of all real numbers that are equal to or greater than zero. Using set notation, we can write

$$\text{Range} = \left\{ y \in \mathbb{R} \mid y \geq 0 \right\}$$

example 21.8   Find the domain and range of the function $f(x) = \dfrac{\sqrt{x}}{x - 2}$.

solution   From the numerator of the function we see that x cannot be a negative number because the square root of a negative number is an imaginary number. From the denominator of the function we see that x cannot equal 2 because this would make the denominator equal zero. Therefore, we see that the domain of the function is the set of all real numbers that are equal to or greater than zero and that are not equal to 2. Using set notation, we can write

$$\text{Domain} = \left\{ x \in \mathbb{R} \mid x \geq 0, x \neq 2 \right\}$$

Finding the range of this function is easier if we graph the function first. We will discuss graphing techniques in later lessons.

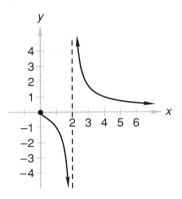

The graph of this function shows that the values of y include zero and all positive and negative real numbers. Therefore, the range of the function is the set of all real numbers. Using set notation, we can write

$$\text{Range} = \left\{ y \in \mathbb{R} \right\}$$

21.C

types of functions   We can think of an algebraic function as a **function machine,** as we show here. The function machine below will accept any real number as the input, will square it, and will add 5 to get the output.

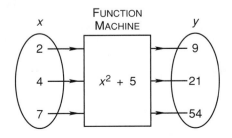

Two squared plus 5 is 9. Thus the function machine takes in a 2 and puts out a 9. We say that the **image** of 2 is 9. Four squared plus 5 is 21, so the output y value is 21 when the x input is 4. Seven squared plus 5 is 54, so the output of this function machine is a y value of 54 when the x value of the input is 7. In other words, the image of 4 is 21, and the image of 7 is 54.

We do not need an algebraic expression to define a function because the function can be described as a *mapping* or a *correspondence*, as we show below.

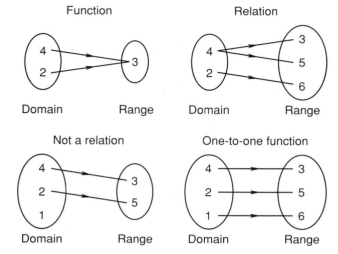

The diagram on the above left defines a function. The members of the domain are the numbers 4 and 2, and both of these numbers are mapped to the number 3. Four maps to 3, so the image of 4 is 3, and 2 maps to 3, so the image of 2 is 3. This is acceptable because two members of the domain can have the same image. The diagram on the above right, however, does not define a function but is merely a relation because 4 has two images, 3 and 5, and only one image is allowed. A **relation** is a mapping or correspondence that maps every member of the domain to one or more members of the range. Note that every function is a relation but not every relation is a function. The diagram on the bottom left is neither a function nor a relation as one member of the domain, 1, does not correspond to any member of the range. Finally, the diagram on the bottom right depicts a **one-to-one function.** First, it is a function. Furthermore, every element of the range corresponds to no more than one member of the domain; because it has this property, we say that the function is **one-to-one.**

The rule for a function may also be stated by a list of ordered pairs such that every first member is paired with exactly one second member. Thus, the following set of ordered pairs defines a *relation* but does not define a function

$$(4, 3), \quad (5, 7), \quad (9, 3), \quad (4, -5), \quad (8, 14), \quad (6, -3)$$

because the first and the fourth pairs have different answers (images) for 4. The following set of ordered pairs *does* define a function.

$$(4, 3), \quad (5, 7), \quad (9, 3), \quad (4, 3), \quad (8, 14), \quad (6, -3)$$

We restate our earlier definition of *function* to include different ways of defining a function.

> **We use the word *function* to describe a mapping from each member of the input set, which is called the *domain*, to exactly one member of the output set, which is called the *range*. Each member of the domain maps to an *image* in the range.** Thus, the word *function* brings to mind the following:
>
> 1. The numbers that are acceptable as inputs and the algebraic rule (if one exists) that can be used to find the unique output that is paired with each input.
> 2. A table of ordered pairs of inputs and outputs where each input member is paired with exactly one output and all equal inputs have the same outputs.
> 3. The graph of the geometric points whose coordinates are the ordered pairs just described.

example 21.9   For each diagram, determine whether or not it designates a function:

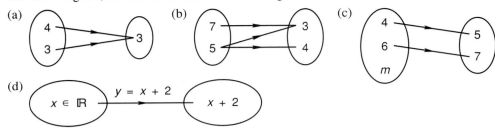

(d)

solution   **Diagrams (a) and (d) designate functions** because both diagrams show exactly one answer for each member of the domain. In (a) the domain is specified to be the numbers 4 and 3, and each member of the domain has one image. The image for 4 is 3, and the image for 3 is 3. Thus both images are the same, but this is acceptable. In (d) a way is given to find any image and for every input there is only one output.

   Diagrams (b) and (c) do not depict functions because in (b) 5 has two images and in (c) no image is designated for *m*. Thus, (c) is not even a relation.

example 21.10   Which of the following sets of ordered pairs are functions?

(a) $\{(1, 2), (2, 3), (3, 4), (4, 5)\}$ (b) $\{(1, 2), (2, 3), (1, 3), (4, 5)\}$

(c) $\{(4, 3), (2, 2), (4, 3), (3, 3)\}$ (d) $\{(1, -1), (4, -1), (-1, -1), (3, -2)\}$

solution   A set of ordered pairs in which every first number is paired with a unique second number is a function. So we look for first numbers that are the same. In set (a), all the first numbers are different and each first number has a second number, so **set (a) describes a function.** Set (b) is not a function because two ordered pairs have 1 as a first number, but the second numbers are different. **Set (c) is a function** because this set has two ordered pairs in which 4 is the first number, but both of these ordered pairs have 3 as the second number. In set (d) three of the second numbers are −1, but **set (d) is a function** because all the first numbers are different.

21.D

tests for functions   We remember that a function has only one value of *y* for each value of *x*. Given a graph, we can determine whether the graph could be that of a function by applying the *vertical line test,* stated below:

VERTICAL LINE TEST

A graph on the coordinate plane represents the graph of a function provided that any vertical line intersects the graph in at most one point.

Therefore, the graph on the left below represents the graph of a function since any vertical line intersects the graph in at most one point. The graph on the right below, however, is not the graph of a function as there are vertical lines that intersect the graph at more than one point.

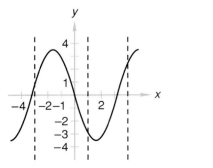

Graph of a function

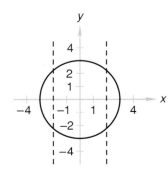

Graph of a relation but not a function

If we are given the graph of a function, we can determine if it is a one-to-one function through a test called the *horizontal line test*.

HORIZONTAL LINE TEST

A function is a one-to-one function provided that any horizontal line intersects its graph in at most one point.

Therefore, the graph on the left represents the graph of a function that is one-to-one and the graph on the right represents the graph of a function that is not one-to-one.

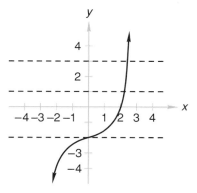

Graph of a one-to-one function   Graph of a function
that is not one-to-one

example 21.11   Determine if each graph represents the graph of a function. If so, determine whether the graph is the graph of a one-to-one function.

(a) 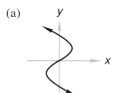   (b) 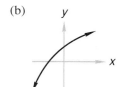   (c) 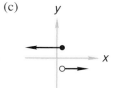   (d)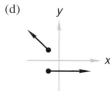

solution   (a) This graph cannot be the graph of a function because it does not pass the vertical line test. That is, a vertical line can be drawn so that it intersects the graph at more than one point. The y axis is one such line.

(b) This graph is the graph of a function since every vertical line drawn intersects the graph in at most one point. Also, every horizontal line drawn intersects the graph in at most one point, so the graph is the graph of a one-to-one function.

(c) On the graph we note the use of the solid point and the open point denoting whether or not the point is on the graph. A solid point indicates that the point is on the graph and an open point indicates that the point is not on the graph. This graph is the graph of a function since every vertical line drawn intersects the graph in at most one point. We note that the graph of a function may be broken, or as mathematicians say, *discontinuous*. The graph is not the graph of a one-to-one function because it does not pass the horizontal line test. That is, a horizontal line can be drawn so that it intersects the graph at more than one point.

(d) This graph cannot be the graph of a function because it does not pass the vertical line test. For example, the two solid points on the graph lie on the same vertical line. Therefore, a vertical line can be drawn so that it intersects the graph at more than one point.

**problem set
21**

1. Sam strained and strained but could only garner $7\frac{1}{8}$. If this was only $\frac{2}{7}$ of what he wanted, how much did he want?

2. Find the equation of the line that passes through $(-2, 5)$ and is perpendicular to the line that passes through $(-4, -2)$ and $(5, 7)$.

3. The number of greens exceeded the sum of the reds and blues by 9. The sum of the blues and greens exceeded 4 times the number of reds by 1. How many of each kind were there if there were 2 more reds than blues?

4. There were 35 nickels, dimes, and silver dollars in the pile, and their value was $12.25. How many coins of each kind were there if there were twice as many silver dollars as nickels?

5. The sum of the digits of a two-digit counting number is 9. When the digits are reversed, the new number is 9 less than the original number. What are the two numbers?

6. How many liters of a solution that is 37% key ingredient should be added to 143 liters of a 73% solution to yield a 51% solution?

7. Which of the following sets of ordered pairs are functions?
   (a) $\{(4, 6), (5, 7), (3, -2), (1, 3)\}$
   (b) $\{(2, 3), (6, 1), (2, -3)\}$
   (c) $\{(1, -1), (4, -1), (-1, -1), (3, -2), (1, 2)\}$
   (d) $\{(1, 2), (2, 3), (4, 4), (7, -2)\}$

8. For each diagram, determine whether or not it designates a function:

   (a)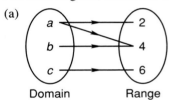
   Domain   Range

   (b)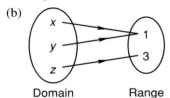
   Domain   Range

9. For functions defined by equations, the domain is the set of all real numbers that can be used as a replacement for x that will result in a unique real number value for $f(x)$. Remember that this excludes values of x that produce square roots of negative numbers and also values of x that indicate division by zero. Find the domain of the function defined by each equation.
   (a) $f(x) = x^2 - 3$ (b) $g(x) = \sqrt{x + 5}$ (c) $h(x) = \sqrt{6 - x}$

10. If $f(x) = x^2 - x + 3$, find $f(4)$.

11. If $g(\theta) = 4\sqrt{3} \cos \theta$, draw the necessary reference triangle and evaluate $g(60°)$. Do not use a calculator.

12. If $h(\theta) = 8 \tan \theta$, draw the necessary reference triangle and evaluate $h(45°)$. Do not use a calculator.

13. In the figure shown, $\overline{RT} \perp \overline{PS}$ and $RT = 49$, $RQ = 21$, $PT = 24$, and $ST = 42$. For $\triangle PQT$ and $\triangle SRT$, write the ratios of the two corresponding sides that form the angle. Determine if $\triangle PQT \sim \triangle SRT$ and justify your answer.

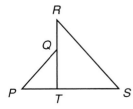

14. Given: $\overline{ED} \parallel \overline{BC}$

    Write a two-column proof to prove:

    $\triangle AED \sim \triangle ABC$

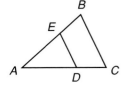

15. Solve: $\begin{cases} xy = 6 \\ x - y = 3 \end{cases}$

Factor:

16. $64a^3b^9 - 8p^3$

17. $27b^9a^6 - 64c^3$

Simplify:

18. $\dfrac{\dfrac{a^3}{x^2y} - \dfrac{6m^2}{y^2x}}{\dfrac{l^2}{y^2} - \dfrac{6t}{x^2}}$

19. $\left(5x^{a-b} + y^{b-a}\right)\left(x^{b-a} - y^{a-b}\right)$

20. $\sqrt{3}\sqrt{2}\sqrt{-3}\sqrt{-2} + \sqrt{3}\sqrt{-9} + 5\sqrt{-16} - 3i$

21. $\dfrac{3 - 2\sqrt{12}}{1 - 3\sqrt{3}}$

22. $\dfrac{5i^2 - 2i^3 + i^4}{-2i^3 + 4i - \sqrt{-16}}$

23. Solve for d: $r = \dfrac{d + 1}{2d - w}$

24. Divide $x^4 + x^2 - x + 1$ by $x^2 + 2$ and check.

25. Convert $25\underline{/130°}$ to rectangular coordinates.

26. Given: $\overline{AB} \cong \overline{DC}$
   $\overline{AD} \cong \overline{BC}$

   Write a two-column proof to prove:

   $\triangle ABD \cong \triangle CDB$

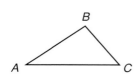

27. In the figure shown, O is the center of the circle that is intersected by a secant and a tangent. Find x.

28. A solid is made up of a right circular cone, right circular cylinder, and hemisphere, as shown. Find the volume of the solid.

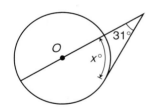

29. If n is a real number, compare: A. $n + 1$ B. $n - 1$

30. In $\triangle ABC$, $BC = 4$ and $AC = 7$.

   Compare: A. AB B. 11

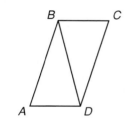

LESSON 22 *Absolute Value • Reciprocal Functions*

22.A

absolute value

We remember that the **absolute value** of a number can be defined to be the **distance** along the x axis from the origin to the graph of the number. The absolute value of zero is zero because the graph of zero is at the origin. The absolute value of every other number is a positive number, as we illustrate here.

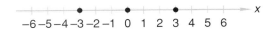

The graphs of both the numbers 3 and -3 are three units from the origin, so the absolute value of both of these numbers is 3.

$$|-3| = 3 \qquad |0| = 0 \qquad |3| = 3$$

Another way to consider absolute value is to say that every real number except zero has two parts, the sign and the absolute value. Both definitions tell us that the absolute value of every number except zero is greater than zero. Thus the inequality $|x| < 0$ has no solution because every real number has an absolute value that is equal to or greater than zero. All real numbers satisfy the inequality $|x| \geq 0$ because every real number has an absolute value that is equal to or greater than zero. The solution to the inequality $|x| \geq 3$ is graphed on the left below. The solution set contains all real numbers that are less than or equal to -3 or that are greater than or equal to 3. The solid circles at -3 and 3 indicate that both of these numbers are members of the solution set.

$$|x| \geq 3 \qquad\qquad\qquad |x| < 3$$

The values of x that satisfy the inequality on the right are all real numbers between -3 and 3. The numbers -3 and 3 are not members of this set, which we indicate with the open circles at -3 and 3.

We can also solve inequalities involving absolute value by thinking of absolute value in terms of distance. If we write that the absolute value of x is less than 4, we are describing all numbers whose graphs are less than 4 units from the origin. If we write that the absolute value of x is greater than 4, we are describing all numbers whose graphs are more than 4 units from the origin.

$$|x| < 4 \qquad\qquad\qquad |x| > 4$$

Similarly, more complicated inequalities such as those shown here

$$|x - 7| > 3 \qquad |x + 4| < 3 \qquad |x - 5| < 3$$

are satisfied by real numbers whose graphs lie in certain regions on the real number line, and it is helpful to have a way to visualize the solution sets of these inequalities without "reinventing the absolute value wheel" every time. We will remember that the numbers that satisfy the inequality on the left below are the numbers whose graphs are within 5 units of the graph of a on the real number line,

$$|x - a| < 5 \qquad |x - a| > 5$$

and that the numbers that satisfy the inequality on the right are the numbers whose graphs are farther than 5 units from the graph of a on the real number line.

Note that if $a = 0$, we have $|x - 0|$ or $|x|$, which denotes the distance from the origin.

example 22.1   Graph $|x| - 2 < 0$ on the real number line.

solution   We begin by isolating $|x|$ by adding 2 to both sides of the inequality.

$$\begin{array}{rcl} |x| - 2 & < & 0 \\ + 2 & & + 2 \\ \hline |x| & < & 2 \end{array}$$

The graph indicates all real numbers a distance less than two units from the origin. The open circles at –2 and 2 tell us that these numbers are not solutions of the inequality because neither has an absolute value that is less than 2.

example 22.2   Graph the set $\{x \in \mathbb{R} \mid |x - 5| < 2\}$ on the real number line.

solution   We are asked to indicate all real numbers that satisfy this inequality. The solution set consists of the numbers strictly less than two units from the point +5 on the real number line.

$$|x - 5| < 2$$

example 22.3   Graph the set $\{x \in \mathbb{R} \mid |x + 2| \geq 3\}$ on the real number line.

solution   We begin by rewriting the inequality as

$$|x - (-2)| \geq 3$$

The solution set of this inequality is the set of all real numbers that are a distance equal to or greater than three units from the point –2 on the real number line, as shown below.

example 22.4   Sketch the graph of the function $y = |x|$.

solution   The graphs in the previous examples were one-dimensional because the only variable was x. This graph will be two-dimensional because there are two variables, x and y. The graph on the left below is the graph of $y = x$, which is the graph of a straight line.

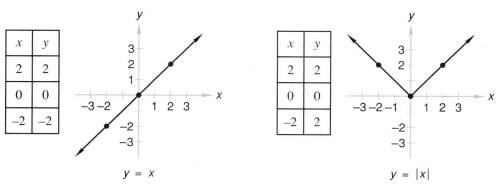

The graph on the right does not go below the x axis because y equals the absolute value of x and the absolute value is never negative. When x equals –2, y equals $|-2|$, which is 2.

22.B
reciprocal functions

If the original function is $y = x$, the reciprocal function is $y = 1/x$ because *reciprocal* means "inverted" or "upside down." A **vertical asymptote** is a vertical line that is approached by the graph of a function as x approaches a fixed point. **The graph of a reciprocal function has a vertical asymptote at every place where the graph of the original function intersects the x axis.** Consider the graph of the function $y = x$ shown on the left below. The graph of the reciprocal function has two parts. One part is the graph of the positive values of x.

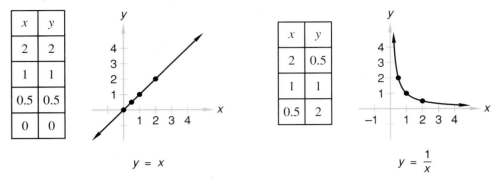

At every point on the graph on the left, y equals x. The line goes through the origin where x equals zero. On the right, when x has a large value, y has a small value because y equals $1/x$. When x equals 2, y equals 1/2, or 0.5. When x equals 1, y equals 1/1, or 1. As x gets even smaller, y gets greater. When x equals 0.5, y equals 1 over 0.5, or 2. As x gets smaller and smaller, y gets greater and greater. The graph continues upward but never touches the y axis. Now let us consider the part of the graph to the left of the origin.

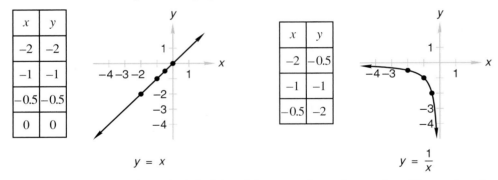

The x and y values on the line to the left of the origin are equal negative numbers. The x and y values of the graph of $y = 1/x$ are also negative numbers, but as x gets closer to zero, y gets further away from zero and the graph approaches the y axis again. If we look at both sides of the graphs,

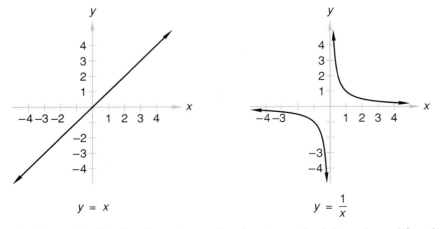

we see that the graph of the line is continuous but that the graph of the reciprocal function has a break or discontinuity at the y axis where the value of x is zero.

example 22.5   Sketch the graph of the function $y = \dfrac{1}{x^2}$.

solution   If x is not zero, x^2 is a positive number. Since y equals $1/x^2$, y will always be positive and the graph will not go below the x axis. We cannot divide by zero, so the graph will have a vertical asymptote at the y axis. The graph looks like a "volcano."

x	x^2	y
-2	4	0.25
-1	1	1
-0.5	0.25	4
0.5	0.25	4
1	1	1
2	4	0.25

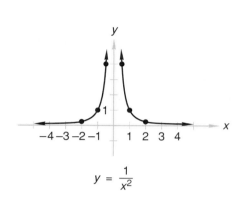

$$y = \dfrac{1}{x^2}$$

problem set 22

1. Find the equation of the line that passes through the point $(5, -2)$ and is perpendicular to the line that passes through the points $(-5, 7)$ and $(-8, -2)$.

2. Problems that involve products of consecutive integers or consecutive even integers or consecutive odd integers often require the solution of a quadratic equation. Find three consecutive even integers such that the product of the second and the third is 4 greater than ten times the first.

3. A cliff is 85 meters above the sea. From the top of the cliff, the angle of depression of a boat measures $43°$. How far is the boat from the base of the cliff?

4. There were 24 pennies, nickels, and quarters in all, and their total value was $1.60. How many of each kind of coin were there if the number of nickels equaled the number of pennies?

5. The sum of the digits of a two-digit counting number is 8. When the digits are reversed, the new number is 36 less than the original number. What are the two numbers?

6. (a) Graph the set $\{x \in \mathbb{R} \mid |x - 3| < 4\}$ on the real number line.
    (b) Graph the set $\{x \in \mathbb{R} \mid |x - 3| \geq 4\}$ on the real number line.

7. Sketch the graph of the function $f(x) = |x|$.

8. The reciprocal of 1 is 1 and the reciprocal of -1 is -1. Thus, the points on the graph of the function whose y coordinates are 1 or -1 will also lie on the graph of the reciprocal function. The graph of the function $f(x) = x + 3$ is shown. We have placed dots at $(-2, 1)$ and $(-4, -1)$ because the y coordinate has a value of 1 or -1 at these points and the graph of the reciprocal function will also pass through these points. The graph of the reciprocal function will have a vertical asymptote at every place where the graph of the original function intersects the x axis. Thus, the graph of the reciprocal function will have a vertical asymptote at $x = -3$, as we have indicated by the dotted line. Make a sketch of the graph of the reciprocal function $g(x) = \dfrac{1}{x + 3}$.

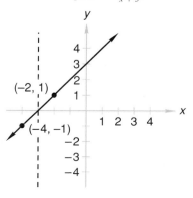

9. For each diagram, determine whether or not it designates a function:

(a)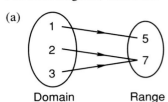

Domain   Range

(b)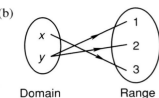

Domain   Range

10. Determine whether each graph represents the graph of a function. If so, determine whether the graph is the graph of a one-to-one function.

(a) 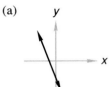   (b) 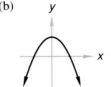   (c) 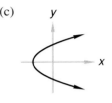   (d)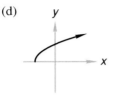

11. Find the domain of the function defined by each equation:

(a) $f(x) = \sqrt{x - 8}$ (b) $g(x) = |x + 3|$ (c) $h(x) = \dfrac{1}{x + 3}$

12. If $f(x) = x^2 + 2x - 3$, find $f(5)$.

13. If $g(\theta) = 2\sqrt{2} \sin \theta$, draw the necessary reference triangle and evaluate $g(60°)$. Do not use a calculator.

14. If $h(\theta) = 3\sqrt{3} \cos \theta$, draw the necessary reference triangle and evaluate $h(30°)$. Do not use a calculator.

15. Given: $\dfrac{AC}{BC} = \dfrac{BC}{DC}$

Write a two-column proof to prove:

$$\triangle ABC \sim \triangle BDC$$

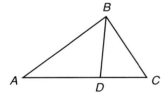

16. Solve: $\begin{cases} x^2 - 2y^2 = -9 \\ x^2 + y^2 = 18 \end{cases}$

17. Simplify by factoring the numerator: $\dfrac{x^4 - y^4}{x - y}$

18. Factor: $8x^3 b^6 - 27p^3$

Simplify:

19. $\dfrac{3s}{2m - \dfrac{z}{1 + \dfrac{k}{l}}}$

20. $\dfrac{6i^3 - 4i^4 - 6i}{-3i^4 - 5i + \sqrt{-25}}$

21. $\dfrac{x^{3a+2}\left(\sqrt{y^3}\right)^{2a}}{y^{2a-4}\left(\sqrt{x}\right)^{2a+1}}$

22. $\dfrac{a^{\frac{5}{2}}b^{-\frac{2}{3}} + a^{-\frac{1}{2}}b^{\frac{1}{3}}}{a^{-\frac{1}{2}}b^{\frac{1}{3}}}$

23. Convert $-9\hat{i} - 10\hat{j}$ to polar coordinates. (Write four forms for this point.)

24. Solve $4x^2 = -5 + 6x$ by completing the square.

25. Given: $\overline{BC} \cong \overline{EF}$
$\overline{BC} \parallel \overline{EF}$
$\overline{AC} \cong \overline{DF}$

Write a two-column proof to prove:
$\triangle ABC \cong \triangle DEF$

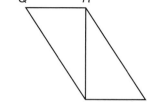

26. Given: $\overline{RP} \perp \overline{PS}$
$\overline{RP} \perp \overline{QR}$
$\overline{PQ} \cong \overline{SR}$

Write a two-column proof to prove:
$\triangle PRQ \cong \triangle RPS$

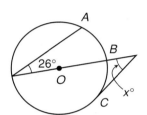

27. In the figure shown, O is the center of a circle that is intersected by a chord, a secant, and a tangent. If $m\overset{\frown}{AB} = m\overset{\frown}{BC}$, find x.

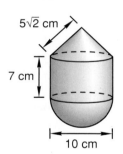

28. A solid is made up of a right circular cone, right circular cylinder, and hemisphere, as shown. Find the volume of the solid.

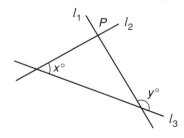

CONCEPT REVIEW PROBLEMS

29. Let a, b, and c be real numbers. If $0 < a < b$, $a < c$, and $c < 5$, compare:
A. 5   B. a

30. In the figure shown, lines l_1, l_2, and l_3 intersect and line l_1 is perpendicular to line l_2 at P.

Compare: A. $y - 90$ B. x

LESSON 23 *The Exponential Function • Sketching Exponentials*

23.A
the exponential function

We can call the following expressions **powers.**

$$3^2 \qquad 4^{10} \qquad 10^5 \qquad 5^{14}$$

The bottom number is called the **base,** and the small raised number is called the **exponent.** The exponent tells how many times the base is to be used as a factor. The expression 10^2 tells us that 10 is to be used as a factor two times, and 10^3 tells us that 10 is to be used as a factor three times. But then, what meaning can $10^{2.5}$ have?

$$10^2 = 10 \cdot 10 = 100$$

$$10^{2.5} = ???$$

$$10^3 = 10 \cdot 10 \cdot 10 = 1000$$

It does not mean that 10 should be used as a factor 2.5 times because this makes no sense. From the pattern we see that the expression should have a value between 100 and 1000. The number 2.5 is a rational number, which means it can be written as a fraction. Since the fractional equivalent of 2.5 is 5/2, we can write

$$10^{2.5} = 10^{\frac{5}{2}}$$

If we use our rules for fractional exponents, we can write this as

$$\left(10^{\frac{1}{2}}\right)^5 \qquad \text{or as} \qquad \left(10^5\right)^{\frac{1}{2}}$$

Both these expressions have the same value. We approximate this number by using a calculator and get

$$316.22777$$

Thus, we see that the expression 10^x has a real-number value if we replace x with any rational number. This investigation can be extended to demonstrate that the expression 10^x also represents a unique real number for every irrational number replacement of x and thus has a value for all real-number values of x, both rational and irrational. Hence, the expressions

$$y = 10^x \qquad \text{and} \qquad f(x) = 10^x$$

express y and $f(x)$ as continuous functions of x and can be graphed. Of course, the base does not have to be the number 10. Other numbers can be used, as shown by the following equations:

$$y = 2^x \qquad f(x) = 7.5^x \qquad y = (0.62)^x \qquad f(x) = \left(\frac{3}{4}\right)^x$$

A power whose base is a constant and whose exponent contains a variable is a special kind of power that is often called an **exponential.** When used with another variable and an equals sign, we can write equations that we call **exponential equations.** Some numbers cannot be used as the base of an exponential function (equation). The numbers 0 and 1 are not used as a base because the result would always be the same regardless of the value of the exponent.

$$y = 1^x \quad \longrightarrow \quad y = 1 \qquad \text{for all } x \qquad x \in \{\text{Reals}\}$$

$$y = 0^x \quad \longrightarrow \quad y = 0 \qquad \text{for all } x \qquad x \in \{\text{Positive reals}\}$$

Negative numbers cannot be used as a base because the y values for some values of x turn out to be complex numbers. For example, suppose we use (-2) as the base:

$$y = (-2)^{\frac{1}{2}} \qquad \text{base is } -2$$

$$y = \sqrt{-2} \qquad \text{equivalent expression}$$

$$y = \sqrt{2}i \qquad \text{simplified}$$

Since we want to define exponential functions to have real-number values for all values of x, we see that negative numbers should not be used as the base of an exponential. Thus, the expression

$$y = b^x$$

has a unique real-number value of y for each real-number value of x if b is a positive number. If b is a positive number less than 1, the graph of the function decreases as x increases. If b is a positive number greater than 1, the graph of the function increases as x increases.

example 23.1   Sketch the graph of the function $y = 2^x$.

solution   We make a table and select several positive values and several negative values for x.

x	-3	-2	0	2	3
y					

Now we compute the matching values for y, complete the table, and graph the function.

If $x = -3$, $\quad y = 2^{-3} = \dfrac{1}{2^3} = \dfrac{1}{8}$

If $x = -2$, $\quad y = 2^{-2} = \dfrac{1}{2^2} = \dfrac{1}{4}$

If $x = 0$, $\quad y = 2^0 = 1$

If $x = 2$, $\quad y = 2^2 = 4$

If $x = 3$, $\quad y = 2^3 = 8$

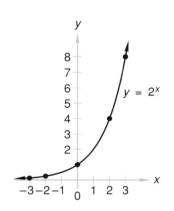

x	-3	-2	0	2	3
y	$\frac{1}{8}$	$\frac{1}{4}$	1	4	8

23.B

sketching exponentials

The point-by-point method of graphing exponentials used in example 23.1 is laborious and time-consuming, especially when a sketch of the curve is usually all we need. We will begin our investigation of the graphs of exponential functions by looking at functions of the form $y = b^x$. The graphs of these functions "look like" a member of one of the two families of curves shown at the top of the next page.

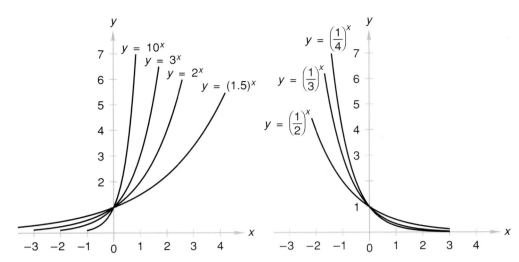

Every exponential function graphed in the left-hand figure has a base that is greater than 1, and we note that the value of y increases when x increases. Every exponential function graphed in the right-hand figure has a base that is greater than 0 but less than 1. For these curves the value of y increases as the value of x decreases. For curve sketching, it is important to note that every one of the curves passes through the point $(0, 1)$ and that there is very little difference in the graphs of the lower end of the different curves. Thus, it is usually not necessary to find values for the curve on the lower end, and usually the coordinates of one point on the other side will suffice to make a sketch.

example 23.2   Sketch the graph of the function $f(x) = 5^x$.

solution   The base is greater than 1, so y increases as x increases. First we put a couple of values on the horizontal and vertical scales and draw the tail of the graph.

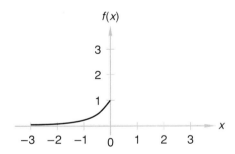

Now we need one or two points on the right. If we let x equal 1, then $f(1)$ will equal 5.

$$f(1) = 5^1 = 5$$

So a point on the curve is $(1, 5)$. We graph this point and sketch the curve.

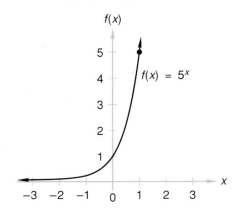

example 23.3   Sketch the graph of the function $y = 0.25^x$.

solution   This time the base is less than 1, so the curve goes the other way. We begin by estimating the tail of the graph.

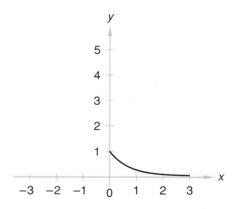

Now we decide to let x equal (a) -1 and (b) -2 and find the paired values of y.

$$\text{(a)} \quad y = (0.25)^{-1} = \frac{1}{0.25} = 4$$

$$\text{(b)} \quad y = (0.25)^{-2} = \frac{1}{(0.25)^2} = 16$$

The coordinates of (b) are $(-2, 16)$. This point falls off our graph, but now we know the curve goes through $(-1, 4)$ and rises quite rapidly thereafter. This is all we need to know to make our sketch.

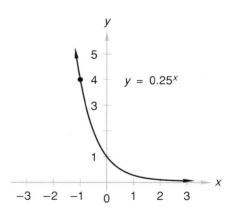

problem set 23

1. Find the equation of the line that passes through the point $(1, 1)$ and is parallel to the line that passes through the points $(5, 2)$ and $(7, -1)$.

2. Federico worked hard, but could only reduce his debt by $3\frac{1}{3}$. If this was only $\frac{2}{9}$ of what he wanted to reduce, how much did he want to reduce it by?

3. Beatrice has a total of 21 coins worth \$2.85. All coins are either nickels, dimes, or quarters. If the number of quarters is twice the number of dimes, how many of each coin does she have?

4. Twice the sum of the number of blues and greens exceeded the number of reds by only 4. The sum of the reds and blues exceeded the number of greens by 7. How many of each kind were there if there were twice as many reds as there were greens?

5. The sum of the digits of a two-digit counting number is 6. When the digits are reversed, the new number is eighteen less than the original number. What are the two numbers?

6. A 27-gallon solution contains 9 gallons of acid and 18 gallons of water. How much water should be added to get a solution that is 25% acid?

7. Sketch the graph of the function $f(x) = 2^x$.

8. Sketch the graph of the function $g(x) = \left(\frac{1}{2}\right)^x$.

9. (a) Graph the set $\{x \in \mathbb{R} \mid |x + 2| > 5\}$ on the real number line.

   (b) Graph the set $\{x \in \mathbb{R} \mid |x + 2| \leq 5\}$ on the real number line.

10. The graph of the function $f(x) = x - 2$ is shown. We have placed dots at (3, 1) and (1, −1) because the y coordinate has a value of 1 or −1 at these points and the graph of the reciprocal function will also pass through these points. The graph of the reciprocal function will have a vertical asymptote at $x = 2$, as we have indicated by the dotted line. Make a sketch of the graph of the reciprocal function $g(x) = \frac{1}{x-2}$.

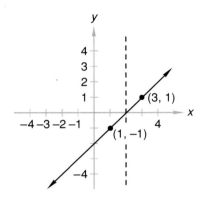

11. Which of the following sets of ordered pairs are functions?

   (a) $\{(2, -1), (5, 2), (3, -2), (2, 1), (6, 1)\}$

   (b) $\{(-1, 2), (8, 3), (5, 1)\}$

   (c) $\{(9, 3), (1, 6), (1, -3)\}$

   (d) $\{(7, 2), (11, 3), (13, -1), (-4, -1)\}$

12. Find the domain of the function defined by each equation:

   (a) $f(x) = x^2 + 4$ (b) $g(x) = |x - 2|$ (c) $h(x) = \dfrac{1}{x - 2}$

13. If $f(\theta) = 2\sqrt{2} \sin \theta$, draw the necessary reference triangle and evaluate $f(45°)$. Do not use a calculator.

14. If $g(\theta) = \tan \theta$, draw the necessary reference triangle and evaluate $8g(60°)$. Do not use a calculator.

15. Find the value of x for which $\triangle ABC \sim \triangle CDE$.

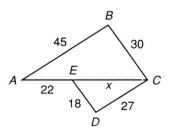

16. Given: $\overline{RQ} \perp \overline{QP}$

   $\overline{RS} \perp \overline{ST}$

   Write a two-column proof to prove:

   $\triangle PQR \sim \triangle TSR$

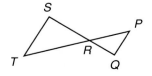

Solve:

17. $\begin{cases} \dfrac{1}{2}x - \dfrac{1}{3}y + z = 1 \\ x - y + z = -2 \\ x + \dfrac{2}{3}z = 0 \end{cases}$

18. $\begin{cases} xy = 9 \\ x + y = 6 \end{cases}$

19. $\dfrac{2x - 5}{x - 6} - \dfrac{x + 4}{x + 5} = \dfrac{3x + 7}{x^2 - x - 30}$

20. Factor: $8a^3b^6 + 27a^9b^3$

Simplify:

21. $\dfrac{2}{1 + \dfrac{3x}{y - \dfrac{z}{k}}}$

22. $\sqrt{5}\sqrt{2}\sqrt{-5}\sqrt{-2} - 3\sqrt{2}i + \sqrt{5}\sqrt{2} - \sqrt{-5}i$

23. $\dfrac{4 + \sqrt{27}}{5 - 2\sqrt{3}}$

24. $(m + n)(m^{-1} + n^{-1})^{-1}$

25. Divide $x^3 + 2x^2 + x$ by $x + 3$ and check.

26. Given: $\angle I \cong \angle L$
   J is the midpoint of $\overline{IL}$

   Write a two-column proof to prove:

   $\triangle HIJ \cong \triangle KLJ$

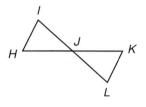

27. In the figure shown, $\overline{AB}$ and $\overline{CD}$ are chords intersecting at P. Find the lengths of chords AB and CD.

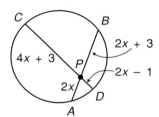

28. A solid is made up of a hemisphere, right circular cylinder, and right circular cone, as shown. Find the surface area of the solid.

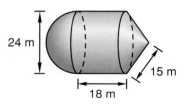

CONCEPT REVIEW PROBLEMS

29. For all real numbers a and b, let $a * b = a + 3b$.

   Compare: A. $(2 * 0) * 5$ B. $2 * (0 * 5)$

30. If x and y are angles as shown, compare: A. 160   B. $x + y$

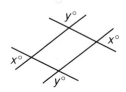

LESSON 24   *Sums of Trigonometric Functions • Combining Functions*

24.A

sums of trigonometric functions

Problems that require the sums of trigonometric functions of 30°, 45°, and 60° provide practice in determining the values of the functions and also provide practice in adding algebraic expressions that contain radicals. Also, drawing the reference triangles will aid long-term retention of the concepts.

example 24.1   Evaluate: $\cos 60° + \sin 45°$

solution   We begin by drawing the reference triangles and then find $\cos 60°$ and $\sin 45°$.

$$\cos \theta = \frac{\text{adj}}{\text{hyp}}$$

$$\cos 60° = \frac{1}{2}$$

$$\sin \theta = \frac{\text{opp}}{\text{hyp}}$$

$$\sin 45° = \frac{1}{\sqrt{2}}$$

REFERENCE TRIANGLES

Therefore, we have

$$\cos 60° + \sin 45° = \frac{1}{2} + \frac{1}{\sqrt{2}}$$

Now we will find a common denominator and add the terms.

$$\frac{1}{2} + \frac{1}{\sqrt{2}} = \frac{\sqrt{2}}{2\sqrt{2}} + \frac{2}{2\sqrt{2}} = \frac{2 + \sqrt{2}}{2\sqrt{2}}$$

Now we multiply $(2 + \sqrt{2})/2\sqrt{2}$ above and below by $\sqrt{2}$ to rationalize the denominator.

$$\frac{2 + \sqrt{2}}{2\sqrt{2}} = \frac{2 + \sqrt{2}}{2\sqrt{2}} \cdot \frac{\sqrt{2}}{\sqrt{2}} = \frac{2\sqrt{2} + 2}{4} = \frac{\sqrt{2} + 1}{2}$$

Therefore, we have

$$\cos 60° + \sin 45° = \frac{\mathbf{\sqrt{2} + 1}}{\mathbf{2}}$$

example 24.2   Evaluate: $\tan 30° + \cos 45°$

solution   We begin by drawing the reference triangles and then find $\tan 30°$ and $\cos 45°$.

$$\tan \theta = \frac{\text{opp}}{\text{adj}}$$

$$\tan 30° = \frac{1}{\sqrt{3}}$$

$$\cos \theta = \frac{\text{adj}}{\text{hyp}}$$

$$\cos 45° = \frac{1}{\sqrt{2}}$$

REFERENCE TRIANGLES

Therefore, we have

$$\tan 30° + \cos 45° = \frac{1}{\sqrt{3}} + \frac{1}{\sqrt{2}}$$

Now we will find a common denominator and add the terms.

$$\frac{1}{\sqrt{3}} + \frac{1}{\sqrt{2}} = \frac{\sqrt{2}}{\sqrt{2}\sqrt{3}} + \frac{\sqrt{3}}{\sqrt{2}\sqrt{3}} = \frac{\sqrt{2} + \sqrt{3}}{\sqrt{6}}$$

Now we multiply $(\sqrt{2} + \sqrt{3})/\sqrt{6}$ above and below by $\sqrt{6}$ to rationalize the denominator.

$$\frac{\sqrt{2} + \sqrt{3}}{\sqrt{6}} = \frac{\sqrt{2} + \sqrt{3}}{\sqrt{6}} \cdot \frac{\sqrt{6}}{\sqrt{6}} = \frac{2\sqrt{3} + 3\sqrt{2}}{6}$$

Therefore, we have

$$\tan 30° + \cos 45° = \frac{2\sqrt{3} + 3\sqrt{2}}{6}$$

example 24.3   Evaluate: $\tan 45° + 2\tan 30°$

solution   We begin by drawing the reference triangles and then find $\tan 45°$ and $\tan 30°$.

REFERENCE TRIANGLES

$$\tan \theta = \frac{\text{opp}}{\text{adj}}$$

$$\tan 45° = \frac{1}{1} = 1$$

$$\tan 30° = \frac{1}{\sqrt{3}}$$

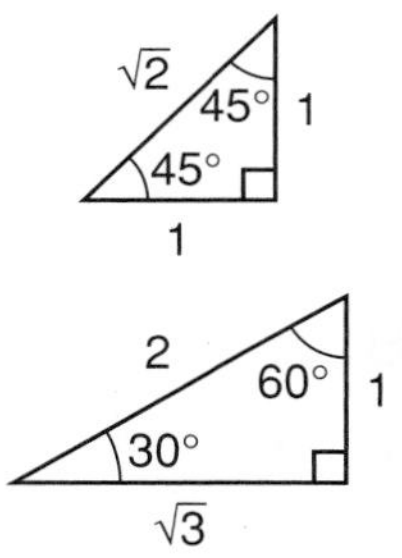

Therefore, we have

$$\tan 45° + 2\tan 30° = 1 + 2\left(\frac{1}{\sqrt{3}}\right)$$

Now we will find a common denominator and add the terms.

$$1 + \frac{2}{\sqrt{3}} = \frac{\sqrt{3}}{\sqrt{3}} + \frac{2}{\sqrt{3}} = \frac{\sqrt{3} + 2}{\sqrt{3}}$$

Now we multiply $(\sqrt{3} + 2)/\sqrt{3}$ above and below by $\sqrt{3}$ to rationalize the denominator.

$$\frac{\sqrt{3} + 2}{\sqrt{3}} = \frac{\sqrt{3} + 2}{\sqrt{3}} \cdot \frac{\sqrt{3}}{\sqrt{3}} = \frac{3 + 2\sqrt{3}}{3}$$

Therefore, we have

$$\tan 45° + 2\tan 30° = \frac{3 + 2\sqrt{3}}{3}$$

example 24.4   Evaluate: $\sqrt{6}\,\sin 30° + \dfrac{1}{\sqrt{2}}\,\tan 60°$

solution   We begin by drawing the reference triangle and then find $\sin 30°$ and $\tan 60°$.

$$\sin \theta = \frac{\text{opp}}{\text{hyp}}$$

$$\sin 30° = \frac{1}{2}$$

REFERENCE TRIANGLE

$$\tan \theta = \frac{\text{opp}}{\text{adj}}$$

$$\tan 60° = \sqrt{3}$$

Therefore, we have

$$\sqrt{6}\,\sin 30° + \frac{1}{\sqrt{2}}\,\tan 60° = \sqrt{6}\left(\frac{1}{2}\right) + \frac{1}{\sqrt{2}}(\sqrt{3})$$

Now we will find a common denominator and add the terms.

$$\frac{\sqrt{6}}{2} + \frac{\sqrt{3}}{\sqrt{2}} = \frac{\sqrt{6}\sqrt{2} + 2\sqrt{3}}{2\sqrt{2}} = \frac{2\sqrt{3} + 2\sqrt{3}}{2\sqrt{2}} = \frac{2\sqrt{3}}{\sqrt{2}}$$

Now we multiply $2\sqrt{3}/\sqrt{2}$ above and below by $\sqrt{2}$ to rationalize the denominator.

$$\frac{2\sqrt{3}}{\sqrt{2}} = \frac{2\sqrt{3}}{\sqrt{2}} \cdot \frac{\sqrt{2}}{\sqrt{2}} = \frac{2\sqrt{6}}{2} = \sqrt{6}$$

Therefore, we have

$$\sqrt{6}\,\sin 30° + \frac{1}{\sqrt{2}}\,\tan 60° = \mathbf{\sqrt{6}}$$

24.B
combining functions

We have found that $f(x)$, $g(x)$, and $h(x)$ are just other symbols for y for single-valued expressions in x. There are other ways that we can use functional notation. The notations

$$f(x) + g(x) \qquad \text{and} \qquad (f + g)(x)$$

are used to denote the **sum** of the f function and the g function. The notations

$$f(x) - g(x) \qquad \text{and} \qquad (f - g)(x)$$

are used to indicate the **difference** of two functions when the g function is subtracted from the f function. The notations

$$f(x) \cdot g(x) \qquad \text{and} \qquad (fg)(x)$$

are used to indicate the **product** of the f function and the g function. The notations

$$\frac{f(x)}{g(x)} \qquad \text{and} \qquad (f/g)(x)$$

are used to designate the **quotient** that results when the f function is divided by the g function. The notations

$$f[g(x)] \qquad \text{and} \qquad (f \circ g)(x)$$

are used to designate the **composition** of the f function and the g function. The composition of two functions can be explained by using two function machines. Consider that

$g(x) = x + 30°$ and $f(x) = \sin x$. If we put x into the g machine, we get an output of $x + 30°$. If we put $x + 30°$ into the f machine, we get an output of $\sin(x + 30°)$.

	g machine	g(x)	f machine	(f ∘ g)(x)
$x \rightarrow$	$x + 30°$	$\rightarrow x + 30° \rightarrow$	$\sin x$	$\rightarrow \sin(x + 30°)$

The last machine would have an output of $\sin x$ for an input of x. But since the input is $x + 30°$, the output is $\sin(x + 30°)$. If the x input is $20°$, we get the following flow diagram:

	g machine	g(x)	f machine	(f ∘ g)(x)
$20° \rightarrow$	$x + 30°$	$\rightarrow 50° \rightarrow$	$\sin x$	$\rightarrow \sin 50°$

example 24.5   If $f(x) = \log x$ and $g(x) = x^2 + 6$, find $(g \circ f)(x)$.

solution   The notation $(g \circ f)(x)$ means to put $f(x)$ into the g machine. Thus

$$(g \circ f)(x) = (\log x)^2 + 6$$

example 24.6   If $f(x) = x + 2$ and $g(x) = x^2 + 3$, find:

(a) $(f + g)(6)$ (b) $(f - g)(6)$ (c) $(fg)(6)$ (d) $(f/g)(6)$

solution   (a) There are two ways to find the sum of $f(6)$ and $g(6)$. The fast way is to find $f(6)$ and $g(6)$ and add these results.

$$f(x) = x + 2 \qquad g(x) = x^2 + 3 \qquad f(6) + g(6) = 8 + 39$$
$$f(6) = 6 + 2 \qquad g(6) = 6^2 + 3 \qquad\qquad\qquad = \mathbf{47}$$
$$= 8 \qquad\qquad\quad = 39$$

The second way is to find the equation for $(f + g)(x)$ and then find $(f + g)(6)$.

$$f(x) = x + 2$$
$$\underline{+\ g(x) = x^2 + 3}$$
$$(f + g)(x) = x^2 + x + 5 \qquad\qquad \text{added to get } (f + g)(x)$$
$$(f + g)(6) = 6^2 + 6 + 5 \qquad\qquad \text{let } x = 6$$
$$= \mathbf{47} \qquad\qquad\qquad\qquad \text{simplified}$$

(b) There are two ways to find the difference of $f(6)$ and $g(6)$. The fast way is to subtract $g(6)$ from $f(6)$. Since $f(6) = 8$ and $g(6) = 39$,

$$f(6) - g(6) = 8 - 39 = \mathbf{-31}$$

The second way is to find the equation for $(f - g)(x)$ and then find $(f - g)(6)$.

$$f(x) = x + 2$$
$$\underline{-\ g(x) = x^2 + 3}$$
$$(f - g)(x) = x + 2 - (x^2 + 3) \qquad\qquad \text{subtracted to get } (f - g)(x)$$
$$= x - x^2 - 1 \qquad\qquad\qquad \text{simplified}$$
$$(f - g)(6) = 6 - 6^2 - 1 \qquad\qquad\qquad \text{let } x = 6$$
$$= \mathbf{-31} \qquad\qquad\qquad\qquad \text{simplified}$$

(c) There are two ways to find the product of $f(6)$ and $g(6)$. The fast way is to multiply $f(6)$ and $g(6)$. Since $f(6) = 8$ and $g(6) = 39$,

$$f(6) \cdot g(6) = 8 \cdot 39 = \mathbf{312}$$

The second way is to find the equation for $(fg)(x)$ and then find $(fg)(6)$.

$$(fg)(x) = (x + 2)(x^2 + 3) = x^3 + 2x^2 + 3x + 6$$

$$(fg)(6) = 6^3 + 2(6)^2 + 3(6) + 6 = \mathbf{312}$$

(d) There are two ways to find the quotient of $f(6)$ and $g(6)$. The fast way is to divide $f(6)$ by $g(6)$. Since $f(6) = 8$ and $g(6) = 39$,

$$\frac{f(6)}{g(6)} = \frac{8}{39}$$

The second way is to find the equation for $(f/g)(x)$ and then find $(f/g)(6)$.

$$(f/g)(x) = \frac{x + 2}{x^2 + 3}$$

$$(f/g)(6) = \frac{6 + 2}{6^2 + 3} = \frac{8}{39}$$

problem set 24

1. Find the equation of the line that passes through the point $(-2, -3)$ and is perpendicular to the line that passes through the points $(5, 2)$ and $(8, -3)$.

2. Find four consecutive even integers such that the sum of the first and second is 70 less than the product of the third and the fourth.

3. There were 14 dimes, quarters, and half-dollars whose total value was $2.50. How many of each kind of coin were there if the number of quarters equaled the number of half-dollars?

4. The total of the numbers of reds and blues was 1 greater than the number of greens. The sum of 3 times the number of reds and twice the number of blues exceeded the number of greens by 9. How many of each color were there if 3 times the number of blues exceeded the number of greens by 2?

5. The sum of the digits of a two-digit counting number is 10. When the digits are reversed, the new number is 36 less than the original number. What are the two numbers?

6. How many ml of a $3\frac{1}{2}\%$ salt solution should be mixed with 176 ml of a $4\frac{3}{4}\%$ salt solution to get a solution that is 4% salt?

7. Sketch the graph of the function $f(x) = 3^x$.

8. Sketch the graph of the function $g(x) = \left(\frac{1}{3}\right)^x$.

9. The equation of the function whose graph is shown is $f(x) = x + 2$. We have placed dots at $(-1, 1)$ and $(-3, -1)$ because the y coordinate has a value of 1 or -1 at these points and the graph of the reciprocal function will also pass through these points. The graph of the reciprocal function will have a vertical asymptote at $x = -2$, as we have indicated by the dotted line. Make a sketch of the graph of the reciprocal function $g(x) = \frac{1}{x + 2}$.

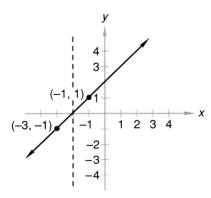

10. For each diagram, determine whether or not it designates a function:

(a)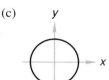

Domain   Range

(b)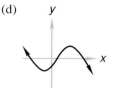

Domain   Range

11. Determine if each graph represents the graph of a function. If so, determine whether the graph is the graph of a one-to-one function.

(a) *y*   (b) *y*   (c) *y*   (d) *y*

12. Find the domain of the function defined by each equation:

(a) $f(x) = \sqrt{x + 6}$ (b) $g(x) = |x + 2|$ (c) $h(x) = \dfrac{1}{x^2}$

13. Draw the necessary reference triangles and evaluate $\frac{\sqrt{3}}{2} \tan 30° + \sqrt{2} \cos 60°$. Do not use a calculator.

14. Let $f(x) = x + 3$ and $g(x) = x^2 + 1$. Evaluate:

(a) $(f + g)(3)$ (b) $(f - g)(3)$ (c) $(f \circ g)(3)$

15. If $f(\theta) = \tan \theta$, draw the necessary reference triangles and evaluate $f(45°) + 2f(30°)$. Do not use a calculator.

16. Find the perimeter of $\triangle DEF$ if $\triangle ABC \sim \triangle DEF$.

17. Solve: $\begin{cases} x^2 + y^2 = 4 \\ 2x + y = 1 \end{cases}$

18. Factor: $4x^{5N+2} + 3x^{8N+3}$

Simplify:

19.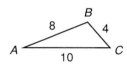

20.

21. $\dfrac{\sqrt[3]{a}\,\sqrt{b}\left(\sqrt[4]{ab}\right)^3}{a^{-2}b^3\left(\sqrt{a}\right)^3 b^{-2}}$

22. $\left(\dfrac{1}{x + y}\right)^{-1}\left(x^{-1} + y^{-1}\right)^{-1}$

23. Convert $5\hat{i} - 8\hat{j}$ to polar coordinates. (Write four forms for this point.)

24. Solve $9x^2 = -3x + 8$ by completing the square.

25. If $f(x) = 2x$, find $f(x + 1)$.

26.   Given: $\overline{BE} \cong \overline{CE}$
$\overline{AE} \cong \overline{DE}$

Write a two-column proof to prove:

$\triangle ABE \cong \triangle DCE$

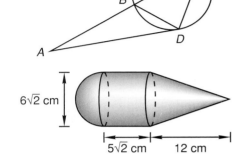

27.   In the figure shown, the circle is intersected by secant *AC* and tangent *AD*. If
$m\angle CBD = 60°$ and $m\angle BDC = 80°$,
find $m\angle ADC$.

28.   A solid is made up of a hemisphere,
right circular cylinder, and right circular cone, as shown. Find the surface
area of the solid.

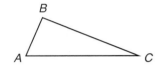

29.   Let *a* and *b* be real numbers. If $a > b$, compare: A. $-a$ B. $-b$

30.   In $\triangle ABC$, $AB = 5$ and $BC = 12$.

Compare: A. 17   B. *AC*

LESSON 25   *Age Problems • Rate Problems*

25.A

age problems   Word problems that consider the ages of two or more people now and the ages of the same
people at some time in the past or in the future are called **age problems.** These problems are
uncomplicated, and their solution is straightforward if subscripted variables are used, as we
see in the next example.

example 25.1   Ten years ago Thomas was twice as old as Patricia. Five years from now, Thomas will be 10
years older than Patricia. How old are both people now?

solution   **The key to this type of problem is the choice of the variables.** We will use P_N for Patricia's
age now and T_N for Thomas' age now. Then

$$P_N + 5 = \text{Patricia's age 5 years from now}$$

$$P_N - 10 = \text{Patricia's age 10 years ago}$$

$$T_N + 5 = \text{Thomas' age 5 years from now}$$

$$T_N - 10 = \text{Thomas' age 10 years ago}$$

The first statement was about their ages 10 years ago.

$$\text{(a)}\quad T_N - 10 = 2(P_N - 10)$$

The second statement was about their ages 5 years from now.

$$\text{(b)}\quad (T_N + 5) - 10 = P_N + 5$$

We simplify the equations and get

$$\text{(a')} \quad T_N - 2P_N = -10$$
$$\text{(b')} \quad T_N - P_N = 10$$

Now we use elimination to solve.

$$(-1)\text{(a')} \quad -T_N + 2P_N = 10$$
$$\text{(b')} \quad \underline{T_N - P_N = 10}$$
$$P_N = \mathbf{20}$$

If we substitute 20 for P_N in either equation (a') or (b'), we find that Thomas' age now is **30**.

25.B
rate problems

Forty miles per hour times 2 hours (hr) equals 80 miles (mi). Forty bottles per minute times 2 minutes (min) equals 80 bottles, and 40 cars per hour times 2 hours equals 80 cars.

$$40 \,\frac{\text{mi}}{\cancel{\text{hr}}} \times 2\,\cancel{\text{hr}} = 80 \text{ mi} \qquad 40 \,\frac{\text{bottles}}{\cancel{\text{min}}} \times 2\,\cancel{\text{min}} = 80 \text{ bottles}$$

$$40 \,\frac{\text{cars}}{\cancel{\text{hr}}} \times 2\,\cancel{\text{hr}} = 80 \text{ cars}$$

From this, we see that rate times time does not have to equal distance; it can also equal bottles, cars, or whatever else is the numerator of the rate. Many rate problems have the form

$$R_1 T_1 + R_2 T_2 = \text{miles, bottles, cars, or whatever}$$

Usually, the problem is stated so that one or both of the rates can be determined. In the next example Joe Frank can wash 3 cars in 5 hours and Myrl can wash 4 cars in 3 hours. These statements allow us to determine both rates by writing the work done over the time. Notice that when the rate is less than 1, the unit is singular, and when the rate is greater than 1, the unit is plural.

$$\text{Rate of Joe Frank} = \frac{3 \text{ cars}}{5 \text{ hr}} = \frac{3}{5}\,\frac{\text{car}}{\text{hr}} \qquad \text{Rate of Myrl} = \frac{4 \text{ cars}}{3 \text{ hr}} = \frac{4}{3}\,\frac{\text{cars}}{\text{hr}}$$

Due to human interaction, the rate of someone working alone would not be the same as that person's rate when he or she works with another person. In these problems, however, we will assume that there is no interaction and that the rates do not change.

example 25.2   Joe Frank can wash 3 cars in 5 hours and Myrl can wash 4 cars in 3 hours. Fifteen cars need to be washed. If Joe Frank works for 2 hours and is then joined by Myrl, how long will Myrl and Joe Frank have to work together to finish washing the 15 cars?

solution   The rates for this problem were found in the preceding paragraph. Now we determine how much Joe Frank accomplished in the 2 hours that he worked alone.

$$\frac{3 \text{ cars}}{5 \,\cancel{\text{hr}}} \times 2\,\cancel{\text{hr}} = \frac{6}{5} \text{ cars}$$

The total job was 15 cars, so now they have only $13\frac{4}{5}$ cars left to wash. We will use the following equation:

$$R_J T_J + R_M T_M = 13\frac{4}{5} \text{ cars}$$

We replace R_J and R_M with the proper rates. Since the times are the same, we can remove the subscripts on the times.

$$\left(\frac{3}{5}\,\frac{\text{car}}{\text{hr}}\right)T + \left(\frac{4}{3}\,\frac{\text{cars}}{\text{hr}}\right)T = \frac{69}{5} \text{ cars}$$

We finish by multiplying every term by 15 and then solving.

$$15\left(\frac{3}{5}\frac{car}{hr}\right)T + 15\left(\frac{4}{3}\frac{cars}{hr}\right)T = (15)\frac{69}{5}\ cars \qquad \text{multiplied}$$

$$\left(9\frac{cars}{hr}\right)T + \left(20\frac{cars}{hr}\right)T = 207\ cars \qquad \text{simplified}$$

$$\left(29\frac{cars}{hr}\right)T = 207\ cars \qquad \text{added}$$

$$T = \frac{207}{29}\ hr \qquad \text{solved}$$

example 25.3 Mayha could empty 2 bottles in 3 hours. Working with Wilbur, she found they could empty 4 bottles in 3 hours. What was Wilbur's rate of emptying bottles?

solution The total work equals the sum of the products of rates and times. The rates are in bottles per hour, and bottles per hour times hours equals bottles. Thus, the work unit is bottles.

$$R_M T_M + R_W T_W = bottles$$

We know that Mayha's rate was two thirds of a bottle per hour and that the time for each person was 3 hours. Since the work done was 4 bottles, we can write

$$\left(\frac{2}{3}\frac{bottle}{hr}\right)(3\ hr) + R_W(3\ hr) = 4\ bottles \qquad \text{substituted}$$

$$(3\ hr)R_W = 2\ bottles \qquad \text{simplified}$$

$$R_W = \frac{2\ bottles}{3\ hr} \qquad \text{solved}$$

In this problem, the unit of work is bottles and the unit of time is hours, and the number of bottles per hour is less than one. Thus, we write our answer as

$$R_W = \frac{2}{3}\frac{bottle}{hr}$$

example 25.4 If 5 workers can do 1 job in 8 days, how many workers would it take to do 3 jobs in 7 days?

solution This rate problem has four variables which are the rate, the number of workers, the length of time, and the number of jobs.

$$\text{Rate} \times \text{workers} \times \text{time} = \text{jobs} \qquad \text{or} \qquad RWT = J$$

These problems are usually stated in two parts. We use the equation and the data in the first part of the sentence to find the rate.

$$RWT = J \qquad \text{equation}$$

$$R(5\ workers)(8\ days) = 1\ job \qquad \text{substituted}$$

$$R = \frac{1\ job}{40\ worker\text{-}days} \qquad \text{divided}$$

To this point in our study of mathematics, a rate has involved just two quantities. In example 25.2, the rates were in cars per hour, and in example 25.3, the rates were in bottles per hour. The rate in this problem involves three quantities: jobs, workers, and days. The rate used is jobs per worker-day. Now we use the basic equation a second time. We use the rate we have found and the information given in the second part of the sentence.

$$RWT = J \qquad \text{equation}$$

$$\left(\frac{1 \text{ job}}{40 \text{ worker-days}}\right)(W)(7 \text{ days}) = 3 \text{ jobs} \qquad \text{substituted}$$

$$W = \frac{120 \text{ worker-days}}{7 \text{ days}} \qquad \text{rearranged}$$

$$W = \mathbf{17.14 \text{ workers}} \qquad \text{solved}$$

Since the use of a decimal number of workers is impossible, it would be necessary to use 18 workers to ensure that the 3 jobs would be completed in 7 days. Nonetheless, the answer to the problem as stated is 17.14 workers.

example 25.5 Mary had 252 gallons (gal) of milk. This would feed 42 infants for 12 days. Then 14 more infants were placed in the nursery and 48 more gallons were provided. How long would the milk last now?

solution This is another four-variable problem.

$$\text{Rate} \times \text{time} \times \text{infants} = \text{gallons} \qquad \text{or} \qquad RTI = G$$

We use the information in the first two sentences to find the rate.

$$RTI = G \qquad \text{equation}$$

$$R(12 \text{ days})(42 \text{ infants}) = 252 \text{ gal} \qquad \text{substituted}$$

$$R = \frac{252 \text{ gal}}{504 \text{ infant-days}} = \frac{1 \text{ gal}}{2 \text{ infant-days}} \qquad \text{divided}$$

Now we use the basic equation a second time. We use the rate we have found and the information in the third sentence.

$$RTI = G \qquad \text{equation}$$

$$\left(\frac{1 \text{ gal}}{2 \text{ infant-days}}\right)(T)(42 + 14) \text{ infants} = (252 + 48) \text{ gal} \qquad \text{substituted}$$

$$T = \frac{300 \,(2 \text{ infant-days})}{56 \text{ infants}} \qquad \text{rearranged}$$

$$T = \mathbf{10.71 \text{ days}} \qquad \text{solved}$$

problem set 25

1. Five years ago, Orville was twice as old as Wilbur. Five years from now, Orville will be $1\frac{1}{2}$ times as old as Wilbur. How old are both now?

2. Emerson can dig 2 holes in 3 hours and Johnna can dig 3 holes in 2 hours. Six holes need to be dug. If Emerson digs for 1 hour and then is joined by Johnna, how long will they work together to finish digging the 6 holes?

3. Sandra could build 3 sandcastles in 5 hours. Working with Frederick, she discovered they could build 3 sandcastles in merely 3 hours. What was Frederick's rate of building sandcastles?

4. Six men can do 1 job in 9 days. How many men would it take to do 15 jobs in 5 days?

5. The sum of the digits of a two-digit counting number is 14, and the ratio of the tens' digit to the units' digit is 0.75. What is the number?

6. Find the equation of the line which passes through point (3, 1) and is parallel to the line which passes through points (−1, 2) and (3, 4).

7. Sketch the graph of the function $f(x) = 4^x$.

8. Sketch the graph of the function $g(x) = \left(\frac{1}{4}\right)^x$.

9. (a) Graph the set $\{x \in \mathbb{R} \mid |x + 3| > 6\}$ on the real number line.

    (b) Graph the set $\{x \in \mathbb{R} \mid |x - 2| \leq 5\}$ on the real number line.

10. Determine if each graph represents the graph of a function. If so, determine whether the graph is the graph of a one-to-one function.

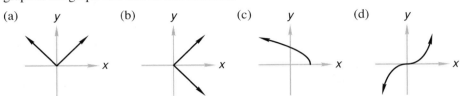

11. Find the domain of the function defined by each equation:

    (a) $f(x) = \sqrt{2x - 1}$ (b) $g(x) = \dfrac{1}{\sqrt{x - 3}}$ (c) $h(x) = \dfrac{2}{(x - 1)(x + 6)}$

12. Draw the necessary reference triangles and evaluate. Do not use a calculator.

    (a) $\sin 60° - \cos 30°$ (b) $\dfrac{\sqrt{2}}{2} \cos 45° - 2 \sin 60°$

13. Let $f(x) = 2x$ and $g(x) = 1 - x^2$. Evaluate:

    (a) $(fg)(2)$ (b) $(f/g)(2)$ (c) $(g \circ f)(2)$

14. If $f(\theta) = \frac{\sqrt{3}}{2} \cos \theta - \frac{1}{2} \sin \theta$, draw the necessary reference triangle and evaluate $f(30°)$. Do not use a calculator.

15. If $m(\theta) = \sin \theta$ and $n(\theta) = \tan \theta$, draw the necessary reference triangle and evaluate $\sqrt{2}m(30°) - 2n(30°)$. Do not use a calculator.

16. Find the perimeter of $\triangle DEF$ if $\triangle ABC \sim \triangle DEF$.

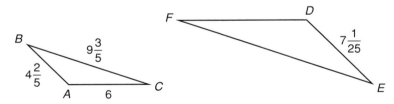

17. Solve: $\begin{cases} x^2 + y^2 = 9 \\ 2x^2 - y^2 = 6 \end{cases}$

18. Simplify by factoring the numerator: $\dfrac{x^{4a} - y^{4a}}{x^a + y^a}$

19. Factor: $8x^3y^6 - 27a^6b^9$

Simplify:

20. $\dfrac{3s}{2 - \dfrac{6l}{m - \dfrac{q}{r}}}$ **21.** $\dfrac{3 - 2\sqrt{12}}{4 + 3\sqrt{3}}$ **22.** $\left(3x^{\frac{1}{2}} - 2z^{\frac{1}{4}}\right)\left(3x^{\frac{1}{2}} + 2z^{\frac{1}{4}}\right)$

23. Divide $x^4 - 6x^3 + 7x^2 - 5$ by $x - 2$ and check.

24. Solve for z: $5s = \dfrac{3k}{m}\left(\dfrac{6t}{z} - \dfrac{4k}{m}\right)$

25. If $f(x) = x^2 + 2x$, find $f(x + 2)$.

26. Given: $\overline{AB} \cong \overline{CB}$

      $\angle ABD \cong \angle CBD$

Write a two-column proof to prove:
$\overline{AD} \cong \overline{CD}$

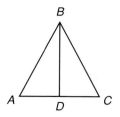

27. In the figure shown, O is the center of the circle that is intersected by a tangent, chord, and secant. If $\overline{AB} \parallel \overline{CD}$ and $m\overset{\frown}{DCE} = 290°$, find x.

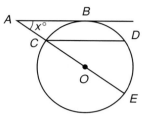

28. The base of a regular pyramid is a regular hexagon, as shown. The volume of this regular pyramid is 13,824 m³. Find the height of the pyramid. Dimensions are in meters.

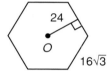 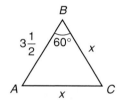

CONCEPT REVIEW PROBLEMS

29. Let a, b, and c be real numbers where $a > 0$, $b > 0$, and $c < 0$. If $ac^2 > bc^2$, compare: A. a B. b

30. Given: $\triangle ABC$

Compare: A. $1\frac{3}{4}$ B. $\frac{x}{2}$

LESSON 26   *The Logarithmic Form of the Exponential • Logarithmic Equations*

26.A

the logarithmic form of the exponential

We remember that any positive number can be written as a positive base raised to a positive power. We will use the letter N to represent the number and will use the letter b to represent the base. **We will use the letter L to represent the logarithm, which is the exponent.**

$$N = b^L$$

We read this by saying "N equals b to the L." We could also read this by saying "The logarithm for b to get N is L."

We abbreviate the word **logarithm** with **log,** and we write this sentence in compact form by writing

$$\log_b N = L$$

We read this as "The logarithm of N to the base b equals L." Thus, we see that

$$N = b^L \qquad \text{and} \qquad \log_b N = L$$

are two ways to write the same thing. Since these equations make the same statement and since N is always positive in the exponential form, it must also be positive in the logarithmic form.

example 26.1 Write $4 = 3^y$ in logarithmic form.

solution We remember that a logarithm is the exponent, and here the exponent is y. Therefore, we begin by writing

$$\log \quad = y$$

Next we indicate the base, which in this case is 3.

$$\log_3 \quad = y$$

Now the only thing left is the number 4. We insert it and have

$$\mathbf{\log_3 4 = y}$$

example 26.2 Write $\log_x 4 = m$ in exponential form.

solution We see that x is the base and that m is the logarithm, or exponent. Thus, we can write

$$x^m$$

and since 4 is the only symbol we have not used, then what we have written equals 4. Now we have as the exponential form

$$\mathbf{x^m = 4}$$

26.B
logarithmic equations

Both these expressions give us the same information.

$$\text{(a) } \log_b N = L \qquad \text{(b) } b^L = N$$

Each expression contains the letters b, L, and N. If we designate values for two of these variables, we can solve the equations for the value of the third variable.

example 26.3 Solve: $\log_b 8 = 3$

solution **We solve logarithmic equations by rewriting them in exponential form.** Then we solve the exponential equation. If we rewrite this equation in exponential form, we get

$$b^3 = 8$$

Now we solve this equation by raising both sides to the $\frac{1}{3}$ power.

$$\left(b^3\right)^{\frac{1}{3}} = (8)^{\frac{1}{3}}$$

$$b = 2$$

example 26.4 Solve: $\log_b 9 = -\frac{1}{2}$

solution First we write the equation in exponential form.

$$b^{-\frac{1}{2}} = 9$$

Now we solve by raising both sides to the -2 power:

$$\left(b^{-\frac{1}{2}}\right)^{-2} = 9^{-2}$$

$$b = \frac{1}{81}$$

example 26.5   Solve: $\log_3 \dfrac{1}{27} = M$

solution   We begin by rewriting the equation in exponential form.

$$3^M = \frac{1}{27}$$

This is a contrived problem and must be recognized as such to be solved without using a calculator. The trick is to write the right-hand side as 3 to some power. We remember that 27 can be written as 3^3, so we make this replacement.

$$3^M = \frac{1}{3^3} \qquad \text{replaced 27 with } 3^3$$

Now we rewrite the right-hand side and get

$$3^M = 3^{-3}$$

and this tells us that M equals -3.

$$M = \mathbf{-3} \qquad \text{solved}$$

We say that the problem just worked was contrived because if the problem had been to solve the equation

$$3^M = \frac{1}{15}$$

we could not have found a solution without using a calculator because 15 cannot be written as a rational power of 3. Problems such as the one we have just worked provide excellent practice in changing the forms of exponential equations, but it is also helpful to remember that they have been carefully contrived so that an easy solution is possible.

example 26.6   Solve: $\log_{1/3} P = -2$

solution   First we rewrite the equation in exponential form. Then we simplify.

$$P = \left(\frac{1}{3}\right)^{-2} \qquad \text{exponential form}$$

$$P = \frac{1}{3^{-2}} \qquad \text{simplified}$$

$$P = \mathbf{9} \qquad \text{solved}$$

example 26.7   Solve: $\log_4 8 = x$

solution   To solve, we first rewrite the equation in exponential form.

$$4^x = 8$$

Now this contrived problem can be solved if we see that 4 can be written as 2^2, and 8 can be written as 2^3.

$$\left(2^2\right)^x = 2^3 \qquad \text{changed form}$$

$$2^{2x} = 2^3 \qquad \text{simplified}$$

$$2x = 3 \qquad \text{equated exponents}$$

$$x = \mathbf{\frac{3}{2}} \qquad \text{solved}$$

**problem set
26**

1. Ten years from now Charlotte will be twice as old as Emily will be then. Five years ago Charlotte was 5 times as old as Emily was then. How old are both now?

2. The daughter can mow the lawn in 30 minutes. Her father can mow the lawn in 40 minutes. The daughter works for 10 minutes before the father begins to help. How long do they work together to complete the job?

3. The larder contained 360 pounds of food. This would feed the 20 men for 10 days. Then 5 more men staggered into camp. Now how many days would the food supply last?

4. Sarah's speed was 20 mph less than that of Donnie. Thus, Donnie could travel 325 miles in half the time it took Sarah to travel 450 miles. Find the speeds and times of both.

5. The pressure of an ideal gas was held constant at 450 millimeters of mercury. The volume was 400 liters and the temperature was 1000 kelvins. What was the volume when the temperature was increased to 2000 kelvins? *Note*: $\frac{P_1 V_1}{T_1} = \frac{P_2 V_2}{T_2}$.

6. (a) Write $k^p = 7$ in logarithmic form.

    (b) Write $\log_k 7 = p$ in exponential form.

7. (a) Write $\log_b 12 = a$ in exponential form.

    (b) Write $b^a = 12$ in logarithmic form.

Solve:

8. $\log_b 27 = 3$ 9. $\log_2 \dfrac{1}{8} = m$ 10. $\log_{1/2} c = -4$

11. Sketch the graphs of the functions:

    (a) $f(x) = 2.5^x$ (b) $g(x) = \left(\dfrac{2}{5}\right)^x$

12. The equation of the function whose graph is shown is $f(x) = x - 3$. We have placed dots at $(4, 1)$ and $(2, -1)$ because the y coordinate has a value of 1 or -1 at these points and the graph of the reciprocal function will also pass through these points. The graph of the reciprocal function will have a vertical asymptote at $x = 3$, as we have indicated by the dotted line. Make a sketch of the graph of the reciprocal function $g(x) = \frac{1}{x-3}$.

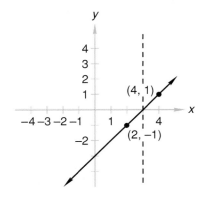

13. Determine if each graph represents the graph of a function. If so, determine whether the graph is the graph of a one-to-one function.

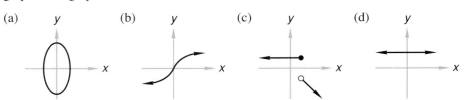

(a)   (b)   (c)   (d)

14. Find the domain of the function defined by each equation:

    (a) $f(x) = \sqrt{1 + 2x}$ (b) $g(x) = \dfrac{\sqrt{x}}{x^2 + 1}$ (c) $h(x) = \dfrac{1}{(2x + 1)(x - 3)}$

Draw the necessary reference triangles and evaluate. Do not use a calculator.

15. $2 \sin 30° \cos 30° - \sin 60°$

16. $\dfrac{\sin 60°}{\cos 60°} - \tan 60°$

17. $\dfrac{\sqrt{3}}{2} \cos 45° - \dfrac{\sqrt{2}}{2} \sin 60°$

18. If $r(\theta) = \tan \theta$, find $\dfrac{\sqrt{2}}{2} r(45°) - \sqrt{3} r(30°)$. Do not use a calculator.

19. Let $f(x) = 1 + x$ and $g(x) = x - x^2$. Evaluate:

    (a) $(f + g)(-1)$ (b) $(fg)(-1)$ (c) $(g \circ f)(-1)$

20. Given: $AC \cdot DC = BC \cdot BC$

    Write a two-column proof to prove:

$$\triangle ABC \sim \triangle BDC$$

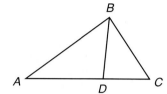

Solve:

21. $\begin{cases} 2x^2 - y^2 = 1 \\ y + 2x = 1 \end{cases}$

22. $\sqrt{x + 6} - x = 4$

23. Simplify by factoring the numerator: $\dfrac{x^3 - y^3}{x - y}$

24. Factor: $64x^{12}y^6 - 27a^6b^9$

25. Convert $-4\hat{i} + 7\hat{j}$ to polar coordinates. (Write four forms for this point.)

26. If $f(x) = \dfrac{x + 1}{x - 2}$, find $f(x - 5)$.

27. In the figure shown, $\overline{AB}$ and $\overline{AC}$ are tangent to circle O. Find x.

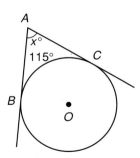

28. A sphere has a surface area of 144π m². If the surface area of the sphere is increased by 880π m², by what amount is the radius of the sphere increased?

CONCEPT REVIEW PROBLEMS

29. If $\dfrac{x}{x + 1} > 1$, compare: A. x B. 0

30. In the figure shown, $ABCDE$ is an inscribed pentagon and $m\overset{\frown}{CD} = 80°$.

    Compare: A. $230°$ B. $m\angle E + m\angle B$

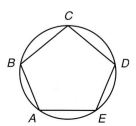

LESSON 27 *Related Angles • Signs of Trigonometric Functions*

27.A
related angles

When we draw the vector $12\underline{/135°}$, we measure the angle from the positive *x* axis, as we show in the left-hand figure.

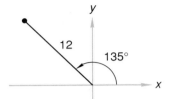 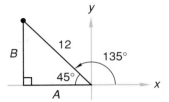

In the right-hand figure, we complete the triangle by drawing a perpendicular from the end of the vector to the *x* axis. We can find the rectangular coordinates of the vector by solving for *A* and *B*.

$$A = 12\cos 45° = 12(0.707) = 8.48$$

$$B = 12\sin 45° = 12(0.707) = 8.48$$

Thus, we have

$$12\underline{/135°} = -8.48\hat{i} + 8.48\hat{j}$$

In this solution, we used the angle 135° to help locate the vector. Then we used the 45° angle to solve the triangle. Many authors call the acute angle between the vector and the *x* axis the **related angle.** In this case, they would say that 45° is the related angle of 135°.

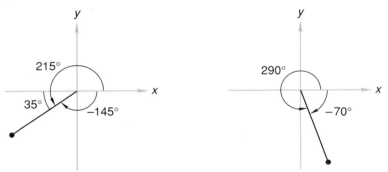

In the left-hand figure, we see that 35° is the related angle of both +215° and −145°. In the right-hand figure, we see that 70° is the related angle of both +290° and −70°. **The related angle is always a positive angle and is the acute angle between the vector and the *x* axis.**

27.B
signs of trigonometric functions

In the beginning of this lesson, we had a vector whose angle was 135°. To find the rectangular components of this vector, we used the related angle, which was 45°, and drew a triangle all sides of which were considered to be positive. We used the cosine of 45° and the sine of 45° to solve this triangle. We did not use the cosine of 135° or the sine of 135°. We will always use this procedure to find the components of vectors.

To discuss trigonometric functions, however, it is necessary to define trigonometric functions of angles that are not first-quadrant angles. **The absolute value of the trigonometric function of any angle is the same as that of the related angle, but the sign (+ or −) of the trigonometric function is determined by the quadrant in which the vector lies.** We determine the sign by considering the signs of the rectangular coordinates of the vector. **The hypotenuse is the length of the vector and is always considered to be positive.**

Below, we shall determine the sign of the various trigonometric functions of angles chosen to lie in the various quadrants. We chose θ, so the triangles that are drawn containing the related angle are identical, except for their orientation. The signs we assign to the horizontal and vertical lengths of the triangles correspond to whether its length is measured along the positive or negative x or y axis, respectively. For example, the horizontal side of a triangle lying in the second quadrant is given a negative value since it lies along the negative x axis.

Note that in the examples shown below θ does not need to lie inside the triangle that is drawn. This is because the absolute value of a trigonometric function evaluated at θ is defined to be the value of the trigonometric function evaluated at the related angle. We show below how we determine the sign of trigonometric functions of θ.

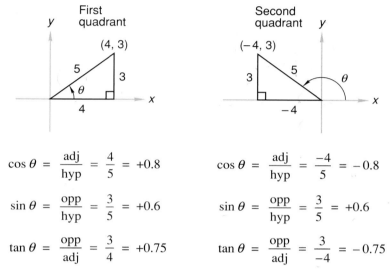

$$\cos \theta = \frac{\text{adj}}{\text{hyp}} = \frac{4}{5} = +0.8 \qquad \cos \theta = \frac{\text{adj}}{\text{hyp}} = \frac{-4}{5} = -0.8$$

$$\sin \theta = \frac{\text{opp}}{\text{hyp}} = \frac{3}{5} = +0.6 \qquad \sin \theta = \frac{\text{opp}}{\text{hyp}} = \frac{3}{5} = +0.6$$

$$\tan \theta = \frac{\text{opp}}{\text{adj}} = \frac{3}{4} = +0.75 \qquad \tan \theta = \frac{\text{opp}}{\text{adj}} = \frac{3}{-4} = -0.75$$

In the first quadrant, we see that the cosine, the sine, and the tangent are all positive. In the second quadrant, the sine is positive and the cosine and tangent are negative.

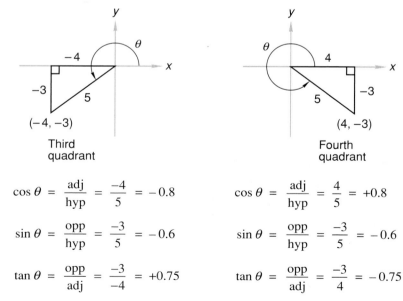

$$\cos \theta = \frac{\text{adj}}{\text{hyp}} = \frac{-4}{5} = -0.8 \qquad \cos \theta = \frac{\text{adj}}{\text{hyp}} = \frac{4}{5} = +0.8$$

$$\sin \theta = \frac{\text{opp}}{\text{hyp}} = \frac{-3}{5} = -0.6 \qquad \sin \theta = \frac{\text{opp}}{\text{hyp}} = \frac{-3}{5} = -0.6$$

$$\tan \theta = \frac{\text{opp}}{\text{adj}} = \frac{-3}{-4} = +0.75 \qquad \tan \theta = \frac{\text{opp}}{\text{adj}} = \frac{-3}{4} = -0.75$$

In the third quadrant, the tangent is positive and both the cosine and sine are negative. In the fourth quadrant, the cosine is positive and both the sine and tangent are negative.

It is important to remember that the sides of a triangle are always positive lengths. We consider negative values only to determine the signs of the trigonometric function values in the various quadrants.

example 27.1   Evaluate: 4 cos 135°

solution   We sketch the problem and note that the related angle of 135° is 45°. We also draw the reference triangle.

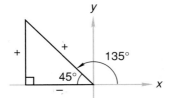

The cosine of 45° is $1/\sqrt{2}$, and the cosine is negative in the second quadrant. Therefore, we can write

$$\cos 135° = -\cos 45° = -\frac{1}{\sqrt{2}}$$

Therefore, we have $\cos 135° = -1/\sqrt{2}$. Since we want 4 cos 135°, we multiply by 4. Then we rationalize the denominator by multiplying above and below by $\sqrt{2}$. Therefore, we have

$$4 \cos 135° = 4\left(-\frac{1}{\sqrt{2}}\right)\left(\frac{\sqrt{2}}{\sqrt{2}}\right) = \frac{-4\sqrt{2}}{2} = -2\sqrt{2}$$

example 27.2   Evaluate: −2 cos (−150°)

solution   We sketch the problem and note that the related angle of −150° is 30°. We also draw the reference triangle.

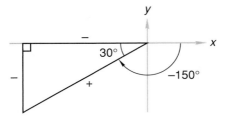
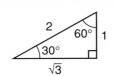

The cosine of 30° is $\sqrt{3}/2$, and the cosine is negative in the third quadrant. Therefore, we can write

$$\cos (-150°) = -\cos 30° = -\frac{\sqrt{3}}{2}$$

Therefore, we have $\cos (-150°) = -\sqrt{3}/2$. Since we want −2 cos (−150°), we multiply by −2. Therefore, we have

$$-2 \cos (-150°) = (-2)\left(-\frac{\sqrt{3}}{2}\right) = \sqrt{3}$$

example 27.3   Evaluate: $\frac{5}{3}$ cos 300°

solution   We sketch the problem and note that the related angle of 300° is 60°. We also draw the reference triangle.

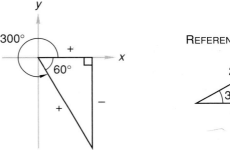
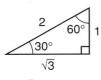

The cosine of 60° is 1/2, and the cosine is positive in the fourth quadrant. Therefore, we can write

$$\cos 300° = \cos 60° = \frac{1}{2}$$

Therefore, we have $\cos 300° = 1/2$. Since we want $5/3 \cos 300°$, we multiply by 5/3. Therefore, we have

$$\frac{5}{3} \cos 300° = \frac{5}{3} \cdot \frac{1}{2} = \frac{5}{6}$$

problem set 27

1. Next year George will be twice as old as Marshall will be then. Five years ago George was 8 times as old as Marshall was then. What are their ages now?

2. Marie can eat the entire cake in 10 minutes. Antoinette joins her after 3 minutes, and together they eat the rest of the cake in 4 minutes. How long would it have taken Antoinette to eat the entire cake alone?

3. Matilda was dismayed when she found out that it would take 2 workers 3 days to do 6 jobs. So she hired 4 more workers. Now how many days will it take all the workers to complete 6 jobs?

4. The number of reds was 11 fewer than the sum of the blues and whites. The number of whites was 3 fewer than the sum of the reds and blues. How many of each were there if the number of whites was 1 greater than the number of blues?

5. Acorns varied directly as walnuts and inversely as squirrels squared. When there were 28 acorns, there were 7 walnuts and 3 squirrels. How many acorns were there when there were 4 walnuts but only 2 squirrels?

6. Find the equation of the line which passes through $(2, -1)$ and is parallel to the line $3y - 2x + 1 = 0$.

7. Write $7 = 3^k$ in logarithmic form.

8. Write $\log_m 8 = n$ in exponential form.

Solve:

9. $\log_b 64 = 3$

10. $\log_3 \frac{1}{27} = n$

11. $\log_{1/2} a = -2$

12. Sketch the graphs of the functions:

   (a) $f(x) = 5^x$

   (b) $g(x) = \left(\frac{1}{5}\right)^x$

13. The equation of the function whose graph is shown is $f(x) = \frac{1}{2}x + 1$. We have placed dots at $(0, 1)$ and $(-4, -1)$ because the y coordinate has a value of 1 or -1 at these points and the graph of the reciprocal function will also pass through these points. The graph of the reciprocal function will have a vertical asymptote at $x = -2$, as we have indicated by the dotted line. Make a sketch of the graph of the reciprocal function $g(x) = \frac{1}{\frac{1}{2}x + 1}$.

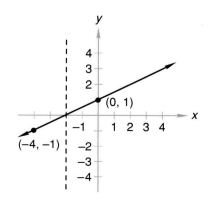

14. Determine if each graph represents the graph of a function. If so, determine whether the graph is the graph of a one-to-one function.

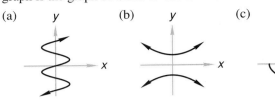 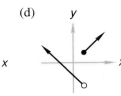

(a)   (b)   (c)   (d)

15. Find the domain of the function defined by each equation:

    (a) $f(x) = \sqrt{2 - 6x}$ (b) $g(x) = \dfrac{\sqrt{x + 10}}{x - 2}$ (c) $h(x) = \dfrac{4}{x^2 + 2x - 3}$

Draw the necessary reference triangles and evaluate. Do not use a calculator.

16. $3 \cos 300°$

17. $\sin 60° + \dfrac{\sqrt{3}}{2} \sin 30°$

18. If $f(x) = -2 \cos x$, find $f(-300°)$. Do not use a calculator.

19. Let $f(x) = 3 - \log_{10} x$ and $g(x) = x^2 + 2$. Evaluate:

    (a) $(f - g)(10)$ (b) $(f/g)(10)$ (c) $(g \circ f)(10)$

20. Solve: $\begin{cases} x^2 + y^2 = 16 \\ y - 3x = 4 \end{cases}$

21. Factor: $3y^{2n+1} + 12y^{3n+2}$

22. Simplify: $\dfrac{\sqrt{-16}i^3 - 4i^2}{1 - \sqrt{-4}}$

23. Solve for a: $2r = \dfrac{1}{25}\left(\dfrac{3z}{a} - \dfrac{k}{p}\right)$

24. Solve $4x^2 - 2x = -2$ by completing the square.

25. If $f(x) = \dfrac{2}{x}$, find $f(x + h)$.

26. Given: C is the midpoint of $\overline{BE}$

        $\angle B \cong \angle E$

    Write a two-column proof to prove:

        $\overline{AC} \cong \overline{DC}$

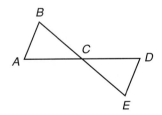

27. In the figure shown, O is the center of the circle. If $\overline{AB} \parallel \overline{CD}$ and $m\overarc{CD} = 48°$, find x.

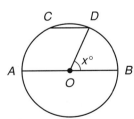

28. A sphere has a volume of 4500π cm³. If the volume of the sphere is decreased by 3528π cm³, by what amount is the radius of the sphere decreased?

CONCEPT REVIEW PROBLEMS

29. If $x^3 = -8$ and $y^3 = -16$, compare: A. x B. y

30. In $\triangle ABC$, $\overline{BD}$ is drawn so that $\angle BDC \cong \angle BCD$.

    If $BC < AB$, compare: A. AB B. BD

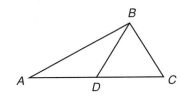

LESSON 28   *Factorial Notation • Abstract Rate Problems*

28.A
factorial notation

When we work problems in mathematical probability, it is often necessary to find the product of a number of positive integers such as

$$(a)\ \ 4 \cdot 3 \cdot 2 \cdot 1$$

$$(b)\ \ 12 \cdot 11 \cdot 10 \cdot 9 \cdot 8 \cdot 7 \cdot 6 \cdot 5 \cdot 4 \cdot 3 \cdot 2 \cdot 1$$

In these examples, the first factor is an integer, and each succeeding factor is the next smaller integer. This pattern continues, and the number 1 is always the last factor. Rather than write the factors out each time, mathematicians have found it convenient to write the first factor and follow it with an exclamation point. If we do this, the products above could be indicated by writing

$$(a)\ \ 4!\ \ \ \ \ \ \ \ (b)\ \ 12!$$

The exclamation point is read as "factorial." Thus, expression (a) is read as "Four factorial" and expression (b) as "Twelve factorial."

example 28.1   Evaluate 5!.

solution   We write out the indicated factors

$$5! = 5 \cdot 4 \cdot 3 \cdot 2 \cdot 1$$

and, if we multiply, we find that

$$5! = \mathbf{120}$$

Most scientific calculators have a factorial key. Use one of these calculators to calculate 5!. Although these calculators employ scientific notation, the factorial product quickly becomes too large for a calculator to handle. What is the largest factorial your calculator can handle?

example 28.2   Evaluate $\dfrac{9!}{3!5!}$ without using a calculator.

solution   We write out the factors and simplify.

$$\frac{9 \cdot 8 \cdot 7 \cdot 6 \cdot 5 \cdot 4 \cdot 3 \cdot 2 \cdot 1}{3 \cdot 2 \cdot 1 \cdot 5 \cdot 4 \cdot 3 \cdot 2 \cdot 1}$$

We note that both the numerator and the denominator have $5 \cdot 4 \cdot 3 \cdot 2 \cdot 1$ as factors. We cancel these.

$$\frac{9 \cdot 8 \cdot 7 \cdot 6 \cdot \cancel{5 \cdot 4 \cdot 3 \cdot 2 \cdot 1}}{3 \cdot 2 \cdot 1 \cdot \cancel{5 \cdot 4 \cdot 3 \cdot 2 \cdot 1}}$$

Now the $3 \cdot 2$ below will cancel the 6 above, so we are left with

$$9 \cdot 8 \cdot 7 = \mathbf{504}$$

example 28.3   Evaluate $\dfrac{14!}{6!11!}$ without using a calculator.

solution   This time we will try a shortcut. We note that 14! can be written with 11! as a factor. Thus, we can write

$$\frac{\overset{7}{\cancel{14}} \cdot 13 \cdot \cancel{12} \cdot \cancel{11!}}{6 \cdot 5 \cdot \cancel{4} \cdot \cancel{3} \cdot \cancel{2} \cdot 1 \cdot \cancel{11!}} = \frac{7 \cdot 13}{30} = \frac{\mathbf{91}}{\mathbf{30}}$$

example 28.4 Use the factorial key on a calculator to help evaluate $11 \cdot 10 \cdot 9 \cdot 8$.

solution There is no key on the calculator for this operation; however, if we multiply above and below by 7!, we get

$$\frac{11 \cdot 10 \cdot 9 \cdot 8 \cdot 7!}{7!} = \frac{11!}{7!}$$

and we can find 11! and 7! on the calculator.

$$\frac{11!}{7!} = \frac{39{,}916{,}800}{5040} = \mathbf{7920}$$

28.B
abstract rate problems

Rate problems that use letters rather than numbers can be used to enhance our understanding of fundamental concepts. In these problems, it is important to keep track of the units. The fundamental equation in distance-rate problems is rate times time equals distance. On the left, we see how the hours cancel when we multiply 60 miles per hour by 2 hours; and on the right, we see how hours cancel when we multiply m miles per hour by h hours to get a distance of mh miles.

$$\text{Rate} \times \text{time} = \text{distance} \qquad\qquad \text{Rate} \times \text{time} = \text{distance}$$

$$60\,\frac{\text{mi}}{\text{hr}} \times 2\,\text{hr} = 120\,\text{mi} \qquad\qquad m\,\frac{\text{mi}}{\text{hr}} \times h\,\text{hr} = mh\,\text{mi}$$

We use the same statements to see how we handle the units when we divide distance by rate to get time.

$$\text{Time} = \frac{\text{distance}}{\text{rate}} \qquad\qquad T = \frac{\text{distance}}{\text{rate}}$$

$$\text{Time} = \frac{120\,\text{mi}}{60\,\frac{\text{mi}}{\text{hr}}} = 2\,\text{hr} \qquad\qquad T = \frac{mh\,\text{mi}}{m\,\frac{\text{mi}}{\text{hr}}} = h\,\text{hr}$$

Abstract rate problems are usually worked in three steps. The statement of the problem defines two of the components, which allows the third to be calculated. Then a change is made in one or two components and the value of the other is requested. We demonstrate this procedure in the next two examples.

example 28.5 The train traveled m miles at p miles per hour and still arrived 1 hour late. How fast should the train have traveled to have arrived on time?

solution The first step is to identify the original values of rate, time, and distance.

$$\text{Distance} = m\,\text{mi} \qquad \text{Rate} = p\,\frac{\text{mi}}{\text{hr}} \qquad \text{Time} = \frac{\text{distance}}{\text{rate}} = \frac{m\,\text{mi}}{p\,\frac{\text{mi}}{\text{hr}}} = \frac{m}{p}\,\text{hr}$$

To arrive on time, the train will have to travel the same distance in 1 hour less. Thus, the new distance will be the same, and the new time will be the old time minus 1 hour.

$$\text{New distance} = m\,\text{mi} \qquad \text{New time} = \left(\frac{m}{p} - 1\right)\text{hr} = \frac{m - p}{p}\,\text{hr}$$

To find the new rate, we divide the new distance by the new time. The new distance is the same as the old distance.

$$\text{New rate} = \frac{\text{new distance}}{\text{new time}} = \frac{m\,\text{mi}}{\frac{m - p}{p}\,\text{hr}} = \mathbf{\frac{mp}{m - p}}\,\frac{\mathbf{mi}}{\mathbf{hr}}$$

example 28.6   The boat traveled k miles in t hours and was 40 miles short of the goal when the gun went off. If the skipper tried again, how long would it take to reach the goal if she increased the rate of travel by 10 mph?

solution   The first step is to identify the rate, time, and distance of the first trip.

$$\text{Distance} = k \text{ miles} \qquad \text{Time} = t \text{ hours} \qquad \text{Rate} = \frac{\text{distance}}{\text{time}} = \frac{k}{t} \frac{\text{mi}}{\text{hr}}$$

In the next trip, the new distance will be $(k + 40)$ miles, and the rate will be 10 mph greater than the old rate.

$$\text{New distance} = (k + 40) \text{ miles} \qquad \text{New rate} = \left(\frac{k}{t} + 10\right)\frac{\text{mi}}{\text{hr}} = \frac{k + 10t}{t} \frac{\text{mi}}{\text{hr}}$$

Now time equals distance divided by rate.

$$\text{Time} = \frac{(k + 40) \text{ mi}}{\dfrac{k + 10t}{t} \dfrac{\text{mi}}{\text{hr}}} = \frac{(k + 40)t}{k + 10t} \textbf{ hours}$$

problem set
28

1. The bus traveled x miles at p miles per hour and still arrived 2 hours late. How fast should the bus have traveled to have arrived on time?

2. Redig ran for T hours at R miles per hour but ended up 20 miles short of the goal. If he tried again and increased his speed by 5 miles per hour, how long would it take him to reach the goal?

3. Seven years from now, Dylan will be 3 times as old as Thomas is now. Dylan's age is twice Thomas' age now. What are their ages now?

4. James can accomplish the entire mission in 20 hours. Irwin joins James after 3 hours. Together, they are able to accomplish the mission in 4 hours. How long would it take Irwin to accomplish the mission alone?

5. Seven workers could do 3 jobs in 5 days. If 3 more workers were hired who worked at the same rate, how long would it take all of them to do 4 jobs?

6. Evaluate $\dfrac{8!}{2!4!}$ without using a calculator.

7. Evaluate $\dfrac{9!}{3!3!}$ without using a calculator.

8. Write $9 = 2^k$ in logarithmic form.

9. Write $\log_m 6 = n$ in exponential form.

Solve:

10. $\log_c 81 = 4$ 11. $\log_2 \dfrac{1}{16} = m$ 12. $\log_{1/4} b = -2$

13. Sketch the graph of each function:

   (a) $f(x) = \left(\dfrac{5}{4}\right)^x$ (b) $g(x) = \left(\dfrac{4}{5}\right)^x$

14. The equation of the function whose graph is shown is $f(x) = \frac{1}{2}x - 1$. We have placed dots at $(4, 1)$ and $(0, -1)$ because the y coordinate has a value of 1 or -1 at these points and the graph of the reciprocal function will also pass through these points. The graph of the reciprocal function will have a vertical asymptote at $x = 2$, as we have indicated by the dotted line. Make a sketch of the graph of the reciprocal function $g(x) = \dfrac{1}{\frac{1}{2}x - 1}$.

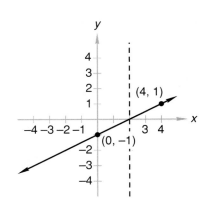

15. Find the domain of the function defined by each equation:

(a) $f(x) = \sqrt{3x + 12}$ (b) $g(x) = \dfrac{1}{x^2 - x}$ (c) $h(x) = \dfrac{\sqrt{x - 4}}{x^2 + 2}$

16. Draw the necessary reference triangle and evaluate $2\cos(-330°)$. Do not use a calculator.

17. If $s(\theta) = \cos\theta$ and $t(\theta) = \sin\theta$, find $s(60°) + \sqrt{2}t(45°)$. Do not use a calculator.

18. Let $f(x) = 2x + 3$ and $g(x) = \frac{1}{2}x - \frac{3}{2}$. Evaluate:

(a) $(f + g)(-3)$ (b) $(f \circ g)(-3)$ (c) $(g \circ f)(-3)$

19. Solve: $\begin{cases} x^2 + y^2 = 4 \\ x^2 - y^2 = 4 \end{cases}$

Simplify:

20. $\dfrac{\dfrac{x^2 y}{ca^3} - \dfrac{y^3 z}{a^2}}{\dfrac{s^2 t}{a^2} - \dfrac{r^2 z}{a^3 c}}$

21. $\dfrac{\sqrt{2}\sqrt{-3}\sqrt{6} + \sqrt{-16} + \sqrt{5}\sqrt{-5}}{1 + \sqrt{-4}i^4}$

22. $\dfrac{4 - 3\sqrt{2}}{2 - 2\sqrt{2}}$

23. $\dfrac{x^{a+2}\left(\sqrt{y^4}\right)^{2a-1}}{y^{3a+2}}$

24. Divide $x^4 - 3x^3 + 2x - 6$ by $x - 1$ and check.

25. If $f(x) = -x^2 - 6x - 8$, find $f(x - 3)$.

26. Given: $\angle 1 \cong \angle 4$
$\angle 2 \cong \angle 3$

Write a two-column proof to prove:

$\overline{QR} \cong \overline{SP}$

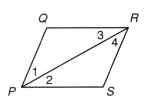

27. In the figure shown, O is the center of the circle. If $m\overarc{AB} = x°$ and $m\overarc{CD} = 130°$, find x, y, and z.

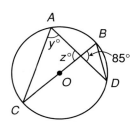

28. The base of a right circular cone has a perimeter of 32π m. The surface area of this right circular cone is 576π m^2. Find the slant height and height of the cone.

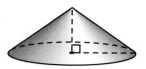

29. If $x^2 + y^2 = 25$ and $x = 3$, compare: A. y B. 0

30. In the figure shown, lines l_1 and l_2 are parallel. Compare: A. AB B. AC

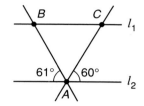

LESSON 29   *The Unit Circle • Very Large and Very Small Fractions • Quadrantal Angles*

29.A
the unit circle   The right triangle shown here has two acute angles, which we have labeled A and B.

The cosine of angle A is the ratio of the length of the side adjacent to angle A to the length of the hypotenuse.

$$\cos A = \frac{4}{5} = 0.8$$

The sine of angle A is the ratio of the length of the side opposite angle A to the length of the hypotenuse.

$$\sin A = \frac{3}{5} = 0.6$$

Below we draw a right triangle with the same acute angles whose hypotenuse is 1 unit long, and we find that the side opposite angle A is 0.6 unit long and the side adjacent to angle A is 0.8 unit long. The cosine of A will be 0.8 over 1, or 0.8, and the sine of A will be 0.6 over 1, or 0.6. Thus, the length of the side adjacent is numerically equal to the cosine of the angle, and the length of the side opposite is numerically equal to the sine of the angle.

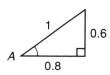

Because of this delightful result, we can use a circle whose center is the origin and whose radius is 1 unit long to help us visualize the values of the cosine and sine of the central angle as the radius rotates counterclockwise from a horizontal position along the *x* axis. The cosine of the angle is the *x* coordinate of the endpoint of the hypotenuse, which indicates the distance to the left or right of the origin. The sine of the angle is the *y* coordinate of the endpoint of the hypotenuse, which indicates the distance above or below the origin.

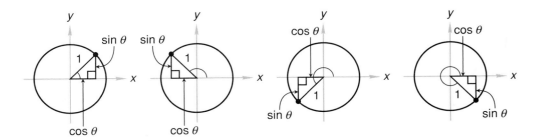

We can use the triangle below and the definitions of cos θ, sin θ, and tan θ to prove that tan θ equals the ratio of sin θ to cos θ.

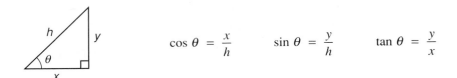

$$\cos \theta = \frac{x}{h} \qquad \sin \theta = \frac{y}{h} \qquad \tan \theta = \frac{y}{x}$$

On the left we write sin θ over cos θ. Next, we replace sin θ with *y* over *h* and cos θ with *x* over *h*.

$$\frac{\sin \theta}{\cos \theta} = \frac{\dfrac{y}{h}}{\dfrac{x}{h}} = \frac{\dfrac{y}{h}}{\dfrac{x}{h}} \cdot \frac{\dfrac{h}{1}}{\dfrac{h}{1}} = \frac{y}{x} = \tan \theta$$

In the middle we multiplied above and below by *h* over 1 and canceled to get *y* over *x*, which equals tan θ.

29.B
very large and very small fractions

If the denominator of a fraction is fixed, the value of the fraction is determined by the value of the numerator. The value of fraction (a) is 0.002. Fraction (b) has the same denominator but has a smaller numerator, so the value of the fraction is the smaller number 0.000002.

$$\text{(a)} \quad \frac{0.008}{4} = 0.002 \qquad \text{(b)} \quad \frac{0.000008}{4} = 0.000002$$

If we make the numerator smaller and smaller, the value of the fraction will be smaller and smaller and will get closer and closer to zero. **We say that the value of the fraction**

$$\frac{x}{4}$$

approaches zero as a limit as the value of *x* gets closer and closer to zero.

If the value of the numerator is fixed, the value of the fraction is determined by the value of the denominator. The value of fraction (c) is 500. Fraction (d) has the same numerator but has a smaller denominator, and the value of this fraction is 500,000.

$$\text{(c)} \quad \frac{4}{0.008} = 500 \qquad\qquad \text{(d)} \quad \frac{4}{0.000008} = 500,000$$

If we make the denominator smaller and smaller, the value of the fraction will get greater and greater. **We say that the value of the fraction (if x is a positive number)**

$$\frac{4}{x}$$

approaches positive infinity as the value of x gets closer and closer to zero. Of course, if x is a negative number, the fraction gets very large negatively as x gets smaller and smaller. We say that the value of the fraction approaches negative infinity as x approaches zero. When we say that a number approaches positive or negative infinity, we mean that the absolute value of the number gets greater and greater and that the sign of this number is positive or negative, respectively. It is important to realize that there is no particular number that has a value of positive infinity or negative infinity. In the fraction above, we can let the denominator get smaller and smaller and closer to zero, but the denominator can never be equal to zero because division by zero is not defined.

29.C
quadrantal angles

The cosine, sine, and tangent of an angle are defined by using the sides of a right triangle. If the angle has a measure of 0°, 90°, 180°, or 270°, there is no triangle, so the definitions are not valid. We call these angles which are multiples of 90° **quadrantal angles.** We define trigonometric functions of quadrantal angles to be the **limit** approached by the trigonometric functions as the angle gets closer and closer to these values.

To find the cosine, sine, and tangent of 0°, we will use the two figures below. In the figure on the left below, we show the radius of the unit circle approaching the positive x axis, where the value of θ will be 0°. The cosine of θ equals the value of x, which approaches one as the angle θ decreases to 0°. The sine of θ equals the value of y, which approaches zero as the angle θ decreases to 0°.

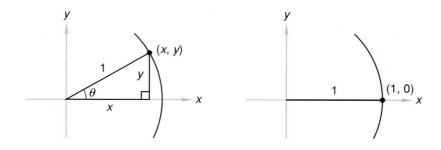

In the figure on the right above, we let θ equal 0° and there is no triangle. The x coordinate of the end of the radius equals the cosine of 0°, which is equal to one. The y coordinate of the end of the radius equals the sine of 0°, which is equal to zero. The tangent of 0° equals sin 0° divided by cos 0°, which is equal to zero. Therefore, the values of the three trigonometric functions of 0° are

$$\cos 0° = 1 \qquad \sin 0° = 0 \qquad \tan 0° = \frac{0}{1} = 0$$

To find the cosine, sine, and tangent of 90°, we will use the two figures below. In the figure on the left below, we show the radius of the unit circle approaching the positive y axis, where the value of θ will be 90°. The cosine of θ equals the value of x, which is approaching zero as the angle θ increases to 90°. The sine of θ equals the value of y, which is approaching one as the angle θ increases to 90°.

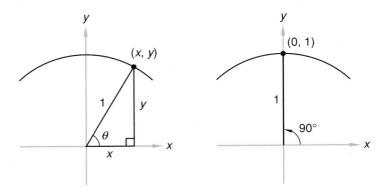

In the figure on the right above, we let θ equal 90° and there is no triangle. The x coordinate of the end of the radius equals the cosine of 90°, which is equal to zero. The y coordinate of the end of the radius equals the sine of 90°, which is equal to one. The tangent of 90° equals sin 90° divided by cos 90°, which is undefined because division by zero is not possible. Therefore, the values of the three trigonometric functions of 90° are

$$\cos 90° = 0 \qquad \sin 90° = 1 \qquad \tan 90° \text{ is undefined}$$

To find the cosine, sine, and tangent of 180°, we will use the two figures below. In the figure on the left below, we show the radius of the unit circle approaching the negative x axis, where the value of θ will be 180°. The cosine of θ equals the value of x, which approaches negative one as the angle θ increases to 180°. The sine of θ equals the value of y, which approaches zero as the angle θ increases to 180°.

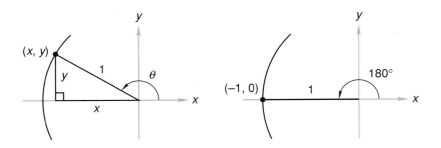

In the figure on the right above, we let θ equal 180° and there is no triangle. The x coordinate of the end of the radius equals the cosine of 180°, which is equal to negative one. The y coordinate of the end of the radius equals the sine of 180°, which is equal to zero. The tangent of 180° equals sin 180° divided by cos 180°, which is equal to zero. Therefore, the values of the three trigonometric functions of 180° are

$$\cos 180° = -1 \qquad \sin 180° = 0 \qquad \tan 180° = \frac{0}{-1} = 0$$

To find the cosine, sine, and tangent of 270°, we will use the two figures below. In the figure on the left below, we show the radius of the unit circle approaching the negative *y* axis, where the value of *θ* will be 270°. The cosine of *θ* equals the value of *x*, which is approaching zero as the angle *θ* increases to 270°. The sine of *θ* equals the value of *y*, which is approaching negative one as the angle *θ* increases to 270°.

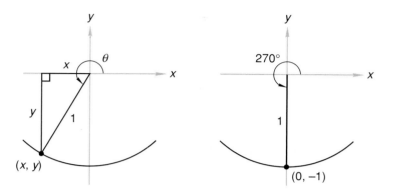

In the figure on the right above, we let *θ* equal 270° and there is no triangle. The *x* coordinate of the end of the radius equals the cosine of 270°, which is equal to zero. The *y* coordinate of the end of the radius equals the sine of 270°, which is equal to negative one. The tangent of 270° equals sin 270° divided by cos 270°, which is undefined because division by zero is not possible. Therefore, the values of the three trigonometric functions of 270° are

$$\cos 270° = 0 \qquad \sin 270° = -1 \qquad \tan 270° \text{ is undefined}$$

example 29.1　　Draw figures as necessary to find 3 tan 180°.

solution　　We being by drawing a triangle that shows the angle *θ* approaching 180°.

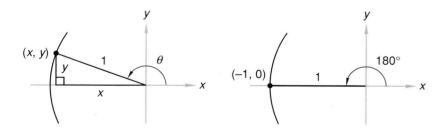

The coordinates of the end of the radius at 180° are (−1, 0). Thus

$$\cos 180° = -1, \quad \sin 180° = 0, \quad \text{and} \quad \tan 180° = \frac{0}{-1} = 0$$

Since tan 180° equals zero, **3 tan 180° also equals zero.**

example 29.2   Draw figures as necessary to find (a) 4 sin 270° and (b) 3 tan 270°.

solution   We begin by drawing a triangle that shows the angle θ approaching 270°.

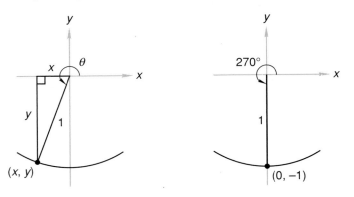

The coordinates of the end of the radius at 270° are (0, –1). Thus

$$\cos 270° = 0 \qquad \sin 270° = -1 \qquad \tan 270° \text{ is undefined}$$

(a) 4 sin 270° = 4(–1) = **–4**

(b) Since tan 270° is undefined, **3 tan 270° is undefined,** and the expression cannot be evaluated.

example 29.3   Evaluate: $\sin(-135°) + 3\sqrt{2}\cos 180°$

solution   In the figure below, we note that the related angle of –135° is 45°. We also draw the reference triangle.

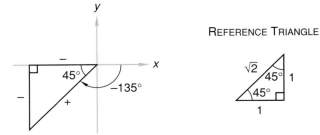

The sine of 45° is $1/\sqrt{2}$, and the sine is negative in the third quadrant. Therefore, we can write

$$\sin(-135°) = -\sin 45° = -\frac{1}{\sqrt{2}}$$

In the figure below, we draw a triangle that shows the angle θ approaching 180°.

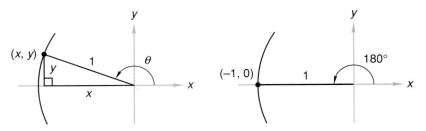

The coordinates of the end of the radius at 180° are (–1, 0). Thus

$$\cos 180° = -1$$

Therefore, we have

$$\sin(-135°) + 3\sqrt{2}\cos 180° = -\sin 45° + 3\sqrt{2}\cos 180° \qquad \text{substituted}$$

$$= -\frac{1}{\sqrt{2}} + 3\sqrt{2}(-1) \qquad \text{sum of functions}$$

$$= -\frac{\sqrt{2}}{2} - \frac{6\sqrt{2}}{2} \qquad \text{common denominator}$$

$$= -\frac{7\sqrt{2}}{2} \qquad \text{added}$$

problem set 29

1. Fox and Bob traveled g miles in x hours. Then they increased their speed by p miles per hour. How far could they go in ax hours at the new rate?

2. Dennis could build 1 henway in 4 days and the order was for 10 henways. Dennis worked for 1 day and then Loretta began to help. If they worked together for 13 days to finish the order, what was Loretta's rate in henways per day?

3. The women all pitched in to do the 10 jobs, and it took 20 women 6 days to do the work. The next time 10 more women volunteered their help. How long would it take the 30 women to complete 20 jobs?

4. Ten years ago Odessa was twice as old as Nat was then. Ten years from now, twice Odessa's age will be 10 less than thrice Nat's age then. How old will each person be 45 years from now?

5. There were 30 nickels, dimes, and pennies in all, and their value was $1.35. If there were twice as many pennies as dimes, how many coins of each kind were there?

6. Evaluate $\dfrac{8!}{2!2!}$ without using a calculator.

7. Evaluate $\dfrac{15!}{8!5!}$ without using a calculator.

8. Write $12 = 3^k$ in logarithmic form.

9. Write $\log_b 5 = 3$ in exponential form.

Solve:

10. $\log_b 49 = 2$ 　　　　　　11. $\log_5 \dfrac{1}{125} = c$ 　　　　　　12. $\log_{1/4} k = -3$

13. Sketch the graph of the function $f(x) = 3 \cdot 2^x$.

14. The equation of the function whose graph is shown is $f(x) = x^2$. We have placed dots at $(1, 1)$ and $(-1, 1)$ because the y coordinate has a value of 1 at these points and the graph of the reciprocal function will also pass through these points. The y axis will be a vertical asymptote for the graph of the reciprocal function because the graph of the original function intersects the x axis at $x = 0$. Make a sketch of the graph of the reciprocal function $g(x) = \dfrac{1}{x^2}$.

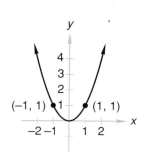

15. Determine if each graph represents the graph of a function. If so, determine whether the graph is the graph of a one-to-one function.

(a) 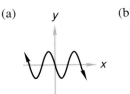   (b)   (c) 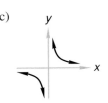   (d)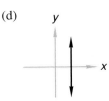

16. Find the domain of the function defined by each equation:

(a) $f(x) = \sqrt{4x - 5}$ (b) $g(x) = \dfrac{2}{\sqrt{4x + 12}}$ (c) $h(x) = \dfrac{\sqrt{5x + 10}}{2x^2 - x - 1}$

Draw the necessary reference triangles and evaluate. Do not use a calculator.

17. $2 \sin 30° \cos 30° - \sin 60° + \cos 90°$

18. $2 \sin 180° - 3 \cos 90° + \cos 270°$

19. If $f(\theta) = \cos \theta$ and $g(\theta) = \sin \theta$, find $3f(60°) + g(180°)$. Do not use a calculator.

20. If $r(\theta) = \dfrac{\sin \theta}{\cos \theta}$ and $s(\theta) = \cos \theta + \sin (\theta - 300°)$, find $\dfrac{\sqrt{3}}{2} r(180°) + s(30°)$. Do not use a calculator.

21. Let $f(x) = \log_4 x$ and $g(x) = 4^x$. Evaluate:

(a) $(f - g)(2)$ (b) $(fg)(2)$ (c) $(f \circ g)(2)$

22. Factor: (a) $4a^{3m+2} - 16a^{3m}$ (b) $8a^3b^3 - 27c^6d^6$

Simplify:

23. $\dfrac{3}{2c + \dfrac{t}{1 + \dfrac{4}{z}}}$ **24.** $\dfrac{\sqrt{5}\sqrt{-5}\sqrt{6}\sqrt{-6} + \sqrt{-25} - \sqrt{-16}}{-3i^2 - \sqrt{-9}i}$

25. Convert $5\hat{i} - 3\hat{j}$ to polar coordinates. (Write four forms for this point.)

26. If $f(x) = \sqrt{x} + x^2$, find $f(x + h)$.

27. Given: $\overline{AC}$ bisects $\angle BAD$

$\angle ABC \cong \angle ADC$

Write a two-column proof to prove:

$\overline{BC} \cong \overline{DC}$

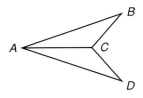

28. Find x and y.

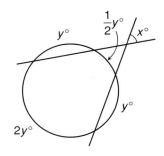

**CONCEPT REVIEW
PROBLEMS**

29. Let x and y be real numbers. If $x + y = 7$ and $x - y = 5$, compare: A. x B. y

30. Given $\triangle ABC$ where $m\angle A > m\angle B$, compare: A. AC B. BC

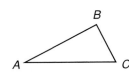

Note: Figure not drawn to scale

LESSON 30 *Addition of Vectors • Overlapping Triangles*

30.A
addition of vectors

A vector has both a magnitude and a direction. A vector can be designated by using either polar coordinates or rectangular coordinates. **Vectors in polar form can be added only if the angles are equal or if they differ by 180°. If the angles are not equal or opposite, the vectors must be rewritten in rectangular form. Then the horizontal components are added to find the horizontal component of the resultant, and the vertical components are added to find the vertical component of the resultant.**

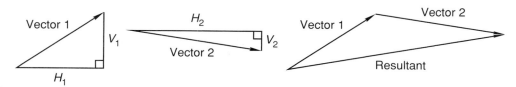

example 30.1   Find the resultant of $4\underline{/20°} + 7\underline{/-230°}$.

solution   A diagram always helps. We will use a calculator to find the components. One component is always $R \cos \theta$ and the other is $R \sin \theta$. Try to develop calculator techniques that will permit a quick and accurate breakdown of vectors.

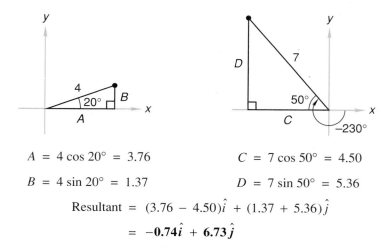

$$A = 4 \cos 20° = 3.76 \qquad\qquad C = 7 \cos 50° = 4.50$$

$$B = 4 \sin 20° = 1.37 \qquad\qquad D = 7 \sin 50° = 5.36$$

$$\text{Resultant} = (3.76 - 4.50)\hat{i} + (1.37 + 5.36)\hat{j}$$

$$= \mathbf{-0.74\hat{i} + 6.73\hat{j}}$$

The resultant can be written in polar form if desired.

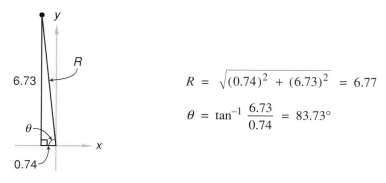

$$R = \sqrt{(0.74)^2 + (6.73)^2} = 6.77$$

$$\theta = \tan^{-1} \frac{6.73}{0.74} = 83.73°$$

The polar angle is measured from the positive x axis and is $180° - \theta$, which is

$$180° - 83.73° = 96.27°$$

The resultant also can be written as $\mathbf{6.77\underline{/96.27°}}$.

example 30.2   The two forces (where lb = pounds) $4\underline{/50°}$ lb and $-6\underline{/170°}$ lb are applied to an object. Find the equilibrant of the forces.

solution   If two forces are applied to a point, the resultant is the sum of the forces. The **equilibrant** is the single force that would be required to negate the applied forces. **The equilibrant has the same magnitude as the resultant but a direction that differs by 180°.** First we will find the resultant.

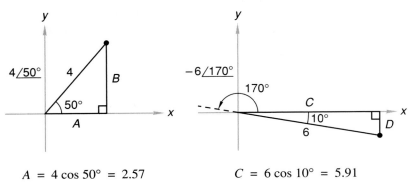

$$A = 4\cos 50° = 2.57 \qquad\qquad C = 6\cos 10° = 5.91$$

$$B = 4\sin 50° = 3.06 \qquad\qquad D = 6\sin 10° = 1.04$$

$$\text{Resultant} = (2.57 + 5.91)\hat{i} + (3.06 - 1.04)\hat{j}$$

$$= 8.48\hat{i} + 2.02\hat{j}$$

The resultant can be written in polar form if desired.

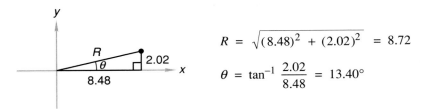

$$R = \sqrt{(8.48)^2 + (2.02)^2} = 8.72$$

$$\theta = \tan^{-1}\frac{2.02}{8.48} = 13.40°$$

Therefore, the polar form of the resultant is $8.72\underline{/13.40°}$. Thus, the resultant is $(8.48\hat{i} + 2.02\hat{j})$ lb, or $8.72\underline{/13.40°}$ lb. The equilibrant is $(-\mathbf{8.48}\hat{i} - \mathbf{2.02}\hat{j})$ **lb,** or $-\mathbf{8.72}\underline{/\mathbf{13.40°}}$ **lb.**

example 30.3   What vector force must be added to a force of $20\underline{/30°}$ newtons to obtain a resultant of $25\underline{/0°}$ newtons?

solution   First we find the horizontal and vertical components of $20\underline{/30°}$

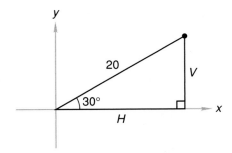

$$H = 20\cos 30° = 17.32 \qquad\qquad V = 20\sin 30° = 10$$

So we have $20\underline{/30°} = 17.32\hat{i} + 10\hat{j}$.

Now we wish to add a vector F to $17.32\hat{i} + 10\hat{j}$ to get a resultant of $25\hat{i} + 0\hat{j}$. This leads to the equation

$$17.32\hat{i} + 10\hat{j} + F = 25\hat{i} + 0\hat{j}$$

We solve this equation by adding $-17.32\hat{i} - 10\hat{j}$ to both sides, and we get

$$F = 25\hat{i} + 0\hat{j} - 17.32\hat{i} - 10\hat{j} \qquad \text{added to both sides}$$

$$F = 7.68\hat{i} - 10\hat{j} \qquad \text{simplified}$$

If we wish, we can write $7.68\hat{i} - 10\hat{j}$ in polar form.

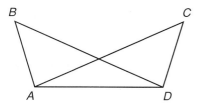

$$R = \sqrt{(7.68)^2 + (10)^2} = 12.61$$

$$\theta = \tan^{-1}\frac{10}{7.68} = 52.48°$$

Thus we have **$(7.68\hat{i} - 10\hat{j})$ newtons $= 12.61\underline{/-52.48°}$ newtons.**

30.B

overlapping triangles

We found one of the proofs of the Pythagorean theorem shown in Lesson 17 was simplified by redrawing the figure so that the triangles of interest were shown separately. We find that proofs concerning figures with overlapping triangles are often made easier if the figure is redrawn with the triangles shown separately. We demonstrate this procedure in the following examples.

example 30.4   Given: $\overline{AB} \cong \overline{DC}$
$\overline{BD} \cong \overline{CA}$

Write a two-column proof to prove:
$\triangle ABD \cong \triangle DCA$

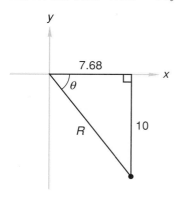

solution   The proof is made easier if we first break out the triangles in which we are interested and use tick marks to identify corresponding congruent parts. We note that $\overline{AD}$ is a side of both triangles.

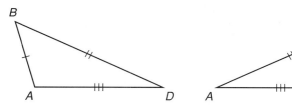

Now we will write a two-column proof to prove $\triangle ABD \cong \triangle DCA$.

STATEMENTS	REASONS
1. $\overline{AB} \cong \overline{DC}$	1. Given
2. $\overline{BD} \cong \overline{CA}$	2. Given
3. $\overline{AD} \cong \overline{AD}$	3. Reflexive axiom
4. $\triangle ABD \cong \triangle DCA$	4. *SSS* congruency postulate

example 30.5   Given: $\overline{PQ} \cong \overline{RQ}$
$\overline{QY} \cong \overline{QX}$

Write a two-column proof to prove:

$\triangle PQY \cong \triangle RQX$

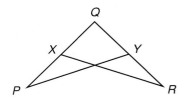

solution   The proof is made easier if we separate the triangles and use tick marks to identify corresponding congruent parts. We note that angle Q is an angle of both triangles.

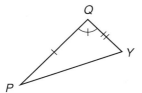 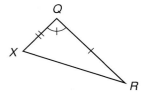

Now we will write a two-column proof to prove $\triangle PQY \cong \triangle RQX$.

STATEMENTS	REASONS
1. $\overline{PQ} \cong \overline{RQ}$	1. Given
2. $\overline{QY} \cong \overline{QX}$	2. Given
3. $\angle Q \cong \angle Q$	3. Reflexive axiom
4. $\triangle PQY \cong \triangle RQX$	4. *SAS* congruency postulate

example 30.6   Given: $\overline{XZ} \cong \overline{YZ}$
$\overline{XV} \perp \overline{YZ}$
$\overline{YU} \perp \overline{XZ}$

Write a two-column proof to prove:

$\overline{XV} \cong \overline{YU}$

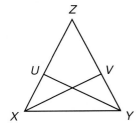

solution   There are four small triangles that have either $\overline{XV}$ or $\overline{YU}$ as sides; and since we are not sure which one to use, we will draw all four triangles separately and use tick marks to identify corresponding congruent parts.

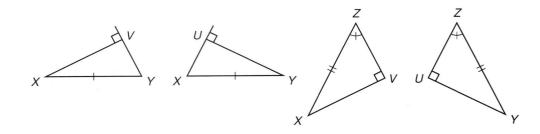

We do not have enough information to use the two triangles on the left. However, we can use the *AAAS* congruency postulate to prove that the two triangles on the right are congruent. Since $\overline{XV}$ and $\overline{YU}$ are corresponding parts of congruent triangles, they are congruent. Now we will write a two-column proof to prove $\overline{XV} \cong \overline{YU}$.

STATEMENTS	REASONS
1. $\angle Z \cong \angle Z$	1. Reflexive axiom
2. $\overline{XV} \perp \overline{YZ}$ and $\overline{YU} \perp \overline{XZ}$	2. Given
3. $\angle ZVX$ and $\angle ZUY$ are right angles.	3. Perpendicular lines intersect to form right angles.
4. $\angle ZVX \cong \angle ZUY$	4. All right angles are congruent.
5. $\angle VXZ \cong \angle UYZ$	5. If two angles in one triangle are congruent to two angles in a second triangle, then the third angles are congruent.
6. $\overline{XZ} \cong \overline{YZ}$	6. Given
7. $\triangle XZV \cong \triangle YZU$	7. *AAAS* congruency postulate
8. $\overline{XV} \cong \overline{YU}$	8. *CPCTC*

problem set 30

1. The number of boys varied inversely as the number of teachers and directly as the number of girls squared. When there were 200 boys, there were 10 girls and 20 teachers. How many boys were there when there were 2 teachers and 8 girls?

2. The sum of the digits of a two-digit counting number is 5. When the digits are reversed, the new number is 27 greater than the original number. What are the two numbers?

3. How many liters of a 90% alcohol solution should be mixed with how many liters of a 58% alcohol solution to make 20 liters of a 78% alcohol solution?

4. How many milliliters of a $13\frac{1}{2}$% iodine solution should be mixed with 370 ml of a 6% iodine solution to get a 10% iodine solution?

5. Find the equation of the line that passes through the point $(-2, 4)$ and is parallel to the line $3x + 2y - 4 = 0$.

6. Find the resultant of $7\underline{/-200°} + 5\underline{/276°}$. Write the answer in polar form.

7. Find the equilibrant of $-14\underline{/130°} + 7\underline{/-30°}$. Write the answer in polar form.

8. Given: $\angle PQR$ and $\angle SRQ$ are right angles
   $\overline{PQ} \cong \overline{SR}$

   Write a two-column proof to prove:
   $\triangle PQR \cong \triangle SRQ$

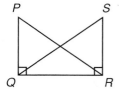

9. Given: $\overline{AB} \cong \overline{DC}$
   $\overline{AC} \cong \overline{DB}$

   Write a two-column proof to prove:
   $\triangle ABC \cong \triangle DCB$

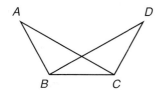

10. Evaluate $\dfrac{7!}{5!2!}$ without using a calculator.

Solve:

11. $\log_b \dfrac{1}{9} = 2$ 12. $\log_9 729 = c$ 13. $\log_{1/5} k = -2$

14. Sketch the graph of the function $f(x) = 0.7^x$.

15. The graph of the function $f(x) = |x|$ is shown. We have placed dots at $(1, 1)$ and $(-1, 1)$ because the y coordinate has a value of 1 at these points and the graph of the reciprocal function will also pass through these points. The y axis will be a vertical asymptote for the graph of the reciprocal function because the graph of the original function intersects the x axis at $x = 0$. Make a sketch of the graph of the reciprocal function $g(x) = \frac{1}{|x|}$.

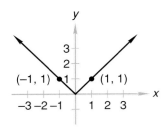

16. Find the domain of the function defined by each equation:

(a) $f(x) = \dfrac{x}{|x|}$ (b) $g(x) = \sqrt{\dfrac{1}{2x + 7}}$ (c) $h(x) = \dfrac{\sqrt{3x - 9}}{9x^2 - 6x + 1}$

17. Draw the necessary reference triangles and evaluate. Do not use a calculator.

(a) $3 \sin 30° \cos 180° - 2 \sin 180° \cos 60°$

(b) $2 \sin 60° + 2 \sin 30° + 2 \sin 45°$

18. If $r(\theta) = 1 + 5 \sin \theta$ and $s(\theta) = \cos \theta \sin \theta$, find $\frac{1}{2}r(270°) + s(45°)$. Do not use a calculator.

19. If $f(\theta) = 2 \sin \theta - 3 \cos \theta$ and $g(\theta) = \frac{\sin \theta}{\cos \theta}$, find $5f(60°) + 2g(45°)$. Do not use a calculator.

20. Let $f(x) = 2x - 1$ and $g(x) = \frac{1}{2}(x + 1)$. Evaluate:

(a) $(f \circ g)(x)$ (b) $(g \circ f)(x)$

21. Solve: $\begin{cases} x^2 - y^2 = 8 \\ 2x^2 + y^2 = 19 \end{cases}$

22. Simplify by factoring the numerator: $\dfrac{x^{2a} - y^{2b}}{x^a - y^b}$

23. Factor: $2x^{3N+1} + 6x^{5N+2}$

Simplify:

24. $\dfrac{k}{a + \dfrac{b}{x + \dfrac{c}{d}}}$ 25. $\dfrac{2i - 4}{3 + 6i}$

26. If $f(x) = x^2 - x$, find $f(x + h)$.

27. In the figure shown, quadrilateral $ABCD$ is inscribed in circle O. If $m\overset{\frown}{CD} = 70°$, find x and y.

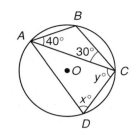

28. The base of a regular pyramid is a square whose perimeter is 128 cm. The volume of this regular pyramid is 4096 cm^3. Find the surface area of the pyramid.

CONCEPT REVIEW PROBLEMS

29. If x is a real number and $0 < x < 1$, compare: A. $x^{\frac{1}{2}}$ B. x

30. In the figure shown, O is the center of the circle with radius r.

Compare: A. Total length of the four darkened line segments

     B. $2r$

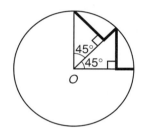

LESSON 31   *Symmetry • Reflections • Translations*

31.A

symmetry   Suppose a point can "see" itself in a mirror. In the diagram on the left, point A is on a line that is perpendicular to the mirror and is 5 units in front of the mirror.

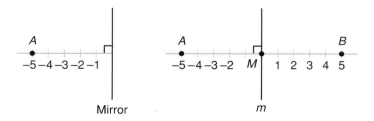

Point A will "see" itself 5 units on the other side of the mirror at point B, as we show on the right. Thus point B is a reflection of point A. If the mirror is very thin and is silvered on both sides, point B will "see" its reflection at point A. We say that points A and B are **reflections** or **mirror images** of each other in line m, which represents the mirror. We say that point M is the **point of symmetry**.

On the left below we show the graph of $y = x^2$. This graph is symmetric with respect to the y axis because every point on one side of this **axis of symmetry** is paired with another point on the other side that is the same perpendicular distance from the y axis. When x equals 2, y equals 2^2, or 4. When x equals -2, y equals $(-2)^2$, or 4. **If replacing x with $-x$ in any equation in x and y results in an equivalent equation, the graph of the equation will be symmetric about the y axis.** The equations $y = x^2$ and $y = (-x)^2$ are equivalent because the value of y will be the same for $+x$ and $-x$. This result will accrue for equations in which every x is raised to an even power. The graph of the equation $y = x^4 + 3x^2$ will be symmetric about the y axis. The equation $y = x^2 + x$ will not be symmetric about the y axis. For example, if x equals 2, the value of y will be 6. If x equals -2, the value of y will be 2.

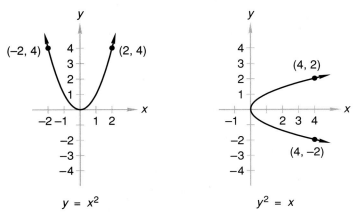

$$y = x^2 \qquad\qquad y^2 = x$$

The axis of symmetry for the equation $y^2 = x$ graphed on the right is the x axis. Every point below the x axis is paired with another point the same perpendicular distance above the x axis. When y equals 2, x equals 2^2, or 4. When y equals -2, x equals $(-2)^2$, or 4. **If replacing y with $-y$ in any equation in x and y results in an equivalent equation, the graph of the equation will be symmetric about the x axis.** The equations $y^2 = x$ and $(-y)^2 = x$ are equivalent equations because the value of x will be the same for $+y$ and $-y$.

In the examples above, the axes of symmetry were the y axis and the x axis. Any line can be an axis of symmetry. Another important axis of symmetry is the line $y = x$. In a later lesson we will discuss that the graph of any function and the graph of its inverse are symmetric about this line.

A graph of an equation in x and y can also be symmetric about a point. The graph of a circle is symmetric about the center of the circle. **If we draw a line through the center of a circle and any point on the circle, there exists another point on the circle the same distance from the center on the same line but in the opposite direction.** The circle shown on the left below has a radius of 10 units. Point B is 10 units away from the center of the circle and is paired with point A, which is on the same line 10 units in the other direction.

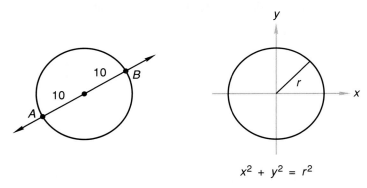

$$x^2 + y^2 = r^2$$

The circle shown on the right is centered at the origin. We note that the graph of the equation of the circle is symmetric about the x axis and about the y axis and is symmetric about the origin. **The graph of any equation in x and y that is symmetric about the x axis and also**

symmetric about the *y* axis will be symmetric about the origin. If replacing *x* with −*x* and replacing *y* with −*y* results in an equivalent equation, the graph of the equation will be symmetric about the origin. The equation $x^2 + y^2 = r^2$ is the equation of a circle centered at the origin, as we will discuss further in a later lesson. If we replace *x* with −*x* and *y* with −*y*, we get $(-x)^2 + (-y)^2 = r^2$, which is an equivalent equation.

31.B
reflections

The general form of the equation of a function is $y = f(x)$. Every value of *y* depends on the function we use and the number we use as a replacement for *x*. If we use $x^2 + 8x + 16$ as our function, we get the equation and the graph shown on the left.

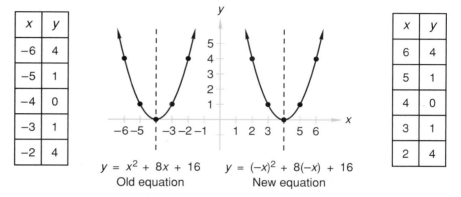

$$y = x^2 + 8x + 16$$
Old equation

$$y = (-x)^2 + 8(-x) + 16$$
New equation

On the right we replaced *x* with −*x* and the graph is a reflection of the original graph in the *y* axis. **If we leave *y* unchanged and replace *x* with −*x* in any equation in *x* and *y*, the graph of the new equation will be a reflection of the old equation in the *y* axis.** Since the old equation defines a function of *x*, we say that the new equation defines a function of −*x*.

OLD EQUATION $y = f(x)$

NEW EQUATION $y = f(-x)$

If we leave the *x* side of the original equation unchanged and change the sign of *y*, the graph of the new equation will be a reflection of the old equation in the *x* axis.

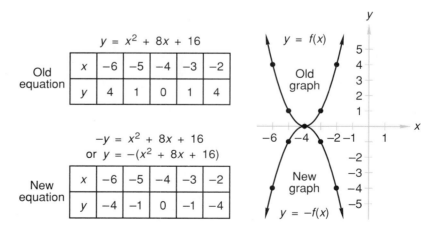

The two equations above the lower box are equivalent, so we see that the old graph was the graph of $y = f(x)$ and that the new graph is the graph of $y = -f(x)$. In the first example we showed that the graph of $y = f(-x)$ was a reflection of the graph of $y = f(x)$ in the *y* axis. In this example we showed that the graph of $y = -f(x)$ is a reflection of the graph of $y = f(x)$ in the *x* axis. **There is a great difference in the meanings of the notations**

$$y = f(-x) \quad \text{and} \quad y = -f(x)$$

31.C

translations   The equation of the parabola graphed in the center figure is $y = x^2 + 2$. The equation of the graph on the left is $y = (x + 8)^2 + 2$ and the equation of the graph on the right is $y = (x - 8)^2 + 2$.

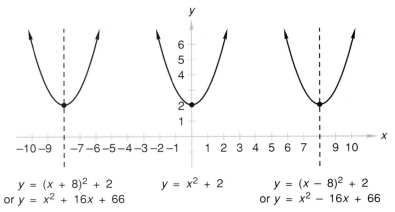

$$y = (x + 8)^2 + 2$$
or $y = x^2 + 16x + 66$

$$y = x^2 + 2$$

$$y = (x - 8)^2 + 2$$
or $y = x^2 - 16x + 66$

If we replace x with $x + 8$ in the equation $y = x^2 + 2$, the graph of the equation is shifted 8 units in the negative x direction. If we replace x with $x - 8$ in the equation $y = x^2 + 2$, the graph of the equation is shifted 8 units in the positive x direction. **In general, if h represents a positive number, replacing x with $x + h$ in any equation in x and y will shift the graph of the original equation h units in the negative x direction. If we replace x with $x - h$ in any equation in x and y, the graph of the original equation is shifted h units in the positive x direction.**

The equation of the parabola graphed in the center figure is $y = x^2 + 2$. The equation of the graph below is $y + 5 = x^2 + 2$ and the equation of the graph above is $y - 5 = x^2 + 2$.

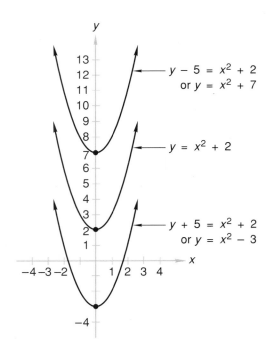

$y - 5 = x^2 + 2$
or $y = x^2 + 7$

$y = x^2 + 2$

$y + 5 = x^2 + 2$
or $y = x^2 - 3$

If we replace y with $y + 5$ in the equation $y = x^2 + 2$, the graph of the equation is shifted 5 units in the negative y direction. If we replace y with $y - 5$ in the equation $y = x^2 + 2$, the graph of the equation is shifted 5 units in the positive y direction. **In general, if k**

represents a positive number, replacing y with $y + k$ in any equation in x and y will shift the graph of the original equation k units in the negative y direction. If we replace y with $y - k$ in any equation in x and y, the graph of the original equation is shifted k units in the positive y direction.

example 31.1   The graph of the equation $y = \sqrt{x}$ is shown on the left below. The graph on the right is the same graph reflected in the y axis. Write the equation of the graph on the right.

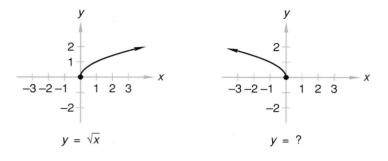

solution   We remember that if we leave y unchanged and replace x with $-x$ in any equation in x and y, the graph of the new equation will be a reflection of the old equation in the y axis. Therefore, we replace x with $-x$ in the equation $y = \sqrt{x}$ and we have $y = \sqrt{-x}$, which is the equation of the graph on the right.

example 31.2   The graph of the equation $y = \sqrt{x}$ is shown on the left below. The graph on the right is the same graph reflected in the x axis and translated 3 units to the left. Write the equation of the graph on the right.

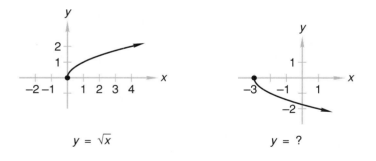

solution   If we replace y with $-y$, we reflect the original graph in the x axis, as we show on the left below.

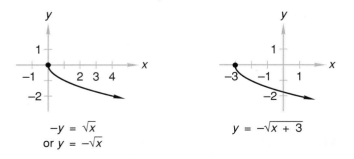

Now, in the diagram on the right, we replace x with $x + 3$ to shift the graph 3 units in the negative x direction. Thus, the equation of this graph is $y = -\sqrt{x + 3}$.

example 31.3   Graph the equation $y = 1/x$. Then write the equation of the graph that has the same shape but is translated 3 units to the left and 4 units down.

solution   On the left we show the graph of the original function $y = x$, which we will use to graph its reciprocal function $y = 1/x$. We place dots at y values of -1 and 1.

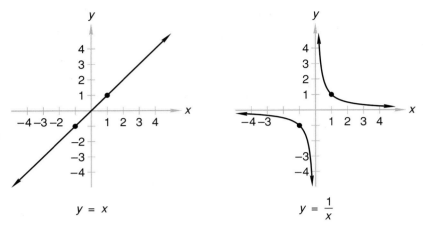

$$y = x \qquad\qquad\qquad y = \frac{1}{x}$$

The graph of the reciprocal function $y = 1/x$ is shown on the right. The graph of the original function crosses the x axis at $x = 0$, so the graph of the reciprocal function has a vertical asymptote at $x = 0$. The graph of the reciprocal function goes through the points where the original function had y values of -1 and 1. To shift this graph 3 units to the left, we replace x with $x + 3$. To shift the graph 4 units down, we replace y with $y + 4$.

$$y = \frac{1}{x} \qquad\qquad \text{reciprocal function}$$

$$y + 4 = \frac{1}{x + 3} \qquad\qquad \text{substituted}$$

$$y = \frac{1}{x + 3} - 4 \qquad\qquad \text{rearranged}$$

The graph of the equation $y = 1/x$ is symmetric about the origin. The graph of the equation $y = \frac{1}{x+3} - 4$ will have the same shape, but its point of symmetry will be $(-3, -4)$.

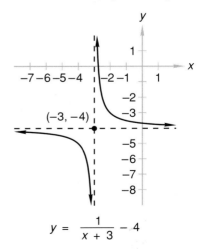

$$y = \frac{1}{x + 3} - 4$$

problem set 31

1. The Austrians marched m miles at p mph and arrived there one hour early. If they had started 5 miles further away, how fast should they have marched to get there on time?

2. Ten years ago, Davout's age was three times Lannes' age. Davout's current age is now only twice Lannes'. How old are they now?

3. Find four consecutive negative integers such that the product of the first and third is 25 greater than the product of -13 and the fourth.

4. The number of blues was two more than the total number of reds and greens. Three times the number of reds added to twice the number of greens was twice the number of blues. If there were 22 total, how many were there of each color?

5. Find the equation of the line passing through $(2, 7)$ and parallel to the line passing through $(1, 1)$ and $(3, -1)$.

6. Determine whether the graph of each equation is symmetric about the x axis, the y axis, and the origin:

(a)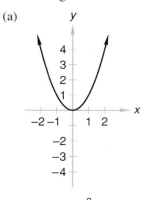

$$y = x^2$$

(b)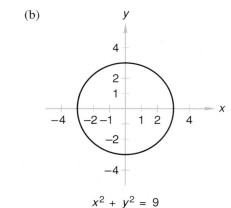

$$x^2 + y^2 = 9$$

7. The graph of the function $f(x) = x^2$ is shown on the left below. The graph on the right is the same graph translated two units to the right. Write the equation of the graph on the right.

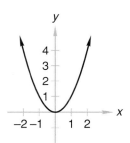 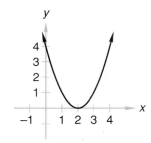

8. The graph of the function $f(x) = |x|$ is shown. Sketch the graph of the function $g(x) = |x - 1|$.

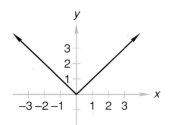

9. Find the resultant of $5\underline{/120°} + 7\underline{/-35°}$. Write the answer in polar form.

10. Given: $\angle Z$ is a right angle

$\qquad \angle ZXV \cong \angle ZYU$

$\qquad \overline{XV} \cong \overline{YU}$

Write a two-column proof to prove:

$\qquad \triangle XZV \cong \triangle YZU$

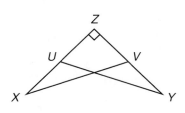

11. Evaluate $\dfrac{7!}{4!3!}$ without using a calculator.

Solve:

12. $\log_a 8 = 3$ **13.** $\log_3 \dfrac{1}{9} = b$ **14.** $\log_3 c = -3$

15. The graph of the function $f(x) = \sqrt{x}$ is shown. We have placed a dot at $(1, 1)$ because the y coordinate has a value of 1 at this point and the graph of the reciprocal function will also pass through this point. The y axis will be a vertical asymptote for the graph of the reciprocal function because the graph of the original function intersects the x axis at $x = 0$. Make a sketch of the graph of the reciprocal function $g(x) = \frac{1}{\sqrt{x}}$.

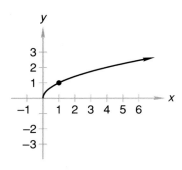

16. Determine if each graph represents the graph of a function. If so, determine whether the graph is the graph of a one-to-one function.

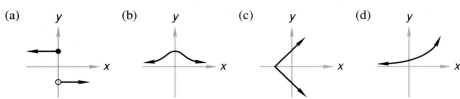

17. Find the domain of the function $f(x) = \dfrac{\sqrt{2x + 6}}{4x^2 - 4x - 3}$.

18. If $f(x) = \sin x$ and $g(x) = \tan x$, find $\sqrt{2}f(45°) - \sqrt{3}g(30°)$. Do not use a calculator.

19. If $r(x) = \tan x$ and $s(x) = \cos x$, find $3r(180°) + 2s(30°)$. Do not use a calculator.

20. Let $f(x) = \cos x$ and $g(x) = \sin x$. Evaluate:

    (a) $(f + g)(180°)$ (b) $(f - g)(180°)$ (c) $(fg)(180°)$

21. Solve: $\begin{cases} x^2 - y^2 = 9 \\ x + y = 9 \end{cases}$ **22.** Factor: $49a^{5n+2} - 7a^{6n+3}$

Simplify:

23. $\dfrac{\dfrac{3a}{b} - \dfrac{2b}{a}}{\dfrac{ab}{c} + \dfrac{c}{a}}$ **24.** $\dfrac{x^{-3}y + y^{-2}}{x^{-2}y}$

25. Divide $2x^3 + x - 1$ by $x + 1$ and check.

26. Solve for x: $y = 3\left(\dfrac{px + 2}{r + 5x}\right)$

27. Solve $4x^2 + 3x - 2 = 0$ by completing the square.

28. If $f(x) = 1 + x^2$, find $f(x + h) - f(x)$.

CONCEPT REVIEW
PROBLEMS

29. If x is a real number and $x < -1$, compare: A. x^3 B. x^2

30. Compare: A. $\sqrt[6]{9\left(\sqrt[3]{3}\right)}$ B. $\sqrt[3]{3\left(\sqrt[6]{9}\right)}$

LESSON 32 *Inverse Functions • Four Quadrant Signs • Inverse Trigonometric Functions*

32.A
inverse functions

We remember that the essence of the word *function* is *single-valued*. The equation

$$y = 2x - 1$$

defines a function because there is exactly one value of y for each value of x. We also remember that the values of x that we can use are those real numbers that will produce a single real number for y. In this equation we can replace x with any real number and get a real-number value for y, so the domain of this function is the set of all real numbers. Also, the range of this function is the set of all real numbers. The diagram below shows the y values that will accrue if we use 2, 4, and 6 for x. We remember that we can think of a function as a function machine which accepts x values at the input and produces the paired y values at the output, as we show here. If we let x equal 2, we get an image of 3. If we let x equal 4, the image is 7, and if we let x equal 6, the image is 11.

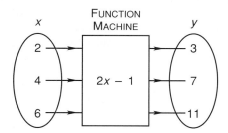

We note that there is only one x value for any value of y, so this function is a one-to-one function. **Every one-to-one function has an inverse function that will let us go the other way.** We want to begin with 3, 7, and 11 and get 2, 4, and 6, the numbers with which we began. To find the inverse function, we solve the original equation for x.

$$y = 2x - 1 \qquad \text{original equation}$$

$$2x = y + 1 \qquad \text{rearranged}$$

$$x = \frac{1}{2}y + \frac{1}{2} \qquad \text{divided by 2}$$

Now we could put the y values in the right-hand end of the backwards function machine and get the paired values of x out the left-hand end. But this makes us begin with y values.

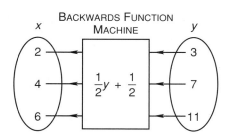

When we discuss functions, we simplify things by always beginning with x and finding the paired values of y. Thus we use the 3, 7, and 11 as inputs, change y to x and x to y, and get our inverse function machine.

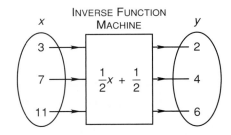

To find the inverse function of a one-to-one function defined by an algebraic equation in which y is a function of x, we will use the two-step procedure:

1. **Solve the original equation for x.**
2. **Replace every x with y and every y with x (that is, exchange x and y).**

The result in this example was

ORIGINAL FUNCTION	SOLVED FOR x	INVERSE FUNCTION (CHANGED x TO y AND y TO x)
$y = 2x - 1$	$x = \dfrac{1}{2}y + \dfrac{1}{2}$	$y = \dfrac{1}{2}x + \dfrac{1}{2}$

If we use x values of 2, 4, and 6, in that order, in the original function, we will get y values of 3, 7, and 11, in that order. If we use x values of 3, 7, and 11, in that order, in the inverse function, we will get y values of 2, 4, and 6, in that order. The two functions are inverses of each other. **Either function can be considered to be the original function and the other function is its inverse.** The graph of a function and its inverse are reflections of each other in the line $y = x$.

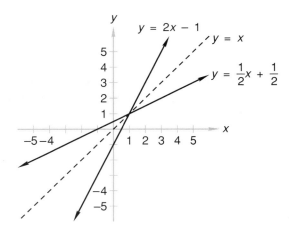

example 32.1   Find the inverse function of $y = 2x + 3$.

solution   We will use the two-step procedure to find the inverse function. First we solve the original equation for x.

$$y = 2x + 3 \qquad \text{original equation}$$

$$2x = y - 3 \qquad \text{rearranged}$$

$$x = \frac{1}{2}y - \frac{3}{2} \qquad \text{divided by 2}$$

Now we interchange x and y in the equation $x = \frac{1}{2}y - \frac{3}{2}$ and we have

$$y = \frac{1}{2}x - \frac{3}{2} \qquad \text{inverse function}$$

We note that the graph of the function $y = 2x + 3$ and the graph of its inverse function $y = \frac{1}{2}x - \frac{3}{2}$ are reflections of each other in the line $y = x$, as shown below.

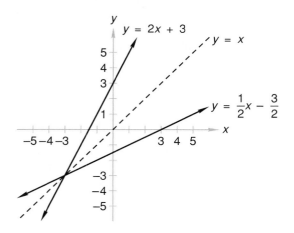

example 32.2   Find the inverse function of $y = -2x + 5$.

solution   We will use the two-step procedure again to find the inverse function. First we solve the original equation for x.

$$y = -2x + 5 \qquad \text{original equation}$$

$$2x = -y + 5 \qquad \text{rearranged}$$

$$x = -\frac{1}{2}y + \frac{5}{2} \qquad \text{divided by 2}$$

Now we interchange x and y in the equation $x = -\frac{1}{2}y + \frac{5}{2}$ and we have

$$y = -\frac{1}{2}x + \frac{5}{2} \qquad \text{inverse function}$$

We note that the graph of the function $y = -2x + 5$ and the graph of its inverse function $y = -\frac{1}{2}x + \frac{5}{2}$ are reflections of each other in the line $y = x$, as shown below.

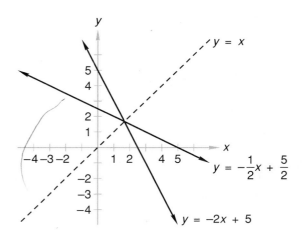

32.B

four quadrant signs

The signs of the trigonometric functions in the four quadrants can be determined by drawing triangles in each of the quadrants, as we show below. In the figures below, plus and minus signs on the horizontal sides of the triangles remind us that the x coordinate of every point to the right of the y axis is positive and the x coordinate of every point to the left of the y axis is negative. The plus and minus signs on the vertical sides of the triangles remind us that the y coordinate of every point above the x axis is positive and the y coordinate of every point below the x axis is negative. The hypotenuse is always positive. We can use these plus and minus signs to help us determine the signs of the cosine, sine, and tangent in the four quadrants. In the first quadrant all three trigonometric functions are positive. The sine is positive in the second quadrant and the other two are negative. The tangent is positive in the third quadrant and the other two are negative. The cosine is positive in the fourth quadrant and the other two are negative.

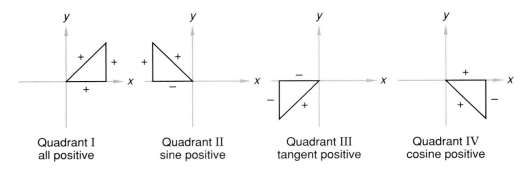

Quadrant I	Quadrant II	Quadrant III	Quadrant IV
all positive	sine positive	tangent positive	cosine positive

The first letters of each word in the sentence

All Students Take Calculus

can be used as a mnemonic to help us remember that **All** three trigonometric functions are positive in the first quadrant, the **S**ine is positive in the second quadrant, the **T**angent is positive in the third quadrant, and the **C**osine is positive in the fourth quadrant. We can use this mnemonic in the figure below to help us remember the quadrants in which each of the three trigonometric functions is positive. This mnemonic is helpful when we consider inverse trigonometric functions.

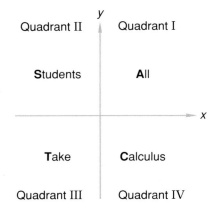

32.C

inverse trigonometric functions

We will now discuss the inverses of the cosine, sine, and tangent functions. In each case we will see that the inverse of any of these trigonometric functions is a relation but not a function since one value in the domain corresponds to more than one value in the range. In order for the inverse relation to be a function, the range of the inverse relation must be severely limited. The particular range of each inverse trigonometric function is accepted by convention.

the inverse cosine function

If we specify an angle, we can write the cosine of the angle at the same time because the cosine of each angle has only one value. Thus, the cosine is a function which we refer to as the *cosine function*. The domain for the cosine function is the set of all angles, since cos θ is defined for any angle θ. Also, the range of the cosine function is the set of all real numbers between −1 and +1 inclusive. We will discuss the graph of the cosine function in a later lesson. Consider domain values of 60° and 300°. We know that the cosine of 60° is $\frac{1}{2}$ and the cosine of 300° is $\frac{1}{2}$.

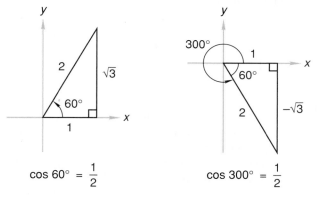

$$\cos 60° = \frac{1}{2} \qquad \cos 300° = \frac{1}{2}$$

We can turn things around and ask for the angle whose cosine is $\frac{1}{2}$ two different ways.

$$\text{arccos}\ \frac{1}{2} = ? \qquad \cos^{-1}\frac{1}{2} = ?$$

Both of these statements refer to the **inverse cosine** of $\frac{1}{2}$. The word *arccosine*, which we abbreviate *arccos*, and the notation cos⁻¹ both mean the same thing (that is, "the angle whose cosine is"). We note that the −1 in the notation cos⁻¹ is **not** an exponent. It is merely part of the conventional notation for the inverse cosine. There are many positive angles whose cosine is $\frac{1}{2}$, such as 60°, 420°, 780°, ..., 300°, 660°, 1020°, ..., etc. This is because 60° plus once around counterclockwise is 420°, and 60° plus twice around counterclockwise is 780°, etc., as shown.

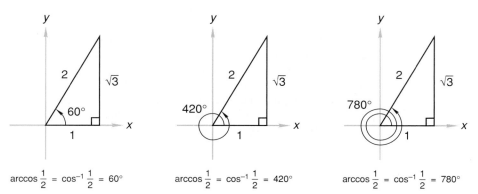

Also, 300° plus once around counterclockwise is 660°, and 300° plus twice around counterclockwise is 1020°, etc., as shown.

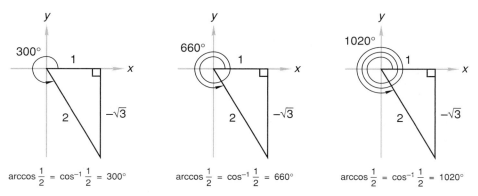

Therefore, we can see that there are multiple angles for every domain value of the inverse cosine, so the inverse cosine is a relation but not a function. In this book, we will use a lowercase "a" in arccos and a lowercase "c" in $\cos^{-1}$ to mean *inverse relation*. The domain for the arccos is the set of all real numbers between −1 and +1 inclusive, and the range is the set of all angles. We will discuss the graph of the inverse cosine relation in a later lesson. Thus, if we choose a domain value of $\frac{1}{2}$ for the inverse cosine relation, then we are considering multiple angles, and we write

$$\text{arccos} \; \frac{1}{2} = 60°, 420°, 780°, \ldots, 300°, 660°, 1020°, \ldots$$

$$\text{or} \qquad \cos^{-1} \frac{1}{2} = 60°, 420°, 780°, \ldots, 300°, 660°, 1020°, \ldots$$

When we ask for the inverse cosine of a number, we would like to have only one answer so that the inverse cosine will be a function. We can do this if we consider only angles between 0° and +180° inclusive, for every positive value of the cosine is associated with some first-quadrant angle, and every negative value of the cosine is associated with some second-quadrant angle.

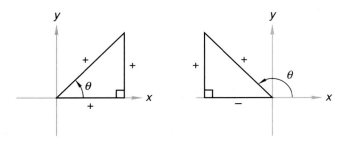

Therefore, when we restrict the range of the inverse cosine to the first and second quadrants, there is only one angle for every domain value of the inverse cosine, so the inverse cosine is a function. In this book, we will use a capital "A" in Arccos and a capital "C" in Cos^{-1} to mean *inverse function*. The domain for the Arccos is the set of all real numbers between −1 and +1 inclusive, and the range is the set of all angles between 0° and +180° inclusive. We will discuss the graph of the inverse cosine function in a later lesson. Thus, if we choose a domain value of $\frac{1}{2}$ for the inverse cosine function, then we are considering only the single angle between 0° and +180° inclusive, and we have

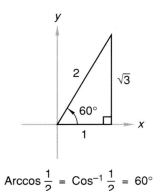

$$\text{Arccos} \; \frac{1}{2} = \text{Cos}^{-1} \frac{1}{2} = 60°$$

Similarly, if we choose a domain value of $-\frac{1}{2}$ for the inverse cosine function, then we are considering only the single angle between $0°$ and $+180°$ inclusive, and we have

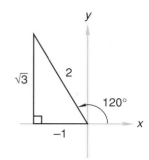

$$\text{Arccos}\left(-\frac{1}{2}\right) = \text{Cos}^{-1}\left(-\frac{1}{2}\right) = 120°$$

the inverse sine function   The sine of each angle has only one value, so the sine is a function which we refer to as the *sine function*. The domain for the sine function is the set of all angles, since $\sin \theta$ is defined for any angle θ. Also, the range of the sine function is the set of all real numbers between -1 and $+1$ inclusive. We will discuss the graph of the sine function in a later lesson. Consider domain values of $30°$ and $150°$. We know that the sine of $30°$ is $\frac{1}{2}$ and the sine of $150°$ is $\frac{1}{2}$.

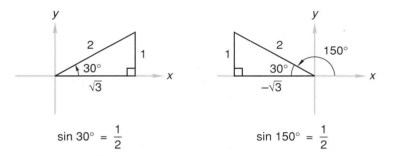

$$\sin 30° = \frac{1}{2} \qquad\qquad \sin 150° = \frac{1}{2}$$

We can turn things around and ask for the angle whose sine is $\frac{1}{2}$ two different ways.

$$\arcsin \frac{1}{2} = ? \qquad \sin^{-1} \frac{1}{2} = ?$$

Both of these statements refer to the **inverse sine** of $\frac{1}{2}$. The word *arcsine*, which we abbreviate *arcsin*, and the notation $\sin^{-1}$ both mean the same thing (that is, "the angle whose sine is"). We note that the -1 in the notation $\sin^{-1}$ is **not** an exponent. It is merely part of the conventional notation for the inverse sine. There are many positive angles whose sine is $\frac{1}{2}$, such as $30°$, $390°$, $750°$, …, $150°$, $510°$, $870°$, …, etc. This is because $30°$ plus once around counterclockwise is $390°$, and $30°$ plus twice around counterclockwise is $750°$, etc., as shown.

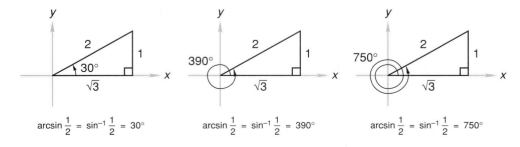

$$\arcsin \frac{1}{2} = \sin^{-1} \frac{1}{2} = 30° \qquad \arcsin \frac{1}{2} = \sin^{-1} \frac{1}{2} = 390° \qquad \arcsin \frac{1}{2} = \sin^{-1} \frac{1}{2} = 750°$$

Also, 150° plus once around counterclockwise is 510°, and 150° plus twice around counterclockwise is 870°, etc., as shown.

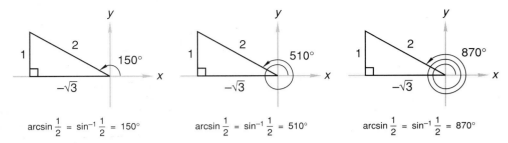

Therefore, we can see that there are multiple angles for every domain value of the inverse sine, so the inverse sine is a relation but not a function. In this book, we will use a lowercase "a" in arcsin and a lowercase "s" in sin^{-1} to mean *inverse relation*. The domain for the arcsin is the set of all real numbers between −1 and +1 inclusive, and the range is the set of all angles. We will discuss the graph of the inverse sine relation in a later lesson. Thus, if we choose a domain value of $\frac{1}{2}$ for the inverse sine relation, then we are considering multiple angles, and we write

$$\text{arcsin } \frac{1}{2} = 30°, 390°, 750°, ..., 150°, 510°, 870°, ...$$

or $\qquad \sin^{-1} \frac{1}{2} = 30°, 390°, 750°, ..., 150°, 510°, 870°, ...$

When we ask for the inverse sine of a number, we would like to have only one answer so that the inverse sine will be a function. We can do this if we consider only angles between −90° and +90° inclusive, for every positive value of the sine is associated with some first-quadrant angle, and every negative value of the sine is associated with some fourth-quadrant angle.

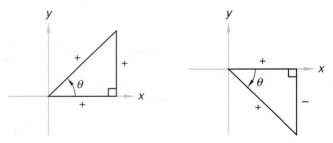

Therefore, when we restrict the range of the inverse sine to the first and fourth quadrants, there is only one angle for every domain value of the inverse sine, so the inverse sine is a function. In this book, we will use a capital "A" in Arcsin and a capital "S" in Sin^{-1} to mean *inverse function*. The domain for the Arcsin is the set of all real numbers between −1 and +1 inclusive, and the range is the set of all angles between −90° and +90° inclusive. We will discuss the graph of the inverse sine function in a later lesson. Thus, if we choose a domain value of $\frac{1}{2}$ for the inverse sine function, then we are considering only the single angle between −90° and +90° inclusive, and we have

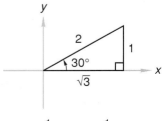

$$\text{Arcsin } \frac{1}{2} = \text{Sin}^{-1} \frac{1}{2} = 30°$$

Similarly, if we choose a domain value of $-\frac{1}{2}$ for the inverse sine function, then we are considering only the single angle between $-90°$ and $+90°$ inclusive, and we have

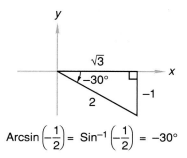

$$\text{Arcsin}\left(-\frac{1}{2}\right) = \text{Sin}^{-1}\left(-\frac{1}{2}\right) = -30°$$

the inverse tangent function

The tangent is a function which we refer to as the *tangent function*. We remember that $\tan\theta$ equals the ratio of $\sin\theta$ to $\cos\theta$.

$$\tan\theta = \frac{\sin\theta}{\cos\theta}$$

When the angle θ is equal to any odd integer multiple of $90°$ (that is, $\theta = \pm90°, \pm270°, \pm450°, \ldots$, etc.), $\cos\theta$ will be equal to zero and, consequently, $\tan\theta$ will be undefined because division by zero is not possible. Therefore, the domain for the tangent function is the set of all angles other than $\pm90°, \pm270°, \pm450°, \ldots$, etc. Also, the range of the tangent function is the set of all real numbers. We will discuss the graph of the tangent function in a later lesson. Consider domain values of $45°$ and $225°$. We know that the tangent of $45°$ is 1 and the tangent of $225°$ is 1.

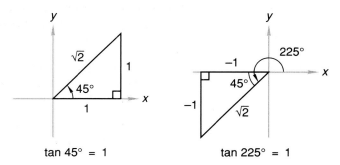

We can turn things around and ask for the angle whose tangent is 1 two different ways.

$$\text{arctan } 1 = ? \qquad \tan^{-1} 1 = ?$$

Both of these statements refer to the **inverse tangent** of 1. The word *arctangent*, which we abbreviate *arctan*, and the notation $\tan^{-1}$ both mean the same thing (that is, "the angle whose tangent is"). We note that the -1 in the notation $\tan^{-1}$ is **not** an exponent. It is merely part of the conventional notation for the inverse tangent. There are many positive angles whose tangent is 1, such as $45°, 405°, 765°, \ldots, 225°, 585°, 945°, \ldots$, etc. This is because $45°$ plus once around counterclockwise is $405°$, and $45°$ plus twice around counterclockwise is $765°$, etc., as shown.

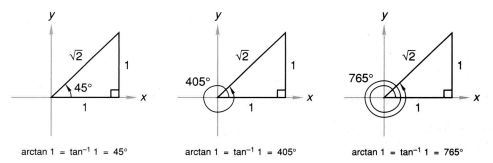

Also, 225° plus once around counterclockwise is 585°, and 225° plus twice around counterclockwise is 945°, etc., as shown.

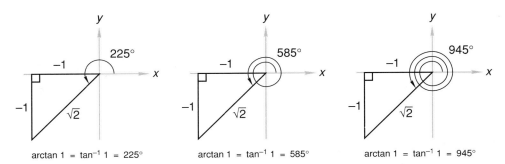

Therefore, we can see that there are multiple angles for every domain value of the inverse tangent, so the inverse tangent is a relation but not a function. In this book, we will use a lowercase "a" in arctan and a lowercase "t" in $\tan^{-1}$ to mean *inverse relation*. The domain for the arctan is the set of all real numbers, and the range is the set of all angles other than ±90°, ±270°, ±450°, ..., etc. We will discuss the graph of the inverse tangent relation in a later lesson. Thus, if we choose a domain value of 1 for the inverse tangent relation, then we are considering multiple angles, and we write

$$\arctan 1 \ = \ 45°, 405°, 765°, ..., 225°, 585°, 945°, ...$$

$$\text{or} \qquad \tan^{-1} 1 \ = \ 45°, 405°, 765°, ..., 225°, 585°, 945°, ...$$

When we ask for the inverse tangent of a number, we would like to have only one answer so that the inverse tangent will be a function. We can do this if we consider only angles between −90° and +90° exclusive, for every positive value of the tangent is associated with some first-quadrant angle, and every negative value of the tangent is associated with some fourth-quadrant angle.

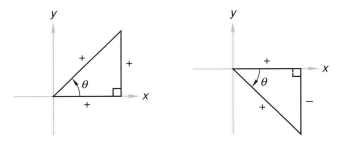

Therefore, when we restrict the range of the inverse tangent to the first and fourth quadrants, there is only one angle for every domain value of the inverse tangent, so the inverse tangent is a function. In this book, we will use a capital "A" in Arctan and a capital "T" in Tan^{-1} to mean *inverse function*. The domain for the Arctan is the set of all real numbers, and the range is the set of all angles between −90° and +90° exclusive. We will discuss the graph of the inverse tangent function in a later lesson. Thus, if we choose a domain value of 1 for the inverse tangent function, then we are considering only the single angle between −90° and +90° exclusive, and we have

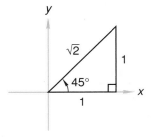

$$\text{Arctan } 1 \ = \ \text{Tan}^{-1} 1 \ = \ 45°$$

Similarly, if we choose a domain value of –1 for the inverse tangent function, then we are considering only the single angle between –90° and +90° exclusive, and we have

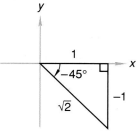

$$\text{Arctan } (-1) = \text{Tan}^{-1} (-1) = -45°$$

example 32.3   Evaluate: $\text{Arcsin } \dfrac{\sqrt{2}}{2}$

solution   We are asked to find the first-quadrant or fourth-quadrant angle whose sine is the positive number given. We begin by changing the form of the number by multiplying above and below by $\sqrt{2}$. We also draw the reference triangle.

$$\frac{\sqrt{2}}{2} \cdot \frac{\sqrt{2}}{\sqrt{2}} = \frac{2}{2\sqrt{2}} = \frac{1}{\sqrt{2}}$$

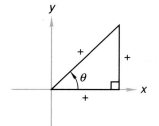   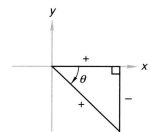   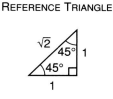

REFERENCE TRIANGLE

The sine of 45° is $1/\sqrt{2}$, and the sine is positive in the first and second quadrants. But the range of the Arcsin is defined to be the set of all angles between –90° and +90° inclusive. So the answer is in the first quadrant. Thus, we have

$$\text{Arcsin } \frac{\sqrt{2}}{2} = \mathbf{45°}$$

example 32.4   Evaluate: $\text{Arctan } \left(-\dfrac{1}{3}\sqrt{3}\right)$

solution   We are asked to find the first-quadrant or fourth-quadrant angle whose tangent is $-\sqrt{3}/3$. We begin by changing the form of the number to a more familiar form by multiplying above and below by $\sqrt{3}$. We also draw the reference triangle.

$$-\frac{1}{3}\sqrt{3} \cdot \frac{\sqrt{3}}{\sqrt{3}} = \frac{-3}{3\sqrt{3}} = -\frac{1}{\sqrt{3}}$$

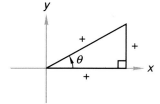   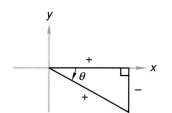   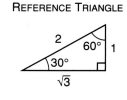

REFERENCE TRIANGLE

The tangent of 30° is $1/\sqrt{3}$, and the tangent is negative in the second and fourth quadrants. But the range of the Arctan is defined to be the set of all angles between –90° and +90° exclusive. So the answer is in the fourth quadrant. Thus, we have

$$\text{Arctan } \left(-\frac{1}{3}\sqrt{3}\right) = \mathbf{-30°}$$

example 32.5   Evaluate: $\cos\left[\text{Arctan}\left(-\dfrac{3}{5}\right)\right]$

solution   We are asked to find the cosine of the first-quadrant or fourth-quadrant angle whose tangent is −3/5. The tangents of fourth-quadrant angles are negative, so this angle is in the fourth quadrant. We now have enough information to draw the triangle.

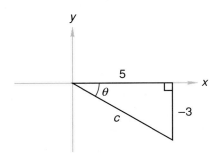

We can use the Pythagorean theorem to find c.

$$c^2 = 5^2 + (-3)^2 \qquad \text{Pythagorean theorem}$$

$$c^2 = 34 \qquad \text{simplified}$$

$$c = \sqrt{34} \qquad \text{solved}$$

Now we see that the cosine of θ is $5/\sqrt{34}$, so we can write

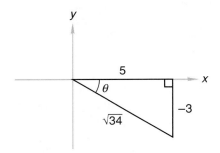

$$\cos\left[\text{Arctan}\left(-\dfrac{3}{5}\right)\right] = \dfrac{5}{\sqrt{34}}$$

$$= \dfrac{5\sqrt{34}}{34}$$

example 32.6   Evaluate: $\sin\left(\text{Arccos}\,\dfrac{2}{3}\right)$

solution   We are asked to find the sine of the first-quadrant or second-quadrant angle whose cosine is 2/3. Since the cosine is positive, our angle must be in the first quadrant. We now have enough information to draw the triangle.

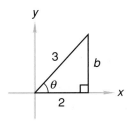

Now we use the Pythagorean theorem to find b.

$$3^2 = 2^2 + b^2 \qquad \text{Pythagorean theorem}$$

$$b^2 = 5 \qquad \text{simplified}$$

$$b = \sqrt{5} \qquad \text{solved}$$

This means that the sine of θ is $\sqrt{5}/3$, so we have

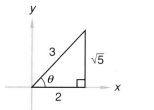

$$\sin\left(\text{Arccos } \frac{2}{3}\right) = \frac{\sqrt{5}}{3}$$

problem set 32

1. Charlie Mac traveled x miles at p miles per hour and arrived 2 hours late. If the distance were increased by 10 miles, how fast would he have to travel to arrive on time?

2. The taskmaster can perform the task in 40 minutes. The apprentice can perform the task in 1 hour. How long will it take both to perform 5 tasks working together if the taskmaster works 1 hour before the apprentice joins in?

3. Thirty workers could do 6 jobs in 4 days. How many days would it take 20 workers to do 4 jobs?

4. A builder needs many boards $5\frac{1}{2}$ feet long. Boards of this type are sold in multiples of 2 feet from 6 feet to 24 feet. The builder has a saw. For minimum waste, the boards should be ordered in what lengths?

5. Ophelia is four fifths as old as Laertes. Ten years ago, Ophelia was three fifths as old as Laertes was then. How old will each person be 20 years from now?

6. Find the inverse function of $y = 3x + 4$.

7. Evaluate. Do not use a calculator.

   (a) $\text{Arcsin } \dfrac{\sqrt{3}}{2}$ (b) $\sin\left[\text{Arccos}\left(-\dfrac{1}{2}\right)\right]$ (c) $\cos\left(\text{Arctan } \dfrac{4}{5}\right)$

8. Determine whether the graph of each equation is symmetric about the x axis, the y axis, and the origin:

   (a)   (b)

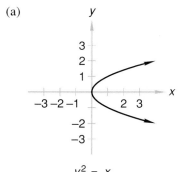

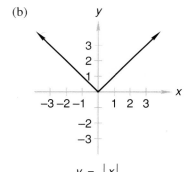

   $y^2 = x$ $y = |x|$

9. The graph of the function $f(x) = x^2$ is shown on the left below. The graph on the right is the same graph translated two units to the left. Write the equation of the graph on the right.

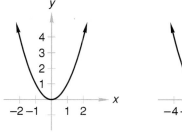

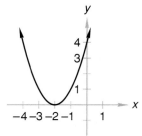

10. The graph of the function $f(x) = |x|$ is shown. Sketch the graph of the function $g(x) = |x + 1|$.

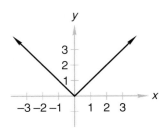

11. Find the equilibrant of $-2\underline{/120°} + 6\underline{/-130°}$. Write the answer in polar form.

12. Given: $\angle BCD \cong \angle EDC$
$\qquad\quad \angle CDB \cong \angle DCE$

Write a two-column proof to prove:
$\qquad\quad \overline{BD} \cong \overline{EC}$

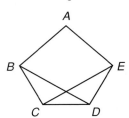

Solve:

13. $\log_a 36 = 2$ **14.** $\log_3 \dfrac{1}{81} = n$ **15.** $\log_{1/3} p = -4$

16. Sketch the graph of the function $f(x) = 2 + \left(\dfrac{1}{4}\right)^x$.

17. The equation of the function whose graph is shown is $f(x) = |x - 2|$. We have placed dots at $(1, 1)$ and $(3, 1)$ because the y coordinate has a value of 1 at these points and the graph of the reciprocal function will also pass through these points. The graph of the reciprocal function will have a vertical asymptote where the graph of the original function intersects the x axis. Make a sketch of the graph of the reciprocal function $g(x) = \frac{1}{|x - 2|}$.

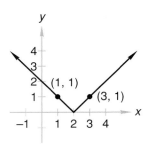

18. Find the domain of the function $f(x) = \dfrac{\sqrt{x}}{|x - 1|}$.

19. Evaluate $-2\sqrt{2} \tan 45° - \sin 45° \cos 45°$ without using a calculator.

20. If $f(x) = \sin x$ and $g(x) = \cos x$, find $2f(-30°) + g(90°)$. Do not use a calculator.

21. Let $f(x) = \log_{1/2} x$ and $g(x) = \left(\frac{1}{2}\right)^x$. Evaluate:
     (a) $(f + g)(4)$ (b) $(f/g)(4)$ (c) $(f \circ g)(4)$

22. Solve: $\begin{cases} y^2 - x^2 = 4 \\ y + 3x = 2 \end{cases}$

Simplify:

23. $\dfrac{2}{6b + \dfrac{3t}{1 + \dfrac{3}{x}}}$ **24.** $\dfrac{\sqrt{3}\sqrt{-3}\sqrt{2}\sqrt{-2} - \sqrt{-16} + \sqrt{-5}\sqrt{5}}{1 - \sqrt{-16}i^2}$

25. $\dfrac{z^{3+b}\left(\sqrt{z^3}\right)^{b+1}}{z^b}$

26. Solve $6x^2 - 2x + 1 = 0$ by completing the square.

27. If $f(x) = x^2 + 3x + 1$, find $f(x + h) - f(x)$.

28. The base of a right circular cone has a
       perimeter of 30π m. The volume of
       this right circular cone is 1500π m^3.
       Find the surface area of the cone.

CONCEPT REVIEW   **29.** Let a and b be real numbers. If $ab = 10$, compare: A. a B. b
PROBLEMS

                    30. If x is a real number and $x > 1$, compare: A. x B. $\dfrac{1}{x}$

LESSON 33 *Quadrilaterals • Properties of Parallelograms •
Types of Parallelograms • Conditions for
Parallelograms • Trapezoids*

33.A
quadrilaterals

A **quadrilateral** is defined simply as a four-sided polygon. There are three distinct categories
of quadrilaterals:

(a) Quadrilaterals none of whose sides are parallel
(b) Quadrilaterals exactly two of whose sides are parallel
(c) Quadrilaterals where both pairs of opposite sides are parallel

We do not have a special name for the class of quadrilaterals described in (a); however,
quadrilaterals described in (b) are called **trapezoids** and quadrilaterals described in (c) are
called **parallelograms.** We show an example from each category of quadrilaterals below. We
remember that we use arrowheads to indicate that sides are parallel.

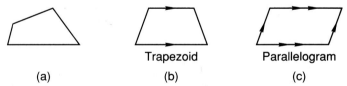

| | Trapezoid | Parallelogram |
| (a) | (b) | (c) |

We are most interested in those quadrilaterals described in (b) and (c), the category of
trapezoids and parallelograms, respectively. We shall examine these types of quadrilaterals in
the succeeding sections.

33.B
properties of parallelograms

We define a parallelogram to be a quadrilateral that has two pairs of parallel sides. From this
definition, we can prove a myriad of properties about parallelograms. We list some of these
properties:

┌───┐
│   PROPERTIES OF PARALLELOGRAMS   │
│   │
│   1. Both pairs of opposite sides are congruent. │
│   2. Both pairs of opposite angles are congruent.│
│   3. The diagonals bisect each other.   │
│   4. Any pair of consecutive angles is supplementary. │
└───┘

All of the properties listed above can be proven. As an example, we shall prove the first
property listed.

example 33.1   Prove that the opposite sides of a parallelogram are congruent.

Given: Parallelogram *ABCD*

Write a two-column proof to prove:

$$\overline{BC} \cong \overline{AD}$$
$$\overline{AB} \cong \overline{DC}$$

solution   We begin by redrawing parallelogram *ABCD* with diagonal *AC* to form two triangles, △*ABC* and △*CDA*. We also label the four angles 1, 2, 3, and 4, as shown.

Now we will write a two-column proof to prove $\overline{BC} \cong \overline{AD}$ and $\overline{AB} \cong \overline{DC}$.

Statements	Reasons
1. *ABCD* is a parallelogram with diagonal *AC*.	1. Given
2. $\overline{BC} \parallel \overline{AD}$ and $\overline{AB} \parallel \overline{DC}$	2. Definition of parallelogram
3. $\angle 1 \cong \angle 2$ and $\angle 3 \cong \angle 4$	3. If two parallel lines are cut by a transversal, then each pair of alternate interior angles is congruent.
4. $\angle B \cong \angle D$	4. If two angles in one triangle are congruent to two angles in a second triangle, then the third angles are congruent.
5. $\overline{AC} \cong \overline{AC}$	5. Reflexive axiom
6. △*ABC* ≅ △*CDA*	6. *AAAS* congruency postulate
7. $\overline{BC} \cong \overline{AD}$ and $\overline{AB} \cong \overline{DC}$	7. *CPCTC*

33.C

types of parallelograms

The set of parallelograms contains two subsets: the set of rectangles and the set of rhombuses. We define a **rectangle** to be a parallelogram one of whose angles is a right angle and a **rhombus** to be a parallelogram in which two consecutive sides are congruent.

Some readers may be puzzled why we did not define a rectangle to be a parallelogram all of whose angles are right angles since a rectangle, as we have learned in elementary school, possesses such a property. The reason is that a definition must be constructed to give the absolute minimum requirements and conditions. The fact that all the angles of a rectangle are right can be proven using the definition of a rectangle.

The two subsets of parallelograms we have identified are not distinct, as their intersection is the set of squares. A **square** is defined to be a parallelogram that is both a rhombus and a rectangle. The diagram below shows what we have discussed in this section.

SET OF PARALLELOGRAMS

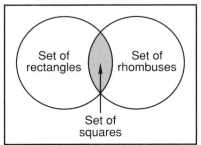

Each of these types of parallelograms has special properties not possessed by all parallelograms. However, all of these types of parallelograms listed have the properties of parallelograms listed in Section B of this lesson since they are all parallelograms.

We list below the properties of rectangles, rhombuses, and squares. All of these properties can be proven. However, in this book we will only state the properties.

PROPERTIES OF RECTANGLES

1. All properties of a parallelogram apply.
2. All angles are right angles.
3. The diagonals are congruent.

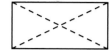

PROPERTIES OF RHOMBUSES

1. All properties of a parallelogram apply.
2. All sides are congruent.
3. The diagonals are perpendicular.
4. The diagonals bisect the angles whose vertices they connect.
5. The intersecting diagonals divide the rhombus into four congruent right triangles.

PROPERTIES OF SQUARES

1. All the properties of a rectangle apply.
2. All the properties of a rhombus apply.
3. The diagonals form four congruent isosceles right triangles.

To help become familiar with the properties of these types of parallelograms, we work the following examples.

example 33.2   The diagonals of a certain parallelogram are of unequal length. Which of the following could the parallelogram be?

A. Rectangle   B. Square   C. Rhombus

solution   A property of rectangles is that their diagonals are of equal length, so the parallelogram cannot be a rectangle. A square is a special type of rectangle, so the parallelogram described cannot be a square. The only choice left is **C.** We can confirm this choice is correct by sketching a rhombus whose diagonals are clearly of different length.

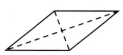

example 33.3 The diagonals of a certain parallelogram are not perpendicular. Which of the following could the parallelogram be?

A. Rectangle   B. Rhombus   C. Square

solution The diagonals of a rhombus are perpendicular, according to the table of properties of a rhombus, so the parallelogram described cannot be a rhombus. Squares are a special type of rhombus and so the parallelogram described cannot be a square. We are left with choice **A.** A quick sketch will confirm that we can find a rectangle whose diagonals are clearly not perpendicular.

33.D

conditions for parallelograms

In the previous sections, we have described the properties of parallelograms in general as well as the properties of particular types of parallelograms. For example, we can prove that a parallelogram has both pairs of opposite sides congruent from the definition of a parallelogram and from other postulates and previously proven theorems. An interesting question is whether a quadrilateral both of whose pairs of opposite sides are congruent is a parallelogram. In other words, is the converse of this property of a parallelogram true? The answer is yes.

We summarize the conditions for a quadrilateral to be a parallelogram.

CONDITIONS FOR A QUADRILATERAL TO BE A PARALLELOGRAM

A quadrilateral is a parallelogram if any of the following conditions are satisfied:

1. Both pairs of opposite sides of the quadrilateral are congruent.
2. One pair of opposite sides of the quadrilateral is congruent and parallel.
3. The diagonals of the quadrilateral bisect each other.
4. Both pairs of opposite angles of the quadrilateral are congruent.

We see that the converse of all the properties of a parallelogram are true. Each of the statements made in the box can be proven though we will not do so here. In general, the converse of a statement is not true. However, in the case of the properties of a parallelogram, they are.

We list below, without proof, conditions for a quadrilateral to be a rhombus and for a quadrilateral to be a rectangle.

CONDITIONS FOR A QUADRILATERAL TO BE A RECTANGLE

If a quadrilateral is a parallelogram and its diagonals are congruent, then the parallelogram is a rectangle.

If all four angles of a quadrilateral are right angles, then the quadrilateral is a rectangle.

CONDITIONS FOR A QUADRILATERAL TO BE A RHOMBUS

If a quadrilateral is a parallelogram and either of its diagonals bisects the angles whose vertices it connects, then the parallelogram is a rhombus.

If the diagonals of a quadrilateral are perpendicular bisectors of each other, then the quadrilateral is a rhombus.

We give an example to provide practice with these conditions.

example 33.4 Given a parallelogram whose diagonals are congruent, which of the following must be true?

  A. All four sides have the same length.

  B. The diagonals are perpendicular bisectors of each other.

  C. All four angles of the parallelogram are right angles.

solution First, we note that a parallelogram whose diagonals are congruent must be a rectangle. Also, all rectangles have diagonals that are congruent. Rectangles can have different dimensions; not all four sides have to be the same length, so A does not necessarily have to be true. If B is true, then the quadrilateral must be a rhombus since B is a condition that guarantees a quadrilateral is a rhombus. However, a rhombus does not have to have diagonals that are congruent, as the following drawing shows.

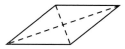

The only choice left is **C,** which must be true as all rectangles satisfy condition C.

33.E
trapezoids

We remember that a **parallelogram** is a four-sided polygon in which **both pairs** of opposite sides are parallel. A **trapezoid** is a four-sided polygon which has **exactly one pair** of parallel sides. Both the figures shown below appear to be trapezoids since in the left-hand figure $\overline{BC}$ appears parallel to $\overline{AD}$ and in the right-hand figure $\overline{FG}$ appears parallel to $\overline{EH}$.

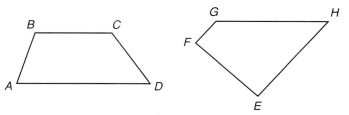

The parallel sides are called the **bases** of the trapezoid, and the nonparallel sides are called the **legs** of the trapezoid. The line segment that connects the midpoints of the legs of a trapezoid is called the **median** of the trapezoid. In the left-hand figure below, line segment *XY* is the median. **An altitude of a trapezoid** is any line segment that connects the bases and is perpendicular to one of the bases. Any number of altitudes can be drawn for a particular trapezoid, and they all have equal lengths. In the center trapezoid below, we show one altitude, and in the trapezoid on the right, we show three altitudes.

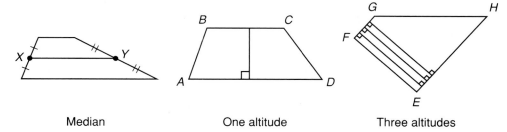

| Median | One altitude | Three altitudes |

We list some properties of trapezoids. The first property listed is proven in example 33.5. The second property is provided without proof.

PROPERTIES OF A TRAPEZOID

1. The area of a trapezoid equals one half the product of the length of the altitude and the sum of the lengths of its bases.
2. The median of a trapezoid is parallel to its bases, and its length is one half the sum of the lengths of its bases.

A special type of trapezoid is an isosceles trapezoid. An **isosceles trapezoid** is a trapezoid whose non-parallel sides have equal length. An isosceles trapezoid is so named because *iso* is a Greek prefix that means "equal" and *skelos* is the Greek word for "leg." In the figure below showing an isosceles trapezoid, $\angle A$ and $\angle D$ are called the **lower base angles** and $\angle B$ and $\angle C$ are called the **upper base angles.**

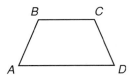

We list the properties of an isosceles trapezoid below.

PROPERTIES OF AN ISOSCELES TRAPEZOID

1. The lower base angles are congruent.
2. The upper base angles are congruent.
3. The diagonals are congruent.
4. Any lower base angle is supplementary to any upper base angle.

Now we will provide some examples about trapezoids.

example 33.5 Derive a general formula for the area of a trapezoid using the figure shown.

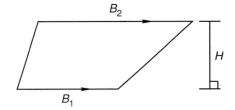

solution The arrows indicate that B_1 is parallel to B_2. The altitude is H. We begin by drawing a diagonal in the left-hand figure below. This divides the trapezoid into the two triangles which we show separately in the center and on the right.

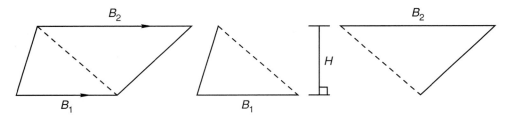

The area of the center triangle is $\frac{1}{2}B_1 H$, and the area of the right-hand triangle is $\frac{1}{2}B_2 H$. The total area is the sum of these areas, so

$$\text{Area} = \frac{1}{2}B_1 H + \frac{1}{2}B_2 H \quad \rightarrow \quad \textbf{Area} = \frac{1}{2}H(B_1 + B_2)$$

example 33.6 The figure shown is a trapezoid whose area is 175 cm^2. Find x. Dimensions are in centimeters.

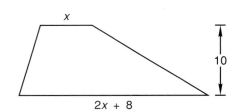

solution   There are two methods for solving this problem. We will show both methods. First we will divide the figure into two triangles and add the areas.

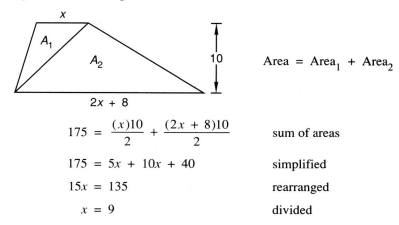

$$175 = \frac{(x)10}{2} + \frac{(2x + 8)10}{2} \qquad \text{sum of areas}$$

$$175 = 5x + 10x + 40 \qquad \text{simplified}$$

$$15x = 135 \qquad \text{rearranged}$$

$$x = 9 \qquad \text{divided}$$

For the second method, we will apply the formula for the area of a trapezoid to work the problem.

$$\text{Area} = \frac{1}{2}H(B_1 + B_2)$$

The area is 175 cm^2, the height is 10 cm, and the lengths of the bases are x and $2x + 8$, respectively. Now we substitute and solve.

$$175 = \frac{1}{2}(10)(x + 2x + 8) \qquad \text{substituted}$$

$$175 = 5(3x + 8) \qquad \text{simplified}$$

$$35 = 3x + 8 \qquad \text{divided}$$

$$3x = 27 \qquad \text{rearranged}$$

$$x = 9 \qquad \text{divided}$$

We see that both approaches yield the same answer. Since dimensions are in centimeters, $x = \mathbf{9\ cm}$.

example 33.7   In the figure shown, $\overline{EF}$ is the median of trapezoid *ABCD*. Find x.

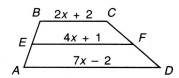

solution   We remember that the length of the median of a trapezoid equals one half the sum of the lengths of the bases. This problem requires that we use that fact since we are given each of these lengths in terms of x.

$$\text{Length of the median} = \frac{1}{2}\left(\text{base}_1 + \text{base}_2\right)$$

Now we substitute and solve.

$$4x + 1 = \frac{1}{2}(2x + 2 + 7x - 2) \qquad \text{substituted}$$

$$4x + 1 = \frac{9x}{2} \qquad \text{simplified}$$

$$8x + 2 = 9x \qquad \text{multiplied both sides by 2}$$

$$x = \mathbf{2} \qquad \text{solved}$$

problem set 33

1. Clanton looked in his pocket and found eleven coins worth $1.55. He noticed that twice the number of quarters was one more than the sum of the nickels and dimes. If all coins were either nickels, dimes, or quarters, how many of each did he have?

2. Fifteen gourmands could put away 45 pounds of food in 2 hours. How many pounds of food could 25 gourmands put away in 10 hours?

3. Find the equation of the line which passes through $(2, 2)$ and is perpendicular to the line $4x - 2y + 3 = 0$.

4. All four sides of a certain quadrilateral have the same length. Which of the following must the quadrilateral be?

   A. Rectangle   B. Square   C. Rhombus   D. Trapezoid

5. Find the area of this trapezoid.

   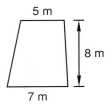

   5 m

   8 m

   7 m

6. Find the inverse function of $y = -4x + 7$.

7. Evaluate. Do not use a calculator.

   (a) $\text{Arctan } \sqrt{3}$ (b) $\sin\left(\text{Arccos } \dfrac{1}{2}\right)$ (c) $\tan\left[\text{Arcsin}\left(-\dfrac{3}{5}\right)\right]$

8. Determine whether the graph of each equation is symmetric about the x axis, the y axis, and the origin:

   (a)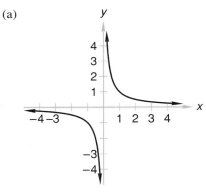

   $yx = 1$

   (b)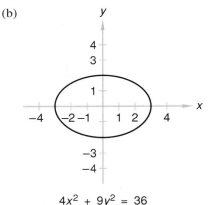

   $4x^2 + 9y^2 = 36$

9. The graph of the function $f(x) = |x|$ is shown on the left below. The graph on the right is the same graph translated three units up. Write the equation of the graph on the right.

   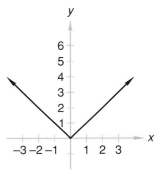

   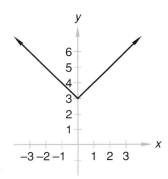

10. The graph of the function $f(x) = x^2$ is shown. Sketch the graph of the function $g(x) = x^2 + 2$.

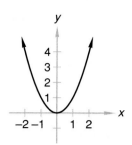

11. Find the resultant of $-2\underline{/140°} + 3\underline{/-120°}$. Write the answer in polar form.

12. Evaluate $\dfrac{12!}{4!8!}$ without using a calculator.

Solve:

13. $\log_d 216 = 3$

14. $\log_2 \dfrac{1}{64} = m$

15. $\log_{1/2} p = -3$

16. Sketch the graph of the function $f(x) = \left(\dfrac{1}{3}\right)^x - 2$.

17. The equation of the function whose graph is shown is $f(x) = (x - 2)^2$. We have placed dots at $(1, 1)$ and $(3, 1)$ because the y coordinate has a value of 1 at these points and the graph of the reciprocal function will also pass through these points. The graph of the reciprocal function will have a vertical asymptote where the graph of the original function intersects the x axis. Make a sketch of the graph of the reciprocal function $g(x) = \frac{1}{(x-2)^2}$.

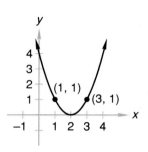

18. Find the domain of the function $f(x) = \dfrac{\sqrt{x^2 - 4}}{|2x - 6|}$.

19. If $f(x) = \cos x$ and $g(x) = \tan x$, find $f(-180°) - \sqrt{2}\, g(-60°)$. Do not use a calculator.

20. Let $f(x) = 3^{x+1}$ and $g(x) = \log_3 x$. Evaluate:

(a) $(f - g)(3)$ (b) $(f \circ g)(3)$ (c) $(g \circ f)(3)$

21. Solve: $\begin{cases} x^2 - y^2 = 4 \\ x + y = 2 \end{cases}$

22. Factor: $4a^{x+2} - 12a^{x+3}$

Simplify:

23. $\dfrac{\dfrac{a^2b}{c^2d^3} - \dfrac{fg^2}{cd^3}}{\dfrac{x^2y}{c^2d} + \dfrac{z^3}{cd^3}}$

24. $\dfrac{\sqrt{2}\sqrt{-3}\sqrt{-2}\sqrt{3} - \sqrt{-16}}{-4i^3 - \sqrt{-16i}}$

25. Solve for g: $h = \dfrac{2d}{f}\left(\dfrac{4s}{g} + \dfrac{2s}{r}\right)$

26. If $f(x) = (x + 1)^2$, find $f(x + h) - f(x)$.

27. Given: $PQRS$ is a rectangle

T is the midpoint of $\overline{QR}$

Write a two-column proof to prove:

$\triangle PQT \cong \triangle SRT$

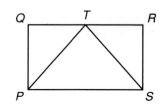

28. Find x, y, and z.

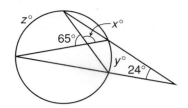

29. Let a and b be real numbers. If $\dfrac{a}{b} = 4$, compare: A. a B. $4b$

30. In $\triangle ABC$, $AB = BC$.

Compare: A. x B. y

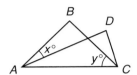

LESSON 34   *Summation Notation • Linear Regression • Decomposing Functions*

34.A

summation notation

Summation notation provides a convenient way to designate the sum of a specified list of numbers. The notation consists of the Greek capital letter **sigma,** which is written Σ, with the **variable of summation,** as shown below. Sigma is used because it is the Greek version of S, the first letter of the word *sum*. The least value of the variable of summation is the integer below the sigma, and the greatest value is the integer above the sigma. The expression to the right of the sigma is called a **typical element** of the list.

$$\text{Greatest value} \longrightarrow 4$$
$$\sum_{y=1} y^2 \longleftarrow \text{Typical element}$$
$$\text{Variable of summation} \longrightarrow y=1$$
$$\text{Least value} \longrightarrow$$

Here the variable of summation is y, and the typical element is y^2. **The variable of summation will take on the values of the integers above and below Σ and all integers between these numbers. Then we add all these values.** Thus, the notation above has a value of 30.

$$\sum_{y=1}^{4} y^2 = (1)^2 + (2)^2 + (3)^2 + (4)^2 = 30$$

Any letter can be used for the variable of summation, but the ones that seem to be used most often are x, y, i, j, and k. **Any symbol other than the variable of summation is assumed to be a constant.** Thus, the summation of ik, where i is the variable of summation, is shown here.

$$\sum_{i=2}^{5} ik = 2k + 3k + 4k + 5k = 14k$$

In this example, the letter k is not the variable of summation and is treated as a constant.

example 34.1   Evaluate: $\displaystyle\sum_{i=1}^{5} 3$

solution   In this problem the variable of summation is i, but i is not a factor of the typical element. To make our overall summation notation consistent, we assume an i whose exponent is zero, as

$$\sum_{i=1}^{5} 3i^0$$

Now we can write our sum as

$$\sum_{i=1}^{5} 3i^0 = 3(1)^0 + 3(2)^0 + 3(3)^0 + 3(4)^0 + 3(5)^0 = 15$$

In practice, it is not customary to record the i factors. Instead, we let the least and greatest value of the variable of summation tell us that there are five terms in the sum. So we write simply

$$\sum_{i=1}^{5} 3 = 3 + 3 + 3 + 3 + 3 = \mathbf{15}$$

The necessity for this definition of the sum of a constant will become evident in an elementary statistics course.

example 34.2   Evaluate: $\displaystyle\sum_{x=1}^{4} 2x$

solution   The variable of summation is x. If we let x take on the values 1 to 4, we get

$$\sum_{x=1}^{4} 2x = 2(1) + 2(2) + 2(3) + 2(4) = \mathbf{20}$$

example 34.3   Evaluate: $\displaystyle\sum_{j=0}^{3} \frac{2^j}{j+1}$

solution   The variable of summation is j and it will take on the values 0, 1, 2, and 3, in turn.

$$\sum_{j=0}^{3} \frac{2^j}{j+1} = \frac{2^0}{0+1} + \frac{2^1}{1+1} + \frac{2^2}{2+1} + \frac{2^3}{3+1} = 1 + 1 + \frac{4}{3} + 2 = \mathbf{\frac{16}{3}}$$

example 34.4   Evaluate: $\displaystyle\sum_{y=4}^{6} \frac{1}{y}$

solution   The variable of summation is y. There are three terms as y takes on the values 4, 5, and 6.

$$\sum_{y=4}^{6} \frac{1}{y} = \frac{1}{4} + \frac{1}{5} + \frac{1}{6} = \mathbf{\frac{37}{60}}$$

34.B
linear regression

Graphs of experimental data often indicate a linear relationship between two variables. This is the reason that we spend so much time studying the equation of a straight line. We remember that all lines in mathematics are straight lines, and the use of the word *straight* is a redundancy but is not harmful. In chemistry and physics the theory often indicates a linear relationship and can be confirmed by experiment. But the physical world does not follow the theory exactly and the data points are scattered. In the social sciences, experiments are often conducted to see if the data indicate a linear relationship. Sometimes it does, but sometimes the scatter of the data points is so great that we are less confident that a linear relationship really exists.

example 34.5   The data points from an experiment involving carbon (C) and salt (S) are given here.

Carbon in grams	48	70	90	108	130	132	158
Salt in grams	0.8	2.5	5.4	7.8	6.3	9.4	8.4

The data are graphed in the figure on the left. In the figure on the right, we estimate the position of the line indicated by these data points. Write the equation of the line which will give salt as a function of carbon ($S = mC + b$).

solution   **This is a graph of experimental data and there is no way to determine the exact equation of the line indicated by the data points. If the experiment were repeated, different data points would result and a slightly different equation might be indicated.** Remember that experimental results only allow us to approximate the linear relationship indicated.

To find the slope of the line, we disregard the data points and use any two coordinates on the line. We note that the line appears to have endpoint coordinates of (40, 0) and (160, 10) and note that the line has a positive slope. We begin by using the rise over the run to determine the magnitude of the slope.

$$\text{Slope} = \frac{\text{rise}}{\text{run}} = \frac{10 - 0}{160 - 40} = 0.083$$

Now we write the equation using 0.083 as the slope.

$$S = 0.083C + b$$

Now we can use the coordinates of any point on the line for C and S so we can find b. We decide to use (40, 0).

$$S = 0.083C + b \qquad \text{equation}$$
$$0 = 0.083(40) + b \qquad \text{substituted}$$
$$b = -3.32 \qquad \text{solved}$$

Now we can use –3.32 for b to write the equation.

$$\mathbf{S = 0.083C - 3.32}$$

34.C
decomposing functions

In Lesson 24, we saw how to compose two functions. We have seen that when two functions are composed, the result is one function as the answer. Now we will work backwards and try to express a function as the composition of two functions. There are a multitude of answers that we can get, as we show in the first example. In the second example, we shall decompose a function into the composition of two functions where one of the two functions is given. Unlike the first example, in the second example there is only one answer.

example 34.6   Find two functions f and g such that $(f \circ g)(x) = \sqrt{x^2 + 1}$.

solution   There are a multitude of pairs of functions f and g such that $(f \circ g)(x) = \sqrt{x^2 + 1}$. One such pair is

$$f(x) = x \qquad g(x) = \sqrt{x^2 + 1}$$

This is considered a **trivial** decomposition because the function f simply takes every input and maps it to itself. Since f, as defined, composed with any function equals that function, we call the function f the **identity function.**

Another pair of functions f and g such that $(f \circ g)(x) = \sqrt{x^2 + 1}$ is

$$f(x) = \sqrt{x} \qquad g(x) = x^2 + 1$$

This is an obvious **non-trivial** decomposition.

A not-so-obvious decomposition is

$$f(x) = \sqrt{x + 1} \qquad g(x) = x^2$$

In the problem sets, when we are asked to decompose a function, we shall provide the most obvious non-trivial decomposition as the answer. We note that there may be other, less obvious answers that we have not given.

example 34.7   Find f where $g(x) = x^2 + 1$ and $(f \circ g)(x) = \dfrac{1}{x^2 + 1}$.

solution   There is only one answer for f.

$$f(x) = \frac{1}{x}$$

We check our answer by computing $(f \circ g)$.

$$(f \circ g)(x) = f\big(g(x)\big) = f\big(x^2 + 1\big) = \frac{1}{x^2 + 1}$$

**problem set
34**

1. The bunch trotted m miles at z miles per hour and arrived 3 hours late. How fast should they have trotted to have arrived on time?

2. Ashley, Trevor, and Trey were average-speed eaters, and they consumed a total of 20 concoctions in 5 hours. Then they were joined by Izzy and T.J., who were also average-speed eaters. How long would it take all 5 of them to consume 14 concoctions?

3. Shelby Don could do 2 jobs in 5 hours. Breanna was slower, as it took her 6 hours to do just 1 job. They had 10 jobs to do and both started to work at the same time. How long did it take them to do the 10 jobs?

4. Repairman A received 12 service calls one day, and repairman B received 16 service calls the same day. A charges three halves as much as B charges for each service call. If B earned \$120 that day, how much did A earn that day?

Evaluate:

5. $\displaystyle\sum_{i=1}^{7} 3$

6. $\displaystyle\sum_{j=0}^{2} \frac{3^j}{1 - 2j}$

7. The data points in the table below came from an experiment that involved molybdenum (Mo) and zirconium (Zr). Note that in the graph the horizontal and vertical scales are different. The position of the line that best fits the data points is estimated. Write the equation that expresses molybdenum as a function of zirconium (Mo = mZr + b).

Zr	60	60	73	75	84	85	98	106	115
Mo	860	960	770	870	800	700	600	615	550

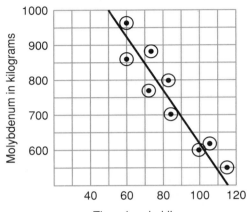

8. The data points in the table below came from an experiment that involved hydrogen (H) and carbon (C). Note that in the graph the horizontal and vertical scales are different. The position of the line that best fits the data points is estimated. Write the equation that expresses hydrogen as a function of carbon (H = mC + b).

C	99.5	101.5	101.5	102.6	102.6	103.7	104.6	106.0
H	82.5	87.5	92.0	102.0	111.5	115.5	117.0	127.5

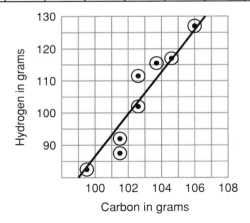

9. Find two functions f and g such that $(f \circ g)(x) = \sqrt{x + 1}$.

10. All four angles of a certain quadrilateral are right angles. Which of the following must the quadrilateral be?

A. Rectangle   B. Square   C. Rhombus   D. Trapezoid

11. In the figure shown, $\overline{EF}$ is the median of trapezoid *ABCD*. Find *x*.

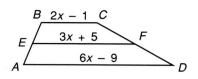

12. Find the inverse function of $y = \dfrac{1}{3}x - \dfrac{5}{6}$.

13. Evaluate. Do not use a calculator.

(a) Arctan 1

(b) $\tan\left(\text{Arcsin } \dfrac{3}{5}\right)$

(c) $\cos\left[\text{Arctan }(-3)\right]$

14. Determine whether the graph of each equation is symmetric about the *x* axis, the *y* axis, and the origin:

(a)

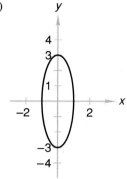

$9x^2 + y^2 = 9$

(b)

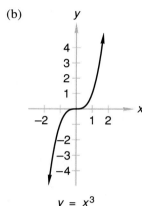

$y = x^3$

15. The graph of the function $f(x) = |x|$ is shown on the left below. The graph on the right is the same graph translated three units down. Write the equation of the graph on the right.

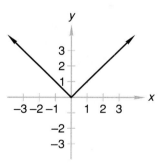

16. The graph of the function $f(x) = x^2$ is shown. Sketch the graph of the function $g(x) = x^2 - 2$.

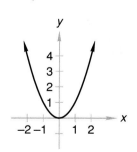

17. Find the equilibrant of $-3\underline{/-135°} - 2\underline{/-140°}$. Write the answer in polar form.

Solve:

18. $\log_b 125 = 3$

19. $\log_2 \dfrac{1}{32} = a$

20. $\log_{1/5} p = -2$

21. Determine if each graph represents the graph of a function. If so, determine whether the graph is the graph of a one-to-one function.

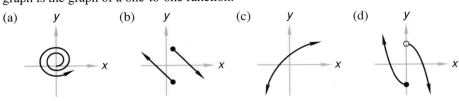

(a)   (b)   (c)   (d)

22. Find the domain of the function $f(x) = \dfrac{\sqrt{x + 11}}{x^2 - x - 12}$.

23. Evaluate $3 \cos 60° \sin 30° - \sin 90° \cos 90°$ without using a calculator.

24. Let $f(x) = 3x - 5$ and $g(x) = 2x^2$. Evaluate:

   (a) $(fg)(2)$ (b) $(gf)(2)$ (c) $(f \circ g)(2)$

25. Solve: $\begin{cases} x^2 + y^2 = 10 \\ 2x^2 - y^2 = 17 \end{cases}$

26. If $f(x) = \dfrac{1}{x}$, find $f(x + h) - f(x)$.

27. Given: $\overline{BD}$ bisects $\overline{AC}$

         $\overline{AB} \cong \overline{CB}$

Write a two-column proof to prove:

         $\angle A \cong \angle C$

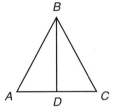

28. The base of a regular pyramid is a regular hexagon whose perimeter is 36 cm. The volume of this regular pyramid is 216 cm^3. Find the surface area of the pyramid. Dimensions are in centimeters.

CONCEPT REVIEW PROBLEMS

29. Let x and y be real numbers with $x \neq 0$. Compare: A. $\dfrac{x + 2y}{x}$ B. $1 + \dfrac{2y}{x}$

30. Let a, b, c, and d be positive real numbers. If $\dfrac{a}{b} = \dfrac{c}{d}$, compare: A. $\dfrac{a + c}{b + d}$ B. $\dfrac{a}{b}$

LESSON 35   *Change in Coordinates • The Name of a Number • The Distance Formula*

35.A
change in coordinates

When we use coordinate geometry, we usually do not encounter expressions such as

$$x_2 - y_1$$

in which the letters are different. Instead, we encounter expressions that contain the same letters but different subscripts.

$$x_1 - x_2 \qquad x_2 - x_1 \qquad y_1 - y_2 \qquad y_2 - y_1$$

These expressions usually represent changes in the values of coordinates as we move from one point to another point. The first entry is the final coordinate, and the last entry is the initial coordinate. If we move one way, the change will be positive. If we move the other way, the change will be negative.

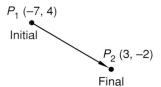

If we move from $P_1\,(x_1, y_1)$ to $P_2\,(x_2, y_2)$, the x coordinate changes from -7 to 3, a change of $+10$; and the y coordinate changes from 4 to -2, a change of -6. **We use a two-step procedure for determining the change in coordinates. The first step is to write down the final coordinate. Then from this number, we subtract the initial coordinate.**

$$x_2 - x_1 = 3 - (-7) = +10 \qquad \text{and} \qquad y_2 - y_1 = -2 - (4) = -6$$

Now, if we turn around and move from P_2 to P_1, we move the same distance but in the opposite direction.

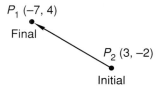

This time the arrowhead is at P_1, so the coordinates of P_1 come first when we write the expressions for the changes in the coordinates.

$$x_1 - x_2 = -7 - (3) = -10 \qquad \text{and} \qquad y_1 - y_2 = 4 - (-2) = +6$$

Thus, notations such as $x_2 - x_1$ and $y_1 - y_2$ represent distances and directions. We can think of each of these notations as representing a **directed distance.**

example 35.1   Given the points $P_1\,(-3, 2)$ and $P_2\,(-4, -5)$, what do we represent by (a) $-3 - (-4)$ and by (b) $-5 - (2)$?

solution   We remember that the first number is the final coordinate.

$$\text{(a) } -3 - (-4) \qquad\qquad \text{(b) } -5 - (2)$$

Thus, expression (a) represents **the change in the x coordinate when we move from P_2 to P_1,** and expression (b) represents **the change in the y coordinate when we move from P_1 to P_2.**

example 35.2 If the coordinates of P_1 are $(-3, -2)$ and the coordinates of P_2 are $(-4, -5)$, what do we represent by (a) $-4 - (-3)$ and by (b) $-2 - (-5)$?

solution When we find the change in coordinates, the first number is always the final coordinate. Thus

$$\text{(a) } -4 - (-3)$$

represents **the change in the x coordinate when we move from P_1 to P_2,** and

$$\text{(b) } -2 - (-5)$$

represents **the change in the y coordinate when we move from P_2 to P_1.**

35.B
the name of a number

We will use the symbol ΔC (read "delta C") to mean **change in coordinate** and will remember that the final coordinate is written first and the initial coordinate is written last. We will use the symbols C_F and C_I to mean the final coordinate and the initial coordinate, respectively.

$$\Delta C = C_F - C_I$$

The coordinate of a point on the number line gives us the distance and direction from the origin to the graph of the number. We can use arrows that represent changes in coordinates to help us solve some interesting problems about the way numbers are arranged in order.

example 35.3 What is the number whose graph is $\frac{2}{3}$ of the way from 3 to -7?

solution We always draw a diagram to help prevent mistakes.

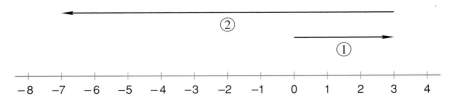

The name of a number gives its directed distance from the origin to the graph of the number on the number line. To find this distance, we will add the directed length of arrow ① to $\frac{2}{3}$ of the directed length of arrow ②.

$$\begin{aligned}
\text{Number} &= 3 + \frac{2}{3}(\Delta C) && \text{equation} \\[2mm]
&= 3 + \frac{2}{3}(C_F - C_I) && \text{substituted in } \Delta C = C_F - C_I \\[2mm]
&= 3 + \frac{2}{3}\left[-7 - (3)\right] && \text{substituted} \\[2mm]
&= 3 + \frac{2}{3}(-10) && \text{simplified} \\[2mm]
&= \frac{9}{3} - \frac{20}{3} && \text{simplified} \\[2mm]
&= -\frac{11}{3} && \text{solved}
\end{aligned}$$

We note that the numbers could be added easily after 3 had been rewritten as $\frac{9}{3}$.

example 35.4   What is the number that is $\frac{3}{7}$ of the way from -4 to $+9$?

solution   We always draw a diagram when possible.

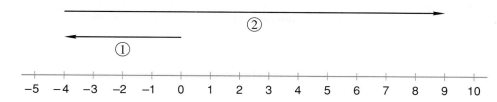

We will add the directed length of arrow ① to $\frac{3}{7}$ of the directed length of arrow ②.

$$\text{Number} = -4 + \frac{3}{7}(\Delta C) \qquad\qquad \text{equation}$$

$$= -4 + \frac{3}{7}(C_F - C_I) \qquad \text{substituted in } \Delta C = C_F - C_I$$

$$= -4 + \frac{3}{7}\left[9 - (-4)\right] \qquad \text{substituted}$$

$$= -4 + \frac{3}{7}(13) \qquad\qquad \text{simplified}$$

$$= -\frac{28}{7} + \frac{39}{7} \qquad\qquad \text{simplified}$$

$$= \frac{11}{7} \qquad\qquad\qquad \text{solved}$$

We note that the numbers could be added easily after -4 had been rewritten as $-\frac{28}{7}$.

example 35.5   Find the number that is $\frac{5}{11}$ of the way from $3\frac{1}{8}$ to $-3\frac{5}{8}$.

solution   A diagram helps prevent errors.

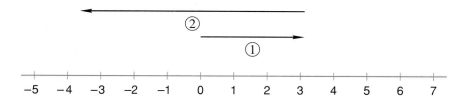

We will add the directed length of arrow ① to $\frac{5}{11}$ of the directed length of arrow ②.

$$\text{Number} = 3\frac{1}{8} + \frac{5}{11}(\Delta C) \qquad\qquad \text{equation}$$

$$= 3\frac{1}{8} + \frac{5}{11}(C_F - C_I) \qquad \text{substituted in } \Delta C = C_F - C_I$$

$$= 3\frac{1}{8} + \frac{5}{11}\left(-3\frac{5}{8} - 3\frac{1}{8}\right) \qquad \text{substituted}$$

$$= 3\frac{1}{8} + \frac{5}{11}\left(-\frac{54}{8}\right) \qquad\qquad \text{simplified}$$

$$= \frac{275}{88} - \frac{270}{88} \qquad\qquad \text{simplified}$$

$$= \frac{5}{88} \qquad\qquad\qquad \text{solved}$$

35.C

the distance formula

We remember that in any right triangle, the square of the length of the hypotenuse equals the sum of the squares of the lengths of the other two sides, and that the statement of this fact is called the **Pythagorean theorem.** The distance between the two points in the figure is the hypotenuse of the right triangle. The length of the horizontal side is the absolute value of the difference of the x coordinates of the two points, and the length of the vertical side is the absolute value of the difference of the y coordinates of the two points.

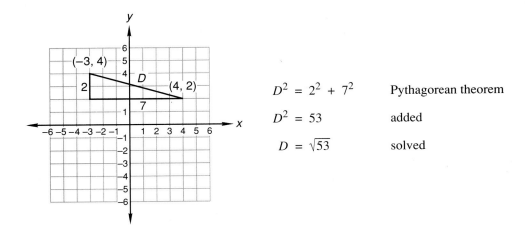

$$D^2 = 2^2 + 7^2 \qquad \text{Pythagorean theorem}$$

$$D^2 = 53 \qquad \text{added}$$

$$D = \sqrt{53} \qquad \text{solved}$$

The distance formula is a general algebraic statement of the Pythagorean theorem. If we take the square root of both sides, the resulting expression gives the distance between the two points and is called the **distance formula.**

PYTHAGOREAN THEOREM   DISTANCE FORMULA

$$D^2 = \left(\text{side}_1\right)^2 + \left(\text{side}_2\right)^2 \quad \longrightarrow \quad D = \sqrt{\left(\text{side}_1\right)^2 + \left(\text{side}_2\right)^2}$$

The formula does not say whether the x side or the y side comes first, and since the coordinates may appear in any order, there are many correct forms of the distance formula. Four of these correct forms are:

$$D = \sqrt{\left(x_1 - x_2\right)^2 + \left(y_2 - y_1\right)^2} \qquad D = \sqrt{\left(y_1 - y_2\right)^2 + \left(x_2 - x_1\right)^2}$$

$$D = \sqrt{\left(y_1 - y_2\right)^2 + \left(x_1 - x_2\right)^2} \qquad D = \sqrt{\left(x_2 - x_1\right)^2 + \left(y_2 - y_1\right)^2}$$

All that is necessary is that the sum of the squares of the differences in the x coordinates and the differences in the y coordinates appear in some order. We will use the distance formula extensively in our study of conic sections.

example 35.6 Use the distance formula to write an expression that gives the distance between the point $(4, -2)$ and some other point (x, y).

solution The distance between the points is the square root of the sum of the squares of the lengths of the sides of the triangle. The length of one side is the magnitude of the difference of the x coordinates of the two points. The length of the other side is the magnitude of the difference of the y coordinates of the two points.

$$D = \sqrt{(4 - x)^2 + (-2 - y)^2} \qquad D = \sqrt{(x - 4)^2 + (y + 2)^2}$$

Although the entries appear to be different, when the terms in the radicands are squared, the radicands will be identical. Thus, both these expressions give us the distance between $(4, -2)$ and (x, y).

problem set 35

1. Four times the number of whites exceeded 9 times the number of reds by 10. The ratio of blues to reds was 3 to 1, and there was a total of 65 of all 3 colors. How many were white, how many were red, and how many were blue?

2. The safe load a beam can support varies jointly as the width and the square of the depth and inversely as the length. If a 2 × 8 inch beam 16 feet long is turned so that the width is 2 inches, it can support 2000 pounds. How much weight can the same beam support if it is turned so that the width is 8 inches?

3. Bean could do 3 jobs in 8 hours. When Zollie helped, they could do 6 jobs in 4 hours. What was Zollie's rate in jobs per hour when she worked alone?

4. The engineer knows that the formula is $T = \sqrt{L/4}$. To get the desired result, she must triple her present value of T. What should she do to the present value of L?

5. What is the number that is $\frac{3}{5}$ of the way from -3 to 9?

6. Find the number that is $\frac{7}{8}$ of the way from $-3\frac{5}{6}$ to $2\frac{1}{6}$.

7. Use the distance formula to write an expression that gives the distance between the points $(3, -2)$ and (x, y).

Evaluate:

8. $\displaystyle\sum_{j=5}^{6} \frac{2}{j}$

9. $\displaystyle\sum_{n=0}^{3} \frac{3^n}{n + 1}$

10. The data points in the table below came from an experiment that involved yttrium (Y) and boron (B). Note that in the graph the horizontal and vertical scales are different. The position of the line which best fits the data points is estimated. Write the equation that expresses yttrium as a function of boron ($Y = mB + b$).

B	92.8	93.6	94.6	95.5	96.6	97.5	98.4	99.3
Y	417	326	228	324	219	170	82	120

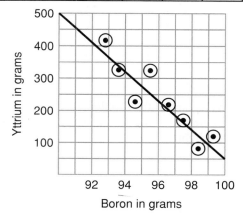

11. Find f where $g(x) = x - 4$ and $(f \circ g)(x) = (x - 4)^2$.

12. A certain parallelogram contains a pair of consecutive sides that are congruent. Which of the following must the parallelogram be?

    A. Rectangle   B. Square   C. Rhombus   D. Trapezoid

13. The figure shown is a trapezoid whose area is 100 cm^2. Find x. Dimensions are in centimeters.

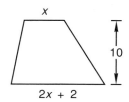

14. Find the inverse function of $y = \dfrac{5}{6}x + \dfrac{4}{3}$.

Evaluate. Do not use a calculator.

15. Arctan $\dfrac{1}{\sqrt{3}}$ **16.** $\cos\left[\text{Arccos}\left(-\dfrac{4}{5}\right)\right]$ **17.** sin (Arctan 2)

18. Determine whether the graph of each equation is symmetric about the x axis, the y axis, and the origin:

(a)

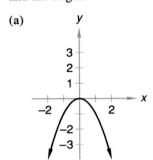

$y = -x^2$

(b)

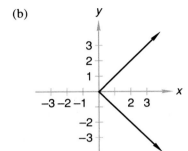

$|y| = x$

19. The graph of the function $f(x) = \sqrt{x}$ is shown on the left below. The graph on the right is the same graph reflected in the x axis. Write the equation of the graph on the right.

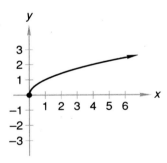   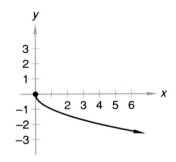

20. The graph of the function $f(x) = x^3$ is shown on the left below. The graph on the right is the same graph translated three units to the right. Write the equation of the graph on the right.

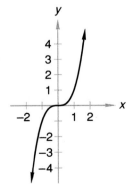   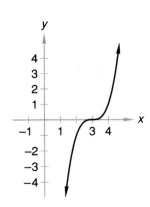

21. Find the resultant of $-2\underline{/120°} - 3\underline{/135°}$. Write the answer in polar form.

22. Solve:

    (a) $\log_a \dfrac{64}{27} = 3$ (b) $\log_9 \dfrac{1}{27} = n$ (c) $\log_{1/3} m = -3$

23. Find the domain and range of each function whose graph is shown:

    (a)

    (b)

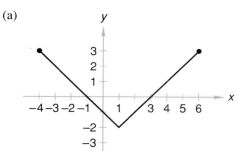
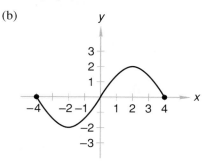

24. If $f(\theta) = \tan \theta$ and $g(\theta) = \cos \theta$, find $f(150°) - g(-90°)$. Do not use a calculator.

25. Let $f(x) = 4x + 5$ and $g(x) = \frac{1}{4}(x - 5)$. Evaluate:

    (a) $(f \circ g)(x)$ (b) $(g \circ f)(x)$

26. If $f(x) = \dfrac{x + 1}{x}$, find $f(x + h) - f(x)$.

27. In the figure shown, O is the center of the circle and $\overline{AC}$ is a diameter. If $m\widehat{AB} = 138°$, find x.

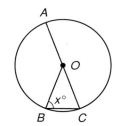

28. Given: $\overline{AC} \cong \overline{EC}$
    $\overline{BC} \cong \overline{DC}$

    Write a two-column proof to prove:
    $\overline{AB} \cong \overline{ED}$

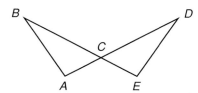

CONCEPT REVIEW PROBLEMS

29. Let a and b be real numbers. If $a < 0$ and $b < 0$, compare: A. $a - b$ B. $a + b$

30. If x is a real number and $x > 1$, compare: A. $\dfrac{1}{x^3}$ B. $\dfrac{1}{x^4}$

LESSON 36 *Angles Greater Than 360°* • *Sums of Trigonometric Functions* • *Boat-in-the-River Problems*

36.A
angles greater than 360°

In polar coordinates, we measure positive angles counterclockwise from the positive x axis and measure negative angles clockwise from the positive x axis. Thus, the positive x axis is the initial side of the angle.

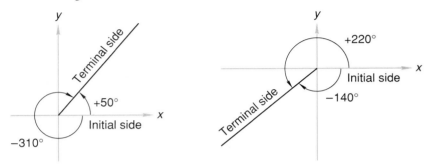

In the left-hand figure, we see that $+50°$ and $-310°$ have the same terminal side, and we say that these angles are **coterminal angles.** In the right-hand figure, we see that $+220°$ and $-140°$ are also coterminal angles. For many purposes, we can think of coterminal angles as being the same angle but with a different name. **Angles that differ by integer multiples of 360° are coterminal angles.** Two times around counterclockwise would be 720°, so angles that differ by 720° are coterminal angles. Three times around counterclockwise would be 1080°, so angles that differ by 1080° are also coterminal angles, as are angles that differ by 1440° for four times around counterclockwise, etc.

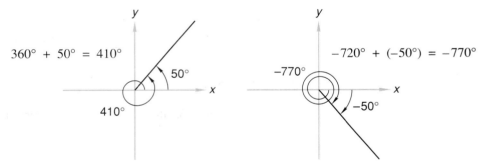

On the left, we see that 50° and 410° are coterminal angles because 410° is once around for 360° plus 50° more. On the right, we see that −50° and −770° are coterminal angles because −770° is twice around for −720° plus another −50°.

36.B
sums of trigonometric functions

Problems that require the addition of trigonometric functions of angles in all quadrants will provide practice that will lead to greater understanding of the values of trigonometric functions and will also give practice in simplifying expressions that contain radicals. The three expressions shown here are equivalent expressions.

$$\text{(a)} \quad -\frac{1}{\sqrt{2}} - \frac{1}{\sqrt{3}} \qquad \text{(b)} \quad -\frac{\sqrt{2}}{2} - \frac{\sqrt{3}}{3} \qquad \text{(c)} \quad \frac{-3\sqrt{2} - 2\sqrt{3}}{6}$$

Many people prefer expressions that do not have radicals in the denominator. In this case, they would prefer expressions (b) and (c). In this book, we will combine the parts as in (c) because of the practice this procedure provides and not because this form of answer is necessarily more desirable.

example 36.1   Evaluate: $\cos 135° + \tan 330°$

solution   It is always helpful to sketch the problem and note the related angles. We also draw the reference triangles.

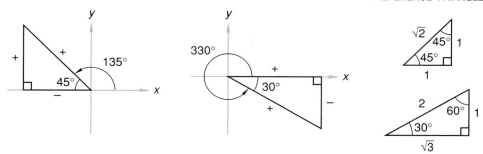

REFERENCE TRIANGLES

The cosine of 45° is $1/\sqrt{2}$, and the cosine is negative in the second quadrant.

$$\cos 135° = -\cos 45° = -\frac{1}{\sqrt{2}}$$

The tangent of 30° is $1/\sqrt{3}$, and the tangent is negative in the fourth quadrant.

$$\tan 330° = -\tan 30° = -\frac{1}{\sqrt{3}}$$

Therefore, we have

$$\cos 135° + \tan 330° = -\cos 45° - \tan 30° \qquad \text{substituted}$$

$$= -\frac{1}{\sqrt{2}} - \frac{1}{\sqrt{3}} \qquad \text{sum of functions}$$

$$= -\frac{\sqrt{2}}{2} - \frac{\sqrt{3}}{3} \qquad \text{rationalized denominators}$$

$$= \frac{-3\sqrt{2} - 2\sqrt{3}}{6} \qquad \text{added}$$

example 36.2   Evaluate: $\cos(-60°) + \cos 210°$

solution   First we sketch the problem and note the related angles. We also draw the reference triangle.

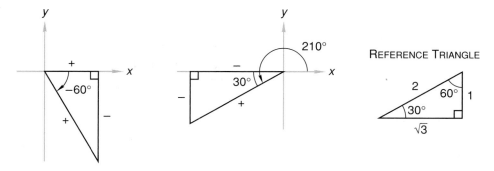

REFERENCE TRIANGLE

The cosine of 60° is 1/2, and the cosine is positive in the fourth quadrant.

$$\cos(-60°) = \cos 60° = \frac{1}{2}$$

The cosine of 30° is $\sqrt{3}/2$, and the cosine is negative in the third quadrant.

$$\cos 210° = -\cos 30° = -\frac{\sqrt{3}}{2}$$

Therefore, we have

$$\cos(-60°) + \cos 210° = \cos 60° - \cos 30° \qquad \text{substituted}$$

$$= \frac{1}{2} - \frac{\sqrt{3}}{2} \qquad \text{sum of functions}$$

$$= \frac{1 - \sqrt{3}}{2} \qquad \text{added}$$

example 36.3   Evaluate: $\cos 570° + \sin(-765°)$

solution   We begin by reducing the absolute values of the angles 360° at a time until we get an angle whose measure is less than 360°.

$$570° - 360° = 210° \qquad\qquad 765° - 360° - 360° = 45°$$

Now we sketch the angles and note the related angles. We also draw the reference triangles.

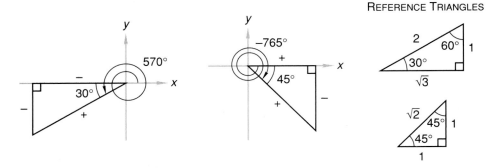

The cosine of 30° is $\sqrt{3}/2$, and the cosine is negative in the third quadrant.

$$\cos 570° = \cos 210° = -\cos 30° = -\frac{\sqrt{3}}{2}$$

The sine of 45° is $1/\sqrt{2}$, and the sine is negative in the fourth quadrant.

$$\sin(-765°) = \sin(-45°) = -\sin 45° = -\frac{1}{\sqrt{2}}$$

Therefore, we have

$$\cos 570° + \sin(-765°) = -\cos 30° - \sin 45° \qquad \text{substituted}$$

$$= -\frac{\sqrt{3}}{2} - \frac{1}{\sqrt{2}} \qquad \text{sum of functions}$$

$$= -\frac{\sqrt{3}}{2} - \frac{\sqrt{2}}{2} \qquad \text{common denominator}$$

$$= \frac{-\sqrt{3} - \sqrt{2}}{2} \qquad \text{added}$$

36.C

boat-in-the-river problems

We have called problems in which boats travel distances with and against the current **boat-in-the-river problems.** There is a downstream equation in which the rate is the still-water speed of the boat plus the speed of the water $(B + W)$. There is also an upstream equation in which the rate is the still-water speed of the boat minus the speed of the water $(B - W)$.

DOWNSTREAM EQUATION   UPSTREAM EQUATION

(a) $(B + W)T_D = D_D$ (b) $(B - W)T_U = D_U$

The same thought process and equations are applicable in problems in which an airplane flies directly against the wind and directly with the wind, as we see in the next example. The setup of this problem is straightforward, but the solution is a little awkward unless a double-variable substitution is used.

example 36.4 One day Selby found that her plane could fly at 5 times the speed of the wind. She flew 396 miles downwind in $\frac{1}{2}$ hour more than it took her to fly 132 miles upwind. What was the speed of her plane in still air and what was the speed of the wind?

solution First we write the equations. We will use A for the speed of the airplane in still air and W for the speed of the wind. Since distance is in miles and time is in hours, the speeds will be in miles per hour.

<table>
<tr><td>DOWNWIND EQUATION</td><td>UPWIND EQUATION</td></tr>
<tr><td>$(A + W)T_D = D_D$</td><td>$(A - W)T_U = D_U$</td></tr>
</table>

Now we substitute $5W$ for A, 396 and 132 for the distances, and $T_U + \frac{1}{2}$ for T_D.

$$(5W + W)\left(T_U + \frac{1}{2}\right) = 396 \qquad (5W - W)T_U = 132$$

Next we multiply, simplify, and get

$$6WT_U + 3W = 396 \qquad 4WT_U = 132$$

Now, if we have worked a problem like this one before, we note that the right-hand equation can be solved for WT_U, and this value can be used for WT_U in the left-hand equation. First we solve the right-hand equation for WT_U.

$$4WT_U = 132 \qquad \text{equation}$$
$$WT_U = 33 \qquad \text{divided by 4}$$

Now we use 33 in place of WT_U in the left-hand equation and solve.

$$6(33) + 3W = 396 \qquad \text{substituted}$$
$$198 + 3W = 396 \qquad \text{multiplied}$$
$$W = \textbf{66 mph} \qquad \text{solved}$$

We were given that A equals $5W$, so

$$A = 5(66)$$
$$A = \textbf{330 mph}$$

problem set 36

1. Bruce found that his plane could only fly at 4 times the speed of the wind. He flew 800 miles downwind in 1 hour more than it took to fly 300 miles upwind. What was the speed of the plane in still air and what was the speed of the wind?

2. Twenty percent of the number of whites exceeded the number of reds by 10. Also, three fifths of the number of blues was exactly equal to 3 times the number of reds. How many of each were there if ten percent of the sum of the reds and blues was 94 less than the number of whites?

3. Erica needed to finish with $3\sqrt{2}$, but her answer was $2/\sqrt{6}$. By what number should she have multiplied her number to get the answer she needed?

4. Jan traveled m miles at p miles per hour and arrived 2 hours early. How fast should she have traveled in order to arrive on time?

5. If the length of a rectangle is increased by 20% and the width of the same rectangle is decreased by 20%, what is the percent change in the area?

6. Find the number that is $\frac{2}{9}$ of the way from $-3\frac{3}{7}$ to $4\frac{2}{7}$.

7. Use the distance formula to write an expression that gives the distance between the points $(-2, 5)$ and (x, y).

8. Evaluate: $\displaystyle\sum_{x=3}^{5} \frac{3}{x + 1}$

9. The data points in the table below relate the number of rabbits per square mile (R) to the number of wolves per ten square miles (W). The position of the line which best fits the data points is estimated. Write the equation that expresses the number of rabbits per square mile as a function of the number of wolves per ten square miles ($R = mW + b$).

Wolves per ten square miles	51.6	52.3	52.6	53.5	53.6	53.7	54.3
Rabbits per square mile	94.8	96.7	92.9	87.2	91.1	81.3	82.9

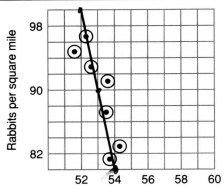

10. Find two functions f and g such that $(f \circ g)(x) = \sqrt{x - 1}$.

11. In the figure shown, $\overline{EF}$ is the median of trapezoid $ABCD$. Find x.

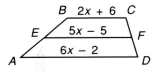

12. Find the inverse function of $y = \dfrac{1}{3}x - \dfrac{7}{3}$.

Evaluate. Do not use a calculator.

13. $\text{Arctan}\left(-\dfrac{1}{3}\sqrt{3}\right)$

14. $\sin\left(\text{Arccos}\ \dfrac{3}{7}\right)$

15. Determine whether the graph of each equation is symmetric about the x axis, the y axis, and the origin:

(a)

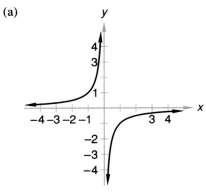

$yx = -1$

(b)

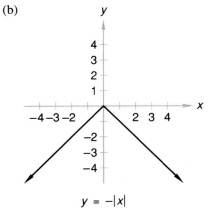

$y = -|x|$

16. The graph of the function $f(x) = \sqrt{x}$ is shown on the left below. The graph on the right is the same graph reflected in the y axis. Write the equation of the graph on the right.

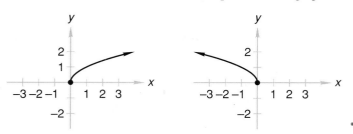

17. The graph of the function $f(x) = x^3$ is shown on the left below. The graph on the right is the same graph translated three units to the left. Write the equation of the graph on the right.

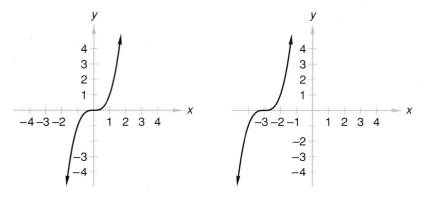

18. Find the equilibrant of $-3\underline{/-135°} + 4\underline{/140°}$. Write the answer in polar form.

19. Evaluate $\dfrac{10!}{2!7!}$ without using a calculator.

20. Solve:

(a) $\log_n 27 = 2$ (b) $\log_2 \dfrac{\sqrt{2}}{64} = t$ (c) $\log_3 k = -2$

21. The equation of the function whose graph is shown is $f(x) = \frac{1}{2}x^2 - 2$. Make a sketch of the graph of the reciprocal function $g(x) = \dfrac{1}{\frac{1}{2}x^2 - 2}$.

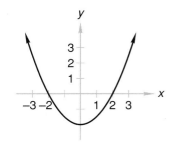

22. Determine if each graph represents the graph of a function. If so, determine whether the graph is the graph of a one-to-one function.

(a)   (b)   (c)   (d)

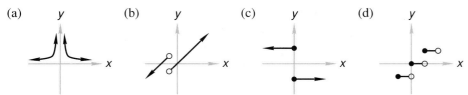

23. Find the domain of the function $f(x) = \dfrac{\sqrt{9 - 3x}}{2x^2 + 9x + 10}$.

24. Evaluate. Do not use a calculator.

    (a) $\cos 225° + \tan (-135°)$ (b) $\sin (-390°) - \cos 495°$

25. If $f(x) = \cos x$ and $g(x) = \tan x$, find $f(90°) - g(420°)$. Do not use a calculator.

26. Let $f(x) = \frac{1}{x}$ and $g(x) = x^3 + 1$. Evaluate:

    (a) $(f/g)(2)$ (b) $(f \circ g)(2)$ (c) $(g \circ f)(2)$

27. If $f(x) = (x - 1)^2$, find $f(x + h) - f(x)$.

28. Given: $\overline{AB} \perp \overline{BC}$ and $\overline{CD} \perp \overline{DA}$

    $\overline{AB} \cong \overline{CD}$

    Write a two-column proof to prove:

    $\overline{BC} \cong \overline{DA}$

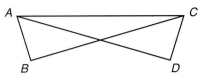

CONCEPT REVIEW
PROBLEMS

29. If $x^2 + y^2 = 8$ and $xy = 4$, compare: A. $(x + y)^2$ B. 16

30. In trapezoid $ABCD$, $\overline{AD} \parallel \overline{BC}$, $m\angle ADC = a°$, and $m\angle ABC = 2a°$. $\overline{BE}$ is drawn so that it bisects $\angle ABC$, as shown.

    Compare: A. AD B. $AB + BC$

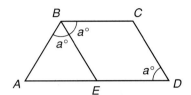

LESSON 37   *The Line as a Locus   •   The Midpoint Formula*

37.A

**the line as
a locus**

The Pythagorean theorem tells us that the area of the square drawn on the hypotenuse of a right triangle equals the sum of the areas of the squares drawn on the other two sides. The lengths of the sides of the right triangle shown on the left are 3 and 4, respectively, and the length of the hypotenuse is 5.

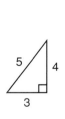

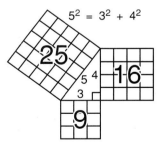

On the right we see that the area of the square drawn on the hypotenuse is 25 square units and this equals the sum of the areas drawn on the other two sides. The distance formula is an algebraic statement of the Pythagorean theorem that uses the coordinates of the endpoints of the hypotenuse. The distance equals the square root of the sum of the squares and is usually written as we show on the right.

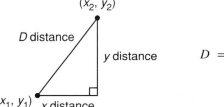

$$D = \sqrt{(x_1 - x_2)^2 + (y_1 - y_2)^2}$$

Many people have difficulty remembering the formula because they cannot remember whether x_1 or x_2 comes first. It doesn't make any difference as long as the x coordinates are separated by a minus sign and squared, as we show here.

$$\left(x_1 - x_2\right)^2 = x_1^2 - 2x_1x_2 + x_2^2$$

$$\left(x_2 - x_1\right)^2 = x_2^2 - 2x_1x_2 + x_1^2$$

The same holds true for the y coordinates.

$$\left(y_1 - y_2\right)^2 = y_1^2 - 2y_1y_2 + y_2^2$$

$$\left(y_2 - y_1\right)^2 = y_2^2 - 2y_1y_2 + y_1^2$$

example 37.1   Write an expression for the distance between $(4, 2)$ and (x, y).

solution   We can use either $(4 - x)^2$ or $(x - 4)^2$ for the x entries and we can use either $(2 - y)^2$ or $(y - 2)^2$ for the y entries.

$$D = \sqrt{(4 - x)^2 + (2 - y)^2}$$

$$D = \sqrt{(x - 4)^2 + (y - 2)^2}$$

We can even use one form for the x's and another form for the y's.

$$D = \sqrt{(x - 4)^2 + (2 - y)^2}$$

The word **locus** is a Latin word which means "place." In mathematics, we use the word *locus* to describe the location of mathematical points. The line, the circle, the parabola, the ellipse, and the hyperbola can all be defined by using the word *locus*. Here we will investigate the locus definition of a line, and we remember that the word *line* in mathematics means a straight line.

DEFINITION OF A LINE

A line is the locus of all points in a plane that are equidistant from two specified points.

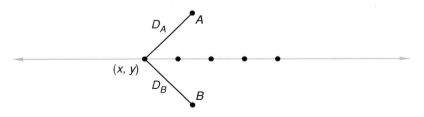

Here we show points A and B and a point (x, y) on a line where D_A equals D_B. The locus of all the points that are equidistant from A and B is the line shown.

example 37.2   Find the equation of the line that is equidistant from the points (4, 2) and (–2, –3). Write the equation in slope-intercept form.

solution   A sketch of the problem is always helpful. We graph the points, estimate the position of the line, and designate point (x, y) on the line. The distances from this point to the points (–2, –3) and (4, 2) are equal.

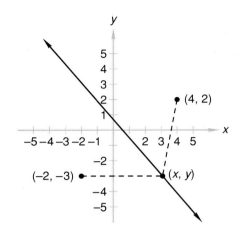

Distance from (x, y) to $(-2, -3)$ = Distance from (x, y) to $(4, 2)$

There are many forms of the distance formula. We will use two different forms of the distance formula to emphasize that any correct form will suffice.

$$\sqrt{[(x) - (-2)]^2 + [(-3) - (y)]^2} = \sqrt{[(4) - (x)]^2 + [(2) - (y)]^2}$$

Now we square both sides to eliminate the radicals, and then simplify to get

$$(x + 2)^2 + (-3 - y)^2 = (4 - x)^2 + (2 - y)^2$$

Now we square the terms as indicated and get

$$x^2 + 4x + 4 + 9 + 6y + y^2 = 16 - 8x + x^2 + 4 - 4y + y^2$$

We find an x^2 and a y^2 on both the left-hand side and the right-hand side, and these can be eliminated by adding $-x^2$ and $-y^2$ to both sides.

$$4x + 4 + 9 + 6y = 16 - 8x + 4 - 4y$$

We finish by collecting like terms and writing the equation of the line.

$$12x + 10y - 7 = 0 \qquad \text{simplified}$$

$$y = -\frac{6}{5}x + \frac{7}{10} \qquad \text{slope-intercept form}$$

example 37.3   Find the equation of the line that is equidistant from the points $(0, -4)$ and $(5, 2)$. Write the equation in slope-intercept form.

solution First we make a sketch. The distance from (x, y) to $(5, 2)$ must equal the distance from (x, y) to $(0, -4)$.

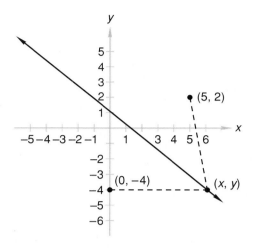

Distance from (x, y) to $(5, 2)$ = Distance from (x, y) to $(0, -4)$

Again we will use different forms of the distance equation to emphasize that any one of the forms is correct.

$$\sqrt{[(y) - (2)]^2 + [(5) - (x)]^2} = \sqrt{[(0) - (x)]^2 + [(y) - (-4)]^2}$$

Now we square both sides to eliminate the radicals, simplify, and get

$$(y - 2)^2 + (5 - x)^2 = (0 - x)^2 + (y + 4)^2$$

Now we perform the indicated multiplications and get

$$y^2 - 4y + 4 + 25 - 10x + x^2 = x^2 + y^2 + 8y + 16$$

As the last step, we collect like terms and write the equation of the line.

$$10x + 12y - 13 = 0 \qquad\qquad \text{simplified}$$

$$y = -\frac{5}{6}x + \frac{13}{12} \qquad\qquad \text{slope-intercept form}$$

37.B
the midpoint formula

There are formulas that can be used to determine the x and y coordinates of the point that lies halfway between two points (x_1, y_1) and (x_2, y_2). These formulas are

$$x = \frac{x_1 + x_2}{2} \qquad \text{and} \qquad y = \frac{y_1 + y_2}{2}$$

We remember that the distance between two points on a number line is the difference in the coordinates of the points, so it seems strange that the signs between x_1 and x_2 and between y_1 and y_2 are plus signs. To find out why, we will look at two points x_1 and x_2 on the number line.

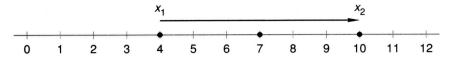

We let x_1 equal 4 and let x_2 equal 10, and we need a formula that will give us the name of the number halfway between. First we find the distance between the points, which is $x_2 - x_1$. To find half this distance, we divide by 2.

$$\text{Half the distance} = \frac{x_2 - x_1}{2} = \frac{10 - 4}{2} = 3$$

Now $10 - 4$ divided by 2 uses the minus sign, but the result is 3, which is not the number halfway between 4 and 10 because that number is 7. The name of a number tells its distance from the origin, so we must add 4 to 3 to get 7. In general, we add the distance from the origin to x_1 to one half the distance from x_1 to x_2.

$$\text{Distance from the origin} = x_1 + \frac{x_2 - x_1}{2}$$

We can simplify this expression by using a common denominator of 2 and adding the terms.

$$\text{Distance from the origin} = \frac{2x_1}{2} + \frac{x_2}{2} - \frac{x_1}{2} \qquad \text{common denominator}$$

$$= \frac{x_1 + x_2}{2} \qquad \text{added}$$

Now the sign between x_1 and x_2 is positive. We see that adding the distance from the origin to x_1 to one half the distance from x_1 to x_2 changed the sign between x_1 and x_2 from negative to positive.

example 37.4   Find the coordinates of the point halfway between $(-2, 6)$ and $(4, -10)$.

solution   We will use the two midpoint formulas.

$$x = \frac{x_1 + x_2}{2} \qquad\qquad y = \frac{y_1 + y_2}{2}$$

$$x = \frac{(-2) + (4)}{2} = 1 \qquad\qquad y = \frac{(6) + (-10)}{2} = -2$$

The coordinates of the midpoint are **(1, –2)**.

problem set 37

1. Sarah's airplane could fly at 6 times the speed of wind. She could fly 700 miles upwind in 3 more hours than it took to fly 560 miles downwind. Find the speed of the plane in still air and the speed of the wind.

2. Three men invested $2000, $3000, and $5000, respectively, when they formed a partnership. The profit at the end of the first year was $1920. How much should the man who invested $2000 receive if the profits are divided in accordance with the amounts invested?

3. The weather was cold, so David had to use 50% of the remaining oil to heat his home that week. If the tank was three fourths full at the beginning of the week, what fractional part of a full tank did he use that week?

4. Six thousand dollars would suffice for 10 people for 15 days. At the same rate, how much money would be required for 20 people for only 5 days?

5. The first leg of the trip was only k miles, and Donnie drove at m miles per hour. He miscalculated and arrived 2 hours late. If the time allotted for the second leg of the trip was the same and the second leg was 10 miles longer, how fast did Donnie have to drive on the second leg to get there on time?

6. Find the equation of the line that is equidistant from the points $(3, 2)$ and $(-4, -3)$. Write the equation in slope-intercept form.

7. Find the coordinates of the point halfway between $(-4, 7)$ and $(3, 2)$.

8. Find the number that is $\frac{3}{7}$ of the way from $-2\frac{2}{5}$ to $-3\frac{1}{5}$.

9. Evaluate: $\displaystyle\sum_{k=2}^{5} \left(k^2 - 2\right)$

10. The data points in the table below relate output (O) to input (I). The position of the line which best fits the data points is estimated. Write the equation that expresses output as a function of input $(O = mI + b)$.

Input in units	21	23	23	25	27	27	29	30
Output in units	33	43	52	62	65	77	84	97

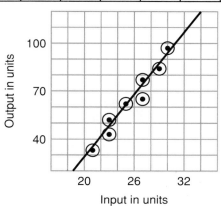

11. Find f where $g(x) = \cos x$ and $(f \circ g)(x) = \sqrt{\cos x}$.

12. A certain parallelogram contains one angle that is a right angle. No information is given about the other three angles. Which of the following must the parallelogram be?

    A. Rectangle   B. Square   C. Rhombus   D. Trapezoid

13. The figure shown is a trapezoid whose area is 180 m^2. Find x. Dimensions are in meters.

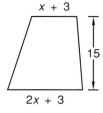

14. Find the inverse function of $y = 4x + \frac{2}{3}$.

15. Evaluate. Do not use a calculator.

    (a) Arctan 0   (b) $\cos\left[\text{Arctan}\,(-2)\right]$

16. Determine whether the graph of each equation is symmetric about the x axis, the y axis, and the origin:

    (a)   (b)

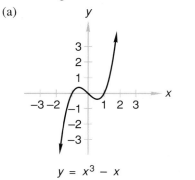

$y = x^3 - x$

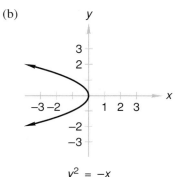

$y^2 = -x$

17. The graph of the function $f(x) = 3^x$ is shown on the left below. The graph on the right is the same graph reflected in the x axis. Write the equation of the graph on the right.

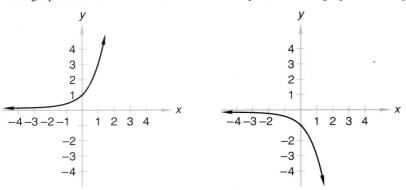

18. The graph of the function $f(x) = 4^x$ is shown on the left below. The graph on the right is the same graph translated three units up. Write the equation of the graph on the right.

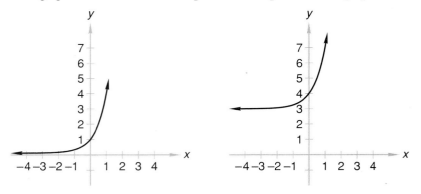

19. Solve:

(a) $\log_m 32 = 5$　　　(b) $\log_3 \dfrac{\sqrt{3}}{81} = n$　　　(c) $\log_{1/2} t = -\dfrac{3}{2}$

20. Find the domain and range of each function whose graph is shown:

(a)　　　　　　　　　　　　　　　(b)

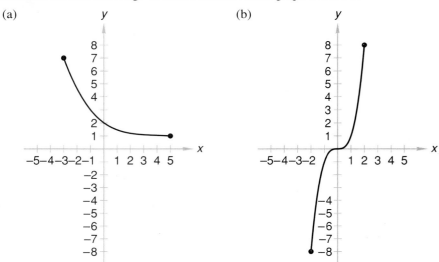

21. Evaluate. Do not use a calculator.

(a) $\sin(-390°) + \cos 495°$　　　　　(b) $\tan(-495°) - \sin 225°$

22. Let $f(x) = 10^x$ and $g(x) = \log_{10} x$. Evaluate:

(a) $(g \circ f)(2)$　　　　　(b) $(g \circ f)(3)$　　　　　(c) $(g \circ f)(4)$

Solve:

23. $\begin{cases} x^2 + y^2 = 4 \\ 2x + y = 2 \end{cases}$

24. $\dfrac{x}{x^2 - 1} - \dfrac{1}{x^2 - x} = \dfrac{1}{x^3 - x}$ (*Hint:* Factor denominators to find a common denominator. Check solutions.)

25. Divide $x^4 - x^3 + x^2 - 1$ by $x - 1$ and check.

26. If $f(x) = x^2 + 1$, find $\dfrac{f(x + h) - f(x)}{h}$.

27. Given: $\overline{PQ} \cong \overline{SR}$
$\quad\quad\quad\ \overline{QS} \cong \overline{RP}$

Write a two-column proof to prove:
$\quad\quad \angle PQS \cong \angle SRP$

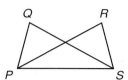

28. A sphere has a surface area of 1764π cm^2. If the surface area of the sphere is decreased by 468π cm^2, by what amount is the volume of the sphere decreased?

CONCEPT REVIEW
PROBLEMS

29. If x is a real number and $0 < x < 1$, compare: A. $\dfrac{1}{x^2}$ B. $\dfrac{1}{x^3}$

30. In polygon $ABCDE$, $m\angle 5 = 90°$.

Compare: A. $540°$
$\quad\quad\quad$ B. $m\angle 1 + m\angle 2 + m\angle 3 + m\angle 4$

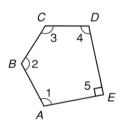

LESSON 38   *Fundamental Counting Principle and Permutations • Designated Roots • Overall Average Rate*

38.A

fundamental counting principle and permutations

The letters A, B, and C can be arranged six different ways. If we put the A first, we can get

| A | B | C | and | A | C | B |

If we put the B first, we can get

| B | A | C | and | B | C | A |

If we put the C first, we can get

| C | A | B | and | C | B | A |

All of the arrangements use the same letters, but the order of the letters is different in each arrangement. We call an arrangement of the members of a set in a definite order without repetition a **permutation** of the members of the set.

We see that any one of the three letters can be put in the first box.

| 3 | | |

Now either of the two remaining letters can be put in the second box.

| 3 | 2 | |

And then the last letter goes in the third box.

| 3 | 2 | 1 |

Thus, any one of the 3 letters can be used first, any one of the 2 letters that remain can be used second, and the remaining letter is used third for a total of 3 times 2 times 1, or 6, ways. This example is a demonstration of the **fundamental counting principle.**

FUNDAMENTAL COUNTING PRINCIPLE

If one choice can be made in A ways and, after the first choice is made, another choice can be made in B ways, then the number of possible choices, in order, is A times B different ways.

If repetition is permitted, the number of possible arrangements is even greater. For example, if the letters A, B, and C can be used more than once, then any of the 3 letters can be used in the first, second, or third position for a total of 3 times 3 times 3, or 27, possible ways.

| 3 | 3 | 3 |

If we list the ways, we get

AAA	AAB	AAC	ABA	ABB	ABC	ACA	ACB	ACC
BBB	BBA	BBC	BAB	BAA	BAC	BCB	BCA	BCC
CCC	CCB	CCA	CBC	CBB	CBA	CAC	CAB	CAA

The fundamental counting principle can be extended to any number of choices in order. If the first choice can be made in 2 ways, the second choice in 3 ways, the third choice in 5 ways, and the fourth choice in 7 ways, then there are

$$2 \cdot 3 \cdot 5 \cdot 7 = 210 \text{ ways}$$

that the choices can be made in order.

example 38.1   How many different ways can the numbers 3, 5, 7, and 8 be arranged in order if no repetition is permitted?

solution   Any one of the 4 numbers can be put in the first box.

| 4 | | | |

Then any one of the remaining 3 numbers can be put in the next box,

| 4 | 3 | | |

then 2 in the next, and 1 in the last.

4	3	2	1

By the fundamental counting principle, there are

$$4 \cdot 3 \cdot 2 \cdot 1 = \textbf{24 ways}$$

that the numbers can be arranged in order if no repetition is permitted. Each of these 24 ways is called a *permutation*.

example 38.2   How many 4-letter signs can be made from the letters in the word EQUAL if repetition is permitted?

solution   Any one of the 5 letters can be used in any of the positions.

5	5	5	5

$\longrightarrow$ $5 \cdot 5 \cdot 5 \cdot 5 = \textbf{625}$

So we have a total of 625 possible arrangements if repetition is permitted.

example 38.3   A multiple choice test has 8 questions, and there are 4 possible choices to each question. How many different sets of answers are possible?

solution   We assume that for each question there are four choices for answers (a), (b), (c), and (d). We know that the same choice may appear more than once in a set of answers. Thus, this is a problem which is asking for the number of arrangements with repetition. Since there are 8 questions with 4 possible choices to each question, we have

4	4	4	4	4	4	4	4

$\longrightarrow$ $4 \cdot 4 \cdot 4 \cdot 4 \cdot 4 \cdot 4 \cdot 4 \cdot 4 = \textbf{65,536}$

Thus, there are 65,536 possible sets of answers to a multiple choice test that has only 8 questions!

example 38.4   How many 3-letter signs can be made from the letters in the word NUMERAL if no repetition is permitted?

solution   This problem is a little different, as only 3 of the 7 letters will be used in each arrangement. So we have only 3 positions, and any one of the 7 letters can be used in the first position.

7		

Now, any one of the 6 that are left can be used in the next position,

7	6	

and any of the 5 that remain can be used in the last position.

7	6	5

$$7 \cdot 6 \cdot 5 = \textbf{210}$$

So 210 three-letter permutations of the 7 letters are possible.

38.B

designated roots

The zero factor theorem tells us that, if the product of two or more quantities equals zero, then one of the quantities must equal zero. For example, if we have the equation

$$(x - 4)(x + 7) = 0$$

then either $x - 4$ equals zero or $x + 7$ equals zero. For $x - 4$ to equal zero, x must equal 4; and for $x + 7$ to equal zero, x must equal -7.

$$x - 4 = 0 \qquad x + 7 = 0$$

$$x = 4 \qquad x = -7$$

We can use the reverse of this procedure to write quadratic equations that have designated roots. We need to be careful as there is an infinite number of quadratic equations that have two designated roots, but only one whose lead coefficient is 1. For example, the quadratic equation below has roots $x = 2$ and $x = 3$.

$$x^2 - 5x + 6 = (x - 2)(x - 3) = 0$$

If we were to multiply this quadratic equation by any nonzero constant, we would get another quadratic equation with the same roots. The new quadratic equation would then have a lead coefficient which is different from 1. Therefore, there are an infinite number of quadratic equations having 2 and 3 as roots, but only one whose lead coefficient is 1. In the examples and problem sets, we will specify that we want the quadratic equation with designated roots that has a lead coefficient of 1.

example 38.5 Write the quadratic equation with a lead coefficient of 1 whose roots are $-\frac{3}{5}$ and $\frac{1}{2}$.

solution If the roots are $-\frac{3}{5}$ and $\frac{1}{2}$, the factors are $\left(x + \frac{3}{5}\right)$ and $\left(x - \frac{1}{2}\right)$. We write the equation and multiply.

$$\left(x + \frac{3}{5}\right)\left(x - \frac{1}{2}\right) = 0 \qquad \text{equation}$$

$$x^2 + \frac{1}{10}x - \frac{3}{10} = 0 \qquad \text{multiplied}$$

example 38.6 Write the quadratic equation with a lead coefficient of 1 whose roots are $1 + \sqrt{2}$ and $1 - \sqrt{2}$.

solution If the roots are as stated, the equation is

$$\left[x - \left(1 + \sqrt{2}\right)\right]\left[x - \left(1 - \sqrt{2}\right)\right] = 0$$

The multiplication is easier if we first simplify within the brackets.

$$\left[x - 1 - \sqrt{2}\right]\left[x - 1 + \sqrt{2}\right] = 0$$

There are nine individual products for this multiplication.

$$x^2 - x + \sqrt{2}x - x + 1 - \sqrt{2} - \sqrt{2}x + \sqrt{2} - 2 = 0$$

Fortunately, this expression can be simplified,

$$x^2 - x + \cancel{\sqrt{2}x} - x + 1 - \cancel{\sqrt{2}} - \cancel{\sqrt{2}x} + \cancel{\sqrt{2}} - 2 = 0$$

and we get

$$x^2 - 2x - 1 = 0$$

38.C

overall average rate

When an object travels over a certain distance d at a constant rate r for a period of time t, we know that

$$d = rt \qquad r = \frac{d}{t} \qquad \text{and} \qquad t = \frac{d}{r}$$

Sometimes, we will need to compute an overall average rate when an object travels at one rate for a certain period of time and at another rate for another period of time. By definition,

$$\text{Overall average rate} = \frac{\text{overall distance}}{\text{overall time}}$$

Usually, when a trip is divided into two or more legs traveled at different individual rates, the overall average rate is **not** the same as the average of the individual rates. We will illustrate this concept below.

example 38.7   Frank and Judy drive for 100 miles at 50 mph. They then drive 180 miles at 60 mph. What is Frank and Judy's overall average rate over the whole trip?

solution   The entire distance traveled is 280 miles (that is, 100 miles plus 180 miles). The time spent on the first leg is equal to the distance traveled, 100 miles, divided by 50 mph.

$$\text{Time spent on first leg} = \frac{\text{distance traveled}}{\text{rate}} = \frac{100 \text{ miles}}{50 \text{ miles/hour}}$$

$$= 2 \text{ hours}$$

Similarly, we compute the time spent on the second leg.

$$\text{Time spent on second leg} = \frac{\text{distance traveled}}{\text{rate}} = \frac{180 \text{ miles}}{60 \text{ miles/hour}}$$

$$= 3 \text{ hours}$$

Thus, the total time spent traveling is 2 hours plus 3 hours, which is 5 hours. We now have enough information to compute the overall average rate.

$$\text{Overall average rate} = \frac{\text{overall distance}}{\text{overall time}} = \frac{280 \text{ miles}}{5 \text{ hours}}$$

$$= \textbf{56 mph}$$

Had we simply averaged the two rates 50 mph and 60 mph, we would have gotten 55 mph, which is close to the actual overall average rate but incorrect.

example 38.8   Frank and Judy drive for 100 miles at 50 mph. They then drive 180 miles at 60 mph. How fast must they drive for the last 120 miles to have an overall average rate of 60 mph for the entire trip?

solution   We divide the trip into three separate legs. By the definition of overall average rate,

$$\text{Overall average rate} = \frac{\text{overall distance}}{\text{overall time}}$$

$$= \frac{100 \text{ miles} + 180 \text{ miles} + 120 \text{ miles}}{\text{overall time}}$$

$$= \frac{400 \text{ miles}}{\text{overall time}}$$

We know that we want the overall average rate to be 60 mph, so by substitution,

$$60 \text{ miles/hour} = \frac{400 \text{ miles}}{\text{overall time}}$$

Thus

$$\text{Overall time} = \frac{400 \text{ miles}}{60 \text{ miles/hour}} = 6\frac{2}{3} \text{ hours}$$

We can compute the times spent on each leg.

$$\text{Time spent on first leg} = \frac{100 \text{ miles}}{50 \text{ miles/hour}} = 2 \text{ hours}$$

$$\text{Time spent on second leg} = \frac{180 \text{ miles}}{60 \text{ miles/hour}} = 3 \text{ hours}$$

The only thing we do not know is the time spent on the third leg. We know that the total time spent was $6\frac{2}{3}$ hours and 5 hours were spent on the first two legs. Therefore, $1\frac{2}{3}$ hours were spent on the third leg. We are asked to find the rate the third leg was traveled. We solve for this rate.

$$\text{Rate of third leg} = \frac{\text{distance of third leg}}{\text{time traveling on third leg}}$$

$$= \frac{120 \text{ miles}}{1\frac{2}{3} \text{ hours}}$$

$$= \textbf{72 mph}$$

problem set 38

1. The tugboat *Gertrude* could steam at 4 times the speed of the current. She could make it 60 miles down the river in 1 more hour than it took her to go 27 miles up the river. What was *Gertrude*'s speed in still water and how fast was the current in the river?

2. On the first leg, Ronkie Boy traveled for T hours at R miles per hour. The next leg was 100 miles longer. How fast did he have to fly in order to cover this distance in only P hours more than he took for the first leg?

3. The average speed for the first 300 miles was 60 mph and for the next 200 miles was 20 mph. What should be the speed for the last 500 miles so that the overall average speed for the trip would be 40 mph?

4. Hortense had a problem. She needed 20 liters of a solution that was 78% alcohol. She had one solution that was 90% alcohol and another that was 75% alcohol. How many liters of each solution should she use?

5. Wilde Oscar worked frantically for 4 hours and called for help because he saw it would take 6 more hours to finish. Calm Sally began to help and they finished the job in 2 more hours. How long would it have taken Sally to do the job alone?

6. How many 3-letter signs can be made from the letters in the word HAMLET if no repetition is permitted?

7. How many 5-letter signs can be made from the letters in the word LEFTY if repetition is permitted?

8. Each question on a survey has three possible answers: yes, no, or maybe. The survey has 5 questions. How many different responses to the survey are possible?

9. Write the quadratic equation with a lead coefficient of 1 whose roots are $-\frac{2}{5}$ and $\frac{4}{3}$.

10. Find the equation of the line that is equidistant from the points $(4, 2)$ and $(-4, 3)$. Write the equation in slope-intercept form.

11. Find the coordinates of the point halfway between $(1, 3)$ and $(6, 5)$.

12. Evaluate: $\displaystyle\sum_{k=-1}^{3}\left(\frac{k^2}{4} - k\right)$

13. The data points in the table below came from an experiment involving vanadium (V) and potassium (K). The position of the line which best fits the data points has been estimated. Write the equation that expresses vanadium as a function of potassium ($V = mK + b$).

K	94.6	95.9	96.8	97.0	98.4	98.6
V	27.2	26.1	23.9	25.0	23.3	21.4

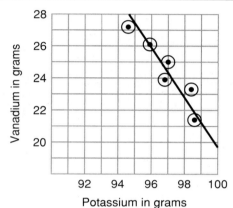

14. Find two functions f and g such that $(f \circ g)(x) = (2x + 3)^3$.

15. The diagonals of a certain quadrilateral are perpendicular bisectors of each other. Which of the following must the quadrilateral be?

A. Rectangle   B. Square   C. Rhombus   D. Trapezoid

16. Find the area of this trapezoid.

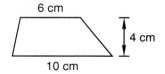

17. Evaluate. Do not use a calculator.

(a) Arctan (-1)

(b) $\sin\left(\text{Arctan }\dfrac{2}{5}\right)$

18. The graph of the function $f(x) = 3^x$ is shown on the left below. The graph on the right is the same graph reflected in the y axis. Write the equation of the graph on the right.

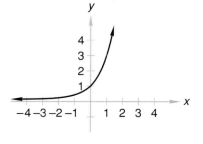
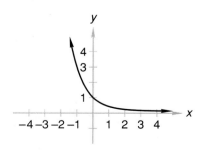

19. The graph of the function $f(x) = 4^x$ is shown on the left below. The graph on the right is the same graph translated three units down. Write the equation of the graph on the right.

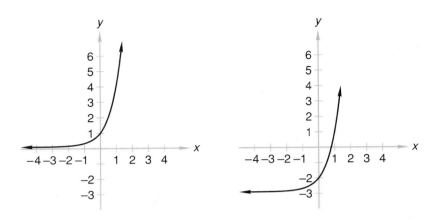

20. Find the resultant of $4\underline{/-45°} + 16\underline{/330°}$. Write the answer in polar form.

21. Solve:

(a) $\log_k \dfrac{1}{8} = -3$ (b) $\log_2 \dfrac{\sqrt[3]{2}}{16} = s$ (c) $\log_{1/3} r = -2$

22. Find the domain of the function $f(x) = \dfrac{\sqrt{100 + x}}{x^2 + 7x + 10}$.

23. Evaluate. Do not use a calculator.

(a) $\sin(-390°) - \tan 495°$ (b) $\sin 90° \cos 135° - \tan 30°$

24. Let $f(x) = \frac{1}{7}(x - 2)$ and $g(x) = 7x + 2$. Evaluate:

(a) $(f \circ g)(x)$ (b) $(g \circ f)(x)$

25. Solve: $\begin{cases} 2y^2 - x^2 = 5 \\ 2y^2 + x^2 = 11 \end{cases}$

26. Solve for g: $x = x_0 + v_0 t + \dfrac{1}{2}gt^2$

27. If $f(x) = x^2 - 2x$, find $\dfrac{f(x + h) - f(x)}{h}$.

28. Given: $ABCD$ is a square

Write a two-column proof to prove:

$\overline{BD} \cong \overline{CA}$

29. If x is a real number and $x < 0$, compare: A. $\dfrac{1}{x}$ B. $\dfrac{1}{x^2}$

30. If $6x - y - 8 = 0$ and $4x - 3y - 7 = 0$, compare: A. $x + y$ B. $\dfrac{1}{4}$

LESSON 39   *Radian Measure of Angles • Forms of Linear Equations*

39.A

radian measure of angles

If a length equal to the radius of a circle is measured on the circle itself, the central angle formed is said to measure 1 radian (rad). The measure of the arc is also said to be 1 radian. **We extend this definition to say that the measure of any arc is the same as the measure of its central angle.**

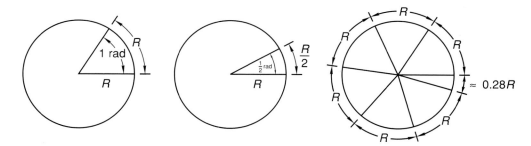

On the left above, we see that an arc that is 1 radius long subtends a central angle whose measure is 1 radian. In the center, we see that an arc that is one half as long as a radius subtends an angle whose measure is $\frac{1}{2}$ radian. On the right, we see that it takes about 6.28 radii to go all the way around a circle. The exact measure of the central angle of a full circle is 2π radians, which equals 360 degrees. The exact measure of the central angle of a semicircle is π radians, which equals 180 degrees. Thus π radians is about 3.14 radians, as we see below.

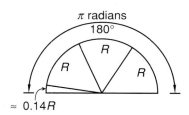

π radians equals 180 degrees

Thus, the unit multipliers necessary to convert degrees to radians and radians to degrees are

$$\frac{\pi \text{ rad}}{180 \text{ deg}} \qquad \text{and} \qquad \frac{180 \text{ deg}}{\pi \text{ rad}}$$

Unless otherwise designated, angles are always assumed to be measured in radians.

example 39.1   Evaluate: $4 \sin \dfrac{\pi}{4} + \sin \left(-\dfrac{\pi}{3} \right)$

solution   If we multiply each of the radian measures by 180 deg/π rad, we convert the radian measures to degrees.

$$\frac{\cancel{\pi \text{ rad}}}{4} \times \frac{180 \text{ deg}}{\cancel{\pi \text{ rad}}} = 45° \qquad\qquad -\frac{\cancel{\pi \text{ rad}}}{3} \times \frac{180 \text{ deg}}{\cancel{\pi \text{ rad}}} = -60°$$

We note that the same numerical result can be achieved if we simply replace π with 180°. Sometimes this shortcut is helpful.

$$\frac{\pi}{4} \;\longrightarrow\; \frac{180°}{4} \;\longrightarrow\; 45° \qquad\qquad -\frac{\pi}{3} \;\longrightarrow\; -\frac{180°}{3} \;\longrightarrow\; -60°$$

Now we use the degree measures and draw the diagrams. We note that the related angle of 45°
is 45° and the related angle of −60° is 60°. We also draw the reference triangles.

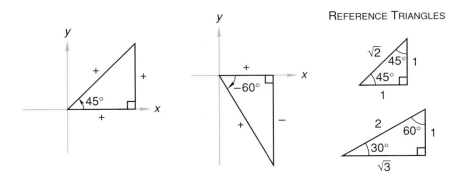

The sine of 45° is $1/\sqrt{2}$, and the sine is positive in the first quadrant. Therefore, we can write

$$\sin \frac{\pi}{4} = \sin 45° = \frac{1}{\sqrt{2}}$$

The sine of 60° is $\sqrt{3}/2$, and the sine is negative in the fourth quadrant. Therefore, we can write

$$\sin \left(-\frac{\pi}{3} \right) = \sin (-60°) = -\sin 60° = -\frac{\sqrt{3}}{2}$$

Therefore, we have

$$4 \sin \frac{\pi}{4} + \sin \left(-\frac{\pi}{3} \right) = 4 \sin 45° + \sin (-60°) \qquad \text{substituted}$$

$$= 4 \sin 45° - \sin 60° \qquad \text{substituted}$$

$$= 4 \cdot \frac{1}{\sqrt{2}} - \frac{\sqrt{3}}{2} \qquad \text{sum of functions}$$

$$= \frac{4\sqrt{2}}{2} - \frac{\sqrt{3}}{2} \qquad \text{common denominator}$$

$$= \frac{\mathbf{4\sqrt{2} - \sqrt{3}}}{\mathbf{2}} \qquad \text{added}$$

It is not necessary to begin by converting radians to degrees, but many people require
considerable experience with radian measure before the use of radian measure is comfortable.
For these people, the conversion to degrees is a recommended first step.

example 39.2   Evaluate: $\sin \dfrac{13\pi}{4} + 3 \cos \left(-\dfrac{5\pi}{3} \right)$

solution   We begin by converting the radian measures to degrees. We will use the shortcut method by
replacing π with 180°.

$$\frac{13\pi}{4} \quad \longrightarrow \quad \frac{13(180°)}{4} \quad \longrightarrow \quad 585° \qquad\qquad -\frac{5\pi}{3} \quad \longrightarrow \quad -\frac{5(180°)}{3} \quad \longrightarrow \quad -300°$$

Now we use the degree measures and draw the diagrams. We note that the related angle of 585° is 45° and the related angle of –300° is 60°. We also draw the reference triangles.

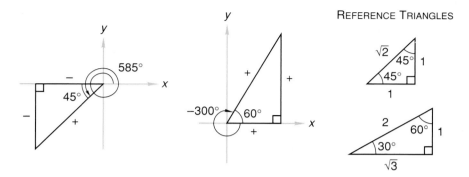

The sine of 45° is $1/\sqrt{2}$, and the sine is negative in the third quadrant. Therefore, we can write

$$\sin \frac{13\pi}{4} = \sin 585° = -\sin 45° = -\frac{1}{\sqrt{2}}$$

The cosine of 60° is 1/2, and the cosine is positive in the first quadrant. Therefore, we can write

$$\cos \left(-\frac{5\pi}{3} \right) = \cos (-300°) = \cos 60° = \frac{1}{2}$$

Therefore, we have

$$\sin \frac{13\pi}{4} + 3 \cos \left(-\frac{5\pi}{3} \right) = \sin 585° + 3 \cos (-300°) \qquad \text{substituted}$$

$$= -\sin 45° + 3 \cos 60° \qquad \text{substituted}$$

$$= -\frac{1}{\sqrt{2}} + 3 \cdot \frac{1}{2} \qquad \text{sum of functions}$$

$$= -\frac{\sqrt{2}}{2} + \frac{3}{2} \qquad \text{common denominator}$$

$$= \frac{-\sqrt{2} + 3}{2} \qquad \text{added}$$

example 39.3   Evaluate: $\cos \left(-\frac{25\pi}{6} \right) - 2 \tan \frac{4\pi}{3}$

solution   We begin by converting the radian measures to degrees. We will use the shortcut method by replacing π with 180°.

$$-\frac{25\pi}{6} \quad \rightarrow \quad -\frac{25(180°)}{6} \quad \rightarrow \quad -750° \qquad\qquad \frac{4\pi}{3} \quad \rightarrow \quad \frac{4(180°)}{3} \quad \rightarrow \quad 240°$$

Now we use the degree measures and draw the diagrams. We note that the related angle of −750° is 30° and the related angle of 240° is 60°. We also draw the reference triangle.

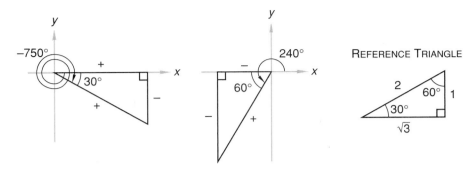

The cosine of 30° is $\sqrt{3}/2$, and the cosine is positive in the fourth quadrant. Therefore, we can write

$$\cos\left(-\frac{25\pi}{6}\right) = \cos\left(-750°\right) = \cos 30° = \frac{\sqrt{3}}{2}$$

The tangent of 60° is $\sqrt{3}/1$, and the tangent is positive in the third quadrant. Therefore, we can write

$$\tan\frac{4\pi}{3} = \tan 240° = \tan 60° = \sqrt{3}$$

Therefore, we have

$$\cos\left(-\frac{25\pi}{6}\right) - 2\tan\frac{4\pi}{3} = \cos\left(-750°\right) - 2\tan 240° \qquad \text{substituted}$$

$$= \cos 30° - 2\tan 60° \qquad \text{substituted}$$

$$= \frac{\sqrt{3}}{2} - 2\sqrt{3} \qquad \text{sum of functions}$$

$$= \frac{\sqrt{3}}{2} - \frac{4\sqrt{3}}{2} \qquad \text{common denominator}$$

$$= -\frac{3\sqrt{3}}{2} \qquad \text{added}$$

example 39.4   The latitude of a point on Earth is the degree measure of the shortest arc from that point to the equator. The latitude of Los Angeles (LA) is 34.05° north of the equator (E). How far is it from Los Angeles to the equator if the diameter of the earth is 7920 miles?

solution   We begin by drawing a diagram of the problem. This diagram is not drawn to scale.

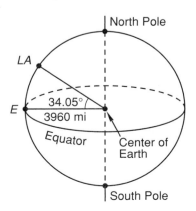

The diameter of the earth is 7920 miles, so the radius is 3960 miles. We note that the distance from Los Angeles to the equator is equal to the length of the arc of the sector with a central angle of 34.05° and radius 3960 miles. **The length of the arc of a sector of a circle is equal to the measure of the central angle in radians times the length of the radius.** Therefore, as a first step, we must convert 34.05° to radians.

$$34.05 \text{ deg} \times \frac{\pi \text{ rad}}{180 \text{ deg}} = 0.594 \text{ rad}$$

Therefore, if the measure of the central angle were 1 radian, the distance from Los Angeles to the equator would be 1 radian times 3960 miles, or 3960 miles. But the measure of the central angle is 0.594 radian, so the distance from Los Angeles to the equator is 0.594 times 3960 miles, or 2352.24 miles.

$$\text{Distance} = 0.594(3960 \text{ miles}) = \textbf{2352.24 miles}$$

example 39.5   Theo measured the angle between the base of the building and the top of the building and received a reading of 0.6°. If Theo was 4000 feet from the base of the building when the measurement was made, how high was the building?

solution   Even a diagram which is not to scale is helpful.

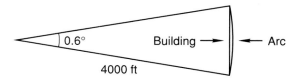

For very small angles, the length of the chord (height of the building) is almost the same as the length of the arc. **The length of the arc is the angle measure in radians times the length of the radius.** As a first step, we convert 0.6° to radians.

$$0.6 \text{ deg} \times \frac{\pi \text{ rad}}{180 \text{ deg}} = 0.010472 \text{ rad}$$

A central angle of 1 radian would yield an arc of 4000 feet, but a central angle of 0.010472 radian yields

$$\text{Length of the arc} = 0.010472(4000 \text{ ft}) = \textbf{41.89 ft} \approx \text{height of the building}$$

39.B
forms of linear equations

The slope-intercept equation of the line whose slope is $-\frac{3}{5}$ and whose y intercept is $\frac{11}{5}$ is

$$y = -\frac{3}{5}x + \frac{11}{5}$$

If many lines share a common characteristic, the lines are said to form a **family of lines.** There is an infinite number of lines whose slope is $-\frac{3}{5}$ and an infinite number of lines whose y intercept is $\frac{11}{5}$. We show a few members of each of these families in the following figures.

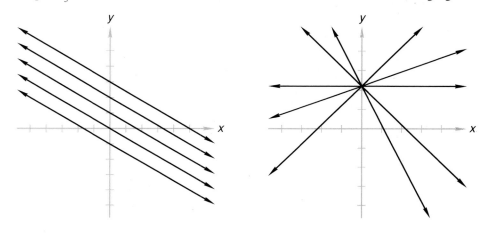

There are other forms of linear equations. Here we show five different forms of the equation on the previous page.

(a) $3x + 5y - 11 = 0$ (b) $y = -\dfrac{3}{5}x + \dfrac{11}{5}$ (c) $\dfrac{x}{\frac{11}{3}} + \dfrac{y}{\frac{11}{5}} = 1$

(d) $y - 1 = -\dfrac{3}{5}(x - 2)$ (e) $y - 1 = \dfrac{-2 - 1}{7 - 2}(x - 2)$

We have concentrated on form (b) because this form is so useful. This form is called the **slope-intercept form** because $-\frac{3}{5}$, the first number, is the slope of the line, and $\frac{11}{5}$, the second number, is the y intercept of the line. The other forms have names and are important because each of them has some characteristic that makes the form desirable for some uses. The letters $A, B, C, a, b, c,$ and m are often used to represent the constants in the equations. The names of the different forms and the constants used are as follows:

GENERAL FORM   SLOPE-INTERCEPT FORM   DOUBLE-INTERCEPT FORM

(a) $Ax + By + C = 0$ (b) $y = mx + b$ (c) $\dfrac{x}{a} + \dfrac{y}{b} = 1$

POINT-SLOPE FORM   TWO-POINT FORM

(d) $y - y_1 = m(x - x_1)$ (e) $y - y_1 = \dfrac{y_2 - y_1}{x_2 - x_1}(x - x_1)$

We will continue to use the slope-intercept form for most applications, but we will practice changing the equations from one form to another form. This practice will help us to recognize the various forms of the equation of a line and will also sharpen a few skills of algebraic manipulation.

example 39.6   Write $y = -\dfrac{7}{3}x + \dfrac{1}{5}$ in general form with integers as the constants.

solution   The general form of the equation is

$$Ax + By + C = 0$$

We need to write the x term first, then the y term, and then the constant. When we do this, we get

$$\frac{7}{3}x + y - \frac{1}{5} = 0$$

Now to eliminate the fractions, we multiply every term by 15, which is the least common multiple (LCM) of 3 and 5, and then cancel the denominators.

$$(15)\frac{7}{3}x + (15)y - (15)\frac{1}{5} = 0 \qquad \text{multiplied}$$

$$\mathbf{35x + 15y - 3 = 0} \qquad \text{simplified}$$

example 39.7   Use the point-slope form to find the equation of the line whose slope is $-\frac{1}{3}$ and that passes through $(-2, 5)$. Then transform the equation to general form.

solution   First we write the point-slope equation,

$$y - y_1 = m(x - x_1)$$

and replace y_1 with 5, x_1 with -2, and m with $-\frac{1}{3}$.

$$y - 5 = -\frac{1}{3}[x - (-2)]$$

Now we simplify and get

$$3y - 15 = -x - 2$$

Then we finish by arranging the result into general form and get

$$x + 3y - 13 = 0$$

example 39.8 Write $2x - 3y + 4 = 0$ in double-intercept form.

solution The double-intercept form has the constant on the right-hand side of the equals sign, and the constant is always 1. So we add -4 to both sides and then divide both sides by -4. Then we simplify.

$$2x - 3y = -4 \qquad \text{added} -4 \text{ to both sides}$$

$$-\frac{x}{2} + \frac{3y}{4} = 1 \qquad \text{divided both sides by} -4$$

Now we rewrite the left-hand side into the required form.

$$\frac{x}{-2} + \frac{y}{\frac{4}{3}} = 1$$

In this form, the values of the x intercept and y intercept can be determined by inspection. We see that if we let $x = 0$, y will equal $\frac{4}{3}$, and that if we let $y = 0$, then x will equal -2.

LET $x = 0$	LET $y = 0$
$\dfrac{0}{-2} + \dfrac{y}{\frac{4}{3}} = 1$	$\dfrac{x}{-2} + \dfrac{0}{\frac{4}{3}} = 1$
so $\quad y = \dfrac{4}{3}$	so $\quad x = -2$

Thus, the constant under x is the x intercept, which we call a, and the constant under y is the y intercept, which we call b.

problem set 39

1. The latitude of Oklahoma City is 35.5° north of the equator. How far is it from Oklahoma City to the equator if the diameter of the earth is 7920 miles?

2. Kim measured the angle between the base of the tree and the top of the tree and received a reading of 1.2°. If Kim was 1500 feet from the base of the tree when the measurement was made, how high was the tree?

3. How many different ways can the letters a, b, c, and d be arranged if no repetition is permitted?

4. Seven boys were to have their pictures taken three at a time. The photographer had three chairs placed in a row. How many ways could the photographer arrange the boys for their pictures?

5. Roselinda rode her bike for 60 miles at 30 miles per hour and then rode 20 miles at 10 miles per hour. How fast would she have to ride for the next 20 miles to have an overall average speed of 20 miles per hour for the entire trip?

6. The red-headed wonder boy ran y yards in s seconds. What would his rate be in yards per second if he ran twice as far in 10 more seconds?

7. Queen Wanatonga was frustrated because the men worked so slowly. It took 5 men 10 days to do the first job, and then 3 men quit. How many days would it take the 2 remaining men to do another job the same size?

8. Use the point-slope form to find a general form of the equation of the line whose slope is $\frac{1}{2}$ and that passes through $(-2, 3)$.

9. Write $3x - 2y + 6 = 0$ in double-intercept form.

Evaluate:

10. $\cos\left(-\dfrac{13\pi}{6}\right) + \sin\dfrac{13\pi}{6}$

11. $\sin\dfrac{\pi}{3}\cos\dfrac{\pi}{3} - \sin\dfrac{\pi}{3}$

12. $\tan\left(-\dfrac{\pi}{4}\right)\cos\dfrac{\pi}{2} + \sin\dfrac{\pi}{6}$

13. Write the quadratic equation with a lead coefficient of 1 whose roots are $-\sqrt{3}$ and $\sqrt{3}$.

14. Find the equation of the line that is equidistant from the points $(5, 1)$ and $(-4, -3)$. Write the equation in slope-intercept form.

15. Find the coordinates of the point halfway between $(-2, 6)$ and $(6, 3)$.

16. Find the number that is $\frac{5}{6}$ of the way from $-3\frac{2}{3}$ to $6\frac{1}{3}$.

17. Evaluate: $\displaystyle\sum_{p=-1}^{3}\dfrac{p^2 - 2}{4}$.

18. The data points in the table below relate the number of books sold (S) to the price per book (P). Note that in the graph the horizontal and vertical scales are different. The position of the line that best fits this data has been estimated. Write the equation that expresses the number of books sold as a function of the price per book $(S = mP + b)$.

Price per book (in dollars)	15.00	16.50	18.25	19.75	21.00	23.50	24.75	25.50	26.00
Number sold (in thousands)	247	236	230	228	213	194	196	188	185

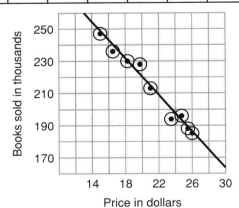

19. Find f where $g(x) = \log_2 x$ and $(f \circ g)(x) = \sqrt{\log_2 x}$.

20. The diagonals of a certain quadrilateral are congruent. Must the quadrilateral be a rectangle? If not, provide an example of a quadrilateral whose diagonals are congruent that is not a rectangle.

21. In the figure shown, $\overline{EF}$ is the median of trapezoid $ABCD$. Find x.

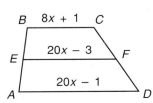

22. Evaluate. Do not use a calculator.

(a) $\operatorname{Arcsin}\left(-\dfrac{\sqrt{2}}{2}\right)$

(b) $\sin\left[\operatorname{Arccos}\left(-\dfrac{1}{5}\right)\right]$

23. Determine whether the graph of each equation is symmetric about the x axis, the y axis, and the origin:

(a)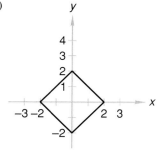

$|x| + |y| = 2$

(b)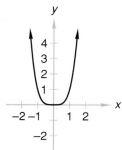

$y = x^4$

24. Solve:

(a) $\log_b \dfrac{1}{27} = -3$

(b) $\log_4 \dfrac{1}{64} = k$

(c) $\log_{1/3} m = -\dfrac{2}{3}$

25. Find the domain and range of each function whose graph is shown:

(a)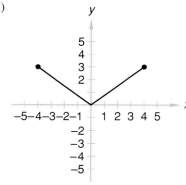

(b)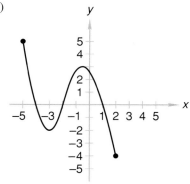

26. Let $f(x) = \dfrac{2}{3}x - \dfrac{4}{3}$ and $g(x) = \dfrac{3}{2}\left(x + \dfrac{4}{3}\right)$. Evaluate:

(a) $(f \circ g)(x)$

(b) $(g \circ f)(x)$

27. Given: $ABCD$ is a rectangle

E is the midpoint of $\overline{BC}$

Write a two-column proof to prove:

$\overline{AE} \cong \overline{DE}$

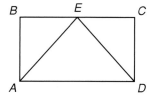

28. A sphere has a volume of $18{,}432\pi$ m³. If the volume of the sphere is increased by $29{,}484\pi$ m³, by what amount is the surface area of the sphere increased?

CONCEPT REVIEW
PROBLEMS

29. Let a and b be real numbers. If $ab > 0$, compare: A. $a^2 + b^2$ B. $(a + b)^2$

30. Let x and y be real numbers. If $x < 0$ and $y > 1$, compare: A. xy B. $\dfrac{x}{y}$

**LESSON 40   *The Argument in Mathematics • The Laws of
Logarithms • Properties of Inverse Functions***

40.A
**the
argument in
mathematics**

Every discipline takes common words and gives them special meanings for use in that discipline. This is also true in mathematics, and the word **argument** is a good example. In common usage, an argument refers to a heated discussion. Mathematicians use the word in this context, and they also give the word three other meanings for use in mathematics. The first meaning comes directly from the Latin word *arguere*, which means "to make clear" or "to prove by showing reasons." For this usage, we say that an argument is a connection of statements or reasons intended to establish or refute a given proposition. The second mathematical use is in the polar form of complex numbers, where the angle is sometimes called the *argument* and the length of the radius vector is called the *modulus*. The third mathematical use of the word *argument* is to designate the input of a function. A function is a set of ordered pairs, and if the same rule is applied to the first member of each pair to get the second member, the first member can be called the **argument of the function.** Here we show three function machines. Each operates on the input in the same way.

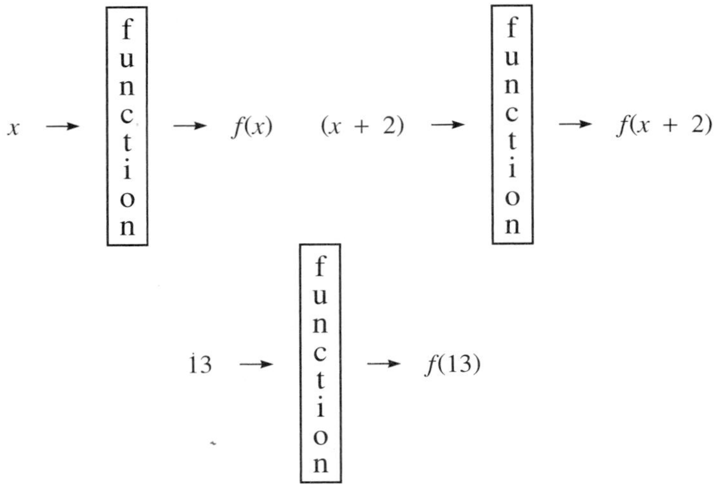

$$x \rightarrow \boxed{\text{function}} \rightarrow f(x) \qquad (x+2) \rightarrow \boxed{\text{function}} \rightarrow f(x+2)$$

$$13 \rightarrow \boxed{\text{function}} \rightarrow f(13)$$

The outputs $f(x)$, $f(x + 2)$, and $f(13)$ tell us that the function machine followed some rule that we designate by the letter f. The inputs (x), $(x + 2)$, and (13) are called **arguments.** If the rule were to take the logarithm of, we would have the following diagrams:

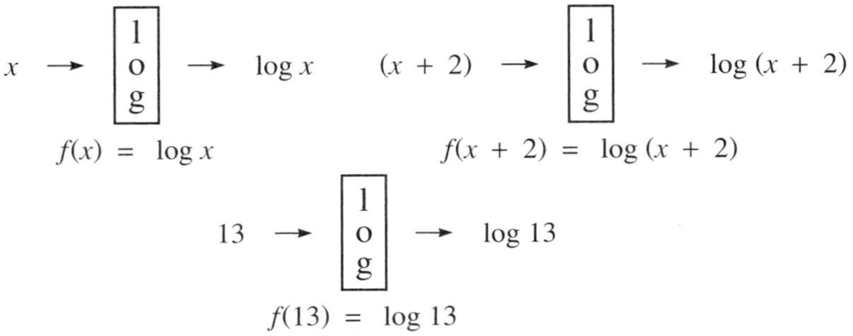

$$x \rightarrow \boxed{\text{log}} \rightarrow \log x \qquad (x+2) \rightarrow \boxed{\text{log}} \rightarrow \log (x+2)$$
$$f(x) = \log x \qquad\qquad\qquad f(x+2) = \log (x+2)$$

$$13 \rightarrow \boxed{\text{log}} \rightarrow \log 13$$
$$f(13) = \log 13$$

We use the word *argument* even if functional notation is not used. In the following expressions, the arguments from left to right are x, $(x + 2)$, and 13, even though these notations do not appear to the left of the equals signs.

$$y = \log x \qquad\qquad y = \log (x+2) \qquad\qquad y = \log 13$$

The word *argument* is used with all functions and especially when discussing trigonometric functions. The arguments in the following trigonometric functions, from left to right, are x, $(2x - \pi)$, and $\left(\frac{\theta}{4} - 30°\right)$.

$$y = \sin x \qquad f(x) = \cos(2x - \pi) \qquad g(\theta) = \tan\left(\frac{\theta}{4} - 30°\right)$$

If the argument consists of more than a single term, it is customary to enclose the argument in parentheses to help avoid confusion.

40.B
the laws of logarithms

Logarithms are exponents. There are three rules for logarithms, and they can be developed by remembering the rules for exponents. To develop the first rule for logarithms, we remember that 100 equals 10^2 and that 1000 equals 10^3.

$$100 = 10^2 \qquad 1000 = 10^3$$

Thus, if 10 is the base, the logarithm (exponent) necessary to get 100 is 2 and the logarithm (exponent) necessary to get 1000 is 3.

$$\log_{10} 100 = 2 \qquad \log_{10} 1000 = 3$$

If we multiply 10^2 by 10^3, we add the exponents.

$$10^2 \cdot 10^3 = 10^{2+3} = 10^5$$

Thus, we see that the logarithm (exponent) of the product of two exponentials is the sum of the individual logarithms (exponents).

$$\log_{10}(10^2 \cdot 10^3) = \log_{10} 10^2 + \log_{10} 10^3 = 5$$

And, if we use 100 instead of 10^2 and 1000 instead of 10^3, we can write

$$\log_{10}(100 \cdot 1000) = \log_{10} 100 + \log_{10} 1000 = 5$$

From this we can generalize and state the product rule of logarithms. We use M to represent the first number and N to represent the second number. We will do a formal proof of this rule in a later lesson.

$$\log_b MN = \log_b M + \log_b N$$

This rule tells us that if we encounter an expression that contains the sum of two logarithms, we know that the arguments were multiplied.

example 40.1 Solve: $\log_a 4 + \log_a 6 = \log_a(x + 4)$

solution On the left-hand side of the equation, we have the sum of the logarithm of 4 and the logarithm of 6, and a is the base for both. This means that 4 and 6 are multiplied, so we can write

$$\log_a 24 = \log_a(x + 4)$$

If the logarithms are equal and the bases are equal, then the arguments are equal. So,

$$x + 4 = 24 \qquad \text{equal arguments}$$

$$x = \mathbf{20} \qquad \text{solved}$$

The argument of a logarithmic function must always be a positive number, so the last step in the solution of a problem of this type must be a check to see that the use of the values found for the variable will result in positive arguments. In this problem we have only one value of the variable to check. When 20 is used in $(x + 4)$, we get 24, a positive number. Thus, 20 is an acceptable value of x in this argument.

To find the quotient rule for logarithms, we note that when we divide 10^3 by 10^2, the logarithm (exponent) of the denominator is subtracted from the logarithm (exponent) of the numerator.

$$\frac{10^3}{10^2} = 10^{3-2} = 10^1$$

Thus, we can write

$$\log_{10} \frac{10^3}{10^2} = \log_{10} 10^3 - \log_{10} 10^2 = 1$$

If we replace 10^3 with M and 10^2 with N, we can generalize and write the quotient rule as

$$\log_b \frac{M}{N} = \log_b M - \log_b N$$

This rule tells us that if an expression is the difference of two logarithms, then we know that the arguments were divided.

example 40.2   Solve: $\log_4 (x + 6) - \log_4 (x - 1) = \log_4 5$

solution   On the left-hand side of the equation, we see the difference of the logarithms of two expressions and that the bases are equal. This tells us that the expressions were divided, so we can write

$$\log_4 \frac{x + 6}{x - 1} = \log_4 5$$

If the logarithms are equal and the bases are equal, then the arguments are equal. We equate the arguments and solve for x.

$$\frac{x + 6}{x - 1} = 5 \qquad \text{equated arguments}$$

$$x + 6 = 5(x - 1) \qquad \text{cross multiplied}$$

$$x + 6 = 5x - 5 \qquad \text{multiplied}$$

$$4x = 11 \qquad \text{simplified}$$

$$x = \frac{11}{4} \qquad \text{divided}$$

To find the power rule for logarithms, we note that

$$\log_{10} 10^2 = 2$$

because the exponent is the logarithm. If we raise 10^2 to the third power, we get 10^6

$$\left(10^2\right)^3 = 10^6$$

and the logarithm of 10^6 is 6. Thus, the log of $\left(10^2\right)^3$ is 3 times the logarithm of 10^2. We generalize and state the power rule for logarithms, using M in place of 10^2 and n in place of 3.

$$\log_b M^n = n \log_b M$$

This rule is probably the most useful of the three rules and is the most difficult to remember. The rule is used two different ways. We can turn an exponent into a coefficient, as

$$\log_b x^5 \xrightarrow{\quad \text{equals} \quad} 5 \log_b x$$

and we can go the other way and turn a coefficient into an exponent.

$$5 \log_b x \xrightarrow{\quad \text{equals} \quad} \log_b x^5$$

example 40.3 Solve: $3 \log_b x = \log_b 8$

solution **On the left-hand side of the equation, we use the power rule to turn the coefficient into an exponent and write**

$$\log_b x^3 = \log_b 8$$

If the logarithms are equal and the bases are equal, then the arguments are equal. We equate the arguments and solve.

$$x^3 = 8 \qquad \text{equated arguments}$$

$$x = \mathbf{2} \qquad \text{solved}$$

example 40.4 Solve: $\log_{12} x = \dfrac{2}{3} \log_{12} 64$

solution **This time we change the coefficient on the right-hand side of the equation to an exponent and write**

$$\log_{12} x = \log_{12} 64^{2/3}$$

If the logarithms are equal and the bases are equal, then the arguments are equal. We equate the arguments and solve.

$$x = 64^{2/3} \qquad \text{equated arguments}$$

$$x = \mathbf{16} \qquad \text{solved}$$

40.C
properties of inverse functions

We remember that two functions f and g can be composed to create a new function. Below, we show $f \circ g$ in terms of function machines.

$$x \rightarrow \boxed{g} \rightarrow g(x) \rightarrow \boxed{f} \rightarrow f(g(x))$$

We also show $g \circ f$ in terms of function machines.

$$x \rightarrow \boxed{f} \rightarrow f(x) \rightarrow \boxed{g} \rightarrow g(f(x))$$

Usually, $f \circ g$ and $g \circ f$ are two very different functions. In other words, inputting x into both series of function machines above usually yields very different answers. However, if in both cases above, x is inputted and the final result is also x, we say that f and g are inverse functions. We state the definition of inverse functions in the box below.

DEFINITION OF INVERSE FUNCTIONS

Two functions f and g are defined to be **inverse functions** if

$$f(g(x)) = x \quad \text{for all } x \text{ in the domain of } g$$
$$\text{and} \quad g(f(x)) = x \quad \text{for all } x \text{ in the domain of } f$$

Though not immediately apparent, the definition above requires that we show that the range of g is contained in the domain of f and that the range of f is contained in the domain of g. In the problem sets and examples that follow, however, we will not worry about these subtle conditions on the domain. We will only perform the algebraic process of showing $f(g(x)) = g(f(x)) = x$.

example 40.5 Show that $f(x) = \frac{1}{3}x - 3$ and $g(x) = 3x + 9$ are inverse functions by computing their compositions.

solution To show f and g are inverse functions, we need to show

$$f(g(x)) = x \qquad \text{and} \qquad g(f(x)) = x$$

We will assume the conditions on the domain required by the definition of inverse functions are already satisfied. First we compute $f(g(x))$.

$$f(g(x)) = f(3x + 9) = \frac{1}{3}(3x + 9) - 3 = x + 3 - 3 = x$$

Now we compute $g(f(x))$.

$$g(f(x)) = g\left(\frac{1}{3}x - 3\right) = 3\left(\frac{1}{3}x - 3\right) + 9 = x - 9 + 9 = x$$

Since $f(g(x)) = g(f(x)) = x$, f and g are inverse functions.

example 40.6 Show that $f(x) = \frac{1}{x-3}$ and $g(x) = \frac{3x+1}{x}$ are inverse functions by computing their compositions.

solution To show f and g are inverse functions, we need to show

$$f(g(x)) = x \qquad \text{and} \qquad g(f(x)) = x$$

We will assume the conditions on the domain required by the definition of inverse functions are already satisfied. First we compute $f(g(x))$.

$$f(g(x)) = f\left(\frac{3x+1}{x}\right) = \frac{1}{\left(\dfrac{3x+1}{x}\right) - 3} = \frac{1}{\dfrac{3x+1}{x} - \dfrac{3x}{x}}$$

$$= \frac{1}{\dfrac{3x+1-3x}{x}} = \frac{1}{\dfrac{1}{x}} = x$$

Now we compute $g(f(x))$.

$$g(f(x)) = g\left(\frac{1}{x-3}\right) = \frac{3\left(\dfrac{1}{x-3}\right) + 1}{\left(\dfrac{1}{x-3}\right)} = \frac{\dfrac{3}{x-3} + \dfrac{x-3}{x-3}}{\dfrac{1}{x-3}}$$

$$= \left(\frac{3+x-3}{x-3}\right)\left(\frac{x-3}{1}\right) = \left(\frac{x}{x-3}\right)\left(\frac{x-3}{1}\right) = x$$

Since $f(g(x)) = g(f(x)) = x$, f and g are inverse functions.

problem set 40

1. A dog tied by a rope to a pole moves through an angle of 35° along a circular arc. How far does the dog move if the rope is 30 feet in length?

2. The average speed for the first 45 miles was 15 mph and the average speed for the next 50 miles was 25 mph. What should be the speed for the next 85 miles so that the overall average speed would be 18 mph?

3. The little red airplane could fly at 6 times the speed of the wind. It could fly 700 miles downwind in 1 hour less than it took to fly 600 miles upwind. What was the speed of the little red airplane in still air and what was the speed of the wind?

4. The correct mixture for the alloy was 16% tin and 84% copper. How much tin must be added to 410 pounds of the correct mixture to get a mixture that is 18% tin?

5. How many 4-letter signs can be made from the letters in the word WESTY if repetition is permitted?

6. Twenty books were available for the display of five books in a row. How many different displays were possible?

Solve for x:

7. $\log_a 3 + \log_a 4 = \log_a (x - 2)$

8. $\log_3 (x + 2) - \log_3 (x - 1) = \log_3 4$

9. $3 \log_c x = \log_c 27$

10. $\log_{12} x = \dfrac{2}{3} \log_{12} 27$

11. Determine if $f(x) = 2x + 3$ and $g(x) = \frac{1}{2}x - \frac{3}{2}$ are inverse functions by computing their compositions.

12. Use the point-slope form to find a general form of the equation of the line whose slope is $-\frac{1}{3}$ and that passes through $(-3, 4)$.

13. Write $2x - 4y + 5 = 0$ in double-intercept form.

Evaluate:

14. $\sin \dfrac{2\pi}{3} \cos \dfrac{2\pi}{3} - \sin \dfrac{4\pi}{3}$

15. $\tan \left(-\dfrac{3\pi}{4} \right) \cos \dfrac{\pi}{2} - \sin \dfrac{\pi}{2}$

16. $\sin \left(-\dfrac{19\pi}{6} \right) + \sin \dfrac{13\pi}{6}$

17. Write the quadratic equation with a lead coefficient of 1 whose roots are $-\dfrac{5}{3}$ and $\dfrac{2}{5}$.

18. Find the equation of the line that is equidistant from the points $(-4, 2)$ and $(5, 3)$. Write your equation in general form.

19. The data points in the table below came from an experiment that measured the radiation emitted (R) from various atoms and the number of neutrons (N) which the atoms contained. The position of the line which best fits the data points has been estimated. Write the equation that expresses the number of neutrons present as a function of the radiation emitted ($N = mR + b$).

R	115	127	132	145	146	147	156	156	176
N	74	53	68	52	32	21	33	17	11

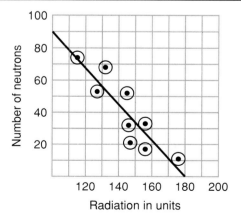

Number of neutrons

Radiation in units

20. Find two functions f and g such that $(f \circ g)(x) = x^2 + 1$.

21. Evaluate. Do not use a calculator.

(a) $\text{Arctan}\left(-\sqrt{3}\right)$

(b) $\cos\left[\text{Arctan}\left(-\dfrac{2}{3}\right)\right]$

22. The graph of the function $f(x) = x^2$ is shown on the left below. The graph on the right is the same graph reflected in the x axis. Write the equation of the graph on the right.

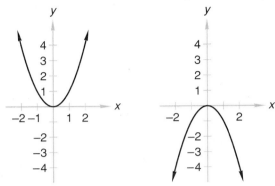

23. The graph of the function $f(x) = 1/x$ is centered at the origin, as shown on the left below. The graph on the right is the same graph translated so that it is centered at $(3, 0)$. Write the equation of the graph on the right.

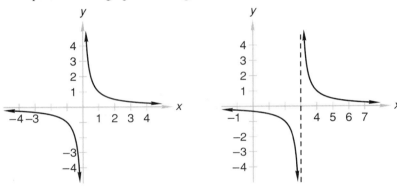

24. Find the domain of the function $f(x) = \dfrac{\sqrt{x}}{x^3 + x^2 - 2x}$.

25. Factor: $125x^3y^6 - 216a^3y^9$

26. If $f(x) = 3x^2 - 4x$, find $\dfrac{f(x + h) - f(x)}{h}$.

27. Given: $\overline{PR}$ bisects $\angle QPS$

$\overline{PR}$ bisects $\angle QRS$

Write a two-column proof to prove:

$\triangle PQR \cong \triangle PSR$

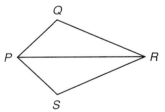

28. A right circular cone of maximum volume is to be cut from a solid wooden right circular cylinder. What fraction of the volume of the cylinder will be discarded?

CONCEPT REVIEW
PROBLEMS

29. Compare: A. $2 \log_3 4$ B. $4 \log_3 2$

30. In $\triangle ABC$, $AB < BC < AC$.

Compare: A. $m\angle C$ B. $60°$

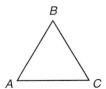

Note: Figure not drawn to scale

LESSON *41* *Reciprocal Trigonometric Functions* • *Permutation Notation*

41.A
reciprocal trigonometric functions

It is convenient to have a name for the reciprocals of the cosine, sine, and tangent. We call these reciprocal functions the secant (sec), cosecant (csc), and cotangent (cot) and define them as follows:

$$\frac{1}{\cos\theta} = \sec\theta \qquad \frac{1}{\sin\theta} = \csc\theta \qquad \frac{1}{\tan\theta} = \cot\theta$$

We can remember the definitions of these ratios if we write the functions vertically and note the pairings.

$$\cos\theta = \frac{adj}{hyp}$$
$$\sin\theta = \frac{opp}{hyp}$$
$$\tan\theta = \frac{opp}{adj}$$
$$\cot\theta = \frac{adj}{opp}$$
$$\csc\theta = \frac{hyp}{opp}$$
$$\sec\theta = \frac{hyp}{adj}$$

We note that the secant (sec) is the ratio of the hypotenuse to the side adjacent to the angle. This is the cosine ratio upside-down. We note that the cosecant (csc) is the ratio of the hypotenuse to the side opposite the angle. This is the sine ratio upside-down. We note also that the cotangent (cot) is the ratio of the side adjacent to the angle to the side opposite the angle. This is the tangent ratio upside-down. If we wanted to, we could use these reciprocal functions to help us solve triangles and add vectors, but we will usually not do so because the cosine, sine, and tangent perform these tasks quite adequately. We will reserve the use of the reciprocal functions to situations where their use is helpful. Problems such as the following will allow us to work with the secant, cosecant, and cotangent so their properties will be as familiar as those of the cosine, sine, and tangent.

example 41.1   Draw the appropriate triangles and evaluate: sec 330° + cot 480°

solution   We draw the diagrams and note that the related angle of 330° is 30° and the related angle of 480° is 60°. We also draw the reference triangle.

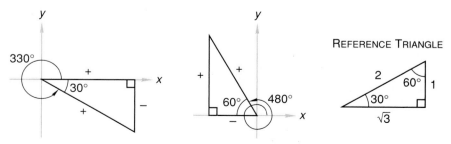

We remember that the secant is the reciprocal of the cosine, and the cosine is positive in the fourth quadrant. So the secant is positive in the fourth quadrant. Therefore, we can write

$$\sec 330° = \sec 30°$$

We remember that the cotangent is the reciprocal of the tangent, and the tangent is negative in the second quadrant. So the cotangent is negative in the second quadrant. Therefore, we can write

$$\cot 480° = -\cot 60°$$

We know sec 30° is the reciprocal of cos 30°, and cot 60° is the reciprocal of tan 60°. Therefore, we have

$$\cos 30° = \frac{\sqrt{3}}{2} \quad \longrightarrow \quad \sec 30° = \frac{1}{\cos 30°} = \frac{2}{\sqrt{3}}$$

$$\tan 60° = \frac{\sqrt{3}}{1} \quad \longrightarrow \quad \cot 60° = \frac{1}{\tan 60°} = \frac{1}{\sqrt{3}}$$

Now we have the values and can add the functions.

$$\sec 330° + \cot 480° = \sec 30° - \cot 60° \qquad \text{substituted}$$

$$= \frac{2}{\sqrt{3}} - \frac{1}{\sqrt{3}} \qquad \text{sum of functions}$$

$$= \frac{1}{\sqrt{3}} \qquad \text{added}$$

$$= \frac{\sqrt{3}}{3} \qquad \text{rationalized denominator}$$

example 41.2   Draw the appropriate triangles and evaluate: $\dfrac{2}{3} \csc\left(-\dfrac{3\pi}{4}\right) - \sec \dfrac{11\pi}{4}$

solution   We draw the diagrams and note that the related angle of $-3\pi/4$ is $\pi/4$ and the related angle of $11\pi/4$ is $\pi/4$. We also draw the reference triangle.

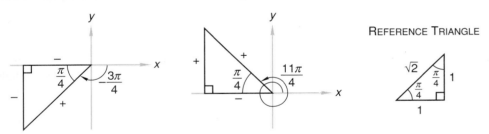

We remember that the cosecant is the reciprocal of the sine, and the sine is negative in the third quadrant. So the cosecant is negative in the third quadrant. Therefore, we can write

$$\csc\left(-\frac{3\pi}{4}\right) = -\csc \frac{\pi}{4}$$

We remember that the secant is the reciprocal of the cosine, and the cosine is negative in the second quadrant. So the secant is negative in the second quadrant. Therefore, we can write

$$\sec \frac{11\pi}{4} = -\sec \frac{\pi}{4}$$

We know csc $\pi/4$ is the reciprocal of sin $\pi/4$, and sec $\pi/4$ is the reciprocal of cos $\pi/4$. Therefore, we have

$$\sin \frac{\pi}{4} = \frac{1}{\sqrt{2}} \quad \longrightarrow \quad \csc \frac{\pi}{4} = \frac{1}{\sin \dfrac{\pi}{4}} = \sqrt{2}$$

$$\cos \frac{\pi}{4} = \frac{1}{\sqrt{2}} \quad \longrightarrow \quad \sec \frac{\pi}{4} = \frac{1}{\cos \dfrac{\pi}{4}} = \sqrt{2}$$

Now we have the values and can add the functions.

$$\frac{2}{3} \csc\left(-\frac{3\pi}{4}\right) - \sec\frac{11\pi}{4} = \frac{2}{3}\left(-\csc\frac{\pi}{4}\right) - \left(-\sec\frac{\pi}{4}\right) \qquad \text{substituted}$$

$$= \frac{2}{3}(-\sqrt{2}) - (-\sqrt{2}) \qquad \text{sum of functions}$$

$$= \frac{-2\sqrt{2}}{3} + \sqrt{2} \qquad \text{simplified}$$

$$= \frac{-2\sqrt{2}}{3} + \frac{3\sqrt{2}}{3} \qquad \text{common denominator}$$

$$= \frac{\sqrt{2}}{3} \qquad \text{added}$$

example 41.3   Draw the appropriate triangles and evaluate: $\sec\dfrac{10\pi}{3} + \csc\left(-\dfrac{7\pi}{2}\right)$

solution   We draw the diagrams and note that the related angle of $10\pi/3$ is $\pi/3$, and the angle $-7\pi/2$ is a quadrantal angle since it is an integer multiple of $\pi/2$. We also draw the reference triangle.

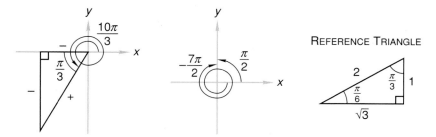

We remember that the secant is the reciprocal of the cosine, and the cosine is negative in the third quadrant. So the secant is negative in the third quadrant. Therefore, we can write

$$\sec\frac{10\pi}{3} = -\sec\frac{\pi}{3}$$

To find the cosecant of $-7\pi/2$, we note that the terminal side of the quadrantal angle $-7\pi/2$ coincides with the positive y axis. We note also that the terminal side of the quadrantal angle $\pi/2$ also coincides with the positive y axis. We remember that angles with the same terminal side are said to be *coterminal angles*. Therefore, $-7\pi/2$ and $\pi/2$ are coterminal angles. Since the trigonometric function values of coterminal angles are equal, the cosecant of $-7\pi/2$ is equal to the cosecant of $\pi/2$. Therefore, we can write

$$\csc\left(-\frac{7\pi}{2}\right) = \csc\frac{\pi}{2}$$

We know sec $\pi/3$ is the reciprocal of cos $\pi/3$, and csc $\pi/2$ is the reciprocal of sin $\pi/2$. Therefore, we have

$$\cos\frac{\pi}{3} = \frac{1}{2} \quad \longrightarrow \quad \sec\frac{\pi}{3} = \frac{1}{\cos\dfrac{\pi}{3}} = 2$$

$$\sin\frac{\pi}{2} = 1 \quad \longrightarrow \quad \csc\frac{\pi}{2} = \frac{1}{\sin\dfrac{\pi}{2}} = 1$$

Now we have the values and can add the functions.

$$\sec \frac{10\pi}{3} + \csc\left(-\frac{7\pi}{2}\right) = -\sec\frac{\pi}{3} + \csc\frac{\pi}{2} \qquad \text{substituted}$$

$$= -2 + 1 \qquad \text{sum of functions}$$

$$= -1 \qquad \text{added}$$

example 41.4   Draw the appropriate triangles and evaluate: $\cot\dfrac{17\pi}{6} - \sqrt{6}\,\csc\left(-\dfrac{9\pi}{4}\right)$

solution   We draw the diagrams and note that the related angle of $17\pi/6$ is $\pi/6$ and the related angle of $-9\pi/4$ is $\pi/4$. We also draw the reference triangles.

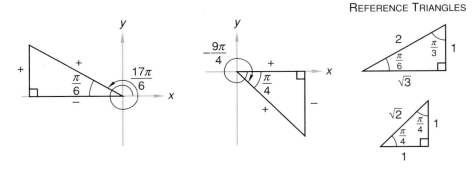

We remember that the cotangent is the reciprocal of the tangent, and the tangent is negative in the second quadrant. So the cotangent is negative in the second quadrant. Therefore, we can write

$$\cot\frac{17\pi}{6} = -\cot\frac{\pi}{6}$$

We remember that the cosecant is the reciprocal of the sine, and the sine is negative in the fourth quadrant. So the cosecant is negative in the fourth quadrant. Therefore, we can write

$$\csc\left(-\frac{9\pi}{4}\right) = -\csc\frac{\pi}{4}$$

We know $\cot\pi/6$ is the reciprocal of $\tan\pi/6$, and $\csc\pi/4$ is the reciprocal of $\sin\pi/4$. Therefore, we have

$$\tan\frac{\pi}{6} = \frac{1}{\sqrt{3}} \quad\longrightarrow\quad \cot\frac{\pi}{6} = \frac{1}{\tan\dfrac{\pi}{6}} = \sqrt{3}$$

$$\sin\frac{\pi}{4} = \frac{1}{\sqrt{2}} \quad\longrightarrow\quad \csc\frac{\pi}{4} = \frac{1}{\sin\dfrac{\pi}{4}} = \sqrt{2}$$

Now we have the values and can add the functions.

$$\cot\frac{17\pi}{6} - \sqrt{6}\,\csc\left(-\frac{9\pi}{4}\right) = -\cot\frac{\pi}{6} - \sqrt{6}\left(-\csc\frac{\pi}{4}\right) \qquad \text{substituted}$$

$$= -\sqrt{3} - \sqrt{6}(-\sqrt{2}) \qquad \text{sum of functions}$$

$$= -\sqrt{3} + 2\sqrt{3} \qquad \text{simplified}$$

$$= \sqrt{3} \qquad \text{added}$$

41.B
permutation notation

We have worked specific permutation problems but have avoided the general notation for this type of problem. The concept and the notation are both helpful and are explained in the following examples.

example 41.5   How many permutations are there of 22 things taken 6 at a time? Generalize this answer to an expression for n things taken r at a time.

solution   We can put 22 things in the first slot, 21 things in the next slot, 20 things in the next slot, etc., until we have all 6 positions filled.

22	21	20	19	18	17

Therefore, we can write

$$22 \cdot 21 \cdot 20 \cdot 19 \cdot 18 \cdot 17 = 53{,}721{,}360$$

Thus, there are **53,721,360** permutations of 22 things taken 6 at a time.

We will now generalize this answer to an expression for n things taken r at a time. In the boxes above, we see that the first number is 22, the second number is 21 (which is 1 less than 22), the third number is 20 (which is 2 less than 22), etc.

$$\begin{array}{cccccc}
(22) & (21) & (20) & (19) & (18) & (17) \\
(22) & (22-1) & (22-2) & (22-3) & (22-4) & (22-5)
\end{array}$$

If we use n for 22 and r for 6, the first factor is n, the next factor is $(n-1)$, the next factor is $(n-2)$, etc.,

$$n(n-1)(n-2)\ldots$$

but the last factor is not $(n-r)$ because $(22-6)$ is 16 and the last entry is 17, which is 1 greater. Thus, we must use $(n-r+1)$ as the last factor. Thus, we write the general expression for the permutation of n things taken r at a time as

$$_nP_r = n(n-1)(n-2)(n-3)\ldots(n-r+1)$$

The notation $_nP_r$ is not the only notation used for the permutation of n things taken r at a time. Some authors use the notation P_r^n and others use $P_{n,r}$ or $P(n, r)$.

example 41.6   Show how $_nP_r$ can be calculated using the concept of factorial.

solution   We will use the formula for $_nP_r$ to obtain a different form for $_nP_r$ that uses the concept of factorial. To do so we will use 22 for n and 6 for r. Now we write the formula for $_{22}P_6$ and then multiply the numerator and denominator by $(22-6)!$ as follows.

$$\begin{aligned}
_{22}P_6 &= 22(22-1)(22-2)(22-3)(22-4)(22-5)\left(\frac{(22-6)!}{(22-6)!}\right) \\
&= \frac{22 \cdot 21 \cdot 20 \cdot 19 \cdot 18 \cdot 17 \cdot 16!}{(22-6)!} \\
&= \frac{22!}{(22-6)!}
\end{aligned}$$

We can use a calculator to evaluate this expression and we get 53,721,360. This is the number of permutations of 22 things taken 6 at a time. We will now generalize this answer to an expression for n things taken r at a time. In the expression above we see that the numerator is 22!, which can be written as $n!$. The denominator is $(22-6)!$, which can be written as $(n-r)!$. Thus, we can also write the general expression for the permutation of n things taken r at a time as

$$_nP_r = \frac{n!}{(n-r)!}$$

example 41.7 Find: $_{12}P_4$

solution This problem asks for the number of permutations of 12 things taken 4 at a time. We know that the permutation of n things taken r at a time can be calculated by using either of the two formulas:

$$_nP_r = n(n-1)(n-2)(n-3) \ldots (n-r+1)$$

$$_nP_r = \frac{n!}{(n-r)!}$$

We will solve this problem by using both formulas.

Using the first formula where $n = 12$ and $r = 4$, we can write

$$_{12}P_4 = 12 \cdot 11 \cdot 10 \cdot 9$$

We can use a calculator to evaluate this expression and we get

$$_{12}P_4 = \mathbf{11{,}880}$$

Using the second formula where $n = 12$ and $r = 4$, we can write

$$_{12}P_4 = \frac{12!}{(12-4)!} = \frac{12!}{8!}$$

We can use a calculator to evaluate this expression and we get

$$_{12}P_4 = \mathbf{11{,}880}$$

**problem set
41**

1. A mouse scurries through an arc of 50° along the edge of a circular swimming pool. If the swimming pool is 70 feet in diameter, how far does the mouse scurry?

2. The average speed for the first 36 miles was 12 mph. The average speed for the next 45 miles was 15 mph. What should be the average speed for the next 54 miles so that the overall average speed would be 15 mph?

3. Four hundred men could do the job in 10 days. Paul had 600 men on the job for 5 days. How many men did he need for the next 5 days to finish the job on time?

4. Bubber strutted with pride because he could do a job in 3 hours that it took Dougan 6 hours to do. Bubber began work at noon and worked for 3 hours and then was joined by Dougan. What time would it be when a total of 4 jobs were completed?

5. The airplane flew m miles in h hours and arrived 3 hours late. How fast should the plane have flown in order to arrive on time?

Evaluate:

6. $\csc(-330°) - \sec 390°$

7. $\sec\left(-\dfrac{\pi}{3}\right) + \cot\left(-\dfrac{13\pi}{6}\right)$

8. Evaluate:

   (a) $_{10}P_4$

   (b) $_{13}P_5$

Solve for x:

9. $\log_4 2 + \log_4 8 = \log_4 (x+3)$

10. $\log_3 (x-2) - \log_3 (x+1) = \log_3 5$

11. $4\log_c x = \log_c 81$

12. $\log_{13} x = \dfrac{3}{4}\log_{13} 16$

13. Determine if $f(x) = 4x - 3$ and $g(x) = \frac{1}{4}x + 3$ are inverse functions by computing their compositions.

14. Use the point-slope form to find a general form of the equation of the line whose slope is $-\frac{1}{3}$ and that passes through $(-2, 3)$.

15. Write $5x - 3y + 6 = 0$ in double-intercept form.

16. Write the quadratic equation with a lead coefficient of 1 whose roots are $-\frac{1}{2}$ and $\frac{2}{3}$.

17. Find the equation of the line that is equidistant from the points $(2, 4)$ and $(-4, 6)$. Write the equation in double-intercept form.

18. Find the number that is $\frac{4}{13}$ of the way from $-3\frac{3}{4}$ to 6.

19. Evaluate: $\displaystyle\sum_{z=-2}^{1} \frac{z^3 - 1}{3}$

20. The data points in the table below relate the number of hypocrites present (H) and the number of sycophants present (S). The position of the line which best fits the data points has been estimated. Write the equation that expresses the number of hypocrites as a function of the number of sycophants $(H = mS + b)$.

Sycophants (in hundreds)	1.5	2.8	3.1	4.0	4.8	5.8	6.9	7.7	9.0
Hypocrites (in hundreds)	1.3	2.2	3.9	3.7	5.9	6.2	6.7	8.6	8.7

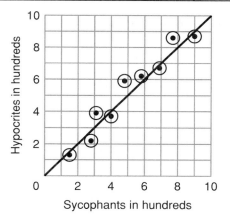

21. One diagonal of a certain parallelogram bisects the angles whose vertices it connects. No information is given about the other diagonal. Which of the following must the parallelogram be?

A. Rectangle B. Square C. Rhombus D. Trapezoid

22. The figure shown is a trapezoid whose area is 60 cm². Find the altitude of the trapezoid.

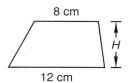

23. Evaluate. Do not use a calculator.

(a) $\text{Arccos}\left(-\dfrac{\sqrt{3}}{2}\right)$

(b) $\cos\left[\text{Arcsin}\left(-\dfrac{2}{3}\right)\right]$

24. The graph of the function $f(x) = 1/x$ is centered at the origin, as shown on the left below. The graph on the right is the same graph translated so that it is centered at $(-3, 0)$. Write the equation of the graph on the right.

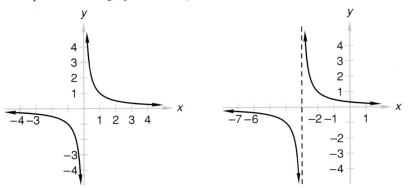

25. The graph of the function $f(x) = |x|$ is shown on the left below. The graph on the right is the same graph translated three units to the right and two units up. Write the equation of the graph on the right.

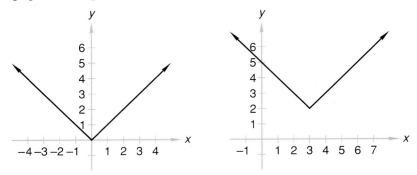

26. Find the resultant of $-2\underline{/140°} + 8\underline{/150°}$. Write the answer in polar form.

27. Find the domain and range of each function whose graph is shown:

(a)   (b)

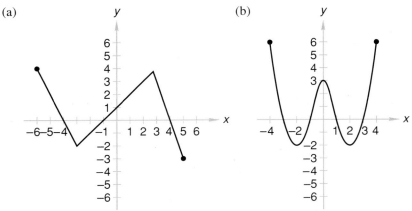

28. If $f(x) = \dfrac{1}{x}$, find $\dfrac{f(x + h) - f(x)}{h}$.

**CONCEPT REVIEW
PROBLEMS**   **29.** Compare: A. $\log_2 6 + \log_2 5$ B. $\log_2 3 + \log_2 10$

30. Let $\triangle ABC$ be an equiangular triangle.

Compare: A. x B. 5

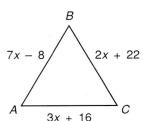

LESSON *42* *Conic Sections • Circles • Constants in Exponential Functions*

42.A
conic sections

A **circular cone** is the surface generated by a line when one point on the line is fixed and another point on the line is moved in a circle. The cone has two parts called **nappes** that are on either side of the fixed point. If the nappes are cut by a plane, the figures formed by the points of intersection of the cone and the plane are called **conic sections.** If the plane is perpendicular to the vertical axis of the cone, the plane will cut only one nappe and the points of intersection form a **circle.** If the plane is tilted slightly, the points of intersection form an **ellipse.**

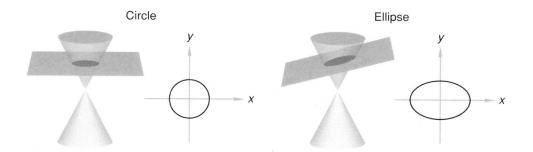

If the plane is tilted even more, the figure formed is a **parabola.** If the plane is tilted so that both nappes are cut, a two-part figure called a **hyperbola** is formed.

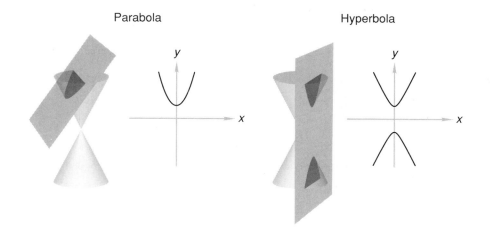

42.B
circles

We remember that in mathematics we use the word *locus* to describe the location of mathematical points. In Lesson 37, we stated that a line is the locus of all points in a plane that are equidistant from two given points. Here we will investigate the locus definition of a circle.

DEFINITION OF A CIRCLE

A circle is the locus of all points in a plane that are equidistant from a point called the *center* of the circle.

Below we show a circle whose center is the origin and whose radius is r. The x coordinate of a point on the circle equals the directed horizontal distance of the point from the center of the circle. The y coordinate of a point on the circle equals the directed vertical distance of the point from the center of the circle. The triangles shown are right triangles, and the Pythagorean theorem lets us write the standard form of the equation of the circle. The **general form** of this equation is also shown.

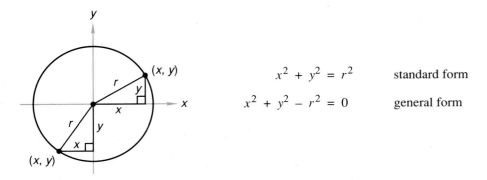

$$x^2 + y^2 = r^2 \qquad \text{standard form}$$
$$x^2 + y^2 - r^2 = 0 \qquad \text{general form}$$

We know we can translate the graph of any equation in x and y four units to the right by replacing x with $x - 4$ and six units down by replacing y with $y + 6$. Therefore, the equation of a circle whose center is $(4, -6)$ and whose radius is 5 is

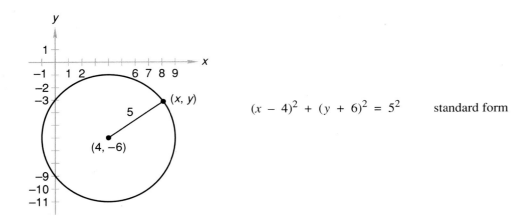

$$(x - 4)^2 + (y + 6)^2 = 5^2 \qquad \text{standard form}$$

If we multiply as indicated and collect like terms, we can write the equation in general form.

$$x^2 - 8x + 16 + y^2 + 12y + 36 = 25 \qquad \text{multiplied}$$
$$x^2 + y^2 - 8x + 12y + 27 = 0 \qquad \text{general form}$$

We can also find the equation of this circle by using the distance formula. The x distance from $(4, -6)$ to (x, y) is $x - 4$. The y distance is $y - (-6)$, or $y + 6$. The distance formula uses the Pythagorean theorem and says the square root of the sum of the squares of the x distance and the y distance equals the direct distance.

$$\sqrt{(x - 4)^2 + [y - (-6)]^2} = 5$$

Now we square both sides and get

$$(x - 4)^2 + (y + 6)^2 = 25$$

This is the same result we obtained by writing the equation of a circle of radius 5 whose center is the origin and translating it four units to the right and six units down.

example 42.1   Find the standard form of the equation of a circle whose center is at (h, k) and whose radius is r.

solution   We begin by sketching the graph of a circle whose center is at (h, k) and whose radius is r.

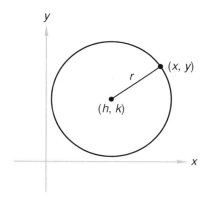

Let (x, y) be a point on the circle. Now we can use the distance formula to describe the distance from (h, k) to (x, y).

$$\sqrt{(x - h)^2 + (y - k)^2} = r$$

Now we square both sides to eliminate the radical and write the result in standard form.

$$(x - h)^2 + (y - k)^2 = r^2$$

example 42.2   Find the standard form of the equation of a circle of radius 4 whose center is at $(-3, 3)$. Then write the general form of the equation.

solution   We begin by sketching the graph of the circle whose center is at $(-3, 3)$ and whose radius is 4.

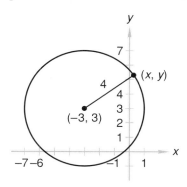

Let (x, y) be a point on the circle. Now we can use the distance formula to describe the distance from $(-3, 3)$ to (x, y).

$$\sqrt{[x - (-3)]^2 + [y - (3)]^2} = 4$$

Now we square both sides to eliminate the radical.

$$[x - (-3)]^2 + [y - (3)]^2 = 4^2$$

Then we simplify and get

$$(x + 3)^2 + (y - 3)^2 = 16 \qquad \text{standard form}$$

Now we perform the indicated multiplications and get

$$x^2 + 6x + 9 + y^2 - 6y + 9 = 16$$

We finish by collecting like terms.

$$x^2 + y^2 + 6x - 6y + 2 = 0 \qquad \text{general form}$$

42.C
constants in exponential functions

The following expressions are called **powers.** In each of these expressions the exponent is a constant.

$$\text{(a) } y = x^2 \quad \text{(b) } y = -(x - 4)^3 \quad \text{(c) } y = x^{1.2} \quad \text{(d) } y = (x - 3)^{1/2}$$

In exponential functions, the exponent contains a variable and the base can be any positive number except 1. Thus, all of the following are exponential functions:

$$\text{(e) } y = 2^x \quad \text{(f) } y = \left(\frac{1}{2}\right)^x \quad \text{(g) } y = 4^{-x} \quad \text{(h) } y = 0.5^{2x} \quad \text{(i) } y = 4^{3x+2}$$

We have been graphing exponential functions similar to (e) and (f). They both have a value of 1 when x equals 0, but in (e) the value of y increases as x increases, and in (f) the value of y decreases as x increases.

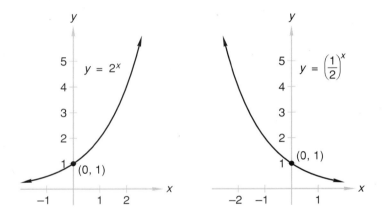

The exponential functions (g), (h), and (i) have the same shape as one of the above with just slight differences. **The trick to graphing one of these exponential functions is to begin by changing the exponential function into a form that is more familiar.**

example 42.3   Sketch the graph of the function $y = 3^{-x}$.

solution   When the exponent is negative, it is helpful to write the exponent with a factor of -1. The result is a simple exponential function whose base is $\frac{1}{3}$. It is graphed below on the right.

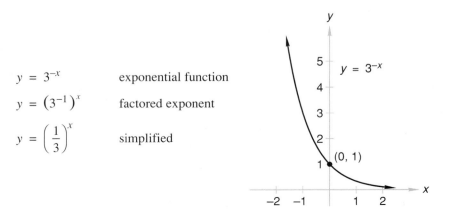

$$y = 3^{-x} \qquad \text{exponential function}$$

$$y = \left(3^{-1}\right)^x \qquad \text{factored exponent}$$

$$y = \left(\frac{1}{3}\right)^x \qquad \text{simplified}$$

example 42.4   Sketch the graph of the function $y = \left(\dfrac{1}{2}\right)^{2x}$.

solution   Again the first step is to work with the exponent. Then we graph the exponential function.

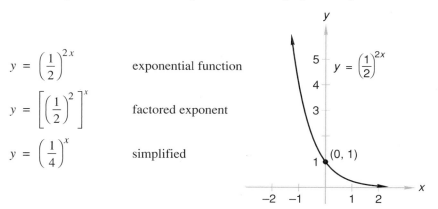

$$y = \left(\frac{1}{2}\right)^{2x} \qquad \text{exponential function}$$

$$y = \left[\left(\frac{1}{2}\right)^{2}\right]^{x} \qquad \text{factored exponent}$$

$$y = \left(\frac{1}{4}\right)^{x} \qquad \text{simplified}$$

example 42.5   Sketch the graph of the function $y = \left(\dfrac{1}{2}\right)^{-x-2}$.

solution   Again we begin by changing the exponential function into a form that is more familiar.

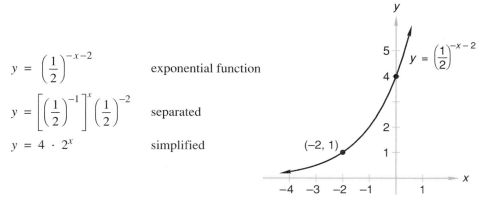

$$y = \left(\frac{1}{2}\right)^{-x-2} \qquad \text{exponential function}$$

$$y = \left[\left(\frac{1}{2}\right)^{-1}\right]^{x}\left(\frac{1}{2}\right)^{-2} \qquad \text{separated}$$

$$y = 4 \cdot 2^{x} \qquad \text{simplified}$$

This curve has the same basic shape as $y = 2^{x}$ except that every y value is multiplied by 4. **It is important to note that if an exponential function has a constant in the exponent that is not a coefficient of x, the value of the exponential function when $x = 0$ is not 1.** Here we show two other examples of this type of exponential function and evaluate each when $x = 0$.

$$y = 4^{x+3} \qquad\qquad y = 3^{2x-3} \qquad\qquad \text{exponential function}$$

$$y = 4^{0} \cdot 4^{3} \qquad\qquad y = 3^{2(0)} \cdot 3^{-3} \qquad \text{let } x = 0$$

$$y = 64 \qquad\qquad\quad y = \frac{1}{27} \qquad\qquad \text{value of } y \text{ when } x = 0$$

**problem set
42**

1. A horse runs through an arc of 40° along a circular racetrack. How far will the horse run if the diameter of the racetrack is 3000 feet?

2. It took Sally 3 hours to go 75 miles downstream and it took her 5 hours to travel back upstream to her starting position. What was the speed of her boat in still water and what was the speed of the current in the river?

3. A runner can run 100 yards in 9.8 seconds and 440 yards in 49 seconds. What is the ratio of her average speed in the 440 to her average speed in the 100?

4. Petunia and Petal worked for 5 hours and completed $1\frac{1}{24}$ jobs. If Petal took 12 hours to do 1 job, how long did it take Petunia to do 2 jobs?

5. Five workers can do 7 jobs in 3 days. How many days will it take 10 workers to do 14 jobs?

6. A furniture salesperson is normally paid $160 for a 40-hour week. During the week of the sale, his hourly pay was increased 25 percent and he was allowed to work 60 hours. How much did he make during the week of the sale?

7. Find the standard form of the equation of a circle whose center is at (3, 4) and whose radius is 3.

Sketch the graph of each of the following functions:

8. $y = \left(\dfrac{1}{2}\right)^{2x}$ 9. $y = \left(\dfrac{1}{2}\right)^{x-2}$

10. Evaluate: $\sec \dfrac{\pi}{4} - \sin \dfrac{13\pi}{6} - \cos\left(-\dfrac{8\pi}{3}\right)$

11. If $f(x) = \csc x$ and $g(x) = \cot x$, find $f\left(\dfrac{-\pi}{6}\right) - g\left(\dfrac{-13\pi}{6}\right)$.

12. Evaluate: $_{10}P_6$

Solve for x:

13. $\log_2 (x + 4) - \log_2 (x - 4) = \log_2 5$

14. $2 \log_7 x = 4$ 15. $4 \log_6 x = \log_6 256$

16. Determine if $f(x) = \frac{x}{2}$ and $g(x) = \frac{2}{x}$ are inverse functions by computing their compositions.

17. Use the point-slope form to find a general form of the equation of the line whose slope is $-\frac{2}{5}$ and that passes through (−1, 3).

18. Write $6x - 5y - 3 = 0$ in double-intercept form.

19. Write the quadratic equation with a lead coefficient of 1 whose roots are $-\frac{1}{2}$ and $\frac{4}{5}$.

20. Find the equation of the line that is equidistant from the points (1, 4) and (−3, 2). Write your equation in general form.

21. The data points in the table below relate people's income (I) with their age (A). The position of the line which best fits the data points is estimated. Write the equation that expresses income as a function of age (I = mA + b).

Age in years	22	25	28	32	35	38	40	43	47	50
Income in thousands of dollars	25	28	30	34	33	35	47	46	47	57

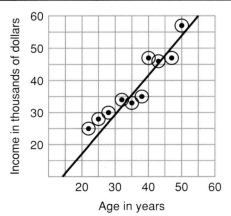

22. The diagonals of a certain quadrilateral do not bisect the angles whose vertices they connect. Which of the following could the quadrilateral be?

    A. Rectangle   B. Square   C. Rhombus

23. The figure shown is a trapezoid whose area is 50 cm^2. Find x. Dimensions are in centimeters.

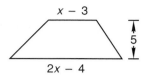

24. Evaluate. Do not use a calculator.

    (a) $\text{Arcsin}\left(-\dfrac{\sqrt{3}}{2}\right)$ (b) $\sin\left[\text{Arccos}\left(-\dfrac{3}{4}\right)\right]$

25. The graph of the function $f(x) = |x|$ is shown on the left below. The graph on the right is the same graph translated three units to the left and two units up. Write the equation of the graph on the right.

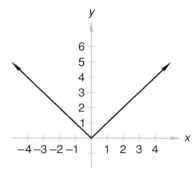 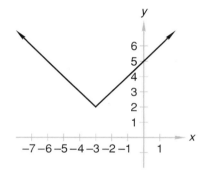

26. Given the function $f(x) = |x|$, write the equation of the function g whose graph is the graph of f translated two units to the right and three units up. Then sketch the graph of the new function g.

27. Find the domain of the function $f(x) = \dfrac{\sqrt{x}}{|2x| - 1}$.

28. Given: $\overline{AD} \cong \overline{BD}$

           $\overline{ED} \cong \overline{CD}$

    Write a two-column proof to prove:

        $\angle A \cong \angle B$

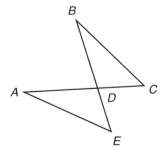

CONCEPT REVIEW
PROBLEMS

29. If $\sqrt{x} + \sqrt{x - 1} = 1$, compare: A. 1 B. x

30. If $x^2 = 4$ and $y^2 = 9$, compare: A. x B. y

LESSON 43 *Periodic Functions • Graphs of Sin θ and Cos θ*

43.A

periodic functions

We tend to concentrate much of our study of functions on functions that will help us understand the world in which we live and help us solve real-world problems. We are fortunate that many of these useful functions are easy to understand and to work with. Three of the most important functions are the linear function, the quadratic function, and the exponential function.

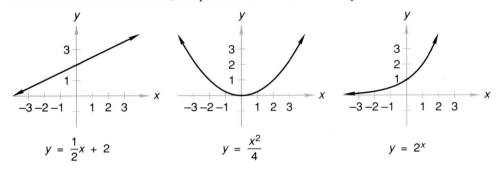

$$y = \frac{1}{2}x + 2 \qquad\qquad y = \frac{x^2}{4} \qquad\qquad y = 2^x$$

In a later lesson we will learn how the exponential function helps us understand the growth of bacteria.

The graphs of some functions have a repeating pattern and these functions are called **periodic functions.** The most important of these periodic functions are the *sine function* and the *cosine function.* The graph of the sine function looks like this. We often use θ instead of x on the horizontal axis, as we do here.

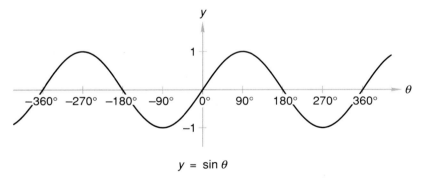

$$y = \sin \theta$$

The Latin suffix *-oid* indicates similarity or likeness. Thus *anthropoid* means "similar to, or like, a man"; *crystalloid* means "similar to, or like, a crystal"; and *planetoid* means "similar to, or like, a planet." In mathematics we use the word **sinusoid** to describe a curve that looks like a sine curve. Thus both the graphs of sin θ and cos θ are sinusoids. A sinusoid can be used to discuss the back-and-forth motion of a pendulum and the back-and-forth motion of any vibrating object. A vibration that slows down and stops can be explained by using the equation of a damped sinusoid, which is the product of an exponential function and a sinusoid, as we show here.

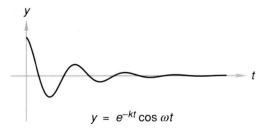

$$y = e^{-kt} \cos \omega t$$

The sinusoids are continuous functions and their importance in the study of vibrating motion is so important that we will devote much attention to the discussion of the sine function and the cosine function in this book. On the graph of a sinusoid, the value of the function for any value of θ equals the directed distance of the graph from the θ axis, as we will explain.

43.B

**graphs of
sin θ and
cos θ**

We remember that the values of the trigonometric functions of an angle depend on the measure of the angle and do not depend on the size of the triangle. Observe the following right triangles that contain a 27° angle.

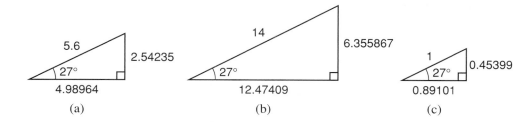

If we find the sine of each of these 27° angles by writing the ratio of the opposite side to the hypotenuse, we get

(a) $\dfrac{2.54235}{5.6} = 0.45399$ (b) $\dfrac{6.355867}{14} = 0.45399$ (c) $\dfrac{0.45399}{1} = 0.45399$

We note that in the last triangle, the length of the vertical side is the same as the sine of the angle. Now let's find the value of cos 27° for each triangle.

(a) $\dfrac{4.98964}{5.6} = 0.89101$ (b) $\dfrac{12.47409}{14} = 0.89101$ (c) $\dfrac{0.89101}{1} = 0.89101$

Again the answers are the same, but this time in (c) the length of the horizontal side equals the cosine of the angle. This is the reason that the unit circle is a valuable aid when we study the graphs of the sine and the cosine.

Let's use the unit circle to study the graph of the sine function. The length of the vertical side of the triangle equals the value of the sine of θ. When θ equals zero, sin θ equals zero. When θ equals 30°, the vertical side of the triangle has a length of 0.5, as we show on the left. When θ equals 60°, the vertical side of the triangle is approximately 0.866, as we show in the center. When θ equals 90°, sin θ equals 1, as we show on the right.

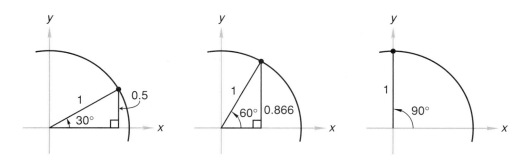

The plot of the vertical sides versus θ looks like this.

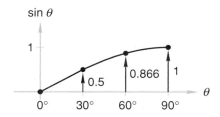

When θ equals 120°, the vertical side of the triangle is approximately 0.866, as we show on the left. When θ equals 150°, the vertical side of the triangle has a length of 0.5, as we show on the right. When θ equals 180°, sin θ equals zero.

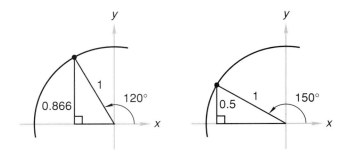

Now our graph looks like this.

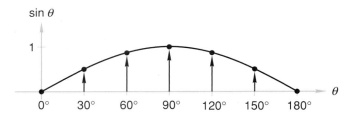

Between 180° and 360° the triangle is below the x axis and the vertical directed distance from the x axis to the point on the unit circle is negative.

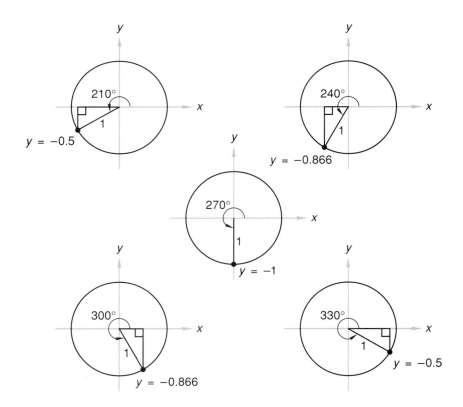

Thus the graph of the sine function from 180° to 360° has the same shape as the first part but is upside down. The graph repeats this pattern along the entire θ axis.

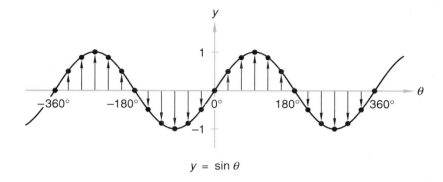

$$y = \sin\theta$$

Thus the vertical directed distance from the θ axis to the graph of the sine function equals the value of sin θ for that value of θ. The maximum distance above and below the horizontal axis is 1, so we say that the **amplitude** of this function is 1. Thus we say that the **range** of the sine function is from −1 to +1 inclusive. **The value of sin θ when θ equals zero is zero and the graph is increasing.** The sine function completes a full up-and-down cycle of values in 360°, or 2π radians. We say that the **period** of this periodic function is 360°, or 2π radians.

The negative of the sine curve has the same characteristics as the positive sine curve, but it begins at the origin by going down instead of going up. It is the sine curve inverted. We remember that the graph of $y = -f(x)$ is a reflection of the graph of $y = f(x)$ in the x axis.

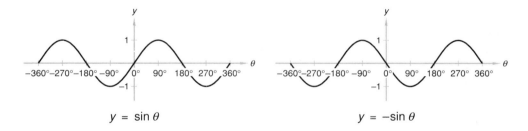

$$y = \sin\theta \qquad\qquad y = -\sin\theta$$

If we look at the horizontal sides of the triangles in the unit circles we drew previously, we see that they represent the values of the cosine. When $\theta = 0°$, the cosine equals 1, and when $\theta = 90°$, the cosine equals 0. Then it decreases to −1 at 180°, goes to 0 at 270°, and returns to 1 at 360°. **A graph of the cosine curve looks exactly like the graph of the sine curve, except the graph of the cosine curve has been shifted horizontally so that it has a y value of +1 when $\theta = 0°$.**

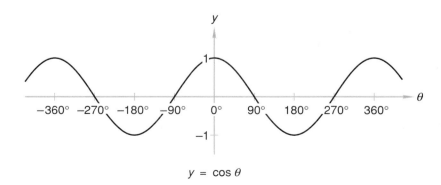

$$y = \cos\theta$$

We can determine whether we are dealing with a positive or negative cosine curve by examining its value when θ equals zero. **The positive cosine curve has its maximum positive value from the centerline when θ equals zero. The negative cosine curve has its maximum negative value from the centerline when θ equals zero.**

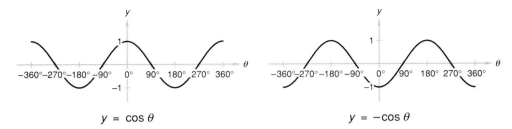

$$y = \cos \theta \qquad\qquad\qquad y = -\cos \theta$$

If the sine or cosine function is multiplied by a constant k, the value of the function for any θ is multiplied by k. For example, the graphs of $y = \sin \theta$ and $y = -\cos \theta$ go 1 unit above and below the centerline. The graphs of $y = 2 \sin \theta$ and $y = -2 \cos \theta$ go 2 units above and below the centerline. Thus we say that the amplitude of both of these functions is 2.

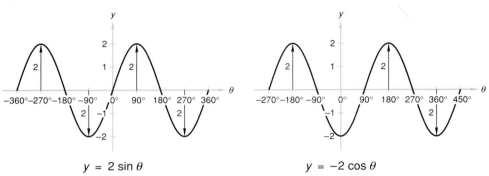

$$y = 2 \sin \theta \qquad\qquad\qquad y = -2 \cos \theta$$

example 43.1   Write the equation for this sinusoid.

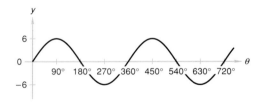

solution   The value of the function when θ equals zero is zero and the graph is increasing, so this is a positive sine function. It goes 6 units above the θ axis and 6 units below, so the equation is

$$y = 6 \sin \theta$$

In this example the Greek letter θ was used as the variable. We also use the letter x as the variable to represent an angle, as we do in the next problem. We can use any symbol as a variable but x, θ, α, and β are the symbols often encountered. The units can be radians or degrees and are not defined by the symbol used.

example 43.2   Write the equation for this sinusoid.

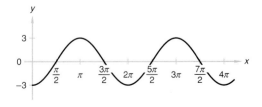

solution   This time we used x instead of θ as the independent variable. The function has a maximum negative value when x equals zero, so it is the graph of a negative cosine function. The graph goes 3 units above and below the x axis, so the equation is

$$y = -3 \cos x$$

problem set 43

1. Andy measured the angle between the base of the building and the top of the building and received a reading of 0.5°. If Andy was 5000 feet from the base of the building when the measurement was made, how high was the building?

2. The tiger trotted through an arc of $\pi/6$ radians along a circular arc of radius 1000 feet. How far did the tiger trot?

3. Ten workers could do the job in 12 days. If 8 workers worked for 5 days and then half of them quit, how long would it take for the rest to complete the job?

4. The standard rate of pay was $560 for a 35-hour week. Hours worked over 40 hours were paid at $1\frac{1}{2}$ times the normal rate. If Sally's pay for 1 week was $880, how many hours did she work?

5. The price of gasoline is $1.30 per gallon plus a federal tax of f cents and a state tax of s cents. How many gallons of gasoline can be purchased for $20?

6. Five times Sally's age now exceeds 3 times John's age by 30. In 10 years, twice Sally's age will exceed John's age by 26. What will be their ages 13 years from now?

Write the equations of the following sinusoids:

7.

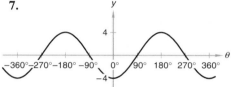

8.

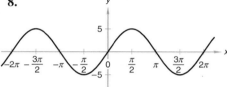

9. Find the standard form of the equation of a circle whose center is at (–2, 3) and whose radius is 4.

10. Sketch the graph of the function $y = \left(\dfrac{1}{3}\right)^{x-1}$.

Evaluate:

11. $\sec\left(-\dfrac{7\pi}{6}\right) + \csc\dfrac{\pi}{3} + \tan\dfrac{8\pi}{3}$

12. $\sec\left(-\dfrac{3\pi}{4}\right) - \cot\dfrac{\pi}{2} + \csc\dfrac{3\pi}{2}$

13. By how much does $_8P_6$ exceed $_8P_5$?

14. Simplify: $\log_3 3^2 + \log_5 5^3 - \log_2 2^4$

Solve for x:

15. $\log_3 6 + \log_3 3 = \log_3 (4x + 2)$

16. $\log_7 (x + 2) - \log_7 (x - 4) = \log_7 2$

17. $2 \log_x 4 = 2$

18. Determine if $f(x) = x^3$ and $g(x) = \sqrt[3]{x}$ are inverse functions by computing their compositions.

19. Write the quadratic equation with a lead coefficient of 1 whose roots are $1 + \sqrt{3}$ and $1 - \sqrt{3}$.

20. Find the equation of the line that is equidistant from the points (–6, 4) and (0, 8). Write the equation in slope-intercept form.

21. Find the coordinates of the point halfway between (–6, 2) and (7, 4).

22. Find the number that is $\frac{1}{3}$ of the way from $2\frac{2}{3}$ to $6\frac{1}{3}$.

23. Evaluate: $\displaystyle\sum_{i=-1}^{3} \left(i^2 - 3\right)$

24. The data points in the table below came from an experiment that involved hydrogen (H) and carbon (C). Note that in the graph the horizontal and vertical scales are different. The position of the line which best fits the data points is estimated. Write the equation that expresses hydrogen as a function of carbon (H = $mC + b$).

C	99.0	101.0	101.5	102.0	102.5	103.0	103.6	104.5	104.6
H	125.0	115.0	110.0	100.0	117.5	96.0	88.0	87.5	82.5

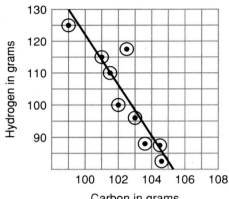

25. Evaluate. Do not use a calculator.

(a) $\text{Arcsin}\left(-\dfrac{1}{2}\right)$

(b) $\sin\left[\text{Arcsin}\left(-\dfrac{3}{5}\right)\right]$

26. Find the domain and range of each function whose graph is shown:

(a)

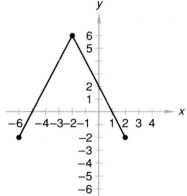

(b)

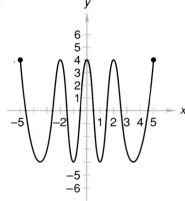

27. The graph of the function $f(x) = x^2$ is shown on the left below. The graph on the right is the same graph translated one unit to the right and one unit down. Write the equation of the graph on the right.

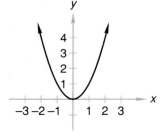

28. Given the function $f(x) = x^2$, write the equation of the function g whose graph is the graph of f translated two units to the right and one unit down. Then sketch the graph of the new function g.

29. Let x be a real number. Compare: A. $\sqrt{x^2}$ B. x

30. If x is a real number and $x > 1$, compare: A. $\dfrac{1}{1 + \dfrac{1}{x}}$ B. $\dfrac{1}{1 + x}$

LESSON *44* *Abstract Rate Problems*

Thus far, we have restricted our investigation of abstract rate problems to problems about distances. We remember we can write rates two different ways. If we can purchase 7 pencils for 10 cents, we can write two rates:

$$\frac{7 \text{ pencils}}{10 \text{ cents}} \quad \longrightarrow \quad \frac{7}{10} \text{ pencil per cent}$$

$$\text{or} \quad \frac{10 \text{ cents}}{7 \text{ pencils}} \quad \longrightarrow \quad \frac{10}{7} \text{ cents per pencil}$$

Problems about price per item and about time to do a job are interesting rate problems. They are worked in the same way that the distance problems are worked. The first step is to identify the original components. The next step is to note the changes that must be made, and the last step is to solve for the unknown component.

example 44.1   Peter purchased p pencils for d dollars. If the p pencils had cost x more dollars, how many pencils could Peter have purchased for $20?

solution   We could write the rate in either of two forms:

$$\text{(a)} \quad \frac{\text{items}}{\text{price}} = \frac{p \text{ pencils}}{d \text{ dollars}} \quad \longrightarrow \quad \frac{p}{d} \frac{\text{pencils}}{\text{dollar}}$$

$$\text{or} \quad \text{(b)} \quad \frac{\text{price}}{\text{items}} = \frac{d \text{ dollars}}{p \text{ pencils}} \quad \longrightarrow \quad \frac{d}{p} \frac{\text{dollars}}{\text{pencil}}$$

Since we want to use the equation

$$\text{Rate} \times \text{price} = \text{pencils}$$

we decide to use rate (a) so that dollars will cancel when we multiply. We begin by identifying the initial values of the pencils, the price, and the rate.

$$\text{Pencils} = p \qquad \text{Price} = d \text{ dollars} \qquad \text{Rate} = \frac{p}{d} \frac{\text{pencils}}{\text{dollar}}$$

If the pencils had cost x more dollars, the price for p pencils would have been $(d + x)$ dollars. Therefore, the new rate is given by

$$\text{Rate} = \frac{p}{d + x} \frac{\text{pencils}}{\text{dollar}}$$

Now, to find the number of pencils we can buy for $20, we multiply the new rate by $20.

$$\frac{p}{d + x} \frac{\text{pencils}}{\text{dollars}} \times 20 \text{ dollars} = \frac{20p}{d + x} \text{ pencils}$$

example 44.2 The coach purchased *b* basketballs for *x* dollars. If each basketball had cost three dollars less, how many basketballs could the coach have purchased for $200?

solution We begin by identifying the initial values of the basketballs, the price, and the rate. We note that the rate is the cost of each basketball.

$$\text{Basketballs} = b \qquad \text{Price} = x \text{ dollars} \qquad \text{Rate} = \frac{x}{b} \frac{\text{dollars}}{\text{basketball}}$$

If each basketball had cost three dollars less, the new cost for each basketball would be $\left(\frac{x}{b} - 3\right) \frac{\text{dollars}}{\text{basketball}}$. Therefore, the new rate is given by

$$\text{Rate} = \left(\frac{x - 3b}{b}\right) \frac{\text{dollars}}{\text{basketball}}$$

We are asked to find how many basketballs the coach could have purchased for $200. We let *N* represent the number of basketballs. Now we substitute and solve.

$$\text{Rate} \times N = \text{price}$$

$$\left(\frac{x - 3b}{b}\right) \frac{\text{dollars}}{\text{basketball}} \times N = \$200$$

$$N = \frac{200 \text{ dollars}}{\left(\frac{x - 3b}{b}\right) \frac{\text{dollars}}{\text{basketball}}}$$

$$N = \frac{200b}{x - 3b} \text{ basketballs}$$

example 44.3 On an assembly line, *m* workers worked *h* hours to produce *c* articles. If *d* workers quit, how many hours would the remaining workers have to work to produce the same number of articles?

solution The rate in this problem is in articles per worker-hour, so the basic equation is

$$\text{Rate} \times \text{workers} \times \text{time} = \text{articles}$$

As the first step, we identify workers, time, articles, and rate.

$$\text{Workers} = m \qquad \text{Time} = h \text{ hours} \qquad \text{Articles} = c \qquad \text{Rate} = \frac{c}{mh} \frac{\text{articles}}{\text{worker-hour}}$$

Now, if *d* workers quit, we have *m* − *d* workers producing *c* articles at the *same rate*. So

$$\text{Workers} = m - d \qquad \text{Articles} = c \qquad \text{Rate} = \frac{c}{mh} \frac{\text{articles}}{\text{worker-hour}}$$

We are asked to find the time. We substitute and solve.

$$\text{Rate} \times \text{workers} \times \text{time} = \text{articles}$$

$$\frac{c}{mh} \frac{\text{articles}}{\text{worker-hour}} \times (m - d) \text{ workers} \times T = c \text{ articles}$$

$$T = \frac{c \text{ articles}}{\frac{c}{mh} \frac{\text{articles}}{\text{worker-hour}} \times (m - d) \text{ workers}}$$

$$T = \frac{mh}{m - d} \text{ hours}$$

example 44.4 Charles had p pounds of food and this would feed m workers for d days. Then 30 more workers showed up. How long would the food feed $m + 30$ workers?

solution The rate is food per worker-day and the equation is

$$\text{Rate} \times \text{workers} \times \text{time} = \text{food}$$

First we identify the initial components.

$$\text{Workers} = m \qquad \text{Time} = d \text{ days} \qquad \text{Food} = p \text{ pounds} \qquad \text{Rate} = \frac{p}{md} \frac{\text{pounds}}{\text{worker-day}}$$

Now, if 30 more workers show up, the components are

$$\text{Workers} = m + 30 \qquad \text{Food} = p \text{ pounds} \qquad \text{Rate} = \frac{p}{md} \frac{\text{pounds}}{\text{worker-day}}$$

We are asked to find the new time.

$$\text{Rate} \times \text{workers} \times \text{time} = \text{food} \quad \longrightarrow \quad \text{Time} = \frac{\text{food}}{\text{workers} \times \text{rate}}$$

Again, we finish by substituting and solving.

$$\text{Time} = \frac{p}{(m + 30)(p/md)} = \frac{md}{m + 30} \text{ days}$$

problem set 44

1. The drummer boy purchased d drums for x dollars. If each drum had cost $5 less, how many drums could the boy have purchased for $100?

2. In the cookie factory, w workers work h hours to produce c cookies. If m more workers are hired, how many hours will they have to work to produce the same number of cookies?

3. Mom had p pounds of cookies and this would feed c children for m minutes. Yet n more children showed up. In how many minutes will p pounds of cookies be devoured by the children?

4. In his search for the fountain, Ponce ambled for 1 year at a leisurely pace and then tripled his pace for the next 10 years. If the total journey was 3100 miles, how far did he amble?

5. How many four-letter signs can be made from the letters in the word JUDGE if no repetition is permitted?

6. The jogger ran through an arc of 60° along a circular track whose diameter is 600 yards. How far did the jogger run?

Write the equations of the following sinusoids:

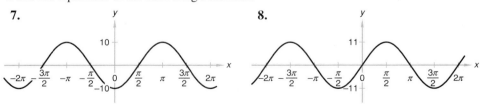

7.

8.

9. Find the standard form of the equation of a circle whose center is (h, k) and whose radius is 5.

10. Sketch the graph of the function $f(x) = 2^{-x-2}$.

Evaluate:

11. $\csc\left(-\dfrac{3\pi}{4}\right) + \cos\left(-\dfrac{13\pi}{3}\right)$

12. $\sec\left(-\dfrac{19\pi}{6}\right) + \csc\left(-\dfrac{\pi}{3}\right) + \cos\dfrac{7\pi}{2}$

13. Simplify: $\log_7 7^3 + \log_{10} 10^4 + \log_5 5 - \log_2 2$

Solve for x:

14. $\log_4 8 + \log_4 6 = \log_4 (3x + 2)$

15. $\log_3 (x + 3) - \log_3 (x - 2) = \log_3 12$

16. $\log_x 16 = 4$

17. $\log_{15} x = \dfrac{2}{3} \log_{15} 8$

18. Determine if $f(x) = \frac{1}{3}x - 3$ and $g(x) = 3x + 9$ are inverse functions by computing their compositions.

19. Write the quadratic equation with a lead coefficient of 1 whose roots are 3 and $-\frac{1}{4}$.

20. Use the point-slope form to find a general form of the equation of the line whose slope is $-\frac{1}{4}$ and that passes through $(-2, 3)$.

21. Find the equation of the line that is equidistant from the points $(-3, -2)$ and $(2, 3)$. Write your equation in general form.

22. Find the coordinates of the point halfway between $(-3, 4)$ and $(8, -3)$.

23. Find the number that is $\frac{4}{5}$ of the way from $1\frac{1}{4}$ to $-6\frac{2}{3}$.

24. The data points in the table below relate the number of fleas per square mile (F) to the number of dogs per square mile (D). The position of the line which best fits the data points is estimated. Write the equation that expresses the number of fleas per square mile as a function of the number of dogs per square mile $(F = mD + b)$.

Dogs per square mile	29.7	30.5	31.4	33.4	33.9	35.5
Fleas per square mile	38	122	167	275	369	421

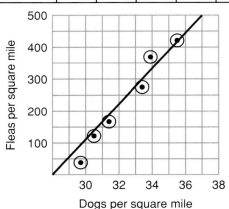

25. Find two functions f and g such that $(f \circ g)(x) = \log_3 (x + 2)$.

26. Evaluate. Do not use a calculator.

(a) $\text{Arccos}\left(\dfrac{\sqrt{2}}{2}\right)$

(b) $\cos\left[\text{Arcsin}\left(-\dfrac{4}{5}\right)\right]$

27. The graph of the function $f(x) = x^2$ is shown on the left below. The graph on the right is the same graph translated three units to the left and one unit down. Write the equation of the graph on the right.

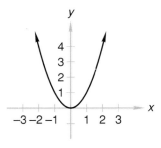 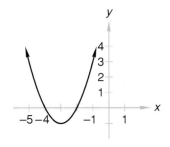

28. If $f(x) = 2x$, find $\dfrac{f(x + h) - f(x - h)}{2h}$.

CONCEPT REVIEW PROBLEMS

29. If $x^2 + y^2 = 40$ and $xy = 16$, compare: A. $(x - y)^2$ B. 12

30. Given: $\triangle ABC$

    Compare: A. 180°

              B. $m\angle 1 + m\angle 2 + m\angle 3$

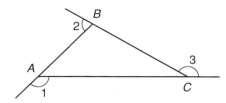

LESSON 45   *Conditional Permutations • Two-Variable Analysis Using a Graphing Calculator*

45.A

conditional permutations

Many problems about permutations (arrangements in a definite order) have conditions attached that make finding the solutions challenging. There is no formula that can be used, for the conditions seem to be different each time. We will find, however, that drawing a diagram is helpful, so the use of diagrams is recommended.

example 45.1   How many odd counting numbers can be formed from the digits 3, 4, and 5 if no repetition of digits is permitted?

solution   We can have one-digit, two-digit, or three-digit odd numbers.

            The one-digit odd numbers are 3 and 5   total 2

The last digit in a two-digit odd number is an odd digit. Both 3 and 5 are odd digits, so there are two possible odd choices for the last digit.

$$\boxed{\,\vert\,2\,}$$

The other digits may be even or odd, and two digits remain that can be used as the first digit.

$$\boxed{2\,\vert\,2}\;\longrightarrow\;2 \cdot 2 = 4 \qquad \text{total 4}$$

For three-digit numbers, we use the same process and get

$$\boxed{1\,\vert\,2\,\vert\,2}\;\longrightarrow\;1 \cdot 2 \cdot 2 = 4 \qquad \text{total 4}$$

$$\text{Grand total} = 4 + 4 + 2 = 10$$

Thus, there are **10** possible odd counting numbers that can be formed using 3, 4, and 5 if no repetition of digits is permitted.

example 45.2   Find the number of odd three-digit counting numbers that are less than 600.

solution   The statement of the problem indicates that repetition of digits is permissible. The 10 digits are 0, 1, 2, 3, 4, 5, 6, 7, 8, and 9, and any of the five odd digits can be used in the last spot.

$$\boxed{\,\vert\,\,\vert\,5}$$

The digit 0 cannot be used in the first box because the resulting number would have only two digits. Also 6, 7, 8, or 9 cannot be used in the first box or the number would not be less than 600. Thus, only 1, 2, 3, 4, or 5 can be used in the first box. There are 10 digits possible for the second box, so we have

$$\boxed{5 \mid 10 \mid 5} \longrightarrow 5 \cdot 10 \cdot 5 = 250$$

Thus, there are **250** odd three-digit counting numbers less than 600.

example 45.3   Five math books and four English books are on a shelf. How many permutations are possible if the math books must be kept together and the English books must be kept together?

solution   If the math books come first, we get

$$\underset{\text{MATH}}{\boxed{5 \mid 4 \mid 3 \mid 2 \mid 1}} \; \underset{\text{ENGLISH}}{\boxed{4 \mid 3 \mid 2 \mid 1}} \longrightarrow 5! \times 4! = 2880$$

If the English books come first, we get

$$\underset{\text{ENGLISH}}{\boxed{4 \mid 3 \mid 2 \mid 1}} \; \underset{\text{MATH}}{\boxed{5 \mid 4 \mid 3 \mid 2 \mid 1}} \longrightarrow 4! \times 5! = 2880$$

If we add the two numbers, we get **5760** possible permutations.

example 45.4   How many different four-digit odd counting numbers can be formed if no repetition of digits is permitted?

solution   The 10 digits are 0, 1, 2, 3, 4, 5, 6, 7, 8, and 9, and five digits are even and five are odd. The number must end with an odd digit, so there are five choices for the last digit.

$$\boxed{ \mid \mid \mid 5}$$

A four-digit number cannot begin with 0 because if it did, it would be at most a three-digit number. Thus, there are only eight choices left for the first digit.

$$\boxed{8 \mid \mid \mid 5}$$

Zero can be the second digit, so there are eight choices for this digit and seven choices for the third digit.

$$\boxed{8 \mid 8 \mid 7 \mid 5} \longrightarrow 8 \cdot 8 \cdot 7 \cdot 5 = 2240$$

Thus, there are **2240** different four-digit odd counting numbers that can be formed if no repetition of digits is permitted.

example 45.5   An elf, a gnome, a fairy, a pixie, and a leprechaun were to sit in a line. How many different ways can they sit if the elf and the gnome insist on sitting next to each other?

solution   Let's begin with the elf and the gnome in the first two seats.

$$\boxed{E \mid G \mid 3 \mid 2 \mid 1} \longrightarrow 3 \times 2 \times 1 = 6$$

$$\boxed{G \mid E \mid 3 \mid 2 \mid 1} \longrightarrow 3 \times 2 \times 1 = 6$$

Now let's put them in the second two seats.

| 3 | E | G | 2 | 1 | $\longrightarrow$ $3 \times 2 \times 1 = 6$

| 3 | G | E | 2 | 1 | $\longrightarrow$ $3 \times 2 \times 1 = 6$

The other possibilities are

| 3 | 2 | E | G | 1 | for 6 | 3 | 2 | 1 | E | G | for 6

| 3 | 2 | G | E | 1 | for 6 | 3 | 2 | 1 | G | E | for 6

There are eight ways the gnome and the elf can sit side by side, and for each of these, there are six ways the other three little people can sit. Since $6 \times 8 = 48$, there are **48** different ways the little people can sit if the elf and the gnome sit next to each other.

45.B
two-variable analysis using a graphing calculator

The data in the table on the left are from an experiment involving silver (Ag) and gold (Au). On the right we have graphed the data points and estimated the position of the line indicated by the data points.

Au	82	87	97	107	107
Ag	9.5	5.5	7.5	1.5	4.6

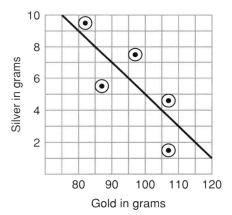

We will use the endpoints of the line (75, 10) and (120, 1) to determine the slope, which we see is negative.

$$\text{Slope} = \frac{\text{rise}}{\text{run}} = \frac{10 - 1}{75 - 120} = \frac{9}{-45} = -0.2$$

Now we find the intercept.

$$\text{Ag} = -0.2\text{Au} + b \qquad \text{equation}$$
$$10 = -0.2(75) + b \qquad \text{used (75, 10) for Au and Ag}$$
$$b = 25 \qquad \text{solved for } b$$

Now we can write the equation that gives silver as a function of gold.

$$\text{Ag} = -0.2\text{Au} + 25$$

The process of estimating the equation of a line that best fits the data is called **linear regression.**[†]

[†]This appellation is a misnomer because it has nothing to do with regression in the usual sense. It was introduced by Sir Francis Galton (1822–1911). Originally, he used the word *reversion*, but in an address in 1877 he used the word *regression*. See *Applied Regression Analysis* by Draper and Smith, John Wiley and Sons, 1966.

Graphing calculators use the *least squares algorithm* to do linear regressions. All you have to do is enter the x data points in one list, enter the y data points in another list, and press the proper key. The TI-82 gives the following display for these data:

$$\text{LinReg}$$
$$y=ax+b$$
$$a=-.2075$$
$$b=25.64$$
$$r=-.7824726541$$

This tells us that the equation of the line that the calculator estimates as the best fit for the data is

$$Ag = -0.21Au + 25.6$$

The last item on the calculator display is r, which is the correlation coefficient. If all the data points lie exactly on the line and the slope of the line is positive, the correlation coefficient r is +1. If all of the data points lie exactly on the line and the slope is negative, the correlation coefficient r is −1. If the data are so scattered that they do not determine a straight line, the correlation coefficient r is 0. For a rule of thumb for scientific data, we would like to have r values between −1 and −0.9 or between 0.9 and 1. For experiments in the social sciences, we would like to have r values between −1 and −0.7 or between 0.7 and 1. Our r value was −0.78. This negative correlation tells us that the amount of silver decreased as the amount of gold increased. We would have hoped for a correlation coefficient between −1 and −0.9. Maybe the relationship is not really linear. We are often not happy with this much scatter in scientific experimental data.

problem set 45

1. How many three-digit counting numbers are there that are less than 300 such that all the digits are even?

2. Six math books and three English books are on a shelf. How many ways can they be arranged if the math books are kept together and the English books are kept together?

3. In the factory k workers worked f hours to produce c articles. If x workers quit, how long would those that remained have to work to produce $c + 10$ articles?

4. The latitude of Princeton, New Jersey, is 40.5° north of the equator. How far is it from Princeton to the equator if the diameter of the earth is 7920 miles?

5. On the 24-mile trip to school, Brandon sauntered at a leisurely pace. Thus, he had to double his speed on the way back to complete the trip in 9 hours. How fast did he travel in each direction, and what were the two times?

6. Four thousand liters of solution was available that was 92% alcohol. How many liters of alcohol had to be extracted so that the solution would be only 80% alcohol?

7. The ratio of greens to blues was 2 to 1, and twice the sum of the number of blues and the number of whites exceeded the number of greens by 10. If there were 35 blues, greens, and whites in all, how many were there of each color?

8. The following data came from an experiment that involved lead (Pb) and copper (Cu). Use a graphing calculator to find the equation of the line which best fits this data and gives copper as a function of lead (Cu = mPb + b). Also, find the correlation coefficient for this scientific data and discuss whether or not the line is a good model for the data.

Pb	160	190	190	194	220
Cu	18	6	16	11	4

9. The following data came from an experiment that involved dysprosium (Dy) and rhodium (Rh). Use a graphing calculator to find the equation of the line which best fits this data and gives rhodium as a function of dysprosium (Rh = mDy + b). Also, find the correlation coefficient for this scientific data and discuss whether or not the line is a good model for the data.

Dy	110	120	130	140	150	160
Rh	80	92	99	105	113	120

Write the equations of the following sinusoids:

10.

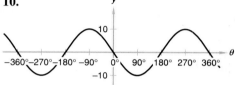

11.

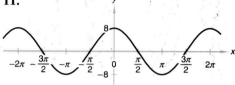

12. Find the standard form of the equation of a circle whose center is (−2, 5) and whose radius is 6.

13. Sketch the graph of the function $f(x) = \left(\dfrac{1}{2}\right)^{-x+1}$.

Evaluate:

14. $\csc \dfrac{3\pi}{4} - \sec \left(-\dfrac{5\pi}{6}\right) + \cos \dfrac{9\pi}{4}$

15. $\sec \left(-\dfrac{19\pi}{6}\right) + \cos \dfrac{7\pi}{2} - \sin \dfrac{10\pi}{3}$

16. By how much does $_6P_3$ exceed $_6P_2$?

17. Simplify: $\log_3 9 - \log_5 5^3 + \log_7 7^2 - \log_{11} 1$

Solve for x:

18. $\log_5 7 + \log_5 8 = \log_5 (2x - 4)$ 19. $\log_3 (x + 1) - \log_3 x = \log_3 15$

20. $\dfrac{3}{4} \log_{10} 10{,}000 = x$

21. Determine if $f(x) = \dfrac{1}{x}$ and $g(x) = \dfrac{1}{x}$ are inverse functions by computing their compositions.

22. Write the quadratic equation with a lead coefficient of 1 whose roots are $2 + \sqrt{5}$ and $2 - \sqrt{5}$.

23. Find the equation of the line that is equidistant from the points $(-4, -3)$ and $(4, 6)$. Write the equation in slope-intercept form.

24. Find f where $g(x) = x^3$ and $(f \circ g)(x) = 2x^3 + 3$.

25. Find the domain of the function $f(x) = \dfrac{\sqrt{x}}{1 - |4x|}$.

26. The graph of the function $f(x) = \sqrt{x}$ is shown on the left below. The graph on the right is the same graph translated two units to the right and three units up. Write the equation of the graph on the right.

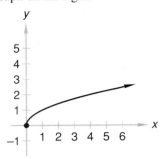 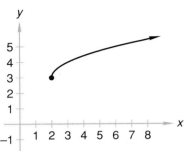

27. Given the function $f(x) = \sqrt{x}$, write the equation of the function g whose graph is the graph of f translated three units to the right and two units up. Then sketch the graph of the new function g.

28. Given: $\overline{PQ} \parallel \overline{ST}$

  R is the midpoint of $\overline{QS}$

Write a two-column proof to prove:

  $\overline{PR} \cong \overline{TR}$

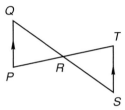

CONCEPT REVIEW
PROBLEMS

29. Let x and y be real numbers. If $x < 1$ and $y > 3$, compare: A. $x + 1$ B. $y - 1$

30. In polygon $ABCD$, $m\angle A = 90°$.

  Compare: A. Area of polygon $ABCD$

    B. 16

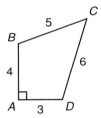

LESSON 46   *Complex Roots • Factoring Over the Complex Numbers*

46.A

complex roots

The set of real numbers is a subset of the set of complex numbers. This is easy to remember if we recall that real numbers such as -7 and 4 are complex numbers whose imaginary part is zero and can also be written as

$$-7 + 0i \qquad \text{and} \qquad 4 + 0i$$

We have been writing quadratic equations with a lead coefficient of 1 whose roots have been designated. For example, if a quadratic equation has roots of -7 and $+4$, the equation can be found by writing the factors and then multiplying, as we show here.

$$(x + 7)(x - 4) = 0 \qquad \text{factored form}$$

$$x^2 + 3x - 28 = 0 \qquad \text{multiplied}$$

The same procedure can be used to write quadratic equations whose roots are designated complex numbers whose imaginary parts are not equal to zero. **For quadratic equations with real-number coefficients, these complex roots always occur in conjugate pairs.**

example 46.1   Write the quadratic equation with a lead coefficient of 1 whose roots are $1 + 2i$ and $1 - 2i$.

solution   First we write an equation that contains a product of factors.

$$[x - (1 + 2i)][x - (1 - 2i)] = 0$$

Next we simplify the signs within the brackets and get

$$[x - 1 - 2i][x - 1 + 2i] = 0$$

There are nine indicated products which must be summed.

$$x^2 - x + 2xi - x + 1 - 2i - 2xi + 2i - 4i^2 = 0$$

Fortunately, we have $+2xi$ and $-2xi$, which sum to zero, as do the terms $+2i$ and $-2i$. If we remember that i^2 equals -1, we can simplify the above expression and get

$$x^2 - 2x + 5 = 0$$

as the quadratic equation that has the required roots.

46.B
factoring over the complex numbers

The quadratic polynomial $2x^2 + 6$ can be written as a product of the number 2 and the two factors that contain the variable x.

$$2x^2 + 6 = 2(x + \sqrt{3}i)(x - \sqrt{3}i)$$

If we use the quadratic formula, we can find that the roots of the equation $2x^2 + 6 = 0$ are $\pm\sqrt{3}i$. These roots can be used to find two of the factors of the polynomial, but we might overlook the constant factor 2. Thus, when we use the quadratic formula to find the roots of a quadratic polynomial, we begin by factoring so that the coefficient of x^2 is unity.

example 46.2   Factor $2x^2 + 4x + 8$ over the set of complex numbers.

solution   The wording of the problem tells us that the factors can contain complex numbers. First we factor out the lead coefficient and then set the resulting polynomial equal to 0.

$$2x^2 + 4x + 8 = 2(x^2 + 2x + 4) \quad \longrightarrow \quad x^2 + 2x + 4 = 0$$

Next we use the quadratic formula to find the roots of the resulting polynomial equation.

$$x = \frac{-2 \pm \sqrt{4 - 4(1)(4)}}{2(1)} \quad \longrightarrow \quad x = -1 \pm \sqrt{3}i$$

Now the roots of the polynomial equation can be used to write two of the factors of the polynomial, and from the initial factorization, the third factor is 2.

$$(2)\left[x - \left(-1 + \sqrt{3}\,i\right)\right]\left[x - \left(-1 - \sqrt{3}\,i\right)\right] \qquad \text{factors}$$

$$(2)(x + 1 - \sqrt{3}i)(x + 1 + \sqrt{3}i) \qquad \text{simplified}$$

example 46.3   Factor: $x^2 + 2x - 5$

solution   Since this polynomial cannot be factored over the integers, we assume that other factors are acceptable. The lead coefficient is 1, so factoring out a constant is not necessary.

$$x^2 + 2x - 5 = 0$$

Now we will use the quadratic formula to find the roots of this equation.

$$x = \frac{-2 \pm \sqrt{4 - 4(1)(-5)}}{2(1)} \qquad \text{quadratic formula}$$

$$= \frac{-2 \pm \sqrt{24}}{2} \qquad \text{simplified}$$

$$= -1 \pm \sqrt{6} \qquad \text{roots}$$

So our roots are $-1 + \sqrt{6}$ and $-1 - \sqrt{6}$. Now we can write the factors of the polynomial.

$$x^2 + 2x - 5 = \left[x - (-1 + \sqrt{6})\right]\left[x - (-1 - \sqrt{6})\right]$$
$$= (x + 1 - \sqrt{6})(x + 1 + \sqrt{6})$$

problem set 46

1. How many three-digit counting numbers that are less than 300 are there such that all the digits are odd?

2. Six literature books and four math books are on a shelf. How many ways can they be arranged if the math books are kept together and the literature books are kept together?

3. The cook had x pounds of food in the storehouse, and this would feed y workers for d days. Then 50 more workers arrived in camp. How many days would the cook's food last since $(y + 50)$ workers must now be fed?

4. The coach purchased b balls for d dollars. If each ball had cost $2 more, how many balls could the coach have purchased for $200?

5. The panther moved 60° along a circular arc of radius 600 meters. How far did the panther move?

6. On the 36-mile trip to the magic fountain, Alice walked at a brisk pace. On the way back, Alice doubled her pace. If the total trip took 6 hours, how fast did Alice travel on the trip to the magic fountain and on the return trip from the magic fountain?

7. One thousand liters of a solution was available, but the solution was 90% alcohol. Jim needed a solution which was 80% alcohol. How many liters of alcohol had to be extracted so that the solution would be 80% alcohol?

8. The ratio of rubies to emeralds was 3 to 1, and the ratio of emeralds to diamonds was 2 to 1. If there were 18 rubies, emeralds, and diamonds in all, how many of each were there?

9. Write the quadratic equation with a lead coefficient of 1 whose roots are $2 - 3i$ and $2 + 3i$.

10. Factor $x^2 + 3x + 6$ over the set of complex numbers.

11. The following data came from an experiment that involved hydrogen (H) and carbon (C). Use a graphing calculator to find the equation of the line which best fits this data and gives carbon as a function of hydrogen ($C = mH + b$). Also, find the correlation coefficient for this scientific data and discuss whether or not the line is a good model for the data.

H	100	150	170	200	220	250
C	40	30	31	28	28	20

Write the equations of the following sinusoids:

12.
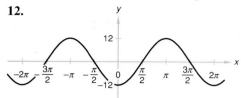

13.
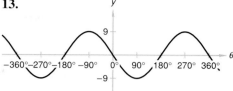

14. Find the standard form of the equation of a circle whose center is (h, k) and whose radius is 6.

15. Sketch the graph of the function $f(x) = \left(\dfrac{1}{3}\right)^{-x+2}$.

16. Evaluate:

(a) $\cos\left(-\dfrac{13\pi}{6}\right) + \sin\dfrac{13\pi}{4} - \cot\dfrac{9\pi}{2}$ (b) $\csc\dfrac{7\pi}{4} - \sec\left(-\dfrac{\pi}{4}\right) + \tan 3\pi$

17. By how much does $_8P_4$ exceed $_8P_2$?

18. Simplify: $3\log_7 7 - \log_5 25 + \log_3 \dfrac{1}{3} + \log_{10} 1$

Solve for x:

19. $\dfrac{5}{2}\log_4 4 = \log_4 (2x - 3)$ **20.** $\log_3 (x + 2) - \log_3 x = \log_3 10$

21. $\log_8 x = \dfrac{3}{4}\log_8 81$

22. Determine if $f(x) = 3x + 1$ and $g(x) = \frac{1}{3}x - \frac{1}{3}$ are inverse functions by computing their compositions.

23. In the figure shown, $\overline{EF}$ is the median of trapezoid $ABCD$. Find x.

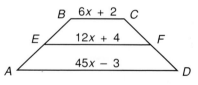

24. Evaluate. Do not use a calculator.

(a) $\sin\left[\text{Arctan}\left(-\dfrac{5}{13}\right)\right]$ (b) $\cos\left[\text{Arcsin}\left(-\dfrac{3}{4}\right)\right]$

25. The graph of the function $f(x) = \sqrt{x}$ is shown on the left below. The graph on the right is the same graph translated one unit to the right and four units down. Write the equation of the graph on the right.

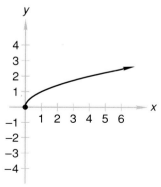
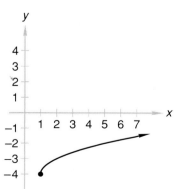

26. Given the function $f(x) = \sqrt{x}$, write the equation of the function g whose graph is the graph of f translated four units to the right and five units down. Then sketch the graph of the new function g.

27. Find the domain and range of each function whose graph is shown:

(a)

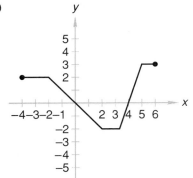

(b)

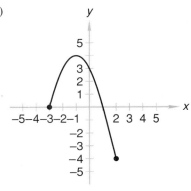

28. If $f(x) = x(1 - x)$, find $\dfrac{f(x + h) - f(x)}{h}$.

29. Let x and y be real numbers with $x + y \neq 0$.

Compare: A. $\dfrac{x^2 + 2xy + y^2}{x + y}$ B. $x + y + 2$

30. In $\triangle ABC$, $AB = 8$.

Compare: A. BC B. 4

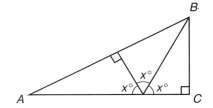

LESSON 47 *Vertical Sinusoid Translations • Arctan*

47.A

vertical sinusoid translations

We remember if k represents a positive number, replacing y with $y - k$ in any equation in x and y will translate the graph of the original equation k units in the positive y direction. If we replace y with $y + k$ in any equation in x and y, the graph of the original equation is translated k units in the negative y direction. The graph of $y = x^2$ is shown on the left. In the center we replaced y with $y - 2$, and every point on the graph was translated 2 units upward. On the right we replaced y with $y + 2$, and every point on the graph was translated 2 units downward.

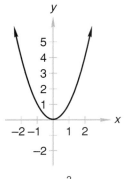

$y = x^2$

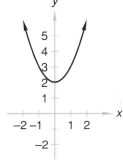

$y - 2 = x^2$
or $y = x^2 + 2$

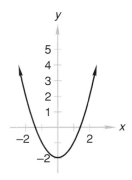

$y + 2 = x^2$
or $y = x^2 - 2$

The graph on the left below is the graph of $y = \sin x$. When x is zero, the value of $\sin x$ is zero. On the right we show the graph of $y = 3 + \sin x$.

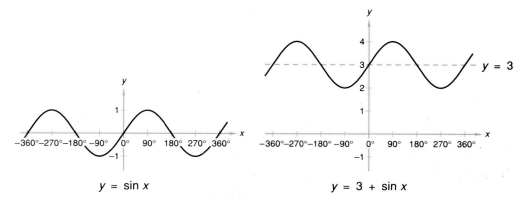

$$y = \sin x \qquad\qquad\qquad y = 3 + \sin x$$

Every point on the graph on the right is 3 units above the corresponding point in the graph on the left. For example, when x equals zero, the value of $3 + \sin x$ is 3. **We note that the centerline of this graph is not the x axis but is the line $y = 3$.** We showed the x axis in this figure, but suppose the equation had been

$$y = 60 + \sin x$$

It would take a very large piece of paper to have a graph that showed the origin and the graph of a sinusoid that was 60 units above the origin. In future problems in this book, we will use a dotted line for the centerline of a sinusoid and will indicate the positive x or θ direction with a small arrow, as we show here.

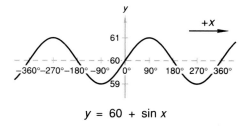

$$y = 60 + \sin x$$

example 47.1   Write the equations of the two sinusoids shown here.

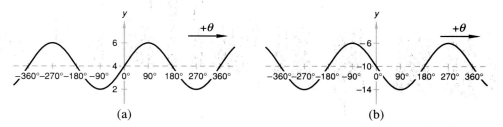

(a)   (b)

solution   **Both are sine curves because the value of each curve when θ equals zero is the value of the centerline.** Curve (a) begins on the centerline and goes up, so it is a positive sine curve. It goes 2 units above and below the centerline, so its amplitude is 2. The centerline is $y = +4$, so the whole curve has been shifted up 4 units. Thus, the equation is

$$\text{(a) } y = 4 + 2 \sin \theta$$

Curve (b) begins on the centerline, so it is a sine curve. It goes down first, so it is a negative sine curve. It goes 4 units above and below the centerline, so it has an amplitude of 4. The centerline is $y = -10$, so the whole curve has been shifted down 10 units. Thus, the equation is

$$\text{(b) } y = -10 - 4 \sin \theta$$

example 47.2   Write the equations of the two sinusoids shown here.

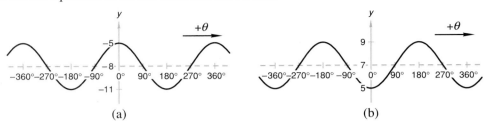

(a)   (b)

solution   **Curve (a) begins at the maximum distance from the centerline, so it is a cosine curve.** It begins a maximum distance above the centerline, so it is a positive cosine curve. It goes 3 units above and below the centerline, so it has an amplitude of 3. The centerline is $y = -8$, so the whole curve has been shifted down 8 units. Thus, the equation is

$$\text{(a) } y = -8 + 3\cos\theta$$

Curve (b) begins at a maximum distance from the centerline, so it is a cosine curve. It begins a maximum distance below the centerline, so it is a negative cosine curve. It goes 2 units above and below the centerline, so it has an amplitude of 2. The centerline is $y = +7$, so the whole curve has been shifted up 7 units. Thus, the equation is

$$\text{(b) } y = 7 - 2\cos\theta$$

47.B
Arctan

When we look at the notation

$$\sin\left(\text{Arctan } \frac{1}{\sqrt{3}}\right)$$

we remember that the capital A in Arctan restricts us to the first-quadrant or fourth-quadrant angle whose tangent is $1/\sqrt{3}$. Thus, the problem simplifies to

$$\sin 30° = \frac{1}{2}$$

Now we will look at another problem that emphasizes the restrictions placed on inverse trigonometric functions to make them single-valued.

example 47.3   Evaluate: Arctan (tan 135°)

solution   This asks for the angle whose tangent is the tangent of 135°. At first glance, one would suspect that the answer is 135°, but let us see. The tangent of 135° is -1.

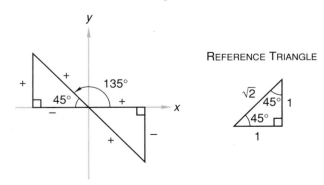

So now we have

$$\text{Arctan } (-1)$$

This asks for the **first-quadrant** or **fourth-quadrant** angle whose tangent is -1, and this angle is $-45°$. So we have

$$\text{Arctan (tan 135°) } = -45°$$

1. How many four-digit counting numbers can be made from the digits 1, 2, 3, and 4 if 2 and 3 must be next to each other and if repetition is not permitted?

2. If m workers can do a job in d days, how long would it take 40 workers to do the same job?

3. On an assembly line, k workers worked d hours to produce x items. If y workers quit, how many hours will the remaining workers have to work to produce the same number of items?

4. Pencils sell at d dollars for 1 dozen. At this price, what would be the total cost of m pencils?

5. Amy walked through an arc of 40° along the rim of a circular swimming pool 40 feet in diameter. How far did she walk?

6. The still-water speed of the *Faerie Queen* was 4 times the speed of the current in the Lazy River. The *Faerie Queen* can travel 100 miles downstream in 1 hour more than she requires to travel 30 miles upstream. What is the still-water speed of the *Faerie Queen* and how fast does the Lazy River flow?

Write the equations of the following sinusoids:

7.

8.

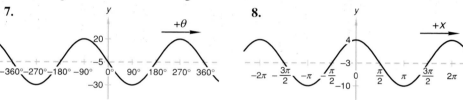

9. Evaluate. Do not use a calculator.
    (a) Arctan (tan 315°)   (b) Arctan (tan 150°)

10. Write the quadratic equation with a lead coefficient of 1 whose roots are $3 + 2i$ and $3 - 2i$.

11. Factor $2x^2 + 4x + 4$ over the set of complex numbers.

12. The following data came from an experiment that involved nitrogen (N) and oxygen (O). Use a graphing calculator to find the equation of the line which best fits this data and gives oxygen as a function of nitrogen ($O = mN + b$). Also, find the correlation coefficient for this scientific data and discuss whether or not the line is a good model for the data.

N	30	36	42	45	50	50	52
O	6	8	9	9	11	12	11

13. Find the standard form of the equation of a circle whose center is (2, 1) and whose radius is 3.

14. Sketch the graph of the function $f(x) = \left(\dfrac{1}{2}\right)^{-x-3}$.

15. Evaluate:
    (a) $\cot\left(-\dfrac{3\pi}{4}\right) - \csc\dfrac{5\pi}{6} + \sin\dfrac{7\pi}{6} - \cos\left(-\dfrac{\pi}{4}\right)$ (b) $\sec\dfrac{13\pi}{6} \cos\dfrac{13\pi}{6}$

16. Simplify: $\log_2 8 + 3\log_3 3 - \log_2 1 + \log_4 \dfrac{1}{4}$

Solve for x:

17. $\log_3 4 + \log_3 5 = \log_3 (4x + 5)$ 18. $\log_7 6 - \log_7 (x - 1) = \log_7 3$

19. $3\log_x 4 = 2$

20. Write $2x - 6y - 3 = 0$ in double-intercept form.

21. Find the coordinates of the point halfway between $(-4, -2)$ and $(6, 4)$.

22. Find the number that is $\frac{4}{5}$ of the way from $-3\frac{2}{3}$ to $4\frac{1}{4}$.

23. Evaluate: $\displaystyle\sum_{k=-1}^{2} \frac{k^2 + 1}{2}$

24. Evaluate. Do not use a calculator.

(a) $\text{Arccos}\left(-\dfrac{\sqrt{3}}{2}\right)$ (b) $\tan\left[\text{Arcsin}\left(-\dfrac{3}{4}\right)\right]$

25. Determine whether the graph of each equation is symmetric about the x axis, the y axis, and the origin:

(a)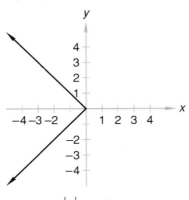

$|y| = -x$

(b)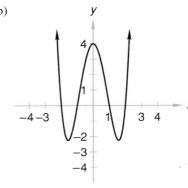

$y = x^4 - 5x^2 + 4$

26. The graph of the function $f(x) = \sqrt{x}$ is shown on the left below. The graph on the right is the same graph translated four units to the left and two units up. Write the equation of the graph on the right.

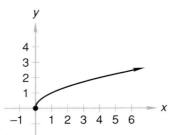

27. Given the function $f(x) = \sqrt{x}$, write the equation of the function g whose graph is the graph of f translated four units to the left and one unit up. Then sketch the graph of the new function g.

28. Let $f(x) = 3x^2$ and $g(x) = x - \frac{2}{x}$. Evaluate:

(a) $(f - g)(3)$ (b) $(f/g)(3)$ (c) $(g \circ f)(3)$

CONCEPT REVIEW
PROBLEMS

29. Let x and y be real numbers. Compare: A. $(x - y)^2$ B. $(y - x)^2$

30. In the figure shown, two parallel lines are intersected by a transversal. If $x - y = 60$, compare: A. y B. 65

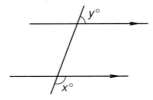

LESSON 48   *Powers of Trigonometric Functions •*
Perpendicular Bisectors

48.A
powers of trigonometric functions

Consider the three notations

$$\sin \theta^2 \qquad (\sin \theta)^2 \qquad \sin^2 \theta$$

The left-hand notation is $\sin \theta^2$. If θ equals 30°, then

$$\sin \theta^2 = \sin (30°)^2 = \sin 900 \text{ deg}^2$$

This notation is almost never used because in trigonometry we seldom find a reason to raise the measure of an angle to a power. This leaves us with the two notations

$$(\sin \theta)^2 \qquad \text{and} \qquad \sin^2 \theta$$

We often raise trigonometric functions to powers and we need a notation to so indicate. The notation on the left is unhandy because it requires the use of parentheses. The notation on the right means the same thing and requires only a superscript to denote the power. Thus, we usually prefer this notation but will sometimes use the other notation when required for clarity.

example 48.1   Evaluate: (a) $\sin^3 (-60°)$ (b) $\cot^2 330°$

solution   First we make the sketches with the related angles. We also draw the reference triangle.

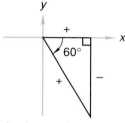
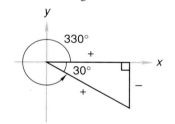
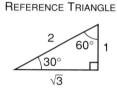

REFERENCE TRIANGLE

sine is negative

$$\sin (-60°) = -\sin 60°$$

tangent and cotangent are negative

$$\cot 330° = -\cot 30°$$

(a) $\sin^3 (-60°) = (-\sin 60°)^3 = \left(-\dfrac{\sqrt{3}}{2}\right)^3 = -\dfrac{3\sqrt{3}}{8}$

(b) $\cot^2 330° = (-\cot 30°)^2 = (-\sqrt{3})^2 = 3$

example 48.2   Evaluate: $\csc^2 (-405°) - \tan^2 45°$

solution   First we make the sketches with the related angles. We also draw the reference triangle.

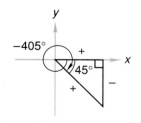
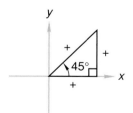
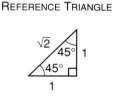

REFERENCE TRIANGLE

sine and cosecant are negative

$$\csc^2 (-405°) = (-\csc 45°)^2$$

tangent is positive

$$\tan^2 45° = (\tan 45°)^2$$

$$\csc^2 (-405°) - \tan^2 45° = \left(-\dfrac{\sqrt{2}}{1}\right)^2 - \left(\dfrac{1}{1}\right)^2 \qquad \text{sum of functions}$$

$$= 2 - 1 \qquad \text{simplified}$$

$$= \mathbf{1} \qquad \text{added}$$

48.B

perpendicular bisectors   Since Lesson 37, we have been using the locus definition and the distance formula to write the equation of a line that is equidistant from two designated points. This line bisects the line segment that connects the two points and is perpendicular to this segment. There is another way to find the equation of a line that is equidistant from two designated points. We can use the midpoint formula to find the coordinates of the point halfway between the two points. Then we write the equation of the line that passes through this point whose slope is the negative reciprocal of the slope of the segment. We will call this method the **midpoint formula method** and will call the other method the **locus definition method.**

example 48.3   Find the equation of the perpendicular bisector of the line segment whose endpoint coordinates are (4, 2) and (8, −3). Use the midpoint formula method.

solution   First we get a picture of the problem by graphing the points and indicating the position of the perpendicular bisector.

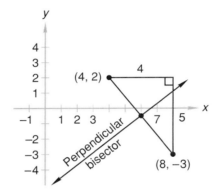

We see that the slope of the line segment is $-\frac{5}{4}$. Now we need to find the coordinates of the midpoint of the line segment.

$$x_m = \frac{x_1 + x_2}{2} \qquad\qquad y_m = \frac{y_1 + y_2}{2}$$

$$x_m = \frac{4 + 8}{2} = 6 \qquad\qquad y_m = \frac{2 + (-3)}{2} = -\frac{1}{2}$$

Since the slope of the perpendicular bisector is the negative reciprocal of the slope of the line segment, the slope of the perpendicular bisector is $\frac{4}{5}$.

$$y = \frac{4}{5}x + b \qquad\qquad \text{equation of perpendicular bisector}$$

Now the perpendicular bisector passes through the midpoint of the segment, which is $\left(6, -\frac{1}{2}\right)$. We use these coordinates for x and y to solve for b.

$$-\frac{1}{2} = \frac{4}{5}(6) + b \qquad\qquad \text{substituted}$$

$$-\frac{5}{10} = \frac{48}{10} + b \qquad\qquad \text{simplified}$$

$$b = -5.3 \qquad\qquad \text{solved}$$

Now we know the y intercept and can write the equation of the perpendicular bisector as

$$y = \frac{4}{5}x - 5.3$$

example 48.4 Write the general form of the perpendicular bisector of the line segment whose endpoints are (4, –3) and (–2, –5). Use the midpoint formula method.

solution First we must find the slope of the line that passes through these two points. This time we will use the slope formula to find the slope and the point-slope form of the equation. First we use the slope formula.

$$m = \frac{y_2 - y_1}{x_2 - x_1} \quad \longrightarrow \quad m = \frac{-5 - (-3)}{-2 - 4} \quad \longrightarrow \quad m = \frac{1}{3}$$

Next we find the coordinates of the midpoint.

$$x_m = \frac{x_1 + x_2}{2} \qquad\qquad y_m = \frac{y_1 + y_2}{2}$$

$$x_m = \frac{4 + (-2)}{2} = 1 \qquad\qquad y_m = \frac{-3 + (-5)}{2} = -4$$

To find the equation of the perpendicular bisector, we use a slope of –3 and the point (1, – 4).

$$y - y_1 = m(x - x_1) \qquad\quad \text{point-slope form}$$

$$y - (-4) = -3(x - 1) \qquad\quad \text{substituted}$$

$$y + 4 = -3x + 3 \qquad\quad \text{simplified}$$

Now we can write the equation of the perpendicular bisector as

$$y = -3x - 1$$

If we write the general form of this equation, we get

$$\mathbf{3x + y + 1 = 0}$$

problem set 48

1. How many odd three-digit counting numbers less than 300 can be found given that the second digit cannot be 2 or 8? Repetition is permitted.

2. How many even three-digit counting numbers can be formed if the second digit is not 0 and the third digit is not 6? Repetition is permitted.

3. The latitude of Cambridge is 42.4° north of the equator. If the diameter of the earth is 7920 miles, how far is Cambridge from the equator?

4. A recipe calls for 12 ounces of cottage cheese and 6 ounces of cream cheese. If there are 216 calories in 8 ounces of cottage cheese and 106 calories in 1 ounce of cream cheese, how many calories are there in 36 ounces of the mixture?

5. A master painter can paint a house in m days and two workers require W_1 and W_2 days each to paint a house alone. If the master can work as fast as the two workers working together, write an expression for m in terms of W_1 and W_2.

6. Michelle had two containers, each containing a mixture of alcohol and disinfectant. One was 40% disinfectant and the other was 80% disinfectant. How much of each should be used to get 600 milliliters of a solution that is 50% disinfectant?

7. The ratio of the number of reds to the number of blues was 2 to 1, and 5 times the sum of the number of reds and blues exceeded 3 times the number of whites by 12. If there were 4 more whites than blues, how many were red, how many were white, and how many were blue?

8. Mr. Lynch owns $\frac{3}{7}$ of the business and his share of the profits for the year was $60,000. Wilbur only owned $\frac{1}{28}$ of the business. What was Wilbur's share of the profits?

Evaluate:

9. $\csc^2 405° - \tan 45°$

10. $\sec^2 (-30°) + \sin^3 90°$

11. Use the midpoint formula method to find the equation of the perpendicular bisector of the line segment whose endpoints are (3, 6) and (8, −4). Write the equation in double-intercept form.

12. Use the midpoint formula method to find the equation of the perpendicular bisector of the line segment whose endpoints are (4, −2) and (−2, 6). Write the equation in slope-intercept form.

Write the equations of the following sinusoids:

13.
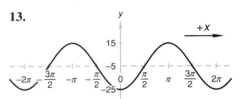

14.
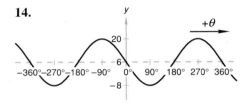

15. Evaluate. Do not use a calculator.

(a) Arctan (tan 240°)

(b) Arctan (tan 330°)

16. Write the quadratic equation with a lead coefficient of 1 whose roots are $1 + 3i$ and $1 - 3i$.

17. Factor $x^2 - 2x + 3$ over the set of complex numbers.

18. The following data came from an experiment performed to determine if there is a relationship between the number of years of education (E) which a person completes and the average yearly income (I) of that person. Use a graphing calculator to find the equation of the line which best fits this data and gives the average yearly income as a function of the number of years of education ($I = mE + b$). Also, find the correlation coefficient for this social science data and discuss whether or not the line is a good model for the data.

Years of education	12	15	16	16	18	20	22
Average yearly income (in thousands)	32	40	52	46	55	85	62

19. Find the standard form of the equation of a circle whose radius is 4 and whose center is (3, 2).

20. Sketch the graph of the function $f(x) = \left(\dfrac{1}{2}\right)^{x-3}$.

21. By how much does $_9P_3$ exceed $_9P_2$?

22. Simplify: $2 \log_4 4 + 3 \log_3 3^2 - \log_4 \dfrac{1}{16} + \log_{10} 10$

Solve for x:

23. $\log_4 5 + \log_4 \dfrac{1}{5} = \log_4 (2x + 1)$

24. $\log_8 (x - 2) - \log_8 3 = \log_8 16$

25. Evaluate. Do not use a calculator.

    (a) Arcsin (-1) (b) $\sin \left[\text{Arccos} \left(-\dfrac{2}{3} \right) \right]$

26. The graph of the function $f(x) = \sqrt{x}$ is shown on the left below. The graph on the right is the same graph translated one unit to the left and three units down. Write the equation of the graph on the right.

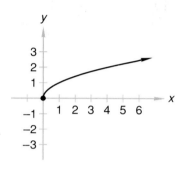 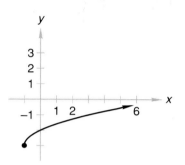

27. Given the function $f(x) = \sqrt{x}$, write the equation of the function g whose graph is the graph of f translated nine units to the left and two units down. Then sketch the graph of the new function g.

28. Given: $\overline{BD}$ is the perpendicular bisector of $\overline{AC}$

    Write a two-column proof to prove:

        $\overline{AB} \cong \overline{CB}$

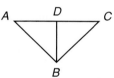

29. Compare: A. $2 \log_2 3 - \log_2 5$ B. $\log_2 9 - \dfrac{1}{2} \log_2 25$

30. Given: $\triangle ABC$

    Compare: A. Area of $\triangle ABC$ B. $\dfrac{1}{2}$

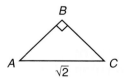

LESSON 49   The Logarithmic Function • Development of the Rules for Logarithms

49.A

the logarithmic function

The two equations

$$N = b^L \qquad \text{and} \qquad L = \log_b N$$

express the same relationship between the variables N and L. In mathematics, we prefer to make our graphs with the independent variable on the horizontal axis and the dependent variable on the vertical axis. If $b = 2$ we get these graphs.

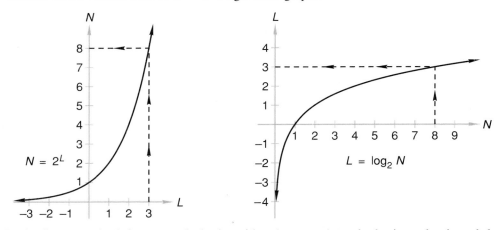

In the figure on the left, we graph the logarithm (exponent) on the horizontal axis and the number on the vertical axis. Now if we are told that the logarithm is 3, we can use the graph to find that the number is 8. In the figure on the right, we graph the number on the horizontal axis and the logarithm (exponent) on the vertical axis. We can use this graph to find that if the number is 8, then the logarithm is 3. We see that both graphs give the same information and that either one can be used, but that if the number (N) is given and we are asked for the logarithm (L), we tend to use the equation

$$L = \log_2 N$$

and the graph on the right. If the logarithm (L) is given and we are asked for the number (N), we tend to use the equation

$$N = 2^L$$

and the graph on the left.

49.B

development of the rules for logarithms

It is reasonable for students to be able to demonstrate a development of the three rules for logarithms. We will review the reasoning involved by using 10^2 and 10^3 and noting that

$$\log_{10} 10^2 = 2 \qquad \text{logarithm is 2}$$
$$\log_{10} 10^3 = 3 \qquad \text{logarithm is 3}$$

Further, we note that when we multiply, we add the logarithms.

$$10^3 \cdot 10^2 = 10^{3+2} \qquad \text{so} \qquad \log_{10} 10^3 10^2 = \log_{10} 10^3 + \log_{10} 10^2$$

When we divide, we subtract the logarithms,

$$\frac{10^3}{10^2} = 10^{3-2} \qquad \text{so} \qquad \log_{10} \frac{10^3}{10^2} = \log_{10} 10^3 - \log_{10} 10^2$$

and when we raise to a power, we multiply the logarithm by the power.

$$\left(10^3\right)^2 = 10^{3 \cdot 2} \qquad \text{so} \qquad \log_{10} \left(10^3\right)^2 = 2 \log_{10} 10^3$$

To develop these ideas in general, we consider that we have two numbers M and N that can be written as a base b to the a power and the same base to the c power.

$$M = b^a \qquad \text{and} \qquad N = b^c$$

so $\qquad \log_b M = a \qquad \text{and} \qquad \log_b N = c$

Now we can write the log of the product MN by replacing M with b^a and replacing N with b^c.

$$\log_b MN = \log_b \left(b^a \cdot b^c\right) = \log_b b^{a+c} = a + c$$

But $a + c$ is the log of M plus the log of N, so we have shown that

$$\log_b MN = \log_b M + \log_b N$$

Next we write the log of the quotient M/N.

$$\log_b \frac{M}{N} = \log_b \frac{b^a}{b^c} = \log_b b^{a-c} = a - c$$

But $a - c$ is the log of M minus the log of N, so we have shown that

$$\log_b \frac{M}{N} = \log_b M - \log_b N$$

Lastly, the log of the power $(N)^x$ is

$$\log_b (N)^x = \log_b \left(b^c\right)^x = \log_b b^{cx} = cx$$

but this is x times the log of N, so we have shown that

$$\log_b N^x = x \log_b N$$

problem set 49

1. How many ways can 4 geometry books and 3 algebra books be arranged in a row if the geometry books must be kept together and the algebra books must be kept together?

2. How many ways can the letters A, B, C, D, E, and F be arranged in a row 4 at a time if neither A nor C can be first or third and D cannot be fourth? Repetition is permitted.

3. The latitude of Wilson, Wyoming, is 43.6° north of the equator. If the diameter of the earth is 7920 miles, how far is Wilson from the equator?

4. Robill can do 2 jobs in 3 days, and Buray can do 5 jobs in 6 days. Robill works for 3 days and then Buray begins to help. How many days will it take to complete a total of 74 jobs?

5. Mugabee thought he was rich because he was paid $240 for a 40-hour week. The next week he received a 20 percent hourly raise, and in addition, he was allowed to work 60 hours. He really celebrated when he saw his paycheck. How much did he get paid?

6. Lorijayne smiled, for she had purchased c cats for only d dollars. Then she frowned, for she still had to purchase p parrots and each parrot cost $\frac{7}{4}$ of the cost of 1 cat. How much did she pay for her parrots?

7. The nurse was aghast. He knew that G gallons of milk would feed S infants for 11 days, but he had $S + 14$ infants to feed. How many days would K gallons of milk last?

8. Let $M = b^a$ and $N = b^c$. Show why $\log_b MN = \log_b M + \log_b N$.

Evaluate:

9. $\sec^2\left(-\frac{13\pi}{6}\right) - \tan^3 \frac{\pi}{4}$

10. $\csc^2\left(-\frac{\pi}{3}\right) + \sec^2 \frac{2\pi}{3} - \tan^2 \frac{5\pi}{6}$

11. Find the equation of the perpendicular bisector of the line segment whose endpoints are $(-2, -4)$ and $(6, 4)$ using the midpoint formula method. Write the equation in general form.

12. Find the equation of the line that is equidistant from the points $(-2, -5)$ and $(3, 4)$ using the midpoint formula method. Write the equation in double-intercept form.

13. Write the equation of the line equidistant from $(1, -1)$ and $(2, -6)$ using the locus definition method. Write the equation in general form.

Write the equations of the following sinusoids:

14.

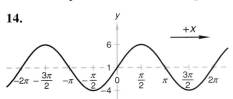

15.

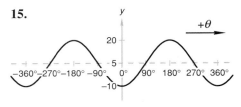

16. Evaluate. Do not use a calculator.

    (a) Arctan (tan 135°)   (b) Arctan (tan 120°)

17. Write the quadratic equation with a lead coefficient of 1 whose roots are $2 + i$ and $2 - i$.

18. Factor $3x^2 - 12x + 24$ over the set of complex numbers.

19. The following data came from an experiment that involved potassium (K) and calcium (Ca). Use a graphing calculator to find the equation of the line which best fits this data and gives calcium as a function of potassium (Ca = mK + b). Also, find the correlation coefficient for this scientific data and discuss whether or not the line is a good model for the data.

K	20	26	30	30	35	37
Ca	18	20	22	20	25	27

20. Find the standard form of the equation of a circle whose radius is 3 and whose center is $(-2, -3)$.

21. Sketch the graph of the function $f(x) = \left(\dfrac{1}{2}\right)^{-x+2}$.

22. Simplify: $4 \log_2 2 + \log_{10} 100 - 5 \log_5 5 + \log_3 \dfrac{1}{3}$

23. Solve for x:

    (a) $\log_{10}(x - 2) - 2 \log_{10} 3 = \log_{10} 4$

    (b) $2 \log_x 9 = 4$

24. The figure shown is a trapezoid whose area is 150 ft^2. Find x. Dimensions are in feet.

25. The graph of the function $f(x) = |x|$ is shown on the left below. The graph on the right is the same graph translated one unit to the right and four units down. Write the equation of the graph on the right.

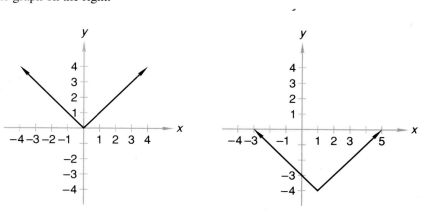

26. Given the function $f(x) = |x|$, write the equation of the function g whose graph is the graph of f translated four units to the right and three units down. Then sketch the graph of the new function g.

27. Find the domain and range of each function whose graph is shown:

(a)

(b)

28. If $f(x) = x^2$, find $\dfrac{f(x + h) - f(x - h)}{2h}$.

**CONCEPT REVIEW
PROBLEMS**

29. Let x be a real number and $x > 1$. Compare: A. $\dfrac{x^2 - 1}{x - 1}$ B. x

30. In $\triangle ABC$, D and E are the midpoints of $\overline{AB}$ and $\overline{BC}$, respectively. Also, $\overline{DE} \parallel \overline{AC}$.

Compare: A. Area of $\triangle DBE$

B. $\frac{1}{4}$ area of $\triangle ABC$

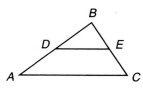

LESSON 50 *Trigonometric Equations*

We know that the sine of 45° equals $+1/\sqrt{2}$ and that the sine of 135° also equals $+1/\sqrt{2}$ because the sine is positive in the first and second quadrants.

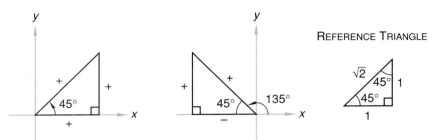

The sine of 405° and the sine of 495° also have a value of $+1/\sqrt{2}$ because these angles are coterminal angles with 45° and 135°. Once around counterclockwise and 45° more equals 405°, and once around counterclockwise and 135° more equals 495°.

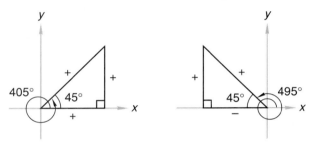

Since twice around counterclockwise, three times around counterclockwise, etc., yields the same result, we find there is an infinite number of angles that have a sine of $1/\sqrt{2}$. If we want to make up a problem that asks which angles have a sine of $1/\sqrt{2}$, and if we wish to restrict the answers to the two angles 45° and 135°, we must make a notation to this effect when we write the problem. We do this by writing

$$0° \leq \theta < 360°$$

to the right of the problem. **This notation tells us that θ is an angle greater than or equal to 0° but less than 360°.**

example 50.1   Solve $\sin \theta = \dfrac{1}{\sqrt{2}}$ given that $0° \leq \theta < 360°$.

solution   This problem asks for the angles whose sine equals $1/\sqrt{2}$. The problem also states that the angles must lie between 0° and 360°. From the discussion above, we know that the angles that satisfy these requirements are 45° and 135°. So

$$\theta = \mathbf{45°, 135°}$$

example 50.2   Solve $2 + \sqrt{3} \sec \theta = 0$ given that $0° \leq \theta < 360°$.

solution   The notation on the right tells us that the value of θ must be between 0° and 360°. First we solve for $\sec \theta$.

$$2 + \sqrt{3} \sec \theta = 0 \qquad \text{equation}$$

$$\sqrt{3} \sec \theta = -2 \qquad \text{added } -2 \text{ to both sides}$$

$$\sec \theta = -\frac{2}{\sqrt{3}} \qquad \text{divided by } \sqrt{3}$$

If sec θ equals $-2/\sqrt{3}$, then cos θ equals $-\sqrt{3}/2$.

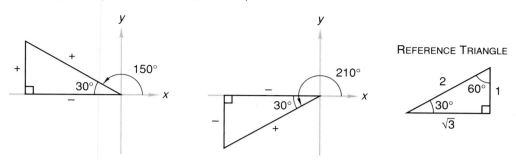

The cosine of 30° is $\sqrt{3}/2$, and the cosine is negative in the second and third quadrants. So the angles are 150° and 210°.

$$\theta = \mathbf{150°, 210°}$$

example 50.3 Solve $3\sqrt{2} + 3 \csc \theta = 0$ given that $0° \le \theta < 360°$.

solution We begin by solving the equation for csc θ.

$$3\sqrt{2} + 3 \csc \theta = 0 \qquad \text{equation}$$

$$3 \csc \theta = -3\sqrt{2} \qquad \text{added } -3\sqrt{2} \text{ to both sides}$$

$$\csc \theta = -\sqrt{2} \qquad \text{divided by 3}$$

If csc $\theta = -\sqrt{2}$, then sin $\theta = -1/\sqrt{2}$.

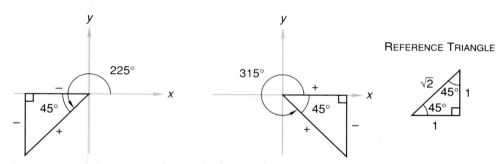

The sine of 45° is $1/\sqrt{2}$ and the sine is negative in the third and fourth quadrants. Thus, the angles that satisfy the given equation are **225°** and **315°**.

problem set 50

1. How many ways can the digits 1, 2, 3, 4, and 5 be arranged in a row of 3 to form an odd counting number if repetition is permitted and if 3 cannot be second and 1 cannot be third?

2. How many positive integers less than 150 are there such that all the digits are odd?

3. The latitude of Oblong, Illinois, is 39.0° north of the equator. If the diameter of the earth is 7920 miles, how far is Oblong from the equator?

4. Three times Sally's age now exceeds 5 times John's age now by 15. In 10 years, twice Sally's age then will be 20 less than 4 times John's age then. How old will they be 15 years from now?

5. The big man could do $\frac{1}{3}$ of a job in 4 hours. The little man could do $\frac{1}{2}$ of a job in 2 hours. If the little man needed to complete 30 jobs and worked for 2 hours alone and then was joined by the big man, how long did it take them both to finish the remaining jobs?

6. Matildabelle found that a quart of milk would serve 4 children or 3 adults. If 16 quarts of milk are available, how much will be left over after 40 children and 12 adults are served?

7. A bus goes d miles in h hours and gets there 4 hours late. At what speed should the bus have been driven to have arrived on time?

Solve the following equations given that $0° \leq \theta < 360°$:

8. $\cos \theta = \dfrac{1}{\sqrt{2}}$

9. $-2 + \sqrt{3} \sec \theta = 0$

10. Let $M = b^a$ and $N = b^c$. Show why $\log_b \dfrac{M}{N} = \log_b M - \log_b N$.

11. Evaluate:

    (a) $\sec^2 \dfrac{3\pi}{4} - \csc^2 \dfrac{\pi}{4} - \cos^2 4\pi$ (b) $\cot^2 \left(-\dfrac{13\pi}{6} \right) - 3 \tan \left(-\dfrac{7\pi}{3} \right)$

12. If $f(x) = \sec^2 x$ and $g(x) = \csc^2 x$, find $f\left(\dfrac{3\pi}{4} \right) - g\left(\dfrac{7\pi}{6} \right)$.

13. Use the midpoint formula method to find the equation of the perpendicular bisector of the line segment whose endpoints are $(-2, 4)$ and $(3, 5)$. Write the equation in general form.

14. Use the locus definition method to write the equation of the line equidistant from $(6, 3)$ and $(3, 2)$. Write the equation in slope-intercept form.

Write the equations of the following sinusoids:

15.

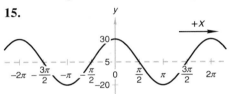

16.

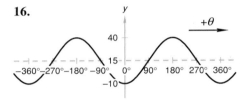

17. Write the quadratic equation with a lead coefficient of 1 whose roots are $1 + \sqrt{3}i$ and $1 - \sqrt{3}i$.

18. Factor $x^2 - 2x + 4$ over the set of complex numbers.

19. The following data came from an experiment performed to determine if there is a relationship between the percentage of blood hemoglobin (H) in dogs and the number of red blood cells (C) they possess. Use a graphing calculator to find the equation of the line which best fits this data and gives the number of red blood cells $\left(\text{in millions per mm}^3\right)$ as a function of the percentage of blood hemoglobin ($C = mH + b$). Also, find the correlation coefficient for this scientific data and discuss whether or not the line is a good model for the data.

Blood hemoglobin %	93	99	96	80	98
Red blood cells	7.3	7.7	7.0	5.1	6.8

20. Find the standard form of the equation of a circle whose radius is 4 and whose center is $(-2, 4)$.

21. Sketch the graph of the function $f(x) = \left(\dfrac{1}{2} \right)^{-x-4}$.

22. Solve for x:

    (a) $\log_3 (x - 3) + \log_3 10 = \log_3 22$ (b) $4 \log_5 3 - \log_5 x = 0$

23. Evaluate: $\displaystyle\sum_{p=1}^{3} \dfrac{p^3 - 2}{p + 1}$

24. Evaluate. Do not use a calculator.

(a) Arccos (cos 150°)

(b) $\sin\left(\text{Arccos } \dfrac{4}{7}\right)$

25. The graph of the function $f(x) = |x|$ is shown on the left below. The graph on the right is the same graph translated three units to the left and three units down. Write the equation of the graph on the right.

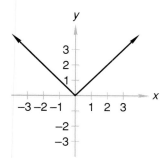
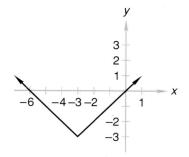

26. Given the function $f(x) = |x|$, write the equation of the function g whose graph is the graph of f translated four units to the left and five units down. Then sketch the graph of the new function g.

27. Find the domain and range of each function whose graph is shown:

(a)

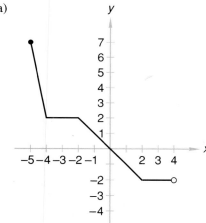

(b)

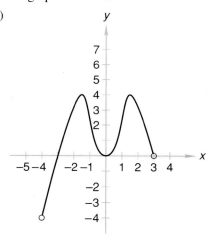

28. Given: $\overline{AB} \parallel \overline{DC}$

$\overline{AD} \parallel \overline{BC}$

Write a two-column proof to prove:

$\overline{AB} \cong \overline{DC}$

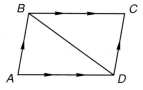

29. Let x and y be real numbers. If $xy = 40$, compare: A. 13 B. $x + y$

30. In the figure shown, one circle is circumscribed around a square with side of length 2 units, and another circle is inscribed in the same square.

Compare: A. Area of smaller circle B. $\frac{1}{\sqrt{2}}$ area of larger circle

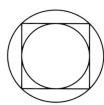

LESSON 51 *Common Logarithms and Natural Logarithms*

We remember that any positive number except 1 can be used as the base of an exponential expression and that the same numbers are the bases of the corresponding logarithmic expressions. We say that the **exponent** is the **logarithm** of the number and that the **number** is the **antilogarithm** of the exponent. Here we use both the exponential form and the logarithmic form to denote that if the base is 10, then 2 is the logarithm of 100 and 100 is the antilogarithm of 2.

$$100 = 10^2 \qquad 2 = \log_{10} 100$$

Logarithms that use 10 as a base are called **common logarithms.** Before slide rules and calculators were invented, most scientific calculations were made by using tables of common logarithms. Common logarithms are still used, and a base of 2 is often used in information theory. The other base most often used is the base e. The number e is an irrational number that is a little greater than 2.71.

$$e = 2.7182818 \ldots$$

Logarithms with a base of e are called **natural logarithms** and are used extensively in calculus, science, engineering, and business.

It is customary to designate that the base is 10 by writing "log" with no subscript. It is customary to designate that the base is e by using the letters "ln" with no subscript. Thus,

$$\log 42 \qquad \text{means} \qquad \log_{10} 42$$
$$\ln 42 \qquad \text{means} \qquad \log_e 42$$

Tables of logarithms give common logarithms and natural logarithms to four or five places, and calculators are accurate to seven or eight places. When accuracy is desired, logarithms can be obtained from these sources, but since beginners often tend to get lost in the arithmetic of logarithm problems, we will round off logarithms to two decimal places and concentrate on understanding rather than on arithmetic accuracy. Thus, for the time being, the logarithm problems will be designed to permit practice in the algebra of logarithms or will be simplified numerical problems designed to let us study the numerical side of logarithmic computations. In time, we will find that our study of these disparate parts will permit us to understand logarithms better.

example 51.1   Write 2.4 as a power with a base of (a) 10 and (b) e.

solution   (a) If we enter 2.4 on a scientific calculator and press the $\boxed{\log}$ key, the 2.4 in the display will change to 0.3802112, which we can round to 0.38. This tells us that 2.4 can also be written as $10^{0.38}$.

$$2.4 = 10^{0.38}$$

(b) If we enter 2.4 on a scientific calculator and press the $\boxed{\ln}$ key, the 2.4 in the display will change to 0.8754687, which we can round to 0.88. This tells us that 2.4 can also be written as $e^{0.88}$.

$$2.4 = e^{0.88}$$

example 51.2   Find (a) log 2.4 and (b) ln 2.4.

solution   "Log" indicates the base 10 exponent and "ln" indicates the base e exponent. From the preceding example, we have

$$2.4 = 10^{0.38} \qquad \text{and} \qquad 2.4 = e^{0.88}$$

so we can write

(a) **log 2.4 = 0.38**   (b) **ln 2.4 = 0.88**

example 51.3   Write 24,000 as a power with a base of 10.

solution   We use a calculator to find log 24,000.

$$\log 24{,}000 = 4.3802112$$

This means we can write that

$$\mathbf{24{,}000 = 10^{4.38}}$$

example 51.4   Write 24,000 as a power whose base is e.

solution   We use a calculator to find ln 24,000.

$$\ln 24{,}000 = 10.085809$$

This means we can write that

$$\mathbf{24{,}000 = e^{10.09}}$$

example 51.5   Write 0.0024 as (a) 10 raised to a power and (b) e raised to a power.

solution   We use a calculator to find log 0.0024 and ln 0.0024.

$$\log 0.0024 = -2.6197888$$

$$\ln 0.0024 = -6.0322865$$

This means we can write that

(a) $\mathbf{0.0024 = 10^{-2.62}}$ (b) $\mathbf{0.0024 = e^{-6.03}}$

problem set 51

1.   How many ways can the letters A, B, C, and D be arranged in a row if B cannot be in the second place and repetition is not allowed?

2.   How many positive integers are there less than 800 such that all the digits are odd?

3.   A lion ran through an arc of $\pi/3$ radians along a circular path of radius 300 meters. How far did the lion run?

4.   The first fellow could finish 7 jobs in 3 hours, and the second fellow could finish 8 jobs in 5 hours. How long would they have to work together to finish 59 jobs?

5.   Use the letter d and the number 100 as required to write an expression that tells the number of 3-cent stamps that can be purchased for d dollars.

6.   A package of raisins weighs 10 ounces. If 3 cups of raisins weighs 1 pound, how many packages will a baker need for a recipe which calls for 15 cups of raisins?

7.   A truck went a distance of d miles in m minutes and arrived 1 hour late. How fast should the truck have been driven to have arrived on time?

8.   Find: (a) log 3.5   (b) ln 3.5

9.   Write 3600 as a power whose base is e.

Solve the following equations given that $0° \le \theta < 360°$:

10. $\sin \theta = -\dfrac{\sqrt{3}}{2}$ 11. $2 + \sqrt{3} \csc \theta = 0$

12.   Let $N = b^c$. Show why $\log_b N^x = x \log_b N$.

13.   Evaluate: $\sec^3 0 - \csc^2 \dfrac{5\pi}{6} + \cos^4 9\pi$

14. Find the coordinates of the point halfway between $(-3, 4)$ and $(6, 2)$.

15. Find the equation of the perpendicular bisector of the line segment whose endpoints are $(-3, 4)$ and $(6, -2)$ using the locus definition method. Write the equation in general form.

16. Find the equation of the line equidistant from $(-2, 1)$ and $(3, 2)$ using the locus definition method. Write the equation in general form.

Write the equations of the following sinusoids:

17.   **18.**

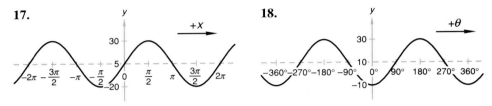

19. Write the quadratic equation with a lead coefficient of 1 whose roots are $3 - i$ and $3 + i$.

20. Factor $4x^2 + 8x + 28$ over the set of complex numbers.

21. The following data came from an experiment performed to determine the relationship between the percent of tricalcium silicate (P) in a sample of cement and the amount of heat in calories per gram of cement (H) produced during hardening. Use a graphing calculator to find the equation of the line which best fits this data and gives the heat as a function of the percentage of cement which is tricalcium silicate $(H = mP + b)$. Also, find the correlation coefficient for this scientific data and discuss whether or not the line is a good model for the data.

Percent of tricalcium silicate	26	29	56	31	52	40
Calories per gram of cement	78.5	74.3	104.3	87.6	95.9	83.8

22. Find the standard form of the equation of a circle whose radius is 5 and whose center is $(-3, 2)$.

23. Sketch the graph of the function $f(x) = \left(\dfrac{1}{2}\right)^{x+2}$.

24. By how much does $_8P_5$ exceed $_8P_3$?

25. Solve for x:

(a) $\log_5 (x + 2) - 2 \log_5 6 = \log_5 1$

(b) $3 \log_7 2 = 2 \log_7 3 + \log_7 x$

26. Determine if $f(x) = \dfrac{1}{x-3}$ and $g(x) = \dfrac{3x+1}{x}$ are inverse functions by computing their compositions.

27. Evaluate. Do not use a calculator.

(a) $\cos \left(\text{Arcsin } \dfrac{3}{4}\right)$ 　　　 (b) $\tan \left[\text{Arcsin } \left(-\dfrac{5}{7}\right)\right]$ 　　　 (c) $\text{Arctan } (\tan 210°)$

28. The graph of the function $f(x) = \sqrt{x}$ is shown on the left below. The graph on the right is the same graph reflected in the x axis and translated two units to the right. Write the equation of the graph on the right.

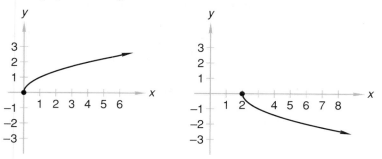

29. Let $f(x) = |x|$ and $g(x) = |x + 6|$. Which of the following statements is true?

  A. The graph of g is the graph of f translated six units to the right.

  B. The graph of g is the graph of f translated six units to the left.

  C. The graph of g is the graph of f translated six units up.

  D. The graph of g is the graph of f translated six units down.

30. If $f(x) = x^2 + x$, find $\dfrac{f(x + h) - f(x - h)}{2h}$.

LESSON 52   *The Inviolable Argument • Arguments in Trigonometric Equations*

52.A

the inviolable argument

The word *inviolable* means "safe from violation or profanation and impregnable to assault or trespass." **The argument of a function is inviolable because the argument cannot be removed from the expression nor changed in form by using standard algebraic techniques. For example, the following procedure is *not* correct because it attempts to change the form of the argument 2θ by the algebraic procedure of dividing both sides of the equation by 2.**

$$\tan 2\theta = 1 \qquad \text{equation}$$

$$\tan \frac{2\theta}{2} = \frac{1}{2} \qquad \text{divided by 2} \qquad \textbf{NO!}$$

$$\tan \theta = \frac{1}{2} \qquad \text{simplified} \qquad \textbf{NO!}$$

If it is necessary to divide both sides of the equation by 2, it is necessary to divide the whole expression by 2.

$$\frac{\tan 2\theta}{2} = \frac{1}{2} \qquad \text{correct}$$

We must always consider that the argument is a thing or an entity that must be retained in the given form unless changed by substituting an equivalent expression. For instance, if $2\theta - \pi = 4x$, then $4x$ could be substituted for $2\theta - \pi$.

$$\cos (2\theta - \pi) = 1 \qquad \text{equation}$$

$$\cos 4x = 1 \qquad \text{substituted}$$

Now we can solve this equation for the value of $4x$, but we cannot find the value of x before we find the value of $4x$. We will demonstrate the proper procedure in the following problems.

52.B
arguments in trigonometric equations

When the argument in a trigonometric equation consists of a variable whose coefficient is a number other than 1, the procedure is to solve the equation to find the value of the argument and then solve for the value of the variable.

example 52.1   Solve: $\tan 3\theta - 1 = 0$ $0° \leq \theta < 360°$

solution   The first step is to find the value of the argument. Had the equation been written $\tan (3\theta - 1) = 0$, the argument would have been $3\theta - 1$. Because the parentheses were not used, we know that the argument is 3θ. We begin by rearranging the equation.

$$\tan 3\theta = 1 \qquad \text{rearranged}$$

The tangent of 45° is 1, and the tangent is positive in the first and third quadrants.

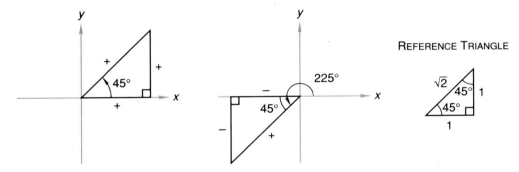

So 3θ equals 45° and 225°. Now we can find θ.

$$3\theta = 45° \qquad\qquad 3\theta = 225°$$

$$\theta = 15° \qquad\qquad \theta = 75°$$

The statement of the problem asked for all values of θ between 0° and 360°, and thus the values of 3θ are between 0° and 3(360°), or between 0° and 1080°. This means that since 3θ can equal 45°, 3θ can also equal 45° + 360° (once around) and 3θ can equal 45° + 2 · 360° (twice around).

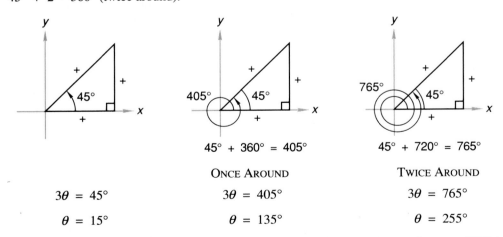

$$45° + 360° = 405° \qquad\qquad 45° + 720° = 765°$$

ONCE AROUND   TWICE AROUND

$$3\theta = 45° \qquad\qquad 3\theta = 405° \qquad\qquad 3\theta = 765°$$

$$\theta = 15° \qquad\qquad \theta = 135° \qquad\qquad \theta = 255°$$

If we check for 3 times around, we find we begin repeating our answers because 375° is 360° + 15°.

$$3 \text{ times around} = 45° + 3(360°) = 1125°$$

$$3\theta = 1125°$$

$$\theta = 375° \quad \text{or} \quad \theta = 15°$$

Now we continue our search for answers and find that 3θ can also equal $225°$, $585°$, and $945°$.

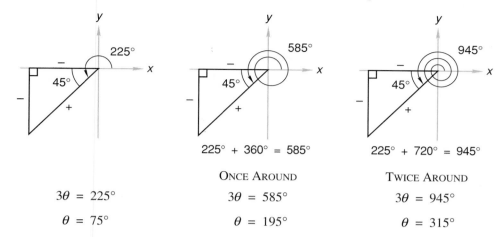

$$225° + 360° = 585° \qquad 225° + 720° = 945°$$

ONCE AROUND TWICE AROUND

$$3\theta = 225° \qquad 3\theta = 585° \qquad 3\theta = 945°$$
$$\theta = 75° \qquad \theta = 195° \qquad \theta = 315°$$

Thus, we find that the equation $\tan 3\theta - 1 = 0$ has six values of θ that satisfy the equation. They are **15°, 75°, 135°, 195°, 255°,** and **315°.**

Had the argument in the above example been 4θ, we would have had to go once around, twice around, and three times around. If the argument had been 5θ, we would have had to go once around, twice around, three times around, and four times around.

example 52.2 Solve: $\cos\dfrac{\theta}{2} + \dfrac{\sqrt{3}}{2} = 0 \qquad 0° \le \theta < 360°$

solution The first step is to rearrange to solve for the value of the argument $\theta/2$.

$$\cos\frac{\theta}{2} = -\frac{\sqrt{3}}{2}$$

Thus, $\dfrac{\theta}{2} = 150° \qquad$ and $\qquad \dfrac{\theta}{2} = 210°$

The angle θ must lie between $0°$ and $360°$. Thus $\theta/2$ must lie between $0°$ and $360°/2$, which is $180°$. Thus we must discard the solution $\theta/2 = 210°$, since $210°$ does not lie between $0°$ and $180°$. Now we solve $\theta/2 = 150°$ for θ and find that $\theta = $ **300°.** Since $300°$ lies between $0°$ and $360°$, **300°** is the solution to the original problem.

problem set 52

1. Given the letters A, B, C, D, E, and F, how many ways can they be arranged in rows of 5 if A is not third and B is fifth? Repetition is allowed.

2. How many positive integers less than 500 are there all of whose digits are odd?

3. The latitude of Washington, D.C., is $38.8°$ north of the equator. If the diameter of the earth is 7920 miles, how far is Washington, D.C., from the equator?

4. Rancie could finish 5 jobs in 4 hours. When Bubba helped, they could complete 12 jobs in 7 hours. How long would it take Bubba to complete 2 jobs if he worked alone?

5. Jimbob worked 40 hours for $200. The week of the fair he received a 40 percent hourly increase, but because of the extra help, he was only able to work 30 hours. What was his paycheck the week of the fair?

6. Sarah bought 50 shares of a company at $60 per share and 2 months later bought 25 shares at $56 per share. What price per share should she pay for 25 more shares so that the average price per share would be $58?

7. A man traveled a distance of D feet in S seconds but arrived 2 minutes late. How fast should he have traveled in feet per second to have arrived on time?

8. The boy could row at twice the speed of the current in the river. He could row 45 miles downstream in 1 more hour than it took to row 10 miles upstream. How fast was the current and how fast could the boy row?

Solve the following equations given that $0° \leq \theta < 360°$:

9. $\cos 2\theta = -\dfrac{1}{2}$

10. $\tan 3\theta - 1 = 0$

11. $\sin \dfrac{\theta}{2} - \dfrac{\sqrt{3}}{2} = 0$

12. Find: (a) $\log 16.3$ (b) $\ln 16.3$

13. Write 3800 as a power whose base is e.

Evaluate:

14. $\sin^2\left(-\dfrac{\pi}{3}\right) - \cos^2 \dfrac{2\pi}{3} + \csc^2 \dfrac{4\pi}{3}$

15. $\csc^2\left(-\dfrac{13\pi}{6}\right) - \sec^2 \dfrac{19\pi}{6} - \cot^2 \dfrac{5\pi}{4}$

16. Use the midpoint formula method to find the equation of the perpendicular bisector of the line segment whose endpoints are $(-4, 8)$ and $(-6, -2)$. Write the equation in double-intercept form.

Write the equations of the following sinusoids:

17.

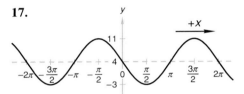

18.

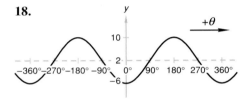

19. Write the quadratic equation with a lead coefficient of 1 whose roots are $-2 + i$ and $-2 - i$.

20. Factor $x^2 + 4x + 5$ over the set of complex numbers.

21. The following data came from an experiment performed to determine whether a person's height (H) is related to his or her weight (W). Use a graphing calculator to find the equation of the line which best fits this data and gives a person's weight as a function of the person's height ($W = mH + b$). Also, find the correlation coefficient for this scientific data and discuss whether or not the line is a good model for the data.

Height in inches	70	73	68	68	67	66
Weight in pounds	190	216	178	119	175	104

22. Find the standard form of the equation of a circle whose radius is r and whose center is (h, k).

23. Sketch the graph of the function $f(x) = \left(\dfrac{1}{4}\right)^{-2x+1}$.

Solve for x:

24. $\log_6 (x - 2) + 2 \log_6 3 = \log_6 2$

25. $2 \log_{1/2} 3 - \log_{1/2} (2x - 3) = 1$

26. Evaluate: $\displaystyle\sum_{k=-1}^{3} \left(k^3 - 2\right)$

27. Determine if $f(x) = \dfrac{x}{x-1}$ and $g(x) = \dfrac{x}{x+1}$ are inverse functions by computing their compositions.

28. The figure shown is a trapezoid whose area is 20 m². Find x. Dimensions are in meters.

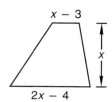

x − 3

x

2x − 4

29. The graph of the function $f(x) = \sqrt{x}$ is shown on the left below. The graph on the right is the same graph reflected in the x axis and translated four units to the left. Write the equation of the graph on the right.

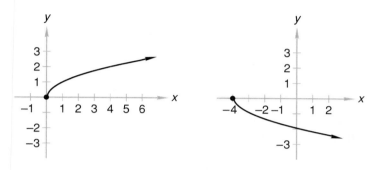

30. Let $f(x) = x^2$ and $g(x) = (x - 5)^2$. Which of the following statements is true?

A. The graph of g is the graph of f translated five units to the right.

B. The graph of g is the graph of f translated five units to the left.

C. The graph of g is the graph of f translated five units up.

D. The graph of g is the graph of f translated five units down.

LESSON 53   *Review of Unit Multipliers • Angular Velocity*

53.A
review of unit multipliers

Unit multipliers are so named because they contain units such as feet, meters, hours, and seconds and also because they have a value of 1. In each of the following fractions, the denominator and the numerator represent the same measure, and thus the value of each of these fractions is 1.

$$\frac{12 \text{ in.}}{1 \text{ ft}} \qquad \frac{3 \text{ ft}}{1 \text{ yd}} \qquad \frac{5280 \text{ ft}}{1 \text{ mi}} \qquad \frac{100 \text{ cm}}{1 \text{ m}} \qquad \frac{1 \text{ liter}}{1000 \text{ cc}}$$

$$\frac{2.54 \text{ cm}}{1 \text{ in.}} \qquad \frac{60 \text{ s}}{1 \text{ min}} \qquad \frac{60 \text{ min}}{1 \text{ hr}} \qquad \frac{24 \text{ hr}}{1 \text{ day}}$$

If any of these fractions is inverted, the value of the fraction will still be 1. Unit multipliers are useful for making unit conversions.

example 53.1   Change 40 miles per hour to meters per second.

solution   First we use unit multipliers to change hours to seconds.

$$\frac{40 \text{ mi}}{1 \text{ hr}} \times \frac{1 \text{ hr}}{60 \text{ min}} \times \frac{1 \text{ min}}{60 \text{ s}}$$

Now we multiply as required to change miles to feet, to inches, to centimeters, to meters.

$$\frac{40 \text{ mi}}{1 \text{ hr}} \times \frac{1 \text{ hr}}{60 \text{ min}} \times \frac{1 \text{ min}}{60 \text{ s}} \times \frac{5280 \text{ ft}}{1 \text{ mi}} \times \frac{12 \text{ in.}}{1 \text{ ft}} \times \frac{2.54 \text{ cm}}{1 \text{ in.}} \times \frac{1 \text{ m}}{100 \text{ cm}}$$

The units cancel as shown and our answer is

$$\frac{40 \times 5280 \times 12 \times 2.54}{60 \times 60 \times 100} \frac{\text{m}}{\text{s}}$$

A calculator can be used to reduce this answer to a single decimal number, if desired.

53.B
angular velocity

Linear velocity is a vector quantity as it has both a magnitude and a direction. **Angular velocity** is also a vector quantity and it measures the rate of rotation of an object. Its direction can be clockwise or counterclockwise. The units of angular velocity are some unit of circular measure per unit of time. Some commonly used units of angular velocity are

$$\frac{\text{deg}}{\text{s}} \qquad \frac{\text{deg}}{\text{min}} \qquad \frac{\text{rad}}{\text{s}} \qquad \frac{\text{rad}}{\text{min}} \qquad \frac{\text{rev}}{\text{s}} \qquad \frac{\text{rev}}{\text{min}}$$

The instantaneous linear velocity of a point on a rotating wheel depends on the rate of rotation and on the distance of the point from the center of the wheel. Consider that the wheel shown here makes 1 revolution (rev) every second.

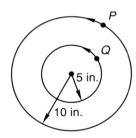

Point P is 10 inches from the center and in 1 second it goes all the way around the outside circle, which has a circumference of $2\pi r$ inches.

$$1 \text{ rotation} = 2(3.14)(10) = 62.8 \text{ in.}$$

Point Q has the same rate of turning or angular velocity, but it is closer to the center of rotation, so in 1 second it travels a different distance.

$$1 \text{ rotation} = 2(3.14)(5) = 31.4 \text{ in.}$$

Thus, while the angular velocities of P and Q are the same, their linear velocities are different.

$$\text{Velocity of } P = 62.8 \frac{\text{in.}}{\text{s}} \qquad \text{Velocity of } Q = 31.4 \frac{\text{in.}}{\text{s}}$$

In general, the linear velocity of a point on a rotating body is

$$v = r\omega$$

where ω (omega) is the angular velocity measured in radians per unit time. If the angular velocity is given in revolutions per unit time or degrees per unit time, the revolutions or degrees must be converted to radians in order to calculate linear velocity.

In the figure on the left the wheel is rotating about its axle, which is attached to the wall. The axle is not moving. The linear velocity of any point on the rim **with respect to the axle** (center of the wheel) is $r\omega$.

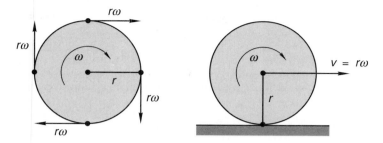

In the figure on the right the wheel is rolling along to the right. **The rim is not moving with respect to the ground at the point of contact with the ground.** The center of the wheel is moving to the right at a velocity of $r\omega$ with respect to the point in contact with the ground. In both cases the linear velocity is $r\omega$. On the left we are interested in the velocity of a point on the rim *with respect to the stationary axle*. On the right we are interested in the velocity of the center of the wheel *with respect to the ground*.

example 53.2   A wheel of a wagon has a radius of 14 inches and is revolving at 40 revolutions per minute (rev/min). How fast is the wagon moving in miles per hour?

solution   **The linear velocity of the center of the wheel with respect to the ground is $r\omega$, where ω is stated in radians per unit time.** Thus, we begin by converting 40 revolutions per minute (rev/min) to radians per minute (rad/min).

$$40 \ \frac{\text{rev}}{\text{min}} \times 2\pi \ \frac{\text{rad}}{\text{rev}} = 80\pi \ \frac{\text{rad}}{\text{min}}$$

Now we can use $v = r\omega$ to find the linear velocity and at the same time convert the answer to miles per hour.

$$v = r\omega = 14 \ \cancel{\text{in.}} \times 80\pi \ \frac{\text{rad}}{\cancel{\text{min}}} \times \frac{1 \ \cancel{\text{ft}}}{12 \ \cancel{\text{in.}}} \times \frac{1 \ \text{mi}}{5280 \ \cancel{\text{ft}}} \times \frac{60 \ \cancel{\text{min}}}{1 \ \text{hr}}$$

$$= \frac{14(80\pi)(60)}{12(5280)} \ \frac{\text{mi}}{\text{hr}}$$

example 53.3   An automobile whose wheels are 30 inches in diameter is traveling at 40 mph. What is the angular velocity of the wheels in revolutions per second?

solution   First we solve for ω.

$$v = r\omega \quad \longrightarrow \quad \omega = \frac{v}{r}$$

We will put the numbers we have into this equation and simplify.

$$\omega = \frac{v}{r} = \frac{40 \ \dfrac{\text{mi}}{\text{hr}}}{15 \ \text{in.}} = \frac{40 \ \text{mi}}{15 \ \text{hr-in.}}$$

All length measurements must be the same. We can convert inches to miles and cancel, or convert miles to inches and cancel. The result will be the same. We decide to convert miles to inches.

$$\omega = \frac{40 \ \cancel{\text{mi}}}{15 \ \text{hr-}\cancel{\text{in.}}} \times \frac{5280 \ \cancel{\text{ft}}}{1 \ \cancel{\text{mi}}} \times \frac{12 \ \cancel{\text{in.}}}{1 \ \cancel{\text{ft}}} = \frac{40(5280)(12)}{15} \ \frac{}{\text{hr}}$$

This answer is really in radians per hour. Radian measure is dimensionless, and the unit *radian* is used as a convenience. Thus, the unit *radian* can be inserted or deleted as is convenient. This is difficult to understand at first and practice with this concept is necessary. In the last step in the preceding example we deleted the unit *radian*. To finish this problem, we will insert the unit *radian*.

$$\omega = \frac{40(5280)(12)}{15} \frac{\text{rad}}{\text{hr}}$$

Now we finish by using unit multipliers to convert radians per hour to revolutions per second.

$$\omega = \frac{40(5280)(12)}{15} \frac{\text{rad}}{\text{hr}} \times \frac{1 \text{ rev}}{2\pi \text{ rad}} \times \frac{1 \text{ hr}}{60 \text{ min}} \times \frac{1 \text{ min}}{60 \text{ s}}$$

$$= \frac{40(5280)(12)}{15(2\pi)(60)(60)} \frac{\text{rev}}{\text{s}}$$

problem set 53

1. If no repetition is permitted, how many ways can the digits 1, 2, 3, 4, 5, and 6 be arranged four at a time to form an even number?

2. A horse runs through an arc of 270° along a circular racetrack whose diameter is 4000 meters. How far does the horse run?

3. Mudog can do 8 jobs in 3 days, and Jimmy can do 5 jobs in 2 days. Thirty-nine jobs need to be done. Mudog works 3 days and then Jimmy joins in. How many days will both of them have to work together to complete the 39 jobs?

4. In a factory, m workers work h hours to do j jobs. If p new workers are hired, how many hours will the work force have to work to do j jobs?

5. Fast Francie could run Y yards in S seconds. What would be her rate in yards per second if she ran 3 times as far in 20 more seconds?

6. Kelly converted 2800 francs to dollars at an exchange rate of 350 francs to the dollar. Then he went to another country and converted back to francs at 400 francs to the dollar. What was his profit in francs?

7. Convert 50 miles per hour to centimeters per minute.

8. Convert 30 liters to cubic inches.

9. An automobile whose wheels are 30 inches in diameter is traveling at 50 miles per hour. What is the angular velocity of the wheels in revolutions per second?

Solve the following equations given that $0° \le \theta < 360°$:

10. $\sin \theta = \dfrac{\sqrt{3}}{2}$

11. $\cos 3\theta - 1 = 0$

12. $\sin \dfrac{\theta}{2} - 1 = 0$

13. Write 6200 as 10 raised to a power.

14. Write 5400 as e raised to a power.

15. If $f(x) = \cot^2 x$ and $g(x) = \sec^2 x$, find $f\left(-\dfrac{\pi}{3}\right) - g(0)$.

16. If $f(x) = \sec^2 x$ and $g(x) = \cos^2 x$, find $f\left(\dfrac{-3\pi}{4}\right) + g\left(\dfrac{13\pi}{6}\right)$.

17. Write the equation of the line equidistant from $(8, 4)$ and $(-3, 4)$ using the locus definition method. Write the equation in general form.

Write the equations of the following sinusoids:

18.

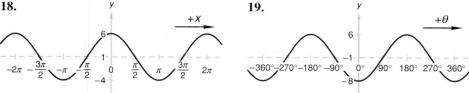

19.

20. Write the quadratic equation with a lead coefficient of 1 whose roots are $-1 + 2\sqrt{2}i$ and $-1 - 2\sqrt{2}i$.

21. The following data came from an experiment to compare a person's body weight (W) with the volume of blood (V) in his or her body. Use a graphing calculator to find the equation of the line which best fits this data and gives the volume of blood as a function of body weight (V = mW + b). Also, find the correlation coefficient for this scientific data and discuss whether or not the line is a good model for the data.

Body weight in kg	34	41	20	37	23
Blood volume in cm³	2320	2810	1660	2560	1550

22. Find the standard form of the equation of a circle whose radius is 5 and whose center is $\left(\sqrt{3}, -2\right)$.

23. Sketch the graph of the function $f(x) = \left(\dfrac{2}{3}\right)^{3x-2}$.

Solve for x:

24. $\log_{15} 4 - \log_{15} \dfrac{2}{x} = 2$

25. $2 \log_7 4 - \log_7 x = \dfrac{2}{3} \log_7 8$

26. Determine if $f(x) = \dfrac{1}{1-x}$ and $g(x) = \dfrac{x-1}{x}$ are inverse functions by computing their compositions.

27. The figure shown is a trapezoid whose area is 6 cm². Find x. Dimensions are in centimeters.

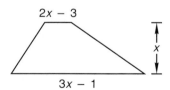

28. The graph of the function $f(x) = x^2$ is shown on the left below. The graph on the right is the same graph reflected in the x axis and translated four units up. Write the equation of the graph on the right.

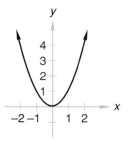

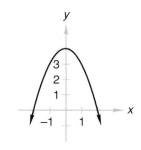

29. Let $f(x) = x^2$ and $g(x) = x^2 - 3$. Which of the following statements is true?

    A. The graph of g is the graph of f translated three units to the right.

    B. The graph of g is the graph of f translated three units to the left.

    C. The graph of g is the graph of f translated three units up.

    D. The graph of g is the graph of f translated three units down.

30. If $f(x) = x^2 - x$, find $\dfrac{f(x + h) - f(x - h)}{2h}$.

LESSON 54 *Parabolas*

In Lesson 42 we noted that the figures formed when a plane cuts a right circular cone are called *conic sections.* If the plane is parallel to the base of the cone, the figure formed is a circle, as we see on the left below. If the plane is tilted as shown on the right, the figure formed is a **parabola.**

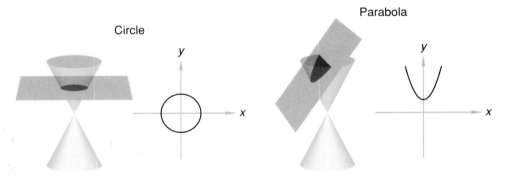

Circle   Parabola

Every parabola has an axis of symmetry, as we see in the following figures. The axis of symmetry can be vertical, horizontal, or inclined to the vertical and the horizontal.

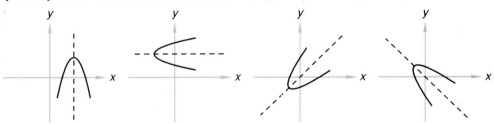

    In this book we will concentrate on parabolas whose axes of symmetry are vertical lines. We remember that the graph of the equation $y = x^2$ is the graph of a parabola that opens upward and whose vertex is at the origin, as we show on the left.

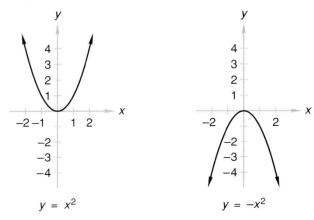

$y = x^2$ $y = -x^2$

This is the graph of a function because for every value of x there is only one point on the graph and hence only one matching value of y. For any function, the graph of $y = -f(x)$ is the graph of the original function reflected in the x axis. Thus the graph of $y = -x^2$ shown on the right is the same graph reflected in the x axis. The vertex of this graph is also at the origin. We remember that the graph of any equation in x and y can be shifted two units to the left by replacing x with $x + 2$ and shifted three units downward by replacing y with $y + 3$.

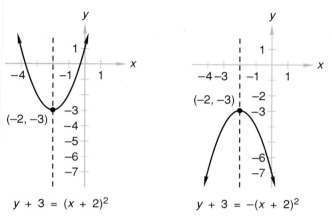

$$y + 3 = (x + 2)^2 \qquad\qquad y + 3 = -(x + 2)^2$$

If we add -3 to both sides of these equations, we get forms of the equations that tell us at a glance whether the parabola opens upward or downward, the equation of the axis of symmetry, and the y coordinate of the vertex.

$$\underbrace{y = +(x + 2)^2 - 3}_{\substack{\text{axis of symmetry} \quad \text{vertex at} \\ \text{is } x = -2 \qquad y = -3}} \qquad\qquad \underbrace{y = -(x + 2)^2 - 3}_{\substack{\text{axis of symmetry} \quad \text{vertex at} \\ \text{is } x = -2 \qquad y = -3}}$$

(opens upward)   (opens downward)

Note that when we have $(x + 2)^2$, the axis of symmetry is $x = -2$ and is not $x = +2$.

Any quadratic equation such as

$$y = x^2 - 4x + 2 \qquad \text{and} \qquad y = -x^2 - 6x - 8$$

can be graphed by making a chart and plotting the graph point by point. This process is very time-consuming and the equation can be graphed in much less time if we use the method of completing the square on the right-hand side of the equation and write the equation in the form

$$y = (x - h)^2 + k$$

In this form we can see whether the parabola opens upward or downward, write the equation of the axis of symmetry, and note the coordinates of the vertex. This information will allow us to graph the parabola quickly and accurately.

example 54.1   Complete the square to graph $y = x^2 - 4x + 2$.

solution   We want to rearrange the right-hand side of the equation into the form

$$y = (x - h)^2 + k$$

so we place parentheses around the x^2 term and the x term.

$$y = \left(x^2 - 4x \quad\right) + 2$$

Now to make the expression inside the parentheses a perfect square, it is necessary to add the square of one half the coefficient of x, which is 4.

$$\left(-4 \cdot \frac{1}{2}\right)^2 = 4$$

Thus, we add +4 inside the parentheses and − 4 outside the parentheses. This addition of +4 and − 4 to the same side of the equation is a net addition of zero.

$$y = \left(x^2 - 4x + 4\right) + 2 - 4$$

Now the term in the parentheses is a perfect square, and we write it as such.

$$y = (x - 2)^2 - 2$$

From this form, we can determine the three things necessary to sketch the curve.

(a) Opens upward
(b) Axis of symmetry is $x = +2$ $\quad y = +(x - 2)^2 - 2$
(c) y coordinate of vertex is -2

We use this information to draw the axis of symmetry and the vertex of the curve, as we show on the left-hand graph below. Now, if we get one more point on the curve, we can make a sketch. Let's let $x = 4$ in the original equation and solve for y.

$$y = (4)^2 - 4(4) + 2 \qquad \text{substituted}$$
$$y = 16 - 16 + 2 \qquad \text{multiplied}$$
$$y = 2 \qquad \text{simplified}$$

Thus, the point $(4, 2)$ lies on the curve. We remember that the curve is symmetric about the line $x = 2$ and complete the sketch.

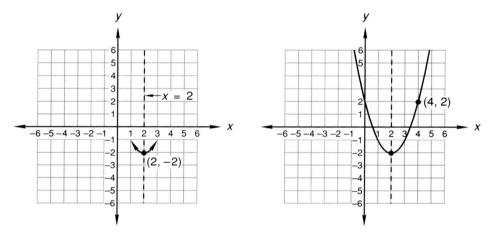

example 54.2   Complete the square to graph $y = -x^2 - 6x - 8$.

solution   **When the coefficient of x^2 is not 1, we begin by factoring the first two terms so that the coefficient of x^2 is 1.**

$$y = -\left(x^2 + 6x \quad\right) - 8 \qquad \text{factored}$$

Now we complete the square inside the parentheses by adding +9. **Since the parentheses are preceded by a minus sign, we have really added −9, so we also add +9 outside the parentheses.** Then we simplify.

$$y = -\left(x^2 + 6x + 9\right) - 8 + 9 \qquad \text{completed the square}$$
$$y = -(x + 3)^2 + 1 \qquad \text{simplified}$$

Now we diagnose the salient features of the graph.

(a) Opens downward
(b) Axis of symmetry is $x = -3$ $\quad y = -(x + 3)^2 + 1$
(c) y coordinate of vertex is $+1$

On the left-hand graph below we use these facts to begin the curve. To find another point on the curve, we replace x with -1 and find that y equals -3.

$$y = -(-1)^2 - 6(-1) - 8 \qquad \text{substituted}$$

$$y = -1 + 6 - 8 \qquad \text{multiplied}$$

$$y = -3 \qquad \text{simplified}$$

Then we use the point $(-1, -3)$ and symmetry to complete the graph.

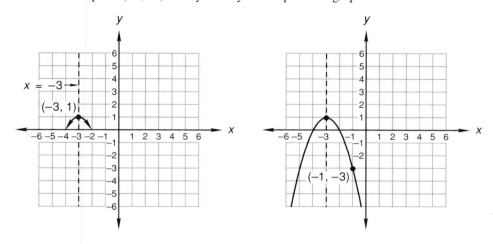

problem set 54

1. A wheel of a big vehicle has a diameter of 3 feet and is revolving at 30 revolutions per minute. What is the velocity of the vehicle in miles per hour?

2. An automobile with a wheel radius of 70 centimeters is traveling at 30 kilometers per hour. What is the angular velocity of the wheels in radians per minute?

3. How many ways can A, B, C, and D be placed in a row of 3 spaces if B cannot be first and D cannot be second? Repetition is permitted.

4. A discombobulated man runs through an arc of 80° along a circle of radius 300 meters. How far does he run?

5. Judy flew R miles in m hours and arrived 2 hours late. How fast should she have flown to have arrived on time?

6. Hortense could complete 1 job in 4 hours while Joe could complete 1 job in 8 hours. If there were $6\frac{1}{4}$ jobs to be completed and Joe worked for 2 hours before Hortense joined him, how long would it take the two of them working together to finish?

7. The vat contained 40 liters of a 5% salt solution. How many liters of a 20% salt solution should be added to get a solution that is 10% salt?

8. Complete the square to graph $y = x^2 - 6x + 4$.

9. Complete the square to graph $y = -x^2 - 4x + 6$.

10. Convert 40 miles per hour to centimeters per second.

11. Convert 12 liters per second to cubic centimeters per hour.

Solve the following equations given that $0° \leq \theta < 360°$:

12. $\cos \theta = -\dfrac{\sqrt{2}}{2}$

13. $\sin 3\theta - \dfrac{1}{2} = 0$

14. $\sec 2\theta - 1 = 0$

15. Write 3100 as 10 raised to a power.

16. Write 3100 as e raised to a power.

17. Evaluate: $\tan^2 \dfrac{19\pi}{6} - \csc^2 \dfrac{\pi}{2} + \sec^2 3\pi$

18. If $f(x) = \sec^2 x$ and $g(x) = \cot^2 x$, find $f\left(-\dfrac{3\pi}{4}\right) - g\left(\dfrac{7\pi}{6}\right)$.

19. Find the coordinates of the point halfway between (6, 7) and (–2, 5).

20. Write the equation of the perpendicular bisector of the line segment which joins (4, 6) and (–4, 8). Use the locus definition method and write the equation in double-intercept form.

Write the equations of the following sinusoids:

21. 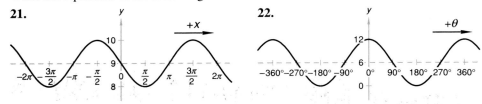 22.

23. Factor $5x^2 + 15x + 45$ over the set of complex numbers.

24. The following data were collected at a power plant and relate the average monthly temperature (T) with the number of pounds of steam (S) a particular generator used each month. Use a graphing calculator to find the equation of the line which best fits this data and gives the pounds of steam used monthly as a function of the average monthly temperature (S = mT + b). Also, find the correlation coefficient for this scientific data and discuss whether or not the line is a good model for the data.

Average monthly temperature in °F	35.3	30.8	58.8	71.3	61.4	48.5
Pounds of steam used monthly	10.98	12.51	8.40	8.73	9.27	9.58

25. Find the standard form of the equation of a circle whose radius is 6 and whose center is (3, 2).

26. Sketch the graph of the function $f(x) = (2)^{-x-3}$.

27. Solve for x:

(a) $\log_5 6 - \log_5 \dfrac{1}{x+1} = \log_5 7$ (b) $2 \ln 5 - \ln x = \dfrac{3}{4} \ln 16$

28. Evaluate: $\displaystyle\sum_{k=-3}^{-1} \dfrac{(k-1)(k+1)}{k}$

29. The graph of the function $f(x) = |x|$ is shown on the left below. The graph on the right is the same graph reflected in the x axis and translated two units down. Write the equation of the graph on the right.

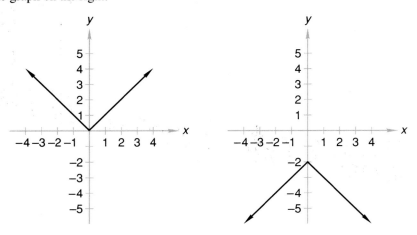

30. Let $f(x) = |x|$ and $g(x) = |x| + 6$. Which of the following statements is true?

    A. The graph of g is the graph of f translated six units to the right.

    B. The graph of g is the graph of f translated six units to the left.

    C. The graph of g is the graph of f translated six units up.

    D. The graph of g is the graph of f translated six units down.

LESSON 55   *Circular Permutations • Distinguishable Permutations*

55.A

circular permutations

When items are arranged in a circle, there is no first place. Thus, the number of permutations is not as great than if the items were arranged in a line. For instance, if the king, the queen, and the prince sit around a circular table with the queen to the king's left, it would look like this.

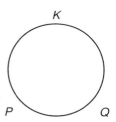

Now if everyone moves to their left one seat or to their right one seat, it would look like one of these.

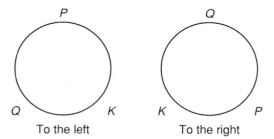

To the left   To the right

In all three diagrams, the queen is seated on the king's left, so all three arrangements are the same. Thus, when three items are arranged in a circle, we consider that there is just one possible entry for the first place instead of the three entries that are possible for the first place of a linear permutation. With three items, the numbers of permutations are

LINEAR PERMUTATIONS

3	2	1

$3 \cdot 2 \cdot 1 = 6$

CIRCULAR PERMUTATIONS

1	2	1

$1 \cdot 2 \cdot 1 = 2$

If we use the letter N to represent the number of objects, we see that there are $N!$ linear permutations but only $(N - 1)!$ circular permutations.

example 55.1   How many ways can 6 different items be arranged in a line and how many ways can 6 different items be arranged in a circle?

solution   For a linear permutation, there are 6 first places, but for a circular permutation, there is only 1 first place. So

LINEAR PERMUTATIONS

6	5	4	3	2	1

$6 \cdot 5 \cdot 4 \cdot 3 \cdot 2 \cdot 1 = \mathbf{720}$

CIRCULAR PERMUTATIONS

1	5	4	3	2	1

$1 \cdot 5 \cdot 4 \cdot 3 \cdot 2 \cdot 1 = \mathbf{120}$

example 55.2   When the chips were down, Ed found that there were 5 chips and each one was a different color. How many ways could Ed place them (a) in a row? (b) in a circle?

solution   (a) There are 5! linear permutations.

5	4	3	2	1

$\longrightarrow \quad 5 \cdot 4 \cdot 3 \cdot 2 \cdot 1 = \mathbf{120}$ linear permutations

(b) In circular permutations there is only 1 first position, so we have only $(5 - 1)!$ permutations.

1	4	3	2	1

$\longrightarrow \quad 1 \cdot 4 \cdot 3 \cdot 2 \cdot 1 = \mathbf{24}$ circular permutations

55.B
distinguishable permutations

If we ask for the number of permutations of the letters in the word *moo*, we have a problem because the two o's look alike. To distinguish between them, we will call them o_1 and o_2 and find

3	2	1

$\longrightarrow \quad 3 \cdot 2 \cdot 1 = 6$

that there are 6 permutations. If we list them, we get

$$\big(\quad mo_1o_2 \qquad mo_2o_1 \quad \big) \qquad \big(\quad o_1mo_2 \qquad o_2mo_1 \quad \big) \qquad \big(\quad o_1o_2m \qquad o_2o_1m \quad \big)$$

Now if we remove the subscripts, we get

$$\big(\quad moo \qquad moo \quad \big) \qquad \big(\quad omo \qquad omo \quad \big) \qquad \big(\quad oom \qquad oom \quad \big)$$

The two permutations in the first oval are exactly alike, and the same is true in the second and third ovals. Thus, there are only three permutations that are different. We call permutations that are different **distinguishable permutations.**

There were 3! permutations in all and 2! ways the o's could be arranged. If we divide 3! by 2!, we eliminate the duplications

$$\frac{3!}{2!} = \frac{3 \cdot 2 \cdot 1}{2 \cdot 1} = 3$$

and find that there are only 3 distinguishable permutations. If there are N items and if a of the items are alike, we find that

$$\text{Number of distinguishable permutations} = \frac{N!}{a!}$$

If there are N items and a of one kind, b of another kind, and c of another kind, we find that

$$\text{Number of distinguishable permutations} = \frac{N!}{a!b!c!}$$

example 55.3   Jojo has 10 marbles; 3 are red, 3 are blue, and 4 are green. How many distinguishable permutations of the 10 marbles can he form?

solution   There are 10! ways that 10 marbles may be arranged, but we can't tell the reds from one another, the blues from one another, or the greens from one another. Thus, we must divide by 3!, 3!, and 4!.

$$\frac{10!}{3!3!4!} = \frac{10 \cdot \overset{3}{\cancel{9}} \cdot \cancel{8} \cdot 7 \cdot \cancel{6} \cdot 5 \cdot \overset{4}{\cancel{4 \cdot 3 \cdot 2 \cdot 1}}}{\cancel{3} \cdot \cancel{2} \cdot 1 \cdot \cancel{3} \cdot \cancel{2} \cdot 1 \cdot \cancel{4 \cdot 3 \cdot 2 \cdot 1}} = \textbf{4200}$$

Thus, while there are 10!, or 3,628,800, permutations in all, only 4200 of them are distinguishable.

example 55.4   How many distinguishable permutations can be formed from the letters in the word *nonsense*?

solution   *Nonsense* has 8 letters, so there are 8! permutations. Yet we must divide by 3! because there are three n's, by 2! for the two e's, and again by 2! for the two s's.

$$\frac{8!}{3!2!2!} = \frac{8 \cdot 7 \cdot 6 \cdot 5 \cdot \cancel{4} \cdot \cancel{3 \cdot 2 \cdot 1}}{\cancel{3 \cdot 2 \cdot 1} \cdot \cancel{2} \cdot 1 \cdot \cancel{2} \cdot 1} = \textbf{1680}$$

Thus, there are 1680 distinguishable permutations.

example 55.5   How many distinguishable seven-digit numbers can be formed from the digits in 2722424?

solution   There are 7 digits in all, but also four 2's and two 4's, so we have

$$\frac{7!}{4!2!} = \frac{7 \cdot \cancel{6} \cdot 5 \cdot \overset{3}{\cancel{4 \cdot 3 \cdot 2 \cdot 1}}}{\cancel{4 \cdot 3 \cdot 2 \cdot 1} \cdot \cancel{2} \cdot 1} = \textbf{105}$$

There are 105 distinguishable permutations of 2722424.

problem set 55

1. How many distinguishable ways can 3 white marbles and 3 red marbles be placed in a row if 2 marbles of the same color cannot be adjacent?

2. The king, queen, duke, and duchess dined at a circular table. How many seating arrangements were possible?

3. How many distinguishable permutations can be formed from the letters in the word *aberrant*?

4. The big-wheel swamp buggy had wheels that were 6 meters in diameter. The swamp buggy was traveling 10 kilometers per hour. What was the angular velocity of the wheels in radians per second?

5. The wheels on the toy car had a diameter of only 1 inch, but they were revolving at 40 radians per second. What was the velocity of the toy car in yards per minute?

6. On the outbound leg of 400 miles, the plane flew at a moderate speed. On the trip back (also 400 miles), the pilot doubled the speed of the plane. How fast did the plane travel on the outbound leg if the total traveling time was 6 hours?

7. There were 2 more reds than there were whites and 1 more red than there were greens. How many of each kind were there if there were 15 reds, whites, and greens in all?

8. Complete the square to graph $y = x^2 - 8x + 12$.

9. Complete the square to graph $y = -x^2 - 2x - 2$.

10. Convert 20 meters per second to miles per hour.

11. Convert 12 liters per hour to cubic inches per minute.

Solve the following equations given that $0° \leq \theta < 360°$:

12. $3 \tan \theta - \sqrt{3} = 0$ **13.** $\tan 3\theta = \dfrac{\sqrt{3}}{3}$ **14.** $\csc 2\theta - 1 = 0$

15. Write 5800 as 10 raised to a power.   **16.** Write 5800 as e raised to a power.

17. Evaluate: $\sec^2\left(-\dfrac{3\pi}{4}\right) - \cot^2\dfrac{7\pi}{6} + 2\tan^2\left(-\dfrac{7\pi}{6}\right)$

18. If $f(x) = \sec^2 x$ and $g(x) = \csc^2 x$, find $f\left(\dfrac{3\pi}{4}\right) - g\left(-\dfrac{4\pi}{3}\right)$.

19. Use the midpoint method to write the equation of the perpendicular bisector of the line segment joining the points $(-2, -3)$ and $(4, 3)$. Write the equation in general form.

Write the equations of the following sinusoids:

20.

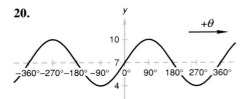

21.

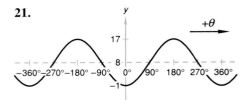

22. Factor $x^2 - 5x + 8$ over the set of complex numbers.

23. The following data were collected by a doctor who was interested in determining if there is a relationship between a person's height (H) and his or her systolic blood pressure (P). Use a graphing calculator to find the equation of the line which best fits this data and gives systolic blood pressure as a function of height ($P = mH + b$). Also, find the correlation coefficient for this scientific data and discuss whether or not the line is a good model for the data.

Height in inches	65	69	71	67	68	70
Systolic blood pressure	120	162	112	112	158	132

24. Find the standard form of the equation of a circle whose radius is 7 and whose center is (2, 5).

25. By how much does $_7P_4$ exceed $_7P_3$?

26. Solve for x:

(a) $\log_{18} 12x - 2\log_{18} 2 = 1$ (b) $\dfrac{2}{3}\ln 8 + 2\ln 3 = \ln(x + 5)$

27. Determine if $f(x) = \dfrac{2x + 1}{3x - 2}$ and $g(x) = \dfrac{2x + 1}{3x - 2}$ are inverse functions by computing their compositions.

28. Evaluate. Do not use a calculator.

(a) $\tan\left[\text{Arccos}\left(-\dfrac{4}{5}\right)\right]$ (b) $\cos\left[\text{Arcsin}\left(-\dfrac{3}{4}\right)\right]$

29. The graph of the function $f(x) = \sqrt{x}$ is shown on the left below. The graph on the right is the same graph reflected in the y axis and translated three units up. Write the equation of the graph on the right.

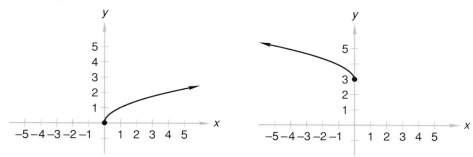

30. Let $f(x) = \sqrt{x}$ and $g(x) = \sqrt{x + 7}$. Which of the following statements is true?

   A. The graph of g is the graph of f translated seven units to the right.

   B. The graph of g is the graph of f translated seven units to the left.

   C. The graph of g is the graph of f translated seven units up.

   D. The graph of g is the graph of f translated seven units down.

LESSON 56   *Triangular Areas • Areas of Segments • Systems of Inequalities*

56.A
triangular areas

The area of any triangle equals one half the product of the base and the altitude, or height.

$$\text{Area} = \frac{\text{base} \times \text{height}}{2}$$

We remember that the **height** of a triangle is the perpendicular distance from the side called the **base** to the opposite vertex. If the height is not known but one of the angles is known, we can draw an auxiliary line to form a right triangle and use trigonometry to find the height.

example 56.1   Find the area of this triangle.

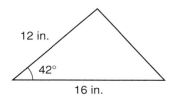

solution   We will draw a perpendicular from the 16-inch side to the opposite vertex and use the triangle formed to find the height.

$$\sin 42° = \frac{H}{12}$$

$$H = 12 \sin 42° = 8.03 \text{ in.}$$

Now we can use 8.03 for H and find the area.

$$\text{Area} = \frac{B \times H}{2} = \frac{16 \text{ in.} \times 8.03 \text{ in.}}{2} = \textbf{64.24 in.}^2$$

example 56.2 Find the area of this triangle.

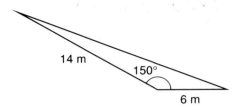

solution We decide to use the side labeled 6 meters as the base. To find the altitude, we must extend this side and erect a perpendicular to the other vertex.

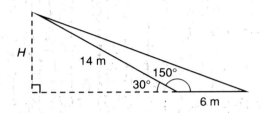

$$\sin 30° = \frac{H}{14}$$

$$H = 14 \sin 30° = 7 \text{ m}$$

Now we can find the area.

$$\text{Area} = \frac{B \times H}{2} = \frac{6 \text{ m} \times 7 \text{ m}}{2} = \textbf{21 m}^2$$

example 56.3 Find the area of this trapezoid.

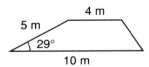

solution We remember that a trapezoid is a four-sided linear figure that has two sides parallel. The parallel sides are called the *bases*. If we draw auxiliary lines, we can find the distance between the bases and then find the area by dividing the trapezoid into triangles.

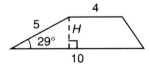   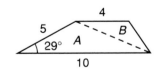

On the left we draw a perpendicular to find the height H, and on the right we draw a diagonal that divides the trapezoid into two triangles A and B. The altitude of both these triangles is H, and the sum of the areas of A and B is the area of the trapezoid.

$$H = 5 \sin 29° = 2.42$$

$$\text{Area } A = \frac{10 \times 2.42}{2} = 12.10 \text{ m}^2 \qquad \text{Area } B = \frac{4 \times 2.42}{2} = 4.84 \text{ m}^2$$

$$\text{Total area} = 12.10 \text{ m}^2 + 4.84 \text{ m}^2 = \textbf{16.94 m}^2$$

56.B
areas of segments

We remember that a **sector** of a circle is the area of the circle bounded by two radii and an arc of the circle. We also remember that the area of the sector is the fractional part of the total area as determined by the central angle of the sector.

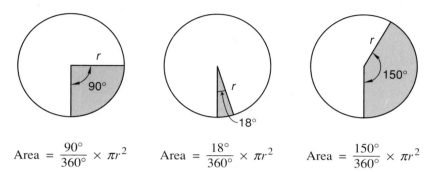

$$\text{Area} = \frac{90°}{360°} \times \pi r^2 \qquad \text{Area} = \frac{18°}{360°} \times \pi r^2 \qquad \text{Area} = \frac{150°}{360°} \times \pi r^2$$

In each case, we see that the area of the sector is the area of the circle multiplied by the fraction formed by the central angle divided by 360°. If the central angle is measured in radians, the procedure is the same except that the fraction is the central angle in radians divided by 2π.

We define a **segment** of a circle to be the area bounded by an arc and a chord that have the same endpoints.

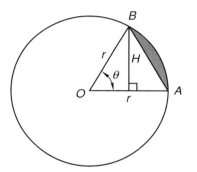

We see that the area of the segment is the area of the sector reduced by the area of triangle OBA. The base of the triangle is r and the altitude H is $r \sin \theta$.

example 56.4 Find the area of the segment shown above if the central angle is 0.6 rad and the radius is 10 ft.

solution First we find the area of the sector.

$$\text{Area of sector} = \left(\pi r^2\right)\left(\frac{0.6}{2\pi}\right) = \frac{100(0.6)}{2} = 30 \text{ ft}^2$$

From this we subtract the area of the triangle. First we find the altitude H. When we evaluate, we are careful to set the calculator to radians.

$$\sin 0.6 = \frac{H}{r} \quad \longrightarrow \quad H = 10 \sin 0.6 = 5.65$$

Now we find the area of the triangle.

$$A_\Delta = \frac{B \times H}{2} = \frac{10 \times 5.65}{2} = 28.25 \text{ ft}^2$$

So the area of the segment is $30 \text{ ft}^2 - 28.25 \text{ ft}^2 = \mathbf{1.75 \text{ ft}^2}$.

56.C

systems of inequalities

We remember that the graph of an equation divides the set of all points in the plane into three disjoint subsets. These are the set of points that lie on the graph and the sets of points that lie on either side of the graph. In this figure we show the graph of the equation $y = -\frac{1}{2}x - 1$. All points whose coordinates satisfy this equation lie on this line. The rest of the points lie on one side of the line or the other side of the line and will satisfy either inequality (a) or inequality (b).

(a) $y > -\frac{1}{2}x - 1$

(b) $y < -\frac{1}{2}x - 1$

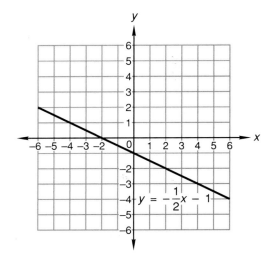

If the coordinates of a point satisfy one of these inequalities, the coordinates of all the points on the same side of the line will satisfy the same inequality. Inequality (a) is read "y is greater than $-\frac{1}{2}x - 1$" and since y is "greater than" as we move up, we surmise that this inequality designates the points that lie above the line. We can always use a test point to check our surmise.

The same thoughts apply to graphs of equations that are not straight lines, as will be demonstrated in the following examples.

example 56.5

The line and the parabola graphed in the figure divide the coordinate system into four distinct regions, which have been labeled $A, B, C,$ and D. Which region contains the coordinates of the points that satisfy the given system of inequalities?

(a) $\begin{cases} y \geq \frac{1}{2}x - 4 & \text{(line)} \\ \\ y \geq -x^2 + 4x - 1 & \text{(parabola)} \end{cases}$

(b)

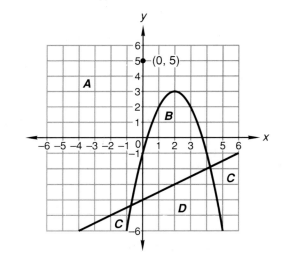

solution Inequality (a) is read "y is greater than or equal to $\frac{1}{2}x - 4$." Since y is "greater than" as we move up, we suspect that this inequality designates the points on or above the line. Inequality (b) reads "y is greater than or equal to $-x^2 + 4x - 1$." Thus, we suspect that this inequality designates the points on or above the parabola. The region above both the line and the parabola is region A. We will use the point $(0, 5)$ as a test point.

Line: $y \geq \frac{1}{2}x - 4$ $\longrightarrow$ $5 \geq \frac{1}{2}(0) - 4$

                                  $\longrightarrow$ $5 \geq -4$ True

Parabola: $y \geq -x^2 + 4x - 1$ $\longrightarrow$ $5 \geq -(0)^2 + 4(0) - 1$

                                  $\longrightarrow$ $5 \geq -1$ True

Thus the solution is **region A, including the bordering points that lie on the line or on the parabola.** The coordinates of any point in area A or on the border will satisfy both of the inequalities given.

example 56.6 In the figure we show the graphs of the given parabola and line. Which region contains the coordinates of the points that will satisfy both inequalities?

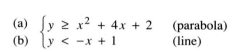

(a) $\begin{cases} y \geq x^2 + 4x + 2 & \text{(parabola)} \\ y < -x + 1 & \text{(line)} \end{cases}$

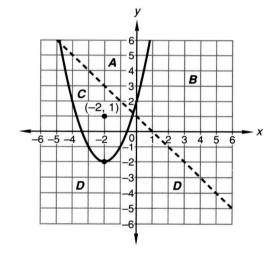

solution The quadratic inequality reads "y is greater than or equal to," which indicates the points above or on the parabola. The linear inequality reads "y is less than," which indicates the points below the line. This indicates region C. We will use the point $(-2, 1)$ as a test point.

Parabola: $y \geq x^2 + 4x + 2$ $\longrightarrow$ $1 \geq (-2)^2 + 4(-2) + 2$

                                    $\longrightarrow$ $1 \geq 4 - 8 + 2$

                                    $\longrightarrow$ $1 \geq -2$ True

Line: $y < -x + 1$ $\longrightarrow$ $1 < -(-2) + 1$

                            $\longrightarrow$ $1 < 2 + 1$

                            $\longrightarrow$ $1 < 3$ True

Thus, the coordinates of all points that lie below the line and on or above the parabola satisfy this system of inequalities, and the answer is **region C.**

example 56.7   Which region contains the coordinates of the points that satisfy the given system of inequalities?

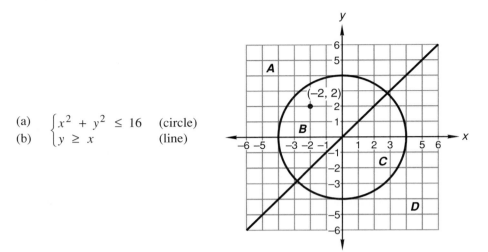

(a) $\begin{cases} x^2 + y^2 \le 16 & \text{(circle)} \\ y \ge x & \text{(line)} \end{cases}$
(b)

solution   The inequality $x^2 + y^2 \le 16$ designates the points that lie on or inside the circle (try a few points to check this out), and the linear inequality designates the points on or above the line. We will use the point $(-2, 2)$ as a test point.

$$\text{Circle:} \quad x^2 + y^2 \le 16 \quad \longrightarrow \quad (-2)^2 + (2)^2 \le 16$$
$$\longrightarrow \quad 4 + 4 \le 16 \qquad \text{True}$$

$$\text{Line:} \quad y \ge x \quad \longrightarrow \quad 2 \ge -2 \qquad \text{True}$$

This verifies our surmise, and thus the region designated is **region B, including the points on the boundary of this area.**

problem set 56

1. How many three-digit positive integers are there such that the first digit is an odd number, the second digit is an even number, and the last digit is an odd number?

2. Twelve people sat in a circle. How many seating arrangements were possible?

3. How many distinguishable permutations can be formed from the letters in the word *arrogator*?

4. The wheels on Susie's car were revolving at 40 revolutions per minute. What was the velocity of the car in centimeters per second if the wheels had a radius of 10 inches?

5. The Formula I car came by at a speed of 260 kilometers per hour. If the wheels had a diameter of 2 feet, what was their angular velocity in revolutions per minute?

6. Hannibal was paid $450 for a 30-hour week. He wanted his wages raised 10 percent and wanted to work more hours. His boss gave him the 10 percent hourly raise and increased his weekly hours to 36. What is his weekly paycheck now?

7. The sum of the digits of a two-digit number is 11. If the digits are reversed, the new number is 27 less than the original number. What was the original number?

8. The ancient one is 40 years older than the youngster. Ten years ago, the age of the ancient one was 22 years greater than 7 times the age of the youngster then. How old are both of them today?

9. Find the area of this triangle. Dimensions are in meters.

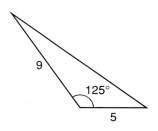

10. Find the area of this triangle. Dimensions are in centimeters.

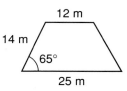

11. Find the area of this trapezoid.

12. The central angle of a sector of a circle is 0.4 radian. Find the area of the sector if the radius is 5 meters.

13. Find the area of the segment bounded by an arc of measure 60° and the chord joining the endpoints of the arc in a circle of radius 10 feet.

14. Designate the region in which the coordinates of the points satisfy the given system of inequalities.

$$\begin{cases} y < x^2 - 3 \\ y \ge x + 1 \end{cases}$$

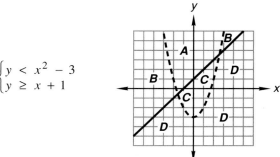

15. Complete the square to graph $y = x^2 - 4x + 6$.

16. Complete the square to graph $y = -x^2 - 6x - 6$.

Solve the following equations given that $0° \le \theta < 360°$:

17. $\tan \theta = -1$

18. $\sin 3\theta + \dfrac{\sqrt{3}}{2} = 0$

19. $\csc 2\theta + 1 = 0$

20. Write 65,000 as 10 raised to a power.

21. Write 65,000 as e raised to a power.

22. If $f(x) = \sec^2 x$ and $g(x) = \tan^2 x$, find $f\left(-\dfrac{2\pi}{3}\right) - g\left(\dfrac{9\pi}{4}\right)$.

23. Use the locus definition method to write the equation of the line which is equidistant from $(-2, 4)$ and $(-4, -4)$. Write the equation in general form.

24. Find the coordinates of the point halfway between $(4, 7)$ and $(12, -3)$.

25. Write the equation of the given sinusoid.

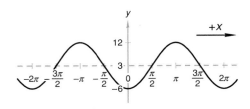

26. Factor $3x^2 + 18x + 30$ over the set of complex numbers.

27. The following data came from an experiment performed to determine whether a person's IQ (I) affects his or her performance (P) on a standardized achievement test. Use a graphing calculator to find the equation of the line which best fits this data and gives performance as a function of IQ ($P = mI + b$). Also, find the correlation coefficient for this social science data and discuss whether or not the line is a good model for the data.

IQ	122	97	106	100	109	79
Performance	66	50	63	68	44	58

28. Find the standard form of the equation of a circle whose radius is 5 and whose center is $(4, 5)$.

29. Solve for x:

(a) $\log_2 128 = x$

(b) $\dfrac{2}{3} \log 27 + \log x = \log 12$

30. If $f(x) = x(x - 2)$, find $\dfrac{f(x + h) - f(x - h)}{2h}$.

LESSON 57   *Phase Shifts in Sinusoids • Period of a Sinusoid*

57.A

phase shifts in sinusoids

We remember that the basic form of a sinusoid is a repeating curve that deviates the same amount above and below its centerline.

For a given value of the centerline, the equation of a sinusoid whose period is 360° (or 2π radians) is determined by the maximum deviation from the centerline (amplitude); by the value when θ equals zero (initial value); and by the direction of the change just to the right of the zero value of θ. A positive sine curve has an initial value of zero and increases as θ increases. A negative sine curve also has an initial value of zero but decreases as θ increases. The positive cosine curve begins at a maximum value and then decreases, and the negative cosine curve begins at a minimum value and then increases.

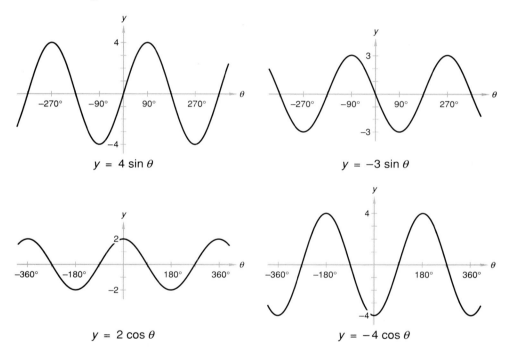

The value of the sinusoid does not have to be zero or its minimum or maximum value when θ equals zero. The initial value can be any value between the minimum value and the maximum value. Observe this curve.

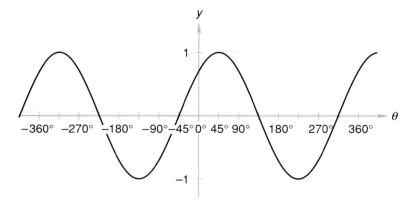

We remember that the graph of any equation in x and y can be translated 2 units to the left by replacing x with $x + 2$. The independent variable in the equation $y = \sin \theta$ is θ. Replacing θ with $\theta + 45°$ will shift the graph 45° to the left. When θ equals $-45°$, the curve has the same value that a sine curve would have when θ equals 0°. We say that the phase angle of this sine curve is $-45°$, but we write the argument with the negative of the phase angle, so we get

$$y = \sin\left[\theta - (-45°)\right] \xrightarrow{\text{so}} y = \sin(\theta + 45°)$$

When θ equals $+45°$, the curve has the same value that a cosine curve would have when θ equals 0°, so the equation for this curve as a cosine function with a phase angle is

$$y = \cos\left[\theta - (45°)\right] \xrightarrow{\text{so}} y = \cos(\theta - 45°)$$

From this discussion, we see that a positive phase angle means the curve has been shifted to the right and that a negative phase angle means the curve has been shifted to the left. We also see that the concept of phase angle can be confusing and that an automatic procedure for writing the phase angle would be helpful. **Thus we note that the phase angle for a sine curve equals the angle nearest the origin where the curve crosses its centerline on the way up. The phase angle for a cosine curve equals the angle nearest the origin where the curve reaches its highest point. Arguments are written as θ minus the phase angle, so an argument of $(\theta - 45°)$ indicates a $+45°$ phase angle and an argument of $(\theta + 45°)$ indicates a $-45°$ phase angle.**

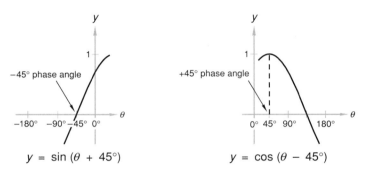

$$y = \sin(\theta + 45°) \qquad\qquad y = \cos(\theta - 45°)$$

example 57.1 Write the equation of the sinusoid shown here as a sine curve with a phase angle and also as a cosine curve with a phase angle.

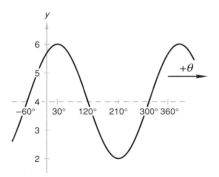

solution The centerline is 4 and the amplitude is 2. These numbers appear in both forms of the equation.

$$y = 4 + 2 \sin(\theta \qquad) \qquad y = 4 + 2 \cos(\theta \qquad)$$

The curve crosses the centerline on the way up at a θ value of $-60°$, so the phase angle for the sine function is $-60°$ and the argument will be $(\theta + 60°)$. The curve has a maximum value when θ equals $+30°$ (our estimate), so the phase angle for the cosine function is $+30°$ and the argument will be $(\theta - 30°)$. Thus our equations are

$$y = 4 + 2 \sin(\theta + 60°) \qquad y = 4 + 2 \cos(\theta - 30°)$$

example 57.2   Write the equation of this function as a sine curve with a phase shift.

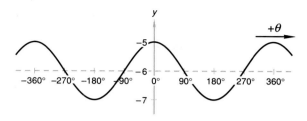

solution   The centerline is − 6 and the amplitude is 1, so we begin by writing

$$y = -6 + \sin (\theta \qquad)$$

We note that the curve crosses its centerline on its way up when θ equals –90°, so our phase angle is –90°. Now we can write the complete equation and remember that the argument contains the negative of the phase angle.

$$\mathbf{y = -6 + \sin (\theta + 90°)}$$

57.B

period of a sinusoid   If the values of the dependent variable of a function repeat at regular intervals as the values of the independent variable increase, the function is called a **periodic function.** Sinusoids are periodic functions since the values of y repeat each time the value of the argument changes 360°, or 2π radians. We say that 360°, or 2π radians, is the **period** of the sinusoid. When the argument is a single variable such as θ or x, the change in the argument equals the change in the variable.

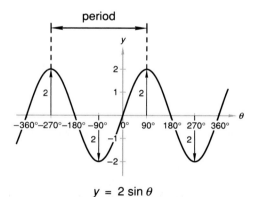

$$y = 2 \sin \theta$$

A phase angle will not change the period of a function. The only effect a phase angle has is to shift the whole curve right or left with respect to the scale on the horizontal axis. If we give the function above a phase angle of − 45°, we will shift the function 45° to the left but leave the period unchanged, as the function still completes a full cycle of values as θ changes 360°.

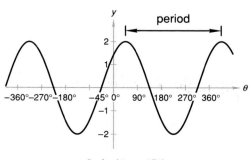

$$y = 2 \sin (\theta + 45°)$$

When the variable θ is multiplied by a nonzero number, the value of the argument is changed for every value of θ and the period is changed. **When the variable is multiplied by 2, the value of the argument changes twice as fast as the change in the variable,**

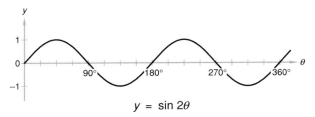

$$y = \sin 2\theta$$

and the function completes a full cycle every time the variable θ goes through 180°. So the period of this function is 180°, or π radians. If the variable is multiplied by 4, the function goes through 4 cycles for every 360° change in the variable, so the period is 90°.

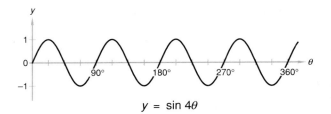

$$y = \sin 4\theta$$

When the variable is multiplied by a number less than 1, the argument changes less for a given change in the variable. **If the variable is multiplied by $\frac{1}{2}$, the argument changes only half as fast as the variable changes, and the period is doubled.**

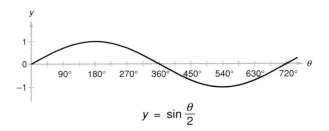

$$y = \sin \frac{\theta}{2}$$

In the same way, when the variable is multiplied by $\frac{1}{4}$, the argument changes only $\frac{1}{4}$ as fast as the variable changes, so the period is 4 times as long. This leads us to the fact that the coefficient of the variable equals 360° divided by the period in degrees, or 2π divided by the period in radians.

$$\text{Coefficient} = \frac{360°}{\text{period in degrees}} \qquad \text{or} \qquad \text{Coefficient} = \frac{2\pi}{\text{period in radians}}$$

example 57.3   Write the equation of the curve.

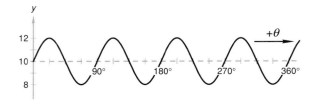

solution   The curve is a sine curve with no phase angle. The centerline is 10 and the amplitude is 2, so we begin by writing

$$y = 10 + 2 \sin k\theta$$

The curve completes a full cycle of values in 90°, so the period is 90°. The coefficient k is 360° divided by the period, so

$$\text{Coefficient } k = \frac{360°}{\text{period}} = \frac{360°}{90°} = 4$$

Thus, the equation we seek is

$$y = 10 + 2 \sin 4\theta$$

example 57.4   Write the equation of the given curve.

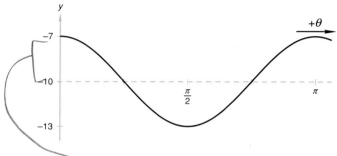

solution   This curve is a cosine curve centered on –10 and it goes up and down 3 units from the centerline. It takes π radians to complete a full cycle, so the coefficient is 2π divided by π, which equals 2. So the equation is as shown.

$$\text{Coefficient} = \frac{2\pi}{\pi} = 2 \qquad \text{so} \qquad y = -10 + 3 \cos 2\theta$$

problem set 57

1. Six red marbles, 4 blue marbles, and 2 white marbles were arranged in a row. How many distinguishable permutations were possible?

2. How many distinguishable permutations can be made from the letters in the word *abracadabra*?

3. Four hundred radians per minute sounds fast, but the wheels on the tiny car had a radius of only 4 centimeters. What was the velocity of the car in miles per hour?

4. Another little car went by at a speed of 40 kilometers per hour. What was the angular velocity of its wheels in radians per second if the diameter of its wheels was 10 centimeters?

5. The tugboat *Mary Beth* could go 24 miles downstream in 1 hour more than it took to go 8 miles upstream. If the speed of the *Mary Beth* in still water was 3 times the speed of the current, what was the still-water speed of the *Mary Beth* and the speed of the current?

6. The latitude of Charleston is 38.3° north of the equator. If the diameter of the earth is 12,000 kilometers, how far is Charleston from the equator?

7. The number of boys who came varied directly with the quality of the food. If 100 boys came when the food quality was 2, how many came when the food quality was increased to 40?

Write the equations of the following sinusoids in terms of the sine function:

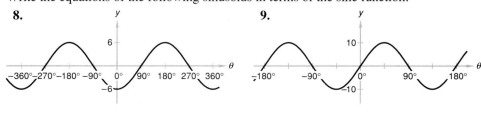

8.

9.

10. Find the area of this triangle.

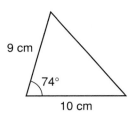

9 cm

74°

10 cm

11. Find the area of this triangle.

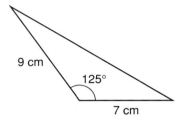

9 cm

125°

7 cm

12. Find the area of this trapezoid.

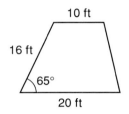

10 ft

16 ft

65°

20 ft

13. The central angle of a sector of a circle is 0.6 radian. Find the area of the sector if the radius is 4 meters.

14. Find the area of the segment bounded by an arc of measure 80° and the chord which joins the endpoints of the arc in a circle of radius 10 centimeters.

15. Sketch the graphs of the equations $y = -x + 1$ and $y = (x - 2)^2 - 3$. Shade the region(s) that satisfies the system of inequalities:

$$\begin{cases} y \leq -x + 1 \\ y \geq (x - 2)^2 - 3 \end{cases}$$

16. Complete the square to graph $y = -x^2 - 4x + 4$.

Solve the following equations given that $0° \leq \theta < 360°$:

17. $2 \cos \theta = 1$ **18.** $2 \cos 3\theta = 1$ **19.** $\cot 3\theta = 0$

20. Write 10,000 as 10 raised to a power.

21. Write 10,000 as e raised to a power.

22. Use the midpoint formula method to write the equation of the line which is the perpendicular bisector of the line segment whose endpoints are $(-4, -6)$ and $(4, 8)$. Write the equation in double-intercept form.

Evaluate:

23. $\text{Arctan} \left(\tan \dfrac{7\pi}{6} \right)$ **24.** $\cot^3 \dfrac{\pi}{4} + \tan^2 \dfrac{8\pi}{3}$

25. Factor $x^2 - 3x + 4$ over the set of complex numbers.

26. Solve for x:

(a) $\dfrac{3}{4} \log_{1/2} 16 - \log_{1/2} (x - 1) = 2$ (b) $\dfrac{1}{2} \ln 25 + \ln (x - 2) = \ln (2x + 3)$

27. Determine if $f(x) = \dfrac{-8}{x + 4}$ and $g(x) = \dfrac{-4x - 8}{x}$ are inverse functions by computing their compositions.

28. The figure shown is a trapezoid whose area is 75 cm². Find x. Dimensions are in centimeters.

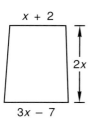

29. The graph of the function $f(x) = \sqrt{x}$ is shown on the left below. The graph on the right is the same graph reflected in the y axis and translated four units to the right. Write the equation of the graph on the right.

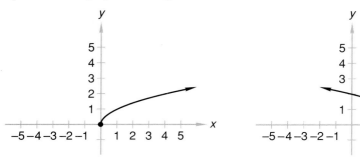

30. Let $f(x) = x^2$ and $g(x) = x^2 - 8$. Which of the following statements is true?

A. The graph of g is the graph of f translated eight units to the right.

B. The graph of g is the graph of f translated eight units to the left.

C. The graph of g is the graph of f translated eight units up.

D. The graph of g is the graph of f translated eight units down.

LESSON 58   *Distance From a Point to a Line • "Narrow" and "Wide" Parabolas*

58.A

distance from a point to a line

The distance from a point to a line is measured along the segment perpendicular to the line that connects the point and the line. If we find the equation of the line that contains the perpendicular segment, we can solve for the coordinates of its intersection with the given line. Then the distance formula can be used to find the distance between the point and the point of intersection. This method of solution is rather primitive, but we will use it because its use affords extensive practice with the fundamental concepts of coordinate geometry. The understanding that will accrue from this practice will permit us to understand and appreciate the development of more elegant methods of solution that will be presented in more advanced courses in mathematics. The use of a calculator is recommended to help with the arithmetic of these problems.

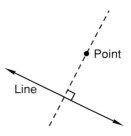

example 58.1 Find the distance between the point (–3, 5) and the line $y = \frac{1}{2}x + 1$.

solution First we will find the equation of the line through the given point that is perpendicular to the given line. We will name the equation for the given line (a). The line perpendicular to the given line has a slope of –2, so

$$y = -2x + b \qquad \text{equation}$$
$$5 = -2(-3) + b \qquad \text{used } (-3, 5)$$
$$b = -1 \qquad \text{solved}$$
$$\text{(b)} \quad y = -2x - 1 \qquad \text{completed equation}$$

Now we will use substitution to find the intersection of lines (a) and (b).

$$\frac{1}{2}x + 1 = -2x - 1 \qquad \text{substitution}$$
$$x + 2 = -4x - 2 \qquad \text{multiplied by 2}$$
$$5x = -4 \qquad \text{rearranged}$$
$$x = -\frac{4}{5} \qquad \text{solved for } x$$

Now we use this value of x in equation (b) to find y.

$$y = -2\left(-\frac{4}{5}\right) - 1 \qquad \text{substituted}$$
$$y = \frac{8}{5} - \frac{5}{5} \qquad \text{simplified}$$
$$y = \frac{3}{5} \qquad \text{solved for } y$$

Now we use the distance formula to find the distance between (–3, 5) and (–0.8, 0.6). We use the decimal form of the numbers, so we can use a calculator.

$$D = \sqrt{[-3 - (-0.8)]^2 + [5 - (0.6)]^2} \qquad \text{distance formula}$$
$$D = \sqrt{(-2.2)^2 + (4.4)^2} \qquad \text{simplified}$$
$$D = \mathbf{4.92} \qquad \text{solved}$$

example 58.2 Find the distance from (–1, 5) to the line $y = -\frac{1}{3}x + 4$.

solution First we find the equation of the line that is perpendicular to the given line and that passes through the given point.

$$y = 3x + b \qquad \text{equation}$$
$$5 = 3(-1) + b \qquad \text{used } (-1, 5)$$
$$b = 8 \qquad \text{solved for } b$$

Thus, the perpendicular line is $y = 3x + 8$. Now we substitute to solve for the point of intersection.

$$-\frac{1}{3}x + 4 = 3x + 8 \qquad \text{substituted}$$
$$-x + 12 = 9x + 24 \qquad \text{multiplied by 3}$$
$$x = -1.2 \qquad \text{solved for } x$$

Now we use the equation of the perpendicular line to find y.

$$y = 3(-1.2) + 8 \qquad \text{substituted}$$

$$y = 4.4 \qquad \text{solved for } y$$

Now we use the distance formula to find the distance between $(-1, 5)$ and $(-1.2, 4.4)$.

$$D = \sqrt{[-1 - (-1.2)]^2 + (5 - 4.4)^2} \qquad \text{distance formula}$$

$$D = \sqrt{(0.2)^2 + (0.6)^2} \qquad \text{simplified}$$

$$D = \mathbf{0.63} \qquad \text{solved}$$

58.B
"narrow" and "wide" parabolas

We remember that when a quadratic equation is written in the form $y = a(x - h)^2 + k$, the sign of a determines whether the graph of the parabola opens up or down. Thus far, we have looked only at equations where the value of a is $+1$ or -1, such as these:

OPENS UPWARD

$$y = +(x - 1)^2 + 2$$

OPENS DOWNWARD

$$y = -(x - 1)^2 + 2$$

If the absolute value of a is greater than 1, the graph of the parabola is "narrowed." If the absolute value of a is less than 1, the graph of the parabola is "widened," as we see in the following figures.

GRAPH IS "NARROWER"

$$y = -3(x - 1)^2 + 2$$

$$y = -(x - 1)^2 + 2$$

GRAPH IS "WIDER"

$$y = -\frac{1}{3}(x - 1)^2 + 2$$

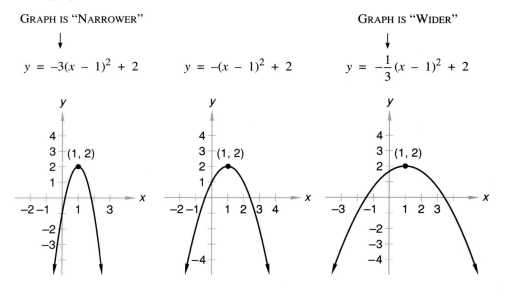

The first step in graphing these parabolas is to write the equation in the form $y = a(x - h)^2 + k$ so that we can determine coordinates of the vertex and determine whether the curve opens up or down. Then the shape of the curve can be determined by finding the coordinates of one more point on the curve. We demonstrate this procedure in the two examples that follow. Note that the procedure for completing the square is just a little more involved because of the necessity of dealing with the nonunity coefficient of the x^2 term.

example 58.3   Complete the square to graph the parabola $3y - x^2 + 2x + 5 = 0$.

solution   We begin by solving the equation for y and we get

$$y = \frac{1}{3}x^2 - \frac{2}{3}x - \frac{5}{3}$$

Next we factor out $\frac{1}{3}$ from the first two terms so that the coefficient of x^2 will be 1.

$$y = \frac{1}{3}\left(x^2 - 2x \qquad\right) - \frac{5}{3}$$

Now we must add +1 inside the parentheses to complete the square. Since the expression within parentheses is multiplied by $\frac{1}{3}$, we have not really added 1 but have added $\frac{1}{3}$ to the right-hand side of the equation. Thus, we must also add $-\frac{1}{3}$ to the right-hand side of the equation.

$$y = \frac{1}{3}\left(x^2 - 2x + 1\right) - \frac{5}{3} - \frac{1}{3} \qquad \text{completed the square}$$

$$y = \frac{1}{3}(x - 1)^2 - 2 \qquad\qquad \text{simplified}$$

From this form we can see that the equation of the axis of symmetry is $x = +1$ and that the parabola opens upward. The y coordinate of the vertex is –2. To get another point on the curve, we let x equal 4 and find that y equals 1.

$$y = \frac{1}{3}[(4) - 1]^2 - 2 \quad\longrightarrow\quad y = \frac{1}{3}(9) - 2 \quad\longrightarrow\quad y = 1$$

We plot the point (4, 1) and the symmetrical point (–2, 1) and complete the sketch. We note that the coefficient $\frac{1}{3}$ made the curve wider than the parabolas that we have graphed previously.

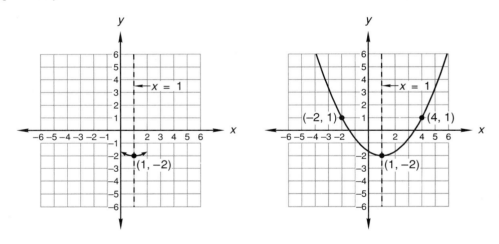

example 58.4   Complete the square to graph the parabola $y + 2x^2 + 12x + 17 = 0$.

solution   As the first step we rearrange the equation to solve for y and get

$$y = -2x^2 - 12x - 17$$

We note that the coefficient of x^2 is not 1. **When the coefficient of x^2 is not 1, we always begin by factoring the first two terms so that the coefficient of x^2 will be 1.** We will factor out –2.

$$y = -2\left(x^2 + 6x \qquad\right) - 17$$

Now we add +9 inside the parentheses and note that since the parentheses is multiplied by –2, we have really added –18. Because we have really added –18, we must add +18 also.

$$y = -2\left(x^2 + 6x + 9\right) - 17 + 18$$

Now we simplify and analyze.

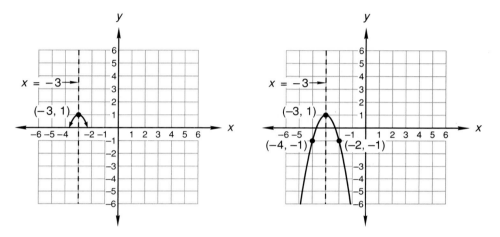

(a) Opens downward

(b) Axis of symmetry is $x = -3$

(c) y coordinate of vertex is $+1$

$$y = -2(x + 3)^2 + 1$$

We use this information to draw the axis of symmetry and the vertex of the curve, as we show in the graph on the left below. To get another point, we let x equal -2 in the original equation and find that $y = -1$.

$$y = -2(-2)^2 - 12(-2) - 17 = -8 + 24 - 17 = -1$$

We graph the point $(-2, -1)$ on the right and complete the sketch, remembering that the parabola is symmetric about its center axis.

problem set 58

1. Nine students sat in a row. How many distinguishable ways could 9 books be distributed to the students if 5 books were of one kind and 4 books were of another kind?

2. There are 5 flags in all. Two are red, 2 are blue, and 1 is yellow. How many different patterns are possible if the flags are displayed vertically on a flagpole?

3. How many ways can 5 different birds be arranged in a circle?

4. Smith couldn't believe his eyes because the wheels on the car were revolving at 525 radians per second. What was the velocity of the car in kilometers per hour if the radius of the wheels was 10 inches?

5. The lone wheel rolled down the mountain until its linear velocity was 100 miles per hour. What was its angular velocity in radians per second if the diameter of the wheel was 80 centimeters?

6. The ratio of the number who were impecunious to the number who were truly destitute was 14 to 3. If there were 4420 standing in line, how many were merely impecunious?

7. There were 4 in the first group and their average quality was 6. There were 10 in the second group and their average quality was 4. What should be the average quality of the last 16 so that the overall average quality would be 8?

8. Use the ideal gas law shown below to find P_2 if P_1 is 4 atmospheres, V_1 is 5 liters, V_2 is 7 liters, T_1 is 400 K, and T_2 is 500 K.

$$\frac{P_1 V_1}{T_1} = \frac{P_2 V_2}{T_2}$$

9. Find the distance between the point $(-2, 4)$ and the line $y = \frac{1}{2}x - 1$.

10. Complete the square to graph the parabola $y = -2x^2 - 8x - 4$.

Write the equations of the following sinusoids in terms of the cosine function:

11.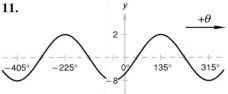

12.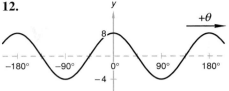

13. Find the area of this triangle.

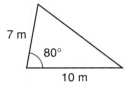

14. Find the area of this trapezoid in square centimeters.

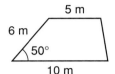

15. The central angle of a sector of a circle is 0.9 radian. Find the area of the sector in square feet if the radius is 1 yard.

16. Find the area in square meters of the segment bounded by an arc of measure $110°$ and the chord which joins the endpoints of the arc in a circle of radius 50 centimeters.

17. Designate the region in which the coordinates of the points satisfy the given system of inequalities.

$$\begin{cases} y \geq x^2 + 4x + 2 \\ y < -x + 1 \end{cases}$$

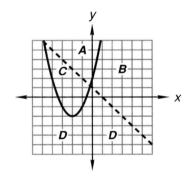

18. Convert 250 kilometers per second to miles per hour.

Solve the following equations given that $0° \leq \theta < 360°$:

19. $2 \cos \theta = \sqrt{3}$　　　　　**20.** $2 \cos 5\theta - \sqrt{3} = 0$　　　　　**21.** $\tan 3\theta = -1$

22. Use the locus definition method to write the equation of the line which is the perpendicular bisector of the line segment joining the points $(-2, 3)$ and $(4, 5)$. Write the equation in general form.

Evaluate:

23. $\cos\left[\operatorname{Arcsin}\left(-\dfrac{1}{4}\right)\right]$　　　　　　　　　　**24.** $\sec^2 \dfrac{3\pi}{4} - 1$

25. $\tan^2 \dfrac{3\pi}{4} + 2 \sec^2 \dfrac{5\pi}{4} + \cos \dfrac{5\pi}{2}$

26. Solve for x:

(a) $\dfrac{2}{3} \log_7 27 - \log_7 (x + 2) = \log_7 3$　　(b) $\dfrac{3}{4} \ln 16 - \ln x = \ln 4$

27. Determine if $f(x) = \dfrac{1}{1 - x}$ and $g(x) = \dfrac{x}{x - 1}$ are inverse functions by computing their compositions.

28. Find the domain and range of each function whose graph is shown:

(a)   (b)

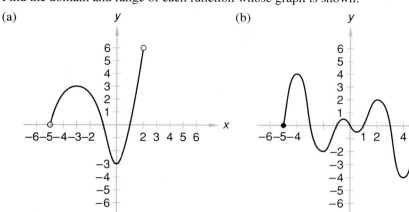

29. The graph of the function $f(x) = \sqrt{x}$ is shown on the left below. The graph on the right is the same graph reflected in the y axis and translated two units down. Write the equation of the graph on the right.

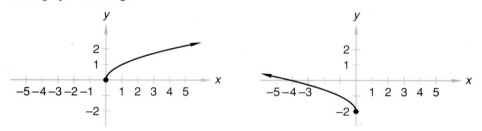

30. Let $f(x) = x^3$ and $g(x) = (x + 4)^3$. Which of the following statements is true?

A. The graph of g is the graph of f translated four units to the right.

B. The graph of g is the graph of f translated four units to the left.

C. The graph of g is the graph of f translated four units up.

D. The graph of g is the graph of f translated four units down.

LESSON 59   *Advanced Logarithm Problems • The Color of the White House*

59.A

advanced logarithm problems

Some of the logarithm problems that we have previously investigated can be reduced to one of the two forms shown here.

$\qquad$ (a) $\log_4 (x + 2) = \log_4 5$ $\qquad\qquad$ (b) $\log_4 (x + 5) = 2$

In (a) the bases are the same, so the logarithm of $x + 2$ equals the logarithm of 5. Thus, $x + 2$ must equal 5.

$$x + 2 = 5$$

$$x = 3$$

We must always check to see that the value of the argument is positive. If we use 3 for x, then

$$(3 + 2) = 5$$

and 5 is greater than 0, so our argument is a positive number.

The other form is shown in (b), where a logarithm on one side equals a constant on the other side. **We can solve this type of equation by rewriting it as an exponential equation and then solving the exponential equation.**

$$\log_4 (x + 5) = 2 \qquad \text{logarithmic equation}$$

$$x + 5 = 4^2 \qquad \text{exponential equation}$$

$$x = 11 \qquad \text{solved}$$

Now we must check to see that using 11 for x will result in a positive argument for the function.

$$x + 5 > 0 \quad \longrightarrow \quad 11 + 5 > 0 \quad \longrightarrow \quad 16 > 0 \qquad \text{check}$$

In this lesson we will look at logarithm problems that are slightly more involved.

example 59.1   Solve: $3 \log_{10} x = \log_{10} 16 - \log_{10} 2$

solution   On the left-hand side we use the power rule and on the right-hand side we use the quotient rule.

$$\log_{10} x^3 = \log_{10} \frac{16}{2} \qquad \text{used rules}$$

$$x^3 = 8 \qquad \text{equated arguments}$$

$$x = \textbf{2} \qquad \text{solved}$$

example 59.2   Solve: $\log_7 (x + 1) + \log_7 (x - 5) = 1$

solution   First we use the product rule.

$$\log_7 (x + 1)(x - 5) = 1$$

Now we rewrite this equation in exponential form. Then we solve the equation.

$$(x + 1)(x - 5) = 7^1 \qquad \text{exponential form}$$

$$x^2 - 4x - 5 = 7 \qquad \text{multiplied}$$

$$x^2 - 4x - 12 = 0 \qquad \text{rearranged}$$

$$(x - 6)(x + 2) = 0 \qquad \text{factored}$$

$$x = 6, -2 \qquad \text{solved}$$

Now we must check to see that $x + 1$ and $x - 5$ are positive for both 6 and –2.

WHEN $x = 6$	WHEN $x = -2$
$x + 1 = 7$ and $x - 5 = 1$	$x + 1 = -1$ and $x - 5 = -7$

Both are greater than 0, so **6** is a solution.

Thus, –2 is not an acceptable solution for the original equation because its use causes at least one argument to be negative.

example 59.3   Solve: $2 \log_3 x - \log_3 (x - 2) = 2$

solution   We first use the power rule on the first term.

$$\log_3 x^2 - \log_3 (x - 2) = 2$$

Now we use the quotient rule.

$$\log_3 \frac{x^2}{x - 2} = 2$$

Next we rewrite the log equation as an exponential equation and solve.

$$3^2 = \frac{x^2}{x - 2} \qquad \text{exponential form}$$

$$9x - 18 = x^2 \qquad \text{simplified}$$

$$x^2 - 9x + 18 = 0 \qquad \text{rearranged}$$

$$(x - 3)(x - 6) = 0 \qquad \text{factored}$$

$$x = \mathbf{3, 6} \qquad \text{solved}$$

Since both x and $x - 2$ are positive when $x = 6$ or $x = 3$, both these numbers are solutions.

59.B
the color of the white house

The color of the white house is white, and the color of the red house is red. The notation

$$5^{\log_5 14}$$

makes a statement that is just as easy to understand. We read this statement as "Five raised to the power that 5 must be raised to in order to get 14." If we raise 5 to that power, the answer will certainly be 14.

$$5^{\log_5 14} = 14$$

The value of the left-hand expression below is $5x^2$ because it is read as "y raised to the exponent that y must be raised to in order to get $5x^2$," and the right-hand expression is read as "Seventeen raised to the exponent that 17 must be raised to in order to get 6," so its value is 6.

$$y^{\log_y 5x^2} = 5x^2 \qquad\qquad 17^{\log_{17} 6} = 6$$

The expressions

$$\text{(a)} \ \log_e e^6 \qquad\qquad \text{(b)} \ \log_5 125$$

can also be simplified by using the word *power* instead of the word *logarithm*. The expression $\log_e e^6$ can be read by saying "The power that e must be raised to in order to get e^6," which is 6.

$$\log_e e^6 = 6$$

The expression $\log_5 125$ can be read as "The power that 5 must be raised to in order to get 125," which is 3 because $5^3 = 125$.

$$\log_5 125 = 3$$

The word *logarithm* means "power" or "exponent." That is all there is to it.

example 59.4   Simplify: $42^{\log_{42} 5}$

solution   We read this as "Forty-two raised to the exponent that 42 must be raised to in order to get 5." So the answer is **5.**

example 59.5   Simplify: $9^{\log_3 5}$

solution   This is a trick problem because we must recognize that 9 can be written as 3^2. Thus, we get

$$3^{2 \log_3 5}$$

which we rewrite as

$$3^{\log_3 5^2}$$

and the answer is $\mathbf{5^2}$, or **25.**

example 59.6   Simplify: $10^{4\log_{10}\sqrt{3}}$

solution   This time we must write $\sqrt{3}$ as $3^{1/2}$ and also use the power rule for logarithms.

$$10^{4\log_{10}\sqrt{3}} = 10^{\log_{10}(3^{1/2})^4} \qquad \text{simplified}$$

$$= 10^{\log_{10}3^2} \qquad \text{multiplied}$$

$$= 3^2 = \mathbf{9} \qquad \text{solution}$$

example 59.7   Simplify: $3^{\log_3 4 + \log_3 5}$

solution   First we use the product rule of logs and get

$$3^{\log_3 4 + \log_3 5} = 3^{\log_3 20} \qquad \text{used product rule}$$

$$= \mathbf{20} \qquad \text{solution}$$

example 59.8   Simplify: $\log_e e^{14}$

solution   The power that e must be raised to in order to get e^{14} is 14.

$$\log_e e^{14} = \mathbf{14}$$

example 59.9   Simplify: $\log_5 25$

solution   The power that 5 must be raised to in order to get 25 is 2 because 5^2 equals 25.

$$\log_5 25 = \mathbf{2}$$

problem set 59

1. How many distinguishable permutations can be formed from the letters in the word *peripatetic*?

2. How many permutations of the letters in the word *vertical* begin with three vowels?

3. Lori is a member of a club that has 10 members. How many ways can a president, a vice president, and a secretary be chosen, in that order, if Lori is not to be president and no member may hold more than one office at a time?

4. The wheel was rolling along at 400 radians per second. What was its velocity in miles per hour if the radius was 1 foot?

5. The truck was traveling at 40 kilometers per hour and its wheels had 16-inch diameters. What was the angular velocity of the wheels in revolutions per minute?

6. Henry could buy $4x + 4$ pencils for $2y$ dollars. How many pencils could he buy for \$10?

7. Uncle Wilbur could do 2 jobs in 3 days and Cousin Harriet could do 4 jobs in 7 days. Cousin Harriet worked for 3 days before Uncle Wilbur joined in. How long would they have to work together to complete a total of 8 jobs?

8. How many gallons of an 80% solvent solution should be mixed with how many gallons of a 20% solvent solution to get 50 gallons of a 56% solvent solution?

Solve for x:

9. $2\log_5 x = \log_5 18 - \log_5 2$

10. $\log_4 (x - 1) + \log_4 (x + 2) = 1$

11. $\log_4 x - \log_4 (2x - 1) = 1$

Simplify:

12. $43^{\log_{43} 6}$

13. $2^{\log_2 5 + \log_2 6}$

14. Find the distance between the point $(2, 1)$ and the line $y = 2x - 1$.

15. Complete the square to graph the parabola $y - 3x^2 + 6x - 5 = 0$.

Write the equations of the following sinusoids in terms of the sine function:

16.
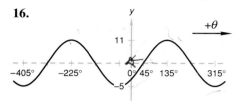

17.
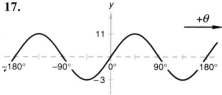

18. Find the area of this triangle in square
centimeters.

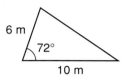

19. Find the area of this trapezoid in
square centimeters.

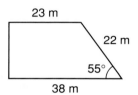

20. Find the area in square meters of the segment bounded by an arc of measure 120° and the
chord which joins the endpoints of the arc in a circle of radius 100 centimeters.

21. Sketch the graphs of the equations $y = x^2 + 2x + 4$ and $y = 2x - 2$. Shade the
region(s) that satisfies the system of inequalities:

$$\begin{cases} y \le x^2 + 2x + 4 \\ y > 2x - 2 \end{cases}$$

22. Convert 30 centimeters per second to kilometers per hour.

Solve the following equations given that $0° \le \theta < 360°$:

23. $\sqrt{3} \tan \theta = 1$ **24.** $\sqrt{3} \tan 3\theta - 1 = 0$

25. Write 20,000 as 10 raised to a power.

26. Write 20,000 as e raised to a power.

27. Evaluate:

(a) $\sin \left[\text{Arcsin} \left(\dfrac{3}{4} \right) \right]$

(b) $\text{Arctan} \left(\tan \dfrac{11\pi}{6} \right)$

(c) $\sin^2 \dfrac{7\pi}{6} + \cos^2 \dfrac{7\pi}{6} - \dfrac{1}{\sec \dfrac{13\pi}{6}} - \cos \dfrac{13\pi}{6}$

28. Find the standard form of the equation of a circle whose radius is 10 and whose center
is $(3, 2)$.

29. The graph of the function $f(x) = \sqrt{x}$ is shown on the left below. The graph on the right is the same graph reflected in the y axis and translated three units to the left. Write the equation of the graph on the right.

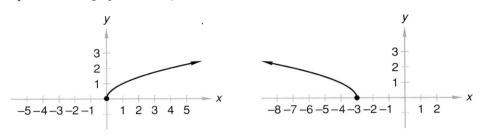

30. Let $f(x) = x^3$ and $g(x) = (x - 1)^3$. Which of the following statements is true?

A. The graph of g is the graph of f translated one unit to the right.

B. The graph of g is the graph of f translated one unit to the left.

C. The graph of g is the graph of f translated one unit up.

D. The graph of g is the graph of f translated one unit down.

LESSON 60   *Factorable Trigonometric Equations • Loss of Solutions Caused by Division*

60.A

factorable trigonometric equations

Both the quadratic equations shown below can be solved by factoring.

$$\text{(a) } x^2 - 1 = 0 \qquad \text{(b) } x^2 + x = 0$$

Equation (a) factors into the product of a sum and a difference. Equation (b) can be solved if we begin by factoring out an x.

$$\text{(a) } (x + 1)(x - 1) = 0 \qquad \text{(b) } x(x + 1) = 0$$
$$x = -1, 1 \qquad\qquad\qquad x = 0, -1$$

We can create interesting trigonometric equations if we replace x in equations like these with trigonometric functions. If we use $\sin x$ and $\tan \theta$, respectively, in equations (a) and (b), we get

$$\sin^2 x - 1 = 0 \qquad \tan^2 \theta + \tan \theta = 0$$

We can factor these equations also, and we get

$$(\sin x + 1)(\sin x - 1) = 0 \qquad (\tan \theta)(\tan \theta + 1) = 0$$

Now the values for x and θ can be found by setting the individual factors equal to zero. In the next three examples we show how some trigonometric equations can be solved by factoring.

example 60.1 Solve $\tan^2 \theta - 1 = 0$ given that $0° \leq \theta < 360°$.

solution This trigonometric equation can be solved by factoring and setting the individual factors equal to zero.

$$(\tan \theta + 1)(\tan \theta - 1) = 0 \qquad \text{factored}$$

$$\tan \theta + 1 = 0 \qquad \tan \theta - 1 = 0 \qquad \text{set factors equal to zero}$$

$$\tan \theta = -1 \qquad\qquad \tan \theta = 1 \qquad \text{solved}$$

The tangent of 45° is 1, and the tangent is positive in the first and third quadrants and negative in the second and fourth quadrants.

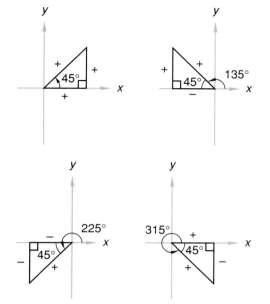

We see that there are four angles that satisfy the equation.

$$\theta = 45°, 135°, 225°, 315°$$

example 60.2   Solve $\sin^2 \theta - \sin \theta = 0$ given that $0° \leq \theta < 360°$.

solution   We begin by factoring and get

$$(\sin \theta)(\sin \theta - 1) = 0$$

Now we set each of the factors equal to zero and solve.

$$\sin \theta = 0 \qquad\qquad\qquad \sin \theta - 1 = 0$$

The only angles between 0° and 360° whose sine is 0 are 0° and 180°, so

$$\theta = 0°, 180°$$

$$\sin \theta = 1$$

The only angle between 0° and 360° whose sine is +1 is 90°, so

$$\theta = 90°$$

We see that there are three values of θ that satisfy the given equation.

$$\theta = 0°, 90°, 180°$$

example 60.3   Solve $\cos^2 \theta = 1$ given that $0° \leq \theta < 360°$.

solution   First we rearrange the equation and factor.

$$\cos^2 \theta - 1 = 0 \qquad \text{rearranged}$$

$$(\cos \theta - 1)(\cos \theta + 1) = 0 \qquad \text{factored}$$

Now we set each of the factors equal to zero and solve.

$$\cos \theta - 1 = 0 \qquad\qquad\qquad \cos \theta + 1 = 0$$

$$\cos \theta = 1 \qquad\qquad\qquad\qquad \cos \theta = -1$$

The only angle between 0° and 360° whose cosine is +1 is 0°, so

$$\theta = 0°$$

The only angle between 0° and 360° whose cosine is −1 is 180°, so

$$\theta = 180°$$

Thus, this trigonometric equation has two solutions.

$$\theta = 0°, 180°$$

60.B
loss of solutions caused by division

The factor method will yield all the solutions of a trigonometric equation and is recommended for this reason. **If an attempt is made to reduce an equation by dividing both sides of the equation by a term containing the unknown, the result may be a defective equation whose solution will not provide all the solutions of the original equation.** For example, if we are asked to solve this equation,

$$2 \sin x \cos x = \sin x \qquad 0° \le x < 360°$$

we might begin by dividing both sides of the equation by $\sin x$. The result would be the defective equation

$$2 \cos x = 1$$

The solutions of this equation are 60° and 300°, but the original equation also has the solutions 0° and 180°, as we see when we use the factor method in the following example.

example 60.4   Solve $2 \sin x \cos x = \sin x$ given that $0° \le x < 360°$.

solution   We rearrange the equation and factor.

$$2 \sin x \cos x - \sin x = 0 \qquad \text{rearranged}$$

$$(\sin x)(2 \cos x - 1) = 0 \qquad \text{factored}$$

Now we set each of the factors equal to zero and solve.

$$\sin x = 0 \qquad\qquad 2 \cos x - 1 = 0$$

$$2 \cos x = 1$$

$$\cos x = \frac{1}{2}$$

The only angles between 0° and 360° whose sine is 0 are 0° and 180°. The cosine of 60° is $\frac{1}{2}$, and the cosine is positive in the first and fourth quadrants.

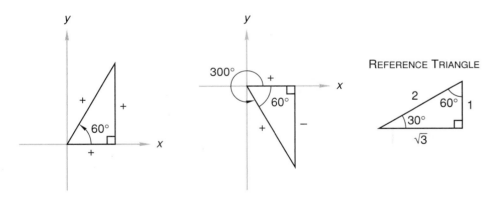

Thus, this trigonometric equation has four solutions.

$$x = \mathbf{0°, 60°, 180°, 300°}$$

problem set 60

1. How many ways can the letters in the word *came* be arranged if a consonant is in the fourth position?

2. How many distinguishable ways can a host and 10 guests be seated in a row if three of the guests are identical triplets?

3. The angular velocity of the wheels on the fire engine was 367 radians per minute. If the radius of the wheels was 16 inches, what was the linear velocity of the fire engine in miles per hour?

4. The linear velocity of the go-cart was 5 kilometers per hour, but its wheels were only 10 centimeters in diameter. What was the angular velocity of the wheels in radians per minute?

5. The jet could fly at 8 times the speed of the wind and thus could travel 1350 miles downwind in 1 hour more than it took to travel 700 miles upwind. What was the speed of the jet in still air and what was the speed of the wind?

6. The ratio of the number of reds to the number of whites was 1 to 2. The ratio of the number of greens to the number of whites was 5 to 4. If the total number of reds, whites, and greens was 22, how many were there of each color?

Solve the following equations given that $0° \leq \theta < 360°$:

7. $\cos^2 \theta - \cos \theta = 0$

8. $\sin^2 \theta - 1 = 0$

Solve for x:

9. $3 \log_6 x = \log_6 24 - \log_6 3$

10. $\log x + \log (x - 3) = 1$

11. $2 \log_2 x - \log_2 \left(x - \dfrac{1}{2} \right) = \log_3 3$

Simplify:

12. $32^{\log_{32} 7}$

13. $3^{\log_3 6 - \log_3 2}$

14. Find the distance between the point $(-4, 6)$ and the line $y = x + 2$.

15. Complete the square to graph the parabola $y = 6x + 3x^2$.

Write the equations of the following sinusoids in terms of the cosine function:

16.
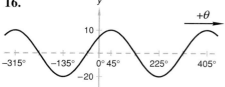

17.
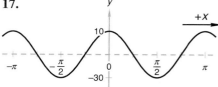

18. Find the area of this triangle. Dimensions are in meters.

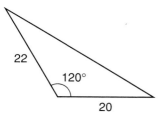

19. Find the area of this trapezoid. Dimensions are in centimeters.

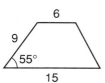

20. The central angle of a sector of a circle is 80°. Find the area of the sector if the radius is 20 centimeters.

21. Find the area in square feet of the segment bounded by an arc of measure 2.4 radians and the chord which joins the endpoints of the arc in a circle of radius 10 inches.

22. Designate the region in which the coordinates of the points satisfy the given system of inequalities.

$$\begin{cases} y \geq -x^2 + 4x - 1 \\ y \geq \dfrac{1}{2}x - 4 \end{cases}$$

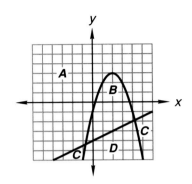

23. Solve $\sin 3\theta - 1 = 0$ given that $0° \leq \theta < 360°$.

24. If $f(x) = \sin^2 x$ and $g(x) = \cos^2 x$, find $f\left(\dfrac{3\pi}{4}\right) + g\left(\dfrac{3\pi}{4}\right)$.

25. Evaluate:

    (a) $\operatorname{Arcsin}\left(\sin \dfrac{\pi}{4}\right)$ (b) $\cos^2\left[\operatorname{Arcsin}\left(-\dfrac{1}{4}\right)\right]$ (c) $\sin^2 \dfrac{3\pi}{4} - \cos^2 \dfrac{3\pi}{4}$

26. Use the locus definition method to find the equation of the line equidistant from $(-2, 4)$ and $(6, 2)$. Write the equation in double-intercept form.

27. Write the quadratic equation with a lead coefficient of 1 whose roots are $-1 - \sqrt{3}i$ and $-1 + \sqrt{3}i$.

28. Determine if $f(x) = \dfrac{5x + 4}{2x - 7}$ and $g(x) = \dfrac{7x + 4}{2x - 5}$ are inverse functions by computing their compositions.

29. The graph of the function $f(x) = -|x - 3|$ is shown below. Write the equation of the function g whose graph is the graph of f reflected in the x axis and translated three units to the left. Then sketch the graph of the new function g.

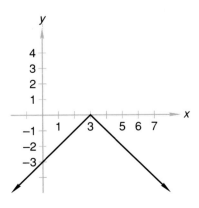

30. If $f(x) = x(x + 3)$, find $\dfrac{f(x + h) - f(x - h)}{2h}$.

LESSON 61 *Single-Variable Analysis • The Normal Distribution • Box-and-Whisker Plots*

61.A
single-variable analysis

In Lesson 45 we discussed linear regression using the graphing calculator. The data were ordered pairs of x and y. We call these data *two-variable data* and note that sometimes their graph indicates a linear relationship between the variables. Single-variable data analysis considers the variation of a single measurement. We customarily use the letter x to represent the variable. The **average** of the measurements is called the **mean.** To compute the mean for a set of measurements, we divide the sum of the measurements by the number of measurements. If the weights of four dogs are 4 pounds, 7 pounds, 9 pounds, and 20 pounds, respectively, the mean weight is 10 pounds. We use the symbol μ (mu) to represent the mean of the measurements.

$$\mu = \text{mean} = \frac{\text{sum}}{\text{number}} = \frac{4 + 7 + 9 + 20}{4} = \frac{40}{4} = 10 \text{ lb}$$

The **standard deviation** is the statistic that mathematicians use to get a feel for how much the measurements are spread out on either side of the mean. To help us understand the method of computing the standard deviation, we will graph the weight of the dogs and draw a vertical line at the mean. All of our measurements lie between 4 and 20, a distance of 16 on the number line. We call this distance the **range** of our set of measurements.

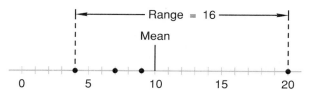

The directed distance from the mean to each measurement is called the **deviation** of the measurement. The measurements of 4, 7, and 9 have negative deviations, and 20 has a positive deviation, as we show in the next figure.

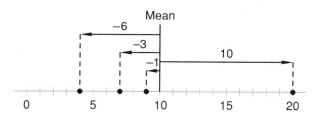

We cannot use the average of the sum of the deviations to tell us how the numbers are spread out because this average is always zero.

$$\text{Average of deviations} = \frac{-6 - 3 - 1 + 10}{4} = \frac{0}{4} = 0$$

We could use the average of the absolute value of the deviations, but mathematicians have found that using the square root of the average of the squares of the deviations is much more useful. The first step is to find the average of the squares of the deviations, which is called the **variance.**

$$\text{Variance} = \frac{(-6)^2 + (-3)^2 + (10)^2 + (-1)^2}{4} = \frac{146}{4} = 36.5$$

The standard deviation is the square root of this average. We will use the symbol σ (sigma) to represent the standard deviation of a sample of measurements. Since the square of any real number is a nonnegative number, we do not need to use negative numbers when we compute standard deviations, as we show here.

$$\sigma = \text{standard deviation} = \sqrt{\frac{6^2 + 3^2 + 10^2 + 1^2}{4}} = \sqrt{36.5} = 6.04$$

example 61.1   The measured distances are 12, 7, 15, and 10. Find the mean and the standard deviation of the distances.

solution   The graphing calculator will compute the mean and the standard deviation quickly, even for long lists of data. Doing practice problems that have a few numbers that are easy to handle will help us understand and remember what the graphing calculator is doing. First we compute the mean.

$$\mu = \frac{12 + 7 + 15 + 10}{4} = \frac{44}{4} = 11$$

Next, we find the average of the square of the differences of each data point and the mean.

$$\frac{1^2 + 4^2 + 4^2 + 1^2}{4} = \frac{34}{4} = 8.5$$

The square root of the average is the standard deviation.

$$\sigma = \sqrt{8.5} = 2.92$$

61.B

the normal distribution

The **normal distribution** is a theoretical frequency distribution that is sometimes approximated by data that is collected experimentally. This distribution is also called a **Gaussian distribution** to honor Carl Friedrich Gauss (1777–1855), a German mathematician who made major contributions to the theory of mathematical statistics. To introduce the normal or Gaussian distribution, we consider an experiment in which 10 coins are placed in a box. We shake the box and record the number of coins that come up heads. Then we shake the box again and record the number of coins that come up heads on the second try. We repeat this procedure 998 more times. We will find out that we get 5 heads about 250 times, or approximately 25% of the time. We will get 4 heads about 210 times (21%) and 6 heads about 210 times (21%). We will get 7 heads about 120 times (12%) and 3 heads about 120 times (12%). For 8 heads and for 2 heads the number will be about 40 (4%), and for 1 head and for 9 heads the number will be about 1 (0.1%). If we graph these data, we get the graph below. This graph is called a **frequency distribution graph,** or a **histogram.** The total area of the graph is 100%, and the area of each box indicates the percent of the time (frequency) that this number of heads occurred.

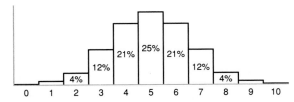

Frequency distribution for the number of heads when ten coins are used

If we increase the number of coins in the box to 20, we can get any number of heads from zero to 20. The graph for 20 coins in the box is shown below. We get 10 heads with 20 coins about 170 times, so the area of the middle box of this graph equals 17% of the total area, which is still 100%.

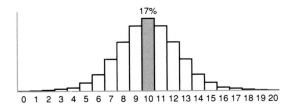

If we increase the number of coins in the box to a large number, say 1000, the graph will approximate the bell-shaped curve shown below. This smooth curve has the same shape to the left and to the right of center.

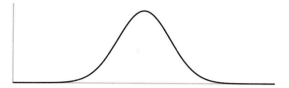

The curves from data from many other experiments also have this shape. If we have 1000 students use a meter stick to measure the length of a rod that is close to 6 meters long, we would not be surprised if the graph of the measurements had the following shape:

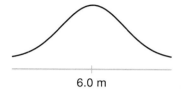

6.0 m

The **mean** (average) of the measurements would be 6.0 meters. About the same number of measurements would be greater than 6.0 meters than are less than 6.0 meters, so the middle measurement, the **median,** would be 6.0 meters. The measurement that occurred the most often, the **mode,** would also be 6.0 meters. **For the normal distribution, the mean, the median, and the mode are the same.** As we see, the normal curve is a smooth, bell-shaped curve. Since this distribution is theoretical, it is possible to compute that about 68% (0.68) of the measurements will lie within one standard deviation of the mean. If the standard deviation is small with respect to the mean, more measurements will be clustered about the mean, and if the standard deviation is larger, the measurements will be more spread out. To illustrate, we show the graph on the left of a normal distribution whose mean is 100 and whose standard deviation σ (sigma) is 3. About 68% of the measurements lie between 97 and 103.

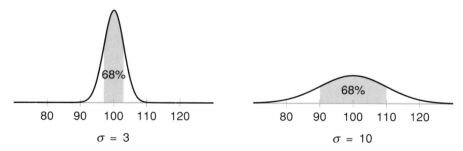

On the right we show the graph of a distribution whose mean is also 100 but whose standard deviation σ (sigma) is 10. Approximately 68% of these measurements lie between 90 and 110. This graph is flatter than the graph on the left.

Approximately 95% (0.95) of the measurements lie within two standard deviations of the mean. Thus, about 95% of the measurements of the graph whose sigma is 3 lie between 94 and 106, as we show on the left, and between 80 and 120, as we show on the right.

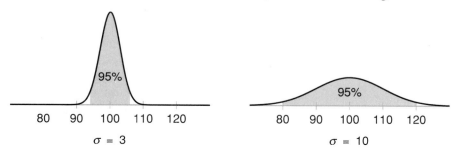

More than 99% of the measurements (almost all) lie within three standard deviations of the mean, as we show in the following graphs.

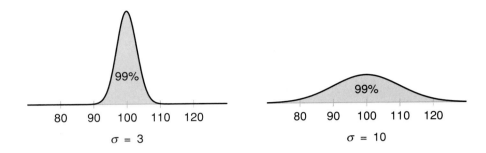

$$\sigma = 3 \qquad\qquad\qquad \sigma = 10$$

example 61.2   The mean of a distribution that is approximately normal is 100 and the standard deviation is 5. Use the standard deviation to tell how the data are distributed with respect to the mean.

solution   Since the distribution is approximately normally distributed, we know that around 68% of the data values lie within one standard deviation of the mean. Thus, about 68% of the values lie between 100 − 5, or 95, and 100 + 5, or 105. Also, about 95% of the data values lie within two standard deviations of the mean, so around 95% of the values lie between 100 − 2(5), or 90, and 100 + 2(5), or 110. Finally, approximately 99% of the data values lie within three standard deviations of the mean, so around 99% of the values lie between 100 − 3(5), or 85, and 100 + 3(5), or 115.

    Many distributions look like normal distributions but are skewed to the left or to the right. The graph on the left below looks like a normal curve that has extra data points to the left of the peak value. We say that this distribution is skewed to the left or is **skewed negatively.** The graph on the right is skewed to the right or is **skewed positively.**

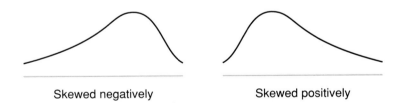

Skewed negatively   Skewed positively

    The graph of some distributions have more than one hump. The French word for *fashionable* is **mode.** Measurements that tend to group in two areas are called **bimodal** because there are two ranges of measurements that are the most popular or the most fashionable. If some students refuse to complete their homework, but many students do complete their homework, the grades on the tests will be bimodal because one group of students will get D's, another group of students will get A's and B's, and few students will get C's.

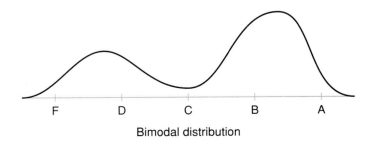

Bimodal distribution

61.C

box-and-whisker plots

Data consists of a list of numbers. For example, a teacher records the grades a class of 32 students received on a test, as we show here.

$$90, 78, 96, 80, 83, 60, 71, 87, 95, 69, 68, 92,$$
$$80, 76, 87, 55, 94, 85, 73, 65, 92, 83, 69, 96,$$
$$60, 83, 88, 78, 96, 63, 83, 71$$

A good first step in analyzing these data is to arrange the numbers in order from the lowest score to the highest. We note that the grades are in the 90s, 80s, 70s, 60s, and 50s, so we put 9, 8, 7, 6, and 5 in a column on the left. The first number in the list above is 90, so we place 0 in the first row to the right of the 9. The second number is 78, so we place 8 in the third row to the right of the 7. The third number is 96, so we place 6 as the second digit in the first row. If we record all the second digits in this manner, we get the following:

STEM	LEAF
9	0, 6, 5, 2, 4, 2, 6, 6
8	0, 3, 7, 0, 7, 5, 3, 3, 8, 3
7	8, 1, 6, 3, 8, 1
6	0, 9, 8, 5, 9, 0, 3
5	5

This method of displaying data is called a **stem-and-leaf plot,** as the first number can be thought of as a branch on a tree and the numbers to the right represent leaves on the branch. As we see, a stem-and-leaf plot gives us a visual image of how the data are grouped. Now, if we arrange the leaves on each stem in order, we get

STEM	LEAF
9	0, 2, 2, 4, 5, 6, 6, 6
8	0, 0, 3, 3, 3, 3, 5, 7, 7, 8
7	1, 1, 3, 6, 8, 8
6	0, 0, 3, 5, 8, 9, 9
5	5

This stem-and-leaf plot has the same shape as the one above, but we can use this plot to record the numbers from the least to the greatest.

$$55, 60, 60, 63, 65, 68, 69, 69, 71, 71, 73, 76,$$
$$78, 78, 80, 80, 83, 83, 83, 83, 85, 87, 87, 88,$$
$$90, 92, 92, 94, 95, 96, 96, 96$$

We know that it is possible to compute the mean (average) and the standard deviation of the scores without arranging the scores in order. But now that the scores are in order, we can find the **range** of the scores.

$$\text{Range} = 96 - 55 = 41$$

We can also find the middle of the scores, which we call the **median.** If there is an odd number of scores, the median is the middle score. If there is an even number of scores, the median is the number halfway between the two middle scores. We have 32 scores and the two scores in the middle are 80 and 83, so the median is 81.5.

$$\text{Median} = \frac{80 + 83}{2} = 81.5$$

We can also separate the scores into four equal groups. This allows us to see how the scores are spread out. In the figure below, we have graphed the scores and have drawn rectangles to group the scores into four equal groups of 8.

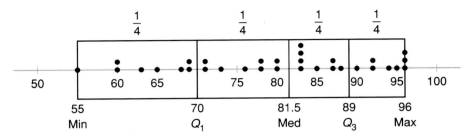

The minimum score is 55. The number halfway between the eighth score of 69 and the next score of 71 is 70, which is called the **first quartile.** We use the symbol Q_1 (q one) to designate this number. The median is 81.5, which we could also call Q_2 (q two). The highest score in the third group is 88, and the number halfway between 88 and the next score is 89, which we call the **third quartile** Q_3 (q three). The highest score in the fourth group is the maximum score 96.

The rectangles do not have the same lengths. The first rectangle is 15 units long, as it begins at 55 and ends at 70. The second rectangle is 11.5 units long, the third is 7.5 units long, and the fourth is 7 units long. The next diagram is called a **box-and-whisker plot,** which is used instead of the four boxes above. The first and last lengths are represented as lines called *whiskers* and the two middle lengths are represented with boxes.

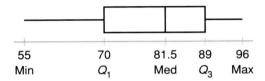

The Latin word for *middle* is *medius* and the Latin word for *fourth* is *quartus.* This is the reason the top of the first fourth of the scores is called the *first quartile*, the middle of all the scores is called the *median*, and the top of the third fourth of the scores is called the *third quartile*. The box-and-whisker plot tells us at a glance how the scores are spread out.

Doing all this with paper and pencil is time consuming. After the data are entered, a graphing calculator will arrange the data from least to greatest in one step. In one more step the calculator will do all of our single-variable analysis. It will display the following information for the problem just completed. For this discussion, we are not interested in the entries marked with an asterisk. The first symbol $\bar{x}$ (bar x) is another notation for the mean.

$$\bar{x} = 79.56\ldots \qquad\qquad n = 32$$
$$*\Sigma x = 2546 \qquad\qquad \text{min}X = 55$$
$$*\Sigma x^2 = 206920 \qquad\qquad Q_1 = 70$$
$$*Sx = 11.85\ldots \qquad\qquad \text{Med} = 81.5$$
$$\sigma x = 11.66\ldots \qquad\qquad Q_3 = 89$$
$$\text{max}X = 96$$

Use this next problem as a class project to develop a foolproof step-by-step procedure to do single-variable analysis. The procedure should detail the methods for clearing a list in the calculator, entering the data in the list, checking the setup, and asking the calculator to do a single-variable analysis of the data. Post one copy on the wall of your classroom and save another copy for yourself.

example 61.3   The measurements are 16, 22, 28, 33, 35, 40, 50, and 120. Use a graphing calculator to find the mean and the standard deviation and to find min x, Q_1, med, Q_3, and max x. Use this data to draw a box-and-whisker plot.

solution   We use a calculator to get

We use these data to draw a box-and-whisker plot.

The data point of 120 is an **outlier** whose relative importance is questionable. An outlier is a data point which lies well outside the range of the majority of the data points. We cannot disregard this data point when we do the calculations above, but we can modify the box-and-whisker plot by not letting either whisker be more than 1.5 times the combined lengths of the two boxes. The two boxes extend from 25 to 45, a distance of 20. Since this is the distance between the quartiles Q_1 and Q_3, we call it the **interquartile range.** If we multiply 20 by 1.5, we get 30. We will let the right-hand whisker be only 30 long so it will end at 75. We place an asterisk at 120 to show it is an outlier.

We believe that this box-and-whisker plot is more descriptive of the data than the plot above that has the whisker extended all the way to 120.

It is interesting to note that the analysis of data is sometimes as much an art as it is a science. And to our dismay, sometimes it is neither. We know that the mean is the average of the data, the median is the middle of the data, and the mode is the data value that is the most popular. Suppose a shipment of animals is composed of very small dogs that weigh about three pounds and one cow that weighs 650 pounds. The weights of the animals are listed here:

2, 2, 2, 2, 2, 2, 2, 2, 2, 3, 3, 3, 3, 3, 3, 3, 3, 4, 4, 650

The 650 data point is an outlier and outliers greatly affect the mean but affect the median no more than any other single data point. The mode is also unaffected.

$$\text{Mean} = \frac{\text{sum}}{\text{number}} = \frac{700}{20} = 35$$

The mode is 2 and the median is 3. The standard deviation is 141.1. The mode and the median make some sense for these data. The mean and standard deviation are almost meaningless.

problem set
61

1. How many ways can a president, a secretary, and a treasurer be chosen from a class of 12 students?

2. How many ways can Tom, Joe, Frank, and Sally sit in a row if Tom refuses to sit next to Sally?

3. To arrive on time, it is necessary to average 40 kilometers per hour. If the wheels have a radius of 14 inches, what should be their average angular velocity in radians per second?

4. A car has wheels that have a radius of 16 centimeters and the wheels turn at 40 revolutions per second. What is the speed of the car in miles per hour?

5. A boat travels downstream m nautical miles at d knots and then travels back upstream m nautical miles at u knots. What is the average speed for the entire trip? (*Note*: A **knot** is a nautical mile per hour.)

6. Mike's wages for a 40-hour week came to $200. The next week he received a 30% hourly raise but was allowed to work only 38 hours. What was his paycheck for that week?

7. Five times Early's age now exceeds 4 times Lucy's age now by 38. In 5 years, twice Early's age will only exceed twice Lucy's age by 8. How old will Early and Lucy be in 13 years?

8. The ratio of the tens' digit to the hundreds' digit in a three-digit counting number was 2 to 1, and twice the tens' digit exceeded 5 times the units' digit by 1. What was the number if the sum of the digits was 15?

9. Every discipline has key words that many neophytes find difficult to remember. Three key words in statistics are *mean*, *median*, and *mode*. Mnemonics are often helpful. We suggest the "mean old average," the "median in the middle," and the "fashionable mode." Find the range, mean, median, mode, variance, and standard deviation for the following data: 3, 4, 5, 7, 8, and 8.

10. The mean of a distribution that is approximately normal is 65 and the standard deviation is 3. Use the standard deviation to tell how the data are distributed with respect to the mean.

11. Given the following data:

$$40, 55, 62, 31, 44, 57, 42, 69, 47, 53, 52, 30$$

Make a stem-and-leaf plot.

12. The measurements are 61, 58, 43, 30, 72, 68, 50, 63, 62, 58, 65, and 60. Use a graphing calculator to find the mean and the standard deviation and to find min x, Q_1, med, Q_3, and max x. Use this data to draw a box-and-whisker plot.

Solve the following equations given that $0° \leq \theta < 360°$:

13. $\cos 3\theta + \dfrac{\sqrt{2}}{2} = 0$ 14. $\sin^2 \theta - \dfrac{1}{4} = 0$ 15. $\cos^2 \theta - \dfrac{1}{2} \cos \theta = 0$

Solve for x:

16. $2 \log_5 x = \log_5 16 - \log_5 4$ 17. $\log x + \log (x - 9) = 1$

18. Simplify: $5^{\log_5 22 - \log_5 2} + 3 \log_2 2^4$

19. Find the distance between the point $(2, 4)$ and the line $y = x - 1$.

20. Complete the square to graph the parabola $y - 2x^2 + 4x = -7$.

Write the equations of the following sinusoids in terms of the sine function:

21.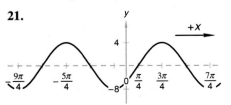

22.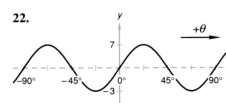

23. Find the area of this triangle in square centimeters.

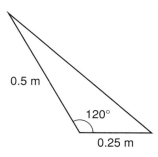

0.5 m

120°

0.25 m

24. The central angle of a sector of a circle is 1.6 radians. Find the area of the sector in square centimeters if the radius of the circle is 1 meter.

25. Find the area of the segment bounded by an arc of measure 150° and the chord which joins the endpoints of the arc in a circle of radius 10 centimeters.

26. Sketch the graphs of the equations $y = x^2$ and $x^2 + y^2 = 4$. Shade the region(s) that satisfies the system of inequalities:

$$\begin{cases} y \le x^2 \\ x^2 + y^2 \le 4 \end{cases}$$

27. If $f(x) = \sin x$ and $g(x) = \cos x$, find $2f\left(\dfrac{13\pi}{6}\right)g\left(\dfrac{13\pi}{6}\right) - f\left(\dfrac{13\pi}{3}\right)$.

Evaluate:

28. $\cot(-450°) - \dfrac{\cos(-450°)}{\sin(-450°)}$

29. $\sin\left[\text{Arctan}\left(-\dfrac{5}{12}\right)\right]$

30. Use the midpoint formula method to find the equation of the line equidistant from $(-4, 2)$ and $(4, 4)$. Write the equation in slope-intercept form.

LESSON 62   *Abstract Coefficients • Linear Variation*

62.A
abstract coefficients

In beginning algebra, we learned that letters can be used in place of unspecified numbers. In this equation

$$2x + 4y = 50$$

the letters x and y are variables. If x takes on the value of 5, then y must equal 10. If x takes on the value of 19, then y equals 3, etc. Thus, while x and y can take on different values in this equation, the symbols 2, 4, and 50 always have the same values, as they represent the constants 2, 4, and 50. At this level of algebra, it is beneficial to begin to place emphasis on problems that use letters to represent constants. If we use a, b, and c in place of the constants 2, 4, and 50 in the equation above, the equation would read

$$ax + by = c$$

Although any letter can be used to represent a constant or a variable, it is customary to use letters from the beginning of the alphabet to represent constants and letters from the end of the alphabet to represent variables. In this lesson we will use letters to represent the constants in systems of linear equations.

example 62.1 Solve for y: $\begin{cases} ax + by = c \\ dx + ey = f \end{cases}$

solution If we multiply every term in the top equation by d and multiply every term in the bottom equation by $(-a)$, the coefficients of x in the resulting equations will be the same except for the signs. Thus, when we add the equations, the x terms will be eliminated.

$$ax + by = c \longrightarrow (d) \longrightarrow adx + bdy = cd$$
$$dx + ey = f \longrightarrow (-a) \longrightarrow \underline{-adx - aey = -af}$$
$$(bd - ae)y = cd - af$$

Note the use of parentheses around $bd - ae$. Now we finish by dividing both sides by $bd - ae$, and we get

$$y = \frac{cd - af}{bd - ae}$$

example 62.2 Solve for x: $\begin{cases} a_1x + b_1y = c_1 \\ a_2x + b_2y = c_2 \end{cases}$

solution Subscripted constants such as these are standard notation for the general study of equations and will be used in later lessons. To eliminate y, we will multiply as required to make the y coefficient equal but opposite in sign. **Be careful with the subscripts.** It is easy to get them mixed up.

$$a_1x + b_1y = c_1 \longrightarrow (b_2) \longrightarrow a_1b_2x + b_1b_2y = c_1b_2$$
$$a_2x + b_2y = c_2 \longrightarrow (-b_1) \longrightarrow \underline{-a_2b_1x - b_1b_2y = -c_2b_1}$$
$$(a_1b_2 - a_2b_1)x = c_1b_2 - c_2b_1$$

To finish, we divide both sides by $a_1b_2 - a_2b_1$ and get

$$x = \frac{c_1b_2 - c_2b_1}{a_1b_2 - a_2b_1}$$

62.B
linear variation

A statement that one variable varies linearly as another variable can sometimes mean the same thing as a statement of direct variation between the two variables. But the two statements may have different meanings, as we explain in the next example.

example 62.3 The total cost varied linearly with the number produced. When 100 were produced, the cost was \$700; and when 400 were produced, the cost was \$2200. Write an equation that gives cost as a function of the number produced.

solution **When a linear relationship is specified, the y intercept may or may not be zero. In general, direct variation can be thought of as linear variation where the y intercept is zero.** The equation implied by this problem is

$$C = mN + b$$

We have been given the coordinates of two points on the line. We will use 100 for N and 700 for C to get one equation and then will use 400 for N and 2200 for C to get the second equation. Then we will solve the equations for m and b.

(a)　　$700 = m100 + b$　→　(4)　→　$2800 = m400 + 4b$

(b)　$2200 = m400 + b$　→　(-1)　→　$\underline{-2200 = -m400 - b}$

$$600 = 3b$$
$$b = 200$$

Now we substitute 200 for b in equation (a) and solve for m.

$$700 = m100 + 200 \qquad \text{substituted 200 for } b$$
$$500 = 100m \qquad \text{added } -200 \text{ to both sides}$$
$$m = 5 \qquad \text{solved}$$

Now we can write the equation of the line, which, as we see, does have a nonzero y intercept.

$$\mathbf{C = 5N + 200}$$

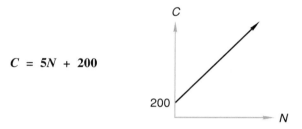

**problem set
62**

1. The total cost varied linearly with the number produced. When 200 were produced, the cost was $2050. When 30 were produced, the cost was $350. Write an equation that gives cost as a function of the number produced.

2. How many ways can 10 boys sit in 5 chairs that are in 1 row?

3. Five red marbles, 4 white marbles, and 2 green marbles are placed in a row. In how many distinguishable ways can they be arranged?

4. How many ways can 4 boys and 1 girl be arranged in a row if the girl insists on sitting in the middle?

5. The wheel had an angular velocity of 723 radians per minute. How fast was the wheel rolling along in feet per second if the radius of the wheel was 20 centimeters?

6. Detia could row 12 miles downstream in 1 hour less than she could row 6 miles upstream. What was the speed of the current in the river, and how fast could Detia row in still water if the speed of the current was one half the speed Detia could row in still water?

7. The pressure of an ideal gas varies inversely as the volume if the temperature is held constant. If the temperature is 1500 K, the pressure is 4 atmospheres when the volume is 500 liters. At the same temperature, what is the pressure when the volume is decreased to 50 liters?

8. The number of reds varied directly as the number of purples and inversely as the number of whites cubed. There were 200 reds when there were 50 purples and 10 whites. How many reds were there when the number of purples was increased to 60 and the number of whites was decreased to 5?

9. Solve for y: $\begin{cases} mx + ny = c \\ dx + ey = f \end{cases}$

10. Find the range, mean, median, mode, variance, and standard deviation for the following data: 1, 2, 3, 4, 7, and 7.

11. The data is normally distributed with a mean of 84 and a standard deviation of 6.

    (a) Give the range of values between which approximately 68% of the data values lie.

    (b) Give the range of values between which approximately 95% of the data values lie.

12. The measurements are 465, 589, 526, 602, 486, 542, 472, 689, and 643. Use a graphing calculator to find the mean and the standard deviation and to find min x, Q_1, med, Q_3, and max x. Use this data to draw a box-and-whisker plot.

Solve the following equations given that $0° \leq \theta < 360°$:

13. $\cos 4\theta - 1 = 0$

14. $\tan^2 \theta = 1$

Solve for x:

15. $3 \log_6 x = \log_6 16 - \log_6 2$

16. $\log_7 (x + 9) - \log_7 x = \log_7 7$

17. Simplify: $6^{2 \log_6 2} + 5 \log_4 4$

18. Find the distance between the point $(3, 1)$ and the line $y = x - 4$.

Write the equations of the following sinusoids in terms of the cosine function:

19.

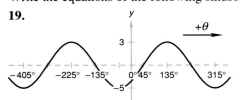

20.

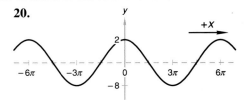

21. Find the area of this trapezoid in square centimeters.

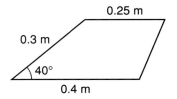

22. The central angle of a sector of a circle is 103°. Find the area of the sector in square centimeters if the radius of the circle is 0.1 meter.

23. Find the area of the segment bounded by an arc of measure 2.44 radians and the chord which joins the endpoints of the arc in a circle whose radius is 8 centimeters.

24. Sketch the graphs of the equations $y = (x + 3)^2$ and $y = -x + 2$. Shade the region(s) that satisfies the system of inequalities:
$$\begin{cases} y \leq (x + 3)^2 \\ y \leq -x + 2 \end{cases}$$

Evaluate:

25. $2 \sin \dfrac{19\pi}{6} \cos \dfrac{19\pi}{6} - \sin \dfrac{19\pi}{3}$

26. $\tan^2 (-390°) + 1$

27. $\tan \left[\text{Arcsin} \left(-\dfrac{5}{13} \right) \right]$

28. Use the locus definition method to find the equation of the line equidistant from $(-4, -4)$ and $(6, 2)$. Write the equation in general form.

29. Let $f(x) = |x|$ and $g(x) = |x + 7| - 5$. Which of the following statements is true?

A. The graph of g is the graph of f translated seven units to the right and five units up.

B. The graph of g is the graph of f translated seven units to the right and five units down.

C. The graph of g is the graph of f translated seven units to the left and five units up.

D. The graph of g is the graph of f translated seven units to the left and five units down.

30. Determine if $f(x) = \dfrac{1}{x - 5}$ and $g(x) = \dfrac{5x + 1}{x}$ are inverse functions by computing their compositions.

LESSON 63   *Circles and Completing the Square*

We review the development of the equation of a circle by using the distance formula to write the equation of a circle of radius 3 whose center is $(2, 4)$.

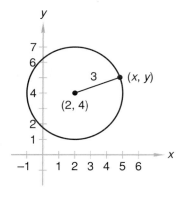

$$\sqrt{(x - 2)^2 + (y - 4)^2} = 3 \qquad \text{distance formula}$$

$$(x - 2)^2 + (y - 4)^2 = 3^2 \qquad \text{standard form}$$

If we do the indicated multiplications and rearrange the terms, we can write the equation of this circle in general form.

$$x^2 - 4x + 4 + y^2 - 8y + 16 = 9 \qquad \text{multiplied}$$

$$x^2 + y^2 - 4x - 8y + 11 = 0 \qquad \text{general form}$$

We note that the standard form is especially useful because, by inspection, we can tell the coordinates of the center of the circle and the length of the radius. If we are given the equation of a circle in general form, we can transform it to standard form by completing the square twice, as we show in the following examples.

example 63.1　　The equation $x^2 + y^2 - 6x + 8y + 21 = 0$ is the equation of a circle. Complete the square to change this equation to the standard form and then graph the circle.

solution　　We group the x terms and the y terms and move the constant to the other side of the equals sign.

$$\left(x^2 - 6x \quad\right) + \left(y^2 + 8y \quad\right) = -21$$

Now we complete the squares inside the parentheses by inserting $+9$ and $+16$. We also add $+9$ and $+16$ to the right-hand side as required by the rules for equations.

$$\left(x^2 - 6x + 9\right) + \left(y^2 + 8y + 16\right) = -21 + 9 + 16$$

Now on the left-hand side we write each term as a quantity squared, and we add on the right-hand side.

$$(x - 3)^2 + (y + 4)^2 = 2^2$$

This is the equation of a circle of radius 2 whose center is $(3, -4)$, as shown in the figure.

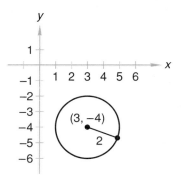

example 63.2   Given the general form of the equation of a circle, $x^2 + y^2 + 4x - 6y + 6 = 0$, complete the square to write the standard form of the equation and then graph the circle.

solution   We use parentheses and group the x terms and the y terms.

$$\left(x^2 + 4x \quad \right) + \left(y^2 - 6y \quad \right) = -6$$

Now we add to complete the squares and remember to add the same numbers to the right-hand side of the equation.

$$\left(x^2 + 4x + 4\right) + \left(y^2 - 6y + 9\right) = -6 + 4 + 9$$

Now we write each grouping on the left-hand side as a squared term and simplify on the right.

$$(x + 2)^2 + (y - 3)^2 = (\sqrt{7})^2$$

This is the equation of a circle whose center is $(-2, 3)$ and whose radius is $\sqrt{7}$.

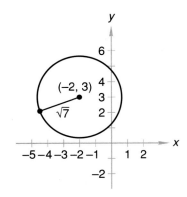

example 63.3   Given the general form of the equation of a circle, $2x^2 + 2y^2 - x + y - 3 = 0$, complete the square to write the standard form of the equation and describe the circle.

solution   We begin by dividing every term by 2 so that the coefficients of x^2 and y^2 are both 1. We get

$$x^2 + y^2 - \frac{1}{2}x + \frac{1}{2}y - \frac{3}{2} = 0$$

Now we rearrange the terms and use parentheses. Then we add as necessary to complete the squares.

$$\left(x^2 - \frac{1}{2}x \quad \right) + \left(y^2 + \frac{1}{2}y \quad \right) = \frac{3}{2} \qquad \text{rearranged}$$

$$\left(x^2 - \frac{1}{2}x + \frac{1}{16}\right) + \left(y^2 + \frac{1}{2}y + \frac{1}{16}\right) = \frac{24}{16} + \frac{1}{16} + \frac{1}{16} \qquad \text{completed squares}$$

$$\left(x - \frac{1}{4}\right)^2 + \left(y + \frac{1}{4}\right)^2 = \left(\frac{\sqrt{26}}{4}\right)^2 \qquad \text{simplified}$$

This is the equation of a circle of radius $\dfrac{\sqrt{26}}{4}$ whose center is $\left(\dfrac{1}{4}, -\dfrac{1}{4}\right)$.

problem set 63

1. The number of reds varied linearly as the number of blues. When there were 2 blues, there were 11 reds. When the blues numbered 8, there were 35 reds. How many reds were there when 6 blues were present?

2. How many distinguishable ways can 4 identical red flags and 3 identical green flags be arranged in a row?

3. How many ways can the letters of the word *vowel* be arranged if the first letter must be a vowel?

4. How many ways can 3 boys and 2 girls sit in a row if boys cannot sit next to one another?

5. The car rolled merrily along at 60 kilometers per hour. If the radius of its wheels was 12 inches, what was the angular velocity of the wheels in radians per second?

6. Marta traveled m miles at a miles per hour, and Kristel traveled the same distance but at a slower rate of b miles per hour. What is the difference in hours between the times of the two girls?

7. Henry traveled a miles in b hours and then increased his rate by c miles per hour. How long would it take him to travel 1000 miles at the new rate?

8. The ratio of onlookers to bystanders was 17 to 4. If 1050 natives were gawking at the spectacle, how many were bystanders and how many were onlookers?

9. The equation $x^2 + y^2 + 8x - 6y - 11 = 0$ is the equation of a circle. Complete the square to change this equation to standard form. Find the radius and the coordinates of the center of the circle and then graph the circle.

10. The equation $x^2 + y^2 - 8x + 2y + 13 = 0$ is the equation of a circle. Complete the square to change this equation to standard form. Find the radius and the coordinates of the center of the circle and then graph the circle.

11. Solve for x: $\begin{cases} ax + by = c \\ mx + ny = f \end{cases}$

12. We know that if the mean (average) of five numbers is 20, the sum of the numbers must be 5 times 20, or 100. If the data points are 24, 16, 18, x, and 28, and the mean is 20, what is the value of the missing data point? Find the range, the median, and the standard deviation, and note that the mode does not exist because no number appears more than once.

13. The distribution of the scores on a test is approximately normal. The mean score is 76 and the standard deviation is 4. Use the standard deviation to tell how the data are distributed with respect to the mean.

14. Given the following data:

   $$89, 76, 70, 62, 83, 67, 56, 78, 80, 63, 81, 72, 65, 74, 64$$

   Make a stem-and-leaf plot.

Solve the following equations given that $0° \le \theta < 360°$:

15. $\cos^2 \theta - \dfrac{1}{4} = 0$

16. $\cos \theta \sin \theta - \sin \theta = 0$

Solve for x:

17. $2 \log_8 x = \log_8 6 + \log_8 2 - \log_8 1$

18. $\log_{1/2} (x + 3) - \log_{1/2} (x - 2) = \log_{1/2} 2$

19. Find the distance between the point $(-2, 4)$ and the line $y - x + 6 = 0$.

20. Complete the square to graph the parabola $y = 2x^2 - 12x + 9$.

Write the equations of the following sinusoids in terms of the sine function:

21.

22.

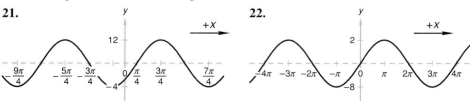

23. Find the area of this triangle in square centimeters.

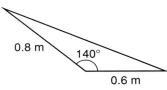

0.8 m   140°

0.6 m

24. The central angle of a sector of a circle is 2.4 radians. Find the area of the sector in square centimeters if the radius of the circle is 0.4 meter.

25. Find the area of the segment bounded by an arc of measure 160° and the chord which joins the endpoints of the arc in a circle whose radius is 10 centimeters.

26. Sketch the graphs of the equations $x^2 + y^2 = 9$, $y = x$, and $y = -x$. Shade the region(s) that satisfies the system of inequalities:

$$\begin{cases} x^2 + y^2 \leq 9 \\ y \geq x \\ y \geq -x \end{cases}$$

Evaluate:

27. $\sin^2 \dfrac{3\pi}{2} + \cos^2 \dfrac{3\pi}{2}$

28. $\cos^2(-405°) - \sin^2(-405°)$

29. $\sin\left[\text{Arccos}\left(-\dfrac{5}{6}\right)\right]$

30. If $f(x) = 8^x$ and $g(x) = 2\log_8 x$, find $(g \circ f)(13)$.

LESSON 64   *The Complex Plane • Polar Form of a Complex Number • Sums and Products of Complex Numbers*

64.A

the complex plane

We can graph complex numbers on a rectangular coordinate system if we use the x axis to graph the real part of the number and the y axis to graph the imaginary part of the number. If we do this, the graph of the complex number $-2 - 4i$ will look exactly like the graph of the vector $-2\hat{i} - 4\hat{j}$. **This is confusing at first, for i indicates up and down for graphs of complex numbers, but $\hat{i}$ indicates right and left for graphs of vectors.**

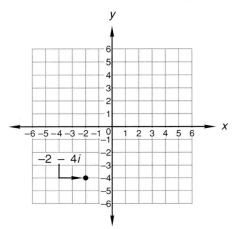

When we graph $-2\hat{i} - 4\hat{j}$, we do not need to put the $\hat{i}$ and $\hat{j}$ on the graph because we can visually determine directions by looking at the graph. When we graph $-2 - 4i$, we do not need to put an i on the graph because we can remember that we use the y direction to graph the imaginary part of a complex number and the x direction to graph the real part of a complex number.

When we graph vectors, we call the system of coordinates a **rectangular coordinate system** or a **Cartesian coordinate system**. Often, it is called simply a **coordinate plane**. When we use the coordinate plane to graph complex numbers, we call the plane the **complex plane** or the **Argand plane**. Some authors replace the letter y on the vertical axis with the word *imaginary*, and others use y as we have in the past. We will continue to use the letter y on the vertical axis and the letter x on the horizontal axis.

64.B
polar form of a complex number

The notations used for the polar form of a vector and the rectangular form of a vector are familiar. The rectangular and polar forms of the vector in the figure are written to the right of the figure.

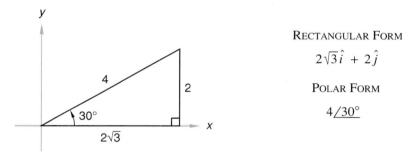

RECTANGULAR FORM

$2\sqrt{3}\,\hat{i} + 2\hat{j}$

POLAR FORM

$4\underline{/30°}$

Unfortunately, the polar forms of the corresponding complex number $2\sqrt{3} + 2i$ can be confusing to the beginner. Some authors use an ordered pair $(4, 30°)$ for the polar form of this number, but the notation used more often is

$$4(\cos 30° + i \sin 30°)$$

Since this is a rather cumbersome notation, many people use the notation cis as a shorthand for $\cos + i \sin$, and they write the polar form as

$$4 \text{ cis } 30°$$

We will use this notation because it closely resembles the notation

$$4\underline{/30°}$$

used for a vector of the same angle and magnitude. **The length of the hypotenuse of the triangle formed when we graph a complex number is called the *absolute value* of the complex number. So the absolute value of $2\sqrt{3} + 2i$ or 4 cis $30°$ is the number 4.**

$$\left| 2\sqrt{3} + 2i \right| = 4$$

	RECTANGULAR FORM	POLAR FORM
Vector	$2\sqrt{3}\,\hat{i} + 2\hat{j}$	$4\underline{/30°}$
Complex number	$2\sqrt{3} + 2i$	4 cis $30°$

From time to time, we will use the notation $4(\cos 30° + i \sin 30°)$ instead of 4 cis $30°$ since the longer notation is used by so many authors.

64.C

sums and products of complex numbers

Complex numbers can be added when they are written in rectangular form by adding real parts to real parts and imaginary parts to imaginary parts. We will demonstrate by adding $\left(2\sqrt{3} + 2i\right)$ and $(2 + 2i)$.

$$\left(2\sqrt{3} + 2i\right) + (2 + 2i) = 2\sqrt{3} + 2i + 2 + 2i = \left(2\sqrt{3} + 2\right) + 4i$$

These numbers cannot be added when they are written in polar form unless the angles are equal or differ by 180°.

$$4 \text{ cis } 30° + 2\sqrt{2} \text{ cis } 45° = \text{cannot be added in this form}$$

Complex numbers can be multiplied in rectangular form or in polar form. To review multiplication of complex numbers in rectangular form, we will multiply $\left(2\sqrt{3} + 2i\right)(2 + 2i)$. We will use the vertical format.

$$
\begin{array}{r}
2\sqrt{3} + 2i \\
2 + 2i \\
\hline
4\sqrt{3} + 4i \\
4\sqrt{3}i + 4i^2 \\
\hline
4\sqrt{3} + 4i + 4\sqrt{3}i - 4 = \left(4\sqrt{3} - 4\right) + \left(4 + 4\sqrt{3}\right)i
\end{array}
$$

To graph this number, we use a calculator to help us get the decimal number equivalent $2.93 + 10.93i$.

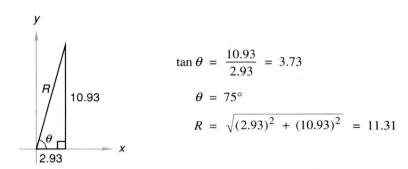

$$\tan \theta = \frac{10.93}{2.93} = 3.73$$

$$\theta = 75°$$

$$R = \sqrt{(2.93)^2 + (10.93)^2} = 11.31$$

So the product obtained this way is 11.31 cis 75°. If we multiply the same numbers in polar form, we get

$$(4 \text{ cis } 30°)\left(2\sqrt{2} \text{ cis } 45°\right) = 8\sqrt{2} \text{ cis } 75° = 11.31 \text{ cis } 75°$$

Thus, to multiply complex numbers in polar form, we multiply the absolute values and add the angles.

example 64.1   Multiply: $\left[5(\cos 20° + i \sin 20°)\right]\left[6(\cos 42° + i \sin 42°)\right]$

solution   First we rewrite the problem using a more familiar notation.

$$(5 \text{ cis } 20°)(6 \text{ cis } 42°)$$

We multiply complex numbers in polar form by multiplying the absolute values and adding the angles.

$$(5 \text{ cis } 20°)(6 \text{ cis } 42°) = \textbf{30 cis 62°}$$

example 64.2   Multiply: (5 cis 280°)(7 cis 300°)

solution   Since the problem is already written in the more familiar notation, we simply multiply the magnitudes and add the angles.

$$(5 \text{ cis } 280°)(7 \text{ cis } 300°) = 35 \text{ cis } 580°$$

$$= \mathbf{35 \text{ cis } 220°}$$

The angles 580° and 220° are coterminal angles, and we normally try to express final results with angles that are between 0° and 360°.

problem set 64

1. The cost varied linearly with the number of workers employed. When there were 10 workers on the job, the weekly cost was $15,000. When there were 20 workers on the job, the weekly cost was $20,000. What was the weekly cost when there were 30 workers on the job?

2. How many three-digit positive integers, all of whose digits are odd, are less than 400?

3. How many distinguishable ways can 4 red marbles and 3 green marbles be arranged in a row?

4. The wheels had a diameter of 20 inches and they revolved at 75 radians per minute. What was the velocity of the car in kilometers per hour?

5. Selby Anne traveled m miles in x hours and then traveled k miles in y hours. If she maintained her overall average rate, how long would it take her to travel 150 miles?

6. The little red car traveled m miles at r miles per hour. The little blue car also traveled m miles but at a slower rate of b miles per hour. How many hours more did it take the blue car to make the trip?

7. Carter bought $k^2 t$ pencils for d dollars. How many pencils could he buy for $100?

8. (a) Convert $6 + 2i$ to polar form.

   (b) Express $5 \text{ cis } 30°$ in the form $a + bi$. Give an exact answer.

9. Multiply $(6 \text{ cis } 300°)(2 \text{ cis } 30°)$ and express the answer in rectangular form. Give an exact answer.

10. Multiply $(3 \text{ cis } 70°)(2 \text{ cis } 110°)$ and express the answer in rectangular form. Give an exact answer.

11. The equation $x^2 + y^2 - 4x = 0$ is the equation of a circle. Complete the square to change this equation to standard form. Find the radius and the coordinates of the center of the circle and then graph the circle.

12. The equation $x^2 + y^2 + 6x - 4y + 9 = 0$ is the equation of a circle. Complete the square to change this equation to standard form. Find the radius and the coordinates of the center of the circle and then graph the circle.

13. Solve for y: $\begin{cases} cx + by = d \\ px + qy = f \end{cases}$

14. The data is normally distributed with a mean of 17 and a standard deviation of 5. Give the range of values between which approximately 95% of the data values lie.

15. The measurements are 12, 15, 32, 26, 19, 48, 28, 33, 37, 26, 41, 32, 35, 17, and 33. Use a graphing calculator to find the mean and the standard deviation and to find min x, Q_1, med, Q_3, and max x. Use this data to draw a box-and-whisker plot.

Solve the following equations given that $0° \le \theta < 360°$:

16. $\sin \theta + 1 = 0$ 17. $\tan^2 \theta - 3 = 0$ 18. $\tan \theta \sin \theta - \sin \theta = 0$

Solve for x:

19. $2 \log_8 x = \log_8 (2x - 1)$ 　　　　　　**20.** $\log_3 (x - 2) + \log_3 x = 1$

21. Simplify: $8^{2 \log_8 13} - 2 \log_7 7^3$

22. Find the distance between the point $(-4, 6)$ and the line $y - x + 4 = 0$.

Write the equations of the following sinusoids in terms of the cosine function:

23.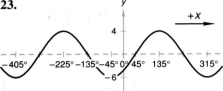

24.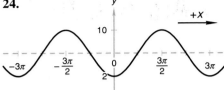

25. Find the area of this trapezoid.

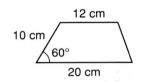

26. Find the area in square centimeters of the segment bounded by an arc of measure $130°$ and the chord which joins the endpoints of the arc in a circle whose radius is 0.3 meter.

27. Sketch the graphs of the equations $y = x^2 - 2$ and $y = 2 - x^2$. Shade the region(s) that satisfies the system of inequalities:

$$\begin{cases} y \geq x^2 - 2 \\ y \leq 2 - x^2 \end{cases}$$

Evaluate:

28. $\cos^2 \dfrac{5\pi}{4} - \sin^2 \dfrac{5\pi}{4} + \tan^2 \dfrac{5\pi}{4}$ 　　　　**29.** $\tan^3 0° - \cot^2 (-405°) + \csc^2 (-315°)$

30. Use the locus definition method to find the equation of the perpendicular bisector of the line segment whose endpoints are $(-4, 6)$ and $(6, 8)$. Write the equation in double-intercept form.

LESSON 65　*Radicals in Trigonometric Equations • Graphs of Logarithmic Functions*

65.A

radicals in trigonometric equations

When radicals are encountered in equations, we can isolate the radical and raise both sides to the power necessary to eliminate the radical. The equation

$$\sqrt{x - 3} - 2 = 0$$

can be solved by isolating the radical and then squaring both sides, as we show here.

$$\sqrt{x - 3} = 2 \qquad \text{isolated radical}$$
$$x - 3 = 4 \qquad \text{squared both sides}$$
$$x = 7 \qquad \text{solved}$$

The same procedure is used when radicals are encountered in trigonometric equations, as we demonstrate in the following example.

example 65.1   Solve $\sin x - \sqrt{1 - \sin^2 x} = 0$ given that $0° \le x < 360°$.

solution   This equation has a radical that we can eliminate by isolating the radical and squaring both sides.

$$\sin x = \sqrt{1 - \sin^2 x} \qquad \text{isolated radical}$$

$$\sin^2 x = 1 - \sin^2 x \qquad \text{squared both sides}$$

$$2\sin^2 x - 1 = 0 \qquad \text{rearranged}$$

Factoring will be easier if we first divide all terms in the equation by 2.

$$\sin^2 x - \frac{1}{2} = 0$$

Now, if we remember that $\frac{1}{2}$ can be written as a product as

$$\frac{1}{2} = \frac{1}{\sqrt{2}} \cdot \frac{1}{\sqrt{2}}$$

we can factor the equation and complete the solution.

$$\left(\sin x - \frac{1}{\sqrt{2}}\right)\left(\sin x + \frac{1}{\sqrt{2}}\right) = 0$$

Next, we equate both factors to zero and solve.

$$\sin x - \frac{1}{\sqrt{2}} = 0 \qquad\qquad \sin x + \frac{1}{\sqrt{2}} = 0$$

$$\sin x = \frac{1}{\sqrt{2}} \qquad\qquad \sin x = -\frac{1}{\sqrt{2}}$$

The sine of $45°$ is $1/\sqrt{2}$, and the sine is positive in the first and second quadrants and negative in the third and fourth quadrants.

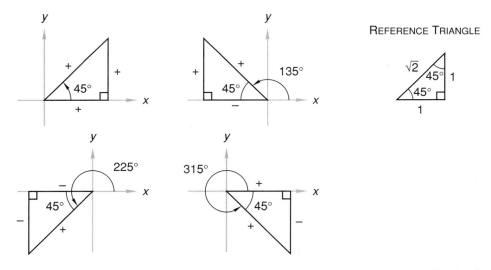

Thus it seems that $45°$, $135°$, $225°$, and $315°$ are solutions. But we must be careful. **In the first step we squared both sides of the equation, and raising both sides of an equation to a power often generates spurious roots in a solution.** If we check all four of these answers, we find that $225°$ and $315°$ are not roots of the original equation. We will use a calculator to provide decimal approximations for the values of the functions.

$$\sin 225° \overset{?}{=} \sqrt{1 - \sin^2 225°} \qquad\qquad \sin 315° \overset{?}{=} \sqrt{1 - \sin^2 315°}$$

$$-0.707 \overset{?}{=} \sqrt{1 - (-0.707)^2} \qquad\qquad -0.707 \overset{?}{=} \sqrt{1 - (-0.707)^2}$$

$$-0.707 \ne 0.707 \qquad\qquad\qquad -0.707 \ne 0.707$$

Thus **45°** and **135°** are the only solutions.

example 65.2   Solve $\left(\tan x - \sqrt{3}\right)(\sin x + 1) = 0$ given that $0 \le x < 2\pi$.

solution   We notice that the statement of this problem implies that we should give our answers in radians. Since we know how to solve for our answers in degrees, we will do that first and then convert the solutions to radians. There is no need to eliminate the radical in this equation because there is no variable in the radicand. In fact, this equation is already in factored form, so all we have to do is to equate each of the factors to zero and solve.

$$\tan x - \sqrt{3} = 0 \qquad\qquad \sin x + 1 = 0$$

$$\tan x = \sqrt{3} \qquad\qquad \sin x = -1$$

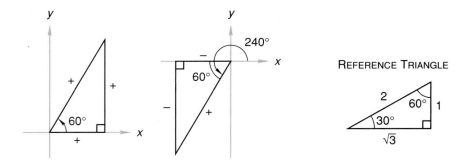

The tangent of $60°$ is $\sqrt{3}$, and the tangent is positive in the first and third quadrants, so two answers are $60°$ and $240°$. It would seem that the third answer would be $270°$ because the sine of $270°$ is -1. But we must be cautious with problems that contain the tangent, cotangent, secant, or cosecant because these functions are not defined for all values of x. If we try to check our solution by using $270°$ for x,

$$\left(\tan 270° - \sqrt{3}\right)(\sin 270° + 1) = 0$$

we cannot evaluate the expression because the tangent of $270°$ is undefined.[†] Thus, there are only two angles that satisfy the stated condition.

$$x = 60°, 240°$$

Now we will convert $60°$ and $240°$ to radians.

$$60° \times \frac{\pi \text{ rad}}{180°} = \frac{\pi}{3} \text{ radians}$$

$$240° \times \frac{\pi \text{ rad}}{180°} = \frac{4\pi}{3} \text{ radians}$$

Therefore,

$$x = \frac{\pi}{3}, \frac{4\pi}{3}$$

[†]Expressions such as this are interesting and will be considered further in more advanced courses. We note that as the value of x gets closer and closer to $270°$, the absolute value of the first factor gets larger and larger. At the same time, the absolute value of the second term gets closer and closer to zero.

65.B
graphs of logarithmic functions

Exponential functions can have as a base any positive number except the number 1. We have been graphing exponential functions whose bases are less than 1 and exponential functions whose bases are greater than 1. We remember that every exponential function can be rewritten as a logarithmic function. Therefore, logarithms also can have bases that are positive numbers less than 1 or greater than 1.

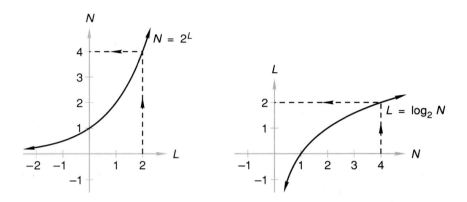

Because logarithms whose bases are less than 1 are rarely encountered, we will restrict our investigation of graphs of logarithmic functions to logarithmic functions whose bases are greater than 1.

When we graph functions, we always graph the independent variable on the horizontal axis and the dependent variable on the vertical axis. In the left-hand figure above, L is the independent variable and N is the dependent variable.

In the right-hand figure above, we graph the same ordered pairs, but change the names of the axes so that N is graphed horizontally and L is graphed vertically. To emphasize that both graphs display the same information, we show on the left how the logarithm 2 is paired with the number 4, and on the right we show that the number 4 is paired with the logarithm 2. **Instead of using N and L in the equations, most mathematics books use x and y, and instead of relabeling the axes, they interchange the meaning of x and y on the graphs and in the equations. Thus, in the left-hand graph shown below, x stands for the logarithm, and in the right-hand graph, x stands for the number!**

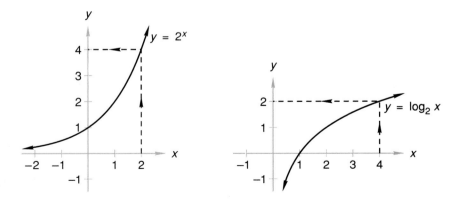

Both graphs present the same information, but because the exponent is the independent variable in the left-hand figure, the graph is considered to be the graph of the exponential function. Since the number is the independent variable in the right-hand figure, this graph is considered to be the graph of the logarithmic function.

If we put both graphs on the same set of axes, we find that the graphs are mirror images in the line $y = x$.

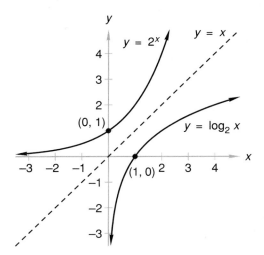

Since we already know how to graph exponentials, we see that we can graph logarithmic functions by graphing the exponential and then drawing its mirror image in the line $y = x$.

example 65.3 Sketch the graph of the function $y = \log_{3.5} x$.

solution We could graph the function directly, but we prefer to sketch the graph of the corresponding exponential equation and then sketch the mirror image in the line $y = x$. On the left we interchange x and y, and on the right we write the exponential form of this equation.

$$x = \log_{3.5} y \qquad\qquad y = 3.5^x$$

Now on the left we sketch the graph of $y = 3.5^x$, and on the right we repeat the sketch, dash in the line $y = x$, and draw the mirror image in this line, which is the logarithmic function $y = \log_{3.5} x$.

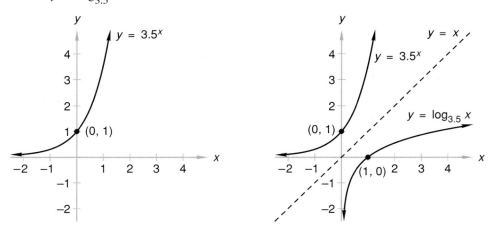

Note how one graph crosses at $(0, 1)$ and the other graph crosses at $(1, 0)$.

problem set 65

1. The cost of doing business varied linearly with the number of hours the store was open. If the store was open 40 hours a week, the cost was $1200; but if the store was open only 20 hours a week, the cost was $800. What would it cost to keep the store open 30 hours a week?

2. How many three-digit counting numbers all of whose digits are even are less than 401?

3. How many distinguishable permutations can be formed from the letters in the word *Mississippi*?

4. The wheels on the car had a 30-centimeter radius, and the car was traveling at 45 kilometers per hour. What was the angular velocity of the wheels in radians per minute?

5. The latitude of Albany is 42.6° north of the equator. What is the distance from Albany to the equator if the diameter of the earth is 7920 miles?

6. Kathie traveled m miles in h hours and then traveled x miles in $h + 4$ hours. At the same overall average rate, how long would it take her to travel 50 miles?

7. Kyle traveled x miles at p miles per hour. Keith also traveled x miles but at a faster rate of R miles per hour. How many more hours did it take Kyle to make the trip?

8. Kerry bought $k^2x + m$ pencils for d dollars. How many pencils could she buy for $500?

9. Solve $\cos x - \sqrt{1 - \cos^2 x} = 0$ given that $0° \le x < 360°$.

10. Solve $\left(\sin x - \dfrac{\sqrt{3}}{2}\right)\left(\sin x + \dfrac{1}{2}\right) = 0$ given that $0 \le x < 2\pi$.

11. Sketch the graph of the function $y = \log_2 x$.

12. (a) Convert $3 + 5i$ to polar form.

    (b) Convert $6 \text{ cis } 60°$ to rectangular form. Give an exact answer.

13. Multiply $(5 \text{ cis } 20°)(6 \text{ cis } 70°)$ and express the answer in rectangular form. Give an exact answer.

14. Multiply $\left[6 \text{ cis } (-30°)\right](3 \text{ cis } 90°)$ and express the answer in rectangular form. Give an exact answer.

15. The equation $x^2 + y^2 + 10x - 75 = 0$ is the equation of a circle. Complete the square to change this equation to standard form. Find the radius and the coordinates of the center of the circle and then graph the circle.

16. Solve for x: $\begin{cases} ax + dy = g \\ cx + fy = h \end{cases}$

17. Find the range, mean, median, mode, variance, and standard deviation for the following data: $7, 9, 5, 3, 1, 9$.

18. The data are normally distributed with a mean of 0 and a standard deviation of 1. Approximately what percentage of the data values lies between -1 and 1?

19. Solve $\cos 3\theta + \dfrac{\sqrt{3}}{2} = 0$ given that $0° \le \theta < 360°$.

Solve for x:

20. $2 \ln x = \ln (6 - x)$ 21. $3 \ln x = \ln 8 + 3 \ln 2$

22. Simplify: $7^{2 \log_7 3} + 8^{\log_8 6 - \log_8 3} - 4 \log_9 9^{1/2}$

Write the equations of the following sinusoids in terms of the sine function:

23.   24.

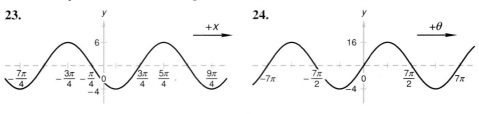

25. Find the area of this triangle in square meters.

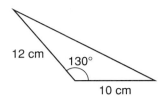

12 cm 130°
10 cm

Evaluate:

26. $\cos\left(\text{Arctan } \dfrac{6}{7}\right)$

27. $\sin^3 \dfrac{\pi}{2} - \cos^2 \dfrac{\pi}{6} + \tan^4\left(\dfrac{-\pi}{4}\right)$

28. Convert 600 kilometers per hour to miles per hour.

29. Factor $x^2 + 3x + 7$ over the set of complex numbers.

30. Let $f(x) = x^2$ and $g(x) = (x + 10)^2 - 2$. Which of the following statements is true?

   A. The graph of g is the graph of f translated ten units to the right and two units up.

   B. The graph of g is the graph of f translated ten units to the right and two units down.

   C. The graph of g is the graph of f translated ten units to the left and two units up.

   D. The graph of g is the graph of f translated ten units to the left and two units down.

LESSON 66 *Formulas for Systems of Equations • Phase Shifts and Period Changes*

66.A
formulas for systems of equations

If we solve a linear system that has abstract coefficients, we can develop formulas that can be used to solve any similar system. To develop a formula for x in a system of two equations and two unknowns, we will solve the system shown below. To solve, we first multiply the top equation by b_2 and the bottom equation by $-b_1$, and then add the resulting equations to eliminate the y terms.

$$\begin{cases} a_1x + b_1y = c_1 \\ a_2x + b_2y = c_2 \end{cases} \begin{array}{c} \rightarrow (b_2) \rightarrow \\ \rightarrow (-b_1) \rightarrow \end{array} \begin{array}{l} a_1b_2x + b_1b_2y = b_2c_1 \\ \underline{-a_2b_1x - b_1b_2y = -b_1c_2} \\ (a_1b_2 - a_2b_1)x = b_2c_1 - b_1c_2 \end{array}$$

We finish by dividing both sides of this equation by the coefficient of x.

$$x = \frac{b_2c_1 - b_1c_2}{a_1b_2 - a_2b_1} \qquad \text{(formula)}$$

Now if we are asked to solve the following system for x,

$$\begin{cases} 3x + 2y = 8 \\ 4x + 5y = 3 \end{cases}$$

we can note the correspondence between the coefficients in the two systems of equations. If, in the formula, we use 3, 2, and 8 for a_1, b_1, and c_1, respectively, and use 4, 5, and 3 for a_2, b_2, and c_2, respectively, we can solve for x.

$$x = \frac{b_2c_1 - b_1c_2}{a_1b_2 - a_2b_1} = \frac{(5)(8) - (2)(3)}{(3)(5) - (4)(2)} = \frac{40 - 6}{15 - 8} = \frac{34}{7}$$

example 66.1 Use abstract coefficients to find a formula for y and then use the formula to solve for y in the system shown here.

$$\begin{cases} 3x + 2y = 8 \\ 4x + 5y = 3 \end{cases}$$

solution To find the formula, we will use the coefficients shown. To solve for y, we will multiply the top equation by $-a_2$ and the bottom equation by a_1.

$$\begin{cases} a_1x + b_1y = c_1 \\ a_2x + b_2y = c_2 \end{cases} \begin{array}{l} \rightarrow (-a_2) \rightarrow -a_1a_2x - a_2b_1y = -a_2c_1 \\ \rightarrow (a_1) \rightarrow \underline{a_1a_2x + a_1b_2y = a_1c_2} \end{array}$$

$$(a_1b_2 - a_2b_1)y = a_1c_2 - a_2c_1$$

We finish by dividing both sides of this equation by the coefficient of y.

$$y = \frac{a_1c_2 - a_2c_1}{a_1b_2 - a_2b_1} \qquad \text{(formula)}$$

Now if we use 3, 2, and 8 for a_1, b_1, and c_1, respectively, and use 4, 5, and 3 for a_2, b_2, and c_2, respectively, we can solve for y.

$$y = \frac{a_1c_2 - a_2c_1}{a_1b_2 - a_2b_1} = \frac{(3)(3) - (4)(8)}{(3)(5) - (4)(2)} = \frac{9 - 32}{15 - 8} = \frac{-23}{7}$$

66.B
phase shifts and period changes

If the dependent variable y of a trigonometric function completes a full cycle of values as the independent variable θ changes 360°, we say that the period of the function is 360°. Thus, the function $y = \sin \theta$ has a period of 360°. If the dependent variable y completes a full cycle of values as the independent variable θ changes 180°, we say that the period of the function is 180°. Thus, the function $y = \sin 2\theta$ has a period of 180°. This reasoning can be used to show that $y = \sin 3\theta$ has a period of 120° and that $y = \sin \frac{1}{2}\theta$ has a period of 720°. Equations and graphs of sine functions that have periods other than 360° and that also have phase shifts are easier to write and to read if the argument is written in factored form. Here we show two forms of the same equation. Both equations tell us that the function has a period of 180° and a phase angle of +45°.

UNFACTORED ARGUMENT   FACTORED ARGUMENT

$y = \sin(2\theta - 90°)$ $y = \sin 2(\theta - 45°)$

In both forms we can see that θ is multiplied by 2, so the period is 180°, but in the unfactored form it is not easy to see that the phase angle is +45°. For this reason, we will concentrate on the factored form of the argument. To write the argument, we determine the period and the phase angle from the graph. **The coefficient of the argument is 360° divided by the period in degrees, or 2π divided by the period in radians.** Thus, if the period is 180°, or π radians, the coefficient is 2.

$$\text{Coefficient} = \frac{360°}{180°} = 2 \qquad \text{or} \qquad \text{Coefficient} = \frac{2\pi}{\pi} = 2$$

We remember that any sinusoid can be expressed either as a sine function with a phase shift or as a cosine function with a phase shift. **The phase angle for a sine function is the angle where the graph of the curve crosses its centerline on the way up. If the curve crosses at +90°, the sine phase angle is +90° and the argument is $C(\theta - 90°)$, where C is the coefficient just defined. The phase angle for a cosine function is the angle for which the value of the function is a maximum. If the maximum value occurs when θ equals +120°, the cosine phase angle is +120° and the cosine argument is $C(\theta - 120°)$.**

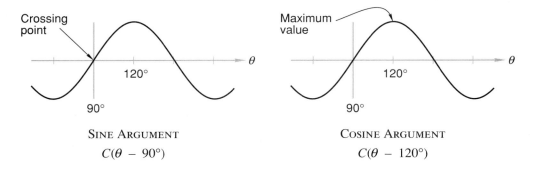

SINE ARGUMENT
$C(\theta - 90°)$

COSINE ARGUMENT
$C(\theta - 120°)$

The general forms of the equations are

$$y = A + B \sin C(\theta - D) \qquad \text{and} \qquad y = A + B \cos C(\theta - D)$$

where A is the value of the centerline, B is the amplitude, C is 360° divided by the period in degrees (or 2π divided by the period in radians), and D is the phase angle. We note again that **the argument always displays the negative of the phase angle.**

example 66.2   Write both the sine and cosine equations of this sinusoid.

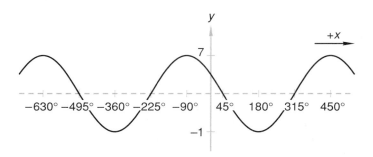

solution   We see that the centerline is +3 and that the amplitude is 4. This graph uses x instead of θ, so our equations are

$$y = 3 + 4 \sin C(x - D) \qquad \text{and} \qquad y = 3 + 4 \cos C(x - D)$$

The period can be measured between any two like points on the curve. We decide to use successive low points and find the distance between −360° and +180° to be 540°. The coefficient of the argument is 360° divided by the period, so

$$\text{Coefficient} = \frac{360°}{540°} = \frac{2}{3}$$

Therefore, our equations are

$$y = 3 + 4 \sin \frac{2}{3}(x - D) \qquad \text{and} \qquad y = 3 + 4 \cos \frac{2}{3}(x - D)$$

The curve crosses its centerline on the way up when x equals $-225°$ and has a maximum value when x equals $-90°$. The negatives of these angles appear in the arguments, so the equations of this function are

$$y = 3 + 4 \sin \frac{2}{3}(x + 225°) \quad \text{and} \quad y = 3 + 4 \cos \frac{2}{3}(x + 90°)$$

The period for this function is $540°$, so the curve repeats itself every $540°$. Thus, the angles in the arguments could be increased or decreased by multiples of $540°$ and still be correct. It is customary to write the phase angle with the least absolute value, as we did in this example.

**problem set
66**

1. The cost of the landfill varied linearly with the loads of dirt required. If 10 loads were used, the cost was $1350. If 20 loads were used, the cost was $2200. What would a landfill of only 5 loads cost?

2. Theresa arranged 6 identical blue ones and 3 identical green ones in a row. How many distinguishable arrangements were possible?

3. How many different ways can 6 chickens be arranged in a circle?

4. The wheels on Danny's Bobcat had a diameter of 26 inches. If he was traveling at 12 miles per hour, what was the angular velocity of the wheels in radians per minute?

5. Ralph traveled k miles in p hours and then traveled z miles in $p + 6$ hours. At the overall average rate, how long would it take Ralph to travel 740 miles?

6. Mumbo traveled m miles at a miles per hour. Jumbo also traveled m miles but at a faster rate of z miles per hour. How much longer did it take Mumbo to make the trip?

7. At the used car sale, Harry purchased p^2k cars for m dollars. How many cars could he have purchased for $10,000?

Write the equation of problem 8 as a cosine function and the equation of problem 9 as a sine function:

8.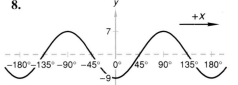

9.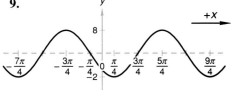

10. Solve $\tan x - \sqrt{1 - 2\tan^2 x} = 0$ given that $0° \leq x < 360°$.

11. Solve $\left(\cos x - \frac{1}{2}\right)\left(\sin x + \frac{1}{2}\right) = 0$ given that $0 \leq x < 2\pi$.

12. Sketch the graph of the function $y = \log_3 x$.

13. (a) Convert $4 + 3i$ to polar form.

    (b) Convert $5 \text{ cis } 150°$ to rectangular form. Give an exact answer.

14. Multiply $(3 \text{ cis } 40°)[2 \text{ cis } (-50°)]$ and express the answer in polar form.

15. Multiply $[8 \text{ cis } (-450°)](2 \text{ cis } 60°)$ and express the answer in rectangular form. Give an exact answer.

16. The equation $x^2 - 8x + y^2 + 6y = -16$ is the equation of a circle. Complete the square to change this equation to standard form. Find the radius and the coordinates of the center of the circle and then graph the circle.

17. Solve for x: $\begin{cases} ax + by = c \\ dx + fy = g \end{cases}$

18. Use the result of problem 17 to solve for x: $\begin{cases} 3x + 2y = 6 \\ 2x - 4y = 12 \end{cases}$

19. Find the range, mean, median, mode, variance, and standard deviation for the following data: 2, 7, 6, 1, 0, 2.

20. The measurements are 102, 136, 253, 328, 491, 111, 316, 222, 191, 347, 381, 401, 262, 270, 300, and 115. Use a graphing calculator to find the mean and the standard deviation and to find min x, Q_1, med, Q_3, and max x. Use this data to draw a box-and-whisker plot.

21. Solve $\sin 3\theta - \dfrac{1}{2} = 0$ given that $0° \leq \theta < 360°$.

Solve for x:

22. $2 \ln x = \ln (6x - 8)$

23. $3 \log_{12} x = \dfrac{3}{4} \log_{12} 16 + \dfrac{3}{2} \log_{12} 4$

24. Simplify: $3^{2 \log_3 7 - 3 \log_3 2} + 4 \log_3 3^3$

25. Find the area of this trapezoid.

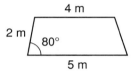

26. Find the area in square centimeters of the segment bounded by an arc of measure $140°$ and the chord which joins the endpoints of the arc in a circle whose radius is 0.4 meter.

Evaluate:

27. $\cot^2 \dfrac{4\pi}{3} - \tan^2 \dfrac{7\pi}{6} - \sec^3 \left(\dfrac{-\pi}{3} \right)$ 28. $\sin^2 (-420°) + \sin^2 420° + \cos^2 270°$

29. Write the quadratic equation with a lead coefficient of 1 whose roots are $2 + \sqrt{5}i$ and $2 - \sqrt{5}i$.

30. If $f(x) = \dfrac{1}{2x}$, find $\dfrac{f(x + h) - f(x - h)}{2h}$.

LESSON 67 *Antilogarithms*

The exponent is the logarithm, and the number is the antilogarithm. If we are given a value and asked for its antilogarithm, we have been given the exponent and asked for the number. The procedure for finding an antilogarithm in base 10 is straightforward since our number system also has a base of 10. This is the reason that base 10 logarithms have been used historically for calculations. Antilogarithms in base e and bases other than 10 are also useful.

example 67.1   If the base is 2, find the antilogarithm of 4.63.

solution   We want to find the value of $2^{4.63}$. We present this problem first because we want to show that we can use the $\boxed{y^x}$ key to find the antilogarithm to any base. **We always estimate as the first step.** The number we seek lies between 16 and 32 because 2^4 equals 16 and 2^5 equals 32.

$$2^4 = 16$$
$$2^{4.63} = ?$$
$$2^5 = 32$$

When we use the y^x key, we enter y first and then press the key. Then we enter x and finish by pressing the equals key.

ENTER	DISPLAY
2	2
y^x	2
4.63	4.63
=	24.76

We accept **24.76** as our antilogarithm because this number is between 16 and 32.

example 67.2   Use a calculator to find the antilogarithm of 4.63 if the base is 10.

solution   We want to find the value of $10^{4.63}$. First we estimate. The number we seek lies between 10^4, or 10,000, and 10^5, or 100,000. We could use the y^x key as we did in the preceding example and use 10 as our value of y. An easier way is to enter 4.63 and then press the inv key and the log key, in that order. If we do, we get

ENTER	DISPLAY
4.63	4.63
inv	4.63
log	42657.95

We accept **42,657.95** as our antilogarithm because this number is between 10,000 and 100,000. When the log key was pressed, the answer might have been in scientific notation as 4.2658   04. Check your calculator instruction manual for an explanation of how to switch back and forth between these two forms of answers.

example 67.3   Use a calculator to find the base e antilogarithm of 4.63.

solution   We want to find the number represented by $e^{4.63}$. Since e is just a little larger than 2.7, we can estimate that the answer lies between 3^4 and 3^5.

$$3^4 = 81$$
$$e^{4.63} = ?$$
$$3^5 = 243$$

The easiest way to get a more exact answer is to enter 4.63 in the calculator and press the inv and ln keys, in that order, and find that the

$$\text{Inverse ln of } 4.63 = \textbf{102.51}$$

example 67.4   Write the value of e to 5 decimal places.

solution   We know the answer is a little greater than 2.7 but its exact value is e^1, which is the inverse logarithm of 1 to the base e. Thus we enter 1 and press the inv and ln keys, in that order, and find

$$e = \textbf{2.71828}$$

example 67.5   Estimate antilog$_e$ (–3.2).

solution   We need to evaluate

$$e^{-3.2} \quad \text{which is} \quad \frac{1}{e^{3.2}}$$

If we use 3^3 as an estimate of $e^{3.2}$, we get

$$\frac{1}{3^3} = \frac{1}{27} \approx \mathbf{0.037}$$

which is reasonably close to the value we get from a calculator, which is

$$e^{-3.2} = 0.0407622$$

problem set 67

1. How many three-digit positive integers can be formed from the digits 1, 2, 3, 4, and 5 if no digits are repeated in the number?

2. The speed of a boat in still water is 16 miles per hour greater than the speed of the current in the river. The boat can travel 48 miles downstream in the same time it takes to travel 32 miles upstream. What is the speed of the boat in still water and what is the speed of the current?

3. Fabian took 3 times as long to fly 1800 miles as it took Hamilcar to fly 1200 miles. Find the rates and times of both if Hamilcar's speed was 200 miles per hour greater than that of Fabian.

4. Three dozen eggs and 5 pounds of flour cost $5.50. Four dozen eggs and 2 pounds of flour cost $5. What is the price of 1 dozen eggs and what is the cost of 1 pound of flour?

5. The tens' digit of a two-digit counting number is 1 greater than the units' digit. If the digits are reversed, the new number is smaller than the original number by an amount equal to the original tens' digit. What was the original number?

6. The units' digit of a two-digit counting number is 1 greater than twice the tens' digit. When the digits are reversed, the sum of the new number and the original number is 77. What was the original number?

7. Use a calculator to find: (a) antilog$_2$ 5.31   (b) antilog$_{10}$ 5.31

8. Estimate: (a) antilog$_e$ 2   (b) antilog$_e$ (–2)

9. Sketch the graph of the function $y = \ln x$.

Write the equation of problem 10 as a sine function and the equation of problem 11 as a cosine function:

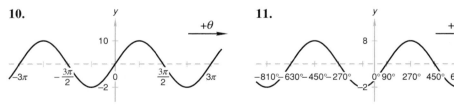

10.

11.

12. (a) Convert $5 - 12i$ to polar form.

    (b) Convert $7 \operatorname{cis} 210°$ to rectangular form. Give an exact answer.

13. Multiply $(4 \operatorname{cis} 20°)(2 \operatorname{cis} 40°)$ and express the answer in rectangular form. Give an exact answer.

14. Multiply $[3 \operatorname{cis} (–200°)](2 \operatorname{cis} 50°)$ and express the answer in rectangular form. Give an exact answer.

15. The equation $x^2 + y^2 - 4x + 6y - 3 = 0$ is the equation of a circle. Complete the square to change this equation to standard form. Find the radius and the coordinates of the center of the circle and then graph the circle.

16. Solve for y: $\begin{cases} cx + fy = a \\ dx + gy = b \end{cases}$

17. Use the result of problem 16 to solve for y: $\begin{cases} 2x - 3y = 5 \\ 3x + 2y = 7 \end{cases}$

18. The data are normally distributed with a mean of 0 and a standard deviation of 1. Approximately what percentage of the data lies between 0 and 2? (*Hint*: A normal distribution is symmetric about the mean and 95% lies between –2 and 2.)

19. Given the data:

$$17, 83, 92, 56, 46, 58, 87, 73, 64, 66, 85,$$
$$75, 70, 82, 71, 68$$

Construct a stem-and-leaf plot. Then use a graphing calculator to obtain the information to do a box-and-whisker plot.

20. Solve $(\tan x + 1)\left(\cos x - \dfrac{1}{2}\right) = 0$ given that $0 \le x < 2\pi$.

Solve the following equations given that $0° \le \theta < 360°$:

21. $\sqrt{\sin \theta} - \dfrac{\sqrt{2}}{2} = 0$

22. $\cos 3\theta + \dfrac{1}{2} = 0$

23. Evaluate: $\tan^2(-405°) - \sec^2(-405°) + \sin^2 495°$

Solve for x:

24. $\ln x + \ln x = \ln(4x - 3)$

25. $3 \log_7 x = \log_7 81 - \log_7 3$

26. Simplify: $2^{\log_2 3} - 3^{2 \log_3 2} + 5^{\log_5 4 + \log_5 6} - 4 \log 10^5$

27. Sketch the graphs of the equations $y = (x - 3)^2 + 2$ and $y = x^2$. Shade the region(s) that satisfies the following system of inequalities:

$$\begin{cases} y \ge (x - 3)^2 + 2 \\ y > x^2 \end{cases}$$

28. Find the area of this triangle.

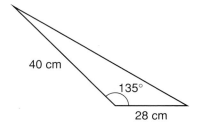

29. Factor $x^2 - 4x + 6$ over the set of complex numbers.

30. Convert 80 kilometers per hour to miles per hour.

LESSON 68 *Locus Definition of a Parabola • Translated Parabolas • Applications • Derivation*

68.A

locus definition of a parabola

We review by remembering that the graph of a quadratic function in x is called a *parabola*. The basic equation of a parabola that opens upward is $y = ax^2$ where a is positive. We show three parabolas with equations of this form below. The parabolas have their vertices at the origin and are all symmetric about the y axis. When a equals 1, the equation is $y = x^2$, as we show on the left. When x equals 1, the point on the graph is 1 unit above the x axis because $(1)^2 = 1$.

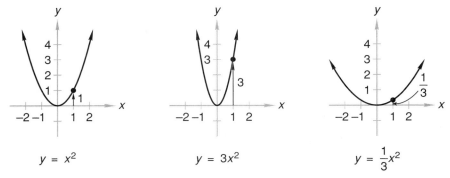

$$y = x^2 \qquad\qquad y = 3x^2 \qquad\qquad y = \frac{1}{3}x^2$$

In the center figure, when x equals 1, the point on the graph is 3 units above the x axis because a in this equation is 3 and $3(1)^2 = 3$. This makes the graph "skinnier" than the graph on the left. In the figure on the right, a equals $\frac{1}{3}$, so when x equals 1, y is equal to $\frac{1}{3}(1)^2$, or $\frac{1}{3}$, and the graph is "fatter."

We remember that the graph of $y = -f(x)$ is the reflection of the graph in the x axis. We can flip all three graphs upside down by placing a minus sign on the right-hand side of the equation, as we show here.

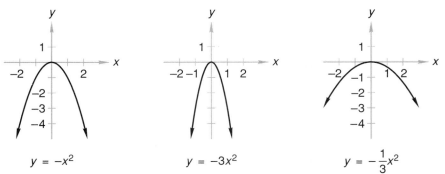

$$y = -x^2 \qquad\qquad y = -3x^2 \qquad\qquad y = -\frac{1}{3}x^2$$

We remember that a line is the locus of all points in a plane that are equidistant from two designated points, as we show on the left. Every point on the line shown is the same distance from points A and B.

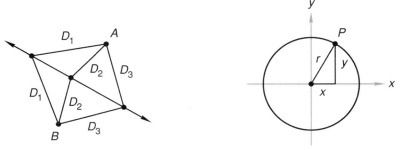

A circle is the locus of all points in a plane that are equidistant from the center of the circle. Thus, for the circle shown on the right, $x^2 + y^2 = r^2$.

Like lines and circles, parabolas can also be defined in terms of a locus of points that satisfy certain conditions, as we show in the box.

LOCUS DEFINITION OF A PARABOLA

A **parabola** is the locus of all points that are equidistant from a given point, called the **focus,** and a given line, called the **directrix.**

Though we will not do so here, we can prove that the graph of any quadratic function satisfies the locus definition of a parabola, and conversely, that the points satisfying the locus definition of any parabola that opens up or down lie on the graph of a quadratic function.

It can be shown that every parabola that opens up or down and whose vertex is at the origin has the form

$$y = \frac{1}{4p}x^2$$

where $(0, p)$ are the coordinates of the focus and $y = -p$ is the equation of the directrix. We show on the left below a parabola where p is positive and on the right a parabola where p is negative.

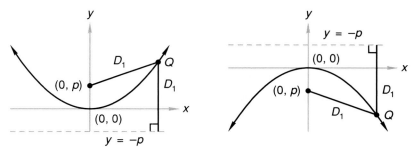

Note that for any point Q on the parabola, the distance from Q to the directrix is the same as the distance from Q to the focus. We can check this easily for the vertex $(0, 0)$. We see that the distance between the focus and the vertex is $|p|$ and that the distance between the vertex and the directrix is also $|p|$.

We summarize these facts about parabolas in the following two boxes:

The graph of the quadratic function $y = ax^2$ is a parabola whose vertex is $(0, 0)$, whose focus is $(0, p)$, and whose directrix is $y = -p$ where $a = \frac{1}{4p}$.

The parabola with vertex $(0, 0)$, focus $(0, p)$, and directrix $y = -p$ has the equation

$$y = \frac{1}{4p}x^2$$

In the problem sets, we may be given only two of the three pieces of information cited in the box (vertex, focus, and directrix). If so, we can use the locus definition of a parabola to find the missing piece of information. For example, if we are given that the focus of a parabola is $(0, 3)$ and that the vertex is the origin, we can deduce, using the graphs of parabolas drawn above, that the parabola opens up and has directrix $y = -3$.

example 68.1   Find the coordinates of the focus and the equation of the directrix for the parabola $y = \frac{3}{7}x^2$.

solution   Remember that the quadratic function $y = ax^2$ is a parabola whose focus is $(0, p)$ and whose directrix has equation $y = -p$ where $a = \frac{1}{4p}$. In this case, $a = \frac{3}{7}$. We solve for p.

$$a = \frac{1}{4p} \qquad \text{equation}$$

$$\frac{3}{7} = \frac{1}{4p} \qquad \text{substituted } \frac{3}{7} \text{ for } a$$

$$4p = \frac{7}{3} \qquad \text{took reciprocals}$$

$$p = \frac{7}{12} \qquad \text{divided by 4}$$

Thus the parabola has focus $\left(0, \frac{7}{12}\right)$ and directrix $y = -\frac{7}{12}$, as we show.

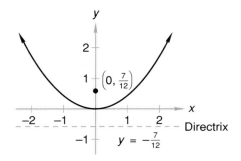

example 68.2   The focus of a parabola has coordinates $\left(0, -\frac{5}{3}\right)$ and the vertex is at the origin. Find the equation of the parabola and sketch it.

solution   Remember that a parabola whose focus is $(0, p)$ and whose vertex is at the origin has a directrix whose equation is $y = -p$. Also, the equation of the parabola is

$$y = \frac{1}{4p}x^2$$

In this case, $p = -\frac{5}{3}$, so the equation of the parabola is

$$y = \frac{1}{4\left(-\frac{5}{3}\right)}x^2 \qquad \text{substituted}$$

$$y = -\frac{3}{20}x^2$$

We graph the focus $\left(0, -\frac{5}{3}\right)$ and note that the directrix is the same distance away from the origin yet above the x axis.

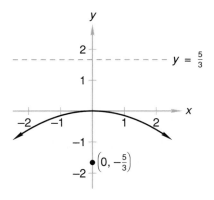

68.B

translated parabolas

So far, we have studied parabolas whose vertices are at the origin and whose axes of symmetry are the y axis. The equations of all such parabolas are of the form

$$y = ax^2$$

Now, we will describe the equations of parabolas whose axes of symmetry are vertical and whose vertices are no longer at the origin. Applying what we learned in Lesson 31 on translation, we describe the equation of a parabola whose graph is the graph of $y = ax^2$ translated h units horizontally from the origin and k units vertically from the origin.

EQUATION OF A TRANSLATED PARABOLA

The equation of a parabola whose graph is the graph of $y = ax^2$ translated h units horizontally and k units vertically is

$$y - k = a(x - h)^2$$

Using this fact, we can make the following statement:

A parabola whose vertex is (h, k) and whose focus is $(h, k + p)$ has as its equation

$$y - k = \frac{1}{4p}(x - h)^2$$

and axis of symmetry

$$x = h$$

We use the following diagrams as a reference. Note that if we know any two of the three pieces of information (vertex, focus, directrix), we can use the diagrams to figure out the third.

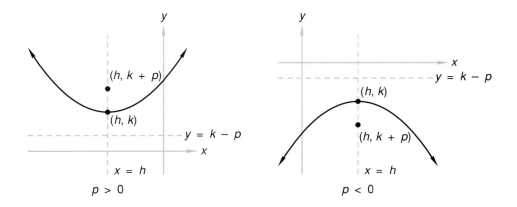

Note that if $p > 0$, then the parabola opens upward, and if $p < 0$, the parabola opens downward. Where the parabola lies on the coordinate plane depends on the location of the point (h, k).

example 68.3   A parabola has a vertex $(-2, 1)$ and focus $(-2, -1)$. Write the equations for the parabola, the directrix, and the axis of symmetry. Sketch the parabola.

solution   The vertex lies directly above the focus, so the parabola resembles the graph of a translated parabola that opens downward, as shown on the previous page. The vertex (h, k) is $(-2, 1)$, so $h = -2$ and $k = 1$. The focus $(h, k + p)$ is $(-2, -1)$, so $k + p = -1$. Using the fact that $k = 1$, we find that $p = -2$. We can now write the equation of the parabola.

$$y - k = \frac{1}{4p}(x - h)^2 \qquad \text{equation}$$

$$y - 1 = \frac{1}{4(-2)}(x - (-2))^2 \qquad \text{substituted}$$

$$y = -\frac{1}{8}(x + 2)^2 + 1 \qquad \text{solved}$$

Using the same graph, where $p < 0$, we find that the directrix is $y = 3$ and the axis of symmetry is $x = -2$.

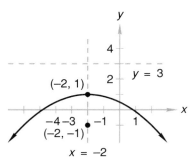

68.C

applications   The locus form of the equation of a parabola whose vertex is at the origin and whose axis is vertical is shown below. If p is positive, the focus is above the x axis and the directrix is the same distance below the x axis.

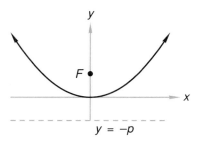

Parabolic reflectors have the shape formed when a parabola is revolved about its axis of symmetry. Parabolic reflectors are used in telescopes, microwave antennae, and searchlights. In the figure on the left below, we see that the surface of a parabolic reflector will reflect light rays that are parallel with the axis through the focus. In the figure on the right, we note that the same reflector will cause the rays from a source of light at the focus to travel outward as parallel rays. This is the way a searchlight is constructed.

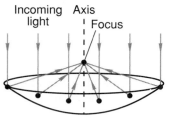

Parabolic reflector

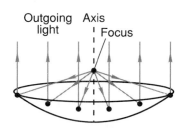

Parabolic reflector

example 68.4   The reflecting surface of a parabolic antenna has the shape formed when the parabola $y = \frac{1}{20}x^2$ is rotated about its axis of symmetry. If the measurements are in feet, how far from the vertex should the receiver be placed if it is to be at the focus?

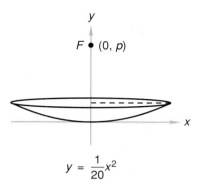

$$y = \frac{1}{20}x^2$$

solution   We see that a equals $\frac{1}{20}$. Thus

$$a = \frac{1}{4p}$$

$$\frac{1}{4p} = \frac{1}{20}$$

$$p = 5$$

Thus the focus is **5 feet** above the vertex and this is where the receiver should be placed.

68.D

derivation   We will use the locus definition of a parabola to derive the equation of a parabola whose vertex is at the origin, whose focus is $(0, p)$, and whose directrix is the line $y = -p$ where p is positive. Other cases can be worked out similarly.

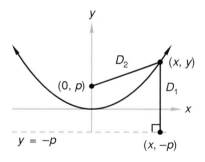

By the locus definition of a parabola, the distance from a point (x, y) on the parabola to the focus at $(0, p)$ is equal to the vertical distance from (x, y) to the directrix $y = -p$.

The vertical distance D_1 from a point (x, y) on the parabola to the directrix $y = -p$ is the distance from the x axis to (x, y), which is y, plus the distance from the x axis to $y = -p$, which is p. Thus $D_1 = y + p$. We use the distance formula to get the distance from (x, y) to the focus $(0, p)$ and find that $D_2 = \sqrt{x^2 + (y - p)^2}$. Thus we have

$$D_1 = D_2 \qquad\qquad \text{locus definition of parabola}$$

$$y + p = \sqrt{x^2 + (y - p)^2} \qquad\qquad \text{substituted}$$

$$y^2 + 2py + p^2 = x^2 + (y - p)^2 \qquad\qquad \text{squared both sides}$$

$$\cancel{y^2} + 2py + \cancel{p^2} = x^2 + \cancel{y^2} - 2py + \cancel{p^2} \qquad\qquad \text{multiplied}$$

$$4py = x^2 \qquad\qquad \text{simplified}$$

$$y = \frac{1}{4p}x^2 \qquad\qquad \text{solved for } y$$

**problem set
68**

1. The cleanup cost at Motel California varies linearly with the number of rooms rented out. When 20 rooms are rented, the cleanup cost is $250 per day; likewise, when 30 rooms are rented, it costs $325 per day. How much is the cleanup cost per day when all 50 rooms are rented out?

2. How many distinguishable ways can 5 identical red marbles and 4 identical white marbles be arranged in a line?

3. How many distinguishable permutations can be made by using the letters in *banana*?

4. The back wheels had an angular velocity of 400 radians per minute. If the wheels rolled along at 15 miles per hour, what was the radius of the wheels in inches?

5. Athos rode *m* miles in *u* hours and then walked *s* miles in *u* + 2 hours. At his average rate, how long did it take Athos to travel 100 miles?

6. When stereos were on sale, Richard purchased w^3a^2 stereos for *g* dollars. How many stereos could he have purchased for $750?

7. Find four consecutive integers such that the product of the second and fourth numbers is three greater than twice the product of the first and third.

8. A parabola has $y = -3$ for its directrix and its focus is at $(0, 3)$. Find the coordinates of the vertex and write the equation for the parabola.

9. The focus of a parabola has coordinates $(0, 3)$ and the vertex is at $(0, 1)$. Find the equations of the directrix, the axis of symmetry, and the parabola. Sketch the parabola.

10. The reflecting surface of a parabolic antenna has the shape formed when the parabola $y = \frac{1}{100}x^2$ is rotated about its axis of symmetry. If the measurements are in feet, how far from the vertex should the receiver be placed if it is to be placed at the focus?

11. The test scores were normally distributed with a mean of 78 and a standard deviation of 4.

    (a) Approximately what percentage of the scores lies between 74 and 82?

    (b) Approximately what percentage of the scores lies between 78 and 82?

12. Given the data:

$$253, 378, 422, 408, 294, 312, 211, 387,$$
$$275, 310, 400, 292, 366, 252, 396, 351$$

    Construct a stem-and-leaf plot. Then use a graphing calculator to help you draw a box-and-whisker plot of the data.

13. Sketch the graph of the function $y = \log_{3/2} x$.

Write the equation of problem 14 as a cosine function and the equation of problem 15 as a sine function. In problem 14, θ is measured in radians.

14.   15.

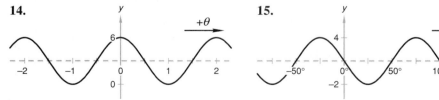

16. Multiply $(3 \text{ cis } 80°)(5 \text{ cis } 310°)$ and express the answer in rectangular form. Give an exact answer.

17. The equation $x^2 + y^2 + 10x - 2y = 1$ is the equation of a circle. Complete the square to change this equation to standard form. Find the radius and the coordinates of the center of the circle and then graph the circle.

18. Solve for *x*: $\begin{cases} ax - dy = s \\ bx + wy = k \end{cases}$

19. Use the result of problem 18 to solve for x: $\begin{cases} 3x - 5y = 10 \\ 4x + 2y = 22 \end{cases}$

20. Solve $(\tan x)(2 \sin x + 1) = 0$ given that $0 \le x < 2\pi$.

Solve the following equations given that $0° \le \theta < 360°$:

21. $\cos \theta - \cos \theta \tan \theta = 0$ **22.** $\sin 4\theta + 1 = 0$

Evaluate:

23. $\text{Arctan}\left[\tan(-120°)\right]$ **24.** $\csc^2\left(-\dfrac{3\pi}{2}\right) + \tan^3 4\pi - \sin^2\left(-\dfrac{3\pi}{2}\right)$

25. If $f(x) = \sec^2 x$ and $g(x) = \tan^2 x$, find $(f - g)(510°)$.

Solve for x:

26. $2 \ln(x - 1) = \ln(3x - 5)$ **27.** $3 \log_2 5 - \log_2 x = \log_2 x$

28. Simplify: $e^{3 \ln 5} - 10^{\log 3 + 2 \log 2} - \ln e^{-3}$

29. Find the area of this triangle in square feet.

30. Find: (a) $\text{antilog}_5 3$ (b) $\text{antilog}_3 4$

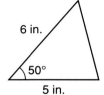

6 in.

50°

5 in.

LESSON 69   *Matrices • Determinants*

69.A

matrices   A **matrix** is a rectangular array of numbers or symbols that stand for numbers.

$$\begin{matrix} 4 & 7 & 5 \\ 2 & 3 & 5 \end{matrix} \qquad \begin{matrix} 4 & 8 \\ 5 & 3 \end{matrix} \qquad \begin{bmatrix} 6 & 1 & 5 & 2 \\ 4 & 2 & 8 & 7 \end{bmatrix} \qquad \begin{bmatrix} 7 & 1 & 8 & 3 & 2 & 5 \\ 5 & 6 & 4 & 3 & 3 & 6 \end{bmatrix}$$
$$\qquad\text{(a)} \qquad\qquad \text{(b)} \qquad\qquad \text{(c)} \qquad\qquad\qquad \text{(d)}$$

$$\begin{bmatrix} a & b & c \\ d & e & f \\ g & h & i \end{bmatrix} \qquad \begin{bmatrix} 4 \\ 7 \\ 3 \end{bmatrix} \qquad \begin{bmatrix} 5 & 2 & 8 \end{bmatrix} \qquad \begin{bmatrix} 7 & 4 \\ 3 & 5 \\ 8 & 6 \\ 9 & 3 \end{bmatrix} \qquad \begin{bmatrix} 3 \end{bmatrix}$$
$$\qquad \text{(e)} \qquad\qquad \text{(f)} \qquad\qquad \text{(g)} \qquad\qquad \text{(h)} \qquad\qquad \text{(i)}$$

The individual **entries** of a matrix are called the **elements** of the matrix and are always arranged regularly in rows and columns. All rows must have the same number of entries and all columns must have the same number of entries. It is customary but not necessary to use brackets to indicate that an array is being considered as a matrix. The **dimensions** (size) of a matrix are given by naming the number of rows and then the number of columns. Thus, (a) is a 2×3 (read "two by three") matrix; (d) is a 2×6 matrix; and (h) is a 4×2 matrix. A matrix may have only one row or one column. We note that (f) is a 3×1 matrix, (g) is a 1×3 matrix, and (i) is a 1×1 matrix.

Two matrices are equal if the entries in one matrix are identical to the entries in the other matrix.

$$\begin{bmatrix} 4 & 7 & 2 \\ 4 & 7 & 2 \end{bmatrix} \qquad \begin{bmatrix} 4 & 7 & 2 \\ 4 & 7 & 2 \end{bmatrix} \qquad \begin{bmatrix} 4 & 2 & 7 \\ 4 & 7 & 2 \end{bmatrix}$$
$$\qquad \text{(a)} \qquad\qquad\quad \text{(b)} \qquad\qquad\quad \text{(c)}$$

Thus, matrices (a) and (b) are equal matrices, but neither of these is equal to matrix (c).

69.B

determinants   If a matrix has the same number of rows as it has columns, the matrix is a **square matrix.** Every square matrix is associated with one real number called the **determinant** of the matrix. **If a matrix is not a square matrix, it does not have a determinant.** The determinant of a matrix is customarily designated by enclosing the matrix within vertical lines.

$$\begin{array}{cc} 4 & 3 \\ 2 & 5 \end{array} \qquad \begin{bmatrix} 4 & 3 \\ 2 & 5 \end{bmatrix} \qquad \begin{vmatrix} 4 & 3 \\ 2 & 5 \end{vmatrix}$$

$$\text{(a)} \qquad\qquad \text{(b)} \qquad\qquad \text{(c)}$$

Array (a) is a square matrix. Array (b) is also a matrix and brackets are used to call attention to the fact that it is a matrix. Array (c) is the same square matrix and we have used vertical lines to designate the determinant of the matrix. We find the determinant of a 2×2 square matrix by adding the product of the entries in one diagonal to the negative of the product of the entries in the other diagonal.

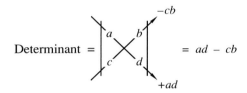

$$\text{Determinant} = \begin{vmatrix} a & b \\ c & d \end{vmatrix} = ad - cb$$

Sometimes one forgets which product is positive and which product is negative. As a memory device, we will superimpose the problem on a map of the United States and associate the minus sign with the cold waters of the North Atlantic and associate the plus sign with the sunshine of the islands of the Caribbean.

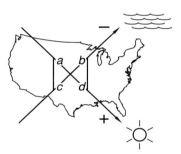

example 69.1   Evaluate: $\begin{vmatrix} -4 & -3 \\ 2 & 7 \end{vmatrix}$

solution   We remember that we use the minus sign with the lower-left to upper-right product.

$$\begin{vmatrix} -4 & -3 \\ 2 & 7 \end{vmatrix} = (-4)(7) - (2)(-3) = -28 - (-6) = \mathbf{-22}$$

example 69.2   Evaluate: $\begin{vmatrix} -7 & 5 \\ 3 & -4 \end{vmatrix}$

solution   The lower-left to upper-right product is preceded by a minus sign.

$$\begin{vmatrix} -7 & 5 \\ 3 & -4 \end{vmatrix} = (-7)(-4) - (3)(5) = 28 - 15 = \mathbf{13}$$

example 69.3   Find x: $\begin{vmatrix} x + 4 & 3 \\ 2 & 4 \end{vmatrix} = 18$

solution   The problem tells us that the value of the determinant is 18 and implies the following equation:

$$(4)(x + 4) - (2)(3) = 18 \qquad \text{equation}$$

$$4x + 16 - 6 = 18 \qquad \text{multiplied}$$

$$4x = 8 \qquad \text{simplified}$$

$$x = 2 \qquad \text{divided}$$

Problems such as this one afford practice with the meaning of the determinant notation and are encountered in more advanced courses in mathematics. They are implemented in computer software in types of problems called *eigenvalue problems.*

example 69.4   Find x: $\begin{vmatrix} x + 4 & 5 \\ 3 & x + 2 \end{vmatrix} = -5$

solution   This is another problem designed to emphasize the meaning of the determinant notation. The equation that results is

$$x^2 + 6x + 8 - 15 = -5 \qquad \text{equation}$$

$$x^2 + 6x - 2 = 0 \qquad \text{simplified}$$

We will use the quadratic formula to solve.

$$x = \frac{-6 \pm \sqrt{36 - 4(1)(-2)}}{2(1)} = \frac{-6 \pm \sqrt{44}}{2} = -3 \pm \sqrt{11}$$

Thus, x is either $-3 + \sqrt{11}$ or $-3 - \sqrt{11}$. If we use $-3 + \sqrt{11}$ for x, we get the determinant on the left. If we use $-3 - \sqrt{11}$ for x, we get the determinant on the right.

$$\begin{vmatrix} 1 + \sqrt{11} & 5 \\ 3 & -1 + \sqrt{11} \end{vmatrix} \qquad \begin{vmatrix} 1 - \sqrt{11} & 5 \\ 3 & -1 - \sqrt{11} \end{vmatrix}$$

Both these determinants have a value of -5.

problem set 69

1. The trip going was arduous, and it took 2 hours longer to cover the 160 miles than it took to come back. If the total time of the round trip was 6 hours, what was the rate going and what was the rate coming back?

2. The variable p varies jointly as the square root of m and as y^2 and varies inversely as x^2. What happens to p when y is doubled, m is quadrupled, and x is halved?

3. Four times the complement of an angle is $40°$ less than 2 times the supplement of the same angle. What is the angle?

4. Matildabelle ran and ran but arrived 20 minutes late. If she ran x miles in k minutes, how fast would she have had to run to get there on time?

5. Each year Darlene received a 20 percent salary increase over what she had been paid the year before. She worked for the company for 3 full years. If her total salary for 3 years was $29,120, how much did she make the first year?

6. Evaluate: $\begin{vmatrix} -4 & 6 \\ 5 & 2 \end{vmatrix}$

7. Solve for x: $\begin{vmatrix} x & 2 \\ 3 & x - 1 \end{vmatrix} = 4$

8. The focus of a parabola has coordinates $\left(0, -\frac{3}{10}\right)$ and the vertex is at the origin. Find the equations of the directrix, the axis of symmetry, and the parabola. Sketch the parabola.

9. A parabola has its vertex at $(-3, 2)$ and its focus at $(-3, -1)$. Write the equations for the parabola, the directrix, and the axis of symmetry.

10. Find the mean, median, mode, variance, and standard deviation for the following data: $-2, 3, -4, 5, -1, 0$.

11. If the data are normally distributed with a mean of 0 and a standard deviation of 1, approximately what percentage of the data lies between −1 and 2? (*Hint*: This is the same as the percentage between −1 and 0 plus the percentage between 0 and 2.)

12. Sketch the graph of the function $y = \log_{5/3} x$.

Write the equation of problem 13 as a cosine function and the equation of problem 14 as a sine function:

13.

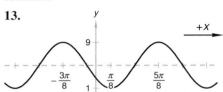

14.

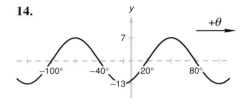

15. Multiply (6 cis 215°)(2 cis 205°) and express the answer in rectangular form. Give an exact answer.

16. (a) Convert $6 - 2i$ to polar form.

(b) Convert $5 \operatorname{cis}\left(-\dfrac{13\pi}{4}\right)$ to rectangular form. Give an exact answer.

17. Solve for y: $\begin{cases} ax + by = c \\ px + qy = d \end{cases}$

18. Graph the solution to the system of inequalities: $\begin{cases} y \geq (x - 3)^2 + 1 \\ y < x \end{cases}$

19. Find the distance between the point (−3, 8) and the line $x - y + 3 = 0$.

20. Find the area in square centimeters of the segment bounded by an arc of measure 110° and the chord which joins the endpoints of the arc in a circle whose radius is 0.6 meter.

Solve the following equations given that $(0 \leq \theta, x < 2\pi)$:

21. $\left(\tan\theta - \sqrt{3}\right)\left(\tan\theta + \sqrt{3}\right) = 0$ **22.** $\sin x + 2\sin^2 x = 0$

23. $\tan^2 x - \dfrac{1}{3} = 0$

Evaluate:

24. Arccos (cos 210°)

25. $\cot^2(-510°) - \csc^3(-510°) - \tan^2(-510°)$

26. Write the quadratic equation with a lead coefficient of 1 whose roots are $\sqrt{2} + i$ and $\sqrt{2} - i$.

27. Find the area of this triangle in square meters.

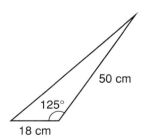

28. Solve for x: $\dfrac{2}{3}\log_4 8 - 3\log_4 x = \log_4 4$

29. Use a calculator to find: (a) antilog$_7$ 2.78 (b) antilog$_{13}$ 2.78

30. Find two functions f and g such that $(f \circ g)(x) = \ln(\log x)$.

LESSON 70   *Percentiles and z Scores*

In statistics we use different symbols for the mean and standard deviation of a population and the mean and standard deviation of a sample from that population. For a sample, $\bar{x}$, pronounced "bar x" or "x bar," stands for the mean of the sample and S_x, pronounced "S sub x," stands for the standard deviation of the sample. Suppose we select one thousand widgets at random in the United States and weigh them one at a time. If the mean of the weights is 10 pounds and the standard deviation is 2 pounds, we can write $\bar{x} = 10$ lb and $S_x = 2$ lb. Now suppose there are 130 million widgets in the United States and the mean weight of all the widgets is 11 pounds and the standard deviation is 3 pounds. We call the 130 million widgets the *population* because that is the total collection of all the widgets. We use the Greek letter μ (mu) to represent the mean of the population (11 lb) and the Greek letter σ (sigma) to represent the standard deviation of the population (3 lb). When we use standardized test scores, we compare the scores of individual students to the scores of the millions of students (the population) who have taken the test previously.

We remember that the mean of a set of data is the value on the x axis just below the peak value of the normal curve. Suppose two million seniors took the same test and that the distribution of the scores was a normal distribution with a mean score of 150. If the standard deviation σ was 10, we know that about 68% of the scores were within one standard deviation of the mean, or between 140 and 160, as we show on the left. About 95% of the scores were within two standard deviations of the mean, or between 130 and 170, as we show on the right.

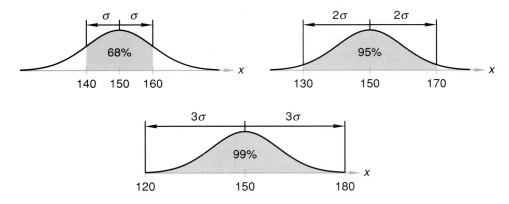

More than 99% of the scores lie within three standard deviations of the mean, as we show above.

Now suppose Charlie Mac and Zollie took the test the next year and their scores were 150 and 171, respectively. When they look at their scores, they do not care how close their scores were to the mean score. They want to know how high their scores were with respect to the scores of the students who took the test last year. Charlie Mac knows he scored higher than 50% of the two million students who took the test because his score equaled their mean score, which is in the middle (the mode, median, and mean are the same for a normal distribution). We say that Charlie Mac's score was at the 50th percentile. But at what percentile was Zollie's score of 171?

We show the equation for the normal curve on the left below. We can use this equation and a calculator to show that the total area under the normal curve is 1.00, or 100%.

$$y = \frac{1}{\sigma\sqrt{2\pi}}\, e^{-\frac{1}{2}\left(\frac{x-\mu}{\sigma}\right)^2} \qquad\qquad y = \frac{1}{10\sqrt{2\pi}}\, e^{-\frac{1}{2}\left(\frac{171-150}{10}\right)^2}$$

To find Zollie's percentile score, we will use the equation on the right. We replace μ with 150, replace σ with 10, and replace x with Zollie's score of 171. We can use a calculator to show that the area to the left of 171 is about 0.9821, so Zollie's score of 171 was higher than 98.21% of the scores. Thus, Zollie's score was just above the 98th percentile.

98.21%

171
Zollie

Instead of having raw scores on the x axis, we find it is more convenient to have a normal distribution whose mean is zero and whose x values are standard deviations to the left and right of the mean. On the left, we show a normal curve whose x values are our raw scores. In the center, we have subtracted the mean score of 150 from the raw scores. Thus, in this figure the mean is zero.

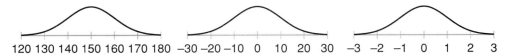

120 130 140 150 160 170 180   −30 −20 −10 0 10 20 30   −3 −2 −1 0 1 2 3

On the right, we have divided the scores in the center figure by the standard deviation, 10. The mean is still zero, and the numbers −3, −2, and −1 represent scores that are 3, 2, and 1 standard deviation to the left of the mean. The numbers 1, 2, and 3 represent scores that are 1, 2, and 3 standard deviations to the right of the mean. These numbers are called *z scores*. Now, to find Zollie's z score, we take her raw score of 171 and subtract the mean, which is 150. Then we divide by the standard deviation of 10.

$$\text{Zollie's } z \text{ score} = \frac{x-\mu}{\sigma} = \frac{171-150}{10} = 2.1$$

This tells us that Zollie's score was 2.1 standard deviations above the mean. The table below gives the decimal fraction of the scores below a given z score. The first digit, 2, of Zollie's z score is found in the z column on the left, and the second part, .1, is found in the z row on the top. We circle the number .9821 at the intersection, which tell us this score is just above the 98th percentile.

Standard Normal Table

z	.0	.1	.2	.3	.4	.5	.6	.7	.8	.9
−3	.0013	.0010	.0007	.0005	.0003	.0002	.0002	.0001	.0001	.0000 +
−2	.0228	.0179	.0139	.0107	.0082	.0062	.0047	.0035	.0026	.0019
−1	.1587	.1357	.1151	.0968	.0808	.0668	.0548	.0446	.0359	.0287
−0	.5000	.4602	.4207	.3821	.3446	.3085	.2743	.2420	.2119	.1841
0	.5000	.5398	.5793	.6179	.6554	.6915	.7257	.7580	.7881	.8159
1	.8413	.8643	.8849	.9032	.9192	.9332	.9452	.9554	.9641	.9713
2	.9772	.9821	.9861	.9893	.9918	.9938	.9953	.9965	.9974	.9981
3	.9987	.9990	.9993	.9995	.9997	.9998	.9998	.9999	.9999	1.0000 −

example 70.1   The mean weight of the babies born in a metropolitan hospital for seven years was 6.8 pounds with a standard deviation of 0.8 pound. If the distribution of the weights were approximately normal, what percent of the babies weighed less than 6.4 pounds?

solution   First we compute the *z* score for a weight of 6.4 pounds. We subtract the mean of 6.8 and divide by the standard deviation of 0.8 to find the *z* score.

$$z \text{ score} = \frac{6.4 - 6.8}{0.8} = -0.5$$

There are two rows that have a zero in the *z* column on the left. We choose the row that is marked with -0 because -0.5 begins with a minus sign. At the intersection of this row and the column headed by .5, we find the entry .3085. Thus, about **30.85%** of the babies weighed less than 6.4 pounds.

example 70.2   For example 70.1, what percent of the babies weighed between 6.0 pounds and 7.0 pounds?

solution   First we compute the *z* scores.

$$\text{For 7.0 lb} \qquad z \text{ score} = \frac{x - \mu}{\sigma} = \frac{7.0 - 6.8}{0.8} = 0.25$$

Now 0.25 is not listed on the table, but 0.2 and 0.3 are listed. We will approximate the percentile associated with 0.25 by averaging the values for 0.2 and 0.3.

$$\text{Percentile for } 0.2 = .5793$$

$$\text{Percentile for } 0.3 = .6179$$

$$\text{Percentile for } 0.25 \approx \frac{.5793 + .6179}{2} = .5986$$

Thus, a *z* score of 0.25 corresponds to the 60th percentile.

$$\text{For 6.0 lb} \qquad z \text{ score} = \frac{x - \mu}{\sigma} = \frac{6.0 - 6.8}{0.8} = -1.0$$

We find .1587 listed on the table under –1.0. Thus, a *z* score of –1.0 is very close to the 16th percentile.

To find the percentage of babies weighing between 6.0 pounds and 7.0 pounds, we subtract the percentiles.

$$.5986 - .1587 = .4399$$

Thus, about **43.99%** of the babies born in the hospital weighed between 6.0 pounds and 7.0 pounds.

example 70.3   In this same hospital, what percentage of the babies weighed more than 7.2 pounds?

solution   First we compute the *z* score.

$$z \text{ score} = \frac{x - \mu}{\sigma} = \frac{7.2 - 6.8}{0.8} = 0.5$$

Looking up 0.5 in the table gives us a value of .6915. About 69.15% of the babies weighed 7.2 pounds or less. We want to know the percentage which weighed 7.2 pounds or more. Thus, our answer is

$$100\% - 69.15\% = \textbf{30.85\%}$$

problem set 70

1. The number of squirrels varied linearly with the number of acorns available. When 1000 acorns were available, there were 20 squirrels, and when 3000 acorns were available, there were 30 squirrels. How many squirrels were there when 6000 acorns were available?

2. Ivy can complete 5 jobs in 4 hours. When Mike helps her, they can complete 9 jobs in 6 hours. How long would it take Mike to complete 1 job?

3. The *Dark Victory* could travel at ten times the speed of the current. Thus, the boat could travel 180 miles upstream in two hours less than it took to travel 264 miles downstream. What was the speed of the boat in still water and how fast was the current?

4. The variable J varies jointly as the square of H and as the cube root of A, and it varies inversely as S. What happens to J when H is doubled, A is multiplied by 8, and S is multiplied by 4?

5. How many distinguishable permutations can be made from the letters in the word *lilliputian?*

6. Gulliver found that the heights of Lilliputians were normally distributed with a mean of five inches and a standard deviation of one half inch. What percentage of the Lilliputians were between 4 inches and $5\frac{1}{2}$ inches in height?

7. The scores of a test are normally distributed with a mean of 75 and a standard deviation of 8. What percent of the test scores are less than 87?

8. Evaluate: $\begin{vmatrix} 5 & 1 \\ 7 & 2 \end{vmatrix}$

9. Solve for x: $\begin{vmatrix} x-2 & 4 \\ 1 & x+1 \end{vmatrix} = 0$

10. A parabola has its vertex at $(2, -1)$ and its focus at $(2, 4)$. Write the equations for the parabola, the directrix, and the axis of symmetry. Graph the parabola.

11. Sketch the graph of the function $y = \log_9 x$.

12. The equation $3x^2 - 12x + 3y^2 + 18y - 24 = 0$ is the equation of a circle. Complete the square to change this equation to standard form. Find the radius and the coordinates of the center of the circle and then graph the circle.

Write the equation of problem 13 as a sine function and the equation of problem 14 as a cosine function.

13.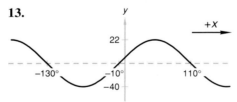

14.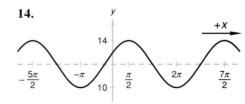

15. Solve for x: $\begin{cases} dx - wy = s \\ kx + jy = a \end{cases}$

16. Multiply $(5 \text{ cis } 72°)\left[-3 \text{ cis } (-312°)\right]$ and express the result in rectangular form. Give an exact answer.

17. Multiply $\left(6 \text{ cis } \frac{4\pi}{3}\right)\left(2 \text{ cis } \frac{\pi}{3}\right)$ and express the answer in rectangular form. Give an exact answer.

Solve the following equations given that $0 \le x < 2\pi$:

18. $(\sqrt{2} \sin x - 1)(\sqrt{3} - 2 \cos x) = 0$

19. $2 \cos^2 x + \cos x - 1 = 0$

Evaluate:

20. $\text{Arctan}\left[\tan(-210°)\right]$

21. $\sec^2 \dfrac{5\pi}{4} - \cos^2 \dfrac{7\pi}{4}$

22. Find the mean, median, mode, variance, and standard deviation for the following data: 1, 1, 3, 4, 7, 8.

23. Graph the solution to the system of inequalities: $\begin{cases} x^2 + y^2 \geq 4 \\ y \geq 2x^2 \end{cases}$

24. Find the area in square feet of the segment bounded by an arc of measure 60° and the chord which joins the endpoints of the arc in a circle whose radius is 8 inches.

25. Write the quadratic equation with a lead coefficient of 1 whose roots are $2\sqrt{3} - 2i$ and $2\sqrt{3} + 2i$.

26. Find the distance between the point (5, 2) and the line $3x - 4y - 2 = 0$.

27. Find the area of the triangle.

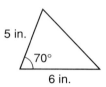

28. Solve for x: $\dfrac{3}{4} \log_7 625 + 2 \log_7 x = 2$

29. Simplify: $2^{\log_2 3 + \log_2 5 - \log_2 7} - \log_5 5$

30. Which of the following graphs most resembles the graph of $f(x) = \sqrt{1 - x^2}$?

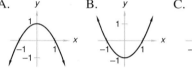 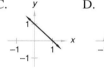

LESSON 71 *The Ellipse (1)*

We remember that a circle is formed when a circular cone is cut by a plane perpendicular to the vertical axis of the cone. If the plane is tilted slightly, the points of intersection of the plane and the cone form an ellipse.

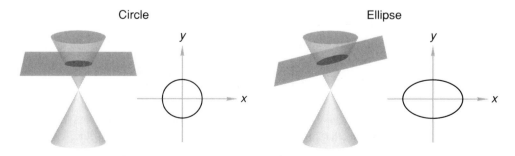

The ellipse can be thought of as a flattened circle. As we see at the top of the next page, the ellipse is formed about two points. Each of the points is called a **focus** of the ellipse, and collectively the points are called the **foci** of the ellipse. **The *ellipse* is the locus of points such that the sum of the distances from a point on the ellipse to the two foci is a constant.**

We can draw an ellipse by attaching the ends of a piece of string at F_1 and F_2 and holding the string taut as a pencil is moved around.

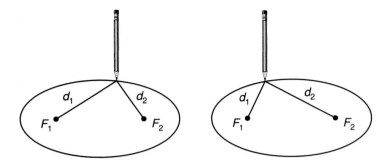

The length of the string is constant. Thus, the lengths d_1 and d_2 change, but their sum always equals the length of the string. The shape of the ellipse can be changed by changing the distance between the foci or by changing the length of the string. As we see in the following figures, if we keep the length of the string constant, the ellipse becomes more circular as the foci get closer together, and the ellipse gets narrower as the foci are moved farther apart.

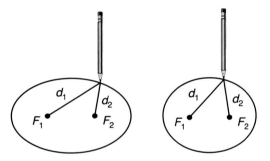

The ellipse has two axes. The axis that passes through the foci is always the longer axis, and it is called the **major axis.** The shorter axis is the **minor axis.** When graphed on a coordinate plane, the major axis can be horizontal, vertical, or inclined.

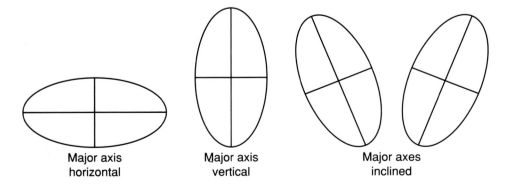

Major axis
horizontal

Major axis
vertical

Major axes
inclined

In this book, we will investigate ellipses whose major axes are vertical or horizontal and reserve the study of ellipses with inclined axes for a later course. It can be shown that the equation of an ellipse whose major axis is vertical or horizontal and whose center is the origin can be written in **standard form** as

$$\frac{x^2}{a^2} + \frac{y^2}{b^2} = 1 \qquad \text{or} \qquad \frac{x^2}{b^2} + \frac{y^2}{a^2} = 1$$

The letter a is always associated with the major axis. In the left-hand equation on the previous page, a^2 is below x^2, so the x axis is the major axis. In the right-hand equation, a^2 is below y^2, so the y axis is the major axis. **In both equations, the letter a represents half the length of the major axis and the letter b represents half the length of the minor axis.** The points $(a, 0)$, $(-a, 0)$, $(0, b)$, and $(0, -b)$ are called the **vertices** of the ellipse.

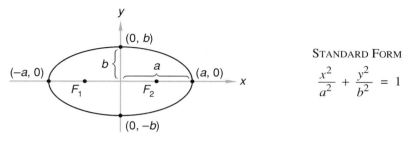

STANDARD FORM

$$\frac{x^2}{a^2} + \frac{y^2}{b^2} = 1$$

example 71.1   Graph the ellipse: $\dfrac{x^2}{25} + \dfrac{y^2}{9} = 1$

solution   First we will find the values of y when x equals 0. To do this, we set $x = 0$ and solve for y.

$$\frac{0}{25} + \frac{y^2}{9} = 1 \qquad \text{substituted } x = 0$$

$$y^2 = 9 \qquad \text{simplified}$$

$$y = \pm 3 \qquad \text{square root}$$

Now we let y equal 0 and find the values of x.

$$\frac{x^2}{25} + \frac{0}{9} = 1 \qquad \text{substituted } y = 0$$

$$x^2 = 25 \qquad \text{simplified}$$

$$x = \pm 5 \qquad \text{square root}$$

We have found the coordinates of the vertices and we can graph the ellipse.

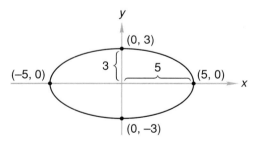

example 71.2   Write the equation in standard form and graph the ellipse: $5x^2 + 2y^2 = 15$

solution   To rewrite this equation of the ellipse in standard form, we must perform operations to make the constant term 1 and to make x^2 and y^2 be the only terms in the numerators. Thus, we begin by dividing each term by 15, and we get

$$\frac{5x^2}{15} + \frac{2y^2}{15} = 1$$

We simplify and rewrite the equation so that x^2 and y^2 are the only terms in the numerators. The standard form of the equation of the ellipse is thus

$$\frac{x^2}{3} + \frac{y^2}{7.5} = 1$$

Now if we let x equal 0, we can solve for y; if we let y equal 0, we can solve for x.

LET $x = 0$ LET $y = 0$

$$\frac{0^2}{3} + \frac{y^2}{7.5} = 1 \qquad\qquad \frac{x^2}{3} + \frac{0^2}{7.5} = 1$$

$$y = \pm\sqrt{7.5} \qquad\qquad\qquad x = \pm\sqrt{3}$$

We use a calculator to get decimal approximations for ease in graphing.

$$y = \pm\sqrt{7.5} = \pm2.74 \qquad x = \pm\sqrt{3} = \pm1.73$$

This time the major axis is vertical.

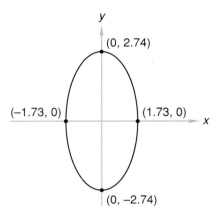

problem set 71

1. The boat could sail at 5 times the speed of the current in the river. Thus, the boat could go 144 miles downstream in 2 hours more than it took to go 64 miles upstream. What was the speed of the boat in still water and how fast was the current in the river?

2. Four times the sum of the number of reds and blues exceeded 3 times the number of whites by 3. Five times the sum of the number of blues and whites exceeded 8 times the number of reds by 13. If there were 5 more whites than blues, how many of each color were there?

3. How many different ways can 5 students sit in 5 chairs in a row if Mark and Ophelia refuse to sit next to each other?

4. Tristan can do 12 jobs in 15 hours; when Isolde helps him, they manage to do 25 jobs in 20 hours. How long does it take Isolde to do one job?

5. If x varies directly as y^2, inversely as z, and inversely as the square root of w, what happens to x when y is multiplied by 3, z is doubled, and w is quadrupled?

6. The sum of the length, width, and height of a rectangular box is 150 centimeters. The length is twice the sum of the width and height, and twice the width is 1 centimeter greater than the height. What are the dimensions of the box?

7. Graph the ellipse: $\dfrac{x^2}{16} + \dfrac{y^2}{9} = 1$

8. Write the equation in standard form and graph the ellipse: $9x^2 + 4y^2 = 36$

9. A doctor believes that the systolic blood pressure of her patients is approximately normally distributed with a mean of 120 and a standard deviation of 10. If she is correct, what percentage of her patients would have a systolic blood pressure greater than 135?

10. Solve for x: $\begin{vmatrix} \dfrac{x+1}{3} & \dfrac{1}{x-1} \\ & 1 \end{vmatrix} = 0$

11. Find the equation of a parabola whose focus is at $(0, -2)$ and whose vertex is at the origin. Also, find the equations of the directrix and the axis of symmetry and sketch the graph.

12. A parabola has its vertex at $(1, 2)$ and its focus at $(1, 4)$. Write the equation of the parabola. Also, find the equations of the directrix and the axis of symmetry and sketch the graph.

13. Sketch the graph of the function $y = \log_{2.2} x$.

14. The equation $x^2 + y^2 + 8x - 12y + 43 = 0$ is the equation of a circle. Complete the square to change this equation to standard form. Find the radius and the coordinates of the center of the circle and then graph the circle.

Write the equations of problems 15 and 16 as cosine functions:

15.

16.

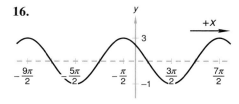

17. (a) Convert $-7 - 8i$ to polar form.

(b) Convert $7 \text{ cis } 270°$ to rectangular form. Give an exact answer.

18. Multiply $(3 \text{ cis } 40°)[2 \text{ cis } (-70°)]$ and express the answer in rectangular form. Give an exact answer.

Solve the following equations given that $(0° \le \theta, x < 360°)$:

19. $(2 \cos \theta + 1)(2 \sin \theta + \sqrt{2}) = 0$ **20.** $\cot^2 x = 3$

21. $\cot^2 x + \cot x = 0$

Evaluate:

22. $\tan^2 \left(-\dfrac{13\pi}{4} \right) - \sec^2 \left(-\dfrac{13\pi}{4} \right)$ **23.** $\sin^2 (-480°) + \cos^2 (-480°)$

24. Find the mean, median, mode, variance, and standard deviation for the following data: $5, 1, 7, 2, 5, 3$.

25. Graph the solution to the system of inequalities: $\begin{cases} x^2 + y^2 \le 9 \\ y \le x^2 \end{cases}$

26. Find the distance between the point $(0, -2)$ and the line $2x - 5y + 4 = 0$.

27. Find the area of this triangle in square feet.

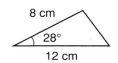

28. Solve for x: $\dfrac{3}{4} \log_8 16 + 2 \log_8 x = \log_8 x + 1$

29. Simplify:

(a) $\ln e - \log 10$ (b) $\ln e^3 + \ln e^{1/2}$ (c) $\log_2 4 + 4^{\log_2 15 - \log_2 5}$

30. Factor $x^2 + 7x + 15$ over the set of complex numbers.

LESSON 72 *One Side Plus Two Other Parts • Law of Sines*

72.A
one side plus two other parts

The Greek word *gonia* means "angle." *Trigonon* means "three angles," and *metron* means "measure." This is the reason we use the word *trigonometry* to describe the study of the measures of triangles.

Triangles have six principal parts: three sides and three angles. **If the length of one side and the measures of two other parts are known, it is possible to solve for the measures of the missing parts. We cannot solve for the missing parts if we do not know the length of at least one side.**

Thus, if the triangle is a right triangle, all we need to know is the length of one side and either the measure of a second angle or the length of a second side.

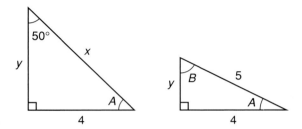

We can solve both of the above right triangles for the missing parts because we know the length of one side and also know the measure of one other part. In the triangle on the left, the other given part is an angle, and in the triangle on the right, the other given part is the length of another side.

A triangle that is not a right triangle is called an **oblique** triangle. **Any oblique triangle can be solved if one side and two other parts are known.** Oblique triangles can be solved by using the law of sines or by using the law of cosines, which we discuss in Lesson 81. The law we use to solve for the missing parts of a particular oblique triangle depends on which three parts of the triangle are known. In this lesson, we will investigate the use of the law of sines. The derivation of the law of sines is more meaningful after the usefulness of the law of sines has been demonstrated and the statement of the law is familiar. Thus, we will reverse the customary procedure by first learning to use the law of sines and postponing the derivation until a later lesson.

72.B
law of sines

A triangle has three sides and three angles. These parts are often labeled by using capital letters for the angles and lowercase letters for the sides opposite the angles, as we show here.

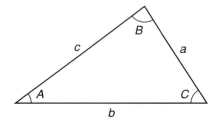

We will consider that an angle and the side opposite the angle constitute a **pair.** The law of sines gives us relationships involving lengths of sides and the sines of the paired angles and is normally stated as we show here.

$$\frac{a}{\sin A} = \frac{b}{\sin B} = \frac{c}{\sin C}$$

This statement is confusing to some because only two of these fractions are ever used at the same time. Thus, to use the law of sines, we will use one of the following forms:

$$\frac{a}{\sin A} = \frac{b}{\sin B} \qquad \frac{a}{\sin A} = \frac{c}{\sin C} \qquad \frac{b}{\sin B} = \frac{c}{\sin C}$$

We can solve any triangle if three parts (one must be a side) are known. If two of the parts constitute a pair, we can use the law of sines to solve for the missing parts.

example 72.1   Solve this triangle for the unknown parts.

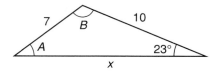

solution   We have a **pair** of knowns and thus can use the law of sines. First, we use the pair to write part of an equation.

$$\frac{7}{\sin 23°} = \underline{\quad\quad}$$

Now on the right-hand side, we must also put the length of a side on top and the sine of its **paired angle** below. We will use 10 and angle A.

$$\frac{7}{\sin 23°} = \frac{10}{\sin A}$$

Problems like this one are good problems for getting practice in the use of scientific calculators. First, we solve algebraically for $\sin A$.

$$\sin A = \frac{10 \sin 23°}{7}$$

Then we use a calculator to find a numerical value for $\sin A$.

$$\sin A = 0.5582$$

There are two angles whose sine is 0.5582. One is a first-quadrant angle, and the other is a second-quadrant angle. The calculator will give us the first-quadrant angle.

First-quadrant angle whose sine is 0.5582 is 33.93°.

Second-quadrant angle whose sine is 0.5582 is 180° − 33.93° = 146.07°.

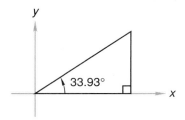

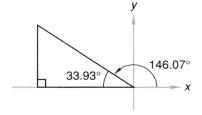

The word *ambiguous* means "capable of being interpreted in two or more ways." **The use of the law of sines to solve for an angle will always result in two possible values for the angle (unless both values are 90°).** Thus, we say that this use of the law of sines always produces an ambiguous result. We will discuss the ambiguity that results from this use of the law of sines in more detail in a later lesson. In this triangle, angle A is obviously less than 90°, so we will use the smaller of the two possible values for angle A.

$$\angle A = \mathbf{33.93°}$$

The sum of the angles is 180°, so

$$\angle B = 180° - 23° - 33.93° = \mathbf{123.07°}$$

Now we know angle B, so we can use the law of sines again to find its paired side, which is x.

$$\frac{7}{\sin 23°} = \frac{x}{\sin 123.07°}$$

We solve for x and get

$$x = \frac{7 \sin 123.07°}{\sin 23°} = \mathbf{15.01}$$

We note that there is no ambiguity when the law of sines is used to solve for a missing side.

example 72.2   Solve this triangle for the unknown parts.

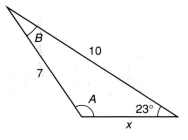

solution   We have a **pair** of knowns and thus can use the law of sines. The pair is the side of length 7 and the 23° angle. We also have the side of length 10, so we write

$$\frac{7}{\sin 23°} = \frac{10}{\sin A}$$

and we solve for the sine of A.

$$\sin A = \frac{10 \sin 23°}{7} = 0.5582$$

Again, there are two angles that have a sine of +0.5582. In the triangle of this example, we are looking for the value of an obtuse angle, so angle A has a value of 146.07°.

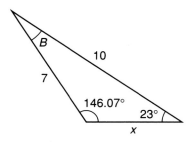

Now we find the value of angle B.

$$\angle B = 180° - 23° - 146.07° = \mathbf{10.93°}$$

The side of length x and the 10.93° angle form a **pair**, so we can solve for x.

$$\frac{7}{\sin 23°} = \frac{x}{\sin 10.93°}$$

$$x = \frac{7 \sin 10.93°}{\sin 23°} = \mathbf{3.40}$$

example 72.3   Solve this triangle for the unknown parts.

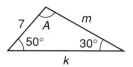

solution   There are 180° in every triangle, so angle A is **100°**. The side of length 7 and the 30° angle constitute a **pair,** and the side of length m and the 50° angle constitute a **pair,** so we can use the law of sines to solve for m and k.

$$\frac{7}{\sin 30°} = \frac{m}{\sin 50°} \qquad\qquad \frac{7}{\sin 30°} = \frac{k}{\sin 100°}$$

$$\frac{7 \sin 50°}{\sin 30°} = m \qquad\qquad \frac{7 \sin 100°}{\sin 30°} = k$$

$$m = \mathbf{10.72} \qquad\qquad k = \mathbf{13.79}$$

problem set 72

1. How many distinguishable linear permutations can be made from the letters in the word *calaboose*?

2. One of the beauties ran for the exit but arrived there 2 minutes late. If she ran y yards in m minutes, how fast should she have run to have arrived at the exit on time?

3. Clausewitz pays m men z marks for w weeks of work. How many men can he hire for one week if he only has 1000 marks?

4. The ratio of beauties to queens at the fair was 14 to 1. If 2550 women attended the fair and all were either beauties or queens, how many beauties attended the fair?

5. The sum of the last two digits of a three-digit counting number is 7. The sum of the first two digits is 5. The middle digit is 4 times the first digit. What is the number?

6. Ten times the complement of an angle exceeds 3 times the supplement of the same angle by 318°. What is the angle?

Solve the following triangles for their unknown parts:

7.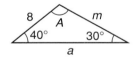

8.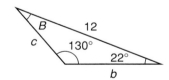

9. Graph the ellipse: $\dfrac{x^2}{16} + \dfrac{y^2}{25} = 1$

10. Write the equation in standard form and graph the ellipse: $4x^2 + 16y^2 = 64$

11. A biologist believes that the lengths of squirrels' tails are normally distributed with a mean of 8 inches and a standard deviation of 0.25 inch. If she is right, what percentage of squirrels have a tail whose length is between 7.6 inches and 8.2 inches?

12. Solve for a: $\begin{vmatrix} a - 1 & 1 \\ 2 & a \end{vmatrix} = 4$

13. Find the coordinates of the focus and the vertex and the equation of the directrix for the parabola $y = -\frac{1}{8}x^2$. Graph the parabola.

14. The reflecting surface of a parabolic radar dish has the shape formed when the parabola $y = \frac{1}{50}x^2$ is rotated about its axis of symmetry. If the measurements are in feet, how far from the vertex should the receiver be placed if it is to be at the focus?

15. Sketch the graph of the function $y = \log_{3.5} x$.

16. Write the equation of the sinusoid as a sine function.

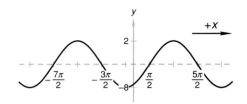

17. Write the equation of the sinusoid whose graph is a sine curve with a centerline value of $y = -10$, an amplitude of 20, and a period of π.

18. (a) Convert $-8 + 6i$ to polar form.

    (b) Convert $3 \operatorname{cis} (-420°)$ to rectangular form. Give an exact answer.

19. Multiply $\left(6 \operatorname{cis} \frac{3\pi}{5}\right)\left(3 \operatorname{cis} \frac{2\pi}{5}\right)$ and express the answer in rectangular form. Give an exact answer.

Solve the following equations given that $(0 \leq x, t, \theta < 2\pi)$:

20. $\sin^2 x \cos x = \cos x$

21. $2 \sin^2 t + \sin t - 1 = 0$

22. $\tan 2\theta - \sqrt{3} = 0$

Evaluate:

23. $\sin^2 \left(-\frac{2\pi}{3}\right) + \cos^2 \left(-\frac{2\pi}{3}\right)$

24. $\cot^3 90° - \sec^2 (-225°) + \csc^2 150°$

25. Find the mean, median, mode, variance, and standard deviation for the following data: 2, 6, 7, 7, 8, 3.

26. Graph the solution to the system of inequalities: $\begin{cases} x^2 + (y + 2)^2 \leq 9 \\ x^2 + (y + 2)^2 \geq 1 \end{cases}$

Solve for x:

27. $2 \log_7 x + \log_7 49 = 5^{\log_5 2}$

28. $\frac{1}{2} \log_8 16 + \log_8 x = 2 \log_8 (x + 1)$

29. Factor $x^2 + 3x + 10$ over the set of complex numbers.

30. Determine if $f(x) = \log (3x + 1)$ and $g(x) = \frac{1}{3}(10^x - 1)$ are inverse functions by computing their compositions.

LESSON 73   *Regular Polygons*

A regular polygon of any number of sides can be inscribed in a circle. The vertices of the polygon will lie on the circle, and the center of the polygon will also be the center of the circle. The same figure can be obtained by beginning with the regular polygon and drawing a circle that passes through every vertex.

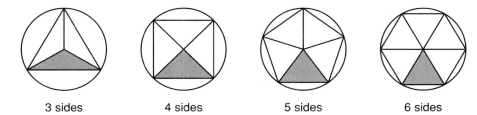

        3 sides   4 sides   5 sides   6 sides

We note that each side of the regular polygon forms the base of an isosceles triangle whose sides are radii of the circle. The area of the regular polygon is the sum of the areas of the triangles. The altitude of each of these triangles is called an **apothem** of the polygon. The apothem is also the radius of the circle that can be inscribed in the regular polygon.

example 73.1   Find the area and the perimeter of a regular pentagon (5 sides) that is inscribed in a circle whose radius is 6 units.

solution   There are 5 sides and 5 triangles. The 360° central angle is divided into 5 angles, each measuring 72°. The apothem bisects this angle and we have a 36° right triangle whose hypotenuse is 6. We can solve for x and the length of the apothem A.

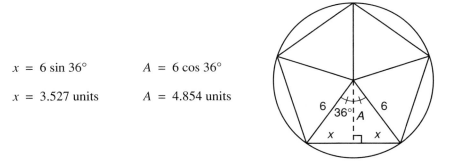

$$x = 6 \sin 36° \qquad A = 6 \cos 36°$$

$$x = 3.527 \text{ units} \qquad A = 4.854 \text{ units}$$

The area of each small triangle is half the product of the base and the altitude.

$$\text{Area} = \frac{3.527 \times 4.854}{2} = 8.560 \text{ square units}$$

There are 10 of these small triangles in the figure, so the area of the whole polygon is 10 times the area of one small triangle, or

$$\text{Area} = (10)(8.560) = \textbf{85.60 square units}$$

Each side of the regular polygon has a length of $2x$, or 2(3.527), which is 7.054 units. The perimeter of the polygon is 5 sides long.

$$\text{Perimeter} = (5)(7.054) = \textbf{35.27 units}$$

example 73.2   The perimeter of a regular polygon of 8 sides is 48. Find the area of the polygon.

solution   The central angle is 360° divided by 8, or 45°, and half of 45° is 22.5°. If the perimeter is 48, each side is 6, and half of 6 is 3. We can solve the triangle for the altitude A.

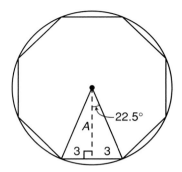

$$A = \frac{3}{\tan 22.5°} = 7.24$$

The area of one small triangle is

$$\frac{3 \times 7.24}{2} = 10.86 \text{ square units}$$

There are 16 of these small triangles, so the total area is

$$16 \times 10.86 = \textbf{173.76 square units}$$

problem set 73

1. Three women were redheads, two were blondes, and two were brunettes. How many distinguishable ways could the women sit in seven chairs if only the color of the hair was considered?

2. M men pledged to contribute equally to the purchase of playground equipment, which cost a total of $1000. If 5 men refused to honor their commitment, how much more did each of the other men have to pay?

3. Ares had h hours of homework to do, but he just worked w hours. What fractional part of his homework remains?

4. The woman is 3 times as old as her son. If she is half as old as her father, her father is how many times older than her son?

5. Three times the lesser of two numbers equals 2 times the greater. If the sum of the numbers is 70, what are the two numbers?

6. If x is an even number, what is the quotient of the next greater even number divided by the next greater odd number?

7. A six-sided regular polygon is inscribed in a circle whose radius is 6 inches. Find the area of the polygon.

8. The length of a side of an 8-sided regular polygon is 10 centimeters. Find the area of the polygon.

9. Two 12-sided polygons are similar. A side of the larger polygon is 9 times as long as the corresponding side of the smaller polygon. What is the ratio of the area of the smaller polygon to the area of the larger polygon?

10. Solve this triangle for the unknown parts.

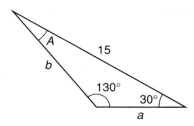

11. Write the equation in standard form and graph the ellipse: $4x^2 + 9y^2 = 36$

12. A manufacturer produces bolts whose lengths are normally distributed with a mean of 4.0 cm and a standard deviation of 0.1 cm. What percentage of the bolts will have a length between 3.94 cm and 4.14 cm?

13. Solve for b: $\begin{vmatrix} b+2 & 1 \\ -12 & b \end{vmatrix} = 12$

14. A parabola has its vertex at $(3, -2)$ and its focus at $(3, 5)$. Write the equations of the parabola, the directrix, and the axis of symmetry. Graph the parabola.

15. Find the coordinates of the focus and the vertex and the equations of the directrix and the axis of symmetry for the parabola $y = \frac{1}{9}x^2$. Graph the parabola.

16. Sketch the graph of the function $y = \log_{7/4} x$.

17. Write the equation of the sinusoid as a cosine function.

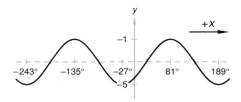

18. Write the equation of the sinusoid whose graph is a sine function with a centerline of $y = -2$, an amplitude of 6, a period of 2π, and a phase angle of $\pi/4$.

19. Multiply $(3 \text{ cis } 420°)(4 \text{ cis } 330°)$ and express the answer in rectangular form. Give an exact answer.

20. Solve for y: $\begin{cases} ax + by = c \\ dx + fy = g \end{cases}$

21. Use the result of problem 20 to solve for y: $\begin{cases} 2x + 6y = 14 \\ x - 4y = 8 \end{cases}$

Solve the following equations given that $(0° \le \theta, x < 360°)$:

22. $\sin \theta - 2 \sin^2 \theta = 0$

23. $\sec^2 \theta - 4 = 0$

24. $2 \cos^2 x - 3 \cos x - 2 = 0$

25. Evaluate: $\tan^2 (-690°) - \sec^2 (-690°) - \cot^2 690°$

26. If $f(x) = \cos^2 x$ and $g(x) = \sin^2 x$, find $f\left(\dfrac{\pi}{4}\right) + g\left(\dfrac{3\pi}{4}\right) f\left(\dfrac{5\pi}{4}\right)$.

27. Graph the solution to the system of inequalities: $\begin{cases} 16 \ge x^2 + y^2 \\ y > x - 2 \end{cases}$

Solve for x:

28. $\dfrac{1}{3} \ln 27 + 2 \ln x = \ln (2 - x)$

29. $\log_8 (x - 2) + \log_8 (x - 3) = \dfrac{1}{3}$

30. Use the locus definition method to find the equation of the line equidistant from the points $(-6, 4)$ and $(4, 9)$. Write the equation in slope-intercept form.

LESSON 74　*Cramer's Rule*

Most mathematicians are intrigued with the study of the patterns that one can obtain from arrays of numbers, and much of the mathematics that we have today is a result of the investigation of these patterns. The study of the patterns of the coefficients in systems of linear equations has evolved into what is known today as *linear algebra*. The first record we have of these investigations is in a letter to L'Hôpital (French) from Leibniz (German) in 1693. Euler (Swiss) and Maclaurin (Scottish) published works on the subject in 1748, and the opus of Gabrielle Cramer (Swiss) was published in 1750. The English mathematician Cayley is given considerable credit for work he did in the nineteenth century in this area.

One of the most famous patterns of coefficients is named for Cramer and is called **Cramer's rule.** It concerns the pattern of the coefficients in the solution of a system of linear equations. We have discovered that we can use elimination to solve a general system of linear equations for x and y, as we show here.

$$\begin{cases} ax + by = e \\ cx + dy = f \end{cases} \quad \begin{matrix} \longrightarrow & (d) & \longrightarrow & dax + dby = de \\ \longrightarrow & (-b) & \longrightarrow & -bcx - bdy = -bf \end{matrix}$$
$$(ad - bc)x = de - bf \quad \longrightarrow \quad x = \frac{de - bf}{ad - bc}$$

$$\begin{cases} ax + by = e \\ cx + dy = f \end{cases} \quad \begin{matrix} \longrightarrow & (-c) & \longrightarrow & -cax - cby = -ce \\ \longrightarrow & (a) & \longrightarrow & acx + ady = af \end{matrix}$$
$$(ad - bc)y = af - ce \quad \longrightarrow \quad y = \frac{af - ce}{ad - bc}$$

If we look carefully at the answers for x and y, we see that the denominators are the same and that the numerators are different. The men mentioned earlier found that these patterns are the same as the patterns we get from the following expressions:

$$x = \frac{\begin{vmatrix} e & b \\ f & d \end{vmatrix}}{\begin{vmatrix} a & b \\ c & d \end{vmatrix}} = \frac{ed - bf}{ad - cb} \qquad y = \frac{\begin{vmatrix} a & e \\ c & f \end{vmatrix}}{\begin{vmatrix} a & b \\ c & d \end{vmatrix}} = \frac{af - ce}{ad - cb}$$

We call this application of the patterns from square matrices *Cramer's rule*. Cramer and the others defined determinants so that the multiplications would produce these patterns. Thus, the rules for determinants were dictated by the requirement that the use of the rules would produce the solutions of the equations. We note that the elements of the determinants in the denominators are the coefficients of x and y in the given equations. For this reason, this matrix is called the **coefficient matrix.** The matrices in the numerators are different. **In the matrices in the numerators, the constants replace the coefficients of x when we solve for x, and the constants replace the coefficients of y when we solve for y.**

example 74.1　Use Cramer's rule to solve: $\begin{cases} 3x + 2y = -1 \\ 4x - 3y = 10 \end{cases}$

solution　The denominator determinant for both variables is composed of the coefficients of x and y as they appear in the equations.

$$x = \frac{\begin{vmatrix} & \\ & \end{vmatrix}}{\begin{vmatrix} 3 & 2 \\ 4 & -3 \end{vmatrix}} \qquad y = \frac{\begin{vmatrix} & \\ & \end{vmatrix}}{\begin{vmatrix} 3 & 2 \\ 4 & -3 \end{vmatrix}}$$

The numerator determinants are the same except that the constants -1 and 10 replace the coefficients of x when we solve for x and replace the coefficients of y when we solve for y.

$$x = \frac{\begin{vmatrix} -1 & 2 \\ 10 & -3 \end{vmatrix}}{\begin{vmatrix} 3 & 2 \\ 4 & -3 \end{vmatrix}} = \frac{3 - 20}{-9 - 8} = 1 \qquad y = \frac{\begin{vmatrix} 3 & -1 \\ 4 & 10 \end{vmatrix}}{\begin{vmatrix} 3 & 2 \\ 4 & -3 \end{vmatrix}} = \frac{30 + 4}{-9 - 8} = -2$$

example 74.2   Use Cramer's rule to solve: $\begin{cases} 5x - 3y = 1 \\ 2x - 7y = -17 \end{cases}$

solution   The denominator determinants are the same, and the numerator determinants are different.

$$x = \frac{\begin{vmatrix} 1 & -3 \\ -17 & -7 \end{vmatrix}}{\begin{vmatrix} 5 & -3 \\ 2 & -7 \end{vmatrix}} = \frac{-7 - 51}{-35 - (-6)} = 2 \qquad y = \frac{\begin{vmatrix} 5 & 1 \\ 2 & -17 \end{vmatrix}}{\begin{vmatrix} 5 & -3 \\ 2 & -7 \end{vmatrix}} = \frac{-85 - 2}{-35 - (-6)} = 3$$

example 74.3   Use Cramer's rule to solve: $\begin{cases} 3x + 2y = 5 \\ 3x + 2y = 8 \end{cases}$

solution   The denominator determinants are the coefficients of x and y. The numerator coefficients are different.

$$x = \frac{\begin{vmatrix} 5 & 2 \\ 8 & 2 \end{vmatrix}}{\begin{vmatrix} 3 & 2 \\ 3 & 2 \end{vmatrix}} = \frac{10 - 16}{6 - 6} = \frac{-6}{0} \qquad y = \frac{\begin{vmatrix} 3 & 5 \\ 3 & 8 \end{vmatrix}}{\begin{vmatrix} 3 & 2 \\ 3 & 2 \end{vmatrix}} = \frac{24 - 15}{6 - 6} = \frac{9}{0}$$

We cannot divide by zero, so Cramer's rule did not provide a solution. **No method will produce a solution because the graphs of the equations are parallel lines and parallel lines never intersect.** Thus, there is no value of x and y that will satisfy both equations.

The determinant of the coefficient matrix of the following system of equations is also zero.

$$\begin{cases} 3x + 2y = 5 \\ 6x + 4y = 10 \end{cases} \qquad \begin{vmatrix} 3 & 2 \\ 6 & 4 \end{vmatrix} = \frac{}{3 \cdot 4 - 6 \cdot 2} = \frac{}{12 - 12} = \frac{}{0}$$

Not only are the lines parallel, they lie on top of each other, so any value of x and y that satisfies one equation will satisfy the other equation. This system has an infinite number of solutions and does not have the single solution we get when the graphs of the two lines intersect in one point. In this example we considered the special case of two equations in two unknowns but the following statement applies to systems of equations in three unknowns or in any number of unknowns.

> **When the determinant of coefficients of a system of linear equations has a value of zero, the system does not have a unique solution.**

problem set 74

1. Galois arranged 8 identical red ones and 4 identical blue ones in a row. How many distinguishable arrangements were possible?

2. A rod is chopped into 3 pieces. The first piece is 3 times as long as the second piece, and the second piece is 3 times as long as the third piece. What fractional part of the rod is the shortest piece?

3. A piece of cloth y yards long had f feet cut from one end and n inches cut from the other end. What is the length in inches of the piece that remains?

4. Sam received $2\frac{1}{2}$ times his regular hourly wage for working on Saturday. On one Saturday he worked $2\frac{1}{2}$ hours and was paid \$40.25. What was his regular hourly wage?

5. Eleanor earned E dollars every month and spent P dollars. What fractional part of her income did she save?

6. A storekeeper sold N items for a total of D dollars and made a total profit of P dollars. How much did he pay for each item?

7. The horse galloped m miles at p miles per hour and then trotted m miles at k miles per hour. What was his average speed for the entire trip?

Use Cramer's rule to solve:

8. $\begin{cases} 2x - 3y = -4 \\ 4x + 2y = 8 \end{cases}$

9. $\begin{cases} 3x + y = -2 \\ x - 2y = -3 \end{cases}$

10. A 12-sided regular polygon is inscribed in a circle whose radius is 10 centimeters. Find the area of the polygon.

11. The length of a side of a 6-sided regular polygon is 4 centimeters. What is the radius of the circle that can be circumscribed about this polygon?

12. Two 14-sided polygons are similar. A side of the larger polygon is $1\frac{1}{2}$ times as long as the corresponding side of the smaller polygon. What is the ratio of the area of the larger polygon to the area of the smaller polygon?

13. Solve this triangle for the unknown parts.

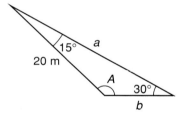

14. Write the equation of the ellipse $25x^2 + 16y^2 = 400$ in standard form and sketch its graph.

15. The scores on a standardized test are normally distributed with a mean of 100 and a standard deviation of 8. What is the percentage of scores that are greater than 120?

16. Solve for x: $\begin{vmatrix} x - 1 & 5 \\ 3 & x \end{vmatrix} = 5$

17. A parabola has its vertex at $(-2, 1)$ and its focus at $(-2, -2)$. Write the equations of the parabola, the directrix, and the axis of symmetry. Graph the parabola.

18. Sketch the graph of the function $y = \log_{8/3} x$.

19. Find the radius and the coordinates of the center of the circle whose equation is $x^2 + 10x + y^2 - 4y + 20 = 0$. Graph the circle.

20. Write the equation of the sinusoid as a sine function.

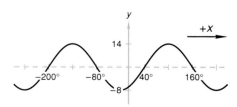

21. Write the equation of the sinusoid whose graph is a sine function with a centerline of $y = -1$, an amplitude of 14, a period of $360°$, and a phase angle of $-45°$.

22. Multiply $\left[4 \operatorname{cis}\left(-\frac{\pi}{3}\right)\right]\left(6 \operatorname{cis} \frac{4\pi}{3}\right)$ and express the answer in rectangular form. Give an exact answer.

23. (a) Convert $2 - 3i$ to polar form.

    (b) Convert $13 \operatorname{cis} \frac{5\pi}{6}$ to rectangular form. Give an exact answer.

Solve the following equations given that $(0 \le t, \theta, x < 2\pi)$:

24. $4 \cos^2 t - 3 = 0$ 25. $2 \cos 2\theta + 1 = 0$

26. $\sec x - \sqrt{2} \sec x - 1 = 0$

27. Evaluate: $\csc^2\left(-\frac{3\pi}{4}\right) - \cot^2\left(-\frac{3\pi}{4}\right) + \sec^2\left(-\frac{3\pi}{4}\right) - \tan^2\left(-\frac{3\pi}{4}\right)$

28. Solve for x: $\frac{1}{4} \ln 16 + 2 \ln x = \ln (6 - x)$

29. Simplify:
    (a) $b^{\log_b 24 - \log_b 6 + 2 \log_b 3}$
    (b) $2 \ln e - 2 \log 10^2$
    (c) $2 \ln e^4 + 4 \ln e^{1/2} - \log 10^5$

30. Factor $x^2 + 20$ over the set of complex numbers.

LESSON 75 *Combinations*

The number of permutations of 10 objects taken 4 at a time is the number of different **ordered sets** of 4 items that can be selected from a set of 10 items. Any one of the 10 can be first; any one of the 9 remaining can be second; etc. Thus we find that there are 5040 permutations.

$$_{10}P_4 = 10 \cdot 9 \cdot 8 \cdot 7 = 5040$$

A *combination* is a selection of items in which order is not considered. In this case, there are

$$4 \cdot 3 \cdot 2 \cdot 1$$

ways that 4 things can be arranged in order, and if we divide as shown here,

$$\frac{10 \cdot 9 \cdot 8 \cdot 7}{4 \cdot 3 \cdot 2 \cdot 1} = 210$$

we find the number of unordered sets of 10 things taken 4 at a time. **Thus, to find the number of combinations of 10 things taken 4 at a time, we first find the number of permutations of 10 things taken 4 at a time, and then we divide by 4! to remove the effect of order in each collection of items.**

We can write the general expression for the number of combinations of n things taken r at a time as the general expression for the number of permutations of n things taken r at a time divided by $r!$ to remove the effect of order.

$$_nC_r = \frac{n(n - 1)(n - 2)(n - 3) \cdots (n - r + 1)}{r!} = \frac{n!}{(n - r)!r!}$$

The expression for the number of combinations of *n* things taken *r* at a time has the same four forms as does the expression for the number of permutations of *n* things taken *r* at a time and has one additional form.

PERMUTATIONS: $_nP_r$ P_r^n $P_{n,r}$ $P(n, r)$

COMBINATIONS: $_nC_r$ C_r^n $C_{n,r}$ $C(n, r)$ $\binom{n}{r}$

The last form, in parentheses with the *n* above the *r*, is used only for combinations. Thus, we could write the expression for the number of combinations of 5 things taken 2 at a time in any of the five following forms:

$$_5C_2 \qquad C_2^5 \qquad C_{5,2} \qquad C(5, 2) \qquad \binom{5}{2}$$

At this point, we will note the way most authors use the words **permutation, arrangement,** and **combination.** The words *arrangement* and *permutation* are used to designate distinct ordered sets, while the word *combination* designates a set or collection without regard to the order of the members of the set.

example 75.1   In how many ways can a committee of 5 students be selected from a group of 12 students?

solution   First we will find the number of permutations of 12 people taken 5 at a time.

$$12 \cdot 11 \cdot 10 \cdot 9 \cdot 8 = 95{,}040$$

Now we divide this product by 5! because there are 5 people in each committee, and order does not count in a committee.

$$\frac{12 \cdot 11 \cdot 10 \cdot 9 \cdot 8}{5 \cdot 4 \cdot 3 \cdot 2 \cdot 1} = \mathbf{792}$$

It is interesting to note that each time we select an unordered set of 5, we leave behind an unordered set of 7. Thus, the number of combinations of 12 things taken 7 at a time should also be 792. It is, as we show here.

$$\frac{12 \cdot 11 \cdot 10 \cdot 9 \cdot 8 \cdot 7 \cdot 6}{7 \cdot 6 \cdot 5 \cdot 4 \cdot 3 \cdot 2 \cdot 1} = 792$$

example 75.2   There are seven points located on a circle, as shown. How many different triangles can be drawn using these points as the vertices?

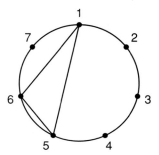

solution   First we will find the number of permutations of 7 things taken 3 at a time.

$$7 \cdot 6 \cdot 5 = 210$$

Every time the same 3 points are used the same triangle results, so the order of the points is not a factor. Thus, we divide by 3! to remove the effect of order.

$$\frac{7 \cdot 6 \cdot 5}{3 \cdot 2 \cdot 1} = 35$$

Thus, it is possible to draw **35** different triangles.

example 75.3   How many different 5-card hands can be dealt from a deck that contains 52 cards?

solution   There are 52 first possibilities, 51 second possibilities, etc., so the following product represents the number of permutations of 52 things taken 5 at a time.

$$52 \cdot 51 \cdot 50 \cdot 49 \cdot 48$$

Now we must divide by 5!, for each combination of 5 cards has 5! possible arrangements or permutations.

$$\frac{52 \cdot 51 \cdot 50 \cdot 49 \cdot 48}{5 \cdot 4 \cdot 3 \cdot 2 \cdot 1} = 2{,}598{,}960$$

There are **2,598,960** possible 5-card hands. We recommend the use of a calculator for calculations like this one.

problem set 75

1.   Amber called Tulsa on the telephone. The cost of the call was $4.40 for the first 3 minutes and $1.10 for each additional minute. Amber talked longer than 3 minutes. In fact, she talked m minutes. What was the cost of her phone call?

2.   There were p pupils in the junior class and they decided to spend D dollars on a school project to which all would contribute equally. Then 20 students refused to donate. How much more did each of the rest of the students have to donate?

3.   If p varies directly as m squared and inversely as the square root of N, what happens to p if m is multiplied by 4 and N is multiplied by 9?

4.   The big car was only averaging 7 miles per gallon of gas, so Bo Willy overhauled the carburetor. Now he uses only one third as much gasoline per mile. How many more miles can he go on 1 gallon of gas?

5.   If 8 points are spaced evenly on a circle, how many different triangles can be drawn using these points as the vertices?

6.   How many ways can a committee of 4 people be selected from a group of 8 students?

7.   Use Cramer's rule to solve: $\begin{cases} 3x - 4y = -3 \\ 2x + 3y = -4 \end{cases}$

8.   A 10-sided regular polygon is inscribed in a circle whose radius is 10 cm. Find the area of the polygon.

9.   The length of a side of an 8-sided regular polygon is 4 cm. What is the area of the polygon? What is the radius of the circle that can be inscribed in the polygon? (*Hint*: Recall that the apothem of a regular polygon is the radius of the circle that can be inscribed in the polygon.)

10.   Two 8-sided polygons are similar. A side of the larger polygon is $2\frac{1}{2}$ times as long as the corresponding side of the smaller polygon. What is the ratio of the area of the larger polygon to the area of the smaller polygon?

11.   Solve this triangle for the unknown parts.

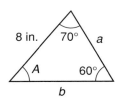

12.   Write the equation of the ellipse $5x^2 + 8y^2 = 40$ in standard form and sketch its graph.

13.   Solve for k: $\begin{vmatrix} 3 & k \\ k+1 & k \end{vmatrix} = 1$

14. Find the coordinates of the focus and the vertex and the equation of the directrix for the parabola $y = -\frac{1}{16}x^2$. Then graph the parabola.

15. Sketch the graph of the function $y = 1 + \log_2 x$.

16. Write the equation of the sinusoid as a cosine function.

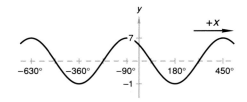

17. Write the equation of the sinusoid whose graph is a sine function with a centerline of $y = 10$, an amplitude of 6, a period of 4π, and a phase angle of $\pi/2$.

18. Multiply $\left[5 \operatorname{cis}(-120°)\right](2 \operatorname{cis} 660°)$ and express the answer in rectangular form. Give an exact answer.

19. (a) Convert $5 + 6i$ to polar form.

    (b) Convert $-7 \operatorname{cis}(-585°)$ to rectangular form. Give an exact answer.

Solve the following equations given that $0° \le \theta < 360°$:

20. $4 \sin^2 \theta - 3 = 0$ 21. $2 \sin \dfrac{\theta}{3} - 1 = 0$ 22. $\sin^2 \theta - 4 \sin \theta + 3 = 0$

23. Evaluate: $\cot^2 \dfrac{14\pi}{3} - \csc^2 \dfrac{14\pi}{3} + \sin^2 \dfrac{14\pi}{3} + \cos^2 \dfrac{14\pi}{3}$

24. Find the mean, median, mode, variance, and standard deviation for the following data: $3, 6, 9, -2, 0, 0$.

25. Graph the solution to the system of inequalities: $\begin{cases} y \le x^2 - 4 \\ x^2 + y^2 \le 9 \end{cases}$

26. Find the distance from the point $(1, 1)$ to the line $y = 3x + 2$.

27. Solve for x: $\dfrac{1}{3} \ln 8 + 2 \ln x = \ln(-3x + 2)$

28. Simplify:

    (a) $h^{3 \log_h 2 - \log_h 2 - \log_h 6}$

    (b) $5 \log 10^3 + 2 \log 10^{1/2} - \ln e^2$

    (c) $\log 10^{1/2} + \ln e^{3/2} - 6 \ln e^{1/3}$

29. Find: (a) $\operatorname{antilog}_6(-2)$ (b) $\operatorname{antilog}_2(-6)$

30. Factor $2x^2 - 5x + 6$ over the set of complex numbers.

LESSON 76   *Functions of (–x) • Functions of the Other Angle • Trigonometric Identities (1) • Rules of the Game*

76.A

functions of (–x)

We remember that the value of a function for a particular value of x equals the **directed distance** from the x axis to the graph of the function. We call this value $f(x)$. We call the directed distance from the x axis to the graph of the function the same distance on the other side of the y axis $f(-x)$. If the directed distance from the x axis to the graph of the function is the same at equal distances to the right and left of the origin, we say the function is an **even function.** In other words, if $f(x) = f(-x)$ for all x in the domain of the function f, we say the function f is **even.**

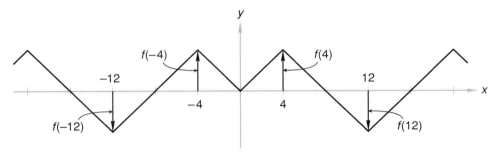

In the graph above, we note that the directed distance from the x axis to the graph is the same when x equals 4 and when x equals -4 because both graphs are the same distance **above** the x axis. Thus $f(4) = f(-4)$. The directed distance from the x axis to the graph is the same when x equals 12 and when x equals -12 because both graphs are the same distance **below** the x axis. Thus $f(12) = f(-12)$. We assume from the graph that $f(x) = f(-x)$ for all x in the domain of the function; therefore, the graph is the graph of an even function. **The graphs of even functions are symmetric about the y axis.**

If the distance from the x axis to the graph is the same **but in the opposite direction** at equal distances to the left and right of the origin, we say that the graph is the graph of an **odd function.**

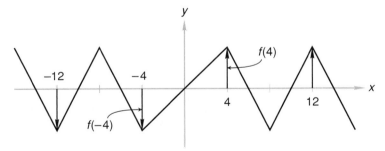

In this graph we note that the y values are the same but in different directions when x equals 4 and -4, so $f(-4) = -f(4)$. The distance from the x axis to the graph is the **same but in the opposite direction.** The same is true for x values of 12 and -12, so $f(-12) = -f(12)$. This is true at equal distances to the right and left of the origin, so the graph is the graph of an odd function. In other words, f is an **odd function** because $f(-x) = -f(x)$ for all values of x in the domain of the function f. **The graphs of odd functions are symmetric about the origin.**

Most functions are neither odd functions nor even functions because most functions are not symmetric. We often use θ as the variable in trigonometry, and we will find that the graph of $y = \sin x$ or $y = \sin \theta$ will show us that the sine function is an odd function and the graph of $y = \cos x$ or $y = \cos \theta$ will show us that this function is an even function. The sine function and the cosine function are the most important odd and even functions.

If we look at the triangles that we use to find the values of functions of 30° and −30°, we see that the sine of 30° equals $\frac{1}{2}$ and the sine of −30° equals $−\frac{1}{2}$.

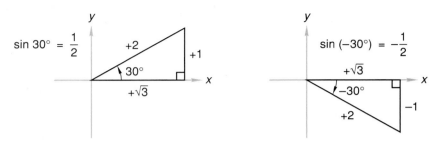

The sine of −30° has the same magnitude as the sine of 30° but has the opposite sign. Thus, we can say that

$$\sin(−30°) = −\sin 30°$$

If we increase θ so that θ is a second-quadrant angle and $−\theta$ is a third-quadrant angle, we get the same relationship between the sines of the angles.

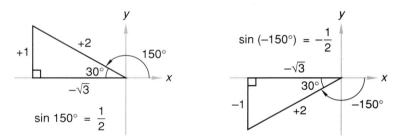

It can be shown that this relationship holds for all values of θ so that, in general, we can say

$$\sin(−\theta) = −\sin \theta$$

We can also see this if we look at the graph of the sine function. If we go a distance θ to the right of 0°, the vertical distance from the axis to the curve represents $\sin \theta$. If we go the same distance to the left of 0°, the vertical distance from the axis to the curve represents the sine of $−\theta$. The vertical distances have the same magnitudes but are measured in opposite directions! Thus, we see that $\sin \theta$ is an odd function.

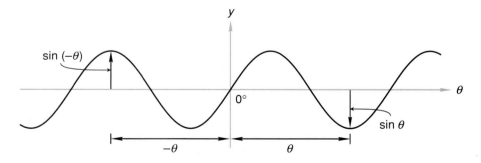

If we go back and look at the four triangles and consider the cosines of ±30° and ±150°, we get

$$\cos 30° = \frac{\sqrt{3}}{2} \qquad \cos(−30°) = \frac{\sqrt{3}}{2}$$

$$\cos 150° = −\frac{\sqrt{3}}{2} \qquad \cos(−150°) = −\frac{\sqrt{3}}{2}$$

Here we see that the cosine of 30° and the cosine of –30° have exactly the same value and that the cosine of 150° and the cosine of –150° are also exactly the same. It can be shown that this relationship holds for any value of the angle and its opposite. In general, we can say

$$\cos(-\theta) = \cos\theta$$

We can also see that $\cos(-\theta) = \cos\theta$ if we look at a graph of the cosine. The distance from the axis to the curve for any value of θ is the same and is in the same direction as it is for $-\theta$. Thus, we see that $\cos\theta$ is an even function.

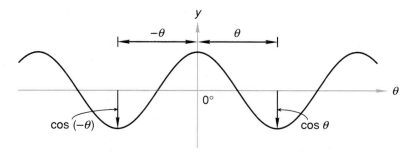

If we go back and look at the four triangles and consider the tangents of the four angles, we get

$$\tan 30° = \frac{1}{\sqrt{3}} \qquad\qquad \tan(-30°) = -\frac{1}{\sqrt{3}}$$

$$\tan 150° = -\frac{1}{\sqrt{3}} \qquad\qquad \tan(-150°) = \frac{1}{\sqrt{3}}$$

This relationship holds for all values of θ, so we can say

$$\tan(-\theta) = -\tan\theta$$

In a future lesson, when we study the graph of the tangent function, we will be able to see this relationship from the graph. Thus, $\sin(-\theta)$ and $\tan(-\theta)$ have opposite signs from $\sin\theta$ and $\tan\theta$, respectively, but $\cos(-\theta)$ has the same value as $\cos\theta$. Since the cosecant, secant, and cotangent are reciprocal functions, their sign relationships will correspond to those for the sine, cosine, and tangent, as we show here.

$$\sin(-\theta) = -\sin\theta \qquad \cos(-\theta) = \cos\theta \qquad \tan(-\theta) = -\tan\theta$$

$$\csc(-\theta) = -\csc\theta \qquad \sec(-\theta) = \sec\theta \qquad \cot(-\theta) = -\cot\theta$$

76.B
functions of the other angle

The sum of the angles in any triangle is 180°. If the triangle is a right triangle, the measure of the right angle equals 90°. Thus, if one acute angle is θ, then the other acute angle must be $90° - \theta$. We remember that if the sum of two angles is 90°, the angles are called **complementary angles,** and thus $90° - \theta$ is often called the **complement of θ.**

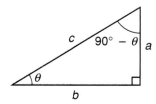

In the right triangle shown here, the sine of θ equals a over c, and the cosine of the other acute angle also equals a over c.

$$\sin\theta = \frac{a}{c} \qquad \cos(90° - \theta) = \frac{a}{c}$$

The cosine of θ equals b over c, and the sine of the other acute angle also equals b over c.

$$\cos \theta = \frac{b}{c} \qquad \sin (90° - \theta) = \frac{b}{c}$$

The tangent and cotangent have similar relationships.

$$\tan \theta = \frac{a}{b} \qquad \cot (90° - \theta) = \frac{a}{b}$$

$$\cot \theta = \frac{b}{a} \qquad \tan (90° - \theta) = \frac{b}{a}$$

The secant and cosecant have similar relationships.

$$\sec \theta = \frac{c}{b} \qquad \csc (90° - \theta) = \frac{c}{b}$$

$$\csc \theta = \frac{c}{a} \qquad \sec (90° - \theta) = \frac{c}{a}$$

Thus, the trigonometric functions of θ have the same values as do the trigonometric cofunctions of $(90° - \theta)$. We can remember this if we always think of $(90° - \theta)$ as the other angle.

$(90° - \theta)$ is the other angle

It is interesting to note that the words *co*sine, *co*tangent and *co*secant are abbreviations for the sine of the complementary angle (the other angle), the tangent of the complementary angle (the other angle), and the secant of the complementary angle (the other angle), respectively. Thus

cosine	**means**	**the sine of the other angle**
cotangent	**means**	**the tangent of the other angle**
cosecant	**means**	**the secant of the other angle**

76.C
trigonometric identities (1)

There is a difference between a conditional equation and an identity. A conditional equation is a true equation only for some specific value(s) of the variable(s), while an identity is true for any value(s) of the variable(s) for which the expression is defined. Consider the conditional equation and the identity shown here.

CONDITIONAL EQUATION   IDENTITY

$$x + 4 = 7 \qquad\qquad 2x - 3 = 3x - x - 3$$

This conditional equation can be transformed into a true equation only by replacing x with 3, which we do on the left below. No other number will satisfy this equation. The identity will be transformed into a true equation with any replacement value of x. We illustrate this on the right below by using -5 as a replacement value for x. Try another number in the identity, for any number will work.

CONDITIONAL EQUATION   IDENTITY

$(3) + 4 = 7$ used 3 for x $2(-5) - 3 = 3(-5) - (-5) - 3$ used -5 for x

$7 = 7$ true $-13 = -13$ true

If we avoid values of the variables that would cause division by zero, the two expressions shown here have identical values.

$$\frac{x}{1 + \dfrac{a}{b + \dfrac{1}{x}}} \qquad\qquad \frac{x(bx + 1)}{bx + 1 + ax}$$

For some purposes the form on the left might be preferred, and for other purposes the form on the right might be preferred.

Some algebraic expressions contain combinations of trigonometric functions, and often the solution of a problem will depend on the ability to change the form of one of these trigonometric expressions to an equivalent form that is more useful. The two forms of the expression have identical values and are called **trigonometric identities.** Learning to change the forms of these expressions can be thought of as a kind of game or puzzle. The solutions to these puzzles have no immediate applications, but the inability to change trigonometric expressions from one form to another can be a serious liability when you take more advanced courses in mathematics.

76.D
rules of the game

We will be demonstrating that an expression can be changed in form to the form of another expression or that two expressions can be transformed into identical forms. It is customary to eschew the use of the rules for solving equations, so we will not add the same quantity to both expressions nor will we multiply both expressions by the same quantity. Thus, we will restrict ourselves to three procedures. We may

1. Substitute an equivalent expression for any part of a given expression.
2. Multiply the top and bottom of any expression or the top and bottom of a part of any expression by the same nonzero quantity.
3. Combine terms that have equal denominators.

To begin identities, we remember that the cotangent, secant, and cosecant are reciprocal functions.

$$\cot \theta = \frac{1}{\tan \theta} \qquad \sec \theta = \frac{1}{\cos \theta} \qquad \csc \theta = \frac{1}{\sin \theta}$$

example 76.1   Show: $\dfrac{\cot x}{\csc x} = \cos x$

solution   A good first step for any trigonometric identity is to replace all tangents, cotangents, secants, and cosecants with equivalent expressions that contain sines and cosines. We will do that, and on the left, we substitute $\sin x$ and $\cos x$ as required and try to algebraically change the left side to $\cos x$.

$$\frac{\cot x}{\csc x} \qquad \text{left side}$$

$$\frac{\dfrac{\cos x}{\sin x}}{\dfrac{1}{\sin x}} \qquad \text{substituted}$$

$$\cos x \qquad \text{simplified}$$

example 76.2   Show: $\sin x \cot x = \dfrac{1}{\sec x}$

solution   We will work with the left side and replace $\cot x$ with $\cos x$ over $\sin x$.

$$\sin x \cot x \qquad \text{left side}$$

$$\sin x \, \frac{\cos x}{\sin x} \qquad \text{substituted}$$

$$\cos x \qquad \text{simplified}$$

$$\frac{1}{\sec x} \qquad \text{substituted}$$

example 76.3   Show: $\cos(-\theta) \sin(90° - \theta) = \cos^2 \theta$

solution   We will work with the left side and replace $\cos(-\theta)$ with $\cos \theta$ and replace $\sin(90° - \theta)$ with $\cos \theta$.

$$\cos(-\theta) \sin(90° - \theta) \qquad \text{left side}$$

$$(\cos \theta)(\cos \theta) \qquad \text{substituted}$$

$$\cos^2 \theta \qquad \text{multiplied}$$

problem set 76

1. There were 10 people present. How many committees of 8 could be selected from the 10 people?

2. A club has 10 members and wants them to pose 6 at a time for group pictures. How many groups of 6 can be formed from the 10 people?

3. The trombone was marked up 20 percent of cost to get a selling price of $480. It did not sell, so the dealer reduced the markup to 15 percent of cost. What was the new selling price? How much did 76 trombones cost at the new selling price?

4. Miranda is 1 year older than Roger. Eight years ago 3 times Miranda's age exceeded twice Roger's age by 6. How old will both of them be in 17 years?

5. Pushmataha ran as fast as he could, but he could only cover y yards in m minutes, so he arrived 15 minutes late. How fast should he have run to have arrived on time?

Show:

6. $\cos x \tan x = \dfrac{1}{\csc x}$

7. $\dfrac{\cot x}{\csc x} = \cos x$

8. $-\sin(-\theta) \cos(90° - \theta) = \sin^2 \theta$

9. Use Cramer's rule to solve: $\begin{cases} 6x - 4y = 5 \\ 3x + 2y = 6 \end{cases}$

10. A 5-sided regular polygon (regular pentagon) is inscribed in a circle whose radius is 12 inches. Find the area of the polygon and the radius of the circle that can be inscribed in the pentagon.

11. The length of a side of an 8-sided regular polygon is 5 inches. What is the radius of the circle that can be circumscribed about this octagon?

12. Solve this triangle for the unknown parts.

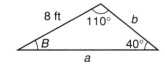

13. Write the equation in standard form and graph the ellipse: $6x^2 + 3y^2 = 36$

14. Ben calculates that the life of a certain type of light bulb is approximately normally distributed with a mean of 750 hours and a variance of 2500 hours^2. Approximately what percentage of the light bulbs will last between 740 and 780 hours? (*Hint*: First compute the standard deviation from the variance.)

15. Solve for a: $\begin{vmatrix} 1 - a & 3 \\ 2 & 2 - a \end{vmatrix} = 0$

16. A parabola has its vertex at $(-3, -2)$ and its focus at $(-3, 5)$. Write the equations of the parabola, the directrix, and the axis of symmetry. Graph the parabola.

17. Sketch the graph of the function $y = -\log_2 x$.

18. Find the radius and the coordinates of the center of the circle whose equation is $2x^2 + 2y^2 - 4x + 4y - 4 = 0$. Graph the circle.

19. Write the equation of the sinusoid as a cosine function.

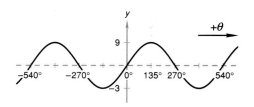

20. Write the equation of the sinusoid whose graph is a sine function with a phase angle of $-30°$, a period of $90°$, an amplitude of $\frac{3}{2}$, and a centerline of $y = -3$.

21. Multiply $\left[6 \operatorname{cis}\left(-\frac{7\pi}{8}\right)\right]\left(3 \operatorname{cis} \frac{13\pi}{8}\right)$ and express the answer in rectangular form. Give an exact answer.

Solve the following equations given that $(0 \le x, \theta < 2\pi)$:

22. $\csc^2 x - 1 = 0$

23. $2 \cos 4\theta + 1 = 0$

24. $\cos^2 x + 4 \cos x + 3 = 0$

25. Evaluate: $\tan^2(-510°) - \sec^2(-510°) + \sin^2(-510°) + \cos^2(-510°)$

26. Find the distance from the point $(2, 3)$ to the line $3x + 2y = 10$.

Solve for x:

27. $\log_7(x + 1) + \log_7(2x - 3) = \log_7 4x$

28. $\dfrac{1}{4} \log_{1/2} 16 - 2 \log_{1/2} x = 3$

29. Simplify:

   (a) $5 \ln e^{-2} - 4 \log 10^{-3} + 2 \log 10^5$ (b) $5 \ln e^{1/3} - 10 \log 10^{1/6} + \ln 1$

30. Use a calculator to find:

   (a) $\operatorname{antilog}_{17} 1.88$ (b) $\operatorname{antilog}_7 1.88$

LESSON 77 *Binomial Expansions (1)*

In mathematics, we often encounter binomials raised to a nonnegative integral power such as the four expressions shown here.

$$(F + S)^2 \qquad (a + b)^7 \qquad (x + y)^5 \qquad (2x + 3m)^4$$

When we perform the indicated multiplications and write the longer equivalent expressions, we say that we have **expanded the binomials.** If we look at the six expansions shown here, we see an interesting pattern.

$$(a + b)^0 = \qquad\qquad 1 \qquad\qquad\qquad \text{1 term}$$
$$(a + b)^1 = \qquad\qquad 1a^1 + 1b^1 \qquad\qquad \text{2 terms}$$
$$(a + b)^2 = \qquad\qquad 1a^2 + 2ab + 1b^2 \qquad \text{3 terms}$$
$$(a + b)^3 = \qquad 1a^3 + 3a^2b + 3ab^2 + 1b^3 \qquad \text{4 terms}$$
$$(a + b)^4 = \qquad 1a^4 + 4a^3b + 6a^2b^2 + 4ab^3 + 1b^4 \qquad \text{5 terms}$$
$$(a + b)^5 = \quad 1a^5 + 5a^4b + 10a^3b^2 + 10a^2b^3 + 5ab^4 + 1b^5 \qquad \text{6 terms}$$

We notice that the number of terms in each expansion is 1 greater than the power of the binomial. The expansion of $(a + b)^2$ has 3 terms, the expansion of $(a + b)^5$ has 6 terms, etc. Further, we note that the first and last terms in the expansions contain only 1 variable and that each of these variables has the same exponent as does the binomial. Also, we note that the exponent of one of the variables increases with each term while the exponent of the other variable decreases, and that the sum of the exponents in each term is a constant. If we use a small box ☐ to represent the coefficient of each term, we can concentrate on the exponents. If we do this for the last line above for the expansion of $(a + b)^5$ and use a^0 and b^0 as necessary to complete the pattern, we get

$$☐\,a^5b^0 + ☐\,a^4b^1 + ☐\,a^3b^2 + ☐\,a^2b^3 + ☐\,a^1b^4 + ☐\,a^0b^5$$

Exponent of a	5	4	3	2	1	0
Exponent of b	0	1	2	3	4	5

A similar pattern of exponents occurs in every expansion. Now, if we disregard the variables and look only at the coefficients in the expansions, we get the following triangular array.

$$(a + b)^0 \qquad\qquad\qquad 1$$
$$(a + b)^1 \qquad\qquad\qquad 1 \quad 1$$
$$(a + b)^2 \qquad\qquad\quad 1 \quad 2 \quad 1$$
$$(a + b)^3 \qquad\qquad 1 \quad 3 \quad 3 \quad 1$$
$$(a + b)^4 \qquad\quad 1 \quad 4 \quad 6 \quad 4 \quad 1$$
$$(a + b)^5 \qquad 1 \quad 5 \quad 10 \quad 10 \quad 5 \quad 1$$
$$(a + b)^6 \quad 1 \quad 6 \quad 15 \quad 20 \quad 15 \quad 6 \quad 1$$

We note that each number is the sum of the two numbers just above it, as we have indicated in three places. This pattern of coefficients is called **Pascal's triangle.** It is easy to reconstruct because the first entry in each row is 1 and the last entry in each row is 1, and there are three 1s at the top.

When we use the patterns just investigated to write the terms of binomial expansions, we do not have to go through the laborious process of multiplying out the binomial expansion. The same patterns always occur, and it is easier to remember the patterns than it is to perform the indicated multiplications.

example 77.1   Write the fourth term of $(x + y)^6$.

solution   First we write the exponents for x and y in order.

Term	①	②	③	④	⑤	⑥	⑦
For x	6	5	4	3	2	1	0
For y	0	1	2	3	4	5	6

Now from the seventh row of Pascal's triangle, we get the coefficients.

Term	①	②	③	④	⑤	⑥	⑦
Coefficient	1	6	15	20	15	6	1

Thus, the fourth term is $\mathbf{20x^3y^3}$.

example 77.2   Write all eight terms of the expansion of $(x + y)^7$.

solution   First we write the exponents.

$$\text{For } x \quad 7 \ 6 \ 5 \ 4 \ 3 \ 2 \ 1 \ 0$$
$$\text{For } y \quad 0 \ 1 \ 2 \ 3 \ 4 \ 5 \ 6 \ 7$$

Now we use the eighth row of Pascal's triangle to write the coefficients and get

$$1 \ \ 7 \ \ 21 \ \ 35 \ \ 35 \ \ 21 \ \ 7 \ \ 1$$

Now we can write the complete expansion.

$$(x + y)^7 = x^7 + 7x^6y + 21x^5y^2 + 35x^4y^3 + 35x^3y^4 + 21x^2y^5 + 7xy^6 + y^7$$

problem set 77

1. How many different 5-player basketball teams could be formed from 9 players? Assume that anyone can play any position.

2. On a 600-mile trip, the traveler traveled at 50 miles per hour for the first one third of the trip and at 40 miles per hour for the rest of the trip. What was the traveler's average speed for the entire trip?

3. Twiddybums sell for $200 each, but students get a 12% discount. If students pay cash, the student price is reduced another 6% of the original price. What would a student who paid cash have to pay for 4 twiddybums?

4. The city has an assessed valuation of $6,400,000. The rate for school taxes is 80¢ per $100 valuation. If all but 2% of the taxes have been collected, how many dollars have not been collected?

5. Find three consecutive positive integers such that the product of the first and the third exceeds the second by 19.

6. If x is an odd number, what is the quotient of the next greater odd number divided by the next greater even number?

7. Write all five terms of $(x + y)^4$.   8. Write the third term of $(x + y)^7$.

Show:

9. $\sin x \sec x = \tan x$ 10. $\sec x \cot x = \csc x$

11. $\sin (-\theta) \tan (90° - \theta) = -\cos \theta$

12. Use Cramer's rule to solve: $\begin{cases} 4x - 2y = 6 \\ 3x - y = 7 \end{cases}$

13. What is the radius of the circle that can be circumscribed about a 6-sided regular polygon (regular hexagon) whose perimeter is 36 centimeters? What is the radius of the circle that can be inscribed inside the regular hexagon?

14. Solve this triangle for angle A and side a.

15. Write the equation of the ellipse $8x^2 + 2y^2 = 16$ in standard form and graph.

16. The scores on a test are normally distributed with a mean of 75 and a standard deviation of 5. What is the percentage of scores that are greater than 82?

17. Solve for s: $\begin{vmatrix} 1 + s & -2 \\ s & 2s - 1 \end{vmatrix} = 0$

18. A parabola has its vertex at $(4, 3)$ and its focus at $(4, 0)$. Write the equations of the parabola, the directrix, and the axis of symmetry. Graph the parabola.

19. Write the equation of the sinusoid as a cosine function.

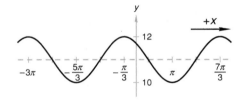

20. Write the equation of the sinusoid whose graph is a sine function with an amplitude of 7, a period of 540°, a centerline of $y = -3$, and a phase angle of 60°.

21. Multiply $\left[4 \text{ cis} (-30°)\right]\left[2 \text{ cis} (-270°)\right]$ and express the answer in rectangular form. Give an exact answer.

Solve the following equations given that $(0° \le x, \theta < 360°)$:

22. $3 \cot^2 x - 1 = 0$

23. $\sqrt{3} \tan 4\theta - 1 = 0$

24. If $f(x) = \csc^2 x$ and $g(x) = \cot^2 x$, find $f\left(\dfrac{19\pi}{3}\right) - g\left(\dfrac{19\pi}{3}\right)$.

25. Find the distance from the point $(1, -4)$ to the line $x - y + 2 = 0$.

26. Graph the solution to the system of inequalities: $\begin{cases} x^2 + y^2 - 6x + 4y + 12 \le 0 \\ 2x^2 + 2y^2 + 8y \le 10 \end{cases}$

27. Find x.

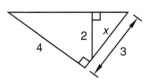

28. Solve for x: $\log_8 (x - 1) - \log_8 (x - 2) = 2 \log_8 3$

29. Simplify:

    (a) $3 \log_7 7 + 7^{2 \log_7 3 - \log_7 3}$

    (b) $4 \log 10^2 - 2 \log 10 + \ln e^{-2}$

    (c) $2 \ln e^{2/3} - \log 10^{1/2} - 4 \log_3 3^{1/12}$

30. If $f(x) = 2x^2 - 3x + 1$, find $\dfrac{f(x + h) - f(x)}{h}$.

LESSON 78   *The Hyperbola*

We remember that an ellipse is the locus of all points such that the **sum of the distances** from any point on the ellipse to two fixed points is a constant. The fixed points are called the foci of the ellipse. The standard form of the equation of an ellipse is shown.

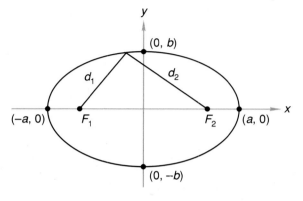

STANDARD FORM
OF THE EQUATION OF AN ELLIPSE
WITH CENTER AT THE ORIGIN

$$\frac{x^2}{a^2} + \frac{y^2}{b^2} = 1$$

$$d_1 + d_2 = \text{constant}$$

Note that the distance a is one half the length of the major axis of the ellipse and that the distance b is one half the length of the minor axis.

The hyperbola is another type of conic section whose locus definition and equation are similar to those of the ellipse. However, its graph is very different. The **hyperbola** is defined to be the locus of all points such that the **absolute value of the difference of the distances** from any point on the hyperbola to two fixed points is a constant.

$$\left| \text{Distance}_1 - \text{distance}_2 \right| = \text{constant}$$

A hyperbola is formed from two curves, each the mirror image of the other. It can be shown that the equation of a hyperbola whose center is at the origin and whose foci are on the x axis can be written as follows:

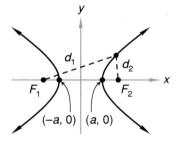

STANDARD FORM
OF THE EQUATION OF A HYPERBOLA
WITH CENTER AT THE ORIGIN AND FOCI
ON THE X AXIS

$$\frac{x^2}{a^2} - \frac{y^2}{b^2} = 1$$

Note that in this equation the minus sign goes with the y^2 term. If the minus sign goes with the x^2 term, as in the next equation, we find that the orientation of the figure is changed.

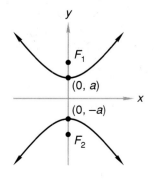

STANDARD FORM
OF THE EQUATION OF A HYPERBOLA
WITH CENTER AT THE ORIGIN AND FOCI
ON THE Y AXIS

$$\frac{y^2}{a^2} - \frac{x^2}{b^2} = 1$$

In the examples we will show how to sketch various hyperbolas whose equations are given. Associated with each hyperbola are two intersecting lines called **asymptotes.** Asymptotes of a hyperbola are straight lines that the graph of the hyperbola approaches but never quite reaches.

example 78.1   Sketch the hyperbola $\dfrac{x^2}{9} - \dfrac{y^2}{4} = 1$, and find the equations of the asymptotes.

solution   We let $y = 0$ and solve for x.

$$\frac{x^2}{9} - \frac{0}{4} = 1$$

$$x^2 = 9$$

$$x = \pm 3$$

Thus we see that when $y = 0$, x can be either $+3$ or -3, so the hyperbola passes through the points $(3, 0)$ and $(-3, 0)$. From the graph of the hyperbola that we will draw, we will see that these points are the **vertices** of the hyperbola. Now we let $x = 0$ and solve for y.

$$\frac{0}{9} - \frac{y^2}{4} = 1$$

$$y^2 = -4$$

$$y = \pm 2i$$

The points $(0, 2i)$ and $(0, -2i)$ cannot be graphed on a real-number rectangular system. Yet, it can be shown that the points $(0, -2)$ and $(0, 2)$ and the points $(-3, 0)$ and $(3, 0)$ can be used to form a rectangle whose diagonals are the asymptotes of the hyperbola.

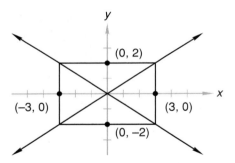

Now we can sketch the hyperbola. The graph goes through the points $(-3, 0)$ and $(3, 0)$ and gets closer and closer to the asymptotes as we get farther and farther from the center of the figure.

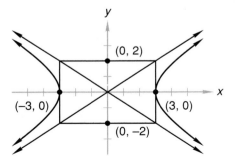

The coordinates of the upper right-hand corner of the rectangle are $(3, 2)$ and the asymptote that passes through this point also passes through the origin. We can use this information to write the equation of this asymptote as $y = \frac{2}{3}x$. The other asymptote passes through the origin and the point $(-3, 2)$. This information allows us to find that the equation of that asymptote is $y = -\frac{2}{3}x$.

example 78.2   Sketch the hyperbola $\dfrac{y^2}{4} - \dfrac{x^2}{25} = 1$, and find the equations of the asymptotes.

solution   To find the coordinates of the vertices, we set $x = 0$ and solve for y.

$$\frac{y^2}{4} - \frac{0}{25} = 1$$

$$y^2 = 4$$

$$y = \pm 2$$

Thus, the coordinates of the vertices are $(0, 2)$ and $(0, -2)$. To find the coordinates on the other sides of the asymptote rectangle, we set $y = 0$ and solve for x.

$$\frac{0}{4} - \frac{x^2}{25} = 1$$

$$x = \pm 5i$$

Thus, the other coordinates on the asymptote rectangle are $(5, 0)$ and $(-5, 0)$. We graph the points, draw the asymptotes, and then sketch the hyperbola.

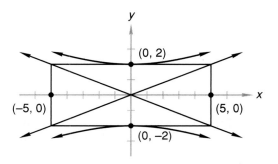

The coordinates of the upper right-hand corner of the rectangle are $(5, 2)$, and the asymptote that passes through this point also passes through the origin. We use this information to write the equation of this asymptote as $\boldsymbol{y = \frac{2}{5}x}$. The other asymptote passes through the point $(-5, 2)$, and thus the equation of the other asymptote is $\boldsymbol{y = -\frac{2}{5}x}$.

example 78.3   Given the hyperbola $4y^2 - 9x^2 - 36 = 0$, write the equation in standard form and find the vertices and the equations of the asymptotes. Graph the hyperbola.

solution   We begin by writing the equation in standard form. We do this by moving the constant term to the other side of the equation and dividing by it to get a constant term of 1. We then simplify so that the x^2 and y^2 terms are in the numerators.

$$4y^2 - 9x^2 = 36 \qquad \text{moved constant to right-hand side}$$

$$\frac{4y^2}{36} - \frac{9x^2}{36} = 1 \qquad \text{divided by 36}$$

$$\frac{y^2}{9} - \frac{x^2}{4} = 1 \qquad \text{simplified}$$

Now if we let x equal 0, we can solve for y; if we let y equal 0, we can solve for x.

Let $x = 0$ $\qquad\qquad\qquad$ Let $y = 0$

$$\frac{y^2}{9} - \frac{(0)^2}{4} = 1 \qquad\qquad \frac{(0)^2}{9} - \frac{x^2}{4} = 1$$

$$y = \pm 3 \qquad\qquad\qquad x = \pm 2i$$

Setting $x = 0$ gives us the coordinates of the vertices of the hyperbola: **(0, 3)** and **(0, –3).** The complex values of x obtained by setting $y = 0$ give us two points on the asymptote rectangle: (2, 0) and (–2, 0). We graph the points, draw the asymptotes, and sketch the hyperbola.

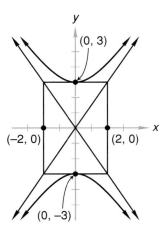

From the graph, we can write the equations of the asymptotes.

$$y = \frac{3}{2}x \qquad \text{and} \qquad y = -\frac{3}{2}x$$

**problem set
78**

1. How many different committees of 5 can be formed from 3 boys and 6 girls?

2. Travis was happy because he had taken 4 tests and still had a 72 average. Then disaster struck because he took the fifth test and his overall average dropped to 70. What grade did he make on the fifth test?

3. The average temperature for 5 days was 80°. Then the sixth day was so hot that the average temperature for all 6 days was 83°. What was the temperature on the sixth day?

4. Jennifer bought K articles for a cents each. To pay for the articles, she gave the clerk Q quarters. How many cents did she get in change?

5. Speedy could complete 5 jobs in 3 hours and Slowpoke could complete 2 jobs in 3 hours. Slowpoke worked for 2 hours and then was joined by Speedy. How long did they have to work together if they had to complete a total of 6 jobs?

6. Lance put some money in Bank A at 6% simple yearly interest and put the rest in Bank B at 8% simple yearly interest. If his total interest after one year was $220 and the total invested was $3000, how much money did he put in each bank?

7. Given the hyperbola $\frac{x^2}{16} - \frac{y^2}{4} = 1$, find the coordinates of the vertices and the equations of the asymptotes. Graph the hyperbola.

8. Given the hyperbola $4y^2 - 9x^2 = 36$, write the equation in standard form and find the coordinates of the vertices and the equations of the asymptotes. Graph the hyperbola.

9. Write all six terms of $(a + b)^5$.

10. Write the fifth term of $(a + b)^6$.

Show:

11. $\sin \theta \csc (90° - \theta) = \tan \theta$ 12. $\sec (90° - \theta) \tan \theta = \sec \theta$

13. Use Cramer's rule to solve: $\begin{cases} 4x - 3y = 5 \\ 2x - 4y = -3 \end{cases}$

14. The perimeter of a 10-sided regular polygon (regular decagon) is 50 centimeters. What is the length of one of the sides of the polygon? What is the radius of the circle that can be circumscribed about the polygon?

15. Two 5-sided polygons (pentagons) are similar. The ratio of a side of the larger pentagon to a corresponding side of the smaller pentagon is 5 to 3. What is the ratio of the area of the smaller polygon to the area of the larger polygon?

16. Solve this triangle for the unknown parts.

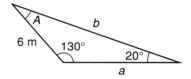

17. Write the equation in standard form and graph the ellipse: $49x^2 + 4y^2 = 196$

18. Solve for d: $\begin{vmatrix} d+2 & 3d-1 \\ d-4 & d+2 \end{vmatrix} = 0$

19. A parabola has its vertex at $(-2, -6)$ and its focus at $(-2, 4)$. Write the equations of the parabola, the directrix, and the axis of symmetry. Graph the parabola.

20. Sketch the graph of the function $y = -\log_{10} x$.

21. Find the radius and the coordinates of the center of the circle whose equation is $3x^2 + 6x + 6y + 3y^2 - 33 = 0$. Graph the circle.

22. Write the equation of the sinusoid whose graph is a sine function that has been shifted $3\pi/2$ to the right and that has an amplitude of 4, a period of 3π, and a centerline of $y = 5$.

23. Multiply $\left(3 \text{ cis } \frac{10\pi}{9}\right)\left(2 \text{ cis } \frac{5\pi}{9}\right)$ and express the answer in rectangular form. Give an exact answer.

Solve the following equations given that $0 \le \theta < 2\pi$:

24. $\cos 3\theta + 1 = 0$

25. $(\cos 2\theta)(\csc \theta - 1) = 0$

26. Evaluate: (a) Arccos (cos 240°) (b) Arcsin $\left(\sin \dfrac{5\pi}{3}\right)$

27. Find the mean, median, mode, variance, and standard deviation for the following data: 5, 2, 7, 1, 5, 3.

28. Find the distance from the point $(-1, -2)$ to the line $\dfrac{x}{4} + y = 1$.

Solve for x:

29. $2 \ln x - \ln\left(x - \dfrac{1}{4}\right) = \ln 4$

30. $2 \log_2 x + \log_2 5 = 2 \log_2 3$

LESSON 79 *De Moivre's Theorem • Roots of Complex Numbers*

79.A
De Moivre's theorem

We remember that when we multiply two complex numbers written in polar form, the absolute values are multiplied together and the angles are added. Therefore,

$$(r_1 \operatorname{cis} \theta_1)(r_2 \operatorname{cis} \theta_2) = (r_1 r_2) \operatorname{cis} (\theta_1 + \theta_2)$$

If $z = r \operatorname{cis} \theta$, we apply this rule to get

$$z^2 = (r \operatorname{cis} \theta)(r \operatorname{cis} \theta) = r^2 \operatorname{cis} 2\theta$$

$$z^3 = (r \operatorname{cis} \theta)(r \operatorname{cis} \theta)(r \operatorname{cis} \theta) = r^3 \operatorname{cis} 3\theta$$

$$z^4 = (r \operatorname{cis} \theta)(r \operatorname{cis} \theta)(r \operatorname{cis} \theta)(r \operatorname{cis} \theta) = r^4 \operatorname{cis} 4\theta$$

If we repeatedly multiply z by itself, we find that

$$z^n = (r \operatorname{cis} \theta)^n = r^n \operatorname{cis} n\theta$$

where n is a positive integer. This fact, considered to be one of the most important in the study of complex numbers, is known as **De Moivre's theorem.** This theorem is named after Abraham De Moivre (1667–1754), a French refugee who lived in London.

example 79.1   Find $(2 \operatorname{cis} 30°)^5$.

solution   By De Moivre's theorem,

$$(2 \operatorname{cis} 30°)^5 = 2^5 \operatorname{cis} (5 \cdot 30°) = \mathbf{32 \ cis \ 150°}$$

example 79.2   Use De Moivre's theorem to find $(1 + i)^{13}$. Express the answer in rectangular form.

solution   To use De Moivre's theorem, we first need to put our complex number into polar form. We compute r and θ.

$$r = \sqrt{1^2 + 1^2} = \sqrt{2}$$

Tan $\theta = \frac{1}{1} = 1$ and the number lies in the first quadrant, so

$$\theta = 45°$$

Thus, $1 + i = \sqrt{2} \operatorname{cis} 45°$. Applying De Moivre's theorem and remembering that cis of an angle equals cis of an integer multiple of 360° added to that angle, we get

$$(1 + i)^{13} = \left(\sqrt{2} \operatorname{cis} 45°\right)^{13}$$

$$= \left(\sqrt{2}\right)^{13} \operatorname{cis} (13 \cdot 45°)$$

$$= 2^{13/2} \operatorname{cis} (13 \cdot 45°)$$

$$= 2^6 \, 2^{1/2} \operatorname{cis} 585°$$

$$= 64\sqrt{2} \operatorname{cis} (360° + 225°)$$

$$= 64\sqrt{2} \operatorname{cis} 225°$$

Converting back to rectangular form gives us the final answer.

$$64\sqrt{2} \operatorname{cis} 225° = 64\sqrt{2}\left(-\frac{\sqrt{2}}{2} - \frac{\sqrt{2}}{2}i\right)$$

$$= \mathbf{-64 - 64}i$$

79.B
roots of complex numbers

If we use 2 as a factor three times, the product is 8.

$$2 \cdot 2 \cdot 2 = 8$$

This is the reason we say that a third root of 8 is 2. Also, we can write

$$\sqrt[3]{8} = 2$$

Because the notation $8^{1/3}$ means the same thing as $\sqrt[3]{8}$, this expression also has a value of 2.

$$8^{1/3} = 2$$

There are really three different cube roots of 8, two of which are complex. In fact, every non-zero number has n distinct roots. In this section, we will learn how to determine all n roots of a number. Above, when we used the cube root notation, $\sqrt[3]{}$, and wrote $8^{1/3}$, we understood the answer to be 2 instead of either of the complex third roots. This is because, by convention, we assume that the nth root notation when applied to a real number refers to the real nth root. Should there be a positive and negative choice of real roots, the nth root notation refers to the positive real root. For example, the number 4 has two square roots, but when we write $\sqrt{4}$, we mean the positive square root, 2.

Now we will illustrate how to find all the roots of a complex number expressed in polar form. Suppose we use the complex number 2 cis 12° as a factor three times. The product is 8 cis 36°

(a)   (2 cis 12°)(2 cis 12°)(2 cis 12°) = 8 cis 36°

because we multiply complex numbers in polar form by multiplying the numerical coefficients and adding the angles. Thus, a third root of 8 cis 36° is 2 cis 12°.

There are two other third roots of 8 cis 36°.

(b)   (2 cis 132°)(2 cis 132°)(2 cis 132°) = 8 cis 396° = 8 cis (360° + 36°)
$$= 8 \text{ cis } 36°$$

(c)   (2 cis 252°)(2 cis 252°)(2 cis 252°) = 8 cis 756° = 8 cis (720° + 36°)
$$= 8 \text{ cis } 36°$$

In (b) the angle of the product is 396°, which is once around (360°) and 36° more. In (c) the angle of the product is 756°, which is twice around (720°) and 36° more. Thus, the three third roots of 8 cis 36° are

$$2 \text{ cis } 12° \qquad 2 \text{ cis } 132° \qquad 2 \text{ cis } 252°$$

To get the first root, we took the third root of 8 and divided the angle by 3. The angle of the next root is 360°/3, or 120°, greater, and the angle of the next root is 2(360°/3), or 240°, greater.

$$\text{A third root of 8 cis } 36° = 8^{1/3} \text{ cis } \frac{36°}{3} = 2 \text{ cis } 12°$$

$$\text{A second third root of 8 cis } 36° = 8^{1/3} \text{ cis } \left(\frac{36°}{3} + 120° \right) = 2 \text{ cis } 132°$$

$$\text{A third third root of 8 cis } 36° = 8^{1/3} \text{ cis } \left(\frac{36°}{3} + 240° \right) = 2 \text{ cis } 252°$$

If we continue the process, the roots will begin to repeat. The next step would be to add 3 × 120°, or 360°. If we do this, the result is 2 cis 12° again.

$$8^{1/3} \text{ cis } \left(\frac{36°}{3} + 360° \right) = 2 \text{ cis } 372° = 2 \text{ cis } 12°$$

Every complex number except zero has two square roots, three cube roots, four fourth roots, five fifth roots, and, in general, n nth roots. The angles of the third roots differ by 360°/3, or 120°. The angles of the fourth roots differ by 360°/4, or 90°. The angles of the fifth roots differ by 360°/5, or 72°; etc. The angles of the nth roots differ by 360°/n.

example 79.3   Find the four fourth roots of 16 cis 60°. Check the answers by multiplying.

solution   The first root is $16^{1/4}$ cis (60°/4) = **2 cis 15°**. Angles in the polar form of the fourth roots differ by 360°/4, or 90°, so the other three roots are

2 cis 105°, 2 cis 195°, 2 cis 285°

Now we check:

(2 cis 15°)(2 cis 15°)(2 cis 15°)(2 cis 15°) = 16 cis 60°

(2 cis 105°)(2 cis 105°)(2 cis 105°)(2 cis 105°) = 16 cis 420°

= 16 cis (60° + 360°) = 16 cis 60°

(2 cis 195°)(2 cis 195°)(2 cis 195°)(2 cis 195°) = 16 cis 780°

= 16 cis (60° + 720°) = 16 cis 60°

(2 cis 285°)(2 cis 285°)(2 cis 285°)(2 cis 285°) = 16 cis 1140°

= 16 cis (60° + 1080°) = 16 cis 60°

example 79.4   Find five fifth roots of i.

solution   **We write a complex number in polar form with a positive coefficient to find the roots.**

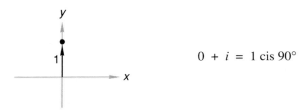

$$0 + i = 1 \text{ cis } 90°$$

The real fifth root of 1 is 1, so we get

$$\text{A fifth root of } i = 1^{1/5} \text{ cis } \frac{90°}{5} = \textbf{1 cis 18°}$$

Successive angles of the polar form of the fifth roots differ by 360°/5, or 72°, so the other roots are

1 cis 90°, 1 cis 162°, 1 cis 234°, 1 cis 306°

Now we check the angles.

5 × 18° = 90°   check

5 × 90° = 450° = 90° + 360°   check

5 × 162° = 810° = 90° + 720°   check

5 × 234° = 1170° = 90° + 1080°   check

5 × 306° = 1530° = 90° + 1440°   check

example 79.5   Find two square roots of 1.

solution   The polar form of $1 + 0i$ is 1 cis 0°.

$$1 + 0i = 1 \text{ cis } 0°$$

The positive real square root (known as the **principal square root**) of 1 is 1, so we get

$$\text{A square root of } 1 \ = \ 1^{1/2} \text{ cis } \frac{0°}{2} \ = \ \textbf{1 cis 0°}$$

The angles of square roots of complex numbers differ by 360°/2, or 180°, so the other square root of 1 cis 0° is **1 cis 180°.** Now we check our answers.

$$(1 \text{ cis } 0°)(1 \text{ cis } 0°) \ = \ 1 \text{ cis } 0° \qquad\qquad\qquad\qquad \text{check}$$

$$(1 \text{ cis } 180°)(1 \text{ cis } 180°) \ = \ 1 \text{ cis } 360° \ = \ 1 \text{ cis } (0° \ + \ 360°) \ = \ 1 \text{ cis } 0° \quad \text{check}$$

Of course, if we wish, we could write the answers in rectangular form as 1 and –1.

example 79.6   Find three third roots of –1.

solution   **We always begin by writing the complex number in polar form with a positive coefficient.**

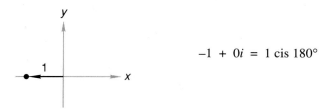

$$-1 \ + \ 0i \ = \ 1 \text{ cis } 180°$$

The first angle is 180°/3, or 60°. The angles of the third roots differ by 120°, so the three roots are as shown.

$$\text{The three third roots of } -1 \ = \ \textbf{1 cis 60°, 1 cis 180°, 1 cis 300°}$$

These roots can also be written in rectangular form as

$$\frac{1}{2} \ + \ \frac{\sqrt{3}}{2}i, \ -1 \ + \ 0i, \ \frac{1}{2} \ - \ \frac{\sqrt{3}}{2}i$$

example 79.7   Find the four fourth roots of 42 cis 40°.

solution   We use the root key on the calculator to find that $42^{1/4}$ is about 2.55. The angles of the fourth roots differ by 360°/4, or 90°, so the four fourth roots are as shown.

2.55 cis 10°, 2.55 cis 100°, 2.55 cis 190°, 2.55 cis 280°

problem set 79

1. There were 12 people present. How many committees of 9 could be selected from the 12 people?

2. How many distinguishable ways can 8 flags be lined up along a wall if 2 of the flags are identical?

3. The cost of finishing the contract varied linearly with the number of men who worked. If 10 men worked, the cost was $5100. If only 5 men worked, the cost was $2600. What would be the cost if only 2 men worked?

4. The still-water speed of the boat was 3 times the speed of the current in the river. If the boat could go 16 miles downstream in 2 hours less than it took to go 32 miles upstream, how fast was the boat in still water and what was the speed of the current in the river?

5. A crew of 81 workers can do 1 job in 24 days. In order to finish on time, the contractor increased the size of the work force by one third. How many days will be saved by adding the additional workers?

6. Find $(3 \text{ cis } 35°)^3$ and write the answer in polar form.

7. Use De Moivre's theorem to find $\left(1 \ - \ \sqrt{3}\,i\right)^5$. Write the answer in rectangular form. Give an exact answer.

8. Find the three cube roots of $8i$ and express them in polar form.

9. Find the two square roots of -1 and express them in rectangular form. Give an exact answer.

10. Given the hyperbola $\frac{x^2}{16} - \frac{y^2}{9} = 1$, find the vertices and the equations of the asymptotes. Graph the hyperbola.

11. Given the hyperbola $9x^2 - 4y^2 = 36$, write the equation in standard form and find the coordinates of the vertices and the equations of the asymptotes. Graph the hyperbola.

12. Write all seven terms of $(x + y)^6$.   13. Write the sixth term of $(a + b)^9$.

Show:

14. $\dfrac{\tan \theta}{\sec \theta} = \sin \theta$

15. $\sin (90° - \theta) \sec (90° - \theta) = \cot \theta$

16. Use Cramer's rule to solve: $\begin{cases} 5x - 3y = 8 \\ 4x + 2y = 5 \end{cases}$

17. What is the radius of the circle that can be circumscribed about a 7-sided regular polygon (regular heptagon) whose perimeter is 49 feet?

18. The perimeter of a 12-sided regular polygon is 96 feet. What is the length of one of the sides of the polygon? What is the area of the polygon?

19. Solve this triangle for the unknown parts.

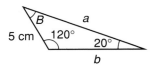

20. Write the equation in standard form and graph the ellipse: $16x^2 + 4y^2 = 64$

21. The birth weights of babies at a particular hospital are found to be approximately normally distributed with a mean of 6.8 pounds and a standard deviation of 0.2 pound. What is the approximate percentage of babies born at this hospital who weigh more than 6.9 pounds?

22. Solve for x: $\begin{vmatrix} x + 2 & 2x \\ x - 1 & x - 3 \end{vmatrix} + 8 = 0$

23. A parabola has its vertex at $(-4, 2)$ and its focus at $(-4, 6)$. Write the equations of the parabola, the directrix, and the axis of symmetry. Graph the parabola.

24. Write the equation of the sinusoid as a cosine function.

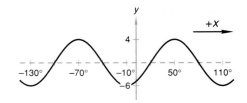

25. Multiply $\left[4 \text{ cis } (-300°)\right](2 \text{ cis } 30°)$ and express the answer in rectangular form. Give an exact answer.

Solve the following equations given that $0° \le \theta < 360°$:

26. $2\sqrt{2} \sin^2 \theta - 12 \sin \theta + 5\sqrt{2} = 0$ 27. $2 \cos 4\theta + 1 = 0$

28. Find the distance from the point $(1, 3)$ to the line $x - 3y + 5 = 0$.

29. Solve for x: $\ln (x + 2) - \ln (3x - 4) = \ln 3$

30. Use the midpoint formula method to find the equation of the perpendicular bisector of the line segment with endpoints $(-6, -2)$ and $(4, -8)$. Write the equation in slope-intercept form.

LESSON 80   Trigonometric Identities (2)

To begin this lesson, we list the basic trigonometric relationships that we have used thus far.

$$\sin\theta \;=\; \frac{1}{\csc\theta} \qquad\qquad \cos\theta \;=\; \frac{1}{\sec\theta} \qquad\qquad \tan\theta \;=\; \frac{1}{\cot\theta}$$

$$\csc\theta \;=\; \frac{1}{\sin\theta} \qquad\qquad \sec\theta \;=\; \frac{1}{\cos\theta} \qquad\qquad \cot\theta \;=\; \frac{1}{\tan\theta}$$

$$\sin(-\theta) = -\sin\theta \qquad \cos(-\theta) = \cos\theta \qquad \tan(-\theta) = -\tan\theta$$

$$\csc(-\theta) = -\csc\theta \qquad \sec(-\theta) = \sec\theta \qquad \cot(-\theta) = -\cot\theta$$

Now we add three more relationships that are most useful.

(a) $\sin^2\theta + \cos^2\theta = 1$ (b) $1 + \cot^2\theta = \csc^2\theta$ (c) $\tan^2\theta + 1 = \sec^2\theta$

We begin by proving (a). Though the relationship stated in (a) is true for all angles θ, we will prove (a) only for the case where $0 < \theta < 90°$. In other words, we will consider only values of θ that lie in the first quadrant. We draw a right triangle with θ as one of its acute angles. We state beside the triangle the Pythagorean theorem and the values of the trigonometric functions in terms of the lengths of the sides of the triangle.

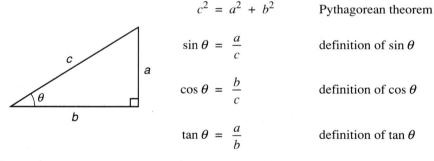

$$c^2 = a^2 + b^2 \qquad\qquad \text{Pythagorean theorem}$$

$$\sin\theta = \frac{a}{c} \qquad\qquad \text{definition of } \sin\theta$$

$$\cos\theta = \frac{b}{c} \qquad\qquad \text{definition of } \cos\theta$$

$$\tan\theta = \frac{a}{b} \qquad\qquad \text{definition of } \tan\theta$$

To prove (a), we write the equation and then substitute for $\sin^2\theta$ and $\cos^2\theta$.

$$\sin^2\theta + \cos^2\theta = \left(\frac{a}{c}\right)^2 + \left(\frac{b}{c}\right)^2 \qquad\qquad \text{substituted}$$

$$= \frac{a^2}{c^2} + \frac{b^2}{c^2} \qquad\qquad \text{simplified}$$

$$= \frac{a^2 + b^2}{c^2} \qquad\qquad \text{added}$$

$$= \frac{c^2}{c^2} \qquad\qquad a^2 + b^2 = c^2$$

$$= 1 \qquad\qquad \text{simplified}$$

The argument above can be extended to θ lying in quadrants other than the first. If we do so, we will find that the values of sine, cosine, and tangent differ by at most a sign from those listed next to the figure. Since these trigonometric quantities are squared, we see that relationship (a) still is true for θ in quadrants other than the first.

We prove (b) and (c) using the same figure, a similar procedure, and a trick.

To Prove (b)	To Prove (c)	

$$1 + \cot^2 \theta = 1 + \left(\frac{b}{a}\right)^2 \qquad\qquad \tan^2 \theta + 1 = \left(\frac{a}{b}\right)^2 + 1 \qquad\qquad \text{substituted}$$

$$= \left(\frac{a}{a}\right)^2 + \left(\frac{b}{a}\right)^2 \qquad\qquad = \left(\frac{a}{b}\right)^2 + \left(\frac{b}{b}\right)^2 \qquad\qquad \begin{array}{l}\text{(trick)} \\ \text{substituted } \frac{a}{a} \text{ and } \frac{b}{b} \text{ for } 1\end{array}$$

$$= \frac{a^2 + b^2}{a^2} \qquad\qquad\qquad = \frac{a^2 + b^2}{b^2} \qquad\qquad\qquad \text{added}$$

$$= \frac{c^2}{a^2} \qquad\qquad\qquad\quad = \frac{c^2}{b^2} \qquad\qquad\qquad\quad a^2 + b^2 = c^2$$

$$= \left(\frac{c}{a}\right)^2 \qquad\qquad\qquad = \left(\frac{c}{b}\right)^2 \qquad\qquad\qquad \text{simplified}$$

$$= \csc^2 \theta \qquad\qquad\qquad = \sec^2 \theta \qquad\qquad\qquad \begin{array}{l}\text{definition of} \\ \csc \theta \text{ and } \sec \theta\end{array}$$

The three equations (a), (b), and (c) have three forms each.

(a) $\sin^2 \theta + \cos^2 \theta = 1 \qquad\qquad \sin^2 \theta = 1 - \cos^2 \theta \qquad\qquad \cos^2 \theta = 1 - \sin^2 \theta$

(b) $1 + \cot^2 \theta = \csc^2 \theta \qquad\qquad \cot^2 \theta = \csc^2 \theta - 1 \qquad\qquad 1 = \csc^2 \theta - \cot^2 \theta$

(c) $\tan^2 \theta + 1 = \sec^2 \theta \qquad\qquad \tan^2 \theta = \sec^2 \theta - 1 \qquad\qquad 1 = \sec^2 \theta - \tan^2 \theta$

These nine forms are difficult to memorize because they are so similar. If we can remember the form

$$\text{(a) } \sin^2 \theta + \cos^2 \theta = 1$$

we can easily develop the basic form of (b) and (c). To develop (b), we divide every term of (a) by $\sin^2 \theta$.

$$\text{(b) } \frac{\sin^2 \theta}{\sin^2 \theta} + \frac{\cos^2 \theta}{\sin^2 \theta} = \frac{1}{\sin^2 \theta} \quad\longrightarrow\quad 1 + \cot^2 \theta = \csc^2 \theta$$

To develop (c), we divide every term of (a) by $\cos^2 \theta$.

$$\text{(c) } \frac{\sin^2 \theta}{\cos^2 \theta} + \frac{\cos^2 \theta}{\cos^2 \theta} = \frac{1}{\cos^2 \theta} \quad\longrightarrow\quad \tan^2 \theta + 1 = \sec^2 \theta$$

There are no set procedures for proving trigonometric identities, and often there are two or three ways to do the same proof. These problems are standard in all trigonometry books and were contrived to give students practice in transforming trigonometric expressions. We often begin by looking for forms for which we can substitute, such as $\csc^2 x - \cot^2 x$ or $1 + \tan^2 x$. Also, if the expressions contain fractions, it is sometimes helpful to add the fractions.

example 80.1 Show: $\dfrac{\sec^2 x - \tan^2 x}{1 + \cot^2 x} = \sin^2 x$

solution We could work with either side. We decide to take the left side and change its form to $\sin^2 x$. First we replace $\sec^2 x - \tan^2 x$ with 1 and replace $1 + \cot^2 x$ with $\csc^2 x$.

$$\frac{\sec^2 x - \tan^2 x}{1 + \cot^2 x} \quad\longrightarrow\quad \frac{1}{\csc^2 x}$$

Now $\csc^2 x$ equals $1/\sin^2 x$, so we can write

$$\frac{1}{\csc^2 x} \quad\longrightarrow\quad \frac{1}{\dfrac{1}{\sin^2 x}} \quad\longrightarrow\quad \sin^2 x$$

Now we have changed the left side to $\sin^2 x$ and the identity has been proved.

example 80.2 Show: $\dfrac{1}{\tan A} + \tan A = \sec A \csc A$

solution We will work with the left side. We will replace tan A with sin A/cos A.

$$\dfrac{1}{\dfrac{\sin A}{\cos A}} + \dfrac{\sin A}{\cos A} \longrightarrow \dfrac{\cos A}{\sin A} + \dfrac{\sin A}{\cos A}$$

Next we will find a common denominator and add.

$$\dfrac{\cos A}{\sin A} \cdot \dfrac{\cos A}{\cos A} + \dfrac{\sin A}{\cos A} \cdot \dfrac{\sin A}{\sin A} \longrightarrow \dfrac{\cos^2 A + \sin^2 A}{\cos A \sin A}$$

But $\cos^2 A + \sin^2 A = 1$, so we have

$$\dfrac{1}{\cos A \sin A} \longrightarrow \dfrac{1}{\cos A} \cdot \dfrac{1}{\sin A}$$

But these expressions equal sec A and csc A, so

$$\dfrac{1}{\cos A} \cdot \dfrac{1}{\sin A} \longrightarrow \sec A \csc A$$

example 80.3 Show: $\dfrac{1}{1 + \cos A} + \dfrac{1}{1 - \cos A} = 2 \csc^2 A$

solution On the left side we have two fractional expressions that can be added. We will begin by adding these fractional expressions.

$$\dfrac{1 - \cos A}{(1 + \cos A)(1 - \cos A)} + \dfrac{1 + \cos A}{(1 - \cos A)(1 + \cos A)} \longrightarrow \dfrac{2}{1 - \cos^2 A}$$

But $1 - \cos^2 A$ equals $\sin^2 A$, which is the reciprocal of $\csc^2 A$.

$$\dfrac{2}{1 - \cos^2 A} \longrightarrow \dfrac{2}{\sin^2 A} \longrightarrow 2 \csc^2 A$$

example 80.4 Show: $\dfrac{\cos A}{1 + \sin A} + \dfrac{1 + \sin A}{\cos A} = 2 \sec A$

solution Again we will add the fractions.

$$\dfrac{\cos A}{1 + \sin A} \cdot \dfrac{\cos A}{\cos A} + \dfrac{1 + \sin A}{\cos A} \cdot \dfrac{1 + \sin A}{1 + \sin A} = \dfrac{\cos^2 A + 1 + \sin A + \sin A + \sin^2 A}{(\cos A)(1 + \sin A)}$$

The top reduces to $2 + 2 \sin A$ because $\cos^2 A + \sin^2 A = 1$.

$$\dfrac{2 + 2 \sin A}{(\cos A)(1 + \sin A)} \longrightarrow \dfrac{2(1 + \sin A)}{(\cos A)(1 + \sin A)} \longrightarrow 2 \sec A$$

problem set 80

1. How many ways can 5 boys sit in a row if Thomas insists on sitting in the middle?

2. Shay and Kassady stop for lunch after they have traveled for h hours at m miles per hour. If the total distance to be traveled is 300 miles, how far do they have to go after lunch?

3. Dinah is in a quandary. She has only $\frac{1}{2}$ cup of white sugar, and the recipe calls for $\frac{3}{4}$ cup of white sugar. How much brown sugar must she use if 1 cup of brown sugar is equivalent to $\frac{3}{4}$ cup of white sugar?

4. The pressure was such that it required 2 hours to fill four sevenths of the empty pool. How much more time would it take to fill the pool completely?

5. If M workers can do 50 jobs in 1 day, how many days will it take 10 workers to do 20 jobs?

6. The sum of the digits in a three-digit counting number was 17. The tens' digit was 5 less than the hundreds' digit. Twice the units' digit exceeded 4 times the tens' digit by 8. What was the number?

Show:

7. $\dfrac{\sec^2 x - \tan^2 x}{1 + \cot^2 x} = \sin^2 x$

8. $\dfrac{\cos A}{1 + \sin A} + \dfrac{1 + \sin A}{\cos A} = 2 \sec A$

9. $\dfrac{1}{\tan A} + \tan A = \sec A \csc A$

10. Find $(2 \operatorname{cis} 300°)^6$ and write the answer in polar form.

11. Find the three cube roots of $27 \operatorname{cis} 36°$ and express them in polar form.

12. Find the four fourth roots of -16 and express them in rectangular form. Give exact answers.

13. Given the hyperbola $16x^2 - 25y^2 = 400$, write the equation in standard form and find the coordinates of the vertices and the equations of the asymptotes. Graph the hyperbola.

14. Write all four terms of $(a + b)^3$.   15. Write the third term of $(x + y)^6$.

16. Use Cramer's rule to solve: $\begin{cases} 4x - 2y = 7 \\ 3x + 4y = 9 \end{cases}$

17. The perimeter of a 13-sided regular polygon is 39 inches. What is the length of one of the sides of the polygon? What is the area of the polygon? What is the radius of the circle that can be circumscribed about the polygon?

18. Solve this triangle for the unknown parts.

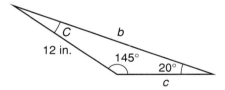

19. Write the equation in standard form and graph the ellipse: $9x^2 + 25y^2 = 225$

20. Solve for k: $\begin{vmatrix} 2 - k & -1 \\ -4 & 1 - 3k \end{vmatrix} = 0$

21. A parabola has its vertex at the origin and its focus at $\left(0, \frac{7}{5}\right)$. Write the equations of the parabola, the directrix, and the axis of symmetry. Graph the parabola.

22. Sketch the graph of the function $y = -\log_6 x$.

23. Find the radius and the coordinates of the center of the circle whose equation is $3x^2 + 3y^2 + 6x - 12y - \frac{4}{3} = 0$.

24. Write the equation of the sinusoid whose graph is a cosine function shifted $110°$ to the left and which has a period of $240°$, an amplitude of 6, and a centerline of $y = -4$.

25. Multiply $\left(3 \operatorname{cis} \frac{\pi}{6}\right)\left(4 \operatorname{cis} \frac{4\pi}{3}\right)$ and express the answer in rectangular form. Give an exact answer.

Solve the following equations given that $(0 \le x, \theta < 2\pi)$:

26. $\sqrt{3} \cos x - \sqrt{2 - \cos^2 x} = 0$

27. $\sqrt{3} \tan \dfrac{\theta}{4} - 1 = 0$

28. Evaluate: $\tan \left[\operatorname{Arccos} \left(-\dfrac{3}{5} \right) \right]$

29. Solve for x: $\log_7 (2x - 1) - \log_7 (3x - 3) = \log_7 5$

30. Simplify: $2 \log_6 6 + 6^{2 \log_6 3 - \log_6 3}$

LESSON 81   *Law of Cosines*

Every triangle has three sides and three angles for a total of six parts. **If we know one side and two other parts, we can solve for the values of the missing parts.**

1. If the triangle is a right triangle, the unknown parts can be found by using the sine, cosine, or tangent.
2. If the triangle is not a right triangle and the **values of a pair** (angle and side opposite) **are known,** the **law of sines** can be used.
3. If the triangle is not a right triangle and the **values of a pair are not known,** the **law of cosines** can be used.

The proof of the law of cosines is given in detail in the appendix. The law of cosines is normally written in one of the following forms:

$$a^2 = b^2 + c^2 - 2bc \cos A$$

$$b^2 = a^2 + c^2 - 2ac \cos B$$

$$c^2 = a^2 + b^2 - 2ab \cos C$$

The many letters used in these forms can be confusing to the beginner, so we will use another form. **We remember that if we had a pair (side and angle opposite), we would use the law of sines. But we do not have a pair, so we use the law of cosines. In the formula, we will use p and P to represent the pair we do not have and a and b to represent the other two sides and write**

$$p^2 = a^2 + b^2 - 2ab \cos P$$

We can remember the law of cosines without difficulty because it looks so much like the Pythagorean theorem with $-2ab \cos P$ attached.

PYTHAGOREAN THEOREM   LAW OF COSINES
$$c^2 = a^2 + b^2 \qquad\qquad p^2 = a^2 + b^2 - 2ab \cos P$$

The use of a calculator is recommended for finding solutions to problems that are solved by using the law of cosines.

example 81.1   Solve the triangle for its unknown parts.

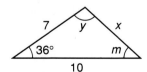

solution   We have one side and two other parts given but we do not have a pair (angle and side opposite), so we will use the law of cosines.

$$p^2 = a^2 + b^2 - 2ab \cos P$$

The pair we wish we had is side x and the 36° angle, so we replace p with x and P with 36° and use 7 and 10 for the two sides.

$$x^2 = 7^2 + 10^2 - 2(7)(10) \cos 36°$$

$$x^2 = 49 + 100 - 113.26$$

$$x^2 = 35.74$$

$$x = \mathbf{5.98}$$

Note that as the last step, we took only the positive square root since x must be positive.

Now we have a pair and we can use the law of sines to solve for *y* and *m*.

$$\frac{5.98}{\sin 36°} = \frac{10}{\sin y} \qquad\qquad \frac{5.98}{\sin 36°} = \frac{7}{\sin m}$$

$$\sin y = \frac{10 \sin 36°}{5.98} \qquad\qquad \sin m = \frac{7 \sin 36°}{5.98}$$

$$\sin y = 0.9829 \qquad\qquad \sin m = 0.6880$$

$$\text{so} \quad y = 79.39° \text{ or } 100.61° \qquad \text{so} \quad m = 43.47° \text{ or } 136.53°$$

When we look at the triangle, we see that angle *y* is greater than 90° and angle *m* is less than 90°, so

$$y = \mathbf{100.61°} \qquad \text{and} \qquad m = \mathbf{43.47°}$$

When we sum the angles, we get 100.61° + 43.47° + 36° = 180.08°. This small difference is a result of rounding results at several points in the solution.

example 81.2   Solve the triangle for its unknown parts.

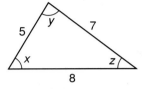

solution   We are given three parts and one of the parts is a side, so the triangle can be solved. **We do not have a pair, so we use the law of cosines.**

$$p^2 = a^2 + b^2 - 2ab \cos P$$

We decide that the pair we wish we had is angle *x* and the side of length 7. So we replace *p* with 7 and replace *P* with *x*. Then we use 5 and 8 for *a* and *b*.

$$7^2 = 5^2 + 8^2 - 2(5)(8) \cos x$$

$$49 = 25 + 64 - 80 \cos x$$

$$40 = 80 \cos x$$

$$0.5 = \cos x$$

$$\text{so} \quad x = 60°, 300°$$

From the diagram we see that *x* is less than 90°, so

$$x = \mathbf{60°}$$

Now we can use the law of sines to find another angle. We choose to find *y*.

$$\frac{7}{\sin 60°} = \frac{8}{\sin y}$$

$$\sin y = \frac{8 \sin 60°}{7}$$

$$\sin y = 0.9897$$

$$\text{so} \quad y = 81.77° \text{ or } 98.23°$$

From the diagram we see that *y* is less than 90°, so

$$y = \mathbf{81.77°}$$

Since the angles must add to 180°,

$$180° = 60° + 81.77° + z$$

$$z = \mathbf{38.23°}$$

example 81.3   Solve the triangle for its unknown parts.

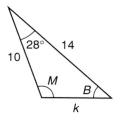

solution   We do not have a pair, so we will use the law of cosines.

$$p^2 = a^2 + b^2 - 2ab \cos P \qquad \text{law of cosines}$$

We will use 10 and 14 for sides a and b and will use 28° and k for the pair we wish we had. We will use a calculator so that the computation can be accomplished quickly and accurately. We must avoid getting bogged down in the arithmetic of these problems.

$$k^2 = 10^2 + 14^2 - 2(10)(14) \cos 28° \qquad \text{substituted}$$

$$k^2 = 100 + 196 - 247.23 \qquad \text{simplified}$$

$$k^2 = 48.77 \qquad \text{simplified}$$

$$k = \textbf{6.98} \qquad \text{solved}$$

Now we have an interesting problem. When we know the lengths of all three sides of a triangle, we can find any of the missing angles by using the law of cosines, so we could use the law of cosines to find either M or B. But we have a pair, so we could also use the law of sines to find M or B.

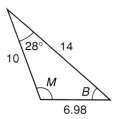

On the left below we show that the sine of 30° is 0.5 and the cosine of 30° is approximately 0.866. On the right we show that the sine of 150° is 0.5 and the cosine of 150° is −0.866 because 150° is an obtuse angle and its terminal side is in the second quadrant.

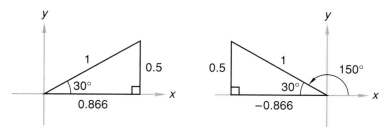

This diagram reminds us that the sine of any angle in a triangle is the same as the sine of its supplement. Thus, knowing the sine of an angle is not enough to determine what that angle is. If you ask a calculator for the angle whose sine is 0.5, it will always give you the first quadrant angle, which is 30°, since the Arcsin function is defined to give values between −90° and 90° only. This is the reason we say that using the law of sines to find an angle is ambiguous. The calculator cannot tell the difference between the sine of an acute angle and the sine of the related obtuse angle. But it can tell the difference between the cosine of 30° and the cosine of 150° because the cosine of 30° is a positive number and the cosine of 150° is a negative number. In fact, for each number between −1 and 1, there is one and only one angle between 0° and 180° whose cosine is that number. Therefore, if we know the cosine of an angle in a triangle, we can determine the angle precisely. **We know the lengths of all three sides in our triangle and we will use the law of cosines to find one of the missing angles because the use of the law of cosines always gives us the correct angle.** We decide to solve for angle M.

$$p^2 = a^2 + b^2 - 2ab \cos P \qquad \text{law of cosines}$$

$$14^2 = 10^2 + 6.98^2 - 2(10)(6.98) \cos M \qquad \text{substituted}$$

$$196 = 100 + 48.72 - 139.6 \cos M \qquad \text{simplified}$$

$$196 - 148.72 = -139.6 \cos M \qquad \text{simplified}$$

$$-0.3387 = \cos M \qquad \text{divided}$$

$$M = \mathbf{109.80°} \qquad \text{inverse cosine}$$

The calculator knows that if the cosine of an angle is a negative number, the angle is a second quadrant angle. The law of cosines never gives us an ambiguous answer.

The sum of the angles in a triangle is always 180° and we use this fact to find the measure of angle B.

$$109.80° + 28° + B = 180° \qquad \text{sum is } 180°$$

$$B = \mathbf{42.20°} \qquad \text{solved}$$

example 81.4 The figure shows two cables that are attached to a vertical tower from a point on the ground. The angle between the cables is 15°. The longer cable is 150 feet long and is attached to the top of the tower. The shorter cable is attached to a point 50 feet below the top of the tower. Find the length of the shorter cable.

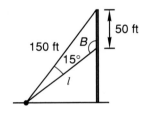

solution In the upper triangle we have a pair, so we will use the law of sines to solve for angle B.

$$\frac{150}{\sin B} = \frac{50}{\sin 15°} \qquad \text{law of sines}$$

$$\sin B = \frac{150 \sin 15°}{50} \qquad \text{rearranged}$$

$$\sin B = 0.7765 \qquad \text{used calculator}$$

$$B = 50.94° \qquad \text{inverse sine}$$

We must beware of ambiguity when we use the law of sines to find an angle. Angle B is certainly not an acute angle, so it must be the second quadrant angle that has the same sine.

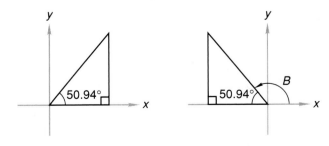

$$B = 180° - 50.94° = 129.06°$$

The sum of the angles of the triangle is 180° and we use this fact to find the angle at the top, which we will call L to match side l.

$$129.06° + 15° + L = 180° \quad \text{sum is } 180°$$

$$L = 35.94° \quad \text{solved}$$

Now we will use the law of sines again to find length l. **There is no ambiguity when we use the law of sines to find the length of a side.**

$$\frac{l}{\sin 35.94°} = \frac{50}{\sin 15°} \quad \text{law of sines}$$

$$l = \frac{50 \sin 35.94°}{\sin 15°} \quad \text{rearranged}$$

$$l = \textbf{113.39 ft} \quad \text{solved}$$

problem set 81

1. The coach had a problem. There are six people on a volleyball team, and he had 10 players. How many different teams could he form from these players?

2. Harry averaged 70 for four straight games, and then disaster struck because after the fifth game his average had dropped all the way to 60. What was his score in the fifth game?

3. The number 150 was written as the sum of two numbers. The first number was divided by 27. This quotient was added to the second number divided by 23, and the total was 6. What were the two numbers?

4. The sum of the angles in any triangle is 180°. Matildabelle had a triangle in which the second angle was 10° greater than the first angle and the third angle was 25° greater than the second angle. What was the measure of each of the angles of Matildabelle's triangle?

5. Five workers can do three jobs in 2 days. How many workers would it take to do 18 jobs in 10 days?

Solve the following triangles for their unknown parts:

6.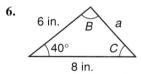

7.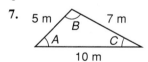

8. Two cables are attached to a vertical tower from a point on the ground, as shown. The angle between the cables is 20°. The longer cable is 120 feet long and is attached to the top of the tower. The shorter cable is attached to a point 60 feet below the top of the tower. Find the length of the shorter cable.

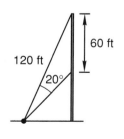

Show:

9. $\dfrac{1 - \cos^2 x}{\sec^2 x - 1} = \cos^2 x$

10. $\dfrac{1}{1 + \sin A} + \dfrac{1}{1 - \sin A} = 2 \sec^2 A$

11. Use De Moivre's theorem to find $(-1 - i)^6$. Write the answer in rectangular form. Give an exact answer.

12. Write the three cube roots of $8 \operatorname{cis} 45°$ in polar form.

13. Write the four fourth roots of -81 in rectangular form. Give exact answers.

14. Given the hyperbola $4x^2 - 25y^2 = 100$, write the equation in standard form and find the coordinates of its vertices and the equations of the asymptotes. Graph the hyperbola.

15. Write all five terms of $(m + n)^4$.

16. Write the fourth term of $(x + y)^7$.

17. The perimeter of a 12-sided regular polygon is 36 inches. What is the area of the polygon? What is the radius of the circle that can be circumscribed about the polygon?

18. Write the equation in standard form and graph the ellipse: $4x^2 + 25y^2 = 100$

19. A rancher decides that the heights of her horses (measured at the shoulder) are approximately normally distributed with a mean of 62 inches and a standard deviation of 2.5 inches. What is the approximate percentage of her horses that are between 60 inches and 63 inches tall?

20. A parabola has its vertex at $(4, 2)$ and its focus at $(4, -2)$. Write the equations of the parabola, its directrix, and its axis of symmetry. Graph the parabola.

21. Sketch the graph of the function $y = \log_2 (x - 1)$.

22. Write the equation of the sinusoid in terms of the sine function.

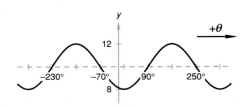

23. Multiply $(2 \text{ cis } 30°)\left[4 \text{ cis } (-90°)\right]$ and express the answer in rectangular form. Give an exact answer.

Solve the following equations given that $0° \le \theta < 360°$:

24. $\sqrt{3} \tan 3\theta + 1 = 0$ **25.** $\cos \theta + 2 \cos \theta \csc \theta = 0$

26. Evaluate: $\cos \left[\text{Arcsin} \left(-\dfrac{4}{5} \right) \right]$

27. Graph the solution to the system of inequalities: $\begin{cases} 2x^2 + 2y^2 - 4x + 8y - 8 \ge 0 \\ y < -(x - 1)^2 - 2 \end{cases}$

Solve for x:

28. $\log_{1/2} (3x - 2) - \log_{1/2} (x + 2) = -\log_{1/2} 4$

29. $\log 10(x - 1) = 0$

30. Simplify: $\dfrac{2 \log_9 6 - \log_9 12}{4 \log_9 3}$

LESSON 82 *Taking the Logarithm of • Exponential Equations*

82.A

taking the logarithm of

Taking the logarithm of is an operation just as raising to a power is an operation. We can raise the number 100 to the one-half power by writing either

$$100^{\frac{1}{2}} \qquad \text{or} \qquad \sqrt{100}$$

and the value of both of these expressions is 10. We can raise x to the one-half power by writing

$$x^{\frac{1}{2}} \qquad \text{or} \qquad \sqrt{x}$$

and, of course, no further simplification is possible unless we have a numerical value for x. **To take the logarithm of a number or an expression, we simply write the abbreviation for the word *logarithm* in front of the number or the expression.** To take the common logarithm of 100, we write either log or log_{10} in front of the number.

$$\log 100 \qquad \text{or} \qquad \log_{10} 100$$

When the abbreviation "log" is used and the base is not indicated, a base of 10 is understood, so the above expressions mean the same thing. Both have a value of 2. To take the common logarithm of x, we would write either

$$\log x \qquad \text{or} \qquad \log_{10} x$$

If we are asked to take the natural logarithm of 100, we would write either

$$\ln 100 \qquad \text{or} \qquad \log_e 100$$

because the letters "ln" mean that the base is e. The approximate numerical value of both these expressions is 4.605. To take the natural logarithm of x, we would write either

$$\ln x \qquad \text{or} \qquad \log_e x$$

82.B

exponential equations

We remember that expressions that consist of a base and an exponent are called **powers.** All of the following expressions are powers.

$$\text{(a) } 5^{2.3} \qquad \text{(b) } (3y)^4 \qquad \text{(c) } x^2 \qquad \text{(d) } 2^x \qquad \text{(e) } 3^{2x+4}$$

The expressions (d) and (e) are considered to be special forms of powers because in each expression the base is a positive real number (not 1) and the exponent contains a variable. We call these powers **exponentials** and call an equation that contains an exponential an **exponential equation.**

We have been solving logarithmic equations by rewriting them as exponential equations. Thus we can find the value of x in this logarithmic equation

$$\log_{1/2} x = 2$$

by rewriting the equation in exponential form and then solving.

$$\left(\frac{1}{2}\right)^2 = x \qquad \qquad \text{exponential form}$$

$$\frac{1}{4} = x \qquad \qquad \text{simplified}$$

We remember that when we take the logarithm of a power, the exponent becomes a coefficient, as we show here.

$$\log 10^x = x \log 10$$

$$\ln 4^x = x \ln 4$$

Now we find that many exponential equations can be solved by taking the logarithm of both sides of the equation as the first step because the resulting expression no longer has the variables in the exponents. When we work these problems, it is important to remember that the logarithm is the exponent, so $\log_{10} 10^1$ is 1 and $\log_e e^1$ is 1.

example 82.1   Solve: $10^{-2x+2} = 8$

solution   First we take the logarithm of both sides to the base 10. **We remember that, if we write** *log* **and do not designate a base, the base is understood to be 10.**

$$\log 10^{-2x+2} = \log 8 \qquad \text{log of both sides}$$

On the left-hand side we will use the power rule for logs, and on the right-hand side we will use a calculator to find the log of 8.

$$(-2x + 2) \log 10 = 0.9031$$

But log 10 is 1, so we end up with a simple algebraic equation, which we solve.

$$-2x + 2 = 0.9031 \qquad \text{equation}$$

$$-2x = -1.0969 \qquad \text{added } -2 \text{ to both sides}$$

$$x = \textbf{0.5485} \qquad \text{divided}$$

example 82.2   Solve: $e^{-2x+3} = 5$

solution   The variable is in the exponent and we do not want it in the exponent. This time, because the base is e, we will take the natural logarithm of both sides.

$$\ln e^{-2x+3} = \ln 5 \qquad \text{ln of both sides}$$

Now we will use the power rule for logarithms on the left-hand side and use a calculator on the right-hand side to find the natural log of 5.

$$(-2x + 3) \ln e = 1.6094$$

We remember that the natural logarithm of e (written "ln e") is 1. This is the reason that we used base e instead of base 10 in this problem. Thus, we get

$$-2x + 3 = 1.6094 \qquad \text{simplified}$$

$$-2x = -1.3906 \qquad \text{added } -3 \text{ to both sides}$$

$$x = \textbf{0.6953} \qquad \text{divided}$$

example 82.3   Solve: $5^{2x-1} = 6^{x-2}$

solution   Again we find variables in the exponents, which is undesirable. We solve exponential equations by taking the logarithm of both sides so that variables are no longer in the exponents. In this equation, neither base is 10 or e, so there is no advantage to taking either the common logarithm or the natural logarithm. We decide to take the common logarithm.

$$\log 5^{2x-1} = \log 6^{x-2}$$

Next we use the power rule on both sides.

$$(2x - 1) \log 5 = (x - 2) \log 6$$

Now we use a calculator to find log 5 and log 6 and use these values.

$$(2x - 1)(0.6990) = (x - 2)(0.7782)$$

Now we multiply and complete the solution.

$1.398x - 0.6990 = 0.7782x - 1.5564$	multiplied
$0.6198x = -0.8574$	simplified
$x = -1.3833$	divided

example 82.4   Solve: $4 = 6e^{2x+3}$

solution   Again we find the variable in the exponent. We will remove it from the exponent by taking the logarithm of both sides. Because the base is e, we will take the natural logarithm of both sides. We remember that the logarithm of the product $6e^{2x+3}$ equals the sum of the logarithm of 6 and the logarithm of e^{2x+3}.

$4 = 6e^{2x+3}$	equation
$\ln 4 = \ln\left(6e^{2x+3}\right)$	ln of both sides
$\ln 4 = \ln 6 + \ln e^{2x+3}$	ln of a product
$1.3863 = 1.7918 + 2x + 3$	used a calculator
$-0.4055 - 3 = 2x$	simplified
$\dfrac{-3.4055}{2} = x$	simplified
$x = -1.7028$	divided

problem set 82

1. There were 20 marbles in a line. Ten were identical red marbles, 6 were identical blue marbles, and 4 were identical white marbles. How many distinguishable linear patterns could be formed?

2. The general expressions for consecutive multiples of 11 are $11N$, $11(N + 1)$, $11(N + 2)$, etc., where N is an integer. Find three consecutive multiples of 11 such that 4 times the sum of the first and the third is 66 less than 10 times the second.

3. The three dimensions of a rectangular box are height, length, and width. The sum of the dimensions is 18 feet. The height equals four fifths the sum of the length and the width and equals 4 times the difference of the length and the width. What are the dimensions of the box?

4. Sherry had to make a trip of t miles. She arose early and drove at r miles per hour for h hours and then stopped for lunch. How many miles did she have to drive after lunch?

5. Seven women could do 3 jobs in 5 days. How many days would it take for 9 women to do 27 jobs?

6. The first crew could do a jobs in 3 days. The second crew could do 3 jobs in b days. How long would it take both crews working together to do 13 jobs?

Solve:

7. $6^{3x+2} = 4^{2x-1}$

8. $10^{-3x-4} = 5^{2x-1}$

Solve the following triangles for their unknown parts:

9.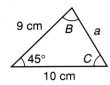

10.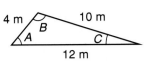

Show:

11. $\dfrac{\sin A}{1 + \cos A} + \dfrac{1 + \cos A}{\sin A} = 2\csc A$ **12.** $\dfrac{\csc^2\theta - \cot^2\theta}{1 + \cot^2\theta} = \sin^2\theta$

13. $\dfrac{\sin x}{\csc x} + \dfrac{\cos x}{\sec x} = 1$

14. Find $(1 \text{ cis } 12°)^{30}$ and write the answer in polar form.

15. Write the four fourth roots of $16 \text{ cis } 60°$ in polar form.

16. Write the three cube roots of -1 in rectangular form. Give exact answers.

17. Given the hyperbola $9x^2 - 36y^2 = 324$, write the equation in standard form and find the coordinates of the vertices and the equations of the asymptotes. Graph the hyperbola.

18. Write all six terms of $(p + q)^5$.

19. Write the sixth term of $(x + 1)^{10}$.

20. The perimeter of a 14-sided regular polygon is 42. Find the radius of the circle that can be circumscribed about the polygon and the radius of the circle that can be inscribed in the polygon.

21. Write the equation in standard form and graph the ellipse: $9x^2 + 36y^2 = 324$

22. A parabola has its focus at $(0, 6)$ and its vertex at the origin. Write the equations of the parabola, its directrix, and its axis of symmetry. Graph the parabola.

23. Find the radius and the coordinates of the center of the circle whose equation is $2x^2 + 2y^2 - 12y + 4x + 1 = 0$.

24. Write the equation of the sine curve that is shifted $\pi/8$ to the right and that has a period of $\pi/2$, an amplitude of 9, and a centerline of $y = 2$.

Solve the following equations given that $0 \le \theta < 2\pi$:

25. $\csc^2\theta - 4 = 0$ **26.** $(\sqrt{2}\cos\theta - 1)(\sqrt{2}\cos\theta + 1) = 0$

27. Find the mean, median, mode, variance, and standard deviation for the following data: $-2, 0, 0, 0, 2, 4$.

28. Find the distance from the point $(2, 1)$ to the line $2x + y = 3$.

29. Solve for x: $\dfrac{2}{3}\log_7 8 + \log_7 x - \log_7 (x - 2) = \log_7 9$

30. A meteorologist determines that the annual rainfall in his hometown is normally distributed with a mean of 40.0 inches and a standard deviation of 2.5 inches. What percentage of years will have an annual rainfall measuring between 38.0 inches and 41.5 inches?

LESSON 83 *Simple Probability • Independent Events • Replacement*

83.A
simple probability

Probability theory had its genesis in the study of games of chance such as rolling dice, drawing cards at random from a deck of cards, or flipping a coin. Problems from games of chance still provide the best models on which to base a study of elementary probability, and we will concentrate on these problems.

The study of probability is based on the study of outcomes that have an equal chance of occurring. A fair coin should come up heads as often as it comes up tails if we flip it enough times. We will assume that our coins are fair coins. A fair die (singular of *dice*) has 6 faces. If we roll it enough times, each face should come up approximately one sixth of the time. We will assume that our dice are fair dice. We will also assume that each card in a deck has the same chance of being selected and that individual marbles have equal chances of being drawn from an urn.

It is customary to call activities such as flipping coins, rolling dice, blindly selecting cards from a deck, or drawing marbles from an urn **experiments** and to call the individual results **outcomes.** We will call the set of outcomes of an experiment the **sample space** of the experiment, and we will call designated subsets of the sample space **events.** We will define the **probability of a particular event** as the number of outcomes that satisfy the requirement divided by the total number of outcomes in the sample space. If we flip a fair coin, it can come up either heads or tails. Thus, our sample space is

If the event is getting a head, the probability of getting a head is

$$P(\text{H}) = \frac{\text{number of outcomes that are H}}{\text{total number of outcomes in the sample space}} = \frac{1}{2}$$

If we roll a single die, the sample space is

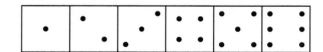

If we define the event as getting a 5, the probability of getting a 5 is

$$P(5) = \frac{\text{number of outcomes that are 5}}{\text{total number of outcomes in the sample space}} = \frac{1}{6}$$

The probability of rolling a number greater than 4 is

$$P(>4) = \frac{\text{number of outcomes that are greater than 4}}{\text{total number of outcomes in the sample space}} = \frac{2}{6} = \frac{1}{3}$$

example 83.1   Two fair dice are rolled. What is the probability of getting (a) a 7 and (b) a number greater than 8?

solution   First we draw a diagram of our sample space. The outcomes are the sums of the values on the individual dice, and there are 36 outcomes in our sample space.

OUTCOME OF SECOND DIE

	1	2	3	4	5	6
1	2	3	4	5	6	7
2	3	4	5	6	7	8
3	4	5	6	7	8	9
4	5	6	7	8	9	10
5	6	7	8	9	10	11
6	7	8	9	10	11	12

OUTCOME OF FIRST DIE

(a) The event is rolling a 7, and we see that 6 of these outcomes are 7, so

$$P(7) = \frac{\text{number of outcomes that equal 7}}{\text{total number of outcomes in the sample space}} = \frac{6}{36} = \frac{1}{6}$$

Thus, we find that the probability of rolling a 7 is $\frac{1}{6}$.

(b) The event is rolling a number greater than 8, and we see that 10 of these outcomes are greater than 8, so

$$P(>8) = \frac{\text{number of outcomes that are greater than 8}}{\text{total number of outcomes in the sample space}} = \frac{10}{36} = \frac{5}{18}$$

Thus, the probability of rolling a number greater than 8 is $\frac{5}{18}$.

We have defined probability so that the probability of any event lies between 0 and 1, inclusive.

$$0 \le P(E) \le 1$$

The sample space for the possible outcomes of a single roll of a pair of dice is always the sample space diagrammed in the last example. If we look at this sample space, we see that there are no outcomes of 146, so the probability of rolling a 146 is 0.

$$P(146) = \frac{\text{number of outcomes that are 146}}{\text{total number of outcomes in the sample space}} = \frac{0}{36} = 0$$

The probability of rolling a number that is less than 146 is 1 because every one of the 36 outcomes is less than 146.

$$P(<146) = \frac{\text{number of outcomes that are less than 146}}{\text{total number of outcomes in the sample space}} = \frac{36}{36} = 1$$

This numerical example demonstrates that the least probability possible for an event is 0 and that the greatest probability possible is 1. Thus, we see that negative probabilities or probabilities greater than 1 are impossible. **Further, we see that a declaration that a probability of a particular event is 4.6 or $-3\frac{1}{2}$ makes no sense because the probability of any event must be a number between 0 and 1, inclusive.**

83.B

independent events

We say that events that do not affect one another are **independent events.** If Danny flips a dime and Paul flips a penny, the outcome of Danny's flip does not affect the outcome of Paul's flip. Thus, we say that these events are independent events. **The probability of independent events occurring in a designated order is the product of the probabilities of the individual events.**

A tree diagram can always be used to demonstrate the probability of independent events occurring in a designated order. This diagram shows the possible outcomes if a coin is tossed three times.

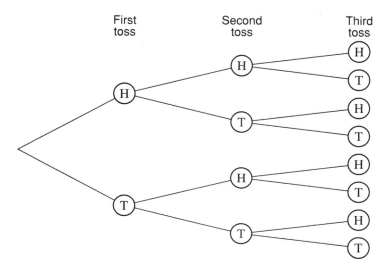

The first toss can be heads or tails and the second and third tosses can be heads or tails. Thus, there are 8 possible ordered outcomes, and the probability of each of these outcomes is $\frac{1}{8}$.

example 83.2   A fair coin is tossed 3 times. What is the probability that it comes up heads every time?

solution   Coin tosses are independent events because the result of one toss has no effect on the result of the next toss. Since the probability of independent events occurring in a designated order is the product of the individual probabilities, we have

$$P(3 \text{ heads}) \;=\; \frac{1}{2} \cdot \frac{1}{2} \cdot \frac{1}{2} \;=\; \frac{1}{8}$$

example 83.3   A fair coin is tossed 4 times and it comes up heads each time. What is the probability it will come up heads on the next toss?

solution   The results of past coin tosses do not affect the outcome of future coin tosses. Thus, the probability of getting a head on the next toss is $\frac{1}{2}$.

83.C

replacement

When we make successive random selections of cards from a deck or of marbles from an urn, the probability of a certain outcome on the second draw is affected by whether or not the item selected on the first draw is returned before the second draw is made.

example 83.4   An urn contains two black marbles and two white marbles. A marble is drawn at random and replaced. Then a second marble is randomly drawn. (a) What is the probability that both marbles are black? (b) If the first marble is not replaced before the second marble is drawn, what is the probability that both marbles are black?

solution   (a)   The probability of a black marble on the first draw is $\frac{1}{2}$. Since the first marble is replaced, the probability of a black marble on the second draw is also $\frac{1}{2}$, so

$$P(\text{both black}) \;=\; \frac{1}{2} \cdot \frac{1}{2} \;=\; \frac{1}{4}$$

(b)   The probability of a black marble on the second draw is not the same because the first marble was not replaced. The diagram shows the possibilities:

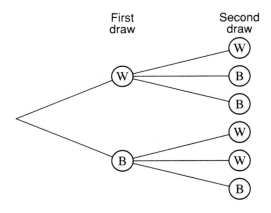

We see that if the first draw was black, then the probability of a black marble on the second draw is $\frac{1}{3}$ because only 3 marbles remain. Thus, the probability of 2 black marbles when there is no replacement between draws is

$$P(\text{both black}) \;=\; \frac{1}{2} \cdot \frac{1}{3} \;=\; \frac{1}{6}$$

example 83.5   Two cards are drawn from a 52-card deck without replacement. What is the probability that the first one is red and the second one is black?

solution   The probability of the second draw changes because there is no replacement.

$$P(\text{red, then black}) \;=\; \frac{26}{52} \cdot \frac{26}{51} \;=\; \frac{13}{51}$$

problem set 83

1.   Two cables are attached to a vertical tower from a point on the ground. The angle between the cables is 10°. The longer cable is 150 feet long and is attached to the top of the tower. The shorter cable is attached to the tower 70 feet below the top of the tower. Find the length of the shorter cable.

2.   The cost varied linearly with the number of workers that were employed. When 10 workers were employed the cost was $450, and when 20 workers were employed the cost was $850. What would it cost if only 2 workers were employed?

3.   If M men could do J jobs in 1 day, how many days would it take 5 fewer men to do k jobs?

4.   Two fair dice are rolled. What is the probability of getting a number greater than 9?

5.   An urn contains 5 red marbles and 12 white marbles. A marble is drawn at random and replaced. Then another marble is randomly drawn. What is the probability that the first marble will be red and the second marble will be white?

6.   In problem 5, what is the probability that the first marble will be red and the second will be white if the first marble drawn is not replaced before the second marble is drawn?

Solve:

7. $7^{2x-4} = 5^{3x+2}$

8. $10^{3x-1} = 5^{4x-2}$

Solve the following triangles for their unknown parts:

9.

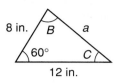

8 in. / B \ a

60° C

12 in.

10.

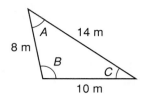

A 14 m

8 m

B

10 m

Show:

11. $\dfrac{\sin A}{1 - \cos A} + \dfrac{1 - \cos A}{\sin A} = 2 \csc A$

12. $\dfrac{\sec^2 \theta - \tan^2 \theta}{\tan^2 \theta + 1} = \cos^2 \theta$

13. $\dfrac{1}{\tan (-x)} + \tan (-x) = -\sec x \csc x$

14. Use De Moivre's theorem to find $(-1 + i)^{10}$. Write the answer in rectangular form. Give an exact answer.

15. Write the five fifth roots of $32 \operatorname{cis} 60°$ in polar form.

16. Write the four fourth roots of 1 in rectangular form. Give exact answers.

17. Given the hyperbola $9y^2 - 16x^2 = 144$, write the equation in standard form and find the coordinates of its vertices and the equations of the asymptotes. Graph the hyperbola.

18. Write the middle term of $(x + z)^6$.

19. Use Cramer's rule to solve: $\begin{cases} 5x + 3y = -1 \\ 4x + 5y = 7 \end{cases}$

20. The perimeter of a 12-sided regular polygon is 96 centimeters. Find the area of the polygon and the radius of the circle that can be inscribed in the polygon.

21. Write the equation of the ellipse $16x^2 + 9y^2 = 144$ in standard form and sketch its graph.

22. Write the equation of the sinusoid as a cosine function.

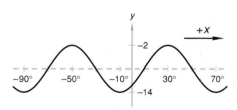

Solve the following equations given that $0° \le \theta < 360°$:

23. $\sec^2 \theta + \sec \theta - 2 = 0$

24. $\csc 2\theta - 2 = 0$

25. Evaluate: $\tan \left[\operatorname{Arccos} \left(-\dfrac{4}{5} \right) \right]$

26. Graph the solution to the system of inequalities: $\begin{cases} y^2 + x^2 + 2x - 6y \ge 6 \\ 8y - x^2 - 2x \ge -63 \end{cases}$

27. Find the distance from the point (4, 2) to the line $3x - 2y = 1$.

28. Solve for x: $\log_8 16 - \log_8 4 = x$

29. Simplify: $\log_5 10 - \log_5 2 + 5^{3 \log_5 2 - \log_5 4}$

30. Factor $x^2 + 27$ over the set of complex numbers.

LESSON 84 *Factorable Expressions • Sketching Sinusoids*

84.A

factorable expressions

Calculus books are rife with problems whose solutions require the factoring of trigonometric expressions such as the ones shown below. Practice with these factorable expressions will improve our ability to change the form of trigonometric expressions and will lessen the intimidation when these expressions are encountered in calculus and in other advanced mathematics courses. For the present, we can consider these problems as puzzles whose solutions have no immediate applications but will be of great value in the future.

EXPRESSION	FACTORED FORM
$\sin^3 x$	$\longrightarrow$ $(\sin x)(\sin^2 x)$
$\tan^2 \theta - 1$	$\longrightarrow$ $(\tan \theta + 1)(\tan \theta - 1)$
$1 - \tan^2 \theta$	$\longrightarrow$ $(1 + \tan \theta)(1 - \tan \theta)$
$\csc^2 x - 1$	$\longrightarrow$ $(\csc x + 1)(\csc x - 1)$
$\sin x - \sin x \cos^2 x$	$\longrightarrow$ $(\sin x)(1 - \cos^2 x)$
$\csc^4 P - \cot^4 P$	$\longrightarrow$ $(\csc^2 P + \cot^2 P)(\csc^2 P - \cot^2 P)$
$1 - 2\sin^2 x + \sin^4 x$	$\longrightarrow$ $(1 - \sin^2 x)(1 - \sin^2 x)$
$\sin^3 x - \cos^3 x$	$\longrightarrow$ $(\sin x - \cos x)(\sin^2 x + \sin x \cos x + \cos^2 x)$

The last two are especially tricky because they must be recognized as having the same form as

$$1 - 2x + x^2 \longrightarrow (1 - x)(1 - x)$$

$$x^3 - y^3 \longrightarrow (x - y)(x^2 + xy + y^2)$$

Look over the forms shown because when one of these forms appears in an identity, it is necessary to recognize that it can be factored.

example 84.1 Show: $\sin x - \sin x \cos^2 x = \sin^3 x$

solution First we will factor the left-hand side and get

$$(\sin x)(1 - \cos^2 x) \qquad \text{factored}$$

But $1 - \cos^2 x$ equals $\sin^2 x$, so we have

$$(\sin x)(\sin^2 x) = \sin^3 x$$

example 84.2 Show: $\dfrac{\sec^4 x - \tan^4 x}{\sec^2 x + \tan^2 x} + \tan^2 x = \sec^2 x$

solution We begin by factoring $\sec^4 x - \tan^4 x$ and we get

$$\frac{(\sec^2 x + \tan^2 x)(\sec^2 x - \tan^2 x)}{\sec^2 x + \tan^2 x} + \tan^2 x \qquad \text{factored}$$

$$\sec^2 x - \tan^2 x + \tan^2 x = \sec^2 x \qquad \text{canceled and added}$$

example 84.3   Show: $\dfrac{\csc^2 x - 1}{\tan x} = \cot^3 x$

solution   Factoring won't always work. If we factor in this problem, we get

$$\frac{(\csc x + 1)(\csc x - 1)}{\tan x}$$

and this time factoring did not help. So we remember that $\csc^2 x - 1$ equals $\cot^2 x$ and that $1/\tan x$ equals $\cot x$. We get

$$\frac{\csc^2 x - 1}{\tan x} = \cot^2 x \cdot \frac{1}{\tan x} = \left(\cot^2 x\right)(\cot x) = \cot^3 x$$

84.B

sketching sinusoids

Sinusoids can be sketched quickly and accurately if the curve is drawn first and then the labels added. The crucial label for the sine function is the phase angle, which is the opposite of the angle in the factored argument. The curve crosses its centerline when θ equals the phase angle. Other crossing points are found by adding or subtracting multiples of half the period to the phase angle. The crucial label for the cosine function is the phase angle, which again is the opposite of the angle in the factored argument. A positive cosine curve reaches its maximum value when θ equals the phase angle. The values of θ for other extreme values of the curve are found by adding or subtracting multiples of half the period to the phase angle.

example 84.4   Sketch the graph of $y = -10 + 2 \sin 3(x - 45°)$.

solution   As the first step we will sketch a sinusoid, and to the left of the curve we draw a vertical scale on which we indicate the value of the centerline and the maximum and minimum values of the curve.

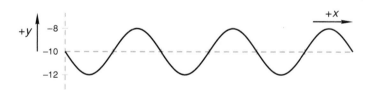

Next, from $(x - 45°)$, we see that the phase angle is $+45°$ because the angle in the argument is the opposite of the phase angle. Thus, one crossing point is the phase angle, which is $+45°$. This curve will cross its centerline every half period. The period for this function is $360°$ divided by 3, or $120°$. Half the period is $60°$, so we label the other crossing points $60°$ apart to the left and right of $+45°$.

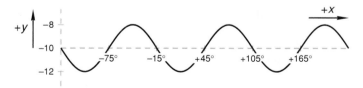

This graph is adequate, but it could be improved slightly by indicating the location of the y axis. We note that $0°$ will lie between $-15°$ and $+45°$ and will be exactly one fourth of the way from $-15°$ to $+45°$. We indicate the location of the y axis to complete the graph.

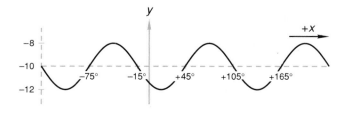

example 84.5 Sketch the graph of $y = -2 + 4 \cos 2\left(x + \dfrac{2\pi}{3}\right)$.

solution This time we will begin by determining the values of x for which the curve is a maximum. The phase angle is $-2\pi/3$, and this is one maximum point. The period is π radians, so the curve will have a maximum value every π radians to the right and the left of this point. We draw a sinusoid and label the centerline and the maximum values.

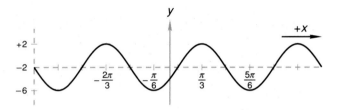

The minimum points occur regularly one half period, or $\pi/2$ radians, to the right and left of the maximum points. We label the minimum points and locate the position of the y axis to complete the graph.

problem set 84

1. A fair coin was flipped 3 times. What is the probability that the first two tosses come up heads and the third toss then comes up tails?

2. The urn contained 7 marbles. Four were white and 3 were blue. Two marbles were randomly drawn. What is the probability that both were white (a) with replacement? (b) without replacement?

3. The average temperature for 5 days was $100°$, and then it was cold for 1 day. That brought the average down to 90 degrees for the 6-day period. What was the temperature on the sixth day?

4. Frankie ran the k yards in p minutes and arrived at the party m minutes early. How fast should Frankie have run to have arrived at the party on time?

5. Ten workers could do p jobs in 5 days. This was too slow, so the contractor hired 5 more workers. How many days would it take the new work force to complete k jobs?

6. Donny found that he could do 4 jobs in 3 days. When Donny worked with Christopher, they found they could finish 11 jobs in 6 days. How many jobs could Christopher complete in 4 days working alone?

Sketch the graphs of the following:

7. $y = -2 + 4 \cos \dfrac{1}{2}(x + 30°)$

8. $y = -1 + 8 \sin 2(x - 45°)$

Show:

9. $\dfrac{\csc^4 x - \cot^4 x}{\csc^2 x + \cot^2 x} + \cot^2 x = \csc^2 x$

10. $\cos x - \cos x \sin^2 x = \cos^3 x$

11. $\dfrac{\sec^2 \theta - 1}{\cot \theta} = \tan^3 \theta$

12. $\cos(-\theta)\csc(-\theta) = \cot(-\theta)$

Solve:

13. $8^{3x-1} = 5^{2x+1}$

14. $2 \cdot 10^{2x-3} = 4^{2x+1}$ $\left[\textit{Hint: } \log\left(2 \cdot 10^{2x-3}\right) = \log 2 + \log 10^{2x-3}\right]$

15. Solve this triangle for its unknown parts.

16. Find q.

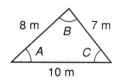

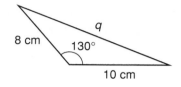

17. Find $\left(\dfrac{1}{2} \text{ cis } 100°\right)^3$ and express the answer in polar form.

18. Write the four fourth roots of 16 cis 120° in rectangular form. Give exact answers.

19. Write the three third roots of 8 in rectangular form. Give exact answers.

20. Given the hyperbola $4x^2 - 25y^2 = 400$, write the equation in standard form and find the coordinates of its vertices and the equations of the asymptotes. Graph the hyperbola.

21. Write all eight terms of $(a + c)^7$.

22. The perimeter of a 10-sided regular polygon (regular decagon) is 60 centimeters. Find the radius of the circle that can be circumscribed about the regular decagon and the area of the regular decagon.

23. Write the equation in standard form and graph the ellipse: $2x^2 + 25y^2 = 50$

24. Find the radius and the coordinates of the center of the circle whose equation is $x^2 + y^2 + 6x - 4y - 15 = 0$. Graph the circle.

25. Multiply (5 cis 205°)(2 cis 155°) and express the answer in rectangular form. Give an exact answer.

Solve the following equations given that $(0 \leq \theta, x < 2\pi)$:

26. $2 \cos \dfrac{\theta}{3} + \sqrt{3} = 0$

27. $3 \sec^2 x - 4 = 0$

28. Find the distance from the point $(0, 0)$ to the line $y = 3x + 1$.

29. Solve for x: $\dfrac{3}{2} \log_8 4 + 2 \log_8 x = \log_8 16$

30. A graduate student in education looks at several high school math textbooks and records the number of pages each contains. She then decides that the data are normally distributed with a mean of 700 pages and a standard deviation of 40 pages. If the student is correct, what percentage of high school math textbooks would have at least 728 pages?

LESSON 85 Advanced Trigonometric Equations •
Clock Problems

85.A

advanced trigonometric equations

We work with trigonometric equations to give us practice with the signs and values of the trigonometric functions in the four quadrants. We can devise trigonometric equations that contain two different trigonometric functions that also will give us practice in using these three identities.

$$\sin^2 \theta + \cos^2 \theta = 1 \qquad \tan^2 \theta + 1 = \sec^2 \theta \qquad 1 + \cot^2 \theta = \csc^2 \theta$$

example 85.1 Solve $3 \tan^2 \theta = 7 \sec \theta - 5$ given that $0° \le \theta < 360°$.

solution This equation contains a $\tan^2 \theta$ term and a $\sec \theta$ term. If we replace $\tan^2 \theta$ with $\sec^2 \theta - 1$ from the middle identity above, we will have an equation whose only variable is $\sec \theta$.

$$3(\sec^2 \theta - 1) = 7 \sec \theta - 5 \qquad \text{substituted}$$

$$3 \sec^2 \theta - 3 = 7 \sec \theta - 5 \qquad \text{multiplied}$$

$$3 \sec^2 \theta - 7 \sec \theta + 2 = 0 \qquad \text{rearranged}$$

This equation has the same form as $3s^2 - 7s + 2 = 0$, which can be factored as $(3s - 1)(s - 2) = 0$. Thus, we can factor the secant variable equation, set each of the factors equal to zero, and solve.

$$(3 \sec \theta - 1)(\sec \theta - 2) = 0$$

If $3 \sec \theta - 1 = 0$ If $\sec \theta - 2 = 0$

$3 \sec \theta = 1$ $\sec \theta = 2$

$\sec \theta = \dfrac{1}{3}$

If the secant has a value of $\frac{1}{3}$, the cosine has a value of 3. This is impossible because the cosine is never greater than 1, and thus we discard this solution. If the secant has a value of 2, the cosine equals $\frac{1}{2}$.

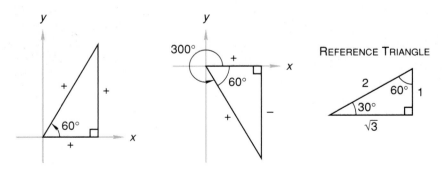

The cosine of 60° is $\frac{1}{2}$ and the cosine is positive in the first and fourth quadrants. Thus our answers are 60° and 300°.

$$\theta = 60°, 300°$$

example 85.2   Solve $2 \sin^2 x = 3 + 3 \cos x$ given that $0° \le x < 360°$.

solution   Since $\sin^2 x + \cos^2 x = 1$, we will replace $\sin^2 x$ in the given equation with $1 - \cos^2 x$.

$$2(1 - \cos^2 x) = 3 + 3 \cos x \qquad \text{substituted}$$

$$2 - 2 \cos^2 x = 3 + 3 \cos x \qquad \text{multiplied}$$

$$2 \cos^2 x + 3 \cos x + 1 = 0 \qquad \text{rearranged}$$

Now we factor, set each of the factors equal to zero, and solve.

$$(2 \cos x + 1)(\cos x + 1) = 0$$

If $2 \cos x + 1 = 0$	If $\cos x + 1 = 0$
$2 \cos x = -1$	$\cos x = -1$
$\cos x = -\dfrac{1}{2}$	

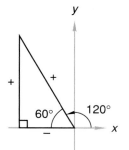 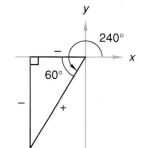 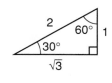

REFERENCE TRIANGLE

The cosine of $60°$ is $\frac{1}{2}$ and the cosine is negative in the second and third quadrants. Also, the angle whose cosine is -1 is $180°$.

$$x = \mathbf{120°, 180°, 240°}$$

example 85.3   Solve $2 \tan^2 \theta = \sec \theta - 1$ given that $0° \le \theta < 360°$.

solution   We will begin by substituting $\sec^2 \theta - 1$ for $\tan^2 \theta$.

$$2(\sec^2 \theta - 1) = \sec \theta - 1 \qquad \text{substituted}$$

$$2 \sec^2 \theta - 2 = \sec \theta - 1 \qquad \text{multiplied}$$

$$2 \sec^2 \theta - \sec \theta - 1 = 0 \qquad \text{rearranged}$$

This equation has the same form as $2x^2 - x - 1 = 0$, which can be factored as $(2x + 1)(x - 1) = 0$. We will factor the secant variable equation, set each of the factors equal to zero, and solve.

$$(2 \sec \theta + 1)(\sec \theta - 1) = 0$$

If $2 \sec \theta + 1 = 0$	If $\sec \theta - 1 = 0$
	$\sec \theta = 1$
$\sec \theta = -\dfrac{1}{2}$	

If the secant equals $-\frac{1}{2}$, then the cosine equals -2. But this is impossible because the values of the cosine lie between -1 and $+1$. Thus, we discard this result. On the right, if the secant equals 1, the cosine also equals 1. The cosine is 1 at $\theta = 0°$ and for no other values of $0° \le \theta < 360°$, so our answer is

$$\theta = \mathbf{0°}$$

85.B

clock problems

In some rate problems, it is convenient to measure distances in spaces and rate in spaces per unit time. In these problems, rate times time equals spaces. For instance, if one thing moved at 20 spaces per second, it would move 100 spaces in 5 seconds.

$$\text{Rate} \times \text{time} = \text{spaces}$$

$$20 \, \frac{\text{spaces}}{\cancel{s}} \times 5\cancel{s} = 100 \text{ spaces}$$

Problems about the hands of a clock fall into this category. The spaces are the 60 one-minute spaces around the face. The rate of the minute hand is 1 space per minute, and the rate of the hour hand is 5 spaces per 60 minutes, or $\frac{1}{12}$ space per minute.

example 85.4   The hands of a clock point in the same direction. In how many minutes will they point in opposite directions?

solution   The little hand will move through S spaces and the big hand will move through $S + 30$ spaces so that it will be 30 spaces ahead. The equations are

$$R_L T_L = S \qquad R_B T_B = S + 30 \qquad R_B = 1 \qquad R_L = \frac{1}{12} \qquad T_L = T_B$$

We note that the presence of five unknowns required that we write five equations to get a unique solution. We begin by substituting into the first two equations and get

$$\frac{T_L}{12} = S \qquad T_B = S + 30$$

The right-hand equation tells us that $S = T_B - 30$. We equate the two values of S and eliminate the subscripts on T because the times are equal. Then we solve.

$$\frac{T_L}{12} = T_B - 30 \qquad \qquad \text{both equal } S$$

$$\frac{T}{12} = T - 30 \qquad \qquad T_L = T_B = T$$

$$T = 12T - 360 \qquad \qquad \text{multiplied}$$

$$11T = 360 \qquad \qquad \text{simplified}$$

$$T = 32\frac{8}{11} \text{ min} \qquad \qquad \text{solved}$$

example 85.5   It is three o'clock. In how many minutes will the two hands of the clock point in the same direction?

solution   The hands are 15 spaces apart, so the little hand will travel S spaces and the big hand will have to travel $S + 15$ spaces to catch up. The equations are

$$R_L T_L = S \qquad R_B T_B = S + 15 \qquad R_L = \frac{1}{12} \qquad R_B = 1 \qquad T_L = T_B$$

Since the times are equal, we can delete the subscripts on T. We begin by substituting into the first two equations and get

$$\frac{T}{12} = S \qquad T = S + 15$$

We solve the right-hand equation for S, substitute, and solve for T.

$$\frac{T}{12} = T - 15 \qquad \text{substituted}$$

$$T = 12T - 180 \qquad \text{multiplied}$$

$$11T = 180 \qquad \text{simplified}$$

$$T = 16\frac{4}{11} \text{ min} \qquad \text{solved}$$

problem set 85

1. It is high noon and the crowd is waiting for the time when the big hand and the little hand will be pointing in opposite directions. How long will they have to wait?

2. It is nine o'clock. How long will it be before both hands are pointing in the same direction?

3. The first time Henry made the trip he drove at 10 miles per hour and arrived 5 hours late. The next time he drove at 25 miles per hour and arrived 1 hour early. How many miles long was the trip? (*Hint*: The correct time is the time for the first trip minus 5 hours. Also, the correct time is the time for the second trip plus 1 hour.)

4. An urn contains 4 red marbles and 3 white marbles. Two marbles are drawn at random and replaced. Both marbles are red. What is the probability the next marble randomly drawn will be red?

5. Two fair dice are rolled. What is the probability that an even number less than 10 is rolled?

6. Four boys and two girls sit in six chairs placed in a circle. How many seating arrangements are possible?

7. Two cables are attached to a vertical tower from a point on the ground. The angle between the cables is 25°. The longer cable is 215 feet long and attached to the top of the tower. The shorter cable is attached to the tower 95 feet below the top of the tower. Find the length of the shorter cable.

8. Find three consecutive even integers such that the product of the first and the second equals the product of the third and the number 3.

Solve the following equations given that $0° \le \theta < 360°$:

9. $3 \tan^2 \theta = 7 \sec \theta - 5$

10. $2 \sin^2 \theta = 3 + 3 \cos \theta$

11. $2 \tan^2 \theta = \sec \theta - 1$

Sketch the graphs of the following:

12. $y = -2 + 5 \sin 3\left(x - \dfrac{\pi}{3}\right)$

13. $y = 3 + 5 \cos \dfrac{1}{2}(x - 90°)$

Show:

14. $\dfrac{\cos^4 x - \sin^4 x}{\cos^2 x - \sin^2 x} = 1$

15. $\tan x + \cot x = \sec x \csc x$

16. $\dfrac{1}{1 + \cos x} + \dfrac{1}{1 - \cos x} = 2 \csc^2 x$

Solve:

17. $10^{3x-2} = 7^{2x+3}$

18. $5^{4x+2} = 3^{6x-1}$

19. Solve this triangle for its unknown parts.

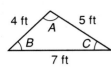

4 ft   5 ft
A
B   C
7 ft

20. Find p and the area of the triangle.

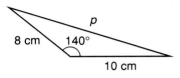

8 cm   140° p
10 cm

21. Use De Moivre's theorem to find $(1 - \sqrt{3}i)^4$. Write the answer in rectangular form.

22. Write the four fourth roots of 16 cis 240° in rectangular form. Give exact answers.

23. Given the hyperbola $4y^2 - 9x^2 = 144$, write the equation in standard form and find the coordinates of its vertices and the equations of the asymptotes. Graph the hyperbola.

24. Use Cramer's rule to solve: $\begin{cases} 2x - 3y = -4 \\ x + 2y = 8 \end{cases}$

25. The perimeter of an 8-sided regular polygon (regular octagon) is 32 cm. What is the area of the polygon? What is the radius of the circle that can be circumscribed about the polygon?

26. Write the equation in standard form and graph the ellipse: $9x^2 + 4y^2 = 72$

27. Multiply $\left(6 \text{ cis } \frac{2\pi}{3}\right)\left(3 \text{ cis } \frac{5\pi}{6}\right)$ and express the answer in rectangular form. Give an exact answer.

28. Find the mean, median, mode, variance, and standard deviation for the following data: $-2, -2, 1, 3, 0$.

29. Solve for x: $\log_3 (x + 2) - \log_3 (3x + 2) = \log_3 4$

30. Find the area of the segment bounded by an arc of measure 50° and the chord joining the endpoints of the arc in a circle whose radius is 10 centimeters.

LESSON 86 *Arithmetic Progressions and Arithmetic Means*

The English word **sequence** comes from the Latin word *sequi*, which means "to follow." **If a group of numbers is arranged in a definite order so that one number follows another number, we say the numbers have been arranged *sequentially* and that the numbers form a *sequence*.** On the left, we show six numbers in a random pattern. We say that these numbers are arranged nonsequentially. On the right, we show two of the many ways these six numbers can be arranged sequentially.

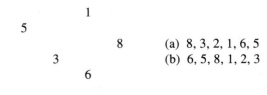

1
5
8   (a) 8, 3, 2, 1, 6, 5
3   (b) 6, 5, 8, 1, 2, 3
6
2

If a sequence has a finite number of members, we say that the sequence is a **finite sequence.** Sequences (a) and (b) have six members and are finite sequences. We write three dots after the last entry to indicate that a sequence has no end, as we show in sequence (c) below.

(c) 1, 2, 3, 4, 5, ...

Sequences with no end are called **infinite sequences.**

Subscripted variables are often used to designate the members of a sequence. The letters most often used for the variables are x, y, a, s, and t. When t is used, the authors often indicate that the letter is an abbreviation for the word *term*. We could use t to indicate the terms of an 8-term sequence by writing

$$t_1, t_2, t_3, t_4, t_5, t_6, t_7, t_8$$

or use the letter a and write

$$a_1, a_2, a_3, a_4, a_5, a_6, a_7, a_8$$

The English word **progression** comes from the Latin word *progredi*, which means "to go forward." In mathematics, we use this word to describe a sequence in which each term depends in some way on the term that precedes it. An **arithmetic progression** (arithmetic sequence) is formed by choosing a first term and then adding the same constant to form each succeeding term. Thus, each term in an arithmetic progression is greater (or less) than the one that precedes it by a given amount. We call the difference between terms the **common difference**, and **any sequence that has a common difference between the terms is an *arithmetic sequence*.** Each term in (a) is 3 greater than the preceding term. Thus, the **common difference** is +3.

(a) 7, $\underline{10}$, $\underline{13}$, $\underline{16}$, $\underline{19}$, 22

(b) 7, $\underline{3}$, $\underline{-1}$, $\underline{-5}$, $\underline{-9}$, $\underline{-13}$, -17

Each term in (b) is 4 less than the preceding term, so the common difference is -4. The terms between the end terms in a finite arithmetic sequence are called the **arithmetic means.** In (a) and (b) above the means are underlined. Sequence (a) has 6 terms and 4 means, and sequence (b) has 7 terms and 5 means. If we look at (a) and (b), we note that the second term uses the difference once. The third term uses the difference twice, the fourth term uses the difference three times, etc.

	①	②	③	④	⑤
(a)	7,	7 + (3),	7 + (3 + 3),	7 + (3 + 3 + 3),	7 + (3 + 3 + 3 + 3)
(b)	7,	7 + (−4),	7 + (−4 − 4),	7 + (−4 − 4 − 4),	7 + (−4 − 4 − 4 − 4)

Each term equals the first term plus the difference one fewer times than the number of the term. If we use a_1 for the first term and n for the number of the nth term, we have, in general,

①	②	③	④	⑤		ⓝ
a_1,	$a_1 + d$,	$a_1 + 2d$,	$a_1 + 3d$,	$a_1 + 4d$,	...,	$a_1 + (n - 1)d$

example 86.1   Write the first four terms of an arithmetic sequence whose first term is -14 and whose common difference is 10.

solution   We begin with -14 and add 10 to get each succeeding term.

①	②	③	④
-14,	$-14 + (10)$,	$-14 + (10 + 10)$,	$-14 + (10 + 10 + 10)$

Our sequence is

$$\mathbf{-14, -4, 6, 16, ...}$$

example 86.2   Find the twenty-fifth term of an arithmetic sequence whose first term is 12 and whose common difference is -6.

solution   The *first* term is 12. The *second* term is $12 + \underline{1}(-6)$. The *third* term is $12 + \underline{2}(-6)$, etc., until the twenty-fifth term, which will be

$$12 + \underline{24}(-6) = \mathbf{-132}$$

example 86.3   Insert three arithmetic means between 2 and -4.

solution   We always draw diagrams of problems when possible because diagrams aid understanding and help prevent mistakes. A useful diagram for this type of problem is to write the sequence twice, once using the given numbers and again using variables. There are 3 means, so each sequence has 5 terms. Often we find that we know enough to equate two pairs of corresponding terms in the two sequences. Then we can solve the resulting equations to find out what we want to know.

$$\begin{array}{ccccc}
① & ② & ③ & ④ & ⑤ \\
2, & \_\_\_, & \_\_\_, & \_\_\_, & -4 \\
a_1, & a_1 + d, & a_1 + 2d, & a_1 + 3d, & a_1 + 4d
\end{array}$$

From these sequences we see that the first terms imply equation (a) and the fifth terms imply equation (b).

$$\text{(a) } a_1 = 2 \qquad \text{(b) } a_1 + 4d = -4$$

We use substitution to solve these equations for d.

$$\begin{array}{ll}
2 + 4d = -4 & \text{substituted} \\
4d = -6 & \text{added } -2 \\
d = -1.5 & \text{divided by 4}
\end{array}$$

Now we can find the three means by adding -1.5 progressively to form the terms. Our sequence, with the means underlined, is

$$\textbf{2, \underline{0.5}, \underline{-1}, \underline{-2.5}, -4}$$

example 86.4   Write the first five terms of an arithmetic sequence in which $a_{17} = -40$ and $a_{28} = -73$.

solution   We begin with a diagram that shows the sequence twice.

$$\begin{array}{ccccc}
① & & ⑰ & & ㉘ \\
?, & \ldots, & -40, & \ldots, & -73 \\
a_1, & \ldots, & a_1 + 16d, & \ldots, & a_1 + 27d
\end{array}$$

In this problem we see that our equations will come from the seventeenth and the twenty-eighth terms.

$$\begin{array}{lllll}
⑰ & a_1 + 16d = -40 & \rightarrow & (-1) & \rightarrow & -a_1 - 16d = +40 \\
㉘ & a_1 + 27d = -73 & \rightarrow & (1) & \rightarrow & a_1 + 27d = -73 \\
\end{array}$$
$$\begin{array}{l}
\qquad\qquad\qquad\qquad\qquad\qquad\qquad\qquad\quad 11d = -33 \\
\qquad\qquad\qquad\qquad\qquad\qquad\qquad\qquad\quad\ d = -3
\end{array}$$

Now we use -3 for d in the top equation to find a_1.

$$\begin{array}{ll}
a_1 + 16(-3) = -40 & \text{substituted} \\
a_1 - 48 = -40 & \text{multiplied} \\
a_1 = 8 & \text{added}
\end{array}$$

Now we can write the first five terms.

$$\textbf{8, 5, 2, -1, -4}$$

example 86.5   Find the tenth term of an arithmetic sequence in which the first term is $3x + 2y$ and the sixth term is $8x + 12y$.

solution   We begin with a diagram that shows the sequence twice.

$$\overset{\text{①}}{3x + 2y}, \quad \overset{\text{②}}{\underline{\hspace{1cm}}}, \quad \overset{\text{③}}{\underline{\hspace{1cm}}}, \quad \overset{\text{④}}{\underline{\hspace{1cm}}}, \quad \overset{\text{⑤}}{\underline{\hspace{1cm}}}, \quad \overset{\text{⑥}}{8x + 12y}, \quad \dots, \quad \overset{\text{⑩}}{\underline{\hspace{1cm}}}$$

$$a_1, \quad a_1 + d, \quad a_1 + 2d, \quad a_1 + 3d, \quad a_1 + 4d, \quad a_1 + 5d, \quad \dots, \quad a_1 + 9d$$

In this problem our two equations come from the first and the sixth terms.

$$\text{①} \qquad a_1 = 3x + 2y \qquad \text{equated the first terms}$$
$$\text{⑥} \qquad a_1 + 5d = 8x + 12y \qquad \text{equated the sixth terms}$$
$$(3x + 2y) + 5d = 8x + 12y \qquad \text{substituted}$$
$$5d = 5x + 10y \qquad \text{added}$$
$$d = x + 2y \qquad \text{simplified}$$

Since the tenth term equals $a_1 + 9d$, we get

$$a_{10} = (3x + 2y) + 9(x + 2y) = \mathbf{12x + 20y}$$

problem set 86

1. Now it is six o'clock. In how many minutes will the little hand and the big hand be at right angles to each other?

2. One card is randomly drawn from a deck of 52 cards and not replaced. Then a second card is drawn at random. What is the probability that the first card will be a spade and the second card will not be a spade?

3. A pair of dice is rolled. What is the probability that the sum of the numbers on the dice is greater than 8?

4. The output varied linearly with the quality of the input. When the input quality was 10, the output was 45. When the input quality fell to 8, the output only fell to 37. Write a linear equation which describes output as a function of input.

5. Anne averaged 30 kilometers per hour, but arrived at the flower market 2 hours late. The next day she increased her average speed to 64 kilometers per hour and arrived at the flower market on time. How far was it to the flower market?

6. Find three consecutive even integers such that the product of the first and the third is 18 greater than the product of -1 and the third.

7. Write the first five terms of an arithmetic sequence whose first term is -10 and whose common difference is 6.

8. Find the thirtieth term of an arithmetic sequence whose first term is 5 and whose common difference is -4.

9. Insert three arithmetic means between 3 and -13.

10. Write the first five terms of an arithmetic sequence whose tenth term is -30 and whose twentieth term is 40.

11. Find the eighth term of an arithmetic sequence in which the first term is $2x + 3y$ and the sixth term is $7x + 8y$.

Solve the following equations given that $(0 \le x, \theta < 2\pi)$:

12. $2 \sin^2 x + 3 \sin x + 1 = 0$

13. $2 \tan^2 \theta = 3 \sec \theta - 3$

14. $-1 - \sqrt{3} \tan \dfrac{\theta}{2} = 0$

Sketch the graphs of the following:

15. $y = 4 + 7 \sin 2\left(x + \dfrac{\pi}{6}\right)$

16. $y = 1 + 5 \cos \dfrac{1}{3}(x - 105°)$

Show:

17. $\dfrac{\sec^2 x}{\sec^2 x - 1} = \csc^2 x$

18. $\dfrac{\cos^2 \theta}{\sin \theta} + \sin \theta = \csc \theta$

19. $\dfrac{\cos (-x)}{\sin (-x) \cot (-x)} = 1$

Solve:

20. $10^{3x-2} = 5^{2x-1} \cdot 10$

21. $3^{5x-3} = 9^{2-x}$

22. Find c.

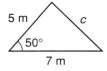

23. Solve this triangle for its unknown parts.

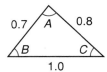

24. Write the three cube roots of 8 cis 270° in rectangular form. Give exact solutions.

25. Given the hyperbola $16x^2 - 9y^2 = 144$, write the equation in standard form and find the coordinates of its vertices and the equations of the asymptotes. Graph the hyperbola.

26. Write all four terms of $(r + s)^3$.

27. Spica took an art aptitude test and scored 435. The test scores were normally distributed with a mean of 300 and a standard deviation of 90. Was Spica's score in the upper 10% of the test scores? Justify your answer.

28. Graph the solution to the system of inequalities: $\begin{cases} \dfrac{x^2}{16} + \dfrac{y^2}{4} \le 1 \\ \dfrac{x^2}{4} + \dfrac{y^2}{16} \le 1 \end{cases}$

29. Find the distance from the point $(0, 0)$ to the line $x + y = 4$.

30. Solve for x: $\dfrac{2}{3} \log_5 8 - \log_5 (x - 4) = 1$

LESSON 87 *Sum and Difference Identities • Tangent Identities*

87.A

sum and difference identities

Unfortunately, the trigonometric functions of sums and products of angles cannot be determined by adding or multiplying the functions of the individual angles. For example, the values of the sines of 30° and 60° are

$$\sin 30° = \frac{1}{2} \qquad \sin 60° = \frac{\sqrt{3}}{2}$$

But as we show here, the sine of (2 × 30°) is not twice the sine of 30°, and the sine of (30° + 60°) is not the sine of 30° plus the sine of 60°.

$$\sin (2 \times 30°) \ne 2 \times \frac{1}{2} \qquad \text{because} \qquad \sin 60° = \frac{\sqrt{3}}{2}$$

$$\sin (30° + 60°) \ne \frac{1}{2} + \frac{\sqrt{3}}{2} \qquad \text{because} \qquad \sin 90° = 1$$

To find the functions of combinations of angles such as these, it is necessary to use trigonometric identities. There are other uses for trigonometric identities, and there are about 25 trigonometric identities that should be memorized because their use is required in calculus and in other upper-division mathematics courses. The ability to recall and use these identities permits a straightforward solution to problems whose solution is otherwise troublesome. Most people have difficulty remembering the identities because there are so many and because many identities look alike. Fortunately, if a few of the identities are memorized, the rest can be developed quickly and accurately when needed. The six key identities that should be memorized are

$$\text{(a)} \quad \sin (A + B) = \sin A \cos B + \cos A \sin B$$

$$\text{(b)} \quad \sin (A - B) = \sin A \cos B - \cos A \sin B$$

$$\text{(c)} \quad \cos (A + B) = \cos A \cos B - \sin A \sin B$$

$$\text{(d)} \quad \cos (A - B) = \cos A \cos B + \sin A \sin B$$

$$\text{(e)} \quad \tan \theta = \frac{\sin \theta}{\cos \theta}$$

$$\text{(f)} \quad \sin^2 \theta + \cos^2 \theta = 1$$

The derivations of (a), (b), (c), and (d) are difficult to follow unless one is familiar with the identities. So for now, we will concentrate on memorizing these identities. Their proofs can be found in the appendix. The identities (e) and (f) are used often and are easy to remember. To memorize the other four, it is helpful to look for patterns. The first pattern is that in each identity the letters A and B alternate A, B, A, B, A, B all the way across. The second thing to note is if the left-hand side begins with "sin," the right-hand side also begins with "sin," and if the left-hand side begins with "cos," the right-hand side also begins with "cos." In addition, we note that (b) is exactly the same as (a) except the signs in the middle are different, and that (d) is exactly the same as (c) except the signs in the middle are different. So if we can memorize the following

$$\sin (A + B) = \sin A \cos B + \cos A \sin B$$
$$(\quad - \quad) = \qquad\qquad -$$
$$\cos (A + B) = \cos A \cos B - \sin A \sin B$$
$$(\quad - \quad) = \qquad\qquad +$$

and remember that on the left the signs from top to bottom are $+, -, +, -$ and that on the right the middle signs from top to bottom are $+, -, -, +$, the four key identities can be reproduced. We suggest writing down these identities several times a day and that they be written down as a first step in taking any test that requires the use of trigonometric identities.

example 87.1   Simplify: $\sin \left(\theta + \dfrac{\pi}{4} \right)$

solution   This is the sine of a sum and requires the use of the identity for $\sin (A + B)$.

$$\sin (A + B) = \sin A \cos B + \cos A \sin B$$

Now replace A with θ and replace B with $\pi/4$.

$$\sin \left(\theta + \frac{\pi}{4} \right) = \sin \theta \cos \frac{\pi}{4} + \cos \theta \sin \frac{\pi}{4}$$

Both the sine and cosine of $\pi/4$ equal $1/\sqrt{2}$, so we get

$$\sin \left(\theta + \frac{\pi}{4} \right) = \sin \theta \cdot \frac{1}{\sqrt{2}} + \cos \theta \cdot \frac{1}{\sqrt{2}}$$

$$= \frac{\sqrt{2}}{2} \sin \theta + \frac{\sqrt{2}}{2} \cos \theta$$

$$= \frac{\sqrt{2}}{2} (\sin \theta + \cos \theta)$$

example 87.2   Find cos 15° by using a trigonometric identity and the fact that $15° = 60° - 45°$.

solution   We will use the identity for cos $(A - B)$.

$$\cos (A - B) = \cos A \cos B + \sin A \sin B$$

Now we replace A with 60° and B with 45°.

$$\cos (60° - 45°) = \cos 60° \cos 45° + \sin 60° \sin 45°$$

$$\cos 15° = \frac{1}{2} \cdot \frac{1}{\sqrt{2}} + \frac{\sqrt{3}}{2} \cdot \frac{1}{\sqrt{2}} = \frac{1}{2\sqrt{2}} + \frac{\sqrt{3}}{2\sqrt{2}} = \frac{\sqrt{2}}{4} + \frac{\sqrt{6}}{4} = \frac{\sqrt{2} + \sqrt{6}}{4}$$

example 87.3   Simplify: $\cos \left(\theta + \dfrac{\pi}{2} \right)$

solution   For this we will use the identity for cos $(A + B)$.

$$\cos (A + B) = \cos A \cos B - \sin A \sin B$$

We replace A with θ and B with $\pi/2$ and get

$$\cos \left(\theta + \frac{\pi}{2} \right) = \cos \theta \cos \frac{\pi}{2} - \sin \theta \sin \frac{\pi}{2}$$

Now cos $(\pi/2)$ is 0 and sin $(\pi/2)$ is 1, so we get

$$\cos \left(\theta + \frac{\pi}{2} \right) = (\cos \theta)(0) - (\sin \theta)(1) = -\sin \theta$$

87.B
tangent identities

The tangent of an angle equals the sine of the angle divided by the cosine of the angle.

$$\tan \theta = \frac{\sin \theta}{\cos \theta}$$

The argument does not have to be a single variable. If the argument is $4x - 3\pi$, we can write

$$\tan (4x - 3\pi) = \frac{\sin (4x - 3\pi)}{\cos (4x - 3\pi)}$$

Some people find it helpful to use empty parentheses, to write

$$\tan (\quad) = \frac{\sin (\quad)}{\cos (\quad)}$$

and to remember that the same entry must be made in all three parentheses.

example 87.4   Develop an identity for tan $(A + B)$.

solution   We know that tan $(A + B)$ equals sin $(A + B)$ divided by cos $(A + B)$.

$$\tan (A + B) = \frac{\sin (A + B)}{\cos (A + B)} = \frac{\sin A \cos B + \cos A \sin B}{\cos A \cos B - \sin A \sin B}$$

There are many forms of tangent identities. We will concentrate on forms in which the first entry in the denominator is the number 1. To change cos A cos B to 1, we must divide it by itself. We do this but also divide every other term in the whole expression by cos A cos B so that the value of the expression will be unchanged.

$$\tan (A + B) = \frac{\dfrac{\sin A \cos B}{\cos A \cos B} + \dfrac{\cos A \sin B}{\cos A \cos B}}{\dfrac{\cos A \cos B}{\cos A \cos B} - \dfrac{\sin A \sin B}{\cos A \cos B}}$$

We cancel as shown and end up with

$$\tan (A + B) = \frac{\tan A + \tan B}{1 - \tan A \tan B}$$

example 87.5   Develop an identity for $\tan (A - B)$.

solution   The procedure is the same except we use the identities for $(A - B)$ instead of for $(A + B)$.

$$\tan (A - B) = \frac{\dfrac{\sin A \cos B}{\cos A \cos B} - \dfrac{\cos A \sin B}{\cos A \cos B}}{\dfrac{\cos A \cos B}{\cos A \cos B} + \dfrac{\sin A \sin B}{\cos A \cos B}}$$

We cancel as shown and end up with

$$\tan (A - B) = \frac{\tan A - \tan B}{1 + \tan A \tan B}$$

example 87.6   Evaluate $\tan (\theta + 45°)$.

solution   We will use the identity for $\tan (A + B)$.

$$\tan (A + B) = \frac{\tan A + \tan B}{1 - \tan A \tan B}$$

We substitute θ for A and $45°$ for B and get

$$\tan (\theta + 45°) = \frac{\tan \theta + \tan 45°}{1 - \tan \theta \tan 45°}$$

Now $\tan 45°$ equals 1, so we get

$$\tan (\theta + 45°) = \frac{\tan \theta + 1}{1 - (\tan \theta)(1)} = \frac{\tan \theta + 1}{1 - \tan \theta}$$

problem set 87

1. Nate looked at his watch when the sun appeared and saw that it was exactly five o'clock. He could not begin until both hands on his watch pointed in the same direction. How long did he have to wait?

2. A pair of dice is rolled. What is the probability that the number rolled will be greater than 10 or less than 6?

3. An urn contains 4 red marbles, 2 white marbles, and 3 green marbles. Two marbles are drawn at random. What is the probability that the first is white and the second is green if the marbles are drawn (a) with replacement?   (b) without replacement?

4. Jimbob averaged 60 kilometers per hour from his home to the office, but arrived 1 hour late. The next day he increased his speed to 90 kilometers per hour and arrived 1 hour early. How far was it from his home to the office?

5. The panther ran a distance of x yards in y minutes but arrived k minutes late to the feast. How fast would the panther have had to run to have arrived on time?

6. Find three consecutive multiples of 3 such that 3 times the sum of the first and the third exceeds 4 times the second by 42.

7. Find $\sin 15°$ by using a trigonometric identity and the fact that $15° = 60° - 45°$. Use exact values.

8. Simplify $\cos \left(\theta - \dfrac{\pi}{4} \right)$ by using sum and difference identities. Use exact values.

9. Develop the identity for $\tan (A + B)$ by using the identities for $\sin (A + B)$ and $\cos (A + B)$.

10. Find $\tan 75°$ by using a trigonometric identity and the fact that $75° = 30° + 45°$. Use exact values.

11. Find the tenth term of an arithmetic sequence whose first term is 6 and whose common difference is -3.

12. Find the four arithmetic means between 6 and 106.

13. Write the first four terms of an arithmetic sequence in which the tenth term is 39 and the fourth term is 15.

Solve the following equations given that $(0° \leq x, \theta < 360°)$:

14. $2 \cos^2 x + \sin x + 1 = 0$ **15.** $\tan^2 x - 3 \sec x + 3 = 0$

16. $1 + 2 \cos 2\theta = 0$

Sketch the graphs of the following:

17. $y = -4 - 2 \cos (x - 45°)$ **18.** $y = -2 + 3 \sin \frac{2}{3}(x + 90°)$

Show:

19. $\sec x + \sec x \tan^2 x = \sec^3 x$ **20.** $\dfrac{\sin^2 x}{\cos x} + \cos x = \sec x$

21. $\dfrac{\tan (-\theta) \cos (-\theta)}{\sin (-\theta)} = 1$

Solve:

22. $3^{3x+2} = 5^{6x-1}$ **23.** $\dfrac{6^{2x-4}}{10^{3x+1}} = 1$

24. Solve this triangle for its unknown parts.

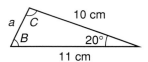

25. Write the four fourth roots of 16 cis 40° in polar form.

26. Given the hyperbola $25y^2 - 4x^2 = 100$, write the equation in standard form and find the coordinates of its vertices and the equations of the asymptotes. Graph the hyperbola.

27. Use Cramer's rule to solve: $\begin{cases} 4x - 5y = 3 \\ 3x + 2y = -10 \end{cases}$

28. A six-sided regular polygon (regular hexagon) has a perimeter of 30 inches. What is the area of the regular hexagon? What is the radius of the circle that can be inscribed in the regular hexagon?

Solve for x:

29. $\log (x + 1) + \log (x - 2) = 1$ **30.** $\log_3 7x + \frac{2}{3} \log_3 27 = 4$

LESSON 88 Exponential Functions (Growth and Decay)

Exponential equations of the form

$$A_t = A_0 e^{kt}$$

are important because they can be used to help us understand many everyday problems such as the growth of bacteria in biology, the voltage across a capacitor in engineering, radioactive decay in physics, and the growth of money in banking. The independent variable is t and is plotted on the horizontal axis. The dependent variable is A_t and is plotted on the vertical axis. The letters A_0 and k are constants whose values must be determined for each problem. Real-world problems often begin when time equals zero, so negative time has no meaning in these problems. Thus, the graphs begin when t is zero.

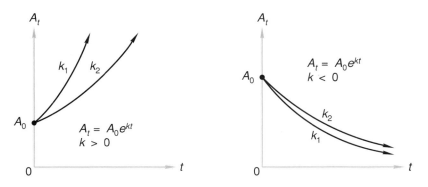

We use A_0 to designate the value of A_t when time is zero and call this value the **initial value** or the **initial amount.** In the left-hand figure, A_t equals A_0 when time is zero, and A_t increases as time increases because k is positive. In the right-hand figure, A_t equals A_0 when time is zero and decreases as time increases because k is negative. In each figure, the curves show that the change is faster for k_1 than for k_2. This is true if $|k_1|$ is greater than $|k_2|$.

We remember that direct and inverse variation problems are two-step problems and that the first step is to solve for the value of the constant of proportionality k. Exponential growth or decay problems are also two-step problems in which the first step is to solve for the value of the constant k in the exponent. We will solve for k by taking the logarithm of both sides of the equation. Next we will replace k in the equation with the proper value.

Then we will do the second part of the solution. **If time is given and the amount is the unknown, a simple evaluation is required. If the amount is given and time is the unknown, we must again take the logarithm of both sides to find t.** The scientific calculator will enable quick and accurate solutions to these problems.

example 88.1   The number of bacteria present at noon was 400, and 9 hours later the bacteria numbered 800. Assume exponential growth and find the number of bacteria present at noon the next day.

solution   We begin by writing the exponential equation for the number of bacteria present at some time t. We use the symbol A_t to represent this number.

$$A_t = A_0 e^{kt}$$

For this problem time began at noon. The number of bacteria was 400 when time equaled 0 (noon), so A_0 equals 400. Now we have

$$A_t = 400 e^{kt}$$

Solving for k always requires that we take the natural logarithm of both sides of the equation. To solve for k, we use 9 for t and 800 for A_t. Next we divide both sides of the equation by 400 to isolate the exponential. Then we take the natural logarithm of both sides so we can solve for k. Then we use this value of k in the equation.

$$A_t = 400e^{kt} \qquad \text{equation}$$

$$800 = 400e^{9k} \qquad \text{substituted}$$

$$2 = e^{9k} \qquad \text{divided by 400}$$

$$0.693 = 9k \qquad \text{ln of both sides}$$

$$0.077 = k \qquad \text{solved for } k$$

$$A_t = 400e^{0.077t} \qquad \text{replaced } k \text{ with } 0.077$$

Now that we have k, we can complete the second part of the solution. We are asked for A_{24}, which is the value of A_t when t equals 24. All that is required is an evaluation of the exponential when t is replaced with 24.

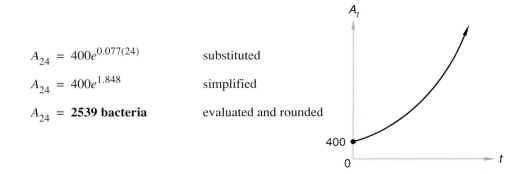

$$A_{24} = 400e^{0.077(24)} \qquad \text{substituted}$$

$$A_{24} = 400e^{1.848} \qquad \text{simplified}$$

$$A_{24} = \textbf{2539 bacteria} \qquad \text{evaluated and rounded}$$

The sketch shown at the right is accurate enough for most purposes. It shows that time is plotted horizontally and the amount is plotted vertically. It also shows the amount when time equals zero and indicates that the amount increases exponentially as time increases.

example 88.2   The number of bacteria present when the experiment began was 1200. After 100 hours there were 2700 bacteria present. Assume exponential growth and find the time required for the number of bacteria to increase to 30,000. Sketch the curve.

solution   First we must find the constant k for this problem and insert this number into the equation. We begin with the equation and use 1200 for A_0. Next we replace A_t with 2700 and t with 100. Then we divide to isolate the exponential and take the natural logarithm of both sides to solve for k.

$$A_t = 1200e^{kt} \qquad \text{used 1200 for } A_0$$

$$2700 = 1200e^{100k} \qquad \text{substituted}$$

$$2.25 = e^{100k} \qquad \text{divided by 1200}$$

$$0.81093 = 100k \qquad \text{ln of both sides}$$

$$0.00811 = k \qquad \text{solved for } k$$

$$A_t = 1200e^{0.00811t} \qquad \text{substituted}$$

Now that we have the value for k, we can solve for the time when the amount present is 30,000. **To solve for t, we must again take the natural logarithm of both sides of the equation.**

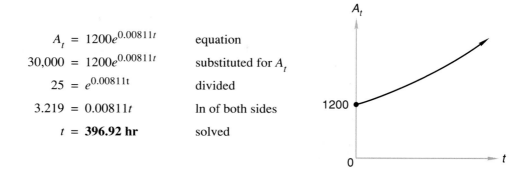

$A_t = 1200e^{0.00811t}$	equation	
$30{,}000 = 1200e^{0.00811t}$	substituted for A_t	
$25 = e^{0.00811t}$	divided	
$3.219 = 0.00811t$	ln of both sides	
$t = \mathbf{396.92\ hr}$	solved	

The sketch shown is sufficient. It shows the initial amount and indicates that the amount increases exponentially as time increases.

example 88.3   The amount of substance initially present was 400 grams, and after 90 hours only 380 grams remained. Assume an exponential decrease and determine the half-life of the substance. Make a sketch of the graph.

solution   The **half-life** is the time required for the amount to decrease to half the original amount. Thus, we are asked to find the time required for the amount present to decrease from 400 grams to 200 grams. **We begin as always by substituting, isolating the exponential, and then taking the natural logarithm of both sides to find k.**

$A_t = 400e^{kt}$	equation
$380 = 400e^{90k}$	substituted
$0.95 = e^{90k}$	divided
$-0.051 = 90k$	ln of both sides
$-0.00057 = k$	solved
$A_t = 400e^{-0.00057t}$	substituted

Now that we have the value for k, we can solve for the time required to have only 200 grams remaining.

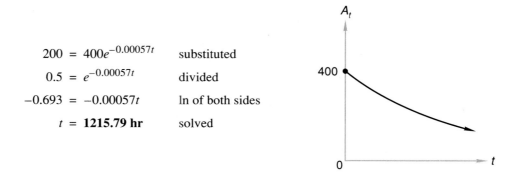

$200 = 400e^{-0.00057t}$	substituted
$0.5 = e^{-0.00057t}$	divided
$-0.693 = -0.00057t$	ln of both sides
$t = \mathbf{1215.79\ hr}$	solved

The graph shows all that we want to know. It shows the amount when t equals 0 and indicates that the amount decreases exponentially with time. The amount present always decreases with time when k is a negative number.

example 88.4   A radioactive substance decays exponentially. After 100 years, 500 grams is left, and after 200 years, only 300 grams remains. Find the amount of the substance that was initially present and its half-life.

solution   Unlike all the earlier examples, we are not given the value of A_0. Doing what we have done for the earlier examples will not work; therefore, we approach this problem differently. We will use the information given to write two exponential equations. Then we will divide one equation by the other to yield an exponential equation that we can solve for k. First we begin with the exponential equation describing the decay of the substance.

$$A_t = A_0 e^{kt}$$

After 100 years, 500 grams remains.

$$500 = A_0 e^{k(100)} = A_0 e^{100k}$$

After 200 years, 300 grams remains.

$$300 = A_0 e^{k(200)} = A_0 e^{200k}$$

This gives us a system of two exponential equations to solve. We will begin by dividing the second exponential equation by the first.

$$\frac{300}{500} = \frac{A_0 e^{200k}}{A_0 e^{100k}} \qquad \text{divided}$$

$$0.6 = e^{100k} \qquad \text{simplified}$$

We take the natural log of both sides.

$$\ln(0.6) = 100k \qquad \text{ln of both sides}$$

$$k = \frac{\ln(0.6)}{100} = -0.005 \qquad \text{solved for } k$$

Now we substitute this back into the first equation to find A_0.

$$500 = A_0 e^{100(-0.005)} = A_0 e^{-0.5} \qquad \text{substituted}$$

so $\qquad A_0 = (500)e^{0.5} = \textbf{824.36 g} \qquad$ solved

Finally, to find the half-life, we set $A_t = \frac{1}{2}A_0 = \frac{1}{2}(824.36)$. Now we solve for t in the equation below.

$$\frac{1}{2}(824.36) = 824.36e^{-0.005t} \qquad \text{substituted}$$

$$\frac{1}{2} = e^{-0.005t} \qquad \text{divided by 824.36}$$

$$\ln\frac{1}{2} = -0.005t \qquad \text{ln of both sides}$$

$$t = \frac{-\ln\frac{1}{2}}{0.005} = \textbf{138.63 years} \qquad \text{solved}$$

problem set 88

1. The number of bacteria at noon was 400 and 10 hours later the number was 4000. Assume exponential growth and write the exponential equation describing the number of bacteria present as a function of time. Then find the number of bacteria present at midnight. Sketch the graph.

2. There was 40 grams of mixture in the bowl when Billie walked in. Fifty minutes later only 20 grams was left. If the decay was exponential, write the exponential equation describing the amount of mixture in the bowl as a function of time and then find the amount remaining after another 50 minutes.

3. At a certain instant, 100 grams of a radioactive substance is present. After 4 years, 20 grams remains. Write the exponential equation describing the amount of radioactive substance present as a function of time and then find the half-life of the substance. Sketch the graph.

4. Jim sees that it is exactly three o'clock, so it is not yet time to go. It will be time to go the first time the hands are pointing in the same direction. What will be the time on the clock when it is time to go?

5. Two cards are drawn randomly from a full deck without replacement. What is the probability that both cards are red?

6. A pair of dice is rolled twice. What is the probability that both rolls of the dice yield numbers less than 5?

7. Find four consecutive nonnegative integers such that twice the product of the first and fourth is eight more than the product of the second and third numbers.

8. Find $\cos 75°$ by using a trigonometric identity and the fact that $75° = 45° + 30°$. Use exact values.

9. Simplify $\sin\left(\theta - \dfrac{\pi}{6}\right)$ by using sum and difference identities. Use exact values.

10. Develop the identity for $\tan(A - B)$ by using the identities for $\sin(A - B)$ and $\cos(A - B)$.

11. Find the twentieth term of an arithmetic sequence whose first term is 2 and whose common difference is -4.

12. Write the first three terms of an arithmetic sequence in which the eighth term is -8 and the tenth term is -12.

Solve the following equations given that $(0 \le x, \theta < 2\pi)$:

13. $\sqrt{3}\tan^2 x + 2\tan x - \sqrt{3} = 0$ $\left[\textit{Hint:}\ \sqrt{3}x^2 + 2x - \sqrt{3} = \left(\sqrt{3}x - 1\right)\left(x + \sqrt{3}\right)\right]$

14. $\tan^2 \theta - \tan \theta = 0$ $\qquad\qquad$ **15.** $\sec 4\theta = 1$

Sketch the graphs of the following:

16. $y = 2 + 3\cos \dfrac{1}{3}(x + \pi)$ $\qquad\qquad$ **17.** $y = -7 + 10\sin \dfrac{9}{5}x$

Show:

18. $\dfrac{\cos \theta}{1 - \sin \theta} - \dfrac{\cos \theta}{1 + \sin \theta} = 2\tan \theta$ $\qquad$ **19.** $(1 - \sin \theta)(1 + \sin \theta) = \cos^2 \theta$

20. $\dfrac{\cos^3 x + \sin^3 x}{\cos x + \sin x} = 1 - \sin x \cos x$ $\quad$ (*Hint:* Factor the numerator by noting that it is the sum of two cubes.)

Solve:

21. $4^{3x-1} = 8^{x+1}$ $\qquad\qquad\qquad\qquad$ **22.** $\dfrac{9^{8x-3}}{5^{2x-3}} = 1$

23. Solve this triangle for a. Find the area in square meters.

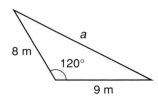

24. Write the three cube roots of 27 cis 30° in polar form.

25. Use Cramer's rule to solve: $\begin{cases} 3x - 4y = 2 \\ 2x + 3y = 4 \end{cases}$

26. The perimeter of a regular pentagon is 30 cm. What is the area of the pentagon? What is the area of the circle that can be circumscribed about the pentagon?

27. Shenandoah plans to attend college. The college of his choice only accepts students who score in the upper 5% on the college board exam. The scores on the exam are normally distributed with a mean of 400 and a standard deviation of 100. If Shenandoah scored a 590 on the college board exam, did he meet the requirement to be accepted to the college? Justify your answer.

Solve for x:

28. $\dfrac{2}{3} \log_2 27 + \log_2 (3x + 2) = 2$

29. $2 \log_3 2 + \log_3 (x - 1) = \log_3 (x + 2)$

30. Simplify: $4^{2 \log_2 3} - 3 \log_2 4$

LESSON 89   *The Ellipse (2)*

An ellipse is symmetric about its two axes, as we show in the figures below. Beside these figures we show the standard forms of the equations of ellipses whose major and minor axes are the coordinate axes. In these equations a is always greater than b. If the major axis (the axis through the foci) is the x axis, as shown in the top figure, a^2 is below x^2. If the major axis is the y axis, as shown in the bottom figure, a^2 is below y^2.

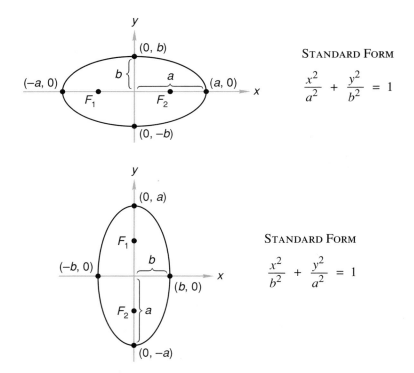

STANDARD FORM

$$\frac{x^2}{a^2} + \frac{y^2}{b^2} = 1$$

STANDARD FORM

$$\frac{x^2}{b^2} + \frac{y^2}{a^2} = 1$$

We remember that the sum of the distances from any point on an ellipse to the two foci is a constant. With the aid of the imaginary piece of string used to draw an ellipse, we can reason that the value of the constant is $2a$, which equals the length of the string and equals the length of the major axis of the ellipse.

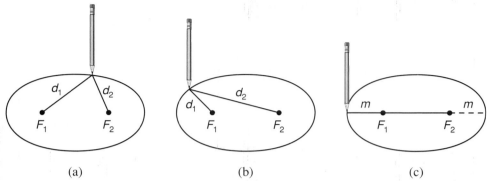

(a)   (b)   (c)

We begin at (a) and trace the ellipse by moving the pencil counterclockwise (b) until we get to the vertex in (c). Now the string goes from F_2 to the pencil and back through distance m to F_1. The string covers the distance m twice. If we mentally remove a piece of string m units long, we can use it to cover the distance m on the right. Thus, our piece of string stretches from vertex to vertex and has a length of $2a$. Now if we move the pencil to the end of the minor axis, we have the following figure.

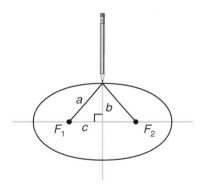

The length of the string is $2a$, so half its length is a. We have formed a right triangle whose hypotenuse is a and whose legs are b and c, as shown. The length of one side is the distance from the origin to the focus, and the length of the other side equals half the length of the minor axis. We can use the Pythagorean theorem and write

$$a^2 = c^2 + b^2$$

We can use this relationship and the standard form of the equation of an ellipse to solve some interesting problems. In the next example, we are given values for c and a and must solve for b.

example 89.1   Write the standard form of the equation of the ellipse with vertices at $(\pm 5, 0)$ and foci at $(\pm 4, 0)$.

solution   **We always begin with a diagram.** The foci of an ellipse always lie on the major axis, so the x axis is the major axis.

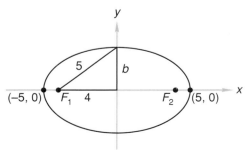

We see that the length of the major axis is 10, so half the major axis is 5. We draw the triangle and get

$$5^2 = 4^2 + b^2$$

$$9 = b^2$$

$$3 = b$$

The equation of an ellipse whose major axis lies along the x axis and whose center is at the origin is

$$\frac{x^2}{a^2} + \frac{y^2}{b^2} = 1$$

Thus, since in this problem $a = 5$ and $b = 3$, the equation of the ellipse in standard form is

$$\frac{x^2}{25} + \frac{y^2}{9} = 1$$

example 89.2   Write the standard form of the equation of the ellipse with vertices at $(0, \pm 6)$ and foci at $(0, \pm 5)$.

solution   **We always begin with a diagram.** We remember that the foci are always on the major axis.

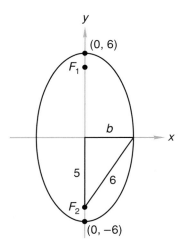

From the triangle, we get

$$6^2 = 5^2 + b^2$$

$$36 = 25 + b^2$$

$$\sqrt{11} = b$$

The length of the minor axis is $2\sqrt{11}$. This time the major axis lies along the y axis, so the equation is

$$\frac{x^2}{b^2} + \frac{y^2}{a^2} = 1$$

Since $a = 6$ and $b = \sqrt{11}$, the equation of the ellipse in standard form is

$$\frac{x^2}{11} + \frac{y^2}{36} = 1$$

example 89.3 A horizontal ellipse has a major axis of length 10 and a minor axis of length 4. If its center is at the origin, find the coordinates of the foci and write the equation in standard form. Graph the ellipse.

solution **Again, we begin with a diagram.**

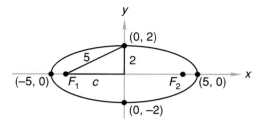

From our diagram, we get

$$5^2 = c^2 + 2^2$$

$$25 = c^2 + 4$$

$$21 = c^2$$

$$\sqrt{21} = c$$

Thus, the coordinates of the foci are $\left(\sqrt{21}, 0\right)$ and $\left(-\sqrt{21}, 0\right)$. Since $a = 5$ and $b = 2$, the equation of the ellipse in standard form is

$$\frac{x^2}{25} + \frac{y^2}{4} = 1$$

problem set 89

1. When the experiment began, there were 40 rabbits. Six years later there were 2000 rabbits. Assume exponential growth and write the exponential equation describing the number of the rabbits as a function of time. Then find the number of rabbits after 8 years. Sketch the graph.

2. When Kris walked into the room, there were 40,000. Ten hours later, there were only 30,000. Assume exponential decay and write the exponential equation describing the number in the room as a function of time. Then find the half-life of the things. Sketch the graph.

3. At 8 p.m. things looked just fine because Jill didn't have much longer to wait. She could proceed on her journey when the clock hands pointed in opposite directions. How long did she have to wait?

4. Three cards were drawn at random from a deck without replacement. What is the probability that two cards were black and one card was red?

5. The urn held 4 black marbles and 3 white marbles. A marble was drawn randomly and then replaced. Then a second was drawn at random and put aside, and then another was randomly drawn. What is the probability that all 3 were white?

6. The sum of the first and the third of three consecutive even counting numbers is 6 greater than the second. What are the numbers?

7. An ellipse has vertices at $(\pm 4, 0)$ and foci at $(\pm 3, 0)$. Write the equation in standard form. Graph the ellipse.

8. An ellipse has vertices at $(0, \pm 7)$ and foci at $(0, \pm 5)$. Write the equation in standard form. Graph the ellipse.

9. A vertical ellipse has a major axis of length 10 and a minor axis of length 4. If its center is at the origin, write the equation in standard form. Graph the ellipse.

10. Simplify $\sin\left(x - \dfrac{\pi}{2}\right)$ by using sum and difference identities.

11. Find tan 75° by using sum and difference identities and the fact that $75° = 45° + 30°$. Use exact values.

12. Find tan 15° by using sum and difference identities and the fact that $15° = 60° - 45°$. Use exact values.

13. Find the sixteenth term of an arithmetic sequence whose first term is 3 and whose common difference is –3.

14. Write the first four terms of an arithmetic sequence in which the ninth term is – 46 and the fourth term is –16.

Solve the following equations given that $0° \le x < 360°$:

15. $\sqrt{3}\cot^2 x + 2\cot x - \sqrt{3} = 0$

16. $3\sec^2 x + 5\sec x - 2 = 0$

17. $\csc 4x + 2 = 0$

Sketch the graphs of the following:

18. $y = 2\cos\left(x - \dfrac{\pi}{2}\right)$

19. $y = -3 + 10\sin 3(x - 20°)$

Show:

20. $\dfrac{\sin\theta}{1 - \cos\theta} - \dfrac{\sin\theta}{1 + \cos\theta} = 2\cot\theta$

21. $\dfrac{\tan^3 x + 1}{\tan x + 1} = \sec^2 x - \tan x$

Solve:

22. $9^{3-2x} = 27^{x+4}$

23. $\dfrac{8^{3x-1}}{4^{2x-1}} = \dfrac{1}{2}$

24. Find $m\angle A - m\angle B$.

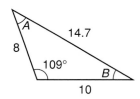

25. Use De Moivre's theorem to find $\left(\dfrac{1}{2} + \dfrac{\sqrt{3}}{2}i\right)^9$. Write the answer in rectangular form. Give an exact answer.

26. Write the two square roots of $-16i$ in rectangular form. Give exact answers.

27. The length of a side of a five-sided regular polygon is 5 cm. What is the radius of the circle that can be circumscribed about this regular pentagon? What is the radius of the circle that can be inscribed inside this regular pentagon?

Solve for x:

28. $\dfrac{3}{4}\ln 16 + 2\ln x = \ln(2x + 1)$

29. $-\dfrac{1}{2}\log_2(x - 1) = 1 + \log_2 5$

30. Let $f(x) = (2x + 3)^2 + 1$ and $g(x) = x^2 - 1$. Find $(f \circ g)(x)$.

LESSON *90*   *Double-Angle Identities • Half-Angle Identities*

90.A
**double-angle
identities**

We begin by repeating our key identities. They include the sine and cosine sum and difference identities.

$$\text{(a) } \sin (A + B) = \sin A \cos B + \cos A \sin B$$

$$\text{(b) } \sin (A - B) = \sin A \cos B - \cos A \sin B$$

$$\text{(c) } \cos (A + B) = \cos A \cos B - \sin A \sin B$$

$$\text{(d) } \cos (A - B) = \cos A \cos B + \sin A \sin B$$

$$\text{(e) } \tan \theta = \frac{\sin \theta}{\cos \theta}$$

$$\text{(f) } \sin^2 \theta + \cos^2 \theta = 1$$

The double-angle identities can be quickly developed from key identities (a) and (c), as we will show.

example 90.1   Develop the identity for (a) $\sin 2A$ and (b) $\cos 2A$.

solution   (a) To develop the identity for $\sin 2A$, we write the identity for $\sin (A + B)$.

$$\sin (A + B) = \sin A \cos B + \cos A \sin B$$

Now the trick is to let angle B be equal to angle A. If B equals A, then we can replace B everywhere with A.

$$\sin (A + A) = \sin A \cos A + \cos A \sin A$$

On the left, we have $\sin 2A$, and both terms on the right are the product of $\sin A$ and $\cos A$. Thus we have

$$\mathbf{\sin 2A = 2 \sin A \cos A}$$

Now look again at the identity for $\sin (A + B)$ and try to visualize the result of replacing B with A.

$$\sin (A + B) = \sin A \cos B + \cos A \sin B$$

You should be able to look at this identity and write the expression for $\sin 2A$ without the intervening steps.

(b) A similar procedure is used to develop the identity for $\cos 2A$. First we write the identity for $\cos (A + B)$.

$$\cos (A + B) = \cos A \cos B - \sin A \sin B$$

Next we replace B with A and get

$$\cos (A + A) = \cos A \cos A - \sin A \sin A$$

which simplifies to

$$\mathbf{\cos 2A = \cos^2 A - \sin^2 A}$$

Now look again at the identity for $\cos (A + B)$ and try to visualize the result of replacing B with A.

$$\cos (A + B) = \cos A \cos B - \sin A \sin B$$

You should be able to look at this identity and write the expression for $\cos 2A$ without the intervening steps.

We remember that $\sin^2 A + \cos^2 A = 1$. This equation can be written in two other forms.

$$\cos^2 A = 1 - \sin^2 A \qquad\qquad \sin^2 A = 1 - \cos^2 A$$

We can use these two equations and substitution to get two other identities for cos 2A. To get the first one, we use the basic identity for cos 2A and replace $\cos^2 A$ with $1 - \sin^2 A$.

$$\cos 2A = \cos^2 A - \sin^2 A \qquad\qquad \text{basic identity}$$
$$\cos 2A = \left(1 - \sin^2 A\right) - \sin^2 A \qquad\qquad \text{substituted}$$
$$\mathbf{\cos 2A = 1 - 2\sin^2 A} \qquad\qquad \text{simplified}$$

We get the third form of cos 2A by replacing $\sin^2 A$ with $1 - \cos^2 A$. **We must be careful with the negative sign.**

$$\cos 2A = \cos^2 A - \sin^2 A \qquad\qquad \text{basic identity}$$
$$\cos 2A = \cos^2 A - \left(1 - \cos^2 A\right) \qquad\qquad \text{substituted}$$
$$\mathbf{\cos 2A = 2\cos^2 A - 1} \qquad\qquad \text{simplified}$$

example 90.2 Begin with the identities for $\sin(A + B)$ and $\cos(A + B)$ and develop the identity for tan 2A.

solution We begin by developing the identities for sin 2A and cos 2A. These identities can be memorized but can also be forgotten—especially when they are needed. Practice in developing them now will make the developments automatic later on. We can do both developments in one step.

$$\sin(A + B) = \sin A \cos B + \cos A \sin B$$

And by inspection

$$\sin 2A = 2\sin A \cos A$$

Also,

$$\cos(A + B) = \cos A \cos B - \sin A \sin B$$

And by inspection

$$\cos 2A = \cos^2 A - \sin^2 A$$

Now the tangent of ( ) equals the sine of ( ) divided by the cosine of ( ). Thus, tan (2A) equals sin (2A) divided by cos (2A).

$$\tan 2A = \frac{\sin 2A}{\cos 2A} = \frac{2\sin A \cos A}{\cos^2 A - \sin^2 A}$$

We remember that we concentrate on tangent identities in which the first term in the denominator is the number 1. To get this form, we divide every term above and below by $\cos^2 A$. On top we write $\cos^2 A$ as $(\cos A)(\cos A)$.

$$\tan 2A = \frac{\dfrac{2\sin A \cos A}{\cos A \cos A}}{\dfrac{\cos^2 A}{\cos^2 A} - \dfrac{\sin^2 A}{\cos^2 A}}$$

$$= \frac{\mathbf{2\tan A}}{\mathbf{1 - \tan^2 A}}$$

90.B

half-angle identities By using the double-angle identities that we developed above, we can derive formulas for $\sin \frac{1}{2}x$ and $\cos \frac{1}{2}x$. These are called the **half-angle identities.**

example 90.3 Develop the identities for $\sin \frac{1}{2}x$ and $\cos \frac{1}{2}x$.

solution This development requires the second and third forms of the identity for cos 2A. **Rather than trust our memory, we will go back to the basic identity for cos (A + B). We can develop the two forms quickly and accurately, and we try never to depend on memory if it is not necessary.**

$$\cos (A + B) = \cos A \cos B - \sin A \sin B$$

By inspection

$$\cos 2A = \cos^2 A - \sin^2 A$$

Now we can get the other two forms by using $\sin^2 A + \cos^2 A = 1$ and substituting.

USING $\cos^2 A = 1 - \sin^2 A$ | USING $\sin^2 A = 1 - \cos^2 A$

$$\cos 2A = \left(1 - \sin^2 A\right) - \sin^2 A \qquad \cos 2A = \cos^2 A - \left(1 - \cos^2 A\right)$$

$$\cos 2A = 1 - 2\sin^2 A \qquad\qquad \cos 2A = 2\cos^2 A - 1$$

Now we have the two forms of cos 2A that we need. We solve the equation on the left for $\sin^2 A$ and solve the equation on the right for $\cos^2 A$.

$$\cos 2A - 1 = -2\sin^2 A \qquad\qquad \cos 2A + 1 = 2\cos^2 A$$

$$-\cos 2A + 1 = 2\sin^2 A \qquad\qquad 2\cos^2 A = 1 + \cos 2A$$

$$\mathbf{\sin^2 A = \frac{1 - \cos 2A}{2}} \qquad\qquad \mathbf{\cos^2 A = \frac{1 + \cos 2A}{2}}$$

This intermediate step is in boldface because we have identities for $\sin^2 A$ and $\cos^2 A$ that are sometimes required. To finish the half-angle development requires two steps. The first step is to take the square root of both sides and remember the $\pm$ signs that accrue.

$$\sin A = \pm\sqrt{\frac{1 - \cos 2A}{2}} \qquad\qquad \cos A = \pm\sqrt{\frac{1 + \cos 2A}{2}}$$

The final step is to replace A with $\frac{x}{2}$. This type of variable change makes some people uncomfortable when first encountered, but it is a legitimate technique, and it is used whenever it is convenient. When we substitute under the radical, the expression cos 2A becomes $\cos 2\left(\frac{x}{2}\right)$, or cos x.

$$\mathbf{\sin \frac{x}{2} = \pm\sqrt{\frac{1 - \cos x}{2}}} \qquad\qquad \mathbf{\cos \frac{x}{2} = \pm\sqrt{\frac{1 + \cos x}{2}}}$$

This development will be required in future problem sets because it provides excellent practice in changing the forms of trigonometric expressions.

problem set 90

1. When the year began, there were only 80, but their growth was exponential. Two years later, there were 400. Find A_0 and k and write the exponential equation that gives the number as a function of time. How long would it take for the number to increase to 2000? Sketch the graph.

2. At the outset, there were 2000 and the decay was exponential. Four years later, there were 500. Write the equation that gives their number as a function of time.

3. John drew one card at random from a full deck of 52 cards and then replaced it. Then John randomly drew another card. What is the probability that both cards were spades?

4. Natalie rolled a fair die 3 times. What was the probability of getting a 6, a 4, and a number greater than 3, in that order?

5. Chuck flipped a fair coin 3 times. It came up heads every time. What is the probability that the next flip also will come up heads?

6. Ten men, 20 women, and 30 children receive $38,250 for 5 days work. If 1 man receives as much as 1 woman or 2 children, how much does each man receive for a day's work?

7. Develop the identity for cos 2A by using the identity for cos (A + B).

8. Develop the identity for sin 2A by using the identity for sin (A + B).

9. Develop the identity for tan 2A by using the identities for sin 2A and cos 2A.

10. An ellipse has vertices at (±5, 0) and foci at (±3, 0). Write the equation in standard form. Graph the ellipse.

11. An ellipse has vertices at (0, ±8) and foci at (0, ±4). Write the equation in standard form. Graph the ellipse.

12. A horizontal ellipse has a major axis of length 12 and a minor axis of length 4. If its center is at the origin, write the equation of the ellipse in standard form. Graph the ellipse.

13. Find sin 105° by using sum and difference identities and the fact that 105° = 60° + 45°. Use exact values.

14. Find the eighteenth term of the arithmetic sequence whose first term is 4 and whose common difference is 2.

15. Write the first three terms of the arithmetic sequence whose tenth term is –22 and whose third term is – 8.

Solve the following equations given that $(0 \leq y, x < 2\pi)$:

16. $2 \cos^2 y - 9 \sin y + 3 = 0$ 17. $\sec 2x + 2 = 0$

Sketch the graph of each of the following:

18. $y = -3 \sin \left(x - \dfrac{\pi}{4} \right)$ 19. $y = -2 + 5 \cos 4(\theta - 40°)$

Show:

20. $\sec^2 x \sin^2 x + \sin^2 x \csc^2 x = \sec^2 x$ 21. $\sin^2 \theta + \tan^2 \theta + \cos^2 \theta = \sec^2 \theta$

22. Find the measure of the largest angle.

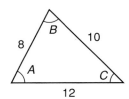

23. Use Cramer's rule to solve: $\begin{cases} 5x + 2y = -6 \\ 3x - 4y = 2 \end{cases}$

24. Graph the solution to the system of inequalities: $\begin{cases} x^2 + 2x + y^2 + 4y \leq 11 \\ x - y < 3 \\ x - y > 0 \end{cases}$

Solve for x:

25. $27^{2-3x} = 81^{x-5}$ 26. $7^{2x-1} = 8^{3x+2}$ 27. $\ln x + \ln x = 2 \ln 2$

28. Simplify: $2^{\log_2 9 - 2 \log_2 6 + 4 \log_2 2} + 3 \log_2 2$

29. Find: (a) $\text{antilog}_4 (-1)$ (b) $\text{antilog}_{1/3} (-1)$

30. A statistician decides that the batting averages of major league baseball players are normally distributed with a mean of 0.270 and a standard deviation of 0.015. What percentage of major league baseball players have batting averages of 0.300 or greater?

LESSON 91   *Geometric Progressions*

We recall that if we begin with a first number and develop a sequence by **adding the same amount** to form each succeeding entry, then the sequence is an **arithmetic sequence** or an **arithmetic progression.** The amount added is called the **common difference.** We can tell that this sequence is an arithmetic sequence because each term is 5 greater than the term to its left.

$$-10, -5, 0, 5, 10$$

Thus the common difference is +5. The second term is the sum of the first term and the common difference; the third term is the sum of the first term and two common differences; etc. If we use a_1 for the first term and d for the difference, we can write a general expression for an arithmetic sequence as

   ①   ②   ③   ④   ⓷

$$a_1, \quad a_1 + d, \quad a_1 + 2d, \quad a_1 + 3d, \quad \dots, \quad a_1 + (n - 1)d$$

In each entry, we note that the difference is used one fewer times than the number of the term.

If we begin with a number and form the succeeding terms in a sequence by **multiplying by the same factor,** then the sequence formed is called a **geometric sequence** or a **geometric progression.** The factor used as a multiplier is called the **common ratio.** If we begin with 8 and use 2 as a common ratio to form a five-term sequence, we get

   ①   ②   ③   ④   ⑤

$$8, \quad 8 \cdot 2, \quad 8 \cdot 2 \cdot 2, \quad 8 \cdot 2 \cdot 2 \cdot 2, \quad 8 \cdot 2 \cdot 2 \cdot 2 \cdot 2$$
$$8, \quad \underline{16}, \quad \underline{32}, \quad \underline{64}, \quad 128$$

We call the terms between the first term and the last term of a finite geometric sequence the **geometric means** of the sequence. **If the common ratio is a negative number, the terms in the sequence will alternate in sign.** If we begin with 8 and use –2 as a common ratio to form a five-term sequence, we get

   ①   ②   ③   ④   ⑤

$$8, \quad 8(-2), \quad 8(-2)(-2), \quad 8(-2)(-2)(-2), \quad 8(-2)(-2)(-2)(-2)$$
$$8, \quad \underline{-16}, \quad \underline{32}, \quad \underline{-64}, \quad 128$$

The three geometric means between 8 and 128 shown here are not the same as the three geometric means in the example above. **Thus, we see that when we say that geometric means are between 8 and 128, 8 is the first term and 128 is the last term, but the means do not necessarily lie between these numbers on the number line.**

example 91.1   Find the fifth term in a geometric sequence whose first term is –2 and whose common ratio is –3.

solution   The terms are as shown here.

   ①   ②   ③   ④   ⑤

$$-2, \quad -2(-3), \quad -2(-3)(-3), \quad -2(-3)(-3)(-3), \quad -2(-3)(-3)(-3)(-3)$$

Thus, the fifth term can be written as

$$-2(-3)^4 = -162$$

We note that –3 was a factor one time in the second term, twice in the third term, etc., and in general, $(n - 1)$ times in the nth term. If we use a_1 for the first term and r for the common ratio, the general expression for the terms in a geometric sequence can be written as

   ①   ②   ③   ④   ⓷

$$a_1, \quad a_1 r, \quad a_1 r^2, \quad a_1 r^3, \quad \dots, \quad a_1 r^{n-1}$$

and the general expression for the nth term is

$$a_n = a_1 r^{n-1}$$

example 91.2   Find three geometric means between 4 and 64.

solution   Making a diagram of the problem enhances understanding and makes memorizing formulas unnecessary. We know that the first term is 4 and the last term is 64.

$$\underset{①}{} \quad \underset{②}{} \quad \underset{③}{} \quad \underset{④}{} \quad \underset{⑤}{}$$

$$4, \quad \underline{\quad}, \quad \underline{\quad}, \quad \underline{\quad}, \quad 64$$

$$a_1, \quad a_1 r, \quad a_1 r^2, \quad a_1 r^3, \quad a_1 r^4$$

We can get one equation (a) from the first terms and one equation (b) from the fifth terms.

$$(a)\ a_1 = 4 \qquad (b)\ a_1 r^4 = 64$$

Now we use substitution and solve for r.

$$4r^4 = 64 \qquad \text{substituted}$$

$$r^4 = 16 \qquad \text{divided by 4}$$

$$r = \pm 2 \qquad \text{root of both sides}$$

If $r = 2$, our sequence is   If $r = -2$, our sequence is

$$\textbf{4, } \underline{\textbf{8}}\textbf{, } \underline{\textbf{16}}\textbf{, } \underline{\textbf{32}}\textbf{, 64} \qquad\qquad \textbf{4, } \underline{\textbf{-8}}\textbf{, } \underline{\textbf{16}}\textbf{, } \underline{\textbf{-32}}\textbf{, 64}$$

and the three geometric means are underlined in each sequence.

example 91.3   Find two geometric means between 2 and $\dfrac{1}{4}$.

solution   We begin by drawing a diagram of the problem.

$$\underset{①}{} \quad \underset{②}{} \quad \underset{③}{} \quad \underset{④}{}$$

$$2, \quad \underline{\quad}, \quad \underline{\quad}, \quad \dfrac{1}{4}$$

$$a_1, \quad a_1 r, \quad a_1 r^2, \quad a_1 r^3$$

This time the first equation comes from the first terms and the other equation comes from the fourth terms.

$$(a)\ a_1 = 2 \qquad (b)\ a_1 r^3 = \dfrac{1}{4}$$

We use substitution to solve. Since $a_1 = 2$ and $a_1 r^3 = \dfrac{1}{4}$, we get

$$2r^3 = \dfrac{1}{4} \qquad \text{substituted}$$

$$r^3 = \dfrac{1}{8} \qquad \text{divided by 2}$$

$$r = \dfrac{1}{2} \qquad \text{root of both sides}$$

The cube root of a positive number is a positive number, so there is only one possible common ratio. Thus, our sequence is

$$\textbf{2, } \underline{\textbf{1}}\textbf{, } \underline{\dfrac{\textbf{1}}{\textbf{2}}}\textbf{, } \dfrac{\textbf{1}}{\textbf{4}}$$

and the two geometric means are underlined.

example 91.4 Find three geometric means between −16 and −1.

solution We begin with a diagram of the problem.

$$
\begin{array}{ccccc}
① & ② & ③ & ④ & ⑤ \\
-16, & \underline{\quad}, & \underline{\quad}, & \underline{\quad}, & -1 \\
a_1, & a_1 r, & a_1 r^2, & a_1 r^3, & a_1 r^4
\end{array}
$$

From the first and fifth terms we see that $a_1 = -16$ and $a_1 r^4 = -1$. We combine these equations to get our basic equation.

$$-16r^4 = -1 \qquad \text{equation}$$

$$r^4 = \frac{1}{16} \qquad \text{divided by } -16$$

$$r = \pm\frac{1}{2} \qquad \text{root of both sides}$$

If $r = \dfrac{1}{2}$, the sequence is   If $r = -\dfrac{1}{2}$, the sequence is

$-16, \underline{-8}, \underline{-4}, \underline{-2}, -1$ $-16, \underline{8}, \underline{-4}, \underline{2}, -1$

and the geometric means are underlined in each sequence.

problem set 91

1. It was exactly eight o'clock. How long did Aaron, Bryce, and Sammie have to wait until the hands of the clock pointed in the same direction?

2. Beaver lost one eighth of his marbles and then 5000 marbles fell into a hole. Next, half the rest were mislaid, so he had only 4500 left. How many marbles did he have when he began?

3. A fair die was rolled 3 times. What is the probability of getting a 2, a 5, and a number greater than 2, in that order?

4. When the snow melted, they began to increase exponentially. They began with 30, and in 3 months their number had increased to 900. Find A_0 and k and write the exponential equation that gives the number present as a function of time. Sketch the graph.

5. Initially the mass was 42 grams. After only 10 years, 7 grams remained. Assume exponential decay and write the equation that gives the mass remaining as a function of time. How long did it take for the mass to decrease to 30 grams? Sketch the graph.

6. One pipe can fill one cistern in 20 hours and another pipe can fill one cistern in 30 hours. How long will it take to fill one cistern if both pipes are used?

7. Find the sixth term of a geometric sequence whose first term is − 4 and whose common ratio is −2.

8. Find two geometric means between 4 and 108.

9. Find three geometric means between 2 and 32.

10. Develop the identity for $\sin \frac{1}{2}A$ by using the identity for $\cos 2A$.

11. Find $\sin 15°$ by using the half-angle identify for $\sin \frac{1}{2}x$ and letting $x = 30°$. Use exact values.

12. Develop the identity for $\cos \frac{1}{2}A$ by using the identity for $\cos 2A$.

13. Find $\cos 15°$ by using the half-angle identity for $\cos \frac{1}{2}x$ and letting $x = 30°$. Use exact values.

14. An ellipse has vertices at $(\pm 6, 0)$ and foci at $(\pm 2, 0)$. Write the equation in standard form. Graph the ellipse.

15. A vertical ellipse has a major axis of length 14 and a minor axis of length 10. If its center is at the origin, write the equation of the ellipse in standard form. Graph the ellipse.

16. Find $\cos 105°$ by using sum and difference identities and the fact that $105° = 45° + 60°$. Use exact values.

17. Find the first four terms of the arithmetic sequence whose first term is 6 and whose tenth term is -30.

Solve the following equations given that $(0° \leq y, \theta < 360°)$:

18. $2 \sin^2 y - 9 \cos y + 3 = 0$

19. $\sqrt{3} + 2 \cos 3\theta = 0$

Sketch the graphs of the following:

20. $y = 2 - 3 \cos (x + 40°)$

21. $y = \dfrac{3}{2} + \dfrac{3}{2} \sin 2\left(x + \dfrac{\pi}{6} \right)$

Show:

22. $\dfrac{1 - \cos^2 \theta}{1 + \tan^2 \theta} = \sin^2 \theta \cos^2 \theta$

23. $\csc^2 y \sec^2 y - \sec^2 y = \csc^2 y$

24. Solve this triangle for A and B.

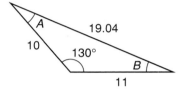

25. The perimeter of a regular hexagon (6-sided regular polygon) is 48 inches. What is the radius of the circle that can be circumscribed about the regular hexagon? What is the area of the regular hexagon?

26. Find the distance from the point $(2, 2)$ to the line $y = 3x - 1$.

Solve for x:

27. $16^{3x-4} = 4^{2x+1} \cdot 8$

28. $\ln (2x + 3) - \ln 3x = \dfrac{2}{3} \ln 27$

29. $\log (2x + 1) = 3 \log 2 - \log 4$

30. Simplify: $3^{\log_3 4 - 2 \log_3 8 + 4 \log_3 2} - \dfrac{1}{2} \log_3 3^2$

LESSON 92 *Probability of Either • Notations for Permutations and Combinations*

92.A
probability of either

When a coin is flipped and comes up heads, it does not come up tails. When a red card is drawn from a deck, the card is not black. When a white marble is drawn from an urn, the marble is not green. These events are called **mutually exclusive events** because when one event occurs, the other event is excluded and cannot occur. The probability of either of two mutually exclusive events occurring is the sum of the individual probabilities. If we have 3 red marbles, 4 blue marbles, and 6 white marbles in an urn, the probability of drawing a red marble is $\frac{3}{13}$, the probability of drawing a blue marble is $\frac{4}{13}$, and the probability of drawing a white marble is $\frac{6}{13}$.

The probability of drawing a marble that is either red or blue is $\frac{7}{13}$.

$$P(R \text{ or } B) = P(R) + P(B) = \frac{3}{13} + \frac{4}{13} = \frac{7}{13}$$

We often use the word **union** instead of using the word **or,** and we use the symbol $\cup$ to stand for *union.* Thus,

$$P(R \text{ or } B) = P(R \text{ union } B) = P(R \cup B)$$

In the same way, we often use the word **intersection** instead of using the word **both,** and we invert the union symbol $\cap$ to designate *intersection.*

$$P(\text{both } R \text{ and } B) = P(R \text{ intersect } B) = P(R \cap B)$$

The probability for both is always zero for mutually exclusive events, as we can see from the diagram on the previous page, for a marble cannot be both red and blue at the same time.

Some events are not mutually exclusive. As an example, we consider the case of 7 boys and 4 redheads. If we ask for the number who are either boys or who are redheads, the number is not necessarily 11 because if some of the boys are redheads, we would have counted them twice. This Venn diagram demonstrates the case of 2 redheaded boys and shows a total of 9 people who either are boys or are redheads.

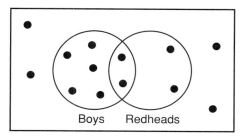

The diagram shows that the events are not mutually exclusive, and the number who either are boys or are redheads is not the sum of the number of boys and the number of redheads because this procedure counts the redheaded boys twice. To correct for this, we must subtract the number of redheaded boys.

$$N(\text{boys or redheads}) = N(\text{boys}) + N(\text{redheads}) - N(\text{redheaded boys})$$

If we select one person blindly from the above grouping, the probability of a boy is $\frac{7}{13}$, the probability of a redhead is $\frac{4}{13}$, and the probability of a redheaded boy is $\frac{2}{13}$. From this example, we can see that **the probability of a person being either redheaded or a boy is**

$$P(R \cup B) = P(R) + P(B) - P(R \cap B)$$

because we must not consider the redheaded boys twice.

example 92.1   A card is drawn from a full deck. What is the probability that the card is an ace or a black card?

solution   We must not count the two black aces twice, so if A means *ace* and B means *black,*

$$P(A \cup B) = P(A) + P(B) - P(A \cap B)$$

$$= \frac{4}{52} + \frac{26}{52} - \frac{2}{52} = \frac{7}{13}$$

example 92.2   An urn contains 4 white balls and 3 black balls. Two of the white balls are rough and one of the black balls is rough. What is the probability of drawing a ball that is either rough or white?

solution   We must not count the rough white balls twice.

$$P(R \cup W) = P(R) + P(W) - P(R \cap W)$$

$$= \frac{3}{7} + \frac{4}{7} - \frac{2}{7} = \frac{5}{7}$$

92.B
notations for permutations and combinations

Earlier in this book we introduced the following formulas for computing the number of permutations and combinations.

$$_nP_r = \frac{n!}{(n-r)!} \qquad\qquad _nC_r = \frac{n!}{r!(n-r)!}$$

Students may be confused by these notations and may think that they magically produce the desired answers. Our earlier discussions of permutations in Lesson 41 and of combinations in Lesson 75 showed that the formulas for computing the number of permutations and combinations are not magical but arise naturally. In the following example, we will show how we do a concrete development of the formulas.

example 92.3 Take the permutations and combinations of 7 things taken 3 at a time to do a concrete development of the formulas for $_nP_r$ and $_nC_r$.

solution The number of permutations of 7 things taken 3 at a time is $7 \cdot 6 \cdot 5$.

$$_7P_3 = 7 \cdot 6 \cdot 5$$

To use a factorial notation for this problem, we can multiply above and below by 4 factorial and get

$$_7P_3 = \frac{(7 \cdot 6 \cdot 5) \cdot 4!}{4!}$$

$$= \frac{7!}{4!}$$

But 4 equals $7 - 3$, and if we make this replacement, we get

$$_7P_3 = \frac{7!}{(7-3)!}$$

Now we can get a general expression for $_nP_r$ by replacing 7 with n and replacing 3 with r.

$$_nP_r = \frac{n!}{(n-r)!}$$

To find the combination of 7 things taken 3 at a time, we would divide by 3! to remove the effect of order in the combinations. We show this below on the left. On the right we replace 7 with n and replace 3 with r to write the general expression for the combination of n things taken r at a time.

$$_7C_3 = \frac{7!}{3!(7-3)!} \qquad\qquad _nC_r = \frac{n!}{r!(n-r)!}$$

problem set 92

1. It was exactly 9:00. How long did Rasputin have to wait until the hands of the clock pointed in opposite directions?

2. Under the onslaught of the horde of kids, the pile of cookies decreased exponentially. They decreased from 10,000 to 9000 in only 40 minutes. Write an exponential equation which expresses cookies as a function of time. What is the half-life of the pile of cookies?

3. The number who wanted increased exponentially with the time. In the beginning, only 100 wanted. After 6 months there were 1000 who wanted. Write the exponential equation which expresses the number who wanted as a function of time, and find how long it will take for 2000 to want.

4. The number who succeeded varied linearly with the number who tried. When 10 tried, 8 succeeded, but when 20 tried, the number of successes rose to 13. How many succeeded when only 8 tried?

5. Find three consecutive even integers such that the product of the first and third is twenty more than five times the second number.

6. A card is drawn at random from a full deck of 52 cards. What is the probability the card drawn will be either a king or a black card?

7. Take the permutations and combinations of 8 things taken 5 at a time to do a concrete development of the formulas for $_nP_r$ and $_nC_r$.

8. Find the fourth term of a geometric sequence whose first term is 2 and whose common ratio is $-\frac{1}{2}$.

9. Find two geometric means between 2 and -16.

10. Begin with the identity for $\cos (A + B)$ and develop an identity for $\sin \frac{1}{2}A$.

11. Find $\sin 165°$ by using the identity for $\sin \frac{1}{2}x$. Use exact values.

12. Use the sum identities as required to find an expression for $\cos \left(x + \frac{\pi}{2}\right)$.

13. A vertical ellipse has a major axis of length 10 and a minor axis of length 8. If its center is at the origin, write the equation of the ellipse in standard form. Graph the ellipse.

14. Find the first four terms of the arithmetic sequence whose fourth term is -2 and whose tenth term is 10.

Solve the following equations given that $0 \le \theta < 2\pi$:

15. $\tan^2 \theta - \sec \theta - 1 = 0$

16. $\sin 3\theta = 0$

17. Sketch the graph of $y = -3 + 5 \cos \frac{1}{2}\left(x - \frac{3}{2}\pi\right)$.

Show:

18. $\dfrac{\sin^4 \theta - \cos^4 \theta}{\sin^2 \theta - \cos^2 \theta} = 1$

19. $\dfrac{\sec^2 x}{\sec^2 x - 1} = \csc^2 x$

20. Find $m\angle B - m\angle A$.

21. Find c.

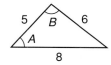

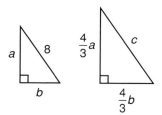

22. Write the four fourth roots of $16 \operatorname{cis} 120°$ in rectangular form. Give exact answers.

23. Given the hyperbola $16x^2 - 25y^2 = 800$, write the equation in standard form and find the coordinates of its vertices and the equations of the asymptotes. Graph the hyperbola.

24. The perimeter of a 10-sided regular polygon (regular decagon) is 40 cm. Find the area of this regular decagon. What is the perimeter of the circle that can be inscribed inside this regular decagon?

25. Principal Larson has decided to give awards to the 5% of all students who have the fewest absences. He decides that students' absences are normally distributed with a mean of 7 and a standard deviation of 3. Smith has 3 absences. Will Smith get an award from Principal Larson? Justify your answer.

Solve for x:

26. $\dfrac{16^{3x-2}}{2^{4x-1}} = 4$

27. $\dfrac{2}{3} \log_7 8 - \log_7 (x - 1) = 1$

28. $\log x + \log (x + 2) = \dfrac{1}{2} \log 9$

29. Simplify: $8^{2\log_8 3 - \log_8 4} + \dfrac{9}{4} \log_8 8^{1/3}$

30. Find: (a) $\operatorname{antilog}_5 (-2)$ (b) $\operatorname{antilog}_{1/5} (-2)$

LESSON 93 *Advanced Trigonometric Identities • Triangle Inequalities (2)*

93.A

advanced trigonometric identities

Many trigonometric identities can be simplified by manipulations that spring from insight or game-playing ability. This ability will increase as more of these problems are worked and as successful thought patterns are practiced.

example 93.1   Show: $\dfrac{1 + \sin B}{\cos B} = \dfrac{\cos B}{1 - \sin B}$

solution   We look at $\cos B$ on the left and note that if it were $\cos^2 B$, we could replace it with $1 - \sin^2 B$, which can be factored. To get $\cos^2 B$ on the bottom, we multiply above and below by $\cos B$.

$$\frac{\cos B}{\cos B} \cdot \frac{1 + \sin B}{\cos B} = \frac{(\cos B)(1 + \sin B)}{\cos^2 B}$$

Now we can replace $\cos^2 B$ with $1 - \sin^2 B$.

$$\frac{(\cos B)(1 + \sin B)}{1 - \sin^2 B}$$

We finish by factoring $1 - \sin^2 B$ and canceling.

$$\frac{(\cos B)(1 + \sin B)}{(1 - \sin B)(1 + \sin B)} = \frac{\cos B}{1 - \sin B}$$

example 93.2   Show: $\dfrac{\tan B + 1}{\tan B - 1} = \dfrac{\sec B + \csc B}{\sec B - \csc B}$

solution   These expressions have the same forms. Two terms are above with a positive sign and two terms are below with a negative sign. The lower left-hand term in the expression on the left is $\tan B$. We can change $\tan B$ to $\sec B$ by multiplying it by $1/\sin B$.

$$\frac{1}{\sin B} \cdot \tan B = \frac{1}{\sin B} \cdot \frac{\sin B}{\cos B} = \frac{1}{\cos B} = \sec B$$

Let's multiply everything on the left side (both top and bottom) by $1/\sin B$ and see if we get the desired changes. First we write $\tan B$ as $\sin B/\cos B$.

$$\frac{\left(\dfrac{\sin B}{\cos B} + 1\right)\left(\dfrac{1}{\sin B}\right)}{\left(\dfrac{\sin B}{\cos B} - 1\right)\left(\dfrac{1}{\sin B}\right)} = \frac{\dfrac{1}{\cos B} + \dfrac{1}{\sin B}}{\dfrac{1}{\cos B} - \dfrac{1}{\sin B}} = \frac{\sec B + \csc B}{\sec B - \csc B}$$

We were able to change the left expression to the desired form by multiplying each part by $1/\sin B$.

example 93.3   Show: $(x \sin \theta + y \cos \theta)^2 + (x \cos \theta - y \sin \theta)^2 = x^2 + y^2$

solution   This problem provides practice in squaring binomials that have two variables and also in factoring and recognizing that $\sin^2 \theta + \cos^2 \theta = 1$. First we multiply out each squared term.

$$\begin{array}{r}
x \sin \theta + y \cos \theta \\
\underline{x \sin \theta + y \cos \theta} \\
x^2 \sin^2 \theta + xy \sin \theta \cos \theta \qquad\qquad \\
\underline{xy \sin \theta \cos \theta + y^2 \cos^2 \theta} \\
x^2 \sin^2 \theta + 2xy \sin \theta \cos \theta + y^2 \cos^2 \theta
\end{array}$$

$$x \cos \theta - y \sin \theta$$

$$\underline{x \cos \theta - y \sin \theta}$$

$$x^2 \cos^2 \theta - \quad xy \sin \theta \cos \theta$$

$$\underline{\quad - \quad xy \sin \theta \cos \theta + y^2 \sin^2 \theta}$$

$$x^2 \cos^2 \theta - 2xy \sin \theta \cos \theta + y^2 \sin^2 \theta$$

Now we add.

$$\left(x^2 \sin^2 \theta + 2xy \sin \theta \cos \theta + y^2 \cos^2 \theta\right) + \left(x^2 \cos^2 \theta - 2xy \sin \theta \cos \theta + y^2 \sin^2 \theta\right)$$

$$= x^2 \sin^2 \theta + y^2 \cos^2 \theta + x^2 \cos^2 \theta + y^2 \sin^2 \theta$$

$$= x^2\left(\sin^2 \theta + \cos^2 \theta\right) + y^2\left(\sin^2 \theta + \cos^2 \theta\right)$$

$$= x^2 + y^2$$

93.B

triangle inequalities (2)

In Lesson 3 we stated without proof the Pythagorean theorem and triangle inequalities. Later we presented two proofs of the Pythagorean theorem in Lesson 17. The first inequality we learned was called the **triangle inequality postulate.** As a postulate, it is a mathematical statement that is made without proof. The postulate states that in any triangle, the sum of the lengths of any two sides is greater than the length of the third side. The triangle inequality postulate can be restated as the well-known postulate that the shortest path between two points is the line segments joining them. Thus in the figure shown, the shortest path between M and N is the segment MN, so we can write

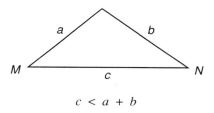

$$c < a + b$$

The other triangle inequalities have to do with the sum of the squares of the lengths of the short sides of a triangle and the square of the length of the longest side of the triangle. On the left below we show a right triangle. For this triangle, the square of the hypotenuse equals the sum of the squares of the two sides.

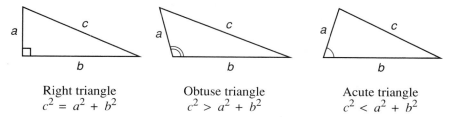

Right triangle   Obtuse triangle   Acute triangle
$c^2 = a^2 + b^2$ $c^2 > a^2 + b^2$ $c^2 < a^2 + b^2$

In the center figure, the shorter sides have the same lengths as before, but the angle formed by them is greater than 90°. In this case, we shall show $c^2 > a^2 + b^2$. In the right-hand figure, the shorter sides have the same lengths as before, but the angle formed by them is less than 90°. In this case, we shall show $c^2 < a^2 + b^2$.

To prove the center inequality shown above, we erect a perpendicular to the base, as we show here.

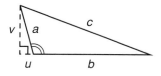

Now we use the Pythagorean theorem.

(1) $c^2 = v^2 + (u + b)^2$ Pythagorean theorem

(2) $c^2 = v^2 + u^2 + 2ub + b^2$ expanded

(3) $c^2 = (v^2 + u^2) + b^2 + 2ub$ rearranged

(4) $c^2 = a^2 + b^2 + 2ub$ substituted using $v^2 + u^2 = a^2$

In step 4 we used the Pythagorean theorem and the small triangle to allow us to substitute a^2 for $v^2 + u^2$. Also, from step 4 we see that c^2 is greater than $a^2 + b^2$ by $2ub$. Thus, we are justified in writing for the center triangle

$$c^2 > a^2 + b^2$$

To prove the inequality on the right on the previous page, we erect a perpendicular to the base as we show here.

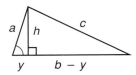

Now we use the Pythagorean theorem on the small triangle on the right.

$c^2 = h^2 + (b - y)^2$ Pythagorean theorem

$c^2 = h^2 + b^2 - 2by + y^2$ expanded

$c^2 = (h^2 + y^2) + b^2 - 2by$ rearranged

$c^2 = a^2 + b^2 - 2by$ substituted using $h^2 + y^2 = a^2$

This final step tells us that c^2 is less than $a^2 + b^2$ by $2by$, so we may write

$$c^2 < a^2 + b^2$$

On the previous page, we showed three triangles and three corresponding inequalities. What we have shown is if a triangle is a right triangle, an obtuse triangle, or an acute triangle, then the corresponding inequality is true. It turns out that the converses of what we have shown are also true; that is, if the inequalities shown below the figures on the previous page are true, then the triangle is the type listed. We will not give proofs of these converse statements because they are beyond the scope of this book. We will, however, apply these statements in the examples below.

example 93.4   Is the triangle whose sides are 3, 4, and 5 a right triangle, an acute triangle, or an obtuse triangle?

solution   **If the sum of the squares of the two short sides of a triangle equals the square of the longest side, the triangle is a right triangle. If the sum is less than the square of the longest side, the triangle is an obtuse triangle. If the sum is greater than the square of the longest side, the triangle is an acute triangle.** In this case, we have

$$3^2 + 4^2 \; ? \; 5^2$$

$$9 + 16 \; ? \; 25$$

$$25 = 25$$

and since the sum equals the square of the long side, the triangle is a **right triangle.**

example 93.5   Classify the triangle whose sides are 4, 7, and 5.

solution   We check the sum of the squares of the two shortest sides.

$$4^2 + 5^2 \; ? \; 7^2$$

$$16 + 25 \; ? \; 49$$

$$41 \; < \; 49$$

Since the sum of the squares of the short sides is less than the square of the long side, the triangle is an **obtuse triangle.**

problem set 93

1. There are 4 green marbles and 5 white marbles in an urn. Two of the green marbles have red spots and 3 of the white marbles have red spots. What is the probability of randomly selecting a marble that is green or a marble that has red spots?

2. The sample of the compound disintegrated exponentially. In the beginning there was 400 grams of it in the beaker, but 30 hours later only 300 grams remained. Write an exponential equation that expresses the mass of the compound as a function of time and find the half-life of the compound.

3. The mother was exasperated because the mess in the kids' room increased exponentially. Only 10 items were out of place at 9 a.m., but 40 minutes later 80 items were out of place. How many items were out of place by 11 a.m.?

4. Diogenes held his lantern high so he could see the clock clearly. It was between four and five o'clock, and the big hand was exactly five minutes ahead of the little hand. What time was it?

5. Take the permutations and combinations of 9 things taken 6 at a time to do a concrete development of the formulas for $_nP_r$ and $_nC_r$.

Show:

6. $\dfrac{1 + \sin B}{\cos B} = \dfrac{\cos B}{1 - \sin B}$

7. $\dfrac{\tan B + 1}{\tan B - 1} = \dfrac{\sec B + \csc B}{\sec B - \csc B}$

8. $(y \sin \theta + x \cos \theta)^2 + (y \cos \theta - x \sin \theta)^2 = x^2 + y^2$

9. Find three geometric means between 2 and 162.

10. Find the first four terms of the arithmetic sequence whose fifth term is 12 and whose thirteenth term is -4.

11. Begin with the identity for $\cos (A + B)$ and develop an identity for $\cos \frac{1}{2}A$.

12. Use the difference identity to find an expression for $\sin \left(x - \frac{\pi}{4}\right)$. Use exact values.

13. Use the identity for $\sin (A + B)$ and the fact that $285° = 240° + 45°$ to find $\sin 285°$. Use exact values.

14. A vertical ellipse has a major axis of length 8 and a minor axis of length 6. If its center is at the origin, write the equation of the ellipse in standard form. Graph the ellipse.

Solve the following equations given that $0° \le x < 360°$:

15. $2 \sin^2 x + 7 \cos x + 2 = 0$

16. $\sqrt{3} \cot 3x + 1 = 0$

Sketch the graphs of the following:

17. $y = 2 + 5 \sin \dfrac{5}{4}(x + 38°)$

18. $y = 4 + 6 \cos \dfrac{1}{2}\left(x - \dfrac{3\pi}{2}\right)$

19. Solve this triangle for a.

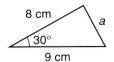

20. Write the five fifth roots of 32 cis 20° in polar form.

21. Given the hyperbola $9x^2 - 4y^2 = 72$, write the equation in standard form and find the coordinates of its vertices and the equations of the asymptotes. Graph the hyperbola.

22. Use Cramer's rule to solve: $\begin{cases} x + 3y = 9 \\ 7x - 2y = -4 \end{cases}$

23. Find the distance from the point $(3, -7)$ to the line $x = -1$.

Solve for x:

24. $\dfrac{3}{4} \log_8 16 + \log_8 (3x - 2) = 2$ **25.** $27^{2x+3} = 3^{x-4}$

26. $\dfrac{1}{4} \log_3 81 - \log_3 (4x - 1) = \log_3 27$

27. Simplify: $e^{-\ln 3 + \frac{1}{2} \ln 9 - \frac{1}{3} \ln 8} - \ln e$

28. Find: (a) antilog$_6$ 2 (b) antilog$_6$ (−2)

29. Factor $x^2 + 9x + 35$ over the set of complex numbers.

30. The scores on a test were normally distributed with a mean of 75 and a standard deviation of 10. What was the percentage of the scores that were greater than 92?

LESSON 94 *Graphs of Secant and Cosecant • Graphs of Tangent and Cotangent*

94.A
graphs of secant and cosecant

The sine function and the cosine function are periodic functions, and their graphs are especially useful. The graphs are continuous and have values for every input value of the independent variable. The cosecant function and the secant function are the reciprocal functions of the sine function and the cosine function, respectively, and thus are also periodic functions. Their graphs are not as useful and are seldom encountered because the cosecant is undefined at values of θ where the sine has a value of zero and the secant is undefined where the cosine has a value of zero. The graphs of these functions are distinctive and are easily identified because the graphs look like a series of equally spaced U's that alternately open up and down. The equations of these functions can be written with no difficulty if we first sketch and identify the related sinusoid, which can be drawn by using the given graphs as guides, as we show in the following examples.

example 94.1   Write the equations of these trigonometric functions.

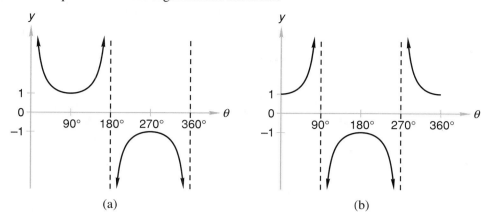

(a)   (b)

solution   As the first step, we will sketch and identify the sinusoids.

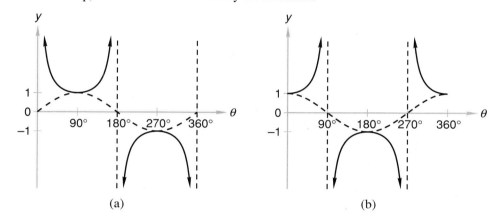

(a)   (b)

We see that the sinusoid on the left is a sine curve whose equation is $y = \sin \theta$. Thus the equation of the solid curve is

$$y = \csc \theta$$

The equation of the sinusoid graphed on the right is

$$y = \cos \theta \qquad \text{or} \qquad y = \sin (\theta + 90°)$$

Thus, the equation of the solid curve is

$$y = \sec \theta \qquad \text{or} \qquad y = \csc (\theta + 90°)$$

example 94.2   Write the equations of these trigonometric functions.

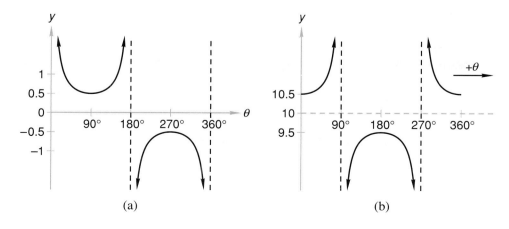

(a)   (b)

solution   We draw in the sinusoids whose extreme values are the same as the peak values of the solid curves in the graphs on the previous page. Then we write the equations of the sinusoids and replace each trigonometric function with its reciprocal function.

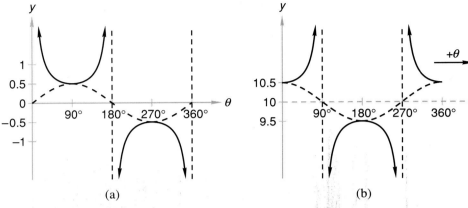

(a)   (b)

The sinusoid on the left is

$$y = 0.5 \sin \theta$$

so the graph of the solid curve is

$$y = \textbf{0.5 csc } \theta$$

The sinusoid on the right is

$$y = 10 + 0.5 \cos \theta$$

so the graph of the solid curve is

$$y = \textbf{10 + 0.5 sec } \theta$$

On the left we replaced $\sin \theta$ with its reciprocal, $\csc \theta$, and left the constant 0.5 alone. Note that we did not replace 0.5 $\sin \theta$ with its reciprocal, which is 2 $\csc \theta$. Similarly, on the right we left the constants 10 and 0.5 alone; we simply replaced $\cos \theta$ with $\sec \theta$.

94.B

graphs of tangent and cotangent

The graphs of the tangent function and cotangent function are also easy to identify because of their distinctive shapes. On the left below, we show the graph of the tangent function from 0° to 90°. The value of the tangent of 0° is 0. The value of the tangent of 30° is about 0.58, of 45° is 1, and of 60° is about 1.7. The value increases without limit as 90° is approached. We graph these points and sketch the curve in the figure on the left. A reflected image of this pattern occurs for negative values of θ, as we show in the figure on the right.

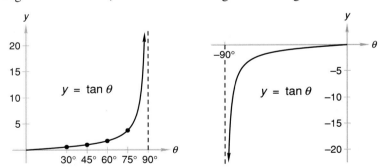

The period of the tangent function is 180°, so this pattern repeats every 180°, as we show here.

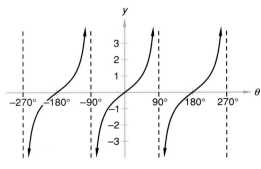

$$y = \tan \theta$$

The graph of the cotangent function has a similar appearance but the curves flex the other way. The cotangent function is the reciprocal of the tangent function, so the cotangent function has a value of 0 at values of θ where the tangent function is undefined, and is undefined at values of θ where the tangent function equals 0.

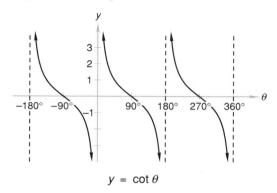

$$y = \cot \theta$$

It may be interesting to investigate graphs of tangent functions and cotangent functions such as $y = -2 \tan \theta$ or $y = \frac{1}{2} \cot (\theta + 30°)$. The sign changes in front of the function will turn the graph upside-down. Adding a constant to the argument will shift the crossing points to the left or the right. Multiplying the argument variable by a constant will change the period. Adding a constant to the function will shift the graph up or down.

example 94.3   Sketch the graph of $y = -2 \tan \theta$.

solution   The constant 2 in front of $\tan \theta$ vertically "stretches" the graph of $y = \tan \theta$. For example, whereas $\tan 45° = 1$, $2 \tan 45° = 2$. The negative sign turns the graph of $y = 2 \tan \theta$ upside down. The resulting graph is shown.

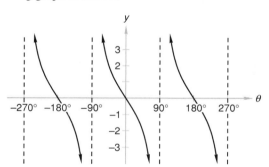

problem set 94

1. Four green marbles and 6 red marbles are in an urn. Three green marbles have white spots and 4 red marbles have white spots. What is the probability of randomly drawing a green marble or a marble with white spots?

2. Four quick bugs nested in a tree and plotted to increase exponentially. Twenty days later there were 200 quick bugs. Write the exponential equation which expresses the number of quick bugs as a function of time.

3. Radium has quite a long half-life. Madame put 1 ounce of radium in the bowl and 100 years later only 0.95817 ounce remained. What is the half-life of radium?

4. The Praetorian Guard was the body of soldiers in ancient Rome whose sole duty was to protect the life of the emperor. Over time, the members acquired a reputation for venality and corruptibility. How many distinguishable permutations can be made from the letters in the word *praetorian*?

5. Rudolph was observant, as he noted that it took X men 9 days to do P jobs. Then he calculated how long it would take Y men to do 20 jobs. What was his answer?

6. Graph: (a) $y = \tan x$ (b) $y = \cot x$

7. Write the equations of these trigonometric functions:

(a)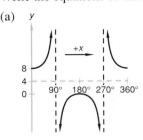

(b)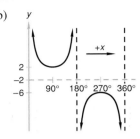

Show:

8. $\dfrac{1 + \cos x}{\sin x} = \dfrac{\sin x}{1 - \cos x}$

9. $\dfrac{\tan B + 1}{\tan B - 1} = \dfrac{\sec B + \csc B}{\sec B - \csc B}$

10. $(1 + \sin x)^2 + (1 - \sin x)^2 = 4 - 2\cos^2 x$

11. Develop the identity for $\tan 2A$ by using the identities for $\cos(A + B)$ and $\sin(A + B)$.

12. Find $\sin 75°$ by using the half-angle identity for $\sin \frac{1}{2}x$. Use exact values.

13. Find $\cos(-285°)$ by using the identity for $\cos(x + y)$ and the fact that $285° = 240° + 45°$ to find $\cos 285°$. Then note that $\cos(-x) = \cos x$. Use exact values.

14. Use a trigonometric identity to find an expression for $\cos(\pi - x)$.

Solve the following equations given that $0 \le x < 2\pi$:

15. $2\cos^2 x + 7\sin x + 2 = 0$

16. $\sqrt{3}\cot \dfrac{x}{2} - 1 = 0$

17. Sketch the graph of $y = -3 + 2\sin \dfrac{5}{3}(x - 27°)$.

18. Solve this triangle for c.

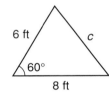

19. Write the four fourth roots of $81 \operatorname{cis} 24°$ in polar form.

20. Find two geometric means between -2 and 16.

21. Find the first three terms of the arithmetic sequence whose eighth term is 19 and whose tenth term is 25.

22. A horizontal ellipse has a major axis of length 10 and a minor axis of length 8. If its center is at the origin, write the equation of the ellipse in standard form. Graph the ellipse.

23. Find the perimeter and the area of the regular hexagon that can be inscribed in a circle whose radius is 20 inches.

24. Find the distance from the point $(-1, 2)$ to the line $3x + 4y = 2$.

Solve for x:

25. $12^{2x-2} = 4^{3x+1}$

26. $\dfrac{2}{3}\log_3 27 - \log_3(2x - 1) = 1$

27. $\dfrac{1}{3}\log_5 8 - 2\log_5 x = 0$

28. Find: (a) $\operatorname{antilog}_2(-3)$ (b) $\operatorname{antilog}_3(-2)$

29. Factor $x^2 + 10x + 30$ over the set of complex numbers.

30. If $g(x) = e^x$, find $g(2\ln 3 - \ln 2)$.

LESSON 95   *Advanced Complex Roots*

We have restricted our work with the roots of complex numbers to problems where the number is written in polar form or can be easily written in polar form. A calculator will permit us to find the roots of any complex number if we remember that the first step is to write the complex number in polar form.

example 95.1   Find the four fourth roots of $6 + 4i$. Express the roots in polar form.

solution   **We begin by writing the number in polar form.** We will use a calculator and round our answers.

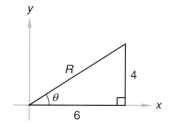

$$R = \sqrt{6^2 + 4^2} \qquad \tan \theta = \frac{4}{6}$$

$$R = 7.21 \qquad\qquad \theta = 33.69°$$

So we find that $6 + 4i = 7.21 \text{ cis } 33.69°$. Now the first of our fourth roots is $(7.21)^{1/4} \text{ cis } (33.69°/4)$. We use the y^x key or the $\sqrt[x]{y}$ key to find the fourth root of 7.21.

$$(7.21)^{1/4} = 1.64$$

Next, we divide 33.69 by 4 to get the angle, so now we have

One fourth root of $7.21 \text{ cis } 33.69° = 1.64 \text{ cis } 8.42°$

Now we add 360°/4, or 90°, to get the second root, add 180° to get the third root, and add 270° to get the fourth root; our four roots are

1.64 cis 8.42°, 1.64 cis 98.42°, 1.64 cis 188.42°, 1.64 cis 278.42°

example 95.2   Find the five fifth roots of $-17 - 14i$. Express the roots in polar form.

solution   The first step is to write the complex number in polar form.

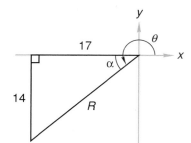

$$R = \sqrt{17^2 + 14^2} \qquad \tan \alpha = \frac{14}{17}$$

$$R = 22.02 \qquad\qquad \alpha = 39.47°$$

Therefore, since θ lies in the third quadrant,

$$\theta = 180° + 39.47° = 219.47°$$

Now we restate the problem as

One fifth root of $22.02 \text{ cis } 219.47° = 22.02^{1/5} \text{ cis } \dfrac{219.47°}{5} = 1.86 \text{ cis } 43.89°$

There are four more roots, which we get by adding $\dfrac{n \cdot 360}{5}$ to 43.89° ($n = 1, 2, 3, 4$).

1.86 cis 43.89°, 1.86 cis 115.89°, 1.86 cis 187.89°, 1.86 cis 259.89°, 1.86 cis 331.89°

**problem set
95**

1. There were 90 people in the room. Half were girls and one third were redheads. Two thirds of the people either were redheads or were girls. If one person is chosen at random, what is the probability of choosing a redheaded girl?

2. An urn contains 4 green marbles, 3 white marbles, and 3 blue marbles. A marble is drawn at random and then replaced. Then 2 more marbles are randomly drawn without replacement. What is the probability that all 3 are white?

3. There were 600 at first, but they increased exponentially. After 60 minutes there were 1000. How many minutes had elapsed before there were 5000?

4. In another room there were also 600, but they decreased exponentially. After 60 minutes, they had decreased in number to only 580. What was the half-life of these creatures?

5. Rondo could carry the 140 liters on his back. If the solution was 20% alcohol, how much pure alcohol must he add to get a solution that is 44% alcohol?

6. Find the four fourth roots of $3 + 4i$ and express the roots in polar form.

7. Find the three third roots of $2 + 3i$ and express the roots in polar form.

Sketch the graphs of the following:

8. $y = 3 + 11 \cos \dfrac{3}{2}(x - 100°)$ 9. (a) $y = \sec x$ (b) $y = \csc x$

10. Write the equations of these trigonometric functions:

(a)

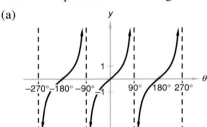

(b)

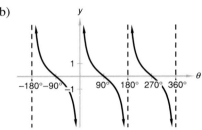

Show:

11. $\dfrac{\sin x}{1 + \cos x} + \dfrac{1 + \cos x}{\sin x} = 2 \csc x$ 12. $(1 + \tan x)^2 = \sec^2 x + 2 \tan x$

13. $\dfrac{\sin^4 x - \cos^4 x}{2 \sin^2 x - 1} = 1$

14. Develop the identity for $\cos \frac{1}{2}x$ by using the identity for $\cos (A + B)$.

15. Find $\cos 285°$ by using the sum identity for the cosine function and the fact that $285° = 240° + 45°$. Use exact values.

16. Use a sum identity to find an expression for $\sin \left(x + \frac{\pi}{4}\right)$. Use exact values.

Solve the following equations given that $0° \le x < 360°$:

17. $3 \tan^2 x + 5 \sec x + 1 = 0$ 18. $-1 + \tan 4x = 0$

19. Find the angle with the smallest measure in the triangle shown.

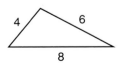

20. Compute $_7P_2$ and $_7C_2$.

21. Find the two geometric means between 3 and –24.

22. Find the first five terms of the arithmetic sequence whose fourth term is 4 and whose thirteenth term is 28.

23. A horizontal ellipse has a major axis of length 10 and a minor axis of length 4. If its center is at the origin, write the equation of the ellipse in standard form. Graph the ellipse.

24. Given the hyperbola $32x^2 - 18y^2 = 288$, write the equation in standard form and find the coordinates of its vertices and the equations of the asymptotes. Graph the hyperbola.

25. A seven-sided regular polygon has a perimeter of 35 inches. What is the area of the polygon?

Solve for x:

26. $\dfrac{9^{3x-2}}{3^{2x-1}} = 3$

27. $\dfrac{1}{3}\log_2 27 - \log_2(2x - 1) = 2$

28. $x = \log_{1/3} 18 - \log_{1/3} 6$

29. Simplify: $5^{\log_5 7 - \log_5 3} - \log_5 5^2$

30. Let $f(x) = \sqrt[3]{x}$ and $g(x) = x - 1$. Find $(g \circ f)(x)$.

LESSON 96   *More Double-Angle Identities • Triangle Area Formula • Proof of the Law of Sines • Equal Angles Imply Proportional Sides*

96.A

more double-angle identities

We have memorized identities for the sine and cosine of the sum of two angles and have practiced using these identities to write identities for the sine, cosine, and tangent of 2θ. **When we are proving identities, we must remember that these double-angle identities are available and use them whenever the identity contains $\sin 2\theta$, $\cos 2\theta$, or $\tan 2\theta$.**

example 96.1   Show: $(\sin x + \cos x)^2 = 1 + \sin 2x$

solution   We will work with the left-hand side and show that it equals the right-hand side.

$$(\sin x + \cos x)^2 = \sin^2 x + 2\sin x \cos x + \cos^2 x \qquad \text{multiplied}$$
$$= 1 + 2\sin x \cos x \qquad\qquad \sin^2 x + \cos^2 x = 1$$
$$= 1 + \sin 2x \qquad\qquad\qquad 2\sin x \cos x = \sin 2x$$

example 96.2   Show: $\dfrac{\cos^4 x - \sin^4 x}{\cos 2x} = 1$

solution   We will work with the left-hand side and show that it equals the right-hand side. We note that the numerator is the difference of two squares and can be factored.

$$\frac{\cos^4 x - \sin^4 x}{\cos 2x} = \frac{(\cos^2 x - \sin^2 x)(\cos^2 x + \sin^2 x)}{\cos 2x} \qquad \text{factored}$$

$$= \frac{\cos^2 x - \sin^2 x}{\cos 2x} \qquad\qquad \sin^2 x + \cos^2 x = 1$$

We remember that there are three identities for $\cos 2x$, and that one of these is $\cos^2 x - \sin^2 x$. We make this substitution and find that we have almost completed the proof.

$$= \frac{\cos 2x}{\cos 2x} \qquad\qquad \cos^2 x - \sin^2 x = \cos 2x$$

$$= 1 \qquad\qquad \text{simplified}$$

96.B

triangle area formula

The area of any triangle equals half the product of any two sides and the sine of the angle between them. Here we show triangle ABC three times.

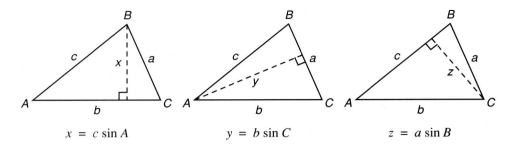

$$x = c \sin A \qquad\qquad y = b \sin C \qquad\qquad z = a \sin B$$

In the left-hand figure, we consider side b as the base and show the altitude x. In the center figure, we consider side a as the base and show altitude y. In the right-hand figure, we consider side c as the base and show altitude z. Below each figure we have used the sine of the angle to determine the length of the altitude. We remember that the area of a triangle equals half the product of the base and the altitude. If we substitute the values we have for the base and the altitude for the three triangles shown above, we get

$$\text{Area} = \frac{1}{2}(b)(c \sin A) \qquad \text{Area} = \frac{1}{2}(a)(b \sin C) \qquad \text{Area} = \frac{1}{2}(c)(a \sin B)$$

and if we remove the parentheses we get

$$\text{Area} = \frac{1}{2}bc \sin A \qquad \text{Area} = \frac{1}{2}ab \sin C \qquad \text{Area} = \frac{1}{2}ca \sin B$$

In each case, we see that the area equals one half the product of two sides and the sine of the angle between them. This proof uses an acute triangle. The same result can be obtained by using an obtuse triangle or a right triangle.

96.C

proof of the law of sines

There are several ways to prove the law of sines. We will prove it by using the area formulas above and substitution and then by rearranging the result. We begin with the following two equations.

$$\text{Area} = \frac{1}{2}bc \sin A \qquad \text{and} \qquad \text{Area} = \frac{1}{2}ab \sin C$$

If we equate these two expressions for the area, we get

$$\frac{1}{2}bc \sin A = \frac{1}{2}ab \sin C$$

If we divide both sides by $\frac{1}{2}b$, we get the expression

$$c \sin A = a \sin C$$

and we can now get the desired form by dividing both sides by $\sin A \sin C$. Since no angle in a triangle can have a measure of $0°$ or $180°$, we know that neither angle A nor angle C equals $0°$ or $180°$, so neither $\sin A$ nor $\sin C$ equals zero. Thus the division by $\sin A \sin C$ is permissible.

$$\frac{c \sin A}{\sin A \sin C} = \frac{a \sin C}{\sin A \sin C} \quad \longrightarrow \quad \frac{c}{\sin C} = \frac{a}{\sin A}$$

We can get the other equality we need by using the third area equation with either of the others. We do this and get

$$\frac{1}{2}ca \sin B = \frac{1}{2}ab \sin C$$

This time we will get the desired form in one step by dividing both sides by $\frac{1}{2}a \sin B \sin C$.

$$\frac{\frac{1}{2}ca \sin B}{\frac{1}{2}a \sin B \sin C} = \frac{\frac{1}{2}ab \sin C}{\frac{1}{2}a \sin B \sin C} \quad \rightarrow \quad \frac{c}{\sin C} = \frac{b}{\sin B}$$

Since all three ratios are equal, we can write the law of sines as

$$\frac{a}{\sin A} = \frac{b}{\sin B} = \frac{c}{\sin C}$$

96.D

equal angles imply proportional sides

Corresponding sides of similar triangles are proportional. This means that the ratios of all pairs of corresponding sides equal the same constant. Given that the triangles shown here are similar triangles,

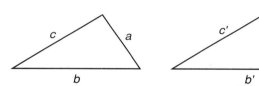

then the ratios of the lengths of corresponding sides equal the same constant, which we will call *SF* for scale factor.

$$\frac{a}{a'} = SF \qquad \frac{b}{b'} = SF \qquad \frac{c}{c'} = SF$$

If we are given two triangles in which corresponding angles are equal, we can use the law of sines to illustrate the fact that the sides are proportional. We remember that the ratio of each side to the sine of the opposite angle is a constant.

$$\frac{a}{\sin A} = \frac{b}{\sin B} = \frac{c}{\sin C} = k$$

If the corresponding angles in the following triangles are equal as indicated, we can use the law of sines to illustrate the fact that the corresponding sides are proportional because we can show that the ratios of corresponding sides all equal the same constant.

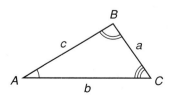
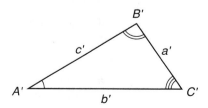

For the left-hand triangle,   For the right-hand triangle,

$$\frac{a}{\sin A} = k$$ $$\frac{a'}{\sin A'} = k'$$

Dividing, we get

$$\frac{\dfrac{a}{\sin A}}{\dfrac{a'}{\sin A'}} = \frac{k}{k'} = P \qquad \text{(another constant)}$$

And since angle A equals angle A', the sines of the angles are equal. Thus, we can simplify and write

$$\frac{a}{a'} = P$$

If we repeat the procedure for angles B and C, we can get the following.

$$\frac{a}{a'} = P \qquad \frac{b}{b'} = P \qquad \frac{c}{c'} = P$$

We have illustrated the fact that the ratios of the lengths of all pairs of corresponding sides equal the same constant, and this implies that the corresponding sides are proportional.

problem set 96

1. There were 500 present initially, and they increased exponentially. If the constant k in the exponent was 0.005, how long did it take them to increase to a total of 4000 present?

2. The number in the stadium decreased exponentially. There were 60,000 when the gun went off, and 5 minutes later only 50,000 remained. How long would it take before only 10,000 remained?

3. It was exactly four o'clock when the bell rang. How long did Fred have to wait before the hands on the clock formed a 90° angle?

4. Water flows down the Niger River at 4 mph. If Kunta rows steadily, he can go 27 miles downstream in the same time it takes him to go 3 miles upstream. How fast can Kunta row in still water?

Show:

5. $\dfrac{\cos^4 x - \sin^4 x}{\cos 2x} = 1$

6. $(\sin x + \cos x)^2 = 1 + \sin 2x$

7. $\dfrac{1 - \cos x}{\sin x} = \dfrac{\sin x}{1 + \cos x}$

8. Solve this triangle for angle A and find its area.

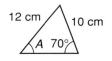

Sketch the graphs of the following:

9. (a) $y = \tan x$ (b) $y = \cot x$

10. (a) $y = \sec x$ (b) $y = \csc x$

11. $y = 11 + \sin \dfrac{3}{4}\left(x + \dfrac{\pi}{3}\right)$

12. Find $\sin(-15°)$ by using the difference identity for the sine function and the fact that $-15° = 30° - 45°$. Use exact values.

13. Use a sum identity to find an expression for $\cos\left(x - \frac{3\pi}{2}\right)$.

Solve the following equations given that $(0 \le x, \theta < 2\pi)$:

14. $2\tan^2 x + 3\sec x = 0$

15. $\sqrt{3} - 2\sin 2\theta = 0$

16. Find the two square roots of $3 + 4i$ and express the roots in polar form.

17. Find the three cube roots of $1 - i$ and express the roots in polar form.

18. Compute $_8P_3$ and $_8C_3$.

19. Find two geometric means between -5 and 625.

20. Find the first three terms of the arithmetic sequence whose third term is −8 and whose fifth term is 0.

21. An ellipse has foci at $(0, \pm 6)$ and vertices at $(0, \pm 10)$. Write the equation of the ellipse in standard form and find the lengths of the major and minor axes. Graph the ellipse.

22. Given the hyperbola $16y^2 - 9x^2 = 144$, write the equation in standard form and find the coordinates of its vertices and the equations of the asymptotes. Graph the hyperbola.

23. Use Cramer's rule to solve: $\begin{cases} 5x + 3y = 11 \\ 3x - 2y = -7 \end{cases}$

24. A 12-sided regular polygon has a perimeter of 72 cm. What is the area of the polygon?

25. What is the area of a sector whose central angle is $\pi/3$ radians in a circle of diameter 12 inches?

Solve for x:

26. $12^{4x+2} = 8^{2x-3}$

27. $\log_3 (x + 2) = 1 - \log_3 x$

28. $\dfrac{2}{3} \log_{12} 8 - \log_{12} (3x - 2) = \dfrac{1}{2} \log_{12} 10{,}000$

Simplify:

29. $2e^{\ln 2} + e^{2 \ln 8 - \ln 2}$

30. $7^{\log_7 (x-y) + \log_7 (x+y)}$

LESSON 97 *The Ambiguous Case*

A triangle has three angles and three sides for a total of six primary parts. **When we know the length of one side and the measures of two other parts, the measures of the three unknown parts can be found.** When we know the values of an angle and the side opposite (a pair), we can use the law of sines for our solution. If our third known value is an angle, then we also know the third angle, and the triangle can be drawn. For instance, if we are given $a = 6$, $A = 30°$, and $B = 70°$, we have a pair (a and A); and we know that angle C equals $80°$ because the sum of the three angles must be $180°$. We know enough to draw the triangle.

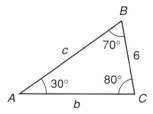

Now we can use the law of sines to find that b equals 11.28 and c equals 11.82.

$$\frac{b}{\sin 70°} = \frac{6}{\sin 30°} \qquad\qquad \frac{c}{\sin 80°} = \frac{6}{\sin 30°}$$

$$b = \frac{6 \sin 70°}{\sin 30°} = 11.28 \qquad\qquad c = \frac{6 \sin 80°}{\sin 30°} = 11.82$$

If we are given the values of a pair and the third value given is another side and no drawing of the triangle is provided, we have a problem. It might be possible to use the given values to draw one triangle, two triangles, or no triangles. We say that this is an **ambiguous case,** because the word *ambiguous* means "capable of two or more interpretations."

example 97.1 Given: $A = 40°$, $a = 4$, and $c = 9$. Draw the triangle and solve for the values of the other side and angles.

solution We have been given the measure of angle A, the length of the side opposite this angle, and the length of another side. **We have not been given a figure.** There are five possible figures that can be drawn, and which figure(s) applies depends on the length of side a.

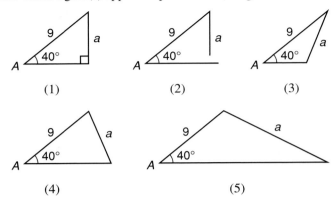

(1)   (2)   (3)

(4)   (5)

The first step is to use figure (1) to determine the value of the altitude H. If the given length a **equals H,** we have a right triangle, (1). If the given length a is **less than H,** we do not get a triangle at all, (2). If the given length a is **greater than H but less than 9,** two different triangles are possible, (3) and (4). If the given length a is **greater than H and greater than 9,** only one triangle is possible, (5). We begin by solving for H.

$$\sin 40° = \frac{H}{9} \qquad \text{equation}$$

$$9 \sin 40° = H \qquad \text{multiplied by 9}$$

$$5.79 = H \qquad \text{solved}$$

The length we were given for side a was 4, and this length is not as long as H, as we show in figure (2) above, so there is no triangle.

example 97.2 Draw the triangle and find the missing parts if $A = 27°$, $a = 5$, and $b = 7$.

solution We use the data given to draw the triangle. Now we solve to see how long side H must be for the triangle to be a right triangle.

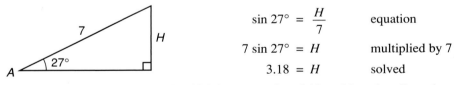

$$\sin 27° = \frac{H}{7} \qquad \text{equation}$$

$$7 \sin 27° = H \qquad \text{multiplied by 7}$$

$$3.18 = H \qquad \text{solved}$$

The length we were given for a is 5, which is greater than 3.18 and less than 7, so there are two possible triangles. We draw them and then solve. We note that the solutions for angle B are the same even though the triangles are different.

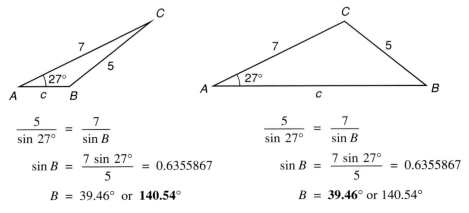

$$\frac{5}{\sin 27°} = \frac{7}{\sin B}$$

$$\sin B = \frac{7 \sin 27°}{5} = 0.6355867$$

$$B = 39.46° \text{ or } \mathbf{140.54°}$$

$$\frac{5}{\sin 27°} = \frac{7}{\sin B}$$

$$\sin B = \frac{7 \sin 27°}{5} = 0.6355867$$

$$B = \mathbf{39.46°} \text{ or } 140.54°$$

We see that both solutions yield the same answers for angle B. Angle C and the length of side c will be different, depending upon which value of B we use.

If $B = 140.54°$

$$C = 180° - 27° - 140.54° = \mathbf{12.46°}$$

$$\frac{c}{\sin 12.46°} = \frac{5}{\sin 27°}$$

$$c = \frac{5 \sin 12.46°}{\sin 27°}$$

$$c = \mathbf{2.38}$$

If $B = 39.46°$

$$C = 180° - 27° - 39.46° = \mathbf{113.54°}$$

$$\frac{c}{\sin 113.54°} = \frac{5}{\sin 27°}$$

$$c = \frac{5 \sin 113.54°}{\sin 27°}$$

$$c = \mathbf{10.10}$$

problem set 97

1. A card is drawn at random from a full deck of 52 cards. What is the probability that the card is a 10 or a spade?

2. The first urn contained 3 red marbles and 4 green marbles. The second urn contained 3 red marbles and 7 green marbles. One marble is randomly drawn from each urn. What is the probability that both marbles are green?

3. Their number was only 50 at the beginning, but the increase was exponential. After thirty minutes they numbered 300. How long did it take for them to increase their number to 1500?

4. The number of horses, sheep, and cows totals 128. One half the number of sheep plus 12 equals the number of cows, and one half the number of cows plus 12 equals the number of horses. How many of each kind of animal are there?

5. A mason built a wall for \$500. If he had received \$5 more per yard, he would have been paid \$750. How many yards of wall did he build?

6. A triangle has a 27° angle. A side adjacent to this angle has length 7 and the side opposite the angle has length 5. Draw the triangle(s) described and find the length(s) of the missing side(s).

7. A triangle has a 40° angle. A side adjacent to the 40° angle has a length of 10, and the side opposite the 40° angle has a length of 5. Draw the triangle(s) described and find the length(s) of the missing side(s).

Show:

8. $\cos 2x + 2 \sin^2 x = 1$

9. $\dfrac{\cos x}{1 - \sin x} - \dfrac{\cos x}{1 + \sin x} = 2 \tan x$

10. $\dfrac{2 \sin x}{\sin 2x} = \sec x$

11. Solve this triangle for c and find the area in square feet.

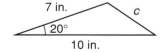

Sketch the graphs of the following:

12. $y = 1 + \tan x$

13. $y = -1 + \cot x$

14. $y = 3 + 4 \cos \dfrac{2}{3}(x + 90°)$

15. Find $2 \sin 15° \cos 15°$ by using the double-angle identity for the sine function.

Solve the following equations given that $(0° \le x, \theta < 360°)$:

16. $2 \cos^2 x = 1 - \sin x$

17. $-2 + \sec 3\theta = 0$

18. Find the three cube roots of $-5 + 8i$ and express the roots in polar form.

19. Find three geometric means between 2 and 32.

20. Find the first three terms of the arithmetic sequence whose fifth term is 0 and whose eighth term is 9.

21. An ellipse has foci at $(0, \pm4)$ and vertices at $(0, \pm5)$. Write the equation of the ellipse in standard form and find the lengths of the major and minor axes. Graph the ellipse.

22. Given the hyperbola $x^2 - y^2 = 4$, write the equation in standard form and find the coordinates of its vertices and the equations of the asymptotes. Graph the hyperbola.

23. The central angle of a sector of a circle is $30°$. Find the area of the sector in square centimeters if the radius is 5 meters.

24. What is the perimeter of the regular pentagon that can be inscribed in a circle whose radius is 12 cm?

Solve for x:

25. $10^{2 \log 5} - e^{3 \ln 2} = \log_2 x$ 26. $2 \log x - \log (x - 1) = \log 4$

27. $\dfrac{3}{4} \ln 16 - \ln (2x - 4) = \ln 3$ 28. $10^{2x-4} = 100^{3x}$

29. Find: (a) $\text{antilog}_6 (-3)$ (b) $\text{antilog}_{1/6} (-3)$

30. Factor $x^2 + 5x + 17$ over the set of complex numbers.

LESSON 98 *Change of Base • Contrived Logarithm Problems*

98.A

change of base

We remember that any positive number except 1 can be used as the base for logarithms. Logarithms with a base of 10 are especially useful for involved numerical calculations and historically have been used extensively for this purpose. Logarithms whose base is e possess certain qualities that make them useful in calculus and in other higher mathematics courses. Base e logarithms are studied to prepare for these courses. Many mathematics books have tables of base 10 logarithms and tables of base e logarithms, and most scientific calculators have log keys for base 10 logarithms and ln keys for base e logarithms.

Sometimes it is necessary to find a logarithm to a base other than e or 10. Fortunately, this can be done easily if base 10 or base e values are available. There is a formula that can be used to change the base, but it is easy to forget. **We prefer to compute logarithms whose base is neither 10 nor e by first writing a logarithmic equation, rewriting the equation as an exponential equation, and then taking the base 10 or base e logarithm of both sides and solving.** It is a simple procedure and is easy to remember.

example 98.1   Find $\log_5 15$.

solution   We begin by writing a logarithmic equation.

$$y = \log_5 15$$

Now we rewrite this equation as an exponential equation.

$$5^y = 15$$

Next we take the log of both sides. We can use either base 10 or base e. We decide to do both to show that the results would be the same.

USING BASE 10

$y \log 5 = \log 15$ took log of both sides

$y = \dfrac{\log 15}{\log 5}$ divided

$y = \dfrac{1.1761}{0.69897}$ log values

$y = 1.6826$ divided

USING BASE e

$y \ln 5 = \ln 15$ took ln of both sides

$y = \dfrac{\ln 15}{\ln 5}$ divided

$y = \dfrac{2.70805}{1.6094}$ ln values

$y = 1.6826$ divided

In both examples, we find the same value for the base 5 logarithm of 15.

$$\log_5 15 = \mathbf{1.6826} \qquad \text{which means} \qquad 5^{1.6826} = 15$$

example 98.2   Find $\log_7 82$.

solution   We will write a log equation, change it to an exponential equation, take the $\log_{10}$ of both sides, and solve.

$$y = \log_7 82 \qquad\qquad \text{log equation}$$

$$7^y = 82 \qquad\qquad \text{exponential equation}$$

$$y \log_{10} 7 = \log_{10} 82 \qquad\qquad \text{took log of both sides}$$

$$y = \frac{\log_{10} 82}{\log_{10} 7} \qquad\qquad \text{divided by } \log_{10} 7$$

$$y = \frac{1.9138}{0.8451} = 2.2646 \qquad\qquad \text{evaluated}$$

Thus, we have

$$\log_7 82 = \mathbf{2.26} \qquad \text{which means} \qquad 7^{2.26} = 82$$

98.B

contrived logarithm problems

Algebra books contain problems designed to give the reader meaningful practice in fundamental concepts. Some of the problems develop understanding that can be applied directly to real-world problems in science and business. Other problems have no direct applications, but the problems are useful because they provide practice that encourages a more comprehensive understanding of basic concepts. In this lesson, we will investigate some logarithm problems that fall into this category.

We have learned that when a variable is raised to a rational power such as

$$x^{3/2} = 8$$

the solution can be found by raising both sides to the reciprocal of the power. In this example, the reciprocal of the power is $\frac{2}{3}$.

$$\left(x^{3/2}\right)^{2/3} = 8^{2/3} \quad \longrightarrow \quad x = 4$$

We have learned to recognize that the sum of the logarithms or the difference of logarithms means that numbers have been multiplied or divided, respectively.

$$\log (x + 2) + \log (x - 3) \qquad \text{equals} \qquad \log (x + 2)(x - 3)$$

$$\log (x + 2) - \log (x - 3) \qquad \text{equals} \qquad \log \frac{x + 2}{x - 3}$$

The problems discussed in this lesson are designed to help us to remember the following:

1. The logarithm of an exponential equals the exponent times the logarithm of the base of the exponential.

$$\log x^n \qquad \text{equals} \qquad n \log x$$

2. Exponential equations can often be solved by taking the log of both sides. To demonstrate, we solve the following equation for x by taking the log of both sides and then dividing by $\log (n - 4)$.

$$(n - 4)^x = k \quad \longrightarrow \quad x \log (n - 4) = \log k \quad \longrightarrow \quad x = \frac{\log k}{\log (n - 4)}$$

   Division by divisors that contain a variable is valid if we exclude values of the variable that cause the divisor to equal zero. Since any nonzero base raised to the zero power has a value of 1, the logarithm of 1 to any nonzero base is 0.

$$b^0 = 1 \qquad \text{therefore} \qquad \log_b 1 = 0$$

   The argument of a logarithm can never be negative. In this example, we have the added restriction that the argument cannot equal 1 because this will cause the divisor to equal zero. Thus, n must be greater than 4, and also n cannot equal 5.

$$x = \frac{\log k}{\log (n - 4)} \qquad (n > 4, n \neq 5)$$

3. Logarithmic equations can often be solved by rewriting them as exponential equations. We can rewrite the following logarithmic equation to solve for x, as we show here.

$$\log x = 4 \qquad \text{logarithmic equation}$$
$$x = 10^4 \qquad \text{exponential form}$$
$$x = 10,000 \qquad \text{simplified}$$

example 98.3 Solve: $\log x^2 = (\log x)^2$

solution We will show two different ways to solve this problem. The first way involves division by an expression, $\log x$, that contains a variable. **The solution is acceptable if, as the last step, we check the original equation with the value(s) of the variable that would cause the divisor to equal 0.** This last step ensures that we do not inadvertently discard a valid root when we divide by $\log x$. We begin the solution by rewriting $\log x^2$ as $2 \log x$.

$$\log x^2 = (\log x)^2 \qquad \text{equation}$$
$$2 \log x = (\log x)^2 \qquad \text{rewritten}$$
$$2 \log x = (\log x)(\log x) \qquad \text{expanded}$$

Here we wrote $(\log x)^2$ in a more basic form as $(\log x)(\log x)$. Now, if we exclude the possibility that $\log x = 0$, we can divide both sides by $\log x$ and get

$$2 = \log x$$

To finish, we rewrite this log equation as an exponential equation and get

$$x = 10^2 \qquad \text{exponential equation}$$
$$x = 100 \qquad \text{solved}$$

As the last step, we must see if 1 is a solution to the original equation because we divided by $\log x$ and $\log x$ has a value of 0 if x equals 1. **This division by $\log x$ is invalid when $\log x$ equals 0, and this division might have caused us to overlook a valid solution.**

$$\log 1^2 = (\log 1)^2 \qquad \text{let } x = 1$$
$$0 = 0 \qquad \text{evaluated}$$

Thus we see that 1 is also a solution, so the equation has two solutions.

$$x = 1 \qquad\qquad x = 100$$

For the second method of solution, we begin by writing $\log x^2$ as $2 \log x$, and then we rearrange the equation and factor to solve.

$$\log x^2 = (\log x)^2 \qquad\qquad \text{equation}$$

$$2 \log x = (\log x)^2 \qquad\qquad \text{power rule}$$

$$(\log x)^2 - 2 \log x = 0 \qquad\qquad \text{rearranged}$$

$$(\log x)(\log x - 2) = 0 \qquad\qquad \text{factored}$$

$$\log x = 0 \qquad\qquad \log x - 2 = 0 \qquad\qquad \text{set factors equal to zero}$$

$$\log x = 2 \qquad\qquad \text{rearranged}$$

$$x = 10^0 \qquad\qquad x = 10^2 \qquad\qquad \text{exponent form}$$

$$x = 1 \qquad\qquad x = 100 \qquad\qquad \text{solved}$$

We see that the factor method also gives both solutions.

example 98.4   Solve: $\log \sqrt{x} = \sqrt{\log x}$

solution   We will only show one method of solution—the method that involves factoring. The other method involves division by $\log x$, which may cause us to inadvertently omit a root. Because of this, the method involving factoring is considered to be better. To begin, we replace the radicals with fractional exponents, and then on the left-hand side we rewrite $\log x^{1/2}$ as $\frac{1}{2} \log x$.

$$\log x^{1/2} = (\log x)^{1/2} \qquad\qquad \text{replaced radicals}$$

$$\frac{1}{2} \log x = (\log x)^{1/2} \qquad\qquad \text{power rule}$$

Next, we eliminate the fractional exponent on the right-hand side by squaring both sides, and we get

$$\frac{1}{4} (\log x)^2 = \log x \qquad\qquad \text{squared both sides}$$

Now we can complete the solution by factoring.

$$\frac{1}{4} (\log x)^2 - \log x = 0 \qquad\qquad \text{rearranged}$$

$$(\log x)\left(\frac{1}{4} \log x - 1 \right) = 0 \qquad\qquad \text{factored}$$

$$\log x = 0 \qquad\qquad \log x = 4$$

$$x = 1 \qquad\qquad x = 10{,}000 \qquad\qquad \text{solved}$$

example 98.5   Solve: $\log (\log x) = 3$

solution   We will solve this logarithmic equation by first rewriting it as an exponential equation.

$$\log x = 10^3$$

$$\log x = 1000$$

Now we solve this logarithmic equation by rewriting it as an exponential equation.

$$x = 10^{1000}$$

example 98.6　Solve: $x^{\sqrt{\log x}} = 10^8$

solution　This is an exponential equation, so we will take the log of both sides.

$$\sqrt{\log x}\,\log x = 8 \log 10$$

The right-hand side equals 8 and $(\log x)^{1/2}(\log x)^1$ equals $(\log x)^{3/2}$, so

$$(\log x)^{3/2} = 8$$

Now we raise both sides to the $\frac{2}{3}$ power, and as the last step, we rewrite the logarithmic equation as an exponential equation.

$\left[(\log x)^{3/2}\right]^{2/3} = 8^{2/3}$	raised both sides to $\frac{2}{3}$ power
$\log x = 4$	simplified
$x = 10^4$	exponential equation
$x = \mathbf{10{,}000}$	10^4 equals 10,000

problem set 98

1. One card is randomly drawn from a full deck and is replaced. Then a second card is randomly drawn. What is the probability that no hearts are drawn?

2. The amount present was initially 400, but it decreased exponentially. If 300 remained after 60 minutes, how much remained after 3 hours?

3. There are 10 people waiting patiently in line to sit in the 5 chairs along the wall. How many different ways can they sit in the chairs?

4. A man working alone can do a job in m hours, and his friend working alone can do the same job in f hours. How long will it take the man and his friend to do the job if they work together?

5. Rachel roared along for m miles in h hours and proudly arrived 2 hours early. How fast should she have roared along to get there 1 hour late?

6. Robert ran for the March of Dimes and was paid $1350. If he had been paid $2 more for each lap, he would have been paid $2250. How many laps did Robert run?

7. Take the permutations and combinations of 7 things taken six at a time to do a concrete development of the formulas for $_nP_r$ and $_nC_r$.

8. Use a calculator to aid in finding $\log_6 81$ to two decimal places.

Solve for x:

9. $x^{\sqrt{\log x}} = 10^8$　　　　10. $\log_2(\log_2 x) = 3$　　　　11. $\log_3 \sqrt{x} = \sqrt{\log_3 x}$

12. A triangle has a 45° angle. A side adjacent to this angle is 8 units long and the side opposite this angle is 4 units long. Find the length(s) of the other side.

13. A triangle has a 20° angle. A side adjacent to this angle has length 10 and the side opposite this angle has length 6. Draw the triangle(s) described and find the measure of the missing side.

Show:

14. $\dfrac{2 \cos 2x}{\sin 2x} = \cot x - \tan x$　　　　15. $2 \csc 2x \cos x = \csc x$

16. $\dfrac{2 \tan x}{1 + \tan^2 x} = \sin 2x$

17. Solve this triangle for angles A, B, and C.

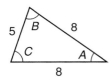

Sketch the graphs of the following:

18. $y = -1 + 5 \cos 3(x - 50°)$ **19.** $y = 2 + \sec x$

20. $y = -3 + \csc x$

21. Find $\cos^2 15° - \sin^2 15°$ by using the double-angle identity for the cosine function. Use exact values.

Solve the following equations given that $(0 \le x, \theta < 2\pi)$:

22. $2 \cos^2 x - \sqrt{3} \cos x = 0$ **23.** $2 - \sqrt{3} \sec 2\theta = 0$

24. Find the three cube roots of $6 - 2i$ and express the roots in polar form.

25. Find the fourth term of the geometric sequence whose first term is 2 and whose common ratio is 4.

26. Given the ellipse $25x^2 + 36y^2 = 1800$, write the equation in standard form and find the lengths of the major and minor axes. Graph the ellipse.

27. Find the perimeter of the square which can be circumscribed about a circle whose radius is 2 inches.

28. Two pentagons are similar. The length of one side of the larger pentagon is $\frac{3}{4}$. The corresponding side of the smaller pentagon is $\frac{2}{3}$. What is the ratio of the area of the larger pentagon to the area of the smaller pentagon?

29. Find the distance from the point $(1, 3)$ to the line $2x - 4y + 2 = 0$.

30. Which of the following graphs most resembles the graph of $f(x) = -\sqrt{x^2 - 9}$?

A.   B. C.   D. 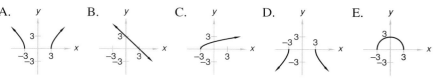   E.

LESSON 99   *Sequence Notations • Advanced Sequence Problems • The Arithmetic and Geometric Means*

99.A

sequence notations

We have used a_1 for the first term of a sequence, d for the common difference of an arithmetic sequence, and r for the common ratio of a geometric sequence. Thus, our general expressions for the nth term of an arithmetic progression and the nth term of a geometric progression are

nth TERM (ARITHMETIC) nth TERM (GEOMETRIC)

$$a_n = a_1 + (n - 1)d$$ $$a_n = a_1 r^{(n-1)}$$

We note that $n - 1$ appears in both expressions because in the arithmetic progression the difference is used one fewer times than the number of the term, and in the geometric progression the common ratio is used one fewer times than the number of the term. Other authors use other notations. We show several here.

nth TERM (ARITHMETIC) nth TERM (GEOMETRIC)

$$t_n = a + (n - 1)d$$ $$t_n = ar^{(n-1)}$$

$$\ell_n = a + (n - 1)d$$ $$\ell_n = ar^{(n-1)}$$

99.B

advanced sequence problems

Geometric progression problems are straightforward and are easy to solve. We will look at three of them in this lesson. In the first problem, we will use the fact that the common ratio can be found by dividing any term by the term that precedes it. If the geometric progression is $2x^2$, $8x^5$, $32x^8$, ..., we can find the common ratio by dividing the second term by the first term or by dividing the third term by the second term.

$$r = \frac{8x^5}{2x^2} = 4x^3 \qquad \text{also} \qquad r = \frac{32x^8}{8x^5} = 4x^3$$

In general, if the geometric progression is

$$t_1, t_2, t_3, t_4, t_5, t_6, \cdots$$

any fraction formed by dividing a term by the preceding term equals r. Thus, these fractions are equal to each other.

$$r = \frac{t_2}{t_1} = \frac{t_3}{t_2} = \frac{t_4}{t_3} = \frac{t_5}{t_4} = \frac{t_6}{t_5} = \cdots = \frac{t_n}{t_{n-1}}$$

example 99.1 Find the tenth term in the geometric progression that begins x, $\sqrt{2}x^2$, $2x^3$, ...

solution The first term is x, and the common ratio is found by dividing any term by the term that precedes it. In this problem, we can divide the second term by the first term and check by dividing the third term by the second term.

$$r = \frac{\sqrt{2}x^2}{x} = \sqrt{2}x \qquad \text{also} \qquad r = \frac{2x^3}{\sqrt{2}x^2} = \sqrt{2}x$$

Thus x is the first term, and r is $\sqrt{2}x$. Therefore,

$$a_{10} = x(\sqrt{2}x)^9 = \mathbf{2^{9/2}x^{10}}$$

example 99.2 Find the fourth term in the geometric progression that begins $2 + \sqrt{6}$, $6 + 2\sqrt{6}$, $12 + 6\sqrt{6}$, ...

solution To find r, we will divide the second term by the first term. Then we multiply above and below to rationalize the expression.

$$r = \frac{6 + 2\sqrt{6}}{2 + \sqrt{6}} \cdot \frac{2 - \sqrt{6}}{2 - \sqrt{6}} = \frac{-2\sqrt{6}}{-2} = \sqrt{6}$$

To find the fourth term, we multiply the third term by $\sqrt{6}$.

$$\left(12 + 6\sqrt{6}\right)\left(\sqrt{6}\right) = \mathbf{36 + 12\sqrt{6}}$$

example 99.3 A ball is dropped from a height of 81 inches. On each bounce, the ball rebounds two fifths of the distance it fell. How far does the ball fall on its sixth fall?

solution We will draw a picture of the problem (not to scale) and let each term represent the distance the ball fell.

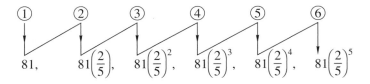

$$81, \qquad 81\left(\frac{2}{5}\right), \qquad 81\left(\frac{2}{5}\right)^2, \qquad 81\left(\frac{2}{5}\right)^3, \qquad 81\left(\frac{2}{5}\right)^4, \qquad 81\left(\frac{2}{5}\right)^5$$

From the diagram we see that on the sixth fall the distance D traveled was

$$D = 81\left(\frac{2}{5}\right)^5 = \mathbf{0.82944 \ inch}$$

99.C

the arithmetic and geometric means

We have learned that we can find any counting number of arithmetic and geometric means between two given numbers. Sometimes a problem will ask that we find **the** arithmetic or **the** geometric mean of two numbers. When this happens, we are asked to find *one mean*. **The arithmetic mean** is often called the **average** of the two numbers, and **the geometric mean** is sometimes called the **mean proportional.**

example 99.4   Find the arithmetic mean of x and y.

solution   We want to find **one** arithmetic mean between x and y. A diagram will help.

$$
\begin{array}{ccc}
① & ② & ③ \\
x, & \underline{\qquad}, & y \\
a_1, & a_1 + d, & a_1 + 2d
\end{array}
$$

We see that a_1 is x and $a_1 + 2d$ equals y. We replace a_1 with x and solve for d.

$$x + 2d = y \qquad \text{replaced } a_1 \text{ with } x$$

$$2d = y - x \qquad \text{added } -x$$

$$d = \frac{y - x}{2} \qquad \text{divided}$$

The mean is the first term plus the difference, or

$$x + \frac{y - x}{2} \qquad \text{add first term and difference}$$

$$\frac{2x}{2} + \frac{y - x}{2} \qquad \text{common denominator}$$

$$\frac{x + y}{2} \qquad \text{added}$$

We will use this last expression as a general expression for the arithmetic mean. **It is important to note and to remember that the arithmetic mean of two numbers is commonly called the *average* of the two numbers.**

example 99.5   Find the geometric mean (mean proportional) of x and y.

solution   We want to find **one** geometric mean. **A diagram always helps,** so we will use one.

$$
\begin{array}{ccc}
① & ② & ③ \\
x, & \underline{\qquad}, & y \\
a_1, & a_1 r, & a_1 r^2
\end{array}
$$

Our diagram tells us that $a_1 = x$ and $a_1 r^2 = y$. We substitute and solve for r.

$$xr^2 = y \qquad \text{equation}$$

$$r^2 = \frac{y}{x} \qquad \text{divided by } x$$

$$r = \pm\sqrt{\frac{y}{x}} \qquad \text{square root of both sides}$$

Now the second term is the product of the first term and the common ratio.

$$a_1 r \qquad \text{second term}$$

$$x\left(\pm\sqrt{\frac{y}{x}}\right) \qquad \text{substituted}$$

$$\pm\sqrt{xy} \qquad \text{simplified}$$

We will use this last expression in example 99.5 as a general expression for the geometric mean of two numbers. We see that we can have either a positive or a negative geometric mean of two given numbers. **The requirement to recall the expression for the geometric mean occurs from time to time, and it is helpful to commit this expression to memory.**

example 99.6   The positive geometric mean of two numbers is 8, and the difference between the numbers is 30. Find the numbers.

solution   We will use L for the larger number and S for the smaller number. We get two equations.

$$(a)\ L - S = 30 \qquad (b)\ \sqrt{LS} = 8$$

First we will square both sides of (b) and then substitute $L - 30$ for S.

$LS = 64$	squared both sides
$L(L - 30) = 64$	substituted
$L^2 - 30L = 64$	multiplied
$L^2 - 30L - 64 = 0$	simplified
$L = \dfrac{30 \pm \sqrt{900 - 4(1)(-64)}}{2(1)}$	quadratic formula
$L = -2, 32$	solved

Thus we find that both -2 and 32 are solutions for the larger number. If we use these numbers one at a time in equation (a), we find that the corresponding smaller numbers are -32 and 2. So the ordered pairs of (L, S) are **$(-2, -32)$** and **$(32, 2)$**.

problem set 99

1. There were 60 people in the room and 20 had blue eyes. Fifty of the people had dyed their hair green, and 10 people who had blue eyes also had dyed green hair. If one person was selected at random, what was the probability of that person having either blue eyes or green hair or both?

2. After 10 years only 500 remained, and after 20 years only 400 remained. If they decayed exponentially, what was their half-life?

3. An English professor has five books that she wishes to place upon her shelf. If the two volumes of Shakespeare's plays must always be next to one another, how many different ways can she line up the books?

4. Franklin ran the F miles at r miles per hour. If he increased his speed by 4 miles per hour, how long would it take him to run $F + 6$ miles?

5. Billy Bob could do m jobs in 4 hours; when Sally Sue helped, they could do 2 jobs in t hours. What was Sally Sue's rate of doing jobs?

6. The value of the purchase varied directly as the square of the satisfaction factor and the square root of the envy factor. What happened to the value of the purchase when the satisfaction factor was multiplied by 3 and the envy factor was multiplied by 4?

7. A ball is dropped from a height of 128 feet. After each bounce, it rebounds one half of the distance it fell. How far does the ball fall on its fourth fall?

8. The positive geometric mean of two numbers is 9, and the difference of the two numbers is 24. Find the numbers.

9. Find the fourth term in the geometric progression that begins $1 + \sqrt{2},\ 3 + 2\sqrt{2},\ \ldots$.

10. Find both the arithmetic and geometric mean for 8 and 22.

11. Use a calculator to aid in finding $\log_5 60$ to two decimal places.

12. Use a calculator to aid in finding $\log_6 50$ to two decimal places.

Solve for x:

13. $\log_2 (\log_2 x) = 2$ **14.** $\log_2 x^2 = 2(\log_2 x)^2$

15. $\log_3 \sqrt[3]{x} = \sqrt{\log_3 x}$

16. A triangle has a 55° angle. A side adjacent to this angle is 10 units long, and the side opposite is 9 units long. Find the length(s) of the other side.

Show:

17. $\dfrac{\cos^3 x - \sin^3 x}{\cos x - \sin x} = 1 + \dfrac{1}{2} \sin 2x$ **18.** $\dfrac{\cos 2x}{\cos^2 x} = 1 - \tan^2 x$

19. $\tan 2x = \dfrac{2}{\cot x - \tan x}$

20. Solve this triangle for a in centimeters. Then find the area in square centimeters.

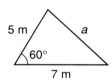

Sketch the graphs of the following:

21. $y = -\tan x$ **22.** $y = -\cot x$

23. Write the equations of the following trigonometric functions:

(a) 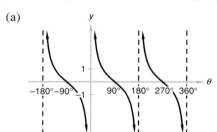   (b)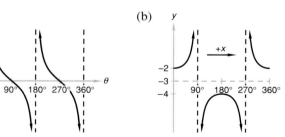

24. Find $2 \cos^2 15° - 1$ by using the double-angle identity for the cosine function. Use exact values.

Solve the following equations given that $(0° \le x, \theta < 360°)$:

25. $\sin x = \cos x$ **26.** $2 + \sqrt{3} \sec 4\theta = 0$

27. Find the four fourth roots of $-3 - 2i$ and express the roots in polar form.

28. An ellipse has foci at $(\pm 2, 0)$ and vertices at $(\pm 5, 0)$. Write the equation of the ellipse in standard form. Graph the ellipse.

29. Find the area of the regular octagon whose perimeter is 16 cm.

30. Factor $x^2 + x + 1$ over the set of complex numbers.

LESSON 100 *Product Identities • More Sum and Difference Identities*

100.A

product identities

There are four identities that involve the products of sines and cosines of angles. The first two are really equivalent, as they involve the product of the sine of one angle and the cosine of another angle. We begin our list with identity (g), since identities (a) to (f) were listed in Lesson 87 and Lesson 90.

$$\text{(g)} \quad \sin A \cos B = \frac{1}{2}\left[\sin (A + B) + \sin (A - B)\right]$$

$$\text{(h)} \quad \cos A \sin B = \frac{1}{2}\left[\sin (A + B) - \sin (A - B)\right]$$

$$\text{(i)} \quad \sin A \sin B = \frac{1}{2}\left[\cos (A - B) - \cos (A + B)\right]$$

$$\text{(j)} \quad \cos A \cos B = \frac{1}{2}\left[\cos (A + B) + \cos (A - B)\right]$$

These identities are difficult to memorize and retain because they are so alike. But they can be developed accurately and without effort by looking at the four key identities for the sine and cosine of the sums and differences of angles, as we will show in the following examples.

example 100.1   Develop the identity for $\sin A \cos B$.

solution   **Whenever one of the identities above is required, an excellent first step is to write down all four key identities. By looking at these identities, the necessary identity can be written without error.**

$$\text{(a)} \quad \sin (A + B) = \sin A \cos B + \cos A \sin B$$

$$\text{(b)} \quad \sin (A - B) = \sin A \cos B - \cos A \sin B$$

$$\text{(c)} \quad \cos (A + B) = \cos A \cos B - \sin A \sin B$$

$$\text{(d)} \quad \cos (A - B) = \cos A \cos B + \sin A \sin B$$

Now we need an identity for $\sin A \cos B$. We look at identities (a) to (d) and see that $\sin A \cos B$ appears in both (a) and (b). If we add identities (a) and (b), we get

$$\sin (A + B) + \sin (A - B) = 2 \sin A \cos B$$

The $\cos A \sin B$ terms had opposite signs and added to zero. Now we have an expression for $2 \sin A \cos B$, and we want only $\sin A \cos B$, so we complete the development by multiplying both sides by $\frac{1}{2}$ and we get the identity we seek.

$$\frac{1}{2}\left[\sin (A + B) + \sin (A - B)\right] = \sin A \cos B$$

example 100.2   Develop the identity for $\cos A \sin B$.

solution   We search the key identities and find $\cos A \sin B$ in identities (a) and (b), but they have opposite signs. We decide to change the signs in (b) so that the result will be positive. To do this, we multiply both sides of (b) by -1 and add the equations.

$$\text{(a)} \qquad \sin (A + B) = \quad \sin A \cos B + \cos A \sin B$$

$$-\text{(b)} \quad -\sin (A - B) = -\sin A \cos B + \cos A \sin B$$

$$\overline{\sin (A + B) - \sin (A - B) = 2 \cos A \sin B}$$

Now we complete the development by multiplying both sides by $\frac{1}{2}$, and we get

$$\frac{1}{2}\big[\sin (A + B) - \sin (A - B)\big] = \cos A \sin B$$

example 100.3   Develop the identity for $\cos A \cos B$.

solution   We find $\cos A \cos B$ in key identities (c) and (d), and we begin by adding these identities. The sum is

$$\cos (A + B) + \cos (A - B) = 2 \cos A \cos B$$

We finish by multiplying both sides by $\frac{1}{2}$, and we get

$$\frac{1}{2}\big[\cos (A + B) + \cos (A - B)\big] = \cos A \cos B$$

example 100.4   Develop the identity for $\sin A \sin B$.

solution   **This development is a little tricky because of the care that must be taken with the minus signs.** We find $\sin A \sin B$ in key identities (c) and (d). If we change the signs in (d), we will end up with $-2 \sin A \sin B$ when we add. So we decide to change the signs in (c) by multiplying every term by -1.

$$-(c) \quad -\cos (A + B) = -\cos A \cos B + \sin A \sin B$$
$$\underline{\quad (d) \qquad \cos (A - B) = \quad \cos A \cos B + \sin A \sin B \quad}$$
$$\cos (A - B) - \cos (A + B) = 2 \sin A \sin B$$

We complete the development by multiplying both sides by $\frac{1}{2}$, and we get

$$\frac{1}{2}\big[\cos (A - B) - \cos (A + B)\big] = \sin A \sin B$$

100.B

more sum and difference identities

There are four rather involved identities for the sums and differences of sines and cosines of two angles. The appearance of these identities is intimidating, but their development by using the key identities is even easier than the four developments in the preceding section. The identities are as follows:

$$(k) \quad \sin x + \sin y = 2 \sin \frac{x + y}{2} \cos \frac{x - y}{2}$$

$$(l) \quad \sin x - \sin y = 2 \cos \frac{x + y}{2} \sin \frac{x - y}{2}$$

$$(m) \quad \cos x + \cos y = 2 \cos \frac{x + y}{2} \cos \frac{x - y}{2}$$

$$(n) \quad \cos x - \cos y = -2 \sin \frac{x + y}{2} \sin \frac{x - y}{2}$$

We note that these identities use the variables x and y rather than the variables A and B. This is because in their development we use a change of variable. We use x to represent $A + B$ and y to represent $A - B$.

$$A + B = x \qquad\qquad A - B = y$$

If we add these equations in their present form, we can solve for A in terms of x and y.

$$A + B = x \qquad \text{left-hand equation}$$
$$\underline{A - B = y} \qquad \text{right-hand equation}$$
$$2A = x + y \qquad \text{added}$$
$$A = \frac{x + y}{2} \qquad \text{divided}$$

If we multiply one of the equations by -1 and add the equations, we can solve for B in terms of x and y.

$$A + B = x \qquad \text{left-hand equation}$$
$$\underline{-A + B = -y} \qquad \text{right-hand equation multiplied by } -1$$
$$2B = x - y \qquad \text{added}$$
$$B = \frac{x - y}{2} \qquad \text{divided}$$

example 100.5 Develop the identity for $\sin x + \sin y$.

solution We begin by writing the four key identities. Then, over each $A + B$ we write x, and over each $A - B$ we write y. Over each A we write $\frac{x+y}{2}$, and over each B we write $\frac{x-y}{2}$.

(a) $\sin (A + B) = \sin A \, \cos B + \cos A \, \sin B$

(b) $\sin (A - B) = \sin A \, \cos B - \cos A \, \sin B$

(c) $\cos (A + B) = \cos A \, \cos B - \sin A \, \sin B$

(d) $\cos (A - B) = \cos A \, \cos B + \sin A \, \sin B$

Now we see that we can get $\sin x + \sin y$ by adding equations (a) and (b).

$$\sin x + \sin y = 2 \sin \frac{x + y}{2} \cos \frac{x - y}{2}$$

example 100.6 Develop the identity for $\sin x - \sin y$.

solution We see that we can get $\sin x - \sin y$ by adding the negative of identity (b) to identity (a). We do this mentally and get

$$\sin x - \sin y = 2 \cos \frac{x + y}{2} \sin \frac{x - y}{2}$$

example 100.7 Develop the identity for $\cos x + \cos y$.

solution We can get this identity in one step by adding identities (c) and (d). We do this and get

$$\cos x + \cos y = 2 \cos \frac{x + y}{2} \cos \frac{x - y}{2}$$

example 100.8   Develop the identity for $\cos x - \cos y$.

solution   The identity can be obtained by adding the negative of identity (d) to identity (c). **Be careful with the signs.** We do this and get

$$\cos x - \cos y = -2 \sin \frac{x + y}{2} \sin \frac{x - y}{2}$$

Of course, there are many identities for sums, differences, and products of trigonometric functions. Problems in the problem sets that refer to *the* identity for a sum, difference, or product of trigonometric functions are referring to the identities developed above. If the development of these identities is practiced once or twice a day for a period of several weeks, the process will become automatic. Then, in the future, these identities can be developed quickly whenever they are needed.

problem set 100

1. A ball is dropped from a height of 81 feet. After each bounce, it rebounds two thirds of the distance it fell. How far does the ball fall on its fourth fall?

2. The whistle blew to signal high noon. Rumblat didn't quit because his lunch hour began the next time the clock hands formed a 90° angle. How long did Rumblat have to wait for lunch?

3. Joe Willy ran m miles at R miles per hour and arrived on time. Then the distance was increased 5 miles. How fast did he have to run to travel the new distance in the same amount of time?

4. Sally Sue bought m of the items for d dollars. If the price were increased k dollars per item, how many items could Sally Sue buy for $14?

5. The number of greens varied directly as the square root of the number of reds and inversely as the number of whites squared. What happens to the number of greens if the number of reds is multiplied by 16 and the number of whites is doubled?

6. Take the permutations and combinations of 11 things taken 4 at a time to do a concrete development of the formulas for $_nP_r$ and $_nC_r$.

Develop the identity for each of the following:

7. $\cos A \cos B$ 8. $\sin A \sin B$

9. $\sin x - \sin y$ 10. $\sin x + \sin y$

11. Find both the arithmetic and the geometric mean of 9 and 21.

12. The positive geometric mean of two numbers is 8, and the difference of the two numbers is 12. Find the numbers.

13. Use a calculator to aid in finding $\log_8 50$ to two decimal places.

14. Use a calculator to aid in finding $\log_5 70$ to two decimal places.

Solve for x:

15. $\log_3 \left(\log_3 x \right) = 2$ 16. $\log_3 x^2 = \log_3 x$

17. $\frac{2}{3} \ln 8 + \ln x - \ln (3x - 2) = \ln 3$

18. A triangle has a 35° angle. A side adjacent to this angle has length 8 and the side opposite this angle has length 4. Draw the triangle(s) described and find the length(s) of the missing side.

Show:

19. $2 \csc 2x = \cot x + \tan x$

20. $\dfrac{\sin 2x}{\tan x} = 2 \cos^2 x$

21. $\left(\tan^2 x\right)\left(1 + \cot^2 x\right) = \dfrac{1}{1 - \sin^2 x}$

22. Solve this triangle for angle A and angle B.

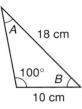

18 cm

100°

B

10 cm

Sketch the graphs of the following:

23. $y = 3 + 2 \sin \dfrac{1}{2}(x - \pi)$

24. $y = -\csc x$

25. Find $\cos 110° \cos 50° + \sin 110° \sin 50°$ by using the identity for the cosine of the difference of two angles.

Solve the following equations given that $(0 \le x, \theta < 2\pi)$:

26. $2 \sin^2 x + 15 \cos x - 9 = 0$

27. $\sqrt{3} - \cot 2\theta = 0$

28. Find the four fourth roots of $4 - 3i$ and express the roots in polar form.

29. Use Cramer's rule to solve: $\begin{cases} 4x - 2y = 10 \\ -2x + 3y = -4 \end{cases}$

30. Simplify: $x3^{\log_3 (x+1) - \log_3 (x^2 + x)}$

LESSON 101 *Zero Determinants • 3 × 3 Determinants • Determinant Solutions of 3 × 3 Systems • Independent Equations*

101.A

zero determinants

We remember that a determinant is a number that is associated with a particular square matrix. A matrix that is not square does not have a determinant.

$$\begin{matrix} 4 & 2 \\ 2 & 1 \end{matrix} \qquad \begin{matrix} 8 & 5 & 6 \\ 4 & 7 & 3 \end{matrix}$$

The matrix on the left above is a square matrix and has a determinant. The matrix on the right is not square, so it does not have a determinant. While the determinant is a number, we also call the notation

$$\begin{vmatrix} 4 & 2 \\ 2 & 1 \end{vmatrix}$$

a determinant because it represents the number. A determinant can be zero or any other number. The value of the determinant above is zero.

$$\begin{vmatrix} 4 & 2 \\ 2 & 1 \end{vmatrix} = 4 \cdot 1 - 2 \cdot 2 = 0$$

When using Cramer's rule, zero determinants in the denominator tell us that the equations do not have a single common solution. The equations shown here are the equations of parallel lines and thus have no common solution. If we attempt to solve this system by using the elimination method,

$$\begin{cases} 4x + 2y = 8 \\ 2x + y = 14 \end{cases} \quad \begin{array}{c} \rightarrow \\ \rightarrow \end{array} \quad \begin{array}{c} (1) \\ (-2) \end{array} \quad \begin{array}{c} \rightarrow \\ \rightarrow \end{array} \quad \begin{array}{r} 4x + 2y = 8 \\ -4x - 2y = -28 \\ \hline 0 = -20 \end{array}$$

the attempt degenerates into the false equation $0 = -20$. If we attempt a solution of the same system by using Cramer's rule,

$$x = \frac{\begin{vmatrix} 8 & 2 \\ 14 & 1 \end{vmatrix}}{\begin{vmatrix} 4 & 2 \\ 2 & 1 \end{vmatrix}} = \frac{-20}{0} \qquad y = \frac{\begin{vmatrix} 4 & 8 \\ 2 & 14 \end{vmatrix}}{\begin{vmatrix} 4 & 2 \\ 2 & 1 \end{vmatrix}} = \frac{40}{0}$$

we see that the denominator determinants are zero. Thus, Cramer's rule cannot be used to solve systems that cannot be solved by using the elimination method because a solution does not exist.

101.B
3 × 3 determinants

If we use the elimination method to solve the following system of equations for x,

$$\begin{cases} a_1 x + b_1 y + c_1 z = k_1 \\ a_2 x + b_2 y + c_2 z = k_2 \\ a_3 x + b_3 y + c_3 z = k_3 \end{cases}$$

the answer will be

$$x = \frac{(k_1 b_2 c_3 + b_1 c_2 k_3 + c_1 k_2 b_3) - (k_3 b_2 c_1 + b_3 c_2 k_1 + c_3 k_2 b_1)}{(a_1 b_2 c_3 + b_1 c_2 a_3 + c_1 a_2 b_3) - (a_3 b_2 c_1 + b_3 c_2 a_1 + c_3 a_2 b_1)}$$

If we are going to use Cramer's rule to solve this system, the solution will be

$$x = \frac{\begin{vmatrix} k_1 & b_1 & c_1 \\ k_2 & b_2 & c_2 \\ k_3 & b_3 & c_3 \end{vmatrix}}{\begin{vmatrix} a_1 & b_1 & c_1 \\ a_2 & b_2 & c_2 \\ a_3 & b_3 & c_3 \end{vmatrix}}$$

Now we must find some system of evaluating these determinants so that we get the same answer that we found when we used elimination. There are many methods that could be used. One method is the method of cofactors, and it can be used for any determinant larger than 2×2. We will study cofactors in a later lesson. **In this lesson, we will use a method that is applicable only to 3 × 3 determinants.** Given the determinant on the left, we repeat the entries on the right and **repeat the first two columns as columns 4 and 5.**

$$\begin{vmatrix} 3 & -2 & 1 \\ -1 & 4 & 10 \\ 2 & -3 & 5 \end{vmatrix}$$

$$-\left[8 \quad -90 \quad 10 \right]$$

$$\begin{array}{ccccc} 3 & -2 & 1 & 3 & -2 \\ -1 & 4 & 10 & -1 & 4 \\ 2 & -3 & 5 & 2 & -3 \end{array}$$

$$+\left[60 \quad -40 \quad 3 \right]$$

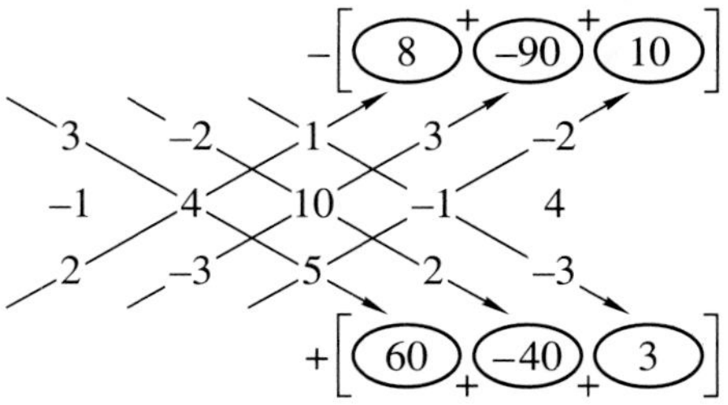

Then we multiply on the diagonals, as shown. After we multiply, we sum the products and remember to use the negative of the sum of the upper products.

$$\begin{vmatrix} 3 & -2 & 1 \\ -1 & 4 & 10 \\ 2 & -3 & 5 \end{vmatrix} = (60 - 40 + 3) - (8 - 90 + 10) = 95$$

101.C
determinant solutions of 3 × 3 systems

Cramer's rule is the same for systems of three equations in three unknowns as it is for two equations in two unknowns. **The denominator determinants are composed of the coefficients of the variables in the equations. In the numerator determinants, the coefficients of x, y, and z are replaced in turn with the constants from the right-hand side of the equations.**

> It is easy to make numerical mistakes when using determinants to solve 3 × 3 equations manually. Work these problems with one or two partners.

example 101.1   Use Cramer's rule to solve for x, y, and z: $\begin{cases} 2x + y + 2z = 7 \\ x + y - z = -2 \\ 3x - y + 2z = 16 \end{cases}$

solution   First we will evaluate the denominator determinant.

$$\begin{vmatrix} 2 & 1 & 2 \\ 1 & 1 & -1 \\ 3 & -1 & 2 \end{vmatrix} \rightarrow$$

$$\rightarrow (4 - 3 - 2) - (6 + 2 + 2) = -11$$

Now we solve for x.

$$x = \frac{\begin{vmatrix} 7 & 1 & 2 \\ -2 & 1 & -1 \\ 16 & -1 & 2 \end{vmatrix}}{-11} \rightarrow$$

$$\rightarrow \frac{(14 - 16 + 4) - (32 + 7 - 4)}{-11} = \frac{-33}{-11} = 3$$

Now we solve for y.

$$y = \frac{\begin{vmatrix} 2 & 7 & 2 \\ 1 & -2 & -1 \\ 3 & 16 & 2 \end{vmatrix}}{-11} \rightarrow$$

$$\rightarrow \frac{(-8 - 21 + 32) - (-12 - 32 + 14)}{-11} = \frac{33}{-11} = -3$$

Now we solve for z.

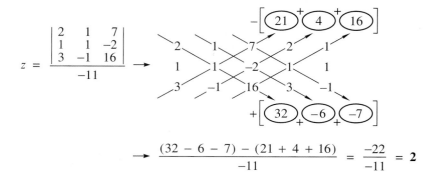

$$z = \frac{\begin{vmatrix} 2 & 1 & 7 \\ 1 & 1 & -2 \\ 3 & -1 & 16 \end{vmatrix}}{-11}$$

$$\longrightarrow \frac{(32 - 6 - 7) - (21 + 4 + 16)}{-11} = \frac{-22}{-11} = \mathbf{2}$$

example 101.2   Use Cramer's rule to solve for z: $\begin{cases} 3x + 2y + z = 9 \\ 2y + 3z = 14 \\ x + 2y = 3 \end{cases}$

solution   Two of the equations have zeros as coefficients for one variable. This will simplify the solution a little, as we will see.

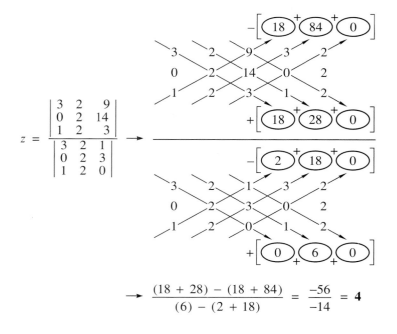

$$z = \frac{\begin{vmatrix} 3 & 2 & 9 \\ 0 & 2 & 14 \\ 1 & 2 & 3 \end{vmatrix}}{\begin{vmatrix} 3 & 2 & 1 \\ 0 & 2 & 3 \\ 1 & 2 & 0 \end{vmatrix}}$$

$$\longrightarrow \frac{(18 + 28) - (18 + 84)}{(6) - (2 + 18)} = \frac{-56}{-14} = \mathbf{4}$$

101.D

independent equations   A system of two linear equations in two unknowns is called a *2 × 2 system*. For the linear system to have a unique solution, the two equations must be **independent.** A system of three linear equations in three unknowns is called a *3 × 3 system*. For the system to have a unique solution, the three linear equations must be independent. A system of n linear equations in n unknowns is called an *n × n system*. For the system to have a unique solution, all n of the equations must be independent. A 2 × 2 linear system of equations is independent if the terms with variables in one equation are not multiples of the terms with variables in another equation.

If we multiply the x and y terms of the top equation in the system on the left below by 2, we get the x and y terms of the second equation. These are the equations of parallel lines. Parallel lines do not intersect and there is no value of x and y that will satisfy both equations.

$$\begin{cases} 4x + 3y = 1 \\ 8x + 6y = 42 \end{cases} \qquad \begin{cases} 4x + 3y = 1 \\ 8x + 6y = 2 \end{cases}$$

If we multiply every term in the top equation on the right on the previous page by 2, we get the bottom equation. These are the equations of parallel lines that lie on top of each other because the graphs are identical. These parallel lines have an infinite number of solutions and thus do not have a unique solution. The determinant of the matrix of coefficients of both systems is zero.

$$\begin{vmatrix} 4 & 3 \\ 8 & 6 \end{vmatrix} = 24 - 24 = 0 \qquad \begin{vmatrix} 4 & 3 \\ 8 & 6 \end{vmatrix} = 24 - 24 = 0$$

An $n \times n$ system of linear equations is an independent system (a) if no row in the coefficient matrix is a product of a constant and the members of another row and (b) if no row of the coefficient matrix can be formed by adding multiples of two or more rows. The 3×3 system of equations on the left is not independent because the second row of coefficients can be formed by multiplying the first row of coefficients by 3.

$$\begin{cases} x + 3y + 2z = 1 \\ 3x + 9y + 6z = 3 \\ x - 4y + 2z = 2 \end{cases} \qquad \begin{cases} 2x + y - z = 4 \\ -x + 3y + 2z = 8 \\ x + 4y + z = 2 \end{cases}$$

The 3×3 system of equations on the right is not independent because the sum of the x, y, and z coefficients in the first two rows are the x, y, and z coefficients of the third row. Because neither system has a unique solution, the determinant of the matrix of coefficients of both systems equals zero.

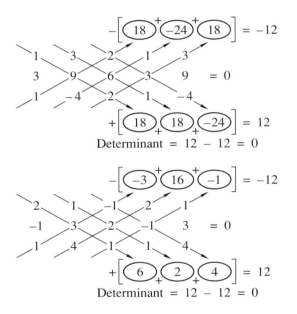

1. A ball is dropped from a height of 256 feet. After each bounce, the ball rebounds three fourths of the distance it fell. How far does the ball fall on its fifth fall?

2. Two of the three pots contained only brass coins, but one of the pots contained 5 silver coins, 4 gold coins, and 2 alloy coins. Harriet randomly selected a pot and then drew 1 coin. What was the probability that the coin was a gold coin? Assume each pot has the same chance of being selected.

3. Adrian counted 800 of the little furry creatures at the outset, and after 20 minutes of exponential decay, only 760 of them remained. What was the half-life of the little furry creatures?

4. The tugboat *Golden Hind* could travel 3 times the speed of the current. She could go 120 miles downstream in only 2 more hours than it took her to go 48 miles upstream. What was *Golden Hind*'s speed in still water and how fast was the current?

5. The 360-mile trip out was made by car, and the 360-mile trip back was made by plane at twice the speed of the trip out. If the round trip took a total of 9 hours, what was the speed on the trip out?

6. The ratio of reds to greens was 4 to 3, and altogether there were 63 of them lying around the house. How many of them were red?

7. Evaluate: $\begin{vmatrix} 2 & 0 & -1 \\ 0 & 3 & -2 \\ 3 & 4 & -1 \end{vmatrix}$

8. Use Cramer's rule to solve for z: $\begin{cases} 2x + 3y + z = 2 \\ y + 2z = 5 \\ x + 2y = -1 \end{cases}$

Develop the identity for each of the following:

9. $\cos A \sin B$

10. $\sin A \cos B$

11. The positive geometric mean of two numbers is 4 and the arithmetic mean of the two numbers is 5. What are the two numbers?

12. The negative geometric mean of two numbers is -10, and the difference of the two numbers is 15. Find the numbers.

13. Use a calculator to aid in determining:

(a) $\log_5 35$

(b) $\log_6 40$

Solve for x:

14. $x^{\ln x} = e^4$

15. $\log_4 (x + 3) + \log_4 (x - 3) = 2$

16. $\log_4 \sqrt[4]{x} = \sqrt{\log_4 x}$

17. A triangle has a 20° angle. A side adjacent to this angle has length 8 and the side opposite this angle has length 4. Draw the triangle(s) described and find the length(s) of the missing side.

Show:

18. $\dfrac{\sec 2x - 1}{2 \sec 2x} = \sin^2 x$

19. $(\cot^2 x)(1 + \tan^2 x) = \dfrac{1}{1 - \cos^2 x}$

20. $\csc 2x = \dfrac{1}{2} \cot x \sec^2 x$

21. A triangular plot of land has sides of lengths 80 meters, 100 meters, and 150 meters, respectively. Find the area of the plot.

Sketch the graph of each of the following:

22. $y = 10 + 2 \sin 4\left(x + \dfrac{\pi}{6}\right)$

23. $y = -\sec x$

24. Find $\cos 75°$ by using the half-angle identity for the cosine function with $x = 150°$. Use exact values.

Solve the following equations given that $0° \le x < 360°$:

25. $2 \csc 3x + 4 = 0$

26. $2 \cos^2 x + 15 \sin x - 9 = 0$

27. Find the three cube roots of $-4 + 2i$ and express the roots in polar form.

28. Find the distance from the point $(0, 1)$ to the line $x - y = 5$.

29. Find: (a) $\text{antilog}_4 (-3)$ (b) $\text{antilog}_{1/4} (-3)$

30. The heights of $2\frac{1}{2}$ year olds in a central Oklahoma town are normally distributed with a mean of 3 feet and a standard deviation of 2 inches. Max is a $2\frac{1}{2}$ year old who is 32 inches tall. What is the approximate percentage of $2\frac{1}{2}$ year olds who are shorter than Max?

LESSON *102* *Binomial Expansions (2)*

The binomial expansions investigated thus far have involved expressions such as the four shown here.

$$(a + b)^{10} \qquad (m + n)^7 \qquad (x + y)^4 \qquad (p + q)^6$$

The coefficient of each variable is +1, and the coefficients in the expansion will be the same as the numbers in Pascal's triangle (see Lesson 77). The exponents of the variables in the binomials are 1, so the exponents in the expansions will increase and decrease in the familiar patterns. When the coefficients and/or the exponents are not 1, the patterns in the expansions will not be so obvious.

example 102.1   Find the fourth term of $\left(-3x + 2y^2\right)^4$.

solution   We will replace $-3x$ with F (for first term) and replace $2y^2$ with S (for second term), and then expand $(F + S)^4$. To do this, we need to find the exponents for F and S in the fourth term and the coefficient of the fourth term. We remember the pattern for the exponents, and we get the coefficients from the fifth row of Pascal's triangle.

Term number	①	②	③	④	⑤
Exponents of F	4	3	2	1	0
Exponents of S	0	1	2	3	4
Coefficients	1	4	6	4	1

So the fourth term of $(F + S)^4$ is $4FS^3$. If we replace F with $-3x$ and S with $2y^2$, we get

$$4(-3x)\left(2y^2\right)^3 = \mathbf{-96xy^6}$$

example 102.2   Expand $\left(2a^2 - x^3\right)^4$.

solution   We will use F to represent the first term $\left(2a^2\right)$ in the binomial and will use S to represent the second term $\left(-x^3\right)$ in the binomial, and then expand $(F + S)^4$. We look at the exponents of F and S and at the fifth row in Pascal's triangle.

Term number	①	②	③	④	⑤
Exponents of F	4	3	2	1	0
Exponents of S	0	1	2	3	4
Coefficients	1	4	6	4	1

Now we write the expansion of $(F + S)^4$.

$$(F + S)^4 = F^4 + 4F^3S + 6F^2S^2 + 4FS^3 + S^4$$

Now we replace F with $2a^2$ and S with $-x^3$.

$$\left(2a^2 - x^3\right)^4 = \left(2a^2\right)^4 + 4\left(2a^2\right)^3\left(-x^3\right) + 6\left(2a^2\right)^2\left(-x^3\right)^2 + 4\left(2a^2\right)\left(-x^3\right)^3 + \left(-x^3\right)^4$$

Finally, we simplify every term and get

$$\left(2a^2 - x^3\right)^4 = \mathbf{16a^8 - 32a^6x^3 + 24a^4x^6 - 8a^2x^9 + x^{12}}$$

example 102.3   Find the third term of $\left(-3x + 2y^2\right)^5$.

solution   First we will use F for $-3x$ and S for $2y^2$ and write the exponents and the coefficients for $(F + S)^5$.

Term number	①	②	③	④	⑤	⑥
Exponents of F	5	4	3	2	1	0
Exponents of S	0	1	2	3	4	5
Coefficients	1	5	10	10	5	1

The third term of $(F + S)^5$ is $10F^3S^2$, and if we replace F with $-3x$ and S with $2y^2$, we get

$$\text{Third term} = 10(-3x)^3\left(2y^2\right)^2$$
$$= -1080x^3y^4$$

1. A ball is dropped from a height of 243 feet. After each bounce, the ball rebounds one third of the distance it fell. How far does the ball fall on its fourth fall?

2. Donny peeked around the corner and quickly drew one card at random from a full deck. He looked at the card and smiled. What was the probability that Donny's card was a 2 or was red or was a red 2?

3. The level of the milk in the magic pitcher increased exponentially. When Greselda first looked, the level was 0.04 centimeter. Twenty seconds later the level was 2.6 centimeters. How long would it take for the level to increase to 16 centimeters?

4. The *Gerta Sue* could huff and puff her way 33 miles down the Old Swampy in 1 hour less than it took her to huff and puff 20 miles up the Old Swampy. If the *Gerta Sue*'s speed was twice the speed of the current, what was the *Gerta Sue*'s speed in still water and what was the speed of the current?

5. Wanatobe is 5 times as old as little Pete. Five years ago, Wanatobe's age exceeded 6 times the age of little Pete by 19 years. How old will both of them be in 17 years?

6. Four times the complement of angle 1 is 40° less than the supplement of angle 2. Find the measures of angle 1 and angle 2 if the sum of the measures of the two angles is 80°.

7. Find the fourth term of $(x - y)^7$.   8. Expand $\left(2a^2 - b^3\right)^3$.

9. Evaluate: $\begin{vmatrix} 0 & 1 & 2 \\ 3 & 0 & 1 \\ 1 & 5 & 6 \end{vmatrix}$

10. Use Cramer's rule to solve for x: $\begin{cases} 3x - y + z = 0 \\ 3y + 2z = 4 \\ x + 2y = 5 \end{cases}$

Develop the identity for each of the following:

11. $\cos x + \cos y$ 12. $\cos x - \cos y$

13. The negative geometric mean of two numbers is -12. The arithmetic mean of the two numbers is 20. Find the two numbers.

14. Use a calculator to aid in finding: (a) $\log_7 40$ (b) $\log_3 40$

Solve for x:

15. $\sqrt{\log_{81} x} = 2\log_{81} x$ 16. $\log_2 (x + 1) - \log_2 (x - 1) = 1$

17. $\ln x + \ln (x - 1) = \ln 20$

18. A triangle has a 50° angle. A side adjacent to this angle has length 10 and the side opposite this angle has length 9. Draw the triangle(s) described and find the length(s) of the missing side.

Show:

19. $\dfrac{\sin^2 x}{1 - \cos x} - \dfrac{1}{\sec x} = 1$ **20.** $\dfrac{\cos 2x}{\sin^2 x} = \cot^2 x - 1$

21. $\dfrac{1 + \sin x}{\cos x} + \dfrac{\cos x}{1 + \sin x} = \dfrac{4 \sin x}{\sin 2x}$

22. Solve this triangle for angle A. Then find the area in square centimeters.

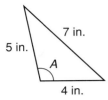

23. Sketch the graph of $y = 2 \tan x$.

24. Write the equations of the following trigonometric functions:

(a)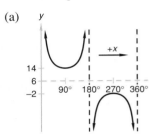

(b)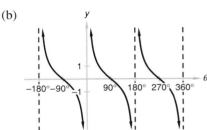

Solve the following equations given that $(0 \le \theta, x < 2\pi)$:

25. $\tan 5\theta = 0$ **26.** $3 \tan^2 x - 5 \sec x + 1 = 0$

27. Find the five fifth roots of $-2 + 8i$ and express the roots in polar form.

28. The perimeter of a regular hexagon is 30 feet. Find the area of the regular hexagon.

29. Factor $x^3 + 5x^2 + 10x$ over the set of complex numbers.

30. If $f(x) = x^3$ and $g(x) = 2x^2 - 1$, find $(f - g)(2)$.

LESSON 103 · *Calculations with Logarithms • Power of the Hydrogen*

103.A

calculations with logarithms

Problems that involve multiplication, division, and taking roots can be performed by writing the numbers as powers and using the rules for exponents. For example, we can multiply 10,000 by 100 by writing both numbers as powers of 10.

$$10^4 \cdot 10^2 = 10^6$$

We see that the answer is 10^6, which equals 1 million. When we do this multiplication by using logarithms, we just use the exponents.

$$\log (10,000)(100) = \log 10,000 + \log 100 = 4 + 2 = 6$$

The antilogarithm of 6 is 1 million, so the answer is the same as the answer above. To take the cube root of 1 million by using exponents, we could write

$$\left(10^6\right)^{\frac{1}{3}}$$

One million is 10^6, and we use the one-third power to indicate the cube root. If we do this,

$$\left(10^6\right)^{\frac{1}{3}} = 10^2$$

we find that the cube root of 1 million is 100. To do the same thing using logs, we remember that

$$\log x^N = N \log x$$

which in this problem gives us

$$\log \left(10^6\right)^{\frac{1}{3}} = \frac{1}{3} \log 10^6 = \frac{1}{3}(6) = 2$$

and the antilog of 2 is 10^2, or 100.

In the past, complicated arithmetic problems involving multiplication, division, or exponentiation were often solved by applying these properties of logarithms. With the advent of calculators, these arithmetic problems can now be solved directly. Although calculators have obviated the need to use logarithms to perform complex arithmetic calculations, logarithms are still needed in higher-level courses like calculus. In the following examples, we will practice applying the properties of logarithms to algebraic expressions.

example 103.1   Write the following expression as a single logarithm:

$$3 \ln \left(x^2 - 1\right) - 2 \ln y - 4 \ln (x + 1) + \frac{2}{3} \ln \left(y^2 + y\right)$$

solution   We begin by using the power rule to "change" the coefficient of each term to an exponent.

$$\ln \left(x^2 - 1\right)^3 - \ln y^2 - \ln (x + 1)^4 + \ln \left(y^2 + y\right)^{\frac{2}{3}}$$

Next, we will apply the product rule and the quotient rule for logarithms to rewrite the sum above into a single logarithmic expression.

$$\ln \left(\frac{\left(x^2 - 1\right)^3 \left(y^2 + y\right)^{\frac{2}{3}}}{(x + 1)^4 y^2}\right)$$

Finally, we simplify the argument.

$$\ln \left(\frac{(x - 1)^3 (x + 1)^3 y^{\frac{2}{3}} (y + 1)^{\frac{2}{3}}}{(x + 1)^4 y^2}\right) = \ln \left(\frac{(x - 1)^3 (y + 1)^{\frac{2}{3}}}{(x + 1) y^{\frac{4}{3}}}\right)$$

example 103.2   Expand the following into the sum of logarithmic expressions, each of whose argument is linear:

$$\log \left(\frac{xy^3}{\sqrt{(x + 1)z^3}}\right)$$

solution $\log\left(\dfrac{xy^3}{\sqrt{(x+1)z^3}}\right) = \log\left(\dfrac{xy^3}{(x+1)^{\frac{1}{2}}z^{\frac{3}{2}}}\right)$

$$= \log\left(xy^3\right) - \log\left((x+1)^{\frac{1}{2}}z^{\frac{3}{2}}\right) \qquad \text{quotient rule}$$

$$= \log x + \log y^3 - \left(\log(x+1)^{\frac{1}{2}} + \log z^{\frac{3}{2}}\right) \qquad \text{product rule}$$

$$= \log x + 3\log y - \left(\frac{1}{2}\log(x+1) + \frac{3}{2}\log z\right) \qquad \text{power rule}$$

$$= \mathbf{\log x + 3\log y - \frac{1}{2}\log(x+1) - \frac{3}{2}\log z}$$

103.B
power of the hydrogen

The relative acidity of a liquid is determined by the concentration of the hydrogen ions in the liquid. As the concentration of the hydrogen ions in the liquid increases, the acidity of a liquid increases. The relationship between the acidity and the concentration of hydrogen ions was defined as an exponential or logarithmic relationship by the Danish chemist Sören Sörenson in 1909. He used the symbol pH to represent the relative acidity (*power* of the *h*ydrogen) and used the symbol H^+ to represent the concentration of the hydrogen ions. The pH of liquids ranges from about 0 to +14, and the pH of water, which is considered to be neutral, is +7. This topic is studied in-depth in chemistry. We are studying algebra and will concern ourselves only with the two forms of the relationship.

<table>
<tr><td>EXPONENTIAL FORM</td><td>LOGARITHMIC FORM</td></tr>
<tr><td>$10^{-pH} = H^+$</td><td>$pH = -\log H^+$</td></tr>
</table>

We will find pH when we are given the concentration of hydrogen ions in moles per liter, and we will find the concentration of hydrogen ions in moles per liter when we are given pH. We will not concern ourselves with units such as moles per liter and will just use the numbers and assume that the units are correct.

example 103.3   Find the pH of a liquid if H^+ is 4.03×10^{-6} mole per liter.

solution   We can use either

$$\text{(a) } 10^{-pH} = H^+ \qquad \text{or} \qquad \text{(b) } pH = -\log H^+$$

We are given H^+ and asked to determine pH, so we will use (b) and substitute 4.03×10^{-6} for H^+.

$$pH = -\log\left(4.03 \times 10^{-6}\right) \qquad \text{substituted}$$
$$pH = 5.3947 \qquad \text{used calculator}$$
$$pH = \mathbf{5.4} \qquad \text{rounded}$$

example 103.4   Find the concentration of hydrogen ions $\left(H^+\right)$ if the pH of the liquid is 7.05.

solution   We can use either

$$\text{(a) } 10^{-pH} = H^+ \qquad \text{or} \qquad \text{(b) } pH = -\log H^+$$

This time we are given the pH and asked to find H^+, so we use (a) and substitute.

$$10^{-7.05} = H^+ \qquad \text{substituted}$$
$$H^+ = \mathbf{8.9 \times 10^{-8}} \qquad \text{used calculator}$$

problem set 103

1. A ball is dropped from a height of 128 feet. On each bounce, the ball rebounds one fourth of the distance it fell. How far does the ball rebound on the fourth bounce?

2. Burt tossed a fair coin 4 times. What is the probability that all 4 tosses came up heads?

3. The onlookers gazed in wonder as the size of the thing decreased exponentially. When it was first observed, it measured 42 cubits. But in only 30 minutes, its measure had decreased to 39 cubits. How long would it take before the thing measured only 12.5 cubits?

4. The pressure of an ideal gas varies inversely with the volume if the temperature is constant. When the temperature was 500 K, the pressure was 4 atmospheres and the volume was 10 liters. At the same temperature, what was the pressure when the volume was reduced to 2 liters?

5. Kateri ran k miles in p hours. Then she increased her speed s miles per hour. How long would it take her to cover 12 miles at the new speed?

6. How much pure acid must be added to 180 milliliters of a 35% acid solution to produce a solution that is 50% acid?

7. Write as a single logarithm: $\dfrac{3}{5} \log_3 x + \dfrac{1}{4} \log_3 y - 3 \log_3 z$

8. Use a calculator to compute: $\dfrac{\sqrt[6]{525,000}}{(6300)^{1.5}}$

9. Find the pH of a liquid if the concentration of hydrogen ions (H^+) is 5.3×10^{-5} mole per liter.

10. Find the concentration of hydrogen ions (H^+) in a liquid if the pH of the liquid is 6.5.

11. Find the middle term of $(x - y)^8$.   **12.** Expand $(3a^2 - b^3)^4$.

13. Use Cramer's rule to solve for x: $\begin{cases} 2x + y + 3z = -3 \\ 3y + 4z = 5 \\ x + 2y = 3 \end{cases}$

Develop the identity for each of the following:

14. $\cos x - \cos y$ **15.** $\sin A \sin B$

16. Use a calculator to aid in determining:

    (a) $\log_5 22$ (b) $\log_{12} 22$

Solve for x:

17. $\log_5 \sqrt{x^2 + 16} = 1$ **18.** $\dfrac{2}{3} \log_4 8 - \log_4 (3x - 2) = 2$

19. $4 \log_3 \sqrt[4]{x} = \log_3 (3x - 1)$ **20.** $\log_2 (\log_2 x) = 1$

21. A triangle has a 25° angle. A side adjacent to this angle is 8 units long and the side opposite the angle is 5 units long. Find the length(s) of the missing side.

Show:

22. $\dfrac{\cos 2x + 1}{2} = \cos^2 x$ **23.** $\dfrac{2 \cot x}{\tan 2x} = \csc^2 x - 2$

24. Find the area of the triangle in square meters. Then find a.

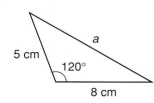

25. Sketch the graph of $y = \dfrac{1}{2}\cot x$.

26. Find the exact value of $\cos 345°$ by using the identity for $\cos(x + y)$ and the fact that $345° = 120° + 225°$.

Solve the following equations given that $(0° \leq \theta, x < 360°)$:

27. $1 + \tan 3\theta = 0$ **28.** $\sqrt{2}\sec x = \sqrt{\sec x + 1}$

29. Find the three cube roots of $-5 + 12i$ and express the roots in polar form.

30. Simplify: $(x + 1)4^{2\log_4 x - \log_4(x^2 + x)}$

LESSON *104* *Arithmetic Series • Geometric Series*

104.A

arithmetic series

A *series* is the indicated sum of a sequence. Here we show the first 10 terms of an arithmetic sequence whose first term is 11 and whose common difference is 3.

$$①\quad②\quad③\quad④\quad⑤\quad⑥\quad⑦\quad⑧\quad⑨\quad⑩$$
$$11,\quad 14,\quad 17,\quad 20,\quad 23,\quad 26,\quad 29,\quad 32,\quad 35,\quad 38, \ldots$$

If we put a plus sign between each of the members of this arithmetic sequence, we turn the arithmetic sequence into an arithmetic series.

$$①\quad②\quad③\quad④\quad⑤\quad⑥\quad⑦\quad⑧\quad⑨\quad⑩$$
$$11 + 14 + 17 + 20 + 23 + 26 + 29 + 32 + 35 + 38 + \cdots$$

Thus, we see that an *arithmetic series* is the same thing as an arithmetic sequence that has a plus sign between every entry. Sometimes we find it necessary to find the sum of a number of terms in a series. We will indicate the sum by using a subscripted capital S. The subscript tells us how many terms of the series we are adding. We can show the sum of 4, 6, or n terms of this series by writing

$$S_4 = 11 + 14 + 17 + 20 = 62$$

$$S_6 = 11 + 14 + 17 + 20 + 23 + 26 = 111$$

$$S_n = 11 + 14 + 17 + 20 + 23 + 26 + 29 + 32 + \cdots + a_n = \,?$$

We can develop a formula for the sum of n terms of an arithmetic series by using a specific series which has **an even number of terms** to get the pattern and then generalizing. Using the first 8 terms of the series S_n above,

$$⑪ + ⑭ + ⑰ + ⑳ + ㉓ + ㉖ + ㉙ + ㉜$$

we see that the sum of the first term and the last term is $11 + 32 = 43$. The sum of the second term and the next-to-the-last term is $14 + 29 = 43$. The sums of the other two pairs are also 43. There are 8 terms in all, and thus there are 4 pairs of terms. The value of each pair is the same as the sum of the first term and the eighth term, so the sum of this 8-term series is

$$\text{Sum of all 8 terms} = \frac{8}{2}(\text{first term} + \text{eighth term})$$

If we use n for the number of terms instead of 8 and a_1 for the first term and a_n for the nth term, we get a formula for the sum of n terms.

$$S_n = \frac{n}{2}(a_1 + a_n)$$

We used a series with an even number of terms to develop this formula. The formula will also work for the sum of an odd number of terms because the value of the middle term equals half the sum of the first term and the last term. To demonstrate, we will find the sum of the 9 terms of this arithmetic series by adding, and then we will use the formula to see if the formula gives the same result.

$$\begin{array}{ccccccccc} \textcircled{1} & \textcircled{2} & \textcircled{3} & \textcircled{4} & \textcircled{5} & \textcircled{6} & \textcircled{7} & \textcircled{8} & \textcircled{9} \end{array}$$

$$S_9 = 11 + 14 + 17 + 20 + 23 + 26 + 29 + 32 + 35 = 207$$

Now we will use the formula.

$$S_9 = \frac{9}{2}(11 + 35) \qquad \text{substituted}$$

$$S_9 = (4.5)(46) \qquad \text{simplified}$$

$$S_9 = 207 \qquad \text{multiplied}$$

We see that the formula gives us the same result as we get when we add the individual terms.

Formulas are difficult to remember, and putting numbers into formulas to find a numerical answer is a task that brings few rewards. Thus, in the problem sets we will have problems, such as the next example, which require the development of this formula as well as its use.

example 104.1   An arithmetic sequence has a first term of -10 and a common difference of $+20$. Use the first 4 terms of this sequence to write a series and develop the formula for the sum. Then use the formula to find the sum of the first 11 terms of the sequence.

solution   First we write the first 4 terms of the sequence and then insert the plus signs to form a series.

$$\begin{array}{cccc} \textcircled{1} & \textcircled{2} & \textcircled{3} & \textcircled{4} \end{array}$$

| Sequence | -10 | 10 | 30 | 50 |

Series $-10 + 10 + 30 + 50$

We see that the sum of the first term and the last term is 40 and that the other two terms also sum to 40. There is one half of four pairs, so our formula for the sum of 4 terms is

$$S_4 = \frac{4}{2}(\text{first} + \text{fourth})$$

If we use n instead of 4 and a_1 and a_n instead of first and fourth, respectively, we get

$$S_n = \frac{n}{2}(a_1 + a_n)$$

In this problem we are told that the first term is -10, and we compute the value of the eleventh term to be 190, which is the sum of the first term and 10 times the difference. Now we can use the formula to find the sum of the first 11 terms.

$$S_{11} = \frac{11}{2}(-10 + 190) = (5.5)(180) = \mathbf{990}$$

104.B

geometric series

A *geometric series* **is formed by placing plus signs between the terms of a geometric sequence.** To develop a formula for the sum of the terms of a geometric sequence, we will subtract one series from another to get rid of all terms between the first term and the last term. We begin by writing the general expression for a geometric sequence. Note how we write the general form of the next-to-last term.

$$\underset{a_1}{①} \quad \underset{a_1 r}{②} \quad \underset{a_1 r^2}{③} \quad \underset{a_1 r^3}{④} \quad \cdots \quad \underset{a_1 r^{n-2}}{(n-1)} \quad \underset{a_1 r^{n-1}}{(n)}$$

Now if we place a plus sign between each term, we will have a geometric series. We set this series equal to S_n to indicate the sum of n terms.

$$\text{(a)} \quad S_n = a_1 + a_1 r + a_1 r^2 + a_1 r^3 + \cdots + a_1 r^{n-2} + a_1 r^{n-1}$$

The next step is to multiply each term on both sides by r.

$$\text{(b)} \quad r S_n = a_1 r + a_1 r^2 + a_1 r^3 + a_1 r^4 + \cdots + a_1 r^{n-1} + a_1 r^n$$

Now if we multiply both sides of equation (b) by -1 and add the result to equation (a), we can eliminate the middle terms in both equations.

$$\text{(a)} \qquad S_n = a_1 + a_1 r + a_1 r^2 + a_1 r^3 + \cdots + a_1 r^{n-2} + a_1 r^{n-1}$$
$$(-1)\text{(b)} \qquad -r S_n = \quad\quad - a_1 r - a_1 r^2 - a_1 r^3 - \cdots - a_1 r^{n-2} - a_1 r^{n-1} - a_1 r^n$$
$$\overline{S_n - r S_n = a_1 \qquad\qquad\qquad\qquad\qquad\qquad\qquad\qquad\qquad\qquad - a_1 r^n}$$

Next, we factor out S_n on the left-hand side and a_1 on the right-hand side. We finish by dividing both sides by the coefficient of S_n.

$$S_n(1 - r) = a_1(1 - r^n) \qquad\qquad \text{factored}$$

$$S_n = \frac{a_1(1 - r^n)}{1 - r} \qquad\qquad \text{divided by } 1 - r$$

This is a simple formula, and using it to produce numerical results teaches us little. Thus, the homework problems will request the development of this formula. The development gives practice in the use of sequence and series notation and will be beneficial in later courses.

example 104.2   Develop the formula for the sum of the first n terms in a geometric series and use the formula to find the sum of the first 9 terms in a geometric series whose first term is –8 and whose common ratio is –2.

solution   The development on the previous page should be repeated to find that

$$S_n = \frac{a_1(1 - r^n)}{1 - r}$$

If we make the required substitutions, we get

$$S_9 = \frac{-8\left[1 - (-2)^9\right]}{1 - (-2)}$$

$$S_9 = \frac{-8\left[1 - (-512)\right]}{3}$$

$$S_9 = \frac{-4104}{3} = \mathbf{-1368}$$

example 104.3 Find the sum of the first 10 terms of the geometric series in the preceding example.

solution We will use the formula again, but this time n will be 10.

$$S_n = \frac{a_1(1 - r^n)}{1 - r}$$

$$S_{10} = \frac{-8[1 - (-2)^{10}]}{1 - (-2)}$$

$$S_{10} = \frac{-8(1 - 1024)}{3} = \textbf{2728}$$

It is interesting to note that the sum of 9 terms of this series is a negative number, and the sum of 10 terms of the same series is a positive number. The terms in the series alternate in sign, and each time another term is included in the sum the sign of the sum changes. This pattern of alternating sign changes of the sum always occurs in a geometric series in which r is a number that is less than –1. It is also interesting to note that if r is not zero and is greater than –1, the sum of any number of terms in the series has the same sign as the first term in the series. Take a particular series and see if you can understand why this statement is true.

problem set
104

1. A single card is randomly drawn from a deck of 52 cards. What is the probability that the card is an 8 or is a black card or is a black 8?

2. The price of gasoline was $1.40 per gallon plus a federal tax of f cents per gallon and a state tax of s cents per gallon. How many gallons could Beetle purchase for $42?

3. Sixty percent of the number of blues exactly equaled the number of whites. Five times the number of reds was 10 greater than twice the number of whites. If the total of all three colors was 140, how many were white, how many were red, and how many were blue?

4. The digits of a two-digit counting number were reversed and the new number was 9 greater than the original number. What was the original number if the sum of its digits was 9?

5. (a) Develop a formula for the sum of n terms of an arithmetic series with a_1 as the first term and a_n as the last term.

   (b) Using the formula developed in (a), find the sum of the following arithmetic series: $2 + 4 + 6 + \cdots + 98 + 100$.

6. (a) Develop the formula for the sum of n terms of a geometric series whose first term is a and whose common ratio is r.

   (b) Using the formula developed in (a), find the sum of the first 5 terms of the geometric series whose first term is 2 and whose common ratio is –2.

7. Expand as the sum of individual logarithms, each of whose argument is linear:

$$\log_4\left(\frac{\sqrt[3]{(s - 1)^2(t + 2)}}{\sqrt{s^3}}\right)$$

8. Use a calculator to compute: $\dfrac{\sqrt[3]{53,000}}{(3200)^{2.5}} + \sqrt[5]{(75,000)^2}$

9. Find the pH of a liquid if H^+ is 6.2×10^{-4} mole per liter.

10. Find the concentration of hydrogen ions (H^+) in a liquid if the pH of the liquid is 8.5.

11. Find the fourth term of $(x + 2y)^6$.   12. Expand $(x^2 - 2y)^3$.

13. Use Cramer's rule to solve for x: $\begin{cases} 2x + 3y + z = 0 \\ x + 2z = 4 \\ y - 3z = -4 \end{cases}$

14. Evaluate: $\begin{vmatrix} 7 & -2 & 3 \\ 0 & 4 & 4 \\ 0 & 1 & 1 \end{vmatrix}$

Develop the identity for each of the following:

15. $\cos x + \cos y$ **16.** $\cos x \cos y$

17. The positive geometric mean of two numbers is 6. The arithmetic mean of the two numbers is 10. What are the two numbers?

18. Use a calculator to aid in finding: (a) $\log_6 45$ (b) $\log_{36} 45$

Solve for x:

19. $\sqrt{\log_2 x} = \frac{1}{2}\log_2 x$ **20.** $\ln x + \ln x - \ln(2x - 2) = \ln 2$

21. $\log_2 (\log_3 x) = 1$

Show:

22. $\dfrac{1 - \cos 2x}{2} = \sin^2 x$ **23.** $\dfrac{1 - 3\cos x - 4\cos^2 x}{\sin^2 x} = \dfrac{1 - 4\cos x}{1 - \cos x}$

Sketch the graph of each of the following:

24. $y = -1 + \sin \dfrac{1}{2}(x - 90°)$ **25.** $y = 3 \sec x$

26. Find the three cube roots of i and write the roots in rectangular form. Give exact answers.

Solve the following equations given that $(0 \le \theta, x < 2\pi)$:

27. $-1 + \sqrt{2} \sin 3\theta = 0$ **28.** $3 \tan^2 x - 2 \sec x + 2 = 0$

29. Simplify: $te^{-\ln t}$

30. Factor $x^2 + x + 3$ over the set of complex numbers.

LESSON *105*   *Cofactors • Expansion by Cofactors*

105.A

cofactors   If we use the elimination method to solve the following system of equations for x,

$$a_1 x + b_1 y + c_1 z = k_1$$
$$a_2 x + b_2 y + c_2 z = k_2$$
$$a_3 x + b_3 y + c_3 z = k_3$$

the answer will be the expression shown here.

$$x = \frac{(k_1 b_2 c_3 + b_1 c_2 k_3 + c_1 k_2 b_3) - (k_3 b_2 c_1 + b_3 c_2 k_1 + c_3 k_2 b_1)}{(a_1 b_2 c_3 + b_1 c_2 a_3 + c_1 a_2 b_3) - (a_3 b_2 c_1 + b_3 c_2 a_1 + c_3 a_2 b_1)}$$

We have found that we can get the same result from Cramer's rule by evaluating the following determinants.

$$x = \frac{\begin{vmatrix} k_1 & b_1 & c_1 \\ k_2 & b_2 & c_2 \\ k_3 & b_3 & c_3 \end{vmatrix}}{\begin{vmatrix} a_1 & b_1 & c_1 \\ a_2 & b_2 & c_2 \\ a_3 & b_3 & c_3 \end{vmatrix}}$$

We develop methods of evaluating determinants so we can get the same answer for x by using determinants that we get when we use elimination. How we get the result does not matter as long as the result is the same. Now we will look at the cofactor/minor method to see why it will also give the same result. To do this we will look at the denominator of the fraction above, which is

$$(a_1b_2c_3 + b_1c_2a_3 + c_1a_2b_3) - (a_3b_2c_1 + b_3c_2a_1 + c_3a_2b_1)$$

We begin by removing the parentheses to get

$$a_1b_2c_3 + b_1c_2a_3 + c_1a_2b_3 - a_3b_2c_1 - b_3c_2a_1 - c_3a_2b_1$$

Now we rearrange the terms so that the terms with a_1 are first; then come the terms with a_2, and then the terms with a_3.

$$a_1b_2c_3 - b_3c_2a_1 + c_1a_2b_3 - c_3a_2b_1 + b_1c_2a_3 - a_3b_2c_1$$

Now we factor out a_1 from the first two terms, factor out $-a_2$ from the third and fourth terms, and factor out a_3 from the last two terms.

$$a_1(b_2c_3 - b_3c_2) - a_2(b_1c_3 - b_3c_1) + a_3(b_1c_2 - b_2c_1)$$

Now this is exactly the same thing as

$$a_1 \begin{vmatrix} b_2 & c_2 \\ b_3 & c_3 \end{vmatrix} - a_2 \begin{vmatrix} b_1 & c_1 \\ b_3 & c_3 \end{vmatrix} + a_3 \begin{vmatrix} b_1 & c_1 \\ b_2 & c_2 \end{vmatrix}$$
$$\text{(M)} \qquad\qquad \text{(N)} \qquad\qquad \text{(P)}$$

If we go back to the original determinant three times,

$$\begin{matrix} \cancel{a_1} & \cancel{b_1} & \cancel{c_1} \\ \cancel{a_2} & b_2 & c_2 \\ \cancel{a_3} & b_3 & c_3 \end{matrix} \qquad \begin{matrix} \cancel{a_1} & b_1 & c_1 \\ \cancel{a_2} & \cancel{b_2} & \cancel{c_2} \\ \cancel{a_3} & b_3 & c_3 \end{matrix} \qquad \begin{matrix} \cancel{a_1} & b_1 & c_1 \\ \cancel{a_2} & b_2 & c_2 \\ \cancel{a_3} & \cancel{b_3} & \cancel{c_3} \end{matrix}$$
$$\text{(Q)} \qquad\qquad\qquad \text{(R)} \qquad\qquad\qquad \text{(S)}$$

we see that we can get (M) from (Q) by crossing out the row and column of a_1, (N) from (R) by crossing out the row and column of a_2, and (P) from (S) by crossing out the row and column of a_3. Further, we see that the original development of this method required no great insight but did require persistence, patience, and a certain fascination with playing with patterns. One knew the required end pattern and had the starting determinant. The rest was just trial and error.

The advantage of this system is that it can be used to find the determinants of square matrices of any size by breaking them down to expressions which contain smaller square matrices which can also be broken down, etc. When we cross out the row and the column of an entry, we call the smaller determinant that results the **minor** of the entry. If the proper sign is appended to the minor, the combination is called the **cofactor** of the element. As we saw above, not all cofactor signs are positive. It can be shown that the signs of the cofactors are in the form of a checkerboard matrix of positive and minus signs in which the sign in the upper left-hand corner is positive.

$$\text{Matrix of Cofactor Signs} \qquad \begin{bmatrix} + & - & + & - & + \\ - & + & - & + & - \\ + & - & + & - & + \\ - & + & - & + & - \\ + & - & + & - & + \end{bmatrix}$$

example 105.1   Find the cofactor of 7 in the following determinant: $\begin{vmatrix} 4 & 7 & 3 \\ 2 & 5 & 6 \\ 2 & 1 & 5 \end{vmatrix}$

solution   To find the minor of 7, we cross out the row and column of 7.

$$\begin{vmatrix} 4 & 7 & 3 \\ 2 & 5 & 6 \\ 2 & 1 & 5 \end{vmatrix}$$

The minor element of 7 is thus

$$\begin{vmatrix} 2 & 6 \\ 2 & 5 \end{vmatrix}$$

and the sign of the 7 in the checkerboard pattern is a minus sign.

$$\begin{array}{ccc} + & \ominus & + \\ - & + & - \\ + & - & + \end{array}$$

So the cofactor is

$$-\begin{vmatrix} 2 & 6 \\ 2 & 5 \end{vmatrix}$$

105.B

expansion by cofactors   **The value of a determinant can be found by summing the products of the elements in any row or column with their respective cofactors.** This means that each term in the sum has three factors. The first factor is the element. The second factor is the sign from the checkerboard, and the third factor is the minor of the element.

example 105.2   Use cofactors to evaluate this determinant: $\begin{vmatrix} -4 & 2 & 1 \\ 1 & 3 & -2 \\ -1 & 2 & -3 \end{vmatrix}$

solution   We could expand using any row or any column. We decide to use the third row.

$$\begin{vmatrix} -4 & 2 & 1 \\ 1 & 3 & -2 \\ -1 & 2 & -3 \end{vmatrix} \qquad \begin{vmatrix} -4 & 2 & 1 \\ 1 & 3 & -2 \\ -1 & 2 & -3 \end{vmatrix} \qquad \begin{vmatrix} -4 & 2 & 1 \\ 1 & 3 & -2 \\ -1 & 2 & -3 \end{vmatrix}$$

There will be three factors in each term. They are the element that is crossed out, the sign from the checkerboard, and the minor of the element.

$$(-1)(+)\begin{vmatrix} 2 & 1 \\ 3 & -2 \end{vmatrix} + (2)(-)\begin{vmatrix} -4 & 1 \\ 1 & -2 \end{vmatrix} + (-3)(+)\begin{vmatrix} -4 & 2 \\ 1 & 3 \end{vmatrix}$$

Now we simplify these expressions and add to evaluate the determinant.

$$-\big[(-4) - (3)\big] - 2\big[(8) - (1)\big] - 3\big[(-12) - (2)\big] \qquad \text{evaluated minors}$$

$$= 7 - 14 + 42 \qquad\qquad\qquad\qquad\qquad \text{simplified}$$

$$= \mathbf{35} \qquad\qquad\qquad\qquad\qquad\qquad\qquad \text{added}$$

example 105.3   Use cofactors to evaluate: $\begin{vmatrix} -3 & 1 & 2 \\ 2 & -3 & -4 \\ 0 & 4 & -5 \end{vmatrix}$

solution   If an element in a matrix is 0, then the product of this element and its cofactor is 0. Thus, the easiest solution is to expand using the row or column that contains the most 0s. In this problem, we note that there is a 0 in the first column and also in the third row, so we could use either. We decide to use the third row.

$$(0)(+)\begin{vmatrix} 1 & 2 \\ -3 & -4 \end{vmatrix} + (4)(-)\begin{vmatrix} -3 & 2 \\ 2 & -4 \end{vmatrix} + (-5)(+)\begin{vmatrix} -3 & 1 \\ 2 & -3 \end{vmatrix}$$

This simplifies as

$$0 - 4(12 - 4) + (-5)(9 - 2) \qquad \text{evaluated minors}$$

$$= 0 - 32 + (-35) \qquad \text{simplified}$$

$$= -67 \qquad \text{added}$$

example 105.4   Use cofactors to evaluate: $\begin{vmatrix} -3 & 1 & 2 \\ 2 & -3 & -4 \\ 1 & 4 & 0 \end{vmatrix}$

solution   This time we decide to use the third column for our expansion,

$$(2)(+)\begin{vmatrix} 2 & -3 \\ 1 & 4 \end{vmatrix} + (-4)(-)\begin{vmatrix} -3 & 1 \\ 1 & 4 \end{vmatrix} + (0)(+)\begin{vmatrix} -3 & 1 \\ 2 & -3 \end{vmatrix}$$

and this simplifies to

$$(2)(+)(8 + 3) + (-4)(-)(-12 - 1) + (0)(+)(9 - 2) \qquad \text{evaluated minors}$$

$$= 22 + (-52) + 0 \qquad \text{simplified}$$

$$= -30 \qquad \text{added}$$

problem set 105

1. A ball is dropped from a height of 256 feet. On each bounce, the ball rebounds one fourth of the distance it fell. How far does it rebound after its fourth fall?

2. When Ida Jane looked the first time, there were 4200 of the things in the bowl, and they were decreasing. She looked again 20 minutes later, and there were only 4100 of them left. If the decrease was exponential, what was the half-life of the things?

3. The grandfather clock in the hall bonged 7 times for seven o'clock. How long did Sammy Lee have to wait if he wanted to see the clock hands pointing in opposite directions?

4. Paul found that K workers can do 40 jobs in h hours. How many workers would it take to do m jobs in 14 hours?

5. Ten people came out for the tennis team. If there were 6 players on a team, how many different teams could the coach form?

6. The number who succeeded varied linearly as the number who tried. When 40 tried, 2 succeeded; when 80 tried, 12 succeeded. How many succeeded when 60 tried?

Use cofactors to evaluate:

7. $\begin{vmatrix} -2 & 0 & 1 \\ 3 & 1 & 2 \\ 1 & 1 & 0 \end{vmatrix}$

8. $\begin{vmatrix} -2 & 0 & 3 \\ 0 & 1 & 2 \\ 3 & 1 & -1 \end{vmatrix}$

9. (a) Develop a formula for the sum of n terms of an arithmetic series whose first term is a_1 and whose last term is a_n.

    (b) Using the formula developed in (a), find: $-2 + 4 + 10 + \cdots + 46$.

10. (a) Develop the formula for the sum of n terms of a geometric series whose first term is a and whose common ratio is r.

    (b) Using the formula developed in (a), find the sum of the first 6 terms of the geometric series whose first term is 1 and whose common ratio is $-\frac{1}{2}$.

11. Use a calculator to compute: $\left(\dfrac{3300 \times 10^7}{2200 \times 10^3} \right) \sqrt[4]{4400 \times 10^{11}}$

12. Find the pH of a liquid if H^+ is 4.4×10^{-4} mole per liter.

13. Find the fifth term of $(x - 2y)^6$.   **14.** Expand $(3x - 2y)^3$.

15. Use Cramer's rule to solve for y: $\begin{cases} 2x + y + z = 0 \\ 2y + 3z = 5 \\ x + 3y = 1 \end{cases}$

16. Develop the identity for $\sin x - \sin y$.

17. Compute $\cos 75° \sin 15°$ by using the identity for $\cos A \sin B$. Use exact values.

Solve for x:

18. $\sqrt{\log_3 x} = \dfrac{1}{2} \log_3 x$ **19.** $\log_3 \left(\log_2 x \right) = 1$

20. $\ln (2x + 6) - \ln (x - 3) = \ln x$

Show:

21. $\dfrac{1}{2} \sin 2x \sec x = \sin x$ **22.** $\dfrac{1 + \cos 2x}{\sin 2x} = \cot x$

23. Find the area of this triangle.

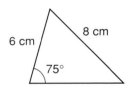

24. Sketch the graph of $y = 2 \csc x$.

25. Write the equations of the following trigonometric functions:

    (a)   (b)

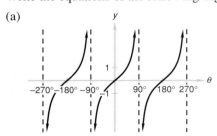   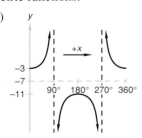

Solve the following equations given that $(0° \le x, \theta < 360°)$:

26. $1 - \sqrt{2} \cos 3x = 0$ **27.** $\sec^2 \theta = 2 \tan \theta$

28. Find the four fourth roots of -1 and write the roots in rectangular form. Give exact answers.

29. Given the hyperbola $8x^2 - 50y^2 = -200$, write the equation in standard form and find the coordinates of its vertices and the equations of the asymptotes. Graph the hyperbola.

30. Find the distance from the point $(1, 2)$ to the line $x - 3y + 5 = 0$.

LESSON *106*   *Translations of Conic Sections   •   Equations of the Ellipse   •   Equations of the Hyperbola*

106.A

translations of conic sections

In Lesson 42, we learned that a circle with center at the origin and radius r has the equation

$$x^2 + y^2 = r^2$$

If we translate this circle centered at the origin h units horizontally and k units vertically to give the circle the center (h, k), the equation of this new circle would be

$$(x - h)^2 + (y - k)^2 = r^2$$

In other words, if we are given the equation of a circle centered at the origin and want the equation of this same circle centered at (h, k), we can replace x with $x - h$ and y with $y - k$ in the equation of the circle whose center is the origin. This technique also applies to ellipses and hyperbolas. If we are given the equation of an ellipse centered at the origin,

$$\frac{x^2}{a^2} + \frac{y^2}{b^2} = 1$$

then the equation of this same ellipse translated h units horizontally and k units vertically so that its new center is (h, k) is

$$\frac{(x - h)^2}{a^2} + \frac{(y - k)^2}{b^2} = 1$$

Similarly, if we are given the equation of a hyperbola centered at the origin,

$$\frac{x^2}{a^2} - \frac{y^2}{b^2} = 1$$

then the equation of this same hyperbola translated h units horizontally and k units vertically so that its new center is (h, k) is

$$\frac{(x - h)^2}{a^2} - \frac{(y - k)^2}{b^2} = 1$$

In general, when we translate the graph of a relation h units horizontally and k units vertically, the equation of the translated graph is the equation of the original graph where x is replaced by $x - h$ and y is replaced by $y - k$.

106.B

equations of the ellipse

On the left below, we show the standard form of the equation of an ellipse whose center is the origin, whose major axis is horizontal and is 8 units long, and whose minor axis is vertical and is 6 units long. On the right, we show the equation of the same ellipse, but this time its center is $(3, -4)$.

$$\text{(a)} \quad \frac{x^2}{4^2} + \frac{y^2}{3^2} = 1 \qquad\qquad \text{(b)} \quad \frac{(x - 3)^2}{4^2} + \frac{(y + 4)^2}{3^2} = 1$$

To change equation (b) from the standard form to the **general form,** we first clear the denominators by multiplying every number by $16 \cdot 9$.

$$\frac{\cancel{16} \cdot 9(x - 3)^2}{\cancel{16}} + \frac{16 \cdot \cancel{9}(y + 4)^2}{\cancel{9}} = 16 \cdot 9$$

Next, we expand the binomials and get

$$9\left(x^2 - 6x + 9\right) + 16\left(y^2 + 8y + 16\right) = 144$$

We finish by multiplying and rearranging and get

$$9x^2 + 16y^2 - 54x + 128y + 193 = 0 \qquad \text{general form}$$

The **general form** of the equation of a conic section is the equation written in the form

$$Ax^2 + Bxy + Cy^2 + Dx + Ey + F = 0$$

For almost all the conic sections we will study, $B = 0$.

In the following example, we show how this process can be reversed by beginning with the general form of the equation and completing the square twice to write the equation in standard form.

example 106.1   Describe the ellipse $3x^2 + 2y^2 - 6x + 8y + 5 = 0$. Begin by writing the equation in standard form.

solution   We rearrange the terms and use parentheses.

$$\left(3x^2 - 6x \qquad\right) + \left(2y^2 + 8y \qquad\right) = -5$$

Next, we factor out a 3 from the first set of parentheses and a 2 from the second set of parentheses.

$$3\left(x^2 - 2x \qquad\right) + 2\left(y^2 + 4y \qquad\right) = -5$$

Next, we complete the square by inserting a 1 in the first set of parentheses and a 4 in the second set of parentheses.

$$3\left(x^2 - 2x + 1\right) + 2\left(y^2 + 4y + 4\right) = -5 + \underline{\qquad}$$

On the right, we must add 3 and 8 because we have added 3 and 8 to the left-hand side.

$$3\left(x^2 - 2x + 1\right) + 2\left(y^2 + 4y + 4\right) = -5 + 3 + 8$$

Now we simplify and get

$$3(x - 1)^2 + 2(y + 2)^2 = 6$$

Finally, we make the constant term 1 by dividing every term by 6, and we get

$$\frac{3(x - 1)^2}{6} + \frac{2(y + 2)^2}{6} = \frac{6}{6}$$

$$\text{or} \quad \frac{(x - 1)^2}{(\sqrt{2})^2} + \frac{(y + 2)^2}{(\sqrt{3})^2} = 1$$

This is the equation of an ellipse whose center is $(1, -2)$, whose major axis is vertical of length $2\sqrt{3}$, and whose minor axis is horizontal of length $2\sqrt{2}$.

106.C

equations of the hyperbola

On the left, we show the standard form of an equation of a hyperbola whose vertices are $(\pm 3, 0)$, whose asymptote rectangle is 6 units wide and 8 units high, and whose center is the origin. On the right, we show the equation that would result if the center of this hyperbola were shifted to $(-2, 3)$.

$$\text{(a)} \quad \frac{x^2}{9} - \frac{y^2}{16} = 1 \qquad \text{(b)} \quad \frac{(x + 2)^2}{9} - \frac{(y - 3)^2}{16} = 1$$

We can write equation (b) in the general form if we perform the indicated multiplications and multiply every term by $9 \cdot 16$ to clear the denominators.

$$\frac{\cancel{9} \cdot 16(x^2 + 4x + 4)}{\cancel{9}} - \frac{9 \cdot \cancel{16}(y^2 - 6y + 9)}{\cancel{16}} = 1 \cdot 9 \cdot 16$$

Now, if we simplify this expression, we can write the general form of the equation as

$$16x^2 - 9y^2 + 64x + 54y - 161 = 0$$

In the following example, we show how this process can be reversed by beginning with the general equation of a hyperbola and completing the square twice to write the equation in standard form.

example 106.2 Complete the square twice to change the form of $9x^2 - 4y^2 + 18x - 16y - 43 = 0$ to the standard form. Graph the equation. Find the equation of the asymptotes.

solution First we rearrange the equation and use parentheses.

$$\left(9x^2 + 18x \qquad\right) + \left(-4y^2 - 16y \qquad\right) = 43$$

Now we factor out a 9 from the first set of parentheses and a -4 from the second.

$$9\left(x^2 + 2x \qquad\right) - 4\left(y^2 + 4y \qquad\right) = 43$$

Next, we complete the square inside each set of parentheses and add $+9$ and -16 to the right-hand side because we added $+9$ and -16 to the left-hand side.

$$9\left(x^2 + 2x + 1\right) - 4\left(y^2 + 4y + 4\right) = 43 + 9 - 16$$

Now we simplify the expressions.

$$9(x + 1)^2 - 4(y + 2)^2 = 36$$

Since the right-hand side must equal 1, we divide every term by 36 and get the standard form.

$$\frac{(x + 1)^2}{4} - \frac{(y + 2)^2}{9} = 1$$

We will graph this equation by first graphing the sister equation.

$$\frac{x^2}{(2)^2} - \frac{y^2}{(3)^2} = 1$$

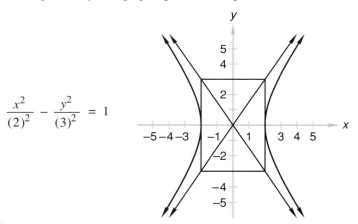

The graph that we need is exactly the same except that its center is $(-1, -2)$ instead of the origin. We merely have to relabel the horizontal and vertical axes and note the coordinates of two corners of the rectangle.

$$\frac{(x + 1)^2}{4} - \frac{(y + 2)^2}{9} = 1$$

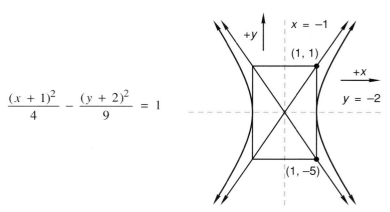

We see that both asymptotes go through the point (−1, −2). We can use the lengths of the sides of the rectangle to find that the coordinates of the upper right-hand corner are (1, 1) and the coordinates of the lower right-hand corner are (1, −5). We can use these points to find the equations of the asymptotes.

$$y = \frac{3}{2}x + b \qquad \text{slope } \frac{3}{2} \qquad\qquad y = -\frac{3}{2}x + b \qquad \text{slope } -\frac{3}{2}$$

$$1 = \frac{3}{2}(1) + b \qquad \text{used } (1, 1) \qquad\qquad -5 = -\frac{3}{2}(1) + b \qquad \text{used } (1, -5)$$

$$b = -\frac{1}{2} \qquad\qquad \text{solved} \qquad\qquad b = -\frac{7}{2} \qquad\qquad \text{solved}$$

$$y = \frac{3}{2}x - \frac{1}{2} \qquad \text{asymptote} \qquad\qquad y = -\frac{3}{2}x - \frac{7}{2} \qquad \text{asymptote}$$

problem set 106

1. Susie Bee piled the coals to the fire, but still the things decreased exponentially. At first they numbered 400, but in 20 minutes they numbered only 380. What was their half-life?

2. How many ways can Arthur, Guinevere, and seven knights be seated at the round table?

3. The wheels whined at 300 radians per minute. Hudson hung on for dear life because the radius of the wheels was 1 full meter and Hudson was on the rim. What was Hudson's speed in miles per minute?

4. Frank Boy owned three sevenths of the business, and his share of the profits was $12,600. Judy Girl was not downcast as she owned four twenty-first parts of the business. What was Judy Girl's share of the profits?

5. Binibo bumped out 72 miles and then walked back home at one third of his bumping speed. If the total time for his trip was 24 hours, how fast could he bump?

6. The general form of the equation of an ellipse is $x^2 + 16y^2 - 10x + 32y + 25 = 0$. Write the equation of this ellipse in standard form and give the coordinates of the center, the length of the major axis, and the length of the minor axis. Then graph the ellipse.

7. The general form of the equation of an ellipse is $9x^2 + 4y^2 + 54x - 8y + 49 = 0$. Write the equation of this ellipse in standard form and give the coordinates of the center, the length of the major axis, and the length of the minor axis. Then graph the ellipse.

8. The general form of the equation of a hyperbola is $-x^2 + y^2 - 2x - 4y + 4 = 0$. Write the equation of this hyperbola in standard form and give the coordinates of the center, the coordinates of the vertices, and the equations of the asymptotes. Then graph the hyperbola.

9. The general form of the equation of a hyperbola is $4x^2 - y^2 + 8x - 4y - 4 = 0$. Write the equation of this hyperbola in standard form and give the coordinates of the center, the coordinates of the vertices, and the equations of the asymptotes. Then graph the hyperbola.

10. Write the equation of the circle shown in standard form and in general form.

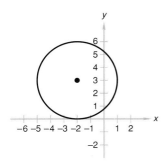

11. Use cofactors to evaluate: $\begin{vmatrix} 1 & 2 & 1 \\ 0 & 1 & 0 \\ 1 & 2 & 2 \end{vmatrix}$

12. (a) Develop a formula for the sum of n terms of an arithmetic series whose first term is a_1 and whose last term is a_n.

   (b) Using the formula developed in (a), find the sum of the following arithmetic series: $-8 + (-4) + 0 + \cdots + 24$.

13. (a) Develop the formula for the sum of n terms of a geometric series whose first term is a and whose common ratio is r.

   (b) Using the formula developed in (a), find the sum of the first 7 terms of the geometric sequence: $4, -8, 16, \ldots$.

14. Write as a single logarithm: $\dfrac{3}{2} \log x^6 - \dfrac{2}{3} \log y^3 + \dfrac{3}{4} \log z^2 - \log xy$

15. The pH of a solution is 3.5. What is the concentration of hydrogen ions in moles per liter of the solution?

16. Find the third term of $(3x - 2y)^6$.

17. Use Cramer's rule to solve for z. Use cofactors to evaluate the determinants.

$$\begin{cases} 2x + y + 2z = 2 \\ 2y + z = 5 \\ x + 3y = 2 \end{cases}$$

18. Develop the identity for $\sin x \cos y$.

19. Compute $\cos 195° \cos 105°$ by using the appropriate identity. Use exact values.

Solve for x:

20. $\dfrac{1}{2} \log_3 25 - \log_3 (2x - 5) = 2$ **21.** $\log_2 3 = 2 \log_2 x$

22. $\sqrt{\ln x} = 3 \ln \sqrt{x}$

Show:

23. $\dfrac{\sin^3 x + \cos^3 x}{\sin x + \cos x} = 1 - \dfrac{1}{2} \sin 2x$ **24.** $\dfrac{\cot x + 1}{\cot x - 1} = \dfrac{\csc x + \sec x}{\csc x - \sec x}$

Sketch the graph of each of the following:

25. $y = \tan \dfrac{1}{2} x$ **26.** $y = -7 + 4 \sin \dfrac{3}{8}\left(x - \dfrac{2\pi}{3}\right)$

27. Solve $2 \sin^2 x + \sqrt{3} \sin x = 0$ given that $0° \leq x < 360°$.

28. Find the four fourth roots of $-6 + 4i$ and write the roots in polar form.

29. A regular pentagon has a perimeter of 25 cm. What is the area of the regular pentagon?

30. Simplify: $\left(t^2 + t\right) 10^{-2 \log (t + 1)}$

LESSON *107* *Convergent Geometric Series*

We remember that we can derive the formula for the sum of the first n terms of a geometric series by using only four steps. The first step is to write the general expression for the sum of the first n terms (a). Then we multiply every term on both sides by $-r$ and add the two equations to get (b). Note how the terms on the right are shifted one place to the right so that like terms can be aligned vertically.

$$
\begin{array}{ll}
\text{(a)} & S_n = a_1 + a_1r + a_1r^2 + a_1r^3 + \cdots + a_1r^{n-2} + a_1r^{n-1} \\
-r\text{(a)} & \underline{-rS_n = \quad\; - a_1r - a_1r^2 - a_1r^3 - \cdots - a_1r^{n-2} - a_1r^{n-1} - a_1r^n} \\
\text{(b)} & S_n - rS_n = a_1 \hspace{8cm} - a_1r^n
\end{array}
$$

Now we factor out S_n on the left-hand side and factor out a_1 on the right-hand side. Then we divide both sides by the coefficient of S_n.

$$S_n(1 - r) = a_1(1 - r^n) \qquad \text{factored}$$

$$S_n = \frac{a_1(1 - r^n)}{1 - r} \qquad \text{divided by } 1 - r$$

Now let's look at the $(1 - r^n)$ on top. If r^n is very, very small, then $(1 - r^n)$ almost equals 1. Let's let r^n be 0.000001. Then we get

$$S_n = \frac{a_1(1 - 0.000001)}{1 - r} = \frac{a_1(0.999999)}{1 - r}$$

But 0.999999 is almost the same as 1, and if we let r^n get smaller and smaller, then the value of $1 - r^n$ gets even closer to 1. In calculus, we use the word **limit** to say that $1 - r^n$ approaches 1 as a limit as r^n gets smaller. It never is exactly equal to 1, but if we use the value of 1 for $1 - r^n$, our error will be extremely small. If r is a number between -1 and 0 or between 0 and $+1$,

$$-1 < r < 0 \qquad \text{or} \qquad 0 < r < 1$$

then as n increases, r^n gets very small. For instance, if $r = \frac{1}{2}$, the value of r^n when $n = 12$ is

$$\left(\frac{1}{2}\right)^{12} = \frac{1}{4096} = 0.0002441$$

and $(1 - r^n) = 0.9997559$, a number very close to 1.

If we use 1 for $1 - r^n$, the formula becomes

$$S = \frac{a_1}{1 - r}$$

We can use this formula to find the exact sum of an infinite geometric series if $|r|$ is less than 1. If $|r|$ is less than 1, we say that the series is a *convergent geometric series*. If $|r|$ is greater than or equal to 1, the series is a *divergent series*. The sum of a divergent series cannot be found.

example 107.1   Find the sum of this infinite geometric series: $5 + \dfrac{5}{2} + \dfrac{5}{4} + \dfrac{5}{8} + \cdots$

solution   We see that a_1 is 5 and r is $\frac{1}{2}$. Since $|r|$ is less than 1, the series is a convergent series, and we can find the sum of an infinite convergent series.

$$S = \frac{a_1}{1 - r} = \frac{5}{1 - \dfrac{1}{2}} = \mathbf{10}$$

Thus, the sum of this series gets closer and closer to 10 as the number of terms increases. The sum is never greater than 10 no matter how many terms are used.

example 107.2   A ball is dropped from a height of 12 feet and rebounds two fifths of the fall distance on each succeeding bounce. (a) How far will the ball fall on the tenth fall? (b) What will be the total distance the ball will travel?

solution   This problem is used in almost every algebra book. **We always draw a diagram of a problem when we can. Diagrams aid understanding and help prevent mistakes.**

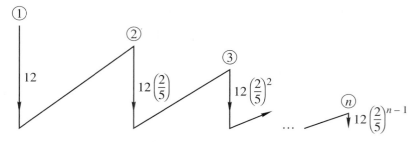

(a) The sequence that describes the distance the ball falls is

$$\overset{①}{12}, \quad \overset{②}{12\left(\frac{2}{5}\right)}, \quad \overset{③}{12\left(\frac{2}{5}\right)^2}, \quad \overset{④}{12\left(\frac{2}{5}\right)^3}, \quad \dots, \quad \overset{⑩}{12\left(\frac{2}{5}\right)^{n-1}}$$

On the second fall, the ball falls $12\left(\frac{2}{5}\right)$; on the third fall, $12\left(\frac{2}{5}\right)^2$; and so on the tenth fall:

$$\text{Tenth fall} = 12\left(\frac{2}{5}\right)^9 = 12(0.0002621) = \mathbf{0.0031452 \text{ ft}}$$

(b) Now we will find the sum of the distances the ball falls,

$$12 + 12\left(\frac{2}{5}\right) + 12\left(\frac{2}{5}\right)^2 + \cdots$$

and we have a formula for the sum of this infinite geometric series.

$$S = \frac{a_1}{1 - r} = \frac{12}{1 - \frac{2}{5}} = \frac{12}{\frac{3}{5}} = 20 \text{ ft}$$

This is the sum of the distances the ball fell. It rebounded the distances the ball fell less the distance of the first fall, which was 12 feet.

$$\text{Distance rebounded} = 20 - 12 = 8 \text{ ft}$$

Thus, the sum of its ups and downs is 20 feet plus 8 feet, which is **28 feet.**

example 107.3   A rabbit runs 2 miles in the first minute, 0.8 mile in the next minute, 0.32 mile in the next minute, and 0.4 times this distance in the next minute. How far will the rabbit travel in all if he continues this process indefinitely?

solution   If we divide 0.8 by 2 and divide 0.32 by 0.8, we get 0.4 both times.

$$\frac{0.8}{2} = 0.4 \qquad \frac{0.32}{0.8} = 0.4$$

So we see that we have been asked to find the sum of an infinite geometric series whose first term is 2 and whose common ratio is 0.4.

$$\overset{①}{a_1} + \overset{②}{a_1 r} + \overset{③}{a_1 r^2} + \overset{④}{a_1 r^3} + \cdots + \overset{⑩}{a_1 r^{n-1}} + \cdots$$
$$2 + 2(0.4) + 2(0.4)^2 + 2(0.4)^3 + \cdots + 2(0.4)^{n-1} + \cdots$$

We can find the sum of this infinite series because $|r|$ is less than 1.

$$S = \frac{a_1}{1 - r} = \frac{2}{1 - 0.4} = \frac{2}{0.6} = \mathbf{\frac{10}{3}}$$

So the rabbit will run only $\frac{10}{3}$ miles if he runs forever.

problem set
107

1. It was exactly 6 p.m. and the hands of the clock pointed in opposite directions. What time would it be the next time both hands pointed in the same direction?

2. If Link and Ellen work together, they can complete the job in 2 days. If Link works alone, he can complete the job in x days. How long would it take Ellen to complete the job alone?

3. The average of two numbers is A. If one of the numbers is m, what is the other number?

4. Salvatore was amazed at the size of x. The overall average of 1.0, 0.8, 0.2, and x was exactly 0.6. How large was x?

5. At the class picnic, the sum of 10 percent of the girls and 20 percent of the boys was 16. If the ratio of girls to boys was 2 to 3, how many boys came to the class picnic?

6. Find the sum of this infinite geometric series: $4 + \dfrac{4}{3} + \dfrac{4}{9} + \dfrac{4}{27} + \cdots$

7. A hare runs 4 miles in the first minute, 2 miles in the next minute, 1 mile in the next minute, and so on. How far will the hare travel in all if he runs forever?

8. The general form of the equation of an ellipse is $9x^2 + 4y^2 + 54x - 8y + 49 = 0$. Write the equation of this ellipse in standard form and give the coordinates of the center, the length of the major axis, and the length of the minor axis. Then graph the ellipse.

9. The general form of the equation of a hyperbola is $x^2 - y^2 - 14x - 8y + 29 = 0$. Write the equation of this hyperbola in standard form and give the coordinates of the center, the coordinates of the vertices, and the equations of the asymptotes. Then graph the hyperbola.

10. Write the equation of the circle shown in standard form and in general form.

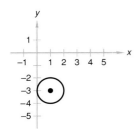

11. Use cofactors to evaluate: $\begin{vmatrix} 2 & 3 & -1 \\ 0 & 4 & 1 \\ 1 & 3 & 3 \end{vmatrix}$

12. Use Cramer's rule to solve this system of equations. Use cofactors to evaluate the determinants.
$$\begin{cases} -2x + y - z = 7 \\ 2y + 3z = 1 \\ x - 3y = -8 \end{cases}$$

13. The first term of an arithmetic sequence is a_1 and the common difference is d. (a) What is the nth term of the arithmetic sequence? (b) What is the sum of the first n terms if we use the expression found in (a) for the last term of the sequence?

14. The pH of a solution is 8.5. What is the concentration of hydrogen ions in moles per liter of the solution?

15. Use a calculator to compute: $\sqrt[4]{42{,}000} \sqrt[3]{2300} - \sqrt[5]{540}$

16. Find the fifth term of $(2x - 1)^7$.

17. (a) Develop the identity for $\cos A \sin B$.

    (b) Find $\cos 75° \sin 15°$ by using the identity found in (a). Use exact values.

18. (a) Develop the identity for $\sin x + \sin y$.

    (b) Find $\sin 15° + \sin 75°$ by using the identity found in (a). Use exact values.

19. Express ln 22 in terms of common logarithms. Do not find a numerical answer.

Solve for x:

20. $2^{3x-2} = 4$

21. $\log_3\left(\log_2 x\right) = 2$

22. $\log_6 (x - 1) + \log_6 (x - 2) = 2 \log_6 \sqrt{6}$

Show:

23. $\sec x - \sin x \tan x = \cos x$

24. $\sec 2x = \dfrac{\sec^2 x}{2 - \sec^2 x}$

25. Solve the triangle for c and find the area in square centimeters.

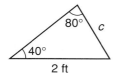

Sketch the graph of each of the following:

26. $y = \cot 2x$

27. $y = 2 + \sin \dfrac{3}{2}(x + 40°)$

28. Find $\sin 105°$ by using the sum identity for the sine function. Use exact values.

29. Solve $\sqrt{3} \tan \dfrac{3\theta}{4} - 1 = 0$ given that $0° \le \theta < 360°$.

30. Write the three cube roots of $-i$ in rectangular form. Give exact answers.

LESSON *108* *Matrix Addition and Multiplication*

We review our discussion of matrices in Lesson 69 by remembering that a matrix is a rectangular array of numbers or symbols that represent numbers. The individual symbols or numbers are called the **entries** or **elements** of the matrix. All of the following arrays can be called matrices because all of them have a rectangular shape.

A	B	C	D	E
$\begin{pmatrix} 4 & 2 \\ 5 & 6 \end{pmatrix}$	$\begin{matrix} 7 & 4 & 3 & 6 \\ 8 & 9 & 5 & 2 \end{matrix}$	$\begin{pmatrix} x \\ m \\ p \end{pmatrix}$	$\begin{bmatrix} 4 \\ 1 \\ 6 \end{bmatrix}$	$[2 \quad 3 \quad 4 \quad 5]$
2×2	2×4	3×1	3×1	1×4

It is customary to enclose a rectangular array in parentheses or brackets when we are considering the array as a matrix. Array B above can be considered to be a matrix even though parentheses or brackets are not used.

The size of a matrix is called the **order** of the matrix and is defined by first indicating the number of rows and then indicating the number of columns, as we show above. Matrix A has 2 rows and 2 columns and is a 2×2 matrix. Matrix B has 2 rows and 4 columns and is a 2×4 matrix. Matrices C and D are 3×1 matrices, and matrix E is a 1×4 matrix. It is customary to use capital letters to name matrices, as we have done here. Mathematicians have devised an algebra of matrices that follows many of the rules that we use in the algebra of real numbers. Matrices can be added and multiplied and we can solve many equations that contain matrices just as we have solved equations that contain real numbers.

In Lessons 66, 69, and 74 we showed how the patterns of the constants in linear equations lead to the definition of the determinant of a square matrix and to Cramer's rule. The rules for the algebra of matrices also come from an investigation of the patterns of constants in an area of mathematics called *linear algebra*. A consideration of this investigation is beyond the scope of this book. We will just state the rules for the addition and multiplication of matrices. We can add two matrices only if they have the same order (are the same size). We will demonstrate matrix addition by adding two 2×3 matrices that we call matrix A and matrix B.

$$
\underset{\text{A}}{\begin{bmatrix} 4 & 2 & 3 \\ 1 & 0 & 5 \end{bmatrix}} + \underset{\text{B}}{\begin{bmatrix} 6 & -3 & 4 \\ 6 & 2 & 0 \end{bmatrix}} = \underset{\text{A + B}}{\begin{bmatrix} (4 + 6) & (2 - 3) & (3 + 4) \\ (1 + 6) & (0 + 2) & (5 + 0) \end{bmatrix}} = \underset{\text{A + B}}{\begin{bmatrix} 10 & -1 & 7 \\ 7 & 2 & 5 \end{bmatrix}}
$$

To find the six members of matrix A + B, we added the members of matrix A to the corresponding members of matrix B. For example, to find the entry 10 in the upper left-hand corner of matrix A + B, we added the 4 in the upper left-hand corner of matrix A to the 6 in the upper left-hand corner of matrix B.

If we exchange the order of addition of real numbers, the sum is the same, as we illustrate by adding 6 and 4.

$$6 + 4 = 10 \qquad 4 + 6 = 10$$

The Latin word for "exchange" is *commutare,* so we say that the addition of real numbers is a **commutative operation** because either number can be first. In the example above, we found the sum of matrices A and B, in that order. The sum of B + A is the same as the sum of A + B, so we say that the addition of matrices is also a commutative operation, or that matrix addition is **commutative.**

$$
\underset{\text{B}}{\begin{bmatrix} 6 & -3 & 4 \\ 6 & 2 & 0 \end{bmatrix}} + \underset{\text{A}}{\begin{bmatrix} 4 & 2 & 3 \\ 1 & 0 & 5 \end{bmatrix}} = \underset{\text{B + A}}{\begin{bmatrix} (6 + 4) & (-3 + 2) & (4 + 3) \\ (6 + 1) & (2 + 0) & (0 + 5) \end{bmatrix}} = \underset{\text{B + A}}{\begin{bmatrix} 10 & -1 & 7 \\ 7 & 2 & 5 \end{bmatrix}}
$$

To have a workable algebraic system, the system must have an **additive identity** and a **multiplicative identity.** The sum of a number and zero is identically the number itself, so **zero** is the additive identity for the real numbers.

$$6 + 0 = 6 \qquad \text{and} \qquad 0 + 6 = 6$$

The additive identity of a matrix is a matrix of the same order (size) all of whose entries are zero. For example, the additive identity of a 3×2 matrix is a 3×2 matrix all of whose entries are zero. The sum of a matrix and its additive identity is identically the matrix itself. Since matrix addition is commutative, the identity matrix can be in front of or behind the other matrix, as we show here.

$$
\begin{bmatrix} 4 & 2 \\ 1 & 0 \\ 3 & 5 \end{bmatrix} + \begin{bmatrix} 0 & 0 \\ 0 & 0 \\ 0 & 0 \end{bmatrix} = \begin{bmatrix} 4 & 2 \\ 1 & 0 \\ 3 & 5 \end{bmatrix} \qquad \text{and} \qquad \begin{bmatrix} 0 & 0 \\ 0 & 0 \\ 0 & 0 \end{bmatrix} + \begin{bmatrix} 4 & 2 \\ 1 & 0 \\ 3 & 5 \end{bmatrix} = \begin{bmatrix} 4 & 2 \\ 1 & 0 \\ 3 & 5 \end{bmatrix}
$$

A matrix can be multiplied by a number, and a matrix can also be multiplied by another matrix. Since a number is often called a *scalar*, we call the product of a number and a matrix a **scalar product.** To multiply a matrix by a number, we multiply every entry in the matrix by the number. On the left we multiply a 3×2 matrix by –2. On the right we multiply a 1×4 matrix by 3.

$$
-2 \begin{bmatrix} 4 & 1 \\ 6 & -5 \\ 2 & -2 \end{bmatrix} = \begin{bmatrix} -8 & -2 \\ -12 & 10 \\ -4 & 4 \end{bmatrix} \qquad\qquad 3 \begin{bmatrix} 1 & 3 & 6 & 2 \end{bmatrix} = \begin{bmatrix} 3 & 9 & 18 & 6 \end{bmatrix}
$$

We can multiply two matrices if the number of columns of the first matrix is the same as the number of rows of the second matrix. This is true if the last number of the order of the first matrix is the same as the first number of the order of the second matrix. These are the "inside" numbers.

$$\overset{\text{YES}}{3 \times 2} \text{ times } 2 \times 2 \qquad\qquad \text{multiplication possible}$$
$$\underset{\text{NO}}{2 \times 4} \text{ times } 2 \times 4 \qquad\qquad \text{multiplication not possible}$$

The product of two matrices is a matrix whose order is determined by the two "outside" numbers.

$$3 \times 2 \text{ times } 2 \times 2 \longrightarrow \text{ a } 3 \times 2 \text{ matrix}$$
$$2 \times 5 \text{ times } 5 \times 3 \longrightarrow \text{ a } 2 \times 3 \text{ matrix}$$

The rule for multiplying matrices is difficult to state in words because each entry in the product matrix is the sum of products of selected entries in the matrices being multiplied. It is helpful to remember that when we are playing with matrices we are playing a **row-column** game. We always name the row first. In the 2×3 matrix on the left below, we use subscripted a's to name the entries and note that the first subscript of every entry in the first row is the number 1. The second subscript tells the number of the column. Thus the entry in the circle is in the first row and the second column and is called a_{12}. The entry in the box is in the second row and the third column and is called a_{23}.

$$\overset{2 \times 3}{\begin{bmatrix} a_{11} & \boxed{a_{12}} & a_{13} \\ a_{21} & a_{22} & \boxed{a_{23}} \end{bmatrix}} \qquad \overset{1 \times 4}{\left(b_{11} \ \ b_{12} \ \ b_{13} \ \ \boxed{b_{14}} \right)}$$

In the 1×4 matrix on the right, the entry in the box is in the first row and the fourth column, so we call it b_{14}.

If we multiply the following 3×2 matrix by the 2×2 matrix, as indicated, we know that the product matrix will be a 3×2 matrix. Each entry in the product matrix will be a sum of products, which we indicate by using the letters SP.

$$\overset{3 \times 2}{\begin{bmatrix} 1 & 2 \\ 3 & 4 \\ 5 & 6 \end{bmatrix}} \cdot \overset{2 \times 2}{\begin{bmatrix} 7 & 8 \\ 9 & -2 \end{bmatrix}} = \overset{3 \times 2}{\begin{bmatrix} SP_{11} & SP_{12} \\ SP_{21} & SP_{22} \\ SP_{31} & SP_{32} \end{bmatrix}}$$

By a delightful accident, the standard row-column designation of the entries tells us that SP_{11} is the sum of the products of the first row of the left-hand matrix and the first column of the right-hand matrix. The entry SP_{12} is the sum of the products of the first row in the left-hand matrix and the second column of the right-hand matrix. We show the way the entries in the product matrix are found in the following diagram.

$$\overset{3 \times 2}{\begin{bmatrix} 1 & 2 \\ 3 & 4 \\ 5 & 6 \end{bmatrix}} \cdot \overset{2 \times 2}{\begin{bmatrix} 7 & 8 \\ 9 & -2 \end{bmatrix}} = \overset{3 \times 2}{\begin{bmatrix} \begin{array}{c} 1 \cdot 7 \\ + 2 \cdot 9 \end{array} & \begin{array}{c} 1 \cdot 8 \\ + 2 \cdot (-2) \end{array} \\ \begin{array}{c} 3 \cdot 7 \\ + 4 \cdot 9 \end{array} & \begin{array}{c} 3 \cdot 8 \\ + 4 \cdot (-2) \end{array} \\ \begin{array}{c} 5 \cdot 7 \\ + 6 \cdot 9 \end{array} & \begin{array}{c} 5 \cdot 8 \\ + 6 \cdot (-2) \end{array} \end{bmatrix}} = \overset{3 \times 2}{\begin{bmatrix} 25 & 4 \\ 57 & 16 \\ 89 & 28 \end{bmatrix}}$$

We can picture the process by drawing boxes around the numbers of the first row of the first matrix and connecting the boxes as if they were wagons.

$$\boxed{1}\!-\!\boxed{2}$$

Then we pull these numbers to the right, make a 90-degree turn, and pull them down so that they are paired with the members of the first column of the second matrix.

$$
\begin{array}{l}
\boxed{1}\cdot 7 = 7 \\
\boxed{2}\cdot 9 = \underline{+18} \\
\phantom{\boxed{2}\cdot 9 = +}25
\end{array}
\qquad
\begin{bmatrix} 25 & \\ & \end{bmatrix}
$$

Then we multiply the paired numbers and add the products to find the entry 25 in the first row and the first column of the product matrix.

Next, we multiply the first row by the second column to get the second entry in the first row of the product.

$$
\begin{array}{l}
\boxed{1}\cdot 8 = 8 \\
\boxed{2}\cdot (-2) = \underline{-4} \\
\phantom{\boxed{2}\cdot (-2) = }4
\end{array}
\qquad
\begin{bmatrix} 25 & 4 \\ & \end{bmatrix}
$$

Next, we multiply the members of the second row by the members of the two columns to get the entries in the second row of the product matrix.

$$
\begin{array}{l}
\boxed{3}\cdot 7 = 21 \\
\boxed{4}\cdot 9 = \underline{+36} \\
\phantom{\boxed{4}\cdot 9 = +}57
\end{array}
\qquad
\begin{array}{l}
\boxed{3}\cdot 8 = 24 \\
\boxed{4}\cdot (-2) = \underline{-8} \\
\phantom{\boxed{4}\cdot (-2) = }16
\end{array}
\qquad
\begin{bmatrix} 25 & 4 \\ 57 & 16 \end{bmatrix}
$$

The last step is to repeat the procedure by multiplying the members of the third row and the members of the two columns.

If we multiply matrix A and matrix B and write matrix A first, we call the product A · B. If we multiply the same two matrices and write matrix B first, we call the product B · A. For most matrices the products will not be the same. Because the products are not always the same, we say that **matrix multiplication is not commutative.** We will demonstrate this by finding the product of two 2 × 2 matrices. First we find A · B.

$$
\overset{\text{A}}{\begin{bmatrix} 4 & 1 \\ 3 & 2 \end{bmatrix}} \cdot \overset{\text{B}}{\begin{bmatrix} 1 & 2 \\ 3 & 4 \end{bmatrix}} = \overset{\text{A · B}}{\begin{bmatrix} 4+3 & 8+4 \\ 3+6 & 6+8 \end{bmatrix}} = \overset{\text{A · B}}{\begin{bmatrix} 7 & 12 \\ 9 & 14 \end{bmatrix}}
$$

Now we reverse the order of the matrices and find B · A.

$$
\overset{\text{B}}{\begin{bmatrix} 1 & 2 \\ 3 & 4 \end{bmatrix}} \cdot \overset{\text{A}}{\begin{bmatrix} 4 & 1 \\ 3 & 2 \end{bmatrix}} = \overset{\text{B · A}}{\begin{bmatrix} 4+6 & 1+4 \\ 12+12 & 3+8 \end{bmatrix}} = \overset{\text{B · A}}{\begin{bmatrix} 10 & 5 \\ 24 & 11 \end{bmatrix}}
$$

The number one is the multiplicative identity for real-number multiplication because the product of any real number and the number one is identically the real number itself.

$$4 \cdot 1 = 4 \qquad 1 \cdot 6 = 6 \qquad -3 \cdot 1 = -3 \qquad 5 \cdot 1 = 5$$

Every square matrix has an identity matrix that has a diagonal of 1's and every other entry is zero. From left to right, we show the identity matrices for multiplication for 2×2, 3×3, 4×4, and 5×5 matrices.

$$2 \times 2 \qquad 3 \times 3 \qquad 4 \times 4 \qquad 5 \times 5$$

$$\begin{bmatrix} 1 & 0 \\ 0 & 1 \end{bmatrix} \qquad \begin{bmatrix} 1 & 0 & 0 \\ 0 & 1 & 0 \\ 0 & 0 & 1 \end{bmatrix} \qquad \begin{bmatrix} 1 & 0 & 0 & 0 \\ 0 & 1 & 0 & 0 \\ 0 & 0 & 1 & 0 \\ 0 & 0 & 0 & 1 \end{bmatrix} \qquad \begin{bmatrix} 1 & 0 & 0 & 0 & 0 \\ 0 & 1 & 0 & 0 & 0 \\ 0 & 0 & 1 & 0 & 0 \\ 0 & 0 & 0 & 1 & 0 \\ 0 & 0 & 0 & 0 & 1 \end{bmatrix}$$

The product of any matrix and its identity matrix is the matrix itself. The identity matrix can be written first or second, as we show here, because multiplication by the identity matrix is commutative.

$$\begin{bmatrix} 4 & 1 \\ 2 & 3 \end{bmatrix} \cdot \begin{bmatrix} 1 & 0 \\ 0 & 1 \end{bmatrix} = \begin{bmatrix} (4+0) & (0+1) \\ (2+0) & (0+3) \end{bmatrix} = \begin{bmatrix} 4 & 1 \\ 2 & 3 \end{bmatrix}$$

$$\begin{bmatrix} 1 & 0 \\ 0 & 1 \end{bmatrix} \cdot \begin{bmatrix} 4 & 1 \\ 2 & 3 \end{bmatrix} = \begin{bmatrix} (4+0) & (1+0) \\ (0+2) & (0+3) \end{bmatrix} = \begin{bmatrix} 4 & 1 \\ 2 & 3 \end{bmatrix}$$

example 108.1   Simplify: $\begin{bmatrix} 4 & 2 & -2 \\ 6 & 3 & 5 \end{bmatrix} - \begin{bmatrix} 3 & 5 & -4 \\ 4 & -2 & 6 \end{bmatrix}$

solution   To subtract real numbers, we add the opposite.

$$4 - 6 \qquad \text{means that} \qquad 4 + (-6) = -2$$

To subtract matrices, we add the opposite of the second matrix.

$$\begin{bmatrix} 4 & 2 & -2 \\ 6 & 3 & 5 \end{bmatrix} - \begin{bmatrix} 3 & 5 & -4 \\ 4 & -2 & 6 \end{bmatrix} = \begin{bmatrix} 4 & 2 & -2 \\ 6 & 3 & 5 \end{bmatrix} + \begin{bmatrix} -3 & -5 & 4 \\ -4 & 2 & -6 \end{bmatrix} = \begin{bmatrix} \mathbf{1} & \mathbf{-3} & \mathbf{2} \\ \mathbf{2} & \mathbf{5} & \mathbf{-1} \end{bmatrix}$$

example 108.2   Multiply: $\begin{bmatrix} 2 & -3 \\ 3 & 1 \\ 4 & 5 \end{bmatrix} \cdot \begin{bmatrix} 1 & 2 \\ 4 & -5 \end{bmatrix}$

solution   We are asked to multiply a 3×2 matrix and a 2×2 matrix.

$$(3 \times ②)(② \times 2)$$

This multiplication is possible because the inside numbers are the same. The order of the product matrix is determined by the outside numbers and will be 3×2, as we show below.

$$\begin{bmatrix} SP_{11} & SP_{12} \\ SP_{21} & SP_{22} \\ SP_{31} & SP_{32} \end{bmatrix}$$

The subscripts of the entries designate the products to be summed. For example, the entry in the upper left-hand corner is the sum of the products of the entries in the first row of the left-hand matrix and the entries in the first column of the right-hand matrix.

$$\begin{bmatrix} 2 \cdot 1 + (-3) \cdot 4 & 2 \cdot 2 + (-3) \cdot (-5) \\ 3 \cdot 1 + 1 \cdot 4 & 3 \cdot 2 + 1 \cdot (-5) \\ 4 \cdot 1 + 5 \cdot 4 & 4 \cdot 2 + 5 \cdot (-5) \end{bmatrix} = \begin{bmatrix} \mathbf{-10} & \mathbf{19} \\ \mathbf{7} & \mathbf{1} \\ \mathbf{24} & \mathbf{-17} \end{bmatrix}$$

example 108.3   Multiply: $\begin{bmatrix} 0 & 1 & 2 \\ -1 & 0 & -2 \\ 3 & 4 & 0 \end{bmatrix} \cdot \begin{bmatrix} 1 & 0 & 1 \\ -1 & 0 & -2 \\ 0 & 1 & 3 \end{bmatrix}$

solution   We are asked to multiply two 3×3 matrices.

$$(3 \times ③)(③ \times 3)$$

This multiplication is possible because the inside numbers are the same. The order of the product matrix is determined by the outside numbers and will be 3×3, as we show below.

$$\begin{bmatrix} SP_{11} & SP_{12} & SP_{13} \\ SP_{21} & SP_{22} & SP_{23} \\ SP_{31} & SP_{32} & SP_{33} \end{bmatrix}$$

The subscripts of the entries designate the products to be summed. For example, the entry in the upper left-hand corner is the sum of the products of the entries in the first row of the left-hand matrix and the entries in the first column of the right-hand matrix.

$$SP_{11} = 0 \cdot 1 + 1 \cdot (-1) + 2 \cdot 0$$

The other entries are determined similarly, giving us the following matrix.

$$\begin{bmatrix} 0 \cdot 1 + 1 \cdot (-1) + 2 \cdot 0 & 0 \cdot 0 + 1 \cdot 0 + 2 \cdot 1 & 0 \cdot 1 + 1 \cdot (-2) + 2 \cdot 3 \\ (-1) \cdot 1 + 0 \cdot (-1) + (-2) \cdot 0 & (-1) \cdot 0 + 0 \cdot 0 + (-2) \cdot 1 & (-1) \cdot 1 + 0 \cdot (-2) + (-2) \cdot 3 \\ 3 \cdot 1 + 4 \cdot (-1) + 0 \cdot 0 & 3 \cdot 0 + 4 \cdot 0 + 0 \cdot 1 & 3 \cdot 1 + 4 \cdot (-2) + 0 \cdot 3 \end{bmatrix}$$

Thus,

$$\begin{bmatrix} 0 & 1 & 2 \\ -1 & 0 & -2 \\ 3 & 4 & 0 \end{bmatrix} \cdot \begin{bmatrix} 1 & 0 & 1 \\ -1 & 0 & -2 \\ 0 & 1 & 3 \end{bmatrix} = \begin{bmatrix} -1 & 2 & 4 \\ -1 & -2 & -7 \\ -1 & 0 & -5 \end{bmatrix}$$

problem set 108

1. A card is drawn at random from a standard 52-card deck and a fair die is rolled. What is the probability that a diamond is drawn or a 6 is rolled on the die or both?

2. If money is compounded continuously at an annual rate of $r\%$, the amount of money in an account after t years is given by $A = A_0 e^{(r/100)(t)}$, where $A_0 = $ initial amount. Use this fact to find the annual interest rate if an initial amount of $10,000 is placed in an account which is compounded continuously and, five years later, the account is worth $15,000.

3. Nancy knew that W workers could build a swimming pool in 3 days. How long would it take if p extra workers helped?

4. Three years ago, Jerri was four times as old as Kelly was then. Five years from now, Jerri will be twice as old as Kelly will be. How old will each one be ten years from now?

Find $A + B$, $A - B$, and $2A$ where A and B are defined as follows:

5. $A = \begin{bmatrix} 3 & 7 \\ 1 & 4 \end{bmatrix}, B = \begin{bmatrix} 1 & 0 \\ -2 & 3 \end{bmatrix}$

6. $A = \begin{bmatrix} 1 & 0 & 1 \\ 0 & 2 & 3 \\ 1 & 1 & 0 \end{bmatrix}, B = \begin{bmatrix} -2 & 1 & 0 \\ 3 & 2 & 0 \\ 4 & 4 & 0 \end{bmatrix}$

Determine whether $A \cdot B$ and $B \cdot A$ exist. If a product exists, compute it.

7. $A = \begin{bmatrix} 1 & 1 \\ 2 & 3 \end{bmatrix}, B = \begin{bmatrix} 3 & 2 \\ -1 & 1 \end{bmatrix}$

8. $A = \begin{bmatrix} 1 \\ 1 \\ 1 \end{bmatrix}, B = \begin{bmatrix} 0 & 2 & 0 \\ 3 & 1 & 4 \end{bmatrix}$

9. Find the sum of the infinite geometric series: $3 - \dfrac{3}{2} + \dfrac{3}{4} - \dfrac{3}{8} + \cdots$

10. The general form of the equation of an ellipse is $5x^2 + 3y^2 + 20x - 18y + 32 = 0$. Write the equation of this ellipse in standard form and give the coordinates of the center, the length of the major axis, and the length of the minor axis. Also, determine whether the major axis is horizontal or vertical and graph the ellipse.

11. The general form of the equation of a hyperbola is $9x^2 - 4y^2 - 18x - 8y - 31 = 0$. Write the equation of this hyperbola in standard form and give the coordinates of the center, the coordinates of the vertices, and the equations of the asymptotes. Then graph the hyperbola.

12. Use cofactors to evaluate: $\begin{vmatrix} 6 & 8 & 5 \\ 0 & 0 & 4 \\ -3 & 2 & 4 \end{vmatrix}$

13. Use Cramer's rule to solve this system of equations for z: $\begin{cases} 2x - y + 3z = 5 \\ x + 2y - z = 10 \\ 3x - 3y + z = 8 \end{cases}$

14. The first term of an arithmetic sequence is 5 and the fourth term is 12. What is the nth term of the arithmetic sequence?

15. The concentration of hydrogen ions in the solution is 8.3×10^{-9} mole per liter. What is the pH of the solution?

16. Expand as the sum of individual logarithms, each of whose argument is linear:

$$\log_6 \left(\frac{36\sqrt[3]{x^5 y^4}}{z^{-3}} \right)$$

17. Find the last term of $(3x^2 + y)^9$.

18. (a) Develop the identity for $\cos A \cos B$.

(b) Find $\cos 105° \cos 75°$ by using the identity found in (a). Use exact values.

19. (a) Develop the identity for $\cos x - \cos y$.

(b) Find $\cos 165° - \cos 75°$ by using the identity found in (a). Use exact values.

20. Express $\log_7 50$ in terms of natural logarithms. Do not find a numerical answer.

Solve for x:

21. $\log (\ln x)^2 = 2$ **22.** $e^{4x-1} = 3$

23. $2 \log_3 (x + 2) + \log_3 (x - 1) = 3 \log_3 x$

24. Show: $\sec \theta - \cos \theta = \sin \theta \tan \theta$

Sketch the graph of each of the following:

25. $y = \csc \frac{1}{2} x$ **26.** $y = -7 - 2 \cos 2\left(x + \frac{\pi}{3} \right)$

27. $y = \sec 2x$

28. Solve $\cos^2 \theta - \sin^2 \theta = 1$ given that $0° \le \theta < 360°$.

29. Write the five fifth roots of $9 - 9i$ in polar form.

30. Graph the solution to the system of inequalities: $\begin{cases} x^2 + 4x + y^2 + 6y + 13 \ge 16 \\ 6y - 4x + 24 > 0 \\ 4x > 6y - 60 \end{cases}$

LESSON *109* *Rational Numbers*

A **common fraction** is the ratio of two integers. A **rational number** is a number that **can be** written as a common fraction. Any terminating decimal number **can be** written as a common fraction. The numbers shown here are terminating decimal numbers

(a) 0.023   (b) 0.0023   (c) 0.000023

and thus **can be** written as a common fraction. We do this by multiplying above and below by the appropriate power of 10. For (a), we multiply above and below by 1000.

$$\text{(a)}\quad 0.023\left(\frac{1000}{1000}\right) = \frac{23}{1000}$$

For fraction (b), we use 10,000 over 10,000 because the decimal point must be moved four places. In (c), we must move the decimal point six places, so we multiply by 1,000,000 over 1,000,000.

$$\text{(b)}\quad 0.0023\left(\frac{10,000}{10,000}\right) = \frac{23}{10,000} \qquad \text{(c)}\quad 0.000023\left(\frac{1,000,000}{1,000,000}\right) = \frac{23}{1,000,000}$$

Decimal numbers whose digits repeat indefinitely in a pattern are also rational numbers because these numbers can be written as common fractions. We use a bar over the repeating digits to indicate that they repeat. Thus,

$0.00\overline{23}$ means $0.0023232323\ldots$

There are several methods that can be used to find a common fraction that has the same value as one of these repeaters. One way is to recognize that these numbers can be expressed as the sum of an infinite geometric series and then to use the formula for the sum of an infinite series to help find the fraction.

example 109.1   Use an infinite geometric series as an aid in writing $0.00\overline{23}$ as a common fraction.

solution   We always draw the best diagram of the problem that we can. We begin by writing the number expanded.

$$0.0023\ 23\ 23\ 23\ 23\ \ldots$$

Now we show that this can be written as a sum.

0.0023	23×10^{-4}
+ 0.000023	$+\ 23 \times 10^{-4} \times 10^{-2}$
+ 0.00000023	$+\ 23 \times 10^{-4} \times 10^{-2} \times 10^{-2}$
+ 0.0000000023	$+\ 23 \times 10^{-4} \times 10^{-2} \times 10^{-2} \times 10^{-2}$
+ $\cdots$	+ $\cdots$

This can be written as an infinite geometric series whose first term is 23×10^{-4} and in which r is 10^{-2}.

$$0.0023 + 0.0023\left(10^{-2}\right) + 0.0023\left(10^{-2}\right)^2 + 0.0023\left(10^{-2}\right)^3 + \cdots$$

Since $|r|$ is less than 1, we can use the formula for the sum of a convergent infinite geometric series.

$$S = \frac{a_1}{1 - r}$$

$$= \frac{23 \times 10^{-4}}{1 - 0.01}$$

$$= \frac{23 \times 10^{-4}}{0.99}$$

To get rid of the 10^{-4}, we multiply above and below by 10^4 and get our fraction of integers.

$$\frac{23 \times 10^{-4}}{0.99} \cdot \frac{10^4}{10^4} = \frac{23}{9900}$$

example 109.2   Use an infinite geometric series as an aid in showing that $5.\overline{013}$ is a rational number by writing it as a common fraction.

solution   Again we begin by drawing a diagram. First we write the number expanded.

$$5.\overline{013} \quad \text{means} \quad 5.013 \ 013 \ 013 \ 013$$

$$5 + 0.013 \qquad\qquad\qquad 5 + 0.013$$
$$+ \ 0.000013 \qquad\qquad\qquad + \ 0.013(10^{-3})$$
$$+ \ 0.000000013 \qquad\qquad + \ 0.013(10^{-3})^2$$
$$+ \ 0.000000000013 \qquad + \ 0.013(10^{-3})^3$$
$$+ \ \cdots \qquad\qquad\qquad\qquad + \ \cdots$$

This can be written as 5 plus a geometric series whose first term is 0.013 and in which r is 10^{-3}.

$$5 + \left[0.013 + 0.013(10^{-3}) + 0.013(10^{-3})^2 + 0.013(10^{-3})^3 + \cdots\right]$$

Now we use $\dfrac{a_1}{1 - r}$ for the sum of the series.

$$5 + \frac{a_1}{1 - r} = 5 + \frac{0.013}{1 - 0.001} \qquad \text{substituted}$$

$$= 5 + \frac{0.013}{0.999} \qquad \text{simplified}$$

$$= 5 + \frac{13}{999} \qquad \text{simplified}$$

$$= \frac{4995}{999} + \frac{13}{999} \qquad \text{common denominator}$$

$$= \frac{5008}{999} \qquad \text{added}$$

It seems reasonable to induce from the results of the preceding two examples that when we have 2 digits that repeat, r is 10^{-2}; when we have 3 digits that repeat, r is 10^{-3}; when we have 4 digits that repeat, r is 10^{-4}; etc.

problem set 109

1.   The urn contained 4 red marbles and 3 green marbles. Roy drew a marble at random and did not put it back. Then he randomly drew another marble. What is the probability that both marbles were green?

2.   Twenty hours into the hard part, the exponential decay had reduced their number to 1400. Forty hours into the hard part, their number was found to be only 1300. How many of them would remain 200 hours into the hard part?

3.   Marie sold the first n of them for a total of d dollars. Then she realized she was losing money and increased the price of each one $3. How many could Faye buy at the new price if Faye had $400 to spend?

4.   Mark could do 5 jobs in H hours. When Rachel helped, they could do 10 jobs in 3 hours. What was Rachel's rate in jobs per hour?

5. Ten years ago, Mary's age exceeded twice Jim's age by 6. Ten years from now, 3 times Mary's age will exceed 4 times Jim's age by 30. How old will Mary and Jim be in 15 years?

6. Use an infinite geometric series as an aid for expressing $0.000\overline{31}$ as a common fraction.

7. Use an infinite geometric series as an aid for expressing $6.0\overline{17}$ as a common fraction.

8. A ball is dropped from a height of 132 feet and rebounds one fourth the distance it falls after each bounce. What will be the total distance the ball travels?

9. Let $A = \begin{bmatrix} 2 & 3 & 1 \\ 4 & 0 & 2 \\ 1 & 1 & 1 \end{bmatrix}$ and $B = \begin{bmatrix} 0 & -1 & 2 \\ 3 & 5 & 7 \\ -2 & 0 & 6 \end{bmatrix}$. Find $A + B$ and $A \cdot B$.

10. The equation $9x^2 + 25y^2 - 36x + 150y + 260 = 0$ is the general form of the equation of an ellipse. Write the equation of this ellipse in standard form and give the coordinates of the center, the length of the major axis, and the length of the minor axis. Then graph the ellipse.

11. The general form of the equation of a hyperbola is $4x^2 - y^2 + 24x + 4y + 28 = 0$. Write the equation of this hyperbola in standard form and give the coordinates of the center, the coordinates of the vertices, and the equations of the asymptotes. Then graph the hyperbola.

12. Use cofactors to evaluate: $\begin{vmatrix} 9 & 3 & 0 \\ 1 & 5 & 2 \\ 0 & -3 & 7 \end{vmatrix}$

13. Use Cramer's rule to solve this system of equations for y:

$$\begin{cases} x + y - 2z = 1 \\ 2x - 3y + 3z = -1 \\ 5x + 2y - 8z = 1 \end{cases}$$

14. Write the following as a single logarithm. Simplify your answer.

$$\log_5 (x + 1) - 2 \log_5 x - \log_5 (x^2 - 1) + \log_5 (x^2 + x)$$

15. The first term of a geometric sequence is 2 and the common ratio is –2. (a) What is the twelfth term of the sequence? (b) What is the sum of the first 12 terms?

16. The pH of a solution is 6.5. What is the concentration of hydrogen ions in moles per liter of the solution?

17. Find the fourth term of $(3a + bc)^5$.

18. (a) Develop the identity for $\sin x - \sin y$.

    (b) Find $\sin 255° - \sin 15°$ using the identity found in (a). Use exact values.

19. Express $\ln 42$ in terms of common logarithms. Do not find a numerical answer.

Solve for x:

20. $x^{\sqrt{\log x}} = 10^{27}$

21. $\dfrac{3}{4} \log_5 16 - \log_5 (3x - 2) = -\log_5 (2x + 1)$

Show:

22. $(\sin x - \cos x)^2 = 1 - \sin 2x$

23. $\dfrac{\tan^2 x}{\sec x + 1} = \sec x - 1$

24. Solve this triangle for angle A. Then find the area of the triangle.

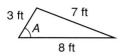

25. Sketch the graph of $y = -3 + 5 \cos(x + 2\pi)$.

26. Find the equations of the following trigonometric functions:

(a)

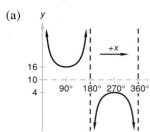

(b)

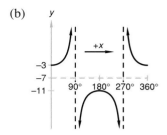

27. Solve $(\sqrt{2} - 2 \cos 3x)(\sin x + 1) = 0$ given that $0 \le x < 2\pi$.

28. Find the three cube roots of $1 - i$ and write the roots in polar form.

29. Find the distance from the point $(0, 0)$ to the line $5x + y + 13 = 0$.

30. Let $f(x) = 2 - x^3$ and $g(x) = x + 1$. Find $(f \circ g)(x)$.

LESSON 110   *Graphs of arcsine and arccosine • Graphs of arcsecant and arccosecant • Graphs of arctangent and arccotangent*

110.A

graphs of arcsine and arccosine

In Lesson 32, we discussed inverse trigonometric relations. We also discussed how an inverse trigonometric relation could be made into a function by restricting the range of the relation. For example, we recall that

$$\sin 30° = \frac{1}{2} \qquad \cos 60° = \frac{1}{2}$$

Yet, when we ask for the arcsine and arccosine of $\frac{1}{2}$, we get a multitude of answers.

$$\arcsin \frac{1}{2} = 30°, 150°, 390°, \dots$$

$$\arccos \frac{1}{2} = 60°, 300°, 420°, \dots$$

We remember that to make these relations into functions, we must restrict the range of these inverse relations. We use a capital letter "A" in the names of these functions, Arcsine and Arccosine, to distinguish them from the relations. By convention, the range of the Arcsine function is restricted to values between $-90°$ and $90°$ inclusive, and the range of the Arccosine function is restricted to values between $0°$ and $180°$ inclusive.

In our earlier discussion of the inverse trigonometric functions, we used degrees as our measure for angles. In calculus and other advanced mathematics courses, radian measure is more useful and common. Therefore, we will use radian measure in this lesson. So, instead of saying

$$\sin 30° = \frac{1}{2} \quad \text{and} \quad \arcsin \frac{1}{2} = 30°, 150°, 390°, \ldots$$

we shall say,

$$\sin \frac{\pi}{6} = \frac{1}{2} \quad \text{and} \quad \arcsin \frac{1}{2} = \frac{\pi}{6}, \frac{5\pi}{6}, \frac{13\pi}{6}, \ldots$$

Also, we note that the range of the Arcsine function is restricted to values between $-\frac{\pi}{2}$ and $\frac{\pi}{2}$ inclusive, and that the range of the Arccosine function is restricted to values between 0 and π inclusive.

Below, we graph the relations

$$\theta = \arcsin x \quad \text{and} \quad \theta = \arccos x$$

The graph of the arcsine displays the ordered pairs of θ and sine θ, where θ is treated as the dependent variable. The values of θ are graphed on the vertical axis, and the values of sine θ are graphed on the horizontal axis. In the same way, the graph of the arccosine has the values of θ graphed vertically and has the values of cosine θ graphed horizontally.

The graphs of the inverse functions $\theta = \text{Arcsin } x$ and $\theta = \text{Arccos } x$ are shown by the heavy lines in the graphs of $\theta = \arcsin x$ and $\theta = \arccos x$, respectively. Note that the values of θ for the Arcsine function are between $-\frac{\pi}{2}$ and $\frac{\pi}{2}$ inclusive, while the values of θ for the Arccosine function are between 0 and π inclusive.

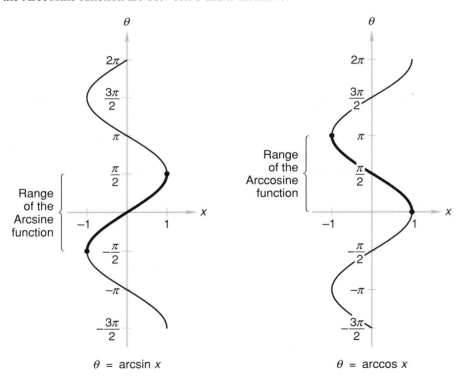

$\theta = \arcsin x$ $\theta = \arccos x$

110.B

graphs of arcsecant and arccosecant

The graphs of the secant and cosecant are graphs of the ordered pairs of $(\theta, \sec \theta)$ and $(\theta, \csc \theta)$ with the first variable plotted on the horizontal axis. The graphs of $\text{arcsec } \theta$ and $\text{arccsc } \theta$ are graphs of the same pairs, but with the order reversed—$(\sec \theta, \theta)$ and $(\csc \theta, \theta)$. The first variable is again graphed on the horizontal axis, so the curves repeat vertically instead of horizontally as before. To consider these relations as functions, there can be only one image for each value of $\sec \theta$ and only one image for each value of $\csc \theta$. Thus, for the function $\theta = \text{Arcsec } x$, the values of θ are restricted between 0 and π inclusive, as shown by the heavy lines in the figure on the left below, and $\theta = \frac{\pi}{2}$ must be excluded. For the function $\theta = \text{Arccsc } x$, the values of θ are restricted between $-\frac{\pi}{2}$ and $\frac{\pi}{2}$ inclusive, as shown by the heavy lines in the figure on the right, and $\theta = 0$ must be excluded.

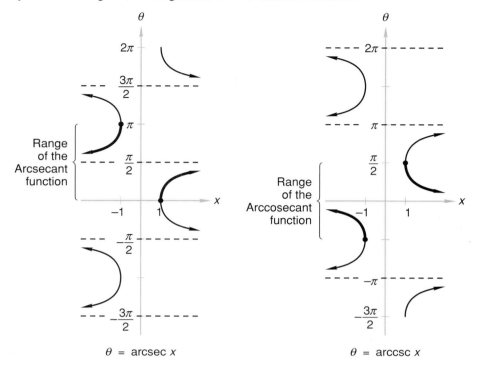

$\theta = \text{arcsec } x$ $\theta = \text{arccsc } x$

110.C

graphs of arctangent and arccotangent

The graphs of the arctangent and the arccotangent are graphs of the same pairs of coordinates as in the graphs of the tangent and cotangent, but the order is reversed. The values of θ are graphed vertically, and the values of $\tan \theta$ or $\cot \theta$ are graphed horizontally, so the curves are horizontal instead of vertical as before. If the pairing is to be a single-valued relationship, there can be only one value of θ for any specified value of $\tan \theta$ or $\cot \theta$; these values are designated by the heavy lines in the graphs. For Arctan θ, the values of θ considered lie between $-\frac{\pi}{2}$ and $\frac{\pi}{2}$ exclusive; for Arccot θ, they lie between 0 and π exclusive.

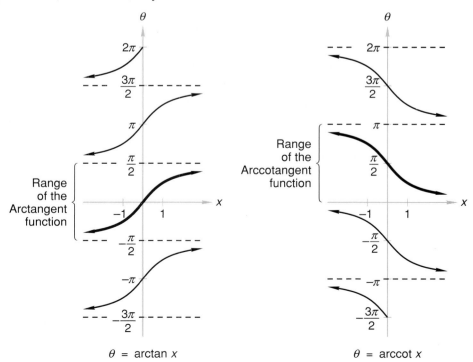

$\theta = \text{arctan } x$ $\theta = \text{arccot } x$

example 110.1   Sketch the graph of $f(x) = \text{Arctan } x$. State the domain and range of the function. Then evaluate Arctan x at $x = -1, 0$, and 1.

solution   To graph the function, we look back at the graph of the relation $\theta = \arctan x$. We see that the "middle piece" of the graph corresponds to the graph of Arctan x.

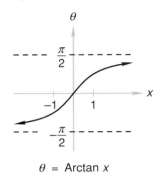

$$\theta = \text{Arctan } x$$

From the graph we see that

$$\text{Domain of Arctan } x = \{x \in \mathbb{R}\}$$

and

$$\text{Range of Arctan } x = \left\{\theta \in \mathbb{R} \,\middle|\, -\frac{\pi}{2} < \theta < \frac{\pi}{2}\right\}$$

To evaluate Arctan x at a particular value of x, we must find the angle θ where $-\frac{\pi}{2} < \theta < \frac{\pi}{2}$ such that $\tan \theta = x$. For example, Arctan (-1) is the angle θ such that $-\frac{\pi}{2} < \theta < \frac{\pi}{2}$ and $\tan \theta = -1$. By applying what we learned in Lesson 32, we find that the angle θ is $-\frac{\pi}{4}$. Thus,

$$\text{Arctan }(-1) = -\frac{\pi}{4}$$

Similarly,

$$\text{Arctan } 0 = 0 \quad \text{and} \quad \text{Arctan } 1 = \frac{\pi}{4}$$

problem set 110

1. Kenny is going to randomly draw a card from a deck of 52 cards. What is the probability that the card will be a queen or a black card or both?

2. The increase was exponential. After 5 hours they numbered 120, and after 10 hours there were 400 of them. How many were there after 30 hours?

3. At 6 a.m. the clock hands pointed in opposite directions. How long would it be before both hands pointed in the same direction?

4. The *Mary Ann* can go 48 miles downstream in 1 hour less than it takes her to go 32 miles upstream. If the speed of the *Mary Ann* in still water is 3 times the speed of the current, what is the speed of the current and the still-water speed of the *Mary Ann*?

5. One pipe can fill a tank in 10 hours and a second pipe can fill a tank in 8 hours. The first pipe is used for 2 hours, and then the second pipe is also used. How long will both pipes take to finish filling the tank?

6. (a) Graph the relation $\theta = \arcsin x$. Indicate on the graph the portion that is the graph of the function $\theta = \text{Arcsin } x$. State the domain and range of $\theta = \text{Arcsin } x$. Find Arcsin $\frac{\sqrt{3}}{2}$.

   (b) Graph the relation $\theta = \arccos x$. Indicate on the graph the portion that is the graph of the function $\theta = \text{Arccos } x$. State the domain and range of $\theta = \text{Arccos } x$. Find Arccos $\left(-\frac{1}{2}\right)$.

   (c) Graph the relation $\theta = \arctan x$. Indicate on the graph the portion that is the graph of the function $\theta = \text{Arctan } x$. State the domain and range of $\theta = \text{Arctan } x$. Find Arctan $\left(-\frac{\sqrt{3}}{3}\right)$.

7. Use an infinite geometric series as an aid for expressing $0.00\overline{241}$ as a common fraction.

8. Find the sum of the following geometric series:

$$\left(\frac{1}{4}\right) + \left(-\frac{3}{16}\right) + \left(\frac{9}{64}\right) + \left(-\frac{27}{256}\right) + \cdots$$

9. Let $A = \begin{bmatrix} 1 & 0 & 1 \\ -2 & 4 & 3 \\ 6 & 2 & 0 \end{bmatrix}$ and $B = \begin{bmatrix} 2 & 2 & 4 \\ 1 & 1 & 0 \\ -2 & 3 & -1 \end{bmatrix}$. Find $A + B$ and $B \cdot A$.

10. The equation $25x^2 + 9y^2 - 200x + 18y + 184 = 0$ is the general form of the equation of an ellipse. Write the equation of the ellipse in standard form and give the coordinates of the center, the length of the major axis, and the length of the minor axis. Also, determine whether the major axis is horizontal or vertical and graph the ellipse.

11. The general form of the equation of a hyperbola is $x^2 - 4y^2 + 4x + 32y - 96 = 0$. Write the equation of the hyperbola in standard form and give the coordinates of the center, the coordinates of the vertices, and the equations of the asymptotes. Then graph the hyperbola.

12. Use Cramer's rule to solve this system of equations for x: $\begin{cases} 3x + 2y = 0 \\ x - 3z = 5 \\ x + y + z = -2 \end{cases}$

13. The first term of a geometric sequence is 4 and the common ratio is 2. What is the fifteenth term of the sequence?

14. Find the geometric mean and the arithmetic mean of 7 and 12.

15. Use a calculator to compute: $10^{\sqrt{\left(\frac{100}{9}\right)\left(\frac{16}{36}\right)}}$

16. Find all the terms of $\left(x^2 - 2y\right)^3$.

17. (a) Develop the identity for $\sin x \cos y$.

    (b) Find $\sin 225° \cos 15°$ using the identity found in (a). Use exact values.

18. Express $\log_4 8$ in terms of common logarithms. Do not find a numerical answer.

Solve for x:

19. $\sqrt{\log_2 x} = \log_2 x - 2$

20. $\log \sqrt[3]{x^2} + \log \sqrt[3]{x^4} = \log 2^{-4}$

Show:

21. $\dfrac{1}{2} \sec x \csc (-x) = -\dfrac{1}{\sin 2x}$

22. $\dfrac{\cos x}{\sec x - 1} - \dfrac{\cos x}{\sec x + 1} = 2 \cos^3 x \csc^2 x$

23. Solve this triangle for the largest angle.

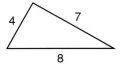

Sketch the graph of each of the following:

24. $y = \tan\left(x + \dfrac{\pi}{2}\right)$

25. $y = -4 + 3 \sin \dfrac{1}{3}(x - 2\pi)$

26. $y = \cot\left(x - \dfrac{\pi}{2}\right)$

27. Solve $-2 \sin 3x = 1$ given that $0° \le x < 360°$.

28. Find the three cube roots of 1 in rectangular form. Give exact answers.

29. Find the perimeter of a ten-sided regular polygon that can be inscribed in a circle whose radius is 1 inch.

30. Factor $x^3 - 1$ over the set of complex numbers. [*Hint*: Recall the factorization $a^3 - b^3 = (a - b)(a^2 + ab + b^2)$.]

LESSON *111*   *Logarithmic Inequalities: Base Greater Than 1 •*
Logarithmic Inequalities: Base Less Than 1

111.A
logarithmic inequalities: base greater than 1

Most of the problems that we have worked using logarithms were designed to help us understand the rules for logarithms and to help us remember that exponential functions and logarithmic functions are two ways to express the same relationships. Sometimes we encounter exercises that are designed to test our knowledge of a single fact. If we recognize this and if we know the fact, then the problems are simple. Most logarithmic inequality problems fall into this category. First, we will investigate logarithms whose bases are greater than 1. We will use 5 as a base to demonstrate.

$$5^2 = 25 \qquad 5^3 = 125 \qquad 5^4 = 625$$

When the logarithm is 3, the number is 5^3, which is 125. When the logarithm is less than 3, the number is less than 5^3. When the logarithm is greater than 3, the number is greater than 5^3. If we are given the inequality

$$\log_5 N < 3$$

we must carefully consider the meaning of the inequality. Since $\log_5 N$ is an exponent, the inequality says

$$\text{The exponent} < 3$$

Now we investigate the result when the exponent equals 3.

$$\log_5 N = 3 \qquad \text{which says} \qquad 5^3 = N$$

The given inequality says the logarithm (exponent) is less than 3. If this is true, then certainly N will be less than 5^3.

$$N < 5^3$$

Care must be taken with the "greater than" and "less than" symbols, for, of course, it would be incorrect to write

$$5^3 < N \qquad \text{incorrect}$$

example 111.1   Solve for x: $\log_4 (x - 2) < 3$

solution   If the logarithm (exponent) of $x - 2$ is less than 3, then $x - 2$ must be less than 4^3.

$$x - 2 < 4^3 \qquad \text{inequality}$$
$$x < 66 \qquad \text{simplified}$$

But the argument of a logarithm must be a positive number, so $x - 2$ must be greater than zero. This means x must be greater than 2. Thus, the final solution is

$$x > 2 \qquad \text{and} \qquad x < 66$$

which we can express in one compound statement by writing

$$\mathbf{2 < x < 66}$$

111.B
logarithmic inequalities: base less than 1

To investigate exponentials whose bases are less than 1, we look at three expressions whose bases are $\frac{1}{2}$.

$$\left(\frac{1}{2}\right)^2 = \frac{1}{4} \qquad \left(\frac{1}{2}\right)^3 = \frac{1}{8} \qquad \left(\frac{1}{2}\right)^4 = \frac{1}{16}$$

In the center we see that when the logarithm (exponent) is 3, the number is $\frac{1}{8}$. On the left we see that when the logarithm (exponent) is less than 3, the number is greater than $\frac{1}{8}$. On the right we see that when the logarithm (exponent) is greater than 3, the number is less than $\frac{1}{8}$. Thus, if we look at the inequality

$$\log_{1/2} N < 3$$

we know that if the logarithm is less than 3, the number must be greater than $\left(\frac{1}{2}\right)^3$.

$$N > \left(\frac{1}{2}\right)^3$$

In general, if the base is less than 1, we turn the inequality sign around when we change to the exponential form.

example 111.2   Solve: $\log_{1/3} (x - 6) > 4$

solution   The log of $x - 6$ is greater than 4, which means that $x - 6$ equals $\frac{1}{3}$ raised to some exponent greater than 4. This means that $x - 6$ must be less than $\left(\frac{1}{3}\right)^4$.

$$x - 6 < \left(\frac{1}{3}\right)^4 \qquad \text{equation}$$

$$x - 6 < \frac{1}{81} \qquad \text{expanded}$$

$$x < 6 + \frac{1}{81} \qquad \text{solved}$$

From this we see that x must be less than $6\frac{1}{81}$. Also, we remember that the argument of any logarithm must be a positive number (a number greater than 0), so $x - 6$ must be greater than 0 and thus x must be greater than 6,

$$x > 6 \qquad \text{and} \qquad x < 6\frac{1}{81}$$

which we can express compactly by writing

$$6 < x < 6\frac{1}{81}$$

**problem set
111**

1. A ball is dropped from a height of 256 feet. After each bounce the ball rebounds three fourths of the distance it fell. How far will the ball rebound after the fourth bounce?

2. Keeth and Tammy were amazed that the first toss of the coin came up heads. What is the probability that the next two tosses will also come up heads?

3. Marie began with 10 grams of radioactive material, but after 2 days, she had only 6 grams left. If the material is decaying exponentially, how much material will she have left after 5 days?

4. One of the elephants lumbered toward the water hole at f feet per hour for t hours but still arrived 2 hours late. How fast should the elephant have lumbered to have arrived at the water hole on time?

5. Twice the supplement of an angle exceeds 5 times the complement of the angle by 30°. What is the angle?

6. Compute $_8P_6$ and $_8C_6$.

Solve for x:

7. $\log_3 (x - 2) < 3$

8. $\log_{1/2} (x - 3) > 3$

9. Sketch the graph of each of the following functions. For each graph, give the domain and the range of the function.

   (a) $f(x) = \text{Arcsec } x$ (b) $g(x) = \text{Arccsc } x$ (c) $h(x) = \text{Arccot } x$

10. Use an infinite geometric series as an aid for expressing $0.00\overline{431}$ as a common fraction.

11. Let $A = \begin{bmatrix} 2 & 0 & 3 \\ 1 & 3 & 5 \\ 2 & 2 & 1 \end{bmatrix}$ and $B = \begin{bmatrix} 5 & 3 & 1 \\ 0 & 2 & 4 \\ 2 & 4 & 8 \end{bmatrix}$. Find $2A - B$ and $B \cdot A$.

12. The general form of the equation of an ellipse is $25x^2 + 9y^2 + 50x - 36y - 164 = 0$. Write the equation of the ellipse in standard form and give the coordinates of the center, the length of the major axis, and the length of the minor axis. Also, determine whether the major axis is horizontal or vertical and graph the ellipse.

13. The equation $4x^2 - 36y^2 - 40x + 216y - 368 = 0$ is the general form of the equation of a hyperbola. Write the equation of the hyperbola in standard form and give the coordinates of the center, the coordinates of the vertices, and the equations of the asymptotes. Then graph the hyperbola.

14. Use Cramer's rule to solve for x: $\begin{cases} 3x + 4y + z = 10 \\ x - y + z = 0 \\ x + 2y + 3z = 10 \end{cases}$

15. Write the following as a single logarithm. Simplify your answer.

$$2 \log (x - 1) - 3 \log x + \log (x^2 + x) - \log (x^2 - 1)$$

16. Use a calculator to compute: $\dfrac{\left(\sqrt[3]{203 \times 10^4} \right)^2}{\sqrt{804 \times 10^{16}}}$

17. Find all the terms of $(2x + y)^4$.   18. Solve for x: $\begin{vmatrix} x & 0 & 1 \\ 0 & 2 & 4 \\ 4 & 0 & x \end{vmatrix} = 0$

19. Find $\sin 255° + \sin 15°$ by using the identity for $\sin x + \sin y$. Use exact values.

Solve for x:

20. $\ln (\ln x) = 1$ 21. $4^{x+2} = 2^{3x} \cdot 8$

Show:

22. $\sec x \csc x = 2 \csc 2x$ 23. $\dfrac{2 \tan \theta}{1 + \tan^2 \theta} = \sin 2\theta$

24. Solve this triangle for a.

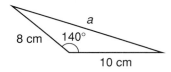

Sketch the graph of each of the following:

25. $y = 2 + 4 \sin \dfrac{1}{3}(x - 20°)$ 26. $y = \cos \left(x - \dfrac{\pi}{2} \right)$

Solve the following equations given that $0 \le x < 2\pi$:

27. $\tan^2 3x = 1$ 28. $\sec^2 2x - 1 = 0$

29. Find the four fourth roots of 16 and write the roots in rectangular form. Give exact answers.

30. Factor $x^3 + 27$ over the set of complex numbers.

LESSON 112 *Binomial Theorem*

We have been using Pascal's triangle to find the coefficients of the terms of the expansions of expressions such as $(a + b)^n$. Pascal's triangle is satisfactory for expansions when n is a small number such as 4, 5, or 6, but its use is inconvenient when n is a larger number such as 15, 27, or 50. A triangle of 51 rows with a bottom row of 51 entries would take a long time to construct. An identity called the **binomial theorem** allows one to compute the coefficient of any particular term of an expansion without knowing the entries in the row above. If n is a positive integer, the general form of the expansion of $(a + b)^n$ is as follows:

$$(a + b)^n = a^n + \frac{n}{1} \cdot a^{n-1}b + \frac{n}{1} \cdot \frac{n-1}{2}a^{n-2}b^2 + \frac{n}{1} \cdot \frac{n-1}{2} \cdot \frac{n-2}{3}a^{n-3}b^3$$

$$+ \cdots + \frac{n}{1} \cdot \frac{n-1}{2} \cdot \frac{n-2}{3} \cdots \frac{n-[k-2]}{k-1}a^{n-(k-1)}b^{k-1} + \cdots + b^n$$

In this notation, k represents the number of a particular term in the expansion. If we use factorial notation, the expression for the kth term of an expansion can be written in a form that is easier to remember. Instead of a and b, we will use F for the first term in the binomial and will use S for the second term in the binomial. To use this expression, we must say that the value of 0! is 1.

> If n is a positive integer and k is a positive integer less than or equal to $n + 1$, the kth term of $(F + S)^n$ is
> $$\frac{n!}{(n - k + 1)!(k - 1)!}F^{n-k+1}S^{k-1}$$

The binomial theorem looks complicated but is especially easy to remember if we can recall that *n* factorial is the numerator of the coefficient, that the sum of the exponents is *n*, and that these exponents always appear as factorials in the denominator of the coefficient.

example 112.1   Find the eighth term of the expansion of $(F + S)^{12}$.

solution   The easy way is to begin with the exponent of S. In the first term, the exponent of S is 0; in the second term, the exponent is 1; etc.

$$\text{Terms:} \qquad ① ② ③ ④ ⑤ \cdots$$
$$\text{Exponent of } S: \quad S^0 \ S^1 \ S^2 \ S^3 \ S^4 \cdots$$

so we see that the exponent of S in the eighth term will be 7. Now the exponent of F must add to 7 to make 12, so the exponent of F must be 5. Thus, the variables are

$$F^5S^7$$

Now the numerator of the coefficient is $(5 + 7)!$, which is 12!, and the denominator of the coefficient is 5!7!. Using this information, we can write the eighth term of the expansion of $(F + S)^{12}$ as follows:

$$\frac{12!}{5!\,7!}F^5S^7 = \mathbf{792}F^5S^7$$

If we use the general expression for the kth term given in the box above and use 12 for n and 8 for k, we will get the same result.

$$\frac{n!}{(n-k+1)!(k-1)!}F^{n-k+1}S^{k-1} = \frac{12!}{(12-8+1)!(8-1)!}F^{12-8+1}S^{8-1}$$

$$= \frac{12!}{5!\,7!}F^5S^7$$

$$= 792F^5S^7$$

example 112.2   Find the tenth term of the expansion of $(F + S)^{14}$.

solution   We begin by finding the exponent of S for the tenth term.

$$\text{Term:} \qquad ①\;②\;③\;④\;⑤\;\dots$$
$$\text{Exponent of }S\text{:}\quad S^0\;\;S^1\;\;S^2\;\;S^3\;\;S^4\;\;\dots$$

We see that the exponent of S in the tenth term will be 9. Since the exponent of F must add to 9 to get 14, the exponent of F must be 5. Thus we can write

$$F^5S^9$$

Now we remember that the numerator of the coefficient is $(5 + 9)!$, and the denominator of the coefficient is $5!9!$, so we can write the tenth term of $(F + S)^{14}$ as

$$\frac{14!}{5!9!}F^5S^9 = 2002F^5S^9$$

example 112.3   Find the tenth term of the expansion of $\left(2x^3 - y\right)^{15}$.

solution   We will begin by finding the tenth term of the expansion of $(F + S)^{15}$. Then we will replace F with $2x^3$ and replace S with $-y$. The exponent of the variable S in the tenth term is 9, so the exponent of F must be 6.

$$F^6S^9$$

Now we remember the pattern and write the coefficient.

$$\text{Tenth term } = \frac{15!}{6!9!}F^6S^9 = 5005F^6S^9$$

We finish by replacing F with $2x^3$ and replacing S with $-y$ and then we simplify.

$$5005\left(2x^3\right)^6(-y)^9 = 5005\left[64x^{18}(-y)^9\right] = -320{,}320x^{18}y^9$$

problem set 112

1. A ball is dropped from a height of 128 feet. After each bounce the ball rebounds one third of the distance it fell. What is the total distance the ball will travel?

2. An urn contains balls and cubes which are either red or green. The probability of randomly choosing a red object is 0.6, the probability of randomly choosing a ball is 0.4, and the probability of randomly choosing a red ball is 0.2. What is the probability of randomly selecting either a ball or a red object?

3. The photographer could take a picture of only 3 people at one time. If 7 cheerleaders were to be photographed, how many different groups of three were possible?

4. Wakulla called Tallahassee on the phone. The cost of the call was $2.20 for the first 3 minutes and $0.90 for each additional minute. Wakulla talked longer than 3 minutes. In fact, she talked p minutes. What was the cost of her call?

5. The rug was marked up 80 percent of cost, so its selling price was $900. It did not sell, so the markup was reduced to 50 percent of cost. What was the new selling price?

6. A city had an assessed valuation of $8,000,000. The rate for school taxes was 60 cents per $100 valuation. If all but 4 percent of the taxes had been collected, how many dollars were still owed to the city?

7. Find the fourth term in the expansion of $\left(2x^2 - y\right)^{10}$.

8. Find the middle term in the expansion of $\left(a^2 - 2b\right)^8$.

Solve for x:

9. $\log_5 (x - 2) < 3$ 10. $\log_{1/3} (x + 1) < 2$

11. Sketch the graph of $f(x) = \text{Arcsin } x$. State the domain and range of the function. Then evaluate Arcsin x at $x = -\frac{1}{2}, \frac{1}{2}$, and -1.

12. Use an infinite geometric series as an aid for expressing $0.00\overline{7}$ as a common fraction.

13. Let $A = \begin{bmatrix} 2 & 0 \\ 1 & 4 \end{bmatrix}$ and $B = \begin{bmatrix} 5 & 2 \\ 3 & 4 \end{bmatrix}$. Find $2A + 3B$ and $A \cdot 2B$.

14. The equation of an ellipse is $16y^2 + x^2 - 128y + 20x + 292 = 0$. Write the equation of the ellipse in standard form and give the coordinates of the center, the length of the major axis, and the length of the minor axis. Also, determine whether the major axis is horizontal or vertical and graph the ellipse.

15. The equation of a hyperbola is $x^2 - y^2 - 6x - 10y = 0$. Write the equation of the hyperbola in standard form and give the coordinates of the vertices and the equations of the asymptotes. Then graph the hyperbola.

16. Expand as the sum of individual logarithms, each of whose argument is linear. Simplify your answer.

$$\log \left(\frac{\sqrt[4]{x^3 y z^5}}{x^2 \sqrt{yz}} \right)$$

17. Use Cramer's rule to solve for y: $\begin{cases} 3x + 2y + z = 1 \\ x - 5y - 4z = 2 \\ 2x + y = 3 \end{cases}$

18. Use the identity for $\cos A \sin B$ to find $\cos 75° \sin 15°$. Use exact values.

Solve for x:

19. $x^{\sqrt{\ln x}} = e$ 20. $\log (\ln x) = 2$

21. Show that $\tan 2x = \frac{2 \tan x}{1 - \tan^2 x}$ by using the double-angle identities for sine and cosine.

22. Show: $\dfrac{1 + \cos \theta}{\sin \theta} + \dfrac{\sin \theta}{\cos \theta} = \dfrac{\cos \theta + 1}{\sin \theta \cos \theta}$

23. Solve this triangle for a.

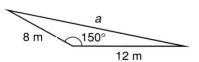

Sketch the graph of each of the following:

24. $y = 1 - 2 \cos \dfrac{1}{2}\left(x + \dfrac{\pi}{3}\right)$ 25. $y = \csc (x - \pi)$

Solve the following equations given that $0° \le x < 360°$:

26. $2 \sin^2 x + 3 \sin x = -1$ 27. $\cos^2 x - \sin^2 x = \dfrac{1}{2}$

28. Find the three third roots of $4 + 3i$ and write the roots in polar form.

29. Find the distance from the point $(1, 0)$ to the line $y - x = 2$.

30. Factor $x^4 - 16$ over the set of complex numbers. [*Hint:* $x^4 - 16 = \left(x^2\right)^2 - 4^2$]

LESSON *113* *Synthetic Division • Zeros and Roots*

113.A
synthetic division

In mathematics we use the word **algorithm** to describe a repetitive computational procedure. Thus, the way we do long division can be called a **long division algorithm.** On the left below, we use the standard long division algorithm to divide $x^4 + x^2 + 2x - 1$ by $x + 3$. On the right, we repeat the problem, but this time we omit the variables.

$$
\begin{array}{r}
x^3 - 3x^2 + 10x - 28 \\
x + 3 \overline{)\, x^4 + 0x^3 + x^2 + 2x - 1} \\
\underline{x^4 + 3x^3} \\
-3x^3 + x^2 \\
\underline{-3x^3 - 9x^2} \\
10x^2 + 2x \\
\underline{10x^2 + 30x} \\
-28x - 1 \\
\underline{-28x - 84} \\
83 \text{ (remainder)}
\end{array}
\qquad
\begin{array}{r}
1 - 3 + 10 - 28 \\
1 + 3 \overline{)\, 1 + 0 + 1 + 2 - 1} \\
\underline{① + 3} \\
-3 + 1 \\
\underline{(-3) - 9} \\
10 + 2 \\
\underline{⑩ + 30} \\
-28 - 1 \\
\underline{(-28) - 84} \\
83 \text{ (remainder)}
\end{array}
$$

We focus our attention on the numbers that have been circled and note that they are repetitions of the numbers in the line directly above them. Furthermore, each of the circled numbers is a repetition of the coefficients of the variables in the quotient. These numbers are the keys to this division process. If we omit the number 1 in the divisor and other non-key numbers, we can write the whole process in compact form, as we show on the left.

$$
\begin{array}{r|rrrrr}
3 & 1 & 0 & 1 & 2 & -1 \\
  &   & 3 & -9 & 30 & -84 \\
\hline
  & 1 & -3 & 10 & -28 & 83 \\
\end{array}
\qquad
\begin{array}{r|rrrrr}
-3 & 1 & 0 & 1 & 2 & -1 \\
   &   & -3 & 9 & -30 & 84 \\
\hline
   & 1 & -3 & 10 & -28 & 83 \\
\end{array}
$$

(Remainder: 83)   (Remainder: 83)

The entries in the bottom line on the left were obtained by subtracting. If we change the sign of the divisor to –3, we can obtain the same bottom line by adding, as we show on the right. This algorithm for division is called **synthetic division.** We restrict its use to linear divisors of the form $x - a$. Our synthetic divisor will always be equal to a. We recall that a linear divisor such as $x + 3$ can be written as $x - (-3)$, so $a = -3$.

example 113.1 Use synthetic division to divide $-4x^2 + 13 + x^3$ by $-3 + x$.

solution Before we begin, we restate the problem with the polynomials written in descending powers of the variable.

$$x^3 - 4x^2 + 13 \qquad \text{divided by} \qquad x - 3$$

We will use +3 as a synthetic divisor because we are dividing by $x - 3$. We record the coefficients of the polynomial and use zero as the coefficient of the missing x term. Then we bring down the first coefficient.

$$
\begin{array}{r|rrrr}
3 & 1 & -4 & 0 & 13 \\
\hline
  & 1 \\
\end{array}
\qquad \text{bring down 1}
$$

The rest of the steps are **multiply, record,** and **add** steps. We multiply 1 by 3, record under the – 4, and add.

$$
\begin{array}{r|rrrr}
3 & 1 & -4 & 0 & 13 \\
  &   & 3 \\
\hline
  & 1 & -1 \\
\end{array}
\qquad \text{multiply, record, add}
$$

Now we multiply −1 by 3, record, and add.

$$\begin{array}{r|rrrr} 3 & 1 & -4 & 0 & 13 \\ & & 3 & -3 & \\ \hline & 1 & -1 & -3 & \end{array}$$ multiply, record, add

Now we multiply −3 by 3, record, and add.

$$\begin{array}{r|rrrr} 3 & 1 & -4 & 0 & 13 \\ & & 3 & -3 & -9 \\ \hline & 1 & -1 & -3 & 4 \end{array}$$ multiply, record, add

The first three numbers in the bottom row are the coefficients of the quotient polynomial, and the last number is the remainder. **The quotient polynomial has a degree which is always 1 less than the degree of the original polynomial,** and the quotient polynomial is sometimes called the **depressed polynomial.** Thus our result is

$$\frac{x^3 - 4x^2 + 13}{x - 3} = x^2 - x - 3 + \frac{4}{x - 3}$$

example 113.2   Divide $2x^4 + x^2 + 2x - 1$ by $x + 3$.

solution   First we check to ensure that both polynomials are written in descending powers of the variable. They are, so we record **a synthetic divisor of −3** and remember to write a zero as the coefficient of x^3. **We begin by bringing down** the first coefficient.

$$\begin{array}{r|rrrrr} -3 & 2 & 0 & 1 & 2 & -1 \\ & & & & & \\ \hline & 2 & & & & \end{array}$$ bring down 2

Now we **multiply, record,** and **add** until the process is complete.

$$\begin{array}{r|rrrrr} -3 & 2 & 0 & 1 & 2 & -1 \\ & & -6 & 18 & -57 & 165 \\ \hline & 2 & -6 & 19 & -55 & 164 \end{array}$$

Thus we get

$$\frac{2x^4 + x^2 + 2x - 1}{x + 3} = 2x^3 - 6x^2 + 19x - 55 + \frac{164}{x + 3}$$

113.B
zeros and roots

The words **zero** and **root** can be confusing because they mean almost the same thing. The word **zero** is used with the word **polynomial,** and the word **root** is used with the word **equation.** On the left below, we show a polynomial, and on the right, we use the same polynomial to write a polynomial equation.

Polynomial	Polynomial Equation
$x^2 + 5x + 6$	$x^2 + 5x + 6 = 0$

We can write each of the polynomials as a product of factors, as we show here.

$$(x + 3)(x + 2) \qquad\qquad (x + 3)(x + 2) = 0$$

If we replace x with either −3 or −2, the expression on the left will equal 0, and the equation on the right will be a true equation. We will demonstrate this by replacing x with −3.

$$(-3 + 3)(-3 + 2) \qquad\qquad (-3 + 3)(-3 + 2) = 0$$
$$(0)(-1) \qquad\qquad\qquad (0)(-1) = 0$$
$$0 \qquad\qquad\qquad\qquad 0 = 0$$

Thus, we say that −3 is a *zero* **of the polynomial** because replacing x with −3 gives the polynomial a value of zero. Also, −3 is a *root* **of the equation** because replacing x with −3 makes the equation a true equality. The difference might seem trivial, but it is not trivial because polynomials do not have roots and equations do not have zeros. It is the other way around.

If we perform the division shown here,

$$\frac{x^2 + 5x + 6}{x + 3} = x + 2$$

we get a quotient of $x + 2$ with no remainder because $x + 3$ is a factor of $x^2 + 5x + 6$, and therefore -3 is a zero of the polynomial. If we use synthetic division to do the division, we see that the remainder is zero.

$$
\begin{array}{r|rrr}
-3 & 1 & 5 & 6 \\
   &   & -3 & -6 \\
\hline
   & 1 & 2 & 0 \qquad \text{remainder of zero}
\end{array}
$$

This zero remainder tells us that -3 is a zero of the polynomial. This demonstrates the way we use synthetic division to see if a given number is a zero of a polynomial.

example 113.3 Use synthetic division to see if -2 is a zero of $x^4 - 2x^3 + 5x - 10$.

solution We divide by -2.

$$
\begin{array}{r|rrrrr}
-2 & 1 & -2 & 0 & 5 & -10 \\
   &   & -2 & 8 & -16 & 22 \\
\hline
   & 1 & -4 & 8 & -11 & 12
\end{array}
$$

The remainder is not zero, so -2 is not a zero of the polynomial.

example 113.4 Use synthetic division to see if -3 is a root of the polynomial equation $2x^4 - 32x = 0$.

solution The first step is to bring down the coefficient of x^4. Then we repeatedly multiply, record, and add.

$$
\begin{array}{r|rrrrr}
-3 & 2 & 0 & 0 & -32 & 0 \\
   &   & -6 & 18 & -54 & 258 \\
\hline
   & 2 & -6 & 18 & -86 & 258
\end{array}
$$

The remainder is not 0, but 258, so -3 is not a root of the polynomial equation.

problem set 113

1. An urn contains 7 red marbles and 4 white marbles. Two marbles are drawn at random, one after the other, without replacement. What is the probability that the marbles are red and white, in that order?

2. The half-life of the things was 14 years. If they began with 10,000, how long would it take until only 4000 were still alive?

3. After traveling h hours at k miles per hour, the caravan stopped for a rest. If the entire trip was 400 miles, how far did the caravan still have to go?

4. The radius of the wheel was k inches. The wheel had an angular velocity of r radians per second. What was the linear speed of the wheel in meters per hour?

5. The trip out was 600 miles. The trip back was also 600 miles, but it took longer because the return speed was only one third of the outgoing speed. If the round trip took 40 hours, what were the two speeds?

6. Use synthetic division to divide $x^3 - 5x^2 + 12$ by $x - 2$.

7. Use synthetic division to divide $4x^4 - 4x^3 + x^2 - 3x + 2$ by $x + 2$.

8. Use synthetic division to see if -1 is a zero of $x^3 + 2x^2 - 3x - 4$.

9. Use synthetic division to see if -2 is a root of the following polynomial equation:
$$2x^3 - x^2 + 2x - 4 = 0$$

10. Use synthetic division to see if 5 is a root of the following polynomial equation:
$$x^4 - 10x^2 - 40x - 175 = 0$$

11. Find the fifth term in the expansion of $\left(2x^2 - y^3\right)^{15}$.

12. Find the fourth term in the expansion of $\left(3x^3 - y^2\right)^8$.

Solve for x:

13. $\log_4 (2x - 1) < 2$

14. $\log_{1/3} (2x + 1) < 2$

15. Sketch the graph of $f(x) = \text{Arccos } x$. State the domain and range of the function. Then evaluate Arccos x at $x = -\frac{1}{2}, \frac{1}{2}$, and -1.

16. Use an infinite geometric series as an aid for expressing $0.0\overline{13}$ as a common fraction.

17. The equation of an ellipse is $36x^2 + 9y^2 = 216x$. Write the equation of the ellipse in standard form and give the coordinates of the center, the length of the major axis, and the length of the minor axis. Also, determine whether the major axis is horizontal or vertical and graph the ellipse.

18. Use Cramer's rule to solve for z: $\begin{cases} x - z = 1 \\ 2x + y + 2z = 5 \\ 3x + 3y + 4z = 7 \end{cases}$

19. Write the following as a single logarithm. Simplify your answer.
$$\ln (xy - x) - \ln \left(x^2 z\right) + 2 \ln z - \ln \left(y^2 - 1\right)$$

20. Use the identity for $\sin A \sin B$ to find $\sin 285° \sin 15°$. Use exact values.

21. Solve for x: $\sqrt{\ln x} = \ln \sqrt{x}$

22. Show: $\dfrac{\tan x}{\tan x - 1} - \dfrac{\cot x}{\cot x + 1} = \dfrac{\tan x + \cot x}{\tan x - \cot x}$

23. Solve this triangle for a.

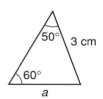

24. Sketch the graph of $y = \sec \left(x + \frac{\pi}{2}\right)$.

25. Solve $2 \sin^2 x - \left(2\sqrt{2} + \sqrt{3}\right) \sin x + \sqrt{6} = 0$ given that $0 \le x < 2\pi$.

26. Find the six sixth roots of 1 and write the roots in rectangular form. Give exact answers.

27. Simplify: $(a + 3)5^{\log_5 \left(a^2 - 5a + 6\right) - \log_5 \left(a^2 - 9\right)}$

28. Graph the solution to the system of inequalities: $\begin{cases} x^2 + y^2 \le 9 \\ y^2 - x^2 \ge 1 \end{cases}$
(*Hint*: Check all regions.)

29. Find the distance from the point $(4, -1)$ to the line $x + y = 5$.

30. Factor $x^4 + 2x^2 + 1$ over the set of complex numbers. [*Hint*: Use the factorization $x^4 + 2x^2 + 1 = \left(x^2 + 1\right)^2$.]

LESSON *114* *Graphs of Factored Polynomial Functions*

Our experience has shown that first-degree polynomial functions (linear functions) and second-degree polynomial functions (quadratic functions) are easy to graph. There are shortcuts that can be used, but if other approaches fail, these functions can always be graphed point by point by choosing values of x and using the equation to find the paired values of y. The point-by-point method can also be used to graph higher-order polynomial functions.

Graphing of higher-order polynomial functions can be facilitated if we begin by considering the number of **turning points,** the **sign** of the highest degree term in the polynomial function, and the location of the **zeros** of the polynomial function.

turning points A **turning point** is the point at the top of a "hump" in the graph of a function or at the bottom of a "valley" in the graph of a function. We have placed dots to mark the turning points of the function in the graph shown here.

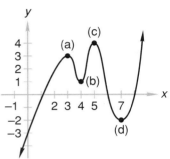

Turning points (a) and (c) are also called **local maximum points** of the function because the y coordinate of each of these points is greater than the y coordinates of nearby points on the curve. Turning points (b) and (d) are also called **local minimum points** of the function because the y coordinate of each of these points is less than the y coordinate of nearby points on the curve.

To consider turning points, we will use the **turning-point theorem** whose proof will not be given as it is a bit advanced for the level of this book. **The turning-point theorem tells us that a polynomial function has fewer turning points than the degree of the polynomial.** Thus, a third-degree polynomial function has **at most** two turning points, a fourth-degree polynomial function has **at most** three turning points, etc. Here we show the graphs of a second-degree, a third-degree, and a fourth-degree polynomial function. The graph of the second-degree polynomial function has one turning point. Graphs of second-degree polynomial functions always have exactly one turning point.

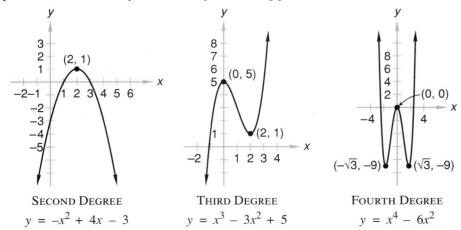

SECOND DEGREE	THIRD DEGREE	FOURTH DEGREE
$y = -x^2 + 4x - 3$	$y = x^3 - 3x^2 + 5$	$y = x^4 - 6x^2$

The graph of the third-degree polynomial function above has two turning points, the most that it can have. The graph of the fourth-degree polynomial function above has three turning points, the most that it can have.

dominant term   The term of highest degree in a polynomial is the **dominant term** because, for large absolute values of x, the value of the highest-degree term will be greater than the absolute value of the sum of all the other terms in the equation. The greater the absolute value of x, the greater the dominance of the highest-degree term becomes. **Thus, the value of the polynomial for large absolute values of x can be determined by looking at the exponent of the highest-degree term and looking at the sign of the coefficient of this term.** In the graph of the second-degree polynomial function on the previous page, the $-x^2$ term is dominant. Since $-x^2$ is negative for any real value of x, the graph will continue smoothly downward in both the positive and negative x directions, as shown.

In the center graph on the previous page, the dominant term is x^3. This term is negative for negative values of x and positive for positive values of x. In this graph, we see that for large positive values of x, the y values of the function are positive, and for large negative values of x, the y values of the function are negative. The graph will continue to increase and decrease smoothly in the positive and negative x directions, respectively.

The graph of the fourth-degree polynomial function on the right on the previous page shows that the function has increasingly large values of y in both directions because if x is not zero, x^4 is always positive, and the coefficient of x^4 is +1. If the coefficient of x^4 had been negative, then the y values would have increased negatively for large absolute values of x.

The graph of a quadratic function is always the graph of a parabola that opens either upward or downward, as we have discussed. When we look at the equation of a cubic function or a quartic function, it is nice to have some idea of the possible shapes the graph of the function could have. The general cubic equation has the form

$$f(x) = ax^3 + bx^2 + cx + d$$

The graph of a cubic function can have a **flex point** or can have a flex point and two turning points. Flex points, called *inflection points* by mathematicians, are difficult to formally define. They can be roughly described as the point on a graph where the graph switches from being "face up" to "face down," or vice versa. Mathematicians would say the same thing by saying that the flex or inflection point is the point where the graph switches from being "concave up" to "concave down," or vice versa.

Returning to our discussion of the graph of cubic functions, we note that if the x^3 term is preceded by a plus sign (a is a positive number), the graph will have one of the two forms shown on the left below. We have placed T's at the turning points and F's at the flex points. If the x^3 term is preceded by a minus sign (a is a negative number), the graphs are flipped upside down, as shown on the right below.

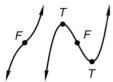 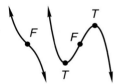

The shape of a graph is determined by the values of the coefficients a, b, and c. The vertical position of the graph can be changed by changing the value of d.

The general equation of a quartic function is

$$y = ax^4 + bx^3 + cx^2 + dx + e$$

The first term is the dominant term, and the value of x^4 is a positive number for any value of x. If a is a positive number, the graph will "open up," as in the graphs below.

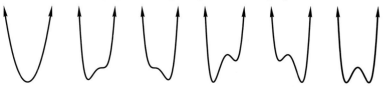

The graph of a quartic function can resemble the graph of a quadratic function, as we show on the left above. It can have one turning point and two flex points, as shown in the next two graphs. The graph can also have three turning points and two flex points, as shown in the three graphs on the right. The shape of the graph is determined by the values of the coefficients a, b, c, and d, and the vertical position of the graph is determined by the value of the constant e. If the coefficient a of the first term is a negative number, the graphs will be upside-down forms of the graphs on the previous page, as we show here.

An in-depth study of polynomial functions will reveal several interesting but seldom discussed properties of polynomials. The general form of an nth-degree polynomial function is

$$f(x) = ax^n + bx^{n-1} + cx^{n-2} + \cdots + k$$

The sum of all real and complex roots is $-b/a$, and the product of all real and complex roots is k/a if the degree of the polynomial is even and is $-k/a$ if the degree of the polynomial is odd. The average value of all the roots is

$$\text{Average of all roots} = \bar{x} = \frac{-b}{na}$$

For a quadratic polynomial, $\bar{x}$ equals the x value of the vertex. For a cubic polynomial, $\bar{x}$ equals the x value of the flex point. For a quartic polynomial, the value of $\bar{x}$ will give us a good idea of the x value of the "center" of the graph.

the zero factor theorem

Some mathematical truths are so obvious that they are easily overlooked. The **zero factor theorem** is an example. Simply stated, the zero factor theorem tells us that **if the product of two factors is zero, then at least one of the factors must be zero.** Consider the following notation:

$$(4)(\ ) = 0$$

The only possible correct entry for the second set of parentheses is zero.

$$(4)(0) = 0$$

In the same way, if we have an indicated multiplication of two factors equal to zero,

$$(\ )(\ ) = 0$$

then either the first factor must equal zero or the second factor must equal zero or both factors must equal zero. The formal statement of this theorem is as follows:

ZERO FACTOR THEOREM

If p and q are any real numbers and if $p \cdot q = 0$, then either $p = 0$ or $q = 0$, or both.

This theorem can be extended to the product of any number of factors. So if we have the equation

$$(x - 4)(x + 3)(x - 15) = 0$$

we know that at least one of the factors must equal zero. If we let x equal 4, the first factor equals zero. If x equals -3, the second factor equals zero, and if x equals 15, the third factor equals zero. Thus, the numbers 4, -3, and 15 are the only numbers that are solutions to the equation because if x has any other value, the product will not equal zero. **The zeros of a polynomial function are the values of x that cause $f(x)$ to equal zero. The graph of the function intersects the x axis at these values of x.**

The polynomial function

$$y = x^3 - 2x^2 - 5x + 6$$

can be written in factored form as

$$y = (x + 2)(x - 1)(x - 3)$$

To graph this function, it is helpful to know the values of x that make y equal zero because at these values of x the graph crosses the x axis. So we replace y with zero and get

$$0 = (x + 2)(x - 1)(x - 3)$$

We can look at the factors and use the zero factor theorem to see that if x equals -2, the first factor equals zero. If x equals 1, the second factor equals zero, and if x equals 3, the third factor equals zero. On the x axis in the figure on the left below, we place dots at x values of -2, 1, and 3. Then in the figure on the right we show the completed graph of the function.

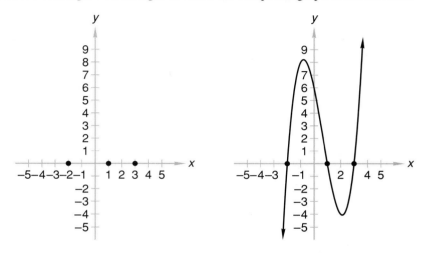

We will restrict our introduction to the graphs of higher-order polynomials to third- and fourth-degree polynomial functions that are presented in factored form, as we show in the next four examples.

example 114.1 Sketch the graph of $f(x) = x(1 - x)(x + 1)$.

solution There are three factors and each contains an x, so the degree of this function is three. We can check this by performing the indicated multiplication to get

$$f(x) = (x - x^2)(x + 1) = x^2 - x^3 + x - x^2 = -x^3 + x$$

We know that a cubic can have two turning points and a flex point or no turning points and a single flex point. It must have one of the following shapes.

The sign of the dominant term x^3 is negative, so for x values far to the left, the value of $f(x)$ will be positive, and for x values far to the right, $f(x)$ will be negative. This eliminates the two graphs on the left, so our graph must look like one of the two on the right.

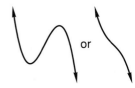

The factored polynomial is $f(x) = x(1 - x)(x + 1)$, so by inspection we see that the graph must intersect the x axis when x equals -1, 0, and 1. We graph these three points on the number line and draw the graph with two humps.

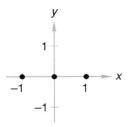 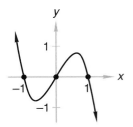

To get a more accurate sketch, we could substitute other values of x into the equation and calculate the paired values of $f(x)$. We just need a rough sketch, so we will do it for only one x value, say 0.5, and see how this helps us.

$$f(x) = x(1 - x)(x + 1)$$

$$f(0.5) = (0.5)(1 - 0.5)(0.5 + 1)$$

$$= 0.5(0.5)(1.5)$$

$$= 0.375$$

Now our sketch will look like this.

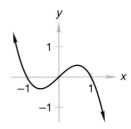

example 114.2 Sketch the graph of $p(x) = (x + 1)(x - 2)^2$.

solution The first factor $x + 1$ is called a **linear factor** because $y = x + 1$ is the equation of a line. The second factor is also called a linear factor because $y = x - 2$ is the equation of a line. The zero factor theorem tells us that this function has a value of zero when x equals -1 and also when x equals 2. The graph of the function **crosses** the x axis at $x = -1$ and will touch the x axis at $x = 2$ but will not cross it because $(x - 2)^2$ is always a positive number. Thus this function has the same sign when x is a little less than 2 as it has when x is a little greater than 2. **When a linear factor of a polynomial is raised to the second, fourth, sixth, or any even power, the graph of the polynomial does not cross the x axis at the zero caused by that linear factor.**

With this in mind, we can proceed with the graph. First we multiply the factors to find the degree of the polynomial function.

$$p(x) = (x + 1)(x - 2)^2$$

$$p(x) = (x + 1)(x^2 - 4x + 4)$$

$$p(x) = x^3 - 4x^2 + 4x + x^2 - 4x + 4$$

$$p(x) = x^3 - 3x^2 + 4$$

This is the cubic equation that crosses the x axis at $x = -1$ and "bumps" the x axis at $x = 2$.

The dominant term is x^3, which is negative for large negative values of x and positive for large positive values of x. Now we have

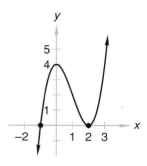

To get a better graph, we evaluate the function when x equals 1.

$$p(x) = x^3 - 3x^2 + 4$$

$$p(1) = (1)^3 - 3(1)^2 + 4$$

$$p(1) = 1 - 3 + 4$$

$$p(1) = 2$$

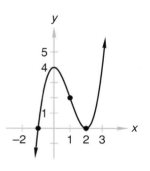

example 114.3   Which of the following graphs most resembles the graph of $g(x) = x(3 - x)(x + 2)^2$?

A.

B.

C.
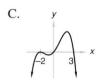

D.

solution   First we note that the graph "bumps" the x axis at $x = -2$ and crosses at $x = 3$ and $x = 0$. Next we multiply to find the degree of the polynomial function

$$g(x) = \left(3x - x^2\right)(x + 2)^2 = -x^4 - x^3 + 8x^2 + 12x$$

which is a fourth-degree polynomial function. The graph can have as many as three turning points, so this is no help. The dominant term is $-x^4$, which is negative for large negative values of x and negative for large positive values of x. This eliminates A, B, and D. **The graph of C appears to be the correct graph.** It bumps the x axis at $x = -2$ and crosses at $x = 0$ and $x = 3$.

example 114.4   Which of the following graphs most resembles the graph of $h(x) = (x - 1)^2(x + 1)$?

A.

B.

C.

D.

solution   The factors of the polynomial are $(x - 1)^2$ and $x + 1$. The graph of the polynomial function will touch the x axis $\left(h(x) = 0\right)$ when $x = 1$ and $x = -1$. The graph will cross the x axis at $x = -1$ and will "bump" the x axis at $x = 1$ because the factor $(x - 1)^2$ is raised to an even power. Graphs B and C cross at $x = -1$, so it must be one of these. If we multiply the factors, we get

$$h(x) = \left(x^2 - 2x + 1\right)(x + 1)$$
$$h(x) = x^3 - 2x^2 + x + x^2 - 2x + 1$$
$$h(x) = x^3 - x^2 - x + 1$$

The dominant term is x^3, so $h(x)$ is negative for large negative values of x and positive for large positive values of x. Graph B satisfies this condition and graph C does not, **so the answer is B.**

**problem set
114**

1. Three fair dice are rolled. What is the probability that the numbers that come up sum to 3?

2. How many positive even numbers are there that are less than 200?

3. The number sold varied linearly with the number produced. When 1300 were produced, 900 were sold, and when 2600 were produced, 1900 were sold. How many were sold when 6500 were produced?

4. Toni can translate 30 pages of Spanish in 2 hours. Mary can translate 54 pages in 3 hours. Working together, how many pages of Spanish can they translate in 4 hours?

Sketch the graphs of the following polynomial functions. Use dots to indicate the locations where the graph intersects the x axis.

5. $y = x(x - 3)(x + 3)$ 6. $y = x^2(x + 3)$

7. $y = (x - 1)(4 - x)(x + 2)$

8. Which of the following graphs most resembles the graph of $f(x) = x(x - 1)(x + 2)$?

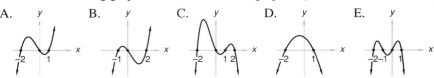

9. The graph of $h(x) = (x - 2)(x - 3)(1 - x)$ most resembles which of the following graphs?

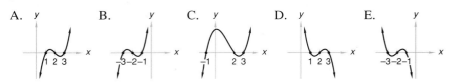

10. Use synthetic division to divide $3x^5 - 2x^3 - 20x - 40$ by $x - 2$.

11. Use synthetic division to divide $2x^3 - x$ by $x + 3$.

12. Use synthetic division to see if -4 is a root of the following polynomial equation:
$$x^4 + x^3 - x^2 + x - 172 = 0$$

13. Write all the terms in the expansion of $\left(2x - y^3\right)^4$.

14. Solve for x: $\log_{1/10}(x - 1) < 2$

15. Sketch the graph of $f(x) = \text{Arctan } x$. State the domain and range of the function. Then evaluate Arctan x at $x = -\sqrt{3}, \sqrt{3}$, and 1.

16. The equation $60x^2 + 15y^2 - 120x - 60y - 120 = 0$ is the general form of the equation of an ellipse. Write the equation of the ellipse in standard form and give the coordinates of the center, the length of the major axis, and the length of the minor axis. Also, determine whether the major axis is horizontal or vertical and graph the ellipse.

17. The equation $3x^2 - 6x - 3y^2 - 6y + 48 = 0$ is the equation of a hyperbola. Write the equation of the hyperbola in standard form and give the coordinates of the center, the coordinates of the vertices, and the equations of the asymptotes. Then graph the hyperbola.

18. Use Cramer's rule to solve for x: $\begin{cases} 3x + 2y + z = 4 \\ 4x - 3y - 2z = 9 \\ x + y + z = 3 \end{cases}$

19. Write the following as a single logarithm. Simplify your answer.
$$\log (a + b) + 2 \log c - \log \left(a^2c - b^2c\right)$$

20. Find $\cos 105° + \cos 15°$ using the identity for $\cos x + \cos y$. Use exact values.

21. Solve for x: $\ln (x + 8) - \ln (x - 1) = \ln x$

22. Show: $\sec^4 x = \tan^4 x + 2 \sec^2 x - 1$

Sketch the graph of each of the following:

23. $y = -1 + 2 \cos 3(x + \pi)$ **24.** $y = \tan (x - \pi)$

25. Solve $\cos 2x - \sin x = 1$ given that $0° \le x < 360°$.

26. (a) Find the concentration of hydrogen ions in moles per liter in a liquid if the pH of the liquid is 7.4.

(b) Find the pH of a liquid if H^+ is 7.7×10^{-7} mole per liter.

27. The third term of an arithmetic sequence is 7 and the twelfth term is 106. What is the one hundredth term of the sequence?

28. Find two numbers whose arithmetic mean is 10 and whose geometric mean is $4\sqrt{6}$.

29. Simplify: $3^{\log_3 12 + 2 \log_3 2 - \log_3 6}$

30. Factor $x^4 - 125x$ over the set of complex numbers.

LESSON *115* *The Remainder Theorem*

If we divide the polynomial $x^3 + 4x + 2$ by $x + 1$, we can make some interesting observations that can be generalized. We will use synthetic division.

$$\begin{array}{r|rrrr} -1 & 1 & 0 & 4 & 2 \\ & & -1 & 1 & -5 \\ \hline & 1 & -1 & 5 & -3 \end{array}$$

We note that the remainder is –3. Thus, we can write

$$x^3 + 4x + 2 = \left(x^2 - x + 5\right)(x + 1) - 3$$

Now, if we replace x on the left-hand side with –1, we get the value of $x^3 + 4x + 2$ when $x = -1$. If we replace x on the right-hand side with –1, we will get –3 because $(-1 + 1)$ is zero.

$$(-1)^3 + 4(-1) + 2 = \left[(-1)^2 - (-1) + 5\right](-1 + 1) - 3$$

$$-1 - 4 + 2 = [7](0) - 3$$

$$-3 = -3$$

If we use $f(x)$ to designate a polynomial, we use the symbol $f(-1)$ for the value of the polynomial when $x = -1$. We see that this value is –3, the remainder when we used synthetic division.

If we use synthetic division to divide by $x - 3$,

$$
\begin{array}{r|rrrr}
3 & 1 & 0 & 4 & 2 \\
  &   & 3 & 9 & 39 \\
\hline
  & 1 & 3 & 13 & 41 \\
\end{array}
$$

we get a remainder of 41. This means that

$$x^3 + 4x + 2 = (x^2 + 3x + 13)(x - 3) + 41$$

Now, if we replace x with 3 everywhere on the left-hand side, we get $f(3)$, and the right-hand side equals 41.

$$f(3) = (\text{some number})(3 - 3) + 41$$

$$f(3) = (\text{some number})(0) + 41$$

$$f(3) = 41$$

We can generalize this observation for evaluating a polynomial $P(x)$.

$$P(x) = Q(x)(x - c) + R$$

Now, if we replace x everywhere with c, on the left-hand side we get $P(c)$, and on the right-hand side we get R.

$$P(c) = Q(c)(c - c) + R$$

$$P(c) = Q(c)(0) + R$$

$$P(c) = R$$

This means that the remainder after division of a polynomial $P(x)$ by $x - c$ is $P(c)$. This provides us with an expeditious manner of evaluating polynomials. The general development shown here is difficult for some students, but a development using a particular polynomial is more reasonable. Thus, the problem sets will contain requests for the development using a designated polynomial, as in the next example.

example 115.1   Use the polynomial equation $f(x) = x^2 + x + 4$ and a divisor of $x - 3$ to do a specific development of the remainder theorem by showing that in this case the remainder equals $f(3)$.

solution   We begin by dividing $x^2 + x + 4$ by $x - 3$.

$$
\begin{array}{r|rrr}
3 & 1 & 1 & 4 \\
  &   & 3 & 12 \\
\hline
  & 1 & 4 & 16 \\
\end{array}
$$

We can use the results to write

$$f(x) = x^2 + x + 4 = (x + 4)(x - 3) + 16$$

Now, if we replace x everywhere with 3, we get

$$f(3) = (3)^2 + (3) + 4 = (3 + 4)(3 - 3) + 16$$

$$f(3) = 16 = (7)(0) + 16$$

$$f(3) = 16 = 16$$

We see that on the left, $f(3)$ is 16, and on the right, the remainder is 16.

example 115.2   Use the remainder theorem to evaluate $2x^3 - 8x^2 + 3x + 5$ when x equals -4.

solution   If we use synthetic division and a "divisor" of -4, the remainder will be $P(-4)$.

$$
\begin{array}{r|rrrr}
-4 & 2 & -8 & 3 & 5 \\
   &   & -8 & 64 & -268 \\
\hline
   & 2 & -16 & 67 & -263 \\
\end{array}
$$

Thus, the value of $2x^3 - 8x^2 + 3x + 5$ when x equals -4 is -263, so

$$P(-4) = \mathbf{-263}$$

example 115.3 Use the remainder theorem to evaluate $x^7 - 4x^4 + x - 3$ when $x = 2$.

solution If we use synthetic division and a divisor of 2, the remainder will be $P(2)$.

$$
\begin{array}{r|rrrrrrrr}
2 & 1 & 0 & 0 & -4 & 0 & 0 & 1 & -3 \\
  &   & 2 & 4 & 8 & 8 & 16 & 32 & 66 \\
\hline
  & 1 & 2 & 4 & 4 & 8 & 16 & 33 & 63
\end{array}
$$

The remainder is 63, so

$$P(2) = 63$$

problem set 115

1. A card was drawn from a full deck of 52 cards. What is the probability that the card was either a 2 or a spade or was the 2 of spades?

2. Peoria ran as hard as she could but could only average k miles per hour for the m miles. As a consequence, she arrived p hours late. How fast should she have run to have arrived on time?

3. The radius of the wheel was 35 centimeters, and the wheel was rolling at 60 feet per second. What was the angular velocity of the wheel in radians per minute?

4. The number of reds exceeded 4 times the number of whites by 2, and 7 times the number of whites was 14 less than 4 times the number of purples. If 4 times the sum of the whites and purples was 6 greater than 3 times the number of reds, how many were there of each color?

5. Rex and Tobi had $200 between them. Rex spent half of his and Tobi spent one tenth of hers, and they still had $124 left. How much did each person have at the beginning?

6. Use the polynomial equation $f(x) = 3x^3 - 9x^2 - 3x + 4$ and a divisor of $x + 2$ to do a specific development of the remainder theorem by showing that the remainder equals $f(-2)$.

7. Use the remainder theorem to evaluate $x^5 - 3x^4 + 3x - 4$ when $x = 2$.

8. Use synthetic division to see if 2 is a zero of $x^2 - 4x + 6$.

9. Use synthetic division to divide $x^6 - 5x^5 + 4x^3 - 2x + 1$ by $x - 1$.

Graph the following polynomial functions. Use dots to indicate locations where the graph intersects the x axis.

10. $y = x(x - 1)(x - 2)$

11. $y = (x + 1)^2(x - 1)$

12. Which of the following graphs most resembles the graph of $f(x) = x(x - 2)^2$?

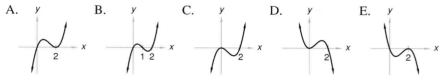

13. Find the seventh term in the expansion of $\left(x^4 - y^3\right)^{10}$.

14. Solve for x: $\log_{1/3}(3x - 2) > 1$

15. Sketch the graph of $f(x) = \text{Arcsin } x$. State the domain and range of the function. Then evaluate Arcsin x at $x = \frac{\sqrt{3}}{2}$, 1, and $-\frac{\sqrt{3}}{2}$.

16. Find the sum of the following infinite geometric series:

$$\frac{1}{4} + \frac{2}{12} + \frac{4}{36} + \cdots$$

17. Compute the arithmetic mean and the geometric mean of 6 and 24.

18. Expand as the sum of individual logarithms, each of whose argument is linear:

$$\ln\left(\frac{\sqrt[4]{(x+1)^2(y-2)^3}}{x(y+2)}\right)$$

19. Use a calculator to compute: $\dfrac{\sqrt{90\times10^5}}{\sqrt[3]{40\times10^4}}-3\sqrt[4]{9\times10^7}$

20. Find $\cos 75°$ by using the identity for $\cos(x+y)$ and the fact that $75° = 30° + 45°$. Use exact values.

Solve for x:

21. $\log_2\left(\log_3 x\right) = 2$

22. $\log_2\sqrt{x} = \sqrt{\log_2 x}$

23. Show: $\dfrac{\cot x}{\cot x - 1} - \dfrac{\tan x}{\tan x + 1} = \dfrac{\cot x + \tan x}{\cot x - \tan x}$

24. Find angle A in this triangle. Then compute the area of the triangle in square yards.

Sketch the graph of each of the following:

25. $y = \cot(x + \pi)$

26. $y = 4 - \cos 4\left(x - \dfrac{\pi}{4}\right)$

Solve the following equations given that $0° \le \theta < 360°$:

27. $\sqrt{2} - 2\sin\dfrac{3\theta}{2} = 0$

28. $\sin 2\theta - \cos 2\theta = 0$

29. Find the five fifth roots of $-1 - i$ and write the roots in polar form.

30. Use Cramer's rule to solve for x and y: $\begin{cases} 2x + y - z = 0 \\ 2y + 3z = 7 \\ 2x - 3y = 7 \end{cases}$

LESSON 116 *The Region of Interest*

In Lesson 114, we studied graphs of various polynomial functions. We saw that the graphs of the polynomial functions twist and turn through a subset of values of x and then begin to increase or decrease smoothly as the dominance of the term of highest degree becomes more pronounced. We call the spread of values of x in which these changes of direction take place the **region of interest.** We are indeed fortunate that this region can be determined by inspecting the coefficients of what is called the **normalized polynomial equation.** The normalized polynomial equation of a polynomial function is the equation of the polynomial function divided by the coefficient of the term with the highest degree.

To determine the region of interest, we select from the normalized polynomial equation the constant of the greatest absolute value and increase this absolute value by 1. If this number is used as the radius of a circle with its center at the origin of the complex plane, the circle will contain on the real axis all x values that are real roots of the equation, all x values of the turning points (local maxima or local minima points), and all x values of all flex points. In addition, the circle will contain all those points whose coordinates are the complex roots of the equation.

Here we show two equations (a) and (b) and the normalized form of each equation (a′) and (b′).

EQUATION

(a) $3x^4 - 11x^3 + 9x^2 + 13x - 10 = 0$

NORMALIZED FORM

(a′) $x^4 - \dfrac{11}{3}x^3 + 3x^2 + \dfrac{13}{3}x - \dfrac{10}{3} = 0$

EQUATION

(b) $3x^4 + 2x^3 - 2x - 4 = 0$

NORMALIZED FORM

(b′) $x^4 + \dfrac{2}{3}x^3 - \dfrac{2}{3}x - \dfrac{4}{3} = 0$

The radii of the regions of interest for equations (a) and (b) are

$$\text{Radius for (a)} = \left(\left|\frac{13}{3}\right| + 1\right) = \frac{16}{3} \qquad \text{Radius for (b)} = \left(\left|-\frac{4}{3}\right| + 1\right) = \frac{7}{3}$$

We use these values of the radius to draw the circle that contains the region of interest for each polynomial. Remember that the circle drawn is in the complex plane, so the vertical axis is measured in terms of i.

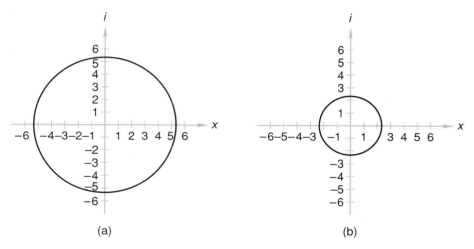

All the roots of equation (a) are contained in circle (a) on the left, and the x values of all turning points and flex points of the graph of the equation lie between $-\frac{16}{3}$ and $+\frac{16}{3}$. All the roots of equation (b) are contained in circle (b), and the x values of all turning points and flex points of the graph of the equation lie between $-\frac{7}{3}$ and $+\frac{7}{3}$.

example 116.1   Graph: $y = x^3 - 3x^2 + x + 1$

solution   There are at most two turning points, and the x^3 term is the dominant term. For positive values of x, this term has a positive value, so outside the region of interest, y will increase as x increases. For negative values of x, this term is negative, so outside the region of interest, y will increase negatively as x takes on larger negative values. The region of interest is bounded by the x values $\pm(|-3| + 1)$, or ±4. We will select a few values of x within these limits and use synthetic division and the remainder theorem to find the matching values of y. We decide to use x values of $-2, -1, 0, 1, 2, 3,$ and 4. We begin by letting x equal zero and find that y equals 1. This gives us the point $(0, 1)$. Next, we will use synthetic division with the other values of x.

$\begin{array}{r|rrrr} -2 & 1 & -3 & 1 & 1 \\ & & -2 & 10 & -22 \\ \hline & 1 & -5 & 11 & -21 \end{array}$

$\begin{array}{r|rrrr} -1 & 1 & -3 & 1 & 1 \\ & & -1 & 4 & -5 \\ \hline & 1 & -4 & 5 & -4 \end{array}$

$\begin{array}{r|rrrr} 1 & 1 & -3 & 1 & 1 \\ & & 1 & -2 & -1 \\ \hline & 1 & -2 & -1 & 0 \end{array}$

$\begin{array}{r|rrrr} 2 & 1 & -3 & 1 & 1 \\ & & 2 & -2 & -2 \\ \hline & 1 & -1 & -1 & -1 \end{array}$

$\begin{array}{r|rrrr} 3 & 1 & -3 & 1 & 1 \\ & & 3 & 0 & 3 \\ \hline & 1 & 0 & 1 & 4 \end{array}$

$\begin{array}{r|rrrr} 4 & 1 & -3 & 1 & 1 \\ & & 4 & 4 & 20 \\ \hline & 1 & 1 & 5 & 21 \end{array}$

The ordered pairs are $(0, 1)$, $(-2, -21)$, $(-1, -4)$, $(1, 0)$, $(2, -1)$, $(3, 4)$, and $(4, 21)$. We can graph five of these ordered pairs, as we show on the left below.

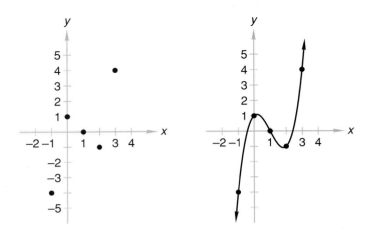

On the right, we connect the points with a smooth curve to complete the graph. We see that this third-degree polynomial equation has two turning points, so all the turning points have been found. The turning points are not necessarily exactly where we show them, but our sketch is a reasonable approximation.

example 116.2   Graph: $y = x^3 + 4x^2 + x - 6$

solution   There are at most two turning points and the x^3 term is the dominant term. From this term, we decide that y has large positive values for large positive values of x and large negative values for large negative values of x. The region of interest is bounded by the x values of -7 and 7. If we let x equal 0, we find that the paired value of y is -6. This gives us the point $(0, -6)$. To find coordinates of other points on the curve, we select x values of -4, -2, 2, and 4 and use synthetic division and the remainder theorem to find the paired values of y.

$$
\begin{array}{r|rrrr}
-4 & 1 & 4 & 1 & -6 \\
   &   & -4 & 0 & -4 \\
\hline
   & 1 & 0 & 1 & -10
\end{array}
\qquad
\begin{array}{r|rrrr}
-2 & 1 & 4 & 1 & -6 \\
   &   & -2 & -4 & 6 \\
\hline
   & 1 & 2 & -3 & 0
\end{array}
$$

$$
\begin{array}{r|rrrr}
2 & 1 & 4 & 1 & -6 \\
  &   & 2 & 12 & 26 \\
\hline
  & 1 & 6 & 13 & 20
\end{array}
\qquad
\begin{array}{r|rrrr}
4 & 1 & 4 & 1 & -6 \\
  &   & 4 & 32 & 132 \\
\hline
  & 1 & 8 & 33 & 126
\end{array}
$$

Now if we try to graph our points, we see that we still do not know much about the shape of the curve.

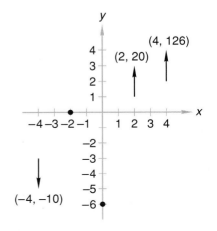

We see that when x equals -4, 2, or 4, we are off the graph, and we cannot tell anything from the other two points. So let's set x equal to -3, -1, and 1 and see what happens.

$$
\begin{array}{r|rrrr}
-3 & 1 & 4 & 1 & -6 \\
   &   & -3 & -3 & 6 \\
\hline
   & 1 & 1 & -2 & 0
\end{array}
\qquad
\begin{array}{r|rrrr}
-1 & 1 & 4 & 1 & -6 \\
   &   & -1 & -3 & 2 \\
\hline
   & 1 & 3 & -2 & -4
\end{array}
\qquad
\begin{array}{r|rrrr}
1 & 1 & 4 & 1 & -6 \\
  &   & 1 & 5 & 6 \\
\hline
  & 1 & 5 & 6 & 0
\end{array}
$$

Now we graph these points and make a couple of guesses as to the shape of the curve.

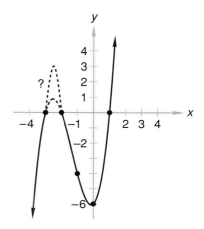

The minimum point may not be exactly as shown on the graph, and we still need a point between the x values of -2 and -3. We will let x equal -2.5 and will use a calculator to help with the arithmetic.

$$
\begin{array}{r|rrrr}
-2.5 & 1 & 4 & 1 & -6 \\
     &   & -2.5 & -3.75 & 6.875 \\
\hline
     & 1 & 1.5 & -2.75 & 0.875
\end{array}
$$

It seems that the lower of the two curves is a better guess because the point $(-2.5, 0.875)$ lies on the graph. This method of random selection of x values from the region of interest is rather primitive, but we will use it because of the practice it provides in graphing and in the evaluation of polynomials.

problem set 116

1. The urn contained 6 red marbles and 3 green marbles. Long Sam drew a marble at random and did not put it back. Then he randomly drew another marble. What is the probability that the first marble was red and the second marble was green?

2. At first there were many of them, but after 7 hours of exponential decay, they numbered only 1400. After 24 hours, they numbered only 1300. How many would remain after 60 hours of decay?

3. The race began at four o'clock and lasted until the hands on the clock pointed in the same direction. How long did the race last?

4. Five men and w women could do 2 jobs in 7 hours. How long would it take m men and 4 women to do c jobs if the men could work just as fast as the women?

5. The number who succeeded varied linearly with the number who gave it a good try. When 20 gave it a good try, 15 succeeded. When 40 gave it a good try, 25 succeeded. How many succeeded when 100 gave it a good try?

For the following polynomial functions, determine the radius of the "region of interest." Then choose various x values within the region of interest and find the corresponding y values. Apply knowledge of the basic shape of the graph from Lesson 114 and use the coordinates of points found on the graph to sketch the graph.

6. $y = x^3 - 5x + 1$

7. $y = x^3 - 2x^2 - 5x + 6$

Sketch the graphs of the following polynomial functions. Indicate the locations where the graph intersects the x axis with a dot.

8. $y = x(x - 3)(x - 4)$

9. $y = (x - 1)(x + 2)^2$

10. Which of the following graphs most resembles the graph of $f(x) = (x - 2)^2(x + 1)$?

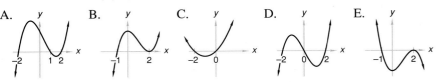

A.   B.   C.   D.   E.

11. Use synthetic division to divide $x^4 - 3x^3 + 2x^2 - 3x + 4$ by $x - 3$.

12. Use synthetic division to divide $x^5 - 1$ by $x + 1$.

13. Use the remainder theorem to evaluate $x^4 - 3x^3 + 2x - 1$ when $x = 3$.

14. Write the sixth term in the expansion of $\left(x^3 - 2y^3\right)^{12}$.

Solve for x:

15. $\log_3 (2x + 1) < 4$

16. $2 \log (x + 1) > 4$

17. Sketch the graph of $f(x) = \text{Arccos } x$. State the domain and range of the function. Then evaluate Arccos x at $x = \frac{\sqrt{3}}{2}, -\frac{\sqrt{3}}{2}$, and 0.

18. Use an infinite geometric series as an aid for expressing $2.\overline{15}$ as a common fraction.

19. What is the sum of all the terms of this geometric sequence?

$$-\frac{1}{3}, \ \frac{2}{9}, \ -\frac{4}{27}, \ \dots$$

20. Let $A = \begin{bmatrix} 2 & 0 & 0 \\ 3 & 1 & 1 \\ 4 & 0 & 2 \end{bmatrix}$ and $B = \begin{bmatrix} 5 & -1 & -1 \\ 0 & 0 & 0 \\ 2 & -3 & 2 \end{bmatrix}$. Find $B \cdot (A - B)$.

21. The equation of a hyperbola is $4x^2 - 9y^2 - 24x - 36y = 36$. Write the equation of the hyperbola in standard form and find the coordinates of the vertices and the equation of the asymptotes. Then graph the hyperbola.

22. Use Cramer's rule to solve for x and z: $\begin{cases} -x + 2y + z = 9 \\ y - 2z = 0 \\ 2x + 3y = -2 \end{cases}$

23. (a) Find the concentration of hydrogen ions in moles per liter in a solution if the pH of the solution is 9.2.

     (b) Find the pH of a solution if the concentration of hydrogen ions is 1.3×10^{-8} mole per liter.

Solve for x:

24. $2 \log_3 x - \log_3 \left(\frac{2}{3}x - \frac{1}{3}\right) = 1$

25. $x^{\sqrt{\log x}} = x$

26. Show: $\dfrac{\cos^2 x}{1 - \sin x} = \dfrac{1 + \csc x}{\csc x}$

27. Find tan 75° by using the identity for $\tan (a + b)$ and the fact that $75° = 30° + 45°$. Use exact values.

28. Solve $-\sqrt{2} - 2 \sin 3\theta = 0$ given that $0 \le \theta < 2\pi$.

29. Sketch the graph of $y = -1 - \csc x$.

30. Find the distance from the point $(1, 5)$ to the line $y = 3$.

LESSON *117*   *Prime and Relatively Prime Numbers • Rational Roots Theorem*

117.A

prime and relatively prime numbers

If a counting number can be composed as the product of two other counting numbers that are both greater than 1, we say that the counting number is a **composite number.** The number 6 is a composite number because it can be composed by multiplying 3 and 2.

$$3 \times 2 = 6$$

Some numbers have only themselves and the number 1 as factors and thus cannot be composed as a product of two other counting numbers. These numbers are called **prime numbers.** The number 7 is a prime number because 7 and 1 are its only counting number factors.

$$7 \times 1 = 7$$

A fraction is reducible if the numerator and the denominator contain a common prime factor. The fraction $\frac{10}{14}$ is reducible because 10 and 14 both have 2 as a factor.

$$\frac{10}{14} = \frac{\cancel{2} \cdot 5}{\cancel{2} \cdot 7} = \frac{5}{7}$$

A fraction cannot be reduced if the numerator and the denominator do not have a common prime factor. Although the numerator and the denominator of $\frac{10}{21}$ are composite numbers, the fraction cannot be reduced because there are no common factors.

$$\frac{10}{21} = \frac{2 \cdot 5}{3 \cdot 7}$$

We often use the words **relatively prime** to describe two counting numbers that do not have common factors other than the number 1. Thus, we could say that 10 and 21 are relatively prime. We normally think of composite numbers when we hear the words *relatively prime.* The numbers do not have to be composite numbers, however, because two different prime numbers do not have common factors other than the number 1. Thus, any two different prime numbers are also relatively prime.

Counting numbers have a property that is not immediately obvious. A statement of this property is called the **fundamental theorem of arithmetic. Each time a counting number is written as a product of prime factors, the same factors must be used.** The order of the factors may be changed, but the factors must be the same. For example, there are three ways that we can write 12 as a product of prime factors,

$$2 \cdot 2 \cdot 3 \qquad 2 \cdot 3 \cdot 2 \qquad 3 \cdot 2 \cdot 2$$

but the same factors must be used each time. This fact is sometimes useful in proofs. For instance, if we have the equation

$$5(12) = kp$$

we know immediately that kp can be written as $5 \cdot 2 \cdot 2 \cdot 3$ because the prime factors of the left-hand side must be the same as the prime factors of the right-hand side. In the same way, if J is an integer and P and Q have no common factors, and if

$$PJ = -8QQQ$$

then P must be one of the factors of -8.

$$(P)(\text{factors of } J) = (\text{factors of} -8)(\text{factors of } QQQ)$$

All the prime factors of *P* and *J* must also appear on the right-hand side because they appear on the left-hand side. Since *P* and *Q* have no factors in common, *P* must be a factor of − 8.

117.B
rational roots theorem

Polynomials are classified by the values of the coefficients of the terms of the polynomial. Some polynomials have complex numbers as coefficients and are called **complex polynomials.** We will not consider these polynomials and will restrict our observation to polynomials that have real number coefficients. We call a polynomial whose coefficients are real numbers a **real polynomial.** When we use an equals sign to set a polynomial equal to zero, we call the equation a *polynomial equation.* A polynomial equation in which the highest power of the variable is 2 is a quadratic equation. We remember that the values of the variable that make a polynomial equation a true equation are called **solutions** to the equation or **roots** of the equation. We have learned to solve quadratic equations by factoring, by completing the square, and by using the quadratic formula. Thus, we can find the roots of any quadratic equation quickly and easily. Unfortunately, the search for the roots of higher-order equations such as

$$3x^4 + 9x^2 - 5x + 2 = 0$$

is a task that is considerably more complex. In advanced algebra courses, we will learn to prove theorems that will help us find the solutions. One of these theorems is

Every polynomial equation of degree *n* has exactly *n* roots.

Therefore, this theorem allows us to state that the fourth-degree equation above has exactly four roots. The *n* roots do not have to be distinct. A root may be repeated; for example, we say that the polynomial equation $x^2 - 2x + 1 = 0$ has the root $x = 1$ twice. Another important theorem is

If a real polynomial equation has $a + bi$ as a root, then it has $a - bi$ as a root.

This theorem tells us that complex roots of real polynomial equations always occur in conjugate pairs. If a root of a polynomial equation does not have an imaginary part, then the root is a real number.

Every real number is either a rational number or an irrational number. Recall that a rational number is a number that can be written as the ratio of two integers. The **rational roots theorem** allows us to say that if the equation

$$3x^4 + 9x^2 - 5x + 2 = 0$$

has a rational root, then this root is one of the possible quotients of an integral factor of 2 (the constant term) divided by an integral factor of 3 (the leading coefficient), as we show here.

INTEGRAL FACTORS   POSSIBLE QUOTIENTS

$$\frac{\{1, -1, 2, -2\}}{\{1, -1, 3, -3\}} \;\longrightarrow\; 1, -1, 2, -2, \frac{1}{3}, -\frac{1}{3}, \frac{2}{3}, -\frac{2}{3}$$

We don't know if any of these numbers is a root, for we don't know if the equation even has a rational root. Yet we do know that if the equation has a rational root, then it must be one of these numbers. This is not much information, but it is better than no information at all. It gives us a starting point in our search for roots. If we are given the equation

$$6x^7 - 3x + 5 = 0$$

we can tell by inspection that if this equation has rational roots, they must be one of the following combinations of an integral factor of 5 divided by an integral factor of 6.

$$1, -1, \frac{1}{2}, -\frac{1}{2}, \frac{1}{3}, -\frac{1}{3}, \frac{1}{6}, -\frac{1}{6}, \frac{5}{2}, -\frac{5}{2}, \frac{5}{3}, -\frac{5}{3}, \frac{5}{6}, -\frac{5}{6}, 5, -5$$

In general, each of the possible rational roots of a polynomial equation whose coefficients are integers is a fraction whose numerator is some integral factor of the constant term divided by some integral factor of the leading coefficient.

$$\text{Rational root} = \frac{\text{An integral factor of the constant}}{\text{An integral factor of the leading coefficient}}$$

The proof is interesting, as you will see in the following example.

example 117.1   Use the polynomial equation $2x^3 + 3x^2 + 2x + 5 = 0$ to develop a specific proof of the rational roots theorem.

solution   We begin by assuming that the polynomial equation given has a rational root p/q, where p and q are integers that do not have a common factor. If so, we can replace x^3 with p^3/q^3, x^2 with p^2/q^2, and x with p/q.

$$2\frac{p^3}{q^3} + 3\frac{p^2}{q^2} + 2\frac{p}{q} + 5 = 0$$

We can eliminate the denominators if we multiply every term by q^3. We do this and get

(a) $2p^3 + 3p^2q + 2pq^2 + 5q^3 = 0$

Now we move $5q^3$ to the right-hand side and factor out a p on the left.

$$p(2p^2 + 3pq + 2q^2) = -5q^3$$

Since p and q are integers, the expression in the parentheses must also be an integer. We have

$$p(\text{some integer}) = -5qqq$$

All the factors on the left must appear on the right, and since p and q do not have a common factor, p must be a factor of –5.

Now we rearrange equation (a) so that all terms on the left have q as a factor.

(b) $3p^2q + 2pq^2 + 5q^3 = -2p^3$

Next, we factor out q.

$$q(3p^2 + 2pq + 5q^2) = -2p^3$$

$$q(\text{some integer}) = -2ppp$$

Now since p and q do not have a common factor and all the factors on the left must appear on the right, q must be a factor of –2. Thus, we have shown that if a rational root p/q exists, then p must be a factor of –5 (and hence of 5) and q must be a factor of –2 (and hence of 2).

example 117.2   Apply the rational roots theorem to list the possible rational roots of the equation $4x^{14} + 3x^8 + 7x + 3 = 0$.

solution   We do not know if this equation has a rational root, but if it does, the numerator of the root must be a factor of 3 and the denominator of the root must be a factor of 4. Therefore, any rational root of the given equation must be one of the following rational numbers:

$$\pm 1, \ \pm\frac{1}{2}, \ \pm\frac{1}{4}, \pm 3, \ \pm\frac{3}{2}, \ \pm\frac{3}{4}$$

problem set 117

1. The probability of reds was 0.4, and the probability of sunshine was 0.7. If the probability of having both reds and sunshine was 0.25, what was the probability of having reds or sunshine or both reds and sunshine?

2. A pair of dice is rolled. What is the probability that the number rolled will be either a 7 or an 11?

3. The wheel rolls merrily along at m miles per hour. If the radius of the wheel is c centimeters, what is its angular velocity in radians per second?

4. Four workers could do k jobs in m hours. If 3 more workers were hired, how long would it take them to do 35 jobs?

5. Sowega ran m miles in h hours. Then he ran k miles in m minutes. At the same overall average rate, how many minutes would it take Sowega to run 30 miles?

6. Are 136 and 81 relatively prime? If not, what common factor do both numbers share?

7. Are two consecutive positive integers always relatively prime?

8. Apply the rational roots theorem to list the possible rational roots of the equation $2x^2 + 3x + 5 = 0$.

9. Apply the rational roots theorem to list the possible rational roots of the equation $4x^{15} - 2x^9 + 6x + 3 = 0$.

For the following polynomial functions, determine the radius of the "region of interest." Then choose various x values within the region of interest and find the corresponding y values. Apply knowledge of the basic shape of the graph from Lesson 114 and use the coordinates of points found on the graph to sketch the graph.

10. $y = x^3 - 3x^2 - x + 3$ 11. $y = -x^3 + 2x - 2$

Sketch the graphs of the following polynomial functions. Indicate the locations where the graph intersects the x axis with a dot. For problem 13, factor the polynomial by first considering it as a quadratic polynomial $\left(\text{let } z = x^2\right)$. It can then be expressed as the product of two quadratics, each of which is factorable.

12. $y = -x^2(x - 1)(x + 1)$ 13. $y = x^4 - 5x^2 + 4$

14. Which of the following graphs most resembles the graph of $f(x) = x(x - 2)$?

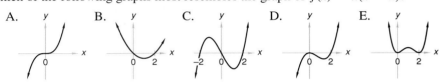

15. Use synthetic division to divide $2x^4 - 3x^2 - 4x + 1$ by $x - 2$.

16. Use the remainder theorem to evaluate $4x^3 + 2x^2 + 3x + 1$ when $x = -1$.

17. Write all the terms in the expansion of $\left(x^2 + 2y\right)^5$.

18. Solve for x: $\log_2 (3x - 1) > 4$

19. Sketch the graph of $f(x) = \text{Arctan } x$. State the domain and range of the function. Then evaluate Arctan x at $x = \frac{\sqrt{3}}{3}, -\frac{\sqrt{3}}{3}$, and -1.

20. Sketch the graph of $y = 1 + 2 \sec x$.

21. Let $A = \begin{bmatrix} 2 & 3 \\ 1 & 0 \\ 2 & 1 \end{bmatrix}$ and $B = \begin{bmatrix} -5 & 2 & 1 \\ 3 & 7 & 0 \end{bmatrix}$. Compute $A \cdot B$.

22. Expand as the sum of individual logarithms, each of whose argument is linear. Simplify your answer.

$$\log_2 \left(\frac{(x + 1)^5 \sqrt[3]{y}}{\sqrt{y + 2} \, (x + 1)^2} \right)$$

23. (a) Find the pH of a liquid if the concentration of hydrogen ions is 5.2×10^{-8} mole per liter.

    (b) Find the concentration of hydrogen ions in a liquid in moles per liter if the pH of the liquid is 10.4.

24. The equation of an ellipse is $5x^2 + 4y^2 + 10x - 16y = -1$. Write the equation of the ellipse in standard form and give the coordinates of the center, the length of the major axis, and the length of the minor axis. Then determine whether the major axis is horizontal or vertical. Graph the ellipse.

25. Use Cramer's rule to solve for y and z: $\begin{cases} 2x - y + z = 4 \\ 2y - z = -3 \\ 3x - 2y = 5 \end{cases}$

26. The geometric mean of two numbers is 15. The arithmetic mean of the two numbers is 39. Find the two numbers.

27. Solve for x: $3 \log_2 x + 2 = 2 \log_2 x - 3$

28. Show: $\dfrac{\csc x + \cot x}{\tan x + \sin x} = \cot x \csc x$

29. Solve $3 \sec^2 x - 2\sqrt{3} \tan x - 6 = 0$ given that $0° \le x < 360°$.

30. Factor $x^2 + x + 2$ over the set of complex numbers.

LESSON 118   *Roots of Polynomial Equations*

Every first-degree polynomial equation has one root. Every second-degree polynomial equation has two roots. Every third-degree polynomial equation has three roots. Every fourth-degree polynomial equation has four roots; and, if n is a counting number, every nth-degree polynomial equation has n roots.

$$x^{14} - 3x^5 - 2x = 0 \qquad\qquad -x^3 + 3 = 0 \qquad\qquad x^5 - 2x^4 + 6x - 2 = 0$$

$$\text{has 14 roots} \qquad\qquad\qquad \text{has 3 roots} \qquad\qquad\qquad \text{has 5 roots}$$

To use this statement, we must allow for equal roots as necessary. To illustrate, we will build a third-degree polynomial by multiplying the following three factors.

$$(x + 2)(x + 2)(x - 3) = 0 \qquad\qquad \text{factored form}$$

$$x^3 + x^2 - 8x - 12 = 0 \qquad\qquad \text{multiplied}$$

The numbers -2 and $+3$ are solutions to the equation. To get the required three roots, we must agree to count -2 as a root twice. Some authors handle this difficulty by saying that a third-degree polynomial equation has **at most** three distinct roots and that this equation has only two distinct roots.

We remember that if we use synthetic division and the remainder theorem and discover a root, the bottom row of numbers in the division will give us the coefficients of a polynomial whose degree is 1 less than that of the original polynomial. To illustrate, we will use synthetic division and a synthetic divisor of -2.

$$
\begin{array}{r|rrrr}
-2 & 1 & 1 & -8 & -12 \\
   &   & -2 & 2 & 12 \\
\hline
   & 1 & -1 & -6 & 0
\end{array}
$$

The zero tells us that -2 is a root, and the numbers 1, -1, and -6 are the coefficients of the **depressed polynomial** $x^2 - x - 6$. We now can write the original polynomial as a product of the factor $x + 2$ and the depressed polynomial.

$$x^3 + x^2 - 8x - 12 = (x + 2)\left(x^2 - x - 6\right)$$

Now we can find the zeros of the quadratic polynomial by using the quadratic formula.

$$x = \frac{1 \pm \sqrt{1 - 4(1)(-6)}}{2(1)} = \frac{1 \pm 5}{2} = 3, -2$$

To discuss cubic equations that have complex roots, we decide to construct a polynomial that has $1 + i$ and $1 - i$ as zeros. To do so, we use these numbers to write factors and get

$$\left[x - (1 + i)\right]\left[x - (1 - i)\right] = (x - 1 - i)(x - 1 + i) = x^2 - 2x + 2$$

Next, we decide to give the polynomial a zero of +3, so we use $x - 3$ as a factor.

$$(x^2 - 2x + 2)(x - 3) = x^3 - 5x^2 + 8x - 6$$

Now to write an equation we set our polynomial equal to 0.

$$x^3 - 5x^2 + 8x - 6 = 0$$

We have constructed a cubic equation with specified roots. Now we assume we do not know what the roots are and try to go backward and find the roots.

To begin, we use the rational roots theorem to list the possible rational roots as follows:

$$\text{Possible rational roots} = \{\pm 1, \pm 2, \pm 3, \pm 6\}$$

Next we use synthetic division with +1, −1, +2, and −2 as synthetic divisors and get a nonzero remainder each time. Then we try +3.

$$
\begin{array}{r|rrrr}
3 & 1 & -5 & 8 & -6 \\
  &   & 3 & -6 & 6 \\
\hline
  & 1 & -2 & 2 & 0
\end{array}
$$

This time we get a remainder of 0, so we know that +3 is a root. The bottom row of numbers gives us the coefficients of the depressed polynomial. This allows us to write the cubic in factored form.

$$x^3 - 5x^2 + 8x - 6 = (x - 3)(x^2 - 2x + 2)$$

Now we will use the quadratic formula to find the roots of the quadratic factor.

$$x = \frac{2 \pm \sqrt{4 - 4(1)(2)}}{2(1)} = \frac{2 \pm \sqrt{-4}}{2} = 1 \pm i$$

Thus, we have found that the roots are 3, $1 + i$, and $1 - i$.

example 118.1 Find the roots of $2x^3 + 3x^2 - 7x - 3 = 0$.

solution We begin by using the rational roots theorem to make a list of the possible rational roots. The list is

$$+1, -1, +3, -3, +\frac{1}{2}, -\frac{1}{2}, +\frac{3}{2}, -\frac{3}{2}$$

Next, we use synthetic division to see if any member of this list is really a root.

$$
\begin{array}{r|rrrr}
1 & 2 & 3 & -7 & -3 \\
  &   & 2 & 5 & -2 \\
\hline
  & 2 & 5 & -2 & -5
\end{array}
\qquad
\begin{array}{r|rrrr}
-1 & 2 & 3 & -7 & -3 \\
   &   & -2 & -1 & 8 \\
\hline
   & 2 & 1 & -8 & 5
\end{array}
$$

$$
\begin{array}{r|rrrr}
3 & 2 & 3 & -7 & -3 \\
  &   & 6 & 27 & 60 \\
\hline
  & 2 & 9 & 20 & 57
\end{array}
\qquad
\begin{array}{r|rrrr}
-3 & 2 & 3 & -7 & -3 \\
   &   & -6 & 9 & -6 \\
\hline
   & 2 & -3 & 2 & -9
\end{array}
$$

$$
\begin{array}{r|rrrr}
\frac{1}{2} & 2 & 3 & -7 & -3 \\
  &   & 1 & 2 & -\frac{5}{2} \\
\hline
  & 2 & 4 & -5 & -\frac{11}{2}
\end{array}
\qquad
\begin{array}{r|rrrr}
-\frac{1}{2} & 2 & 3 & -7 & -3 \\
   &   & -1 & -1 & 4 \\
\hline
   & 2 & 2 & -8 & 1
\end{array}
$$

$$
\begin{array}{r|rrrr}
\frac{3}{2} & 2 & 3 & -7 & -3 \\
  &   & 3 & 9 & 3 \\
\hline
  & 2 & 6 & 2 & 0
\end{array}
$$

Since the remainder of the synthetic division by $\frac{3}{2}$ is 0, we know that $\frac{3}{2}$ is a root of the polynomial equation and can use the results of the division by $\frac{3}{2}$ to write the polynomial in factored form as

$$\left(x - \frac{3}{2}\right)\left(2x^2 + 6x + 2\right) = 0$$

or $\qquad \left(x - \frac{3}{2}\right)(2)\left(x^2 + 3x + 1\right) = 0$

Next, we will use the quadratic formula to find the roots of the quadratic polynomial equation.

$$x = \frac{-3 \pm \sqrt{9 - 4(1)(1)}}{2(1)}$$

$$x = -\frac{3}{2} \pm \frac{\sqrt{5}}{2}$$

Thus, the roots of the given cubic equation are

$$\frac{3}{2}, -\frac{3}{2} + \frac{\sqrt{5}}{2}, -\frac{3}{2} - \frac{\sqrt{5}}{2}$$

example 118.2   Find the roots of $x^3 + 2x^2 + 6x + 5 = 0$.

solution   First, we list the possible rational roots.

$$\pm 1, \pm 5$$

Now we use synthetic division to check these possible roots.

$$\begin{array}{r|rrrr} 1 & 1 & 2 & 6 & 5 \\ & & 1 & 3 & 9 \\ \hline & 1 & 3 & 9 & 14 \end{array} \qquad \begin{array}{r|rrrr} -1 & 1 & 2 & 6 & 5 \\ & & -1 & -1 & -5 \\ \hline & 1 & 1 & 5 & 0 \end{array}$$

The remainder when we use a synthetic divisor of −1 is 0, so we know −1 is a root. It is not necessary to try to use a synthetic divisor of +5 and −5, as we can already write the polynomial in factored form as

$$(x + 1)\left(x^2 + x + 5\right) = 0$$

Now we use the quadratic formula.

$$x = \frac{-1 \pm \sqrt{1 - 4(1)(5)}}{2(1)}$$

$$x = -\frac{1}{2} \pm \frac{\sqrt{19}}{2}i$$

So the roots are

$$-1, -\frac{1}{2} + \frac{\sqrt{19}}{2}i, -\frac{1}{2} - \frac{\sqrt{19}}{2}i$$

problem set 118

1. A single die is rolled twice. What is the probability that the first number rolled will be greater than 4 and also that the second number rolled will be less than 4?

2. The increase was exponential. Fourteen years after the Big Crash there were 400 grams, and 40 years after the Big Crash there were 2800 grams. How many years after the Big Crash would it be before there were 5000 grams?

3. Widlo's speed was 20 miles per hour less than Bridgett's speed. Thus, Widlo could travel 400 miles in one half the time it took Bridgett to travel 1120 miles. Find the speeds of both and the times of both.

4. One pipe could fill 2 tanks in 3 hours, and the other pipe could fill 1 tank in 4 hours. If both pipes were used, how long would it take to fill an empty tank?

5. Some were fast and the rest were slow. Ten times the number of fast was 180 less than twice the number of slow. Also, one half the number of slow exceeded 3 times the number of fast by 40. How many were fast and how many were slow?

6. One zero of $y = x^3 - 2x^2 - 9x + 18$ is 3. What are the other two zeros?

7. One root of $4x^3 - 13x + 6 = 0$ is –2. What are the other two roots?

8. Find the roots of the polynomial equation $4x^3 - 4x^2 - 5x + 3 = 0$.

9. Are 96 and 60 relatively prime? If not, what common factor do both numbers share?

10. Apply the rational roots theorem to list the possible rational roots of the equation $4x^7 - 8x^3 + 2x - 6 = 0$.

For the following polynomial functions, determine the radius of the "region of interest." Then choose various x values within the region of interest and find the corresponding y values. Apply knowledge of the basic shape of the graph from Lesson 114 and use the coordinates of points found on the graph to sketch the graph.

11. $y = 4x^3 - 4x^2 - 5x + 3$ **12.** $y = x^4 - x^2 + 1$

Sketch the graphs of the following polynomial functions. Indicate the locations where the graph intersects the x axis with a dot. For problem 14, note that the term $(x - 2)$ can be factored from the first two and last two terms.

13. $y = (1 - x)(1 + x)(x - 3)$ **14.** $y = x^3 - 2x^2 - 9x + 18$

15. Which of the following graphs most resembles the graph of $f(x) = x(x - 2)(x + 2)$?

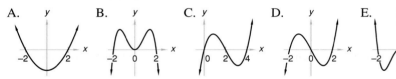

16. Use the remainder theorem to evaluate $x^6 - 3x^4 + 2x^2 - 1$ when $x = -1$.

17. Use synthetic division to divide $3x^5 - 7x^4 + 9x^3 - 12x + 2$ by $x + 1$.

18. Write all the terms in the expansion of $\left(x^3 - y^2\right)^5$.

19. Solve for x: $3 \log_{1/2} (x - 2) < 9$

20. Use an infinite geometric series to express $0.42\overline{3}$ as a common fraction.

21. Sketch the graph of $f(x) = $ Arcsin x. State the domain and range of the function. Then evaluate Arcsin x at $x = \frac{\sqrt{2}}{2}, -\frac{\sqrt{2}}{2}$, and 0.

22. Let $A = \begin{bmatrix} 2 & 1 & 3 \\ 1 & 0 & 1 \\ 2 & 0 & 2 \end{bmatrix}$ and $B = \begin{bmatrix} 1 & 0 \\ 1 & 0 \\ 1 & 1 \end{bmatrix}$. Compute $2A \cdot B$.

23. The equation of a hyperbola is $25y^2 + 100y - 9x^2 - 54x = 206$. Write the equation of the hyperbola in standard form and give the coordinates of the vertices and the equations of the asymptotes. Then graph the hyperbola.

24. Find the third term in the expansion of $\left(2x^2 - \dfrac{1}{x}\right)^7$.

25. Expand as the sum of individual logarithms, each of whose argument is linear:

$$\log_3\left(\frac{(x + 1)^2 \sqrt[3]{x + 2}}{(x - 3)}\right)$$

Solve for x:

26. $\log_2 \left(\log_2 x \right) = 4$ **27.** $4^{x+2} = 2^{3x-1}$

28. Show: $\cos 2x + \sin 2x + 2\sin^2 x = (\sin x + \cos x)^2$

29. Sketch the graph of $y = -3 + 5 \csc x$.

30. Solve $2\cot^2 x + 3\csc x = 0$ given that $0 \leq x < 2\pi$.

LESSON *119* *Descartes' Rule of Signs • Upper and Lower Bound Theorem • Irrational Roots*

119.A
Descartes' rule of signs

There is no single direct method of finding the roots of polynomial equations, and the simplest way to find these roots often involves ingenuity as well as skill. The task is simplified somewhat by mustering all the knowledge that we have concerning the roots of these equations.

In the preceding lesson, we again noted that every nth-degree equation has exactly n roots. Now we show that the number of positive real roots of a polynomial with real coefficients can be estimated by counting the number of sign changes in the polynomial when the terms of the polynomial are written in descending powers of the variable. We say *estimated* because pairs of complex roots also cause sign changes, and we don't know how many sign changes are caused by the real roots and how many are caused by pairs of complex roots. Thus, three sign changes could indicate three positive real roots or one positive real root, with the other two sign changes caused by a pair of complex roots. If we encounter five sign changes, we could have five positive roots or three positive roots in addition to one pair of complex roots, or one positive root in addition to two pairs of complex roots. The same reasoning process tells us that six sign changes would indicate that we have six positive roots, four positive roots, two positive roots, or no positive roots. Since complex roots always occur in pairs, one change in sign tells us that we have one real root. If the factors are $x + 2$ and $x - 3$, the only positive real root is $+3$. We note that the polynomial equation formed by multiplying these factors and equating the product to zero has one change in sign, indicated below by the symbol ©:

$$x^2 - x - 6 = 0$$
$$+ \quad \text{©} - \quad \quad -$$

The polynomial in the following equation

$$x^4 - 2x^3 + 3x^2 + 4x - 7 = 0$$
$$+ \text{©} - \text{©} + \quad + \text{©} -$$

has three changes in sign, so this equation has either three positive real roots or one positive real root. When sign changes are counted, the fact that the term of a particular power is missing is not considered. The next polynomial does not have an x^3 term, but this is not considered. This polynomial

$$x^6 - 4x^5 + 3x^4 - 2x^2 - 3x + 4 = 0$$
$$+ \text{©} - \text{©} + \text{©} - \quad - \text{©} +$$

has four sign changes. The four sign changes tell us that there are four positive real roots *or* two positive real roots *or* zero positive real roots. **The number of positive real roots of a polynomial equation with real coefficients equals the number of sign changes in the polynomial $p(x)$, or that number less 2, or less 4, or less 6, etc.**

If we consider the original polynomial to be $p(x)$, then we can find $p(-x)$ by replacing x everywhere with $-x$. The resulting polynomial will be exactly the same as the original polynomial except that the signs of the terms whose exponents are odd will be the opposite of the signs of these terms in $p(x)$.

$$p(x) = x^4 - 2x^3 + 2x - 5 \qquad p(-x) = (-x)^4 - 2(-x)^3 + 2(-x) - 5$$
$$= x^4 + 2x^3 - 2x - 5$$

We see that in this example $p(-x)$ is the same as $p(x)$ except that the signs of the x^3 term and the x^1 term are changed. **The number of negative real roots of a polynomial equation with real coefficients equals the number of sign changes in $p(-x)$, or that number less 2, or less 4, or less 6, etc.**

example 119.1   Discuss the number of possible positive real roots of $x^5 - 2x^4 + 3x^3 - 5x^2 + x - 2 = 0$.

solution   To find the number of positive real roots, we count the number of sign changes in $p(x)$.

$$p(x) = x^5 - 2x^4 + 3x^3 - 5x^2 + x - 2$$
$$+\,ⓒ\,-\,ⓒ\,+\,ⓒ\,-\,ⓒ\,+\,ⓒ\,-$$

There are five sign changes in $p(x)$, so **the given equation has five positive real roots, or three positive real roots, or one positive real root.**

example 119.2   Discuss the number of negative real roots of $2x^5 + 3x^4 + 4x^3 + 5x^2 + x + 2 = 0$.

solution   We begin by writing $p(-x)$ and counting the sign changes.

$$p(-x) = -2x^5 + 3x^4 - 4x^3 + 5x^2 - x + 2$$
$$-\,ⓒ\,+\,ⓒ\,-\,ⓒ\,+\,ⓒ\,-\,ⓒ\,+$$

We count five sign changes in $p(-x)$, so **the original equation has five negative real roots, or three negative real roots, or one negative real root.**

119.B
upper and lower bound theorem

The constants in some polynomial equations are such that the region of interest as determined by the method of Lesson 116 is not sufficiently restrictive to be of much use. The equation of the function graphed below is $y = x^4 - 13x^2 + 35$. We see that all real zeros for this polynomial lie between -5 and 5, but the region-of-interest method gives us bounds of -36 and 36. We can get more restrictive bounds for this equation by using the upper and lower bound theorem.

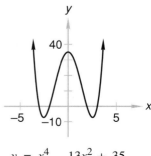

$$y = x^4 - 13x^2 + 35$$

To determine an upper bound for real roots of a polynomial equation, we use synthetic division and use positive integers (integers for convenience) as divisors. If every nonzero number in the bottom row is positive or if every nonzero number in the bottom row is negative, there is no real root greater than the positive integer used as the divisor. For the polynomial of this example, we will illustrate by using $+1$, $+3$, and $+4$ as synthetic divisors.

```
1│ 1   0  -13    0   35        3│ 1   0  -13    0   35
       1    1  -12  -12               3    9  -12  -36
   ─────────────────────           ─────────────────────
   1   1  -12  -12   23           1   3   -4  -12   -1


              4│ 1   0  -13    0   35
                     4   16   12   48
                 ─────────────────────
                 1   4    3   12   83
```

When we use 1 as a synthetic divisor, we get a remainder of 23 and two sign changes. The nonzero remainder tells us that 1 is not a root, and the sign changes tell us that 1 is not necessarily an upper bound. When we use 3 as a synthetic divisor, the nonzero remainder tells us that 3 is not a root, and the sign change tells us that 3 is not necessarily an upper bound. Finally, when we use 4 as a synthetic divisor, we get a nonzero remainder and a bottom row with no sign changes. This tells us that 4 is not a root and that there is no root greater than 4, so 4 is an upper bound.

To determine a lower bound, we again use synthetic division, but use negative integers as synthetic divisors. For lower bounds we look for alternating signs because a bottom row of alternating signs tells us that the divisor is a lower bound and that there are no real roots less than this negative divisor. If a zero appears in the bottom row, we can consider the zero to be positive or negative in order to get alternating signs. For the problem under consideration, we will try divisors of −1, −3, and −4.

```
-1│ 1    0  -13    0   35       -3│ 1    0  -13    0   35
        -1    1   12  -12              -3    9   12  -36
    ─────────────────────           ─────────────────────
    1   -1  -12   12   23           1   -3   -4   12   -1


            -4│ 1    0  -13    0   35
                   -4   16  -12   48
               ─────────────────────
               1   -4    3  -12   83
```

When we use −1 and −3 as synthetic divisors, we do not get alternating signs, so neither of these numbers is guaranteed to be a lower bound. But the synthetic divisor of −4 gives us the alternating signs we seek, and thus we know that there is no real root less than −4. So −4 is a lower bound.

example 119.3   Use the upper and lower bound theorem to find an upper and a lower bound for the real roots of the equation $x^2 - x - 21 = 0$.

solution   **To find an upper bound, we use synthetic division with positive integers as divisors and look for a bottom row in which all nonzero numbers have the same signs.** We will use 1, 2, 3, 4, 5, 6, …, as synthetic divisors.

```
1│ 1  -1  -21       2│ 1  -1  -21       3│ 1  -1  -21
       1    0              2    2              3    6
   ─────────────      ─────────────      ─────────────
   1   0  -21         1   1  -19         1   2  -15


4│ 1  -1  -21       5│ 1  -1  -21       6│ 1  -1  -21
       4   12              5   20              6   30
   ─────────────      ─────────────      ─────────────
   1   3   -9         1   4   -1         1   5    9
```

The divisor of 6 gives us a row of all positive numbers, so we know there are no real roots greater than 6.

To find a lower bound, we will use negative integers as divisors and look for a bottom row in which the signs alternate. For synthetic divisors we will use $-1, -2, -3, -4, -5, \ldots$.

$$
\begin{array}{r|rrr}
-1 & 1 & -1 & -21 \\
   &   & -1 & 2 \\
\hline
   & 1 & -2 & -19
\end{array}
\qquad
\begin{array}{r|rrr}
-2 & 1 & -1 & -21 \\
   &   & -2 & 6 \\
\hline
   & 1 & -3 & -15
\end{array}
\qquad
\begin{array}{r|rrr}
-3 & 1 & -1 & -21 \\
   &   & -3 & 12 \\
\hline
   & 1 & -4 & -9
\end{array}
$$

$$
\begin{array}{r|rrr}
-4 & 1 & -1 & -21 \\
   &   & -4 & 20 \\
\hline
   & 1 & -5 & -1
\end{array}
\qquad
\begin{array}{r|rrr}
-5 & 1 & -1 & -21 \\
   &   & -5 & 30 \\
\hline
   & 1 & -6 & 9
\end{array}
$$

When we use -5 as a divisor, we get a bottom row of alternating signs, so we know there are no real roots less than -5. **Thus, we know that all real roots lie between -5 and 6.**

example 119.4   Use the upper and lower bound theorem to find an upper and a lower bound for the real roots of the equation $x^3 - 21x + 20 = 0$.

solution   We begin by using a synthetic divisor of $+1$.

$$
\begin{array}{r|rrrr}
1 & 1 & 0 & -21 & 20 \\
  &   & 1 & 1 &   \\
\hline
  & 1 & 1 & -20 &
\end{array}
$$

This is enough to see that 1 is not an upper bound because the divisor must be large enough to overcome the -21 in the third step to get all positive numbers in the bottom row. For this reason, we decide to skip 2 and 3 and try 4 and 5 as synthetic divisors.

$$
\begin{array}{r|rrrr}
4 & 1 & 0 & -21 & 20 \\
  &   & 4 & 16 &   \\
\hline
  & 1 & 4 & -5 &
\end{array}
\qquad
\begin{array}{r|rrrr}
5 & 1 & 0 & -21 & 20 \\
  &   & 5 & 25 & 20 \\
\hline
  & 1 & 5 & 4 & 40
\end{array}
$$

We terminated the division by 4 as soon as we got a sign change (-5). **The division by 5 yields all positive numbers in the bottom row, so we know there are no roots of the polynomial that are greater than 5.** For a lower bound, we play a hunch and begin with $-4, -5,$ and -6.

$$
\begin{array}{r|rrrr}
-4 & 1 & 0 & -21 & 20 \\
   &   & -4 & 16 &   \\
\hline
   & 1 & -4 & -5 &
\end{array}
\qquad
\begin{array}{r|rrrr}
-5 & 1 & 0 & -21 & 20 \\
   &   & -5 & 25 & -20 \\
\hline
   & 1 & -5 & 4 & 0
\end{array}
$$

$$
\begin{array}{r|rrrr}
-6 & 1 & 0 & -21 & 20 \\
   &   & -6 & 36 & -90 \\
\hline
   & 1 & -6 & 15 & -70
\end{array}
$$

We find that -5 is a root and that there are no real roots less than -5 because a zero in the bottom row can be considered as either positive or negative. We consider this 0 to be negative to get a row of alternating signs. We also use -6 as a divisor and note that the last row also contains alternating signs, as we would have predicted.

119.C
irrational roots

We have restricted our investigation of the real roots of polynomial equations to roots that are rational numbers. The list of possible rational roots can be determined by using the rational roots theorem. Unfortunately, there is no similar theorem for finding a list of possible irrational roots, and these roots can only be estimated by using other numerical methods. If the value of a polynomial is positive for some value of x and negative for another value of x, we know that the polynomial will have a value of zero for some x between these two values. For example, suppose we know the coordinates of two points on the graph of a polynomial function as shown. We then know the polynomial will have a value of zero for some x value between 2 and 3.

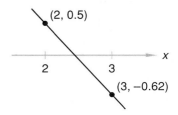

The procedure used in the past for finding irrational roots required paper-and-pencil calculations and was long and involved. Now we can use a computer or a graphing calculator to find a very good estimate quickly and easily.

problem set 119

1. A ball is dropped from a height of 100 ft. After each bounce it rebounds $\frac{1}{5}$ of the distance it fell. What is the total distance the ball will travel?

2. One card is drawn from a full deck. What is the probability that the card will be red or will be an ace or will be a red ace?

3. The decrease was exponential. Five years after the decrease began, Tim found that only 800 remained, and to his dismay, only 500 remained after 7 years. How many remained after 10 years had gone by?

4. Cordan's speed was 20 miles an hour greater than that of Wilda. Thus, Cordan could travel 240 miles in 2 hours less than it took Wilda to travel 160 miles. Find the speeds and times of both.

5. Some were red and the rest were blue. Ten times the number of reds exceeded twice the number of blues by 26. If the number of blues exceeded the number of reds by 7, how many were red and how many were blue?

Use Descartes' rule of signs to determine the possible number of:

6. Positive real roots of $x^4 - 2x^3 + 3x^2 + 4x - 7 = 0$

7. Negative real roots of $3x^4 - 4x^3 + 2x^2 + 5x - 2 = 0$

8. Positive real roots of $6x^5 - 17x^4 - 3x^3 + 22x^2 - 7x + 20 = 0$

9. Negative real roots of $2x^5 - 3x^4 - 5x^3 + 11x^2 - 4x + 5 = 0$

Use synthetic division with integers as divisors and the upper and lower bound theorem to find upper and lower bounds for the real roots of the following polynomial equations:

10. $x^3 - 3x + 19 = 0$ 11. $x^4 - 2x^3 - 7x + 5 = 0$

Find the roots of the following polynomial equations:

12. $x^3 + 2x^2 - x - 2 = 0$ 13. $x^3 - 3x^2 + 4x - 12 = 0$

14. One zero of $y = x^3 - 6x^2 + 13x - 10$ is 2. What are the other two zeros?

15. One zero of $y = 3x^3 - x^2 + 2x - 4$ is 1. What are the other two zeros?

16. Apply the rational roots theorem to list the possible rational roots of the equation $8x^7 - 5x^3 + 3 = 0$.

17. Are 102 and 35 relatively prime? If not, what common factor do both numbers share?

For the following polynomial functions, determine the radius of the "region of interest." Then choose various x values within the region of interest and find the corresponding y values. Apply knowledge of the basic shape of the graph from Lesson 114 and use the coordinates of points found on the graph to sketch the graph.

18. $y = x^3 + 2x^2 - x - 2$ **19.** $y = -x^4 + x^2 + 2$

Sketch the graphs of the following polynomial functions. Indicate the locations where the graph intersects the x axis with a dot. For problem 21, note that the term $(x + 2)$ can be factored from the first two and last two terms.

20. $y = (x - 2)(x + 1)^2$ **21.** $y = x^3 + 2x^2 - x - 2$

22. Use the remainder theorem to evaluate $x^5 - 3x$ when $x = -2$.

23. Write all the terms in the expansion of $\left(x + \dfrac{1}{x} \right)^3$.

24. Solve for x: $x^{2 \ln x} = x$

25. Sketch the graph of $y = 1 + \dfrac{1}{2} \tan x$.

26. Show: $\sin^2 \theta = \cos^2 \theta \left(\dfrac{1 - \cos 2\theta}{1 + \cos 2\theta} \right)$

27. Solve $\sec^2 x + \tan^2 x = 3$ given that $0° \le x < 360°$.

28. Solve for x: $\log (x - 2) > 2$

29. Write the four fourth roots of $-i$ in polar form.

30. Express $\log_6 72$ in terms of base 10 logarithms. Do not find a numerical answer.

LESSON 120 *Matrix Algebra • Finding Inverse Matrices*

120.A

matrix algebra

We have solved systems of linear equations by using the substitution method, the elimination method, or Cramer's rule. We can also use matrix algebra to solve systems of linear equations. As the first step, we review matrix multiplication by multiplying a 2×2 matrix of numbers by a 2×1 matrix whose members are x and y.

$$\begin{bmatrix} 4 & 1 \\ 11 & 3 \end{bmatrix} \cdot \begin{bmatrix} x \\ y \end{bmatrix} = \begin{bmatrix} 4x + y \\ 11x + 3y \end{bmatrix}$$

The products of the first row of the left matrix and the only column of the second matrix are $4x$ and y, and their sum is $4x + y$. The sum of the products of the second row of the left matrix and the only column of the second matrix is $11x + 3y$. This is important because it shows us that the 2×2 system of linear equations

$$\begin{cases} 4x + y = 7 \\ 11x + 3y = 20 \end{cases}$$

can be written as a matrix equation

$$\begin{bmatrix} 4 & 1 \\ 11 & 3 \end{bmatrix} \cdot \begin{bmatrix} x \\ y \end{bmatrix} = \begin{bmatrix} 7 \\ 20 \end{bmatrix}$$

and then we can use the algebra of matrices to solve for x and y. Because the 2×2 matrix is composed of the coefficients of x and y, we call this matrix the **coefficient matrix.** To show how the algebra of matrices is almost exactly the same as the algebra of real numbers, we will preface the solution of this matrix equation with the solution of a very simple real-number algebraic equation that contains x as its only variable. We will be able to compare the solution of the simple equation with the solution of the matrix equation and see that the procedures are very similar.

To solve the following equation for x, we want to get rid of the 4 on the left-hand side and leave the x all by itself.

$$4x = 12$$

If we multiply 4 by $\frac{1}{4}$, the product is 1. If we multiply one side of the equation by $\frac{1}{4}$, we must also multiply the other side by $\frac{1}{4}$.

$$\left(\frac{1}{4}\right)4x = \left(\frac{1}{4}\right)(12) \qquad \text{multiplied by } \frac{1}{4}$$

$$1x = 3 \qquad\qquad \text{simplified}$$

One fourth is called the **multiplicative inverse** of 4 because the product of these two numbers is the number 1. Every number except zero has its own multiplicative inverse. If the left-hand side of the equation had been $5x$, we would have multiplied by $\frac{1}{5}$ and again the result would have been $1x$. Now if we multiply x by 1, the product is x.

$$1x = 3 \qquad \text{equation}$$

$$x = 3 \qquad \text{multiplied}$$

We say that the number 1 is the **identity for multiplication** because the product of 1 and any number is identically the number itself. The product of 1 and x is identically x.

To solve the matrix equation above, we would like to get rid of the 2×2 matrix in front of the matrix with x and y as entries and get a solution for x and y. We remember from Lesson 74 that if the determinant of a matrix of coefficients is zero, the system of equations does not have a unique solution, and if the determinant is not zero, a unique solution exists. We want to use the inverse matrix to find a solution, so it should not surprise us to find that **every square matrix whose determinant is not zero has an inverse matrix for multiplication.** The product of a square matrix and its inverse matrix is the identity matrix, just as the product of 4 and $\frac{1}{4}$ equals 1, the identity for real numbers. Also, the order of multiplication of a matrix and its inverse does not matter, unlike the usual case when the product of matrices is involved. Therefore, the product of a matrix and its inverse matrix and the product of these two matrices in reverse order both equal the identity matrix. The determinant of our square matrix is $4 \cdot 3 - 11 \cdot 1$, which equals 1. Since the determinant of our matrix is not zero, this 2×2 matrix does have an inverse matrix. We will show how to find the inverse matrix of a square matrix in the next section of this lesson. For the problem at hand, we will just provide the inverse matrix so we can use it in our solution.

To get rid of the 2×2 matrix in front of the x-and-y matrix, we multiply both sides of the equation by the inverse of the 2×2 matrix, as we show here.

$$\underset{\substack{\text{INVERSE} \\ \text{MATRIX}}}{\begin{bmatrix} 3 & -1 \\ -11 & 4 \end{bmatrix}} \cdot \underset{\substack{\text{COEFFICIENT} \\ \text{MATRIX}}}{\begin{bmatrix} 4 & 1 \\ 11 & 3 \end{bmatrix}} \cdot \begin{bmatrix} x \\ y \end{bmatrix} = \underset{\substack{\text{INVERSE} \\ \text{MATRIX}}}{\begin{bmatrix} 3 & -1 \\ -11 & 4 \end{bmatrix}} \cdot \begin{bmatrix} 7 \\ 20 \end{bmatrix}$$

When we multiply the first two matrices on the left, we get the identity matrix in the same way we got 1 when we multiplied 4 by $\frac{1}{4}$.

$$\begin{bmatrix} 1 & 0 \\ 0 & 1 \end{bmatrix} \cdot \begin{bmatrix} x \\ y \end{bmatrix} = \begin{bmatrix} 3 & -1 \\ -11 & 4 \end{bmatrix} \cdot \begin{bmatrix} 7 \\ 20 \end{bmatrix}$$

The product of the identity matrix and the matrix with x and y is identically the matrix with x and y as entries. The product of the two matrices on the right on the previous page is a 2×1 matrix, as we show here.

$$\begin{bmatrix} x \\ y \end{bmatrix} = \begin{bmatrix} 1 \\ 3 \end{bmatrix}$$

Finally, we remove the brackets and see that the solution to our 2×2 system of linear equations is

$$x = 1 \quad \text{and} \quad y = 3$$

120.B
finding inverse matrices

We can develop formulas that can be used to find the inverse matrix for multiplication for a 2×2 matrix, a 3×3 matrix, or for a square matrix of any number of rows and columns. The formula for a 2×2 square matrix is shown here. We use the letters a, b, c, and d to represent the entries in the original matrix and in the inverse matrix.

ORIGINAL   INVERSE
MATRIX   MATRIX

$$\begin{bmatrix} a & b \\ c & d \end{bmatrix} \qquad \begin{bmatrix} \dfrac{d}{ad-cb} & \dfrac{-b}{ad-cb} \\ \dfrac{-c}{ad-cb} & \dfrac{a}{ad-cb} \end{bmatrix}$$

We note that the denominator of each entry in the inverse matrix is the determinant of the original matrix. It is difficult to remember this form for the inverse matrix, so many books show the inverse matrix as a scalar product of the reciprocal of the determinant of the original matrix and the original matrix with a and d interchanged and with minus signs before b and c, as we show here.

$$\frac{1}{ad-bc} \begin{bmatrix} d & -b \\ -c & a \end{bmatrix}$$

We see that both forms require division by $ad - bc$, which is the determinant of the original matrix. This division by the determinant is also required when we find the inverse of larger square matrices. Division by zero is not permissible, and this is the reason that we say that every square matrix has an inverse as long as it has a non-zero determinant.

To develop the formula for the inverse matrix of a 2×2 matrix which has entries a, b, c, and d, we note that the product of the matrix and its inverse must be the identity matrix.

ORIGINAL INVERSE   IDENTITY
MATRIX MATRIX   MATRIX

$$\begin{bmatrix} a & b \\ c & d \end{bmatrix} \cdot \begin{bmatrix} m & n \\ p & q \end{bmatrix} = \begin{bmatrix} 1 & 0 \\ 0 & 1 \end{bmatrix}$$

When we multiply the two matrices on the left, we get a matrix product that must equal the identity matrix on the right, as we show here.

$$\begin{bmatrix} am + bp & an + bq \\ cm + dp & cn + dq \end{bmatrix} = \begin{bmatrix} 1 & 0 \\ 0 & 1 \end{bmatrix}$$

For matrices to be equal matrices, the corresponding entries must be equal. If we set the entries in the matrix on the left equal to the corresponding entries in the matrix on the right, we get four equations whose variables are m, n, p, and q, as we show here.

$$(1) \quad am + bp = 1$$

$$(2) \quad an + bq = 0$$

$$(3) \quad cm + dp = 0$$

$$(4) \quad cn + dq = 1$$

We want to solve for m, n, p, and q, which are the entries in the inverse matrix. If we solve equation (3) for m, we can replace m in equation (1) with this value.

$$(5) \qquad m = \frac{-dp}{c} \qquad \text{solved equation (3) for } m$$

$$\frac{-adp}{c} + bp = 1 \qquad \text{replaced } m \text{ in equation (1)}$$

Next, we factor out a p and solve for p.

$$p\left(\frac{-ad}{c} + b\right) = 1 \qquad \text{factored}$$

$$p = \frac{1}{b - \dfrac{ad}{c}} \qquad \text{divided}$$

$$p = \frac{1}{\dfrac{bc - ad}{c}} \qquad \text{simplified}$$

$$p = \frac{c}{bc - ad} \qquad \text{simplified}$$

$$(6) \qquad p = \frac{-c}{ad - bc} \qquad \text{multiplied by } -1 \text{ over } -1$$

This is the entry for p in the lower left-hand entry in the inverse matrix. If we replace p in equation (5) with the value of p in equation (6), we get the required entry for m in the inverse matrix. Now we can use the same procedure with equations (2) and (4) to solve for the entries in the inverse matrix for n and q.

We are indeed fortunate that a graphing calculator can be used quickly and easily to find the inverse matrix of a larger square matrix whose determinant is not zero. The problems that require matrix multiplication in the homework problem sets will involve 2×2 matrices for which the inverse matrices can be easily calculated, as in the next example. We can always use a graphing calculator to do the arithmetic of matrices for problems in which the arithmetic requires tedious calculations.

example 120.1   Use matrix algebra to find x and y: $\begin{cases} 5x + 8y = -4 \\ 6x + 10y = -6 \end{cases}$

solution   We begin by writing the system of equations as a matrix equation. The first matrix is the matrix of coefficients.

$$\begin{bmatrix} 5 & 8 \\ 6 & 10 \end{bmatrix} \cdot \begin{bmatrix} x \\ y \end{bmatrix} = \begin{bmatrix} -4 \\ -6 \end{bmatrix}$$

To find the inverse matrix for any 2×2 matrix, we interchange the entries on the diagonal from the upper left to the lower right and change the signs on the other entries.

$$\begin{matrix} \text{ORIGINAL} & & \text{FIRST} \\ \text{MATRIX} & & \text{STEP} \end{matrix}$$

$$\begin{bmatrix} 5 & 8 \\ 6 & 10 \end{bmatrix} \quad \longrightarrow \quad \begin{bmatrix} 10 & -8 \\ -6 & 5 \end{bmatrix}$$

Then we multiply this result by the reciprocal of the determinant of the original matrix. This determinant equals $5 \cdot 10 - 6 \cdot 8$, or 2, so we multiply by $\frac{1}{2}$.

$$\begin{matrix} \text{SECOND} & & \text{INVERSE} \\ \text{STEP} & & \text{MATRIX} \end{matrix}$$

$$\frac{1}{2}\begin{bmatrix} 10 & -8 \\ -6 & 5 \end{bmatrix} = \begin{bmatrix} 5 & -4 \\ -3 & 2.5 \end{bmatrix}$$

Now to solve the matrix equation, we multiply both sides of the matrix equation by the inverse matrix.

$$\begin{bmatrix} 5 & -4 \\ -3 & 2.5 \end{bmatrix} \cdot \begin{bmatrix} 5 & 8 \\ 6 & 10 \end{bmatrix} \cdot \begin{bmatrix} x \\ y \end{bmatrix} = \begin{bmatrix} 5 & -4 \\ -3 & 2.5 \end{bmatrix} \cdot \begin{bmatrix} -4 \\ -6 \end{bmatrix}$$

If we multiply the first two matrices, we are multiplying a matrix by its inverse and the result is always the identity matrix. We get

$$\begin{bmatrix} 1 & 0 \\ 0 & 1 \end{bmatrix} \cdot \begin{bmatrix} x \\ y \end{bmatrix} = \begin{bmatrix} 5 & -4 \\ -3 & 2.5 \end{bmatrix} \cdot \begin{bmatrix} -4 \\ -6 \end{bmatrix}$$

The product of the two matrices on the left is the x-and-y matrix. We multiply the two matrices on the right to get the product matrix, whose entries are 4 and -3.

$$\begin{bmatrix} x \\ y \end{bmatrix} = \begin{bmatrix} -20 + 24 \\ +12 - 15 \end{bmatrix} = \begin{bmatrix} 4 \\ -3 \end{bmatrix}$$

Thus the answer is

$$x = \mathbf{4} \quad \text{and} \quad y = \mathbf{-3}$$

**problem set
120**

1. Two cards are drawn at random from a standard 52-card deck. What is the probability that neither card is a diamond?

2. The half-life of absurdium is 2 days and it decays exponentially. If Denise begins with 10 g of absurdium, how long will it take until only 2 g remain?

3. Ten women and eight men apply for three offices. If the first office must be held by a woman, in how many different ways can the offices be filled?

4. Herb can dig a ditch in H_1 hours and Albert can dig a ditch in H_2 hours. If Herb digs for one hour before Albert joins him, how long must they work together to finish digging the ditch?

Find the inverse matrix for each of the following:

5. $\begin{bmatrix} 1 & 2 \\ 3 & 4 \end{bmatrix}$

6. $\begin{bmatrix} -3 & 2 \\ -2 & -4 \end{bmatrix}$

Solve the following systems by using inverse matrices:

7. $\begin{cases} x + 2y = 4 \\ 3x + 4y = 6 \end{cases}$

8. $\begin{cases} -3x + 2y = -11 \\ -2x - 4y = 14 \end{cases}$

In problems 9 and 10, use Descartes' rule of signs to determine the possible number of:

9. (a) Positive real zeros of $x^4 + x^3 - 3x^2 - x + 2$
   (b) Negative real zeros of $x^4 + x^3 - 3x^2 - x + 2$

10. (a) Positive real zeros of $3x^3 - 4x^2 - 2x - 3$
    (b) Negative real zeros of $3x^3 - 4x^2 - 2x - 3$

11. Use synthetic division with integers as divisors and the upper and lower bound theorem to find upper and lower bounds for the real roots of the polynomial equation $x^4 + x^3 - 3x^2 - x + 2 = 0$.

12. Find the roots of the polynomial equation $x^4 + x^3 - 3x^2 - x + 2 = 0$.

13. One zero of $y = x^3 - x^2 - 4x + 4$ is 2. What are the other two zeros?

14. Determine the radius of the "region of interest" of the polynomial function $y = -x^4 - x^3 + 3x^2 + x - 2$. Determine the coordinates of some points on the graph and sketch the graph using knowledge about its basic shape from Lesson 114.

15. Sketch the graph of the polynomial function $y = x^2(x - 1)(x + 2)$. Indicate the locations where the graph intersects the x axis with a dot.

16. Find the third term in the expansion of $\left(3xy - 2a^4\right)^4$.

17. Solve for x: $2 \log_3 x > \log_3 x$

18. Sketch the graph of each of the following functions. State the domain and range of each function.
    (a) $f(x) = \text{Arccos } x$ (b) $g(x) = \text{Arctan } x$ (c) $h(x) = \text{Arcsin } x$

19. Use an infinite geometric series as an aid for expressing $2.0\overline{11}$ as a common fraction.

20. Let $A = \begin{bmatrix} 2 & 0 & 1 \\ 0 & 1 & 1 \\ 3 & 5 & 0 \end{bmatrix}$ and $B = \begin{bmatrix} 5 & 6 & 2 \\ 1 & 7 & -3 \\ 4 & 1 & 2 \end{bmatrix}$. Compute $A - B$ and $A \cdot B$.

Solve for x:

21. $3 \log_2 x - 2 = 2 \log_2 x + 3$ 22. $\ln\left(x^{\ln x}\right) = 1$

23. Show: $\sec^2\left(\dfrac{\pi}{2} - \theta\right) + \csc^2\left(\dfrac{\pi}{2} - \theta\right) = \sec^2 \theta \csc^2 \theta$

24. Solve this triangle for c.

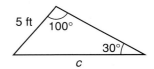

Sketch the graph of each of the following:

25. $y = -3 + \cot(x - \pi)$ 26. $y = -10 + 8 \cos 4\left(x + \dfrac{\pi}{3}\right)$

27. Solve $2 \sin^2 \dfrac{\theta}{4} = 1$ given that $0 \leq \theta < 2\pi$.

28. Express $\log_5 10$ in terms of natural logarithms. Do not find a numerical answer.

29. Find the six sixth roots of $-64i$ in polar form.

30. Find the radius of a circle that circumscribes a regular hexagon whose perimeter is 18 inches.

LESSON *121* *Piecewise Functions • Greatest Integer Function*

121.A

**piecewise
functions**

Most of the functions that we have considered can be defined by a single algebraic expression. Some functions require that we use one algebraic expression to describe one "piece" of the function and one or more other expressions to describe other "pieces" of the function. These multipart functions are called **piecewise functions.** The domain for each piece of the function must be specified, as we show in the next three examples.

example 121.1   Write the equations for this function.

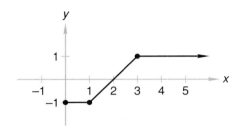

solution   Between $x = 0$ and $x = 1$, the function has a value of -1, so

$$y = -1 \qquad \text{if } 0 \le x \le 1$$

Between $x = 1$ and $x = 3$, the slope is 2 over 2, or 1, and the line $y = x$ is shifted 2 units to the right, so

$$y = x - 2 \qquad \text{when } 1 \le x \le 3$$

To the right of $x = 3$, the function has a value of $+1$, so

$$y = 1 \qquad \text{when } x \ge 3$$

Now we will write the three parts of the description.

$$\begin{cases} \boldsymbol{y = -1} & \textbf{if } \boldsymbol{0 \le x \le 1} \\ \boldsymbol{y = x - 2} & \textbf{if } \boldsymbol{1 \le x \le 3} \\ \boldsymbol{y = 1} & \textbf{if } \boldsymbol{x \ge 3} \end{cases}$$

example 121.2   Write the equations for this function.

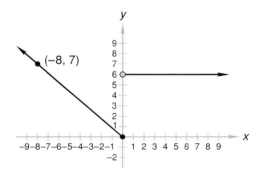

solution   The slope of the first part is $-\frac{7}{8}$ and the y intercept is 0, so we can write

$$y = -\frac{7}{8}x \qquad \text{if } x \le 0$$

To the right of the origin y equals 6, so

$$y = 6 \qquad \text{if } x > 0$$

The solid dot at the origin indicates $y = 0$ when $x = 0$. The open circle on the second piece indicates the graph of the second piece begins when $x > 0$ and not when $x = 0$. Thus, our function is

$$\begin{cases} \boldsymbol{y = -\dfrac{7}{8}x} & \textbf{if } \boldsymbol{x \le 0} \\ \boldsymbol{y = 6} & \textbf{if } \boldsymbol{x > 0} \end{cases}$$

example 121.3   Graph the function:
$$\begin{cases} y = 2 & \text{if } -\infty < x \le 0 \\ y = x & \text{if } 0 < x \le 2 \\ y = 3 - x & \text{if } 2 < x < \infty \end{cases}$$

solution   The graph is in three pieces.

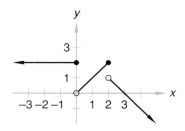

The notation used in the statement of this example is slightly different from the notation used in the statement of the previous examples. In this example, we use "∞" and "−∞" when describing intervals. The symbols ∞ and −∞ are not numbers so that the variable must be strictly less than ∞ or strictly greater than −∞. Generally, the interval described remains the same whether or not the ∞ and −∞ symbols are used. For example, the interval described by $-\infty < x < 1$ is the same as the interval described by $x < 1$; both describe the set of all real numbers strictly less than 1.

Now we return to our problem and examine the graph of the piecewise function. To the left of 0, the graph is horizontal and $y = 2$. From $x = 0$ to $x = 2$, the graph is that of $y = x$. The empty circle at $x = 0$ indicates that the graph of the second piece begins when $x > 0$ and not at $x = 0$. The solid circle at $x = 2$ indicates that when $x = 2$, $y = 2$. The empty circle at $x = 2$ indicates that the graph of the third piece begins when x is greater than 2.

121.B

greatest integer function

The **greatest integer function** is a function for which a notation has been devised. It is

$$f(x) = [x]$$

The value of the function is the value of the greatest integer less than or equal to the value of x. The graph of this function is shown here.

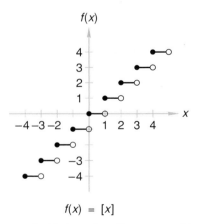

$$f(x) = [x]$$

Let's check a few values. The greatest integer less than or equal to 4 is 4, so 4 has a solid circle. The greatest integer less than or equal to 3.9 is 3, so on the graph from $x = 3$ to $x = 4$ but not including 4, the value of the function $f(x)$ is 3. A check of other values of x will show that the value of y increases only when the value of x gets to the next larger integral value. All functions can be shifted right or left and up or down by changing the equation, and this function is no exception. As an example, we note that the graph could be shifted 40 units to the right by adding − 40 to the argument. In addition, the graph could be shifted up 10 units by adding +10 to the function. If we do this, we would get

$$y = [x - 40] + 10$$

**problem set
121**

1. A pair of dice is rolled. What is the probability that the number rolled will be either 5 or 9?

2. The amount of substance initially present was 600 grams, and after 60 hours only 280 grams remained. Assuming the amount of substance decreases exponentially, determine the half-life of the substance.

3. A disk is rotating at a constant angular speed of 191 revolutions per minute. A point on the rim of the disk has a linear speed of 85 meters per second. What is the diameter of the disk?

4. The pressure of an ideal gas varies inversely as the volume if the temperature is held constant. When the temperature was 200°C, the pressure and the volume of an amount of gas were 8 atmospheres and 60 liters, respectively. What would be the pressure if the volume were increased to 112 liters and the temperature remained at 200°C?

5. Write the equations for the functions shown.

(a)
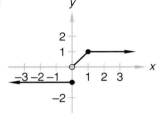

(b)
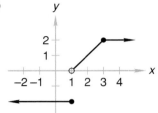

6. Graph the piecewise function: $\begin{cases} y = -\dfrac{1}{2}x & \text{if } x \le 4 \\ y = x - 7 & \text{if } 4 < x < 10 \end{cases}$

7. Graph the piecewise function: $\begin{cases} y = -3 & \text{if } -\infty < x < -3 \\ y = x & \text{if } -3 < x < 3 \\ y = 3 & \text{if } 3 < x < \infty \end{cases}$

8. Sketch the graph of the function $y = [x] + 3$.

9. For the following system, find the associated inverse matrix and then use it to solve for x and y:

$$\begin{cases} 4x + 2y = 7 \\ 3x - y = 2 \end{cases}$$

10. Use Descartes' rule of signs to determine the possible number of:
    (a) Positive real zeros of $4x^3 + 8x^2 - x - 2$
    (b) Negative real zeros of $4x^3 + 8x^2 - x - 2$

11. Use synthetic division with integers as divisors and the upper and lower bound theorem to find upper and lower bounds for the real roots of the polynomial equation $4x^3 + 8x^2 - x - 2 = 0$.

12. Apply the rational roots theorem to list the possible rational roots of the equation $4x^3 + 8x^2 - x - 2 = 0$.

13. Find the roots of the polynomial equation $4x^3 + 8x^2 - x - 2 = 0$.

14. Are 128 and 87 relatively prime? If not, what common factor do both numbers share?

15. Use the remainder theorem to evaluate $x^6 - 2x^4 + x^3 - 3x^2 - 30x + 2$ when $x = 2$.

16. Determine the radius of the "region of interest" of the polynomial function $y = 4x^3 + 8x^2 - x - 2$. Determine the coordinates of some points on the graph and sketch the graph using knowledge about its basic shape from Lesson 114.

17. Sketch the graph of the polynomial function $y = (x - 3)^2(x + 1)(1 - x)$. Indicate the locations where the graph intersects the x axis with a dot.

18. Use synthetic division to divide $x^5 - 2x^3 - 4x + 1$ by $x - 3$.

19. Write the fourth term in the expansion of $\left(1 - \dfrac{2}{p}\right)^{12}$.

20. Solve for x: $\log_{1/2}(3x + 2) > 2$

21. What is the sum of all the terms of this infinite geometric sequence?

$$7, \ -\frac{21}{4}, \ \frac{63}{16}, \ -\frac{189}{64}, \ ...$$

22. Solve for x: $\sqrt{\log_6 x} = \log_6 \sqrt[3]{x}$

Show:

23. $\dfrac{1 + \sin\theta}{1 - \sin\theta} = (\sec\theta + \tan\theta)^2$ **24.** $\dfrac{1 - \tan^2 x}{1 + \tan^2 x} = \cos 2x$

Sketch the graph of each of the following:

25. $\theta = \text{Arccos } x$ **26.** $y = \dfrac{3}{2} - 4\cos\left(\theta - \dfrac{7\pi}{4}\right)$

Solve the following equations given that $(0° \leq x, \theta < 360°)$:

27. $3\csc^2 x - 2\sqrt{3}\cot x - 6 = 0$ **28.** $6\sin^2\theta - 3 = 0$

29. Write the three cube roots of 64 cis 270° in rectangular form. Give exact answers.

30. Determine if $f(x) = \dfrac{2x + 1}{x}$ and $g(x) = \dfrac{x}{2x - 1}$ are inverse functions by computing their compositions.

LESSON 122 *Graphs of Rational Functions • Graphs That Contain Holes*

122.A
graphs of rational functions

We remember that a polynomial is a single term or an algebraic sum of terms each of which can be written in the form ax^N, where a is a real number and N is a whole number. A rational function is an algebraic function that can be written as a fraction of polynomials. The function

$$f(x) = \frac{3}{x}$$

is a rational function because 3 can be written as $3x^0$ and x can be written as $1x^1$. The following function is a general expression for a rational function whose numerator has degree 3 and whose denominator has degree 4.

$$f(x) = \frac{a_1 x^3 + a_2 x^2 + a_3 x + a_4}{b_1 x^4 + b_2 x^3 + b_3 x^2 + b_4 x + b_5}$$

Every polynomial of degree n can be factored into the product of a constant and exactly n linear factors of the form $(x + a)$, where a can be complex. We will restrict this discussion to polynomials whose linear factors are all real linear factors. Thus, it is possible to factor the numerator into a product of a constant a_1 and three linear factors of the form $(x + a)$. The denominator can be factored into the product of b_1 and four linear factors.

$$f(x) = \frac{a_1(x + a)(x + b)(x + c)}{b_1(x + d)(x + e)(x + f)(x + g)}$$

The zeros of the numerator are the zeros of the function, and the zeros of the denominator are the *poles* of the function.

We will investigate the graphs of rational functions by considering the special case of functions that are factored into linear real factors that occur only once each and that have more factors in the denominator than in the numerator. This last stipulation will ensure that the x axis is the horizontal asymptote.

Since a rational function that is composed of unique nonrepeating linear factors changes signs at every zero of the numerator and the denominator, the graph must cross the x axis at every zero and must jump across the x axis at every pole.

The graphs of these functions can be sketched quickly if we begin by drawing vertical dotted lines at the poles and placing dots on the x axis at the zeros. Next, we determine whether the function is positive or negative for large positive values of x. Then we work our way from right to left, crossing the x axis at the zeros and going off the paper vertically at the poles.

Suppose we have a function that has a small positive value when x is a large positive number, and the zeros and the vertical asymptotes are as shown below.

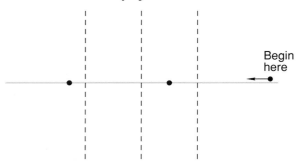

We will begin on the right at a small positive value of y and move to the left. The graph cannot cross the x axis because there is no zero, so it goes off the figure vertically at the asymptote.

The graph went off the figure in the up direction at the right asymptote. Thus, the graph must reappear from the down direction on the left side of this asymptote. It sees a crossing point, so it crosses the x axis and goes off the figure again in the up direction.

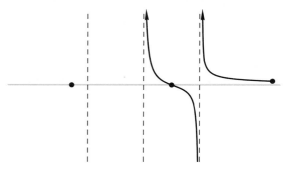

Now it must reappear from the down direction on the left side of the second asymptote. This time it sees no zero, so it must not touch the x axis. Thus, it turns around and goes back down. In calculus, we will learn how to find the x and y values of the turning point.

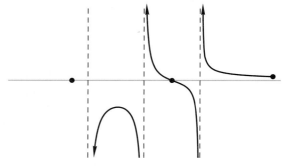

The graph must reappear on the left side of the left asymptote from above. Then it crosses at the zero and then comes back to approach the horizontal asymptote, which is the x axis.

Note that we started the graph at a dot and moved leftward. In reality, the graph has no starting point and continues to the right of the dot without end. We use the starting dot and selectively drawn arrows on the graph to illustrate the method of graphing of rational functions. The final graph, as shown below, will exclude the starting dot and will use arrows whenever the graph continues without end.

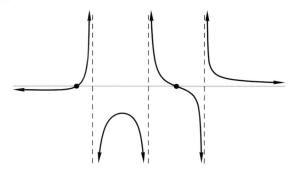

example 122.1   Graph: $f(x) = -\dfrac{x(x - 7)}{(x + 5)(x + 2)(x - 2)(x - 5)}$

solution   First we plot the zeros and the vertical asymptotes.

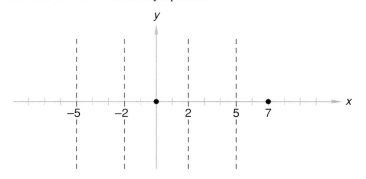

Next, we must determine the starting point for the right-hand end of the graph. The term of highest degree in a polynomial is the dominant term, because for large absolute values of x, the value of the highest-degree term will be greater than the absolute value of the sum of all the other terms in the polynomial. Thus, if x is a large positive number, we can estimate the value of a rational function whose denominator is of higher degree than the numerator by considering only the lead terms in the numerator and denominator, as shown.

$$f(x) = \frac{-x^2 + (\text{other terms})}{x^4 + (\text{other terms})}$$

As x takes on larger and larger positive values, both x^2 and x^4 are large positive numbers, and since x^4 is in the denominator and since there is a minus sign in front, the value of the fraction is a small negative number. This gives us our starting point on the right-hand end of the graph. We begin at the starting dot, which is not shown in the final sketch of the graph below, and move leftward. As the last step, we extend the graph to the right of the starting dot. The graph approaches the x axis as we move rightward since the x axis is the horizontal asymptote.

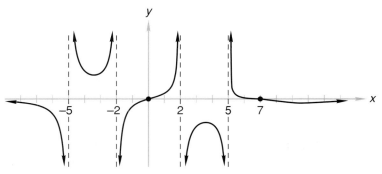

122.B

graphs that contain holes

If we are asked to graph the function

$$y = \frac{x^2 - x - 6}{x - 3}$$

the first thing we should note is that the denominator will equal zero if x equals 3, so this value of x cannot be used. Next, we should try to simplify the function. Let's try to factor the numerator.

$$y = \frac{(x - 3)(x + 2)}{x - 3} = x + 2 \quad (x \neq 3)$$

We were able to cancel the common factor $x - 3$, and the equation reduced to the equation of the line $y = x + 2$. **But the x value of 3 still cannot be used because this value of x would cause the original function to have a denominator of zero.** Since division by zero is not permitted, our simplification is not permissible when $x = 3$. We note this by drawing the graph of the line $y = x + 2$ and drawing an empty circle at the x value of 3.

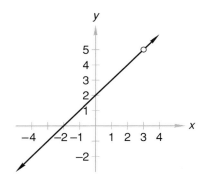

Thus, the graph of this function is not the whole line but a line with a hole in it!

example 122.2   Graph: $y = \dfrac{-x^2 - 5x - 6}{x + 2}$

solution   First we note that the function is not defined when x equals -2 because this value of x causes the denominator to equal zero. Next, we factor the numerator and cancel.

$$y = \frac{(-1)(x + 3)\cancel{(x + 2)}}{\cancel{x + 2}} = -x - 3 \quad (x \neq -2)$$

Now we graph the function and get a graph of the line $y = -x - 3$ with a hole in it at the x value of -2.

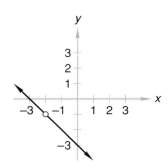

example 122.3   Graph: $y = \dfrac{(x + 5)(x - 3)(x - 1)}{(x - 4)(x + 2)(x + 4)(x - 1)}$

solution First we simplify the expression by canceling the $x - 1$ factors above and below, and we will remember to put a hole in the graph when $x = 1$ because the function is not defined at that point. Then we plot the zeros and the vertical asymptotes. We begin our sketch on the right-hand end at the starting dot (not shown) by noting that when x is a large positive number, y is a small positive number because the ratio of the lead polynomial terms is $+x^2/x^3$. We move leftward, completing the graph, and extend the graph to the right of the starting dot.

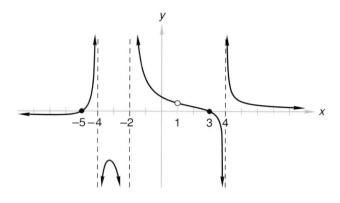

problem set 122

1. An urn contains 6 black marbles and 4 white marbles. Two marbles are drawn at random. What is the probability that both are black?

2. The increase was exponential. One day after the increase began, Jayne found that she had six, and after six days, she had 192. How many did Jayne start with?

3. Cordelia managed the k miles to court in only p hours, but still arrived two hours early. What should her speed have been to have arrived on time if the court were 5 miles further away?

4. Find four consecutive nonnegative odd integers such that twice the product of the first and fourth numbers is one less than the product of the second and third numbers.

Sketch the graphs of the following functions, showing clearly all x intercepts and asymptotes. Other than these features, the graphs need not be precisely drawn.

5. $y = \dfrac{4x}{x^2 - 1}$

6. $y = \dfrac{(x + 1)(x - 2)}{x(x + 3)(x + 2)(x - 4)}$

7. $y = \dfrac{x^2 - x}{(x - 1)(x + 1)(x - 5)}$

8. Graph the piecewise function: $\begin{cases} y = 2x^2 & \text{if } -1 < x < 1 \\ y = 5 - x & \text{if } 1 \le x < \infty \end{cases}$

9. Write the equations for the functions shown:

(a)

(b)

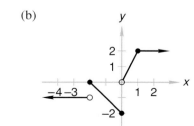

10. For the following system, find the associated inverse matrix and use it to solve for x and y:

$$\begin{cases} 4x + 2y = 10 \\ 7x - 5y = 9 \end{cases}$$

In problems 11 and 12, use Descartes' rule of signs to determine the possible number of:

11. (a) Negative real zeros of $5x^3 + 4x - 9$

    (b) Positive real zeros of $5x^3 + 4x - 9$

12. (a) Negative real zeros of $5x^3 + 3x^2 + 6x + 8$

    (b) Positive real zeros of $5x^3 + 3x^2 + 6x + 8$

Use synthetic division with integers as divisors and the upper and lower bound theorem to find upper and lower bounds for the real roots of the following polynomial equations:

13. $x^3 - 3x^2 - 6x + 8 = 0$ **14.** $3x^3 - 5x^2 + 6x - 10 = 0$

Find the roots of the following polynomial equations:

15. $5x^3 - 2x^2 - 5x + 2 = 0$ **16.** $5x^3 + 3x^2 + 6x + 8 = 0$

17. One zero of $y = x^3 + 4x^2 + 3x - 8$ is 1. What are the other two zeros?

18. One root of $x^4 - 3x^2 - 4 = 0$ is $-i$. What are the other three roots? (*Hint*: If all the coefficients are real, complex roots always occur in conjugate pairs.)

19. Are 120 and 195 relatively prime? If not, what common factor do both numbers share?

20. Determine the radius of the "region of interest" of the polynomial function $y = -x^3 - 2x^2 + 5x + 6$. Determine the coordinates of some points on the graph and sketch the graph using knowledge about its basic shape from Lesson 114.

21. Sketch the graph of the polynomial function $y = x(x - 2)^2(x + 2)$. Indicate the locations where the graph intersects the x axis with a dot.

22. Which of the following graphs most resembles the graph of $f(x) = x^2(1 - x)^2$?

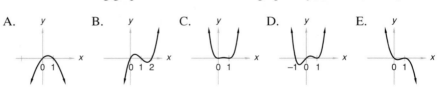

  A.   B.   C.   D.   E.

23. Use the remainder theorem to evaluate $3x^6 - 5x^4 + x^2$ when $x = 1$.

24. Write all the terms in the expansion of $\left(2x + \dfrac{3}{x^2}\right)^3$.

25. Solve for x: $\log_5(x - 5) < 1$

26. Use an infinite geometric series as an aid for expressing $3.\overline{1}$ as a common fraction.

Solve for x:

27. $\log x^3 = (\log x)^2$ **28.** $2 \log x - \log(x - 1) = \log 4$

29. Show: $\cos 3x = 4\cos^3 x - 3\cos x$ $\left[\text{\textit{Hint}: } \cos 3x = \cos(2x + x)\right]$

30. Solve $\cos 2x - \cos x = 0$ given that $0 \le x < 2\pi$.

LESSON 123   *The General Conic Equation*

The general equation of all conic sections is the equation

$$ax^2 + bxy + cy^2 + dx + ey + f = 0$$

If the coefficients b and c are zero and the coefficients a and e are not zero, then the result is an equation such as

$$x^2 + 4x - y + 1 = 0 \qquad \text{PARABOLA}$$

which is the equation of a parabola. We can change the form of this equation by completing the square and can write the equation in standard form as

$$y = (x + 2)^2 - 3 \qquad \text{PARABOLA}$$

If b equals zero and the constants a and c are equal and nonzero, we get an equation such as

$$x^2 + y^2 - 8x - 4y + 11 = 0 \qquad \text{CIRCLE}$$

This is the equation of a circle and can be rewritten in standard form. The standard form of this equation is

$$(x - 4)^2 + (y - 2)^2 = 9 \qquad \text{CIRCLE}$$

If $b = 0$, a and c are both positive or both negative, and a is not equal to c, the equation is the equation of an ellipse.

$$4x^2 + 3y^2 + 4x - 2y = 0 \qquad \text{ELLIPSE}$$

If $b = 0$ and a and c have opposite signs, the equation is the equation of a hyperbola. In the following equation, the coefficients 4 and –3 have opposite signs, so the equation is the equation of a hyperbola.

$$4x^2 - 3y^2 + 4x - 3y + 7 = 0 \qquad \text{HYPERBOLA}$$

In all the cases we shall study, we will assume that values of the coefficients are chosen so that the conic is not **degenerate. Degenerate conic sections** are one of the following: a point, a line, two parallel lines, two intersecting lines, or no graph at all. For example, the equation $x^2 + y^2 = 0$ represents a degenerate conic; it is the equation of a circle of radius zero. There is only one point (0, 0) that satisfies its equation.

If b is not zero, the equation will have an xy term. If a conic equation contains an xy term, we know that the graph of the equation is inclined to the x and y axes, which is the same thing as saying that the axes of the equation have been rotated. The equations of some of these rotated figures are similar to the equation shown below.

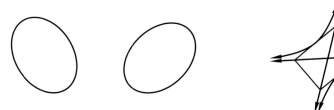

$$3x^2 + 4xy \pm 2y^2 - 4x + 3y + 7 = 0 \qquad \text{rotated conic}$$

With one exception, we will reserve the study of rotated figures until another course. The exception is the conic whose equation contains only an xy term and a constant such as

$$xy = 5 \qquad \text{or} \qquad xy = -5$$

These equations are often encountered. They are equations of hyperbolas that lie in the first and third quadrants or in the second and fourth quadrants. The asymptotes for these hyperbolas are the x and y axes.

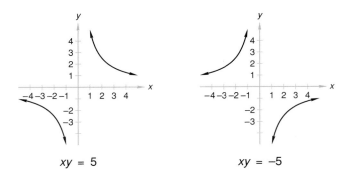

example 123.1   Graph: $xy = -4$

solution   We recognize this as the equation of a hyperbola that has the x and y axes as asymptotes. We begin by making a table and selecting values of x.

x	1	2	-2	4	-4	-1
y						

Now we use the equation to find the paired values of y.

If $x = 1$	If $x = 2$	If $x = -2$
$(1)y = -4$	$(2)y = -4$	$(-2)y = -4$
$y = -4$	$y = -2$	$y = 2$

If $x = 4$	If $x = -4$	If $x = -1$
$(4)y = -4$	$(-4)y = -4$	$(-1)y = -4$
$y = -1$	$y = 1$	$y = 4$

We graph these points and sketch the curve.

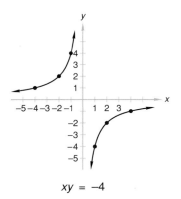

xy = −4

If the equation had been $xy = 4$, the curves would have been graphed in the first and third quadrants. Try a few points and see.

example 123.2 The following equations are the equations of a circle, a parabola, an ellipse, and a hyperbola, not necessarily in that order. Tell which is which and why, and then write the equation of the ellipse in standard form and describe it.

$$\text{(a) } x^2 + 2y + 3x + 5 = 0$$

$$\text{(b) } 2x^2 + 3x - 2y + 2y^2 - 3 = 0$$

$$\text{(c) } 2x^2 - 3y^2 + 7x + 4y + 5 = 0$$

$$\text{(d) } 9x^2 + 4y^2 + 36x - 24y + 36 = 0$$

solution **Equation (a) is a parabola** because it has only one squared term. **Equation (b) is a circle** because there is no xy term and the coefficients of x^2 and y^2 are equal. **Equation (c) is a hyperbola** because the signs of the x^2 term and the y^2 term are different. **Equation (d) is the equation of an ellipse** because the coefficients of the x^2 term and the y^2 term have the same sign but different absolute values. We use parentheses to help us complete the squares.

$9x^2 + 4y^2 + 36x - 24y + 36 = 0$	equation of an ellipse
$(9x^2 + 36x \quad) + (4y^2 - 24y \quad) = -36$	rearranged
$9(x^2 + 4x \quad) + 4(y^2 - 6y \quad) = -36$	factored
$9(x^2 + 4x + 4) + 4(y^2 - 6y + 9) = -36 + 36 + 36$	completed the square twice
$9(x + 2)^2 + 4(y - 3)^2 = 36$	simplified
$\dfrac{(x + 2)^2}{4} + \dfrac{(y - 3)^2}{9} = 1$	divided by 36

This is the equation of an ellipse whose major axis is vertical and has a length of 6, whose minor axis has a length of 4, and whose center is at (–2, 3).

problem set 123

1. The hubbub varied linearly with the number who joined in. When 4 joined in, the hubbub measured 60 units; it only measured 30 units when 2 joined in. What would the hubbub measure if 10 joined in?

2. The big container contained a solution that was 10% glycerine. The little container contained a solution that was 40% glycerine. How much should be used from each container to get 300 milliliters of a solution that is 30% glycerine?

3. The sports car was twice as fast as the truck and made the trip in 3 fewer hours than did the truck. If the truck traveled at 50 miles per hour, then the trip was how many miles long?

4. Find three consecutive even integers such that the product of the first and the third is 24 less than 9 times the second.

5. Bob's age 10 years ago equaled the current age of John, but 10 years from now, 3 times Bob's age will be 16 less than 4 times John's age. How old are both people now?

6. Graph the following hyperbolas:
   (a) $xy = 4$ (b) $xy = -4$

7. Listed are the equations of conic sections, none of which are degenerate. Indicate whether each equation represents a circle, a parabola, an ellipse, or a hyperbola.
   (a) $x^2 + y^2 - 4x = 0$
   (b) $4x^2 + 9y^2 = 1$
   (c) $4x^2 - y^2 = 4$
   (d) $x^2 + 2x - 8y - 3 = 0$
   (e) $x^2 + y^2 + 8x - 6y - 15 = 0$

8. Write equation (e) of problem 7 in standard form and graph the conic section that the equation represents.

9. Listed are the equations of conic sections, none of which are degenerate. Indicate whether each equation represents a circle, a parabola, an ellipse, or a hyperbola.

   (a) $4x^2 + 36y^2 + 40x - 288y + 532 = 0$

   (b) $24x^2 - 16y^2 - 100x - 96y - 444 = 0$

   (c) $x^2 + y^2 - 10x - 8y + 16 = 0$

   (d) $y = -2x^2 + 12x - 16$

   (e) $x^2 + y^2 - 10x + 8y + 5 = 0$

10. Write equation (d) of problem 9 in standard form and graph the conic section that the equation represents.

Sketch the graphs of the following functions, showing clearly all x intercepts and asymptotes. Other than these features, the graphs need not be precisely drawn.

11. $y = \dfrac{(x + 2)(x - 3)}{(x - 1)(x + 3)(x - 5)}$ 12. $y = \dfrac{x^2 + 2x}{(x - 1)(x + 2)(x + 3)}$

13. Graph the piecewise function: $\begin{cases} y = 2 & \text{if } -\infty < x < 0 \\ y = 0 & \text{if } x = 0 \\ y = x + 1 & \text{if } 0 < x < \infty \end{cases}$

14. Sketch the graph of the function $y = [x - 1]$.

15. Write the equations for the functions shown:

   (a) 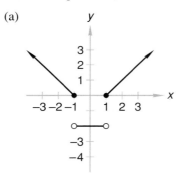   (b)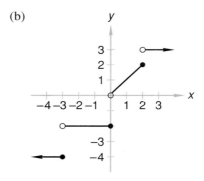

16. For the following system, find the associated inverse matrix and use it to solve for x and y:

$$\begin{cases} 2x + 6y = -2 \\ 6x + 2y = 10 \end{cases}$$

17. Use Descartes' rule of signs to determine the possible number of:

   (a) Positive real zeros of $2x^4 + x^3 - 15x^2 - 8x + 20$

   (b) Negative real zeros of $2x^4 + x^3 - 15x^2 - 8x + 20$

18. Use synthetic division with integers as divisors and the upper and lower bound theorem to find upper and lower bounds for the real roots of the polynomial equation $2x^4 + x^3 - 15x^2 - 8x + 20 = 0$.

19. Find the roots of the polynomial equation $2x^4 + x^3 - 15x^2 - 8x + 20 = 0$.

20. Determine the radius of the "region of interest" of the polynomial function $y = x^4 - 5x^3 + 6x^2$. Determine the coordinates of some points on the graph and sketch the graph using knowledge about its basic shape from Lesson 114.

21. Sketch the graph of the polynomial function $y = x^2(2 - x)$. Indicate the locations where the graph intersects the x axis with a dot.

22. Use synthetic division to divide $x^4 - 3x^2 - 2x + 1$ by $x - 1$.

23. Find the middle term in the expansion of $\left(1 - \dfrac{1}{m}\right)^{12}$.

Solve for x:

24. $\log_{1/2}(x - 3) < 3$ **25.** $x^{\log x} = 10$

26. Show: $\dfrac{\cot^2 x + \sec^2 x + 1}{\cot^2 x} = \sec^4 x$

27. Solve this triangle for a.

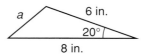

28. Sketch the graph of $y = 6 + 2\cos\frac{1}{5}(x - 40°)$.

29. Solve $-\sqrt{3} - \tan 3\theta = 0$ given that $0° \leq \theta < 360°$.

30. Factor $x^4 + x^3 + 3x^2 + 2x + 2$ over the set of complex numbers.
[*Hint*: Use the factorization $x^4 + x^3 + 3x^2 + 2x + 2 = (x^2 + 2)(x^2 + x + 1)$]

LESSON 124 *Point of Division Formulas*

We remember that when we move from one point to another point on a number line, the coordinate change is the final coordinate minus the initial coordinate. If we move from 4 to -6, the coordinate change is -10, as we see in the following diagram.

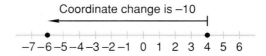

Coordinate change is -10

$$\text{Coordinate change} = (\text{final coordinate}) - (\text{initial coordinate})$$

$$= (-6) - (4) = -10$$

If we had moved only $\frac{3}{5}$ of the way from 4 to -6, the coordinate change would have been -6, which is three fifths of the difference in the two coordinates. From this problem, we can generalize and say that if we move $\frac{n}{d}$ (where n stands for "numerator" and d stands for "denominator") of the way from point (x_1, y_1) to point (x_2, y_2), the coordinate change in x is $\frac{n}{d}$ times $x_2 - x_1$ and the coordinate change in y is $\frac{n}{d}$ times $y_2 - y_1$. We will use the symbol Δx to indicate the change in the x coordinate and the symbol Δy to indicate the change in the y coordinate.

$$\Delta x = \frac{n}{d}(x_2 - x_1)$$

$$\Delta y = \frac{n}{d}(y_2 - y_1)$$

example 124.1   Find general equations for the coordinates of the point F that lies two fifths of the way from point P_1 to point P_2, where $P_1 = (x_1, y_1)$ and $P_2 = (x_2, y_2)$.

solution   We begin by drawing a diagram.

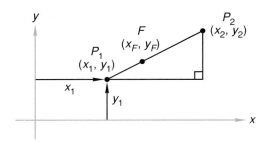

The coordinates of point F give the total distance and direction from the origin to point F. Thus, the x coordinate is x_1 plus the change in x, and the y coordinate is y_1 plus the change in y.

$$x_F = x_1 + \Delta x \qquad\qquad\qquad y_F = y_1 + \Delta y$$

$$= x_1 + \frac{2}{5}(x_2 - x_1) \qquad\qquad = y_1 + \frac{2}{5}(y_2 - y_1)$$

$$= x_1 + \frac{2}{5}x_2 - \frac{2}{5}x_1 \qquad\qquad = y_1 + \frac{2}{5}y_2 - \frac{2}{5}y_1$$

$$= \frac{3x_1 + 2x_2}{5} \qquad\qquad\qquad = \frac{3y_1 + 2y_2}{5}$$

example 124.2   Find general equations for the coordinates of the point F that lies three sevenths of the way from point P_1 to point P_2, where $P_1 = (x_1, y_1)$ and $P_2 = (x_2, y_2)$.

solution   We begin by drawing a diagram.

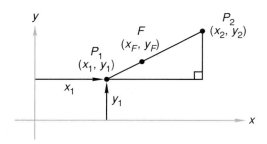

The coordinates x_F and y_F give the total x distance of point F from the origin and the total y distance of point F from the origin. These distances are $x_1 + \Delta x$ and $y_1 + \Delta y$, respectively.

$$x_F = x_1 + \Delta x \qquad\qquad\qquad y_F = y_1 + \Delta y$$

$$= x_1 + \frac{3}{7}(x_2 - x_1) \qquad\qquad = y_1 + \frac{3}{7}(y_2 - y_1)$$

$$= x_1 + \frac{3}{7}x_2 - \frac{3}{7}x_1 \qquad\qquad = y_1 + \frac{3}{7}y_2 - \frac{3}{7}y_1$$

$$= \frac{4}{7}x_1 + \frac{3}{7}x_2 \qquad\qquad\qquad = \frac{4}{7}y_1 + \frac{3}{7}y_2$$

$$= \frac{4x_1 + 3x_2}{7} \qquad\qquad\qquad = \frac{4y_1 + 3y_2}{7}$$

1. The decrease was exponential. After 40 minutes, there were 1460 in the bowl. After 400 minutes, there were only 440 in the bowl. What was the half-life of the things in the bowl?

2. The *River Belle* could steam 3 times as fast as the current in the river. She could steam 90 miles down the river in 1 hour less than she could steam 48 miles up the river. What was her speed in still water, and what was the speed of the current in the river?

3. The pressure of an ideal gas varies inversely as the volume if the temperature is held constant. When the temperature was 400°C, the pressure and the volume of an amount of gas were 5 atmospheres and 40 liters, respectively. What will the pressure be if the volume is decreased to 1 liter and the temperature remains at 400°C?

4. The ratio of reds to blues was 1 to 2, and the greens outnumbered the reds by 7. If the sum of the reds and the blues was 1 greater than the number of greens, how many were there of each color?

5. Four times the complement of angle A exceeds twice the supplement of angle B by 40°. If the supplement of angle A exceeds twice the complement of angle B by 70°, find the measure of both angles.

6. Find the coordinates of the point that lies three fourths of the way from $P_1 = (x_1, y_1)$ to $P_2 = (x_2, y_2)$.

7. Find the coordinates of the point that lies four elevenths of the way from $P_1 = (x_1, y_1)$ to $P_2 = (x_2, y_2)$.

8. Find the coordinates of the point that lies one fourth of the way from $(2, 4)$ to $(6, 6)$.

9. Find the coordinates of the point that lies three fifths of the way from $(-2, -3)$ to $(-5, 4)$.

10. Listed are the equations of conic sections, none of which are degenerate. Indicate whether each equation represents a circle, a parabola, an ellipse, or a hyperbola.

(a) $x^2 + 10x + y^2 + 2y = 5$

(b) $16x^2 - 49y^2 - 200x - 100 = 98y$

(c) $-y^2 + 9x^2 - 90x + 4y + 302 = 0$

(d) $y = x^2 - 4x + 3$

(e) $16x^2 + 25y^2 + 500 = 300y$

11. Write equation (e) of problem 10 in standard form and graph the conic section that the equation represents.

12. Listed are the equations of conic sections, none of which are degenerate. Indicate whether each equation represents a circle, a parabola, an ellipse, or a hyperbola.

(a) $x^2 + y^2 - 12x - 4y + 8 = 0$

(b) $12x^2 - y^2 = 48$

(c) $9x^2 + 81y^2 + 18x - 162y - 100 = 0$

(d) $16x^2 - 9y^2 + 144 = 0$

(e) $10y = -x^2$

13. Write equation (d) of problem 12 in standard form and graph the conic section that the equation represents.

Sketch the graphs of the following functions, showing clearly all x intercepts and asymptotes. Other than these features, the graphs need not be precisely drawn.

14. $y = \dfrac{3x}{(x - 2)(x + 1)(x + 3)}$

15. $y = \dfrac{x - 2}{x^2 - 3x + 2}$ \qquad (*Hint*: Factor the polynomial in the denominator first.)

16. Graph the piecewise function:
$$\begin{cases} y = -x & \text{if } -\infty < x \le -1 \\ y = 1 & \text{if } -1 < x < 1 \\ y = x & \text{if } 1 < x < \infty \end{cases}$$

17. Write the equations for the functions shown:

(a)

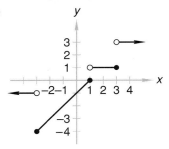

(b)

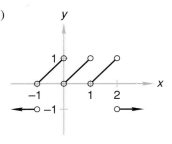

18. For the following system, find the associated inverse matrix and use it to solve for x and y:
$$\begin{cases} 5x - 7y = 3 \\ 12x + 3y = -51 \end{cases}$$

19. Use Descartes' rule of signs to determine the possible number of:
(a) Positive real zeros of $3x^3 - 7x^2 - 12x + 28$
(b) Negative real zeros of $3x^3 - 7x^2 - 12x + 28$

20. Use synthetic division with integers as divisors and the upper and lower bound theorem to find upper and lower bounds for the real roots of the polynomial equation $3x^3 - 7x^2 - 12x + 28 = 0$.

21. Find the roots of the polynomial equation $3x^3 - 7x^2 - 12x + 28 = 0$.

22. Determine the radius of the "region of interest" of the polynomial function $y = -2x^4 + 8x^2$. Determine the coordinates of some points on the graph and sketch the graph using knowledge about its basic shape from Lesson 114.

23. Sketch the graph of the polynomial function $y = \frac{1}{25}(x - 2)(x + 3)(x - 5)^2$. Indicate the locations where the graph intersects the x axis with a dot.

Solve for x:

24. $\log_5 (x - 2) > 2$

25. $\sqrt{\log_3 x} = \log_3 \sqrt[4]{x}$

26. Show: $\sin 3x = 3 \sin x - 4 \sin^3 x$ $\left[\textit{Hint}: \sin 3x = \sin (x + 2x)\right]$

Sketch the graph of each of the following:

27. $\theta = \text{Arctan } x$

28. $y = \dfrac{1}{2} + 2 \sin (x - 10°)$

29. Solve $2 \cos^2 2\theta - 1 = 0$ given that $0 \le \theta < 2\pi$.

30. Simplify: $\log 10^{y^2 - 5xy} + 4^{\log_4 5xy}$

LESSON 125 *Using the Graphing Calculator to Graph •*
Solutions of Systems of Equations Using the
Graphing Calculator • Roots

125.A
using the graphing calculator to graph

We can use a graphing calculator to graph functions without having to use synthetic division, as we demonstrate in the next example. We will use a Texas Instruments' (TI) graphing calculator—a TI-82 graphing calculator model, in particular. In the foreseeable future, newer TI graphing calculator models will share the same features as are used in this lesson. If you have a different brand calculator, consult the instruction manual.

example 125.1   Use a graphing calculator to graph the function $y = x^3 + 4x^2 + x - 6$. Use the [TRACE] key and the cursor to estimate the coordinates of the turning points.

solution   We begin by using the [Y=] key to enter the function. We use the [X,T,θ] key to enter x, the [^] key to enter the exponents, the [+] key to enter the plus sign, and the [−] key to enter the minus sign. Now we press [ZOOM]. The window will show what is called a menu of choices. The choices provide different ways the graph can be displayed. We select ZStandard, which shows x and y coordinate values ranging from −10 to 10.

Next, we press [TRACE] and the graph appears with a moveable cursor somewhere on the graph. The trace feature allows us to trace out selected points on the graph. The x and y coordinates of the cursor are displayed at the bottom of the screen. If we use the left and right arrow keys, we can move the cursor to the leftmost turning point, as we show in the figure on the right.

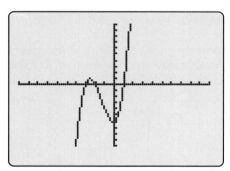
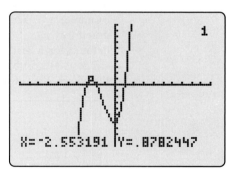

The window settings are important when we graph functions on a graphing calculator. Changing the window settings allows us to focus in on different portions of the graph. For example, if we press [WINDOW], move the cursor to Xmin and set it at −5, move the cursor to Xmax and set it at 5, and then press [GRAPH], we get the graph on the left below.

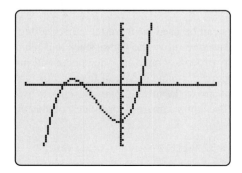
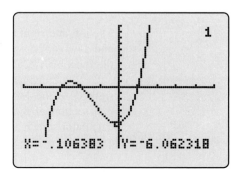

If we use [TRACE] and move the cursor to the rightmost turning point, we get the graph in the figure on the right.

Next, we will show how the **CALCULATE** menu can be used to approximate the points of intersection of two graphs and the roots of functions.

125.B
solutions of systems of equations using the graphing calculator

A solution to a system of two equations in x and y is an ordered pair (x, y) that will satisfy both equations. If the graphs of the equations intersect at any one point, the coordinates of that point will satisfy both equations. Thus, points where two graphs intersect are solutions to a system of equations.

We began by studying systems of equations whose solutions were integers. Then we found that the solutions to many systems were fractions, and some systems had irrational solutions such as $4 + \sqrt{2}$. The problems in this book were carefully contrived so that the numbers were relatively easy to handle and did not cause undue confusion. Computers and graphing calculators can handle difficult numbers with ease. We can use a graphing calculator to graph functions and find the coordinates of the places where the graphs of the two functions intersect.

example 125.2   Use a graphing calculator to find the solution to this system of equations: $\begin{cases} y = x^{2.3} \\ y = x + 1.44 \end{cases}$

solution   The window settings are crucial when the graphing calculator is used. Turn the calculator on and press ⌐ZOOM⌐. Then select ZStandard from the list of choices and the coordinate system appears. If we press ⌐WINDOW⌐, we see that both the x and y scales go from -10 to 10 and the scale marks for both are 1 unit apart. We will consider problems such as this one for which the zoom standard settings are adequate. Now press ⌐Y=⌐, ⌐X,T,θ⌐ to enter x, and ⌐^⌐ ⌐2⌐ ⌐.⌐ ⌐3⌐ to enter the first equation. Then use the down arrow key to move the cursor to Y₂= and enter $x + 1.44$. Now press ⌐TRACE⌐ and the functions will be graphed. (*Note:* The graphing of fractional powers of x by a graphing calculator may not be accurate as the graphing calculator may not graph for negative values of x when it should. For example, $y = x^{2/3}$ is defined for all values of x, but the TI-82 graphing calculator will only graph for $x \geq 0$. In this case, for $y = x^{2.3}$, which can be written as $y = x^{23/10}$, y is only defined for $x \geq 0$ and is correctly graphed.) The 1 in the upper right-hand corner of the window tells us that the moveable cursor is on the graph of Y₁. The cursor is hard to see, but the coordinates of the cursor, $x = 0$ and $y = 0$, appear at the bottom of the screen.

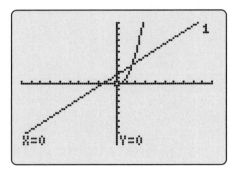   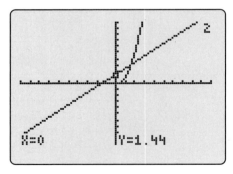

The left and right arrow keys can be used to move the cursor along the function Y₁. The up and down arrow keys can be used to move the cursor back and forth from the function Y₁ to the function Y₂. Press the up arrow key once and the cursor will jump up to the graph of Y₂ and a 2 will appear in the upper right-hand corner of the screen, as we see in the figure on the right. Use the left and right arrow keys to move the cursor as close as you can to the intersection of the graphs. The approximate coordinates of the intersection appear on our calculator screen as

X=1.7021277   Y=3.1421277

The TI-82 has the ability to use the equations of the functions to calculate the ordered pairs of the x and y values that satisfy both equations. To do this, press ⌐2nd⌐[CALC] and the **CALCULATE** menu appears. Select intersect. The calculator will ask you to select the first curve, select the second curve, and then guess where you think the point of intersection is. In this case, all this can be accomplished by pressing [ENTER] three times. The coordinates of the intersection of the graphs appear at the bottom of the screen as

X=1.6281064   Y=3.0681064

125.C

roots

A similar process can be used to find the roots of polynomial equations, as we show in the next example.

example 125.3   Find the roots of the polynomial equation $x^3 + 4x^2 + x - 4 = 0$.

solution   The roots of this equation are the x coordinates of the points where the graph of the function

$$y = x^3 + 4x^2 + x - 4$$

crosses the x axis. We use the [Y=] key and enter the function. Then we press [TRACE] and the graph on the left appears.

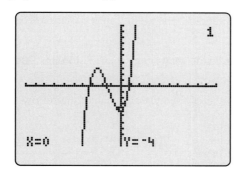
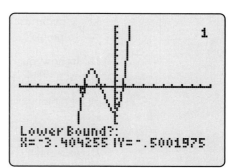

We can see that this cubic polynomial has three real roots because its graph crosses the x axis in three points. To calculate the x value of the crossing points, we press [2nd][CALC]. Select root from the menu of choices. The calculator asks for a lower bound, which is an x value just to the left of the crossing point. We decide to begin by finding the x value of the leftmost crossing point, so we use the left and right arrow keys as necessary to move the cursor just to the left of the x value of the crossing point. (The up and down arrow keys will not do this because they shift the cursor between functions and we have only one function). Then we press [ENTER] and the calculator asks for an upper bound, which is an x value just to the right of the x value of the crossing point. We use the right arrow key to move the cursor just above the crossing point and press [ENTER] twice. The calculator then tells us that the x value of the crossing point is $x = -3.342923$ and the y value is $y = 9 \times 10^{-13}$, or almost zero. The x value is the calculator's approximation of this root. If we use the same procedure to find the middle root, we get $x = -1.470 \ldots$, and for the root on the right, we get $x = 0.8136 \ldots$.

example 125.4   Use the graphing calculator to find the zeros of the polynomial $x^2 + 1$.

solution   The zeros of the polynomial are the roots of the polynomial equation $x^2 + 1 = 0$, which are the x coordinates of the points where the graph of the function $y = x^2 + 1$ crosses the x axis. We press [Y=] and enter $x^2 + 1$. Then we press [TRACE] and the graph and cursor appear.

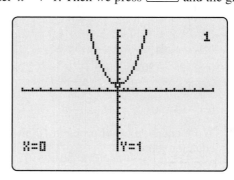

The graph of $y = x^2 + 1$ does not cross the x axis, so the equation $x^2 + 1 = 0$ has no real roots and the polynomial $x^2 + 1$ has no real zeros. The polynomial equation does have a pair of imaginary roots, which are $-i$ and $+i$, because

$$x^2 + 1 = 0 \qquad \text{equation}$$
$$\left(x + \sqrt{-1}\right)\left(x - \sqrt{-1}\right) = 0 \qquad \text{factored}$$
$$x = \pm\sqrt{-1} \qquad \text{solved}$$
$$x = \pm i$$

problem set 125

1. A radioactive substance decayed exponentially. Three days after the experiment began there were 10 grams remaining, while two days later only 6 grams remained. How much of the substance was present when the experiment began and what is the half-life of the substance?

2. Tamsen's clock read 6:00. How long would she have to wait until the hands pointed in the same direction?

3. A circle has 15 points marked on it. How many triangles can be formed using these 15 points?

4. In how many distinguishable ways can Cherith, Jordan, Dee, and Allen sit around a round table?

Use a graphing calculator to sketch the graph of each of the following:

5. $y = 2x^3 + 4x$

6. $y = x^3 + 2x^2 - x - 4$

7. $y = 0.04(x - 2)(x + 3)(x - 5)^2$

8. $y = \dfrac{3x}{(x - 2)(x + 1)(x + 3)}$

9. $y = \dfrac{x + 2}{(x - 1)(x - 5)}$

Use a graphing calculator to find the points of intersection of each of the following systems of equations. Write the points of intersection to four decimal places.

10. $\begin{cases} y = x^4 - 2x^2 + x \\ y = x + 1 \end{cases}$

11. $\begin{cases} y = e^x + 1 \\ y = x^2 \end{cases}$

12. $\begin{cases} y = x^3 - 2x^2 + 2 \\ y = e^x \end{cases}$

13. $\begin{cases} y = x^3 + 2x^2 \\ y = 8 - x^2 \end{cases}$

Use a graphing calculator to find to four decimal places all the real roots of the following polynomial equations:

14. $-x^4 + x^2 + 2 = 0$

15. $x^3 - 3x^2 + x + 1 = 0$

16. $x^4 + 3x^3 - 2x - 3 = 0$

17. $x^4 + x^3 - 3x^2 - 4x - 4 = 0$

18. Find the coordinates of the point five eighths of the way from $(-4, 7)$ to $(5, 2)$.

19. The equations below are equations of conic sections, none of which are degenerate. Indicate whether each equation represents a circle, a parabola, an ellipse, or a hyperbola.

(a) $4y = -2x - 7 + x^2$

(b) $y + 4x^2 = 20x - 16$

(c) $-y^2 + 20x + 100 - 2y = -25x^2$

(d) $36x^2 + 9y^2 - 288x = -90y - 553$

(e) $-14y + y^2 + 48 = -x^2$

20. Write equation (a) of problem 19 in standard form and graph the conic section that the equation represents.

21. Graph the following hyperbolas:

(a) $xy = 8$ (b) $xy = -8$

Sketch the graphs of the following functions, showing clearly all x intercepts and asymptotes. Other than these features, the graphs need not be precisely drawn.

22. $y = \dfrac{x^2 - 3x}{(x + 1)(x - 3)(x - 2)}$ **23.** $y = \dfrac{x - 2}{x^2 - x - 2}$

24. Graph the piecewise function: $\begin{cases} y = 1 & \text{if } -\infty < x \le -1 \\ y = |x| & \text{if } -1 < x < 1 \\ y = 1 & \text{if } 1 \le x < \infty \end{cases}$

25. Write the equations for the functions shown:

(a) 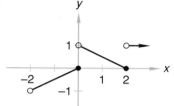   (b)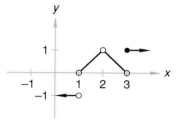

26. Use Descartes' rule of signs to determine the possible number of:

(a) Positive real roots of $8x^3 + 18x^2 + 7x - 3 = 0$

(b) Negative real roots of $8x^3 + 18x^2 + 7x - 3 = 0$

27. Use synthetic division with integers as divisors and the upper and lower bound theorem to find upper and lower bounds for the real roots of the polynomial equation $8x^3 + 18x^2 + 7x - 3 = 0$.

28. Without using a graphing calculator, find the roots of the polynomial equation $8x^3 + 18x^2 + 7x - 3 = 0$.

29. One zero of $y = x^4 - 2x^3 + x^2 + 2x - 2$ is -1. Without using a graphing calculator determine what are the other three zeros.

30. Solve $\sin 2x - \cos x = 0$ given that $0° \le x < 360°$.

APPENDIX *Proofs*

AP.A

proof of the law of cosines

We will prove the law of cosines for an acute triangle and an obtuse triangle separately. We begin with the case of an acute triangle first and use the triangle on the left below. On the right, we draw a segment from vertex C that is perpendicular to side c.

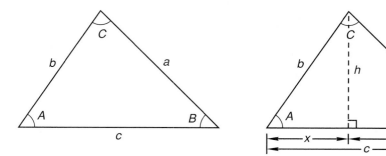

We use the small triangle in the right-hand figure whose side is x to write the following:

$$\frac{x}{b} = \cos A \quad \rightarrow \quad x = b \cos A$$

We will use this equivalence for x in the last step. Next, we use the Pythagorean theorem in both the small triangles in the right-hand figure.

$$b^2 = x^2 + h^2 \qquad (c - x)^2 + h^2 = a^2$$

We leave the equation on the left as it is. Then we expand $(c - x)^2$ in the right-hand equation and rearrange this equation to solve for $x^2 + h^2$.

$$b^2 = x^2 + h^2 \qquad c^2 - 2cx + x^2 + h^2 = a^2 \qquad \text{expanded}$$

$$x^2 + h^2 = a^2 - c^2 + 2cx \qquad \text{rearranged}$$

Now we substitute b^2 for $x^2 + h^2$ in the right-hand equation and get

$$b^2 = a^2 - c^2 + 2cx$$

and rearrange

$$a^2 = b^2 + c^2 - 2cx$$

We finish by replacing x with $b \cos A$ in this equation.

$$a^2 = b^2 + c^2 - 2bc \cos A$$

685

The proof of the law of cosines for an obtuse triangle is similar. This time, in the right-hand figure below, we label the new distance as x.

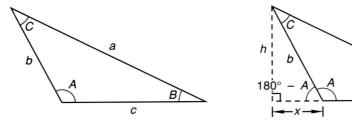

We begin with the small right triangle in the right-hand figure.

$$\cos(180° - A) = \frac{x}{b} \quad \longrightarrow \quad b\cos(180° - A) = x$$

$$\text{but} \quad \cos(180° - A) = -\cos A \quad \text{so} \quad x = -b\cos A$$

Now we use the Pythagorean theorem in both the small right triangle and the large right triangle in the right-hand figure.

$$x^2 + h^2 = b^2 \quad \text{and} \quad (x + c)^2 + h^2 = a^2$$

We leave the left-hand equation as it is and expand and rearrange the right-hand equation.

$$x^2 + h^2 = b^2 \qquad x^2 + 2xc + c^2 + h^2 = a^2 \qquad \text{expanded}$$

$$x^2 + h^2 + c^2 + 2xc = a^2 \qquad \text{rearranged}$$

Now we substitute b^2 for $x^2 + h^2$ in the right-hand equation and get

$$a^2 = b^2 + c^2 + 2xc \qquad \text{substituted}$$

Finally, from the first step, we know that $x = -b\cos A$, so

$$a^2 = b^2 + c^2 - 2bc\cos A \qquad \text{substituted}$$

We can use the law of cosines to "prove" that if the sides of one triangle are proportional to the corresponding sides in another triangle, then the corresponding angles have equal measures. We use quotation marks because this "proof" uses circular reasoning in that the definition of the cosine of an angle includes the assumption that the lengths of sides are proportional in two right triangles whose other angles have equal measures. Note that the word *proof* was avoided on page 555 in a similar development that used the law of sines. Regard the following triangles whose sides are proportional. We use the letter m for the scale factor, or constant of proportionality.

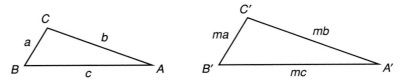

The length of each side in the triangle on the right is m times the length of the corresponding side in the triangle on the left. We would like to show that the corresponding angles have equal measures. As the first step we write the law of cosines for both triangles, using angles A and A' in the statements.

$$a^2 = b^2 + c^2 - 2bc\cos A \qquad m^2a^2 = m^2b^2 + m^2c^2 - 2mbmc\cos A'$$

Next, we rearrange both equations to solve for $\cos A$ and $\cos A'$.

$$\cos A = \frac{b^2 + c^2 - a^2}{2bc} \qquad \cos A' = \frac{m^2b^2 + m^2c^2 - m^2a^2}{2m^2bc}$$

Every term in the expression for cos A' contains m^2. If we factor out m^2, we can cancel and get the same value we found for cos A.

$$\cos A' = \frac{\cancel{m^2}(b^2 + c^2 - a^2)}{\cancel{m^2}(2bc)} = \frac{b^2 + c^2 - a^2}{2bc}$$

Angles A and A' are both positive and less than 180°, and their cosines are equal. This tells us that these angles have equal measures. The same process can be used to show that angles B and B' have equal measures and that angles C and C' also have equal measures. Thus, we have shown that if the corresponding sides of two triangles are proportional, then the corresponding angles have equal measures.

We can also use the law of cosines to illustrate that if two sides of one triangle are proportional to two sides of another triangle, and if the angles included by these sides have equal measures, then the third sides are also proportional and thus the triangles are similar. In the two triangles shown here,

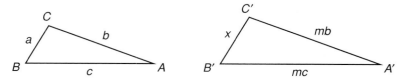

angles A and A' have equal measures and the scale factor for the sides that form these angles is m. If we can show that side x equals ma, then we have shown that the third sides are also proportional and the triangles are similar. If we write the law of cosines for each triangle, we get

$$a^2 = b^2 + c^2 - 2bc \cos A \qquad x^2 = m^2 b^2 + m^2 c^2 - 2m^2 bc \cos A'$$

If we multiply both sides of the left-hand equation by m^2, we get

$$m^2 a^2 = m^2 b^2 + m^2 c^2 - 2m^2 bc \cos A$$

Remembering that the measures of angles A and A' are equal, we see that the right-hand side of this equation is exactly the same as the expression for x^2, so we can write

$$x^2 = m^2 a^2 \qquad \text{and thus} \qquad x = ma$$

Thus, we see that the triangles are similar by the *SSS* similarity postulate. Since the law of cosines is applicable to all triangles, this illustration is also applicable regardless of whether angle A is a right angle, an acute angle, or an obtuse angle.

AP.B
proof of cos (A − B) and cos (A + B) identities

There are four identities to prove. We will prove them by first proving the identity

$$\cos (A - B) = \cos A \cos B + \sin A \sin B$$

and using this identity to prove the other three identities. We begin by reviewing the fact that the coordinates of a point on a unit circle equal the cosine of the angle and the sine of the angle.

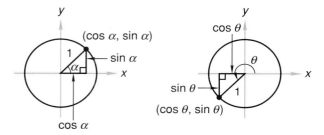

The circles are unit circles, so the length of the hypotenuse of each triangle is 1. The x coordinate of the point on the circle on the left above is cos α and the y coordinate is sin α, so the coordinates of the point are (cos α, sin α). The same is true for the circle on the right, except this time the angle is θ and thus the x and y coordinates are (cos θ, sin θ).

In the circle shown below, we show angle α, angle θ, and angle $\alpha + \theta$ and indicate the coordinates of the points where the terminal sides of the angles intersect the unit circle.

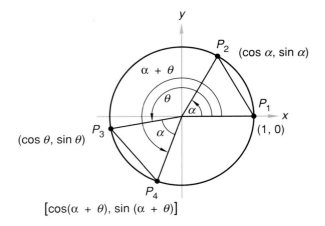

$$[\cos(\alpha + \theta),\ \sin(\alpha + \theta)]$$

The proof is a little long but involves only the use of the distance formula and a few straightforward algebraic manipulations. The angles marked α have equal measures, and thus the length of chord P_1P_2 equals the length of chord P_3P_4. We use the distance formula to make this statement of equality.

$$\sqrt{(\cos \alpha - 1)^2 + (\sin \alpha - 0)^2} = \sqrt{[\cos(\alpha + \theta) - \cos \theta]^2 + [\sin(\alpha + \theta) - \sin \theta]^2}$$

Now we square both sides to remove the radical signs.

$$(\cos \alpha - 1)^2 + (\sin \alpha - 0)^2 = [\cos(\alpha + \theta) - \cos \theta]^2 + [\sin(\alpha + \theta) - \sin \theta]^2$$

Next, the two terms on the left must be squared and the two terms on the right must be squared. We get

$$\cos^2 \alpha - 2\cos \alpha + 1 + \sin^2 \alpha = \cos^2(\alpha + \theta) - 2\cos(\alpha + \theta)\cos \theta + \cos^2 \theta$$
$$+ \sin^2(\alpha + \theta) - 2\sin(\alpha + \theta)\sin \theta + \sin^2 \theta$$

Using the fact that $\cos^2 x + \sin^2 x = 1$, we can simplify on both sides to get

$$2 - 2\cos \alpha = 2 - 2\cos(\alpha + \theta)\cos \theta - 2\sin(\alpha + \theta)\sin \theta$$

Now we add -2 to both sides to eliminate the constants and get

$$-2\cos \alpha = -2\cos(\alpha + \theta)\cos \theta - 2\sin(\alpha + \theta)\sin \theta$$

Next, we divide each term on both sides by -2 and get

$$\cos \alpha = \cos(\alpha + \theta)\cos \theta + \sin(\alpha + \theta)\sin \theta$$

Now we finish by using a change of variable. We let $\alpha = A - B$ and $\theta = B$, and we get

$$\cos(A - B) = \cos(A - B + B)\cos B + \sin(A - B + B)\sin B$$

which simplifies to

$$\mathbf{\cos(A - B) = \cos A \cos B + \sin A \sin B}$$

Now to get the identity for $\cos(A + B)$, we replace B with $-B$ and get

$$\cos[A - (-B)] = \cos A \cos(-B) + \sin A \sin(-B)$$

If we simplify the left-hand side, we get

$$\cos(A + B) = \cos A \cos(-B) + \sin A \sin(-B)$$

Now we remember the basic identities $\cos(-\theta) = \cos\theta$ and $\sin(-\theta) = -\sin\theta$, so we can replace $\cos(-B)$ with $\cos B$ and replace $\sin(-B)$ with $-\sin B$, and we get

$$\cos(A + B) = \cos A \cos B + (\sin A)(-\sin B)$$

$$\mathbf{\cos(A + B) = \cos A \cos B - \sin A \sin B}$$

AP.C
proof of
sin (*A* + *B*)
and
sin (*A* − *B*)
identities

We begin by restating the identity for $\cos(A - B)$.

$$\cos(A - B) = \cos A \cos B + \sin A \sin B$$

This identity is true for all angles A and B. Now to review another basic identity, we draw a right triangle. Since θ and the other angle must sum to $90°$, the other angle must be $90° - \theta$.

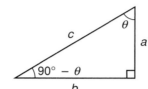

$$\sin\theta = \frac{b}{c} \qquad \cos(90° - \theta) = \frac{b}{c}$$

$$\cos\theta = \frac{a}{c} \qquad \sin(90° - \theta) = \frac{a}{c}$$

Thus, we see from the figure that $\sin\theta = \cos(90° - \theta)$ and that $\cos\theta = \sin(90° - \theta)$. This figure shows θ to be an acute angle. To show that these formulas are valid for all values of θ, we replace A with $90°$ and B with θ in the identity for $\cos(A - B)$ stated above and get

$$\cos(90° - \theta) = \cos 90° \cos\theta + \sin 90° \sin\theta$$

But the value of $\cos 90°$ is 0 and that of $\sin 90°$ is 1. So

$$\cos(90° - \theta) = 0 \cdot \cos\theta + 1 \cdot \sin\theta$$

$$\mathbf{\cos(90° - \theta) = \sin\theta} \qquad \text{for all } \theta$$

Now if we replace θ with $90° - \theta$, we get

$$\mathbf{\cos\theta = \sin(90° - \theta)} \qquad \text{for all } \theta$$

Next, to prove the identity for $\sin(A + B)$, we replace θ with $A + B$.

$$\cos\big[90° - (A + B)\big] = \sin(A + B)$$

$$\cos\big[(90° - A) - B\big] = \sin(A + B)$$

Now on the left in this equation we use the identity for $\cos(A - B)$ and substitute $90° - A$ for A and substitute B for B.

$$\cos(90° - A)\cos B + \sin(90° - A)\sin B = \sin(A + B)$$

But $\cos(90° - A) = \sin A$ and $\sin(90° - A) = \cos A$. Therefore,

$$\mathbf{\sin A \cos B + \cos A \sin B = \sin(A + B)}$$

Now to prove the identity for $\sin(A - B)$, we replace B with $-B$ and get

$$\sin A \cos(-B) + \cos A \sin(-B) = \sin\big[A + (-B)\big]$$

but $\cos(-B) = \cos B$ and $\sin(-B) = -\sin B$. Therefore,

$$\sin A \cos B + (\cos A)(-\sin B) = \sin(A - B)$$

and thus

$$\mathbf{\sin A \cos B - \cos A \sin B = \sin(A - B)}$$

Answers to Odd-Numbered Problems

problem set 1

1. $30°$ **3.** $40°$ **5.** 36 **7.** $-\dfrac{87}{8}$ **9.** $\dfrac{1}{y^2 m} - \dfrac{3x^2 m^2}{y}$ **11.** -3

13. $4x^3 + 10x^2 + 10x + 6$ **15.** $N_P = 40;\ N_D = 10$

17. Two line segments are congruent if the segments have equal length.

19. $x = 36;\ y = 108$ **21.** $A = 20;\ B = 50;\ C = 40$ **23.** $2\pi^2$ cm   **25.** $18\sqrt{2}$ cm

27. 288π cm^2 **29.** A

problem set 2

1. $40°$ **3.** $N_R = 5;\ N_B = 8$ **5.** 2025 gallons   **7.** -15 **9.** $c^2 d^2 f - cd^2$ **11.** -1

13. $N_R = 20;\ N_B = 50$ **15.** 24 **17.** $x = 145;\ y = 29$

19. $A = 55;\ B = 14;\ C = 110$ **21.** $4\sqrt{3}$ m   **23.** 180π m^2 **25.** 12 cm

27. $(80 + 12\pi)$ m$^3 = 117.70$ m^3 **29.** A

problem set 3

1. $20°$ **3.** 700 **5.** Obtuse triangle   **7.** $x = \dfrac{45}{7};\ y = \dfrac{35}{3}$

9. $a = 12;\ b = 24;\ c = 15$ **11.** $\dfrac{7p^7}{q^7}$ **13.** $x = 3;\ y = 3$ **15.** $-\dfrac{4}{7}$

17. $4x^5 - 3x^4 - 4x^3 + 8x^2 - 5$ **19.** 24 **21.** $\dfrac{7\pi}{3}$ cm^2 **23.** $(4 - \pi)$ in.$^2 = 0.86$ in.^{2}

25. $(48 + 4\pi)$ ft $= 60.57$ ft   **27.** 3888π cm^3 **29.** C

problem set 4

1. $25°$ **3.** 825 **5.** $N_O = 28;\ N_B = 16$ **7.** Refer to Lesson 4.

9. Refer to Lesson 4.   **11.** Refer to Lesson 4.   **13.** $\dfrac{1}{15}$ **15.** $\dfrac{-x^2 + 4x + 3}{x^2(x + 1)}$

17. $\dfrac{19}{2}$ **19.** $a = 4;\ b = 10;\ c = 8$ **21.** $a = 4\sqrt{10};\ b = 4\sqrt{15};\ h = 4\sqrt{6}$

23. $(36 + \pi)$ m $= 39.14$ m   **25.** 18π m^3

27. $V = \dfrac{4000\pi}{3}$ m$^3 = 4188.80$ m^3; $A_{\text{surface}} = 400\pi$ m$^2 = 1256.64$ m^2 **29.** A

problem set 5

1. $52°$ **3.** $N_Q = 10;\ N_D = 14$ **5.** $N_B = 42;\ N_W = 30$ **7.** $x^{\frac{7}{4}} y^{\frac{7}{4}}$ **9.** $a^{\frac{-7x}{2}} y^{\frac{2+3x}{2}}$

11. $4\sqrt{6}$ **13.** $\sqrt{2} - (1 + \sqrt{2})\sqrt{x} + x$ **15.** $1 - i$ **17.** $(4 + 3\sqrt{2})i$ **19.** $\sqrt{13 + n^2}$

21. $\dfrac{7\pi}{6}$ m^2 **23.** $a = 4\sqrt{5};\ b = \dfrac{3\sqrt{5}}{2};\ c = \dfrac{11}{2}$ **25.** Refer to Lesson 4.

27. $\left(24\sqrt{7} + 12\pi\right)$ m$^3 = 101.20$ m^3 **29.** A

problem set 6

1. $N_R = 40$; $N_B = 100$ **3.** $N_R = 40$; $N_G = 128$ **5.** $-\dfrac{6}{23}$ **7.** 19   **9.** 36

11. $x = 1$; $y = -1$; $z = 2$ **13.** $a^{\frac{8}{15}} b^{\frac{59}{15}}$ **15.** $\dfrac{-73\sqrt{21}}{21}$ **17.** $2\sqrt{2} - 2x - \sqrt{2}\sqrt{x} + x\sqrt{x}$

19. $-3 - 2\sqrt{2}\,i$ **21.** Refer to Lesson 4.   **23.** Refer to Lesson 4.

25. $x = 2\sqrt{11}$; $y = \sqrt{77}$; $z = 2\sqrt{7}$ **27.** 80 cm^3 **29.** C

problem set 7

1. If the animal is an elephant, then it is a large animal.

3. If an animal is a seal, then it is not green.   **5.** Invalid.   **7.** $N_R = 80$; $N_G = 220$

9. 22, 24, 26   **11.** $x = \dfrac{1}{2}$; $y = \dfrac{1}{4}$ **13.** $x = 1$; $y = 1$; $z = -1$

15. $2 + 2\sqrt{2}\sqrt{x} + x$ **17.** $x + 2x^{\frac{1}{2}} y^{\frac{1}{2}} + y$ **19.** $10 - 10i$ **21.** $\dfrac{9}{1}$

23. Refer to Lesson 4.   **25.** Refer to Lesson 4.   **27.** 24 m^2 **29.** B

problem set 8

1. $N_G = 50$; $N_P = 40$ **3.** $N_N = 160$; $N_Q = 13$ **5.** Invalid.

7. If it is blue, then it is a dog. Valid.   **9.** $\triangle XYZ \sim \triangle XMY$ so $\dfrac{XY}{XM} = \dfrac{YZ}{MY}$

11. $\dfrac{16}{3}$ **13.** $x = 3$; $y = 2$; $z = 1$ **15.** $-\dfrac{31}{7}$ **17.** $\dfrac{73\sqrt{10}}{10}$ **19.** $x^{\frac{a-8b+4}{4}} y^{\frac{3c+1}{2}}$

21. $-10 - i$ **23.** Refer to Lesson 4.   **25.** $a = 7$; $b = 10$

27. $V = \dfrac{256\pi}{3} \text{ cm}^3 = 268.08 \text{ cm}^3$; $A_{\text{surface}} = 64\pi \text{ cm}^2 = 201.06 \text{ cm}^2$ **29.** 5

problem set 9

1. $N_G = 80$; $N_B = 200$

3. If two angles of a triangle are congruent, then the sides opposite these angles are congruent.

5. If the light is on, then the switch is not on. Invalid.   **7.** $\dfrac{9}{16}$

9. (a) *AAAS* congruency postulate   (b) *SAS* congruency postulate
   (c) *SSS* congruency postulate   (d) *HL* congruency postulate

11. $\triangle ABC \cong \triangle ADC$ by *SSS* congruency postulate; $\angle ABC \cong \angle ADC$ by *CPCTC*

13. $(2 - \sqrt{2})i$ **15.** $x^{\frac{-5a-6}{2}} y^{\frac{-b-9}{6}}$ **17.** $\dfrac{-19}{4}$ **19.** $x = 4$; $y = 2$; $z = -2$

21. $\triangle ABC \sim \triangle BDC$ so $\dfrac{AB}{BD} = \dfrac{AC}{BC}$ **23.** Refer to Lesson 4.   **25.** $x = 20$; $y = 10$

27. $a = 3\sqrt{5}$; $b = 2\sqrt{5}$; $c = 5$ **29.** -28

problem set 10

1. $N_B = 680$; $N_S = 240$ **3.** $\dfrac{1}{8}$ **5.** $y = -x + 1$ **7.** $3 - 5i$ **9.** $\dfrac{4}{13} + \dfrac{7}{13}i$

11. $-4 - 2\sqrt{3}$ **13.** $-\dfrac{1}{6} \pm \dfrac{\sqrt{59}}{6}i$

15. (a) *SSS* congruency postulate   (b) *SAS* congruency postulate
   (c) *AAAS* congruency postulate   (d) *SAS* congruency postulate

17. $\triangle ADC \cong \triangle BDC$ by *SAS* congruency postulate; $\angle A \cong \angle B$ by *CPCTC*

19. $a = 2$; $b = \sqrt{5}$; $c = \sqrt{5}$ **21.** 8   **23.** $\dfrac{x^3 y^6 + x^6}{y^8}$ **25.** Refer to Lesson 4.

27. 378 m^2 **29.** A

problem set 11

1. $N_I = 8$; $N_E = 14$ **3.** 52, 54, 56, 58 **5.** $x = 38$; $y = 25$ **7.** $x = 4$; $y = 15$

9. $-\dfrac{1}{3} \pm \dfrac{\sqrt{14}}{3}i$ **11.** $y = \dfrac{1}{3}x - 3$ **13.** $\dfrac{-24 - 13\sqrt{3}}{23}$ **15.** $\dfrac{1}{3} \pm \dfrac{\sqrt{22}}{3}$ **17.** 8

19. (a) *HL* congruency postulate (b) *AAAS* congruency postulate
(c) *AAAS* congruency postulate (d) *SSS* congruency postulate

21. $\triangle ABC \cong \triangle EDC$ by *AAAS* congruency postulate; $\overline{BC} \cong \overline{DC}$ by *CPCTC*

23. $\dfrac{5}{2}$ **25.** Refer to Lesson 4. **27.** $x^{\frac{10a+3}{2}} y^{4-2a}$ **29.** B

problem set 12

1. 119 **3.** 305 grams **5.** 27 **7.** $x = 160$; $y = 60$; $z = 140$

9. $x = \dfrac{-b \pm \sqrt{b^2 - 4ac}}{2a}$ (See Lesson 11.) **11.** $-\dfrac{1}{3} \pm \dfrac{\sqrt{11}}{3}i$ **13.** $2 - 6i$

15. $-\dfrac{1}{6} \pm \dfrac{\sqrt{71}}{6}i$ **17.** $x = 9$; $y = 4$; $z = 2$ **19.** $-24 - 22i$ **21.** $\dfrac{xy^4 + x^4}{y^{10}}$

23. $\triangle AYX \cong \triangle CZX$ by *AAAS* congruency postulate

25. $x = 2\sqrt{14}$; $y = 2\sqrt{10}$; $z = 2\sqrt{35}$ **27.** Refer to Lesson 4. **29.** C

problem set 13

1. 96 **3.** 0, 2, 4 **5.** 15 **7.** 4 **9.** Interior: $1440°$; Exterior: $360°$

11. $x = 60$; $y = 30$ **13.** 1 **15.** $\dfrac{3}{4} \pm \dfrac{\sqrt{41}}{4}$ **17.** $y = 3x - 3$ **19.** $\dfrac{10}{3}$

21. 3 **23.** $-\dfrac{1}{2}i$ **25.** $\triangle PQR \cong \triangle RSP$ by *SAS* congruency postulate

27. Refer to Lesson 4. **29.** C

problem set 14

1. $N_U = 70$; $N_D = 50$ **3.** Interior: $2700°$; Exterior: $360°$

5. $4.11\underline{/318.05°}$; $4.11\underline{/-41.95°}$; $-4.11\underline{/138.05°}$; $-4.11\underline{/-221.95°}$ **7.** $0.75\hat{i} + 8.57\hat{j}$

9. $x = 28$; $y = 20$ **11.** $x = 50$; $y = 130$ **13.** $-\dfrac{1}{4} \pm \dfrac{\sqrt{19}}{4}i$ **15.** $\dfrac{1}{3} \pm \dfrac{\sqrt{11}}{3}i$

17. $y = -\dfrac{3}{2}x - \dfrac{7}{2}$ **19.** $a^{\frac{7x-2}{2}} b^{2x+y}$ **21.** $\dfrac{b^7 + a^8 b^5}{a^9}$ **23.** $\dfrac{7 + 3\sqrt{3}}{2}$

25. $x = 3$; $y = 4$; $z = 4$ **27.** $a = 2\sqrt{13}$; $b = 3\sqrt{13}$; $h = 6$ **29.** A

problem set 15

1. $-11, -9, -7, -5$ **3.** $y = x + 9$ **5.**

STATEMENTS	REASONS
1. $\overline{AC} \cong \overline{BC}$	1. Given
2. $\angle ACD \cong \angle BCD$	2. Given
3. $\overline{CD} \cong \overline{CD}$	3 Reflexive axiom
4. $\triangle ACD \cong \triangle BCD$	4. *SAS* congruency postulate

7. $8.23\underline{/149.32°}$; $8.23\underline{/-210.68°}$; $-8.23\underline{/329.32°}$; $-8.23\underline{/-30.68°}$

9. $-13.59\hat{i} - 6.34\hat{j}$ **11.** $\dfrac{20}{7}$ **13.** $\dfrac{1}{2} \pm \dfrac{\sqrt{39}}{6}i$ **15.** $-\dfrac{5}{6} \pm \dfrac{\sqrt{71}}{6}i$

17. $x = 4$; $y = 6$; $z = 1$ **19.** $2 + \sqrt{2}$ **21.** $-6 - 25i$ **23.** $9x - 4z^{\frac{1}{2}}$

25. $m\angle A = 84°$; $m\angle C = 96°$ **27.** $\sqrt{58 + x^2}$ **29.** A

problem set 16

1. $N_C = 5$; $N_R = 8$ **3.** $y = -\dfrac{3}{2}x - 4$ **5.** $\dfrac{cx + cab}{c - ka}$ **7.** $\dfrac{apc + am}{xpc + xm + cy}$

9. $c = \dfrac{bx}{xy - ma}$ **11.**

Statements	Reasons
1. $\angle A \cong \angle B$	1. Given
2. $\angle ACD \cong \angle BCE$	2. Vertical angles are congruent.
3. $\angle D \cong \angle E$	3. If two angles in one triangle are congruent to two angles in a second triangle, then the third angles are congruent.
4. $\overline{CD} \cong \overline{CE}$	4. Given
5. $\triangle ACD \cong \triangle BCE$	5. *AAAS* congruency postulate

13. $7.21 \underline{/303.69°}$; $7.21 \underline{/-56.31°}$; $-7.21 \underline{/123.69°}$; $-7.21 \underline{/-236.31°}$

15. $1.09\hat{i} - 4.06\hat{j}$ **17.** $\dfrac{1}{3} \pm \dfrac{\sqrt{14}}{3}i$ **19.** Line A: $x = -4$; Line B: $y = -4x + 10$ **21.** 9

23. $\dfrac{-21 - 11\sqrt{3}}{104}$ **25.** $\dfrac{a^6 + a^8 b^6}{b^5}$ **27.** $a = 4\sqrt{2}$; $b = 4\sqrt{14}$; $h = 2\sqrt{7}$ **29.** B

problem set 17

1. $-8, -6, -4$ and $4, 6, 8$ **3.** $y = 4x - 5$ **5.** $\triangle GHI \sim \triangle JKL$ by *SSS* similarity postulate

7. $\triangle ABC \sim \triangle DEF$ by *AAA*   **9.** $\dfrac{a^2 cx - abx^2}{bxc^3 + b^2 c^2}$ **11.** $k = \dfrac{b}{2a - b}$

13. $x^2 - 3x + 11 - \dfrac{34}{x + 3}$

15. $8.60 \underline{/54.46°}$; $8.60 \underline{/-305.54°}$; $-8.60 \underline{/234.46°}$; $-8.60 \underline{/-125.54°}$ **17.** $-3.47\hat{i} - 19.70\hat{j}$

19. Line A: $y = -3x + 3$; Line B: $x = -3$ **21.** $\dfrac{1}{4}$ **23.** $\dfrac{-7 + \sqrt{5}}{4}$ **25.** $x^{-a+3} b^{\frac{4y - 9a}{6}}$

27. $AD = 5$; $DC = 7$ **29.** D

problem set 18

1. $N_B = 2$; $N_W = 3$; $N_G = 6$ **3.** 10   **5.** 49   **7.** 891.43 grams   **9.** $\dfrac{m^2 x + 7a^2 y}{ap^2 - 3x}$

11. $c = \dfrac{kbx}{x^2 + kba}$ **13.** $x^2 + 1 - \dfrac{1}{x^2 - 1}$

15. $15.30 \underline{/168.69°}$; $15.30 \underline{/-191.31°}$; $-15.30 \underline{/348.69°}$; $-15.30 \underline{/-11.31°}$ **17.** $-20.57\hat{i} + 24.51\hat{j}$

19. $\dfrac{5}{6} \pm \dfrac{\sqrt{23}}{6}i$ **21.** $x = 2$; $y = -2$; $z = 3$ **23.** $\dfrac{-18 - 10\sqrt{3}}{3}$ **25.** $\dfrac{7}{4}$

27. $(50\pi - 100)$ cm^2 = 57.08 cm^2 **29.** B

problem set 19

1. $\dfrac{16}{1}$ **3.** $N_N = 8$; $N_D = 30$; $N_Q = 12$ **5.** 108   **7.** 40 ml of 10%, 10 ml of 40%

9. $(1, 2\sqrt{2}), (1, -2\sqrt{2}), (-1, 2\sqrt{2}), (-1, -2\sqrt{2})$ **11.** $2x^{3n+1}(2x - 3x^n)$

13. $(3x^4 y^2 - z^3)(9x^8 y^4 + 3x^4 y^2 z^3 + z^6)$

15. $\triangle UVW \sim \triangle XYZ$ by *SAS* similarity postulate   **17.** $\dfrac{17}{25} - \dfrac{19}{25}i$ **19.** $-\dfrac{11}{41} - \dfrac{17}{41}i$

21. $x^{2c-1-d} y^{2-3d-c}$ **23.** $z = \dfrac{36s^2 nt + 24m}{5n}$

25.

Statements	Reasons
1. $\overline{HK} \cong \overline{IJ}$	1. Given
2. $\overline{HI} \cong \overline{KJ}$	2. Given
3. $\overline{IK} \cong \overline{IK}$	3. Reflexive axiom
4. $\triangle HIK \cong \triangle JKI$	4. *SSS* congruency postulate

27. 60   **29.** C

problem set 20

1. 226.58 m   **3.** $N_R = 20$; $N_G = 80$ **5.** $N_N = 5$; $N_D = 3$; $N_Q = 4$ **7.** 12 lb

9. $3\sqrt{6}$ **11.** $4\sqrt{3}$ **13.**

STATEMENTS	REASONS
1. $\overline{AB} \parallel \overline{DE}$	1. Given
2. $\angle BAC \cong \angle EDF$	2. If two parallel lines are cut by a transversal, then each pair of corresponding angles is congruent.
3. $\overline{BC} \parallel \overline{EF}$	3. Given
4. $\angle BCA \cong \angle EFD$	4. If two parallel lines are cut by a transversal, then each pair of corresponding angles is congruent.
5. $\angle B \cong \angle E$	5. $AA \rightarrow AAA$
6. $\triangle ABC \sim \triangle DEF$	6. AAA

15. $\left(-\dfrac{2}{5} + \dfrac{2\sqrt{11}}{5}, \dfrac{1}{5} + \dfrac{4\sqrt{11}}{5}\right), \left(-\dfrac{2}{5} - \dfrac{2\sqrt{11}}{5}, \dfrac{1}{5} - \dfrac{4\sqrt{11}}{5}\right)$

17. $(3xy^2 + 2p)(9x^2y^4 - 6xy^2p + 4p^2)$ **19.** $\dfrac{3tx + xs}{6yt + 2ys - 6zt}$

21. $(7\sqrt{7} - 5\sqrt{5} - 4)i$ **23.** $x^2 + 1 - \dfrac{5}{x^2 - 1}$ **25.** $-\dfrac{5}{6} \pm \dfrac{\sqrt{71}}{6}i$ **27.** 12 m **29.** A

problem set 21

1. $\dfrac{399}{16}$ **3.** $N_R = 4$; $N_B = 2$; $N_G = 15$ **5.** 54, 45 **7.** (a), (d)

9. (a) $\{x \in \mathbb{R}\}$ (b) $\{x \in \mathbb{R} \mid x \geq -5\}$ (c) $\{x \in \mathbb{R} \mid x \leq 6\}$ **11.** $2\sqrt{3}$

13. $\triangle PQT \sim \triangle SRT$ by SAS similarity postulate

15. $\left(\dfrac{3 + \sqrt{33}}{2}, \dfrac{-3 + \sqrt{33}}{2}\right), \left(\dfrac{3 - \sqrt{33}}{2}, \dfrac{-3 - \sqrt{33}}{2}\right)$

17. $(3b^3a^2 - 4c)(9b^6a^4 + 12b^3a^2c + 16c^2)$ **19.** $4 - 5x^{a-b}y^{a-b} + x^{b-a}y^{b-a}$

21. $\dfrac{33 - 5\sqrt{3}}{26}$ **23.** $d = \dfrac{wr + 1}{2r - 1}$ **25.** $-16.07\hat{i} + 19.15\hat{j}$ **27.** 59 **29.** A

problem set 22

1. $y = -\dfrac{1}{3}x - \dfrac{1}{3}$ **3.** 91.15 m **5.** 62, 26 **7.**

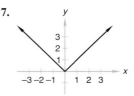

9. (a) Function (b) Not a function

11. (a) $\{x \in \mathbb{R} \mid x \geq 8\}$ (b) $\{y \in \mathbb{R}\}$ (c) $\{x \in \mathbb{R} \mid x \neq -3\}$ **13.** $\sqrt{6}$

15.

STATEMENTS	REASONS
1. $\dfrac{AC}{BC} = \dfrac{BC}{DC}$	1. Given
2. $\angle C \cong \angle C$	2. Reflexive axiom
3. $\triangle ABC \sim \triangle BDC$	3. SAS similarity postulate

17. $(x^2 + y^2)(x + y)$

19. $\dfrac{3sl + 3sk}{2ml + 2mk - zl}$ **21.** $x^{2a+\frac{3}{2}}y^{a+4}$

23. $13.45\underline{/228.01°}$; $13.45\underline{/-131.99°}$; $-13.45\underline{/48.01°}$; $-13.45\underline{/-311.99°}$

25.

STATEMENTS	REASONS
1. $\overline{BC} \cong \overline{EF}$	1. Given
2. $\overline{BC} \parallel \overline{EF}$	2. Given
3. $\angle ACB \cong \angle DFE$	3. If two parallel lines are cut by a transversal, then each pair of corresponding angles is congruent.
4. $\overline{AC} \cong \overline{DF}$	4. Given
5. $\triangle ABC \cong \triangle DEF$	5. SAS congruency postulate

27. 38 **29.** A

problem set 23

1. $y = -\dfrac{3}{2}x + \dfrac{5}{2}$ **3.** $N_N = 9;\ N_D = 4;\ N_Q = 8$ **5.** $42, 24$ **7.**

9. (a)   (b)

11. (b), (d)   **13.** 2 **15.** 33 **17.** $x = -2;\ y = 3;\ z = 3$

19. $-2 \pm 2\sqrt{3}$ **21.** $\dfrac{2(yk - z)}{yk - z + 3xk}$ **23.** $\dfrac{38 + 23\sqrt{3}}{13}$

25. $x^2 - x + 4 - \dfrac{12}{x + 3}$ **27.** $AB = 9;\ CD = 11$ **29.** B

problem set 24

1. $y = \dfrac{3}{5}x - \dfrac{9}{5}$ **3.** $N_D = 10;\ N_Q = 2;\ N_H = 2$ **5.** $73, 37$

7.   **9.**

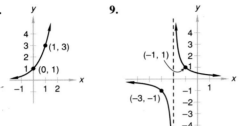

11. (a) Not a function   (b) Function, not 1 to 1   (c) Not a function   (d) Function, not 1 to 1

13. $\dfrac{1 + \sqrt{2}}{2}$ **15.** $1 + \dfrac{2\sqrt{3}}{3}$ **17.** $\left(\dfrac{2 + \sqrt{19}}{5}, \dfrac{1 - 2\sqrt{19}}{5}\right), \left(\dfrac{2 - \sqrt{19}}{5}, \dfrac{1 + 2\sqrt{19}}{5}\right)$

19. $\dfrac{ac^3 - 6m^3xy}{xy^2d^2 - gx^3y}$ **21.** $a^{\frac{19}{12}}b^{\frac{1}{4}}$

23. $9.43\underline{/302.01°};\ 9.43\underline{/-57.99°};\ -9.43\underline{/122.01°};\ -9.43\underline{/-237.99°}$

25. $2x + 2$ **27.** $120°$ **29.** B

problem set 25

1. Orville $= 25$ yr; Wilbur $= 15$ yr   **3.** $\dfrac{2}{5} \dfrac{\text{sandcastles}}{\text{hr}}$ **5.** 68 **7.**

9. (a)   (b)

11. (a) $\left\{x \in \mathbb{R} \mid x \geq \dfrac{1}{2}\right\}$ (b) $\{x \in \mathbb{R} \mid x > 3\}$
   (c) $\{x \in \mathbb{R} \mid x \neq 1, -6\}$

13. (a) -12 (b) $-\dfrac{4}{3}$ (c) -15 **15.** $\dfrac{\sqrt{2}}{2} - \dfrac{2\sqrt{3}}{3}$ **17.** $\left(\sqrt{5}, 2\right), \left(\sqrt{5}, -2\right), \left(-\sqrt{5}, 2\right), \left(-\sqrt{5}, -2\right)$

19. $\left(2xy^2 - 3a^2b^3\right)\left(4x^2y^4 + 6xy^2a^2b^3 + 9a^4b^6\right)$ **21.** $\dfrac{-48 + 25\sqrt{3}}{11}$

23. $x^3 - 4x^2 - x - 2 - \dfrac{9}{x - 2}$ **25.** $x^2 + 6x + 8$ **27.** 35 **29.** A

problem set 26

1. Charlotte $= 30$ yr; Emily $= 10$ yr   **3.** 8 days   **5.** 800 liters

7. (a) $b^a = 12$ (b) $\log_b 12 = a$ **9.** -3 **11.** (a)   (b)

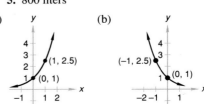

13. (a) Not a function   (b) Function, 1 to 1   (c) Function, not 1 to 1   (d) Function, not 1 to 1

15. 0   **17.** 0   **19.** (a) -2 (b) 0   (c) 0   **21.** $x = 1; y = -1$ **23.** $x^2 + xy + y^2$

25. $8.06\underline{/119.74°}$; $8.06\underline{/-240.26°}$; $-8.06\underline{/299.74°}$; $-8.06\underline{/-60.26°}$ **27.** 65   **29.** B

problem set 27

1. Marshall = 6 yr; George = 13 yr   **3.** 1 day   **5.** 36 acorns   **7.** $\log_3 7 = k$

9. 4   **11.** 4   **13.**

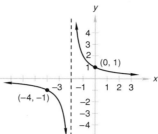

15. (a) $\left\{ x \in \mathbb{R} \mid x \le \dfrac{1}{3} \right\}$ (b) $\{ x \in \mathbb{R} \mid x \ge -10, x \ne 2 \}$ (c) $\{ x \in \mathbb{R} \mid x \ne -3, 1 \}$

17. $\dfrac{3\sqrt{3}}{4}$ **19.** (a) -100 (b) $\dfrac{1}{51}$ (c) 6   **21.** $3y^{2n+1}\left(1 + 4y^{n+1} \right)$

23. $a = \dfrac{3zp}{50pr + k}$ **25.** $\dfrac{2}{x + h}$ **27.** 66   **29.** A

problem set 28

1. $\dfrac{xp}{x - 2p} \dfrac{\text{mi}}{\text{hr}}$ **3.** Thomas = 7 yr; Dylan = 14 yr   **5.** $\dfrac{14}{3}$ days   **7.** 10,080

9. $m^n = 6$ **11.** -4 **13.** (a)   (b)

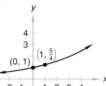
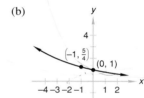

15. (a) $\{ x \in \mathbb{R} \mid x \ge -4 \}$ (b) $\{ x \in \mathbb{R} \mid x \ne 0, 1 \}$ (c) $\{ x \in \mathbb{R} \mid x \ge 4 \}$

17. $\dfrac{3}{2}$ **19.** $(2, 0), (-2, 0)$ **21.** $6 + 3i$ **23.** $x^{a+2} y^{a-4}$

25. $1 - x^2$ **27.** $x = 60; y = 65; z = 85$ **29.** D

problem set 29

1. $(ag + pax)$ mi   **3.** 8 days   **5.** $N_P = 10; N_N = 15; N_D = 5$ **7.** 270,270

9. $b^3 = 5$ **11.** -3 **13.**   **15.** (a) Function, not 1 to 1   (b) Not a function

                                          (c) Function, 1 to 1   (d) Not a function

17. 0   **19.** $\dfrac{3}{2}$ **21.** (a) $-15\dfrac{1}{2}$ (b) 8   (c) 2   **23.** $\dfrac{3z + 12}{2cz + 8c + tz}$

25. $5.83\underline{/329.04°}$; $5.83\underline{/-30.96°}$; $-5.83\underline{/149.04°}$; $-5.83\underline{/-210.96°}$

27.

Statements	Reasons
1. $\overline{AC}$ bisects $\angle BAD$	1. Given
2. $\angle BAC \cong \angle DAC$	2. A bisector divides an angle into two congruent angles.
3. $\angle ABC \cong \angle ADC$	3. Given
4. $\angle ACB \cong \angle ACD$	4. If two angles in one triangle are congruent to two angles in a second triangle, then the third angles are congruent.
5. $\overline{AC} \cong \overline{AC}$	5. Reflexive axiom
6. $\triangle ABC \cong \triangle ADC$	6. AAAS congruency postulate
7. $\overline{BC} \cong \overline{DC}$	7. CPCTC

29. A

problem set 30

1. 1280 boys   **3.** 12.5 liters of 90%, 7.5 liters of 58%   **5.** $y = -\dfrac{3}{2}x + 1$

7. 20.72$\underline{/136.64°}$ **9.**

STATEMENTS	REASONS
1. $\overline{AB} \cong \overline{DC}$	1. Given
2. $\overline{AC} \cong \overline{DB}$	2. Given
3. $\overline{BC} \cong \overline{BC}$	3. Reflexive axiom
4. $\triangle ABC \cong \triangle DCB$	4. *SSS* congruency postulate

11. $\dfrac{1}{3}$

13. 25   **15.**   **17.** (a) $-\dfrac{3}{2}$ (b) $\sqrt{3} + 1 + \sqrt{2}$ **19.** $5\sqrt{3} - \dfrac{11}{2}$

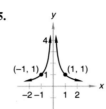

21. $(3, 1), (3, -1), (-3, 1), (-3, -1)$ **23.** $2x^{3N+1}\left(1 + 3x^{2N+1}\right)$ **25.** $\dfrac{2}{3}i$

27. $x = 70;\ y = 75$ **29.** A

problem set 31

1. $\dfrac{pm + 5p}{m + p}\ \dfrac{\text{mi}}{\text{hr}}$ **3.** $-14, -13, -12, -11$ **5.** $y = -x + 9$

7. $y = (x - 2)^2$ **9.** 3.25$\underline{/5.56°}$ **11.** 35   **13.** -2 **15.**

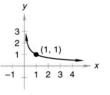

17. $\left\{ x \in \mathbb{R} \mid x \geq -3,\ x \neq -\dfrac{1}{2}, \dfrac{3}{2} \right\}$ **19.** $\sqrt{3}$ **21.** $x = 5;\ y = 4$ **23.** $\dfrac{3a^2c - 2b^2c}{a^2b^2 + bc^2}$

25. $2x^2 - 2x + 3 - \dfrac{4}{x + 1}$ **27.** $-\dfrac{3}{8} \pm \dfrac{\sqrt{41}}{8}$ **29.** B

problem set 32

1. $\dfrac{xp + 10p}{x - 2p}\ \dfrac{\text{mi}}{\text{hr}}$ **3.** 4 days   **5.** Laertes $= 40$ yr; Ophelia $= 36$ yr

7. (a) $60°$ (b) $\dfrac{\sqrt{3}}{2}$ (c) $\dfrac{5\sqrt{41}}{41}$ **9.** $y = (x + 2)^2$ **11.** 6.94$\underline{/65.70°}$ **13.** 6

15. 81   **17.**   **19.** $-2\sqrt{2} - \dfrac{1}{2}$ **21.** (a) $-\dfrac{31}{16}$ (b) -32 (c) 4

23. $\dfrac{2x + 6}{6bx + 18b + 3tx}$ **25.** $z^{\frac{3}{2}b + \frac{9}{2}}$ **27.** $h^2 + 2xh + 3h$ **29.** D

problem set 33

1. $N_N = 3;\ N_D = 4;\ N_Q = 4$ **3.** $y = -\dfrac{1}{2}x + 3$ **5.** 48 m^2

7. (a) $60°$ (b) $\dfrac{\sqrt{3}}{2}$ (c) $-\dfrac{3}{4}$ **9.** $y = |x| + 3$ **11.** 3.88$\underline{/270.47°}$ **13.** 6   **15.** 8

17.

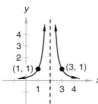

19. $\sqrt{6} - 1$ **21.** $x = 2$; $y = 0$ **23.** $\dfrac{a^2 b - fg^2 c}{x^2 yd^2 + cz^3}$

25. $g = \dfrac{8dsr}{hfr - 4ds}$

27.

STATEMENTS	REASONS
1. $PQRS$ is a rectangle.	1. Given
2. $\angle PQT$ and $\angle SRT$ are right angles.	2. A rectangle contains four right angles.
3. $\angle PQT \cong \angle SRT$	3. All right angles are congruent.
4. T is midpoint of $\overline{QR}$.	4. Given
5. $\overline{QT} \cong \overline{RT}$	5. A midpoint divides a segment into two congruent segments.
6. $\overline{PQ} \cong \overline{SR}$	6. Opposite sides of a rectangle are congruent.
7. $\triangle PQT \cong \triangle SRT$	7. SAS congruency postulate

29. C

problem set 34

1. $\dfrac{mz}{m - 3z} \dfrac{\text{mi}}{\text{hr}}$ **3.** $\dfrac{300}{17}$ hr   **5.** 21   **7.** Mo $= -7.5Zr + 1375$

9. $f(x) = \sqrt{x}$; $g(x) = x + 1$ **11.** 10   **13.** (a) $45°$ (b) $\dfrac{3}{4}$ (c) $\dfrac{\sqrt{10}}{10}$

15. $y = |x| - 3$ **17.** $5\underline{/223°}$ **19.** -5

21. (a) Not a function (b) Not a function (c) Function, 1 to 1 (d) Function, not 1 to 1

23. $\dfrac{3}{4}$ **25.** $(3, 1), (3, -1), (-3, 1), (-3, -1)$

27.

STATEMENTS	REASONS
1. $\overline{BD}$ bisects $\overline{AC}$	1. Given
2. $\overline{AD} \cong \overline{CD}$	2. A bisector divides a segment into two congruent segments.
3. $\overline{AB} \cong \overline{CB}$	3. Given
4. $\overline{BD} \cong \overline{BD}$	4. Reflexive axiom
5. $\triangle ABD \cong \triangle CBD$	5. SSS congruency postulate
6. $\angle A \cong \angle C$	6. $CPCTC$

29. C

problem set 35

1. $N_W = 25$; $N_R = 10$; $N_B = 30$ **3.** $\dfrac{9}{8} \dfrac{\text{jobs}}{\text{hr}}$ **5.** $\dfrac{21}{5}$ **7.** $\sqrt{(x - 3)^2 + (y + 2)^2}$

9. $\dfrac{49}{4}$ **11.** $f(x) = x^2$ **13.** 6   **15.** $30°$ **17.** $\dfrac{2\sqrt{5}}{5}$

19. $y = -\sqrt{x}$ **21.** $4.96\underline{/309.01°}$

23. (a) Domain $= \{x \in \mathbb{R} \mid -4 \le x \le 6\}$; Range $= \{y \in \mathbb{R} \mid -2 \le y \le 3\}$

(b) Domain $= \{x \in \mathbb{R} \mid -4 \le x \le 4\}$; Range $= \{y \in \mathbb{R} \mid -2 \le y \le 2\}$

25. (a) x (b) x **27.** 69   **29.** A

problem set 36

1. Plane $= 240$ mph; wind $= 60$ mph   **3.** $3\sqrt{3}$ **5.** Decreased by 4%

7. $\sqrt{(x + 2)^2 + (y - 5)^2}$ **9.** R $= -10W + 620$ **11.** 7   **13.** $-30°$

15. (a) x axis, no; y axis, no; origin, yes (b) x axis, no; y axis, yes; origin, no

17. $y = (x + 3)^3$ **19.** 360   **21.**

23. $\left\{ x \in \mathbb{R} \mid x \le 3, x \ne -\dfrac{5}{2}, -2 \right\}$

25. $-\sqrt{3}$

27. $h^2 + 2xh - 2h$

29. C

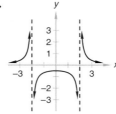

problem set 37

1. Plane = 120 mph; wind = 20 mph　**3.** $\dfrac{3}{8}$　**5.** $\dfrac{mk + 10m}{k - 2m}\ \dfrac{\text{mi}}{\text{hr}}$　**7.** $\left(-\dfrac{1}{2}, \dfrac{9}{2}\right)$

9. 46　**11.** $f(x) = \sqrt{x}$　**13.** 6　**15.** (a) 0°　(b) $\dfrac{\sqrt{5}}{5}$

17. $y = -(3^x)$　**19.** (a) 2　(b) $-\dfrac{7}{2}$　(c) $2\sqrt{2}$　**21.** (a) $\dfrac{-1 - \sqrt{2}}{2}$　(b) $\dfrac{2 + \sqrt{2}}{2}$

23. $(0, 2), \left(\dfrac{8}{5}, -\dfrac{6}{5}\right)$　**25.** $x^3 + x + 1$

27.

STATEMENTS	REASONS
1. $\overline{PQ} \cong \overline{SR}$	1. Given
2. $\overline{QS} \cong \overline{RP}$	2. Given
3. $\overline{PS} \cong \overline{PS}$	3. Reflexive axiom
4. $\triangle PQS \cong \triangle SRP$	4. *SSS* congruency postulate
5. $\angle PQS \cong \angle SRP$	5. *CPCTC*

29. B

---

problem set 38

1. Boat = 12 mph; current = 3 mph　**3.** 50 mph　**5.** 5 hr　**7.** 3125

9. $x^2 - \dfrac{14}{15}x - \dfrac{8}{15} = 0$　**11.** $\left(\dfrac{7}{2}, 4\right)$　**13.** V = −1.54K + 173.7　**15.** C

17. (a) −45°　(b) $\dfrac{2\sqrt{29}}{29}$　**19.** $y = 4^x - 3$　**21.** (a) 2　(b) $-\dfrac{11}{3}$　(c) 9

23. (a) $\dfrac{1}{2}$　(b) $-\dfrac{\sqrt{2}}{2} - \dfrac{\sqrt{3}}{3}$　**25.** $(\sqrt{3}, 2), (\sqrt{3}, -2), (-\sqrt{3}, 2), (-\sqrt{3}, -2)$

27. $h + 2x - 2$　**29.** B

---

problem set 39

1. 2453.58 mi　**3.** 24　**5.** 20 mph　**7.** 25 days　**9.** $\dfrac{x}{-2} + \dfrac{y}{3} = 1$　**11.** $-\dfrac{\sqrt{3}}{4}$

13. $x^2 - 3 = 0$　**15.** $\left(2, \dfrac{9}{2}\right)$　**17.** $\dfrac{5}{4}$　**19.** $f(x) = \sqrt{x}$　**21.** $\dfrac{1}{2}$

23. (a) *x* axis, yes; *y* axis, yes; origin, yes　(b) *x* axis, no; *y* axis, yes; origin, no

25. (a) Domain = $\{x \in \mathbb{R} \mid -4 \le x \le 4\}$; Range = $\{y \in \mathbb{R} \mid 0 \le y \le 3\}$
(b) Domain = $\{x \in \mathbb{R} \mid -5 \le x \le 2\}$; Range = $\{y \in \mathbb{R} \mid -4 \le y \le 5\}$

27.

STATEMENTS	REASONS
1. *ABCD* is a rectangle.	1. Given
2. $\angle B$ and $\angle C$ are right angles.	2. A rectangle contains four right angles.
3. $\angle B \cong \angle C$	3. All right angles are congruent.
4. $\overline{AB} \cong \overline{CD}$	4. Opposite sides of a rectangle are congruent.
5. *E* is the midpoint of $\overline{BC}$.	5. Given
6. $\overline{BE} \cong \overline{CE}$	6. A midpoint divides a segment into two congruent segments.
7. $\triangle ABE \cong \triangle DCE$	7. *SAS* congruency postulate
8. $\overline{AE} \cong \overline{DE}$	8. *CPCTC*

29. B

---

problem set 40

1. 18.33 ft　**3.** Plane = 120 mph; wind = 20 mph　**5.** 625　**7.** 14　**9.** 3　**11.** Yes

13. $\dfrac{x}{-\dfrac{5}{2}} + \dfrac{v}{\dfrac{5}{4}} = 1$　**15.** −1　**17.** $x^2 + \dfrac{19}{15}x - \dfrac{2}{3} = 0$　**19.** N = $-\dfrac{9}{8}$R + 202.5

21. (a) −60°　(b) $\dfrac{3\sqrt{13}}{13}$　**23.** $y = \dfrac{1}{x - 3}$　**25.** $y^6(5x - 6ay)(25x^2 + 30xay + 36a^2y^2)$

27.

Statements	Reasons
1. $\overline{PR}$ bisects $\angle QPS$	1. Given
2. $\overline{PR}$ bisects $\angle QRS$	2. Given
3. $\angle QPR \cong \angle SPR$	3. A bisector divides an angle
$\angle QRP \cong \angle SRP$	into two congruent angles.
4. $\overline{PR} \cong \overline{PR}$	4. Reflexive axiom
5. $\angle Q \cong \angle S$	5. If two angles in one triangle
	are congruent to two angles
	in a second triangle, then the
	third angles are congruent.
6. $\triangle PQR \cong \triangle PSR$	6. AAAS congruency postulate

29. C

problem set 41

1. 30.54 ft   **3.** 200 men   **5.** $\dfrac{m}{h-3}\dfrac{\text{mi}}{\text{hr}}$ **7.** $2 - \sqrt{3}$ **9.** 13   **11.** 3   **13.** No

15. $\dfrac{x}{-\frac{6}{5}} + \dfrac{y}{2} = 1$ **17.** $\dfrac{x}{-\frac{8}{3}} + \dfrac{y}{8} = 1$ **19.** -4 **21.** C

23. (a) $150°$ (b) $\dfrac{\sqrt{5}}{3}$ **25.** $y = |x - 3| + 2$

27. (a) Domain $= \{x \in \mathbb{R} \mid -6 \le x \le 5\}$; Range $= \{y \in \mathbb{R} \mid -3 \le y \le 4\}$
(b) Domain $= \{x \in \mathbb{R} \mid -4 \le x \le 4\}$; Range $= \{y \in \mathbb{R} \mid -2 \le y \le 6\}$

29. C

problem set 42

1. 1047.20 ft   **3.** 0.88   **5.** 3 days   **7.** $(x - 3)^2 + (y - 4)^2 = 3^2$

9.

11. $-2 + \sqrt{3}$ **13.** 6   **15.** 4   **17.** $2x + 5y - 13 = 0$

19. $x^2 - \dfrac{3}{10}x - \dfrac{2}{5} = 0$ **21.** $I = 1.22A - 7.1$ **23.** 9 cm   **25.** $y = |x + 3| + 2$

27. $\left\{x \in \mathbb{R} \mid x \ge 0,\, x \ne \dfrac{1}{2}\right\}$ **29.** C

problem set 43

1. 43.63 ft   **3.** 20 days   **5.** $\dfrac{2000}{130 + f + s}$ gal   **7.** $y = -4\cos\theta$

9. $(x + 2)^2 + (y - 3)^2 = 4^2$ **11.** $-\sqrt{3}$ **13.** 13,440   **15.** 4   **17.** 4

19. $x^2 - 2x - 2 = 0$ **21.** $\left(\dfrac{1}{2}, 3\right)$ **23.** 0   **25.** (a) $-30°$ (b) $-\dfrac{3}{5}$

27. $y = (x - 1)^2 - 1$ **29.** D

problem set 44

1. $\dfrac{100d}{x - 5d}$ drums   **3.** $\dfrac{mc}{c + n}$ min   **5.** 120   **7.** $y = -10\cos x$

9. $(x - h)^2 + (y - k)^2 = 5^2$ **11.** $-\sqrt{2} + \dfrac{1}{2}$ **13.** 7   **15.** $\dfrac{27}{11}$ **17.** 4

19. $x^2 - \dfrac{11}{4}x - \dfrac{3}{4} = 0$ **21.** $x + y = 0$ **23.** $\dfrac{-61}{12}$ **25.** $f(x) = \log_3 x$; $g(x) = x + 2$

27. $y = (x + 3)^2 - 1$ **29.** B

problem set 45

1. 25   **3.** $\dfrac{fk(c + 10)}{c(k - x)}$ hr   **5.** $R_O = 4$ mph; $T_O = 6$ hr; $R_B = 8$ mph; $T_B = 3$ hr

7. $N_G = 20$; $N_B = 10$; $N_W = 5$ **9.** Rh $= 0.7686$Dy $- 2.2571$; $r = 0.9944$; good correlation

11. $y = 8 \cos x$ **13.**   **15.** $-\dfrac{\sqrt{3}}{6}$ **17.** 1   **19.** $\dfrac{1}{14}$

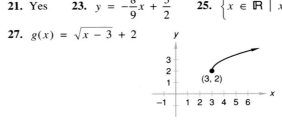

21. Yes   **23.** $y = -\dfrac{8}{9}x + \dfrac{3}{2}$ **25.** $\left\{ x \in \mathbb{R} \mid x \geq 0, x \neq \dfrac{1}{4} \right\}$

27. $g(x) = \sqrt{x - 3} + 2$ **29.** B

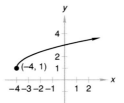

problem set 46

1. 25   **3.** $\dfrac{dy}{y + 50}$ days   **5.** 628.32 m   **7.** 500 liters   **9.** $x^2 - 4x + 13 = 0$

11. C $= -0.1138$H $+ 50.1680$; $r = -0.9439$; good correlation   **13.** $y = -9 \sin \theta$

15.   **17.** 1624   **19.** $\dfrac{35}{2}$ **21.** 27   **23.** $\dfrac{1}{3}$ **25.** $y = \sqrt{x - 1} - 4$

27. (a) Domain $= \{x \in \mathbb{R} \mid -4 \leq x \leq 6\}$; Range $= \{y \in \mathbb{R} \mid -2 \leq y \leq 3\}$
(b) Domain $= \{x \in \mathbb{R} \mid -3 \leq x \leq 2\}$; Range $= \{y \in \mathbb{R} \mid -4 \leq y \leq 4\}$

29. B

problem set 47

1. 12   **3.** $\dfrac{dk}{k - y}$ hr   **5.** 13.96 ft   **7.** $y = -5 - 25 \sin \theta$

9. (a) $-45°$ (b) $-30°$ **11.** $2(x + 1 - i)(x + 1 + i)$ **13.** $(x - 2)^2 + (y - 1)^2 = 3^2$

15. (a) $\dfrac{-3 - \sqrt{2}}{2}$ (b) 1   **17.** $\dfrac{15}{4}$ **19.** 8   **21.** (1, 1)   **23.** 5

25. (a) x axis, yes; y axis, no; origin, no   (b) x axis, no; y axis, yes; origin, no

27. $g(x) = \sqrt{x + 4} + 1$ **29.** C

problem set 48

1. 80   **3.** 2930.48 mi   **5.** $m = \dfrac{W_1 W_2}{W_1 + W_2}$ **7.** $N_R = 4$; $N_B = 2$; $N_W = 6$ **9.** 1

11. $\dfrac{x}{\frac{7}{2}} + \dfrac{y}{-\frac{7}{4}} = 1$ **13.** $y = -5 - 20 \cos x$ **15.** (a) $60°$ (b) $-30°$

17. $(x - 1 - \sqrt{2}i)(x - 1 + \sqrt{2}i)$ **19.** $(x - 3)^2 + (y - 2)^2 = 4^2$ **21.** 432   **23.** 0

25. (a) $-90°$ (b) $\dfrac{\sqrt{5}}{3}$ **27.** $g(x) = \sqrt{x + 9} - 2$ **29.** C

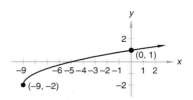

problem set 49

1. 288   **3.** 3013.42 mi   **5.** \$432   **7.** $\dfrac{11KS}{G(S + 14)}$ days   **9.** $\dfrac{1}{3}$

11. $x + y - 2 = 0$ **13.** $x - 5y - 19 = 0$ **15.** $y = 5 - 15 \cos \theta$

17. $x^2 - 4x + 5 = 0$ **19.** Ca $= 0.5176$K $+ 6.6444$; $r = 0.9352$; good correlation

21.

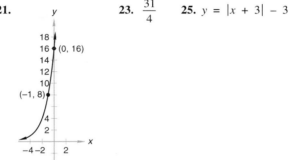

23. (a) 38 (b) 3   **25.** $y = |x - 1| - 4$

27. (a) Domain $= \{x \in \mathbb{R} \mid -2 < x \le 4\}$; Range $= \{y \in \mathbb{R} \mid -3 < y \le 3\}$
(b) Domain $= \{x \in \mathbb{R} \mid -3 \le x < 6\}$; Range $= \{y \in \mathbb{R} \mid -4 \le y \le 5\}$

29. A

problem set 50

1. 40   **3.** 2695.49 mi   **5.** $\dfrac{177}{2}$ hr   **7.** $\dfrac{d}{h - 4}$ $\dfrac{\text{mi}}{\text{hr}}$ **9.** $30°, 330°$

11. (a) -1 (b) $3 + 3\sqrt{3}$ **13.** $5x + y - 7 = 0$ **15.** $y = 5 + 25 \cos x$

17. $x^2 - 2x + 4 = 0$ **19.** C $= 0.1178$H $- 4.1948$; $r = 0.9112$; good correlation

21.   **23.** $\dfrac{31}{4}$ **25.** $y = |x + 3| - 3$

27. (a) Domain $= \{x \in \mathbb{R} \mid -5 \le x < 4\}$; Range $= \{y \in \mathbb{R} \mid -2 \le y \le 7\}$
(b) Domain $= \{x \in \mathbb{R} \mid -4 < x < 3\}$; Range $= \{y \in \mathbb{R} \mid -4 < y \le 4\}$

29. D

problem set 51

1. 18   **3.** 314.16 m   **5.** $\dfrac{100d}{3}$ stamps   **7.** $\dfrac{60d}{m - 60}$ mph

9. $e^{8.1887}$ **11.** $240°, 300°$ **13.** -2 **15.** $6x - 4y - 5 = 0$ **17.** $y = 5 + 25 \sin x$

19. $x^2 - 6x + 10 = 0$ **21.** H $= 0.8072$P $+ 55.9193$; $r = 0.9111$; good correlation

23.   **25.** (a) 34 (b) $\dfrac{8}{9}$ **27.** (a) $\dfrac{\sqrt{7}}{4}$ (b) $-\dfrac{5\sqrt{6}}{12}$ (c) $30°$ **29.** B

problem set 52

1. 1080   **3.** 2681.66 mi   **5.** \$210   **7.** $\dfrac{D}{S - 120}$ $\dfrac{\text{ft}}{\text{s}}$

9. $60°, 120°, 240°, 300°$ **11.** $120°, 240°$ **13.** $e^{8.2428}$ **15.** $\dfrac{5}{3}$ **17.** $y = 4 - 7 \sin x$

19. $x^2 + 4x + 5 = 0$ **21.** $W = 13.4787H - 761.8723$; $r = 0.7815$; not a good correlation

23.   **25.** $\dfrac{21}{2}$ **27.** No   **29.** $y = -\sqrt{x + 4}$

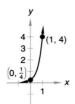

problem set 53

1. 180   **3.** 6 days   **5.** $\dfrac{3Y}{S + 20} \dfrac{\text{yd}}{\text{s}}$ **7.** $\dfrac{(50)(5280)(12)(2.54)}{60} \dfrac{\text{cm}}{\text{min}}$

9. $\dfrac{(50)(5280)(12)}{(15)(60)(60)(2\pi)} \dfrac{\text{rev}}{\text{s}}$ **11.** $0°, 120°, 240°$ **13.** $10^{3.7924}$ **15.** $-\dfrac{2}{3}$

17. $2x - 5 = 0$ **19.** $y = -1 - 7\cos\theta$

21. $V = 59.88W + 323.76$; $r = 0.9815$; good correlation   **23.**

25. 4   **27.** 2   **29.** D

problem set 54

1. $\dfrac{(1.5)(30)(60)(2\pi)}{5280} \dfrac{\text{mi}}{\text{hr}}$ **3.** 36   **5.** $\dfrac{R}{m - 2} \dfrac{\text{mi}}{\text{hr}}$ **7.** 20 liters

9. $y = -(x + 2)^2 + 10$ **11.** $(12)(10)^3(60)(60) \dfrac{\text{cm}^3}{\text{hr}}$

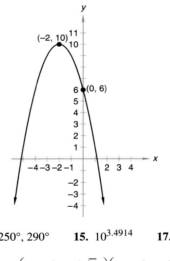

13. $10°, 50°, 130°, 170°, 250°, 290°$ **15.** $10^{3.4914}$ **17.** $\dfrac{1}{3}$ **19.** $(2, 6)$

21. $y = 9 - \sin x$ **23.** $5\left(x + \dfrac{3}{2} - \dfrac{3\sqrt{3}}{2}i\right)\left(x + \dfrac{3}{2} + \dfrac{3\sqrt{3}}{2}i\right)$

25. $(x - 3)^2 + (y - 2)^2 = 6^2$ **27.** (a) $\dfrac{1}{6}$ (b) $\dfrac{25}{8}$ **29.** $y = -|x| - 2$

problem set 55

1. 2   **3.** 10,080   **5.** $\dfrac{(0.5)(40)(60)}{36} \dfrac{\text{yd}}{\text{min}}$ **7.** $N_R = 6$; $N_W = 4$; $N_G = 5$

9. $y = -(x + 1)^2 - 1$ **11.** $\dfrac{(12)(10)^3}{(2.54)^3(60)} \dfrac{\text{in.}^3}{\text{min}}$

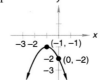

13. $10°, 70°, 130°, 190°, 250°, 310°$ **15.** $10^{3.7634}$ **17.** $-\frac{1}{3}$ **19.** $x + y - 1 = 0$

21. $y = 8 - 9\cos\theta$ **23.** $P = 1.057H + 60.43; \ r = 0.1018; \ \text{not a good correlation}$

25. 630 **27.** Yes   **29.** $y = \sqrt{-x} + 3$

problem set 56

1. 125 **3.** $15,120$ **5.** $\dfrac{(260)(1000)(100)}{(60)(2.54)(12)(2\pi)} \ \dfrac{\text{rev}}{\text{min}}$ **7.** 74 **9.** $14.74 \ \text{m}^2$

11. $234.73 \ \text{m}^2$ **13.** $9.06 \ \text{ft}^2$ **15.** $y = (x - 2)^2 + 2$

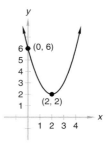

17. $135°, 315°$ **19.** $135°, 315°$ **21.** $e^{11.0821}$ **23.** $x + 4y + 3 = 0$

25. $y = 3 - 9\cos x$ **27.** $P = 0.0996I + 47.9949; \ r = 0.1503; \ \text{not a good correlation}$

29. (a) 7 (b) $\dfrac{4}{3}$

problem set 57

1. $13,860$ **3.** $\dfrac{(4)(400)(60)}{(2.54)(12)(5280)} \ \dfrac{\text{mi}}{\text{hr}}$ **5.** $B = 6 \ \text{mph}; \ W = 2 \ \text{mph}$ **7.** $2000 \ \text{boys}$

9. $y = 10\sin 2\theta$ **11.** $25.80 \ \text{cm}^2$ **13.** $4.80 \ \text{m}^2$ **15.**

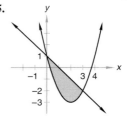

17. $60°, 300°$ **19.** $30°, 90°, 150°, 210°, 270°, 330°$ **21.** $e^{9.210}$ **23.** $\dfrac{\pi}{6}$

25. $\left(x - \dfrac{3}{2} - \dfrac{\sqrt{7}}{2}i \right)\left(x - \dfrac{3}{2} + \dfrac{\sqrt{7}}{2}i \right)$ **27.** Yes   **29.** $y = \sqrt{-(x - 4)}$

problem set 58

1. 126 **3.** 24 **5.** $\dfrac{(100)(5280)(12)(2.54)}{(60)(60)(40)} \ \dfrac{\text{rad}}{\text{s}}$ **7.** 11 **9.** $\dfrac{12\sqrt{5}}{5}$

11. $y = -3 + 5\cos(\theta - 135°)$ **13.** $34.47 \ \text{m}^2$ **15.** $4.05 \ \text{ft}^2$ **17.** C **19.** $30°, 330°$

21. $45°, 105°, 165°, 225°, 285°, 345°$ **23.** $\dfrac{\sqrt{15}}{4}$ **25.** 5 **27.** No   **29.** $y = \sqrt{-x} - 2$

problem set 59

1. $2,494,800$ **3.** 648 **5.** $\dfrac{(40)(1000)(100)}{(2.54)(60)(8)(2\pi)} \ \dfrac{\text{rev}}{\text{min}}$ **7.** $\dfrac{66}{13} \ \text{days}$ **9.** 3 **11.** $\dfrac{4}{7}$

13. 30 **15.** $y = 3(x - 1)^2 + 2$ **17.** $y = 4 + 7\sin 2\theta$

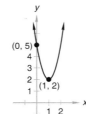

19. 5,496,510.22 cm^2 **21.**

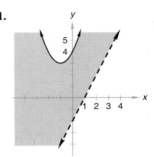

23. 30°, 210°   **25.** 10$^{4.3010}$

27. (a) $\dfrac{3}{4}$ (b) $-\dfrac{\pi}{6}$ (c) $1 - \sqrt{3}$ **29.** $y = \sqrt{-(x + 3)}$

problem set 60

1. 12   **3.** $\dfrac{(16)(367)(60)}{(12)(5280)} \dfrac{\text{mi}}{\text{hr}}$ **5.** $J = 400$ mph; $W = 50$ mph   **7.** 0°, 90°, 270°

9. 2   **11.** 1   **13.** 3   **15.** $y = 3(x + 1)^2 - 3$

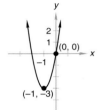

17. $y = -10 + 20 \cos 2x$ **19.** 77.41 cm^2 **21.** 0.60 ft^2 **23.** 30°, 150°, 270°

25. (a) $\dfrac{\pi}{4}$ (b) $\dfrac{15}{16}$ (c) 0   **27.** $x^2 + 2x + 4 = 0$

29. $g(x) = |x|$

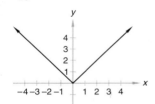

problem set 61

1. 1320   **3.** $\dfrac{(40)(1000)(100)}{(2.54)(60)(60)(14)} \dfrac{\text{rad}}{\text{s}}$ **5.** $\dfrac{2ud}{u + d}$ knots   **7.** $E = 35$ yr; $L = 31$ yr

9. Range = 5; mean = 5.83; median = 6; mode = 8; variance = 3.81; standard deviation = 1.95

11.

Stem	Leaf
3	1, 0
4	0, 4, 2, 7
5	5, 7, 3, 2
6	2, 9

13. 45°, 75°, 165°, 195°, 285°, 315°   **15.** 60°, 90°, 270°, 300°

17. 10   **19.** $\dfrac{3\sqrt{2}}{2}$ **21.** $y = -2 + 6 \sin\left(x - \dfrac{\pi}{4}\right)$ **23.** 541.27 cm^2

25. 105.90 cm^2 **27.** 0   **29.** $-\dfrac{5}{13}$

problem set 62

1. $C = 10N + 50$ **3.** 6,930   **5.** $\dfrac{(20)(723)}{(2.54)(12)(60)} \dfrac{\text{ft}}{\text{s}}$ **7.** 40 atm   **9.** $y = \dfrac{mf - cd}{me - nd}$

11. (a) 78 to 90   (b) 72 to 96   **13.** 0°, 90°, 180°, 270°   **15.** 2   **17.** 9

19. $y = -1 + 4 \cos(\theta - 135°)$ **21.** 626.72 cm^2 **23.** 57.43 cm^2

25. 0   **27.** $-\dfrac{5}{12}$ **29.** D

problem set 63

1. $N_R = 27$ **3.** 48   **5.** $\dfrac{(60)(100)(1000)}{(2.54)(12)(60)(60)} \dfrac{\text{rad}}{\text{s}}$ **7.** $\dfrac{1000b}{a + bc}$ hr

9. $(x + 4)^2 + (y - 3)^2 = 6^2$; center = $(-4, 3)$; radius = 6

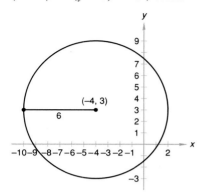

11. $x = \dfrac{cn - bf}{an - mb}$

13. 68% of the data lie between 72 and 80; 95% of the data lie between 68 and 84; 99% of the data lie between 64 and 88.

15. 60°, 120°, 240°, 300°   **17.** $2\sqrt{3}$ **19.** $6\sqrt{2}$ **21.** $y = 4 + 8 \sin\left(x - \dfrac{\pi}{4}\right)$

23. 1542.69 cm²   **25.** 122.53 cm²   **27.** 1   **29.** $\dfrac{\sqrt{11}}{6}$

problem set 64

1. $25,000   **3.** 35   **5.** $\dfrac{150(x + y)}{m + k}$ hr   **7.** $\dfrac{100k^2 t}{d}$ pencils   **9.** $6\sqrt{3} - 6i$

11. $(x - 2)^2 + y^2 = 2^2$; center = $(2, 0)$; radius = 2

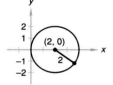

13. $y = \dfrac{cf - dp}{cq - bp}$

15. Mean = 28.93; standard deviation = 9.67;

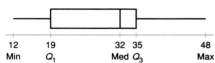

17. 60°, 120°, 240°, 300°   **19.** 1   **21.** 163   **23.** $y = -1 + 5\cos(x - 135°)$

25. 138.56 cm²   **27.**

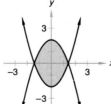

   29. 1

problem set 65

1. $1000   **3.** 34,650   **5.** 2944.30 miles   **7.** $\dfrac{Rx - px}{Rp}$ hr   **9.** 45°, 315°

11.   **13.** 30i

15. $(x + 5)^2 + y^2 = 10^2$; center $= (-5, 0)$; radius $= 10$

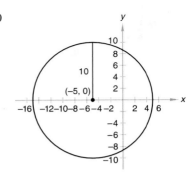

17. Range $= 8$; mean $= 5.67$; median $= 6$; mode $= 9$; variance $= 8.89$;
standard deviation $= 2.98$

19. $50°, 70°, 170°, 190°, 290°, 310°$ **21.** 4 **23.** $y = 1 + 5 \sin\left(x - \dfrac{3\pi}{4}\right)$ **25.** 0.0046 m^2

27. $\dfrac{5}{4}$ **29.** $\left(x + \dfrac{3}{2} - \dfrac{\sqrt{19}}{2}i\right)\left(x + \dfrac{3}{2} + \dfrac{\sqrt{19}}{2}i\right)$

**problem set
66**

1. $925   **3.** 120 **5.** $\dfrac{740(2p + 6)}{k + z}$ hr   **7.** $\dfrac{10,000\,p^2 k}{m}$ cars

9. $y = 3 + 5 \sin\left(x - \dfrac{3\pi}{4}\right)$ **11.** $\dfrac{\pi}{3}, \dfrac{7\pi}{6}, \dfrac{5\pi}{3}, \dfrac{11\pi}{6}$

13. (a) $5 \text{ cis } 36.87°$ (b) $-\dfrac{5}{2}\sqrt{3} + \dfrac{5}{2}i$ **15.** $8\sqrt{3} - 8i$ **17.** $x = \dfrac{cf - bg}{af - bd}$

19. Range $= 7$; mean $= 3$; median $= 2$; mode $= 2$; variance $= 6.67$; standard deviation $= 2.58$

21. $10°, 50°, 130°, 170°, 250°, 290°$ **23.** $x = 4$ **25.** 8.86 m^2 **27.** -8

29. $x^2 - 4x + 9 = 0$

**problem set
67**

1. 60 **3.** $R_H = 400$ mph; $T_H = 3$ hr; $R_F = 200$ mph; $T_F = 9$ hr   **5.** 98

7. (a) 39.67 (b) $204,173.79$ **9.**

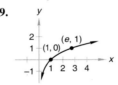

11. $y = 3 + 5 \cos \dfrac{1}{2}(x - 270°)$ **13.** $4 + 4\sqrt{3}i$

15. $(x - 2)^2 + (y + 3)^2 = 4^2$; center $= (2, -3)$; radius $= 4$

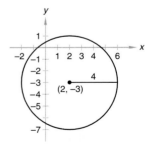

17. $-\dfrac{1}{13}$

19.

STEM	LEAF
1	7
2	
3	
4	6
5	6, 8
6	4, 6, 8
7	3, 5, 0, 1
8	3, 7, 5, 2
9	2

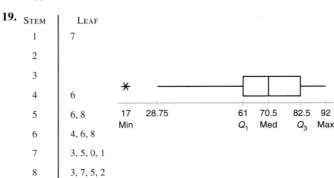

21. 30°, 150°   **23.** $-\dfrac{1}{2}$ **25.** 3   **27.**

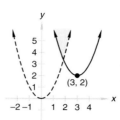

29. $(x - 2 - \sqrt{2}i)(x - 2 + \sqrt{2}i)$

problem set 68

1. \$475   **3.** 60   **5.** $\dfrac{100(2u + 2)}{m + s}$ hr   **7.** 0, 1, 2, 3

9. Directrix: $y = -1$; axis of symmetry: $x = 0$; parabola: $y = \dfrac{1}{8}x^2 + 1$

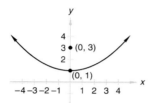

11. (a) 68%   (b) 34%

13.   **15.** $y = 1 - 3\sin\dfrac{18}{5}x$

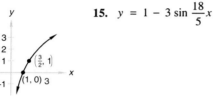

17. $(x + 5)^2 + (y - 1)^2 = \sqrt{27}^2$; center $= (-5, 1)$; radius $= \sqrt{27}$

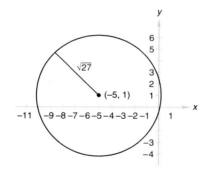

19. $x = 5$ **21.** 45°, 225°   **23.** 60°   **25.** 1   **27.** $5\sqrt{5}$ **29.** 0.080 ft^2

problem set 69

1. $R_G = 40$ mph; $R_B = 80$ mph   **3.** 20°   **5.** \$8000   **7.** $\dfrac{1 \pm \sqrt{41}}{2}$

9. Parabola: $y = -\dfrac{1}{12}(x + 3)^2 + 2$; directrix: $y = 5$; axis of symmetry: $x = -3$

11. 81.5%   **13.** $y = 5 + 4\cos 2\left(x + \dfrac{3\pi}{8}\right)$ **15.** $6 + 6\sqrt{3}i$ **17.** $y = \dfrac{ad - pc}{aq - pb}$

19. $4\sqrt{2}$ **21.** $\dfrac{\pi}{3}, \dfrac{2\pi}{3}, \dfrac{4\pi}{3}, \dfrac{5\pi}{3}$ **23.** $\dfrac{\pi}{6}, \dfrac{5\pi}{6}, \dfrac{7\pi}{6}, \dfrac{11\pi}{6}$ **25.** $\dfrac{32}{3}$

27. 0.037 m^2 **29.** (a) 223.55   (b) 1249.58

problem set 70

1. 45 squirrels   **3.** $B = 20$ mph; $W = 2$ mph   **5.** 1,108,800   **7.** 93.32%   **9.** 3, –2

11.

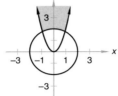

13. $y = -9 + 31 \sin \frac{3}{2}(x + 10°)$

15. $x = \dfrac{js + aw}{jd + kw}$ **17.** $6 - 6\sqrt{3}i$ **19.** $\dfrac{\pi}{3}, \pi, \dfrac{5\pi}{3}$ **21.** $\dfrac{3}{2}$

23.

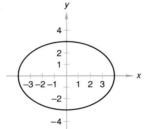

25. $x^2 - 4\sqrt{3}x + 16 = 0$ **27.** 14.10 in.^{2} **29.** $\dfrac{8}{7}$

problem set 71

1. $B = 20$ mph; $W = 4$ mph   **3.** 72   **5.** is multiplied by $\dfrac{9}{4}$

7.

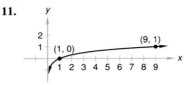

9. 6.68%

11. Parabola: $y = -\dfrac{1}{8}x^2$; directrix: $y = 2$; axis of symmetry: $x = 0$

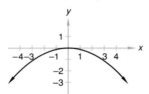

13.

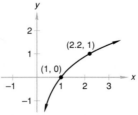

15. $y = -3 + 8 \cos \dfrac{1}{4}(x - 180°)$

17. (a) 10.63 cis 228.81°   (b) $0 - 7i$ **19.** 120°, 225°, 240°, 315°

21. 90°, 135°, 270°, 315°   **23.** 1   **25.**

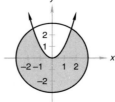

27. 0.024 ft^2

29. (a) 0   (b) $\dfrac{7}{2}$ (c) 11

problem set 72

1. 90,720   3. $\dfrac{1000wm}{z}$ men   5. 143   7. $A = 110°$; $a = 15.04$; $m = 10.28$

9.
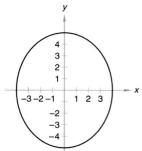

11. 73.33%   13. Focus $= (0, -2)$; vertex $= (0, 0)$; directrix: $y = 2$

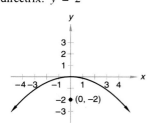

15.
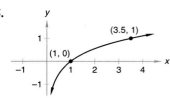

17. $y = -10 + 20 \sin 2x$ 19. $-18 + 0i$

21. $\dfrac{\pi}{6}, \dfrac{5\pi}{6}, \dfrac{3\pi}{2}$ 23. 1

25. Mean $= 5.5$; median $= 6.5$; mode $= 7$; variance $= 4.92$; standard deviation $= 2.22$

27. 1   29. $\left(x + \dfrac{3}{2} - \dfrac{\sqrt{31}}{2}i \right)\left(x + \dfrac{3}{2} + \dfrac{\sqrt{31}}{2}i \right)$

problem set 73

1. 210   3. $\dfrac{h - w}{h}$ 5. 28, 42   7. 93.53 in.^{2} 9. $\dfrac{1}{81}$

11. $\dfrac{x^2}{9} + \dfrac{y^2}{4} = 1$ 13. $-2, 0$

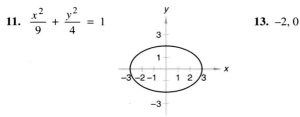

15. Focus $= \left(0, \dfrac{9}{4} \right)$; directrix: $y = -\dfrac{9}{4}$; vertex $= (0, 0)$; axis of symmetry: $x = 0$

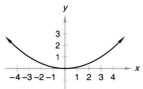

17. $y = -3 + 2 \cos \dfrac{5}{3}(x - 81°)$ 19. $6\sqrt{3} + 6i$ 21. $y = -\dfrac{1}{7}$

23. $60°, 120°, 240°, 300°$ 25. -4 27.   29. 4

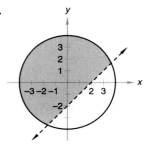

problem set 74

1. 495   **3.** $(36y - 12f - n)$ in.   **5.** $\dfrac{E - P}{E}$ **7.** $\dfrac{2pk}{k + p}$ mph   **9.** $x = -1;\ y = 1$

11. 4 cm   **13.** $A = 135°;\ a = 28.28;\ b = 10.35$ **15.** 0.62%

17. Parabola: $y = -\dfrac{1}{12}(x + 2)^2 + 1$; directrix: $y = 4$; axis of symmetry: $x = -2$

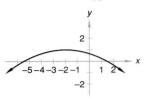

19. $(x + 5)^2 + (y - 2)^2 = 3^2$; center $= (-5, 2)$; radius $= 3$ **21.** $y = -1 + 14 \sin (x + 45°)$

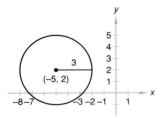

23. (a) 3.61 cis 303.69°   (b) $-\dfrac{13\sqrt{3}}{2} + \dfrac{13}{2}i$ **25.** $\dfrac{\pi}{3}, \dfrac{2\pi}{3}, \dfrac{4\pi}{3}, \dfrac{5\pi}{3}$

27. 2   **29.** (a) 36   (b) -2 (c) 5

problem set 75

1. $\$1.10 + \$1.10m$ **3.** p is multiplied by $\dfrac{16}{3}$ **5.** 56 triangles

7. $x = -\dfrac{25}{17};\ y = -\dfrac{6}{17}$ **9.** Area $= 77.25$ cm^2; radius $= 4.83$ cm

11. $A = 50°;\ a = 7.08;\ b = 8.68$ **13.** 1   **15.**

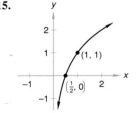

17. $y = 10 + 6 \sin \dfrac{1}{2}\left(x - \dfrac{\pi}{2}\right)$ **19.** (a) 7.81 cis 50.19°   (b) $\dfrac{7\sqrt{2}}{2} - \dfrac{7\sqrt{2}}{2}i$ **21.** 90°

23. 0   **25.**

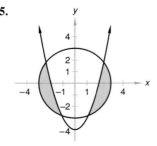

27. $\dfrac{1}{2}$ **29.** (a) $\dfrac{1}{36}$ (b) $\dfrac{1}{64}$

problem set 76

1. 45 committees   **3.** \$460; \$34,960   **5.** $\dfrac{y}{m - 15}\ \dfrac{\text{yards}}{\text{minutes}}$

7. $\dfrac{\cot x}{\csc x} = \dfrac{\dfrac{\cos x}{\sin x}}{\dfrac{1}{\sin x}} = \dfrac{\cos x}{\sin x} \cdot \dfrac{\sin x}{1} = \cos x$ **9.** $x = \dfrac{17}{12};\ y = \dfrac{7}{8}$ **11.** 6.53 in.

13. $\dfrac{x^2}{6} + \dfrac{y^2}{12} = 1$

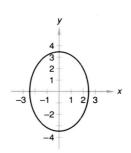

15. $-1, 4$ **17.**

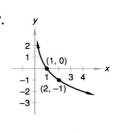

19. $y = 3 + 6 \cos \dfrac{2}{3}(\theta - 135°)$ **21.** $-9\sqrt{2} + 9\sqrt{2}i$

23. $\dfrac{\pi}{6}, \dfrac{\pi}{3}, \dfrac{2\pi}{3}, \dfrac{5\pi}{6}, \dfrac{7\pi}{6}, \dfrac{4\pi}{3}, \dfrac{5\pi}{3}, \dfrac{11\pi}{6}$ **25.** 0 **27.** 3 **29.** (a) 12 (b) 0

problem set 77

1. 126 teams   **3.** \$656   **5.** 4, 5, 6   **7.** $x^4 + 4x^3y + 6x^2y^2 + 4xy^3 + y^4$

9. $\sin x \sec x = \sin x \dfrac{1}{\cos x} = \dfrac{\sin x}{\cos x} = \tan x$

11. $\sin (-\theta) \tan (90° - \theta) = (-\sin \theta) \cot \theta = (-\sin \theta)\left(\dfrac{\cos \theta}{\sin \theta}\right) = -\cos \theta$

13. Radius of circumscribed circle $= 6$ cm; radius of inscribed circle $= 5.20$ cm

15. $\dfrac{x^2}{2} + \dfrac{y^2}{8} = 1$

17. $\dfrac{-3 \pm \sqrt{17}}{4}$

19. $y = 11 + \cos\left(\dfrac{3}{4}\left(x + \dfrac{\pi}{3}\right)\right)$ **21.** $4 + 4\sqrt{3}i$

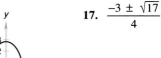

23. $7.5°, 52.5°, 97.5°, 142.5°, 187.5°, 232.5°, 277.5°, 322.5°$ **25.** $\dfrac{7\sqrt{2}}{2}$

27. $\dfrac{5}{2}$ **29.** (a) 6 (b) 4 (c) $\dfrac{1}{2}$

problem set 78

1. 126 committees   **3.** $98°$ **5.** 2 hr

7. Vertices $= (4, 0)$; $(-4, 0)$; asymptotes: $y = \dfrac{1}{2}x$; $y = -\dfrac{1}{2}x$

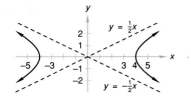

9. $a^5 + 5a^4b + 10a^3b^2 + 10a^2b^3 + 5ab^4 + b^5$

11. $\sin \theta \csc (90° - \theta) = \sin \theta \sec \theta = \sin \theta \dfrac{1}{\cos \theta} = \tan \theta$

13. $x = \dfrac{29}{10}$; $y = \dfrac{11}{5}$ **15.** $\dfrac{9}{25}$ **17.** $\dfrac{x^2}{4} + \dfrac{y^2}{49} = 1$

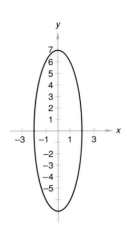

19. Parabola: $y = \dfrac{1}{40}(x + 2)^2 - 6$; directrix: $y = -16$; axis of symmetry: $x = -2$

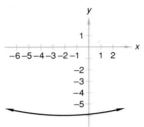

21. $(x + 1)^2 + (y + 1)^2 = (\sqrt{13})^2$; center $= (-1, -1)$; radius $= \sqrt{13}$

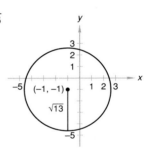

23. $3 - 3\sqrt{3}i$ **25.** $\dfrac{\pi}{4}, \dfrac{\pi}{2}, \dfrac{3\pi}{4}, \dfrac{5\pi}{4}, \dfrac{7\pi}{4}$

27. Mean $= 3.83$; median $= 4$; mode $= 5$; variance $= 4.14$; standard deviation $= 2.03$

29. $2 \pm \sqrt{3}$

problem set 79

1. 220 committees **3.** \$1100 **5.** 6 days **7.** $16 + 16\sqrt{3}i$ **9.** i; $-i$

11. $\dfrac{x^2}{4} - \dfrac{y^2}{9} = 1$; vertices $= (2, 0)$; $(-2, 0)$; asymptotes: $y = \dfrac{3}{2}x$; $y = -\dfrac{3}{2}x$ **13.** $126a^4b^5$

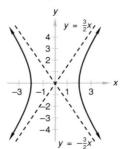

15. $\sin (90° - \theta) \sec (90° - \theta) = \cos \theta \csc \theta = \cos \theta \cdot \dfrac{1}{\sin \theta} = \dfrac{\cos \theta}{\sin \theta} = \cot \theta$

17. 8.07 ft **19.** $B = 40°$; $a = 12.66$ cm; $b = 9.40$ cm **21.** 30.85%

23. Parabola: $y = \frac{1}{16}(x + 4)^2 + 2$; directrix: $y = -2$; axis of symmetry: $x = -4$

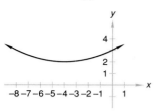

25. $8i$ **27.** 30°, 60°, 120°, 150°, 210°, 240°, 300°, 330°   **29.** $\frac{7}{4}$

problem set 80

1. 24   **3.** $\frac{1}{3}$ cup   **5.** $\frac{M}{25}$ days   **7.** $\frac{\sec^2 x - \tan^2 x}{1 + \cot^2 x} = \frac{1}{\csc^2 x} = \sin^2 x$

9. $\frac{1}{\tan A} + \tan A = \frac{1 + \tan^2 A}{\tan A} = \frac{\sec^2 A}{\tan A} = \frac{\frac{1}{\cos^2 A}}{\frac{\sin A}{\cos A}} = \frac{1}{\cos^2 A} \cdot \frac{\cos A}{\sin A}$

$$= \frac{1}{\cos A} \cdot \frac{1}{\sin A} = \sec A \csc A$$

11. 3 cis 12°; 3 cis 132°; 3 cis 252°

13. $\frac{x^2}{25} - \frac{y^2}{16} = 1$; vertices = (5, 0); (–5, 0); asymptotes; $y = \frac{4}{5}x$; $y = -\frac{4}{5}x$

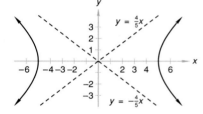

15. $15x^4y^2$ **17.** Side = 3 in.; area = 118.67 in.²; radius = 6.27 in.

19. $\frac{x^2}{25} + \frac{y^2}{9} = 1$

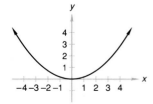

21. Parabola: $y = \frac{5}{28}x^2$; directrix: $y = -\frac{7}{5}$; axis of symmetry: $x = 0$

23. $(x + 1)^2 + (y - 2)^2 = \left(\frac{7}{3}\right)^2$; center = (–1, 2); radius = $\frac{7}{3}$

25. $-12i$ **27.** $\frac{2\pi}{3}$ **29.** $\frac{14}{13}$

problem set 81

1. 210 teams   **3.** 81 and 69   **5.** 6 workers   **7.** $A = 40.54°$; $B = 111.80°$; $C = 27.66°$

9. $\dfrac{1 - \cos^2 x}{\sec^2 x - 1} = \dfrac{\sin^2 x}{\tan^2 x} = \dfrac{\sin^2 x}{\dfrac{\sin^2 x}{\cos^2 x}} = \dfrac{\sin^2 x}{1} \cdot \dfrac{\cos^2 x}{\sin^2 x} = \cos^2 x$

11. $-8i$ **13.** $\dfrac{3\sqrt{2}}{2} + \dfrac{3\sqrt{2}}{2}i;\ -\dfrac{3\sqrt{2}}{2} + \dfrac{3\sqrt{2}}{2}i;\ -\dfrac{3\sqrt{2}}{2} - \dfrac{3\sqrt{2}}{2}i;\ \dfrac{3\sqrt{2}}{2} - \dfrac{3\sqrt{2}}{2}i$

15. $m^4 + 4m^3n + 6m^2n^2 + 4mn^3 + n^4$ **17.** Area = 100.77 in.²; radius = 5.80 in.

19. 44.35%   **21.**

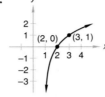

   23. $4 - 4\sqrt{3}i$ **25.** 90°, 270°

27.

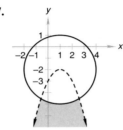

   29. $\dfrac{11}{10}$

problem set 82

1. 38,798,760 patterns   **3.** Height = 8 ft; length = 6 ft; width = 4 ft   **5.** 35 days

7. -1.91 **9.** $= 74.74°$; $C = 60.26°$; $a = 7.33$ cm

11. $\dfrac{\sin A}{1 + \cos A} + \dfrac{1 + \cos A}{\sin A} = \dfrac{\sin^2 A + (1 + \cos A)^2}{(1 + \cos A)\sin A} = \dfrac{\sin^2 A + 1 + 2\cos A + \cos^2 A}{(1 + \cos A)\sin A}$

$= \dfrac{2 + 2\cos A}{(1 + \cos A)\sin A} = \dfrac{2(1 + \cos A)}{(1 + \cos A)\sin A} = \dfrac{2}{\sin A} = 2\csc A$

13. $\dfrac{\sin x}{\csc x} + \dfrac{\cos x}{\sec x} = \dfrac{\sin x}{\dfrac{1}{\sin x}} + \dfrac{\cos x}{\dfrac{1}{\cos x}} = \sin^2 x + \cos^2 x = 1$

15. 2 cis 15°; 2 cis 105°; 2 cis 195°; 2 cis 285°

17. $\dfrac{x^2}{36} - \dfrac{y^2}{9} = 1$; vertices = (6, 0); (–6, 0); asymptotes: $y = \dfrac{1}{2}x$; $y = -\dfrac{1}{2}x$

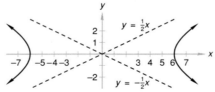

19. $252x^5$ **21.** $\dfrac{x^2}{36} + \dfrac{y^2}{9} = 1$

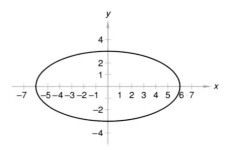

23. $(x + 1)^2 + (y - 3)^2 = \left(\dfrac{\sqrt{38}}{2}\right)^2$; center $= (-1, 3)$; radius $= \dfrac{\sqrt{38}}{2}$

25. $\dfrac{\pi}{6}, \dfrac{5\pi}{6}, \dfrac{7\pi}{6}, \dfrac{11\pi}{6}$

27. Mean $= \dfrac{2}{3}$; median $= 0$; mode $= 0$; variance $= 3.56$; standard deviation $= 1.89$

29. $\dfrac{18}{5}$

problem set 83

1. 82.75 ft   **3.** $\dfrac{Mk}{J(M - 5)}$ days   **5.** $\dfrac{60}{289}$ **7.** -11.75

9. $B = 79.11°$; $C = 40.89°$; $a = 10.58$ in.

11. $\dfrac{\sin A}{1 - \cos A} + \dfrac{1 - \cos A}{\sin A} = \dfrac{\sin^2 A + (1 - \cos A)^2}{(1 - \cos A)\sin A} = \dfrac{\sin^2 A + 1 - 2\cos A + \cos^2 A}{(1 - \cos A)\sin A}$

$$= \dfrac{2 - 2\cos A}{(1 - \cos A)\sin A} = \dfrac{2(1 - \cos A)}{(1 - \cos A)\sin A} = \dfrac{2}{\sin A} = 2\csc A$$

13. $\dfrac{1}{\tan(-x)} + \tan(-x) = \dfrac{1}{-\tan x} - \tan x = \dfrac{-1 - \tan^2 x}{\tan x} = \dfrac{-(1 + \tan^2 x)}{\tan x} = \dfrac{-\sec^2 x}{\tan x}$

$$= \dfrac{-\dfrac{1}{\cos^2 x}}{\dfrac{\sin x}{\cos x}} = -\dfrac{1}{\cos^2 x} \cdot \dfrac{\cos x}{\sin x} = -\dfrac{1}{\cos x} \cdot \dfrac{1}{\sin x} = -\sec x \csc x$$

15. 2 cis $12°$; 2 cis $84°$; 2 cis $156°$; 2 cis $228°$; 2 cis $300°$

17. $\dfrac{y^2}{16} - \dfrac{x^2}{9} = 1$; vertices $= (0, 4)$; $(0, -4)$; asymptotes: $y = \dfrac{4}{3}x$; $y = -\dfrac{4}{3}x$

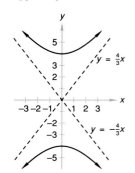

19. $x = -2$; $y = 3$ **21.** $\dfrac{x^2}{9} + \dfrac{y^2}{16} = 1$ **23.** $0°, 120°, 240°$

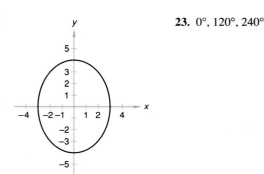

25. $-\dfrac{3}{4}$ **27.** $\dfrac{7\sqrt{13}}{13}$ **29.** 3

problem set 84

1. $\dfrac{1}{8}$ **3.** $40°$ **5.** $\dfrac{10k}{3p}$ days **7.**

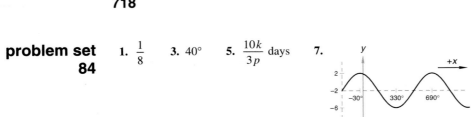

9. $\dfrac{\csc^4 x - \cot^4 x}{\csc^2 x + \cot^2 x} + \cot^2 x = \dfrac{(\csc^2 x + \cot^2 x)(\csc^2 x - \cot^2 x)}{\csc^2 x + \cot^2 x} + \cot^2 x$

$= \csc^2 x - \cot^2 x + \cot^2 x = \csc^2 x$

11. $\dfrac{\sec^2 \theta - 1}{\cot \theta} = \dfrac{\tan^2 \theta}{\cot \theta} = \dfrac{\tan^2 \theta}{\dfrac{1}{\tan \theta}} = \tan^3 \theta$

13. 1.22 **15.** $A = 44.05°$; $B = 83.33°$; $C = 52.62°$ **17.** $\dfrac{1}{8}$ cis $300°$

19. 2; $-1 + \sqrt{3}i$; $-1 - \sqrt{3}i$

21. $a^7 + 7a^6 c + 21a^5 c^2 + 35a^4 c^3 + 35a^3 c^4 + 21a^2 c^5 + 7ac^6 + c^7$

23. $\dfrac{x^2}{25} + \dfrac{y^2}{2} = 1$

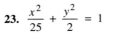

25. 10 **27.** $\dfrac{\pi}{6}, \dfrac{5\pi}{6}, \dfrac{7\pi}{6}, \dfrac{11\pi}{6}$ **29.** $\sqrt{2}$

problem set 85

1. $32\dfrac{8}{11}$ min **3.** 100 mi **5.** $\dfrac{7}{18}$ **7.** 167.13 ft **9.** $60°, 300°$ **11.** $0°$

13.

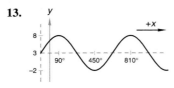

15. $\tan x + \cot x = \dfrac{\sin x}{\cos x} + \dfrac{\cos x}{\sin x} = \dfrac{\sin^2 x + \cos^2 x}{\cos x \sin x} = \dfrac{1}{\cos x \sin x} = \sec x \csc x$

17. 3.46 **19.** $A = 101.54°$; $B = 44.42°$; $C = 34.04°$ **21.** $-8 + 8\sqrt{3}i$

23. $\dfrac{y^2}{36} - \dfrac{x^2}{16} = 1$; vertices $= (0, 6)$; $(0, -6)$; asymptotes: $y = \dfrac{3}{2}x$; $y = -\dfrac{3}{2}x$

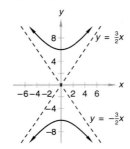

25. Area $= 77.25$ cm^2; radius $= 5.23$ cm **27.** $-18i$ **29.** $-\dfrac{6}{11}$

problem set 86

1. $16\frac{4}{11}$ minutes   **3.** $\frac{5}{18}$ **5.** $112\frac{16}{17}$ km   **7.** $-10, -4, 2, 8, 14$ **9.** $-1, -5, -9$

11. $9x + 10y$ **13.** 0 **15.**

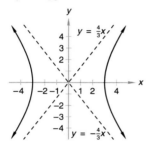

17. $\dfrac{\sec^2 x}{\sec^2 x - 1} = \dfrac{\sec^2 x}{\tan^2 x} = \dfrac{\dfrac{1}{\cos^2 x}}{\dfrac{\sin^2 x}{\cos^2 x}} = \dfrac{1}{\cos^2 x} \cdot \dfrac{\cos^2 x}{\sin^2 x} = \dfrac{1}{\sin^2 x} = \csc^2 x$

19. $\dfrac{\cos(-x)}{\sin(-x)\cot(-x)} = \dfrac{\cos x}{(-\sin x)(-\cot x)} = \dfrac{\cos x}{\sin x\left(\dfrac{\cos x}{\sin x}\right)} = 1$ **21.** 1

23. $A = 83.33°$; $B = 52.62°$; $C = 44.05°$

25. $\dfrac{x^2}{9} - \dfrac{y^2}{16} = 1$; vertices $= (3, 0)$; $(-3, 0)$; asymptotes: $y = \dfrac{4}{3}x$; $y = -\dfrac{4}{3}x$

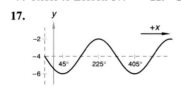

27. Yes, percentile $= 0.9332$ **29.** $2\sqrt{2}$

problem set 87

1. $27\frac{3}{11}$ min   **3.** (a) $\frac{2}{27}$ (b) $\frac{1}{12}$ **5.** $\dfrac{x}{y-k}\dfrac{\text{yd}}{\text{min}}$ **7.** $\dfrac{\sqrt{6} - \sqrt{2}}{4}$

9. Refer to Lesson 87.   **11.** -21 **13.** $3, 7, 11, 15$ **15.** $0°, 60°, 300°$

17.

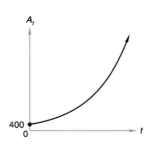

19. $\sec x + \sec x \tan^2 x = \sec x \left(1 + \tan^2 x\right) = \sec x \sec^2 x = \sec^3 x$

21. $\dfrac{\tan(-\theta)\cos(-\theta)}{\sin(-\theta)} = \dfrac{-\tan\theta\cos\theta}{-\sin\theta} = \dfrac{\dfrac{\sin\theta}{\cos\theta}\cdot\cos\theta}{\sin\theta} = \dfrac{\sin\theta}{\sin\theta} = 1$ **23.** -2.85

25. $2\,\text{cis}\,10°$; $2\,\text{cis}\,100°$; $2\,\text{cis}\,190°$; $2\,\text{cis}\,280°$

27. $x = -\dfrac{44}{23}$; $y = -\dfrac{49}{23}$ **29.** 4

problem set 88

1. $A_t = 400e^{0.23t}$; 6320 bacteria

3. $A_t = 100e^{-0.40t}$; half-life = 1.73 yr

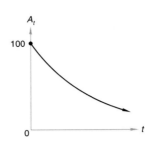

5. $\dfrac{25}{102}$ **7.** 2, 3, 4, 5

9. $\dfrac{\sqrt{3}}{2} \sin \theta - \dfrac{1}{2} \cos \theta$ **11.** −74   **13.** $\dfrac{\pi}{6}, \dfrac{2\pi}{3}, \dfrac{7\pi}{6}, \dfrac{5\pi}{3}$ **15.** $0, \dfrac{\pi}{2}, \pi, \dfrac{3\pi}{2}$

17.

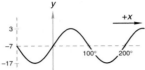

19. $(1 - \sin \theta)(1 + \sin \theta) = 1 - \sin^2 \theta = \cos^2 \theta$

21. $\dfrac{5}{3}$ **23.** $a = 14.73$ m; area = 31.18 m^2 **25.** $x = \dfrac{22}{17}$; $y = \dfrac{8}{17}$

27. Yes, percentile = 0.9713   **29.** 2

problem set 89   **1.** $A_t = 40e^{0.65t}$; 7251 rabbits

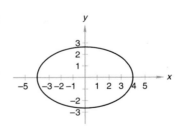

3. $10\dfrac{10}{11}$ min   **5.** $\dfrac{3}{49}$

7. $\dfrac{x^2}{16} + \dfrac{y^2}{7} = 1$

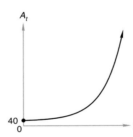

9. $\dfrac{x^2}{4} + \dfrac{y^2}{25} = 1$

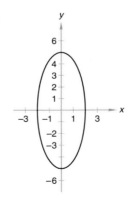

11. $2 + \sqrt{3}$ **13.** −42

15. 60°, 150°, 240°, 330°   **17.** 52.5°, 82.5°, 142.5°, 172.5°, 232.5°, 262.5°, 322.5°, 352.5°

19.

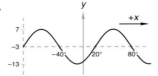

21. $\dfrac{\tan^3 x + 1}{\tan x + 1} = \dfrac{(\tan x + 1)(\tan^2 x - \tan x + 1)}{\tan x + 1} = \sec^2 x - \tan x$ **23.** 0   **25.** −1

27. Radius of circumscribed circle = 4.25 cm; radius of inscribed circle = 3.44 cm   **29.** $\dfrac{101}{100}$

problem set 90

1. $A_0 = 80;\ k = 0.80;\ A_t = 80e^{0.80t};\ t = 4.02$ yr   **3.** $\dfrac{1}{16}$

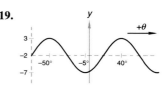

5. $\dfrac{1}{2}$ **7.** Refer to Lesson 90.

9. Refer to Lesson 90.

11. $\dfrac{x^2}{48} + \dfrac{y^2}{64} = 1$ **13.** $\dfrac{\sqrt{6} + \sqrt{2}}{4}$ **15.** −4, −6, −8

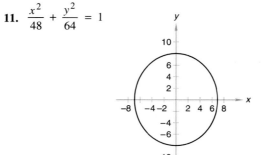

17. $\dfrac{\pi}{3},\ \dfrac{2\pi}{3},\ \dfrac{4\pi}{3},\ \dfrac{5\pi}{3}$

19.

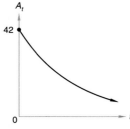

21. $\sin^2 \theta + \tan^2 \theta + \cos^2 \theta = 1 + \tan^2 \theta = \sec^2 \theta$ **23.** $x = -\dfrac{10}{13};\ y = -\dfrac{14}{13}$

25. 2   **27.** 2   **29.** (a) $\dfrac{1}{4}$ (b) 3

problem set 91

1. $43\dfrac{7}{11}$ min   **3.** $\dfrac{1}{54}$ **5.** $A_t = 42e^{-0.18t};\ t = 1.87$ yr

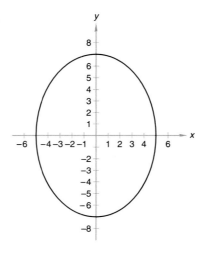

7. 128   **9.** 4, 8, 16 or −4, 8, −16   **11.** $\dfrac{\sqrt{2 - \sqrt{3}}}{2}$ **13.** $\dfrac{\sqrt{2 + \sqrt{3}}}{2}$

15. $\dfrac{x^2}{25} + \dfrac{y^2}{49} = 1$ **17.** 6, 2, −2, −6

19. 50°, 70°, 170°, 190°, 290°, 310°   **21.**

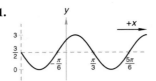

23. $\csc^2 y \sec^2 y - \sec^2 y = \sec^2 y \left(\csc^2 y - 1\right) = \sec^2 y \cot^2 y$

$$= \frac{1}{\cos^2 y} \cdot \frac{\cos^2 y}{\sin^2 y} = \frac{1}{\sin^2 y} = \csc^2 y$$

25. Radius = 8 in.; area = 166.28 in.²   **27.** $\dfrac{21}{8}$ **29.** $\dfrac{1}{2}$

**problem set
92**

1. $16\dfrac{4}{11}$ min   **3.** $A_t = 100e^{0.38t}$; 7.88 mo   **5.** 6, 8, 10

7. $_8P_5 = \dfrac{8!}{3!} = 6720$; $_8C_5 = \dfrac{8!}{3!5!} = 56$ **9.** −4, 8   **11.** $\dfrac{\sqrt{2-\sqrt{3}}}{2}$

13. $\dfrac{x^2}{16} + \dfrac{y^2}{25} = 1$ **15.** $\dfrac{\pi}{3}, \pi, \dfrac{5\pi}{3}$

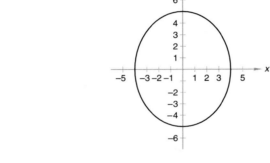

17.

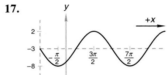

19. $\dfrac{\sec^2 x}{\sec^2 x - 1} = \dfrac{\sec^2 x}{\tan^2 x} = \dfrac{\frac{1}{\cos^2 x}}{\frac{\sin^2 x}{\cos^2 x}} = \dfrac{1}{\cos^2 x} \cdot \dfrac{\cos^2 x}{\sin^2 x} = \dfrac{1}{\sin^2 x} = \csc^2 x$ **21.** $\dfrac{32}{3}$

23. $\dfrac{x^2}{50} - \dfrac{y^2}{32} = 1$; vertices: $\left(5\sqrt{2}, 0\right)$; $\left(-5\sqrt{2}, 0\right)$; asymptotes: $y = \dfrac{4}{5}x$; $y = -\dfrac{4}{5}x$

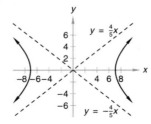

25. No, Smith is not in the top 5%.   **27.** $\dfrac{11}{7}$ **29.** 3

**problem set
93**

1. $\dfrac{7}{9}$ **3.** 5120   **5.** $_9P_6 = \dfrac{9!}{3!} = 60{,}480$; $_9C_6 = \dfrac{9!}{3!6!} = 84$

7. $\dfrac{\tan B + 1}{\tan B - 1} = \dfrac{\dfrac{\sin B}{\cos B} + 1}{\dfrac{\sin B}{\cos B} - 1} \cdot \dfrac{\dfrac{1}{\sin B}}{\dfrac{1}{\sin B}} = \dfrac{\dfrac{1}{\cos B} + \dfrac{1}{\sin B}}{\dfrac{1}{\cos B} - \dfrac{1}{\sin B}} = \dfrac{\sec B + \csc B}{\sec B - \csc B}$

9. 6, 18, 54 or –6, 18, –54   **11.** Refer to Lesson 90.   **13.** $\dfrac{-\sqrt{6} - \sqrt{2}}{4}$

15. 120°, 240°   **17.**

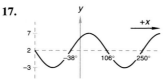

19. 4.50 cm

21. $\dfrac{x^2}{8} - \dfrac{y^2}{18} = 1$; vertices = $(2\sqrt{2}, 0)$; $(-2\sqrt{2}, 0)$; asymptotes: $y = \dfrac{3}{2}x$; $y = -\dfrac{3}{2}x$ **23.** 4

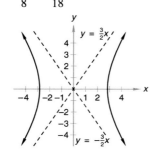

25. $-\dfrac{13}{5}$ **27.** $-\dfrac{1}{2}$ **29.** $\left(x + \dfrac{9}{2} + \dfrac{\sqrt{59}}{2}i\right)\left(x + \dfrac{9}{2} - \dfrac{\sqrt{59}}{2}i\right)$

problem set 94

1. $\dfrac{4}{5}$ **3.** 1622.15 yr   **5.** $\dfrac{180X}{PY}$ days   **7.** (a) $y = 4 + 4\sec x$ (b) $y = -2 + 4\csc x$

9. $\dfrac{\tan B + 1}{\tan B - 1} = \dfrac{\dfrac{\sin B}{\cos B} + 1}{\dfrac{\sin B}{\cos B} - 1} \cdot \dfrac{\dfrac{1}{\sin B}}{\dfrac{1}{\sin B}} = \dfrac{\dfrac{1}{\cos B} + \dfrac{1}{\sin B}}{\dfrac{1}{\cos B} - \dfrac{1}{\sin B}} = \dfrac{\sec B + \csc B}{\sec B - \csc B}$

11. Refer to Lesson 90.   **13.** $\dfrac{\sqrt{6} - \sqrt{2}}{4}$ **15.** $\dfrac{7\pi}{6}, \dfrac{11\pi}{6}$ **17.**

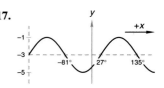

19. 3 cis 6°; 3 cis 96°; 3 cis 186°; 3 cis 276°   **21.** –2, 1, 4

23. Perimeter = 120 in.; area = 1039.23 in.^{2} **25.** 7.84

27. $\sqrt{2}$ **29.** $(x + 5 - \sqrt{5}i)(x + 5 + \sqrt{5}i)$

problem set 95

1. $\dfrac{1}{6}$ **3.** 249.04 min   **5.** 60 liters   **7.** 1.53 cis 18.77°; 1.53 cis 138.77°; 1.53 cis 258.77°

9. (a)

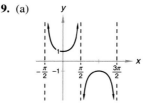

(b)

11. $\dfrac{\sin x}{1 + \cos x} + \dfrac{1 + \cos x}{\sin x} = \dfrac{\sin^2 x + (1 + \cos x)^2}{(1 + \cos x)\sin x} = \dfrac{\sin^2 x + 1 + 2\cos x + \cos^2 x}{(1 + \cos x)\sin x}$

$$= \dfrac{2 + 2\cos x}{(1 + \cos x)\sin x} = \dfrac{2(1 + \cos x)}{(1 + \cos x)\sin x} = 2\csc x$$

13. $\dfrac{\sin^4 x - \cos^4 x}{2\sin^2 x - 1} = \dfrac{(\sin^2 x + \cos^2 x)(\sin^2 x - \cos^2 x)}{2\sin^2 x - 1} = \dfrac{\sin^2 x - (1 - \sin^2 x)}{2\sin^2 x - 1}$

$$= \dfrac{2\sin^2 x - 1}{2\sin^2 x - 1} = 1$$

15. $\dfrac{\sqrt{6} - \sqrt{2}}{4}$ **17.** $120°, 240°$ **19.** $28.96°$ **21.** $-6, 12$

23. $\dfrac{x^2}{25} + \dfrac{y^2}{4} = 1$

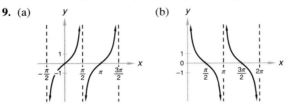

25. 90.85 in.^{2} **27.** $\dfrac{7}{8}$ **29.** $\dfrac{1}{3}$

problem set 96

1. 415.89 units of time   **3.** $5\dfrac{5}{11}$ min

5. $\dfrac{\cos^4 x - \sin^4 x}{\cos 2x} = \dfrac{(\cos^2 x + \sin^2 x)(\cos^2 x - \sin^2 x)}{\cos^2 x - \sin^2 x} = \cos^2 x + \sin^2 x = 1$

7. $\dfrac{1 - \cos x}{\sin x} \cdot \dfrac{(1 + \cos x)}{(1 + \cos x)} = \dfrac{1 - \cos^2 x}{\sin x(1 + \cos x)} = \dfrac{\sin^2 x}{\sin x(1 + \cos x)} = \dfrac{\sin x}{1 + \cos x}$

9. (a)   (b)   **11.**

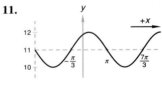

13. $-\sin x$ **15.** $\dfrac{\pi}{6}, \dfrac{\pi}{3}, \dfrac{7\pi}{6}, \dfrac{4\pi}{3}$

17. $1.12\text{ cis }105°;\ 1.12\text{ cis }225°;\ 1.12\text{ cis }345°$ **19.** $25, -125$

21. $\dfrac{x^2}{64} + \dfrac{y^2}{100} = 1$; length of major axis $= 20$; length of minor axis $= 16$

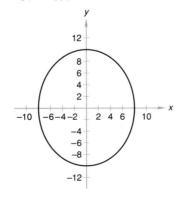

23. $x = \dfrac{1}{19};\ y = \dfrac{68}{19}$ **25.** 18.85 in.^{2} **27.** 1 **29.** 36

problem set 97

1. $\dfrac{4}{13}$ **3.** 56.95 min   **5.** 50 yd   **7.** No such triangle exists.

9. $\dfrac{\cos x}{1 - \sin x} - \dfrac{\cos x}{1 + \sin x} = \dfrac{\cos x(1 + \sin x) - \cos x(1 - \sin x)}{1 - \sin^2 x} = \dfrac{2 \cos x \sin x}{\cos^2 x} = 2 \tan x$

11. $c = 4.18$ in.; area $= 0.083$ ft^2 **13.**   **15.** $\dfrac{1}{2}$

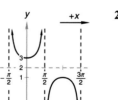

17. $20°, 100°, 140°, 220°, 260°, 340°$ **19.** 4, 8, 16 or $-4, 8, -16$

21. $\dfrac{x^2}{9} + \dfrac{y^2}{25} = 1$; length of major axis $= 10$; length of minor axis $= 6$

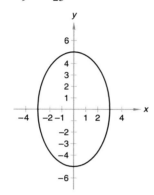

23. 65,449.85 cm^2 **25.** 2^{17} **27.** $\dfrac{10}{3}$ **29.** (a) $\dfrac{1}{216}$ (b) 216

problem set 98

1. $\dfrac{9}{16}$ **3.** 30,240   **5.** $\dfrac{m}{h + 3}$ mph   **7.** $_7P_6 = \dfrac{7!}{1!} = 5040$; $_7C_6 = \dfrac{7!}{6!1!} = 7$

9. 10^4 **11.** 1, 81   **13.** 4.47; 14.33

15. $2 \csc 2x \cos x = \dfrac{2 \cos x}{\sin 2x} = \dfrac{2 \cos x}{2 \sin x \cos x} = \dfrac{1}{\sin x} = \csc x$

17. $A = 36.42°$; $B = 71.79°$; $C = 71.79°$ **19.**   **21.** $\dfrac{\sqrt{3}}{2}$

23. $\dfrac{\pi}{12}, \dfrac{11\pi}{12}, \dfrac{13\pi}{12}, \dfrac{23\pi}{12}$ **25.** 128   **27.** 16 in.   **29.** $\dfrac{4\sqrt{5}}{5}$

problem set 99

1. 1   **3.** 48   **5.** $\dfrac{8 - mt}{4t} \dfrac{\text{jobs}}{\text{hr}}$ **7.** 16 ft   **9.** $17 + 12\sqrt{2}$

11. 2.54   **13.** 16   **15.** $1, 3^9$

17. $\dfrac{\cos^3 x - \sin^3 x}{\cos x - \sin x} = \dfrac{(\cos x - \sin x)(\cos^2 x + \cos x \sin x + \sin^2 x)}{\cos x - \sin x}$

$= 1 + \cos x \sin x = 1 + \dfrac{1}{2} \sin 2x$

19. $\dfrac{2}{\cot x - \tan x} = \dfrac{2}{\dfrac{1}{\tan x} - \tan x} = \dfrac{2}{\dfrac{1 - \tan^2 x}{\tan x}} = \dfrac{2 \tan x}{1 - \tan^2 x} = \tan 2x$

21.

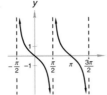

23. (a) $y = \cot \theta$ (b) $y = -3 + \sec x$ **25.** $45°, 225°$

27. $1.38 \text{ cis } 53.42°; \ 1.38 \text{ cis } 143.42°; \ 1.38 \text{ cis } 233.42°; \ 1.38 \text{ cis } 323.42°$ **29.** 19.31 cm^2

problem set 100

1. 24 ft   **3.** $\dfrac{R(m + 5)}{m} \ \dfrac{\text{mi}}{\text{hr}}$ **5.** No change in number of greens

7. Refer to Lesson 100.   **9.** Refer to Lesson 100.

11. Arithmetic mean = 15; geometric mean = $\pm 3\sqrt{21}$ **13.** 1.88   **15.** 3^9 **17.** $\dfrac{6}{5}$

19. $\cot x + \tan x = \dfrac{\cos x}{\sin x} + \dfrac{\sin x}{\cos x} = \dfrac{\cos^2 x + \sin^2 x}{\cos x \sin x} = \dfrac{1}{\cos x \sin x} = \dfrac{2}{2} \cdot \dfrac{1}{\cos x \sin x}$

$= \dfrac{2}{2 \cos x \sin x} = \dfrac{2}{\sin 2x} = 2 \csc 2x$

21. $(\tan^2 x)(1 + \cot^2 x) = \tan^2 x \csc^2 x = \dfrac{\sin^2 x}{\cos^2 x} \cdot \dfrac{1}{\sin^2 x} = \dfrac{1}{\cos^2 x} = \dfrac{1}{1 - \sin^2 x}$

23.

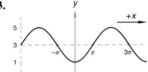

25. $\dfrac{1}{2}$

27. $\dfrac{\pi}{12}, \dfrac{7\pi}{12}, \dfrac{13\pi}{12}, \dfrac{19\pi}{12}$ **29.** $x = \dfrac{11}{4}; \ y = \dfrac{1}{2}$

problem set 101

1. 81 ft   **3.** 270.27 min   **5.** 60 mph   **7.** 19   **9.** Refer to Lesson 100.   **11.** 2 and 8

13. (a) 2.21   (b) 2.06   **15.** 5   **17.** 4.60; 10.44

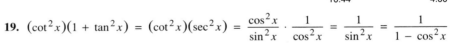

19. $(\cot^2 x)(1 + \tan^2 x) = (\cot^2 x)(\sec^2 x) = \dfrac{\cos^2 x}{\sin^2 x} \cdot \dfrac{1}{\cos^2 x} = \dfrac{1}{\sin^2 x} = \dfrac{1}{1 - \cos^2 x}$

21. 3697.89 m^2 **23.**

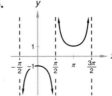

25. $70°, 110°, 190°, 230°, 310°, 350°$

27. $1.65 \text{ cis } 51.14°; \ 1.65 \text{ cis } 171.14°; \ 1.65 \text{ cis } 291.14°$ **29.** (a) $\dfrac{1}{64}$ (b) 64

problem set 102

1. 9 ft   **3.** 28.71 s   **5.** $W = 47 \text{ yr}; \ P = 23 \text{ yr}$ **7.** $-35x^4 y^3$ **9.** 13

11. Refer to Lesson 100.   **13.** 4 and 36   **15.** 1, 3   **17.** 5

19. $\dfrac{\sin^2 x}{1 - \cos x} - \dfrac{1}{\sec x} = \dfrac{1 - \cos^2 x}{1 - \cos x} - \dfrac{1}{\sec x} = \dfrac{(1 + \cos x)(1 - \cos x)}{1 - \cos x} - \cos x$

$= 1 + \cos x - \cos x = 1$

21.
$$\frac{1 + \sin x}{\cos x} + \frac{\cos x}{1 + \sin x} = \frac{(1 + \sin x)^2 + \cos^2 x}{\cos x(1 + \sin x)} = \frac{1 + 2\sin x + \sin^2 x + \cos^2 x}{\cos x(1 + \sin x)}$$
$$= \frac{2 + 2\sin x}{\cos x(1 + \sin x)} = \frac{2(1 + \sin x)}{\cos x(1 + \sin x)} = \frac{2}{\cos x} \cdot \frac{2\sin x}{2\sin x}$$
$$= \frac{4\sin x}{2\sin x \cos x} = \frac{4\sin x}{\sin 2x}$$

23.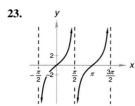

25. $0, \dfrac{\pi}{5}, \dfrac{2\pi}{5}, \dfrac{3\pi}{5}, \dfrac{4\pi}{5}, \pi, \dfrac{6\pi}{5}, \dfrac{7\pi}{5}, \dfrac{8\pi}{5}, \dfrac{9\pi}{5}$

27. $1.52 \operatorname{cis} 20.81°$; $1.52 \operatorname{cis} 92.81°$; $1.52 \operatorname{cis} 164.81°$; $1.52 \operatorname{cis} 236.81°$; $1.52 \operatorname{cis} 308.81°$

29. $\left(x + \dfrac{5}{2} - \dfrac{\sqrt{15}}{2}i\right)\left(x + \dfrac{5}{2} + \dfrac{\sqrt{15}}{2}i\right)x$

problem set 103

1. $\dfrac{1}{2}$ ft   **3.** 490.61 min   **5.** $\dfrac{12p}{k + sp}$ hr   **7.** $\log_3 \dfrac{x^{\frac{3}{5}} y^{\frac{1}{4}}}{z^3}$ **9.** 4.28 **11.** $70x^4 y^4$

13. $-\dfrac{13}{7}$ **15.** Refer to Lesson 100.   **17.** ± 3 **19.** $\dfrac{1}{2}$

21. 3.57; 10.93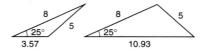

23.
$$\frac{2\cot x}{\tan 2x} = \frac{2\cot x}{\dfrac{2\tan x}{1 - \tan^2 x}} = 2\cot x \cdot \frac{1 - \tan^2 x}{2\tan x} = 2\cot x \cdot \frac{(1 - \tan^2 x)}{\dfrac{2}{\cot x}}$$
$$= \cot^2 x(1 - \tan^2 x) = \cot^2 x - 1 = \csc^2 x - 1 - 1 = \csc^2 x - 2$$

25. 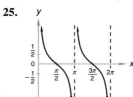   **27.** $45°, 105°, 165°, 225°, 285°, 345°$

29. $2.35 \operatorname{cis} 37.54°$; $2.35 \operatorname{cis} 157.54°$; $2.35 \operatorname{cis} 277.54°$

problem set 104

1. $\dfrac{7}{13}$ **3.** $N_W = 45$; $N_R = 20$; $N_B = 75$ **5.** (a) Refer to Lesson 104.   (b) 2550

7. $\dfrac{2}{3}\log_4(s - 1) + \dfrac{1}{3}\log_4(t + 2) - \dfrac{3}{2}\log_4 s$ **9.** 3.2 **11.** $160x^3 y^3$ **13.** $\dfrac{8}{3}$

15. Refer to Lesson 100.   **17.** 2 and 18 **19.** $1, 16$ **21.** 9

23.
$$\frac{1 - 3\cos x - 4\cos^2 x}{\sin^2 x} = \frac{1 - 3\cos x - 4\cos^2 x}{1 - \cos^2 x} = \frac{(1 - 4\cos x)(1 + \cos x)}{(1 - \cos x)(1 + \cos x)}$$
$$= \frac{1 - 4\cos x}{1 - \cos x}$$

25. 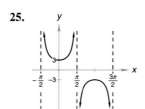   **27.** $\dfrac{\pi}{12}, \dfrac{\pi}{4}, \dfrac{3\pi}{4}, \dfrac{11\pi}{12}, \dfrac{17\pi}{12}, \dfrac{19\pi}{12}$ **29.** 1

problem set 105

1. 1 ft **3.** $5\frac{5}{11}$ min **5.** 210 teams **7.** 6 **9.** (a) Refer to Lesson 104. (b) 198

11. 68,699,634.76 **13.** $240x^2y^4$ **15.** $\frac{11}{17}$ **17.** $\frac{2 - \sqrt{3}}{4}$

19. 8 **21.** $\frac{1}{2}\sin 2x \sec x = \frac{1}{2} 2 \sin x \cos x \frac{1}{\cos x} = \sin x$ **23.** 20.48 cm^2

25. (a) $y = \tan\theta$ (b) $y = -7 + 4\sec x$ **27.** 45°, 225°

29. $\frac{y^2}{4} - \frac{x^2}{25} = 1$; vertices $= (0, 2)$; $(0, -2)$; asymptotes: $y = \frac{2}{5}x$; $y = -\frac{2}{5}x$

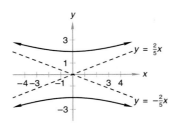

problem set 106

1. 270.27 min **3.** $\frac{300(100)}{(2.54)(12)(5280)} \frac{\text{mi}}{\text{min}}$ **5.** 12 mph

7. $\frac{(x + 3)^2}{4} + \frac{(y - 1)^2}{9} = 1$; center $= (-3, 1)$; length of major axis $= 6$;

length of minor axis $= 4$

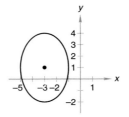

9. $\frac{(x + 1)^2}{1} - \frac{(y + 2)^2}{4} = 1$; center $= (-1, -2)$; vertices $= (0, -2)$; $(-2, -2)$;

asymptotes: $y = 2x$; $y = -2x - 4$

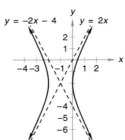

11. 1 **13.** (a) Refer to Lesson 104. (b) 172

15. $3.16 \times 10^{-4} \frac{\text{mole}}{\text{liter}}$ **17.** $\frac{7}{3}$ **19.** $\frac{1}{4}$ **21.** $\sqrt{3}$

23. $\frac{\sin^3 x + \cos^3 x}{\sin x + \cos x} = \frac{(\sin x + \cos x)(\sin^2 x - \sin x \cos x + \cos^2 x)}{\sin x + \cos x}$

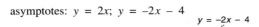

$= 1 - \sin x \cos x = 1 - \frac{1}{2}\sin 2x$

25. **27.** 0°, 180°, 240°, 300° **29.** 43.01 cm^2

problem set 107

1. $6:32\dfrac{8}{11}$ p.m.   **3.** $2A - m$ **5.** 60 boys   **7.** 8 mi

9. $\dfrac{(x-7)^2}{4} - \dfrac{(y+4)^2}{4} = 1$; center $= (7, -4)$; vertices $= (9, -4)$; $(5, -4)$;

asymptotes: $y = x - 11$; $y = -x + 3$

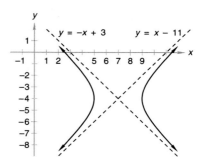

11. 25   **13.** (a) $a_n = a_1 + (n-1)d$ (b) $\dfrac{n}{2}\big[2a_1 + (n-1)d\big]$ **15.** 185.45

17. (a) Refer to Lesson 100.   (b) $\dfrac{2 - \sqrt{3}}{4}$ **19.** $\dfrac{\log 22}{\log e}$ **21.** 2^9

23. $\sec x - \sin x \tan x = \dfrac{1}{\cos x} - \sin x\,\dfrac{\sin x}{\cos x} = \dfrac{1 - \sin^2 x}{\cos x} = \dfrac{\cos^2 x}{\cos x} = \cos x$

25. $c = 1.31$ ft; area $= 1053.98$ cm^2 **27.**

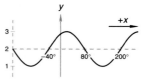

29. $40°, 280°$

problem set 108

1. $\dfrac{3}{8}$ **3.** $\dfrac{3W}{W+p}$ days   **5.** $A + B = \begin{bmatrix} 4 & 7 \\ -1 & 7 \end{bmatrix}$; $A - B = \begin{bmatrix} 2 & 7 \\ 3 & 1 \end{bmatrix}$; $2A = \begin{bmatrix} 6 & 14 \\ 2 & 8 \end{bmatrix}$

7. $A \cdot B = \begin{bmatrix} 2 & 3 \\ 3 & 7 \end{bmatrix}$; $B \cdot A = \begin{bmatrix} 7 & 9 \\ 1 & 2 \end{bmatrix}$ **9.** 2

11. $\dfrac{(x-1)^2}{4} - \dfrac{(y+1)^2}{9} = 1$; center $= (1, -1)$; vertices $= (3, -1)$; $(-1, -1)$;

asymptotes: $y = \dfrac{3}{2}x - \dfrac{5}{2}$; $y = -\dfrac{3}{2}x + \dfrac{1}{2}$

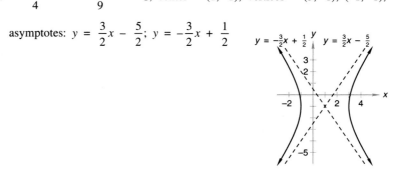

13. -1 **15.** 8.08   **17.** y^9 **19.** (a) Refer to Lesson 100.   (b) $-\dfrac{\sqrt{6}}{2}$ **21.** e^{10}

23. $\dfrac{2\sqrt{3}}{3}$ **25.**   **27.**

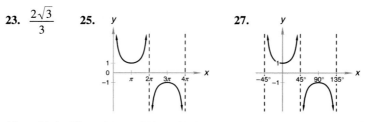

29. $1.66\text{ cis }63°$; $1.66\text{ cis }135°$; $1.66\text{ cis }207°$; $1.66\text{ cis }279°$; $1.66\text{ cis }351°$

problem set 109

1. $\dfrac{1}{7}$ 3. $\dfrac{400n}{d + 3n}$ 5. $M = 63$ yr; $J = 41$ yr   7. $\dfrac{5957}{990}$

9. $A + B = \begin{bmatrix} 2 & 2 & 3 \\ 7 & 5 & 9 \\ -1 & 1 & 7 \end{bmatrix}$; $A \cdot B = \begin{bmatrix} 7 & 13 & 31 \\ -4 & -4 & 20 \\ 1 & 4 & 15 \end{bmatrix}$

11. $\dfrac{(x + 3)^2}{1} - \dfrac{(y - 2)^2}{4} = 1$; center $= (-3, 2)$; vertices $= (-2, 2)$; $(-4, 2)$;

asymptotes: $y = 2x + 8$; $y = -2x - 4$

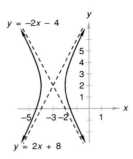

13. 2   15. (a) $2(-2)^{11}$ (b) -2730 17. $90a^2 b^3 c^3$ 19. $\dfrac{\log 42}{\log e}$ 21. No solution

23. $\dfrac{\tan^2 x}{\sec x + 1} = \dfrac{\sec^2 x - 1}{\sec x + 1} = \dfrac{(\sec x + 1)(\sec x - 1)}{\sec x + 1} = \sec x - 1$

25.

27. $\dfrac{\pi}{12}, \dfrac{7\pi}{12}, \dfrac{3\pi}{4}, \dfrac{5\pi}{4}, \dfrac{17\pi}{12}, \dfrac{3\pi}{2}, \dfrac{23\pi}{12}$ 29. $\dfrac{\sqrt{26}}{2}$

problem set 110

1. $\dfrac{7}{13}$ 3. $32\dfrac{8}{11}$ min   5. $\dfrac{32}{9}$ hr   7. $\dfrac{241}{99,900}$

9. $A + B = \begin{bmatrix} 3 & 2 & 5 \\ -1 & 5 & 3 \\ 4 & 5 & -1 \end{bmatrix}$; $B \cdot A = \begin{bmatrix} 22 & 16 & 8 \\ -1 & 4 & 4 \\ -14 & 10 & 7 \end{bmatrix}$

11. $\dfrac{(x + 2)^2}{36} - \dfrac{(y - 4)^2}{9} = 1$; center $= (-2, 4)$; vertices $= (4, 4)$; $(-8, 4)$;

asymptotes: $y = \dfrac{1}{2}x + 5$; $y = -\dfrac{1}{2}x + 3$

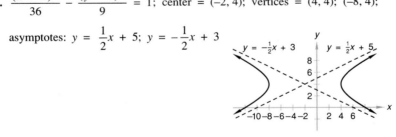

13. 65,536   15. 166.81   17. (a) Refer to Lesson 100.   (b) $-\dfrac{\sqrt{3}}{4} - \dfrac{1}{4}$ 19. 16

21. $\dfrac{1}{2} \sec x \csc (-x) = -\dfrac{1}{2} \sec x \csc x = -\dfrac{1}{2} \dfrac{1}{\cos x} \dfrac{1}{\sin x} = -\dfrac{1}{2 \sin x \cos x} = -\dfrac{1}{\sin 2x}$

23. $88.98°$ 25.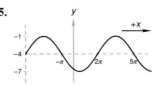

27. $70°, 110°, 190°, 230°, 310°, 350°$ 29. 6.18 in.

**problem set
111**

1. 81 ft   **3.** 2.79 g   **5.** 40°   **7.** $2 < x < 29$

9. (a) Domain = $\{x \in \mathbb{R} \mid x \le -1 \text{ or } 1 \le x\}$

Range = $\left\{ y \in \mathbb{R} \mid 0 \le y < \dfrac{\pi}{2} \text{ or } \dfrac{\pi}{2} < y \le \pi \right\}$

(b) Domain = $\{x \in \mathbb{R} \mid x \le -1 \text{ or } 1 \le x\}$

Range = $\left\{ y \in \mathbb{R} \mid -\dfrac{\pi}{2} \le y < 0 \text{ or } 0 < y \le \dfrac{\pi}{2} \right\}$

(c) Domain = $\{x \in \mathbb{R}\}$

Range = $\left\{ y \in \mathbb{R} \mid 0 < y < \pi \right\}$

11. $2A - B = \begin{bmatrix} -1 & -3 & 5 \\ 2 & 4 & 6 \\ 2 & 0 & -6 \end{bmatrix}$; $B \cdot A = \begin{bmatrix} 15 & 11 & 31 \\ 10 & 14 & 14 \\ 24 & 28 & 34 \end{bmatrix}$

13. $\dfrac{(x-5)^2}{36} - \dfrac{(y-3)^2}{4} = 1$; center = $(5, 3)$; vertices = $(11, 3)$; $(-1, 3)$;

asymptotes: $y = \dfrac{1}{3}x + \dfrac{4}{3}$; $y = -\dfrac{1}{3}x + \dfrac{14}{3}$

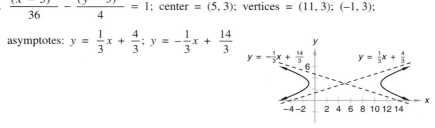

15. $\log \dfrac{x-1}{x^2}$ **17.** $16x^4 + 32x^3y + 24x^2y^2 + 8xy^3 + y^4$ **19.** $-\dfrac{\sqrt{2}}{2}$ **21.** 1

23. $\dfrac{2 \tan \theta}{1 + \tan^2 \theta} = \dfrac{\dfrac{2 \sin \theta}{\cos \theta}}{\sec^2 \theta} = \dfrac{\dfrac{2 \sin \theta}{\cos \theta}}{\dfrac{1}{\cos^2 \theta}} = \dfrac{2 \sin \theta}{\cos \theta} \cdot \dfrac{\cos^2 \theta}{1} = 2 \sin \theta \cos \theta = \sin 2\theta$

25.

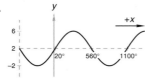

27. $\dfrac{\pi}{12}, \dfrac{\pi}{4}, \dfrac{5\pi}{12}, \dfrac{7\pi}{12}, \dfrac{3\pi}{4}, \dfrac{11\pi}{12}, \dfrac{13\pi}{12}, \dfrac{5\pi}{4}, \dfrac{17\pi}{12}, \dfrac{19\pi}{12}, \dfrac{7\pi}{4}, \dfrac{23\pi}{12}$ **29.** 2; $2i$; -2; $-2i$

**problem set
112**

1. 256 ft   **3.** 35 groups   **5.** $750   **7.** $-15{,}360x^{14}y^3$ **9.** $2 < x < 127$

11. Domain = $\{x \in \mathbb{R} \mid -1 \le x \le 1\}$

Range = $\left\{ y \in \mathbb{R} \mid -\dfrac{\pi}{2} \le y \le \dfrac{\pi}{2} \right\}$

$\text{Arcsin} \left(-\dfrac{1}{2} \right) = -\dfrac{\pi}{6}$; $\text{Arcsin } \dfrac{1}{2} = \dfrac{\pi}{6}$; $\text{Arcsin } (-1) = -\dfrac{\pi}{2}$

13. $2A + 3B = \begin{bmatrix} 19 & 6 \\ 11 & 20 \end{bmatrix}$; $A \cdot 2B = \begin{bmatrix} 20 & 8 \\ 34 & 36 \end{bmatrix}$

15. $\dfrac{(y+5)^2}{16} - \dfrac{(x-3)^2}{16} = 1$; center $= (3,-5)$; vertices $= (3,-1)$; $(3,-9)$;   **17.** $\dfrac{27}{7}$

asymptotes: $y = x - 8$; $y = -x - 2$

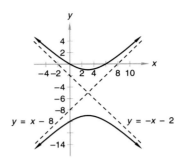

19. e **21.** $\tan 2x = \dfrac{\sin 2x}{\cos 2x} = \dfrac{2\sin x \cos x}{\cos^2 x - \sin^2 x} \cdot \dfrac{\dfrac{1}{\cos^2 x}}{\dfrac{1}{\cos^2 x}} = \dfrac{2\dfrac{\sin x}{\cos x}}{1 - \dfrac{\sin^2 x}{\cos^2 x}} = \dfrac{2\tan x}{1 - \tan^2 x}$

23. 19.35 m   **25.** y 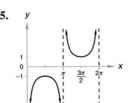   **27.** $30°, 150°, 210°, 330°$ **29.** $\dfrac{3\sqrt{2}}{2}$

problem set 113

1. $\dfrac{14}{55}$ **3.** $(400 - hk)$ mi   **5.** $R_O = 60$ mph; $R_B = 20$ mph

7. $4x^3 - 12x^2 + 25x - 53 + \dfrac{108}{x+2}$ **9.** No   **11.** $2{,}795{,}520x^{22}y^{12}$ **13.** $\dfrac{1}{2} < x < \dfrac{17}{2}$

15. Domain $= \{x \in \mathbb{R} \mid -1 \le x \le 1\}$

Range $= \{y \in \mathbb{R} \mid 0 \le y \le \pi\}$

$\text{Arccos}\left(-\dfrac{1}{2}\right) = \dfrac{2\pi}{3}$; $\text{Arccos}\,\dfrac{1}{2} = \dfrac{\pi}{3}$; $\text{Arccos}\,(-1) = \pi$

17. $\dfrac{(x-3)^2}{9} + \dfrac{(y-0)^2}{36} = 1$; center $= (3, 0)$; length of major axis $= 12$;

length of minor axis $= 6$; vertical

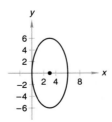

19. $\ln \dfrac{z}{x(y+1)}$ **21.** $1, e^4$ **23.** 2.65 cm

25. $\dfrac{\pi}{3}, \dfrac{2\pi}{3}$ **27.** $a - 2$ **29.** $\sqrt{2}$

problem set 114

1. $\dfrac{1}{216}$ **3.** 4900   **5.** 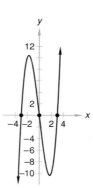   **7.** 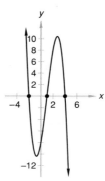   **9.** D

11. $2x^2 - 6x + 17 - \dfrac{51}{x + 3}$ **13.** $16x^4 - 32x^3y^3 + 24x^2y^6 - 8xy^9 + y^{12}$

15. Domain $= \{x \in \mathbb{R}\}$

Range $= \left\{ y \in \mathbb{R} \mid -\dfrac{\pi}{2} < y < \dfrac{\pi}{2} \right\}$

Arctan $\left(-\sqrt{3}\right) = -\dfrac{\pi}{3}$; Arctan $\sqrt{3} = \dfrac{\pi}{3}$; Arctan $1 = \dfrac{\pi}{4}$

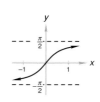

17. $\dfrac{(y + 1)^2}{16} - \dfrac{(x - 1)^2}{16} = 1$; center $= (1, -1)$; vertices $= (1, -5)$; $(1, 3)$;

asymptotes: $y = x - 2$; $y = -x$

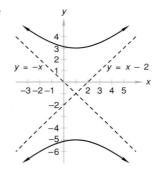

19. $\log \dfrac{c}{a - b}$ **21.** 4   **23.**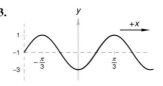

25. $0°, 180°, 210°, 330°$ **27.** 1074   **29.** 8

problem set 115

1. $\dfrac{4}{13}$ **3.** $\dfrac{(60)(60)(12)(2.54)}{35} \dfrac{\text{rad}}{\text{min}}$ **5.** $R = \$140$; $T = \$60$ **7.** -14

9. $x^5 - 4x^4 - 4x^3 - 2 - \dfrac{1}{x - 1}$ **11.** 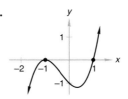   **13.** $210x^{16}y^{18}$

15. Domain = $\{x \in \mathbb{R} \mid -1 \le x \le 1\}$

Range = $\left\{y \in \mathbb{R} \mid -\dfrac{\pi}{2} \le y \le \dfrac{\pi}{2}\right\}$

Arcsin $\dfrac{\sqrt{3}}{2} = \dfrac{\pi}{3}$; Arcsin $1 = \dfrac{\pi}{2}$; Arcsin $\left(-\dfrac{\sqrt{3}}{2}\right) = -\dfrac{\pi}{3}$

17. Arithmetic mean = 15; geometric mean = ±12   **19.** –251.48   **21.** 81

23. $\dfrac{\cot x}{\cot x - 1} - \dfrac{\tan x}{\tan x + 1} = \dfrac{\cot x \tan x + \cot x - \tan x \cot x + \tan x}{\cot x \tan x + \cot x - \tan x - 1} = \dfrac{\cot x + \tan x}{\cot x - \tan x}$

25.   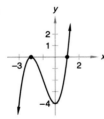   **27.** 30°, 90°, 270°, 330°

29. 1.07 cis 45°; 1.07 cis 117°; 1.07 cis 189°; 1.07 cis 261°; 1.07 cis 333°

problem set 116   **1.** $\dfrac{1}{4}$ **3.** $21\dfrac{9}{11}$ min   **5.** 55   **7.** $r = 7$

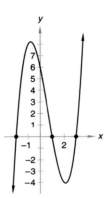

9.   **11.** $x^3 + 2x + 3 + \dfrac{13}{x - 3}$ **13.** 5   **15.** $-\dfrac{1}{2} < x < 40$

17. Domain = $\{x \in \mathbb{R} \mid -1 \le x \le 1\}$

Range = $\{y \in \mathbb{R} \mid 0 \le y \le \pi\}$

Arccos $\dfrac{\sqrt{3}}{2} = \dfrac{\pi}{6}$; Arccos $\left(-\dfrac{\sqrt{3}}{2}\right) = \dfrac{5\pi}{6}$; Arccos $0 = \dfrac{\pi}{2}$

19. $-\dfrac{1}{5}$

21. $\dfrac{(x-3)^2}{9} - \dfrac{(y+2)^2}{4} = 1$; center = (3, –2); vertices = (6, –2); (0, –2);

asymptotes: $y = \dfrac{2}{3}x - 4$; $y = -\dfrac{2}{3}x$

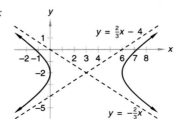

23. (a) $6.31 \times 10^{-10} \dfrac{\text{mole}}{\text{liter}}$ (b) 7.89   **25.** 1, 10   **27.** $2 + \sqrt{3}$ **29.**

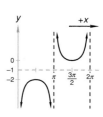

problem set 117

1. 0.85   **3.** $\dfrac{m(5280)(12)(2.54)}{c(60)(60)} \dfrac{\text{rad}}{\text{s}}$ **5.** $\dfrac{1800h + 30m}{m + k}$ min   **7.** Yes

9. $\pm 1, \pm 3, \pm \dfrac{1}{2}, \pm \dfrac{3}{2}, \pm \dfrac{1}{4}, \pm \dfrac{3}{4}$ **11.** $r = 3$

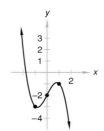

13. $(x - 2)(x + 2)(x - 1)(x + 1)$

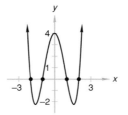

15. $2x^3 + 4x^2 + 5x + 6 + \dfrac{13}{x - 2}$ **17.** $x^{10} + 10x^8y + 40x^6y^2 + 80x^4y^3 + 80x^2y^4 + 32y^5$

19. Domain = $\{x \in \mathbb{R}\}$

Range = $\left\{ y \in \mathbb{R} \mid -\dfrac{\pi}{2} < y < \dfrac{\pi}{2} \right\}$

Arctan $\dfrac{\sqrt{3}}{3} = \dfrac{\pi}{6}$; Arctan $\left(-\dfrac{\sqrt{3}}{3} \right) = -\dfrac{\pi}{6}$; Arctan $(-1) = -\dfrac{\pi}{4}$

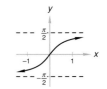

21. $\begin{bmatrix} -1 & 25 & 2 \\ -5 & 2 & 1 \\ -7 & 11 & 2 \end{bmatrix}$ **23.** (a) 7.28   (b) $3.98 \times 10^{-11} \dfrac{\text{mole}}{\text{liter}}$

25. $y = -1$; $z = 1$ **27.** $\dfrac{1}{32}$ **29.** $60°, 150°, 240°, 330°$

problem set 118

1. $\dfrac{1}{6}$ **3.** $R_W = 50$ mph; $T_W = 8$ hr; $R_B = 70$ mph; $T_B = 16$ hr   **5.** $N_F = 10$; $N_S = 140$

7. $\dfrac{1}{2}, \dfrac{3}{2}$ **9.** No, they have the factor of 12 in common.

11. $r = \dfrac{9}{4}$ **13.**   **15.** D

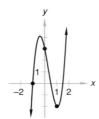

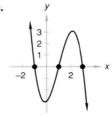

17. $3x^4 - 10x^3 + 19x^2 - 19x + 7 - \dfrac{5}{x + 1}$ **19.** $x > \dfrac{17}{8}$

21. Domain $= \{x \in \mathbb{R} \mid -1 \leq x \leq 1\}$

Range $= \left\{ y \in \mathbb{R} \mid -\dfrac{\pi}{2} \leq y \leq \dfrac{\pi}{2} \right\}$

$\text{Arcsin } \dfrac{\sqrt{2}}{2} = \dfrac{\pi}{4}$; $\text{Arcsin } \left(-\dfrac{\sqrt{2}}{2} \right) = -\dfrac{\pi}{4}$; $\text{Arcsin } 0 = 0$

23. $\dfrac{(y + 2)^2}{9} - \dfrac{(x + 3)^2}{25} = 1$; vertices $= (-3, -5)$; $(-3, 1)$;

asymptotes: $y = \dfrac{3}{5}x - \dfrac{1}{5}$; $y = -\dfrac{3}{5}x - \dfrac{19}{5}$

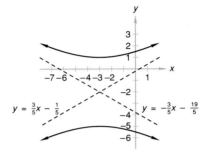

25. $2 \log_3 (x + 1) + \dfrac{1}{3} \log_3 (x + 2) - \log_3 (x - 3)$ **27.** 5   **29.**

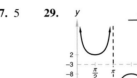

problem set 119

1. 150 ft   **3.** 247.05   **5.** $N_R = 5$; $N_B = 12$ **7.** 1   **9.** 1

11. Upper bound $= 3$; lower bound $= -1$ **13.** 3, 2i, $-2i$ **15.** $-\dfrac{1}{3} + \dfrac{\sqrt{11}}{3}i$, $-\dfrac{1}{3} - \dfrac{\sqrt{11}}{3}i$

17. Yes   **19.** $r = 3$

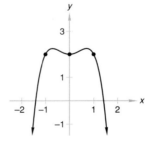

21. $y = (x + 2)(x + 1)(x - 1)$ **23.** $x^3 + 3x + \dfrac{3}{x} + \dfrac{1}{x^3}$

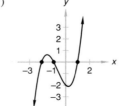

25.   **27.** 45°, 135°, 225°, 315°

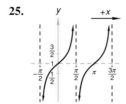

29. cis 67.5°; cis 157.5°; cis 247.5°; cis 337.5°

problem set 120

1. $\dfrac{19}{34}$ 3. 2720   5. $\begin{bmatrix} -2 & 1 \\ \frac{3}{2} & -\frac{1}{2} \end{bmatrix}$ 7. $x = -2;\ y = 3$ 9. (a) 0 or 2   (b) 0 or 2

11. Upper bound $= 2$; lower bound $= -3$ 13. $-2, 1$ 15.

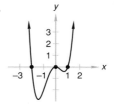

17. $x > 1$ 19. $\dfrac{181}{90}$ 21. 32

23. $\sec^2\left(\dfrac{\pi}{2} - \theta\right) + \csc^2\left(\dfrac{\pi}{2} - \theta\right) = \csc^2\theta + \sec^2\theta = \dfrac{1}{\sin^2\theta} + \dfrac{1}{\cos^2\theta}$

$$= \dfrac{\cos^2\theta + \sin^2\theta}{\sin^2\theta\cos^2\theta} = \dfrac{1}{\sin^2\theta\cos^2\theta} = \sec^2\theta\csc^2\theta$$

25. 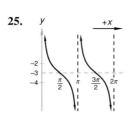   27. π

29. $2\operatorname{cis}45°;\ 2\operatorname{cis}105°;\ 2\operatorname{cis}165°;\ 2\operatorname{cis}225°;\ 2\operatorname{cis}285°;\ 2\operatorname{cis}345°$

problem set 121

1. $\dfrac{2}{9}$ 3. $\dfrac{(85)(60)(2)}{(191)(2\pi)}$ m

5. (a) $\begin{cases} y = -1 & \text{if } x \le 0 \\ y = x & \text{if } 0 < x \le 1 \\ y = 1 & \text{if } x \ge 1 \end{cases}$ (b) $\begin{cases} y = -2 & \text{if } x \le 1 \\ y = x - 1 & \text{if } 1 < x \le 3 \\ y = 2 & \text{if } x \ge 3 \end{cases}$

7.    9. $\begin{bmatrix} \frac{1}{10} & \frac{1}{5} \\ \frac{3}{10} & -\frac{2}{5} \end{bmatrix};\ x = \dfrac{11}{10};\ y = \dfrac{13}{10}$

11. Upper bound $= 1$; lower bound $= -3$ 13. $-2, -\dfrac{1}{2}, \dfrac{1}{2}$ 15. -30

17. 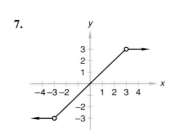   19. $-\dfrac{1760}{p^3}$ 21. 4

23. $(\sec\theta + \tan\theta)^2 = \sec^2\theta + 2\sec\theta\tan\theta + \tan^2\theta = \dfrac{1}{\cos^2\theta} + \dfrac{2\sin\theta}{\cos^2\theta} + \dfrac{\sin^2\theta}{\cos^2\theta}$

$$= \dfrac{1 + 2\sin\theta + \sin^2\theta}{1 - \sin^2\theta} = \dfrac{(1 + \sin\theta)(1 + \sin\theta)}{(1 + \sin\theta)(1 - \sin\theta)} = \dfrac{1 + \sin\theta}{1 - \sin\theta}$$

25.

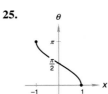

27. $30°, 120°, 210°, 300°$ **29.** $4i;\; -2\sqrt{3} - 2i;\; 2\sqrt{3} - 2i$

**problem set
122**

1. $\dfrac{1}{3}$ **3.** $\dfrac{k + 5}{p + 2}$ mph   **5.**

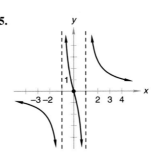

7.

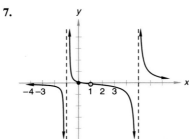

9. (a) $\begin{cases} y = x + 1 & \text{if } -\infty < x \le -1 \\ y = -2 & \text{if } -1 < x < 1 \\ y = x - 1 & \text{if } 1 \le x < \infty \end{cases}$ (b) $\begin{cases} y = -1 & \text{if } -\infty < x < -2 \\ y = -x - 2 & \text{if } -2 \le x \le 0 \\ y = 2x & \text{if } 0 < x \le 1 \\ y = 2 & \text{if } 1 \le x < \infty \end{cases}$

11. (a) 0   (b) 1   **13.** Upper bound $= 5$; lower bound $= -2$ **15.** $-1, \dfrac{2}{5}, 1$

17. $-\dfrac{5}{2} \pm \dfrac{\sqrt{7}}{2}i$ **19.** No, 15 is a common factor.   **21.**

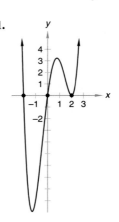

23. -1 **25.** $5 < x < 10$ **27.** $1, 1000$

29. $\cos 3x = \cos(2x + x) = \cos 2x \cos x - \sin 2x \sin x = (2\cos^2 x - 1)\cos x - 2\sin x \cos x \sin x$

$$= 2\cos^3 x - \cos x - 2\cos x \sin^2 x = 2\cos^3 x - \cos x - 2\cos x(1 - \cos^2 x)$$

$$= 2\cos^3 x - \cos x - 2\cos x + 2\cos^3 x = 4\cos^3 x - 3\cos x$$

problem set 123

1. 150 units   **3.** 300 mi   **5.** B = 46 yr; J = 36 yr

7. (a) Circle (b) Ellipse (c) Hyperbola (d) Parabola (e) Circle

9. (a) Ellipse (b) Hyperbola (c) Circle (d) Parabola (e) Circle

11.

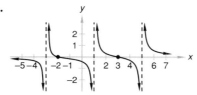

13.

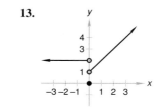

15. (a) $\begin{cases} y = -x - 1 & \text{if } -\infty < x \le -1 \\ y = -2 & \text{if } -1 < x < 1 \\ y = x - 1 & \text{if } 1 \le x < \infty \end{cases}$ (b) $\begin{cases} y = -4 & \text{if } -\infty < x \le -3 \\ y = -2 & \text{if } -3 < x \le 0 \\ y = x & \text{if } 0 < x \le 2 \\ y = 3 & \text{if } 2 < x < \infty \end{cases}$

17. (a) 0 or 2 (b) 0 or 2   **19.** $-2, -2, 1, \dfrac{5}{2}$ **21.**

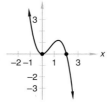

    23. $\dfrac{924}{m^6}$

25. $10, \dfrac{1}{10}$ **27.** 3.13 in.   **29.** 40°, 100°, 160°, 220°, 280°, 340°

problem set 124

1. 208.05 min   **3.** 200 atm   **5.** A = 10°; B = 40°   **7.** $\left(\dfrac{7}{11}x_1 + \dfrac{4}{11}x_2, \dfrac{7}{11}y_1 + \dfrac{4}{11}y_2 \right)$

9. $\left(-\dfrac{19}{5}, \dfrac{6}{5} \right)$ **11.** $\dfrac{x^2}{25} + \dfrac{(y - 6)^2}{16} = 1$

13. $\dfrac{y^2}{16} - \dfrac{x^2}{9} = 1$

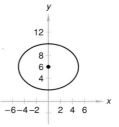

15.

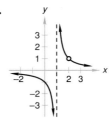

17. (a) $\begin{cases} y = -1 & \text{if } -\infty < x < -3 \\ y = x - 1 & \text{if } -3 \le x \le 1 \\ y = 1 & \text{if } 1 < x \le 3 \\ y = 3 & \text{if } 3 < x < \infty \end{cases}$ (b) $\begin{cases} y = -1 & \text{if } -\infty < x < -1 \\ y = x + 1 & \text{if } -1 < x < 0 \\ y = x & \text{if } 0 < x < 1 \\ y = x - 1 & \text{if } 1 < x < 2 \\ y = -1 & \text{if } 2 < x < \infty \end{cases}$

19. (a) 0 or 2 (b) 1   **21.** $-2, 2, \dfrac{7}{3}$ **23.**   **25.** $1, 3^{16}$

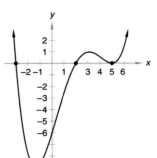

27.

29. $\dfrac{\pi}{8}, \dfrac{3\pi}{8}, \dfrac{5\pi}{8}, \dfrac{7\pi}{8}, \dfrac{9\pi}{8}, \dfrac{11\pi}{8}, \dfrac{13\pi}{8}, \dfrac{15\pi}{8}$

problem set 125

1. 21.52 g; 2.71 days   **3.** 455   **5.**   **7.**

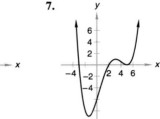

9.   **11.** $(-1.1478, 1.3173)$ **13.** $(1.3553, 6.1632)$

15. $-0.4142, 1, 2.4142$ **17.** $-2, 2$

19. (a) Parabola (b) Parabola (c) Hyperbola (d) Ellipse (e) Circle

21. (a)   (b)   **23.**

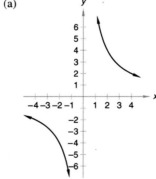
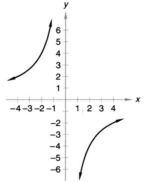
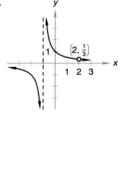

25. (a) $\begin{cases} y = \dfrac{1}{2}x & \text{if } -2 < x \le 0 \\ y = -\dfrac{1}{2}x + 1 & \text{if } 0 < x \le 2 \\ y = 1 & \text{if } 2 < x < \infty \end{cases}$ (b) $\begin{cases} y = -1 & \text{if } -\infty < x < 1 \\ y = x - 1 & \text{if } 1 < x < 2 \\ y = 3 - x & \text{if } 2 < x < 3 \\ y = 1 & \text{if } 3 \le x < \infty \end{cases}$

27. Upper bound = 1; lower bound = -3 **29.** $1, 1 + i, 1 - i$

Index

TRIGONOMETRIC RELATIONSHIPS

LAW OF SINES

$$\frac{a}{\sin A} = \frac{b}{\sin B} = \frac{c}{\sin C}$$

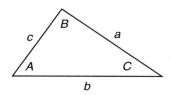

LAW OF COSINES

$$c^2 = a^2 + b^2 - 2ab \cos C$$

BASIC IDENTITIES

$$\sin \theta = \frac{1}{\csc \theta} \qquad \cos \theta = \frac{1}{\sec \theta} \qquad \tan \theta = \frac{1}{\cot \theta}$$

$$\csc \theta = \frac{1}{\sin \theta} \qquad \sec \theta = \frac{1}{\cos \theta} \qquad \cot \theta = \frac{1}{\tan \theta}$$

$$\sin(-\theta) = -\sin \theta \qquad \cos(-\theta) = \cos \theta \qquad \tan(-\theta) = -\tan \theta$$

$$\csc(-\theta) = -\csc \theta \qquad \sec(-\theta) = \sec \theta \qquad \cot(-\theta) = -\cot \theta$$

PYTHAGOREAN IDENTITIES

$$\sin^2 \theta + \cos^2 \theta = 1 \qquad \tan^2 \theta + 1 = \sec^2 \theta \qquad 1 + \cot^2 \theta = \csc^2 \theta$$

HALF-ANGLE IDENTITIES

$$\sin \frac{x}{2} = \pm\sqrt{\frac{1 - \cos x}{2}}$$

$$\cos \frac{x}{2} = \pm\sqrt{\frac{1 + \cos x}{2}}$$

SUM AND DIFFERENCE IDENTITIES

$$\sin(A + B) = \sin A \cos B + \cos A \sin B$$

$$\sin(A - B) = \sin A \cos B - \cos A \sin B$$

$$\cos(A + B) = \cos A \cos B - \sin A \sin B$$

$$\cos(A - B) = \cos A \cos B + \sin A \sin B$$

$$\tan(A + B) = \frac{\tan A + \tan B}{1 - \tan A \tan B}$$

$$\tan(A - B) = \frac{\tan A - \tan B}{1 + \tan A \tan B}$$

DOUBLE-ANGLE IDENTITIES

$$\sin(2A) = 2 \sin A \cos A$$

$$\cos(2A) = \cos^2 A - \sin^2 A$$

$$= 2 \cos^2 A - 1$$

$$= 1 - 2 \sin^2 A$$

$$\tan(2A) = \frac{2 \tan A}{1 - \tan^2 A}$$

$$\sin x + \sin y = 2 \sin \frac{x + y}{2} \cos \frac{x - y}{2}$$

$$\sin x - \sin y = 2 \cos \frac{x + y}{2} \sin \frac{x - y}{2}$$

$$\cos x + \cos y = 2 \cos \frac{x + y}{2} \cos \frac{x - y}{2}$$

$$\cos x - \cos y = -2 \sin \frac{x + y}{2} \sin \frac{x - y}{2}$$

ABBREVIATIONS

U.S. Customary		Metric	
Unit	Abbreviation	Unit	Abbreviation
inch	in.	meter	m
foot	ft	centimeter	cm
yard	yd	millimeter	mm
mile	mi	kilometer	km
ounce	oz	gram	g
pound	lb	kilogram	kg
degree(s) Fahrenheit	°F	degree(s) Celsius	°C
pint	pt	liter	L
quart	qt	milliliter	mL
gallon	gal		

Time	
second	s
hour	hr

UNIT EQUIVALENCES

Length	
U.S. Customary	Metric
12 in. = 1 ft	10 mm = 1 cm
3 ft = 1 yd	1000 mm = 1 m
5280 ft = 1 mi	100 cm = 1 m
1760 yd = 1 mi	1000 m = 1 km

Weight	Mass
U.S. Customary	Metric
16 oz = 1 lb	1000 g = 1 kg
2000 lb = 1 ton	

Liquid Measure	
U.S. Customary	Metric
16 oz = 1 pt	1000 mL = 1 L
2 pt = 1 qt	
4 qt = 1 gal	

Conversion
2.54 cm = 1 in.
3600 s = 1 hr